SIXTH EDITION

MANAGERIAL ECONOMICS in a GLOBAL ECONOMY

DOMINICK SALVATORE

Fordham University

New York   Oxford
OXFORD UNIVERSITY PRESS
2007

Oxford University Press, Inc., publishes works that further
Oxford University's objective of excellence in research, scholarship,
and education.

Oxford   New York
Auckland   Cape Town   Dar es Salaam   Hong Kong   Karachi
Kuala Lumpur   Madrid   Melbourne   Mexico City   Nairobi
New Delhi   Shanghai   Taipei   Toronto

With offices in
Argentina   Austria   Brazil   Chile   Czech Republic   France   Greece
Guatemala   Hungary   Italy   Japan   Poland   Portugal   Singapore
South Korea   Switzerland   Thailand   Turkey   Ukraine   Vietnam

Library of Congress Cataloging-in-Publication Data

Salvatore, Dominick.
    Managerial economics in a global economy / Dominick Salvatore.—6th ed.
        p. cm.
    Includes index.
    ISBN: 978-0-19-530719-1 (cloth : alk. paper)
    1. Managerial economics. I. Title.

HD30.22.S247 2006
338.5024'658—dc22

                                                            2006007418

Printing number: 9 8 7 6 5 4 3

Printed in the United States of America
on acid-free paper

To Madeleine

CONTENTS IN BRIEF

Appendixes   611

CONTENTS

PART FOUR

Market Structure and Pricing Practices   327

PART FIVE
Regulation, Risk Analysis, and Capital Budgeting   491

Appendixes   611

PREFACE

This is a textbook for the traditional course in managerial economics offered in most business and economics programs. The organization of the text and the topics covered follow the traditional way the course is being taught, but they have been greatly extended in many new and exciting directions to reflect modern managerial tools and methods.

The primary aims of this text are:

To provide a unifying theme of managerial decision making around the theory of the firm. This text shows how managerial economics is not the study of unrelated topics but the *synthesis* of economic theory, decision sciences, and the various fields of business administration studies, and it examines how they interact with one another as the firm attempts to reach optimal managerial decisions in the face of constraints.

To present many new topics and managerial tools not discussed at all or discussed only superficially in other managerial texts. These include firm architecture, the evolution of the creative company, Porter's strategic framework, the virtual corporation, relationship enterprises, firm governance, business ethics, electronic commerce, the economics of information, international risks, the new (international) economies of scale, and learning curves, as well as total quality management, reengineering, benchmarking, the learning organization, the new digital factory, bundling, the effect of taxation on business decisions, and the business use of the Internet.

To introduce an international dimension into managerial economics to reflect the globalization of tastes, production, and distribution in today's world. Other managerial economics texts include only a few examples or an isolated chapter on the international aspects of managerial economics. This text, on the other hand, fully integrates and discusses, in each chapter and for each topic, the international ramifications of managerial economics in today's global economy. This is essential because many of the commodities we consume are imported, and firms today purchase many inputs abroad and sell an increasing share of their outputs overseas. Even more important, domestic firms face more and more competition from foreign producers.

To show how managerial decisions are actually made in the real world. The text includes 129 *real-world Case Studies (far more than other texts),* as well as six longer *Integrating Case Studies* at the end of each of the five parts of the text. These Case Studies are substantial rather than just a few lines as in many other texts. Since managerial economics is by nature an applied field, this feature can hardly be overstated. The Case Studies in this text cover a broad range of topics, such as: electronic commerce, eBay and competition on the Internet, benchmarking at Xerox, reengineering at General Electric, Gillette's introduction of the Sensor and Mach3 razors, virtual management, General Motors' decision that small is better, the new U.S. digital firm, how firms get new technologies, logistics at Hewlett-Packard, the euro and the international competitiveness of European firms, the exchange rate of the dollar and the profitability of U.S. firms, Wal-Mart's preemptive marketing strategy, transfer pricing by multinational corporations, price discrimination by Con Edison, pricing at Priceline, the Microsoft antitrust case, RiskMetrics, spreading risks in the choice of a portfolio, and the Enron–Andersen and other financial disasters.

OTHER UNIQUE FEATURES

The text has other unique features, among which are the following:

- It offers *complete coverage of all the topics* usually encountered in actual managerial decision making and covered in any managerial economics course. Thus, the text allows a great deal of *flexibility in the choice of the topics* that any instructor may wish to cover.
- *The text can be used in courses with or without calculus.* In-depth coverage of the full range of optimization techniques used in managerial decision making is presented in Chapter 2. The calculus of optimization is introduced in the appendix to Chapter 2 and used only in the mathematical appendixes at the end of most chapters and in footnotes.
- *While applied in nature, this text rests on sound analytical foundations.* This addresses the common criticism that texts in this field are either overly theoretical, or are applied in nature but rest on weak theoretical foundations.

NEW TO THE SIXTH EDITION

Among the new sections added are: Section 1-2 on the basic process of decision making, 4-2 on virtual shopping and virtual management, 6-8 on the innovation process, 9-3 on Porter's strategic framework, 9-6 on the evolution of the creative company, 12-7 on the effect of taxation on business decisions, 13-8 on the principle–agent problem, and 13-8 on auctions. Appendixes were also added to Chapters 4 and 5, showing how to use Microsoft Excel for simple and multiple regression analyses and for forecasting fluctuations in time-series data. The calculus of optimization was also shifted from Chapter 2 to the appendix to Chapter 2.

About a quarter of the more than 125 case studies included in the text are brand new, and half of the others have been subject to major revisions to update them and make them more relevant. Among the new case studies are: Case Study 1-1 on Peter Drucker—the man who invented management, 1-13 on changes in demand and supply and coffee prices, 4-3 on reaching consumers in the vanishing mass market, 8-4 on the dollar exchange rate and the profitability of U.S. firms, 9-6 on the globalization of the automobile industry, 11-5 on transfer pricing in advanced countries, 12-11 on corporate taxes around the world, 12-12 on U.S. border taxes and export subsidies, 13-9 on golden parachutes rewarding failures, and 13-10 on the auctioning of airwaves.

In addition two longer integrating case studies were added on "The Education of Michael Dell" and on "eBay and Competition on the Internet" and other case studies, supplementary readings, and Internet site addresses have been thoroughly revised and expanded. The Web site for this text has also been updated. It now includes 16 case studies and applications and a chapter on "Linear Programming."

THE SUBJECT MATTER OF MANAGERIAL ECONOMICS

Managerial economics refers to the application of economic theory and the tools of analysis of decision science to examine how a firm can make optimal managerial decisions in the face of the constraints it faces.

This is a text for the standard upper-level undergraduate and graduate course in managerial economics offered in most business and some economics programs. This text uses the theory of the firm to integrate and link economic theory (microeconomics and macroeconomics), decision sciences (mathematical economics and econometrics), and the functional areas of business (accounting, finance, marketing, personnel or human resource management, and production) and shows how all of these topics are crucial components of managerial decision making. The functional areas of business administration studies examine the business environment in which the firm operates and, as such, they provide the background for managerial decision making. Economic theory provides the analytical framework for optimal decision making, while decision science provides the tools for optimization and for the estimation of economic relationships. As an overview course, managerial economics integrates and links all of these topics and shows their crucial importance in managerial decision making.

As stated above, the text exhibits *four unique features. First,* it uses the theory of the firm as the unifying theme to examine the managerial decision-making process. *Second,* it introduces a global view into managerial economics to reflect the internationalization of tastes, production, and distribution and competition in today's rapidly globalizing world. *Third,* it introduces many exciting topics into the study of managerial economics, such as firm architecture, the evolution of the creative firm, Porter's strategic framework, business ethics, electronic commerce, and risk management, as well as international economies of scale, the virtual corporation, reengineering, benchmarking, the learning organization, and the digital factory. *Fourth,* it shows how managerial decisions are actually made today with more than 125 real-world case studies (more than any other text) as well as six more extensive integrating case studies at the end of each of the five parts of the text.

ORGANIZATION OF THE BOOK

The text is organized into five parts.

Part One (Chapters 1 and 2) examines the nature and scope of managerial economics, presents the theory of the firm, and reviews optimization techniques. Chapter 1 shows in a clearer and more convincing manner than in other texts how the theory of the firm provides the unifying theme to the study of managerial economics and why a global view of managerial economics is required as a result of the rapidly increasing trend toward the internationalization of tastes, production, distribution, and competition in the world today. A brief review of the basics of demand and supply is also included. Chapter 2 then reviews optimization techniques, or the way a firm seeks to achieve its aims and objectives, subject to some constraints, most efficiently. Chapter 2 also discusses several of the new managerial tools.

Part Two (Chapters 3 to 5) analyzes demand. Separate chapters deal with demand theory, the empirical estimation of demand, and demand forecasting. Other texts generally do not have a separate chapter for each of these important topics and are, as a result, less comprehensive.

Part Three (Chapters 6 and 7) presents the theory and measurement of the firm's production and costs. The presentation of input substitution in production in Chapter 6 and the discussion of short-run and long-run cost curves in Chapter 7 are all more complete and clearer than in any other text. A brand new chapter on linear programming is included in the Web site for this text.

Part Four (Chapters 8 to 11) brings together demand analysis (examined in Part Two) and production and cost analysis (examined in Part Three) in order to analyze how price and output are determined under various forms of market organization. Chapter 8 deals with perfect competition, monopoly, and monopolistic competition; Chapter 9 examines oligopoly and firm architecture; Chapter 10 deals with game theory and strategic behavior; while Chapter 11 deals with pricing practices under various forms of market organization.

Part Five (Chapters 12 to 14) examines regulation and antitrust, the role of government in the economy, risk analysis, long-term investment decisions, and capital budgeting.

PEDAGOGICAL FEATURES

In addition to the more than 125 real-world case studies presented in the text (six to thirteen per chapter), an extensive, integrating real-world case study at the end of each of the five parts provides an overview of the type of managerial decision making examined in the particular part.

Important pedagogical features of the text are as follows:

- The sections of each chapter are numbered for easy reference, and longer sections are broken into two or more subsections.
- All of the graphs and diagrams are carefully explained in the text and then summarized in the captions.
- Diagrams are generally drawn on numerical scales to allow the reading of the answers in actual numbers rather than simply as distances.
- Important terms are presented in boldface in the chapters, and a glossary giving the definition of each important term, arranged alphabetically, is provided at the end of the book.

Each chapter also contains the following teaching aids:

1. An *Outline* of each chapter as well as the key terms introduced in each chapter, giving an overview of the material.
2. A *Summary,* which reviews the main points covered in the text.
3. *Discussion Questions* The ability to answer the fifteen questions for each chapter indicates that the student has fully absorbed the material covered in the chapter.
4. *Problems* The fifteen problems in each chapter ask the student to actually apply and put to use what he or she has learned from the chapter. Answers to selected problems,

marked by an asterisk (*), are provided at the end of the book for the type of quick feedback that is so essential to effective learning.

5. *Supplementary Readings* These include the most important references on the various topics covered in each chapter. A separate subject index is included at the end of the book.

6. *Internet Site Addresses* These provide the most important Internet site addresses for the topics presented in each chapter.

7. *Web Site* This presents additional material (cases, theoretical points, or applications) for each chapter in the text that is frequently updated. The Web site also includes a chapter on linear programming and PowerPoint® slides of the tables and charts in the text.

FOR THE INSTRUCTOR

The following ancillaries are available to the instructor:

1. An *Instructor's Manual* provides the answers to all end-of-chapter questions and problems. The *Manual* was prepared by the author with as much care as the text itself and is the most extensive of any text presently on the market. It is available in a print version (ISBN: 978-0-19-531415-1) and on CD.

2. *The Test Bank,* which contains a total of 1,200 items (800 multiple-choice questions with answers, 150 true-and-false questions with answers, and 250 numerical problems fully worked out), is available in a print version (ISBN: 978-0-19-531967-5) and on CD. This comprehensive *Test Bank* is more extensive than for any competing text on the market.

3. *PowerPoint® Presentations.* For professors who wish to use the textbook's graphs, figures, and tables in overhead lecture presentations, the figures are now available on the Web site and on CD. Professors can download the figures by accessing the Oxford University Web site. All of the PowerPoint figures can also be edited so that professors can customize their presentations as they please or print them on overhead transparencies.

4. *Instructor Resources on the Web site.* The Web site contains essential resources for instructors in downloadable format: PowerPoint® slides including lecture notes with animated charts and all important tables and charts contained in the text. The Web site also provides a Web chapter on linear programming.

FOR THE STUDENT

The student will find the following supplements invaluable:

1. A *Study Guide,* prepared by Professor Robert Brooker of Gannon University, can be purchased from Oxford University Press to assist students in reviewing and applying the material covered in the text (ISBN: 978-0-19-531969-9).

2. A *Web site,* prepared by the author, presents additional material (cases, theoretical points, or applications) for each chapter in the text and is constantly updated. The Web site also includes a chapter on linear programming.

ACKNOWLEDGMENTS

This text grew out of the undergraduate and graduate courses in managerial economics that I have been teaching for over two decades at Fordham University in New York and at the Business and Economics University of Vienna and Krems. I was fortunate to have had many excellent students, who with their questions and comments contributed much to the clarity and exposition of this text.

I owe a great intellectual debt to my brilliant former teachers: William Baumol (New York and Princeton Universities), Victor Fuchs (Stanford University and the National Bureau of Economic Research), Jack Johnston (University of California at Irvine), and Lawrence Klein (University of Pennsylvania and the Wharton School of Business). It is incredible how many of the insights that one gains as a student of a superb economist and teacher live on for the rest of one's life.

Many of my colleagues in the School of Business and Department of Economics at Fordham University made suggestions that significantly improved the final product. Among these are Victor M. Borun, John Malindretos, James A. F. Stoner, David P. Stuhr, and Robert M. Wharton from the Business School; and Joseph Cammarosano, Fred Campano, Clive Daniel, Edward Dowling, Nicholas Gianaris, Duncan James, Derrick Reagle, and Greg Winczewski from the Department of Economics. My former colleague, Frank Fabozzi, also made many valuable suggestions.

The following professors have made many valuable suggestions for the present edition of the text:

Robert Brooker, Dahlkemper School of Business, Gannon University
Ananish Chaudhuri, Business and Economics, Washington State University
Wilfrid Csaplar, Economics Department, Bethany College
Jayoti Das, Department of Economics, Love School of Business
Denise Dimon, Director, International Business and International MBA, University of San Diego
Satyajit Ghosh, Chair, Economics and Finance Department, Kania School of Management, University of Scranton
Luba Habodaszova, School of Business, Indiana University at Kokomo
Robert Johnson, School of Business Administration, University of San Diego
Philip LeBel, Department of Economics and Finance, School of Business, Montclair State University
Matthew Roelofs, College of Business and Economics, Western Washington University
Lucjan Orlowski, Faculty of Financial Studies, Sacred Heart University
Rupert Rhodd, Department of Economics and Business, Florida Atlantic University
Stuart Rosenberg, School of Business, Dowling College
Mehmet Tosun, College of Business Economics, West Virginia University

Other American professors made valuable contributions that helped make this one of the leading texts in managerial economics all over the world. These are: Robert Brooker, Gannon University; Denise Dimon and Bob Johnson, University of San Diego; Otis Gilley, Louisiana Technical University; Jack Hou, California State University at Long Beach; Brad Kamp, University of South Florida; Carl Kogut, Northeast Louisiana University; David Miller, Gannon University; Marc Nyeland, University of Copenhagen; Lucjan Orlowski, Sacred Heart University; Robert Pennington, University of Central Florida; and David Saurman, San Jose State University. The following professors teaching managerial economics around the world have also made some valuable suggestions that were included in the present edition of this text: Fritz Breuss, Gerhard Fink, and Stefan Griller, Business and Economics University of Vienna; Ove Hedegaard, Copenhagen School of Business; Fatimah Wati Ibrahim and Shaharuddin Tahir, University of Utara in Indonesia; Wasif Siddiqui, Foreman Christian College in Lahore; Hans Stoessel, University of Ho Chi Min City; Sooraj B. Swami, University College of Bahrain; Chin-Fan Tai, Shih-Hsin University in Taipei; and Cecilio Tamarit, University of Valencia. To all of them I am very grateful.

The following professors reviewed previous editions of the text and made many useful suggestions for improvements: Dean Baim, Pepperdine University; Saul Barr, University of Tennessee; John Beck, Indiana University, South Bend; Trent E. Boggess, Plymouth State College; Robert Brooker, Gannon University; Barrington K. Brown, Bowie State University; John Bungum, Gustavas Adolphus College; John E. Connor, LaSalle University; John Gregor, Plymouth State College; Simon Hakim, Temple University; Richard Hannah, Middle Tennessee State University; Dean Hiebert, Illinois State University; James Horner, Cameron University; Nicholas Karatjas, Indiana University of Pennsylvania; Demitrius Karenteli, Assumption College; Douglas J. Lamdin, University of Maryland, Baltimore; Mary Lesser, Iona College; Louis Lopilato, Marcy College; Wilfred McAloon, Fairleigh Dickinson University; Warren Machone, University of Central Florida; Philip S. Mahoney, University of Northern Colorado; Daniel Marsh, University of Dallas; Don Maxwell, Central State University; Marshall H. Medoff, California State University, Long Beach; Dean Hiebert, Illinois State University; Robert Nicholson, University of Richmond; Patrick O'Sullivan, State University of New York, Old Westbury; Robert Pennington, University of Central Florida; Walter Rice, California Polytech Institute; David Riefel, University of North Carolina at Charlotte; Janet M. Rives, University of Northern Iowa; John Rodgers, University of North Carolina, Greensboro; William J. Simeone, Providence College; Michael Szenberg, Pace University; John Wade, Western Carolina University; James N. Wetzel, Virginia Commonwealth University; and Richard Winkelman, Arizona State University.

Valuable suggestions were also made by Dr. Michael Halloran (Partner at Ernst & Young), Dr. Reza Barazesh (Head of Predictive Science at Equifax), Dr. Jeffrey Shafer (Managing Director of Solomon Smith Barney and Vice-Chairman of Solomon Smith Barney International), Dr. Robert Himmelberg (Dean of The Graduate Business School at Fordham University), Dr. Anthonly Bisceglio (Chief Financial Officer at Simsbury Bank), and Dr. Khosrow Fatemi (President of Eastern Oregon University).

I am grateful to the literary executor of the estate of the late Sir Ronald A. Fisher, F.R.S., to Dr. Frank Yates, F.R.S., and to the Longman Group Ltd., London, for permission to reprint Table C-2 from their book, *Statistical Tables for Biological, Agricultural and Medical Research,* 6th ed. (1974).

Finally, I would like to express my gratitude to the entire staff of Oxford University Press, especially to Terry Vaughn and Catherine Rae for their kind and skillful assistance, Noel Hernandez, Meghan Hennessy, and Candace Marriott (my graduate assistants), and to Angela Bates and Josephine Cannariato (the departmental secretaries at Fordham) for their efficiency and cheerful dispositions.

Dominick Salvatore

ABOUT THE AUTHOR

Dominick Salvatore is Professor of Economics and Business at Fordham University. He was chairman of the New York Academy of Sciences and is consultant to the Economic Policy Institute in Washington, the United Nations, and various multinational banks and corporations. He is the author, co-author, or editor of 44 books, among which are: *Income Distribution* (2006), *Introduction to International Economics* (2005), *International Economics* (8th ed., 2004), *Microeconomics Theory and Applications* (5th ed., 2003), *The Dollarization Debate* (2003), *Protectionism and World Welfare* (1993), and *The Japanese Competitive Challenge and the U.S. Response* (1990). He is the co-editor of the *Journal of Policy Modeling* and the *Open Economies Review,* and associate editor of the *American Economist.* His research has been published in more than 100 journal articles in leading business and economics journals and presented at numerous national and international conferences.

PART ONE

Introduction

Part One (Chapters 1 and 2) examines the nature and scope of managerial economics and presents the optimization techniques that will be used throughout the text. Chapter 1 defines the subject matter of managerial economics and examines its relationship to other fields of study; it discusses the basic process of decision making; it presents the theory of the firm and examines the nature and function of profits; it discusses ethics in business; finally, it examines the importance of introducing an international dimension into managerial economics and of using the Internet.

Chapter 1 Appendix reviews the basics of demand, supply, and equilibrium. Chapter 2 presents the techniques for maximizing or minimizing an objective function, such as profits or costs, and examines new management theories.

CHAPTER 1 — The Nature and Scope of Managerial Economics

CHAPTER OUTLINE

KEY TERMS (in the order of their appearance)

Managerial economics
Economic theory
Microeconomics
Macroeconomics
Model
Mathematical economics
Econometrics
Functional areas of business
    administration studies

Firm
Transaction costs
Circular flow of economic activity
Theory of the firm
Value of the firm
Constrained optimization
Principal–agent problem
Satisficing behavior
Business profit

Explicit costs
Economic profit
Implicit costs
Business ethics
Sarbanes–Oxley Act
Globalization of economic activity
Internet
Information superhighway

I n this chapter we examine the nature and scope of managerial economics. We begin with a definition of managerial economics and a discussion of its relationship to other fields of study. We then go on to discuss the basic process of decision making and examine the theory of the firm. Here, we discuss the reason for the existence of firms and their functions, and we define the value of the firm, point out the constraints faced by firms, and examine the limitations of the theory of the firm, including the *principal–agent problem.* Then, we examine the nature of profits by distinguishing between economic and business profits and by analyzing their function in a free-enterprise system. Subsequently, we discuss business ethics. Finally, we examine the importance of introducing an international dimension into managerial economics to reflect the globalization of production and distribution in today's world, as well as the importance of using the Internet as a crucial source of information and data for managerial economics. In the Chapter Appendix, we review the basics of demand, supply, and equilibrium.

Each section of the chapter includes one or more real-world case studies, which clearly illustrate the major concept introduced in the particular section. This is an important chapter because it defines the subject matter of managerial economics, it clearly shows its relationship to other fields of study, and it examines the great importance and relevance of managerial economics in all business and economic decision-making situations and programs in today's global economy.

1-1   THE SCOPE OF MANAGERIAL ECONOMICS

In this section we define the function of managerial economics and examine its relationship to economic theory, management decision sciences, and functional areas of business administration studies.

Definition of Managerial Economics

Managerial economics* refers to the application of economic theory and the tools of analysis of decision science to examine how an organization can achieve its aims or

---

* The definition of all boldfaced terms, arranged alphabetically, is provided in the Glossary at the end of the book.

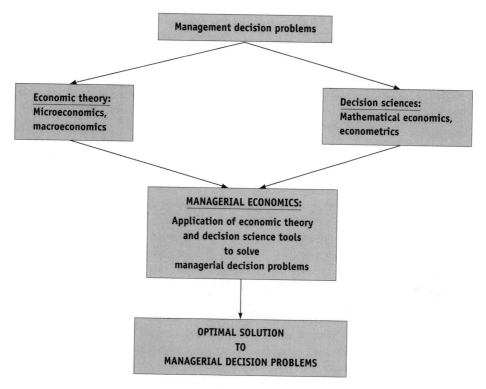

FIGURE 1-1   The Nature of Managerial Economics*
* Managerial economics *refers to the application of economic theory and decision science tools to find the optimal solution to managerial decision problems.*

objectives most efficiently. The meaning of this definition can best be examined with the aid of Figure 1-1.

Management decision problems (see the top of Figure 1-1) arise in any organization—be it a firm, a not-for-profit organization (such as a hospital or a university), or a government agency—when it seeks to achieve some goal or objective subject to some constraints. For example, a firm may seek to maximize profits subject to limitations on the availability of essential inputs and in the face of legal constraints. A hospital may seek to treat as many patients as possible at an "adequate" medical standard with its limited physical resources (physicians, technicians, nurses, equipment, beds) and budget. The goal of a state university may be to provide an adequate education to as many students as possible, subject to the physical and financial constraints it faces. Similarly, a government agency may seek to provide a particular service (which cannot be provided as efficiently by business firms) to as many people as possible at the lowest possible cost. In all these cases, the organization faces management decision problems as it seeks to achieve its goal or objective, subject to the constraints it faces. The goals and constraints may differ from case to case, but the basic decision-making process is the same.

Relationship to Economic Theory

The organization can solve its management decision problems by the application of economic theory and the tools of decision science. **Economic theory** refers to microeconomics and macroeconomics. **Microeconomics** is the study of the economic behavior of *individual* decision-making units, such as individual consumers, resource owners, and business firms, in a free-enterprise system. **Macroeconomics,** on the other hand, is the study of the total or aggregate level of output, income, employment, consumption, investment, and prices for the economy *viewed as a whole.* Although the (microeconomic) theory of the firm is the single most important element in managerial economics, the general macroeconomic conditions of the economy (such as the level of aggregate demand, rate of inflation, and interest rates) within which the firm operates are also very important.

Economic theories seek to predict and explain economic behavior. Economic theories usually begin with a **model.** This abstracts from the many details surrounding an event and seeks to identify a few of the most important determinants of the event. For example, the theory of the firm assumes that the firm seeks to maximize profits, and on the basis of that it predicts how much of a particular commodity the firm should produce under different forms of market structure or organization. While the firm may have other (multiple) aims, the profit-maximization model accurately predicts the behavior of firms, and, therefore, we accept it. Thus, the methodology of economics (and science in general) is to accept a theory or model if it predicts accurately and if the predictions follow logically from the assumptions.[1]

Relationship to the Decision Sciences

Managerial economics is also closely related to the decision sciences. These use the tools of mathematical economics and econometrics (see Figure 1-1) to construct and estimate decision models aimed at determining the optimal behavior of the firm (i.e., how the firm can achieve its goals most efficiently). Specifically, **mathematical economics** is used to formalize (i.e., to express in equational form) the economic models postulated by economic theory. **Econometrics** then applies statistical tools (particularly regression analysis) to real-world data to estimate the models postulated by economic theory and for forecasting.

For example, economic theory postulates that the quantity demanded (Q) of a commodity is a function of or depends on the price of the commodity (P), the income of consumers (Y), and the price of related (i.e., complementary and substitute) commodities (P_C and P_S, respectively). Assuming constant tastes, we may postulate the following formal (mathematical) model:

$$Q = f(P, Y, P_C, P_S) \tag{1-1}$$

---

[1] See M. Friedman, "The Methodology of Positive Economics," in *Essays in Positive Economics* (Chicago: University of Chicago Press, 1953); and M. Blaug, *The Methodology of Economics and How Economists Explain* (Cambridge, England: Cambridge University Press, 1980).

By collecting data on Q, P, Y, P_C, and P_S for a particular commodity, we can then estimate the empirical (econometric) relationship. This will permit the firm to determine how much Q would change by a change in P, Y, P_C, and P_S, and to forecast the future demand for the commodity. This information is essential in order for management to achieve the goal or objective of the firm (profit maximization) most efficiently.

To conclude, *managerial economics* refers to the application of economic theory and decision science tools to find the optimal solution to managerial decision problems.

Relationship to the Functional Areas of Business Administration Studies

Having defined the subject matter of managerial economics and its function, we can now examine the relationship between managerial economics and the **functional areas of business administration studies.** The latter include accounting, finance, marketing, personnel or human resource management, and production. These disciplines study the business environment in which the firm operates and, as such, they provide the background for managerial decision making. Thus, managerial economics can be regarded as an overview course that *integrates* economic theory, decision sciences, and the functional areas of business administration studies; and it examines how they interact with one another as the firm attempts to achieve its goal most efficiently.

Most students taking managerial economics are likely to have some knowledge (from other courses) of some of the topics presented and tools of analysis used in managerial economics. While reviewing these topics and studying the others, the student should pay particular attention to the overall decision-making process by which the firm can achieve its objective, since this is the ultimate goal of managerial economics.

In short, managerial economics is not the study of a number of independent topics but the use of economic theory and management science tools to examine how a firm can achieve its objective most efficiently within the business environment in which it operates. If all students in a managerial economics course had already taken courses in microeconomic and macroeconomic theory, in mathematical economics and econometrics, and in the functional areas of business, then managerial economics could concentrate exclusively on its integrating and synthesizing role in analyzing the decision-making process. As it is, most students have had some of those courses but not all. Thus, a managerial economics course, while stressing the process of reaching optimal managerial decisions, must also present the theories and tools required to make such optimal managerial decisions.

1-2   THE BASIC PROCESS OF DECISION MAKING

Regardless of the type, all decision-making processes involve or can be subdivided into five basic steps, as shown in Figure 1-2.

> 1. **Define the Problem**
> 2. **Determine the Objective**
> 3. **Identify Possible Solutions**
> 4. **Select the Best Possible Solution**
> 5. **Implement the Decision**

FIGURE 1-2   The Decision-Making Process   The five basic steps of the decision-making process.

The first step involves defining the problem that the firm or organization faces. For example, in 1979 the Xerox Corporation, which invented the copying machine in 1959 and had no competition until 1969, found itself unable to compete with Japanese copiers, which were of better quality and cheaper.

The second step in the decision-making process is for the firm or organization to determine the objective of the firm. In the case of Xerox, the company had to decide whether to try to meet the competition or leave the copier market to the Japanese and move on to develop and produce some other more technologically advanced product. Xerox decided to stay in the market by trying to meet the competition head on.

The third step is to identify the options or range of possible solutions to the problem defined in step one in order to achieve the objective set in step two. In the case of Xerox, the range of choices included trying to improve quality while reducing the costs of production in its American plants, import from Japan those parts and components that could be produced better and more cheaply in Japan, or transfer its entire production of copiers to Fuji Xerox, its Japanese subsidiary.

The fourth step in the decision-making process is for the firm or organization to select the best possible solution or course of action among the choices identified in step three. In the case of Xerox, this required reorganization and integration of development and production, and an ambitious companywide quality-control effort in its domestic plants with the direct involvement of Fuji Xerox, as well as the importation of parts or components that Fuji Xerox could best produce in Japan.

The fifth and final step is the implementation of the best possible solution identified in step four. To continue with our example, Xerox greatly increased employee involvement, brought suppliers into the early stages of product design, greatly reduced inventories and the number of suppliers, and used Fuji Xerox to produce in Japan those parts or components that could be better supplied from Japan and, more importantly, to monitor progress in the companywide quality-control program and customer satisfaction. By taking these drastic actions, Xerox was able to reverse the trend toward loss of market share to Japanese competitors (Xerox's experience is reported in greater detail in Case Study 6-7).

The decision-making process analyzed above was, for the most part, introduced by Peter Drucker (see Case Study 1-1) and is now being revolutionized by the rapid globalization of the world economy and by the widespread use of computers and information technology (see Case Study 1-2).

CASE STUDY 1-1
Peter Drucker—The Man Who Invented Management

Many of the management theories and ideas examined in this and other management books have been introduced by Peter F. Drucker, who has been justly called "the man who invented management." He was certainly the most important management thinker of the past century. (Drucker passed away in November 2005 at the age of 95.) Many of the management theories and ideas which we now consider conventional wisdom or commonplace were in fact first introduced by Peter Drucker, and he strongly influenced most business leaders (such as Bill Gates of Microsoft, Andrew Grove of Intel, and Jack Welch of General Electric) and many political leaders (such as President George Bush and Newt Gingrich, the former leader of the House of Representatives) not only in the United States but throughout the world.

His 1945 landmark study of General Motors, *The Concept of the Corporation,* Drucker introduced decentralization as a principle of organization, which by the 1980s had been adopted by more than three-quarters of American companies. In his 1954 book, *The Practice of Management,* he asked the seemingly naïve but fundamental questions: "What business are we in?" "Who are our costumers?" "What does the costumer consider value?" In the same book Drucker emphasized the importance of managers and corporations setting clear long-term objectives and then translating them into more immediate and achievable goals. In *The Effective Executive* (1966), Drucker says that managers should focus on important matters in order to avoid wasting time on nonessentials, to focus on substance rather than style and on institutionalized practices over charismatic or cult leaders.

It was a result of the following question that Drucker asked Jack Welch soon after the latter became the CEO (Corporate Executive Officer) of General Electric (GE) in 1981: "If you were not in a business, would you enter it today, and if the answer is no, what are you going to do about it?" that Welch decided that GE either had to be No. 1 or the No. 2 in the particular line of business or get out of it. And it was this one principle that Jack Welch followed during his 15-year tenure as GE's CEO which was responsible for the spectacular performance of GE during those years.

Some of the other basic management principles introduced by Drucker are: (1) the necessity of "empowering" workers and treating them as resources rather than just as costs in a profit-generating machine; (2) the world was moving from an "economy of goods" to an "economy of knowledge," where value is created more by brainpower and knowledge workers than by the sweat of laborers; (3) the corporation is a human community built on trust and respect and satisfying workers' desire for continuous training and learning; (4) change should be exploited as an opportunity rather than viewed as a threat; (5) every decision is risky, and risk can be minimized if managers know when a decision is necessary, how to clearly define and directly tackle it, and that a decision has not been made until a way is found to implement it.

Source: "Peter F. Drucker, a Pioneer in Social and Management Theory," *The New York Times* (November 12, 1995), p. 13; "Trusting the Teacher in the Gray-Flannel Suit," *The Economist* (November 19, 2005), pp. 71–73; and "The Man Who Invented Management," *BusinessWeek* (November 28, 2005), pp. 97–106.

CASE STUDY 1-2
The Management Revolution

Business and society are today in the midst of a revolution comparable to the Industrial Revolution in both scale and consequence. Today's revolution has four components: the globalization of markets, the spread of information technology and computer networks, the dismantling of traditional managerial hierarchies, and the creation of a new information economy. These four components are all occurring quickly and simultaneously, and are affected by and affect one another.

Globalization (the first component of today's revolution) once meant simply exporting some goods and services to other nations and maybe setting up a few production facilities abroad. Today, globalization means that more and more managerial decisions must consider the world as a whole, rather than the region or the nation, as the relevant marketplace. Because of the tremendous improvement in communications and transportation, tastes are converging internationally, many more products than in the past are now imported and most others have parts of components made abroad, and domestic producers face ever-growing competition from abroad.

The second component of today's revolution is the spread of the information technology and computer networks. Practically every bank teller, post office worker, retail clerk, telephone operator, bill collector, and so on works with a computer today. This greatly speeds up the delivery of goods and services, cuts waste, reduces inventory, and generally increases productivity.

The computer has also dismantled traditional managerial hierarchies and decimated the ranks of middle management (the third component of today's revolution). In the past, middle managers were the transmission lines for information between top management and workers. Today, information can in most instances be transmitted from top management directly to workers and vice-versa by a simple tap of a computer key and without any need of middle management. Surviving middle managers are today assuming more important roles and are increasingly being used to shelter senior managers from the day-to-day operations of the firm so that the latter can concentrate their energies on the strategic management of the firm.

The fourth component of today's revolution is the rapid spread of the information economy, where the creation of value is increasingly based on knowledge and communications rather than as in the past on natural resources and physical labor. For example, many auto repairs will soon be made not by a mechanic with a wrench but by a technician who fixes an engine knock by reprogramming a computer chip, and goods and services will increasingly be marketed and distributed electronically. Today's four-pronged revolution affects drastically not only how traditional products and services are produced and distributed but also the entire organization of production, consumption, and management in ways that are not yet fully evident or understood.

Source: "Welcome to the Revolution," *Fortune* (December 13, 1993), pp. 66–78; "Management's New Paradigm," *Forbes* (October 5, 1998), pp. 152–176; Q. N. Huy, "In Praise of Middle Managers," *Harvard Business Review* (September 2001), pp. 72–79; "A Management Revolution Still in the Making," *The New York Times* (March 12, 2002), p. 5; "In Defence of Globalization," *IMF Survey* (March 1, 2004), pp. 63–64; and "More Employers Plan to Hire Middle Managers," *The Wall Street Journal* (February 1, 2005), p. B6.

1-3   THE THEORY OF THE FIRM

In this section, we examine first the reason for the existence of firms and their principal functions. Then we define the value of the firm and the constraints under which it operates. Finally, we discuss the limitations of the theory of the firm. This is a most important section since the theory of firm behavior is the centerpiece and central theme of managerial economics.

Reasons for the Existence of Firms and Their Functions

A **firm** is an organization that combines and organizes resources for the purpose of producing goods and/or services for sale. There are millions of firms in the United States. These include proprietorships (firms owned by one individual), partnerships (firms owned by two or more individuals), and corporations (owned by stockholders). Firms produce more than 80 percent of all goods and services consumed in the United States. The remainder is produced by the government and not-for-profit organizations, such as private colleges, hospitals, museums, and foundations.

Firms exist because it would be very inefficient and costly for entrepreneurs to enter into and enforce contracts with workers and owners of capital, land, and other resources for each separate step of the production and distribution process. Instead, entrepreneurs usually enter into longer-term, broader contracts with labor to perform a number of tasks for specific wages and fringe benefits. Such a general contract is much less costly than numerous specific contracts and is highly advantageous both to the entrepreneurs and to the workers and other resource owners. The firm exists in order to save on such **transaction costs.** By internalizing many transactions (i.e., by performing many functions within the firm), the firm also saves on sales taxes and avoids price controls and other government regulations that apply only to transactions among firms.

Firms, however, do not continue to grow larger and larger indefinitely because of limitations on management's ability to effectively control and direct the operation of the firm as it becomes larger and larger. It is true that up to a point, a firm can overcome these internal disadvantages of large size or diseconomies of scale by establishing a number of semiautonomous divisions (i.e., by decentralizing). Eventually, however, the increased communication traffic that is generated, coupled with the further and further distancing of top management from the operation of each division, imposes sufficient diseconomies of scale to limit the growth of the firm. Furthermore, the firm will reach a point where the cost of supplying additional services within the firm exceeds the cost of purchasing these services from other firms. An example is provided by some highly technical (legal, medical, or engineering) service that the firm may need only occasionally.

The function of firms, therefore, is to purchase resources or inputs of labor services, capital, and raw materials in order to transform them into goods and services for sale. Resource owners (workers and owners of capital, land, and raw materials) then use the income generated from the sale of their services or other resources to firms to purchase the goods and services produced by firms. The **circular flow of economic activity** is thus complete.[2] In the process of supplying the goods and services that society demands, firms provide employment to workers and pay taxes, which the government uses to provide services (such as national defense, education, and fire protection) that firms could not provide at all or as efficiently.

The Objective and Value of the Firm

Managerial economics begins by postulating a theory of the firm, which it then uses to analyze managerial decision making. Originally, the theory of the firm was based on the

---

[2] For a more extensive discussion, see D. Salvatore, *Microeconomics: Theory and Applications,* 4th ed. (New York: Oxford University Press, 2003), pp. 7–8.

assumption that the goal or objective of the firm was to maximize current or short-term profits. Firms, however, are often observed to sacrifice short-term profits for the sake of increasing future or long-term profits. Some examples of this are expenditures on research and development, new capital equipment, and an enhanced promotional campaign.[3] Since both short-term as well as long-term profits are clearly important, the **theory of the firm** now postulates that the primary goal or objective of the firm is to maximize the wealth or **value of the firm.** This is given by the present value of all expected future profits of the firm. Future profits must be discounted to the present because a dollar of profit in the future is worth less than a dollar of profit today.[4]

Formally stated, the wealth or value of the firm is given by

$$PV = \frac{\pi_1}{(1 + r)^1} + \frac{\pi_2}{(1 + r)^2} + \cdots + \frac{\pi_n}{(1 + r)^n} \qquad [1\text{-}2]$$

$$= \sum_{t=1}^{n} \frac{\pi_t}{(1 + r)^t} \qquad [1\text{-}2a]$$

where PV is the present value of all expected future profits of the firm, $\pi_1, \pi_2, \ldots, \pi_n$ represent the expected profits in each of the n years considered, and r is the appropriate discount rate used to find the present value of future profits. In Equation 1-2a, $\sum$ refers to "the sum of" and t assumes the values from 1 up to the n years considered. Thus, $\sum_{t=1}^{n}$ means "sum or add" all the $\pi_t/(1 + r)^t$ terms resulting from substituting the values of 1 to n for t. Hence, Equation 1-2a is an abbreviated but equivalent form of Equation 1-2. The introduction of the time dimension in Equations 1-2 and 1-2a also allows for the consideration of uncertainty. For example, the more uncertain the stream of expected future profits is, the higher is the discount rate that the firm will use, and, therefore, the smaller is the present value of the firm.[5]

Since profits are equal to total revenue (TR) minus total costs (TC), Equation 1-2a can be rewritten as

$$\text{Value of firm} = \sum_{t=1}^{n} \frac{TR_t - TC_t}{(1 + r)^t} \qquad [1\text{-}3]$$

Equation 1-3 provides a unifying theme for the analysis of managerial decision making and, indeed, for this entire text. Specifically, TR depends on sales or the demand for the firm's output and the firm's pricing decisions. These are the major responsibility of

---

[3] Many managers, however, complain that the pressure to report profits every year or every quarter forces them to take actions that are detrimental to the long-term profitability of the firm.

[4] A $1 investment today at 10 percent interest will grow to $1.10 in one year. Therefore, $1 is defined as the present value of $1.10 due in one year. For the purpose of this chapter, this is all that needs to be known. A detailed presentation of the concepts of present value and compound interest, which are required for understanding Chapter 13 on risk analysis and Chapter 14 on long-run investment decisions, is given in Appendix A at the end of the book.

[5] "Valuing Old and New Companies," *Financial Times* (May 28, 2001), p. 2; and "Bringing the Future into Play," *Business Week* (March 11, 2002), pp. 70–71.

the marketing department and are discussed in detail in Part Two (Chapters 3 through 5) and Part Four (Chapters 8 through 11), respectively. The *TC* depends on the technology of production and resource prices. These are the major responsibility of the production and personnel or human resources departments and are discussed in detail in Part Three (Chapters 6 and 7). The discount rate (*r*) depends on the perceived risk of the firm and on the cost of borrowing funds. These are the major responsibility of the finance department and are discussed in detail in Chapters 13 and 14 (in Part Five).

Equation 1-3 can also be used to organize the discussion of how the various departments within the firm interact with one another. For example, the marketing department can reduce the cost associated with a given level of output by promoting off-season sales. The production and human resources departments can stimulate sales by quality improvements and the development of new products. The accounting department can provide more timely information on sales and costs. All these activities increase the efficiency of the firm and reduce its risk, thereby allowing the firm to use a lower discount rate to determine the present value of its expected future profits (which increases the value of the firm).

Constraints on the Operation of the Firm

We have seen that the goal or objective of the firm is to maximize wealth or the value of the firm. In trying to do this, however, the firm faces many constraints. Some of these constraints arise from limitations on the availability of essential inputs. Specifically, a firm might not be able to hire as many skilled workers as it wants, especially in the short run. Similarly, the firm might not be able to acquire all the specific raw materials it demands. It might also face limitations on factory and warehouse space and in the quantity of capital funds available for a given project or purpose. Government agencies and not-for-profit organizations also face similar resource constraints. Besides resource constraints, the firm also faces many legal constraints. These take the form of minimum wage laws, health and safety standards, pollution emission standards, as well as laws and regulations that prevent firms from employing unfair business practices. In general, society imposes these constraints on firms in order to modify their behavior and make it more nearly consistent with broad social welfare goals.

So important and pervasive are the constraints facing firms that we speak of **constrained optimization.**[6] That is, the primary goal or objective of the firm is to maximize wealth or the value of the firm subject to the constraints it faces. The existence of these constraints restricts the range of possibilities or freedom of action of the firm and limits the value of the firm to a level that is lower than in the absence of such constraints (unconstrained optimization). Within these constraints, however, the firm seeks to maximize wealth or its value. While government agencies and not-for-profit organizations may have goals other than wealth or value maximization, they also face constraints in achieving their goals or objectives, whatever these goals or objectives might be. Most of the discussion in the rest of the text will be in terms of constrained optimization, and we will develop and use powerful techniques to examine how the firm achieves constrained optimization.

---

[6] We refer to "optimization" rather than "maximization" in order to allow for cases where the firm wants to *minimize* costs and other objectives, subject to the constraints it faces.

Limitations of the Theory of the Firm

The theory of the firm, which postulates that the goal or objective of the firm is to maximize wealth or the value of the firm, has been criticized as being much too narrow and unrealistic. In its place, broader theories of the firm have been proposed. The most prominent among these are models that postulate that the primary objective of the firm is the maximization of sales, the maximization of management utility, and satisficing behavior.[7]

According to the sales-maximization model introduced by William Baumol and others, managers of modern corporations seek to maximize sales after an adequate rate of profit has been earned to satisfy stockholders.[8] Indeed, some early empirical studies found a strong correlation between executives' salaries and sales, but not between salaries and profits. More recent studies, however, found the opposite.

Oliver Williamson and others have introduced a model of management utility maximization, which postulates that with the advent of the modern corporation and the resulting separation of management from ownership, managers are more interested in maximizing their utility, measured in terms of their compensation (salaries, fringe benefits, stock options, etc.), the size of their staff, the extent of control over the corporation, lavish offices, etc., than in maximizing corporate profits.[9] This is referred to as the **principal–agent problem.** That is, the agent (manager) may be more interested in maximizing his or her benefits than maximizing the principal's (the owner's) interest. This principal–agent problem can be resolved by tying the manager's reward to the firm's performance in relation to other firms in the same industry. Managers who maximize their own interests rather than the corporation's profits or value are also more likely to be replaced either by the stockholders of the corporation or as a result of the corporation's being taken over by (merged with) another firm that sees the unexploited profit potential of the first. The principal–agent problem will be examined in greater detail in Section 13-8.

Finally, Richard Cyert and James March, building on the work of Herbert Simon, pointed out that because of the great complexity of running the large modern corporation—a task often complicated by uncertainty and a lack of adequate data—managers are not able to maximize profits but can only strive for some satisfactory goal in terms of sales, profits, growth, market share, and so on. Simon called this **satisficing behavior.** That is, the large corporation is a satisficing, rather than a maximizing, organization.[10] This, however, is not necessarily inconsistent with profit or value maximization; presumably, with more and better data and search procedures, the modern corporation could conceivably approach profit or value maximization.

---

[7] Still other objectives might be to take advantage of economies of scale or scope, to pay lower prices for inputs (pecuniary economics of scale), to better face risks, to raise capital more effectively (the corporate form), to gain technological advantage, and so on.

[8] See W. J. Baumol, *Business Behavior, Value and Growth* (New York: Macmillan, 1959).

[9] See O. E. Williamson, "A Model of Rational Managerial Behavior," in R. M. Cyert and J. G. March, eds., *A Behavioral Theory of the Firm* (Englewood Cliffs, N.J.: Prentice-Hall, 1963).

[10] See R. M. Cyert and J. G. March, eds., *A Behavioral Theory of the Firm* (Englewood Cliffs, N.J.: Prentice-Hall, 1963); and H. A. Simon, "Theories of Decision-Making in Economics," *American Economic Review,* vol. 49 (June 1949).

Although these alternative and broader theories of the firm stress some relevant aspect of the operation of the modern corporation, they do not provide a satisfactory alternative to the theory of the firm postulated in Section 1-3. Indeed, the stiff competition prevailing in most product and resource markets as well as in managerial and entrepreneurial talent today forces managers to pay close attention to profits—lest the firm go out of business or they be replaced. As a result, we retain our theory of the firm (in terms of profit or value maximization) in the rest of the text as the basis for analyzing managerial decisions, because it is from this vantage point that the behavior of the firm can be studied most fruitfully. The assumptions of the theory may be somewhat unrealistic, but the theory predicts the behavior of the firm more accurately than any of its alternatives (see Case Study 1-3).

CASE STUDY 1-3
The Objective and Strategy of Firms in the Cigarette Industry

Until the rash of recent legal suits and court rulings on the health damages of cigarette smoking, the objective of firms in the cigarette industry seemed to be the maximization of long-run profits or firm value, as postulated by the theory of the firm. Different firms, however, pursued these goals differently. The doubling of the federal excise tax on each pack of cigarettes on January 1, 1983, as well as the rise in other state taxes since then, resulted in a sharp increase in cigarette prices and a reduction in consumption. In order to lure customers from rivals and maintain profit levels, the weaker three of the nation's six major producers introduced generic cigarettes. These contain cheaper tobacco, come in plain black-and-white packages, are advertised very little, and sell at less than half the price of name brands.

The other three major producers, instead, followed the more traditional marketing strategy of brand proliferation. That is, they introduced a large number of new brands to appeal to every conceivable taste or consumer group and spent hundreds of millions of dollars on advertising. They resisted the introduction of generic cigarettes because these cigarettes have very low profit margins. But as sales of generic cigarettes rose, these other major producers responded with the introduction of discounts—brand-name cigarettes that cost more than generics

but less than the traditional brands. Then on Friday, April 2, 1993 (which became known as the infamous Marlboro Friday), Philip Morris took the unusual step of cutting the price of Marlboro cigarettes (one of the world's best-known and most profitable brands) and its other premium brands by 20 percent (about 40 cents per pack) in an effort to contain continued loss of market share to generic cigarettes. RJR Nabisco, Philip Morris's main competitor, quickly matched the price cut.

At the same time, both groups of cigarette producers greatly expanded sales abroad. With the antismoking campaign going global, however, and with a Worldwide Anti-Smoking Treaty signed in February 2004, severely restricting advertising and marketing practices, international sales of American cigarettes also slowed down.

In recent years and as a result of the rash of lawsuits on the harmful health effects of smoking, cigarette companies have been forced to change their strategy to that of containing potential financial losses from adverse court rulings. Thus, in November 1998 they agreed to pay $246 billion over 25 years to settle the high-profile national effort on the part of 46 states to recoup public-health costs linked to smoking. This added 42.5 cents to each pack sold by Big Tobacco and resulted in their loss of

Continued . . .

market share to the three Minors (that were not part of the settlement) from 99.6 percent to 91.9 percent. In 2005, the U.S. Justice Department also asked for a $10 billion penalty from tobacco companies (scaled down from $130 billion recommended by a government witness) to finance a stop-smoking campaign at the conclusion of a long-run case filed in 1999 that charged them with conspiracy to promote smoking and misleading the public on the dangers of smoking.

Source: "Big Tobacco's Toughest Road," *U.S. News & World Report* (April 17, 1989), p. 26; "Philip Morris Cuts Cigarette Prices, Stunning Market," *The New York Times* (April 3, 1993), p. 1; "Cigarette Makers and States Draft a $206 Billion Deal," *The New York Times* (November 14, 1998), p. 1; "Major Makers of Cigarettes Raise Prices," *The Wall Street Journal* (August 31, 1999), p. A3; "Worldwide Anti-Tobacco Treaty Takes Effect," *The New York Times* (February 28, 2004), p. 8; "Tobacco Trustbuster," *Forbes* (February 28, 2005), pp. 86–89; "The High Cost of Nicotine Withdrawal," *Newsweek* (May 23, 2005), p. 40; and "Limit for Award in Tobacco Case Sets Off Protests," *The New York Times* (June 9, 2005), p. 1.

1-4   THE NATURE AND FUNCTION OF PROFITS

In this section we examine the nature and function of profits. We distinguish between business and economic profits, present various theories of profits, and examine the function of profits in a free-enterprise economy.

Business versus Economic Profit

To the general public and the business community, profit or **business profit** refers to the revenue of the firm minus the explicit or accounting costs of the firm. **Explicit costs** are the actual out-of-pocket expenditures of the firm to purchase or hire the inputs it requires in production. These expenditures include the wages to hire labor, interest on borrowed capital, rent on land and buildings, and the expenditures on raw materials. To the economist, however, **economic profit** (or above-normal profit) equals the revenue of the firm minus its explicit costs and implicit costs. **Implicit costs** refer to the value of the inputs owned and used by the firm in its own production processes.

Specifically, implicit costs include the salary that the entrepreneur could earn from working for someone else in a similar capacity (say, as the manager of another firm) and the return that the firm could earn from investing its capital and renting its land and other inputs to other firms. The inputs owned and used by the firm in its own production processes are not free to the firm, even though the firm can use them without any actual or explicit expenditures. Their implicit costs are what these same inputs could earn in their best alternative use outside the firm. Accordingly, economists include both explicit and implicit costs in their definition of costs. That is, they include a normal return on owned resources as part of costs, so that economic profit is revenue minus explicit and implicit costs. While the concept of business profit may be useful for accounting and tax purposes, it is the concept of economic profit that must be used in order to reach correct investment decisions.

For example, suppose that a firm reports a business profit of $30,000 during a year, but the entrepreneur could have earned $35,000 by managing another firm and $10,000 by lending out his capital to another firm facing similar risks. To the economist this entrepreneur is actually incurring an economic loss of $15,000 because, from the *business* profit of

$30,000, he would have to subtract the implicit or opportunity cost of $35,000 for his wages and $10,000 for his capital. A business profit of $30,000, thus, corresponds to an economic loss of $15,000 per year. Even if the entrepreneur owned no capital, he would still incur an economic loss of $5,000 per year by continuing to operate his own firm and earning a business profit of $30,000 rather than working for someone else in a similar capacity for $35,000. Thus, the entrepreneur should close his firm and work in his best alternative occupation. In other words, it is the economic, rather than the business, concept of profit that is important in directing resources to different sectors of the economy. In the rest of the text we will use the term *profit* to mean economic profit and *cost* to mean the sum of explicit and implicit costs.

Theories of Profit

Profit rates usually differ among firms in a given industry and even more widely among firms in different industries. Firms in such industries as steel, textiles, and railroads generally earn very low profits both absolutely and in relation to the profits of firms in pharmaceutical, office equipment, and other high-technology industries. Several theories attempt to explain these differences.

RISK-BEARING THEORIES OF PROFIT   According to risk-bearing theories, above-normal returns (i.e., economic profits) are required by firms to enter and remain in such fields as petroleum exploration with above-average risks. Similarly, the expected return on stocks has to be higher than on bonds because of the greater risk of the former. This will be discussed in greater detail in Chapter 13.

FRICTIONAL THEORY OF PROFIT   This theory stresses that profits arise as a result of friction or disturbances from long-run equilibrium. That is, in long-run, perfectly competitive equilibrium, firms tend to earn only a normal return (adjusted for risk) or zero (economic) profit on their investment. At any time, however, firms are not likely to be in long-run equilibrium and may earn a profit or incur a loss. For example, at the time of the energy crisis in the early 1970s, firms producing insulating materials enjoyed a sharp increase in demand, which led to large profits. With the sharp decline in petroleum prices in the mid-1980s, many of these firms began to incur losses. When profits are made in an industry in the short run, more firms are attracted to the industry in the long run, and this tends to drive profits down to zero (i.e., it leads to firms earning only a normal return on investment). On the other hand, when losses are incurred, some firms leave the industry. This leads to higher prices and the elimination of the losses.

MONOPOLY THEORY OF PROFIT   Some firms with monopoly power can restrict output and charge higher prices than under perfect competition, thereby earning a profit. Because of restricted entry into the industry, these firms can continue to earn profits even in the long run. Monopoly power may arise from the firm's owning and controlling the entire supply of a raw material required for the production of the commodity, from economies of large-scale production, from ownership of patents, or from government restrictions that prohibit competition. The causes, effects, and control of monopoly are examined in detail in Chapters 8, 11, and 12.

INNOVATION THEORY OF PROFIT   The innovation theory of profit postulates that (economic) profit is the reward for the introduction of a successful innovation. For example, Steven Jobs, the founder of the Apple Computer Company, became a millionaire in the course of a few years by introducing the Apple Computer in 1977. Indeed, the U.S. patent system is designed to protect the profits of a successful innovator in order to encourage the flow of innovations. Inevitably, as other firms imitate the innovation, the profit of the innovator is reduced and eventually eliminated. This is, in fact, what happened to the Apple Computer Company in the early 1980s.

MANAGERIAL EFFICIENCY THEORY OF PROFIT   This theory rests on the observation that if the average firm tends to earn only a normal return on its investment in the long run, firms that are more efficient than the average would earn above-normal returns and (economic) profits.

   All of these theories of profit have some element of truth, and each may be more applicable to some industries. Indeed, profits often arise from a combination of factors, including differential risk, market disequilibrium, monopoly power, innovation, and above-average managerial efficiency. This was, for example, the case of the Apple Computer Company when it was established and is the case for Dell now.

   In the fast-paced Internet world, where barriers to entry are very low, trying to become profitable too quickly may suggest that the company's management is not aggressive enough in pursuing growth and market share. As the Web bookseller Amazon.com has shown, a company can be both healthy and unprofitable. Profits matter, but only eventually. In the meantime, the best strategy for Internet start-ups is to grow rapidly and grab as much market share as fast as possible. Venture capitalists believe that when profits eventually come, they will be huge.[11] At least so it was believed until the technological bubble burst in 2000 and many Internet start-ups went out of business.

Function of Profit

Profit serves a crucial function in a free-enterprise economy, such as our own. High profits are the signal that consumers want more of the output of the industry. High profits provide the incentive for firms to expand output and for more firms to enter the industry in the long run. For a firm of above-average efficiency, profits represent the reward for greater efficiency. On the other hand, lower profits or losses are the signal that consumers want less of the commodity and/or that production methods are not efficient. Thus, profits provide the incentive for firms to increase their efficiency and/or produce less of the commodity, and for some firms to leave the industry for more profitable ones. Profits, therefore, provide the crucial signals for the reallocation of society's resources to reflect changes in consumers' tastes and demand over time (see Case Study 1-4).

   To be sure, the profit system is not perfect, and governments in free-enterprise economies often step in to modify the operation of the profit system to make it more nearly consistent with broad societal goals. For example, governments invariably regulate the

---

[11] See "Rethinking a Quaint Idea: Profits," *The Wall Street Journal* (May 19, 1999), p. B1.

CASE STUDY 1-4
Profits in the Personal Computer Industry

In 1976, Steven Jobs, then 20 years old, dropped out of college and, with a friend, developed a prototype desktop computer. With financing from an independent investor, the Apple Computer Company was born, revolutionizing the computer industry. Sales of Apple Computers jumped from $3 million in 1977 to more than $1.9 billion in 1986, with profits of more than $150 million. The immense success of Apple was not lost on potential competitors, and by 1984 more than 75 companies had jumped into the market. Even IBM, which had originally chosen not to enter the market, soon put all its weight and muscle behind the development of its own version of the personal computer—the IBM PC.

Because of increased competition, however, many of the early entrants had dropped out by 1986 and profits fell sharply. For example, profit margins for the 11 largest U.S. computer companies averaged 11.5 percent from 1980 to 1985 but only 6.5 percent from 1986 to 1990. Since 1991, PC makers have been engaged in a brutal price war in which PC prices fell by as much as 20 to 40 percent per year, and this cut profit margins even further. PCs have now become practically a commodity, and as such, provide only a meager operating margin of about 5 percent. Notebooks are following in the same direction.

In 1985, Jobs was ousted after a nasty power struggle with John Scully, Apple president at the time. After unsuccessfully trying a comeback with his NeXT computer in 1986, the 43-year-old Jobs was called back to lead Apple in 1997, after it had suffered years of losses and several CEO changes. Jobs revived Apple by simplifying its confusing product line to a few basic models and by introducing its successful iMac in 1998, a new line of notebook computers in 1999, its sleek PowerMac G4 Cube in 2000, the iPod in 2001, the new iMac in 2002, and the iTunes Music Store in 2003, which merged computing and entertainment.

This is a classic example of the source, function, and importance of profits in our economy. Jobs's huge rewards from the setting up of Apple resulted from correctly anticipating, promoting, and satisfying an important type of market demand. Competitors, attracted by the huge early profits, were quick to follow, thereby causing profits in the industry to fall sharply. In the process, however, more and more of society's resources were attracted to the computer industry, which supplied consumers with rapidly improving personal computers at sharply declining prices.

Source: "Steve Jobs Vision So on Target at Apple, Now Is Falling Short," *The Wall Street Journal* (May 25, 1993), p. A1; "The Second Coming," *Fortune* (November 1998), pp. 86–100; "Apple and PC Given for Dead Are Rising Anew," *The New York Times* (April 6, 1999), p. C1; "Apple," *Business Week* (July 31, 2000), pp. 102–113; "The New iMac," *Fortune* (June 10, 2002), p. 2; "How Low Can a PC Go?" *U.S. News & World Report* (November 4, 2002), p. 62; "I.B.M. Division Headed to China Has Made No Profit in 3½ Years," *The New York Times* (December 31, 2004), p. C4; and "Notebooks without Wide Margins," *BusinessWeek* (September 5, 2005), p. 38.

prices charged for electricity by public utility companies to provide shareholders with only a normal return on their investment. Governments also pass minimum wage legislation and pollution emission controls to internalize to polluting firms the social cost of the pollution they create. While not perfect, the profit system is the most efficient form of resource allocation available. In societies such as the former Soviet Union and the People's Republic of China, where profits were not allowed, a committee of the ruling party performed this function in a much less efficient manner.

1-5   BUSINESS ETHICS

Business ethics seeks to proscribe behavior that businesses, firm managers, and workers should not engage in. Ethics is a source of guidance beyond enforceable law. It is clear and uncontroversial that firms and their workers should not engage in unlawful acts, such as selling harmful or defective products, and ignorance of the law cannot be used as a justification for unlawful actions. Business and management ethics goes beyond the law to provide guidelines as to what is acceptable behavior in business transactions. Being based on values, however, it is often not clear what ethical behavior is and what it is not, since different people may have different values.

For example, should you report to your supervisor an affair between two of your co-workers? Some people would say yes, but others would think that it is none of their business. What about selling a product abroad that has been found to be harmful to health and is not allowed to be sold in the United States? Or buying foreign products made with child labor? Or polluting abroad in a way that is not allowed at home? These issues are important to the firm because, independent of its ethical stand, they could seriously affect its bottom line if, for example, they lead angry consumers to boycott the firm.

Today, most large companies have established codes of ethical behavior for the firm's personnel and have created "ethics officers" or guardians of corporate rectitude with the mission of keeping employees' conduct more upright than the law requires. A company with such a code of behavior and an ethics officer is more likely to hear of unethical behavior in the firm before it becomes a legal problem or before it leads to consumer reaction, both of which can harm the image and profitability of the firm. There have been many such cases, such as when it became known that Nestlé (the Swiss multinational and largest food company in the world) pushed infant formula in many poor countries when the mother's milk would have been healthier for the infant, or when Nike was exposed for paying poverty wages in many developing countries to workers making its high-priced sneakers.

An important additional incentive for many firms establishing codes of conduct for their employees and creating ethics officers was the establishment of sentencing guidelines by the courts in 1991 (revised in November 2003) that reduced fines for white-collar crimes committed by employees of companies that had established comprehensive ethics programs. Such ethics programs attempt to indicate as clearly as possible behavior that the firm regards as unethical and that employees are asked to avoid not only domestically but around the world. These include using the company's telephone for personal use, taking office supplies home, lying about being sick for missing work, not reporting illegal behavior by other employees, giving or accepting gifts, and many others (see Case Study 1-5). Since it is practically impossible to list all types of hypothetical behavior that a company would regard as unethical and come up with a universally accepted code of conduct, after listing many such examples, some companies provide the broad guideline of "don't do it if it doesn't feel right or if you would be embarrassed reading about it in the local newspaper or hearing about it on the local evening news."

Today, professions such as medicine, law, and accounting have professional codes of ethics. Despite this, a number of spectacular financial frauds were exposed, starting with the Enron–Arthur Andersen case at the end of 2001 and spilling into most of 2002, which clearly demonstrated that firms' officers sometimes behave not just unethically, but downright illegally (see Case Study 1-6).

CASE STUDY 1-5
Business Ethics at Boeing

For its program called "Questions of Integrity: The Boeing Ethics Challenge," the large Seattle-based aerospace company compiled a large number of ethical situations that employees might face. Supervisors present each situation and then ask employees to choose among four possible responses, after which the correct response is discussed. Following is an example regarding the proper use of the company's resources:

You are a manager, and one of your employees is selling Amway products to co-workers. The employee shows catalogs and takes orders during lunch. He also leaves an order form on a table in the break room and collects money and distributes products during lunch and after work. As the employee's manager, should you say anything about this?

A. No. Place your order.
B. No. The employee appears not to be disrupting the workplace.
C. Yes. Employees are not permitted to use company premises for outside business activities.
D. Yes. You should tell your employee that he may only continue the business on the premises with your approval and discuss with him the way the business is being conducted at the workplace.

Preferred answer: C

Rationale

A. As a manager, you should set a good example and stop this type of activity.
B. It could be difficult to restrict this activity to break and lunch periods. There is a possibility that it will escalate and disrupt the workday.
C. Sales for personal gain on company premises are strictly prohibited. The distributor is also taking advantage of a "captive audience."
D. Even a manager cannot authorize for-profit sales on company property. However, the manager can permit nonprofit activities, such as Girl Scout cookies or candies, as long as it doesn't interfere with work.

Despite its ethics program, a Boeing manager misused Lockheed documents to win a government contract and was fired in 2003, and in 2005 Boeing's chief executive, who had spearheaded the drive to restore the company's reputation after a series of ethics scandals, was himself ousted for having an office affair.

Source: "Charting a Course for Ethical Profits," *The New York Times* (February 8, 1998), sec. 3, p. 1; "The Ethics Policy: Mind Over Matter," *The New York Times* (July 16, 2000), sec. 3, p. 4; "Boeing Probe Gets to Grips with Ethics," *Financial Times* (August 25, 2003), p. 19; "Ethics: This Time Is Personal," *Financial Times* (March 24, 2005), p. 7; and "The New Ethics Enforcer," *Business Week* (February 13, 2006), pp. 76–77.

Better would be to change the structure or architecture of the corporation so as to foster ethical behavior. This might include rewarding the company's CEO more with stock options that tie rewards to the company's *long-run* profitability than with salary ties to current profits; requiring founders of the company to retain a large position in the stock of the company to ensure that their interests are consistent with those of new investors; rewarding production workers for both quality and quantity and not just for quantity; providing bonuses for the sales force for having satisfied customers and not just for maximizing sales; and rewarding rather than punishing employees exposing illegal behavior at the firm.

CASE STUDY 1-6
Enron–Andersen and Other Financial Disasters

Before its collapse at the end of 2001, Enron, the Houston-based energy-trading company, was the seventh largest corporation in the United States with revenues of nearly $140 billion. It was also the most admired of the online wonders at the height of the Internet euphoria. Then everything quickly unraveled and Enron became the largest bankruptcy (superseded by WorldCom's bankruptcy in July 2002) and one of the biggest business scandals in U.S. history. Although it owned some pipelines and power plants, what Enron really offered was a vision. It dazzled investors, analysts, and management gurus alike by creating trendy markets in everything and making money in trading in those markets. *Fortune* magazine voted Enron "the most innovative company of the year" in 2000 and *The Economist* wrote in June 2001, "Enron has created what may be the most successful Internet venture of any company in any industry anywhere." At its height in fall 2000, Enron stock sold for $400; by the end of 2001, it was worth practically nothing. How did it all happen?

Enron was so good at selling itself that it led to unrealistic expectations about its growth and profitability. In trying to live up to these unrealistic expectations, Enron started to falsify financial reports. It inflated earnings by using outside partnerships to monetize assets (and counting the proceeds as earnings) and to move its debt off its balance sheet. But deceit required growing falsification until it all became unsustainable. Enron was then forced to restate its earnings sharply downward, and this caused its stock to collapse. By giving its auditor's stamp of approval, and then quickly shredding the evidence once Enron's troubles began, Andersen, the huge consulting firm with worldwide offices, also collapsed. Enron was Andersen's second-largest client with consulting and auditing fees in excess of $52 million in the year 2000. This proves how inconsistent it is for the same accounting firm to provide consulting services to companies whose books it also audits.

The question then became how pervasive in the accounting profession was the type of Andersen's auditing failure at Enron. How objective can auditors be if they also provide consulting services to the same company? How many Enrons are out there? That question was answered during the spring and summer 2002 when many other fraudulent accounting practices were exposed at some leading U.S. companies such as WorldCom, Global Crossing, Tyco, and many others. The financial scandals greatly undermined the accounting profession's reputation for providing a true and fair view of a company's financial condition. Accounting, ordinarily a pillar of capitalism, was misused by Enron, WorldCom, Global Crossing, Tyco, Adelphia, Quest, and even Xerox to prop up profits and the frauds were often certified by accounting firms keen on retaining a large client.

The result was that Congress swiftly passed the **Sarbanes–Oxley Act** in July 2002 providing much tougher regulations on corporate governance and accounting oversight. Among other things, the new law prohibits accounting firms from providing consulting and some auditing services to the same client, it increased penalties for securities fraud and destroying evidence, and it requires CEOs and CFOs to certify the firm's financial reports. The importance of adopting stricter accounting standards can hardly be exaggerated. How else could investors properly evaluate their investment opportunities, regain confidence in the financial system, and decide in what company to invest? Scandals, however, continue on Main Street and Wall Street.

Source: "Lights Out: Enron's Failed Power Play," *Newsweek* (January 21, 2002), pp. 16–24; "The Biggest Casualty of Enron's Collapse: Confidence," *The New York Times* (February 10, 2002), sec. 4, p. 1; "Governance Bill Has Major Consequences for Many," *The Wall Street Journal* (July 2, 2002), p. A4; "Wall Street Banks to Pay $1.4 Billion in Historic Deal on Analyst Abuses," *The Financial Times* (December 21, 2002), p. 1; "Merk Hit as $2.5 bn Painkiller Withdrawn," *Financial Times* (October 1, 2004), p. 1; "Crackdown Puts Corporations, Executives in New Legal Peril," *The Wall Street Journal* (June 20, 2005), p. A1; and "Ebbers Is Sentenced to 25 Years for $11 Billion WorldCom Fraud," *The Wall Street Journal* (July 14, 2005), p. A1.

Many consumer groups would like corporations to go further and have a social conscience, using some of their resources to redress social ills, for example, by aiding the poor, promoting education, funding crime-prevention programs, reducing general environmental pollution, financing public projects, and so on. Some of these actions can directly benefit the bottom line of the firm. By helping local schools, for example, the firm gets better trained workers than otherwise (thus saving on its training expenses), or it can benefit the firm indirectly by establishing a reputation for the firm as a "good citizen" (thus attracting more customers and leading to more sales). Going beyond that, however, would impose an economic burden on the firm and represent, in a way, double taxation for the firm and its investors, and it would only reduce the value of the firm.[12]

1-6   THE INTERNATIONAL FRAMEWORK OF MANAGERIAL ECONOMICS

Many of the commodities we consume today are imported, and American firms purchase many inputs abroad and sell an increasing share of their products overseas. Even more important, domestic firms face increasing competition from foreign firms in the U.S. market and around the world. The international flow of capital, technology, and skilled labor has also reached unprecedented dimensions. In short, there is a rapid movement toward the globalization of production, consumption, and competition. Thus, it is essential to introduce a global dimension in the study of managerial economics to reflect these realities.

Specifically, as consumers, we purchase Japanese Toyotas and German Mercedes, Italian handbags and French perfumes, Hong Kong clothes and Taiwanese hand calculators, British scotch and Swiss chocolates, Canadian fish and Mexican tomatoes, Costa Rican bananas and Brazilian coffee. Often, we are not even aware that the products, or parts of them, are made abroad. For example, imported cloth is used in American-made suits, many American brand-name shoes are entirely manufactured abroad, and a great deal of the orange juice we drink is imported. American multinational corporations produce and import many parts and components from abroad and export an increasing share of their output.

For example, most of the parts and components of the IBM PC are manufactured abroad, and almost two-thirds of IBM's revenues and profits are now generated abroad. The competition faced by Boeing in commercial aircraft production is from European Airbus Industrie. General Motors and Ford face increasing competition from Toyota, Nissan, and DaimlerChrysler. U.S. steel companies almost collapsed during the 1980s as a result of increasing foreign competition and rising steel imports, and survived only after merging with foreign steel producers, mostly Japanese and French. Case Study 1-7 gives a sample of global corporations and the proportion of their sales outside the home country, as well as an overall index of their "transnationality."

---

[12] See "Curse of the Ethical Executive," *The Economist* (November 17, 2001), p. 70; "Make Your Value Mean Something," *Harvard Business Review* (July 2002), pp. 113–117; "The Good Company," *The Economist* (January 22, 2005), p. 11; and "Defining the Value of Doing Good Business," *Financial Times* (June 3, 2005), pp. 2–3.

CASE STUDY 1-7
The Rise of the Global Corporation

One of the most significant business and economic trends of the late twentieth century was the rise of global or *stateless* corporations. These are companies that have research and production facilities in many countries, are run by an international team of managers, and sell their products, finance their operation, and employ workers in many parts of the world. The trend toward global corporations is unmistakable and is accelerating. Going global has become an essential competitive strategy. Global corporations maintain a balance between functioning as a global organism and customizing products to local tastes. Both geographic and product managers report to top managers at the companies' headquarters, who reconcile differences. Companies that were

entirely domestic and merely exported some of their output as late as a decade ago are now finding that in order to remain competitive, they have to become global players. They need to be insiders in most major world markets rather than mere exporters. Even smaller companies are often finding it necessary to form joint ventures with foreign companies in order to expand abroad and remain competitive at home. Today a large number of corporations with headquarters in the United States, Europe, and Japan sell more of their products and earn more profits abroad than in the country where the corporations' headquarters are located. Table 1-1 shows a sample of such corporations with yearly sales in excess of $60 billion.

TABLE 1-1 Global Corporations in 2003

Company	Country	Total Sales (billions of dollars)	Foreign Sales (%)	Foreign Assets (%)	Foreign Employment (%)	Trans-nationality Index* (%)	Number of Foreign Affiliates	Internation-alization Index†
Vodafone Group	United Kingdom	$ 59.9	83.6	92.8	79.0	85.1	71	35.3
British Petroleum	United Kingdom	232.6	82.9	79.7	83.6	82.1	60	51.3
Total	France	118.1	80.2	88.4	55.0	74.1	419	69.6
Nestlé	Switzerland	65.3	67.8	56.7	97.8	74.1	471	94.0
Honda	Japan	70.4	77.0	68.3	70.7	72.0	102	76.7
Royal Dutch/Shell	UK/Netherlands	201.7	64.4	67.0	84.0	71.8	454	48.9
ExxonMobil	United States	237.1	70.4	67.0	60.9	66.1	218	74.2
Siemens AG	Germany	83.8	77.0	59.6	59.2	65.3	753	74.5
ChevronTexaco	United States	120.0	60.2	62.4	55.0	59.2	93	46.3
Sony	Japan	64.7	68.6	41.5	59.5	56.6	236	78.9
Volkswagen	Germany	98.4	72.4	38.5	47.9	52.9	203	71.7
IBM	United States	89.1	62.1	39.2	56.5	52.6	315	92.1
Hewlett Packard	United States	73.1	60.0	43.0	51.5	51.5	179	83.3
Carrefour SA	France	79.8	49.3	65.6	33.0	50.6	128	55.4

Source: United Nations, World Investment Report 2005 (New York: United Nations, 2005), pp. 267–269.

*Transnationality Index calculated as the average of the three ratios: foreign sales to total sales, foreign assets to total assets, and foreign employment to total employment.

†*Internationalization Index* calculated as the number of foreign affiliates divided by the number of all affiliates.

CASE STUDY 1-8
The Global Business Leader

Besides the traditional hard skills of accounting, marketing, and finance, the global business executive is a leader and a visionary rather than merely a manager. She has a global outlook and is knowledgeable about information systems and technology, she capitalizes on diversity and is a master of teamwork, she is creative and shows initiative, she is able to discern patterns and opportunities in apparent chaos and has the ability to synthesize information rather than just analyze it, and, above all, she is strong on interpersonal skills and is able to communicate effectively. In short, being smart and well trained in traditional business areas is no longer enough for the business leader of the twenty-first century.

Specifically, the global business leader must be cross-functional, or have the ability to combine disparate skills to solve problems. She must be a visionary and a leader; that is, she must combine hard work and a deep understanding of the business she is in with the ability to inspire others to also work hard to make the vision a reality. She must work effectively on teams, be accepted by others as the person with the best sense of the challenge confronting the group, and be able to break problems into manageable, status-free tasks that others are willing to focus on. She must have a deep understanding of global issues and the ethical aspects of her business decisions. She must be familiar with and be able to use information

technology and be comfortable with technology in general. She does not have to be a scientist, but she must understand in detail how the technology incorporated in the product or service that the firm sells works and avoid calling the experts every time she has to make a decision. She must have some experience with excellence—in whatever field—so as to recognize it and encourage it in others when she sees it.

Sounds impossible? Maybe it is, but those who come closer to this ideal will rise to the pinnacles of business leadership. Having an M.B.A. from a good school is important, but in today's world no one is automatically impressed. The global business leader must sell herself and, above all, must perform. Today's corporations have enormous expectations from their newly minted M.B.A.s, often expecting them to have talents and abilities that few chief executives possess. Most of the 700 or so business schools, from Harvard to the most modest, understand this and are reengineering the training of M.B.A.s to reflect the qualifications that the global business leader must possess for the new, competitive, dynamic world of the twenty-first century. The difficulty is that many of the newly required skills are hard to measure and teach in the classroom, and that is why many business schools are taking in students who already have some business and real-world experience.

Source: "Learning to Manage in Global Workplace," *The Wall Street Journal* (June 2, 1998), p. B1; V. Condivarajan and A. K. Gupta, "Building an Effective Global Business Team," *MIT Sloan Management Review* (Summer 2001), pp. 63–71; M. W. McCall and G. P. Hollenbeck, *Developing Global Executives* (Cambridge, Mass.: Harvard University Press, 2002). "Global-Trotters," *The Wall Street Journal* (May 31, 2005), p. B1; "Hired Guns of the Global Economy," *Fortune* (July 25, 2005), p. 208; and Glenn Rifkin, "Building Better Global Managers," *Harvard Management Update* (March 2006), pp. 1–4.

In view of such a **globalization of economic activity,** it would be unrealistic to study managerial economics in an international vacuum, as if U.S. firms did not face serious and increasing competition from foreign firms and as if foreign firms did not face competition from U.S. firms. This requires the training of a new type of global executive, who requires many new skills that are not easy to acquire (see Case Study 1-8). Case Study 1-9 provides a list of the world's most admired companies.

CASE STUDY 1-9
Global Most Admired Companies

Table 1-2 lists the 25 most admired companies in the world in 2005 prepared by *Fortune* magazine. To make the list, a company needs managers of genius, innovative products, financial stamina, global reach, and devotion to shareholders. The ranking was compiled from the answers of senior executives and outside directors in each industry, as well as from the answers of financial analysts whose job it is to eval-uate competitors in each industry. They were asked to rank each company on nine criteria: (1) overall management quality, (2) product or service quality, (3) innovativeness, (4) value as a long-term invest-ment, (5) financial strength, (6) responsibility to the community, (7) responsibility to the environment, (8) wise use of corporate assets, and (9) effectiveness in conducting business globally.

TABLE 1-2 Global Most Admired Companies in 2005

Rank	Company	Country	Industry
1	General Electric	United States	Electronics
2	Wal-Mart Stores	United States	General merchandisers
3	Dell	United States	Computers
4	Microsoft	United States	Computers
5	Toyota Motor	Japan	Motor vehicles
6	Procter & Gamble	United States	Household and personal products
7	Johnson & Johnson	United States	Pharmaceuticals
8	FedEx	United States	Delivery
9	IBM	United States	Computers
10	Berkshire Hathaway	United States	Insurance: P & C
11	BMW	Germany	Motor vehicles
12	Intel	United States	Semiconductors
13	United Parcel Service	United States	Delivery
14	Home Depot	United States	Specialty retailers
15	Sony	Japan	Electronics
16	PepsiCo	United States	Consumer food products
17	Pfizer	United States	Pharmaceuticals
18	Citigroup	United States	Megabanks
19	Honda Motors	Japan	Motor vehicles
20	Coca-Cola	United States	Beverages
21	Target	United States	General merchandisers
22	British Petroleum	Britain	Petroleum refining
23	Nestlé	Switzerland	Consumer food products
24*	Costco Wholesale	United States	Specialty retailers
25*	Walgreen	United States	Food and drug stores

Source: http://www.fortune.com/lists/globaladmired/index.html.

*A tie.

CASE STUDY 1-10
Globalization and Terrorism

The September 11, 2001, terrorist attacks in New York City and Washington, DC, sharply reduced domestic and international air travel, as well as international trade and financial transactions, in the weeks and months following the attacks. Even though some degree of normality had returned by the spring of 2002, the danger and fear of other terrorist attacks in the United States and abroad has had some lasting effects. Surveillance of offices, schools, and public places, such as stadiums and theme parks, has increased in the United States as never before during peacetime. The energy, transportation, and telecommunications systems as well as the nation's municipal water supplies are now much more closely guarded. Air travelers routinely can expect to be scanned from head to toe at airports. Metal detectors and inspections of bags are now routine in order to access many public places.

Terrorism and the fear of terrorism have not reversed the trend toward globalization in the world economy, however. It only slowed it down by making all sorts of transactions more costly and time consuming. It is clear that the cost of all sorts of international transactions (from tourism, international trade, and international financial transactions) has increased in order to pay for the added security, and insurance costs have skyrocketed. Furthermore, some investments that before September 11 flowed into directly productive activities are being diverted and spent on security. The effect of this is like the impo-

sition of a tariff, of say 10 percent, or other obstruction to the flow of international trade and investments. Globalization is simply here to stay. The reason is that economic efficiency requires it and technological advances make it inevitable. There is simply no alternative model.

Of course, globalization does have its costs or negative effects. For example, it can lead to contagion, whereby a financial and economic crisis in one nation or region of the world can spread and cause havoc in other nations and regions, which until a decade ago were to a large extent shielded by their geographical distance. And globalization did not increase international inequalities (as many antiglobal demonstrators assert). The World Bank has presented clear and undeniable evidence showing that the number of poor people in the world (those that live on less than $1 or $2 per day) has been greatly reduced by globalization. Globalization did not create poverty; without globalization, world poverty would be greater. No one forced Communist China to open to the world, but without such an opening China would not have obtained all the capital, technology, and markets that allowed it to grow very rapidly during the past 10 years. In any event, we are here not interested in analyzing the benefits and costs (and there are costs) of globalization, but only to point out that globalization is here to stay and inevitable, and so it is crucial to analyze its effects on the operation and management of modern firms throughout the world.

Source: "How September 11 Changed America," *The New York Times* (March 8, 2002), p. 31; "Global Companies Face up to a New Risk from Terrorism," *Global Finance* (May 2002), p. 8; "New Study Puts Sept. 11 Payout at $38 Billion," *The New York Times* (September 11, 2004), p. 1; "Airline Passenger Traffic in 2005 Likely to Hit Pre-September 11 Level," *The Wall Street Journal* (March 8, 2005), p. A2; and D. Salvatore, "Growth and Poverty in a Globalizing World," *Journal of Policy Modeling* (June 2004), pp. 543–551.

This text will explicitly introduce and integrate this essential global dimension into the study of managerial decision making and will examine the new skills required of the future business leader. All the topics examined in traditional managerial economics are covered, but the focus is broadened to reflect the globalization of most economic activities and the management revolution taking place in the world today. Terrorism only slowed down, but did not reverse, the trend toward globalization (see Case Study 1-10).

1-7   MANAGERIAL ECONOMICS AND THE INTERNET

The **Internet,** or simply the *Net,* is a collection of nearly 1 billion computers throughout the world linked together in a service called the World Wide Web (WWW). In 2006, more than 200 million individuals in the United States and nearly 1 billion people scattered throughout the world were connected through the WWW, with hundreds of thousands joining every week. In short, the entire world is rapidly becoming a unified **information superhighway** though the Internet.[13] This means that individuals, researchers, firms, and consumers can hook up with libraries, databases, and marketing information and have at their fingertips a vast amount of information as never before. Information technology is being applied to fields as diverse as science, manufacturing, finance, and marketing, and it is revolutionizing the way business is conducted. An individual can use the Internet to send electronic mail (e-mail) and examine thousands of multimedia documents from anywhere in the world, browse through a firm's catalog, and be able (in an increasing number of cases) to click on a "buy" button and fill in an electronic order form, including shipping and credit-card information. (Electronic commerce, or e-commerce, will be examined in detail in Section 3-7 and Case Study 3-10.) The Internet has been around since the 1960s, but only during the past decade has its use been greatly simplified, leading to massive growth.

The Internet is a good place to start the search for information on managerial economics. For example, you can find information on macroeconomic trends in inflation, growth, and unemployment, as well as microeconomic information in specific sectors, industries, and companies. A number of comprehensive as well as specific directories or indexes of economic information are available on the Internet. Each of these will have a particular Internet address classification, known as the "top-level domain name," which appears as the last item in an address. These classifications are ".com" for commercial, ".edu" for educational, ".gov" for government, ".net" for Internet service provider, and ".org" for nonprofit organization. You can often guess an Internet site address by simply using the name of the organization and its domain name, preceded by "http://www," which stands for "hypertext transport protocol: World Wide Web." For example, the site for the Microsoft Corporation is http://www.microsoft.com. For McDonald's, it is http://www.mcdonalds.com. Case Study 1-11 provides the most important Internet site addresses for economic information. Of course, there are many other sites that may interest you (i.e., the list is far from exhaustive).

---

[13] "An Information Superhighway," Business Week (February 1991), p. 28; "The Internet," Business Week (November 14, 1994), pp. 80–88; "Putting the Internet in Perspective," *The Wall Street Journal* (April 16, 1998), p. B12; "Business and the Internet," *The Economist* (June 26, 1999), pp. 1–40; "Reshaping the Global Landscape of IT," *Financial Times* (February 2, 2000), p. 1; and www.computerindustryalmanac.com.

CASE STUDY 1-11
The Most Important Internet Site Addresses for Managerial Economics

General directory and index of economic information:

Yahoo!-Economics: http://dir.yahoo.com/
Social_Science/Economics/

U.S. economic data, indicators, and statistics:

Bureau of Economic Analysis:
http://www.bea.doc.gov/
Bureau of Labor Statistics:
http://www.stats.bls.gov/
Census Bureau: http://www.census.gov/
Department of Commerce:
http://www.commerce.gov/
Department of the Treasury:
http://www.ustreas.gov/
Economic Indicators Monthly:
http://www.access.gpo.gov/index.html

Economic analysis and forecasts:

Citicorp Market Information:
http://www.web.da-us.citibank.com/us/
Index.html
J.P. Morgan: http://www.adr.com

Financial data and financial market information:

Board of Governors, Federal Reserve
System:
http://www.federalreserve.gov/rnd.html
Federal Reserve:
http://www.research.stlouisfed.org/fred2

Yahoo! Finance:http://finance.yahoo.com
U.S. stock markets: http://www.money.cnn.
com/markets/us_markets.html
World stock market indexes: http://www.money.
cnn.com/markets/world_markets.html
Currency exchange rates: http://www.money.
cnn.com/markets/currencies.html

International economic data, indicators, and statistics:

International Monetary Fund: http://www.imf.org
Organisation for Economic Cooperation and
Development: http://www.oecd.org
World Bank: http://www.worldbank.org
World Trade Organization: http://www.wto.org

Current national and international business news:

Bloomberg Business News:
http://www.bloomberg.com/
Financial Times: http://www.news.ft.com/home/us
The Wall Street Journal interactive edition:
http://online.wsj.com/public/us
Business Week: http://www.businessweek.com/
Forbes: http://www.forbes.com/
Fortune: http://www.fortune.com
The Economist: http://www.economist.com/

Additional Internet site addresses are listed at the end
of each chapter.

SUMMARY

1. *Managerial economics* refers to the application of economic theory (microeconomics and macroeconomics) and the tools of analysis of decision science (mathematical economics and econometrics) to examine how an organization can achieve its aims or objectives most efficiently. The functional areas of business administration studies (accounting, finance, marketing, human resources, and production) provide the environmental background for managerial decision making.

2. The five steps in the *decision-making process* are: (1) define the problem, (2) determine the objective, (3) identify possible solutions, (4) select the best possible solution, and (5) implement the decision.

3. Firms exist because the economies that they generate in production and distribution confer great benefits to entrepreneurs, workers, and other resource owners. The *theory of the firm* postulates that the primary goal or objective of the firm is to maximize wealth or the value of the firm. This is given by the present value of the expected future profits of the firm. Since the firm usually faces many resource, legal, and other constraints, we speak of *constrained optimization.* Alternative theories of the firm postulate other objectives for the firm, but profit or value maximization predicts the behavior of the firm more accurately than do any of its alternatives.

4. *Business profit* refers to the revenue of the firm minus its explicit costs. The latter are the actual out-of-pocket expenditures of the firm. Economic profit equals the revenue of the firm minus its explicit and implicit costs. The latter refer to the value of the inputs owned and used by the firm in its own production processes. Economic profit can result from one or a combination of the following: risk bearing, frictional disturbances, monopoly power, the introduction of innovations, or managerial efficiency. Profits provide the signal for the efficient allocation of society's resources.

5. *Business ethics* seeks to proscribe behavior that businesses, firm managers, and workers should not engage in. Business and management ethics goes beyond the law to provide guidelines as to what is acceptable behavior in business transactions. Being based on values, however, it is often not clear what ethical behavior is and is not, since different people may have different values. Most large corporations and professional associations have ethics codes and ethics officers.

6. Many of the commodities we consume are imported, and American firms purchase many inputs abroad, sell an increasing share of their output to other nations, and face increasing competition from foreign firms operating in the United States. Furthermore, the international flow of capital, technology, and skilled labor has reached unprecedented dimensions. In view of such a globalization of economic activity, it is essential to introduce a global dimension into the study of managerial economics.

7. A good place to start the search for information on any topic, including managerial economics, is the Internet. This is a collection of more than 100,000 computers to which more than 200 million people scattered throughout the world are connected in a sort of information superhighway. There you can find information on macroeconomic trends in inflation, growth, unemployment, and many other topics, as well as microeconomic information on specific sectors, industries, and companies.

DISCUSSION QUESTIONS

1. What is the relationship between the fields of managerial economics and (*a*) Microeconomics and macroeconomics? (*b*) Mathematical economics and econometrics? (*c*) Accounting, finance, marketing, personnel, and production?

2. Managerial economics is often said to help the business student integrate the knowledge gained in other courses. How is this integration accomplished?

3. What is the methodology of science in general and of managerial economics in particular?

4. What might be the objective of a museum? Of a firm? What are the basic steps in all types of decision-making processes?

5. Why do firms exist? Who benefits from their existence?

6. How does the theory of the firm differ from short-term profit maximization? Why is the former superior to the latter?

7. How does the theory of the firm provide an integrated framework for the analysis of managerial decision making across the functional areas of business?

8. What effect would each of the following have on the value of the firm? (*a*) A new advertising campaign increases the sales of the firm substantially. (*b*) A new competitor enters the market. (*c*) The production department achieves a

technological breakthrough that reduces production costs. (*d*) The firm is required to install pollution-control equipment. (*e*) The workforce votes to unionize. (*f*) The rate of interest rises. (*g*) The rate of inflation changes.

9. How is the concept of a normal return on investment related to the distinction between business and economic profit?

10. What factors should be considered in determining whether profit levels are excessive in a particular industry?

11. What is the difference between unethical and unlawful behavior? What does an ethics officer do?

12. Why does the government regulate telephone and electric power companies if the profit motive serves such an important function in the operation of a free-enterprise system?

13. Why is it crucial to introduce an international dimension into managerial economics?

14. How does the danger and fear of terrorism affect managerial decisions?

15. What is the use of the Internet in managerial economics?

PROBLEMS

1. Find the present value of $100 due in one year if the discount rate is 5 percent, 8 percent, 10 percent, 15 percent, 20 percent, and 25 percent.

2. Find the present value of $100 due in *two* years if the discount rate is 5 percent, 8 percent, 10 percent, 15 percent, 20 percent, and 25 percent.

*3. The owner of a firm expects to make a profit of $100 for each of the next two years and to be able to sell the firm at the end of the second year for $800. The owner of the firm believes that the appropriate discount rate for the firm is 15 percent. Calculate the value of the firm.

4. A firm is contemplating an advertising campaign that promises to yield $120 one year from now for $100 spent now. Explain why the firm should or should not undertake the advertising campaign.

*5. Determine which of two investment projects a manager should choose if the discount rate of the firm is 10 percent. The first project promises a profit of $100,000 in each of the next four years, while the second project promises a profit of $75,000 in each of the next six years.

6. Determine which of the two investment projects of Problem 5 the manager should choose if the discount rate of the firm is 20 percent.

7. Explain the effect that the timing in the receipt of the profits from project 1 and project 2 in Problems 5 and 6 has on the present value of the two investment projects.

*8. The cost of attending a private college for one year is $6,000 for tuition, $2,000 for the room, $1,500 for meals, and $500 for books and supplies. The student could also have earned $15,000 by getting a job instead of going to college and 10 percent interest on expenses he or she incurs at the beginning of the year. Calculate the explicit, implicit, and total economic costs of attending college.

9. A woman managing a photocopying establishment for $25,000 per year decides to open her own duplicating place. Her revenue during the first year of operation is $120,000, and her expenses are as follows:

Salaries to hired help	$45,000
Supplies	15,000
Rent	10,000
Utilities	1,000
Interest on bank loan	10,000

Calculate (*a*) the explicit costs, (*b*) the implicit costs, (*c*) the business profit, (*d*) the economic profit, and (*e*) the normal return on investment in this business.

---

* = answer provided in Appendix D at the end of the book.

10. According to Milton Friedman, "Business has only one social responsibility—to make profits (as long as it stays within the legal and moral rules of the game established by society). Few trends could so thoroughly undermine the very foundations of our society as the acceptance by corporate officials of a social responsibility other than to make as much money for their stockholders as possible." Explain why you agree or disagree with such a statement.

11. Apply the decision-making model developed in this chapter to your decision to attend college.

12. Explain why computer companies remain in the industry even though profits in the industry have been declining over the years.

13. Using the Internet site address: http://www.fortune.com/companies, find the global 20 most admired companies for 2006 and 2007. How many of the companies are American?

*14. From the *Financial Times* newspaper website, identify the world's 20 best M.B.A. programs. How many schools are American?

15. **Integrating Problem**
    Samantha Roberts has a job as a pharmacist earning $30,000 per year, and she is deciding whether to take another job as the manager of another pharmacy for $40,000 per year or to purchase a pharmacy that generates a revenue of $200,000 per year. To purchase the pharmacy, Samantha would have to use her $20,000 savings and borrow another $80,000 at an interest rate of 10 percent per year. The pharmacy that Samantha is contemplating purchasing has additional expenses of $80,000 for supplies, $40,000 for hired help, $10,000 for rent, and $5,000 for utilities. Assume that income and business taxes are zero and that the repayment of the principal of the loan does not start before three years.
    (*a*) What would be the business and economic profit if Samantha purchased the pharmacy? Should Samantha purchase the pharmacy?
    (*b*) Suppose that Samantha expects that another pharmacy will open nearby at the end of three years and that this will drive the economic profit of the pharmacy to zero. What would the revenue of the pharmacy be in three years? (*c*) What theory of profit would account for profits being earned by the pharmacy during the first three years of the operation? (*d*) Suppose that Samantha expects to sell the pharmacy at the end of three years for $50,000 more than the price she paid for it and that she requires a 15 percent return on her investment. Should she still purchase the pharmacy?

APPENDIX TO CHAPTER 1: THE BASICS OF DEMAND, SUPPLY, AND EQUILIBRIUM

In this appendix, we present an overview of the functioning of markets. We begin by reviewing the concepts of market demand and market supply curves and then show how the equilibrium price is determined at their intersection. Afterward, we examine the effect on the equilibrium price resulting from a change in demand and/or supply. This appendix may be skipped by students who remember all of this from their principles of economics course.

The Demand Side of the Market

Every market has a demand side and a supply side. The demand side can be represented by a *market demand curve,* which shows the amount of the commodity buyers would like to purchase at different prices. For example, the market demand curve for aluminum in Figure 1-3 shows that 4 million pounds of aluminum would be demanded annually at the price of $1.50 per pound (point *A*), 6 million pounds would be demanded at the price of $1.00 per pound (point *E*), and 8 million pounds would be demanded at the price of $0.50 per pound (point *B*). Note that more aluminum would be demanded annually at lower prices; that is, the demand curve for aluminum slopes downward to the right. This is

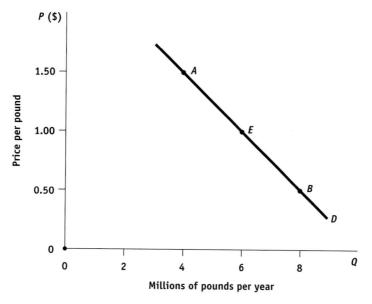

FIGURE 1-3   The Market Demand Curve for Aluminum   The market demand curve for aluminum shows that at lower aluminum prices, buyers would purchase more aluminum.

true for practically all commodities and is referred to as the *law of demand.* Demand curves are drawn on the assumption that buyers' tastes, buyers' incomes, the number of consumers in the market, and the price of related commodities (substitutes and complements) are unchanged. Changes in any of these factors will cause a demand curve to shift. For example, if consumers' tastes for aluminum products or consumers' incomes increase, the entire demand curve for aluminum shifts to the right, indicating that buyers will purchase more aluminum at each price annually. More will be said on market demand in Chapter 3.

The Supply Side of the Market

The supply side of a market can be represented by the *market supply curve.* This shows the amount of a commodity that sellers would offer for sale at various prices. For example, the market supply curve for aluminum in Figure 1-4 shows that 2 million pounds of aluminum would be offered for sale annually at the price of $0.50 per pound (point *C*), 6 million pounds would be offered at the price of $1.00 per pound (point *E*), and 10 million pounds at the price of $1.50 (point *F*). Note that a higher aluminum price will induce sellers to sell more (i.e., the supply curve of aluminum slopes upward to the right). This is usually true for most products. Supply curves are drawn on the assumption of constant technology and input or resource (labor, capital, and land) prices. An improvement in technology and/or a reduction in input prices would make it possible to produce a commodity, such as aluminum, at a lower cost and cause the entire supply curve of aluminum to shift to the right, indicating that sellers would be willing to sell more aluminum annually at each price. On the other hand, an increase in resource prices would cause the supply curve to shift to the left. More will be said on production, costs, and supply in Chapters 6–8.

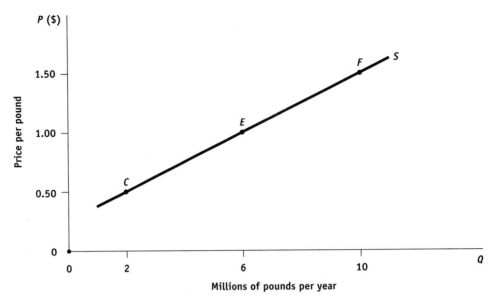

FIGURE 1-4   The Market Supply Curve for Aluminum   The market supply curve for aluminum shows that at higher aluminum prices, sellers would sell more aluminum.

The Equilibrium Price

The *equilibrium price* of a commodity is determined at the intersection of the market de-mand curve and the market supply curve of the commodity. For example, in Figure 1-5 the equilibrium price of aluminum is $1.00 per pound and is given at point *E,* where the market demand curve for alu-minum (from Figure 1-3) and the market supply curve (from Figure 1-4) intersect. At the price of $1.50, the quantity supplied of aluminum exceeds the quantity demanded, and the resulting *excess supply or surplus* (*AF* = 6 million pounds) induces sellers to lower their price to get rid of unwanted aluminum inventories. On the other hand, at the price of $0.50 per pound, the quantity demanded of aluminum ex-ceeds the quantity supplied, and the resulting *excess demand or shortage* (*CB* = 6 million pounds) al-lows sellers to increase their price. Only at the price of $1.00 per pound does the quantity demanded of aluminum match the quantity supplied and there is no tendency for the price to change. Thus, the equi-librium price of aluminum is $1.00 per pound. This is the price that would persist in time as long as the demand and/or the supply curves of aluminum do not change (shift). At a particular point in time, the actual or observed market price may or may not be the equilibrium price. We know, however, that mar-ket forces always push the market price toward the equilibrium level. This may occur rapidly or slowly. Before a market price reaches a particular equilibrium level, the demand curve and/or the supply curve may shift, defining a new equilibrium price.

Shift in the Demand Curve and Equilibrium

If the demand curve for a commodity increases or shifts to the right as a result, for example, of growth in the economy, the equilibrium price will rise. For example, Figure 1-6 shows that an increase in the demand curve for aluminum from *D* to *D′* results in an excess demand of

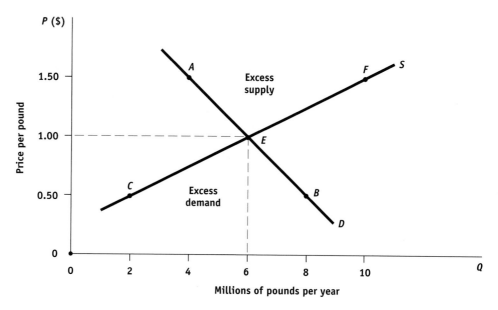

FIGURE 1-5   The Equilibrium Price for Aluminum   The equilibrium price of aluminum is $1.00 per pound and is given at the intersection of the market demand and the market supply curve of aluminum.

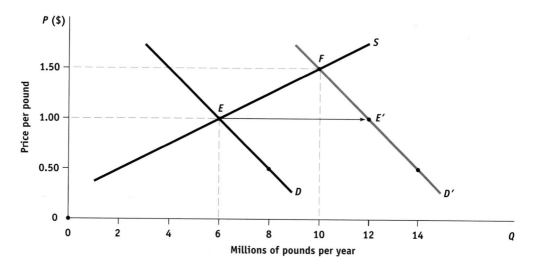

FIGURE 1-6   The Effect of a Rightward Shift of the Demand Curve for Aluminum   A rightward shift in the demand curve of aluminum results in an increase in the equilibrium price of aluminum.

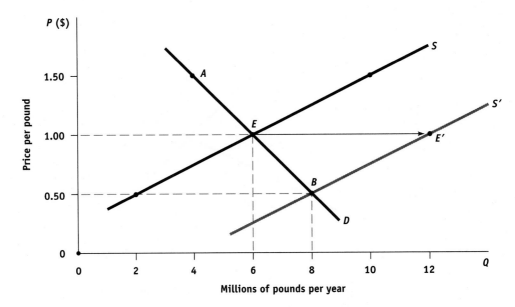

FIGURE 1-7   The Effect of a Rightward Shift of the Supply Curve for Aluminum   A rightward shift in the supply curve of aluminum results in a reduction in the equilibrium price of aluminum.

aluminum of $EE' = 6$ million pounds per year at the original equilibrium price of $1.00 per pound. As a result, the equilibrium price of aluminum rises from $1.00 to $1.50 per pound and is determined at the intersection of D' and S at point F. The opposite occurs for a reduction in demand.

Shift in the Supply Curve and Equilibrium

If the supply curve of a commodity increases or shifts to the right as a result, for example, of an improvement in technology or a reduction in resource prices, the equilibrium price will fall. For example, Figure 1-7 shows that an increase in the supply curve of aluminum from S to S' results in an excess supply of aluminum of $EE' = 6$ million pounds per year at the original equilibrium price of $1.00 per pound. As a result, the equilibrium price of aluminum falls from $1.00 to $0.50 per pound and is determined at the intersection of D and S' at point B. The opposite occurs for a reduction in supply. If both the demand and the supply the curves of aluminum shift to the right to D' and S', respectively, the equilibrium price of aluminum will remain at $1.00 per pound, but the equilibrium quantity increases from 6 million pounds to 12 million pounds. (You should be able to sketch this on Figure 1-7.) Case Study 1-12 examines changes in demand and supply and their effect on the price of PCs, while Case Study 1-13 does the same for coffee prices.

CASE STUDY 1-12
Changes in Demand and Supply and the Price of PCs

From 1986 to 2006, the demand for personal computers (PCs) increased sharply in the United States, but the supply increased much more. As a result, the price of PCs adjusted for inflation and quality changes fell sharply in the United States. This can be visualized with Figure 1-8, where D and S are the U.S. demand and supply curves of PCs, respectively, in 1986, and D' and S' are the U.S. demand and supply curves of PCs in 2006. D and S intersect at point E in Figure 1-8 and give the equilibrium price of P_E in the United States in 1986, while D' and S' intersect at point E' and give the much lower equilibrium price of P'_E in 2006. We can expect the trend toward more computing power at lower prices to continue and even accelerate in the future.

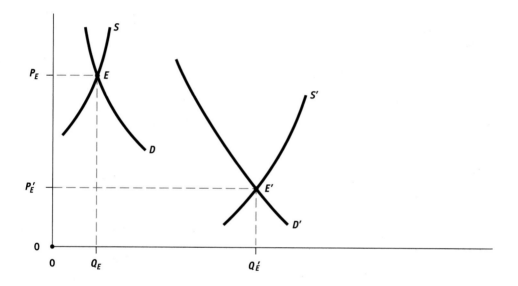

FIGURE 1-8   Shifts in Demand and Supply and the Price of PCs   With D and S, the equilibrium price of PCs in the United States is P_E in 1986. With D' and S', the equilibrium price of PCs in the United States is P'_E in 2006.

Source: "The Big Squeeze in the PC Market," *Business Week* (September 20, 1999), p. 40; "Personal Computers: Are the Glory Days Over?" *Business Week* (February 14, 2000), p. 50; "As PC Industry Slumps, IBM Hands Off Manufacturing of Desktops," *The New York Times* (January 9, 2002), p. B1; and "I.B.M. Division Headed to China Has Made No Profit in 3½ Years," *The New York Times* (December 31, 2004), p. C4.

CASE STUDY 1-13
Changes in Demand and Supply and Coffee Prices

Changes in demand and supply of coffee explain why world wholesale coffee prices fell by nearly one-half from 1998 to 2004, reaching their lowest level in three decades. The sharp decline in coffee prices threw millions of small coffee farmers and their families in coffee-producing developing countries into extreme poverty, while multinational food companies (such as Nestlé) and coffee shops (such as Starbucks) posted very high profits from coffee sales.

The problem in the coffee market arose from the fact that the supply of coffee increased faster than its demand, causing coffee prices to fall. Since coffee prices fell faster than quantities increased, the earnings of coffee farmers also declined. From 1998 to 2004, the supply of coffee increased at twice the rate of the increase in demand as a result of new countries (such as Viet Nam) starting to produce and export coffee on a large scale and others (such as Indonesia and Brazil) increasing exports sharply. This caused

the price of coffee that growers received to fall from $1.40 per pound in 1998 to as low as $0.48 in June 2002, which is lower than the production costs of many poor small farmers. As more efficient larger farmers increased their production to make up for the reduction in price, the market supply curve for coffee shifted even more to the right, causing coffee prices to fall even lower from 2002 to 2004.

A plan drawn up in May 2000 by the 28-member Association of Coffee Producing Countries (ACPC) sponsored by Brazil and Colombia (the world's largest and third largest coffee exporters, respectively) failed to reduce coffee exports and stabilize prices. But then bad weather in coffee-producing nations came to the rescue of coffee producers. This reduced the supply of coffee on the world market so much that, in the face of demand also rising, it led to coffee prices rising to $1.20 in May 2005.

Source: "Drowning in Cheap Coffee," *The Economist* (September 29, 2001), pp. 43–44; "Crisis Call to Coffee Growers," *Financial Times* (April 16, 2002), p. 23; and "Coffee Reaches Five-Year Highs on Signs of Smaller Brazil Crop," *The Wall Street Journal* (February 24, 2005), p. 4.

APPENDIX PROBLEMS

1. Draw a figure similar to Figure 1-5. Show on it the change in the equilibrium price of aluminum resulting from a parallel leftward shift in the market demand curve for aluminum of 4 million pounds.

2. Draw a figure similar to Figure 1-5. Show on it the change in the equilibrium price of aluminum resulting from a parallel leftward shift in the market supply curve for aluminum of 3 million pounds.

3. Draw a figure similar to Figure 1-5. Show on it the change in the equilibrium price of aluminum resulting from a shift in the market demand curve of aluminum from D to D' (as in Figure 1-6) and in the market supply curve of aluminum from S to S' (as in Figure 1-7).

SUPPLEMENTARY READINGS

For a general description of the scope of managerial economics and its relationship to other fields of study, see:

Bazerman, M., *Judgment in Managerial Decision Making* (New York: Wiley, 1997), chap. 1 and 9.

A discussion of the theories of the firm is found in:

Bolton, Patrick, and David F. Scharfstein, "Corporate Finance, the Theory of the Firm, and Organizations," *Journal of Economic Perspectives,* vol. 12 (Fall 1998), pp. 95–114.

Holstrom, Bent, and John Roberts, "The Boundaries of the Firm Revisited," *Journal of Economic Perspectives,* vol. 12 (Fall 1998), pp. 73–94.

Lamoreaux, Naomi R., "Partnerships, Corporations and the Theory of the Firm," *American Economic Review,* vol. 88 (May 1988), pp. 66–71.

Rajan, R., and L. Zingales, "The Firm as a Dedicated Hierarchy: A Theory of the Origins and Growth of Firms," *Quarterly Journal of Economics* (August 2001), pp. 805–851.

On the theories of profit, see:

Solomon, David, "Economic and Accounting Concepts of Income," *The Accounting Review,* vol. 36 (July 1961).

Wong, Robert E., "Profit Maximization and Alternative Theories: A Dynamic Reconciliation," *American Economic Review,* vol. 65 (September 1975).

Business ethics is discussed in:

Arce, M. D., "Conspicuous by Its Absence: Ethics and Managerial Economics," *Journal of Business Ethics,* no. 54 (2004), pp. 261–277.

Badaracco, J. L., *Leading Quietly: An Unorthodox Guide to Doing the Right Thing* (Boston, Mass.: Harvard Business School Press, 2002).

Donaldson, Thomas, "Defining the Value of Doing Good Business," in *Mastering Corporate Governance, Financial Times* (June 3, 2005), pp. 2–3.

McWilliams, A., and D. Siegel, "Corporate Social Responsibility: A Theory of the Firm's Perspective," *Academy of Management Review* (January 2001), pp. 117–127.

For the globalization of managerial decision making and qualification for the future business leader, see:

Barlett, Christopher A., and Samantra Ghoshal, *Managing Across Borders* (Boston, Mass.: Harvard Business School Press, 1998).

Karahan, R. S., " Toward an Eclectic Theory of Firm Globalization," *International Journal of Management* (January 2001), pp. 523–532.

Kuemmerle, Walter, "The Entrepreneur's Path to Global Expansion," *MIT Sloan Management Review* (Winter 2005), pp. 42–49.

Salvatore, Dominick, *Introduction to International Economics* (Hoboken, N.J.: Wiley, 2005), chap. 1.

Trompenaars, Fons, *Did the Pedestrian Die?* (London: Capstone, 2003).

INTERNET SITE ADDRESSES

For the list of the Fortune 500, the Global 500, and America's Most Admired companies, see:

http://www.fortune.com/companies

For the ranking of the Fortune 500 companies' key industries by revenues, profits, assets, shareholder equity, and return to investors, or any combination of these factors, see:

http://www.fortune.com/lists/f500/index.html

For a comprehensive Website about economics, firms, markets, government regulation, and much more, see:

http://www.economics.about.com/money/economics

For general information, data, and trends about the Internet, see:

http://www.InternetIndicators.com
http://www.forrester.com

CHAPTER 2

Optimization Techniques and New Management Tools

CHAPTER OUTLINE

KEY TERMS (in the order of their appearance)

Marginal cost	Reengineering	Pricing power
Marginal revenue	Learning organization	Process management
Marginal analysis	Broadbanding	Small-world model
Constrained optimization	Direct business model	Strategic development
Benchmarking	Networking	Virtual integration
Total quality management (TQM)	Performance management	Virtual management

I n Chapter 1, we defined *managerial economics* as the application of economic theory and the tools of decision science to examine how an organization can achieve its aims and objectives most efficiently. In the case of a business firm, the objective is usually to maximize profits or the value of the firm or to minimize costs, subject to some constraints. Accordingly, in this chapter we present optimization techniques, or methods for maximizing or minimizing the objective function of a firm or other organization. These techniques are very important and will be used frequently in the rest of the text. In this chapter we also describe many of the new management tools that have been introduced during the past two decades and examine how they are revolutionizing the way firms are managed.

The first step in presenting optimization techniques is to examine ways to express economic relationships. This is done in Section 2-1. In Section 2-2, we examine the relationship between total, average, and marginal concepts and measures, such as revenue, product, cost, or profit. Section 2-3 examines the process of unconstrained optimization and Section 2-4 the process of constrained optimization by the firm. Section 2-5 then discusses many of the new management tools that are revolutionizing the way firms are managed, Section 2-6 presents some other management tools or ideas for optimization, while Section 2-7 examines their relationship to the traditional functional areas of managerial economics.

The Chapter Appendix reviews differential calculus and shows how it is used for optimization. We discuss the concept of the derivative, the rules of differentiation, and apply the rules of differential calculus to find the optimal solution to unconstrained and constrained optimization problems. The Appendix can be omitted for courses in which calculus is not used. In the rest of the text, more advanced material utilizing calculus is presented only in footnotes and appendices.

At the end of the chapter, there is an extensive integrating real-world case study, which illustrates, integrates, and shows the relationship among the various concepts presented in this chapter and in Chapter 1.

2-1   METHODS OF EXPRESSING ECONOMIC RELATIONSHIPS

Economic relationships can be expressed in the form of equations, tables, or graphs. When the relationship is simple, a table and/or graph may be sufficient. When the relationship is complex, however, expressing the relationship in equational form may be necessary.

TABLE 2-1	The Total-Revenue Schedule of the Firm	
Q	$100Q - 10Q^2$	TR
0	$100(0) - 10(0)^2$	$ 0
1	$100(1) - 10(1)^2$	90
2	$100(2) - 10(2)^2$	160
3	$100(3) - 10(3)^2$	210
4	$100(4) - 10(4)^2$	240
5	$100(5) - 10(5)^2$	250
6	$100(6) - 10(6)^2$	240

For example, suppose that the relationship between the total revenue (TR) of a firm and the quantity (Q) of the good or service that the firm sells over a given period of time, say, one year, is given by

$$TR = 100Q - 10Q^2 \qquad\qquad [2\text{-}1]$$

By substituting into Equation 2-1 various hypothetical values for the quantity sold, we generate the total-revenue schedule of the firm, shown in Table 2-1.

Plotting the TR schedule of Table 2-1, we get the TR curve in Figure 2-1. Note that the TR curve in Figure 2-1 rises up to $Q = 5$ and declines thereafter. Thus, we see that the

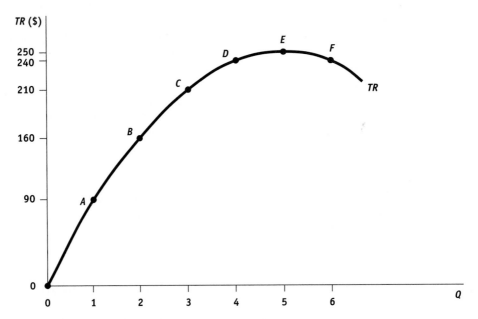

FIGURE 2-1   The Total Revenue Curve of a Firm   The total-revenue curve shows the total revenue (TR) of the firm at each quantity sold (Q). It is obtained by plotting the total-revenue schedule of Table 2-1. Note that TR rises to $Q = 5$ and declines thereafter.

relationship between the total revenue of the firm and its sales volume can be expressed in equational, tabular, or graphical form.

2-2   TOTAL, AVERAGE, AND MARGINAL RELATIONSHIPS

The relationship between total, average, and marginal concepts and measures is crucial in optimization analysis. This relationship is basically the same whether we deal with revenue, product, cost, or profit. In what follows, we examine the relationship between total cost, average cost, and marginal cost. This, together with the revenue concepts examined in the previous section, will be utilized in the next section to show how a firm maximizes profits (a most important example of optimizing behavior on the part of the firm).[1] In the following section, we examine the relationship between total, average, and marginal cost, and then we show how average- and marginal-cost curves are derived geometrically from the total-cost curve.

Total, Average, and Marginal Cost

The first two columns of Table 2-2 present a hypothetical total-cost schedule of a firm, from which the average- and marginal-cost schedules are derived (columns 3 and 4 of the table). Note that the total cost (TC) of the firm is $20 when output ($Q$) is zero and rises as the output increases.[2] Average cost (AC) equals total cost divided by output. That is, $AC = TC/Q$. Thus, at $Q = 1$, $AC = TC/1 = \$140/1 = \$140$. At $Q = 2$, $AC = TC/2 = \$160/2 = \$80$, and so on (see the third column of Table 2-2). Note that AC first falls and then rises. Marginal cost (MC), on the other hand, equals the change in total cost per unit change in output. That is, $MC = \Delta TC/\Delta Q$, where the symbol Δ (delta) refers to "a change in." Since

TABLE 2-2	Total, Average, and Marginal Costs of a Firm		
Q	**TC**	**AC**	**MC**
0	$ 20	—	—
1	140	$140	$120
2	160	80	20
3	180	60	20
4	240	60	60
5	480	96	240

---

[1] The relationship between total, average, and marginal revenue, product, and profit will be examined in Problems 1 to 6 at the end of the chapter, with the answer to Problem 6 provided at the end of the text, Appendix D.

[2] The reason that the total cost is positive when output is zero is that the firm incurs some costs in the short run, such as rent on buildings during the life of the contract, which are given and fixed whether the firm produces or not. The theory of cost will be examined in detail in Chapter 7. At this point, we are interested only in the relationship between total, average, and marginal concepts and measures in general, as exemplified by the relationship between total, average, and marginal costs.

output increases by 1 unit at a time in column 1 of Table 2-2, *MC* (in the last column of the table) is obtained by subtracting successive values of *TC* shown in the second column of the table. For example, *TC* increases from $20 to $140 when the firm produces the first unit of output. Thus, *MC* = $120. For an increase in output from 1 to 2 units, *TC* increases from $140 to $160, so that *MC* = $20, and so on. Note that, as for the case of *AC*, *MC* also falls first and then rises.

Plotting the total-, average-, and marginal-cost schedules of Table 2-2 gives the corresponding cost curves shown in Figure 2-2. The shape of the *TC* curve (in the top panel)

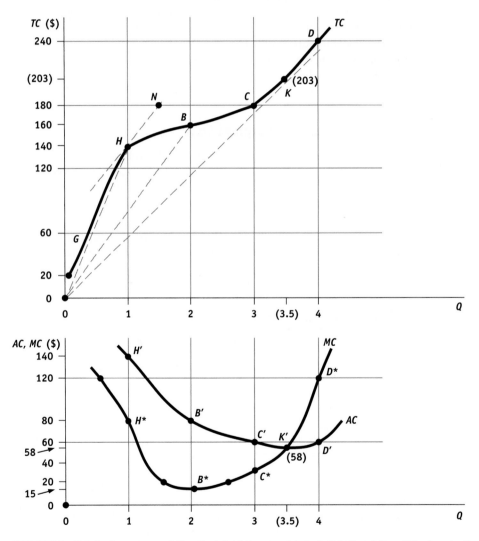

FIGURE 2-2   Total-, Average-, and Marginal-Cost Curves and Their Relationship   *AC* is given by the slope of a ray from the origin to the *TC* curve. Thus, *AC* falls to point *K* (*Q* = 3.5) and rises thereafter. *MC* is given by the slope of the *TC* curve. Thus, *MC* falls to point *B* (the point of inflection at *Q* = 2) and then rises. When *MC* is less than *AC*, *AC* falls; when *MC* is larger than *AC*, *AC* rises; *MC* = *AC* at lowest *AC*.

is explained in Chapter 7. Note that the *AC* curve (in the bottom panel) is U-shaped. Since marginal cost is defined as the change in total cost per unit change in output, the *MC* values of Table 2-2 are plotted (as an approximation) halfway between successive levels of output in the bottom panel of Figure 2-2. Thus, the *MC* of $120, which results from increasing output from 0*Q* to 1*Q* in Table 2-2, is plotted at 0.5*Q* in the bottom panel of Figure 2-2; the *MC* of $20, which results from increasing output from 1*Q* to 2*Q*, is plotted at 1.5*Q*; and so on. Note that the *MC* curve is also U-shaped but reaches the lowest point at a smaller level of output than the *AC* curve, and it intercepts (i.e., it goes through) the lowest point of the *AC* curve. This is always the case (for the reason explained next).

Geometric Derivation of the Average- and Marginal-Cost Curves

The *AC* and *MC* curves in the bottom panel of Figure 2-2 can be derived *geometrically* from the *TC* curve in the top panel. The *AC* corresponding to any point on the *TC* curve is given by the slope of a ray from the origin to the point on the *TC* curve. For example, the *AC* corresponding to point *H* on the *TC* curve in the top panel is given by the slope of ray 0*H,* or $140/1 = $140 (point *H'* in the bottom panel). The *AC* corresponding to point *B* on the *TC* curve is given by the slope of ray 0*B,* or $160/2 = $80 (point *B'* in the bottom panel). The *AC* for both points *C* and *D* on the *TC* curve is given by the slope of ray 0*CD,* or $180/3 = $240/4 = $60 (points *C'* and *D'*, respectively, in the bottom panel). These correspond to the *AC* values shown in Table 2-2. *AC* is minimum at point *K* on the *TC* curve and is given by the slope of ray 0*K,* or $203/3.5 = $58 (point *K'* in the bottom panel). By joining points *H'*, *B'*, *C'*, *K'*, and *D'* in the bottom panel, we generate the *AC* curve corresponding to the *TC* curve in the top panel. Note that the slope of a ray from the origin to the *TC* curve in the top panel falls to point *K* and then rises. Thus, the *AC* curve in the bottom panel falls to point *K'* (at *Q* = 3.5) and then rises.

From the *TC* curve we can also derive geometrically the *MC* curve. The *MC* curve corresponding to any point on the *TC* curve is given by the slope of the tangent *HN* to the *TC* curve at that point. For example, the slope of the tangent to the *TC* curve at point *H* in the top panel, or *MC*, is $80 [from ($180 − 140)/0.5] and is plotted as point *H** in the bottom panel. The slope of the tangent (not shown) to the *TC* curve at points *B, C, K,* and *D,* or *MC,* is $15, $40, $58, and $120, respectively, and is plotted as points *B**, *C**, *K'*, and *D** in the bottom panel. By joining points *H**, *B**, *C**, *K'*, and *D** in the bottom panel, we generate the *MC* curve corresponding to the *TC* curve in the top panel. Note that the slope of the *TC* curve in the top panel declines to point *B* (the inflection point) and rises thereafter. Thus, the *MC* curve in the bottom panel falls to point *B** (at *Q* = 2) and then rises. Note also that the slope of the *TC* curve, or *MC,* at point *K* is equal to the slope of the ray from the origin to point *K* on the *TC* curve, or *AC*. Since this is the lowest *AC,* *MC = AC* at the lowest point on the *AC* curve (see Figure 2-2).

The bottom panel of Figure 2-2 shows an important relationship between the *AC* and *MC* curves. That is, as long as the *MC* curve is below the *AC* curve, the *AC* curve falls, and when the *MC* curve is above the *AC* curve, the *AC* curve rises. When *AC* is neither falling nor rising (i.e., at the point where the *AC* is at its minimum), the *MC* curve intersects the *AC* curve from below, and *AC = MC*. This makes sense. For example, for a student to increase his or her cumulative average test score, he or she must receive a grade on the next (marginal) test that exceeds his or her average. With a lower grade on the next test, the student's average will fall. If the grade on the next test equals the previous average, the average will remain unchanged. Case Study 2-1 examines the total-, average-, and marginal-cost curves of firms in the U.S. steel industry.

In this section we have dealt only with marginal cost. Marginal revenue and marginal profit are similarly defined (as the change in total revenue and total profit, respectively,

CASE STUDY 2-1
Total, Average, and Marginal Cost in the U.S. Steel Industry

The total-cost function of the U.S. steel industry in the 1930s was estimated to be

$$TC = 182 + 56Q \qquad [2\text{-}2]$$

(with all decimals rounded to the nearest whole number), where *TC* is the total cost in millions of dollars, and *Q* is output in millions of tons. Substituting various hypothetical values for *Q* into Equation 2-2, we get the *TC* schedules shown in the third column of Table 2-3. *AC = TC/Q* in the fourth column of the table, and *MC = ΔTC/ΔQ* in the fifth column. The *TC*, *AC*, and *MC* schedules are then plotted in Figure 2-3. Note that the *TC* curve is linear, with fixed costs of $182 million per year, and slope *(MC)* of $56 million for each million tons of steel produced. Thus, the *AC* curve declines continuously, and the *MC* curve

is horizontal. These curves are a simplified version of the average- and marginal-cost curves shown in Figure 2-2. More recently (1989),* the total-cost function for Springs Industries, a leading producer of textile and home furnishings in South Carolina, was estimated to be

$$TC = 10.65 + 0.94S \qquad [2\text{-}2a]$$

where *S* is millions of dollars of sales. Thus, the total-cost curve of Springs is linear, with fixed costs of $10.65 million, declining *AC*, and constant *MC* at 0.94 (i.e., $940,000) per million dollars of additional sales (the slope of the *TC* curve). Thus, these curves look very much like those for steel in Figure 2-3 (the student should be able to sketch the curves for Springs on his or her own).

TABLE 2-3 Total-, Average-, and Marginal-Cost Schedules of the U.S. Steel Industry in the 1930s

Q (in millions of tons)	182 + 56Q	TC (millions of dollars)	AC (millions of dollars)	MC (millions of dollars)
0	182 + 0	$182	—	—
1	182 + 56	238	$238	$56
2	182 + 112	294	147	56
3	182 + 168	350	117	56
4	182 + 224	406	102	56

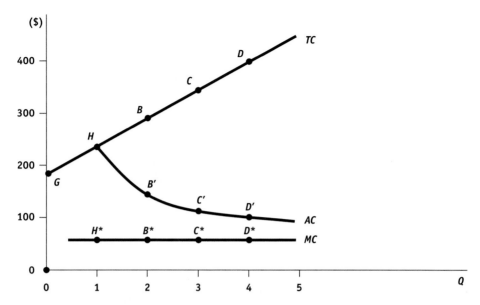

FIGURE 2-3 *TC, AC,* and *MC* Curves of the U.S. Steel Industry   The total-cost curve of the U.S. steel industry in the 1930s was estimated to be linear, with fixed costs of $182 million per year. Thus, *AC* declines continuously and *MC* is constant at $56 million per additional million tons of steel produced (the slope of the *TC* curve).

Source: Based on T. Yntema, in Committee on the Judiciary, U.S. Senate, 85th Congress, *Administered Prices: Steel* (Washington, D.C.: Government Printing Office, 1940).

* Ronald P. Wilder, "Empirical Cost Analysis in Managerial Economics: A Short-Run Cost Estimation Exercise" (November 1989), mimeographed.

per unit change in sales or output) and are equally important. In the next section, we will show how the concept of the margin is crucial in determining the optimal behavior of the firm.

2-3   OPTIMIZATION ANALYSIS

Optimization analysis can best be explained by examining the process by which a firm determines the output level at which it maximizes total profits. We will start by using the total-revenue and total-cost curves of the previous sections in order to set the stage for the subsequent marginal analysis, with which we are primarily concerned.

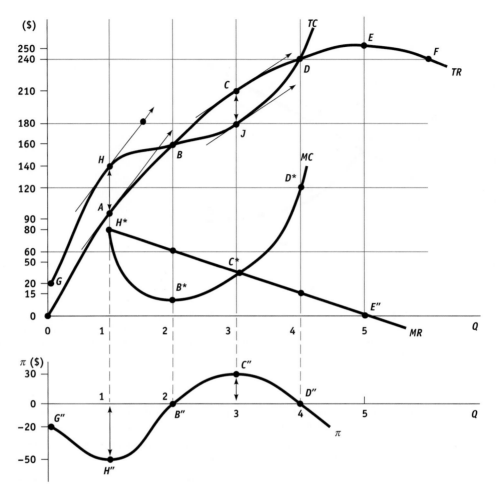

FIGURE 2-4 **Profit Maximization as an Example of Optimization** The firm maximizes total profit at $Q = 3$, where the positive difference between *TR* and *TC* is greatest, $MR = MC$, and the π function is at its highest point.

Profit Maximization by the Total-Revenue and Total-Cost Approach

In the top panel of Figure 2-4, the *TR* curve is that of Figure 2-1 and the *TC* curve is that of Figure 2-2. Total profit (π) is the difference between total revenue and total cost. That is, $\pi = TR - TC$. The top panel of Figure 2-4 shows that at $Q = 0$, $TR = 0$, but $TC = \$20$. Therefore, $\pi = 0 - \$20 = -\$20$ (point G'' on the π function in the bottom panel). This means that the firm incurs a loss of $20 at zero output. At $Q = 1$, $TR = \$90$ and $TC = \$140$. Therefore, $\pi = \$90 - \$140 = -\$50$ (the largest loss, given by point H'' in the bottom panel). At $Q = 2$, $TR = TC = \$160$. Therefore, $\pi = 0$ (point B'' in the bottom panel), and the firm breaks even. The same is true at $Q = 4$, at which $TR = TC = \$240$ and $\pi = 0$ (point D'' in the bottom panel). Between $Q = 2$ and $Q = 4$, *TR* exceeds *TC*, and the firm earns a profit. Total profit is greatest at $Q = 3$, at which the positive difference between TR and TC is greatest. At $Q = 3$, $\pi = \$30$ (point C'' in the bottom panel).

Optimization by Marginal Analysis

While the process by which the firm maximized total profit was determined in the preceding by looking at the total-revenue and total-cost curves, it is more useful to use marginal analysis. Indeed, marginal analysis is one of the most important concepts in managerial economics in general and in optimization analysis in particular. According to marginal analysis, the firm maximizes profits when marginal revenue equals marginal cost. **Marginal cost** (MC) was defined earlier as the change in total cost per unit change in output and is given by the slope of the TC curve. The slope of the TC curve in the top panel of Figure 2-4 falls up to point B (the point of inflection) and rises thereafter. Thus, the MC curve (also in the top panel of Figure 2-4) falls up to point B^* (at $Q = 2$) and then rises (as in Figure 2-2). **Marginal revenue** (MR) is similarly defined as the change in total revenue per unit change in output or sales and is given by the slope of the TR curve. For example, at point A, the slope of the TR curve or MR is $\$80$ (point H^* on the MR curve in the top panel of Figure 2-4). At point B, the slope of the TR curve or $MR = \$60$. At points C and D, the slope of the TR curve or MR is $\$40$ and $\$20$, respectively. At point E, the TR curve is highest or has zero slope, so that $MR = 0$. Past point E, TR declines and MR is negative.

According to marginal analysis, as long as the slope of the TR curve or MR exceeds the slope of the TC curve or MC, it pays for the firm to expand output and sales. The firm would be adding more to its total revenue than to its total costs, and so its total profit would increase. In Figure 2-4, this is true between $Q = 1$ and $Q = 3$. On the other hand, between $Q = 3$ and $Q = 4$, the slope of the TR curve or MR is smaller than the slope of the TC curve or MC, so that the firm would be adding less to its total revenue than to its total cost, and total profits would be less. At $Q = 3$, the slope of the TR curve or MR equals the slope of the TC curve or MC, so that the TR and TC curves are parallel and the vertical distance between them (π) is greatest. At $Q = 3$, $MR = MC$ (point C^* in the top panel of Figure 2-4) and π is at a maximum (point C' in the bottom panel). This is an extremely important concept and is of general applicability. That is, according to **marginal analysis,** as long as the marginal benefit of an activity (such as expanding output or sales) exceeds the marginal cost, it pays for the organization (firm) to increase the activity (expand output). The total net benefit (profit) is maximized when the marginal benefit (revenue) equals the marginal cost. Although the example discussed here involves profit maximization, marginal analysis can also be applied to decisions involving maximization of utility, cost minimization, and so on. Case Study 2-2 applies marginal analysis to optimal pollution control.

Two additional points must be noted with regard to Figure 2-4. The first is that the slope of the TR curve or MR equals the slope of the TC curve or MC (see point H^*) at $Q = 1$ also. However, at $Q = 1$, TC exceeds TR, and the firm incurs a loss. Indeed, at $Q = 1$, the loss is greatest (at $\$50$, see point H'' and the π curve in the bottom panel of Figure 2-4). Thus, for the firm to maximize its total profits, MR must not only be equal to MC but the MC curve must also intersect the MR curve from below, which occurs in Figure 2-4 only at $Q = 3$. This difference between the intersections at $Q = 3$ and $Q = 1$ distinguishes between the profit-maximizing and the loss-maximizing levels of output and leads to our second

CASE STUDY 2-2
Optimal Pollution Control

To a stout environmentalist, the optimal level of pollution is probably zero. However, as long as pollution is a byproduct of the production and consumption of commodities that we want, it does not make much economic sense to try to reduce pollution to zero. The optimal level of pollution is the one at which the marginal *benefit* of pollution (in the form of avoiding more costly methods of waste disposal) equals the marginal cost of pollution (in terms of higher cleaning bills, more respiratory illnesses, and so on).

This is shown in Figure 2-5, where the horizontal axis measures levels of pollution per year and the vertical axis measures the marginal cost and benefit of pollution to society. Note that with increasing levels of pollution, the marginal cost (MC) increases while the marginal benefit (MB) declines. In the absence of any pollution control, firms and individuals would dump wastes until the benefit of pollution equals zero (point A in the figure), and pollution would be excessive. From society's point of view, the optimal level of pollution is Q^* given by point E, where the MB curve intersects the MC curve, and $MB = MC$. While the optimal solution is clearcut, it is often difficult to estimate MB and MC in the real world.

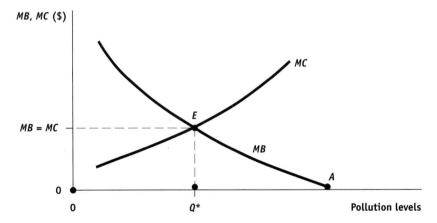

FIGURE 2-5   The Optimal Level of Pollution   The MC curve shows the rising marginal cost or loss to society from increasing levels of pollution. The MB curve shows the declining marginal benefit to the polluter (and to society) by being able to freely dump increasing amounts of waste. Without controls, dumping will take place at point A, where $MB = 0$. The optimal level of dumping is Q^*, at which the MB and MC curves intersect and $MB = MC$.

Source: M. L. Cropper and W. E. Oates, "Environmental Economics: A Survey," *Journal of Economic Literature* (June 1992), pp. 675–740; "Clean Air: Adding It Up," *The New York Times* (December 1, 1996), sec. 3, p. 2; "How Clean Can You Get," *The Economist* (February 17, 1996), p. 37; D. Clement, "Cost v. Benefit: Clearing the Air," *Fed. Res. Bank of Minneapolis Review* (December 2001), pp. 1–21, 48–57; "Files Detail Debate in E.P.A. on Clean Air," *The New York Times* (March 21, 2002), p. 32; and "E. P. A. Sets Rules to Cut Pollution," *The New York Times* (March 11, 2005), p. 1.

point. That is, the slope of the total profit (π) function in the bottom panel of Figure 2-4 is zero both at point H'' (where the total loss of the firm is greatest) and at point C'' (where the firm maximizes total profit). But the π function faces up (so that its slope increases, from being negative to the left of point H'', to zero at point H'', to positive to the right of point H'') where the losses are maximum, while it faces down (so that its slope declines) in the neighborhood of point C'', where the firm maximizes its total profit.

2-4 CONSTRAINED OPTIMIZATION

Until now in this chapter we have examined unconstrained optimization, or the maximization or minimization of an objective function subject to no constraints. Most of the time, however, managers face constraints in their optimization decisions. For example, a firm may face a limitation on its production capacity or on the availability of skilled personnel and crucial raw materials. It may also face legal and environmental constraints. In such cases, we have a **constrained optimization** problem (i.e., the maximizing or minimizing of an objective function subject to some constraints). The existence of such constraints reduces the freedom of action of the firm and usually prevents attainment of its unconstrained optimum. Case Study 2-3 deals with the multiple objectives pursued by global

CASE STUDY 2-3
Pursuing Multiple Objectives under Constraints by Global Corporations

Table 2-4 shows the ranking (from 1 to 16) and the rating (from 0 to 10) of the 16 most important objectives that global corporations believe they will face. They range from customer service, product development, and product quality (the first three, ranked in that order) all the way down to mergers and acquisitions, reliance on consulting services, and political lobbying (the last three). These 16 objectives and their ranking were distilled from the nearly 1,800 responses to a questionnaire listing 65 issues that the American Management Association (AMA) sent to managers of global corporations in 36 countries in 1998. Note that even though political lobbying ranks lowest among the 16 most important objectives, it is still a very important objective—it is the 16th most important objective among the 65 issues, with a rating of 5.26.

Since each of the 16 most important objectives costs money to pursue and firms' resources

are limited, the question faced by top management is how much of a company's resources to devote to each. The optimal solution is for the firm to pursue each activity until the marginal *net* benefit from the activity is zero, subject to the constraints under which it operates. While the firm may not have sufficient data to apply this rule precisely at any point in time, the concept and the rule themselves are very clear. The firm should strive to come as close as possible to the optimal solution and, in the meantime, collect more and better data on the costs and benefits of pursuing each activity under the constraints it faces, so as to be able to get even closer to the optimal solution in the future. In an updated study, security against terrorism would surely be among the most important objectives of global corporations.

Continued . . .

TABLE 2-4	Rating the 16 Most Important Objectives That Global Corporations Believe They Will Face	
Rank	**Objective**	**Average Rating**
1	Customer service	9.06
2	R&D/new product development	8.68
3	Quality control and assurance	8.64
4	Acquiring new technologies	8.55
5	Innovation	8.47
6	Environmentally sound practices	7.96
7	Team-based approach	7.92
8	Manpower planning	7.76
9	Business partnerships and alliances	7.75
10	Study and use of best practices	7.71
11	Outsourcing and contracting	7.03
12	Reengineering business processes	6.96
13	Foreign language training	6.86
14	Mergers and acquisitions	6.66
15	Reliance on consulting services	6.50
16	Political lobbying	5.26

Source: AMA Global Survey on Key Business Issues, (New York: American Management Association, 1998); "Long-Term Effects of Sept. 11 May Be More Costly," *The Wall Street Journal* (June 7, 2002), p. A2; and "Global Strategy Faces Local Constraints," in *Mastering Corporate Governance, Financial Times* (May 27, 2005), pp. 4–5.

corporations under constraints. Constrained optimization problems can best be solved expediently by differential calculus (see the Appendix to this chapter).

2-5   NEW MANAGEMENT TOOLS FOR OPTIMIZATION

During the past two decades many new management tools have revolutionized the way firms are managed. The most important of these tools are benchmarking, total quality management, reengineering, and the learning organization. In this section we discuss each of these, as well as some more recent management tools or ideas and examine how they are related to the traditional functional areas of managerial economics.

Benchmarking

Benchmarking refers to the finding out, in an open and aboveboard way, how other firms may be doing something better (cheaper) so that your firm can copy and possibly improve on its technique. Benchmarking is usually accomplished by field trips to other firms. The technique has now become a standard tool for improving productivity and quality at a large number of American firms, including IBM, AT&T, Ford, Du Pont, and Xerox.

Benchmarking requires (1) picking a specific process that your firm seeks to improve and identifying a few firms that do a better job and (2) sending on the benchmarking mission the people who will actually have to make the changes. Benchmarking can result in dramatic cost reductions. For example, through benchmarking, Xerox was able to cut the cost of processing each order from $95 to $35 and as a result saved tens of billions of dollars. Similarly, benchmarking allowed Ford to reduce the number of employees handling accounts payable from 500 to less than 200 in a few months. Through benchmarking, the Mellon Bank cut complaints by 60 percent and was able to resolve them on the average in 25 days instead of 45 days. Benchmarking has now become a standard tool to increase productivity and minimize costs at many U.S. and foreign firms. The explosion in interest in benchmarking has led to the formation of many benchmarking associations, councils, programs (such as the International Benchmarking Clearinghouse), as well as conferences, courses, data, and consultants.

In recent years, benchmarking has evolved from a rather lengthy and cumbersome set of procedures to a fast and flexible tool that is less elaborate and more tactical; it has come to be called *fast-cycle* or *rapid benchmarking*. Rather than seeking across-the-board operational improvements, the firm looks for "useful analogies" from other companies that may help solve specific problems that the firm faces (see Case Study 2-4).

Total Quality Management

One movement that swept U.S. corporations in the 1980s involved maximizing quality and minimizing costs through **total quality management (TQM).** This refers to constantly improving the quality of products and the firm's processes so as to consistently deliver increasing value to customers. TQM constantly asks, "How can we do this cheaper, faster, or better?" It involves worker teams and benchmarking. In its broader form, TQM applies quality-improvement methods to all the firm's processes from production to customer service, sales and marketing, and even finance. By improving quality and reducing costs in all these areas, Hewlett-Packard achieved spectacular results. Other companies that have successfully used TQM are Xerox, Motorola, General Electric, Marriott, Harley-Davidson, and Ford.

Five rules determine the success of a TQM program:

1. The corporate executive officer (CEO) must strongly and visibly support it with words and actions.
2. The TQM program must clearly show how it benefits customers and creates value for the firm.
3. The TQM program must have a few clear strategic goals; that is, it must ask, "What is the firm trying to accomplish?"
4. The TQM program must provide quick financial returns and compensation—people need to see early and concrete results to continue to support the program.
5. The TQM program should be tailored to a particular firm; that is, one firm cannot simply copy another firm's TQM program.

CASE STUDY 2-4
Benchmarking at Xerox, Ford, and Mobil

The first benchmarking mission by a U.S. firm was undertaken by Xerox in 1979, when it realized that the Japanese were selling copiers for less than Xerox's production costs. At first Xerox management thought the Japanese were dumping (i.e., selling copiers in the United States at prices below their production costs) in order to establish a foothold in the American market. But a benchmarking mission to Japan led Xerox to the shocking realization that Japanese production costs were, in fact, much lower than Xerox's. Responding to the challenge eventually led Xerox to imitate Japanese producers, thus recapturing some of its lost market. Xerox has successfully used benchmarking ever since.

The highly successful Ford Taurus introduced in the early 1980s was also the result of benchmarking. Ford first set out to identify about 400 features that U.S. car buyers considered most important, then it identified the competitive cars (mostly Japanese) that embodied those features, and, finally, it built a car (the Taurus) incorporating those features at competitive costs by copying the production methods of its competitors. The redesigned 1992 Taurus was, once again, based on a new round of benchmarking. Ford benchmarked door handles and fuel economy against the Chevy Lumina, the halogen headlamps and tilt wheel against the Honda Accord, the easy-to-change taillight bulbs and express window control against Nissan's Maxima, and the remote radio controls against the Pontiac Grand Prix.

When the Mobil Corporation (now Exxon-Mobil) wanted to reduce time at the gas pump in remaking its 8,000 service stations, it employed fast-cycle or rapid benchmarking by studying Home Depot to determine why the retail chain's customers were so loyal and examining how the Team Penske auto-racing crew minimized time in the pit. These useful analogies led to creative thinking that resulted in the introduction of Speed Pass, Mobil's wave-at-the-pump credit system that minimized customers' time at the gas pump and increased their loyalty.

Source: "How to Steal the Best Ideas Around," *Fortune* (October 19, 1992), pp. 102–106; "Fast-Cycle Benchmarking," *Harvard Management Update* (April 1999), pp. 1–4; and "Is Your Benchmarking Doing the Right Work?" *Harvard Management Update* (September 2003), pp. 1–5.

Despite some glaring successes from using TQM programs (e.g., Motorola was able to cut $700 million in manufacturing costs over five years), only about a third of American corporations polled indicated that their TQM programs significantly increased the quality of their products, reduced costs, and increased their competitiveness. The most frequent reason for lack of success in TQM programs is the failure of upper management to show a strong personal involvement and commitment to the program. Other reasons for failure were that TQM programs often were not strongly linked to the overall business strategy of the firm or aimed at delivering increasing value to customers.

In recent years, the TQM model was extended to include innovation, knowledge, and the management of partnerships in order to make it more relevant in today's rapidly globalizing world of business. And now a new extension called *Six Sigma* has been added to the TQM vocabulary. (Actually, this was developed at Motorola more than a decade ago, but only recently is it catching on and receiving wider acceptance.) Six Sigma refers to the situation in which everything—from product design to manufacturing to billing—proceeds practically flawlessly, with fewer than 3.4 defects per million widgets or procedures. The name itself means that nondefective products or procedures fall or are encompassed within six standard deviations from the mean. Two sigma would mean that 95 percent of the products or procedures are non-defective. Six sigma means that 99.99966 percent are nondefective, or 3.4 defectives per million— practically perfection! And Six Sigma is not a managerial fad; a growing number of no-nonsense companies from Allied Signal to Motorola and General Electric swear by it (see Case Study 2-5).

Reengineering

Reengineering was the hottest trend in management in the mid-1990s. Reengineering seeks to completely reorganize the firm. It asks, "If this were an entirely new firm, how would you organize it?" or, "If you were able to start all over again, how would you do it?" Then it requires restructuring the firm to conform to that vision. Reengineering involves the radical redesign of all of the firm's processes to achieve major gains in speed, quality, service, and profitability. While total quality management (TQM) seeks how to do something faster, cheaper, or better, reengineering asks first whether something should be done at all, and so it is more likely than TQM to come up with novel solutions.

There are two major reasons to reengineer: (1) fear that competitors may come up with new products, services, or ways of doing business that might destroy your firm or (2) greed, if you believe that by reengineering, your company can obliterate the competition. The best candidates for reengineering are firms that face major shifts in the nature of competition, such as financial and telecommunications firms after deregulation. Reengineering involves reorganizing the firm horizontally around cross-functional core processes managed by teams that seek to maximize customers' satisfaction. Profits are likely to be maximized at dramatically higher levels in the long run if the reengineering is successful. For example, instead of product development being handled by different departments as in traditional firms (where the marketing department comes up with an idea for a product and hands it to the engineering department, which hands it to the production department), in a successfully reengineered horizontal firm a team of key people will handle all aspects of product development, from the idea, to the production, to the marketing of the product, eliminating layers of management, bureaucracy, and waste and providing cheaper and better products to customers.

Although reengineering makes a great deal of sense on paper and is easy to understand in principle, it is extremely difficult to carry out, and not all firms are capable of reengineering or need to reengineer. Indeed, more than two-thirds of the firms that tried it achieved only mediocre or no results. Even companies that have been successful have not completely eliminated functional specializations. That is, there will always be a need for experts in production, finance, marketing, human resource development, and so on. What reengineering does is make them work together in teams. Few firms, however, are likely to

CASE STUDY 2-5
Total Quality Management at Johnson & Johnson, Motorola, General Electric, and Ford

Johnson & Johnson's TQM program identified three quantifiable goals: increasing customer satisfaction, reducing the time it takes to introduce products, and cutting costs. One type of total quality initiative, by encouraging the sharing of responsibility rather than resistance to it, reduced the time required by Johnson & Johnson to prepare customized retail displays for chain drugstores and supermarkets from 120 days to 30 days, and this contributed to an increase in sales from $25 million to $90 million in one year. Motorola's TQM program has had two basic aims: defect prevention and cycle-time reduction (i.e., the time it takes to get a job done). Past success in achieving the first goal led the company to set a goal of about three defects per *million* operations by 2000 (the Six Sigma TQM program). The second goal has led to a reduction in the time required to close the books each month from eleven days five years ago to two days now, and this has led to a 50 percent saving in external auditors' cost. The TQM program at Tenneco was based on sharply cutting internal failures (such as unscheduled downtime), external failures (which resulted in a flood of warranty claims), prevention of defects (project planning), and appraisal (testing and inspection).

When it comes to *Six Sigma,* so firm a believer was John Welch (who retired as General Electric president in 2001), that he spent more than three years and $1 billion to convert all its divisions to the Six Sigma faith, which he credited with raising the company's operating profit margins from 14.4 percent to 16.6 percent. Welch stated that Six Sigma galvanized GE with an intensity he had never seen in his 40 years with the company. For example, GE used 200 people for nearly three years to run 250 separate Six Sigma analyses at a cost of $50 million in developing its $1.25 million superfast diagnostic scanner called the Lightspeed, which can do a full-body scan in only 20 seconds instead of the three minutes it took before. This was crucial because the patient must remain perfectly still during the scan. Welch stated: "Six Sigma lets you approach problems with the assumption that there is a data-oriented fix at the end . . . and that is a radical culture change."

The Ford Motor Company used TQM to turn the company around after the invasion of Japanese automobiles threatened the existence of the entire U.S. automotive industry at the beginning of the 1980s. By successfully applying TQM, Ford was able to turn huge losses to high profits that made Ford the most profitable of the American automakers by 1986 with the introduction of its highly successful Taurus. By 2001, however, Ford was again in trouble with losses of $5.5 billion as a result of the controversy over deadly rollovers of its Explorers, costly recalls of several models, and delays on the introduction of others. And again, Ford embraced TQM and its Six Sigma extension in 2001.

Source: "TQM—More Than a Dying Fad?" *Fortune* (October 18, 1993), pp. 66–72; "Report Card on TQM," *Management Review* (January 1994), pp. 22–25; "Six Sigma Enlightenment," *The New York Times* (December 7, 1998), p. C1; "Making Continuous Improvements Better," *Financial Times* (April 21, 1999), p. 28; "Quality Revival, Part 2: Ford Embraces Six Sigma," *The New York Times* (June 13, 2001), p. C5; "Quality Isn't Just for Widgets," *Business Week* (July 22, 2002), pp. 72–73; "Six Sigma: A Hollywood Studio Learns the G.E. Way," *The New York Times* (September 27, 2004), p. C1; and "Rethinking the Quality Improvement Program," *The Wall Street Journal* (September 19, 2005), p. B3.

ever become entirely horizontal or boundaryless. Most are likely to be hybrids, or less vertically organized than in the past.

During the 1990s, reengineering went from a management fad to a $51 billion consulting industry practically overnight. Today, it is slowly fading—some people would even say that it is dead. There are two reasons for this. First, only a small number of firms that tried it actually succeeded (one of these is GE—see Case Study 2-6). Second is the bad press that it got as a result of the large layoffs and workers' resistance that accompanied the downsizing that took place in the name of reengineering. But reengineering means reinventing the firm in dramatically more productive ways

CASE STUDY 2-6
Reengineering at GE

When Jack Welch became corporate executive officer in 1981, General Electric had a strong balance sheet but modest earnings and technology, and it was almost an entirely nonglobal business. By 1990, Welch had entirely redesigned (read *reengineered*) GE into a much more efficient, dynamic, global, and profitable organization. The reengineering involved first brutally awakening GE to the need to change for survival in the dramatically transformed competitive situation of the 1980s. Second, it involved envisioning a boundaryless firm based on cross-functional teamwork capable of constantly reinventing itself. Finally, it required the actual redesign of the firm into one capable of continual change and one in which information flowed freely across functional and business boundaries, from where it was developed to where it was needed.

Actual reengineering at GE involved adopting a new strategy, revolutionizing its organizational structure, and entirely changing its human resource management. The strategy was for GE to aim for high-growth businesses. This meant that GE had to be number 1 or number 2 in each segment of the market; otherwise it had to fix, sell, or close the business. The organizational structure was reorganized into 13 businesses that shared the best practices and reported to a central CEO team. In human resource management, GE made rewards very flexible, did employee appraisal from below as well as from above, and made training and development a continuous process.

Welch had to overcome tremendous resistance from traditional vested interests all down the chain of command. But he was able to carry out one of the most far-reaching programs of innovation in business history, a program that turned GE into one of the most efficient, dynamic, and admired companies in the world. And by adopting the Six Sigma TQM program in all of its divisions, Welch forced GE to constantly reinvent or reengineer itself (see Case Study 2-5). Other companies that successfully reengineered during the past decade are Intel, IBM, and Boeing.

Source: "Revolutionize Your Company," *Fortune* (December 13, 1993), pp. 114–118; "Reengineering: The Hot New Management Tool," *Fortune* (August 23, 1993), pp. 41–48; "The Horizontal Corporation," *Business Week* (December 20, 1993), pp. 76–81; "Six Sigma Enlightenment," *The New York Times* (December 7, 1998), p. C1; "Reinventing Intel," *Forbes* (May 3, 1999), pp. 154–159; "IBM New Boss," *Business Week* (February 11, 2002), pp. 66–72; "Reengineering 101," *Forbes* (May 13, 2002), pp. 82–88; and "Look First at Failures," *Harvard Business Review* (October 2004), pp. 18–20.

and, although this may involve downsizing, the latter is only part of the story. Nor has reinterpreting it and renaming it *business transformation, organizational agility,* or *value engineering*—to stress the fact that reengineering involves a culture change, the ability of a firm to respond to or anticipate rapid changes, and a strategy for rapid growth—been sufficient to reignite the type of interest that it enjoyed during the early 1990s.

The Learning Organization

The learning organization may be the hot management tool of this decade. A **learning organization** values continuing learning, both individual and collective, and believes that competitive advantage derives from and requires continuous learning in our information age. According to Peter Senge, its intellectual and spiritual champion, a learning organization is based on five basic ingredients:

1. *New mental model*—People must put aside old ways of thinking and be willing to change.
2. *Personal mastery*—Firm employees must learn to be open with others and listen, rather than telling others what to do.
3. *System thinking*—Everyone in the organization must have an understanding of how the firm really works.
4. *Shared vision*—All firm employees must share the same strategy.
5. *Team learning*—The organization must see how all the firm's employees can be made to work and learn together to realize the shared vision and carry out the strategy of the firm.

To be sure, none of these five concepts is new; however, what is original and promises to provide major benefits is how the concepts are linked to create a learning organization.

Although the five ingredients on which the learning organization is based may be clear in theory, they are very difficult to carry out in practice. It is to make the learning organization more accessible to management that Senge formed the Center for Organizational Learning at the Massachusetts Institute of Technology (MIT) in 1990. This research center had 18 sponsors (among them Ford, AT&T, Motorola, and Federal Express), each paying $80,000 per year and striving to create a pilot program for transforming their firm into a learning organization with the help of the center. These leading corporations believed that by becoming learning organizations, they could dramatically increase their efficiency and dynamic competitiveness. The center, however, closed in 1997.

A number of organizations providing organizational learning have sprung up in recent years, among them the Society for Organizational Learning—a nonprofit organization located in Cambridge, Massachusetts; the Program on Social and Organizational Learning—at George Mason University; the Organizational Learning and Instructional Technologies Program—at the University of New Mexico; the Research Program in Social and Organizational Learning—at George Washington University, and the Center for Organizational Learning and Renewal—at the University of St. Louis.

For now, the learning organization is, for the most part, a management vision of the future. It is possible, however, that the concept may storm corporate America during this decade, as total quality management did in the 1980s and reengineering in the 1990s. Case Study 2-7 discusses the application of learning-organization principles at Ford and Southwest Airlines.

CASE STUDY 2-7
Applying Learning-Organization Principles at Ford and Southwest Airlines

One of the earliest successful uses of learning-organization principles was in the launching of a revamped Lincoln Continental at Ford. The first step was to induce people involved in the Lincoln project to come forward early on and admit that they had a problem that needed to be solved. This went smack against Ford's culture, where problems were hidden as long as possible to avoid charges of incompetence. The new openness allowed people working on the Continental project to cooperate more readily, to engage in systems thinking, and to thereby more effectively solve systems problems.

For example, the project manager found that because the engineers who designed the air-conditioning system, the headlights, the power seats, and the CD player traditionally worked separately, they did not realize that the simultaneous operation of these car systems drained the car's battery. Under Ford's traditional management system, when this problem came to light, the engineers from the various departments would fight with one another to determine who had to make the adjustment to lower the power requirement. The impasse would then have to be broken by a decision from the overall project manager. The engineers in the department that had to give in would feel like losers. In addition to the time lost in controversy, the end result was a lot of hard feelings.

When the management shifted to using learning-organization principles, the engineers for the various car systems worked together and realized the power problem early on. They decided to raise the car's idle to increase the battery charge. This, however, required increasing fuel efficiency. Since the engineers working on that problem did not feel like losers but rather that they were working for the good of the car, they solved the problem much more quickly and in a spirit of cooperation and appreciation by all the other departments. By looking at the problem as a systems problem and addressing it by systems thinking, the Lincoln Continental engineers avoided blaming each other and finger pointing, which greatly increased production efficiency.

Southwest Airlines was the first to apply learning-organization principles in the airline industry, thereby gaining a competitive edge over its competitors. Southwest learned sooner than others in the industry how to manage knowledge to find new ways of doing business in order to improve its efficiency on a continuing basis. It was able to change management philosophies and practices, as well as organizational culture and procedures. For example, when one of its employees suggested doing away with tickets in order to reduce costs and loading times, Southwest immediately began experimenting with electronic ticketing on some of its routes and then adopted it exclusively as soon as its advantages were proven.

Source: "The Learning Organization," *Fortune* (October 17, 1994), pp. 147–158; "IT and the Challenge of Organizational Learning," *Mastering Information Technology Section, Financial Times* (April 5, 1999), p. 8; "Turning Knowledge Into Business," *Financial Times* (January 1, 2001), pp. 12–13; "Real-Time Learning," *Harvard Management Update* (January 2005), pp. 9–11; and "A Powerful Idea Whose Time May Still to Come," *Financial Times* (January 25, 2006), p. 1.

2-6 OTHER MANAGEMENT TOOLS FOR OPTIMIZATION

In this section we examine other recent management tools or ideas for optimal decisions by the firm. These are[3]:

- **Broadbanding**—The elimination of multiple salary grades to foster movement among jobs within the firm, thus increasing labor flexibility and lowering costs.
- **Direct business model**—The situation where a firm deals directly with the consumer, thus eliminating the time and cost of third-party distribution (i.e., eliminating distributors, as for example in the selling of Dell PCs).
- **Networking**—The forming of temporary strategic alliances where each firm contributes its best competence, as in the case of virtual integration (see below).
- **Performance management**—The holding of executives and their subordinates accountable for delivering the desired results and superior competitive performance.
- **Pricing power**—The ability of a firm to raise prices faster than the rise in its costs or to lower its costs faster than the fall in the prices at which the firm sells—thus increasing its profits.
- **Process management**—The coordination or integration under a single umbrella of all the firm's performance-improvement initiatives, such as benchmarking, reengineering, TQM, and Six Sigma.
- **Small-world model**—The idea or theory that a corporate giant can be made to operate like a small firm by linking well-connected individuals from each level of the organization to one another, so as to improve the flow of information and the operational efficiency of the firm. This is based on research that we are all connected to one another by a small chain of six people or less, as in the song, "It's a small world after all." The idea is to find the key or well-connected individuals at each level of the firm and establish links among them.
- **Strategic development**—The idea that assessment and action should be under continuous review and provide a direction and an agenda or continuous strategic development, rather than a strategic plan.
- **Virtual integration**—The blurring of the traditional boundaries and roles between the manufacturer and its suppliers, on the one hand, and the manufacturer and its customers, on the other, in the value chain, thus treating suppliers and customers as if they were part of the company. This greatly reduces or eliminates the need for inventories and satisfies consumer demand expeditiously—again, as practiced by Dell.
- **Virtual management**—The ability of a manager to simulate consumer behavior using computer models based on the emerging science or theory of complexity. (Virtual management will be examined in detail in Case Study 4-3.)

---

[3] See, "Cost Consciousness Beats Pricing Power," *The Wall Street Journal* (May 31, 1999), p. A1; "Do the Math—It Is a Small World," *Business Week* (August 17, 1998), pp. 54–55; "The Power of Virtual Integration: An Interview with Michael Dell," *Harvard Business Review* (March–April 1998), pp. 73–84; "Virtual Management," *Business Week* (September 21, 1998), pp. 80–82; "Evolution, Revolution and the Ins and Outs of Business Vocabulary," *The Wall Street Journal* (December 12, 2001), p. B1; M. Hammer, "Process Management and the Future of Six Sigma," *MIT Sloan Management Review* (Winter 2002), pp. 26–32; "Performance Management that Drives Results," *Harvard Management Update* (September 2004), pp. 1–4; and "Making Strategy Development Matter," *Harvard Management Update* (May 2005), pp. 4–6.

The list, of course, does not end here. We also have *skill-based pay, worker empowerment, capturing synergies* (by a firm diversifying into related businesses), *leading through the turmoil, evolutionary change,* and many others—and every year seems to bring an additional crop of new buzzwords or ideas.

2-7 NEW MANAGEMENT TOOLS AND FUNCTIONAL SPECIALIZATION

Companies have introduced new management tools and trendy remedies to improve efficiency and productivity while maximizing profits subject to the constraints faced by the firm. Some of these new management tools are *benchmarking, total quality management (TQM), reengineering,* and the *learning organization.* Others are *broadbanding, direct business model, networking, performance management, pricing power, process management, small-world model, strategic development, virtual integration, virtual management,* as well as *skill-based pay, worker empowerment, capturing synergies, leading through the turmoil,* and *evolutionary change.* The labels abound and so do the promises of major benefits. The results to date, however, have been mixed. Most leading American firms now use benchmarking, but only about a third successfully adopted TQM programs. Fewer have tried reengineering, and the learning organization is for the most part still in its blueprint stage. Failure to receive major benefits by the firms that tried some of these new management tools often resulted from lack of conviction and effort, however. Applied with more conviction, their success rate is likely to increase.[4]

The new management tools and ideas have already changed drastically the way many firms are being managed, and many more firms are likely to be forced to change their management ways in the future. The increasing use of these new management tools, however, is not likely to eliminate functional specializations and the need for specific expertise in production, finance, marketing, human resource development, and so on. One reason for this is that some of the new management tools and ideas do not provide a completely worked out and cohesive set of guidelines that most firms can easily understand and implement. For example, learning-organization principles are based on some brilliant ideas that some firms can implement and some cannot. They can sometimes lead to major benefits, and sometimes cannot. To be sure, under the pressure of global competitiveness, firms will have to be constantly looking for new as well as traditional ways to increase their productivity and competitiveness.

Some universal truths stemming from the new management tools and ideas that would consistently benefit any organization are (1) explaining the firm's corporate strategy to employees, suppliers, and customers, (2) improving and simplifying development

---

[4] "Many Companies Try Management Fads, Only to See Them Flop," *The Wall Street Journal* (July 6, 1993), p. A1; "Total Quality Is Termed Only Partial Success," *The Wall Street Journal* (October 10, 1992), p. B1; "Hopelessly Seeking Synergy," *The Economist* (August 20, 1994), p. 53; "Competition Can Teach You a Lot, but the Lessons Can Hurt," *The New York Times* (July 18, 1999), sec. 3, p. 4; D. Rigby, "Management Tools and Techniques," *California Management Review* (Winter 2001), pp. 139–160; and "Why Most Management Tools Don't Work," *Harvard Business Update* (October 2003), pp. 10–11.

and production processes, and (3) reducing cycle time (i.e., how long it takes to get any task done) by paying more attention to processes and teamwork than to functions and individualism. These management ideas and others are part of the *American business model* that is increasingly being accepted throughout the world (see Case Study 2-8) despite its shortcomings (see Case Study 2-9).

CASE STUDY 2-8
The American Business Model

With the tearing down of the Berlin wall and the collapse of communism in 1989, and with the economic and financial crisis in corporatist Japan and the slow growth in overregulated Europe during the past decade, more and more foreign companies are adopting American business practices. These practices are responsible for the high-tech boom and rapid growth of the United States since the mid-1990s.

Briefly stated, the American business model preaches maximizing the value of the firm, subject to the constraints it faces and shareholder supremacy as defined by the Financial Accounting Standards Board in New York (which was the blueprint for the new International Accounting Standards Board). It involves tools and language. For all of its shortcomings, quarterly reporting makes the company transparent to investors as to its goals, its strategy for achieving them, and its degree of success.

The universal language of global business is English. Most of the professors in the top business schools in the United States and in Europe have degrees from U.S. business schools, and more than one-third of the student body in the top American business schools is made up by foreigners. The number of foreign companies listed on the New York Stock Exchange (NYSE) has more than quadrupled during the past decade, from 96 in 1990 to 464 in 2005. Europe's largest bank, Deutsche Bank, decided to be listed on the NYSE, as did Daimler (now DaimlerChrysler) in 1993, creating a sensation in the European business establishment. The American business model is simply the only business model that works. Globalization during the past decade has meant Americanization.

Inevitably (and enviably), the American business model has come under attack for spreading American influence around the world, for being excessively materialist and looking only at the bottom line, for requiring quarterly reporting and thus overstressing the short run at the expense of the long run, and more recently, for its failure to prevent corporate accounting scandals. But no one is forcing global corporations to adopt American ways. The foreign expansion of American companies after World War II introduced millions of people all over the world to American business practices. But it was not until after the collapse of communism with its nonmarket ways, the failure of the Japanese corporatist model, and the slow growth of overregulated Europe during the past decade that the American model became widely accepted as the best (even if not perfect) business model.

Although some reject it (the London Stock Exchange and Porsche do not accept quarterly reports) and some accept it only grudgingly, the American business model is the only durable business model that works. New legislation passed in July 2002 (the Sarbanes-Oxley Act) improved it so as to prevent future Enrons, and the model does need to be extended to take more clearly into consideration employee welfare and security, local cultures, and environmental concerns. But it is clearly the best game in town.

Source: "How We Got Here," *The Wall Street Journal* (September 27, 1999), p. R6; "Economic Thinking Finds a Free Market," *The New York Times* (January 1, 2000), p. E4; "Attack Offers Lessons on People and Markets," *The Wall Street Journal* (September 20, 2001), p. A1; "The America Way," *Fortune* (November 26, 2001); and "Snow Hits Out at EU Antipathy to Business," *Financial Times* (June 15, 2005), p. 1.

CASE STUDY 2-9
When Governance Rules Fail, Public Trust Is Eroded

Starting at the end of 2001 with the Enron–Andersen scandal (see Case Study 1-6) and spreading like wildfire in 2002, a number of high-profile scandals erupted (Adelphia Communications, Global Crossing, WorldCom, Tyco, Xerox, Merrill Lynch). These scandals eroded public confidence in the American financial system and dampened stock prices. Some major corporations have had to admit that they fabricated revenues, seriously overstated earnings, or otherwise falsified financial reports. Investment-bank analysts confessed that they had promoted shares that they knew to be worthless or nearly so. Merrill Lynch had to pay a $100 million fine to settle a lawsuit regarding the lack of integrity of its analyses at the height of the Internet boom. Accounting malpractice, conflicts of interests, excessive executive compensation, and poor boardroom scrutiny have resulted in American investors losing confidence in Wall Street's ability and willingness to act as an honest broker between them, as providers of capital, and the corporate users of that capital.

Perhaps this was inevitable in a system that lavishly rewards executives and induced them to pursue success, almost at all costs. But the blame for what has happened can be widely spread. Where were board directors when all of this was taking place? Didn't they either condone it or abdicate their responsibility to stockholders? Where were the auditors that were supposed to verify company reports? And why did investors slavishly follow the advice of some Wall Street analysts without realizing that 10- to 20-percent profit rates, year-in and year-out, from new-economy companies with little or no tangible assets, were only fairytale dreams? And where were the Financial Accounting Standards Board and the Security and Exchange Commission, which were supposed to oversee, respectively, that the accounting profession and Wall Street stayed honest? It is taking years and billions of dollars in penalties to settle all the private lawsuits directed against financial services firms for the misleading advice they provided. America's capital markets and business model, for so long the envy of the world, surely got a black eye from all this mess.

The most serious damage arising from the scandals was the loss of investors' trust in financial markets and in Wall Street. The issue that troubled investors the most was the quality of the financial information provided by the companies, which depends on honest accounting and adequate firm governance. It was clear that all of the checks and balances in place were inadequate and needed to be greatly improved. Congress responded swiftly to the crisis by passing the Sarbanes-Oxley Act in July 2002, which greatly tightened accounting standards in order to rebuild investor confidence (see Case Study 1-6).

Source: "Audacious Climb to Success Ended in a Dizzying Plunge," *The New York Times* (January 13, 2002), p. 1; "A Tattered Andersen Fights for Its Future," *The New York Times* (January 13, 2002), p. 3; "Enron: How Governance Rules Failed," *Business Week* (January 21, 2002), pp. 21–22; "When Public Trust Is Eroded," *Financial Times* (June 8, 2002), p. 8; "Governance Bill Has Major Consequences for Many," *The Wall Street Journal* (July 2, 2002), p. A4. "Wall Street Banks to Pay $1.4bn in Historic Deal on Analysts Abuses," *Financial Times* (December 12, 2002), p. 1; "Citigroup Agrees to Pay $2 Billion in Enron Scandal," *The New York Times* (June 11, 2005), p. 1; "J. P. Morgan Settles Enron Lawsuit," *The Wall Street Journal* (June 15, 2005), p. A3; and "Ebbers Is Sentenced to 25 Years for $11 Billion WorldCom Fraud," *The Wall Street Journal* (July 14, 2005), p. A1.

SUMMARY

1. Economic relationships can be expressed in equational, tabular, or graphical form. Expressing an economic relationship in equational form allows the use of the powerful techniques of differential calculus to determine the optimal behavior of the firm.

2. The relationship between total, average, and marginal concepts and measures is crucial in optimization analysis. The relationship is basically the same whether we deal with revenue, product, cost, or profit. The average value is equal to the total value divided by the quantity. The marginal value is equal to the change in the total value per unit change in the quantity.

3. Optimization analysis can best be explained by examining the process of profit maximization by the firm. The firm maximizes its total profit at the output level, at which the positive difference between its total revenue and its total cost is greatest, and its marginal revenue equals its marginal cost. More generally, according to marginal analysis, optimization occurs where the marginal benefit of an activity equals the marginal cost.

4. Firms often face constraints in their optimization decisions. These reduce the freedom of action of the firm and usually prevent the attainment of its unconstrained optimum.

5. During the past two decades many new management tools have been introduced that are revolutionizing the way firms are managed. *Benchmarking* refers to the finding out how other firms may be doing something better so as to copy and possibly improve on it. *Total quality management (TQM)* is the effort to constantly improve the quality of products and the firm's processes by benchmarking and teamwork. *Reengineering* is the radical redesign of all of the firm's processes to achieve major gains in speed, quality, service, and profitability. A *learning organization* is one that values continuing learning and believes that competitive advantage derives from and requires continuous learning in our information age.

6. Other recent management tools or ideas are broadbanding, direct business model, networking, performance management, pricing power, process management, small-world model, strategic development, virtual integration, virtual management, and others.

7. The new management tools and ideas introduced during the past two decades have drastically changed the way many firms are being managed, but they did not eliminate functional specialization and the need for specific expertise in production, finance, marketing, human resource development, and so on.

 DISCUSSION QUESTIONS

1. What is the meaning of average and marginal (*a*) revenue, (*b*) product, (*c*) cost, and (*d*) profit?

2. What is the shape of the marginal-revenue curve if the total-revenue curve has a concave shape?

3. What is the value of the marginal revenue when the total revenue increases, is maximum, or decreases?

4. What is the shape of the marginal-revenue curve if the total-revenue curve is a positively sloped straight line? Why?

5. If the total-product curve first increases at an increasing rate (i.e., it faces up) and then increases at a decreasing rate (i.e., it faces down), what are the shapes of the average-product and the marginal-product curves?

6. What is the relationship between average product and marginal product?

7. What is the relationship between a total-product curve that first increases at an increasing rate and then increases at a decreasing rate and the total-cost curve of Figure 2-2?

8. How does a firm determine the profit-maximizing level of output?

9. How would you react to a sales manager's announcement that he or she has in place a marketing program to maximize sales?

10. How should a firm determine the best level of (*a*) advertising, (*b*) input use, and (*c*) investment?

11. How does the value of a businessperson's time affect his or her decision to fly or drive on a business trip?

12. How much time should a consumer spend on shopping (searching) for lower prices?

13. For which type of good would you expect consumers to spend more time on comparative shopping, or shopping for lower prices?

14. What are the new management tools that have been introduced during the past two decades?

15. Have the new management tools that have been introduced during the past two decades eliminated the need for the functional areas of managerial economics? Why or why not?

PROBLEMS

1. Given the following total-revenue function:

$$TR = 9Q - Q^2$$

(*a*) Derive the total-, average-, and marginal-revenue schedules from $Q = 0$ to $Q = 6$ by 1's.
(*b*) On the same set of axes, plot the total-, average-, and marginal-revenue schedules of part (*a*).

2. With reference to your figure in Problem 1*b*, explain the relationship among the total-, average-, and marginal-revenue curves.

3. Given the following total-product schedule:

Q	0	1	2	3	4	5	6	7	8
TP	0	2	5	9	12	14	15	15	14

Derive the average- and marginal-product schedules.

4. (*a*) On the same set of axes, plot the total-, average-, and marginal-product schedules of Problem 2.
(*b*) What is the relationship between the total-, average-, and marginal-product curves in part (*a*)?

*5. Derive the average- and marginal-profit schedules for the total-profit curve in the bottom panel of Figure 2-4 in the text.

*6. (*a*) Plot the total-profit curve of Figure 2-4, and below it, on a separate set of axes, plot the corresponding average- and marginal-profit schedules that you derived in Problem 5.
(*b*) Explain the relationship among the total-, average-, and marginal-profit curves in part (*a*).

7. Given the following total-cost schedule:

Q	0	1	2	3	4
TC	1	12	14	15	20

Derive the average- and marginal-cost schedules.

8. (*a*) On the same set of axes, plot the total-, average-, and marginal-cost schedules of Problem 7. (*b*) Explain the relationship among the total-, average-, and marginal-cost curves in part (*a*).

9. With the total-revenue curve of Problem 1 and the total-cost curve of Problem 7, derive the total-profit function and show how the firm determines the profit-maximizing level of output.

10. (*a*) Explain what is meant by "constrained optimization." (*b*) Indicate the importance of this in managerial economics.

11. Identify the characteristics of the American business model.

12. Explain the advantages of the American business model over its alternatives.

13. Explain how companies' governance failed in the United States at the beginning of this decade.

14. Explain how public trust in American financial markets was reestablished after companies' governance failed in the United States at the beginning of this decade.

*15. **Integrating Problem**
(*a*) Draw on the same set of axes the marginal-revenue curve derived in Problem 1 and the marginal-cost curve derived in Problem 7, and use them to explain why the best level of output of the firm is 3 units. (*b*) Explain why your answer to part (*a*) is an example of marginal analysis and optimizing behavior in general.

APPENDIX TO CHAPTER 2: DIFFERENTIAL CALCULUS AND OPTIMIZATION TECHNIQUES

This appendix reviews differential calculus and shows how it is used for optimization. We discuss the concept of the derivative, the rules of differentiation, and apply the rules of differential calculus to find the optimal solution to unconstrained and constrained optimization problems.

THE DERIVATIVE AND RULES OF DIFFERENTIATION

Optimization analysis can be conducted much more efficiently and precisely with differential calculus, which relies on the concept of the derivative. In this appendix, we examine the concept of the derivative and present some simple rules of differentiation.

The Concept of the Derivative

The concept of the derivative is closely related to the concept of the margin examined earlier. These can be explained in terms of the *TR* curve of Figure 2-1, reproduced with some modifications in Figure 2-6.

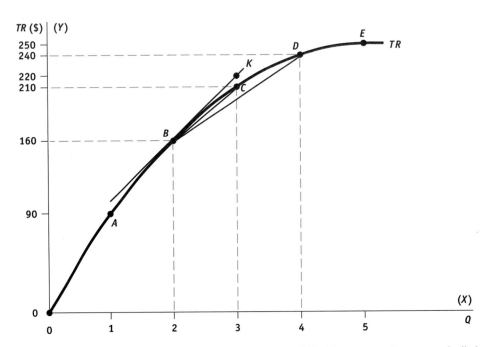

FIGURE 2-6 The Concept of the Derivative The derivative of *TR* with respect to *Q* measures the limit of $\Delta TR/\Delta Q$, as ΔQ approaches zero. Geometrically, this is given by the slope of the *TR* curve, or *MR*, at the point at which we want to find the derivative. More generally, letting $TR = Y$ and $Q = X$, the derivative of Y with respect to X, $dY/dX = \lim_{\Delta X \to 0} \Delta Y/\Delta X$.

In Section 2-3, we defined marginal revenue as the change in total revenue per unit change in output. For example, when output increases from 2 to 3 units, total revenue increases from $160 to $210. Thus,

$$MR = \frac{\Delta TR}{\Delta Q} = \frac{\$210 - \$160}{3 - 2} = \frac{\$50}{1} = \$50$$

This is the slope of chord BC on the total-revenue curve. However, when the quantity is infinitesimally divisible (i.e., when ΔQ assumes values smaller than unity and as small as we want, and even approaching zero in the limit), then MR is given by the slope of shorter and shorter chords, and it approaches the slope of the TR curve at a point, in the limit. Thus, starting from point B, as the change in quantity approaches zero, the change in total revenue or marginal revenue approaches the slope of the TR curve at point B. That is, $MR = \Delta TR/\Delta Q = \$60$ (the slope of tangent BK to the TR curve at point B) as the change in output approaches zero in the limit.

To summarize, between points B and C on the total-revenue curve of Figure 2-6, the marginal revenue is given by the slope of chord BC ($50). This is the *average* marginal revenue *between* 2 and 3 units of output. On the other hand, the marginal revenue at point B is given by the slope of line BK ($60), which is tangent to the total-revenue curve at point B. The marginal revenue or slope of the total-revenue curve varies at every point on the total-revenue curve. For example, at point C, the marginal revenue is $40 and is given by the slope of the tangent (not shown) to the total-revenue curve at point C. Similarly, at point D, $MR = \$20$, while at point E, $MR = \$0$. Thus, MR declines as we move farther up the total-revenue curve to reflect its concave shape and declining slope.

More generally, if we let $TR = Y$ and $Q = X$, the *derivative of Y with respect to X* is given by the change in Y with respect to X, as the change in X approaches zero. That is,

$$\frac{dY}{dX} = \lim_{\Delta X \to 0} \frac{\Delta Y}{\Delta X} \qquad \text{[2-3]}$$

This reads: The derivative of Y with respect to X is equal to the limit of the ratio $\Delta Y/\Delta X$ as ΔX approaches zero. Geometrically, this corresponds to the slope of the curve at the point at which we want to find the limit. Note that the smaller the change in X, the closer is the value of the derivative to the slope of the curve at a point. For example, for ΔX between 2 and 4 in Figure 2-6, the average $dY/dX = \$40$ (the slope of chord BD). For the smaller ΔX between 2 and 3, the average $dY/dX = \$50$ (the slope of chord BC), which is closer to the slope of the curve at point B (that is, $dY/dX = \$60$). The concept of the limit is extremely important in marginal and optimization analysis. However, before we can actually use the concept, we must define the rules by which we can find the derivative of any mathematical function (equation) in general and of any economic function in particular.

Rules of Differentiation

Differentiation is the process of determining the derivative of a function (i.e., finding the change in Y for a change in X, when the change in X approaches zero). In this section, we present the rules of differentiation.[5]

---

[5] A more extensive treatment of these rules as well as their proofs are presented in any introductory calculus text, such as John B. Fraleigh, *Calculus and Analytic Geometry* (Reading, Mass.: Addison-Wesley, 1985).

CONSTANT-FUNCTION RULE The derivative of a constant function, $Y = f(X) = a$, is zero for all values of a (the constant). That is, for the function

$$Y = f(X) = a$$
$$\frac{dY}{dX} = 0$$

For example, for the function

$$Y = 2$$
$$\frac{dY}{dX} = 0$$

This is graphed in the left panel of Figure 2-7. Since Y is defined to be a constant, its value does not change for any value of X, and so dY/dX (the slope of the Y line) is zero.

POWER-FUNCTION RULE The derivative of a power function, $Y = aX^b$, where a and b are constants, is equal to the exponent b multiplied by the coefficient a times the variable X raised to the $b - 1$ power. That is, for the function

$$Y = aX^b$$
$$\frac{dY}{dX} = b \cdot a \cdot X^{(b-1)}$$

For example, given the function $Y = 2X$, where $a = 2$, $b = 1$ (implicit), $dY/dX = 1 \cdot 2 \cdot X^{(1-1)} = 2X^0 = 2(1) = 2$. That is, for

$$Y = 2X$$
$$\frac{dY}{dX} = 2$$

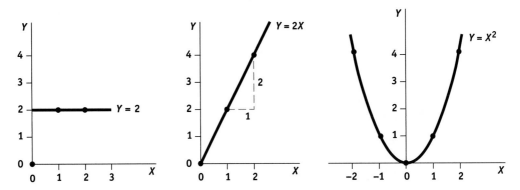

FIGURE 2-7 **Differentiating Constant and Power Functions** The derivative (slope) of the constant function $Y = 2$ is zero. The derivative (slope) of the power function $Y = 2X$ is 2 for any range of X values. For $Y = X^2$, $dY/dX = 2X$. Thus, dY/dX (slope) changes at every value of X and is negative for $X < 0$, is zero for $X = 0$, and is positive for $X > 0$.

This is graphed in the middle panel of Figure 2-7. Note that the slope of the line (dY/dX) is constant at the value of 2 over any range of X values. As another example, for the function $Y = X^2$, $dY/dX = 2 \cdot 1 \cdot X^{(2-1)} = 2X^1 = 2X$. That is, for the function

$$Y = X^2$$

$$\frac{dY}{dX} = 2X$$

This is graphed in the right panel of Figure 2-7. Note that the slope of the curve (dY/dX) varies at every value of X and is negative for $X < 0$, zero at $X = 0$, and positive for $X > 0$.

SUMS-AND-DIFFERENCES RULE   The derivative of a sum (difference) is equal to the sum (difference) of the derivatives of the individual terms. Thus, if

$$U = g(X) \qquad \text{and} \qquad V = h(X)$$

where U is an unspecified function, g of X, while V is another unspecified function, h of X,[6] then for the function

$$Y = U \pm V$$

$$\frac{dY}{dX} = \frac{dU}{dX} \pm \frac{dV}{dX}$$

For example, if $U = g(X) = 2X$ and $V = h(X) = X^2$ so that

$$Y = U + V = 2X + X^2$$

$$\frac{dY}{dX} = 2 + 2X$$

Since $dU/dX = 2$ and $dV/dX = 2X$ (by the power-function rule), the derivative of the total function (dY/dX) is equal to the derivative of the sum of its parts $(2 + 2X)$. As another example, for

$$Y = 0.04X^3 - 0.9X^2 + 10X + 5$$

$$\frac{dY}{dX} = 0.12X^2 - 1.8X + 10$$

Note that the derivatives of the first three terms of the Y function are obtained by the power-function rule, while the derivative of the constant, 5, is equal to zero by the constant-function rule.

PRODUCT RULE   The derivative of a product of two expressions is equal to the first expression multiplied by the derivative of the second, *plus* the second expression times the derivative of the first. Thus, for the function

$$Y = U \cdot V$$

---

[6] In the equations $U = g(X)$ and $V = h(X)$, or more generally, $Y = f(X)$, the variable to the left of the equals sign is called the "dependent variable" while the variable to the right of the equals sign is called the "independent variable." The reason for this terminology is that the value of the dependent or left-hand variable depends on the value of the independent or right-hand variable or variables. On the other hand, the independent or right-hand variable or variables is or are determined outside, or independently, of the relationship expressed by the equation.

where $U = g(X)$ and $V = h(X)$,

$$\frac{dY}{dX} = U\frac{dV}{dX} + V\frac{dU}{dX}$$

For example, for the function

$$Y = 2X^2(3 - 2X)$$

and letting $U = 2X^2$ and $V = 3 - 2X$,

$$\frac{dY}{dX} = 2X^2\left(\frac{dV}{dX}\right) + (3 - 2X)\left(\frac{dU}{dX}\right)$$

$$= 2X^2(-2) + (3 - 2X)(4X)$$

$$= -4X^2 + 12X - 8X^2$$

$$= 12X - 12X^2$$

QUOTIENT RULE The derivative of the quotient of two expressions is equal to the denominator multiplied by the derivative of the numerator, *minus* the numerator times the derivative of the denominator, all divided by the denominator squared. Thus, for the function

$$Y = \frac{U}{V}$$

and letting $U = g(X)$ and $V = h(X)$,

$$\frac{dY}{dX} = \frac{V(dU/dX) - U(dV/dX)}{V^2}$$

For example, for the function

$$Y = \frac{3 - 2X}{2X^2}$$

and letting $U = 3 - 2X$ and $V = 2X^2$,

$$\frac{dY}{dX} = \frac{2X^2(-2) - (3 - 2X)4X}{(2X^2)^2} = \frac{-4X^2 - 12X + 8X^2}{4X^4}$$

$$= \frac{4X^2 - 12X}{4X^4} = \frac{4X(X - 3)}{4X(X^3)} = \frac{X - 3}{X^3}$$

FUNCTION-OF-A-FUNCTION (CHAIN) RULE If $Y = f(U)$ and $U = g(X)$, then the derivative of Y with respect to X is equal to the derivative of Y with respect to U multiplied by the derivative of U with respect to X. That is, if

$$Y = f(U) \qquad \text{and} \qquad U = g(X)$$

then

$$\frac{dY}{dX} = \frac{dY}{dU} \cdot \frac{dU}{dX}$$

For example, if $\qquad Y = U^3 + 10 \qquad$ and $\qquad U = 2X^2$

then $\qquad \dfrac{dY}{dX} = 3U^2 \quad$ and $\quad \dfrac{dU}{dX} = 4X$

Therefore, $\qquad \dfrac{dY}{dX} = \dfrac{dY}{dU} \cdot \dfrac{dU}{dX} = (3U^2)4X$

Substituting the expression for U (that is, $U = 2X^2$) into the previous expression, we get

$$\frac{dY}{dX} = 3(2X^2)^2(4X) = 3(4X^4)4X = 48X^5$$

As another example, to find the derivative of

$$Y = (3X^2 + 10)^3$$

let $\qquad U = 3X^2 + 10 \qquad$ and $\qquad Y = U^3$

Then $\qquad \dfrac{dY}{dX} = 3U^2 \quad$ and $\quad \dfrac{dU}{dX} = 6X$

Thus, $\qquad \dfrac{dY}{dX} = \dfrac{dY}{dU} \cdot \dfrac{dU}{dX} = (3U^2)6X$

Substituting the value of U (that is, $3X^2 + 10$) into the previous expression, we get

$$\frac{dY}{dX} = 3(3X^2 + 10)^2(6X) = 3(9X^4 + 60X^2 + 100)(6X)$$

$$= 162X^5 + 1{,}080X^3 + 1{,}800X = 2X(81X^4 + 540X^2 + 900)$$

Table 2-5 summarizes these rules for differentiating functions.

TABLE 2-5 Rules for Differentiating Functions	
Function	**Derivative**
1. Constant function	
$Y = a$	$\dfrac{dy}{dx} = 0$
2. Power function	
$Y = aX^b$	$\dfrac{dY}{dX} = b \cdot a \cdot X^{(b-1)}$
3. Sums and differences of functions	
$Y = U \pm V$	$\dfrac{dY}{dX} = \dfrac{dU}{dX} \pm \dfrac{dV}{dX}$
4. Product of two functions	
$Y = U \cdot V$	$\dfrac{dY}{dX} = U\dfrac{dV}{dX} + V\dfrac{dU}{dX}$
5. Quotient of two functions	
$Y = \dfrac{U}{V}$	$\dfrac{dY}{dX} = \dfrac{V(dU/dX) - U(dV/dX)}{V^2}$
6. Function of a function	
$Y = f(U)$, where $U = g(X)$	$\dfrac{dY}{dX} = \dfrac{dY}{dU} \cdot \dfrac{dU}{dX}$

OPTIMIZATION WITH CALCULUS

We now examine the process of optimization with calculus. First we examine how we can determine the point at which a function is maximum or minimum. We then show how to distinguish between a maximum and a minimum.

Determining a Maximum or a Minimum by Calculus

Optimization often requires finding the maximum or the minimum value of a function. For example, a firm might want to maximize its revenue, minimize the cost of producing a given output, or, more likely, maximize its profits. For a function to be at its maximum or minimum, the derivative of the function must be zero. Geometrically, this corresponds to the point where the curve has zero slope. For example, for the total-revenue function (Equation 2-1 in Section 2-1),

$$TR = 100Q - 10Q^2$$

$$\frac{d(TR)}{dQ} = 100 - 20Q$$

Setting $d(TR)/dQ = 0$, we get

$$100 - 20Q = 0$$

Therefore,
$$Q = 5$$

That is, for the total-revenue function (Equation 2-1), $d(TR)/dQ = 0$ (i.e., its slope is zero), and the total revenue is maximum at the output level of 5 units (see Figure 2-1). Similarly, the derivative or slope of the marginal-cost and average-cost functions of Figure 2-2 is zero at $Q = 2$ and $Q = 3.5$, respectively, where these functions (curves) are minimum.

Distinguishing between a Maximum and a Minimum: The Second Derivative

We have seen that the derivative (slope) of a function (curve) is zero at both a minimum and a maximum point. To distinguish between a maximum and a minimum point, we use the *second derivative*. For the general function $Y = f(X)$, the second derivative is written as d^2Y/dX^2. The second derivative is the derivative of the derivative and is found by applying again to the (first) derivative the rules of differentiation presented in the previous section and summarized in Table 2-5. For example,

$$Y = X^3$$

$$\frac{dY}{dX} = 3X^2$$

and
$$\frac{d^2Y}{dX^2} = 6X$$

Similarly, for $TR = 100Q - 10Q^2$,

$$\frac{d(TR)}{dQ} = 100 - 20Q$$

and
$$\frac{d^2(TR)}{dQ^2} = -20$$

Geometrically, the derivative refers to the slope of the function, while the second derivative refers to the *change* in the slope of the function. The value of the second derivative can thus be used to determine whether we have a maximum or a minimum at the point at which the first derivative (slope) is zero. The rule is *if the second derivative is positive, we have a minimum, and if the second derivative is negative, we have a maximum.* We have already encountered the geometric equivalent of this rule when dealing with the total profit (π) function at the bottom of Figure 2-4. That function has a zero slope (i.e., $d\pi/dQ = 0$) at $Q = 1$ and $Q = 3$. But in the neighborhood of $Q = 1$, the slope of the π function increases (i.e., $d^2\pi/dQ^2 > 0$) from being negative at $Q < 1$ to zero at $Q = 1$, and positive at $Q > 1$, so that the π function faces up and we have a minimum. On the other hand, in the neighborhood of $Q = 3$, the slope of the π function decreases (i.e., $d^2\pi/dQ^2 < 0$) from being positive first, then zero, and then negative, so that the π function faces down and we have a maximum. A few applications follow.

First, given the following total-revenue function:

$$TR = 45Q - 0.5Q^2$$

Then
$$\frac{d(TR)}{dQ} = 45 - Q$$

Setting the first derivative equal to zero, we find that the *TR* function has a zero slope at $Q = 45$. Since $d^2(TR)/dQ^2 = -1$, this *TR* function reaches a maximum at $Q = 45$.[7]

As another example, consider the following marginal-cost function:

$$MC = 3Q^2 - 16Q + 57$$

Then
$$\frac{d(MC)}{dQ} = 6Q - 16$$

Setting the first derivative equal to zero, we find that the *MC* curve has zero slope at $Q = 2\frac{2}{3}$. Since $d^2(MC)/dQ^2 = 6$, this *MC* curve reaches a minimum at $Q = 2\frac{2}{3}$ so that the *MC* curve looks similar to the *MC* curve in Figure 2-2.

A final, more comprehensive and important example is provided by profit maximization by the firm. Suppose that the total-revenue and total-cost functions of the firm are, respectively,

$$TR = 45Q - 0.5Q^2$$
$$TC = Q^3 - 8Q^2 + 57Q + 2$$

Then
$$\pi = TR - TC$$
$$= 45Q - 0.5Q^2 - (Q^3 - 8Q^2 + 57Q + 2)$$
$$= 45Q - 0.5Q^2 - Q^3 + 8Q^2 - 57Q - 2$$
$$= -Q^3 + 7.5Q^2 - 12Q - 2$$

To determine the level of output at which the firm maximizes π, we proceed as follows:

$$\frac{d\pi}{dQ} = -3Q^2 + 15Q - 12 = 0$$
$$= (-3Q + 3)(Q - 4) = 0$$

----

[7] Note that for the function $TR = 100Q - 10Q^2$ examined earlier, we found that $d(TR)/dQ = 100 - 20Q$. Therefore, $d(TR)/dQ = 0$ at $Q = 5$, and $d^2(TR)/dQ^2 = -20$, so that this *TR* function reaches a *maximum* at $Q = 5$ (see Figure 2-1). If plotted, the above *TR* curve would look like the one in Figure 2-1, but it reaches a maximum at $Q = 45$.

Therefore, $\qquad\qquad\qquad\qquad Q = 1 \qquad$ and $\qquad Q = 4$

$$\frac{d^2\pi}{dQ^2} = -6Q + 15$$

At $Q = 1$, $(d^2\pi/dQ^2) = -6(1) + 15 = 9$, and π is minimum. At $Q = 4$, $(d^2\pi/dQ^2) = -6(4) + 15 = -9$, and π is maximum. Therefore, π is maximized at $Q = 4$, and from the original π function we can determine that

$$\pi = -(4)^3 + 7.5(4)^2 - 12(4) - 2$$
$$= -64 + 120 - 48 - 2$$
$$= \$6$$

The geometric equivalent of this analysis is similar to Figure 2-4.[8]

MULTIVARIATE OPTIMIZATION

In this section, we examine multivariate optimization, or the process of determining the maximum or minimum point of a function of more than two variables. To do this, we first introduce the concept of the partial derivative, and then we use it to examine the process of maximizing a multivariable function.

Partial Derivatives

Until now we have examined the relationship between two variables only. For example, variable Y (say, total revenue, total cost, or total profit) was assumed to be a function of, or to depend on, only the value of variable X (total output or quantity). Most economic relationships, however, involve more than two variables. For example, total revenue may be a function of, or depend on, both output and advertising, total costs may depend on expenditures of both labor and capital, and total profit on sales of commodities X and Y. Thus, it becomes important to determine the marginal effect on the dependent variable, say, total profit, resulting from changes in the quantities of each individual variable, say, the quantities sold of commodity X and commodity Y, *separately*. These marginal effects are measured by the *partial derivative*, which is indicated by the symbol ∂ (as compared to d for the derivative). The partial derivative of the dependent or left-hand variable with respect to each of the independent or right-hand variables is found by the same rules of differentiation presented earlier, except that all independent variables other than the one with respect to which we are finding the partial derivative are held constant.

For example, suppose that the total profit (π) function of a firm depends on sales of commodities X and Y as follows:

$$\pi = f(X,Y) = 80X - 2X^2 - XY - 3Y^2 + 100Y \qquad\qquad\qquad\qquad [2\text{-}4]$$

To find the partial derivative of π with respect to X, $\partial\pi/\partial X$, we hold Y constant and obtain

$$\frac{\partial\pi}{\partial X} = 80 - 4X - Y$$

---

[8] Note that if we set the $d(TR)/dQ$ or MR equal to $d(TC)/dQ$ or MC, we would find that $MR = MC$ at $Q = 1$ and $Q = 4$. However, only at $Q = 4$ does the MC curve intercept the MR curve from below so that π is maximized.

This isolates the marginal effect on π from changes in the quantity sold of commodity X only (i.e., while holding the quantity of commodity Y constant). Note that the derivative of the third term of the π function is $-Y$ (since the implicit exponent of X is 1) and that Y is treated as a constant. The fourth and the fifth terms of the π function drop out in the partial differentiation because they contain no X term. Similarly, to isolate the marginal effect of a change of Y on π, we hold X constant and obtain

$$\frac{\partial \pi}{\partial Y} = -X - 6Y + 100$$

We can visualize geometrically the concept of the partial derivative with a three-dimensional figure, with π on the vertical axis and with the X axis and the Y axis forming the (plane surface, rather than the line) base of the figure. Then, $\partial \pi / \partial X$ measures the marginal effect of X on π, in the cross section of the three-dimensional figure along the X axis. Similarly, $\partial \pi / \partial Y$ examines the marginal effect of Y on π in the cross section of the three-dimensional figure along the Y axis. Note furthermore that the value of $\partial \pi / \partial X$ depends also on the level at which Y is held constant. Similarly, the value of $\partial \pi / \partial Y$ depends also on the level at which X is held constant. This is the reason that the expression for $\partial \pi / \partial X$ found above also contains a Y term, while $\partial \pi / \partial Y$ also has an X term.

Maximizing a Multivariable Function

To maximize or minimize a multivariable function, we must set each partial derivative equal to zero and solve the resulting set of simultaneous equations for the optimal value of the independent or right-hand variables.[9] For example, to maximize the total-profit function (Equation 2-4, repeated here for ease of reference)

$$\pi = 80X - 2X^2 - XY - 3Y^2 + 100Y \qquad [2\text{-}4]$$

we set $\partial \pi / \partial X$ and $\partial \pi / \partial Y$ (found earlier) equal to zero and solve for X and Y. Specifically,

$$\frac{\partial \pi}{\partial X} = 80 - 4X - Y = 0$$

$$\frac{\partial \pi}{\partial Y} = -X - 6Y + 100 = 0$$

Multiplying the first of these expressions by -6, rearranging the second, and adding, we get

$$\begin{aligned} -480 + 24X + 6Y &= 0 \\ 100 - \quad X - 6Y &= 0 \\ \hline -380 + 23X \qquad\quad &= 0 \end{aligned}$$

Therefore, $X = 380/23 = 16.52$.

Substituting $X = 16.52$ into the first expression of the partial derivative set equal to zero, and solving for Y, we get

$$80 - 4(16.52) - Y = 0$$

Therefore, $Y = 80 - 66.08 = 13.92$.

---

[9] The condition for distinguishing between a maximum and a minimum is based on the value of the second-order partial derivative. This condition is much more complex than for a function of a single independent variable and is beyond the scope of this text. In the rest of this book, the context of the problem will tell us whether the point at which all partial derivatives are zero is a maximum or a minimum, and we implicitly assume that the second-order condition for maximization or minimization is satisfied. For the interested reader, the second-order condition to distinguish between a maximum and a minimum for a multivariate function is examined in any calculus text.

Thus, the firm maximizes π when it sells 16.52 units of commodity X and 13.92 units of commodity Y. Substituting these values into the π function, we get the maximum total profit of the firm,

$$\pi = 80(16.52) - 2(16.52)^2 - (16.52)(13.92) - 3(13.92)^2 + 100(13.92)$$
$$= \$1,356.52$$

CONSTRAINED OPTIMIZATION

We have seen in Section 2-4 that when managers face some constraints we have constrained optimization. This reduces the freedom of action of the firm and usually prevents the attainment of its unconstrained optimum. Constrained optimization can be solved by substitution or by the Lagrangian method. These are examined in turn.

Constrained Optimization by Substitution

A constrained optimization problem may be solved by first solving the *constraint equation* for one of the decision variables, and then substituting the expression for this variable into the *objective function* that the firm seeks to maximize or minimize. This procedure converts a constrained optimization problem into an unconstrained one, which can be solved as indicated in the previous section.

For example, suppose that the firm seeks to maximize its total-profit function given by Equation 2-4 (repeated below for ease of reference),

$$\pi = 80X - 2X^2 - XY - 3Y^2 + 100Y \qquad [2\text{-}4]$$

but faces the constraint that the output of commodity X plus the output of commodity Y must be 12. That is,

$$X + Y = 12 \qquad [2\text{-}5]$$

To solve this optimization problem by substitution, we can solve the constraint function for X, substitute the value of X into the objective function (π) that the firm seeks to maximize, and then apply the procedure for maximizing an unconstrained objective function shown in the previous section. Specifically, solving the constraint function for X, we get

$$X = 12 - Y$$

Substituting the constraint expression for X into the objective profit function, we obtain

$$\pi = 80(12 - Y) - 2(12 - Y)^2 - (12 - Y)Y - 3Y^2 + 100Y$$
$$= 960 - 80Y - 2(144 - 24Y + Y^2) - 12Y + Y^2 - 3Y^2 + 100Y$$
$$= 960 - 80Y - 288 + 48Y - 2Y^2 - 12Y + Y^2 - 3Y^2 + 100Y$$
$$= -4Y^2 + 56Y + 672$$

To maximize this (unconstrained) profit function, we find the first derivative of π with respect to Y, set it equal to zero, and solve for Y. That is,

$$\frac{d\pi}{dY} = -8Y + 56 = 0$$

Therefore, $Y = 7$.

Substituting $Y = 7$ into the constraint function, we get $X = 12 - Y = 12 - 7 = 5$. Thus, the firm maximizes total profits when it produces 5 units of commodity X and 7 units of commodity Y (as compared with $X = 16.52$ and $Y = 13.92$ when the firm faced no output constraint—see p. 75). With $X = 5$ and $Y = 7$,

$$\pi = 80(5) - 2(5)^2 - (5)(7) - 3(7)^2 + 100(7)$$
$$= \$868$$

as compared with \$1,356.52 found earlier in the absence of any output constraint.

Constrained Optimization by the Lagrangian Multiplier Method

When the constraint equation is too complex or cannot be solved for one of the decision variables as an explicit function of the other(s), the techniques of substitution to solve a constrained optimization problem can become burdensome or impossible. In such cases we may resort to the *Lagrangian multiplier method*. The first step in this method is to form a *Lagrangian function*. This is given by the original objective function that the firm seeks to maximize or minimize, plus λ (the Greek letter lambda that is conventionally used for the Lagrangian multiplier), times the constraint function set equal to zero. Because it incorporates the constraint function set equal to zero, the Lagrangian function can also be treated as an unconstrained optimization problem, and its solution will always be identical to the original constrained optimization problem.

As an illustration, we show how the constrained profit maximization problem that was solved in the previous section by substitution can be solved by the Lagrangian multiplier method. To do so, we first set the constraint function (i.e., $X + Y = 12$) equal to zero and obtain

$$X + Y - 12 = 0$$

We then multiply this form of the constraint function by λ and add it to the original profit function we seek to maximize (i.e., to $\pi = 80X - 2X^2 - XY - 3Y^2 + 100Y$) to form the Lagrangian function (L_π). That is,

$$L_\pi = 80X - 2X^2 - XY - 3Y^2 + 100Y + \lambda(X + Y - 12) \qquad \text{[2-6]}$$

The Lagrangian function (L_π) can be treated as an unconstrained function in three unknowns: X, Y, and λ. Now, the solution that maximizes L_π also maximizes π.

To maximize L_π, we set the partial derivative of L_π with respect to X, Y, and λ equal to zero, and solve the resulting set of simultaneous equations for the values of X, Y, and λ. Finding the partial derivative of L_π with respect to X, Y, and λ, and setting them equal to zero, we get

$$\frac{\partial L_\pi}{\partial X} = 80 - 4X - Y + \lambda = 0 \qquad \text{[2-7]}$$

$$\frac{\partial L_\pi}{\partial Y} = -X - 6Y + 100 + \lambda = 0 \qquad \text{[2-8]}$$

$$\frac{\partial L_\pi}{\partial \lambda} = X + Y - 12 = 0 \qquad \text{[2-9]}$$

Note that Equation 2-9 is equal to the constraint imposed on the original profit function of the firm (Equation 2-4). Indeed, the Lagrangian function (Equation 2-6) was specifically set up so that when the partial derivative of L_π with respect to λ (the Lagrangian multiplier) is set equal to zero, not only the constraint of the problem is satisfied but the Lagrangian function (L_π) reduces to the original unconstrained profit function (π), so that the optimal solution of both functions is identical.

To find the values of X, Y, and λ that maximize L_π and π, we solve simultaneously Equations 2-7, 2-8, and 2-9. To do this, subtract Equation 2-8 from Equation 2-7 and get

$$-20 - 3X + 5Y = 0 \qquad\qquad [2\text{-}10]$$

Multiplying Equation 2-9 by 3 and adding to it Equation 2-10, we obtain

$$
\begin{array}{r}
3X + 3Y - 36 = 0 \\
-3X + 5Y - 20 = 0 \\
\hline
-8Y - 56 = 0
\end{array}
$$

Therefore, $Y = 7$ and $X = 5$, so that $\pi = \$868$ (as in the previous section). Finally, by substituting the value of $X = 5$ and $Y = 7$ into Equation 2-8, we get the value of λ. That is,

$$-5 - 42 + 100 = -\lambda$$

Thus, $\lambda = -53$.

The value of λ has an important economic interpretation. It is the marginal effect on the objective-function solution associated with a 1-unit change in the constraint. In the preceding problem, this means that a decrease in the output capacity constraint from 12 to 11 units or an increase to 13 units will reduce or increase, respectively, the total profit of the firm (π) by about \$53.

APPENDIX PROBLEMS

1. Find the derivative of the following functions:
   (a) $Y = f(X) = a$
       $TC = f(Q) = 182$
   (b) $Y = 2X^2$
       $Y = -1X^3$
       $Y = \frac{1}{2}X^{-2}$
       $TR = f(Q) = 10Q$
       $TR = f(Q) = -Q^2$

2. Find the derivative of the following functions:
   (a) $Y = 45X - 0.5X^2$
       $Y = X^3 - 8X^2 + 57X + 2$
       $TR = 100Q - 10Q^2$ (Equation 2-1)
       $TC = 182 + 56Q$ (Equation 2-2)
   (b) $Y = X^3 - 2X^2$
       $Y = 8X^4 - 20X^3$
       $Y = 4X^3(2X - 5)$

3. Find the derivative of the following functions:
   (a) $Y = \dfrac{3X^3}{X^2}$

   $Y = \dfrac{5X^3}{4X + 3}$

   (b) $Y = U^5$ and $U = 2X^3 + 3$
       $Y = U^3 + 3U$ and $U = -X^2 + 10X$
       $Y = (2X^3 + 5)^2$

4. For the following total-revenue and total-cost functions of a firm:

   $$TR = 22Q - 0.5Q^2$$
   $$TC = \tfrac{1}{3}Q^3 - 8.5Q^2 + 50Q + 90$$

   (a) Determine the level of output at which the firm maximizes its total profit. (b) Determine the maximum profit that the firm could earn.

5. A firm's total-revenue and total-cost functions are

   $$TR = 4Q$$
   $$TC = 0.04Q^3 - 0.9Q^2 + 10Q + 5$$

   (a) Determine the best level of output.
   (b) Determine the total profit of the firm at its best level of output.

6. Given the following cost function, determine the level of (nonzero) output at which the cost function is minimized, and the level of the costs.

   $$AC = 200 - 24Q + Q^2$$

7. Given the following cost function, determine the level of (nonzero) output at which the cost function is minimized, and the level of the costs.

   $$MC = 200 - 48Q + 3Q^2$$

8. For the following total-profit function of a firm:

$$\pi = 144X - 3X^2 - XY - 2Y^2 + 120Y - 35$$

(*a*) Determine the level of output of each commodity at which the firm maximizes its total profit. (*b*) Determine the value of the maximum amount of the total profit of the firm.

9. **Integrating Problem**

The Warren & Smith Company manufactures commercial zippers of two kinds, kind *X* and kind *Y*. Its production department estimates that the average-cost function of the firm is

$$AC = X^2 + 2Y^2 - 2XY - 2X - 6Y + 20$$

(*a*) The manager of the firm would like to know the level of output of zipper *X* and zipper *Y* at which the average cost of the firm is minimized, and the level of this minimum average cost. (*b*) The firm expects an order that will require it to produce a total output of 6 units of both kinds of zippers (each unit may be a large number of zippers), and so the manager would also like to know how many of each type of zipper the firm must produce to minimize its average cost, and what its minimum average cost would be if it receives the order. The manager gives this assignment to two researchers who use different methods to obtain their answers. (*c*) While the firm expects the order to be of 6 units, it may be as large as 7 units or as small as 5 units. Determine the minimum average cost of the firm with these different order sizes.

SUPPLEMENTARY READINGS

The utilization of popular management tools is discussed in:

Rigby, D., "Management Tools and Techniques: A Survey," *California Management Review* (Winter 2001), pp. 139–160.

Benchmarking is discussed in:

Bogan, Christopher E., and Michael J. English, *Benchmarking for Best Practices: Winning Through Innovative Adaptations* (New York: McGraw-Hill, 1994).

"Is Your Benchmarking Doing the Right Work?" *Harvard Business Update* (September 2003), pp. 1–4.

Total quality management is examined in:

Grant, R. M., R. Shani, and R. Krishnan, "TQM's Challenge to Managerial Theory and Practice," *Sloan Management Review* (Winter 1994), pp. 25–35.

Easton, George S., and Sherry L. Jarrell, "The Effects of Total Quality Management on Corporate Performance: An Empirical Investigation," *Journal of Business*, no. 2 (1998), pp. 253–307.

Rosett, Joshua G., and Richard N. Rosett, "Characteristics of TQM: Evidence from the TIT/USA Today Quality Cup Competition," NBER, *Working Paper 7241* (July 1999).

For reengineering, see:

Hammer, M., "Process Management and the Future of Six Sigma," *MIT Sloan Management Review* (Winter 2002), pp. 26–32.

Hammer, R. M., *Beyond Reengineering: How the Process-Centered Organization Is Changing Our Work and Our Lives* (New York: HarperCollins, 1997).

Hammer, R. M., and J. Champy, *Reengineering the Corporation: A Manifesto for Business Revolution* (New York: HarperBusiness, 1993).

The learning organization is examined in:

Becker, B., M. Huselid, and D. Ulrich, *The HR Scorecard: Linking People, Strategy and Performance* (Boston: Harvard University Press, 2001).

Nevis, E. C., A. J. DiBella, and J. M. Gould, "Understanding Organizations as Learning Systems," *Sloan Management Review* (Winter 1995), pp. 73–85.

Senge, P., *The Fifth Discipline Fieldbook* (New York: Doubleday, 1994).

Senge, P., et al., *The Dance of Change: The Challenge of Sustaining Momentum in a Learning Organization* (New York: Double Currency, 1999).

Storey, J., *Human Resource Management: A Critical Text* (London: Thomson Learning, 2001).

Zack, Michael H., "Rethinking the Knowledge-Based Organization," *Sloan Management Review* (Summer 2003), pp. 67–71.

For a review of differential calculus, see:

Chiang, Alpha, *Fundamental Methods of Mathematical Economics,* 3rd ed. (New York: McGraw-Hill, 1984).

Dowling, Edward T., *Mathematics for Economists* (New York: McGraw-Hill, 2000).

Mathematical and other optimization techniques are presented in:

Baumol, William J., *Economic Theory and Operations Analysis,* 4th ed. (Englewood Cliffs, N.J.: Prentice-Hall, 1977).

Fourer, R., and J. P. Goux, "Optimization as an Internet Resource," *Interfaces* (March–April 2001), pp. 130–150.

Salvatore, Dominick, *Microeconomics: Theory and Applications,* 3rd ed. (New York: Oxford University Press, 2003), mathematical appendix.

Silberberg, Eugene, *The Structure of Economics: A Mathematical Analysis* (New York: McGraw-Hill, 1990).

 INTERNET SITE ADDRESSES

Following are the Internet site addresses for more information and data on the companies discussed in this chapter:

Adelphia Communications: http://www.adelphia.com

AT&T: http://www.att.com

Canon: http://www.usa.canon.com

Citigroup: http://www.citigroup.com

Coca-Cola: http://www.coca-cola.com

Compaq: http://www.compaq.com

Dell: http://www.dell.com

DuPont: http://www.dupont.com

Enron: http://www.enron.com

Ford: http://www.ford.com

GE Information Services: http://www.ge.com

Hewlett-Packard: http://www.hp.com

IBM: http://www.ibm.com

Johnson & Johnson: http://www.jj.com

McDonald's: http://www.mcdonalds.com

Merrill Lynch: http://www.ml.com

Microsoft: http://www.microsoft.com

Mobil: http://www.mobil.com

J. P. Morgan: http://www.jpmorgan.com

Motorola: http://www.mot.com

WorldCom, now MCI: http://www.mci.com

Xerox: http://www.xerox.com

INTEGRATING CASE STUDY 1
The Education of Michael Dell

Introductory Comment: The following selection illustrates most of the concepts presented in this part of the text, and thus it serves as an excellent integrating case study. It clearly shows the nature and scope of managerial decisions in a current real-world situation—the industry for personal computers (PCs). In addition, it illustrates the theory of the firm in actual operation and the importance and function of profits in providing the signal for the efficient allocation of society's resources. It also shows the firm's optimizing behavior as it attempts to minimize costs and maximize profits. Finally, it shows why increased competition lowered profit margins for other U.S. PC makers, but not for Dell, and why Dell is now aggressively pushing sales abroad and moving into other markets, such as printers and storage.

He dropped out of college to start his company. His business model conquered the PC industry. Now, at age 40, Dell takes his place among the nation's most respected executives. The company turned 21 years old in May 2005, and it is now one of the nation's most prominent and respected corporations.

Michael Dell's company has run through the competition like some kind of sports team from Boston. Let's quickly review the recent events of the PC industry: IBM, the company that practically invented the desktop computer, has exited the business by selling out to the Chinese firm Lenovo. Gateway has seen its business crash—its stock, which traded above $80 five years ago, now fetches $4 and change. Compaq wisely sold out to Hewlett-Packard, which unwisely doubled down in this market, giving Dell—as one wag puts it—"a bigger butt to kick." And of course it was HP's bet on Compaq that ultimately cost Carly Fiorina her job. Truly, this is an industry under assault, and in every instance the guy at the other end of the gun is Michael Dell. "You have to just say he has done a hell of a job," says former GE CEO Jack Welch. "No one has pulled the levers of cost, quality, and service better than Dell."

Dell has thrived as downward-spiraling prices and commodification washed over the PC industry, benefiting the company's customers and bashing its competitors. Instead of battling the tide by attempting to erect proprietary systems, as HP and IBM often did, Dell used its low-cost, direct-sales model to ride the wave. Today, by nearly every unit of measure in the computer hardware business Dell is irrefutably the No. 1 company in the U.S. Be it in desktops, notebooks, and servers, or in profits, growth, and margins, Dell is the leader. And it isn't slowing down either. At its mid-February (2005) earnings conference call, Dell announced that technology research firm IDC had determined that it had surpassed HP to become the worldwide leader in PC market share, with 17.6 percent.

Success brings unexpected challenges. For years Michael Dell and company CEO Kevin Rollins—Dell remains chairman but turned over the CEO reins to his right-hand man last year—cultivated a chip-on-the-shoulder mentality at their company. But now, with all the accolades and soaring market share, that could ring hollow. I suggest as much in an interview with Rollins.

Fortune: "You're not an underdog anymore."
Rollins: "Well, we think we are."
Fortune: "You're deluding yourself."
Rollins: "I'll tell you why we think we're an underdog, and that is, we had been a PC company. We've been migrating the last three or four years out of being a PC company. We've moved into servers and

storage, mobility products, services, software peripheral categories, and printers, and became a diversified IT company. If you look at those other categories, we're not the leader, we're not the biggest. So as we've built out a diversified IT portfolio, we're a small guy again, and it keeps this notion of the underdog, gotta struggle, gotta change, gotta do things for the customer."

Sure, it's pep-talk stuff, but Rollins is describing a fundamental shift at Dell. Until recently the company's business model was to be the world's most efficient assembler and distributor of Wintel technology. In other words, if a customer wanted a PC with an Intel chip and Microsoft software, Dell was the optimal machine to purchase. The idea may seem basic, but remember that companies like IBM and DEC spent hundreds of millions of dollars developing alternative operating systems and hardware that didn't pan out.

Obviously, being the premier Wintel vendor has worked like a charm for Dell, but lately growth in the PC business has been slowing down, particularly in the huge but mature U.S. market. Between 1996 and 1999, PC sales in the U.S. climbed on average 16 percent annually. Between 2000 and 2004, sales grew only 3.6 percent per year. True, Dell can still make big market-share gains—unlike Microsoft and Intel—but the graying of the U.S. PC business is nevertheless critical, because Dell derives some 50 percent of its revenue from this market. Looking ahead, Dell and Rollins understood that their company would need new growth drivers, which is why they have pushed into servers and storage, and—in a direct challenge to HP's golden goose—printers.

Michael Dell's Rise

By now you are probably familiar with Michael Dell's star-spangled bio. He began his business tinkering with machines in his University of Texas dorm room, and a mere eight years later cracked the Fortune 500, making him, at 27, the youngest Fortune 500 CEO ever. Doubters said his company would never challenge the big boys, that his model wouldn't work overseas, that he couldn't sell servers—and he has proved them wrong every time. Today the 9.6 percent stake he holds in his company is worth some $10 billion, making him one of the richest men in the world.

There is one key point in Michael Dell's story that is overlooked, however, and that is the extent to which he is almost completely self-taught. Unlike CEOs such as GE's Immelt, Home Depot's Nardelli, and 3M's McNerney, for instance, Michael Dell didn't do time at GE's famed Crotonville, N.Y., training center, soaking up management acumen at the knee of Jack Welch. Dell never went to Wharton or the Harvard Business School either. He didn't even stick around at the University of Texas long enough to collect his undergraduate degree.

Initially the man and his company were perceived as geek and gimmick. Dell knew how to cobble together PCs on the cheap and sell them on the phone—hardly a threat to the technology orthodoxy. After early success, though, it was acknowledged that the man and the company had become players in the PC industry. Dell understood not just the guts of a computer but also what made IBM tick and—more to the point—how to skewer Compaq and why it's not wise to compete with Sony in consumer electronics. And today the man and the company have become global business paradigms, analyzed by management consultants, studied by old-school companies like GM and Lockheed Martin, and naturally the subject of case studies at the Harvard Business School. Sure, Michael Dell has surrounded himself with mentors and consultants when he needed to, but that's not always easy for a founding CEO. "Michael never had an ego problem or a not-invented-here mentality. He had no problem going outside the company to find talent," says Mike Kwatinetz, a general partner with Azure Capital in Silicon Valley who, as a former analyst at Sanford Bernstein, was one of the first on Wall Street to recognize Dell's potential 13 years ago.

The company's ride has not always been smooth, and of course its mistakes have contributed mightily to Michael Dell's business education. In 1989 the company developed a family of high-end products code-named Olympic, which customers rejected out of hand. Dell killed the products hastily rather than allow engineers to convince him that they could be tweaked.

Four years later poor quality derailed Dell's notebook line. Michael Dell brought in John Medica, the man behind Apple's PowerBook, to fix the mess, and at his urging the company focused on the one notebook that worked best and scrapped the rest of the line.

More recently Dell and Rollins discovered that their subordinates perceived them as cold technocrats. Now Dell, Rollins, and the rest of management are working hard on the fuzzy stuff. Employees rate their bosses—including Michael and Kevin—every six months in "Tell Dell" surveys. "If you're a manager and you're not addressing [employee] issues, you're not going to get promoted, you're not going to get compensation," says Dell. "And if you consistently score in the bottom rungs of the surveys, we're going to look at you and say, 'Maybe this isn't the right job for you.'"

Just to give you an idea of how far Dell has come: 21 years ago (when the company was founded in 1984) IBM and HP were voted No. 1 and No. 3, respectively, on America's Most Admired Companies list. (At that point if you had asked the voters, "What's a Dell?" they probably would have told you it was a small, secluded, wooded valley.) As for PC market share, of course, Dell wasn't on the radar screen, while Commodore, with about $1.1 billion in PC sales, was the industry leader with a 27 percent U.S. market share. IBM was No. 2, and Apple and Tandy came in at No. 3 and No. 4. (Atari and Kaypro were big back then, too, remember?) Fast-forward to today (2005) and you'll notice that HP and IBM are no longer in the Most Admired's top ten, though interestingly IBM ranks higher than Dell on the industry list (perhaps because Dell's competitors didn't want to vote for a company that's eating their lunch). As for market share in the U.S., Dell is just above 33 percent, which means that today one in three PCs shipped is a Dell. (Worldwide it's one in six.) Besides the U.S., Dell is now the No. 1 brand in Britain, Canada, and Ireland (all top-ten markets).

Dell's market-share gains would be impressive enough, but the company also has the growth and profitability throttles open all the way. Its worldwide revenues are growing 19 percent now—that's seven percentage points higher than the rest of the industry—while profits are growing even faster. Dell's margins are revealing, in that its gross margin of 18 percent is actually lower than IBM's and HP's. That's because Dell is generally selling lower-margin machines. But a funny thing happens on the way to the bottom line: Dell's net margin checks in at 6 percent, while the others are close to 1 percent. Why is that? Because Dell's operating expenses—i.e., selling, general, and administrative—are so low, a direct result of the cost-effectiveness of selling directly to customers rather than through a middleman.

Dell also spends less on research and development than HP, IBM, and the others, a point that makes the folks at Dell a little prickly and defensive. Dell's competitors say it is evidence that Dell doesn't innovate. The folks at Dell beg to differ. Recently I had dinner in Austin at a place called Kenichi with Jeff Clarke, senior VP of products and head of R&D at Dell. As we order, I point out that Dell spends less than $500 million a year on R&D, or less than 1 percent of sales, while HP and IBM lay out upward of 6 percent. "It means they're spending a lot more money than we are," says Clarke, who's been at Dell for 18 years. "One has to measure effectiveness. One has to measure the value. We tend to be a very efficient and a very effective spender of our dollars." Clarke argues that Dell's R&D effort is focused solely on open-standards-based computing (read Wintel), while the competition spends much of its R&D resources on proprietary systems that often don't cut it in the marketplace.

Dell's Move into Printers

The latest great battle in the PC business isn't in computers but in printers. Dell is now waging war on Hewlett-Packard's vaunted imaging and printing division, which produces some 70 percent of that company's operating profit. To destroy this business would be devastating to HP. Printing is what's known as an installed-base business, much like the famous Gillette razor-blade model. You sell the customer a razor, or in this case a printer, but the real margins are in the blades or, in the case of the printer, the cartridges, and you now have a captive customer who will buy from you for years. Dell began selling printers, both inkjet and lasers, two years ago, and Michael says that so far the effort is coming along fine. "Our goal this past year was to sell five million printers, and we did that," he says.

"We now have about 20 percent of the inkjet-printer market in the U.S., which I think is pretty remarkable. That suggests to me that five or ten years from now this is going to be a very significant business for us in terms of revenues and profits." For now, Dell admits that margins are "not as great as the other businesses," but he insists that his machine's lower price will erode HP's business. (He maintains that a Dell color laser is roughly half the price of an HP and that the toner is 45 percent less.)

Vyomesh Joshi, head of printers and PC business at HP, counters by saying that Dell succeeded in PCs because that business was commodifying, while printers aren't. He also believes that Dell's partners (Dell outsources the making of printers) won't let it get big. Told of this, a Dell executive responded, "Go back and see what HP said about us in servers five years ago. I'm sure they were saying the same kind of thing." Yes, it's true that Lexmark, Fuji, and Kodak are manufacturing Dell's printers, but Dell's engineers are digging into this business to make the machines work seamlessly with Dell PCs, servers, and notebooks. Dell has an ever-improving feature that will alert the customer when he's getting low on ink. Just click to reorder one of those high-margin cartridges! And of course there is no middleman to take a slice of the profit.

Whether or not Dell is an innovator or will reign supreme in printers, what is unassailable is that this company is a manufacturing marvel. A fundamental difference between Dell and the competition is that at Dell, every single machine is made for a specific order. The others are producing machines to match a sales forecast. The advantages that Dell derives from this model on the factory floor are tangible and enormous. For instance, industry sources say Dell now carries only four days of inventory, while IBM has 20 days and HP has 28. Obviously, low inventory frees up mountains of cash for Dell that is otherwise tied up at IBM and HP. Dell's manufacturing prowess doesn't stop there. The company urges its suppliers—everyone from drive makers to Intel—to warehouse inventory as close to its factories as possible. Any cost that can be "shared with" (read "transferred to") those suppliers, is. (Does that remind anyone of a certain large retailer headquartered in Bentonville, Ark.?) Pay a visit to a Dell plant and you can watch workers unload a supplier's components almost right onto the assembly line.

All this is reflected in one eye-catching statistic: In 1998, Dell produced $745,000 of revenue per employee. Now, seven years later, the company does $900,000 of sales per employee (HP comes in at $540,000).

You would be correct, then, if you guessed that Dell's factories are running full-tilt boogie right now. "We challenged our manufacturing guys to triple the throughput, and they did it," says Rollins. Adds Dell: "We need capacity. The plants here are running flat out, seven days a week." But Dell and Rollins saw that coming, and in late 2003 the company began searching for a site for a massive new plant. Where was the most cost-effective location? Taipei? Mumbai? Kuala Lumpur? Would you believe, Winston-Salem?

The notion of building a giant new computer-assembly plant in the U.S.—east of the Mississippi, mind you—is, to put it mildly, counterintuitive. Can Dell really make money manufacturing computers in North Carolina? "Our business in North America continues to grow in increments of $6 billion to $7 billion a year—but where are you going to make all the stuff?" asks Dell. "With our business model, it just does not make sense to go off-shore. The value equation is better building close to the customer."

While the number of employees at the Winston-Salem plant is fairly modest, the state of North Carolina hopes the factory will attract dozens of other businesses to serve Dell and turn into something really large. Might be a pretty good bet. When Michael Dell first appeared on the business horizon a little more than a decade ago, you could see the potential of his business in the same way you can see an 18-wheel truck coming at you ten miles across the Bonneville Salt Flats. You know it's going to take a while, but there's no question it's a big rig and no question it's coming. If there are still any questions, let it be said that Dell, the big rig of the PC business, has arrived.

Source: Adapted and reprinted with permission from Andy Serwer, "The Education of Michael Dell," *Fortune* (March 5, 2005), pp. 73–82. @ Time Inc. All rights reserved.

PART TWO

Demand Analysis

Part Two (Chapters 3 through 5) analyzes demand. This is one of the most important aspects of managerial economics, since no firm could exist or survive if a sufficient demand for its product did not exist or could not be generated. Chapter 3 deals with demand theory and examines the forces that determine the demand for the firm's product. Chapter 4 then shows how a firm can estimate the demand for its product. Finally, Chapter 5 examines how a firm can forecast demand. The increasing importance of global products and global competition, including electronic commerce or *e-commerce,* also is examined.

CHAPTER 3 Demand Theory

CHAPTER OUTLINE

KEY TERMS (in the order of their appearance)

Consumer demand theory
Normal goods
Inferior goods
Individual's demand schedule
Individual's demand curve
Law of demand
Substitution effect
Income effect
Giffen good
Change in the quantity
    demanded
Change in demand
Market demand curve

Market demand function
Bandwagon effect
Snob effect
Monopoly
Perfect competition
Oligopoly
Monopolistic competition
Durable goods
Demand function faced by a firm
Derived demand
Producers' goods
Price elasticity of demand (E_P)
Point price elasticity of demand

Arc price elasticity of demand
Total revenue (TR)
Marginal revenue (MR)
Income elasticity of demand (E_I)
Point income elasticity of demand
Arc income elasticity of demand
Cross-price elasticity of
    demand (E_{XY})
Point cross-price elasticity
    of demand
Arc cross-price elasticity of
    demand
E-commerce

In this chapter, we begin our analysis of consumer demand. Demand is one of the most important aspects of managerial economics, since a firm would not be established or survive if a sufficient demand for its product did not exist or could not be created. That is, a firm could have the most efficient production techniques and the most effective management, but without a demand for its product that is sufficient to cover at least all production and selling costs over the long run, it simply would not survive. Indeed, many firms go out of business soon after being set up because their expectation of a sufficient demand for their products fails to materialize, even with a great deal of advertising. Each year also sees many previously established and profitable firms close as a result of consumers shifting their purchases to different firms and products. Demand is, thus, essential for the creation, survival, and profitability of a firm.

In this chapter we examine *demand theory,* or the forces that determine the demand for a firm's product or service. We also introduce the important concept of elasticity. This measures the responsiveness in the quantity demanded of a commodity to changes in each of the forces that determine demand. The forces that determine consumers' demand for a commodity are the price of the commodity, consumers' incomes, the price of related commodities, consumers' tastes, and all the other important but more specific forces that affect the demand for a particular commodity. In Chapter 4 we will show how a firm can actually estimate the demand for the product it sells, and in Chapter 5, we will examine how the firm can forecast future demand for the product. We will see that in order to properly estimate and forecast demand, we need to be familiar with the theory of demand presented in this chapter as well as with the estimating techniques presented in Chapter 4.

The strength and stability of present and future demand for the firm's product are also crucial in determining the most efficient methods of producing and selling the product, as well as in planning for the expansion of production facilities, and for entering new markets and other product lines. For example, if the demand for the firm's product is forecast to grow but to be unstable, the firm might need to build a larger plant (to meet the growing demand) but might also have to carry larger inventories (because of the volatility of demand), and it might want to increase its promotional effort to make demand less volatile (for example, by trying to increase off-season demand, finding new uses for its product, and so on). In any event, demand analysis is essential to the firm and to its profitability.

THE DEMAND FOR A COMMODITY

In this section, we begin by examining the determinants of an individual's demand for a commodity. By then aggregating or summing up the individual consumer's demands for the commodity, we obtain the market demand curve for the commodity. The share of the total market or industry demand for the product that a particular firm faces depends on the number of firms in the industry and on the structure or the form of market organization of the industry. Finally, in order to show how the abstract concepts of demand theory are applied in the real world, we examine the demand for Big Macs and the demand curve for sweet potatoes in the United States (see Case Studies 3-1 and 3-2).

An Individual's Demand for a Commodity

In managerial economics we are primarily interested in the demand for a commodity faced by the firm. This depends on the size of the total market or industry demand for the commodity, which in turn is the sum of the demands for the commodity of the individual consumers in the market. Thus, we begin by examining the theory of consumer demand in order to learn about the market demand, on which the demand for the product faced by a particular firm depends. The analysis is general and refers to almost any type of commodity (good or service).

The demand for a commodity arises from the consumers' willingness and ability (i.e., from their desire or want for the commodity backed by the income) to purchase the commodity. **Consumer demand theory** postulates that the quantity demanded of a commodity is a function of, or depends on, the price of the commodity, the consumer's income, the price of related (i.e., complementary and substitute) commodities, and the tastes of the consumer. In functional form, we can express this as

$$Qd_X = f(P_X, I, P_Y, T) \qquad\qquad [3\text{-}1]$$

where Qd_X = quantity demanded of commodity X by an individual per time period (year, month, week, day, or other unit of time)

P_X = price per unit of commodity X

I = consumer income

P_Y = price of related (i.e., substitute and complementary) commodities

T = consumer taste

Even the most unsophisticated of managers has probably had occasion to observe that when the firm increases the price of a commodity, sales generally decline. He or she also knows that the firm would probably sell more units of the commodity by lowering the price. Thus, he or she expects an inverse relationship between the quantity demanded of a commodity and its price. That is, when the price rises, the quantity purchased declines, and when the price falls, the quantity sold increases.

On the other hand, when a consumer's income rises, he or she usually purchases more of most commodities (shoes, steaks, movies, travel, education, automobiles, housing, and so on). These are known as **normal goods.** There are some goods and services, however, of which the consumer purchases less as income rises. For example, when a consumer's income rises, the consumer usually consumes fewer potatoes, hot dogs, and hamburgers because he or she can now afford steaks and other higher-quality foods. Potatoes, hot dogs, hamburgers, and similar "cheap" foods are thus **inferior goods** for the consumer. Most goods are normal, however, and we will be dealing primarily with these in the analysis that follows.

The quantity demanded of a commodity by an individual also depends on the price of related commodities. The individual will purchase more of a commodity if the price of a substitute commodity increases or if the price of a complementary commodity falls. For example, a consumer will purchase more coffee if the price of tea (a substitute for coffee) increases or if the price of sugar (a complement of coffee) falls (since the price of a cup of coffee *with sugar* is then lower). Even more importantly, the quantity of a commodity that is purchased depends on an individual's tastes. For example, today's typical consumer purchases leaner meats than he or she did a generation ago because of heightened concern with the level of blood cholesterol and body weight (a change in tastes).

To summarize, then, consumer demand theory postulates that the quantity demanded of a commodity per time period increases with a reduction in its price, with an increase in the consumer's income, with an increase in the price of substitute commodities and a reduction in the price of complementary commodities, and with an increased taste for the commodity. On the other hand, the quantity demanded of a commodity declines with the opposite changes.

For the purpose of analysis it is often useful to examine the relationship between the quantity demanded of a commodity per unit of time and the price of the commodity only (i.e., independently of the other forces that affect demand). This can be accomplished by assuming, for the moment, that the individual's income, the price of related commodities, and tastes are unchanged. The inverse relationship between the price and the quantity demanded of the commodity per time period is then the **individual's demand schedule** for the commodity, and the plot of data (with price on the vertical axis and quantity on the horizontal axis) gives the corresponding **individual's demand curve.**[1]

For example, Table 3-1 gives a very simple hypothetical demand schedule for an individual, and Figure 3-1 presents the corresponding individual's demand curve (d_X). Commodity X could refer, for example, to hamburgers. The table and the figure show that at the price of $2 per unit the individual purchases 1 unit of the commodity per time period. At $P_X = \$1$, the individual purchases 3 units of X, and at $P_X = \$0.50$, $Qd_X = 4.5$. Note that the individual's demand curve, d_X in Figure 3-1, is negatively sloped, indicating that the individual purchases more of the commodity per time period at lower prices (while

TABLE 3-1 An Individual's Demand Schedule for Commodity X			
Price of commodity X per unit (P_X)	$2	$1	$0.50
Quantity demanded of X per time period (Qd_X)	1	3	4.5

---

[1] Note that, by convention, quantity per unit of time (the dependent variable), rather than price (the independent variable), is plotted on the horizontal axis.

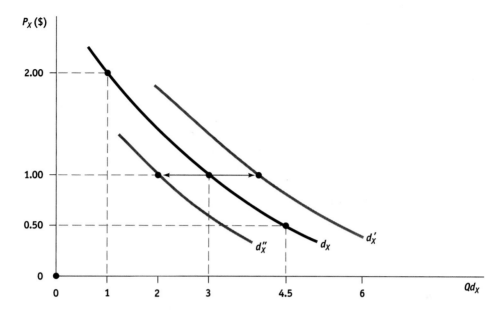

FIGURE 3-1   An Individual's Demand Curve for Commodity X   At the price of $2, the individual purchases 1 unit of the commodity per time period. At $P_X = \$1$, the individual purchases 3 units of X, and at $P_X = \$0.50$, $Qd_X = 4.5$. The inverse relationship between P_X and Qd_X (negative slope of d_X) is called the "law of demand." d_X shifts to the right, say, to d_X', with an increase in the consumer's income, in the price of a substitute commodity, in tastes for the commodity, and with a reduction in the price of a complementary commodity. d_X shifts to the left, say, to d_X'', with the opposite changes.

holding income, the price of related commodities, and tastes constant). The inverse relationship between the price of the commodity and the quantity demanded per time period is referred to as the **law of demand.**

The reason for the negative slope of d_X, or inverse relationship between P_X and Qd_X, is not difficult to find. When P_X falls, the quantity demanded of the commodity by the individual (Qd_X) increases because the individual substitutes in consumption commodity X for other commodities (which are now relatively more expensive). This is called the **substitution effect.** In addition, when the price of a commodity falls, a consumer can purchase more of the commodity with a given money income (i.e., his or her real income increases). This is called the **income effect.** Thus, a fall in P_X leads to an increase in Qd_X (so that d_X is negatively sloped) because of the substitution effect and the income effect.[2]

---

[2] The demand curve shown in Figure 3-1 is derived with indifference curve analysis in the appendix to this chapter. If commodity X were an inferior good, the increase in real income resulting from the reduction of P_X would lead the consumer to purchase less, not more, of commodity X. Thus, the income effect would be negative, while the substitution effect would continue to be positive (i.e., to lead the consumer to purchase more of X when its price declines). Only in the very rare case when the consumer spends so much on commodity X that the negative income effect overwhelms the positive substitution effect will Qd_X fall when P_X falls (so that the demand curve would be positively sloped). Commodity X is then called a **Giffen good** (after the nineteenth-century English economist Robert Giffen, who first discussed it). This is extremely rare in the real world, and we disregard this possibility in what follows.

If any of the things held constant in drawing a demand curve change, the entire demand curve shifts. The individual's demand curve shifts upward or to the right (so that the individual demands more of the commodity at each commodity price) if the consumer's income increases, if the price of a substitute commodity increases or the price of a complementary commodity falls, and if the consumer's taste for the commodity increases. This gives d'_X in Figure 3-1. With opposite changes, d_X shifts to the left to, say, d''_X.[3] To clearly distinguish between a movement along a given demand curve (as a result of a change in the commodity price) from a shift in demand (as a result of a change in income, price of related commodities, or tastes), we refer to the first as a **change in the quantity demanded** and to the second as a **change in demand.**

From Individual to Market Demand

The **market demand curve** for a commodity is simply the *horizontal summation* of the demand curves of all the consumers in the market. For example, in the top part of Figure 3-2, the market demand curve for commodity X is obtained by the horizontal summation of the demand curve of individual 1 (d_1) and individual 2 (d_2), on the assumption that they are the only two consumers in the market. Thus, at $P_X = \$1$, the market quantity demanded of 5 units of commodity X is the sum of the 3 units of X demanded by individual 1 and the 2 units of X demanded by individual 2. If there were 100 individuals in the market instead, each with demand curve d_X, the market demand curve for commodity X would be D_X (see the bottom part of Figure 3-2). D_X has the same shape as d_X, but the horizontal scale refers to hundreds of units of commodity X.[4]

The market demand curve for a commodity shows the various quantities of the commodity demanded in the market per time period (QD_X) at various alternative prices of the commodity, while holding everything else constant. The market demand curve for a commodity (just as an individual's demand curve) is negatively sloped, indicating that price and quantity are inversely related. That is, the quantity demanded of the commodity increases when its price falls and decreases when its price rises. The things held constant in drawing the market demand curve for a commodity are: the number of consumers in the market (N), consumers' incomes (I), the price of related (i.e., substitute and complementary) commodities (P_Y), and tastes (T). A change in any of these will cause the market demand curve of the commodity to shift in the same direction as (and as a result of) the shift in the individuals' demand curves. Thus, we can express the general **market demand function** for commodity X as

$$QD_X = F(P_X, N, I, P_Y, T) \tag{3-2}$$

---

[3] A change in expectations about the future price of a commodity will also result in a shift in the individual's demand curve. For example, if the individual expects prices to be lower in the future, he or she will postpone purchases in anticipation of the lower prices. Thus, the individual's demand curve for the commodity in the current period shifts to the left. On the other hand, if the individual expects prices to rise, his or her demand curve for the present period shifts to the right, as the consumer increases present purchases to avoid future price increases.

[4] Note that the demand curves are curvilinear in the top part of Figure 3-2 but straight lines in the bottom part of the figure. Either form is possible, with the linear form perhaps more common.

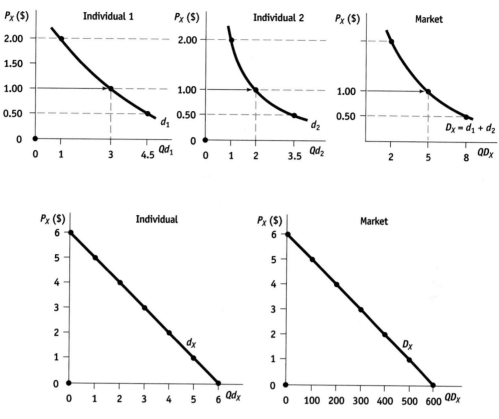

FIGURE 3-2   From Individual to Market Demand   The top part of the figure shows that the market demand curve for the commodity, D_X, is obtained from the horizontal summation of the demand curve of individual 1 (d_1) and individual 2 (d_2). The bottom part of the figure shows an individual's demand curve, d_X, and the market demand curve, D_X, on the assumption that there are 100 individuals in the market with demand curves identical to d_X.

Finally, it must be pointed out that a market demand *curve* is simply the horizontal summation of the individual demand curves *only* if the consumption decisions of individual consumers are independent. This is not always the case. For example, people sometimes demand a commodity because others are purchasing it and in order to be fashionable. The result is a **bandwagon effect** to "keep up with the Joneses." This tends to make the market demand curve flatter than indicated by the simple horizontal summation of the individuals' demand curves. At other times, the opposite, or **snob effect,** occurs as many consumers seek to be different and exclusive by demanding less of a commodity as more people consume it. This tends to make the market demand curve steeper than indicated by the horizontal summation of the individuals' demand curves. For simplicity, however, we assume the absence of such bandwagon and snob effects in what follows.

CASE STUDY 3-1
The Demand for Big Macs

With 36,000 restaurants in 122 countries and serving 47 million people around the world every day in 2005, McDonald's dwarfed the competition in the fast-food burger market (its closest competitor, Burger King, had 11,200 restaurants in 57 countries). In the United States McDonald's has 13,100 outlets, compared with Burger King's 8,400. After nearly three decades of double-digit gains, however, domestic sales at McDonald's have been growing slowly since the mid-1980s as a result of higher prices, changing tastes, demographic changes, increased competition from other fast-food chains, the mad cow disease in Europe, and, more recently, the obesity concern in the United States.

Price increases at McDonald's exceeded inflation in each year since 1986. The average check at McDonald's now exceeds $4—a far cry from the 15-cent hamburger on which McDonald's got rich—and this sent customers streaming to lower-pricing competitors. Concern over cholesterol and calories has also reduced growth. In addition, the proportion of the 15- to 29-year-olds (the primary fast-food customers) in the total population has shrunk from 27.5 to 22.5 percent during the past decade. Increased competition from other fast-food chains (especially Burger King and Wendy's), other fast-food options (pizza, chicken, tacos, and so on), frozen fast foods, mobile units, and the vending machines also slowed down the growth of demand for Big Macs. In 2002, McDonald's was even hit by a highly publicized

multimillion dollar suit for allegedly misleading young consumers about the healthiness of its products (which inspired the movie "Super Size Me" in 2004).

McDonald's did not sit idle but tried to meet its challenges head on by introducing new items on its menu and cutting prices. For example, in 1990 McDonald's introduced a value menu with small hamburgers selling for as little as 59 cents (down from 89 cents) and a combination of burger, French fries, and soft drink for as much as half off. In response to increased public concern about cholesterol and calories, McDonald's began publicizing the nutritional content of its menu offerings, substituted vegetable oils for beef tallow in frying its French fries, replaced ice cream with low-fat yogurt, introduced bran muffins and cereals to its breakfast menu, and, in 1991, introduced the McLean Deluxe—a new reduced-fat, quarter-pound hamburger on which McDonald's spent from $50 to $70 million in development and promotion. Then, in 1995 McDonald's introduced McPizza, in 1996 its Arch Deluxe, in 1999 it introduced the "Made For You" freshly cooked meals, in 2004 it phased out the "super-sized" fries and drinks and introduced main-course salads and bunless versions of beef and chicken sandwiches. In 2006, McDonald's became the first fast-food company to put nutritional labels on its products. All of these menu changes, however, did not alienate McDonald's core burger-eating customers.

Source: "An American Icon Wrestles with a Troubled Future," *The New York Times* (May 12, 1991), sec. 3, p. 1; "Too Skinny a Burger Is a Mighty Hard Sell, McDonald's Learns," *The Wall Street Journal* (April 15, 1994), p. A1; "Fallen Arches," *Fortune* (April 29, 2002), pp. 74–76; "Big Mac Trims Portions as Worry on Waistline Grows," *Financial Times* (March 3, 2004), p. 8; "Part of McDonald's Obesity Suit Is Reinstated by Appeals Court," *The Wall Street Journal* (January 26, 2005), p. D10; "McDonald's Gets Healthier—But Burgers Still Rule," *The Wall Street Journal* (February 23, 2005), p. B7; "McDonald's to Introduce Nutrition Labels," *Financial Times* (October 26, 2005), p. 15; and "Salads or Not, Cheap Burgers Revive McDonald's," *The New York Times* (April 19, 2006), p. 1.

The Demand Faced by a Firm

Since the analysis of the firm is central to managerial economics, we are primarily interested in the demand for a commodity faced by a firm. The demand for a commodity faced by a particular firm depends on the size of the market or industry demand for the commodity, the form in which the industry is organized, and the number of firms in the industry.

If the firm is the sole producer of a commodity for which there are no good substitutes (i.e., if the firm is a monopolist), the firm is or represents the industry, and it faces the industry or market demand for the commodity. **Monopoly** is rare in the real world, and when it does occur, it is usually the result of a government franchise, which is accompanied by government regulation. Examples of this are public transportation and some other public utility companies. At the opposite extreme is the form of market organization called **perfect competition.** Here, there are a large number of firms producing a homogeneous (i.e., identical) product, and each firm is too small to affect the price of the commodity by its own actions. In such a case, each firm is a price taker and faces a horizontal demand curve for the commodity (i.e., the firm can sell any amount of the commodity without affecting its price). This form of market organization is also very rare. The closest we may have come to it in the United States was in the growing of wheat at the turn of the century, when millions of small farmers raised wheat of the same type.

The vast majority of the firms operating in the United States and in other industrial countries today falls between the extremes of monopoly and perfect competition, into the forms of market organization known as oligopoly and monopolistic competition. In **oligopoly,** there are only a few firms in the industry, producing either a homogeneous or standardized product (e.g., cement, steel, and chemicals) or a heterogeneous or differentiated product (e.g., automobiles, cigarettes, and soft drinks). The most striking characteristic of oligopoly is the interdependence that exists among the firms in the industry. Since there are only a few firms in the industry, the pricing, advertising, and other promotional behavior of each firm greatly affect the other firms in the industry and evoke imitation and retaliation. This is a very common form of market organization in the production sector of the economy, where efficiency requires large-scale operation (production).

The other common form of market organization is **monopolistic competition.** Here, there are many firms selling a heterogeneous or differentiated product. As the name implies, monopolistic competition has elements of both competition and monopoly. The competitive element arises from the fact that there are many firms in the industry. The monopoly element arises because each firm's product is somewhat different from the product of other firms. Thus, the firm has some degree of control over the price it charges (i.e., the firm faces a negatively sloped demand curve). However, because the products of the many other firms in the industry are very similar, the degree of control that a firm has over the price of the product it sells is very limited. That is, each firm faces a demand curve that, though negatively sloped, is fairly flat, so that any increase in price would lead to a very large decline in sales. This form of market organization is common in the service sector of the economy—witness the large number of gasoline stations and barber shops in a given area, each selling similar but not identical products or services.

A detailed discussion of market organization will be presented in Chapters 9 and 10, but what has been said here is sufficient to allow us to identify the most important forces that determine the demand for a commodity faced by a firm. Under all forms of market organization, except perfect competition, the firm faces a negatively sloped demand curve for the commodity it sells, and this demand curve shifts with changes in the number of consumers in the market, consumers' incomes, the price of related commodities, and consumers' tastes, as well as with changes in other more specific forces that may affect the firm's demand in the particular industry or market.

These other forces may be price expectations, the level of advertising and other promotional efforts on the part of the firm, the pricing and promotional policies of other firms in the industry (especially in oligopoly), availability of credit, the type of good that the firm sells, and so on. The demand curve for a product faced by a firm will shift to the right (so that the firm's sales increase at a given price) if consumers expect prices to rise in the future, if the firm mounts a successful advertising campaign, or if the firm introduces or increases credit incentives to stimulate the purchase of its product. On the other hand, the demand curve faced by a firm shifts to the left if consumers expect prices to fall in the future or if competitors reduce their prices, undertake a successful advertising campaign of their own, or introduce credit incentives.

The demand for a firm's product also depends on the type of product that the firm sells. If the firm sells **durable goods** (e.g., automobiles, washing machines, and refrigerators that provide services not only during the year when they are purchased but also in subsequent years, or goods that can be stored), the firm will generally face a more volatile or unstable demand than a firm selling nondurable goods. The reason is that consumers can run their cars, washing machines, or refrigerators a little longer by increasing their expenditures on maintenance and repairs, and can postpone the purchase of a new unit until the economy improves and their income rises or credit incentives become available. They can also reduce inventories of storable goods. When the economy improves or credit incentives are introduced, the demand for durable goods can then increase (i.e., shift to the right) substantially.

We can specify the linear form of the **demand function faced by a firm** as

$$Q_X = a_0 + a_1 P_X + a_2 N + a_3 I + a_4 P_Y + a_5 T + \cdots \qquad [3\text{-}3]$$

where Q_X refers to the quantity demanded of commodity X per time period faced by the firm, and $P_X, N, I, P_Y,$ and T refer, as before, to the price of the commodity, the number of consumers in the market, consumers' incomes, the price of related commodities, and consumers' tastes, respectively. The a's represent the coefficients to be estimated by regression analysis, which is the most used technique for estimating demand. Regression analysis will be examined in the next chapter. Here we simply examine the meaning and use of the estimated coefficients (i.e., the a's). The dots in Equation 3-3 refer to the other determinants of demand that are specific to the firm in a given industry and that can be identified only by an in-depth knowledge of the particular industry and firm.[5]

---

[5] If tastes or other determinants of demand remain approximately constant during the period of the analysis, they can safely be omitted from Equation 3-3. This would be particularly useful in the case of tastes since it is often difficult to obtain reliable quantitative measures of changes in tastes. One way to capture changes in tastes is to include a time trend in the estimating regression (see Case Study 3-2).

CASE STUDY 3-2
The Demand for Sweet Potatoes in the United States

Using the technique of regression analysis presented in Chapter 4, Schrimper and Mathia estimated the following demand function for sweet potatoes in the United States for the period of 1949 to 1972:

$$QD_S = 7,609 - 1,606P_S + 59N$$
$$+ 947I + 479P_W - 271t \qquad [3\text{-}4]$$

where QD_S = quantity of sweet potatoes sold per year in the United States per 1,000 hundredweight (cwt)

P_S = real-dollar price of sweet potatoes per hundredweight received by farmers

N = two-year moving average of total U.S. population, in millions

I = real per capita personal disposable income, in thousands of dollars

P_W = real-dollar price of white potatoes per hundredweight received by farmers

t = time trend ($t = 1$ for 1949, $t = 2$ for 1950, up to $t = 24$ for 1972)

This estimated demand function indicates that the quantity demanded of sweet potatoes per year in 1,000-cwt (i.e., in 100,000-pound) units in the United States (QD_S) declines by 1,606 for each $1 increase in its price (P_S), increases by 59 for each 1 million increase in population *(N)*, increases by 947 for each $1,000 increase in real income *(I)*, increases by 479 for each $1 increase in the real price of white potatoes (P_W), but falls by 271 with each passing year (the coefficient of *t,* the time trend variable). Thus, the demand curve for sweet potatoes is negatively sloped, and it shifts to the right with an increase in population, in income, and in the price of white potatoes, but shifts to the left with each passing year. Since the demand for sweet potatoes increases (i.e., shifts to the right) with an increase in income, sweet potatoes are a normal good (even though we usually think of potatoes as being an inferior good). Since QD_S increases with an increase in P_W and declines with a reduction in P_W, white potatoes are a substitute for sweet potatoes. Finally, the negative coefficient of *t* can be taken to reflect the declining tastes for sweet potatoes over time.

If we now substitute into Equation 3-4 the actual values of $N = 150.73$, $I = 1.76$, $P_W = 2.94$, and $t = 1$ for the United States for the year 1949, we get the following equation for the U.S. demand curve for sweet potatoes in 1949:

$$QD_S = 7,609 - 1,606P_S + 59(150.73)$$
$$+ 947(1.76) + 479(2.94) - 271(1)$$
$$= 7,609 - 1,606P_S + 8,893$$
$$+ 1,667 + 1,408 - 271$$
$$= 19,306 - 1,606P_S \qquad [3\text{-}5]$$

By then substituting the value of $7 for P_S into Equation 3-5, we get $QD_S = 8,064$. If $P_S = 5.60$ (the actual real price of sweet potatoes in the United States in 1949), $QD_S = 10,312$. Finally, if $P_S = 4$, $QD_S = 12,882$. This demand schedule is plotted as D_X in Figure 3-3.

On the other hand, if we substitute into Equation 3-4 the values of $N = 208.78$, $I = 3.19$, $P_W = 2.41$, and $t = 24$ for the year 1972, we get Equation 3-6 for the U.S. demand curve for sweet potatoes in 1972:

$$QD'_S = 17,598 - 1,606P_S \qquad [3\text{-}6]$$

By then substituting the same values as above for P_S into Equation 3-6, we get market demand curve D'_X in Figure 3-3. Note that the reduction in tastes for sweet potatoes between 1949 and 1972 and in P_W tends to shift D_X to the left, while the increase in N and I tends to shift D_X to the right. Since the first set of forces overwhelms the second, D'_X is to the left of D_X. In general, it is the average value of the independent or explanatory variables over the entire period that is substituted into the estimated demand equation to get the equation of the *average* demand curve for the period (see Problem 2, with the answer at the end of the text).

Finally, it must be pointed out that each producer of sweet potatoes shares in the total market demand for sweet potatoes. Therefore, for a given change in the market price of potatoes or other variable, the quantity response by a firm will be some fraction of the total market response. Furthermore, in order to estimate demand correctly, a producer would have to include

Continued . . .

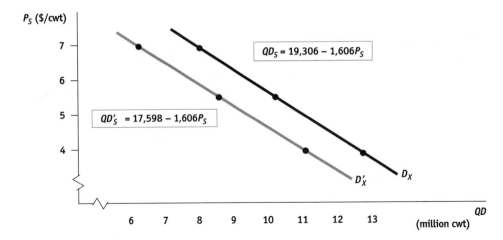

FIGURE 3-3   The Market Demand Curve for Sweet Potatoes in the United States   By substituting into Equation 3-5 the values for P_S of \$7, \$5.60, and \$4 and plotting, we get market demand curve D_X for sweet potatoes in the United States for 1949. On the other hand, by substituting the same values for P_S into Equation 3-6, we get D'_X as the U.S. demand curve for sweet potatoes in 1972. Since the constant term is smaller for 1972 than for 1949, D'_X is to the left of D_X.

explanatory variables in addition to those used to estimate the market demand—as indicated in the previous section. Practically all the available estimates of demand, however, refer to market demand because firms do not want to disclose their knowledge of the market and their strategies and plans to competitors. An example of the demand faced by a firm is given in Problem 2 (with the answer at the end of the text).

Source: Ronald A. Schrimper and Gene A. Mathia, "Reservation and Market Demands for Sweet Potatoes at the Farm Level," *American Journal of Agricultural Economics,* vol. 57 (February 1975).

The demand faced by a firm will then determine the type and quantity of inputs or resources (producers' goods) that the firm will purchase or hire in order to produce or meet the demand for the goods and services that it sells. Since the demand for the inputs or resources that a firm uses depends on the demand for the goods and services it sells, the firm's demand for inputs is a **derived demand.** The greater the demand for the goods and services that the firm sells, the greater will be the firm's demand for the inputs or resources that are required to produce those goods and services. In fact, the firm's demand for **producers' goods,** such as capital equipment and raw materials that can be stored, is also more volatile and unstable than the firm's demand for perishable raw materials. These and other aspects of the demand for inputs or factors of production are examined in Chapter 6 (which deals with production) and in subsequent chapters.

Thus, we have a number of demands. There is the individual's demand for a commodity, the market demand for the commodity, the demand for the commodity that the firm faces, and the firm's derived demand for the inputs it needs to produce final commodities, and it is important to clearly distinguish among these different demand concepts.

3-2   PRICE ELASTICITY OF DEMAND

The responsiveness in the quantity demanded of a commodity to a change in its price is very important to the firm. Sometimes, lowering the price of the commodity increases sales sufficiently to increase total revenues. At other times, lowering the commodity price reduces the firm's total revenues. By affecting sales, the pricing policies of the firm also affect its production costs, and thus its profitability. In this section, we introduce measures of the responsiveness (elasticity) in the quantity demanded of the commodity to a change in its price. We will show how to measure price elasticity at one point as well as over a range (arc) of the demand curve. We will also examine the relationship among price elasticity, the total revenue of the firm, and its marginal revenue. Finally, we discuss the factors affecting the price elasticity of demand and present some real-world estimates of it.

Point Price Elasticity of Demand

The responsiveness in the quantity demanded of a commodity to a change in its price could be measured by the inverse of the slope of the demand curve (i.e., by $\Delta Q/\Delta P$).[6] The disadvantage is that the inverse of the slope ($\Delta Q/\Delta P$) is expressed in terms of the units of measurement. Thus, simply changing prices from dollars to cents would change the value of $\Delta Q/\Delta P$ one hundredfold. Furthermore, a comparison of changes in quantity to changes in prices across commodities would be meaningless. In order to avoid these disadvantages, we use instead the price elasticity of demand.

The **price elasticity of demand (E_P)** is given by the percentage change in the quantity demanded of the commodity divided by the percentage change in its price, holding constant all the other variables in the demand function. That is,

$$E_P = \frac{\Delta Q/Q}{\Delta P/P} = \frac{\Delta Q}{\Delta P} \cdot \frac{P}{Q} \qquad [3\text{-}7]$$

where ΔQ and ΔP refer, respectively, to the change in quantity and the change in price. Note that the inverse of the slope of the demand curve (i.e, $\Delta Q/\Delta P$) is a component, but only a component, of the elasticity formula and that the value of $\Delta Q/\Delta P$ is negative because price and quantity move in opposite directions (i.e., when P rises, Q falls, and vice versa).[7]

Equation 3-7 gives the **point price elasticity of demand,** or the elasticity at a given point on the demand curve. For example, for D_X (the market demand curve for commodity

---

[6] Since price is plotted on the vertical axis and quantity on the horizontal axis, the quantity response to a change in price could be measured by $\Delta Q/\Delta P$, which is the inverse of the slope of the demand curve.

[7] In terms of calculus,

$$E_P = \frac{\partial Q}{\partial P} \cdot \frac{P}{Q}$$

We take the partial rather than the regular derivative of Q with respect to P in order to remind ourselves that the other variables included in the demand function are to be held constant in measuring the effect of a change in P on Q.

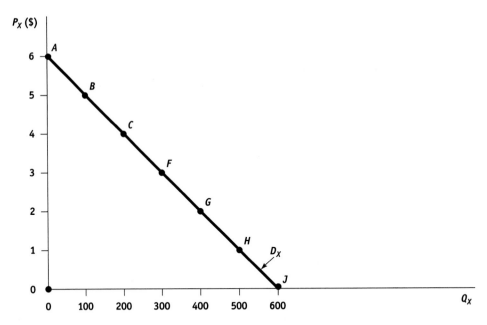

FIGURE 3-4   The Point Price Elasticity of Demand   At point B on D_X,

$$E_P = \frac{\Delta Q}{\Delta P} \cdot \frac{P}{Q} = \frac{-100}{\$1} \cdot \frac{\$5}{100} = -1\left(\frac{5}{1}\right) = -5$$

At point C, $E_P = -1\left(\frac{4}{2}\right) = -2$; at point F, $E_P = -1\left(\frac{3}{3}\right) = -1$; at point G, $E_P = -1\left(\frac{2}{4}\right) = -\frac{1}{2}$; and at point H, $E_P = -1\left(\frac{1}{5}\right) = -\frac{1}{5}$.

X in Figure 3-2, repeated above for ease of reference) in Figure 3-4, $\Delta Q/\Delta P = -100/\$1$ at every point on D_X (since D_X is linear), and so price elasticity at point B is

$$E_P = \frac{\Delta Q}{\Delta P} \cdot \frac{P}{Q} = \frac{-100}{\$1} \cdot \frac{\$5}{100} = -1\left(\frac{5}{1}\right) = -5$$

This means that the quantity demanded declines by 5 percent for each 1 percent increase in price, while holding constant all the other variables in the demand function. At point C on D_X, $E_P = -1\left(\frac{4}{2}\right) = -2$; at point F, $E_P = -1\left(\frac{3}{3}\right) = -1$; at point G, $E_P = -1\left(\frac{2}{4}\right) = -\frac{1}{2}$; and at point H, $E_P = -1\left(\frac{1}{5}\right) = -\frac{1}{5}$.[8]

As these calculations show, the price elasticity of demand is usually different at different points on the demand curve.[9] For a linear demand curve, such as D_X in Figure 3-4, the price elasticity of demand has an absolute value (that is, $|E_P|$) that is greater than 1 (i.e., the demand curve is elastic) above the geometric midpoint of the demand curve;

---

[8] Sometimes the absolute value of E_P (that is, $|E_P|$) is reported. This creates no difficulty as long as we remember that price and quantity move in opposite directions along the demand curve. Note that at point F, $E_P = -1\left(\frac{0}{6}\right) = 0$, while at point A, $E_P = -1\left(\frac{6}{0}\right) = -\infty$. Thus, E_P can range anywhere from 0 to $-\infty$.

[9] Since the slope and its inverse are constant for a linear demand curve, but P and Q vary at different points on the demand curve, E_P varies at different points on the demand curve.

$|E_P| = 1$ at the geometric midpoint (that is, D_X is unitary elastic), and $|E_P| < 1$ below the midpoint (that is, D_X is inelastic). This is confirmed by examining the values of E_P found above for D_X.[10]

Note that the value of $\Delta Q/\Delta P$ is given by a_1, the estimated coefficient of P in regression Equation 3-3.[11] Therefore, the formula for the point price elasticity of demand can be rewritten as

$$E_P = a_1 \cdot \frac{P}{Q} \qquad [3\text{-}8]$$

where a_1 is the estimated coefficient of P in the linear regression of Q on P and other explanatory variables. For example, with $a_1 = -1{,}606$ cwt/$1 in regression Equation 3-4, and $Q_S = 8{,}064$ cwt at $P_S = \$7$, $E_P = -1{,}606(7/8{,}064) = -1.39$. This means that a 1 percent increase in P_S leads to a 1.39 percent decline in Q_S.

Arc Price Elasticity of Demand

More frequently than point price elasticity of demand, we measure **arc price elasticity of demand,** or the price elasticity of demand between two points on the demand curve, in the real world. If we used Formula 3-7 to measure arc price elasticity of demand, however, we would get different results depending on whether the price rose or fell. For example, using Formula 3-7 to measure arc price elasticity for a movement from point C to point F (i.e., for a price decline) on demand curve D_X in Figure 3-4, we would obtain

$$E_P = \frac{\Delta Q}{\Delta P} \cdot \frac{P}{Q} = \frac{100}{-\$1} \cdot \frac{\$4}{200} = -2$$

On the other hand, using Formula 3-7 to measure arc price elasticity for a *price increase* from point F to point C, we would get

$$E_P = \frac{\Delta Q}{\Delta P} \cdot \frac{P}{Q} = \frac{-100}{\$1} \cdot \frac{\$3}{300} = -1$$

To avoid this, we use the average of the two prices and the average of the two quantities in the calculations. Thus, the formula for arc price elasticity of demand (E_P) can be expressed as

$$E_P = \frac{\Delta Q}{\Delta P} \cdot \frac{(P_2 + P_1)/2}{(Q_2 + Q_1)/2} = \frac{Q_2 - Q_1}{P_2 - P_1} \cdot \frac{P_2 + P_1}{Q_2 + Q_1} \qquad [3\text{-}9]$$

---

[10] The point price elasticity of demand can also be obtained geometrically by dividing the price of the commodity (P) at the point on the demand curve at which we want to find the elasticity by $P - A$, where A is the price at which the quantity demanded is zero (i.e., the price at which the demand curve crosses the vertical axis). For a curvilinear demand curve, we draw a tangent to the demand curve at the point at which we want to measure E_P and then proceed as if we were dealing with a linear demand curve (see Problem 5, with the answer at the end of the text).

[11] In terms of calculus, $\Delta Q/\Delta P = \partial Q/\partial P$. Since the exponent of P is 1 in Equation 3-3, $\partial Q/\partial P = a_1$ (the coefficient of P).

where the subscripts 1 and 2 refer to the original and to the new values, respectively, of price and quantity, or vice versa. For example, using Formula 3-9 to measure the arc price elasticity of D_X for a movement from point C to point F, we get

$$E_P = \frac{Q_2 - Q_1}{P_2 - P_1} \cdot \frac{P_2 + P_1}{Q_2 + Q_1} = \frac{300 - 200}{\$3 - \$4} \cdot \frac{\$3 + \$4}{300 + 200} = \frac{7}{-5} = -1.4$$

We now get the same result for the reverse movement from point F to point C:

$$E_P = \frac{Q_2 - Q_1}{P_2 - P_1} \cdot \frac{P_2 + P_1}{Q_2 + Q_1} = \frac{200 - 300}{\$4 - \$3} \cdot \frac{\$4 + \$3}{200 + 300} = \frac{-7}{5} = -1.4$$

This means that *between* points C and F on D_X, a 1 percent change in price results, on average, in a 1.4 percent *opposite* change in the quantity demanded of commodity X. Note that the value of $E_P = -1.4$ for arc price elasticity of demand is between the values of $E_P = -2$ and $E_P = -1$ obtained by the use of Formula 3-7 for the point price elasticity of demand.

While we have been examining the price elasticity of the market demand curve for a commodity, the concept applies equally well to individuals' and firms' demand curves. In general, the price elasticity of the demand curve that a firm faces (i.e., the absolute value of E_P) is larger than the price elasticity of the corresponding market demand curve because the firm faces competition from similar commodities from rival firms, while there are few, if any, close substitutes for the *industry's* product from other industries.

Price Elasticity, Total Revenue, and Marginal Revenue

There is an important relationship between the price elasticity of demand and the firm's total revenue and marginal revenue. **Total revenue (*TR*)** is equal to price (P) times quantity (Q), while **marginal revenue (*MR*)** is the change in total revenue per unit change in output or sales (quantity demanded).[12] That is,

$$TR = P \cdot Q \tag{3-10}$$

$$MR = \frac{\Delta TR}{\Delta Q} \tag{3-11}$$

With a decline in price, total revenue increases if demand is elastic (i.e., if $|E_P| > 1$); *TR* remains unchanged if demand is unitary elastic, and *TR* declines if demand is inelastic.

The reason for this is that if demand is elastic, a price decline leads to a proportionately larger increase in quantity demanded, and so total revenue increases. When demand is unitary elastic, a decline in price leads to an equal proportionate increase in quantity demanded, and so total revenue remains unchanged. Finally, if demand is inelastic, a decline in price leads to a smaller proportionate increase in quantity demanded, and so the total revenue of the firm declines. Since a linear demand curve is elastic above the midpoint, unitary elastic at the midpoint, and inelastic below the midpoint, a reduction in price leads to an increase in *TR* down to the midpoint of the demand curve (where total revenue is

---

[12] Note that $TR/Q = AR = P$, where AR is the average revenue. Thus, the price that the firm receives per unit of the commodity is equal to the average revenue of the firm.

TABLE 3-2	Price Elasticity, Total Revenue, and Marginal Revenue			
(1) P	**(2)** Q	**(3)** E_P	**(4)** $TR = P \cdot Q$	**(5)** $MR = \Delta TR / \Delta Q$
$6	0	$-\infty$	$0	—
5	100	-5	500	
				$5
4	200	-2	800	
				3
3	300	-1	900	
				1
2	400	$-\frac{1}{2}$	800	
				-1
1	500	$\frac{1}{5}$	500	
				-3
0	600	0	0	
				-5

maximum) and to a decline thereafter. *MR* is positive as long as *TR* increases; *MR* is zero when *TR* is maximum, and *MR* is negative when *TR* declines.

For example, suppose that a firm is a monopolist and faces the market demand curve for commodity *X* shown in Figure 3-4. The market demand schedule that the firm faces is then the one given in the first two columns of Table 3-2. The price elasticity of demand at various prices is given in column 3 and equals those found above for demand curve D_X. The total revenue of the firm is given in column 4 and is obtained by multiplying price by quantity. The marginal revenue of the firm is given in column 5 and is obtained by finding the change in total revenue per unit change in output. Note that *TR* increases as long as $|E_P| > 1$, *TR* is maximum when $|E_P| = 1$, and *TR* declines when $|E_P| < 1$. *MR* is positive as long as *TR* increases (i.e., as long as demand is elastic) and negative when *TR* declines (i.e., when demand is inelastic).

The relationship between the price elasticity of demand, the total revenue, and the marginal revenues of the firm given in Table 3-2 is shown graphically in Figure 3-5. Note that since marginal revenue is defined as the change in total revenue per unit change in output or sales, the *MR* values given in column 5 of Table 3-2 are plotted *between* the various levels of output in the bottom panel of Figure 3-5. Note also that the *MR* curve starts at the same point as D_X on the vertical or price axis and at every point bisects (i.e., cuts in half) the distance of D_X from the price axis.[13]

---

[13] In terms of calculus, $MR = d(TR)/dQ$. Given demand function $Q = 600 - 100P$, $P = 6 - Q/100$, and $TR = PQ = (6 - Q/100)Q = 6Q - Q^2/100$. Therefore,

$$\frac{d(TR)}{dQ} = MR = 6 - \frac{Q}{50}$$

Setting

$$\frac{d(TR)}{dQ} = 0$$

we get $Q = 300$. That is, the *TR* curve has zero slope at $Q = 300$. To ensure that *TR* is a maximum rather than a minimum of $Q = 300$, we find

$$\frac{d^2(TR)}{dQ^2}$$

Since this is negative (that is, $-\frac{1}{50}$), *TR* is maximum at $Q = 300$ (see above).

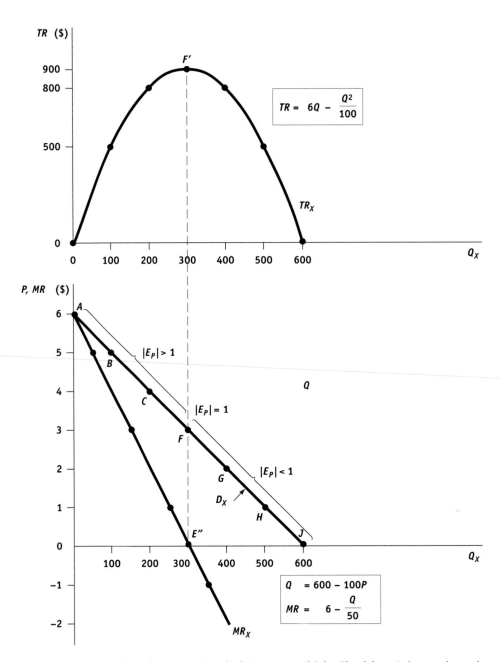

FIGURE 3-5 Demand, Total Revenue, Marginal Revenue, and Price Elasticity   As long as demand is price elastic (i.e., up to 300 units of output), a price reduction increases total revenue (*TR*), and marginal revenue (*MR*) is positive. At *Q* = 300, demand is unitary price elastic, *TR* is maximum, and *MR* = 0. When demand is price inelastic (i.e., for outputs greater than 300), a price reduction reduces *TR*, and *MR* is negative.

There is an important and often-used relationship among marginal revenue, price, and the price elasticity of demand, given by[14]

$$MR = P\left(1 + \frac{1}{E_P}\right)$$ [3-12]

For example, from Table 3-2 we know that when $P = \$4$, $E_P = -2$. Substituting these values into Formula 3-12, we get

$$MR = \$4\left(1 + \frac{1}{-2}\right) = \$4\left(1 - \frac{1}{2}\right) = 2$$

The value of $MR = \$2$ when $P = \$4$ is confirmed by examining Figure 3-5. At $P = \$3$, $E_P = -1$, and

$$MR = \$3\left(1 + \frac{1}{-1}\right) = 0$$

(see the bottom panel of Figure 3-5). At $P = \$2$, $E_P = -\frac{1}{2}$, and

$$MR = \$2\left(1 + \frac{1}{-0.5}\right) = -2$$

(see the bottom panel of Figure 3-5).

The above relationships among E_P, TR, MR, and P hold for both the firm and the industry under any form of market organization. If the firm is a perfect competitor in the product market, it faces a horizontal or infinitely elastic demand curve for the commodity. Then the change in total revenue in selling each additional unit of the commodity (i.e., the marginal revenue) equals price. This is confirmed by using Formula 3-12. That is,

$$MR = P\left(1 + \frac{1}{-\infty}\right) = P$$

For example, in Figure 3-6, if the firm sells 3X, its $TR = \$12$. If it sells 4X, $TR = \$16$. Thus, $MR = P = \$4$, and the demand and marginal revenue curves that the firm faces coincide. (The perfectly competitive model will be examined in Chapter 8.) On the other hand, if the firm faced a vertical demand curve (so that the quantity demanded remains the same regardless of price), $E_P = 0$ throughout the demand curve. This is very rare in the real world.[15]

Factors Affecting the Price Elasticity of Demand

The price elasticity of demand for a commodity depends primarily on the availability of substitutes for the commodity but also on the length of time over which the quantity response

[14] Since $TR = PQ$, in terms of calculus,

$$MR = \frac{d(PQ)}{dQ} = P + Q\frac{dP}{dQ} = P\left(1 + \frac{dP}{dQ} \cdot \frac{Q}{P}\right) = P\left(1 + \frac{1}{E_P}\right)$$

[15] If the demand curve assumes the shape of a rectangular hyperbola (so that total revenue is constant regardless of price), the price elasticity of demand is constant and is equal to 1 throughout the demand curve. For example, if $Q = P^b$, $dQ/dP = bP^{b-1}$ and $E_p = (dQ/dP)(P/Q) = (bP^{b-1})(P/Q) = bP^b/Q$; but since $Q = P^b$, $E_p = b = -1$ (the exponent of P) and is the same throughout the demand curve.

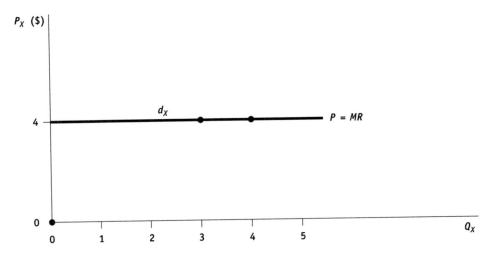

FIGURE 3-6   The Demand Curve Faced by a Perfectly Competitive Firm   The demand curve for the output of a perfectly competitive firm (discussed in Section 8-2) is horizontal or infinitely elastic. Thus, $P = MR$, and the demand curve and the marginal revenue curve of the firm coincide.

to the price change is measured. The size of the price elasticity of demand is larger the closer and the greater is the number of available substitutes for the commodity. For example, the demand for sugar is more price elastic than the demand for table salt because sugar has better and more substitutes (honey and saccharine) than salt. Thus, a given percentage increase in the price of sugar and salt elicits a larger percentage reduction per time period in the quantity demanded of sugar than of salt.

In general, the more narrowly a commodity is defined, the greater is its price elasticity of demand because the greater will be the number of substitutes. For example, the price elasticity for Coke is much greater than the price elasticity for soft drinks in general and still larger than the price elasticity of demand for all nonalcoholic beverages. If a commodity is defined so that it has very close substitutes, its price elasticity of demand is likely to be large indeed and may be close to infinity. For example, if a producer of aspirin tried to increase the price above the general range of market prices for aspirin, he or she would stand to lose a large portion of his or her sales as buyers can readily switch most of their purchases to competitors who sell similar products.

The price elasticity of demand is also larger the longer is the time period allowed for consumers to respond to the change in the commodity price. The reason is that it usually takes some time for consumers to learn of the availability of substitutes and to adjust their purchases to the price change. For example, during the period immediately following the sharp increase in gasoline prices in 1974, the price elasticity of demand for gasoline was very low. Over the period of several years, however, the reduction in the quantity demanded of gasoline was much greater (i.e., the long-run price elasticity of demand for gasoline was much larger) than in the short run as consumers replaced their gas guzzlers with fuel-efficient, compact automobiles, switched to car pools and to public transportation, and took other steps to reduce gasoline consumption. Thus, for a given price change, the quantity response is likely to be much larger in the long run than in the short run, and so the price

CASE STUDY 3-3
Price Elasticities of Demand in the Real World

Table 3-3 gives the estimated absolute value of the short-run and long-run price elasticity of demand (E_P) for selected commodities in the United States and other countries. The table shows that the long-run price elasticity of demand for most commodities is much larger than the corresponding short-run price elasticity.

For example, the table shows that the price elasticity of demand for clothing (the first row in the table) is 0.90 in the short run but becomes 2.90 in the long run. This means that a 1 percent increase in price leads to a reduction in the quantity demanded of clothing of 0.90 percent in the short run but 2.90 percent in the long run. Although the price elasticity of demand for gasoline (the last row in Table 3-3) is about four times higher in the long run than in the short run, the demand for gasoline remains price inelastic.

It should be noted that the estimated price elasticity of demand for any commodity is likely to vary (sometimes widely) depending on the nation under consideration, the time period examined, and the estimation technique used. Thus, estimated price elasticity values should be used with caution.

TABLE 3-3 Estimated Short-Run and Long-Run Price Elasticities of Demand (E_P) for Selected Commodities

Commodity	Elasticity	
	Short Run	Long Run
Clothing (US)[a]	0.90	2.90
Tobacco products (US)[b]	0.46	1.89
Jewelry and watches (US)[b]	0.41	0.67
Beer (US)[c]	1.72	2.17
Cheese (UK)[d]	1.36	—
Wine (Canada)[e]	0.88	1.17
Household natural gas (US)[f]	1.40	2.10
Electricity (household, US)[b]	0.13	1.89
Public transport (England)[g]	0.51	0.69
Public transport (France)[g]	0.32	0.61
Gasoline (US)[g]	0.25	0.92
Gasoline (Canada)[g]	0.15	0.60
Gasoline (Australia)[g]	0.12	0.58

[a]M. R. Baye, D. W. Jansen, and T. W. Lee, "Advertising in Complete Demand Systems," *Applied Economics*, vol. 24 (1992).

[b]H. S. Houthakker and L. S. Taylor, *Consumer Demand in the United States: Analyses and Projections* (Cambridge, Mass.: Harvard University Press, 1970).

[c]C. A. Gallet and J. A. List, "Elasticity of Beer Demand Revisited," *Economic Letters* (October 1998).

[d]D. Harvey, "Major Market Response Concepts and Measures," http://www.staff.ncl.ac.uk/david.harvey/AEF116/1.6/html.

[e]J. A. Johnson, E. H. Oksanen, M. R. Veal, and D. Fretz, "Short-Run and Long-Run Elasticities for Canadian Consumption of Alcoholic Beverages," *Review of Economics and Statistics* (February 1992).

[f]G. R. Lakshmanan and W. Anderson, "Residential Energy Demand in the United States," *Regional Science and Urban Economics* (August 1980).

[g]B. Hagler, "Transportation Elasticities," *TDM Encyclopedia* (Victoria BC, Canada: Victoria Transport Policy Institute, 2005), http://www.vtpi.org/tdm/tdm11.htm.

elasticity of demand is likely to be much greater in the long run than in the short run.[16] Case Study 3-3 gives the estimated short-run and long-run price elasticities of demand for various commodities.

3-3   INCOME ELASTICITY OF DEMAND

The level of consumer income is also a very important determinant of demand. We can measure the responsiveness in the demand for a commodity to a change in consumer income by the **income elasticity of demand (E_I).** This is given by the percentage change in the demand for the commodity divided by the percentage change in income, holding constant all the other variables in the demand function, including price. As with price elasticity, we have point and arc income elasticity. **Point income elasticity of demand** is given by

$$E_I = \frac{\Delta Q/Q}{\Delta I/I} = \frac{\Delta Q}{\Delta I} \cdot \frac{I}{Q} \qquad\qquad [3\text{-}13]$$

where ΔQ and ΔI refer, respectively, to the change in quantity and the change in income. Note that the income elasticity of demand measures the *shift* in the demand curve at each price level.[17]

The value of $\Delta Q/\Delta I$ is given by a_3, the estimated coefficient of I in regression Equation 3-3.[18] Therefore, the formula for the point income elasticity of demand can be rewritten as

$$E_I = a_3 \cdot \frac{I}{Q} \qquad\qquad [3\text{-}14]$$

where a_3 is the estimated coefficient of I in the linear regression of Q on I and other explanatory variables. For example, with $a_3 = 947$ in regression Equation 3-4, at $I = 1.76$ and $QD_S = 10,312$ cwt (obtained by substituting the actual values of $P_S = \$5.60$, $N = 150.73$, $I = 1.76$, $P_W = \$2.94$, and $t = 1$ into Equation 3-4 for the year 1949), we have

$$E_I = 947\left(\frac{1.76}{10,312}\right) = 0.16$$

---

[16] It is also said sometimes that the price elasticity of demand is larger the greater is the number of uses of the commodity, the smaller is the importance of the commodity in consumers' budgets (i.e., the smaller is the proportion of income that consumers spend on the commodity), and the more in the nature of a durable good is the commodity. Not everyone agrees with these statements, and, in fact, they are often contradicted by empirical studies.

[17] In terms of calculus,

$$E_I = \frac{\partial Q}{\partial I} \cdot \frac{I}{Q}$$

[18] That is, $\partial Q/\partial I = a_3$ (the coefficient of I) in Equation 3-3.

This means that a 10 percent increase in income would have resulted in only a 1.6 percent increase in the demand for sweet potatoes in the United States in 1949.

As with point price elasticity of demand, point income elasticity of demand gives different results depending on whether income rises or falls. To avoid this, we usually measure the **arc income elasticity of demand.** This uses the average of the original and new incomes, and the average of the original and new quantities. By doing so, we get the same result whether income rises or falls. Thus, the formula for arc income elasticity of demand can be expressed as

$$E_I = \frac{\Delta Q}{\Delta I} \cdot \frac{(I_2 + I_1)/2}{(Q_2 + Q_1)/2} = \frac{Q_2 - Q_1}{I_2 - I_1} \cdot \frac{I_2 + I_1}{Q_2 + Q_1} \qquad [3\text{-}15]$$

where the subscripts 1 and 2 refer to the original and the new levels of income and quantity, respectively, or vice versa. Thus, arc income elasticity of demand measures the average relative responsiveness in the demand of the commodity for a change in income in the range between I_1 and I_2.

For most commodities, an increase in income leads to an increase in demand for the commodity (that is, $\Delta Q/\Delta I$ is positive), so that E_I is also positive. As pointed out on page 90, these are called *normal goods.* In the real world, most broadly defined goods such as food, clothing, housing, health care, education, and recreation are normal goods. For the first three (necessities), E_I is positive but low (i.e., between zero and 1). For the last three classes of goods (luxuries), E_I is likely to be well above 1. There are some narrowly defined and inexpensive goods, however, of which consumers purchase less as income rises. For these, $\Delta Q/\Delta I$ and hence E_I are negative. These are called *inferior goods.* An example of an inferior good might be flour. Its demand decreases as income rises because consumers can then afford to buy prepared foods or to eat out.

Note that the income elasticity of demand is not as clear-cut and precise a measure as the price elasticity of demand. First, different concepts of income can be used in its measurement (GNP, national income, personal income, personal disposable income, and so on). More importantly, a commodity may be normal for some individuals and at some income levels and inferior for other individuals and at other levels of income. Nevertheless, the concept is very useful to a firm in estimating and forecasting the overall demand for the product it sells in a particular market and for a specific range of consumers' incomes.

One important use of the income elasticity of demand is in forecasting the change in the demand for the commodity that a firm sells under different economic conditions. On one hand, the demand for a commodity with low-income elasticity will not be greatly affected (i.e., will not fluctuate very much) as a result of boom conditions or recession in the economy. On the other hand, the demand for a luxury item, such as vacations in the Caribbean, will increase very much when the economy is booming and fall sharply during recessionary periods. Although somewhat sheltered from changing economic conditions, firms selling necessities may want to upgrade their product to share in the rise of incomes in the economy over time. Knowledge of income elasticity of demand is also important for a firm in identifying more precisely the market for its product (i.e., which types of consumers are most likely to purchase the product) and in determining the most suitable media for its promotional campaign to reach the targeted audience. Case Study 3-4 gives the estimated income elasticity of demand for various commodities.

CASE STUDY 3-4
Income Elasticities of Demand in the Real World

The first and sixth rows of Table 3-4 show, respectively, that the income elasticity of demand is 2.59 for wine in Canada and −0.36 for flour in the United States. This means that a 1 percent increase in consumer income leads to a 2.59 percent increase in expenditures on wine in Canada but to a 0.36 percent *reduction* in expenditures on flour in the United States. Thus, wine is a (strong) luxury good in Canada while flour is a (weak) inferior good in the United States. The table shows that household electricity is also a luxury in the United States and so are

European, Asian, and domestic cars, as well as gasoline, while chicken and cigarettes in the United States and cheese in the United Kingdom are necessities. Beef is on the borderline.

Note that the income elasticities given in Table 3-4 are measured as the percentage change in expenditures on the various commodities (rather than the percentage change in the *quantity* purchased of the various commodities). To the extent that prices are held constant, however, we get the same results as if the percentage change in quantities were used.

TABLE 3-4	Estimated Income Elasticity of Demand (E_I) for Selected Commodities
Commodity	**Income Elasticity**
Wine (Canada)[a]	2.59
Beef (US)[b]	1.06
Cheese (UK)[c]	0.37
Chicken (US)[b]	0.28
Potatoes (UK)[c]	−0.32
Flour (US)[d]	−0.36
Electricity (household, US)[d]	1.94
European cars (US)[e]	1.93
Asian cars (US)[e]	1.65
Domestic cars (US)[e]	1.63
Gasoline (US)[c]	1.20
Cigarettes (US)[f]	0.50

[a]J. A. Johnson, E. H. Oksanen, M. R. Veal, and D. Fretz, op. cit.
[b]D. B. Suits, "Agriculture," in W. Adams and J. Brock, eds., *Structure of American Industry* (Englewood Cliffs, N.J.: Prentice-Hall, 2000).
[c]D. Harvey, op. cit.
[d]H. S. Houthakker and L. S. Taylor, op. cit.
[e]P. S. McCarthy, "Market Price and Elasticities of New Vehicle Demands," *Review of Economics and Statistics* (August 1996), pp. 543–547.
[f]F. Calemaker, "Rational Addictive Behavior and Cigarette Smoking," *Journal of Political Economy* (August 1991).

3-4 CROSS-PRICE ELASTICITY OF DEMAND

The demand for a commodity also depends on the price of related (i.e., substitute and complementary) commodities. On one hand, if the price of tea rises, the demand for coffee increases (i.e., shifts to the right, and more coffee is demanded at each coffee price) as consumers substitute coffee for tea in consumption. On the other hand, if the price of sugar (a complement of coffee) rises, the demand for coffee declines (shifts to the left so that less coffee is demanded at each coffee price) because the price of a cup of coffee *with* sugar is now higher.

We can measure the responsiveness in the demand for commodity X to a change in the price of commodity Y with the **cross-price elasticity of demand (E_{XY}).** This is given by the percentage change in the *demand for commodity X* divided by the percentage change in the *price of commodity Y,* holding constant all the other variables in the demand function, including income and the price of commodity X. As with price and income elasticities, we have point and arc cross-price elasticity of demand. **Point cross-price elasticity of demand** is given by

$$E_{XY} = \frac{\Delta Q_X/Q_X}{\Delta P_Y/P_Y} = \frac{\Delta Q_X}{\Delta P_Y} \cdot \frac{P_Y}{Q_X} \qquad [3\text{-}16]$$

where ΔQ_X and ΔP_Y refer, respectively, to the change in the quantity of commodity X and the change in the price of commodity Y.[19]

Note that the value of $\Delta Q_X/\Delta P_Y$ is given by a_4, the estimated coefficient of P_Y, in regression Equation 3-3.[20] Therefore, the formula for the point cross-price elasticity of demand can be rewritten as

$$E_{XY} = a_4 \cdot \frac{P_Y}{Q_X} \qquad [3\text{-}17]$$

where a_4 is the estimated coefficient of P_Y in the linear regression of Q_X on P_Y and other explanatory variables. For example, with $a_4 = 479$ in regression Equation 3-4, at $P_W = \$2.94$ (P_Y) and $Q_S = 10,312$ cwt (obtained by substituting the actual values of $P_S = \$5.60$, $N = 150.73$, $I = 1.76$, $P_W = \$2.94$, and $t = 1$ into Equation 3-4 for the United States in 1949), we have

$$E_{XY} = 479\left(\frac{2.94}{10,312}\right) = 0.14$$

This means that a 10 percent increase in the price of white potatoes would have resulted in only a 1.4 percent increase in the demand for sweet potatoes in the United States in 1949.

As with point price and income elasticities of demand, point cross-price elasticity of demand gives different results, depending on whether the price of the related commodity

---

[19] In terms of calculus,

$$E_{XY} = \frac{\partial Q_X}{\partial P_Y} \cdot \frac{P_Y}{Q_X}$$

[20] That is, $\partial Q_X/\partial P_Y = a_4$ (the coefficient of P_Y) in Equation 3-3.

(P_Y) rises or falls. To avoid this, we usually measure the **arc cross-price elasticity of demand** with Formula 3-18:

$$E_{XY} = \frac{\Delta Q_X}{\Delta P_Y} \cdot \frac{(P_{Y_2} + P_{Y_1})/2}{(Q_{X_2} + Q_{X_1})/2} = \frac{Q_{X_2} - Q_{X_1}}{P_{Y_2} - P_{Y_1}} \cdot \frac{P_{Y_2} + P_{Y_1}}{Q_{X_2} + Q_{X_1}} \qquad [3\text{-}18]$$

where the subscripts 1 and 2 refer to the original and the new levels of income and quantity, respectively, or vice versa.

If the value of E_{XY} is positive, commodities X and Y are substitutes because an increase in P_Y leads to an increase in Q_X as X is substituted for Y in consumption. Examples of substitute commodities are coffee and tea, coffee and cocoa, butter and margarine, hamburgers and hot dogs, Coca-Cola and Pepsi, and electricity and gas. On the other hand, if E_{XY} is negative, commodities X and Y are complementary because an increase in P_Y leads to a reduction in Q_Y and Q_X. Examples of complementary commodities are coffee and sugar, coffee and cream, hamburgers and buns, hot dogs and mustard, and cars and gasoline. The absolute value (i.e., the value without the sign) of E_{XY} measures the degree of substitutability and complementarity between X and Y. For example, if the cross-price elasticity of demand between coffee and tea is found to be larger than that between coffee and cocoa, this means that tea is a better substitute for coffee than cocoa. Finally, if E_{XY} is close to zero, X and Y are independent commodities. This may be the case with books and beer, cars and candy, pencils and potatoes, and so on.

The cross-price elasticity of demand is a very important concept in managerial decision making. Firms often use this concept to measure the effect of changing the price of a product they sell on the demand of other related products that the firm also sells. For example, the General Motors Corporation can use the cross-price elasticity of demand to measure the effect of changing the price of Chevrolets on the demand for Pontiacs. Since Chevrolets and Pontiacs are substitutes, lowering the price of the former will reduce the demand for the latter. However, a manufacturer of both razors and razor blades can use cross-price elasticity of demand to measure the increase in the demand for razor blades that would result if the firm reduced the price of razors.

A high positive cross-price elasticity of demand is often used to define an industry, since it indicates that the various commodities are very similar. For example, the cross-price elasticity of demand between Chevrolets and Pontiacs is positive and very high and so they belong to the same (auto) industry. This concept is often used by the courts to reach a decision in business antitrust cases. For example, in the well-known *cellophane* case, the Du Pont Company was accused of monopolizing the market for cellophane. In its defense, Du Pont argued that cellophane was just one of many flexible packaging materials that included cellophane, waxed paper, aluminum foil, and many others. Based on the high cross-price elasticity of demand between cellophane and these other products, Du Pont successfully argued that the relevant market was not cellophane but flexible packaging materials. Since Du Pont had less than 20 percent of this market, the courts concluded in 1953 that Du Pont had not monopolized the market. This use of cross-price elasticity of demand is examined in greater detail in Chapter 12, which deals with business regulation and antitrust. Case Study 3-5 gives the estimated cross-price elasticity of demand for various commodities, while Case Study 3-6 examines the substitution between domestic and foreign goods.

CASE STUDY 3-5
Cross-Price Elasticities of Demand in the Real World

The first row of Table 3-5 shows that the cross-price elasticity of demand of margarine with respect to the price of butter is 1.53 percent. This means that a 1 percent increase in the price of butter leads to a 1.53 percent increase in the demand for margarine. Thus, margarine and butter are substitutes in the United States. Rows 2 and 3 show that pork and beef in the United States and mutton/lamb and beef/veal in the United Kingdom are also substitutes, although not as strong as margarine and butter in the United States. On the other hand, pork and beef/veal are unrelated products in the United Kingdom (row 4), while entertainment and food in the United States are complementary (row 8). This means that a 1 percent increase in the price of beef/veal leads to no change in the demand for pork in the United Kingdom, while a 1 percent in the price of food leads to a 0.72 *reduction* in the demand for entertainment in the United States.

TABLE 3-5 Estimated Cross-Price Elasticity of Demand (E_{XY}) between Selected Commodities

Commodity *X*	Commodity *Y*	Cross-Price Elasticity
Margarine (US)	Butter (US)	1.53[a]
Pork (US)	Beef (US)	0.40[a]
Mutton/lamb (UK)	Beef/veal (UK)	0.28[b]
Pork (UK)	Beef/veal (UK)	0.00[b]
Natural gas (US)	Electricity (US)	0.80[c]
Coal (Ireland)	Oil (Ireland)	0.70[d]
Coal (Ireland)	Natural gas (Ireland)	0.40[d]
Entertainment (US)	Food (US)	−0.72[e]
European cars	US domestic & Asian cars	0.76[f]
Asian cars	US domestic & European cars	0.61[f]
US domestic cars	European & Asian cars	0.28[f]
Automobile (Australia)	Bus transportation (Australia)	0.07[b]

[a]D. M. Heien, "The Structure of Food Demand: Interrelatedness and Duality," *American Journal of Agricultural Economics* (May 1982).
[b]D. Harvey, op. cit.
[c]G. R. Lakshmanan and W. Anderson, op. cit.
[d]Competition Authority Decision, 30 January 1998, Stateoil Ireland Ltd./Clare Oil Company Ltd., Decision No. 490, http://www.irlgov.ie/compauth/dec490.
[e]E. T. Fujii et al., "An Almost Ideal Demand System for Visitor Expenditures," *Journal of Transport Economics and Policy* (May 1985).
[f]P. S. McCarthy, op. cit.

CASE STUDY 3-6
Substitution between Domestic and Foreign Goods

Substitution between domestic and foreign goods and services has reached an all-time high in the world and is expected to continue to increase sharply. For homogeneous products such as a particular grade of wheat and steel, and for many industrial products with precise specifications such as computer chips, fiber optics, and specialized machinery, substitutability between domestic and foreign products is almost perfect. Here, a small price difference can lead quickly to large shifts in sales from domestic to foreign sources and vice versa. Even for differentiated products, such as automobiles and motorcycles, computers and copiers, watches and cameras, TV films and TV programs, soft drinks and cigarettes, soaps and detergents, commercial and military aircraft, and most other products that are similar but not identical, substitutability between domestic and foreign products is very high and rising.

Despite the quality problems of the past, U.S.-made automobiles today are highly substitutable for Japanese and European automobiles, and so are most other products. Furthermore, with many parts and components imported from many nations and with production facilities and sales around the world often exceeding sales at home, even the distinction between domestic and foreign products is fast becoming obsolete. Should a Honda Accord produced in Ohio be considered American? What about a Chrysler minivan produced in Canada, especially now that Chrysler is owned by Germany's Daimler-Benz? Is a Kentucky Toyota or Mazda that contains nearly 50 percent imported Japanese parts American? It is clearly becoming more difficult to define an American automobile, even after the American Automobile Labeling Act of 1992, which requires all automobiles sold in the United States to indicate what percentage of the car's parts are domestic or foreign. Indeed, one could even ask if the question is relevant in a world growing more and more interdependent and globalized.

Be that as it may, the increased availability of foreign products greatly increases the choices open to consumers, thus increasing their well-being.

Source: "Honda's Nationality Proves Troublesome for Free-Trade Pact," *The New York Times* (October 9, 1992), p. 1; "Want a U.S. Car? Read the Label," *The New York Times* (September 18, 1994), sec. 3, p. 6; and C. Broda, "Are We Underestimating the Gains from Globalization for the United States?" *Recent Issues in Economics and Finance, Federal Reserve Bank of New York* (April 2005), pp. 1–7.

3-5   USING ELASTICITIES IN MANAGERIAL DECISION MAKING

The analysis of the forces or variables that affect demand and reliable estimates of their quantitative effect on sales are essential for the firm to make the best operating decisions and to plan for its growth. Some of the forces that affect demand are under the control of the firm, while others are not. A firm can usually set the price of the commodity it sells and decide on the level of its expenditures on advertising, product quality, and customer service, but it has no control over the level and growth of consumers' incomes, consumers' price expectations, competitors' pricing decisions, and competitors' expenditures on advertising, product quality, and customer service. The firm can estimate the elasticity of demand with respect to all the forces or variables that affect the demand for the commodity that the firm sells. The firm needs these elasticity estimates in order to determine the optimal operational policies and the most effective way to respond to the policies of competing firms. For example, if the demand for the product is price inelastic, the firm would not want to lower its price since that would reduce its total revenue, increase its total costs (as more units of the commodity will be sold at the lower price) and, thus, give it lower profits. Similarly, if the elasticity of the firm's sales with respect to advertising is positive and higher than for its expenditures on product quality and customer service, then the firm may want to concentrate its sales efforts on advertising rather than on product quality and customer service.

The elasticity of the firm's sales with respect to the variables outside the firm's control is also crucial to the firm in responding most effectively to competitors' policies and in planning the best growth strategy. For example, if the firm has estimated that the cross-price elasticity of the demand for its product with respect to the price of a competitor's product is very high, it will be quick to respond to a competitor's price reduction; otherwise, the firm would lose a great deal of its sales. However, the firm would think twice before lowering its price for fear of starting a price war. Furthermore, if the income elasticity is very low for the firm's product, management knows that the firm will not benefit much from rising incomes and may want to improve its product or move into new product lines with more income-elastic demand.

Thus, the firm should first identify all the important variables that affect the demand for the product it sells. Then the firm should obtain variable estimates of the marginal effect of a change in each variable on demand.[21] The firm would use this information to estimate the elasticity of demand for the product it sells with respect to each of the variables in the demand function. These are essential for optimal managerial decisions in the short run and in planning for growth in the long run.

For example, suppose that the Tasty Company markets coffee brand X and estimated the following regression of the demand for its brand of coffee:

$$Q_X = 1.5 - 3.0P_X + 0.8I + 2.0P_Y - 0.6P_S + 1.2A \qquad [3\text{-}19]$$

where Q_X = sales of coffee brand X in the United States, in millions of pounds per year
   P_X = price of coffee brand X, in dollars per pound
   I = personal disposable income, in trillions of dollars per year
   P_Y = price of the competitive brand of coffee, in dollars per pound
   P_S = price of sugar, in dollars per pound
   A = advertising expenditures for coffee brand X, in hundreds of thousands of dollars per year

Suppose also that this year, $P_X = \$2$, $I = \$2.5$, $P_Y = \$1.80$, $P_S = \$0.50$, and $A = \$1$. Substituting these values into Equation 3-19, we obtain

$$Q_X = 1.5 - 3(2) + 0.8(2.5) + 2(1.80) - 0.6(0.50) + 1.2(1) = 2$$

Thus, this year the firm would sell 2 million pounds of coffee brand X.

---

[21] This can be accomplished by regression analysis, to be discussed in Chapter 4.

The firm can use this information to find the elasticity of the demand for coffee brand X with respect to its price, income, the price of competitive coffee brand Y, the price of sugar, and advertising. Thus,

$$E_P = -3\left(\frac{2}{2}\right) = -3$$

$$E_I = 0.8\left(\frac{2.5}{2}\right) = 1$$

$$E_{XY} = 2\left(\frac{1.8}{2}\right) = 1.8$$

$$E_{XS} = -0.6\left(\frac{0.50}{2}\right) = -0.15$$

$$E_A = 1.2\left(\frac{1}{2}\right) = 0.6$$

The firm can use these elasticities to forecast the demand for its brand of coffee next year. For example, suppose that next year the firm intends to increase the price of its brand of coffee by 5 percent and its advertising expenditures by 12 percent. Suppose also that the firm expects personal disposable income to rise by 4 percent, P_Y to rise by 7 percent, and P_S to fall by 8 percent. Using the level of sales (Q_X) of 2 million pounds this year, the elasticities calculated above, the firm's intended policies for next year, and the firm's expectations about the change in other variables given above, the firm can determine its sales next year (Q_X') as follows:

$$Q_X' = Q_X + Q_X\left(\frac{\Delta P_X}{P_X}\right)E_P + Q_X\left(\frac{\Delta I}{I}\right)E_I + Q_X\left(\frac{\Delta P_Y}{P_Y}\right)E_{XY} + Q_X\left(\frac{\Delta P_S}{P_S}\right)E_{XS} + Q_X\left(\frac{\Delta A}{A}\right)E_A$$

$$= 2 + 2(5\%)(-3) + 2(4\%)(1) + 2(7\%)(1.8) + 2(-8\%)(-0.15) + 2(12\%)(0.6)$$

$$= 2 + 2(0.05)(-3) + 2(0.04)(1) + 2(0.07)(1.8) + 2(-0.08)(-0.15) + 2(0.12)(0.6)$$

$$= 2(1 - 0.15 + 0.04 + 0.126 + 0.012 + 0.072)$$

$$= 2(1 + 0.1)$$

$$= 2(1.1)$$

$$= 2.2, \text{ or } 2{,}200{,}000 \text{ pounds}$$

The Tasty Company could also use this information to determine that it could sell 2 million pounds of its brand of coffee next year (the same as this year) by increasing its price by 8.33 percent instead of by 5 percent (if everything else remained the same). The extra 3.33 percent increase in P_X would result in $2(0.033)(-3) = -0.198$, or 198,000 pounds less coffee sold than the 2.2 million pounds forecast for next year with an increase in P_X of only 5 percent. Case Study 3-7 gives an estimate of the price, income, and cross-price elasticity of demand for alcoholic beverages in the United States that can be used by firms in the market to make the type of managerial decisions we have discussed.

CASE STUDY 3-7
Demand Elasticities for Alcoholic Beverages in the United States

Table 3-6 gives the price, cross, and income (expenditures) elasticities of the U.S. demand for alcoholic beverages (beer, wine, and spirits) estimated from U.S. Department of Agriculture individual and household food-consumption survey data for 1987–1988. From the table, we see that the price elasticity of demand for beer (E_{XP}) is –0.23. This means that a 10 percent *increase* in the price of beer results in a 2.3 percent *reduction* in the quantity of beer demanded by U.S. consumers and thus to an *increase* in consumer expenditures on beer. The price elasticity of wine (E_{YP}) is –0.40 and that of spirits (E_{ZP}) is –0.25, so that an increase in their price also leads consumers to demand a smaller quantity of wine and spirits, but also to spend more on these alcoholic beverages.

Table 3-6 also shows that the cross-price elasticity of demand for beer with respect to wine (E_{XY}) is 0.31 and with respect to spirits (E_{XZ}) is 0.15. This means that wine and spirits are substitutes for beer,

with wine being a better substitute. Thus, a 10 percent increase in the price of wine will lead to a 3.1 percent increase in the demand for beer, while a 10 percent increase in the price of spirits leads to a 1.5 percent increase in the demand for beer. Note that the cross-price elasticity of wine and spirits with respect to beer (i.e., E_{YX} and E_{ZX} in columns 2 and 3 of the table) are somewhat different from the cross-price elasticity of demand for beer with respect to wine and spirits (E_{XY} and E_{XZ} in column 1).

Finally, the table shows that with E_{XI} = –0.09, E_{YI} = 5.03, and E_{ZI} = 1.21, a 10 percent increase in consumer income (expenditure) leads to a 0.9 percent *reduction* in the demand for beer, but to a 50.3 percent *increase* in the demand for wine, and a 12.1 *increase* in the demand for spirits. Thus, beer can be considered an inferior good, while wine and spirits can be regarded as a luxury (with wine being a much stronger luxury than spirits).

TABLE 3-6	Price, Income, and Cross-Price Elasticities of Demand for Beer, Wine, and Spirits in the United States	
Beer	**Wine**	**Spirits**
E_{XP} = –0.23	E_{YP} = –0.40	E_{ZP} = –0.25
E_{XI} = –0.09	E_{YI} = 5.03	E_{ZI} = 1.21
E_{XY} = 0.31	E_{YX} = 0.16	E_{ZX} = 0.07
E_{XZ} = 0.15	E_{YZ} = 0.10	E_{ZY} = 0.09

Legend: X = beer, Y = wine, Z = spirits, I = Income

Source: X. M. Gao, E. J. Wiles, and G. L. Kramer, "A Microeconometric Model of the U.S. Consumer Demand for Alcoholic Beverages," *Applied Economics* (January 1995), pp. 59–69.

3-6   INTERNATIONAL CONVERGENCE OF TASTES

A rapid convergence of tastes is taking place around the world. Tastes in the United States affect tastes in other countries, and tastes abroad strongly influence tastes in the United States. Coca-Cola and McDonald's are only two of the most obvious U.S. products that have become household items around the world. One can see Adidas sneakers and Sony

CASE STUDY 3-8
Gillette Introduces the Sensor and Mach3 Razors—Two Truly Global Products

As tastes become global, firms are responding with truly global products. These are introduced more or less simultaneously in most countries with little or no local variation. This is leading to what has been called the *global supermarket.* For example, in 1990, Gillette introduced its new Sensor razor at the same time in most nations of the world and advertised it with virtually the same TV spots (ad campaign) in 19 countries in Europe and North America. In 1994, Gillette introduced an upgrade of the Sensor razor called SensorExcel with a high-tech edge. By 1998, Gillette had sold more than 400 million of Sensor and SensorExcel razors and more than 8 billion twin-blade cartridges, and it had captured an incredible 71 percent of the global blade market.

Then in April 1998, Gillette unveiled the Mach3, the company's most important new product since the Sensor. It has three blades with a new, revolutionary edge produced with chip-making technology that took five years to develop. Gillette developed its new razor in secrecy at the astounding cost of more than $750 million, and it spent another $300 million to advertise it. Since it went on sale in July 1998, the Mach3 has proved to be an even bigger

success than the Sensor razor. In April 2002, Gillette introduced worldwide the Mach3 Turbo razor and in June 2004 its M3Power razor, as evolutions of its Mach3, and its five-blade Fusion razor in early 2006. The global reach of the M3Power and Fusion are likely to be even greater than for its predecessors with the merger of Gillette with Procter & Gamble.

The trend toward the global supermarket is rapidly spreading in Europe as borders fade and as Europe's single currency (the euro) brings prices closer across the continent. A growing number of companies are creating *Euro-brands*—a single product for most countries of Europe—and advertising them with *Euro-ads,* which are identical or nearly identical across countries, except for language. Many national differences in taste will, of course, remain; for example, Nestlé markets more than 200 blends of Nescafe to cater to differences in tastes in different markets. But the converging trend in tastes around the world is unmistakable, and is likely to lead to more and more global products. This is true not only in foods and inexpensive consumer products but also in automobiles, tires, portable computers, phones, and many other durable products.

Source: "Building the Global Supermarket," *The New York Times* (November 18, 1988), p. D1; "Gillette's World View: One Blade Fits All," *The Wall Street Journal* (January 3, 1994), p. C3; "Gillette Finally Reveals Its Vision of the Future, and It Has 3 Blades," *The Wall Street Journal* (April 4, 1998), p. A1; "Selling in Europe: Borders Fade," *The New York Times* (May 31, 1990), p. D1; "Converging Prices Mean Trouble for European Retailers," *Financial Times* (June 18, 1999), p. 27; "Can Nestlé Be the Very Best?" *Fortune* (November 13, 2001), pp. 353–360. "For Cutting-Edge Dads," *U.S. News & World Report* (June 14, 2004), pp. 80–81; "P&G's $57 Billion Bargain," *Business Week* (July 25, 2005), p. 26; "How Many Blades Is Enough?" *Fortune* (October 31, 2005), p. 40; "Gillette New Edge," *Business Week* (February 6, 2006), p. 44.

Walkman personal stereos on joggers from Central Park in New York City to Tivoli Gardens in Copenhagen. You can eat a Big Mac in Piazza di Spagna in Rome or Gorky's Square in Moscow. We find Japanese cars and VCRs in New York and in New Delhi, French perfumes in Paris and in Cairo, and Perrier in practically every major (and not so major) city around the world. Texas Instruments and Canon calculators, Dell and IBM portable PCs, and Xerox and Minolta copiers are found in offices and homes more or less everywhere. With more rapid communications and more frequent travels, the worldwide convergence of tastes is even accelerating. As a result, firms must increasingly think in

CASE STUDY 3-9
Ford's World Car(s)

In fall 1994, Ford introduced the Ford Contour and Mercury Mystique in the United States—the same basic mid-size car it introduced in Europe in 1993 under the name of Mondeo. Intended to be Ford's world car, it took six years to develop at a cost of $6 billion—twice what Ford spent to develop its vastly successful Taurus and four times more than DaimlerChrysler spent on its Dodge/Plymouth Neon. Ford insisted that by developing and producing a single basic car for Europe and the United States, it saved about 25 percent of developing and producing a separate car for each side of the Atlantic, as it had done in the past. Consumer tastes had converged sufficiently, according to Ford, so that a single car would find lots of buyers everywhere, just as one menu is working around the world for McDonald's. Building a world car is a most ambitious undertaking; in the past, only Volkswagen's classic Beetle and Toyota's Corolla have come close to succeeding.

For the exterior design, Ford commissioned clay models from its design studios in California, Michigan, England, and Italy—from which it developed a consensus model. After showing the model to consumer clinics in the United States, Ford chose to change the front and rear styling and put a larger trunk and more chrome on the U.S. version of the car. Still, the European and American versions have 75 percent of their parts in common. This was a far cry from Ford's previous unsuccessful attempt in 1981 to build a common car for Europe and the United States (the Escort), which resulted in one of the grandest corporate foul-ups ever and led to European and American models that shared only two insignificant parts. Indeed, many experts still feel that a common car for the world market violated the basic marketing wisdom of the 1990s to get closer to customers. Ford, however, was confident that consumer tastes had converged sufficiently during the previous decade as to ensure the success of its world car.

As it turned out, the Mondeo–Contour–Mystique was not very successful. Undeterred, Ford tore up its management structure, abolished its regional companies, and turned itself into a world company that made global cars. Ford spent $2 billion to develop its new world car, the Focus, which it introduced in Europe in 1998 and in the United States in 1999. But this was also not very successful because consumer tastes had shifted toward *sport wagons*—a cross between sedans and sport utility vehicles.

Source: "Ford's $6 Billion Baby," *Fortune* (June 28, 1993), pp. 76–81; "Ford Sets Its Sights on a World Car," *The New York Times* (September 27, 1993), p. D1; "One World, One Ford," *Forbes* (June 20, 1994), pp. 40–41; "The World That Changed the Machine," *The Economist* (March 30, 1996), pp. 63–64; "Ford Hopes Its New Focus Will be a Global Bestseller," *The Wall Street Journal* (October 8, 1998), p. B10; "Ford's Taurus Loses Favor to New-Age 'Sport Wagon'," *The New York Times* (February 7, 2002), p. B1; and "A Hard Lesson in Globalization," *The Economist* (April 30, 2005), p. 63.

terms of global production and marketing to remain competitive. Even small firms must constantly worry that new global products do not wipe out their entire product line overnight.

In a 1983 article "The Globalization of Markets" in the *Harvard Business Review,* Theodore Levitt asserted that consumers from New York to Frankfurt to Tokyo want similar products, and that future success would require more standardized products and pricing around the world. In fact, in country after country, we are seeing the emergence of a middle-class consumer lifestyle based on a taste for comfort, convenience, and speed. In the food business, this means packaged, fast-to-prepare, and ready-to-eat products. This is the inevitable result of the information revolution: people are traveling more, and they are watching the same movies and TV shows.

Market researchers have discovered that similarities in living styles among middle-class people all over the world are much greater than once thought to be, and the similarities are growing with rising incomes and education levels. With the tremendous improvement in telecommunications, transportation, and travel, the cross-fertilization of cultures and convergence of tastes can be expected to accelerate in the future—with important implications for consumers, producers, and sellers of an increasing number and variety of products and services. Case Studies 3-8 and 3-9 provide two important examples of global products.

3-7   ELECTRONIC COMMERCE

Since the mid-1990s, the Internet (see Section 1-7) has given rise to electronic commerce or electronic business, and this is revolutionizing traditional business relationships. **E-commerce** refers to the production, advertising, sale, and distribution of products and services from business to business and from business to consumer through the Internet. This has sharply reduced time and distance barriers between buyers and sellers. In e-commerce, there is no traveling to a traditional "bricks-and-mortar" store, no salesperson, no order book, and no cash register—only the Web site. This offers tremendous advantages to buyers and sellers and represents a fundamental change in the way buyers and sellers interact in the marketplace. The biggest lures for consumers are the convenience of having round-the-clock access to the virtual store and being able to engage in comparative shopping at minimal cost and effort. E-commerce provides even greater benefits for sellers by sharply reducing their cost of executing sales and procuring inputs, reformulating supply chains and logistics, and redefining customer relationship management.

From 1997 to 2005, worldwide business-to-consumer, or retail, e-commerce increased from less than $20 billion to nearly $300 billion. More than half of worldwide retail e-commerce is now in the United States, but this percentage is expected to fall below 50 percent in a few years because of its even more rapid growth outside the United States. Many times larger than retail e-commerce are business-to-business (B2B) sales on the Internet. The reasons for this are that (1) business-to-business spending is far larger than consumer spending and (2) businesses are more willing and able than individuals to use the Internet. Wal-Mart, for one, now conducts all of its business with suppliers over a proprietary B2B network. Nearly half of business-to-business e-commerce is in the computer and electronics industries, while for business-to-consumer e-commerce the largest three categories are travel, PCs, and books. Even though e-commerce accounts for only 15 percent of global gross domestic product (GDP), it is already having a significant effect on large economic sectors such as communications, finance, and retailing. For example, trading securities on the Web reached nearly one-third of all retail equity trades in the United States in 2005, from practically zero in 1995.

Producers and sellers have found that online connections with consumers, on the one hand, and corporate customers and suppliers, on the other, have led to a dramatic fall in the cost of doing business, a cut in reaction times, and an expansion of sales reach. For example, while the banks' cost of processing a paper check averages $1.20 and that of processing a credit-card payment averages $0.50, the cost of processing an electronic payment is as low as $0.01. Another area in which e-commerce is making a significant impact is business procurement of maintenance, repair, and operations (MRO). For example, Ford moved most of its $16 billion-per-year MRO purchases from 3,000 vendors to the Web in 1999, and Sweden's telecommunications maker Ericsson followed in 2001. Even more dramatic is the reorganization of supply chains made possible by e-commerce, which permits moving more and more toward a build-to-order process model with extremely low inventory levels (as, for example, at Dell—refer to Integrating Case Study 1 at the end of Part One).

After missing the first round, traditional or bricks-and-mortar retailers entered e-commerce in droves. The percentage of U.S. companies selling products online increased from 24 in 1998 to more than 60 in 2005. Traditional retailers do come to e-commerce with some formidable advantages, such as strong brand names and nation-wide distribution and service centers, and they do satisfy consumers' needs for human contact, entertainment, and the social activity of "going out." In fact, by integrating their Internet and traditional retailing operations, in what has become known as *click-and-mortar* retailing, traditional sellers can regain the upper hand on Internet-only sellers. For example, Internet shoppers can gather up-to-date information on products and prices on the Web and then physically examine the product and make the actual purchase at a real store on their way home from work. Many companies, such as Wal-Mart, Gap, and Hewlett-Packard, have put major efforts into providing their customers a virtual shopping option, even when physically visiting one of their stores, by installing Internet-enabled devices on their premises. To be sure, it is neither cheap nor easy to fully integrate traditional and online retailing services, but competition is forcing more companies to do so.

E-commerce does provide challenges for Internet sellers. One of the most serious arises from the ability of consumers to do comparison shopping on the Internet (a phenomenon dubbed *frictionless capitalism*), which is likely to greatly squeeze profit margins in many industries. Another challenge for traditional retailers that have not entered online selling or have not yet fully integrated it with their traditional retailing services is that suppliers will themselves market their products on the Internet directly, undermining not only the retailers' traditional business but also their effort to sell on the Internet.

New selling methods, such as auctions, have also become popular on the Internet. An Internet auction model that is growing rapidly lets buyers post a price that they are willing to pay for an item or service, with the site facilitating a match with a seller. For example, Priceline.com uses this technique to sell airline tickets, hotel rooms, car rentals, vacations, home financing, and even cars. This type of auction is now also spreading to the purchase of raw materials, electronic components, and personal items, and it is opening new opportunities for small and mid-size enterprises as never before. E-commerce is also giving rise to a new type of business called *infomediaries,* which are enterprises that collect consumer information and develop detailed consumer profiles for sale to other businesses for the latter's marketing use.

E-commerce is not without problems, however. For one thing, even though the Web is making the Internet easier to use and hundreds of companies are developing software to make it easier still, finding what you want in the ocean of information available on the Internet can be maddeningly slow. Then there is the risk. For example, a file traveling on the Internet could be examined, copied, or altered without the intended recipient being aware of it. The Internet was simply not designed to ensure secure commerce. For example, in 1995 a hacker, or computer expert, tapped into Citibank's computing system and transferred $10 million to various bank accounts throughout the world. Although this computer fraud was quickly discovered and only $400,000 was actually withdrawn, it vividly points out the danger of doing business on the Internet. All of this can be avoided by encrypting the data (i.e., transmitting the data in code) and then unencrypting it upon arrival by the intended recipient. But this still cannot be easily and conveniently done. The Internet also creates problems for publishers because any copyrighted material can easily be copied and transmitted, thus undermining copyright laws. It is likely that all these problems will be overcome in time, but currently they present some thorny problems for Internet users.

Although business-to-business e-commerce continued to grow rapidly, business-to-consumer e-commerce leveled off somewhat in 2000 and 2001, when many e-commerce-only firms faced spectacular failure (such as the Internet-only grocers). Since then, however, very rapid growth has resumed and it is now becoming more and more apparent that retail e-commerce has become another sales channel, alongside department stores and strip malls, but one that is likely to continue to outstrip the growth of traditional commerce.[22] Case Studies 3-10 and 3-11 examine e-commerce at Amazon.com and at eBay, respectively.

---

[22] See "How the Internet Will Reshape Worldwide Business Activity," *Financial Times* (April 7, 1999), p. 1; "Playing Catch-Up at the On-Line Mall," *The New York Times* (February 21, 1999), sec. 3, p. 1; "E-Commerce Report: Conventional Retailers Are Integrating Web Sites with Stores, Improving Service in Both Areas," *The New York Times* (August 16, 1999), p. C6; "The Big Guys Go Online," *Business Week* (September 6, 1999), pp. 30–32; "Citibank Fraud Case Raises Computer Security Questions," *The New York Times* (August 19, 1995), p. 31; B. Fraumeni, "E-Commerce: Measurement and Measurement Issues," *American Economic Review* (May 2001), pp. 318–322; D. Lucking-Reiley and D. F. Spulber, "Business-to-Business Electronic Commerce," *Journal of Economic Perspectives* (Winter 2001), pp. 55–68; "Online Shoppers Choose Price over Convenience," *Financial Times* (February 20, 2002), p. 1; "E-Commerce Takes Off," *The Economist*, May 15, 2004, p. 9; and "Clicks, Bricks and Bargains," *The Economist*, December 3, 2005, pp. 57–58.

CASE STUDY 3-10
E-Commerce at Amazon.com

In July 1995, 31-year-old Jeff Bezos launched Amazon.com, an online bookseller, revolutionizing bookselling and redefining the entire retailing business. With a few clicks of the mouse, an individual can search through the 3.1 million titles offered by Amazon, compared with 175,000 titles available in any Barnes & Noble superstore. And Amazon does all that without the multimillion-dollar expenditures for buildings and the droves of store clerks used by its archrival. Amazon's total sales grew from a few million dollars in 1995 to $542 million in 1998, compared with $3.1 billion for Barnes & Noble. But Amazon reached its sales level with only 1,600 employees against its rival's 27,000, so that sales per employee were a staggering $375,000 at Amazon but only $100,000 at Barnes & Noble (see Table 3-7). Sales growth seems to be running faster at Amazon than at Barnes & Noble by multiples of ten, returns were only 2 percent, and the annual inventory turnover was 24 percent at Amazon compared with 30 percent and 3 percent, respectively, at Barnes & Noble. But Amazon lost $29.2 million in 1998 while Barnes & Noble earned $147.3 million, and yet the book (stock) value of Amazon was $11.1 billion in 1998 compared with a book value of $2.2 billion for B&N.

The immediate question that comes to mind is how can the book value of Amazon, which lost $29.2 million in 1998 be higher than Barnes & Noble's, which is highly profitable? The answer is that investors believe that once Amazon has grown sufficiently large to pay off its initial marketing and technology investment, it is likely to become very profitable because its cost of doing business on the Internet is substantially lower than that for traditional bookstores. Losses also arise from Amazon.com's goal of growing rapidly and establishing a global brand name quickly before competitors can mount a serious challenge. CNN and *USA Today* also ran losses for many years in order to stake their markets before returning a profit. In short, Bezos has defined a new retailing paradigm, which is forcing even retailing giants (including Barnes & Noble) into a mad rush into online marketing. But Amazon is not stopping with books. Toward the end of 1998, Amazon.com debuted a video store and expanded its gift shop, and it is now looking to apply its winning selling strategy to many other retailing fields, from software to apparel, with the goal of becoming the Internet's premier shopping destination.

The secret of Amazon's amazing success is more than making the buying experience irresistibly easy

TABLE 3-7	The Amazon Advantage	
	Amazon	**Barnes & Noble**
Number of stores	1 Web site	1,011
Number of employees	1,600	27,000
Titles per superstore	3.1 million	175,000
Total sales	$542 million	$3.1 billion
Sales per employee per year	$375,000	$100,000
Sales growth (last quarter of 1998)	306%	10%
Book returns	2%	30%
Inventory turnover per year	24%	3%
Operating income in 1998	–$29.2 million	$147.3 million

Source: "Amazon.com: The Wild World of E-Commerce," *Business Week* (December 14, 1998), pp. 104–114.

Continued . . .

and even fun, and in the process drastically cutting selling costs—as crucially important as they are. Another shrewd advantage arises from pioneering the use of "collaborative filtering technology" that allows it to suggest other titles to a customer based on buying histories of other customers with similar tastes. This is a powerful mass-marketing strategy. Still another important advantage of online selling arises from the fact that Amazon.com needs to carry a relatively small inventory. This is possible because Amazon places an order to a publisher only when a customer orders a book. Amazon charges its customers as soon as it ships the book, but it does not have to pay the publisher for 45 to 90 days after ordering the book. Thus, while traditional retailers must carry inventory for several months after paying for it, Amazon and all other online sellers can use their customers' money for as much as a month or two before paying their suppliers. Of course, as more and more traditional retailers enter online selling, they will also gain these benefits. But by being first and by defining the entire process of online selling, Amazon seems able to retain a major advantage over its competitors.

In October 1999, Amazon.com opened its Web site for a nominal fee to merchants of all kinds, thus becoming essentially an Internet shopping bazaar. By 2005, it was selling not only books, videos, and music, but also jewelry, health products, and musical instruments, bringing to 31 the number of categories on its Web site. The company also expanded to Britain, Germany, France, Japan, Canada, and, most recently, to China. Nearly three-quarters of Amazon's revenue, however, are still from books, videos, and music—the first three categories the company entered.

Since 2000, the growth of sales at Amazon slowed down considerably and sales are now less than half those of eBay. From the time of its founding in 1995 until 2002, Amazon.com incurred losses in each year totaling $3.0 billion, before turning a profit of $35 million in 2003 and $589 in 2004 on $6.9 billion in sales (as compared with profits of $132 million on sales of $4.1 billion at archrival B&N). Amazon.com's stock traded in the mid-thirties in 2005, as compared to $55-$85 during 1999. The firm, however, survived the 2001 burst in the Internet bubble with its low costs and large discounts (30 percent on all book purchases of $20 or more and free shipping on orders of $99 or more). But gross margins of only 10 to 12 percent, do not allow Amazon.com much room for error.

Source: "Does Amazon 5 = 2 Barnes & Nobles?" *The New York Times* (July 19, 1998), sec. 3, p. 4; "Amazon.com: The Wild World of E-Commerce," *Business Week* (December 14, 1998), pp. 104–114; "Amazon.com Throws Open the Doors," *Business Week* (October 11, 1999), p. 44; and "A Retail Revolution Turns 10," *The New York Times* (July 10, 2005), sec. 3, p. 1.

CASE STUDY 3-11
eBay and Some Internet Veterans Are Cashing In

By 2002, over 50 of the more than 200 Web companies that survived the shakedown of the previous two years were making money, and more of them did so in 2003–2005. One of the largest, eBay, the dominant Internet auction site, which sells almost everything from junk found in the attic to mint-condition antique cars, has been profitable from its first year of existence and is now the most successful business on the Internet. Among other big hitters

are Yahoo (the search engine), Hotels.com, and Expedia (the travel site).

The interesting thing about these Internet companies is that once they start making money, earnings can increase very rapidly because of operating leverage. That is, once these companies have built their Web site and set up their basic operations, it is very cheap for them to process additional orders, and profits can grow then much faster than revenues. For example, eBay's revenues in the first quarter of 2002 jumped 59 percent to $245 million, while costs rose only by 39 percent to $197 million, so that profits more than doubled from $21 million a year before to nearly $48 million. Over the same period, Hotels.com's revenues increased by 57 percent to $165 million, while profits increased sevenfold to nearly $13 million; for Expedia, revenues rose 103 percent to $103 million and profits were nearly $6 million (as compared with a loss of $20 million in the first quarter of 2001).

One advantage that Hotels.com and Expedia have over Amazon.com is that the former sell travel and hotel reservation services without any product to store or ship. Amazon.com, on the other hand, must buy a book and ship it (or have it shipped) every time a customer makes a purchase. As a result, Amazon's gross margins are much smaller than Hotels.com's and Expedia's. As pointed out in Case Study 3-10, however, Amazon does have some advantages, and it did turn profitable since 2003. Of course, the same operating leverage that helps Internet companies in good times hurts them when the market turns bad. In bad times, even a small reduction in revenues results in losses because of the high fixed costs that these companies face. This is exactly what happened to Yahoo and America Online in 2001.

The star performer of the Internet remains eBay, however. Its stock never experienced the collapse of Amazon and Yahoo, and eBay has been profitable in every quarter of every year since its creation in 1995. Its market capitalization was $57 billion in 2005, its revenue was expected to be $4.4 billion with profits of $1 billion, and its registered users exceed 150 million in 15 countries around the world, with 60 million active users (those that have bid for or listed items within the last year). Millions of collectibles, appliances, computers, furniture, equipment, vehicles, and other miscellaneous items are listed, bought, and sold daily. eBay does not handle the goods or the payment for them (except through its subsidiary PayPal). To encourage honesty, however, eBay maintains, rates, and posts feedback for all transactions and from all users. eBay collects a small fee for each transaction that takes place on its Web site and tens of thousands of people now make their living from trading on it. eBay has simply become an unstoppable business phenomenon, just as McDonald's was in the 1970s and Wal-Mart in the 1980s. At the end of 2005, however, the search engine Google was getting ready to invade eBay's market and spoil the fun.

Source: "If at First You Don't Succeed …," *The Wall Street Journal* (February 11, 2002), p. R6; "The eBay Way of Life," *Newsweek* (June 17, 2002), pp. 51–60; "Finally, the Pot of Gold," *Business Week* (June 24, 2002), pp. 104–106; A. Cohen, *The Perfect Store: Inside eBay* (Boston: Little, Brown and Company, 2002); "Europe Heads for the Mall," *Business Week* (July 12, 2004), p. 51; "eBay to Buy Shopping Site," *Financial Times* (June 2, 2005), p. 19; "Meg and the Power of Many," *The Economist* (June 15, 2005), pp. 65–67; "eBay, with a Global Boost, Beats Wall Street Expectations," *The New York Times* (July 21, 2005), p. C4; and "Google Tests New Service that Could Threaten to Rival eBay," *Financial Times* (October 26, 2005), p. 15.

SUMMARY

1. The demand for a commodity faced by a firm depends on the market or industry demand for the commodity, which, in turn, is the sum of the demands for the commodity of the individual consumers in the market. The demand for the commodity that a firm faces depends on the price of the commodity, the size of (i.e., the number of consumers in) the market, consumer income, the price of related commodities, tastes, price expectations, the promotional efforts of the firm, and competitors' pricing and promotional policies. In general, the quantity response by a firm to a change in the price of the commodity will be some fraction of the total market response. The demand for durable goods is generally less stable than the demand for nondurable goods. The firm's demand for inputs or resources (producers' goods) is derived from the demand for the final commodities produced with the inputs.

2. The price elasticity of demand (E_P) measures the percentage change in the quantity demanded of a commodity divided by the percentage change in its price, while holding constant all other variables in the demand function. We can measure point or arc price elasticity of demand. A linear demand curve is price elastic (that is, $|E_P| > 1$) above its geometric midpoint, is unitary elastic at its midpoint (that is, $|E_P| = 1$), and is inelastic (that is, $|E_P| < 1$) below the midpoint. For a decline in price, total revenue (TR) increases if demand is elastic, remains unchanged if demand is unitary elastic, and declines if demand is inelastic. The elasticity of demand is greater, the more and better are the substitutes available for the commodity and the greater is the length of time allowed for the quantity response by consumers to the price change.

3. The income elasticity of demand (E_I) measures the percentage change in the demand for a commodity divided by the percentage change in consumer income, while holding constant all other variables in the demand function, including price. We can measure point or arc income elasticity of demand. Most goods are normal ($E_I > 0$). For inferior goods, $E_I < 0$. Those normal goods for which $E_I > 1$ are called *luxuries,* while normal goods for which E_I is between zero and 1 are *necessities.*

4. The cross-price elasticity of demand for commodity X with respect to commodity Y (E_{XY}) measures the percentage change in the demand for commodity X divided by the percentage change in the price of commodity Y, while holding constant all other variables in the demand function, including income and the price of commodity X. We can measure point or arc cross-price elasticity. Commodities X and Y are substitutes if E_{XY} is positive, complementary if E_{XY} is negative, and independent if E_{XY} is close to zero. A firm uses the cross-price elasticity of demand to estimate the effect of reducing the price of a commodity on the demand of other related commodities that the firm sells. A high cross-price elasticity of demand is also used to define an industry.

5. For the analysis of demand, the firm should first identify all the important variables that affect the demand for the product it sells. By using regression analysis (discussed in Chapter 4), the firm could obtain reliable estimates of the effect of a change in each of these variables on demand for the product.

6. There is an increasing trend of converging tastes around the world. Tastes in the United States affect tastes around the world, and tastes abroad strongly influence tastes in the United States. While some national differences will surely remain, the information revolution and cross-fertilization of cultures can be expected to accelerate the global convergence of tastes. This has important implications for all firms.

7. Since the mid-1990s, the Internet has given rise to electronic commerce, which is revolutionizing traditional business relationships. E-commerce refers to the production, advertising, sale, and distribution of products and services from business to business and from business to consumer through the Internet. The biggest lures of e-commerce for consumers are the convenience of having round-the-clock access to the virtual store and the ability to engage in comparative shopping at minimal cost and effort. Through e-commerce, sellers can sharply reduce their cost of executing sales and procuring inputs, reformulate supply chains and logistics, and redefine customer relationship management.

DISCUSSION QUESTIONS

1. (*a*) If our main interest in managerial economics is the demand that a firm faces for its product, why do we study consumer demand theory? (*b*) What is the distinction between inferior goods and normal goods? Between the substitution effect and the income effect? Between a change in the quantity demanded and a change in demand?

2. (*a*) How many types of demand functions are there? (*b*) In which type of demand are we most interested in managerial economics? Why? (*c*) Why do we then study the other types of demand?

3. (*a*) What are the most important determinants of the demand function that a firm faces for the commodity it sells? (*b*) What is meant by

producers' goods? By derived demand? (c) Why is the demand for durable goods (both consumers' and producers') less stable than the demand for nondurable goods?

4. (a) What is the advantage of using the price elasticity rather than the slope of the demand curve or its inverse to measure the responsiveness in the quantity demanded of a commodity to a change in its price? (b) Why and how is the formula for arc price elasticity of demand different from the formula for point price elasticity of demand?

5. (a) State the relationship between the total revenue of a firm and the price elasticity of demand for a *price increase* along a linear demand curve. (b) Explain the reason for the relationship that you stated in part (a).

6. (a) Explain why a firm facing a negatively sloped demand curve would never produce in the inelastic portion of the demand curve. (b) When would the firm want to operate at the point where its demand curve is unitary elastic?

7. (a) Would you expect the price elasticity of demand to be higher for Chevrolet automobiles or for automobiles in general? Why? (b) Would you expect the price elasticity of demand for electricity for residential use to be higher or lower than for industrial use? Why? (c) Would you expect the price elasticity of demand for electricity to be higher or lower in the short run as compared with the long run? Why?

8. If the price increases by 10 percent, by how much does the quantity of household (a) natural gas and (b) electricity change in the short run and in the long run? (*Hint:* Use the price-elasticity values in Table 3-3.)

9. If there has been a 10 percent increase in consumer income between two periods, what was the percentage change in the demand for foreign travel? For tobacco products? For flour? (*Hint:* Use the income-elasticity values in Table 3-4.)

10. Agricultural commodities are known to have a price-inelastic demand and to be necessities. How can this information allow us to explain why the income of farmers falls (a) after a good harvest? (b) in relation to the incomes in other sectors of the economy?

11. Suppose that the cross-price elasticity of demand between McIntosh and Golden Delicious apples is 0.8, between apples and apple juice is 0.5, between apples and cheese is 0.4, and between apples and beer is 0.1. What can you say about the relationship between each set of commodities?

12. (a) If the price of pork increases by 10 percent, by how much does the demand for beef change? (b) If the price of clothing increases by 10 percent, by how much does the demand for food change? (*Hint:* Use the cross-price elasticity values in Table 3-5.)

13. (a) What other elasticities of demand are there besides price, income, and cross-price? (b) What is the usefulness to the firm of the elasticity of demand for the variables over which the firm has some control? (c) Of the elasticity of demand over which the firm has no control? (d) Why is it essential for the firm to use the elasticity of all the variables included in the demand function?

14. (a) Why are tastes converging around the world? (b) What is the importance of this for U.S. firms?

15. How is e-commerce revolutionizing the business world?

PROBLEMS

1. John Smith, the research manager for marketing at the Chevrolet Division of the General Motors Corporation, has specified the following general demand function for Chevrolets in the United States:

$$Q_C = f(P_C, N, I, P_F, P_G, A, P_I)$$

where Q_C is the quantity demanded of Chevrolets per year, P_C is the price of Chevrolets, N is

population, I is disposable income, P_F is the price of Ford automobiles, P_G is the price of gasoline, A is the amount of advertising for Chevrolets, and P_I is credit incentives to purchase Chevrolets. Indicate whether you expect each independent or explanatory variable to be directly or inversely related to the quantity demanded of Chevrolets and the reason for your expectation.

*2. Suppose that GM's Smith estimated the following regression equation for Chevrolet automobiles:

$$Q_C = 100,000 - 100P_C + 2,000N + 50I + 30P_F \\ -1,000P_G + 3A + 40,000P_I$$

where Q_C = quantity demanded per year of Chevrolet automobiles

P_C = price of Chevrolet automobiles, in dollars

N = population of the United States, in millions

I = per capita disposable income, in dollars

P_F = price of Ford automobiles, in dollars

P_G = real price of gasoline, in cents per gallon

A = advertising expenditures by Chevrolet, in dollars per year

P_I = credit incentives to purchase Chevrolets, in percentage points below the rate of interest on borrowing in the absence of incentives

(a) Indicate the change in the number of Chevrolets purchased per year (Q_C) for each unit change in the independent or explanatory variables. (b) Find the value of Q_C if the average value of P_C = $9,000, N = 200 million, I = $10,000, P_F = $8,000, P_G = 80 cents, A = $200,000, and if P_I = 1. (c) Derive the equation for the demand curve for Chevrolets. (d) Plot it.

3. Starting with the estimated demand function for Chevrolets given in Problem 2, assume that the average value of the independent variables changes to N = 225 million, I = $12,000, P_F = $10,000, P_G = 100 cents, A = $250,000, and P_I = 0 (i.e., the incentives are phased out). (a) Find the equation of the new demand curve for Chevrolets. (b) Plot this new demand curve, D'_C, and, on the same graph, plot the demand curve for Chevrolets, D_C, found in Problem 2(d). (c) What is the relationship between D_C and D'_C? What explains this relationship?

4. The Ice Cream Parlor is the only ice cream parlor in Smithtown. Michael, the son of the owner, has just come back from college, where he majors in business administration. In his course in managerial economics, Michael has just studied demand analysis, and he decides to apply what he has learned to estimate the demand for ice cream in his father's parlor during his summer vacation. Using regression analysis, Michael estimates the following demand function:

$$Q_I = 120 - 20P_I$$

where the subscript I refers to ice cream portions served per day in his father's parlor, and P_I is the dollar price. Michael then sets out to (a) derive the demand schedule for ice cream and plot it, (b) find the point price elasticity of demand at each dollar price, from P = $6 to P = $0, and (c) find the arc price elasticity of demand between consecutive dollar prices (i.e., between P = $6 and P = $5, P = $5 and P = $4, and so on). Show how Michael would get his results.

*5. Show how Michael could have found the price elasticity of demand (E_P) for ice cream graphically at, say, P_I = $4 for the demand function given in Problem 4. Also show graphically that at P_I = $4, E_P would be the same if the demand curve for ice cream were curvilinear but tangent to the linear demand curve at P_I = $4.

6. For the demand function for ice cream given in Problem 4, (a) construct a table similar to Table 3-2 in the text, showing the quantity demanded, the total revenue, and the marginal revenue schedules of the Ice Cream Parlor. (b) Plot the demand, the total revenue, and the marginal revenue schedules from part (a) in a figure similar to Figure 3-5 in the text and indicate on it the range over which demand is elastic, inelastic, and unitary elastic. (c) Derive the equation for the TR and MR schedules for the parlor.

7. The total operating revenues of a public transportation authority are $100 million while its total operating costs are $120 million. The price of a ride is $1, and the price elasticity of demand for public transportation has been estimated to be −0.4. By law, the public transportation authority must take steps to eliminate its operating deficit. (a) What pricing policy should the transportation authority adopt? Why? (b) What price per ride must the public transportation authority charge to eliminate the deficit if it cannot reduce costs?

*8. The coefficient of income in a regression of the quantity demanded of a commodity on price, income, and other variables is 10. (a) Calculate the income elasticity of demand for this commodity at income of $10,000 and sales of 80,000 units. (b) What would be the income elasticity of demand if sales increased from 80,000 to 90,000 units and income rose from $10,000 to $11,000? What type of good is this commodity?

9. A researcher estimated that the price elasticity of demand for automobiles in the United States is −1.2, while the income elasticity of demand is 3.0. Next year, U.S. auto makers intend to increase the average price of automobiles by 5 percent, and they expect consumers' disposable income to rise by 3 percent. (a) If sales of domestically produced automobiles are 8 million this year, how many automobiles do you expect U.S. auto makers to sell next year? (b) By how much should domestic auto makers increase the price of automobiles if they wish to increase sales by 5 percent next year?

10. The coefficient of the price of gasoline in the regression of the quantity demanded of automobiles (in millions of units) on the price of gasoline (in dollars) and other variables is −14. (a) Calculate the cross-price elasticity of demand between automobiles and gasoline at the gasoline price of $1 per gallon and sales of automobiles of 8 (million units). (b) What would be the cross-price elasticity of demand between automobiles and gasoline if sales of automobiles declined from 8 to 6 with an increase in the gasoline price from $1 to $1.20 per gallon?

11. Suppose that the price elasticity of demand for cigarettes is 0.46 in the short run and 1.89 in the long run, the income elasticity of demand for cigarettes is 0.50, and the cross-price elasticity of demand between cigarettes and alcohol is −0.70. Suppose also that the price of cigarettes, the income of consumers, and the price of alcohol all increase by 10 percent. Calculate by how much the demand for cigarettes will change (a) in the short run and (b) in the long run.

*12. The management of the Mini Mill Steel Company estimated the following elasticities for a special type of steel: $E_P = 2$, $E_I = 1$, and $E_{XY} = 1.5$, where X refers to steel and Y to aluminum. Next year, the firm would like to increase the price of the steel it sells by 6 percent. The management forecasts that income will rise by 4 percent next year and that the price of aluminum will fall by 2 percent. (a) If the sales this year are 1,200 tons of the steel, how many tons can the firm expect to sell next year? (b) By what percentage must the firm change the price of steel to keep its sales at 1,200 tons next year?

*13. (a) Find the marginal revenue of a firm that sells a product at the price of $10 and the price elasticity of the demand for the product it sells is (−)2. (b) Find the price elasticity of demand of another firm that sells a product at $P = 16 and $MR = 12. (c) What would be the marginal cost of the firm in part (b)? (Hint: Refer back to Figure 2-4.)

14. Suppose that a firm maximizes its total profits and has a marginal cost (MC) of production of $8 and the price elasticity of demand for the product it sells is (−)3. Find the price at which the firm sells the product.

15. **Integrating Problem**
The research department of the Corn Flakes Corporation (CFC) estimated the following regression for the demand of the cornflakes it sells:

$$Q_X = 1.0 - 2.0P_X + 1.5I + 0.8P_Y - 3.0P_M + 1.0A$$

where Q_X = sales of CFC cornflakes, in millions of 10-ounce boxes per year
P_X = the price of CFC cornflakes, in dollars per 10-ounce box
I = personal disposable income, in trillions of dollars per year
P_Y = price of competitive brand of cornflakes, in dollars per 10-ounce box
P_M = price of milk, in dollars per quart
A = advertising expenditures of CFC cornflakes, in hundreds of thousands of dollars per year

This year, $P_X = 2, $I = 4, $P_Y = 2.50, $P_M = 1, and $A = 2. (a) Calculate the sales of CFC cornflakes this year. (b) Calculate the elasticity of sales with respect to each variable in the demand function. (c) Estimate the level of sales next year if CFC reduces P_X by 10 percent, increases advertising by 20 percent, I rises by 5 percent, P_Y is reduced by 10 percent, and P_M remains unchanged. (d) By how much should CFC change its advertising if it wants its sales to be 30 percent higher than this year?

APPENDIX TO CHAPTER 3:   BEHIND THE MARKET DEMAND CURVE—THE THEORY OF CONSUMER CHOICE

In this appendix we present the theory of consumer choice. We introduce indifference curves to show a consumer's tastes and the budget line to show the constraints under which the consumer operates. By the interaction of indifference curves (tastes) and the budget line (constraints), we define the consumer's equilibrium, and from consumer-equilibrium points we derive the consumer's demand curve for a commodity. Subsequently, we separate the income effect from the substitution effect of a price change. Finally, we present the theory of consumer choice mathematically. For a more detailed presentation of the theory of consumer choice, consult any text in microeconomic theory, such as my own (see the supplementary readings on the Web site).

The Consumer's Tastes: Indifference Curves

If we assume, for simplicity, that a consumer spends all of his or her income on commodities X and Y, we can represent the tastes of the consumer with indifference curves. An *indifference curve* shows the various combinations of commodity X and commodity Y that yield equal utility or satisfaction to the consumer. For example, in Figure 3-7, indifference curve U_1 shows that 1 unit of commodity X and 4 units of commodity Y (point A) yield the same satisfaction as $2X$ and $2.5Y$ (point B), and $4X$ and $1.5Y$ (point C). On the other hand, points on higher indifference curves (U_2 and U_3) show higher levels of utility or satisfaction. Indifference curves give an ordinal (rank) rather than a cardinal measure of utility. That is, we know that $U_3 > U_2 > U_1$, but not by how much.

Indifference curves are negatively sloped because by consuming more of X, the individual would have to consume less of Y in order to remain on the same indifference curve (i.e., at the

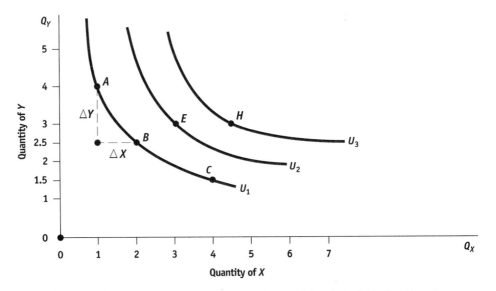

FIGURE 3-7   Indifference Curves   Indifference curve U_1 shows that the individual receives the same level of satisfaction from consuming $1X$ and $4Y$ (point A), $2X$ and $2.5Y$ (point B), and $4X$ and $1.5Y$ (point C). Indifference curve U_2 refers to a higher level of satisfaction than U_1, and U_3 to a still higher level. Indifference curves are negatively sloped, are convex to the origin, and cannot cross.

same level of satisfaction). The amount of Y that the individual would be willing to give up for an additional unit of X is called the *marginal rate of substitution (MRS)*. For example, starting from point A ($1X$, $4Y$) on U_1, the individual is willing to give up $1.5Y$ for an additional unit of X (and reach point B, which has $2X$ and $2.5Y$ and is also on U_1). Thus, the MRS between points A and B on U_1 is 1.5. Note that as we move down an indifference curve, the MRS declines (i.e., the individual is willing to give up less and less of Y for each additional unit of X). Declining MRS is reflected in the convex shape of indifference curves. Not only are indifference curves negatively sloped and convex to the origin, but they also cannot cross. If two indifference curves crossed, it would mean that one of them refers to a higher level of satisfaction than the other at one side of the intersection and to a lower level of satisfaction at the other side of the intersection. This is impossible because all points on the same indifference curve refer to the same level of satisfaction.

The Consumer's Constraints: The Budget Line

The constraints that a consumer faces can be shown graphically by the budget line. The *budget line* shows the various combinations of commodities X and Y that a consumer can purchase, given his or her money income and the prices of the two commodities. For example, suppose that the consumer's money income $M = \$6$, and $P_X = P_Y = \$1$. Figure 3-8 shows that if the consumer spent all of his or her income on either X or Y, he or she could purchase either $6X$ (point F) or $6Y$ (point G). By joining points F and G by a straight line, we define budget line GF. Budget line GF shows all the combinations of X and Y that the individual can purchase, given his or her money income and P_X and P_Y. With M and P_Y unchanged, the budget line would be GF' with $P_X = \$2$ and GF'' with $P_X = \$0.67$.

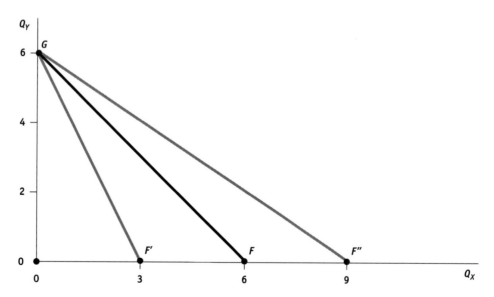

FIGURE 3-8 The Consumer's Budget Line With money income, $M = \$6$, and $P_X = P_Y = \$1$, the consumer could purchase either $6X$ (point F) or $6Y$ (point G), or any combination of X and Y on GF (the budget line). With M and P_Y unchanged, the budget line would be GF' with $P_X = \$2$ and GF'' with $P_X = \$0.67$.

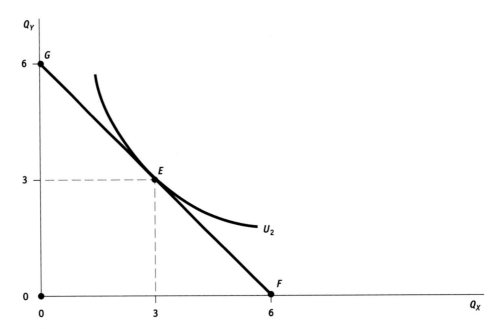

FIGURE 3-9 The Consumer's Equilibrium Given budget line *GF*, the consumer is in equilibrium when he or she consumes 3*X* and 3*Y* (point *E*), where budget line *GF* is tangent to the indifference curve U_2 (the highest indifference curve that the consumer can reach with his or her budget line).

The Consumer's Equilibrium

A consumer is in equilibrium when, given his or her income and commodity prices, the consumer maximizes the utility or satisfaction from his or her expenditures. In other words, a consumer is in equilibrium when he or she reaches the highest indifference curve possible with his or her budget line. For example, Figure 3-9 shows that given $M = \$6$ and $P_X = P_Y = \$1$ (i.e., given budget line *GF*), the consumer is in equilibrium when he or she consumes 3*X* and 3*Y* (point *E*), where budget line *GF* is tangent to indifference curve U_2 (the highest indifference curve that the consumer can reach with his or her budget line).

Derivation of the Consumer's Demand Curve

Given the consumer's money income and the price of commodity *Y*, we can derive the consumer's demand curve for commodity *X* from the consumer's equilibrium points that result from different prices of commodity *X*. This is shown in Figure 3-10. The top panel of the figure shows that with $M = \$6$, $P_Y = \$1$, and $P_X = \$2$ (i.e., with budget line *GF′*), the individual is in equilibrium at point *A* (i.e., by consuming 1*X* and 4*Y*), where budget line *GF′* is tangent to indifference curve U_1. This gives point *A′* ($Q_X = 1$ at $P_X = \$2$) in the bottom panel. With $M = \$6$ and $P_Y = \$1$ but $P_X = \$1$, the individual would be in equilibrium at point *E* (3*X* and 3*Y*), where budget line *GF* is tangent to indifference curve U_2 (as in Figure 3-9). This gives point *E′* ($Q_X = 3$ at $P_X = \$1$) in the bottom panel. Finally, with $M = \$6$ and $P_Y = \$1$ but $P_X = \$0.67$, the individual would be in equilibrium at point *H* (4.5*X* and 3*Y*), where budget line *GF″* is tangent to indifference curve U_3. This gives point *H′* ($Q_X = 4.5$ at $P_X = \$0.67$) in the bottom panel. By joining points *A′*, *E′*, and *H′* in the bottom panel of Figure 3-10, we derive d_X, the individual's demand curve for commodity *X*.

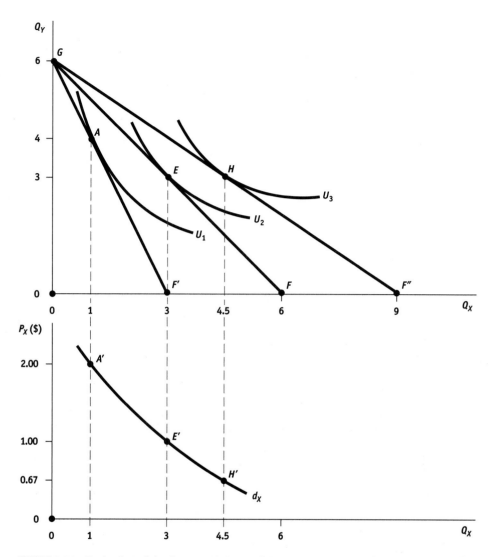

FIGURE 3-10 Derivation of the Consumer's Demand Curve The top panel shows that with $P_X = \$2$, $P_X = \$1$, and $P_X = \$0.67$, we have budget lines GF', GF, and GF'', and consumer equilibrium points A, E, and H, respectively. From equilibrium points A, E, and H in the top panel, we derive points A', E', and H', in the bottom panel. By joining points A', E', and H', we derive d_X, the consumer's demand curve for commodity X.

Income and Substitution Effects of a Price Change

We can use indifference curve analysis to separate the substitution from the income effect of the price change. This is shown in Figure 3-11. As in Figure 3-10, Figure 3-11 shows that with $M = \$6$, $P_Y = \$1$, and $P_X = \$2$, the individual is in equilibrium at point A and demands 1 unit of commodity X. On the other hand, with $M = \$6$, $P_Y = \$1$, and $P_X = \$1$, the individual is in equilibrium at point E and demands 3 units of X. The increase in the demand for commodity X from $1X$ to $3X$ represents the

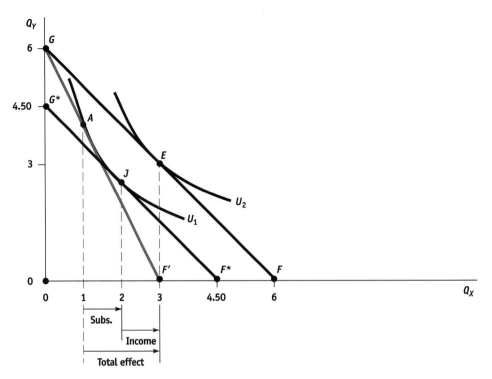

FIGURE 3-11 **Separation of the Substitution from the Income Effect of a Price Change** The individual is in equilibrium at point A with $P_X = \$2$ and at point E with $P_X = \$1$ (as in the top panel of Figure 3-10). To isolate the substitution effect, we draw hypothetical budget line G^*F^*, which is parallel to GF and tangent to U_1 at point J. The movement along U_1 from point A to point J is the substitution effect and results from the relative reduction in P_X only (i.e., with real income constant). The shift from point J on U_1 to point E on U_2 is then the income effect. The total effect $(AE = 2X)$ equals the substitution effect $(AJ = 1X)$ plus the income effect $(JE = 1X)$.

combined effect of the substitution and the income effects. The substitution effect postulates that when the price of X falls, the consumer will substitute X for Y in consumption. On the other hand, the income effect arises because when P_X falls but money income (M) and P_Y do not change, the individual's *real* income increases, and so he or she purchases more of X.

To separate the substitution from the income effect of the price change, we draw hypothetical budget line G^*F^*, which is parallel to budget line GF but tangent to indifference curve U_1 at point J. Hypothetical budget line G^*F^* involves the reduction in money income of $\$1.50 = GG^* = FF^*$ in order to keep the individual at the same level of real income that he or she had before the price change (i.e., in order to keep the individual on indifference curve U_1). The movement along indifference curve U_1 from point A to point J (equals $1X$) is then the substitution effect of the price change, while the shift from point J on U_1 to point E on U_2 (which also equals $1X$) is the income effect. The sum of the substitution and the income effects equals the total effect $(2X)$ of the price change.

To be noted is that while the two effects are equal in Figure 3-11, the substitution effect is usually much larger than the income effect in the real world. The reason is that the consumer usually spends only a small proportion of his or her income on any one commodity. Thus, even a large change in the price of the commodity does not result in a large income effect. On the other hand, the substitution effect can be very large if the commodity has many good substitutes.

The Theory of Consumer Choice Mathematically

Suppose that a consumer spends all of his or her income on commodities X and Y. To reach equilibrium, the consumer must maximize utility (U) subject to his or her budget constraint. That is, the consumer must

$$\text{maximize } U = f(Q_X, Q_Y) \tag{3-20}$$

$$\text{subject to } M = P_X Q_X + P_Y Q_Y \tag{3-21}$$

This constrained maximization problem can be solved by the Lagrangian multiplier method (see page 77).

To do so, we first form the Lagrangian function:

$$L = f(Q_X, Q_Y) + \lambda(M - P_X Q_X - P_Y Q_Y) \tag{3-22}$$

APPENDIX PROBLEMS

1. Given $U = Q_X Q_Y$, $M = \$100$, $P_X = \$2$, and $P_Y = \$5$, derive d_x and d_y by the Lagrangian multiplier method.

2. Show mathematically that if P_X, P_Y, and M in the last section are all multiplied by the constant k, the condition for consumer equilibrium remains unchanged.

To maximize L, we find the partial derivatives of L with respect to Q_X, Q_Y, and λ, and set them equal to zero. That is,

$$\frac{\partial L}{\partial Q_X} = \frac{\partial f}{\partial Q_X} - \lambda P_X = 0 \tag{3-23}$$

$$\frac{\partial L}{\partial Q_Y} = \frac{\partial f}{\partial Q_Y} - \lambda P_Y = 0 \tag{3-24}$$

$$\frac{\partial L}{\partial \lambda} = M - P_X Q_X - P_Y Q_Y = 0 \tag{3-25}$$

Solving Equations 3-23 and 3-24 for λ and setting them equal to each other, we get

$$\lambda = \frac{\partial f / \partial Q_X}{P_X} = \frac{\partial f / \partial Q_Y}{P_Y} \tag{3-26}$$

or

$$\lambda = \frac{MU_X}{P_X} = \frac{MU_Y}{P_Y} \tag{3-27}$$

where MU_X is the marginal or extra utility that the individual receives from consuming the last unit of commodity X and MU_Y is the marginal utility of Y. Thus, Equation 3-27 postulates that in order to maximize utility subject to the budget constraint (i.e., in order to be in equilibrium), the individual must spend his or her income so that the marginal utility of the last dollar spent on X equals the marginal utility of the last dollar spent on Y. Thus, λ is the marginal utility of the last dollar spent on X and Y when the consumer is in equilibrium.

From this equilibrium condition, we get one point on the individual's demand curves for commodity X and commodity Y. By changing the price of X and Y and repeating the process, we obtain other points of consumer equilibrium, and, by joining these, we can derive the individual's demand curve for commodities X and Y (i.e., d_X and d_Y).

SUPPLEMENTARY READINGS

For a more extensive problem-solving approach to demand theory, see:

Salvatore, Dominick, *Theory and Problems of Microeconomic Theory*, 4th ed., Schaum Outline Series (New York: McGraw-Hill, 2006), chaps. 2–5.

The complete presentation of consumer demand theory is found in:

Salvatore, Dominick, *Microeconomic Theory and Applications*, 4th ed. (New York: Oxford University Press, 2003), part II, chaps. 3, 4, and 5.

For consumer demand theory based on the characteristics of goods, see:

Lancaster, Kelvin, *Consumer Demand: A New Approach* (New York: Columbia University Press, 1971).

For e-commerce, see:

Choi, Soon-Yong, Dale O. Stahl, and Andrew B. Whiston, *The Economics of Electronic Commerce* (New York: Macmillan, 1997).

Dinlersoz, E. M. and R. Hernandez-Murillo, "The Diffusion of Electronic Commerce in the United States," *Federal Reserve Bank of St. Louis Review*, (January/February 2005).

Lucas, Henry C., *Strategies for Electronic Commerce and the Internet* (Cambridge, Mass: MIT Press, 2003).

Tapscott, Don, Alex Lowy, David Ticol, and Nata Klym, eds., *Blueprint to the Digital Economy: Wealth Creation in the Era of E-Business* (New York: McGraw-Hill, 1998).

INTERNET SITE ADDRESSES

For more information on the companies examined in this chapter, visit these sites:

McDonald's: http://www.mcdonalds.com

Gillette: http://www.gillette.com

Ford: http://www.ford.com

Amazon: http://www.amazon.com

Barnes & Noble: http://www.bn.com

eBay: http://www.ebay.com

For more information on e-commerce, access these resources:

U.S. Census Bureau: http://www.census.gov/estats

Center for Research in Electronic Commerce at the University of Texas at Austin: http://cism.mmcombs.utexas.edu

On Line Marketing Research Center: http://www.ecommerce-guide.com

Ecommerce Times: http://www.ecommercetimes. com

Web Marketing Today: http://www.wilsonweb.com

Internet.com: http://www.internetnews.com/ec-news

Federal Trade Commission: http://www.ftc.gov/bcp/menu-internet.htm

Financial Times: http://www.news.ft.com/reports/ftit

For data on U.S. Internet retailers with more than $1 billion in sales and their consumer satisfaction scores, see:

http://www.internetretailer.com/article.asp?id=150099

http://www.forreseeresults.com/Press_Top40Retail.html

CHAPTER 4   Demand Estimation

CHAPTER OUTLINE

KEY TERMS (in the order of their appearance)

Identification problem	Least-squares method	Multiple regression analysis
Consumer surveys	Degrees of freedom (df)	Adjusted R^2 ($\bar{R}^2$)
Observational research	Simple regression analysis	Analysis of variance
Consumer clinics	t statistic	F statistic
Market experiments	Significance test	Standard error (SE) of the
Micromarketing	Critical value	regression
Customer relationship	t test	Multicollinearity
management (CRM)	Confidence interval	Heteroscedasticity
Virtual shopping	Coefficient of determination (R^2)	Cross-sectional data
Virtual management	Total variation	Autocorrelation
Scatter diagram	Explained variation	Time-series data
Regression analysis	Unexplained variation	Durbin–Watson statistic (d)
Regression line	Coefficient of correlation	

In this chapter we build on the analysis of consumer demand theory examined in Chapter 3 to show how a firm can estimate the demand for the product it sells. We saw in Chapter 3 that the forces that affect demand are the price of the commodity, consumer incomes, the price of related (i.e., substitute and complementary) commodities, consumers' tastes, and other more specific forces that are important for the particular commodity. We also saw in Chapter 3 that reliable estimates of the quantitative effect on sales of all the significant forces that affect demand are essential for the firm to make the best operating decisions and for planning.

Important questions to which we seek an answer in this chapter are: How much will the revenues of the firm change after increasing the price of the commodity by a certain amount? How much will the quantity demanded of the commodity increase if consumer incomes increase by a specific amount? What if the firm doubles its advertising expenditures and/or it provides a particular credit incentive to consumers? How much would the demand that a firm faces for its product fall if competitors lowered their prices, increased their advertising expenditures, or provided credit incentives? Firms must know the answers to these and other questions to achieve the objective of maximizing their value. The answers are just as important for not-for-profit organizations. For example, it is crucial for a state university to know how much enrollment would decline with a 10 percent increase in tuition, how the socioeconomic composition of its student body would change, and how the number of out-of-state students would be affected.

In this chapter, we begin by examining some general difficulties encountered in deriving the demand curve for a product from market data (the *identification problem*). Then, we briefly discuss some marketing research approaches to demand estimation. Subsequently, we focus on regression analysis as the most useful and common method of demand estimation. Finally, we discuss the estimation of the demand for imports and exports. The Chapter Appendix shows how to run a regression in spreadsheet Excel. In the next chapter, we will examine methods of forecasting demand.

4-1   ## THE IDENTIFICATION PROBLEM

The demand curve for a commodity is generally estimated from market data on the quantity purchased of the commodity at various prices over time (i.e., using time-series data) or for various consuming units or markets at one point in time (i.e., using cross-sectional data). However, simply joining the price-quantity observations on a graph does not generate the demand curve for the commodity. The reason is that each price-quantity observation is given by the intersection of a different (but unobserved) demand and supply curve of the commodity.[1]

Over time or across different individuals or markets, the demand for the commodity shifts or differs because of changes or differences in tastes, incomes, price of related commodities, and so on. Similarly, over time or across different sellers or markets, the supply curve shifts or is different because of changes or differences in technology, factor prices, and weather conditions (for agricultural commodities). The intersection (equilibrium) of the different but unknown demand and supply curves generates the different price-quantity points observed. (If the demand and supply curves did not shift or differ, the commodity price would remain the same.) Therefore, by simply joining the different price-quantity observations, we do not generate the demand curve for the commodity. The demand curve cannot be identified so simply. This is referred to as the **identification problem.**

For example, in Figure 4-1, only price-quantity points E_1, E_2, E_3, and E_4 are observed.[2] Each of these price-quantity observations, however, lies on a different demand and supply curve. These different demand curves result from changes in tastes, incomes, and prices of related commodities over time (with time-series analysis), or from differences in tastes, incomes, and prices of related commodities across different individuals or markets (with cross-sectional data). It is clear, therefore, that simply joining points E_1, E_2, E_3, and E_4 by a line as in Figure 4-1 does not generate the demand curve for the commodity. Thus, the dashed line connecting points E_1, E_2, E_3, and E_4 in Figure 4-1 is not the demand curve for the commodity.

In order to derive the demand curve for the commodity from the observed price-quantity data points, we should allow the supply curve of the commodity to shift or to differ, in an unrestricted manner, as shown in Figure 4-1, while we adjust or correct for the shifts or differences in the demand curve. That is, we must adjust or correct for the effect on the demand for the commodity resulting from changes or differences in consumer incomes, in the price of related commodities, in consumer tastes, and in other factors that cause the demand curve of the particular commodity to shift or to be different, so that we can isolate or identify the effect on the quantity demanded of the commodity resulting only from a change in its price. This price-quantity relationship, *after correction for all the forces that cause the demand curve to shift or to be different,* gives the true demand curve for the commodity (say, D_2, in Figure 4-1).

Note that in Figure 4-1, the demand curves that we seek to identify are flatter or more elastic than the dashed line joining the price-quantity observation points. Which of the

---

[1] From principles of economics and the appendix to Chapter 1, we know that the supply curve of a commodity shows the quantity supplied of the commodity per time period at various prices of the commodity, while holding constant all the other determinants of supply.

[2] To derive a demand curve from market data, we need many more points, but in order to keep the figure simple, we assume that we have only the four price-quantity observations shown in Figure 4-1.

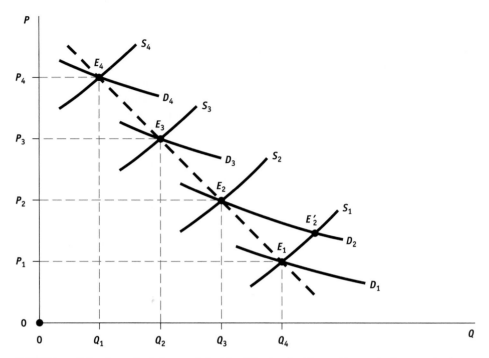

FIGURE 4-1   Price-Quantity Points and the Identification Problem   Observed price-quantity data points E_1, E_2, E_3, and E_4 result, respectively, from the intersection of unobserved demand and supply curves D_1 and S_1, D_2 and S_2, D_3 and S_3, and D_4 and S_4. Therefore, the dashed line connecting observed points E_1, E_2, E_3, and E_4 is not the demand curve for the commodity. To derive a demand curve for the commodity, say, D_2, we allow the supply to shift or to be different and correct, through regression analysis, for the forces that cause demand curve D_2 to shift or to be different (see points E_2 and E_2').

demand curves shown in Figure 4-1 we actually derive depends on the level at which we hold constant consumer incomes, the price of related commodities, consumers' tastes, and other forces that cause the demand curve of the commodity to shift or to be different. For example, demand curve D_3 is above demand curve D_2. This means that consumer incomes and/or the price of substitute commodities are held constant at a higher level, while the price of complementary commodities are held constant at a lower level than along market demand curve D_2. The opposite is true for demand curve D_1.

By including among the independent or explanatory variables the most important determinants of demand, regression analysis allows the researcher to disentangle the independent effects of the various determinants of demand, so as to isolate the effect of the price of the commodity on the quantity demanded of the commodity (i.e., to identify the demand curve for the commodity). Note that nothing is or should be done to correct for shifts or differences in supply. In fact, it is these uncorrected shifts or differences in supply, after having adjusted for shifts or differences in demand, that allow us to derive a particular demand curve. For example, in Figure 4-1, point E_2' on demand curve D_2 is derived by correcting the shifts or differences in demand while allowing the supply curve to shift from S_2 to S_1.

4-2 MARKETING RESEARCH APPROACHES TO DEMAND ESTIMATION

Although regression analysis (to be discussed next) is by far the most useful and used method of estimating demand, marketing research approaches are also used. The most important of these are consumer surveys, consumer clinics, market experiments, and virtual shopping and virtual management. These approaches to demand estimation are discussed in detail in marketing courses. In this section we briefly examine these methods and point out their advantages and disadvantages and the conditions under which they might be useful to managers and economists.

Consumer Surveys and Observational Research

Consumer surveys involve questioning a sample of consumers about how they would respond to particular changes in the price of the commodity, incomes, the price of related commodities, advertising expenditures, credit incentives, and other determinants of demand. These surveys can be conducted by simply stopping and questioning people at a shopping center or by administering sophisticated questionnaires to a carefully constructed representative sample of consumers by trained interviewers.

In theory, consumer questionnaires can provide a great deal of useful information to the firm. In fact, they are often biased because consumers are either unable or unwilling to provide accurate answers. For example, do you know how much your monthly beer consumption would change if the price of beer rose by 10 cents per 12-ounce can or bottle? If the price of sodas fell by 5 cents? If your income rose by 20 percent? If a beer producer doubled its advertising expenditures? If the alcoholic content of beer were reduced by 1 percentage point? Even if you tried to answer these questions as accurately as possible, your reaction might be entirely different if you were actually faced with any of these situations. Sometimes consumers provide a response that they deem more socially acceptable rather than disclosing their true preferences. For example, no one would like to admit that he or she drinks 200 beers a month. Depending on the size of the sample and the elaborateness of the analysis, consumer surveys can also be expensive.

Because of the shortcomings of consumer surveys, many firms are supplementing or supplanting consumer surveys with **observational research.** This refers to the gathering of information on consumer preferences by watching them buying and using products. For example, observational research has led some automakers to conclude that many people think of their cars as art objects that are on display whenever they drive them. Observational research has also shown that consumers prefer to take several cold medicines, not just one. Observational research relies on product scanners, which are increasingly found in stores, and on people meters in homes. These make it possible for a company to learn overnight how a wide variety of products sell and the effectiveness of commercials, as well as television viewing patterns. Scanners and people meters, however, raise legal questions about privacy.

Observational research does not, however, render consumer surveys useless. Sometimes consumer surveys are the only way to obtain information about possible consumers' responses. For example, if a firm is thinking of introducing a new product or changing the quality of an existing one, the only way that the firm can test consumers' reactions is to directly ask them, since no other data are available. From the survey, the researcher then typically tries to determine the demographic characteristics (age, sex, education, income, family size) of consumers who are most likely to purchase the product. The same might be true in detecting changes in consumer tastes and preferences and in determining consumers' expectations about future prices and business conditions. Consumer surveys can also be useful in detecting consumers' awareness of an advertising campaign by the firm. Furthermore, if the survey shows that consumers are unaware of price differences between the firm's product and competitive products, this might be a good indication that the demand for the firm's product is price inelastic. Case Study 4-1 examines micromarketing and customer relationship management, two of the most important new marketing research approaches to demand estimation and marketing.

Consumer Clinics

Another approach to demand estimation is **consumer clinics.** These are laboratory experiments in which the participants are given a sum of money and asked to spend it in a simulated store to see how they react to changes in the commodity price, product packaging, displays, price of competing products, and other factors affecting demand. Participants in the experiment can be selected so as to closely represent the socioeconomic characteristics of the market of interest. Participants have an incentive to purchase the commodities they want the most because they are usually allowed to keep the goods purchased. Thus, consumer clinics are more realistic than consumer surveys. By being able to control the environment, consumer clinics also avoid the pitfall of actual market experiments (discussed next), which can be ruined by extraneous events.

Consumer clinics also face serious shortcomings, however. First, the results are questionable because participants know that they are in an artificial situation and that they are being observed. Therefore, they are not likely to act normally, as they would in a real market situation. For example, suspecting that the researchers might be interested in their reaction to price changes, participants are likely to show more sensitivity to price changes than in their everyday shopping. Second, the sample of participants must necessarily be small because of the high cost of running the experiment. Inferring a market behavior from the results of an experiment based on a very small sample can also be dangerous. Despite these disadvantages, consumer clinics can provide useful information about the demand for the firm's product, particularly if consumer clinics are supplemented with consumer surveys.

Market Experiments

Unlike consumer clinics, which are conducted under strict laboratory conditions, **market experiments** are conducted in the actual marketplace. There are many ways of performing market experiments. One method is to select several markets with similar socioeconomic characteristics and change the commodity price in some markets or stores, packaging in other markets or stores, and the amount and type of promotion in still other markets or stores, then record the responses (purchases) of consumers in the different markets. By using census data or surveys for various markets, a firm can also determine the effect of age, sex, level of education, income, family size, and so forth on the demand for the commodity. Alternatively, the firm could change, one at a time, each of the determinants of demand under its control in a particular market over time and record consumers' responses.

CASE STUDY 4-1
Micromarketing: Marketers Zero in on Their Customers

More and more consumer-product companies are narrowing their marketing strategy from the region and city to the individual neighborhood and single store. The aim of such detailed point-of-sale information, or **micromarketing,** is to identify store by store the types of products with the greatest potential appeal for the specific customers in the area. Using census data and checkout scanners, Market Metrics, a marketing research firm, collects consumer information at more than 30,000 supermarkets around the country.

For example, for a particular grocery store in Georgia, Pennsylvania, Market Metrics found that potential customers were predominantly white, blue collar, and owned two cars, that they lived in households of three or four people and had an average income of $54,421, and that 26 percent of the people were below the age of 15. Based on these demographic and economic characteristics, Market Metrics determined that the strongest sellers in this market would be baby foods and grooming items, baking mixes, desserts, dry dinner mixes, cigarettes, laundry supplies, first-aid products, and milk. Less strong would be sales of artificial sweeteners, tea, books, film, prepared food, yogurt, wine, and liquor. Such store-specific micromarketing is likely to become more and more common and necessary for successful retailing.

As marketers refine their tools, they are increasingly taking aim at the ultimate narrow target: the individual consumer. Indeed, many companies, led by banks, are assembling customer profiles and employing sophisticated technology called *neural networks* in order to set up *one-to-one marketing* (also called relationship marketing or customer relationship management). This seeks to reach the individual consumer and establish a learning relationship with each customer, starting from the most valuable ones. This is exactly what Amazon.com does when it reminds a customer that a book that might interest her has just come

in. One-to-one marketing requires identifying the company's customers, differentiating among them, interacting with them, and customizing the product or service to fit each individual customer's needs.

For example, Merrill Lynch & Co. provides detailed financial information about its customers to its brokers in order to help them promote the company's financial products. Depositing a $10,000 check may eliminate the customer as a likely candidate for a car loan but not for a home mortgage loan. It may even determine whether your telephone call gets answered first (if your profile, which comes up immediately on the bank's computer screen, identifies you as a valued customer) or last. Dell has been selling customized PCs for years, and you can now buy computer-fitted apparel, customized vitamins, customized music compilations on CDs, and so on. Although it is not easy to set up one-to-one marketing, and most companies may not be capable of it or ready for it, it is almost certain that marketing will be getting more and more personalized in the future.

Related to micromarketing is **customer relationship management (CRM),** which refers to the use of business strategy, marketing, and information technology (IT) by which a firm can try to increase business with customers that the firm already has, especially the most profitable ones, while trying to attract new ones. It tries to do this by trying to learn everything possible about the buying habits of customers and making them feel that they are receiving personal attention. A number of companies have sprung up that offer all sorts of IT-based CRM services to their clients, such as setting up call centers, sales force automation, marketing, data analysis, and Web site management. One of the largest of these CRM consultancy companies, Accenture, estimates that with a 10 percent improvement in CRM capabilities a firm can increase its profits by as much as 4 or 5 percent.

Source: "Know Your Customer," *The Wall Street Journal* (June 21, 1999), p. R18; "Is Your Company Ready for One-to-One Marketing?" *Harvard Business Review* (January–February 1999), pp. 151–160; "Winning in Smart Markets," *Sloan Management Review* (Summer 1999), pp. 59–69; "Focus on Customer Relationship Management," *Financial Times* (October 17, 2001), p. 1; and "The Vanishing Mass Market," *BusinessWeek* (July 12, 2004).

The advantages of market experiments are that they can be conducted on a large scale to ensure the validity of the results and that consumers are not aware that they are part of an experiment. Market experiments also have serious disadvantages, however. One of these is that in order to keep costs down, the experiment is likely to be conducted on too limited a scale and over a fairly short period of time, so that inferences about the entire market and for a more extended period of time are questionable. Extraneous occurrences, such as a strike or unusually bad weather, may seriously bias the results in uncontrolled experiments. Competitors could try to sabotage the experiment by also changing prices and other determinants of demand under their control. They could also monitor the experiment and gain useful information that the firm would prefer not to disclose. Finally, a firm might permanently lose customers in the process of raising prices in the market where it is experimenting with a high price.

Despite these shortcomings, market experiments may be useful to a firm in determining its best pricing strategy and in testing different packaging, promotional campaigns, and product qualities. Market experiments are particularly useful in the process of introducing a product for which no other data exist. They may also be useful in verifying the results of other statistical techniques used to estimate demand and in providing some of the data required for these other statistical techniques of demand estimation.

Case Study 4-2 shows how the price elasticity and cross-price elasticity of demand for Florida and California oranges have been estimated by market experiment.

Virtual Shopping and Virtual Management

The past few years have seen the development of the new and exciting marketing tools of virtual shopping and virtual management. In **virtual shopping** a representative sample of consumers shop in a virtual store simulated on the computer screen, instead of in a simulated physical store, as in consumer clinics. By doing so, virtual shopping eliminates the high cost in terms of time and money involved in consumer clinics. Virtual shopping has been made possible by recent advances in computer graphics and three-dimensional (3D) modeling that allow marketers to recreate the atmosphere of an actual retail store, virtually on the computer screen. The consumer can see shelves stocked with all kinds of products, he can view up close any product by touching its image on the screen so as to be able to read its label and check its content, and he can then purchase the product by touching the picture of a shopping cart. The sample consumers are then asked to take a series of trips through the simulated virtual store and shop as they would in a regular retail store. Prices, packaging, displays, and promotions are then changed in subsequent trips and the consumers' reactions recorded. Virtual shopping simulations can be very helpful in making intelligent marketing decisions very quickly and inexpensively. Preliminary tests seem to indicate that virtual shopping can track rather closely the buying behavior of consumers in a real store.

Much more sophisticated is **virtual management.** As defined in Section 2-6, virtual management refers to the ability of a manager to simulate consumer behavior using computer models based on the emerging science or theory of complexity. If successful, such computational models would mimic human behavior sufficiently closely to allow top management to simulate or test the impact of managerial decisions (such as changing the product price or its characteristics) before implementing those decisions in the real world. As

CASE STUDY 4-2
Estimation of the Demand for Oranges
by Market Experiment

In 1962, researchers at the University of Florida conducted a market experiment in Grand Rapids, Michigan, to determine the price elasticity and the cross-price elasticity of demand for three types of Valencia oranges: those from the Indian River district of Florida, those from the interior district of Florida, and those from California. Grand Rapids was chosen as the site for the market experiment because its size, demographic characteristics, and economic base were representative of other midwestern markets for oranges.

Nine supermarkets participated in the experiment, which involved changing the price of the three types of oranges, each day, for 31 consecutive days and recording the quantity sold of each variety. The price changes ranged within 16 cents, in 4-cent increments, around the price of oranges that prevailed in the market at the time of the study. More than 9,250 dozen oranges were sold in the nine supermarkets during the 31 days of the experiment. Each of the supermarkets was provided with an adequate supply of each type of orange so that supply effects could be ignored. The length of the experiment was

also sufficiently short so as to ensure no change in tastes, incomes, population, the rate of inflation, and determinants of demand other than price.

The results, summarized in Table 4-1, indicate that the price elasticity of demand for all three types of oranges was fairly high (the boldface numbers in the main diagonal of the table). For example, the price elasticity of demand for the Indian River oranges of −3.07 indicates that a 1 percent increase in their price leads to a 3.07 percent decline in their quantity demanded. More interestingly, the off-diagonal entries in the table show that while the cross-price elasticities of demand between the two types of Florida oranges were larger than 1, they were close to zero with respect to the California oranges. In other words, while consumers regarded the two types of Florida oranges as close substitutes, they did not view the California oranges as such. In pricing their oranges, therefore, producers of each of the two Florida varieties would have to carefully consider the price of the other (as consumers switch readily among them as a result of price changes) but need not be much concerned about the price of California oranges.

TABLE 4-1 Price Elasticity and Cross-Price Elasticity of Demand for Florida Indian River, Florida Interior, and California Oranges

Type of Orange	Florida Indian River	Florida Interior	California
Florida Indian River	**−3.07**	+1.56	+0.01
Florida Interior	+1.16	**−3.01**	+0.14
California	+0.18	+0.09	**−2.76**

Source: M. B. Godwin, W. F. Chapman, and W. T. Hanley, "Competition between Florida and California Valencia Oranges in the Fruit Market," *Bulletin 704* (Gainesville: University of Florida, December 1965).

contrasted to virtual shopping, virtual management does not rely on actual subjects to simulate actual shopping, but relies instead on consumer behavior that has already been inputted into the program. In virtual management, there are no actual or physical subjects involved at all. Their behavior has already been distilled and incorporated into the program and is ready to be used in managerial simulations. As such, virtual management is much more complex and potentially much more valuable than virtual shopping.

For example, Macy's Department Store in New York City has created an elaborate computer model based on information from consumer research surveys and other database information in which hundreds of synthetic shoppers interact in a virtual shopping experience. Macy's hopes that the system will allow it to determine (1) the number of salespeople needed in each department of the store, (2) how to turn browsers into shoppers, and (3) how to locate service desks and cash registers to maximize sales. But with a sufficiently more elaborate system, management could conceivably simulate almost any type of managerial decision, from customers' reactions to price changes, to the effectiveness of different types of advertisements, to the sales effect of different shelf arrangements, and so on, thus allowing management to maximize the value of the firm and possibly avoid embarrassing mistakes since it operates with a synthetic rather than a real public. Marketing scenarios also lead to dramatic time compression—a marketing day can be simulated in a minute and a month in a few hours.

Some top U.S. corporations, such as Citicorp, Coca-Cola, Shell International Petroleum, and Texas Instruments, are betting hundreds of thousands of dollars by sponsoring research in the field of complexity at the Santa Fe Institute in New Mexico, the foremost research center in this new science. Virtual management harnesses the power of database information, econometrics, and the new information technology in a way that is much easier for management to understand and use than linear programming and operations research—and thus potentially much more useful. The challenge of setting up simulation models that closely duplicate human market behavior, however, remains dauntingly difficult. But this challenge is not less than that encountered by micromarketeers in the face of the vanishing mass market (see Case Study 4-3).

CASE STUDY 4-3
Reaching Consumers in the Vanishing Mass Market

Virtual shopping and virtual management are two potentially fruitful ways of studying consumer tastes and preferences without the invasion of privacy that micromarketing often represents. First of all, today consumers are better informed than ever before through the Internet about products and prices and not easily swayed by micromarketing. For example, Ford found that eight out of ten of its customers have already used the Internet and cell phones to decide what car they want to buy and what price they are willing to pay, even before arriving at the showroom. Secondly, many consumers are rebelling against telemarketing, as indicated by the fact that more than 60 million telephones have been placed out of reach of telemarketing through the "do-not-call registry."

Thirdly, the same technological advances that made micromarketing possible are empowering a new class of digitally savvy consumers with their fingers ready on the zapper, the mouse, or the remote to cut advertisements out of TV and other programs. The device that mass advertisers and TV executives fear most is the personal video recorder (PVR), which allows viewers to watch any program when they want and skip the commercials. Although less than 10 percent of the homes were equipped with a PVR in 2005, this percentage is expected to reach 50 percent in a few years.

Of particular concern to marketers is how to reach the 60-million-strong new generation (those born between 1979 and 1994), who is coming of age in the new millennium. These so-called millennials are famous for frenetic multitasking (i.e., watching two or three TV programs simultaneously, and maybe also playing video games on their laptop while sending SMS messages). They are regarded as hard sells on brands, skeptical about advertising, and extremely difficult to reach and catch their attention, and even more difficult to retain it without being zapped, blocked, or tuned out. Advertisers are responding by weaving promotions into programming, peppering sports events with a blitz of sponsored spots, and otherwise surrounding them with hundreds of Web sites, video games, channels, and billboards—appropriate for their multitasking lifestyles, empowered as they are by countless options. This is why developing virtual shopping and virtual management is so crucial in today's world of micromarketing.

Sources: "Test Marketers Use Virtual Shopping to Gauge Potential of Real Products," *The New York Times* (December 22, 1997), p. D3; "Virtual Management," *Business Week* (September 21, 1998), pp. 80–82; "Power at Last," *The Economist* (April 2, 2005), p. 11; "American Hang Up on Telemarketers," *Fortune* (October 13, 2003), p. 58; "The Vanishing Mass Market," *Business Week* (July 12, 2004), pp. 61–68; and "Channeling the Future," *Business Week* (July 12, 2004), pp. 70–72.

4-3   INTRODUCTION TO REGRESSION ANALYSIS*

In order to introduce regression analysis, suppose that a manager wants to determine the relationship between the firm's advertising expenditures and its sales revenue. The manager wants to test the hypothesis that higher advertising expenditures lead to higher sales for the firm, and, furthermore, she wants to estimate the strength of the relationship (i.e., how much sales increase for each dollar increase in advertising expenditures). To this end, the manager collects data on advertising expenditures and on sales revenue for the firm over the past 10 years. In this case, the level of advertising expenditures (X) is the independent or explanatory variable, while sales revenues (Y) is the dependent variable that the manager seeks to explain. Suppose that the advertising-sales data for the firm in each of the past 10 years that the manager has collected are those in Table 4-2.

If we now plot each pair of advertising-sales values in Table 4-2 as a point on a graph, with advertising expenditures (the independent or explanatory variable) measured along the horizontal axis and sales revenues (the dependent variable) measured along the vertical axis, we get the points (dots) in Figure 4-2. This is known as a **scatter diagram** since it shows the spread of the points in the X–Y plane.

From Figure 4-2 (scatter diagram), we see that there is a positive relationship between the level of the firm's advertising expenditures and its sales revenues (i.e., higher

TABLE 4-2 Advertising Expenditures and Sales Revenues of the Firm (millions of dollars)										
Year (t)	1	2	3	4	5	6	7	8	9	10
Advertising expenditures (X)	10	9	11	12	11	12	13	13	14	15
Sales revenues (Y)	44	40	42	46	48	52	54	58	56	60

* Students familiar with regression analysis can use this and the next three sections as a review or skip them and go on directly to Section 4-7.

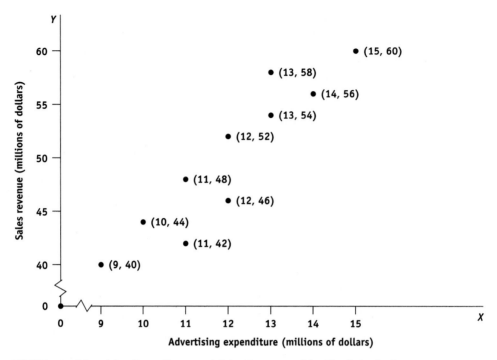

FIGURE 4-2 Advertising Expenditures and Sales Revenues of the Firm in Each of 10 Years
Advertising expenditure (X), the independent variable, is measured along the horizontal axis, while sales revenue (Y), the dependent variable, is measured along the vertical axis. Each point (dot) in the figure represents one of the advertising-sales combinations shown in Table 4-2.

advertising expenditures are associated with higher sales revenues) and that this relationship is approximately linear.

One way to estimate the approximate linear relationship between the firm's advertising expenditures and its sales revenues is to draw in, by visual inspection, the positively sloped straight line that "best" fits between the data points (so that the data points are about equally distant on either side of the line). By extending the line to the vertical axis, we can then estimate the firm's sales revenues with zero advertising expenditures. The slope of the line will then provide an estimate of the increase in the sales revenues that the firm can expect with each $1 million increase in its advertising expenditures. This will give us a rough estimate of the linear relationship between the firm's sales revenues (Y) and its advertising expenditures (X) in the form of Equation 4-1:

$$Y = a + bX \qquad [4\text{-}1]$$

In Equation 4-1, a is the vertical intercept of the estimated linear relationship and gives the value of Y when $X = 0$, while b is the slope of the line and gives an estimate of the increase in Y resulting from each unit increase in X. The manager could use this information to estimate how much the sales revenues of the firm would be if its advertising expenditures were anywhere between $9 million and $15 million per year (the range of the advertising expenditures given in Table 4-2 and shown in Figure 4-2), or if advertising expenditures increased, say, to $16 million per year, or fell to $8 million per year.

The difficulty with the visual fitting of a line to the data points in Figure 4-2 is that different researchers would probably fit a somewhat different line to the same data points and obtain somewhat different results. **Regression analysis** is a statistical technique for obtaining the line that best fits the data points according to an objective statistical criterion, so that all researchers looking at the same data would get exactly the same result (i.e., obtain the same line). Specifically, the **regression line** is the line obtained by minimizing the sum of the squared vertical deviations of each point from the regression line. This method is, therefore, appropriately called the "ordinary least-squares," or OLS, method. The regression line fitted by such a **least-squares method** is shown in Figure 4-3.

In Figure 4-3, Y_1 refers to the actual or observed sales revenue of $44 million associated with the advertising expenditures of $10 million in the first year for which the data were collected (see Table 4-2). The $\hat{Y}_1$ (read: Y hat sub 1) shown in the figure is the corresponding sales revenue of the firm estimated from the regression line for the advertising expenditure of $10 million in the first year. The symbol e_1 in the figure is then the corresponding vertical deviation or error of the actual or observed sales revenue of the firm from the sales revenue estimated from the regression line in the first year. That is,

$$e_1 = Y_1 - \hat{Y}_1 \qquad [4\text{-}2]$$

Errors of this type arise because (1) numerous explanatory variables with only a slight or irregular effect on Y are not included in Equation 4-1, (2) there are possible errors of

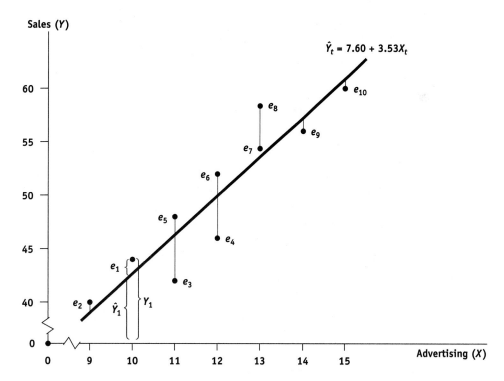

FIGURE 4-3   **Fitting a Regression Line**   The regression line shown in the figure is the line that best fits the data points in the sense that the sum of the squared vertical deviations of the points from the line is a minimum.

measurement in Y, and (3) random human behavior leads to different results (say, different purchases of a commodity) under identical conditions.

Since there are 10 observation points in Figure 4-3, we have 10 such vertical deviations or errors. These are labeled e_1 to e_{10} in the figure. The regression line shown in Figure 4-3 is the line that best fits the data points in the sense that the sum of the squared (vertical) deviations from the line is minimum. That is, each of the 10 e values is first squared and then summed. The regression line is the line for which the sum of these squared deviations is a minimum.[3] How the values of $\hat{a}$ (the vertical intercept) and $\hat{b}$ (the slope coefficient) of the regression line that minimizes the sum of the squared deviations are actually obtained is shown next.

4-4   SIMPLE REGRESSION ANALYSIS

In this section we examine how to (1) calculate the value of a (the vertical intercept) and the value of b (the slope coefficient) of the regression line; (2) conduct tests of significance of parameter estimates; (3) construct confidence intervals for the true parameter; and (4) test for the overall explanatory power of the regression. While all these tasks are usually performed by the computer, we will do these operations by hand at first with very simple numbers in order to show exactly how regression analysis is performed and what it entails.

The Ordinary Least-Squares Method

We have seen in the previous section that a regression line is the line that best fits the data points in the sense that the sum of the squared deviations from the line is a minimum. The objective of regression analysis is to obtain estimates of a (the vertical intercept) and b (the slope) of the regression line:

$$\hat{Y}_t = \hat{a} + \hat{b}X_t \qquad [4\text{-}3]$$

In Equation 4-3, $\hat{Y}_t$ is the estimate of the firm's sales revenues in year t obtained from the regression line for the level of advertising in year t (X_t), and $\hat{a}$ and $\hat{b}$ are estimates of parameters a and b, respectively. The deviation of error (e_t) of each observed sales revenue (Y_t) from its corresponding value estimated from the regression line ($\hat{Y}_t$) is then

$$e_t = Y_t - \hat{Y}_t = Y_t - \hat{a} - \hat{b}X_t \qquad [4\text{-}4]$$

The sum of these squared errors or deviations can thus be expressed as

$$\sum_{t=1}^{n} e_t^2 = \sum_{t=1}^{n} (Y_t - \hat{Y}_t)^2 = \sum_{t=1}^{n} (Y_t - \hat{a} - \hat{b}X_t)^2 \qquad [4\text{-}5]$$

---

[3] The errors are squared before they are added in order to avoid the cancellation of errors of equal size but opposite signs. Squaring the errors also penalizes larger errors relatively more than smaller ones.

where $\sum_{t=1}^{n}$ is the sum of all observations, from time period $t = 1$ to $t = n$. The estimated values of a and b (that is, $\hat{a}$ and $\hat{b}$) are obtained by minimizing the sum of the squared deviations (i.e., by minimizing the value of Equation 4-5).[4] The value of $\hat{b}$ is given by

$$\hat{b} = \frac{\sum_{t=1}^{n}(X_t - \bar{X})(Y_t - \bar{Y})}{\sum_{t=1}^{n}(X_t - \bar{X})^2} \qquad [4\text{-}6]$$

where $\bar{Y}$ and $\bar{X}$ are the mean or average values of Y_t and X_t, respectively. The value of $\hat{a}$ is then obtained from

$$\hat{a} = \bar{Y} - \hat{b}\bar{X} \qquad [4\text{-}7]$$

Table 4-3 shows the calculation to determine the values of $\hat{a}$ and $\hat{b}$ for the advertising-sales data in Table 4-2. Substituting the values obtained from Table 4-3 into Equation 4-6, we get the value of $\hat{b}$:

$$\hat{b} = \frac{\sum_{t=1}^{n}(X_t - \bar{X})(Y_t - \bar{Y})}{\sum_{t=1}^{n}(X_t - \bar{X})^2} = \frac{106}{30} = 3.533$$

TABLE 4-3   **Calculations to Estimate Regression Line for Sales-Advertising Problem**

t Year	X_t Advertising	Y_t Sales	$X_t - \bar{X}$	$Y_t - \bar{Y}$	$(X_t - \bar{X})(Y_t - \bar{Y})$	$(X_t - \bar{X})^2$
1	10	44	−2	−6	12	4
2	9	40	−3	−10	30	9
3	11	42	−1	−8	8	1
4	12	46	0	−4	0	0
5	11	48	−1	−2	2	1
6	12	52	0	2	0	0
7	13	54	1	4	4	1
8	13	58	1	8	8	1
9	14	56	2	6	12	4
10	15	60	3	10	30	9
$n = 10$	$\sum X_t = 120$ $\bar{X} = 12$	$\sum Y_t = 500$ $\bar{Y} = 50$	$\sum(X_t - \bar{X}) = 0$	$\sum(Y_t - \bar{Y}) = 0$	$\sum(X_t - \bar{X})(Y_t - \bar{Y})$ $= 106$	$\sum(X_t - \bar{X})^2$ $= 30$

[4] The values of $\hat{a}$ and $\hat{b}$ are obtained by finding the partial derivative of Equation 4-5 with respect to $\hat{a}$ and $\hat{b}$, setting the resulting two normal equations equal to zero, and solving them simultaneously to obtain Equation 4-6. [See Dominick Salvatore and Derrick Reagle, *Theory and Problems of Statistics and Econometrics,* 2nd ed. (New York: McGraw-Hill, 2002), chap. 6.]

By then substituting the value of $\hat{b}$ found in the preceding equation and the values of $\bar{Y}$ and $\bar{X}$ found in Table 4-3 into Equation 4-7, we get the value of $\hat{a}$:

$$\hat{a} = \bar{Y} - \hat{b}\bar{X} = 50 - 3.533(12) = 7.60$$

Thus, the equation of the regression line is

$$\hat{Y}_t = 7.60 + 3.53X_t \qquad [4\text{-}8]$$

This regression line indicates that with zero advertising expenditures (i.e., with $X_t = 0$), the expected sales revenue of the firm ($\hat{Y}_t$) is $7.60 million. With advertising of $10 million as in the first observation year (i.e., with $X_1 = \$10$ million), $\hat{Y}_1 = \$7.60 + \$3.53(10) = \$42.90$ million. On the other hand, with $X_{10} = \$15$ million, $\hat{Y}_{10} = \$7.60 + \$3.53(15) = \$60.55$ million. Plotting these last two points (10, 42.90) and (15, 60.55) and joining them by a straight line, we obtain the regression line plotted in Figure 4-3.[5]

The estimated regression line could also be used to estimate that the firm's sales revenue with advertising expenditures of $16 million would be $7.60 + \$3.53(16) = \$64.08$ million, or $3.53 million higher than with advertising expenditures of $15 million. Caution should, however, be exercised in using the regression line to estimate the sales revenue of the firm for advertising expenditures very different from those used in the estimation of the regression line itself. Strictly speaking, the regression line should be used only to estimate the sales revenues of the firm resulting from advertising expenditures that were within the range or that at least are near the advertising values that are used in the estimation of the regression line. Thus, not much confidence can usually be attached to the value of the estimated $\hat{a}$ coefficient, since this gives the sales revenues of the firm when advertising expenditures are zero (far off from the observed values). Because of this, we will concentrate our attention on the value of the $\hat{b}$, or slope, coefficient. The value of $\hat{b}$ measures the increase in the firm's sales revenues resulting from each unit (in this case, each $1 million) increase in the advertising expenditures of the firm. That is, $\hat{b} = \Delta Y/\Delta X$. In the terminology of Chapter 2, $\hat{b}$ measures the marginal effect on Y (sales) from each unit change in X (advertising).[6]

Regression analysis is based on a number of crucial assumptions. These are that the error term (1) is normally distributed, (2) has zero expected value or mean, and (3) has constant variance in each time period and for all values of X, and that (4) its value in one time period is unrelated to its value in any other period. These assumptions are required so as to obtain unbiased estimates of the slope coefficient and to be able to utilize probability theory to test for the reliability of the estimates. How this is done is shown next.

Tests of Significance of Parameter Estimates

In the previous section, we estimated the slope coefficient ($\hat{b}$) from one sample of the advertising-sales data of the firm. If we had used a different sample (say, data for a different 10-year period), we would have obtained a somewhat different estimate of b. The greater is the dispersion of (i.e., the more spread out are) the estimated values of b (that we would obtain if we were to actually run many regressions for different data samples), the smaller is the confidence that we have in our single estimated value of the b coefficient.

---

[5] Note that the regression line goes through point ($\bar{X} = 12$, $\bar{Y} = 50$). This is always the case and will be useful in the analysis that follows.

[6] In terms of calculus, b is the derivative of Y with respect to X, or dY/dX.

To test the hypothesis that b is statistically significant (i.e., that advertising positively affects sales), we need to first of all calculate the standard error (deviation) of $\hat{b}$. The standard error of $\hat{b}$ ($s_{\hat{b}}$) is routinely provided as part of the computer printout of the regression analysis, but it is important to know how it is calculated and how it is used in tests of significance. The standard error of $\hat{b}$ is given by

$$s_{\hat{b}} = \sqrt{\frac{\Sigma(Y_t - \hat{Y}_t)^2}{(n-k)\Sigma(X_t - \overline{X})^2}} = \sqrt{\frac{\Sigma e_t^2}{(n-k)\Sigma(X_t - \overline{X})^2}} \qquad [4\text{-}9]$$

where Y_t and X_t are the actual sample observations of the dependent and independent variables in year t, $\hat{Y}_t$ is the value of the dependent variable in year t estimated from the regression line, $\overline{X}$ is the expected value or mean of the independent variable, e is the error term, or $Y_t - \hat{Y}_t$, n is the number of observations or data points used in the estimation of the regression line, and k is the number of estimated coefficients in the regression. The value of $n - k$ is called the **degrees of freedom (df).** Since in simple regression analysis, we estimate two parameters, $\hat{a}$ and $\hat{b}$, the value of k is 2, and the degrees of freedom are $n - 2$.

The value of $s_{\hat{b}}$ for our advertising-sales example can be calculated by substituting the values from Table 4-4 (an extension of Table 4-3) into Equation 4-9. In Table 4-4, the values of $\hat{Y}_t$ in column 4 are obtained by substituting the various advertising expenditures of column 2 into Equation 4-8. Column 5 is obtained by subtracting the values in column 4 from the corresponding values in column 3, column 6 is obtained by squaring the values in column 5, and column 7 is repeated from Table 4-3.

Thus, the value of $s_{\hat{b}}$ is equal to

$$s_{\hat{b}} = \sqrt{\frac{\Sigma e_t^2}{(n-k)\Sigma(X_t - \overline{X})^2}} = \sqrt{\frac{65.4830}{(10-2)(30)}} = \sqrt{0.2728} = 0.52$$

TABLE 4-4	Calculations to Estimate the Standard Error of $\hat{b}$					
(1) Year	(2) X_t	(3) Y_t	(4) $\hat{Y}_t$	(5) $Y_t - \hat{Y}_t = e_t$	(6) $(Y_t - \hat{Y}_t)^2 = e_t^2$	(7) $(X_t - \overline{X})^2$
1	10	44	42.90	1.10	1.2100	4
2	9	40	39.37	0.63	0.3969	9
3	11	42	46.43	−4.43	19.6249	1
4	12	46	49.96	−3.96	15.6816	0
5	11	48	46.43	1.57	2.4649	1
6	12	52	49.96	2.04	4.1616	0
7	13	54	53.49	0.51	0.2601	1
8	13	58	53.49	4.51	20.3401	1
9	14	56	57.02	−1.02	1.0404	4
10	15	60	60.55	−0.55	0.3025	9
$n = 10$	$\Sigma X_t = 120$ $\overline{X} = 12$	$\Sigma Y_t = 500$ $\overline{Y} = 50$			$\Sigma e_t^2 = 65.4830$	$\Sigma(X_t - \overline{X})^2 = 30$

Having obtained the value of $s_{\hat{b}}$, we next calculate the ratio $\hat{b}/s_{\hat{b}}$. This is called the **t statistic,** or *t* ratio. The higher this calculated *t* ratio is, the more confident we are that the true but unknown value of *b* that we are seeking is not equal to zero (i.e., that there is a significant relationship between advertising and sales). For our sales-advertising example, we have

$$t = \frac{\hat{b}}{s_{\hat{b}}} = \frac{3.53}{0.52} = 6.79 \qquad [4\text{-}10]$$

In order to conduct an objective or **significance test** for $\hat{b}$, we compare the calculated *t* ratio to the **critical value** of the *t* distribution with $n - k = 10 - 2 = 8$ df given by Table C-2 on page 626.[7] This ***t* test** of the statistical significance of the estimated coefficient is usually performed at the 5 percent level of significance. Thus, we go down the column headed 0.05 (referring to 2.5 percent of the area or probability in each tail of the *t* distribution, for a total of 5 percent in both tails) in Table C-2 until we reach 8 df. This gives the critical value of $t = 2.306$ for this two-tailed *t* test.

Since our calculated value of $t = 6.79$ exceeds the tabular value of $t = 2.306$ for the 5 percent level of significance with 8 df, we reject the null hypothesis that there is no relationship between X (advertising) and Y (sales) and accept the alternative hypothesis that there is in fact a significant relationship between X and Y. To say that there is a statistically significant relationship between X and Y at the 5 percent level means that we are 95 percent confident that such a relationship exists. In other words, there is less than 1 chance in 20 (i.e., less than a 5 percent chance) of being wrong, or accepting the hypothesis that there is a significant relationship between X and Y, when in fact there is not.

Other Aspects of Significance Tests and Confidence Intervals

In the previous section we showed how to conduct statistical tests to show that the slope coefficient is different from zero at the 5 percent level of significance. Other tests of significance are possible as well. For example, we can construct confidence intervals for the true parameter from the estimated coefficient.

Moreover, we could test the hypothesis that the slope coefficient is different from zero at the 1 percent level of significance rather than at the 5 percent level. In that case, we would be allowing for only 1 chance in 100 of being wrong (i.e., of accepting the alternative hypothesis that there is a relationship between X and Y when in fact no such relationship

---

[7] The *t* distribution is a bell-shaped, symmetrical distribution about its zero mean that is flatter than the standard normal distribution (see the figures on pages 625 and 626 in Appendix C at the end of the book) so that more of its area falls within the tails. While there is a single standard normal distribution, there is a different *t* distribution for each sample size, *n*. However, as *n* becomes larger, the *t* distribution approaches the standard normal distribution until, when $n > 30$, they are approximately equal. Thus, for large sample sizes, we can conduct significance tests using the normal distribution without concerning ourselves with degrees of freedom. In any event, a useful rule of thumb is that an estimated parameter is likely to be statistically significant at the 5 percent level if the calculated *t* statistic for the coefficient is greater than 2. Since in this case we have 10 observations or data points in our advertising-sales example, and we estimate two parameters ($\hat{a}$ and $\hat{b}$), the degrees of freedom are $n - k = 10 - 2 = 8$ and we use the *t* distribution to conduct our significance test.

exists). To test the hypothesis at the 1 percent level, we go down the column headed 0.01 in Table C-2 until once again we reach 8 df. The critical value of t that we get from the t table is 3.355. Since the calculated t value of 6.79 exceeds this critical tabular value, we accept the hypothesis that there is in fact a significant relationship between X and Y at the 1 percent level also.

While tests of significance are sometimes conducted at the 1 percent or even at the 10 percent level of significance, it is more common to use the 5 percent level. Note also that the greater the number of degrees of freedom (i.e., the greater the number of observations or data points in relation to the number of estimated parameters in the regression analysis), the smaller are the critical t values in Table C-2 regardless of the level of significance that we choose. Therefore, the greater the number of degrees of freedom, the more likely it is to accept the hypothesis that a statistically significant relationship exists between the independent variable(s) and the dependent variable.

Note that tests of significance are not usually conducted for the $\hat{a}$ coefficient (the vertical intercept), since this coefficient usually has little or no economic significance. Also note that in our presentation, we have tested only the hypothesis that $\hat{b}$ is significantly different from zero. Since $\hat{b}$ can be significantly different from zero by being either negative or positive, we conducted a two-tailed test. That is, we allowed for the possibility of $\hat{b}$ being significantly positive or significantly negative and examined areas (probabilities) under the t distribution in both tails. We could also test, however, the hypothesis that b is larger or smaller than some specified value. In those cases, we would conduct a single-tailed test and examine the area (probability) that the value of $\hat{b}$ falls only in the right or in the left tail of the t distribution (and look under the column headed 0.10 for the 5 percent test).

The above concepts can also be used to determine **confidence intervals** for the true b coefficient. Thus, using the tabular value of $t = 2.306$ for the 5 percent level of significance (2.5 percent in each tail) and 8 df in our advertising-sales example, we can say that we are 95 percent confident that the true value of b will be between

$$\hat{b} \pm 2.306(s_{\hat{b}})$$
$$3.53 \pm 2.306(0.52)$$
$$3.53 \pm 1.20$$

That is, we are 95 percent confident that the true value of b lies between 2.33 and 4.73. Similarly, we can say that we are 99 percent confident that the true value of b will be between $3.53 \pm 3.355(0.52)$, or 1.79 and 5.27 (the value of $t = 3.355$ is obtained by going down the column headed 0.01 in Table C-2 until we reach 8 df).

Test of Goodness of Fit and Correlation

Besides testing for the statistical significance of a particular estimated parameter, we can also test for the overall explanatory power of the entire regression. This is accomplished by calculating the coefficient of determination, which is usually denoted by R^2. The **coefficient of determination (R^2)** is defined as the proportion of the total variation or dispersion in the dependent variable (about its mean) that is explained by the variation in the independent or explanatory variable(s) in the regression. In terms of our advertising-sales example, R^2 measures how much of the variation in the firm's sales is explained by the variation in its advertising expenditures. The closer the observed data points fall to the regression line, the greater is the proportion of the variation in the firm's sales explained by the variation in its advertising expenditures, and the larger is the value of the coefficient of determination, or R^2.

We can calculate the coefficient of determination (R^2) by defining the total, the explained, and the unexplained or residual variation in the dependent variable (Y). The **total variation** in Y can be measured by squaring the deviation of each observed value of Y from its mean and then summing. That is,

$$\text{Total variation in } Y = \sum_{t=1}^{n} (Y_t - \overline{Y})^2 \qquad [4\text{-}11]$$

Regression analysis breaks up this total variation in Y into two components: the variation in Y that is explained by the independent variable (X) and the unexplained or residual variation in Y. The **explained variation** in Y is given by Equation 4-12:

$$\text{Explained variation in } Y = \sum_{t=1}^{n} (\hat{Y}_t - \overline{Y})^2 \qquad [4\text{-}12]$$

The values of $\hat{Y}$ in Equation 4-12 are obtained by substituting the various observed values of X (the independent variable) into the estimated regression equation. The mean of Y ($\overline{Y}$) is then subtracted from each of the estimated values of Y_t ($\hat{Y}_t$). As indicated by Equation 4-12, these differences are then squared and added to get the explained variation in Y.

Finally, the **unexplained variation** in Y is given by Equation 4-13:

$$\text{Unexplained variation in } Y = \sum_{t=1}^{n} (Y_t - \hat{Y}_t)^2 \qquad [4\text{-}13]$$

That is, the unexplained or residual variation in Y is obtained by first subtracting from each observed value of Y the corresponding estimated value of $\hat{Y}$, and then squaring and summing.

Summarizing, we have

$$\text{Total variation} = \text{explained variation} + \text{unexplained variation}$$

$$\Sigma (Y_t - \overline{Y})^2 = \Sigma (\hat{Y}_t - \overline{Y})^2 + \Sigma (Y_t - \hat{Y}_t)^2 \qquad [4\text{-}14]$$

This breakdown of the total variation in Y into the explained and the unexplained variation is shown in Figure 4-4 for one particular observation or data point for our advertising-sales example.

Now, the coefficient of determination, R^2, is defined as the ratio of the explained variation in Y to the total variation in Y. That is,

$$R^2 = \frac{\text{explained variation in } Y}{\text{total variation in } Y} = \frac{\Sigma (\hat{Y}_t - \overline{Y})^2}{\Sigma (Y_t - \overline{Y})^2} \qquad [4\text{-}15]$$

If all the data points were to fall on the regression line (a most unusual occurrence), all the variation in the dependent variable (Y) would be explained by the variation in the

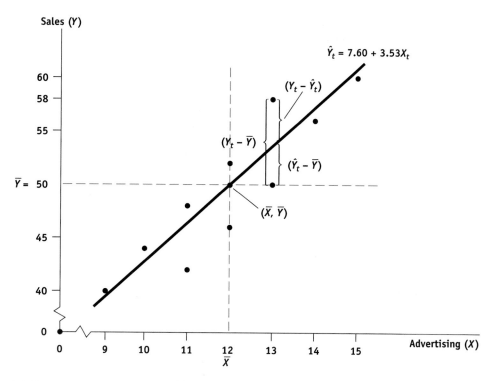

FIGURE 4-4   Total, Explained, and Residual Variation   The total variation in the dependent variable, $\Sigma(Y_t - \bar{Y})^2$, is equal to the explained variation, $\Sigma(\hat{Y}_t - \bar{Y})^2$, plus the unexplained or residual variation, $\Sigma(Y_t - \hat{Y}_t)^2$. For the observation ($X = 13$, $Y = 58$), $Y_t - \bar{Y} = 58 - 50 = 8$, $\hat{Y}_t - \bar{Y} = 53.49 - 50 = 3.49$, and $Y_t - \hat{Y}_t = 4.51$. ($\hat{Y}_t = 53.49$ is the estimated value of Y_t for $X = 13$ in the fourth column of Table 4-4.)

independent or explanatory variable (X), and R^2 would be equal to 1, or 100 percent. At the opposite extreme, if none of the variation in Y were explained by the variation in X, R^2 would be equal to zero. Thus, the value of R^2 can assume any value from 0 to 1.

While the coefficient of determination is also routinely provided in the computer printout of the regression analysis, we will now show how to actually calculate R^2 for our advertising-sales problem. The calculations are shown in Table 4-5. From the bottom of column 4, we see that the total variation in Y (sales) is $440 million. The explained variation is $373.84 million, as shown at the bottom of column 7. Thus, the coefficient of determination for our advertising-sales problem is

$$R^2 = \frac{\$373.84}{\$440} = 0.85$$

This means that 85 percent of the total variation in the firm's sales is accounted for by the variation in the firm's advertising expenditures.

The last column of Table 4-5 gives the unexplained variation in Y (and has been copied from column 6 of Table 4-4). The unexplained variation in Y for our advertising-sales example is $65.48 million. The sum of the explained and unexplained variation in Y

TABLE 4-5 Calculations to Estimate the Coefficient of Determination (R^2)

(1) Year	(2) Y_t	(3) $Y_t - \bar{Y}$	(4) $(Y_t - \bar{Y})^2$	(5) $\hat{Y}_t$	(6) $\hat{Y}_t - \bar{Y}$	(7) $(\hat{Y}_t - \bar{Y})^2$	(8) $(Y_t - \hat{Y}_t)^2$
1	44	−6	36	42.90	−7.10	50.4100	1.2100
2	40	−10	100	39.37	−10.63	112.9969	0.3969
3	42	−8	64	46.43	−3.57	12.7449	19.6249
4	46	−4	16	49.96	−0.04	0.0016	15.6816
5	48	−2	4	46.43	−3.57	12.7449	2.4649
6	52	2	4	49.96	−0.04	0.0016	4.1616
7	54	4	16	53.49	3.49	12.1801	0.2601
8	58	8	64	53.49	3.49	12.1801	20.3401
9	56	6	36	57.02	7.02	49.2804	1.0404
10	60	10	100	60.55	10.55	111.3025	0.3025
$n = 10$	$\sum Y_t = 500$ $\bar{Y} = 50$		$\sum(Y_t - \bar{Y})^2$ $= 440$			$\sum(\hat{Y}_t - \bar{Y})^2$ $= 373.8430$	$\sum(Y_t - \hat{Y}_t)^2$ $= 65.4830$

($\$373.84 + \$65.48 = \$439.32$) is equal to the total variation in Y ($\$440$), except for rounding errors.[8]

Two final things must be pointed out with respect to the coefficient of determination. The first is that in simple regression analysis the square root of the coefficient of determination (R^2) is the (absolute value of the) **coefficient of correlation,** which is denoted by r. That is,

$$r = \sqrt{R^2} \qquad [4\text{-}16]$$

This is simply a measure of the degree of association or covariation that exists between variables X and Y. For our advertising-sales example,

$$r = \sqrt{R^2} = \sqrt{0.85} = 0.92$$

This means that variables X and Y vary together 92 percent of the time. The coefficient of correlation ranges in value between −1 (if all the sample observation points fall on a negatively sloped straight line) and 1 (for perfect positive linear correlation). It should be noted that the sign of the coefficient of correlation (r) is always the same as the sign of the estimated slope coefficient ($\hat{b}$).

As opposed to regression analysis, which implies that the variation in Y results from the variation in X, correlation analysis measures only the degree of association or covariation between the two variables, without any implication of causality or dependence. In short, we can find the correlation coefficient between any two variables, but we run a regression analysis only if we believe that the variation in one variable (the independent variable, X) affects or somehow results in some variation in Y (the dependent variable).

---

[8] Note that once we obtain two of the three values of the total, explained, and unexplained variation in Y, we can obtain the remaining measure simply by subtraction.

This brings us to the second point. That is, although regression analysis implies causality (i.e., that the variation in X causes the variation in Y), only theory can tell us if we can expect the variation in X to result in a variation in Y. In fact, it is possible that a high coefficient of determination (and correlation) between X and Y may be due to some other factor that affects both X and Y, which is not included in the regression analysis. For example, expenditures on food and housing may both depend on the level of consumer income rather than on each other. In such a case, we would simply say that there is *correlation* or covariation between X and Y without identifying one variable (X) as the independent or explanatory variable.

The Chapter Appendix shows how to run a simple regression analysis using the Microsoft Excel program.

4-5 | **MULTIPLE REGRESSION ANALYSIS**

We now extend the simple regression model to multiple regression analysis. We will show how to estimate the regression parameters, how to conduct tests of their statistical significance, and how to measure and test the overall explanatory power of the entire regression.

The Multiple Regression Model

When the dependent variable that we seek to explain is hypothesized to depend on more than one independent or explanatory variable, we have **multiple regression analysis.** For example, the firm's sales revenue may be postulated to depend not only on the firm's advertising expenditures (as examined in Section 4-4) but also on its expenditures on quality control. The regression model can then be written as

$$Y = a + b_1X_1 + b_2X_2 \qquad [4\text{-}17]$$

where Y is the dependent variable referring to the firm's sales revenue, X_1 refers to the firm's advertising expenditures, and X_2 refers to its expenditures on quality control. The coefficients a, b_1, and b_2 are the parameters to be estimated.

The a coefficient is the constant or vertical intercept and gives the value of Y when both X_1 and X_2 are equal to zero. On the other hand, b_1 and b_2 are the slope coefficients. They measure the change in Y per unit change of X_1 and X_2, respectively. Specifically, b_1 measures the change in sales (Y) per unit change in advertising expenditures (X_1), while holding quality-control expenditures (X_2) constant. Similarly, b_2 measures the change in Y per unit change in X_2 while holding X_1 constant. That is, $b_1 = \Delta Y/\Delta X_1$, while $b_2 = \Delta Y/\Delta X_2$.[9] In our sales-advertising and quality-control problem we postulate that both b_1 and b_2 are positive, or that the firm can increase its sales by increasing its expenditures for advertising and quality control.

---

[9] In terms of calculus, $b_1 = \partial Y/\partial X_1$, while $b_2 = \partial Y/\partial X_2$. Thus, b_1 and b_2 are often referred to as the "partial regression coefficients."

TABLE 4-6	Yearly Expenditures on Advertising and Quality Control, and Sales of the Firm (millions of dollars)									
Year (t)	1	2	3	4	5	6	7	8	9	10
Advertising (X_1)	10	9	11	12	11	12	13	13	14	15
Quality control (X_2)	3	4	3	3	4	5	6	7	7	8
Sales revenue (Y)	44	40	42	46	48	52	54	58	56	60

The model can also be generalized to any number of independent or explanatory variables (k'), as indicated in Equation 4-18:

$$Y = a + b_1X_1 + b_2X_2 + \cdots + b'_kX'_k \qquad [4\text{-}18]$$

The only assumptions made in multiple regression analysis in addition to those made for simple regression analysis are that the number of independent or explanatory variables in the regression be smaller than the number of observations and that there be no perfect linear correlation among the independent variables.[10]

The process of estimating the parameters or coefficients of a multiple regression equation is, in principle, the same as in simple regression analysis, but since the calculations are much more complex and time-consuming, they are invariably done with computers. The computer also provides routinely the standard error of the estimates, the t statistics, the coefficient of multiple determination, and several other important statistics that are used to conduct other statistical tests of the results (to be examined later). All that is required is to be able to set up the regression analysis, feed the data into the computer, and interpret the results.

For example, if we regress the firm's sales (Y) on its expenditures for advertising (X_1) and quality control (X_2) using the data in Table 4-6 (an extension of Table 4-2), we obtain the results given in Table 4-7.[11]

From the results shown in Table 4-7, we can write the following regression equation:

$$\hat{Y}_t = 17.944 + 1.873X_{1t} + 1.915X_{2t} \qquad [4\text{-}19]$$

$$t \text{ statistic} \qquad (2.663) \qquad (2.813)$$

These results indicate that for each \$1 million increase in expenditures on advertising and quality control, the sales of the firm increase by \$1.87 million (the estimated coefficient of X_1) and \$1.92 million (the estimated coefficient of X_2), respectively. To perform t tests for the statistical significance of the estimated parameters or coefficients, we need to determine the critical value of t from the table of the t distribution. At the 0.05 level of

---

[10] If the number of independent or explanatory variables (the X's) is equal to or larger than the number of observations, or if there is an exact linear relationship among some or all of the independent or explanatory variables, the regression equation cannot be estimated.

[11] The results given in Table 4-7 are in the form provided by a standard computer program (TSP). Other computer programs (such as SPSS, EViews, and RATS) usually provide the same general information in a similar format. Different computer programs, however, usually give slightly different results because of differences in rounding.

TABLE 4-7	Computer Results of Regression of Y on X_1 and X_2		

SMPL 1 - 10
10 Observations
LS // Dependent variable is Y

	Coefficient	Standard Error	T Statistic
C	17.9437	5.91914	3.03147
X1	1.87324	0.70334	2.66335
X2	1.91549	0.68101	2.81272
R squared	0.930154	Mean of dependent var	50.00000
Adjusted R squared	0.910198	SD of dependent var	6.992061
SE of regression	2.095311	Sum of squared resid	30.73242
Durbin-Watson stat	1.541100	F statistic	46.61000
Log likelihood	−19.80301		

significance for $n - k = 10 - 3 = 7$ df (where k is the number of estimated parameters, including the constant term), this is 2.365, obtained by going down the column headed 0.05 in Table C-2 (for the two-tailed test with 2.5 percent of the area under each tail of the t distribution) until we reach 7 df. Since the value of the calculated t statistic exceeds the critical t value of 2.365, we conclude that both parameters are statistically different from zero at the 5 percent level of significance.[12]

The Coefficient of Determination and Adjusted R^2

As in simple regression analysis, the coefficient of determination measures the proportion of the total variation in the dependent variable that is explained by the variation in the independent or explanatory variables in the regression. From Table 4-7, we see that for our example the coefficient of determination, or R^2, is 0.93. This means that variation in the firm's expenditures on advertising and quality control explain 93 percent of the variation in the firm's sales revenues. This is larger than the R^2 of 0.85 that we obtained on page 157 for the simple regression of sales on advertising expenditures alone. This was to be expected. That is, as more relevant independent or explanatory variables are included in the regression, we generally expect a larger proportion of the total variation in the dependent variable to be "explained."

However, in order to take into consideration that the number of degrees of freedom declines as additional independent or explanatory variables are included in the regression, we calculate the **adjusted R^2 ($\bar{R}^2$)** as

$$\bar{R}^2 = 1 - (1 - R^2)\left(\frac{n - 1}{n - k}\right) \tag{4-20}$$

---

[12] Note that because the t statistics were provided by the computer printout, we have presented those below the estimated coefficients rather than the standard errors (which are used to calculate the t statistics). We will follow this procedure in the rest of the text, unless otherwise indicated.

where n is the number of observations or sample data points and k is the number of parameters or coefficients estimated. For example, in the regression analysis of Y on X_1 and X_2, $n = 10$, $n - k = 10 - 3 = 7$, and $R^2 = 0.930154$. Substituting these values into Equation 4-20, we get the value of $\bar{R}^2 = 0.910198$ (the same as in the computer printout given in Table 4-7). This means that when due consideration is given to the fact that including the firm's expenditures on quality control as an additional explanatory variable in the regression reduces the degrees of freedom, the proportion of the total variation in sales explained by the regression is 91 percent rather than 93 percent. This is still larger than the 85 percent explained by advertising as the single independent variable in the simple regression.[13]

The inclusion of expenditures on quality control in the regression analysis also leads to a very different value of $\hat{b}_1$ (the estimated coefficient of advertising expenditures in the multiple regression), as compared to the value of $\hat{b}$ (the estimated coefficient of advertising expenditures in the simple regression). The value of $\hat{b}$ was found to be 3.53 in Equation 4-8, while the value of $\hat{b}_1$ is 1.87 in Equation 4-19. Thus, omission of an important explanatory variable (expenditures for quality control, in this case) from the simple regression gives biased results for the estimated slope coefficient. Specifically, simple regression analysis attributes a much greater influence of advertising on sales than warranted. In other words, advertising gets credited for some of the influence on sales that is, in fact, due to expenditures on quality control. Thus, it is crucial to include in the regression analysis all *important* independent or explanatory variables.

Analysis of Variance

The overall explanatory power of the entire regression can be tested with the **analysis of variance.** This uses the value of the **F statistic,** or F ratio, which is also provided by the computer printout. Specifically, the F statistic is used to test the hypothesis that the variation in the independent variables (the X's) explains a significant proportion of the variation in the dependent variable (Y). Thus, we can use the F statistic to test the null hypothesis that all the regression coefficients are equal to zero against the alternative hypothesis that they are not all equal to zero.

The value of the F statistic is given by

$$F = \frac{\text{explained variation}/(k-1)}{\text{unexplained variation}/(n-k)} \qquad [4\text{-}21]$$

where, as usual, n is the number of observations and k is the number of estimated parameters or coefficients in the regression. It is because the F statistic is the ratio of two variances that this test is often referred to as the "analysis of variance." The F statistic can also be calculated in terms of the coefficient of determination as follows:

$$F = \frac{R^2/(k-1)}{(1-R^2)/(n-k)} \qquad [4\text{-}22]$$

[13] Note that the adjustment (reduction) in R^2 to obtain $\bar{R}^2$ is smaller the larger the value of n is in relation to k.

Using the values of $R^2 = 0.930154$, $n = 10$, and $k = 3$ for our example, we obtain $F = 46.61$, the same value as in the computer printout in Table 4-7.

To conduct the F test or analysis of variance, we compare the calculated or regression value of the F statistic with a critical value from the table of the F distribution. Two tables of the F distribution are presented in Appendix C at the end of the text. One is for the 5 percent level of significance, and the other is for the 1 percent level. The F distribution for each level of statistical significance is defined in terms of 2 df. These are $k - 1$ for the numerator (see Equations 4-20 and 4-22) and $n - k$ for the denominator. Thus, in our example, the degrees of freedom are $k - 1 = 3 - 1 = 2$ (the number of independent variables in the regression) for the numerator and $n - k = 10 - 3 = 7$ for the denominator.

To determine the critical value of the F distribution, we first move across Table C-3 of the F distribution (provided in Appendix C at the end of the text) until we reach 2 df for the numerator, and then move down in the table until we reach 7 df for the denominator. The critical value of F that we find in the table for the 5 percent level of significance is 4.74. Since the calculated value of the F statistic of 46.61 exceeds the critical value of 4.74 for the F distribution with 2 and 7 df, we reject at the 5 percent level of significance the null hypothesis that there is no statistically significant relationship between the independent variables and the dependent variable (i.e., we accept the alternative hypothesis at the 5 percent level of significance that not all coefficients are equal to zero).[14]

Point and Interval Estimates

The computer printout presented in Table 4-7 also gives the standard error of the entire regression (the value of 2.09531 labeled "*SE* of regression"). This is nothing else than the standard error of the dependent variable (Y) from the regression line.[15] The smaller the value of the **standard error (*SE*) of the regression,** the better is the "fit" of the regression line to the observation or sample points. The *SE* of the regression can be used to estimate confidence intervals for the dependent variable. Specifically, we can use the estimated regression given by Equation 4-19 to find a point estimate, or forecast, of Y, and then use the point estimate, or forecast, and the value of the *SE* of the regression to obtain interval estimates, or forecasts, of Y. For example, for $X_1 = 5$ and $X_2 = 12$, we obtain the point estimate (forecast) of

$$\hat{Y} = 17.944 + 1.873(5) + 1.915(12) = 50.289 \qquad [4\text{-}23]$$

The *approximate* 95 percent confidence interval estimate, or forecast, of Y is then given by

$$50.289 \pm 2(SE)$$
$$50.289 \pm (2)(2.095)$$
$$50.289 \pm 4.190 \qquad [4\text{-}24]$$

---

[14] To test the hypothesis at the 1 percent level of significance, we compare the calculated value of the F statistic to the critical F value from Table C-3 for the 1 percent level of statistical significance, with 2 and 7 df. In simple regression analysis, where there is only one independent variable, it can be shown that the F test is equivalent to the t test.

[15] This is not to be confused with the standard deviation (*SD*) of the dependent variable *itself* from its mean or expected value, which is also reported in Table 4-7.

That is, we are 95 percent confident that the true value of Y will lie between 46.10 and 54.48.[16]

The Chapter Appendix shows how to run the multiple regression analysis using the Microsoft Excel program.

PROBLEMS IN REGRESSION ANALYSIS

Regression analysis may face some serious problems. These are multicollinearity, heteroscedasticity, and autocorrelation. In this section, we discuss each of these in turn by examining the conditions under which they might arise, the tests available to detect their presence, and possible ways to overcome the difficulties that they create.

Multicollinearity

Multicollinearity refers to the situation in which two or more explanatory variables in the regression are highly correlated. For example, suppose that the firm of Table 4-6 had kept its expenditures on quality control nearly constant as a fraction of its advertising expenditures over time (so that both types of expenditures would be highly collinear). In such a case, running a regression of sales on expenditures for advertising and for quality control would very likely have led to exaggerated standard errors and, therefore, to low t values for both estimated coefficients. This could lead to the conclusion that both slope coefficients are statistically insignificant, even though the R^2 may be very high.[17]

Serious multicollinearity can sometimes be overcome or reduced by (1) extending the sample size (i.e., collecting more data); (2) using a priori information (e.g., we may know from a previous study that $b_2 = 2b_1$); (3) transforming the functional relationship; and/or (4) dropping one of the highly collinear variables. An example of the last method may be the elimination of price as an explanatory variable in the regression model by using deflated (i.e., price-adjusted) values of the dependent and independent variables in the regression (see Problem 9). Dropping other variables that theory tells us should be included in the model would, however, lead to specification bias, which is even more serious than the multicollinearity problem.

Heteroscedasticity

Another serious problem that we may face in regression analysis is **heteroscedasticity.** This arises when the assumption that the variance of the error term is constant for all values of the independent variables is violated. This often occurs in **cross-sectional data** (i.e., data on a sample of families, firms, or other economic unit for a given year or other time period), where the size of the error may rise (the more common form) or fall with the

---

[16] The Durbin–Watson statistic, which is also presented in Table 4-7, will be used on pages 166–167.

[17] To be sure, while the test for the statistical significance of the slope coefficients is biased, the value of the estimated coefficients is not (if the regression equation is otherwise properly specified by the inclusion of all important variables). Therefore, the regression results can still be used for forecasting purposes if the pattern of multicollinearity is expected to persist more or less unchanged during the forecasting period.

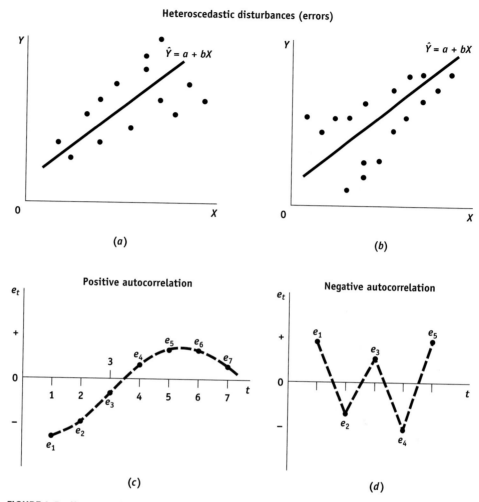

FIGURE 4-5 Heteroscedastic and Autocorrelated Disturbances   Part (*a*) shows heteroscedastic disturbances, where the size of the error or residual increases with the size of the value of *X*. Part (*b*) shows the opposite pattern of heteroscedastic disturbances (which is less common). Part (*c*) shows positive autocorrelation (i.e., a positive or negative error in one period is followed by another positive or negative error term, respectively, in the following period). Part (*d*) shows negative autocorrelation (which is less common).

size of an independent variable (see Figure 4-5*a* and *b*, respectively). For example, the error associated with the expenditures of low-income families is usually smaller than for high-income families because most of the expenditures of low-income families are on necessities, with little room for discretion. Thus, if data on family expenditures were used as an explanatory variable, the regression analysis would likely face the problem of heteroscedasticity.

Heteroscedastic disturbances lead to biased standard errors and, thus, to incorrect statistical tests and confidence intervals for the parameter estimates. When the pattern of errors or residuals points to the existence of heteroscedasticity, the researcher may overcome the problem by using the log of the explanatory variable that leads to heteroscedastic disturbances or by running a weighted least-squares regression. To run a weighted least-squares regression, we first divide the dependent and all independent variables by the variable that is responsible for the heteroscedasticity and then run the regression on the transformed variables.

Autocorrelation

Whenever consecutive errors or residuals are correlated, we have **autocorrelation,** or serial correlation. When consecutive errors have the same sign, we have positive autocorrelation (see Figure 4-5c). When they change sign frequently, we have negative autocorrelation (see Figure 4-5d). Autocorrelation is frequently found in **time-series data** (i.e., data where there is one observation on each variable for each time period). In economics, positive autocorrelation is more common than negative autocorrelation, and so we will deal only with the former in what follows. While estimated coefficients are not biased in the presence of autocorrelation, their standard errors are biased downward (so that the value of their t statistic is exaggerated). As a result, we may conclude that an estimated coefficient is statistically significant when, in fact, it is not. The value of $\bar{R}^2$ and of the F statistic will also be unreliable in the presence of autocorrelation.

Autocorrelation can arise from the existence of trends and cycles in economic variables, from the exclusion of an important variable from the regression, or from nonlinearities in the data. Autocorrelation can be detected by plotting the residuals or errors (as in Figure 4-5c and d) or, more formally, by using the **Durbin–Watson statistic (d).** This is given by Equation 4-25 and is routinely provided in the computer printout of practically all regression packages. In Equation 4-25, e_t and e_{t-1} refer, respectively, to the error term in period t and in the previous time period ($t-1$). The value of d ranges between 0 and 4.

$$d = \frac{\sum\limits_{t=2}^{n} (e_t - e_{t-1})^2}{\sum\limits_{t=1}^{n} (e_t)^2} \qquad\qquad [4\text{-}25]$$

The computed d statistic is then compared to a critical value from the Durbin–Watson (D–W) table (Table C-4) provided at the end of the book. The D–W test can be conducted either at the 5 percent or at the 1 percent level of significance. Across the top of the D–W table, we have k' (the number of explanatory variables in the regression); moving downward on the table, we have n (the number of observations or sample data points). The D–W table starts at $n = 15$; therefore, we cannot use this method of testing for autocorrelation if we have fewer than 15 observations in our sample.

For each value of k' there are two columns in the D–W table, one headed d_L (for the lower value of d) and one headed d_U (for the upper value of d). If the calculated value of the d statistic exceeds the critical value of d_U in the table (for the appropriate values of k' and n), we conclude that there is no evidence of autocorrelation at the 5 or 1 percent level of significance. In general, a value of about $d = 2$ indicates the absence of autocorrelation. If the value of the D–W statistic falls between the critical values of d_L and d_U in the table, the test is inconclusive. Finally, if the value of the d statistic is smaller than the critical value of d_L given in the table, there is evidence of autocorrelation.

If the *D–W* test indicates the presence of autocorrelation, we must then adjust for its effect. The adjustment may involve the inclusion of time as an additional explanatory variable to take into consideration the trend that may exist in the data, the inclusion of an important missing variable into the regression, or the reestimation of the regression in nonlinear form. Sometimes, reestimating the regression for the *change* (i.e., using the first differences) in the dependent and independent variables and omitting the constant term may overcome autocorrelation. More complex methods also exist. These, however, are beyond the scope of this book.

4-7 DEMAND ESTIMATION BY REGRESSION ANALYSIS

Although consumer surveys, consumer clinics, market experiments, and other marketing research approaches to demand estimation may be useful, by far the most common method of estimating demand in managerial economics is regression analysis. This method is usually more objective, provides more complete information, and is generally less expensive than properly conducted marketing approaches to demand estimation.

In this section, we summarize and review the method of estimating demand by regression analysis. Specifically, we discuss the specification of the model to be estimated, the data requirements, the possible functional forms of the demand equation, and the evaluation of the econometric results obtained.

Model Specification

The first step in using regression analysis to estimate demand is to specify the model to be estimated. This involves identifying the most important variables that are believed to affect the demand for the commodity under study. These will usually include the price of the commodity (P_X), consumer income (I), the number of consumers in the market (N), the price of related (i.e., substitute and complementary) commodities (P_Y), consumers' tastes (T), and all the other variables, such as the level of advertising, the availability and level of credit incentives, and consumers' price expectations, that are thought to be important determinants of the demand for the particular commodity under study. These were discussed in detail in Chapter 3. Thus, we can specify the following general function of the demand for the commodity (Q_X), measured in physical units, where the dots at the end of Equation 4-26 refer to the other determinants of demand that are specific to the particular firm and commodity:

$$Q_X = f(P_X, I, N, P_Y, T, \ldots) \qquad [4\text{-}26]$$

The variables that are specific to the demand function being estimated are determined from an in-depth knowledge of the market for the commodity. Thus, the demand function for expensive durable goods, such as automobiles and houses, which are usually purchased by borrowing money, must include credit terms or interest rates among the explanatory variables. The demand function for seasonal equipment, such as skiing equipment, air conditioners, swimming suits, and cold beverages, will have to include weather conditions, while the demand function for capital goods, such as machinery and factory buildings, will very likely have to include rates of profit, capital utilization, and wage increases among the explanatory variables. The researcher must avoid omitting important variables from the demand equation to be estimated; otherwise he or she will obtain biased results. At the same time, including too many explanatory variables (say, more than five or six) may lead to econometric difficulties, such as having too few degrees of freedom (see page 155) and multicollinearity (see page 164).

Collecting Data on the Variables

The second step in using regression analysis to estimate the demand for a particular commodity is to collect the data for the variables in the model. Data can be collected for each variable over time (i.e., yearly, quarterly, monthly, etc.) or for different economic units (individuals, households, etc.) at a particular point in time (i.e., for a particular year, month, week, etc.). As described on page 166, the former are called *time-series data,* while the latter are called *cross-sectional data.* Each type of data has specific advantages but leads to particular estimation problems.

The type of data actually used in demand estimation is often dictated by availability. Lack of data might also force the researcher to use a proxy for some of the variables for which no data are available. For example, a proxy for consumers' price expectations in each period might be the actual price changes from the previous period. The researcher could also try to measure consumers' expectations by consumer surveys. Finally, since it is usually very difficult to find reliable quantitative measures of tastes, the researcher may have to make sure (possibly by consumer surveys) that they have not changed during the period of the analysis. In that case, tastes can be dropped as an explicit explanatory variable from the actual estimation of the demand equation.

The most important sources of general published data that are likely to be useful in gathering the data for demand estimation are the *Survey of Current Business,* the *Statistical Abstract of the United States,* the *Federal Reserve Bulletin,* and the *Annual Economic Report to the President.*

Specifying the Form of the Demand Equation

The third step in estimating demand by regression analysis is to determine the functional form of the model to be estimated. The simplest model to deal with, and the one that is often also the most realistic, is the linear model. For example, Equation 4-25 can be written in explicit linear form as

$$Q_X = a_0 + a_1 P_X + a_2 I + a_3 N + a_4 P_Y + \cdots + e \qquad [4\text{-}27]$$

In Equation 4-27, the a's are the parameters (coefficients) to be estimated, and e is the error term. In such a linear model, the change in (i.e., the marginal effect on) the dependent variable (Q_X) for each one-unit change in the independent or explanatory variables (given by the estimated coefficient for the variables) is constant regardless of the *level* of the particular variable (or other variables included in the demand equation). This leads to easy interpretation of the estimated coefficients of the regression.

There are cases, however, where a nonlinear relationship will fit the data better than the linear form. This may be revealed by plotting on a graph (scatter diagram) the dependent variable against each of the independent variables. The most common nonlinear specification of the demand equation is the power function. A demand equation in the form of a power function (including, for simplicity, only the price of the commodity and consumer income as independent or explanatory variables) is

$$Q_X = a(P_X^{b_1})\,(I^{b_2}) \qquad\qquad [4\text{-}28]$$

In order to estimate the parameters (i.e., coefficients a, b_1, and b_2) of demand Equation 4-28, we must first transform it into double log Equation 4-29, which is linear in the logarithms, and then run the regression on the log of the variables.[18]

$$\ln Q_X = \ln a + b_1 \ln P_X + b_2 \ln I \qquad\qquad [4\text{-}29]$$

The estimated slope coefficients (that is, b_1 and b_2) in Equation 4-29 now represent percentage changes or average elasticities. Specifically, b_1 is the price elasticity of demand (E_P), while b_2 is the income elasticity of demand (E_I) for commodity X.[19] Thus, the advantage of the power formulation of the demand function is that the estimated coefficients give demand elasticities directly.[20] In the real world, both the power and the linear forms of the demand function are usually estimated, and the one that gives better results (i.e., that fits the data better) is reported.

---

[18] That is, first we find the logarithm of each of the variables (the computer usually does this) and then the regression is run on the logarithms of the variables, just as it was done before.

[19] Specifically,

$$E_P = \frac{\partial Q_X}{\partial P_X} \cdot \frac{P_X}{Q_X}$$

For Equation 4-28,

$$\frac{\partial Q_X}{\partial P_X} = b_1[a(P_X^{b_1-1})I^{b_2}]$$

Therefore,

$$E_P = b_1[a(P_X^{b_1-1})I^{b_2}] \cdot \frac{P_X}{Q_X} = \frac{b_1[a(P_X^{b_1})I^{b_2}]}{Q_X} = b_1 \cdot \frac{Q_X}{Q_X} = b_1$$

Similarly,

$$E_I = \frac{\partial Q_X}{\partial I} \cdot \frac{I}{Q_X}$$

For Equation 4-28,

$$\frac{\partial Q_X}{\partial I} = b_2[a(P_X^{b_1})I^{b_2-1}]$$

Therefore,

$$E_I = b_2[a(P_X^{b_1})I^{b_2-1}] \cdot \frac{I}{Q_X} = \frac{b_2[a(P_X^{b_1})I^{b_2}]}{Q_X} = b_2 \cdot \frac{Q_X}{Q_X} = b_2$$

[20] Note that while a_1 (which equals $\Delta Q_X/\Delta P_X$ in linear demand Equation 4-27) is independent of the level of P_X, b_1 (which equals E_P in demand Equation 4-28) depends on the level of P_X and also on the level of I (consumers' incomes). This is often realistic. For example, if commodity X were steaks, it is likely that the higher I is, the lower would be E_P because consumers may already be purchasing a large quantity of steaks at high incomes. Similarly, b_2 in demand Equation 4-28 depends on both the level of P_X and I.

Testing the Econometric Results

The fourth and final step in the estimation of demand by regression analysis is to evaluate the regression results, as discussed in Sections 4-4 to 4-6. First, the sign of each estimated slope coefficient must be checked to see if it conforms to what is postulated on theoretical grounds. Second, t tests must be conducted on the statistical significance of the estimated parameters to determine the degree of confidence that we can have in each of the estimated slope coefficients. The (adjusted) coefficient of determination, $\bar{R}^2$ (see page 161), will then indicate the proportion of the total variation in the demand for the commodity that is "explained" by the independent or explanatory variables included in the demand equation.

Finally, the estimated demand equation must pass other econometric tests to make sure that such problems as multicollinearity, heteroscedasticity, and autocorrelation are not present (see Section 4-6). If any of these problems are detected from the tests, measures (also discussed in Section 4-6) must be applied to try to overcome these problems. In general, heteroscedasticity is more likely to be present if cross-sectional data are used to estimate demand, while autocorrelation is more likely to be prevalent when time-series data are used. Case Study 4-4 gives the results of the actual econometric estimation of the demand for air travel over the Atlantic.

CASE STUDY 4-4
Estimation of the Demand for Air Travel over the North Atlantic

J. M. Cigliano estimated the demand for air travel between the United States and Europe and between Canada and Europe, from 1965 to 1978. In what follows, we examine the demand for air travel between the United States and Europe only. Results are similar for air travel between Canada and Europe. Cigliano estimated the following regression equation (the symbols for the variables have been changed to simplify the presentation):

$$\ln Q_t = 2.737 \qquad\qquad\qquad [4\text{-}30]$$
$$-1.247 \ln P_t + 1.905 \ln GNP_t$$
$$\quad(-5.071)\qquad\quad(7.286)$$
$$\bar{R}^2 = 0.97 \qquad D\text{–}W = 1.83$$

where Q_t = number of passengers per year traveling between the United States and Europe from 1965 to 1978 on IATA (International Air Transport Association) carriers, in thousands

P_t = average yearly airfare between New York and London (weighted by the seasonal distribution of traffic and adjusted for inflation)

GNP_t = U.S. gross national product in each year, adjusted for inflation

The numbers in parentheses below the estimated slope coefficients refer to the estimated t statistics or ratios.

Since all the variables in demand Equation 4-30 have been transformed into natural logarithms (a simple command in the regression package accomplished this) and the regression is run on the transformed variables, the estimated coefficients give demand elasticities directly. Specifically, the estimated coefficient of -1.247 for variable $\ln P_t$ gives the price elasticity of demand, while the estimated coefficient of 1.905 for variable $\ln GNP_t$ gives the GNP (income) elasticity of demand. These indicate, respectively, that a 10 percent increase in real average airfares would reduce the number of airline passengers by 12.47 percent, while a 10 percent rise in real GNP in the United States would increase the number of passengers by 19.05 percent. Thus, the demand for air travel between the United States and Europe is price elastic and is a luxury. Also to be noted is that since most airlines were flying at only $\frac{2}{3}$

to $\frac{4}{5}$ capacity during the period of the analysis, by lowering fares, airlines increased total revenue without incurring much higher costs (they simply filled empty seats), so that their profits increased.

We can have a great deal of confidence in the above regression results because (1) the signs of the estimated slope coefficients (elasticities) are as postulated by demand theory, (2) the very high t statistics reported below the estimated slope coefficients indicate that both are statistically significant at better than the 1 percent level, (3) the adjusted coefficient of determination ($\bar{R}^2$) indicates that airfares and GNP "explain" 97 percent of the variation in the log of the number of passengers flying between New York and London. Furthermore, (4) the multicollinearity problem between

the two independent variables seems to have been avoided by deflating both airfares and GNP by the price index, and (5) the value of the Durbin–Watson (D–W) statistic indicates that the hypothesis of no autocorrelation cannot be rejected.*

Cigliano also found that the price elasticity of demand was much lower for first-class air travel (-0.447) than for economy-class travel (-1.826) and that within the economy class, it was much higher for short trips (-2.181), where good alternatives exist (automobile, bus, train), than for long trips. This meant that airlines increased their total revenues and profits by keeping the class distinctions and by charging relatively lower fares for short trips (to meet the competition from other modes of transportation) than for long trips.

Source: J. M. Cigliano, "Price and Income Elasticities for Airline Travel: The North Atlantic Market," *Business Economics* (September 1980), pp. 17–21.
* Even though the number of observations for each variable is only 14 and Table C-4 in the Appendix starts from 15 observations, one can project that the D–W value obtained by the regression is well outside the critical value of d_U in Table C-4 for $n = 14$ (the number of observations) and $k' = 2$ (the number of explanatory variables).

4-8 ESTIMATING THE DEMAND FOR U.S. IMPORTS AND EXPORTS

Just like the demand for any domestic good or service (see Equation 4-26), the demand for U.S. imports (Q_M) is a function of the dollar price of the imported commodity or service (P_M), U.S. consumers' incomes (I), the number of U.S. consumers (N), the dollar price of related (i.e., substitute and complementary) commodities or services in the United States (P_Y), the tastes of U.S. consumers (T), and all the other variables that are thought to be important determinants of the demand for the particular imported commodity or service under study. That is,

$$Q_M = f(P_M, I, N, P_Y, T, \ldots) \qquad [4\text{-}31]$$

Note, however, that the dollar price of U.S. imports depends on prices in exporting nations (expressed in foreign currencies) and on the rate of exchange between the dollar and foreign currencies. For example, the dollar price of U.S. imports from the United Kingdom depends on the pound price of the commodity or service in the United Kingdom and the exchange rate between the dollar and the pound. If the exchange rate between the U.S. dollar and the British pound sterling (£) is 2, this means that the price of a DVD that costs £10 in the United Kingdom is $20 to U.S. consumers. If the price of the DVD falls to £5 in the United Kingdom, U.S. consumers will have to pay only $10 for the DVD. The price of the British DVD to U.S. consumers can also fall to $10, even if the price remains at £10 in the United Kingdom, if the exchange rate between the dollar and the pound falls from $2 to £1 to $1 to £1. Exchange rates change frequently in the real world.[21]

[21] How exchange rates are determined and the reasons why they change are not important at this point and will be explained in Chapter 8.

What is important is that the *dollar* price of U.S. imports can change because of a change in foreign-currency prices abroad or because of a change in exchange rates. Regardless of the reason for the change in the price of U.S. imports, we can measure the change in the quantity of U.S. imports resulting from a change in their *dollar* price by the price elasticity of demand for imports. Similarly, we can measure the change in the quantity of U.S. exports resulting from a change in their *dollar* price by the price elasticity of demand for exports. In addition, we can measure the increase in the demand for imports of any nation resulting from an increase in the income or GDP in the nation by the income elasticity of demand of imports (see Case Study 4-5).

The demand for U.S. imports and exports also depends on the price of substitute and complementary commodities, as well as tastes in the United States and abroad. The ability to substitute domestic for foreign goods and services at home and abroad has reached an all-time high and is expected to continue to increase in the future because of (1) the decline in transportation costs for most products, (2) increased knowledge of foreign products due to an international information revolution, (3) global advertising campaigns by multinational corporations, (4) the explosion of international travel, and (5) the rapid convergence of tastes internationally.

CASE STUDY 4-5
Price and Income Elasticities of Imports and Exports in the Real World

The price elasticity of demand for U.S. manufactured imports has been estimated to be about 1.06, both in the short run and in the long run. That is, a 1 percent decline in the dollar price of U.S. imports of manufactured goods can be expected to lead to a 1.06 percent increase in the quantity demanded and thus leave their dollar value practically unchanged in the short run, as well as in the long run.

On the other hand, the price elasticity of demand for U.S. exports of manufactured goods was estimated to be 0.48 in the short run and 1.67 in the long run. This means that a 1 percent decline in the price of U.S. exports can be expected to lead to an increase in the quantity of U.S. manufactured goods exports of 0.48 percent within a year or two of the price change and 1.67 percent in the long run (i.e., in a period of five years or so). Thus, a decline in U.S. export prices leads to U.S. earnings from manufactured exports to fall in the short run and to rise in the long run.

Finally, the income elasticity of demand for imports was estimated to be 1.94 in the United States. This means that a 1 percent increase in U.S. income or GNP can be expected to lead to an increase of about 1.94 percent in U.S. imports. Thus, U.S. imports are normal goods and can be regarded as luxuries. The income elasticity of imports for the other six largest industrial countries (Japan, Germany, France, the United Kingdom, Italy, and Canada) ranges from 0.35 for Japan to 2.51 for the United Kingdom. On the other hand, the income elasticity of exports ranges from 0.80 for the United States to 1.60 for Italy.

The price and income elasticities of imports and exports are important to individual consumers and producers in the United States and abroad, and affect the level of economic activity in all the nations engaging in international trade.

Source: D. Salvatore, *International Economics,* 8th ed. (Hoboken, N.J.: Wiley, 2004), chaps. 16 and 17.

CASE STUDY 4-6
The Major Commodity Exports and Imports of the United States

Table 4-8 gives the values of the major commodity exports and imports of the United States in 2004. The major U.S. exports were automotive vehicles, parts, and engines (mostly to Canada, as part of the U.S.–Canada automotive agreement); chemicals; industrial, agricultural, and service machinery; aircraft; agricultural products (a great deal of which were grains); and semiconductors. Other large U.S. exports were metals and nonmetallic products, computers, electric gener-

ating machinery, telecommunications equipment, and scientific equipment. U.S. imports were dominated by automobile imports (mostly from Japan), petroleum products, computers, household appliances, textiles, metals and nonmetallic products, and industrial, agricultural, and service machinery. Also large were imports of agricultural products, chemicals, building materials, TV and video receivers, telecommunications equipment, and aircraft.

TABLE 4-8 Major U.S. Commodity Exports and Imports in 2004 (in billions of dollars)

Exports		Imports	
Product	**Value**	**Product**	**Value**
Automotive vehicles, parts, and engines	$89.3	Automotive vehicles, parts, and engines	$228.2
Chemicals, excluding medicinals	68.6	Petroleum products	180.5
Industrial, agricultural, and service industry machinery	52.9	Computers, peripherals, and parts	88.6
Civilian aircraft, engines, and parts	50.0	Household appliances	87.4
Agricultural products	51.0	Textiles	74.6
of which grains	17.1	Metals and nonmetallic products	72.8
Semiconductors	48.1	Industrial, agricultural, and service industry machinery	62.0
Metals and nonmetallic products	43.0	Agricultural products	46.5
Computers, peripherals, and parts	42.8	Chemicals, excluding medicinals	42.3
Electric generating machinery	31.3	Building materials, except metals	32.0
Telecommunications equipment	24.5	TV and video receivers	30.9
Scientific, hospital, and medical equipment	23.9	Telecommunications equipment	29.4
		Semiconductors	26.7
		Civilian aircraft, engines, and parts	24.3

Source: U.S. Department of Commerce, *Survey of Current Business* (Washington, D.C.: Government Printing Office, July 2005), pp. 96–99.

CASE STUDY 4-7
The Major Trade Partners of the United States

Table 4-9 gives data on the value and the percentage of total U.S. exports and imports of America's top trade partners in 2004. The table shows that Canada, Mexico, Japan, and China are, by far, the largest trade partners of the United States. These four nations accounted for 48.0 percent of total U.S. exports and 50.5 percent of total U.S. imports in 2004. The closeness of Canada and Mexico to the United States goes a long way toward explaining their top rankings. Faraway Japan, on the other hand, is the

world's second largest industrial economy and one of the largest traders. U.S. imports from China, however, have increased so rapidly during the past few years that it now represents the second largest import market for the United States, surpassing Mexico and Japan. Together, the largest 12 U.S. export markets absorbed 72.1 percent of total U.S. exports, while the 12 largest exporters to the United States accounted for 71.3 percent of total U.S. imports in 2004.

TABLE 4-9	America's Top Trade Partners in 2004					
U.S. Exports to				**U.S. Imports from**		
Country	Value (billion dollars)	Percent of Total		Country	Value (billion dollars)	Percent of Total
Canada	$190.0	23.5		Canada	$259.0	17.6
Mexico	110.7	13.7		China	196.7	13.4
Japan	52.3	6.5		Mexico	157.1	10.7
U.K.	35.1	4.3		Japan	129.8	8.8
China	34.6	4.3		Germany	77.1	5.2
Germany	30.8	3.8		S. Korea	46.2	3.1
S. Korea	25.7	3.2		U.K.	46.0	3.1
Netherlands	24.1	3.0		Taiwan	34.6	2.3
Taiwan	21.3	2.6		France	31.6	2.1
France	21.1	2.6		Italy	28.1	1.9
Singapore	19.3	2.4		Venezuela	24.9	1.7
Belgium	17.4	2.2		Brazil	21.2	1.4

Source: U.S. Department of Commerce, *Survey of Current Business* (Washington, D.C.: Government Printing Office, July 2005), pp. 92–94.

For homogeneous products such as a particular grade of wheat and steel, and for many industrial products with precise specifications such as computer chips, fiber optics, and specialized machinery, substitutability between domestic and foreign products is almost perfect. Here, a small price difference can lead quickly to large shifts in sales from domestic to foreign sources, and vice versa. Indeed, so fluid is the market for such products that

CASE STUDY 4-8
The Top U.S. International Exporters

Table 4-10 gives data on the top U.S. industrial exporters in 2003. They range from Ford, IBM, General Electric, and General Motors, each of which exported more than $50 billion in 2003, to United Technologies with $14.3 billion in exports. As a percentage of total company sales, IBM, Dow Chemicals, and Hewlett-Packard came first with exports exceed-ing 60 percent of total sales, while General Motors was last with exports of 27.8 percent of total sales. Note that most U.S. top exporters also have production facilities abroad, so their total sales abroad are much higher than indicated by their exports. In addition, with parts or components of many products being imported, it is impossible to determine the *net* value of exports.

TABLE 4-10	America's Top International Exporters		
Company	**Major Exports**	**Value of Exports (billion dollars)**	**Percent of Total Sales**
Ford Motors	Motor vehicles	60.8	37.0
IBM	Electrical and electronic equipment	55.4	61.0
General Electric	Electrical and electronic equipment	54.1	40.3
General Motors	Motor vehicles	51.6	27.8
Hewlett-Packard	Electrical and electronic equipment	43.8	60.0
Altria Group	Tobacco	34.4	56.6
Procter & Gamble	Chemicals/cosmetics	27.7	53.9
Dow Chemical	Chemicals	19.8	60.7
Pfizer	Pharmaceuticals	18.3	40.6
Motorola	Electronics	18.0	66.5
Du Pont	Chemicals	14.9	55.1
United Technologies	Transport equipment	14.3	45.2

Source: United Nations, *World Investment Report* (New York: United Nations, 2005), pp. 267–269.

governments often step in to protect these industries from foreign competition.[22] Even for differentiated products, such as automobiles and motorcycles, computers and copiers, watches and cameras, TV films and TV programs, soft drinks and cigarettes, soaps and detergents, commercial and military aircraft, and most other products that are similar but not identical, substitutability between domestic and foreign products is very high and rising. Thus, a change in the price of substitute and complementary commodities or tastes at home or abroad will significantly affect the demand for imports and exports.

Case Study 4-6 presents data on the major commodity exports and imports of the United States, Case Study 4-7 gives the major trade partners of the United States, and Case Study 4-8 shows the top U.S. international exporters.

---

[22] D. Salvatore, *International Economics,* 8th ed. (Hoboken, N.J: Wiley, 2004), chaps. 17 and 18.

SUMMARY

1. Joining the price-quantity observations on a graph does not usually generate the demand curve for a commodity. The reason is that each price-quantity observation is the joint result (intersection) of a different (but unobserved) demand and supply curve for the commodity. The difficulty of deriving the demand curve for a commodity from observed price-quantity points is called the *identification problem.* To derive the demand curve for a commodity from the price-quantity data points, we allow the supply curve to shift but correct for the forces that cause the demand curve to shift. This is done by regression analysis.

2. Besides regression analysis, a firm can estimate demand by consumer surveys, consumer clinics, and market experiments. Consumer surveys involve questioning a sample of consumers about how they would respond to particular changes in the price and other determinants of the demand for the commodity. Consumer clinics are laboratory experiments in which the participants are given a sum of money and asked to spend it in a simulated store to see how they react to changes in price, product packaging, displays, price of competing products, and other factors affecting demand. With market experiments, the firm attempts to estimate the demand for the commodity by changing price and other determinants of demand in the actual marketplace. Although these methods are sometimes the only ones available for estimating demand, they face serious shortcomings.

3. Regression analysis is a statistical technique for estimating the quantitative relationship between the economic variable that we seek to explain (the dependent variable) and one or more independent or explanatory variables. When there is only one independent or explanatory variable, we have simple regression analysis. Simple regression analysis usually begins by plotting the set of X and Y values on a scatter diagram and determining by inspection if there exists an approximate linear relationship. However, estimating the regression line by simply drawing a line between the observation points is imprecise and subjective.

4. The objective of regression analysis is to obtain estimates of a (the vertical intercept) and b (the slope) in order to derive the regression line that best fits the data points (in the sense that the sum of the squared vertical deviations of each observed point from the line is a minimum). A parameter estimate is statistically significant if the value of the calculated t statistic exceeds the critical value found from the table of the t distribution, at the appropriate degree of significance (usually 5 percent) and degrees of freedom. The t statistic is given by the estimated value of the parameter divided by the standard error (deviation) of the estimate. The degrees of freedom equal the sample size minus the number of parameters estimated. We can also construct confidence intervals for the true parameter from the estimated parameter. The coefficient of determination (R^2) measures the proportion of the explained to the total variation in the dependent variable in the regression analysis. The coefficient of correlation (r) measures the degree of association or covariation between variables. Regression analysis implies but does not prove causality.

5. When the dependent variable that we seek to explain is hypothesized to depend on more than one independent variable, we have multiple regression analysis. Here the calculations are invariably done with computers, which also provide the statistics to conduct statistical tests. In order to take into consideration the reduction in the degrees of freedom as additional independent variables are included in the regression, we calculate the adjusted R^2, $\bar{R}^2$. The analysis of variance can be used to test the overall explanatory power of the entire regression. This uses the F statistic, which is the ratio of the explained variance divided by $k - 1$ df to the unexplained variance divided by $n - k$ df, where k is the number of estimated parameters and n is the number of observations. If the value of the F statistic exceeds the critical value from the F table with $k - 1$ and $n - k$ df, we accept the hypothesis at the specified level of statistical significance that not all the regression coefficients are zero. The standard error of the regression can be used to make interval estimates or forecasts of the dependent variable.

6. Regression analysis may face some serious problems. Multicollinearity arises when two or more explanatory variables in the regression are highly correlated. This may lead to insignificant

coefficients, even though $\bar{R}^2$ may be very high. This could be overcome by increasing the sample size, using a priori information, transforming the function, or dropping one of the highly collinear variables. Heteroscedasticity arises in cross-sectional data when the error term is not constant. This leads to biased standard errors and incorrect statistical tests. It could be corrected by using the log of the variable that causes the problem or by weighted least squares. Autocorrelation often arises in time-series data when consecutive errors have the same sign or change sign frequently. This leads to exaggerated t statistics and unreliable $\bar{R}^2$ and F statistics. Autocorrelation can be detected by the Durbin–Watson test and may be corrected by including a time trend or an important missing variable in the regression, using a nonlinear form, running the regression on first differences in the variables, or with more complex techniques.

7. The process of estimating a demand equation by regression analysis involves four steps. First, the model must be specified. This involves determining the variables to include in the demand equation. These are dictated by demand theory and knowledge of the market for the commodity. Second, the data on each variable or its proxy must be obtained. Third, the researcher must decide on the functional form of the demand equation. The linear and the power-function formulations are most common, and often both are tried. In the power-function formulation, the estimated slope coefficients refer to elasticities rather than to marginal changes (as in the linear model). Finally, the regression results must be evaluated as to the sign of the estimated slope coefficients, the statistical significance of the coefficients, and the proportion of the total variation explained and to ensure that multicollinearity, heteroscedasticity, and autocorrelation do not bias the results.

8. As in the case of purely domestic goods and services, we can estimate the demand for imports and exports and obtain from them price and income elasticities. The only difference is that the domestic-currency prices of imports depend on foreign-currency prices and the exchange rate. The ability to substitute domestic for foreign goods and services is very high and increasing in today's world.

DISCUSSION QUESTIONS

1. (a) Why is the line connecting the observed price-quantity data points usually not the demand curve for the commodity? (b) How is the demand curve for a commodity derived or identified from observed price-quantity data points?

2. What are the major advantages and disadvantages of estimating demand by consumer surveys?

3. What are the major advantages and disadvantages of estimating demand by consumer clinics?

4. What are the major advantages and disadvantages of estimating demand by market experiments?

5. (a) What are the main advantages of regression analysis over the marketing research approaches of estimating demand? (b) What, if any, residual usefulness to the manager and economist do marketing research approaches have in demand estimation?

6. (a) What steps are usually involved in the estimation of a demand equation by regression analysis? (b) How does the researcher determine the demand model to estimate?

7. (a) How does a researcher go about obtaining the data to estimate a demand equation by regression analysis? (b) What are some of the most useful sources of published data in the United States today?

8. (a) How does the researcher determine the form of the demand equation to be estimated? (b) How are the estimated slope coefficients of the two most common forms of the demand equation interpreted?

9. (a) Why is it important to conduct a significance test of an estimated parameter? (b) How is this conducted? (c) What is meant by a confidence interval? (d) How is it determined?

10. (a) How can we test the overall explanatory power of a regression? (b) What is meant by the total, explained, and unexplained variation in the dependent variable? How are they measured? (c) What is meant by the coefficient of correlation?

11. Does regression analysis imply causality? Explain.

12. (a) What is the use of analysis of variance?
    (b) How is the analysis of variance conducted?
    (c) What is the relationship between the analysis of variance and the coefficient of determination?

13. With respect to multicollinearity, explain (a) what it is and why it is a problem, (b) how it can be detected, and (c) how it can be overcome.

14. With respect to autocorrelation, explain (a) what it is and why it is a problem, (b) how it can be detected, and (c) how it can be overcome.

15. (a) On what does the domestic-currency price of a nation's imports depend? (b) What would happen to the domestic-currency price of a nation's imports if the foreign-currency price of the nation's imports increases and the nation's currency depreciates (i.e., loses value in relation to the foreign currency)?

PROBLEMS

1. With the aid of a figure, show why (a) if the observed price-quantity data points fall more or less downward and to the right, we can derive the demand curve for the commodity, but (b) if the observed price-quantity data points are clustered or bunched together, we cannot derive the demand curve for the commodity.

*2. Draw two figures: (a) one showing that if the demand curve did not shift but the supply curve did, we could derive the demand curve for the commodity by simply connecting the observed price-quantity data points and (b) the other showing that if the supply curve did not shift but the demand curve did, we could derive the supply curve of the commodity by simply connecting the observed price-quantity data points. (c) In which sector of the economy is each of these cases most likely to occur? Why?

*3. From Table 4-1 in the text, which gives the price elasticity of demand for Florida Indian River oranges, Florida interior oranges, and California oranges, as well as the cross-price elasticities among them, determine (a) by how much the quantity demanded of each type of orange would change if its price were reduced by 10 percent, (b) whether the sellers' total revenues would increase, decrease, or remain unchanged with the 10 percent decrease in price, and (c) whether the sellers' profits would increase, decrease, or remain unchanged with the 10 percent decrease in price.

4. From Table 4-1 in the text, determine by how much the demand for Florida Indian River oranges would change as a result of a 10 percent increase in the price of Florida interior oranges, and vice versa.

*5. (a) Estimate by hand calculation the regression equation of the firm's sales revenue (Y) on its quality control expenditure (call it Z) for the data given in Table 4-6. (b) Plot the estimated regression line on a graph that also shows the data points and the errors. (c) What would be the sales revenue of the firm when the firm's expenditure on quality control is $2 million per year? $9 million per year? Why would you expect these results to be greatly biased?

*6. From the following table giving the quantity demanded of a commodity (Y), its price (X_1), and consumer income (X_2) from 1986 to 2005, (a) estimate the regression equation of Y on X_1 and X_2, (b) test at the 5 percent level for the statistical significance of the slope parameters, (c) find the unadjusted and the adjusted coefficients of determination, and (d) test at the 5 percent level for the overall statistical significance of the regression. Show all your results to three decimal places. [If you have not used the computer before, ask a fellow student to show you how to run the regression. If this is not possible, from the answer to part (a) of this question provided at the end of the book, answer parts (b), (c), and (d).]

Year	Y	X_1	X_1
1986	72	$10	$2,000
1987	81	9	2,100
1988	90	10	2,210
1989	99	9	2,305
1990	108	8	2,407
1991	126	7	2,500
1992	117	7	2,610

Year	Y	X_1	X_1
1993	117	9	2,698
1994	135	6	2,801
1995	135	6	2,921
1996	144	6	3,000
1997	180	4	3,099
1998	162	5	3,201
1999	171	4	3,308
2000	153	5	3,397
2001	180	4	3,501
2002	171	5	3,689
2003	180	4	3,800
2004	198	4	3,896
2005	189	4	3,989

7. If the regression of Y on X_1 and X_2 is run in double-log form for the data of Problem 6, the results are as follows:

$$\ln Y_t = -0.533 - 0.389 \ln X_{1t} + 0.769 \ln X_{2t}$$
$$(-3.304) \qquad (4.042)$$
$$\bar{R}^2 = 0.95054 \qquad F = 183.582$$

Compare the above results with those of Problem 6. Which are better? Why?

8. In a study published in 1980, B. B. Gibson estimated the following price and income elasticities of demand for six types of public goods:

State Activity	Price Elasticity	Income Elasticity
Aid to needy people	−0.83	0.26
Pollution control	−0.99	0.77
Colleges and universities	−0.87	0.92
Elementary school aid	−1.16	1.14
Parks and recreational areas	−1.02	1.06
Highway construction and maintenance	−1.09	0.99

Source: B. B. Gibson, "Estimating Demand Elasticities for Public Goods from Survey Data," *American Economic Review* (December 1980), pp. 1068–1076.

(*a*) Do these public goods conform to the law of demand? For which public goods is demand price elastic? (*b*) What types of goods are these public goods? (*c*) If the price or cost of college and university education increased by 10 percent and, at the same time, incomes also increased by 10 percent, what would be the change in the demand for college and university education?

9. Following are the results of four regressions, in which M refers to the imports and Y to the GNP of the United States (both in billions of current dollars) from 1985 to 2000, and P is the consumer price index. Theory postulates that imports are directly related to the level of GNP and domestic prices.

(1) $\hat{M} = -108.20 + 0.045Y + 0.931P$
$$(1.232) \quad (1.844)$$
$$R^2 = 0.9894 \quad \bar{R}^2 = 0.9877 \quad F = 604.621$$

(2) $\hat{M} = -69.97 + 0.112Y$
$$(32.08)$$
$$R^2 = 0.9866 \quad F = 1029.40$$

(3) $\hat{M} = -555.84 - 13.81P$
$$(42.18)$$
$$R^2 = 0.9922 \quad F = 1778.84$$

(4) $\hat{M/P} = -1.39 + 0.202Y/P$
$$(12.22)$$
$$R^2 = 0.9142 \quad F = 149.25$$

Explain (*a*) why the first three regression results indicate the presence of serious multicollinearity and (*b*) how the fourth regression attempts to overcome the multicollinearity problem.

10. In their volume, *Consumer Demand in the United States: Analyses and Projections* (Cambridge, Mass.: Harvard University Press, 1970), p. 119, H. S. Houthakker and L. D. Taylor presented the following results for their estimated demand equation for local bus service over the period from 1929 to 1961 (excluding the 1942 through 1945 war years) in the United States:

$$Q_t = 22.819 + 0.0159X_t - 0.1156P_t$$
$$(12.23) \qquad (16.84)$$
$$-86.106S_t - 0.9841D_t$$
$$(15.83) \qquad (3.22)$$
$$R^2 = 0.996 \qquad D\text{–}W = 1.11$$

where Q_t = per capita personal consumption expenditures on bus transportation during year t, at 1954 prices

X_t = total per capita consumption expenditures during year t, at 1954 prices

P_t = relative price of bus transportation in year t, at 1954 prices

S_t = car stock per capita in year t

D_t = dummy variable to separate pre– from post–World War II years; $D_t = 0$ for years 1929 to 1941 and $D_t = 1$ for years 1946 to 1961

The numbers in parentheses below the estimated slope coefficients refer to the estimated t values.

Evaluate the above results (*a*) in terms of the signs and values of the coefficients, (*b*) for the statistical significance of the coefficients and the explanatory power of the regression, and (*c*) for the presence of possible econometric problems.

Note that a dummy variable is added to (if positive) or subtracted from (if negative) the value of the constant of the regression, thus causing the regression line to shift up or shift down, respectively, for the years to which the dummy variable refers. For a more detailed discussion of dummy variables, see D. Salvatore and D. Reagle, *Statistics and Econometrics,* 2nd ed. (New York: McGraw-Hill, 2002, sec. 8.2), or any other introductory econometrics text.

11. Suppose that during a given year: (1) the price of TV sets increases by 4 percent in Japan, (2) the dollar depreciates by 5 percent with respect to the yen (the Japanese currency), (3) consumer incomes in the United States increase by 3 percent, (4) the price elasticity of demand for imported TV sets in the United States is 1.5, and (5) consumers' income elasticity of demand for TV sets in the United States is 2. (*a*) If the price of the imported TV set was $300 in the United States at the beginning of the year, approximately how much would you expect the price of the same imported TV set to be in the United States at the end of the year? (*b*) By how much would the quantity demanded of imported TV sets in the United States change as a result of the change in price only? (*c*) By how much would the demand for imported TV sets in the United States change as a result of the increase in consumer income alone? (*d*) By how much would the demand for imported TV sets in the United States change as a result of both the change in price and in incomes?

12. Redo Problem 11 for a dollar appreciation (instead of a dollar depreciation) of 5 percent.

13. Suppose that the statistical department of the California Power Company estimated that the price elasticity of demand for household natural gas is

−1.4 in the short run and −2.1 in the long run, the income elasticity of demand is 1.2, the cross-price elasticity of demand for household gas and electricity is 0.8, and the elasticity of demand for household gas with respect to population is 1.0. Determine the change in the demand for household natural gas (*a*) in the short run and (*b*) in the long run if all the variables increase by 10 percent.

14. How much confidence should the management of the California Power Company have in the estimates obtained from the solution of Problem 13? What questions should the management ask of its statistical department regarding the estimates it provided management?

15. **Integrating Problem**

Starting with the data for Problem 6 and the data on the price of a related commodity for the years 1986 to 2005 given below, we estimated the regression for the quantity demanded of a commodity (which we now relabel $\hat{Q}_X$), on the price of the commodity (which we now label P_X), consumer income (which we now label Y), and the price of the related commodity (P_Z), and we obtained the following results. (If you can, run this regression yourself; you should get results identical or very similar to those given below.)

Year	1986	1987	1988	1989	1990
P_Z ($)	14	15	15	16	17
Year	1991	1992	1993	1994	1995
P_Z ($)	18	17	18	19	20
Year	1996	1997	1998	1999	2000
P_Z ($)	20	19	21	21	22
Year	2001	2002	2003	2004	2005
P_Z ($)	23	23	24	25	25

$$\hat{Q}_X = 121.86 - 9.50P_X + 0.04Y - 2.21P_Z$$
$$(-5.12) \quad (2.18) \quad (-0.68)$$
$$R^2 = 0.9633 \quad F = 167.33 \quad D\text{–}W = 2.38$$

(*a*) Explain why you think we have chosen to include the price of commodity Z in the above regression. (*b*) Evaluate the above regression results. (*c*) What type of commodity is Z? Can you be sure?

APPENDIX TO CHAPTER 4: REGRESSION ANALYSIS WITH EXCEL

In this appendix we show how to run the simple and multiple regression analyses discussed in this chapter using the Microsoft Excel Program.

Simple Regression

We will use the data from Table 4-2 in the text to demonstrate how to use Excel to run the simple regression discussed in Section 4-4. Remember that in Table 4-2, we had for our dependent variable the amount of sales revenue and the independent variable was the amount of advertising expenditures.

Step One: Enter the data.   Click on Microsoft Excel on your PC. A worksheet opens up for you to enter the data. The data for both variables should be inputted in to Excel in columns. It is recommended to include labels on top of the data columns (as indicated on the next page).

Step Two: Start the regression program.   There may be a few differences in starting this part, depending on the version of Excel that you are using. But in general they will all follow the same steps: click on Tools, a menu will then drop down; click on Data Analysis, scroll, and look for Regression; then click OK. A dialogue box should appear. The next step will show you how to navigate through it.

Step Three: Selecting the data to be used.   There are two important fields that you have to fill in, "Y Input Range" and "X Input Range." The Y Input Range refers to our dependent variable, which in this case is the amount of sales revenue. To select the data simply click on D2 and highlight the whole area down to D12. The entry in the box should appear as $D$2:$D$12. Since we included the label, we must make sure to click on the label box so that it does not cause us any problems. For the independent variable, the data are located from cells C2 to C12; again we will include the labels. To input the data simply repeat the procedure we did for the dependent variable.

TABLE 4-11	Advertising Expenditure and Sales Revenue of Firms (millions of dollars)

	A	B	C	D	E
1					
2		Year	Advertising Expenditure (X)	Sales Revenue (Y)	
3		1	10	44	
4		2	9	40	
5		3	11	42	
6		4	12	46	
7		5	11	48	
8		6	12	52	
9		7	13	54	
10		8	13	58	
11		9	14	56	
12		10	15	60	
13					
14					
15					

Step Four: Inform the program where to print the output.   Now that it knows the data it will use for the regression, it will then ask you where to place the output. This is also known as "Output Range." You can choose to simply type the cell you want the output to appear (you can also click on the cell) or you can have it put on a separate spreadsheet. A word of caution: if you decide to choose the former option, make sure it does not contain any data that were used to run the regression.

Step Five: Run the regression.   Simply click OK. You will then be directed to the output table from the regression (as shown after the Excel data table).

TABLE 4-12   Simple Regression Printout

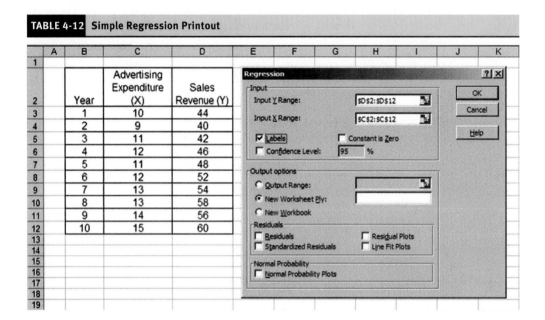

	A	B	C	D	E	F	G	H	I
1	SUMMARY OUTPUT								
2									
3	*Regression Statistics*								
4	Multiple R	0.922611577							
5	R Square	0.851212121							
6	Adjusted R Square	0.832613636							
7	Standard Error	2.860652606							
8	Observations	10							
9									
10	ANOVA								
11		*df*	*SS*	*MS*	*F*	*Significance F*			
12	Regression	1	374.5333333	374.5333333	45.76782077	0.000142813			
13	Residual	8	65.46666667	8.183333333					
14	Total	9	440						
15									
16		*Coefficients*	*Standard Error*	*t Stat*	*P-value*	*Lower 95%*	*Upper 95%*	*Lower 95.0%*	*Upper 95.0%*
17	Intercept	7.6	6.332324481	1.200191181	0.264396906	-7.002375882	22.20237588	-7.002375882	22.20237588
18	Advertising Expenditure (X)	3.533333333	0.522281321	6.76519185	0.000142813	2.32894967	4.737716997	2.32894967	4.737716997
19									

Multiple Regression Analysis

Multiple regression analysis will involve the same steps as when performing a simple regression. In our example, advertising and quality control will be our independent variables, with sales revenue our dependent variable. In inputting the data, all values of our independent values must be in adjacent columns. After bringing up the regression menu, make sure that the highlighted column for the X range is $D$2:$E$12. The regression program recognizes that each column of data is a separate series of the independent variable. Finally, you will then have to choose the output range, after which you execute the program by clicking on OK. Following are the Excel spreadsheet tables of the results for the multiple regression discussed in Section 4-5.

TABLE 4-13 Multiple Regression Printout

	A	B	C	D	E	F	G	H	I	J	K	L
1												
2		Year	Sales Revenue (Y)	Advertising (X1)	Quality Control (X2)	Regression						?|X
3		1	44	10	3	Input						
4		2	40	9	4	Input Y Range:		$C$2:$C$12			OK	
5		3	42	11	3						Cancel	
6		4	46	12	3	Input X Range:		$D$2:$E$12				
7		5	48	11	4							
8		6	52	12	5	☑ Labels		☐ Constant is Zero			Help	
9		7	54	13	6	☐ Confidence Level:	95	%				
10		8	58	13	7							
11		9	56	14	7	Output options						
12		10	60	15	8	○ Output Range:						
13						◉ New Worksheet Ply:						
14						○ New Workbook						
15						Residuals						
16						☐ Residuals		☐ Residual Plots				
17						☐ Standardized Residuals		☐ Line Fit Plots				
18												
19												
20						Normal Probability						
21						☐ Normal Probability Plots						
22												
23												
24												

	A	B	C	D	E	F	G	H	I
1	SUMMARY OUTPUT								
2									
3	*Regression Statistics*								
4	Multiple R	0.96444474							
5	R Square	0.93015365							
6	Adjusted R Square	0.91019755							
7	Standard Error	2.09531431							
8	Observations	10							
9									
10	ANOVA								
11		df	SS	MS	F	Significance F			
12	Regression	2	409.2676056	204.633803	46.6099908	9.0054E-05			
13	Residual	7	30.73239437	4.39034205					
14	Total	9	440						
15									
16		Coefficients	Standard Error	t Stat	P-value	Lower 95%	Upper 95%	Lower 95.0%	Upper 95.0%
17	Intercept	17.943662	5.919135604	3.03146661	0.01907509	3.947140388	31.940184	3.94714039	31.9401836
18	Advertising (X1)	1.87323944	0.703339483	2.66335032	0.03230973	0.210107028	3.5363718	0.21010703	3.53637185
19	Quality Control (X2)	1.91549296	0.681005526	2.81274216	0.02604318	0.305171927	3.525814	0.30517193	3.52581399
20									

SUPPLEMENTARY READINGS

For a classical discussion on demand estimation, see:

Schultz, Henry, *Theory and Measurement of Demand* (Chicago: University of Chicago Press, 1964).

Working, E. J., "What Do Statistical 'Demand Curves' Show?" *Quarterly Journal of Economics* (1927).

The use of regression analysis in demand estimation is discussed in:

Berk, K. N., and P. Carey, *Data Analysis with Microsoft Excel* (Duxbury, Mass: Duxbury Press, 1995).

Pindyck, Robert S., and Daniel L. Rubinfeld, *Econometric Models and Economic Forecasts* (Boston: McGraw-Hill, 1998).

Salvatore, Dominick, and Derrick Reagle, *Theory and Problems of Statistics and Econometrics,* 2nd ed., Schaum Outline Series (New York: McGraw-Hill, 2002), chaps. 7–10.

A discussion of marketing approaches to demand estimation is found in:

DeJong, Douglas V., and Robert Foresythe, "A Prospective on the Use of Laboratory Market Experimentation in Auditing Research," *Accounting Review* (January 1992).

Montgomery, Alan, "Applying Quantitative Marketing Techniques to the Internet," *Interfaces* (March 2001).

Nevin, J. R., "Laboratory Experiments for Establishing Consumer Demand: A Validation Study," *Journal of Marketing Research* (August 1974).

Peppers, Don, Martha Rogers, and Robert Dorf, *The One-to-One Fieldbook: The Complete Toolkit to Implement a 1-to-1 Marketing Program* (New York: Currency/Doubleday, 1999).

Pessemier, E. A., "An Experimental Method for Estimating Demand," *Journal of Business* (October 1960).

For empirical estimates of demand utilizing regression analysis, see:

Houthakker, H. S., and L. D. Taylor, *Consumer Demand in the United States: Analyses and Projections* (Cambridge, Mass.: Harvard University Press, 1970).

For empirical estimates of demand for exports and imports, see:

Salvatore, Dominick, *International Economics,* 8th ed. (Hoboken, N.J.: Wiley, 2003), chaps. 16 and 17.

INTERNET SITE ADDRESSES

For consumer surveys, see the Council of American Survey Research Organization Web site:

http://www.casro.org

For more information on the major commodity exports and imports of the United States and its major trade partners, see the Bureau of Economic Analysis, the Board of Governors of the Federal Reserve System, and the Economic Report of the President, respectively, at:

http://www.bea.doc.gov

http://www.federalreserve.gov

http://www.gpoaccess.gov/eop/index.html

For the major commodity exports and imports, the major trade partners, and the top U.S. industrial exporters, see:

http://www.bea.doc.gov/bea/pub/0402cont.htm

http://www.esds.ac.uk/international/support/user_guides/imf/dots.asp

The Web sites for the companies listed in Table 4-10 are:

http://www.ford.com

http://www.ibm.com

http://www.ge.com

http://www.gm.com

http://www.hp.com

http://www.altria.com

http://www.pg.com/main.jhtml

http://www.dow.com

http://www.pfizer.com/pfizer.main.jsp

http://www.motorola.com

http://www.dupont.com

http://www.utc.com

CHAPTER 5   Demand Forecasting

CHAPTER OUTLINE

KEY TERMS (in the order of their appearance)

Delphi method	Moving average	Diffusion index
Time-series data	Root-mean-square error (*RMSE*)	Endogenous variables
Time-series analysis	Exponential smoothing	Exogenous variables
Secular trend	Barometric forecasting	Structural (behavioral) equations
Cyclical fluctuations	Leading economic indicators	Definitional equations
Seasonal variation	Coincident indicators	Reduced-form equations
Irregular or random influences	Lagging indicators	
Smoothing techniques	Composite indexes	

Most business decisions are made in the face of risk or uncertainty. A firm must decide how much of each product to produce, what price to charge, and how much to spend on advertising, and it must also plan for the growth of the firm. All these decisions are based on some forecast of the level of future economic activity in general and demand for the firm's product(s) in particular. The aim of economic forecasting is to reduce the risk or uncertainty that the firm faces in its short-term operational decision making and in planning for its long-term growth.

Forecasting the demand and sales of the firm's product usually begins with a macroeconomic forecast of the general level of economic activity for the economy as a whole, or *gross national product.* The reason for this is that the demand and sales of most goods and services are strongly affected by business conditions. For example, the demand and sales of new automobiles, new houses, electricity, and most other goods and services rise and fall with the general level of economic activity. General forecasts of economic conditions for the economy as a whole are routinely provided by the President's Council of Economic Advisers, the U.S. Department of Commerce and other government agencies, economists working for private firms, and firms specializing in and selling their forecasting services to their clients (see Case Study 5-7).

The firm uses these *macroforecasts* of general economic activity as inputs for their *microforecasts* of the industry's and firm's demand and sales. The firm's demand and sales are usually forecast on the basis of its historical market (industry) share and its planned marketing strategy (i.e., the introduction of new products and models, changes in relative prices, and promotional effort). From its general sales forecast, the firm can forecast its sales by product line and region. These, in turn, are used to forecast the firm's operational needs for production (raw material, equipment, warehousing, workers), marketing (distributional network, sales force, promotional campaign), finances (cash flow, profits, need for and cost of outside financing), and personnel throughout the firm. The firm uses long-term forecasts for the economy and the industry to forecast expenditures on plant and equipment to meet its long-term growth plan and strategy.

Forecasting techniques range from very naive ones that require little effort to very sophisticated ones that are costly in terms of time and effort. Some forecasting techniques are basically qualitative, while others are quantitative. Some are based on examining only past values of the data series to forecast its future values; others involve the use of complex models based on a great deal of additional data and relationships. Some are performed by the firm itself; others are purchased from consulting firms. In this chapter we examine qualitative forecasts, time-series forecasts, forecasts based on smoothing techniques such as moving averages, barometric forecasts based on leading indicators, econometric forecasts on econometric models, and input-output forecasting. In each case we examine the advantages and limitations of the particular forecasting technique under study.

Some techniques, such as the barometric method, are more useful for short-term (monthly or quarterly) forecasts, while others, such as the input-output method, are more useful for long-term forecasting of one year or longer. Some may be more appropriate for forecasting at the macrolevel, while others are better for forecasting at the microlevel. Which forecasting method a firm chooses depends on (1) the cost of preparing the forecast and the benefit that results from its use, (2) the lead time in decision making, (3) the time period of the forecast (short term or long term), (4) the level of accuracy required, (5) the quality and availability of the data, and (6) the level of complexity of the relationships to be forecast. In general, the greater the level of accuracy required and the more complex the relationships to be forecast, the more sophisticated and expensive will be the forecasting exercise. By considering the advantages and limitations of each forecasting technique, managers can choose the method or combination of methods most useful to the firm.

5-1 QUALITATIVE FORECASTS

Surveys and opinion polls are often used to make short-term forecasts when quantitative data are not available. These qualitative techniques can also be useful for supplementing quantitative forecasts that anticipate changes in consumer tastes or business expectations about future economic conditions. They can also be invaluable in forecasting the demand for a product that the firm intends to introduce. In this section, we briefly examine forecasting based on surveys, opinion polling, and soliciting a foreign perspective.

Survey Techniques

The rationale for forecasting based on surveys of economic intentions is that many economic decisions are made well in advance of actual expenditures. For example, businesses usually plan to add to plant and equipment long before expenditures are actually incurred. Consumers' decisions to purchase houses, automobiles, TV sets, washing machines, furniture, vacations, education, and other major consumption items are made months or years in advance of actual purchases. Similarly, government agencies prepare budgets and anticipate expenditures a year or more in advance. Surveys of economic intentions, thus, can reveal and can be used to forecast future purchases of capital equipment, inventory changes, and major consumer expenditures.

Some of the best-known surveys used to forecast economic activity in general and economic activity in various sectors of the economy are:

1. *Surveys of business executives' plant and equipment expenditure plans.* These are conducted periodically by McGraw-Hill, Inc., the U.S. Department of Commerce, the Securities and Exchange Commission, and the National Industrial Conference Board. For example, the McGraw-Hill survey accounts for more than 50 percent of expenditures on new plant and equipment, is conducted twice yearly, and is published in *Business Week* (a McGraw-Hill publication). The Department of Commerce survey is even more comprehensive: it is conducted quarterly and is published in its *Survey of Current Business.*

2. *Surveys of plans for inventory changes and sales expectations.* These are conducted periodically by the Department of Commerce, McGraw-Hill, Dun & Bradstreet, and the Institute for Supply Management, and they report on business executives' plans for inventory changes and expectations about future sales.

3. *Surveys of consumers' expenditure plans.* These are conducted periodically by the Bureau of the Census and the Survey Research Center of the University of Michigan, and they report on consumer intentions to purchase specific products, including homes, consumer appliances, and automobiles. These results are often used to forecast consumer demand in general and the level of consumer confidence in the economy.

In general, the record of these surveys has been rather good in forecasting actual expenditures, except during periods of unexpected international political upheavals, such as war or threatened war. When used in conjunction with other quantitative methods, surveys can be very useful in forecasting economic activity in specific sectors of the economy and for the economy as a whole. U.S. firms spend more than $1 billion each year to ask more than 50 million consumers for their opinions on a large variety of products and services. A growing number of consumers, however, are refusing to participate in market-research surveys because of the time involved, the loss of privacy, and the pressure from salespeople operating under the guise of market research. This leads to increasing difficulties in obtaining representative samples and to a trend toward the greater use of observational research (see Section 4-2).

Opinion Polls

Although the results of published surveys of expenditure plans of businesses, consumers, and governments are useful, the firm usually needs specific forecasts of its own sales. The firm's sales are strongly dependent on the general level of economic activity and sales for the industry as a whole, but they also depend on the policies adopted by the firm. The firm can forecast its sales by polling experts within and outside the firm. There are several such polling techniques:

1. *Executive polling.* The firm can poll its top management from its sales, production, finance, and personnel departments on their views on the sales outlook for

the firm during the next quarter or year. Although these personal insights are to a large extent subjective, by averaging the opinions of the experts who are most knowledgeable about the firm and its products, the firm hopes to arrive at a better forecast than would be provided by these experts individually. Outside market experts could also be polled. To avoid a bandwagon effect (whereby the opinions of some experts might be overshadowed by some dominant personality in their midst), the **Delphi method** can be used. Here, experts are polled separately, and then feedback is provided without identifying the expert responsible for a particular opinion. The hope is that through this feedback procedure the experts can arrive at some consensus forecast.

2. *Sales force polling.* This is a forecast of the firm's sales in each region and for each product line; it is based on the opinion of the firm's sales force in the field. These are the people closest to the market, and their opinion of future sales can provide valuable information to the firm's top management.

3. *Consumer intentions polling.* Companies selling automobiles, furniture, household appliances, and other durable goods sometimes poll a sample of potential buyers on their purchasing intentions. Using the results of the poll, the firm can forecast its national sales for different levels of consumers' future disposable income.

Soliciting a Foreign Perspective

Many U.S. firms sell an increasing share of their output abroad and face rising competition at home and abroad from foreign firms. Thus, it becomes increasingly important for them to forecast changes in markets and products abroad because these affect not only the firm's exports but also its competitiveness at home. To get such an international perspective, an increasing number of U.S. firms are forming councils of distinguished foreign dignitaries and businesspeople, especially in Europe. The purpose is to get a global perspective on evolving events resulting from economic unification in Western Europe, restructuring in Eastern Europe, and economic liberalization in emerging markets or developing countries. The rationale is that there is no better way to forecast and figure out what is going to happen in Europe than to solicit the ideas of government and business leaders who live there.

For example, General Motors found its European Advisory Council useful in preparing for the first decade of the new century. IBM calls on its advisory councils in Europe, Asia, and Latin America to help develop strategic plans. The advantage of such foreign councils is that they do not have to spend time reviewing budgets or handling other fiduciary duties such as succession planning, but can devote their full attention to international issues that can have enormous impact on the firm's future as a global competitor. Firms' boards are usually so taken up with immediate concerns and are so lacking in knowledge of developments that they are unable to fully evaluate the global situation. The input of such foreign councils becomes an invaluable tool to get a global perspective and plan longer-term domestic and foreign strategies. Case Study 5-1 presents a forecast of the number of McDonald's restaurants worldwide.

CASE STUDY 5-1
Forecasting the Number of McDonald's Restaurants Worldwide

Increased competition and lower profit margins at home have driven McDonald's and other large U.S. fast-food chains to expand abroad, where competition is weaker and profit margins are higher (refer to Case Study 3-1). In fact, by 2005 there were more McDonald's restaurants abroad (17,500) than in the United States (13,100). McDonald's operated in 122 countries, and 4 out of 5 of its new restaurants were abroad.

Using data on each country's population and per capita income, *Fortune* magazine estimated the potential number of restaurants that McDonald's could build in each country if tastes were similar to U.S. tastes. The results for some countries are indicated in Table 5-1. *Fortune* came up with a total worldwide number of 42,000 restaurants. At the time of *Fortune*'s estimate in 1993, there were 3,597 McDonald's

restaurants abroad. By 2005, there were 30,600. Thus, McDonald's is well along reaching the estimated minimum market potential abroad (in Canada and Australia it has already surpassed it).

Some countries in which McDonald's is hardly present are estimated to be able to sustain a large number of its restaurants. For example, *Fortune* estimated that India could sustain at least 489 as compared with the present 56. To be remembered, however, is that *Fortune*'s estimates were based on the assumption that tastes in the rest of the world were the same as in the United States. Although converging, tastes are unlikely to ever become the same, and so these can be regarded only as rough "guesstimates." In 2005, McDonald's predicted that it would reach 50,000 restaurants worldwide during this decade. At that time, it had 600 outlets in China and planned 400 more.

TABLE 5-1 McDonald's Actual and Potential Restaurants around the World

Country	Number of Restaurants in 1993	Number of Restaurants in 2002	Minimum Market Potential
Japan	1,070	3,822	6,100
Canada	694	1,223	1,023
Britain	550	1,010	1,724
Germany	535	1,152	3,235
Australia	411	715	526
France	314	913	2,237
China	23	430	784

Source: "McDonald's Conquers the World," *Fortune* (October 17,1994), p. 104; "Thin Pickings," *The Economist* (July 16, 2005), pp. 60–61; and McDonald's 2005 Web site, http://www.mcdonalds.com.

5-2   TIME-SERIES ANALYSIS

One of the most frequently used forecasting methods is time-series analysis or the analysis of time-series data. **Time-series data,** discussed in Chapter 4, refers to the values of a variable arranged chronologically by days, weeks, months, quarters, or years. The first step in time-series analysis is usually to plot past values of the variable that we seek to forecast (say, the sales of a firm) on the vertical axis and time on the horizontal axis in order to visually inspect the movement of the time series over time. **Time-series analysis** attempts to forecast future values of the time series by examining past observations of the data only. The assumption is that the time series will continue to move as in the past (i.e., the past pattern will continue unchanged or will be similar in the future). For this reason, time-series analysis is often referred to as *naive forecasting*.

In this section, we first examine why most time-series data fluctuate and then examine how to use this information to forecast values of the time series.

Reasons for Fluctuations in Time-Series Data

If we plot most economic time-series data, we discover that they fluctuate or vary over time. This variation is usually caused by secular trends, cyclical fluctuations, seasonal variations, and irregular or random influences. These sources of variation are shown in Figure 5-1 and are briefly examined below:

1. **Secular trend** refers to a long-run increase or decrease in the data series (the solid line in the top panel of Figure 5-1). For example, many time series of sales exhibit rising trends over the years because of population growth and increasing per capita expenditures. Some, such as typewriters, follow a declining trend as more and more consumers switch to personal computers.
2. **Cyclical fluctuations** are the major expansions and contractions in most economic time series that seem to recur every several years (the dashed curved line in the top panel of Figure 5-1). For example, the housing construction industry follows long cyclical swings lasting 15 to 20 years, while the automobile industry seems to follow much shorter cycles.
3. **Seasonal variation** refers to the regularly recurring fluctuation in economic activity during each year (the dashed curved line in the bottom panel of Figure 5-1) because of weather and social customs. Thus, housing starts used to be much more numerous in spring and summer than in autumn and winter (because of weather conditions), while retail sales are greatest during the last quarter of each year (because of the holidays).
4. **Irregular or random influences** are the variations in the data series resulting from wars, natural disasters, strikes, or other unique events. These are shown by the solid line segments in the bottom panel of Figure 5-1.

The total variation in the time series of sales (not shown in Figure 5-1) is the result of all four factors operating together. Thus, the original sales data would show the seasonal and irregular variations superimposed on the cyclical fluctuations around the rising trend (the reader should try to sketch such original sales data). Since cyclical swings or business cycles can be of different duration and can arise from a variety of causes that even today are not yet fully understood, they are usually examined separately with qualitative techniques (see Section 5-4). Similarly, irregular or random influences in time series, by their very nature, cannot be examined systematically or forecast. Thus, in this section we concentrate on forecasting the values of time-series data by using only the long-term trend and the seasonal variations in the data.

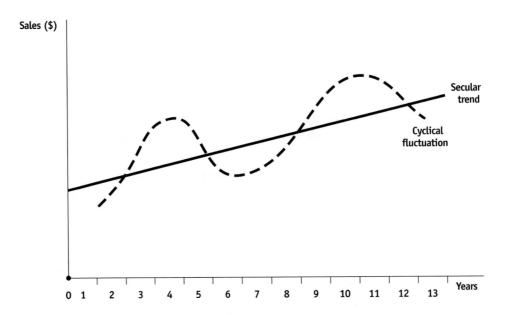

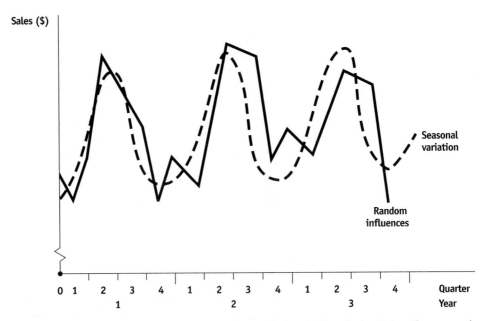

FIGURE 5-1 **Trend, Cyclical, Seasonal, and Random Variations in Time-Series Data** The top panel shows the rising secular trend in the sales of the firm (the solid line) as well as the cyclical fluctuations above and below the trend during the course of several years (dashed line). The bottom panel shows the seasonal variation in the data during each year (dashed line) and the irregular or random influences (solid line). The total variation in the time series is the result of all four forces working together.

TABLE 5-2	Seasonal Demand for (Sales of) Electricity (millions of kilowatt-hours) in a U.S. City, 2003–2006						
Time period	2003.1	2003.2	2003.3	2003.4	2004.1	2004.2	2004.3	2004.4
Quantity	11	15	12	14	12	17	13	16
Time period	2005.1	2005.2	2005.3	2005.4	2006.1	2006.2	2006.3	2006.4
Quantity	14	18	15	17	15	20	16	19

Trend Projection

The simplest form of time-series analysis is projecting the past trend by fitting a straight line to the data either visually or, more precisely, by regression analysis. The linear regression model will take the form of

$$S_t = S_0 + bt \qquad [5\text{-}1]$$

where S_t is the value of the time series to be forecast for period t, S_0 is the estimated value of the time series (the constant of the regression) in the base period (i.e., at time period $t = 0$), b is the absolute amount of growth per period, and t is the time period in which the time series is to be forecast.

For example, fitting a regression line to the electricity sales (consumption) data running from the first quarter of 2003 ($t = 1$) to the last quarter of 2006 ($t = 16$) given in Table 5-2, we get estimated regression Equation 5-2,

$$S_t = 11.90 + 0.394t \qquad R^2 = 0.50 \qquad [5\text{-}2]$$
$$(4.00)$$

Regression Equation 5-2 indicates that electricity sales in the city in the last quarter of 2002 (that is, S_0) are estimated to be 11.90 million kilowatt-hours and increase at the average rate of 0.394 million kilowatt-hours per quarter. The trend variable is statistically significant at better than the 1 percent level (inferred from the value of 4 for the t statistic given in parentheses below the estimated slope coefficient) and "explains" 50 percent in the quarterly variation of electricity consumption in the city (from $R^2 = 0.50$). Thus, based on the past trend, we can forecast electricity consumption (in million kilowatt-hours) in the city to be

$$S_{17} = 11.90 + 0.394(17) = 18.60 \quad \text{in the first quarter of 2007}$$

$$S_{18} = 11.90 + 0.394(18) = 18.99 \quad \text{in the second quarter of 2007}$$

$$S_{19} = 11.90 + 0.394(19) = 19.39 \quad \text{in the third quarter of 2007}$$

$$S_{20} = 11.90 + 0.394(20) = 19.78 \quad \text{in the fourth quarter of 2007}$$

These forecasts are shown by the dots on the dashed portion of the trend line extended into 2007 in Figure 5-2 (disregard for the moment the encircled points above and below the line). Note that the forecast values of electricity sales read off the extended trend line take into consideration only the long-run trend factor in the data. By completely disregarding the significant seasonal variation in the data (see the figure), the forecast values are likely

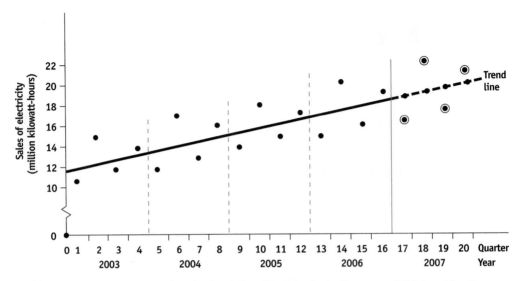

FIGURE 5-2 **Forecasting by Trend Projection** Electricity sales for the first, second, third, and fourth quarters of 2007 can be read off the extended regression (trend) line (the dots on the dashed portion of the trend line) for quarters 17, 18, 19, and 20, respectively.

to be far off their actual future values. In the next subsection, we will see how to incorporate this seasonal variation to significantly improve the forecast of future electricity consumption in the city. Before that, however, we will show how to fit a constant growth (percentage) rate trend to the same data.

Although the assumption of a constant absolute amount of change per time period (here a quarter) may be appropriate in many cases, there are situations (such as the sales of many products) where a constant percentage change is more appropriate (i.e., fits the data better and gives better forecasts).[1] The constant percentage growth rate model can be specified as

$$S_t = S_0(1 + g)^t \qquad\qquad [5\text{-}3]$$

where g is the constant percentage growth rate to be estimated.

To estimate g from Equation 5-3, we must first transform the time-series data into their natural logarithms and then run the regression on the transformed data. The transformed regression equation is linear in the logarithms and is given by

$$\ln S_t = \ln S_0 + t \ln (1 + g) \qquad\qquad [5\text{-}4]$$

Running regression Equation 5-4 for the data on electricity sales given in Table 5-2 transformed into logs,[2] we get

$$\ln S_t = 2.49 + 0.026t \qquad R^2 = 0.50 \qquad [5\text{-}5]$$
$$(4.06)$$

---

[1] Both the linear (i.e., the constant amount growth) and the exponential (constant percentage growth) trends can be tried, and the one that fits the data better is used for forecasting.

[2] For example, the log of 11 (the value in Table 5-2 for the first quarter of 2003) is 2.40 (obtained by simply entering the value of 11 into any hand calculator and pressing the "ln" key).

In this case, the fit of Equation 5-5 is similar to that of Equation 5-2. Because the estimated parameters are now based on the logarithms of the data, however, they must be converted into their antilogs to be able to interpret them in terms of the original data. The antilog of $\ln S_0 = 2.49$ is $S_0 = 12.06$ (obtained by simply entering the value of 2.49 into any pocket calculator and pressing the key e^x for the antilog), and the antilog of $\ln (1 + g) = 0.026$ gives $(1 + g) = 1.026$. Substituting these values back into Equation 5-3, we get

$$S_t = 12.06(1.026)^t \qquad\qquad [5\text{-}6]$$

where $S_0 = 12.06$ million kilowatt-hours is the estimated sales of electricity in the city in the fourth quarter of 2002 (i.e., at $t = 0$) and the estimated growth rate is 1.026, or 2.6 percent, per quarter.

To estimate sales in any future quarter, we substitute into Equation 5-6 the value of t for the quarter for which we are seeking to forecast S and solve for S_t. Thus,

$$S_{17} = 12.06(1.026)^{17} = 18.66 \quad \text{in the first quarter of 2007}$$

$$S_{18} = 12.06(1.026)^{18} = 19.14 \quad \text{in the second quarter of 2007}$$

$$S_{19} = 12.06(1.026)^{19} = 19.64 \quad \text{in the third quarter of 2007}$$

$$S_{20} = 12.06(1.026)^{20} = 20.15 \quad \text{in the fourth quarter of 2007}$$

These forecasts are similar to those obtained by fitting a linear trend.[3]

Seasonal Variations

As we have seen, the forecast values of electricity sales read off from the extended trend line in Figure 5-2 take into consideration only the long-run trend factor in the data. The data for the years 2003 to 2006, however, show strong seasonal variation, with sales in the first and third quarters of each year consistently below the corresponding long-run trend values, while sales in the second and fourth quarters are consistently above the trend values. By incorporating this seasonal variation, we can significantly improve the forecast of electricity sales in the city. We can do this with the ratio-to-trend method or with dummy variables.

To adjust the trend forecast for the seasonal variation by the ratio-to-trend method, we simply find the average ratio by which the actual value of the time series differs from the corresponding estimated trend value in each quarter during the 2003 to 2006 period and then multiply the forecasted trend value by this ratio. The predicted trend value for each quarter in the 2003 to 2006 period is obtained by simply substituting the value of t corresponding to the quarter under consideration into Equation 5-2 and solving for S_t. It is also given in the computer printout for Equation 5-2. Table 5-3 shows the calculations for the

---

[3] Note that the differences in the forecasts obtained using an exponential trend differ by increasing amounts from those obtained with a linear trend as the time series is forecast further into the future. This is usually the case.

TABLE 5-3	Calculation of the Seasonal Adjustment of the Trend Forecast by the Ratio-to-Trend Method		
Year	**Forecast**	**Actual**	**Actual/Forecast**
2003.1	12.29	11.00	0.895
2004.1	13.87	12.00	0.865
2005.1	15.45	14.00	0.906
2006.1	17.02	15.00	0.881
			Average: 0.887
2003.2	12.69	15.00	1.182
2004.2	14.26	17.00	1.192
2005.2	15.84	18.00	1.136
2006.2	17.42	20.00	1.148
			Average: 1.165
2003.3	13.08	12.00	0.917
2004.3	14.66	13.00	0.887
2005.3	16.23	15.00	0.924
2006.3	17.81	16.00	0.898
			Average: 0.907
2003.4	13.48	14.00	1.039
2004.4	15.05	16.00	1.063
2005.4	16.63	17.00	1.022
2006.4	18.20	19.00	1.044
			Average: 1.042

seasonal adjustment of the electricity sales forecast for each quarter of 2003–2006 from the extended trend line examined earlier.

Multiplying the electricity sales forecast earlier (from the simple extension of the linear trend) by the seasonal factors estimated in Table 5-3 (that is, 0.887 for the first quarter, 1.165 for the second quarter, and so on) we get the following new forecasts based on both the linear trend and the seasonal adjustment:

$$S_{17} = 18.60(0.887) = 16.50 \quad \text{in the first quarter of 2007}$$

$$S_{18} = 18.99(1.165) = 22.12 \quad \text{in the second quarter of 2007}$$

$$S_{19} = 19.39(0.907) = 17.59 \quad \text{in the third quarter of 2007}$$

$$S_{20} = 19.78(1.042) = 20.61 \quad \text{in the fourth quarter of 2007}$$

These forecasts are shown by the encircled points in Figure 5-2. Note that with the inclusion of the seasonal adjustment, the forecast values for electricity sales closely replicate the past seasonal pattern in the time-series data along the rising linear trend.

Similar results can be obtained by the inclusion of seasonal dummy variables in Equation 5-1. Taking the last quarter as the base-period quarter and defining dummy variable

D_1 by a time series with 1's in the first quarter of each year and zero in the other quarters, D_2 by a time series with 1's in the second quarter of each year and zero in the other quarters, and D_3 by a time series with 1's in the third quarters and zero in the other quarters, we obtain the following results by running a regression of electricity sales on the seasonal dummy variables and the linear time trend:[4]

$$S_t = 12.75 - 2.375D_{1t} + 1.750D_{2t} - 2.125D_{3t} + 0.375t \qquad R^2 = 0.99 \qquad [5\text{-}7]$$
$$ (-10.83) \quad (8.11) \quad (-9.94) \quad (22.25)$$

Note that the estimated coefficients for the dummy variables and the trend variable are all statistically significant at better than the 1 percent level and that Equation 5-7 "explains" 99 percent of the variation in electricity sales (as compared with only 50 percent for Equation 5-2). Using Equation 5-7 to forecast electricity sales for each quarter of 2007, we get[5]

$$S_{17} = 12.75 - 2.375 + 0.375(17) = 16.75 \quad \text{in the first quarter of 2007}$$

$$S_{18} = 12.75 + 1.750 + 0.375(18) = 21.25 \quad \text{in the second quarter of 2007}$$

$$S_{19} = 12.75 - 2.125 + 0.375(19) = 17.75 \quad \text{in the third quarter of 2007}$$

$$S_{20} = 12.75 + 0.375(20) = 20.25 \quad \text{in the fourth quarter of 2007}$$

These forecast values are similar to those obtained by the ratio-to-trend method. Thus, in this case the two methods are good alternatives for introducing the seasonal variation into the forecasts. It is important to remember, however, that these forecasts are based on the assumption that the past trend and seasonal patterns in the data will persist during 2007. If the pattern changes drastically, the forecasts are likely to be far off the mark. This is more likely the further into the future we attempt to forecast. In addition, it is difficult or impossible to consider cyclical and irregular or random forces. Thus, time-series analysis cannot forecast turning points until they have occurred. Even though these do not seem important in the historical data on electricity sales used in the example, this may not be the situation in other real-world cases. Finally, time-series analysis does not examine the underlying forces that cause the observed time series to fluctuate. In any event, time-series analysis is seldom used alone but is most useful in conjunction with other forecasting methods.[6] Case Study 5-2 shows how housing starts in the United States were forecast with time-series analysis.

---

[4] To be noted is that only three dummy variables are used for the four seasons, with the constant of the regression representing the fourth.

[5] Note that the dummy variable is added to (if positive) or subtracted from (if negative) the value of the constant of the regression (which refers to the fourth quarter, which is taken as the base). For a more detailed discussion of dummy variables, see D. Salvatore and D. Reagle, *Statistics and Econometrics,* 2nd ed. (New York: McGraw-Hill, 2002), sec. 8.2, or any other introductory econometrics text.

[6] There are more sophisticated methods of forecasting time series called ARIMA (autoregressive integrated moving average) models. These are much more complex than the analysis presented above and are beyond the scope of this text. The interested reader is referred to the econometrics texts in the supplementary readings at the end of this chapter.

CASE STUDY 5-2
Forecasting New-Housing Starts with Time-Series Analysis

Table 5-4 gives the number (in thousands) of new-housing units started in the United States from the first quarter of 1999 to the last quarter of 2004. Inspection of the data does not reveal any pattern because of the recession in 2001 and the slow growth of the economy in 2002.

To forecast housing starts in each quarter of 2005, we begin by regressing housing starts (H_t) on time (t) from $t = 1$ (first quarter of 1999) to $t = 24$ (last quarter of 2004) and get

$$H_t = 381.21 + 4.05t \qquad R^2 = 0.59 \qquad [5\text{-}8]$$
$$(5.09)$$

Using these regression results to forecast new-housing starts for each quarter of 2005, we get

$S_{25} = 381.21 + 4.05 (25) = 482.46$
in the first quarter of 2005

$S_{26} = 381.21 + 4.05 (26) = 486.51$
in the second quarter of 2005

$S_{27} = 381.21 + 4.05 (27) = 490.56$
in the third quarter of 2005

$S_{28} = 381.21 + 4.05 (28) = 494.61$
in the fourth quarter of 2005

To adjust the trend forecasts for seasonal variations by the ratio-to-trend method, we find the average ratio by which the actual value of the time series differs from the corresponding estimated trend value

in each quarter during the 1999 to 2004 period and then multiply the forecast trend value by this ratio. The seasonal adjustment factors found by calculations analogous to those shown in Table 5-2 are 1.015, 0.984, 0.991, and 1.001 for the first, second, third, and fourth quarters, respectively.

Multiplying the number of new-housing starts forecast above from the simple extension of the linear trend by the seasonal factors, we get the following new forecasts based on both the linear trend and the seasonal adjustment:

$S_{25} = 482.46 (1.015) = 489.70$
in the first quarter of 2005

$S_{26} = 486.51 (0.984) = 478.73$
in the second quarter of 2005

$S_{27} = 490.56 (0.991) = 486.14$
in the third quarter of 2005

$S_{28} = 494.61 (1.001) = 495.10$
in the fourth quarter of 2005

Very similar results are obtained by using seasonal dummies. The student can check these forecasts against the actual number of new-housing starts in the United States in each quarter of 2005 (published in the *Economic Report of the President of 2006*). The Chapter Appendix shows how to forecast new-housing starts with time-series analysis using Microsoft Excel.

TABLE 5-4	New-Housing Starts in the United States: 1999.1–2004.4 (in thousand units)										
1999.1	439.9	2000.1	417.1	2001.1	402.8	2002.1	429.1	2003.1	436.8	2004.1	485.8
1999.2	397.7	2000.2	396.6	2001.2	406.1	2002.2	420.7	2003.2	436.3	2004.2	479.9
1999.3	415.8	2000.3	376.3	2001.3	400.7	2002.3	425.5	2003.3	470.8	2004.3	492.3
1999.4	422.3	2000.4	384.8	2001.4	393.2	2002.4	435.7	2003.4	508.7	2004.4	489.7

Source: Economic Report of the President (Washington, D.C.: Government Printing Office, various issues).

5-3   SMOOTHING TECHNIQUES

Other methods of naive forecasting are **smoothing techniques.** These predict values of a time series on the basis of some average of its past values only. Smoothing techniques are useful when the time series exhibit little trend or seasonal variations but a great deal of irregular or random variation. The irregular or random variation in the time series is then smoothed, and future values are forecast based on some average of past observations. In this section we examine two smoothing techniques: moving averages and exponential smoothing.

Moving Averages

The simplest smoothing technique is the **moving average.** Here the forecast value of a time series in a given period (month, quarter, year, etc.) is equal to the average value of the time series in a number of previous periods. For example, with a three-period moving average, the forecast value of the time series for the next period is given by the average value of the time series in the previous three periods. Similarly, with a five-period moving average, the forecast for the next period is equal to the average for the previous five periods, and so on. The greater the number of periods used in the moving average, the greater is the smoothing effect because each new observation receives less weight. This is more useful the more erratic or random the time-series data are.

For example, columns 1 and 2 in Table 5-5 present hypothetical data on the market share of a firm for 12 quarters. Note that the data seem to show considerable random

TABLE 5-5 Three-Quarter and Five-Quarter Moving Average Forecasts and Comparison

(1)	(2)	(3)	(4)	(5)	(6)	(7)	(8)
Quarter	Firm's Actual Market Share (A)	Three-Quarter Moving Average Forecast (F)	A – F	$(A - F)^2$	Five-Quarter Moving Average Forecast (F)	A – F	$(A - F)^2$
1	20	—	—	—	—	—	—
2	22	—	—	—	—	—	—
3	23	—	—	—	—	—	—
4	24	21.67	2.33	5.4289	—	—	—
5	18	23.00	−5.00	25.0000	—	—	—
6	23	21.67	1.33	1.7689	21.4	1.6	2.56
7	19	21.67	−2.67	7.1289	22.0	−3.0	9.00
8	17	20.00	−3.00	9.0000	21.4	−4.4	19.36
9	22	19.67	2.33	5.4289	20.2	1.8	3.24
10	23	19.33	3.67	13.4689	19.8	3.2	10.24
11	18	20.67	−2.67	7.1289	20.8	−2.8	7.84
12	23	21.00	2.00	4.0000	19.8	3.2	10.24
				Total: 78.3534			Total: 62.48
13	—	21.33			20.6		

variation but no secular or seasonal variations. Column 3 gives the calculated three-quarter moving average. For example, the value of 21.67 for the fourth quarter (the first value in column 3) is obtained by adding the first three values in column 2 and dividing by 3 [i.e., $(20 + 22 + 23)/3 = 21.67$]. If we had data for only the first three quarters, our three-quarter forecast (F) for the *fourth* quarter would be 21.67. This compares with the actual value (A) of 24 for the firm's market share in the fourth quarter. Dropping the first-quarter observation in column 2 (that is, 20) and adding the fourth observation (i.e., 24) before averaging, we get the value of 23 as our forecast for the firm's fifth-quarter market share (the second value in column 3). This compares with the actual market share of 18 in column 2.

By continuing this way, we forecast the firm's market share to be 21.33 in the thirteenth quarter (this is a real forecast, since no actual data were available for the thirteenth quarter). On the other hand, by averaging the firm's market share in the first five quarters in column 2, we get the five-quarter moving average forecast of 21.4 for the sixth quarter shown in column 6 of the table. This compares with the actual value of 23 in column 2.

Although in Table 5-5 we calculated the three-quarter and the five-quarter moving average forecasts for the firm's market share, moving average forecasts for still other numbers of quarters can be obtained. In order to decide which of these moving average forecasts is better (i.e., closer to the actual data), we calculate the **root-mean-square error** **(RMSE)** of each forecast and use the moving average that results in the smallest *RMSE* (weighted average error in the forecast). The formula for the root-mean-square error (*RMSE*) is

$$RMSE = \sqrt{\frac{\Sigma(A_t - F_t)^2}{n}} \tag{5-9}$$

where A_t is the actual value of the time series in period t, F_t is the forecast value, and n is the number of time periods or observations. The forecast difference or error (that is, $A - F$) is squared in order to penalize larger errors proportionately more than smaller errors.

For example, column 4 in Table 5-5 shows $A_t - F_t$ for the three-quarter moving average forecast in column 3. Column 5 shows $(A_t - F_t)^2$. The *RMSE* for the three-quarter moving average forecast in column 3 is obtained by dividing the total of column 5 by 9 (the number of squared forecast errors) and finding the square root. That is,

$$RMSE = \sqrt{\frac{78.3534}{9}} = 2.95 \tag{5-10}$$

This compares with

$$RMSE = \sqrt{\frac{62.48}{7}} = 2.99 \tag{5-11}$$

for the five-quarter moving average forecast. Thus, the three-quarter moving average forecast is marginally better than the corresponding five-quarter moving average forecast. That is, we are a little more confident in the forecast of 21.33 than 20.6 for the thirteenth quarter (see Table 5-5).

Exponential Smoothing*

A serious criticism of using simple moving averages in forecasting is that they give equal weight to all observations in computing the average, even though intuitively we might expect more recent observations to be more important. Exponential smoothing overcomes this objection and is used more frequently than simple moving averages in forecasting.

With **exponential smoothing,** the forecast for period $t + 1$ (that is, F_{t+1}) is a weighted average of the actual and forecast values of the time series in period t. The value of the time series at period t (that is, A_t) is assigned a weight (w) between 0 and 1 inclusive, and the forecast for period t (that is, F_t) is assigned the weight of $1 - w$.[7] The greater the value of w, the greater is the weight given to the value of the time series in period t as opposed to previous periods.[8] Thus, the value of the forecast of time series in period $t + 1$ is

$$F_{t+1} = wA_t + (1 - w)F_t \qquad [5\text{-}12]$$

Two decisions must be made in order to use Equation 5-12 for exponential smoothing. First, it is necessary to assign a value to the initial forecast (F_t) to get the analysis started. One way to do this is to let F_t equal the mean value of the entire observed time-series data. We must also decide on the value of w (the weight to assign to A_t). In general, different values of w are tried, and the one that leads to the forecast with the smallest root-mean-square error ($RMSE$) is actually used in forecasting.

For example, column 3 in Table 5-6 shows the forecasts for the firm's market share data given in columns 1 and 2 (the same as in Table 5-5) by using the average market share of the firm over the 12 quarters for which we have data (that is, 21.0) for F_1 (to get the calculations started) and $w = 0.3$ as the weight for A_t. Thus, F_2 (the second value in column 3) is

$$F_2 = 0.3(20) + (1 - 0.3)21 = 20.7 \qquad [5\text{-}13]$$

The forecasts for other time periods (rounded off to the first decimal) are similarly obtained, until $F_{13} = 21.0$ for the thirteenth quarter.

On the other hand, starting again with the average market share of the firm for the 12 quarters for which we have data (that is, 21.0) for F_1 but now using $w = 0.5$ as the weight for A_t, we get the exponential forecasts of the firm's market share shown in column 6 of Table 5-6. Thus, F_2 (the second value in column 6) is

$$F_2 = 0.5(20) + (1 - 0.5)21 = 20.5$$

The forecasts for the other time periods are similarly obtained, until $F_{13} = 21.5$ for the thirteenth quarter.

---

* This section is more advanced than the others, but it can be skipped without loss of continuity.

[7] Note that the sum of the weights equals 1. That is, $w + (1 - w) = 1$. This is always the case.

[8] While F_{t+1} is calculated from the value of the time series and its forecast for period t only, the forecast for period t can be shown to depend on all past values of the time series, with weights declining exponentially for values further into the past. It is for this reason that this technique is called "exponential smoothing."

TABLE 5-6	Exponential Forecasts with $w = 0.3$ and $w = 0.5$, and Comparison						
(1)	(2)	(3)	(4)	(5)	(6)	(7)	(8)
Quarter	Firm's Actual Market Share (A)	Forecast with $w = 0.3$ (F)	A – F	(A – F)²	Forecast with $w = 0.5$ (F)	A – F	(A – F)²
1	20	21.0	–1.0	1.00	21.0	–1.0	1.00
2	22	20.7	1.3	1.69	20.5	1.5	2.25
3	23	21.1	1.9	3.61	21.3	1.7	2.89
4	24	21.7	2.3	5.29	22.2	1.8	3.24
5	18	22.4	–4.4	19.36	23.1	–5.1	26.01
6	23	21.1	1.9	3.61	20.6	2.4	5.76
7	19	21.7	–2.7	7.29	21.8	–2.8	7.84
8	17	20.9	–3.9	15.21	20.4	–3.4	11.56
9	22	19.7	2.3	5.29	18.7	3.3	10.89
10	23	20.4	2.6	6.76	20.4	2.6	6.76
11	18	21.2	–3.2	10.24	21.7	–3.7	13.69
12	23	20.2	2.8	7.84	19.9	3.1	9.61
				Total: 87.19			Total: 101.50
13	—	21.0			21.5		

The root-mean-square error (*RMSE*) for the exponential forecasts using $w = 0.3$ is

$$RMSE = \sqrt{\frac{87.19}{12}} = 2.70 \qquad\qquad [5\text{-}14]$$

On the other hand, the *RMSE* for the exponential forecasts using $w = 0.5$ is

$$RMSE = \sqrt{\frac{101.5}{12}} = 2.91 \qquad\qquad [5\text{-}15]$$

Thus, we are more confident in the exponential forecast of 21.0 for the thirteenth quarter obtained by using $w = 0.3$ than in the exponential forecast of 21.5 obtained by using $w = 0.5$ (see Table 5-6). Both exponential forecasts are also better than the three-quarter and the five-quarter moving average forecasts obtained earlier in Section 5-3. Since the best exponential forecast is usually better than the best moving average forecast, the former is generally used.[9] Case Study 5-3 shows how smoothing techniques were used to forecast lumber sales in the United States.

---

[9] If the time-series data exhibit not only random variation but also a secular trend, the double exponential smoothing technique is required. This, however, is beyond the scope of this text. The interested reader can consult C. W. J. Granger, *Forecasting in Business and Economics* (New York: Academic Press, 1989).

CASE STUDY 5-3
Forecasting Lumber Sales with Smoothing Techniques

The second column of Table 5-7 gives the index (with 1984 = 100) of lumber sales (in millions of cubic feet) in the United States per year from 1985 to 1996. Inspection of the data reveals no secular trend (and, of course, there is no seasonal variation) but a great deal of irregular or random variation. Thus, we can use exponential smoothing to forecast lumber consumption in the United States.

Starting with the average lumber delivery from 1985 to 1996 (108) for F_1 and using $w = 0.3$ and $w = 0.7$ as the weights (we could have chosen any other value for w between 0.1 and 0.9) for actual lumber sales in each year (A_t), we get the exponential forecasts (rounded off to the nearest integer) in columns 3 and 6, respectively, by using

Equation 5-12 and using the *RMSE* of these forecasts to compare them.

With $w = 0.3$,

$$RMSE = \sqrt{\frac{803}{12}} = 8.18 \qquad [5\text{-}16]$$

With $w = 0.7$,

$$RMSE = \sqrt{\frac{732}{12}} = 7.81 \qquad [5\text{-}17]$$

Thus, we are much more confident in the exponential forecast of 110 for 1997 obtained by using $w = 0.7$ than in the exponential forecast of 108 obtained with $w = 0.3$.

TABLE 5-7 Exponential Forecasts of Index of Lumber Sales in the United States (1984 = 100)

(1)	(2)	(3)	(4)	(5)	(6)	(7)	(8)
	Actual Lumber Sales	**Forecast with $w = 0.3$**			**Forecast with $w = 0.7$**		
Year	**(A)**	**(F)**	**A − F**	**(A − F)²**	**(F)**	**A − F**	**(A − F)²**
1985	98	108	−10	100	108	−10	100
1986	113	105	8	64	101	12	144
1987	121	107	14	196	109	12	144
1988	120	111	9	81	117	3	9
1989	112	114	−2	4	119	−7	49
1990	105	113	−8	64	114	−9	81
1991	96	111	−15	225	108	−12	144
1992	102	107	−5	25	100	2	4
1993	103	106	−3	9	101	2	4
1994	108	105	3	9	102	6	36
1995	107	106	1	1	106	1	1
1996	111	106	5	25	107	4	16
				Total: 803			Total: 732
1997		108			110		

Source: Statistical Abstract of the United States (Washington, D.C.: Government Printing Office, various issues).

5-4   BAROMETRIC METHODS

Until now we have examined secular trends, seasonal variations, and random influences in time-series data. Little has been said about forecasting cyclical swings in the level of economic activity or business cycles. One way to forecast or anticipate short-term changes in economic activity or turning points in business cycles is to use the index of leading economic indicators. These are time series that tend to precede (lead) changes in the level of general economic activity, much as changes in the mercury in a barometer precede changes in weather conditions (hence the name *barometric methods*). **Barometric forecasting,** as conducted today, is primarily the result of the work conducted at the National Bureau of Economic Research (NBER) and the Conference Board.

A rise in the **leading economic indicators** is used to forecast an increase in general business activity, and vice versa. For example, an increase in building permits can be used to forecast an increase in housing construction. Less obvious—but very important—an increase in stock prices, in general, precedes (i.e., it is a leading indicator for) an upturn in general business activity, since rising stock prices reflect expectations by business managers and others that profits will rise. On the other hand, a decline in contracts for plant and equipment usually precedes a slowdown in general economic activity. Thus, leading indicators are used to forecast turning points in the business cycle.

Although we are primarily interested in leading indicators, some time series move in step or coincide with movements in general economic activity and are therefore called **coincident indicators.** Still others follow or lag movements in economic activity and are called **lagging indicators.** The relative positions of leading, coincident, and lagging indicators in the business cycle are shown graphically in Figure 5-3. The figure shows that leading

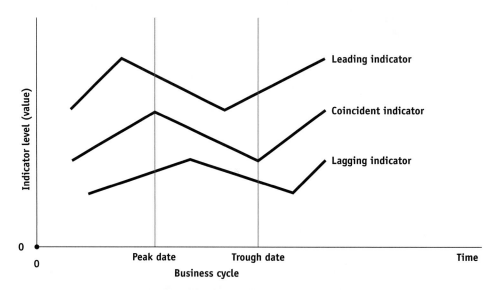

FIGURE 5-3   Economic Indicators   *Leading indicators* precede (lead) business cycles' turning points (i.e., peaks and troughs), *coincident indicators* move in step with business cycles, while *lagging indicators* follow or lag turning points in business cycles.

indicators precede business cycles' turning points (i.e., peaks and troughs), coincident indicators move in step with business cycles, while lagging indicators follow or lag turning points in business cycles.

Time-series data on more than 300 leading, coincident, and lagging indicators are provided in *Business Cycle Indicators,* a monthly publication of the Conference Board. A shorter list of the 21 best indicators (10 leading, 4 coincident, and 7 lagging) is given in Table 5-8. Our interest is primarily in the leading indicators. Table 5-8 also gives the lead (–) and lag (+) times for the **composite indexes** of the 10 leading, the 4 coincident, and the 7 lagging indicators. These are a weighted average of the individual indicators in each

---

TABLE 5-8 Short List of Leading, Coincident, and Lagging Indicators

Leading Indicators (10 Series)

Average weekly hours, manufacturing

Initial claims for unemployment insurance, thousands

Manufacturers' new orders, consumer goods and materials

Vendor performance, slower deliveries diffusion index

Manufacturers' new orders, nondefense capital goods

Building permits, new private housing units

Stock prices, 500 common stocks

Money supply, M2

Interest rate spread, 10-year Treasury bonds less federal funds

Index of consumer expectations

Coincident Indicators (4 Series)

Employees on nonagricultural payrolls

Personal income less transfer payments

Industrial production

Manufacturing and trade sales

Lagging Indicators (7 Series)

Average duration of unemployment, weeks

Ratio, manufacturing and trade inventories to sales

Change in labor cost per unit of output, manufacturing

Average prime rate charged by banks

Commercial and industrial loans outstanding

Ratio, consumer installment credit to personal income

Change in consumer price index for services

Composite Indexes	Leads (–) and Lags (+) (in months)
Composite index of 10 leading indicators	–6
Composite index of 4 coincident indicators	–1
Composite index of 7 lagging indicators	+3

Source: The Conference Board, *Business Cycle Indicators* (New York), various issues.

group, with the indicators that do a better job of forecasting given bigger weights. As such, composite indexes smooth out random variations and provide more reliable forecasts and fewer wrong signals than individual indicators.

Another method for overcoming the difficulty arising when some of the 10 leading indicators move up and some move down is the **diffusion index.** Instead of combining the 10 leading indicators into a composite index, the diffusion index gives the percentage of the 10 leading indicators moving upward. If all 10 move up, the diffusion index is 100. If all move down, its value is 0. If only 7 move up, the diffusion index is 70. We usually forecast an improvement in economic activity when the diffusion index is above 50, and we have greater confidence in our forecast the closer the index is to 100. In general, barometric forecasting employs composite and diffusion indexes rather than individual indicators, except when a firm seeks information about anticipated changes in the market for specific goods and services.

Each month the Conference Board reports changes in the individual and composite indexes. Although not much significance can be attached to individual monthly swings, three or four successive one-month declines in the composite index and a diffusion index of less than 50 percent are usually a prelude to recession (popularly defined as a decline in gross national product for three or more consecutive quarters). This can be seen from Figure 5-4. The top panel shows that the composite index of leading indicators turned down prior to the recessions

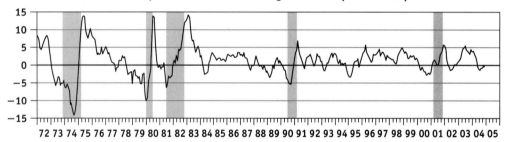

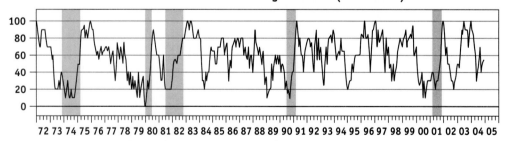

FIGURE 5-4   Composite and Diffusion Indexes of the 10 Leading Indicators   The top panel shows that the composite index of 10 leading indicators turned down prior to (i.e., led) the recessions of 1973–1975, 1980, 1981–1982, 1990–1991, and 2001 (shaded regions). The bottom panel shows that the diffusion index of the 10 leading indicators was generally below 50 percent in the months preceding the recessions (shaded areas).
Source: The Conference Board, *Business Cycle Indicators* (New York, April 2005), p. 4.

of 1973 to 1975, 1980, 1981 to 1982, 1990 to 1991, and 2001 (the shaded regions in the figure). Similarly, the bottom panel shows that the diffusion index for the 10 leading indicators was generally below 50 percent in the months preceding recessions (the shaded areas).

Although the composite and diffusion indexes of leading indicators are reasonably good tools for predicting turning points in business cycles, they face a number of shortcomings. One is that on several occasions they forecast a recession that failed to occur.[10] The variability in lead time can also be considerable. More importantly, barometric forecasting gives little or no indication of the *magnitude* of the forecast change in the level of economic activity (i.e., it provides only a qualitative forecast of turning points). Thus, while barometric forecasting is certainly superior to time-series analysis and smoothing techniques (naive methods) in forecasting short-term turning points in economic activity, it must be used in conjunction with other methods (such as econometric forecasting—discussed in Section 5-5) to forecast the magnitude of change in the level of economic activity. Case Study 5-4 shows the use of composite and diffusion indexes in forecasting the level of economic activity in April 2005 (the reader can check whether the forecast was correct). Case Study 5-5 shows that the index of leading indicators has now gone global.

CASE STUDY 5-4
Forecasting the Level of Economic Activity with Composite and Diffusion Indexes

Table 5-9 gives the monthly composite index (with 1992 = 100) and the diffusion index of the 10 leading indicators from January 2004 through December 2004. Note that the composite index increased in each month—except for June, July, August, and September, thus correctly anticipating continued economic expansion in 2005. Similarly, the diffusion index was above 50 in every month except for February, April, and August through October, thus also signaling continued expansion in 2005.

TABLE 5-9 Composite and Diffusion Indexes for the 10 Leading Indicators from January 2004 to December 2004

Month	Composite Index	Diffusion Index	Month	Composite Index	Diffusion Index
January	114.7	50.0	July	116.0	50.0
February	114.8	45.0	August	115.7	40.0
March	115.7	70.0	September	115.4	40.0
April	115.8	45.0	October	115.1	30.0
May	116.3	60.0	November	115.5	70.0
June	116.2	60.0	December	115.9	60.0

Source: The Conference Board, *Business Cycle Indicators* (New York, March 2005), p. 30.

---

[10] At best, barometric forecasting is only 80 to 90 percent accurate in forecasting turning points.

CASE STUDY 5-5
The Index of Leading Indicators Goes Global

In 1995 the Conference Board began compiling the Index of Leading, Coincident, and Lagging Indicators for the United States on behalf of the U.S. Government. This was the first time that the U.S. government privatized an official statistical series. In 2000, the Conference Board began compiling a global index of leading, coincident, and lagging economic indicators for eight other countries (Japan, Germany, France, United Kingdom, Australia, Spain, Mexico, and Korea) and planned to extend the series to another 6 countries in the future, for a total of 15 countries (including the United States). Subscription to all the series cost $500 per year ($25 for a one-time download of a country's series, except for Australia, for which the data are not available for purchase).

The new global indicators include the same 10 series of the leading indicators, 4 series of the coincident indicators, and 7 series of the lagging indicators as for the U.S. indicators (see Table 5-8), and just as the U.S.

series, the global series are updated each month. For example, on July 7, 2005, the Conference Board published the indicators for Japan for May 2005, which showed a composite index of 98.0 (1990 = 100). This represented a 0.2 percent increase from the previous month, and also a 0.2 percent increase over the previous six months through May. Since the six-month diffusion index was 50.0, the data seemed to indicate that Japan was not going to grow rapidly during the subsequent months (which is in fact what happened). Similarly, on July 20, the Conference Board released the indicators for Germany, which showed a composite index of leading indicators of 104.2 (1990 = 100). This represented a 0.2 percent decline from April but a 0.2 percent increase over the previous six months through May. Since the six-month diffusion index was 75.0 percent, the indicators seemed to show that Germany could expect only moderate growth in the subsequent months, and this is what happened.

Source: A. J. Vogl, "A New Map of the World," *Across the Board* (October 2000), pp. 1–25, and http://www.conference-board.org/economics/bci.

5-5   ECONOMETRIC MODELS

The firm's demand and sales of a commodity, as well as many other economic variables, are increasingly being forecast with econometric models. The characteristic that distinguishes econometric models from other forecasting methods is that they seek to identify and measure the relative importance (elasticity) of the various determinants of demand or other economic variables to be forecast. By attempting to *explain* the relationship being forecast, econometric forecasting allows the manager to determine the optimal policies for the firm. This is to be contrasted with the other forecasting techniques examined in this chapter that forecast demand, sales, or other economic variables on the basis of their past patterns or on the basis of some leading indicator alone.

Econometric forecasting frequently incorporates or uses the best features of other forecasting techniques, such as trend and seasonal variations, smoothing techniques, and leading indicators. Econometric forecasting models range from single-equation models of the demand that the firm faces for its product to large, multiple-equation models describing hundreds of sectors and industries of the economy. Although the concern here is with forecasting the demand for a firm's product, macroforecasts of national income and major sectors of the economy are often used as inputs or explanatory variables in simple single-equation demand models of the firm. Therefore, we discuss both types of forecasting in this section, starting with single-equation models.

Single-Equation Models

The simplest form of econometric forecasting is with a single-equation model. The first step is to identify the determinants of the variable to be forecast. For example, in forecasting the demand for breakfast cereals, the firm will usually postulate that demand (Q) is a function of or depends on the price of breakfast cereals (P), consumers' disposable income (Y), the size of the population (N), the price of muffins (P_S—a substitute), the price of milk (P_C—a complement), and the level of advertising by the firm (A). Thus, we can write the following demand equation to be estimated:

$$Q = a_0 + a_1P + a_2Y + a_3N + a_4P_S + a_5P_C + a_6A + e \qquad [5\text{-}18]$$

Once the model has been estimated (i.e., the values of the a's determined) and evaluated (as discussed in Section 4-7), the firm must obtain forecast values of the independent or explanatory variables of the model for the time period for which the dependent variable is to be forecast. Thus, to forecast Q_{t+1} (i.e., the demand faced by the firm in the next period), the firm must obtain the values for P_{t+1}, Y_{t+1}, N_{t+1}, $P_{S_{t+1}}$, $P_{C_{t+1}}$, and A_{t+1}. By substituting these forecast values of the independent variables into the estimated equation, we obtain the forecast values of the dependent variable (Q_{t+1}). The forecast values of the macroeconomic variables of the model (Y_{t+1} and N_{t+1}) are usually obtained from the Department of Commerce or from many private firms that specialize in making such forecasts (see Case Study 5-6). The microvariables in the model not under the control of the firm

CASE STUDY 5-6
Forecasting the Demand for Air Travel over the North Atlantic

In Case Study 4-4, we reported the following estimated equation for air travel between New York and London for the period from 1965 to 1978:

$$\ln Q_t = 2.737 - 1.247 \ln P_t$$
$$+ 1.905 \ln GNP_t$$
$$\bar{R}^2 = 0.97 \qquad [5\text{-}19]$$

where Q_t = number of passengers per year traveling between the United States and Europe from 1965 to 1978 on IATA (International Air Transport Association) carriers, in thousands

P_t = average yearly airfare between New York and London (weighted by the seasonal distribution of traffic), in dollars, adjusted for inflation

GNP_t = U.S. gross national product in each year, in billions of dollars, adjusted for inflation

Suppose that in 1978 an airline company forecast that in 1979 airfares (adjusted for inflation) between New York and London (that is, P_{t+1}) would be $550 and real GNP (that is, GNP_{t+1}) would be $1,480. The natural log of 550 (i.e., ln 550) is 6.310 and ln 1,480 is 7.300. Substituting these values into Equation 5-19, we get

$$\ln Q_{t+1} = 2.737 - 1.247(6.310)$$
$$+ 1.905(7.300) = 8.775 \qquad [5\text{-}20]$$

The antilog of 8.775 is 6,470, or 6,470,000 passengers forecast for 1979. The accuracy of this forecast depends on the accuracy of the estimated demand coefficients and on the accuracy of the forecast values of the independent or explanatory variables in the demand equation.

($P_{S_{t+1}}$ and $P_{C_{t+1}}$) might be forecast by time-series analysis or smoothing techniques, and the firm can experiment with various alternative forecast values of the independent policy variables under its control (P_{t+1} and A_{t+1}). An example of econometric forecasting with a single-equation model is provided in Case Study 5-6.

Multiple-Equation Models

Although single-equation models are often used by firms to forecast demand or sales, economic relationships may be so complex that a multiple-equation model may be required. This is particularly the case in forecasting macrovariables such as gross national product (*GNP*) or the demand and sales of major sectors or industries. Multiple-equation models may include only a few equations or hundreds of them. To show how multiple-equation models are used in forecasting, we start with a very simple three-equation (5-21, 5-22, and 5-23) model of the national economy that can be used to forecast *GNP*,

$$C_t = a_1 + b_1 GNP_t + u_{1t} \qquad [5\text{-}21]$$

$$I_t = a_2 + b_2 \pi_{t-1} + u_{2t} \qquad [5\text{-}22]$$

$$GNP_t = C_t + I_t + G_t \qquad [5\text{-}23]$$

where C = consumption expenditures
GNP = gross national product in year t
I = investment
π = profits
G = government expenditures
u = stochastic disturbance (random error term)
t = current year
$t-1$ = previous year

Equation 5-21 postulates that consumption expenditures in year t (C_t) are a linear function of *GNP* in the same year (that is, GNP_t). Equation 5-22 postulates that investment in year t (I_t) is a linear function of profits in the previous year (that is, π_{t-1}). Finally, Equation 5-23 defines *GNP* in year t as the sum of consumption expenditures, investment, and government expenditures in the same year.

Variables C_t, I_t, and GNP_t (the left-hand variables, or variables to the left of the equals signs in Equations 5-21, 5-22, and 5-23) are called **endogenous variables.** These are the variables that the model seeks to explain or predict from the solution of the model. **Exogenous variables,** on the other hand, are those determined outside the model. In the above model, π_{t-1} and G_t are the exogenous variables. Their values must be supplied from outside the model in order to be able to estimate the model. When (as in the national economy model) some of the endogenous variables also appear on the right of the equals signs, this means that they both affect and are, in turn, affected by the other variables in the model (i.e., they are simultaneously determined).

Equations 5-21 and 5-22 are called **structural (behavioral) equations** because they seek to explain the relationship between the particular endogenous variable and the other variables in the system. Equation 5-23 is a **definitional equation,** or an *identity,* and is always true by definition. Note that Equation 5-23 has no parameters or coefficients to be estimated. We will see that, given the value of the exogenous variables (π_{t-1} and G_t), we can solve the system and estimate the values of the endogenous variables. A change in the value of an exogenous variable will affect directly the endogenous variable in the equation in which it appears and indirectly the other endogenous variables in the system. For example, an increase in π_{t-1} leads to a rise in I_t directly (Equation 5-22). The induced increase in I_t then leads to an increase in GNP_t and, through it, in C_t as well.

Since the endogenous variables of the system (i.e., C_t, I_t, and GNP_t) are both determined by and in turn determine the value of the other endogenous variables in the model (i.e., they also appear on the right-hand side in Equations 5-21 and 5-23), we cannot use the ordinary least-squares technique (OLS) to estimate the parameters of the structural equations (the a's and the b's in Equations 5-21 and 5-22). More advanced econometric techniques are required to obtain unbiased estimates of the coefficients of the model. These are beyond the scope of this book.[11] By assuming that these coefficients are correctly estimated by the appropriate estimating technique, we can show how the above simple macromodel can be used for forecasting the values of the endogenous variables. To do this, we substitute Equations 5-21 and 5-22 into Equation 5-23 (the definitional equation) and solve. This will give an equation for GNP_t that is expressed only in terms of π_{t-1} and G_t (the exogenous variables of the system). By then substituting the values of π_t (which is known in year $t + 1$) and the predicted or forecast value of G_{t+1} into the solved equation, we get a forecast for GNP_{t+1}. That is, substituting Equation 5-21 into Equation 5-23, we get[12]

$$GNP_t = a_1 + b_1 GNP_t + I_t + G_t \qquad [5\text{-}24]$$

By then substituting Equation 5-22 into Equation 5-24, we get

$$GNP_t = a_1 + b_1 GNP_t + a_2 + b_2 \pi_{t-1} + G_t \qquad [5\text{-}25]$$

Collecting the GNP_t terms to the left in Equation 5-25 and isolating GNP_t, we have

$$GNP_t(1 - b_1) = a_1 + a_2 + b_2 \pi_{t-1} + G_t \qquad [5\text{-}26]$$

Dividing both sides of Equation 5-26 by $1 - b_1$, we finally obtain

$$GNP_t = \frac{a_1 + a_2}{1 - b_1} + \frac{b_2 \pi_{t-1}}{1 - b_1} + \frac{G_t}{1 - b_1} \qquad [5\text{-}27]$$

Equation 5-27 is called a **reduced-form equation** because GNP_t is expressed only in terms of π_{t-1} and G_t (the exogenous variables of the model). By substituting into Equation 5-27 the value of π_t (which is known in year $t + 1$) and the predicted value of G_{t+1}, we obtain the forecast value for GNP_{t+1}. The reduced-form equations for C_t and I_t can similarly be obtained (see Problem 11, with answer at the end of the book).

---

[11] See D. Salvatore and D. Reagle, *Theory and Problems of Statistics and Econometrics,* 2nd ed. (New York: McGraw-Hill, 2002), chap. 10; and W. Baumol, *Economic Theory and Operations Analysis* (Englewood Cliffs, N.J.: Prentice-Hall, 1977), chap. 10.

[12] The stochastic disturbances (i.e., the u's in Equations 5-21 and 5-22) are omitted in the following equations because their expected values are zero.

The simple macromodel we have been using contains three endogenous and two exogenous variables in two structural and one definitional equations. However, most large models of the U.S. economy contain hundreds of variables and equations. They require estimates of tens, if not hundreds, of exogenous variables and provide forecasts of an even greater number of endogenous variables, ranging from *GNP* to consumption, investment, and exports and

CASE STUDY 5-7
Economic Forecasts with Large Econometric Models

Table 5-10 presents quarterly forecasts of real GDP, as well as yearly forecasts for real GDP, CPI (consumer price index or rate of inflation), and the jobless rate for the U.S. economy for the year 2006 prepared in the fall of 2005 by well-known econometric forecasters. Also included in the last row of Table 5-10 are the consensus forecasts (i.e., the average forecasts of all 54 economists included in the survey).

From the table we see that the forecast percentage change in real GDP from the fourth quarter of 2005 to the fourth quarter of 2006 ranges from 3.6 for Moody's Investors to 2.8 for the Conference Board, for an average of 3.5 for the 10 forecasts included in Table 5-10 and 3.3 for the consensus forecast of all 54 economists surveyed. For the rate of inflation, the range is from 3.5 for the National Federation of Independent Businesses to 1.5 for Standard & Poor's, for an average of 2.5 for the 10 forecasts included in Table 5-10 and 2.4 for the consensus forecast. The range for the jobless rate is from 5.2 for the Conference Board to 4.5 for Business Week and Goldman Sachs, for an average of 4.8 for the 10 forecasts included in Table 5-10 and 4.9 for the consensus forecast.

Most forecasts adjust the mechanical output of the econometric model for data revisions, past forecasting errors, feedback from users of the forecast, and for expected events (such as an anticipated strike) not considered by the model. The forecasting errors in these models are generally below 6 percent for GDP and less than 10 percent for the rate of inflation and unemployment. Economic forecasting, however, remains more of an art than a science.

TABLE 5-10   **Macroforecasts for 2006 by Econometric Services**

	Real GDP Growth Quarterly Percentage Change 2006 Annual Rate				Percentage Change 2005 Q4 to 2006 Q4		Jobless Rate 2005 Q4 to 2006 Q4
	I	II	III	IV	Real GDP	CPI	
Bank of America	4.2	4.1	3.6	3.0	3.7	2.0	4.9
Business Week	4.0	3.5	3.0	3.0	3.4	2.8	4.5
Conference Board	2.2	3.7	3.1	2.8	2.9	3.0	5.2
Federal Express	4.7	3.1	2.9	2.9	3.4	3.2	4.8
Goldman Sachs	3.5	4.0	3.5	3.5	3.7	2.4	4.5
J. P. Morgan Chase	3.5	4.0	3.0	3.0	3.4	1.8	4.7
Moody's Investors	3.5	4.5	3.7	3.6	3.8	2.7	4.6
Nat'l Fed. Indep. Bus.	4.0	3.2	3.3	3.5	3.5	3.5	4.9
Standard & Poor's	3.6	3.3	3.0	3.0	3.2	1.5	4.9
U.S. Chamber Comm.	3.7	3.6	3.4	3.3	3.5	2.3	5.0
Average	3.6	3.8	3.9	3.6	3.7	2.4	5.1
Consensus	3.7	3.4	3.1	3.1	3.3	2.4	4.9

Source: Business Week (December 26, 2005), pp. 74–75.

imports by sector, as well as for numerous other real and financial variables. Firms usually obtain (purchase) macroforecasts for the entire economy and its major sectors from companies specializing in making such forecasts, and they use these macroforecasts as inputs in their own specific forecasting of the demand and sales of the firm's product(s). Case Study 5-7 presents some econometric forecasts obtained with large econometric models, while Case Study 5-8 discusses the risks and the reliability of forecasting demand.

CASE STUDY 5-8
Risks in Demand Forecasting

Demand forecasting faces two major risks of grossly overestimating or underestimating demand. One risk arises from entirely unforeseen events, such as war, political upheavals, or natural disasters. The second risk arises from inadequate analysis of the market. For example, between 1983 and 1984, 67 new types of personal computers were introduced in the U.S. market, and most computer companies forecast growth of shipments to be twice as large as those that actually took place. This led to many computer companies going out of business by 1986. Computer companies based their forecast of rapid growth on the fact that there were more than 50 million white-collar workers in the United States in 1983 but only 8 million PCs. More careful market analysis, however, would have shown that two-thirds of white-collar workers either did not require a PC on their jobs or were already connected with inexpensive terminals to mainframe computers.

Another example is provided by the petroleum industry, which invested $500 billion worldwide between 1980 and 1981 in the expectation that demand would grow from 52 million barrels of oil per day in 1979 to 60 million barrels by 1985, and that this would raise petroleum prices 50 percent. Instead, because of increased energy efficiency, the demand for petroleum declined to 46 million barrels per day by 1986, and this resulted in the collapse of petroleum prices and huge losses in drilling, production, refining, and shipping investments. Still another example of a costly but avoidable forecasting error was committed by videogame companies, which projected explosive growth based on the very small (10 percent) overall

market penetration in the United States. More careful analysis with available data, however, would have shown that 75 percent of upper-income families with children between the ages of 6 and 15 (the main target market for video games) already had videogames.

To come closer to the present, no one, not even Alan Greenspan, the topnotch governor of the Federal Reserve Bank, or Fed (the Central Bank), of the United States saw the 2001 recession coming until several months after it officially started in March 2001. Similarly, the consensus forecast in December 2001 was for a growth rate of real GDP in the United States of 0.4 percent in the first quarter of 2002, as compared with the actual growth of 5.6 percent—and this by some of the leading forecasters and only a few months before the first quarter of 2002! Normally, however, forecasters do better.

All these costly forecasting errors could possibly have been avoided by (1) carefully defining the market for the product to include all potential users of the product and considering the possibility of product substitution, (2) dividing total industry demand into its main components and analyzing each component separately, (3) forecasting the main drivers or users of the product in each segment of the market and projecting how they are likely to change in the future, and (4) conducting sensitivity analyses of how the forecast would be affected by changes in any of the assumptions on which the forecast is based. Although uncertainties will remain, a manager who follows this fourfold approach is more likely to anticipate major changes in the demand for his or her product and to make better forecasts.

Source: "Four Steps to Forecast Total Market Demand," *Harvard Business Review* (July–August 1988), pp. 28–37; "Economists Prove Weak Fortune Tellers," *The Wall Street Journal* (April 9, 1998), p. A2; "Few Economists Are Seeing Recession, Survey Finds," *The Wall Street Journal* (February 12, 2001), p. A2; "The Recovery that Defied the Forecasts of Economists," *The New York Times* (March 7, 2002), p. C1; "Crystal Balls," *The Economist* (March 16, 2002), p. 76; and "First-Quarter GDP Is Revised Upward on Housing Surge," *The Wall Street Journal* (June 30, 2005), p. A2.

5-6   INPUT-OUTPUT FORECASTING

A firm can also forecast sales by using input-output tables. An *input-output table* examines the interdependence among the various industries and sectors of the economy. It shows the use of the output of each industry as inputs by other industries and for final consumption, and thus it can be used for forecasting. For example, it shows how an increase in the demand for trucks will lead to (and can be used to forecast) the increase in the demand for steel, glass, tires, plastic, upholstery materials, and so on, and how the increase in the demand for these products will, in turn, lead to an increase in the demand for the inputs required to produce them (including trucks). Input-output analysis allows us to trace through all these interindustry input and output flows throughout the economy and to determine (forecast) the total increase (direct and indirect) of all the inputs required to meet the increased demand for trucks.

The construction of an input-output table is a very time-consuming and expensive undertaking. Most firms using input-output tables for forecasting purposes rely on the input-output tables periodically constructed by the Bureau of Economic Analysis of the U.S. Department of Commerce. As of 2005, the most recent input-output table for the U.S. economy was for the year 2003 (from the 1997 benchmark I-O table) and refers to 85 industries and commodities, with a more detailed table for 498 industries and/or commodities also available.[13] Input-output forecasting has fallen in popularity, and it is not used very much by firms today.

SUMMARY

1. The aim of economic forecasting is to reduce the risk or uncertainty that the firm faces in its short-term operational decision making and in planning for its long-term growth. Forecasting techniques range from naive and inexpensive to sophisticated and expensive. By considering the advantages and limitations of various forecasting techniques, managers can choose the method or combinations of methods that are most suitable to the firm. Qualitative forecasts can be based on surveys of business executives' plans for plant and equipment expenditures, inventory changes and sales expectations, and surveys of consumer expenditure plans. Sales forecasts can be based on polls of a firm's executives, sales force, and consumers. Firms often solicit perspective from councils of foreign dignitaries and businesspeople.

2. One of the most frequently used forecasting methods is time-series analysis. Time-series data usually fluctuate because of secular trends, cyclical fluctuations, seasonal variations, and irregular or random influences. The simplest form of time-series analysis is trend projection. A linear trend assumes a constant absolute amount of change per time period. Sometimes an exponential trend (showing a constant percentage change per period) fits the data better. By incorporating the seasonal variation, we can significantly improve the trend forecast. This can be done by the ratio-to-trend method or by using dummy variables. It must be remembered, however, that time-series analysis is based on the assumption that the past pattern of movements in the data will continue unchanged.

---

[13] See P. Kuhbach and M. A. Planting, "Annual Input-Output Accounts of the U.S. Economy in 1997," *Survey of Current Business* (January 2001), pp. 9–43. For the 1998–2003 I-O tables of the U.S. economy, see: www.bea.gov/bea/pm/Annual_IOMakeUse.XLS.

3. Naive forecasting includes smoothing techniques, such as moving averages and exponential smoothing. These are useful when the time series exhibits little trend or seasonal variation but a great deal of irregular or random variation. With a moving average, the forecast value of a time series in a given period is equal to the average value of the time series in a number of previous periods. With exponential smoothing, the forecast for a given period is a weighted average of the actual and forecast values of the time series in the previous period. The exponential forecast is usually better than the moving average forecast. The weight chosen for the former is the one that minimizes the root-mean-square error (*RMSE*) of the forecast.

4. Turning points in the level of economic activity can be forecast by using the composite index of the best 10 leading economic indicators. These are time series that tend to precede (lead) changes in the level of general economic activity. Composite indexes smooth out random variations and provide more reliable forecasts and fewer wrong signals than individual indicators. The diffusion index is also used. This gives the percentage of the 10 leading indicators that move upward. Barometric forecasting is 80 to 90 percent successful in forecasting turning points in economic activity, the variability in lead time can be considerable, and it cannot predict the magnitude of the changes. Thus, barometric forecasting should be used in conjunction with other methods.

5. Forecasting is increasingly being performed with econometric models. These seek to explain the relationship(s) being forecast and are essential for devising optimal policies. Econometric forecasting models frequently incorporate other forecasting techniques and range from single-equation models forecasting a firm's sales of a product to very large, multiple-equation macromodels of the entire economy. Forecasting with single-equation models involves substituting into the estimated equation the predicted values of the independent or explanatory variables for the period of the forecast and solving for the forecast values of the dependent variable. In multiple-equation models, the estimated values of the exogenous variables (i.e., those determined outside the system) must be substituted into the estimated model to obtain forecasts of the endogenous variables.

6. A firm can also forecast sales by using input-output tables. An input-output table examines the interdependence among the various industries and sectors of the economy. It shows the use of the output of each industry as inputs by other industries and for final consumption, and thus it can be used for forecasting. Input-output forecasting has fallen in popularity and it is not used much by firms today.

DISCUSSION QUESTIONS

1. (*a*) What is forecasting? Why is it so important in the management of business firms and other enterprises? (*b*) What are the different types of forecasting? (*c*) How can the firm determine the most suitable forecasting method to use?

2. (*a*) What are qualitative forecasts? What are the most important forms of qualitative forecasts? (*b*) What is their rationale and usefulness? (*c*) What are the most important surveys of future economic activities? (*d*) What are the most important opinion polls of future economic activities? (*e*) Why is gaining a foreign perspective important? How do firms usually go about gaining this?

3. (*a*) What are time-series data? What are the possible sources of variation in time-series data? (*b*) What is the basic assumption in time-series analysis? (*c*) How are the sources of variation reflected in the time-series data? (*d*) Why does time-series analysis deal primarily with trend and seasonal variations rather than with cyclical and irregular or random variations? (*e*) Why is time-series analysis often referred to as naive forecasting?

4. (*a*) What is trend projection? (*b*) What does a linear trend measure? What is the other most common trend form used in time-series analysis? What does this show? Which is better? (*c*) Why might a forecast obtained by projecting a past trend into the future give poor results even if past patterns remain unchanged?

5. (*a*) What are two methods of incorporating the past seasonal variation in the data into a trend forecast?

(b) How is each accomplished?

(c) Which is better?

6. (a) What are smoothing techniques? (b) When are smoothing techniques useful in forecasting the value of a time series? (c) What are two types of smoothing techniques? How is each undertaken?

7. (a) Which type of smoothing technique is generally better? (b) How do we determine which of two smoothing techniques is better? (c) How can we forecast the values of a time series that contains a secular trend as well as strong seasonal and random variations?

8. By how many months were the troughs of 1974, 1980, 1981, 1991, and 2001 in Figure 5-4 anticipated by (a) the composite index of the 10 leading indicators? (b) the diffusion index of the 10 leading indicators?

9. Is it possible for the composite index of the 10 leading indicators to rise but the diffusion index of the same indicators to be below 50 percent for the same time period? Explain.

10. (a) What is econometric forecasting? How is it conducted? (b) What are the advantages of econometric forecasting over other forecasting techniques?

11. If econometric forecasting is the best forecasting technique, what usefulness remains for other forecasting techniques?

12. (a) What are endogenous and exogenous variables? (b) What are structural, definitional, and reduced-form equations? What is their importance in a multiple-equation model? (c) If multiple-equation models require estimating or predicting the exogenous variables in order to forecast the endogenous variables, why can't we forecast the endogenous variables directly without the need for a model?

13. (a) What is an input-output table? (b) How can it be used for forecasting?

14. How reliable are forecasts of demand or economic activity in the U.S. economy today?

15. Explain why it is still useful to pursue forecasting even though it is often off the mark by wide margins.

PROBLEMS

*1. This table shows gasoline sales in the United States (in thousands of barrels) from the first quarter of 1995 to the last quarter of 1998.

Gasoline Sales in the United States: 1995:1 to 1998:4 (in Thousands of Barrels)			
1995.1	22,434	1996.1	22,662
1995.2	23,766	1996.2	24,032
1995.3	23,860	1996.3	24,171
1995.4	23,391	1996.4	23,803
1997.1	22,776	1998.1	23,302
1997.2	24,491	1998.2	24,045
1997.3	24,751	1998.3	25,437
1997.4	24,170	1998.4	25,272

Source: American Petroleum Institute, *Basic Petroleum Data Book* (Washington, D.C., various issues).

(a) Estimate the linear trend in the data and use it to forecast gasoline sales in the United States in

each quarter of 1999. (b) Estimate the log-linear trend in the data, and use it to forecast gasoline sales in the United States in each quarter of 1999. (c) Which form of the trend fits the historical data better? Why would we expect both forecasts to be rather poor?

2. Adjust the linear trend projection found in Problem 1a for the seasonal variation in the data by using (a) the ratio-to-trend method and (b) dummy variables. (c) On the same graph, plot the original time series, the linear trend forecasts obtained in Problem 1a, and the forecasts obtained after adjustment for the seasonal variation by the ratio-to-trend method and by dummy variables.

*3. Adjust the trend forecasts of housing starts for each quarter of 2005 obtained from regression Equation 5-8 in Case Study 5-2 in the text by the use of dummy variables.

4. (a) Check the forecast of housing starts that was made for the four quarters of 2005 in

Case Study 5-2 against data from the most recent *Survey of Current Business* available in your college library. (*b*) What is the most important reason for the difference between the forecast and the actual number of housing starts in each quarter of 2005?

5. Using the index (with 1985 = 100) on housing starts in the United States per year from 1986 to 1997 given in the table below, forecast the index for 1998 using a three-year and a five-year moving average. Which of your estimates is better if the actual index of housing starts in the United States for 1998 is 163?

Index of Housing Starts in the United States: 1986 to 1997 (with 1985 = 100)

1986	1987	1988	1989	1990	1991
116	122	121	121	111	97
1992	1993	1994	1995	1996	1997
113	125	146	142	156	162

6. (*a*) Forecast the index of housing starts in the United States in 1998 by exponential smoothing with $w = 0.3$ and $w = 0.7$. (*b*) Which of these forecasts gives a better forecast for 1998? Which gives a better forecast on the average? (Skip this problem if "Exponential Smoothing" in Section 5-3 was not covered.)

7. The following table presents data on three leading indicators for a three-month period. Construct the composite index (with each indicator assigned equal weight) and the diffusion index.

Month	Leading Indicator *A*	Leading Indicator *B*	Leading Indicator *C*
1	100	200	30
2	110	230	27
3	120	240	33

8. The following table presents the monthly sales index of breakfast cereals of the Tasty Food Company for 2006 and three other time series for the same period. Indicate which time series is a (*a*) coincident indicator, (*b*) leading indicator (and

the lead time), and (*c*) lagging indicator (and the lag time).

	Month					
	1	2	3	4	5	6
Index of cereal sales	110	130	125	120	130	135
Time series *A*	50	60	56	54	60	62
Time series *B*	140	130	145	150	170	160
Time series *C*	100	100	120	115	110	120

	Month					
	7	8	9	10	11	12
Index of cereal sales	150	140	150	130	120	110
Time series *A*	70	65	70	60	54	50
Time series *B*	165	170	145	143	136	135
Time series *C*	125	120	125	115	110	100

*9. Using estimated regression Equation 3-4 for the demand for sweet potatoes in the United States presented in Case Study 3-2, forecast the demand for sweet potatoes for (*a*) 1972 and (*b*) 1973 if the forecast values of the independent or explanatory variables of the estimated demand equation are those given in the following table:

Year	P_S	N	Y	P_W
1972	4.10	208.78	3.19	2.41
1973	4.00	210.90	3.55	2.40

10. In their volume, *Consumer Demand in the United States: Analyses and Projections* (Cambridge, Mass.: Harvard University Press, 1970, p. 66), H. S. Houthakker and L. D. Taylor reported the following estimated demand equation for shoes in the United States over the period 1929 to 1961 (excluding the war years between 1942 and 1945):

$$Q_t = 19.575 + 0.0289X_t - 0.0923P_t - 99.568C_t - 4.06D_t$$
$$\quad\quad (9.3125) \quad (-1.7682) \quad (-9.8964) \quad (23.50)$$
$$R^2 = 0.857 \quad\quad D\text{-}W = 1.86$$

where Q_t = per capita personal consumption expenditures on shoes and other footwear during year t, at 1954 prices

X_t = total per capita consumption expenditures during year t, at 1954 prices

P_t = relative price of shoes in year t, at 1954 prices

C_t = stock of automobiles per capita in year t

D_t = dummy variable to separate pre– from post–World War II years; $D_t = 0$ for years 1929 through 1941 and $D_t = 1$ for years 1946 to 1961

The numbers in parentheses below the estimated slope coefficients refer to the estimated t statistics.

Using the above estimated regression equation, forecast the demand for shoes for (*a*) 1962 and (*b*) 1972 if the forecast values of the independent or explanatory variables are those given in the following table. (*c*) Why would you expect the error to be larger for the 1972 forecast than for the 1962 forecast?

Year	X	P	C
1962	1,646	20	0.4
1972	2,236	30	0.6

*11. In the simple macromodel given by Equations 5-21, 5-22, and 5-23 in Section 5-5, find the reduced-form equations for (*a*) C_t and (*b*) I_t.

12. Compare the macroforecasts for 2005 by econometric services presented in Table 5-10 in the text with the actual results for 2005 when they are out in the first quarter of 2006. How good were the forecasts?

13. From the last issue of *Business Week* for 2005, prepare a table similar to Table 5-10 in the text with the macroforecasts of the U.S. economy for 2006.

14. (*a*) Compare the macroforecasts for 2006 that you reported for Problem 13 with the actual results for 2006 when they are out in the first quarter of 2007. How good were the forecasts? (*b*) Were the forecasts for 2006 better or worse than the forecasts for 2005 in comparison with the actual results? To what do you attribute the difference in forecasting accuracy in the two years?

15. **Integrating Problem**
In their article, "The Demand for Coffee in the United States: 1963–1977" (*Quarterly Review of Economics and Business,* Summer 1980, pp. 36–50), C. J. Huang, J. J. Siegfried, and

F. Zardoshty estimated the following regression equation using quarterly data for the 58 quarters running from the first quarter of 1963 through the second quarter of 1977:

$$\ln Q_t = 1.2789 - 0.1647 \ln P_t + 0.5115 \ln I_t + 0.1483 \ln P'_t$$
$$\qquad\qquad (-2.14) \qquad\quad (1.23) \qquad\quad (0.55)$$
$$- 0.0089T - 0.0961D_{1t} - 0.1570D_{2t} - 0.0097D_{3t}$$
$$(-3.36) \quad (-3.74) \quad\quad (-6.03) \quad\quad (-0.37)$$
$$R^2 = 0.80 \quad D\!-\!W = 2.08$$

where Q_t = quantity (in pounds) of coffee consumed per capita (for population over 16 years of age) in quarter t

P_t = relative price of coffee per pound in quarter t, at 1967 prices

I_t = per capita disposable personal income in quarter t, in thousands of 1967 dollars

P'_t = relative price of tea per quarter pound in quarter t, at 1967 prices

T = time trend; $T = 1$ for first quarter of 1963 to $T = 58$ for second quarter of 1977

D_{1t} = dummy variable equal to 1 for first quarter (spring) and 0 otherwise

D_{2t} = dummy variable equal to 1 for second quarter (summer) and 0 otherwise

D_{3t} = dummy variable equal to 1 for third quarter (fall) and 0 otherwise

The numbers in parentheses below the estimated coefficients are t statistics.

Using the above estimated regression equation for the seasonal demand for coffee in the United States and predicting that the values of the independent or explanatory variables in the demand equation from the third quarter of 1977 to the second quarter of 1978 are those indicated in the following table, forecast the demand for coffee for (*a*) the third quarter of 1977, (*b*) the fourth quarter of 1977, (*c*) the first quarter of 1978, and (*d*) the second quarter of 1978. (*e*) How much confidence can we have in these forecasts? What could cause the forecasting error to be very large?

Quarter	P	Y	P'
1977.3	1.86	3.57	1.10
1977.4	1.73	3.60	1.08
1978.1	1.60	3.63	1.07
1978.2	1.46	3.67	1.05

APPENDIX TO CHAPTER 5: FORECASTING FLUCTUATIONS IN TIME-SERIES ANALYSIS USING EXCEL

In this appendix we show how to forecast new-housing starts with time-series analysis using Microsoft Excel. We will do so by showing how the results of Case Study 5-2 on forecasting new-housing starts were obtained. The results are slightly different because of rounding.

Forecasting New-Housing Starts with Regression Analysis

TABLE 5-11 Forecasting New-Housing Starts in the United States: 1999.1–2004.4 (in thousand units)

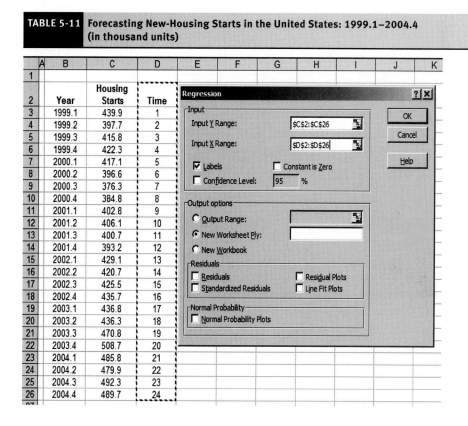

	Year	Housing Starts	Time
3	1999.1	439.9	1
4	1999.2	397.7	2
5	1999.3	415.8	3
6	1999.4	422.3	4
7	2000.1	417.1	5
8	2000.2	396.6	6
9	2000.3	376.3	7
10	2000.4	384.8	8
11	2001.1	402.8	9
12	2001.2	406.1	10
13	2001.3	400.7	11
14	2001.4	393.2	12
15	2002.1	429.1	13
16	2002.2	420.7	14
17	2002.3	425.5	15
18	2002.4	435.7	16
19	2003.1	436.8	17
20	2003.2	436.3	18
21	2003.3	470.8	19
22	2003.4	508.7	20
23	2004.1	485.8	21
24	2004.2	479.9	22
25	2004.3	492.3	23
26	2004.4	489.7	24

Regression dialog box:
- Input
  - Input Y Range: $C$2:$C$26
  - Input X Range: $D$2:$D$26
  - ☑ Labels   ☐ Constant is Zero
  - ☐ Confidence Level: 95 %
- Output options
  - ☐ Output Range:
  - ☉ New Worksheet Ply:
  - ☐ New Workbook
- Residuals
  - ☐ Residuals   ☐ Residual Plots
  - ☐ Standardized Residuals   ☐ Line Fit Plots
- Normal Probability
  - ☐ Normal Probability Plots
- OK   Cancel   Help

TABLE 5-11 *(continued)*

	A	B	C	D	E	F	G	H	I
1	SUMMARY OUTPUT								
2									
3	*Regression Statistics*								
4	Multiple R	0.76589969							
5	R Square	0.58660233							
6	Adjusted R Square	0.56781153							
7	Standard Error	24.5923764							
8	Observations	24							
9									
10	ANOVA								
11		*df*	*SS*	*MS*	*F*	*Significance F*			
12	Regression	1	18879.88883	18879.8888	31.21752283	1.2873E-05			
13	Residual	22	13305.2695	604.784977					
14	Total	23	32185.15833						
15									
16		*Coefficients*	*Standard Error*	*t Stat*	*P-value*	*Lower 95%*	*Upper 95%*	*Lower 95.0%*	*Upper 95.0%*
17	Intercept	381.210507	10.36200974	36.7892442	2.97006E-21	359.7209912	402.700023	359.720991	402.7000232
18	Time	4.05182609	0.725189617	5.58726434	1.2873E-05	2.547873258	5.55577892	2.54787326	5.555778916

	A	B	C	D	E	F
1						
2		Year	Housing Starts	Time		Forecast
3		1999.1	439.9	1		385.3
4		1999.2	397.7	2		389.3
5		1999.3	415.8	3		393.4
6		1999.4	422.3	4		397.4
7		2000.1	417.1	5		401.5
8		2000.2	396.6	6		405.5
9		2000.3	376.3	7		409.6
10		2000.4	384.8	8		413.6
11		2001.1	402.8	9		417.7
12		2001.2	406.1	10		421.7
13		2001.3	400.7	11		425.8
14		2001.4	393.2	12		429.8
15		2002.1	429.1	13		433.9
16		2002.2	420.7	14		437.9
17		2002.3	425.5	15		442.0
18		2002.4	435.7	16		446.0
19		2003.1	436.8	17		450.1
20		2003.2	436.3	18		454.1
21		2003.3	470.8	19		458.2
22		2003.4	508.7	20		462.2
23		2004.1	485.8	21		466.3
24		2004.2	479.9	22		470.4
25		2004.3	492.3	23		474.4
26		2004.4	489.7	24		478.5
27		2005.1		25		482.5
28		2005.2		26		486.6
29		2005.3		27		490.6
30		2005.4		28		494.7

Adjusting the Trend Forecasts of New-Housing Starts for Seasonal Variations by the Ratio-to-Trend Method

TABLE 5-12   Adjusting Trend Forecasts of New-Housing Starts for Seasonal Variation by Ratio-to-Trend Method

	A	B	C	D	E	F	G
1			Ratio to Trend				
2							
3		Year	Actual	Forecasted			Actual / Forecast
4		1999.1	439.9	385.3			1.142
5		2000.1	417.1	401.5			1.039
6		2001.1	402.8	417.7			0.964
7		2002.1	429.1	433.9			0.989
8		2003.1	436.8	450.1			0.970
9		2004.1	458.8	466.3			0.984
10						ave	1.015
11		1999.2	397.7	389.3			1.022
12		2000.2	396.6	405.5			0.978
13		2001.2	406.1	421.7			0.963
14		2002.2	420.7	437.9			0.961
15		2003.2	436.3	454.1			0.961
16		2004.2	479.9	470.4			1.020
17						ave	0.984
18		1999.3	415.8	393.4			1.057
19		2000.3	376.3	409.6			0.919
20		2001.3	400.7	425.8			0.941
21		2002.3	425.5	442			0.963
22		2003.3	470.8	458.2			1.027
23		2004.3	492.3	474.4			1.038
24						ave	0.991
25		1999.4	422.3	397.4			1.063
26		2000.4	384.8	413.6			0.930
27		2001.4	393.2	429.8			0.915
28		2002.4	435.7	446			0.977
29		2003.4	508.7	462.2			1.101
30		2004.4	489.7	478.5			1.023
31						ave	1.001

	A	B	C	D	E	F
1						
2						
3		Year	Time	Original Forecast	Ratio-to-Trend Adjustment	Forecast with Ratio-to-Trend Adjustment
4		2005.1	27	482.5	1.015	489.7
5		2005.2	28	486.6	0.984	478.8
6		2005.3	29	490.6	0.991	486.2
7		2005.4	30	494.7	1.001	495.2
8						

TABLE 5-12 *(continued)*

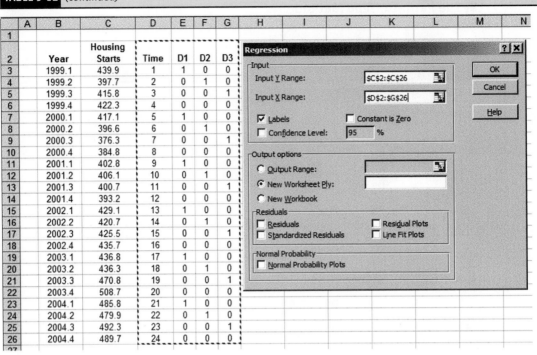

	Year	Housing Starts	Time	D1	D2	D3
3	1999.1	439.9	1	1	0	0
4	1999.2	397.7	2	0	1	0
5	1999.3	415.8	3	0	0	1
6	1999.4	422.3	4	0	0	0
7	2000.1	417.1	5	1	0	0
8	2000.2	396.6	6	0	1	0
9	2000.3	376.3	7	0	0	1
10	2000.4	384.8	8	0	0	0
11	2001.1	402.8	9	1	0	0
12	2001.2	406.1	10	0	1	0
13	2001.3	400.7	11	0	0	1
14	2001.4	393.2	12	0	0	0
15	2002.1	429.1	13	1	0	0
16	2002.2	420.7	14	0	1	0
17	2002.3	425.5	15	0	0	1
18	2002.4	435.7	16	0	0	0
19	2003.1	436.8	17	1	0	0
20	2003.2	436.3	18	0	1	0
21	2003.3	470.8	19	0	0	1
22	2003.4	508.7	20	0	0	0
23	2004.1	485.8	21	1	0	0
24	2004.2	479.9	22	0	1	0
25	2004.3	492.3	23	0	0	1
26	2004.4	489.7	24	0	0	0

Regression input dialog:
- Input Y Range: $C$2:$C$26
- Input X Range: $D$2:$G$26
- ☑ Labels ☐ Constant is Zero
- ☐ Confidence Level: 95 %
- Output options: ☐ Output Range: ; ⦿ New Worksheet Ply: ; ☐ New Workbook
- Residuals: ☐ Residuals ☐ Residual Plots ☐ Standardized Residuals ☐ Line Fit Plots
- Normal Probability: ☐ Normal Probability Plots
- OK / Cancel / Help

SUMMARY OUTPUT

Regression Statistics	
Multiple R	0.784322518
R Square	0.615161812
Adjusted R Square	0.534143247
Standard Error	25.53230977
Observations	24

ANOVA

	df	SS	MS	F	Significance F
Regression	4	19799.08033	4949.770083	7.592849939	0.000786059
Residual	19	12386.078	651.8988421		
Total	23	32185.15833			

	Coefficients	Standard Error	t Stat	P-value	Lower 95%	Upper 95%	Lower 95.0%	Upper 95.0%
Intercept	381.5266667	14.92421202	25.56427543	3.52663E-16	350.2899222	412.763411	350.2899222	412.7634111
Time	4.11	0.762923677	5.387170593	3.37305E-05	2.513181895	5.7068181	2.513181895	5.706818105
D1	8.513333333	14.91771051	0.570686321	0.574900379	-22.7098033	39.73647	-22.7098033	39.73646997
D2	-7.96333333	14.81984562	-0.53734253	0.597268684	-38.98163633	23.0549697	-38.9816363	23.05496967
D3	-4.72333333	14.76081524	-0.31999136	0.752467008	-35.61808429	26.1714176	-35.6180843	26.17141763

Adjusting the Trend Forecasts of New-Housing Starts for Seasonal Variations by Using Seasonal Dummies

TABLE 5-13 **Adjusting Trend Forecasts of New-Housing Starts for Seasonal Variation with Seasonal Dummies**

	A	B	C	D	E	F	G	H	I
1									
2		Year	Housing Starts	Time	D1	D2	D3		Forecast
3		1999.1	439.9	1	1	0	0		394.2
4		1999.2	397.7	2	0	1	0		381.8
5		1999.3	415.8	3	0	0	1		389.1
6		1999.4	422.3	4	0	0	0		398.0
7		2000.1	417.1	5	1	0	0		410.6
8		2000.2	396.6	6	0	1	0		398.2
9		2000.3	376.3	7	0	0	1		405.6
10		2000.4	384.8	8	0	0	0		414.4
11		2001.1	402.8	9	1	0	0		427.0
12		2001.2	406.1	10	0	1	0		414.7
13		2001.3	400.7	11	0	0	1		422.0
14		2001.4	393.2	12	0	0	0		430.8
15		2002.1	429.1	13	1	0	0		443.5
16		2002.2	420.7	14	0	1	0		431.1
17		2002.3	425.5	15	0	0	1		438.5
18		2002.4	435.7	16	0	0	0		447.3
19		2003.1	436.8	17	1	0	0		459.9
20		2003.2	436.3	18	0	1	0		447.5
21		2003.3	470.8	19	0	0	1		454.9
22		2003.4	508.7	20	0	0	0		463.7
23		2004.1	485.8	21	1	0	0		476.4
24		2004.2	479.9	22	0	1	0		464.0
25		2004.3	492.3	23	0	0	1		471.3
26		2004.4	489.7	24	0	0	0		480.2
27		2005.1		25	1	0	0		492.8
28		2005.2		26	0	1	0		480.4
29		2005.3		27	0	0	1		487.8
30		2005.4		28	0	0	0		496.6

SUPPLEMENTARY READINGS

A discussion of the forecasting techniques examined in this chapter is found in:

Berk, K. N., and P. Carey, *Data Analysis with Microsoft Excel* (Duxbury, Mass: Duxbury Press, 1995).

Campbell, John Y., Andrew W. Lo, and A. Graig MacKinlay, *The Econometrics of Financial Markets* (Princeton, N.J.: Princeton University Press, 1997).

Dukarat, James R., "Forecasting Demand," *Utility Business* (May 2001).

Granger, C. W., *Forecasting in Economics and Business* (New York: Academic Press, 1989).

Jain, C. L., "Forecasting Practices in Corporate America," *Journal of Business Forecasting Methods & Systems* (Summer 2001).

Pindyck, Robert S., and Daniel L. Rubenfeld, *Econometric Models and Economic Forecasts* (Boston: McGraw-Hill, 1997).

For qualitative forecasting, see:

Bertrand, M., and S. Mullainathan, "Do People Mean What They Say? Implications for Subjective

Survey Data," *American Economic Review* (May 2001).

Dunkelberg, W. C., "The Use of Survey Data in Forecasting," *Business Economics,* vol. 21 (January 1986).

For a discussion of barometric methods, see:

Conference Board, *Business Cycle Indicators* (New York, monthly).

U.S. Department of Commerce, Bureau of Economic Analysis: *Survey of Current Business* (Washington, D.C.: Government Printing Office, monthly).

Walsh, John F., "Sales Forecasting in Cyclical Markets," *Business Economics* (July 1998).

For more advanced techniques for estimating simultaneous equation models, see:

Diebold, Francis X., "The Past, Present, and Future of Macroeconomic Forecasts," *The Journal of Economic Perspectives* (Spring 1998).

Green, William, *Econometric Analysis* (Upper Saddle River, N.J.: Prentice-Hall, 1997), chap. 18.

Salvatore, D., and D. Reagle, *Theory and Problems of Statistics and Econometrics,* 2nd ed. (New York: McGraw-Hill, 2002), chap. 10.

For input-output analysis and forecasting, see:

Mohn, N. C., et al., "Input-Output Modeling: New Sales Forecasting Tool," *University of Michigan Business Review* (July 1986).

U.S. Department of Commerce, Bureau of Economic Analysis, "Benchmark Input-Output Accounts for the U.S. Economy, 1997: Requirements Tables," *Survey of Current Business* (December 2002).

 INTERNET SITE ADDRESSES

For general conditions of economic activity and forecasts, see the *Survey of Current Business,* the *Federal Reserve Bulletin,* and the *Economic Report of the President* at:

http://www.bea.doc.gov/bea/pubs.htm

http://www.federalreserve.gov/pubs/bulletin/default.htm

http://www.gpoaccess.gov/eop

For qualitative forecasting, see the Institute for Supply Management, the University of Michigan's Survey Research Center, and the Livingston Survey of the Philadelphia Federal Research Bank, respectively, at:

http://www.ism.ws

http://www.isr.umich.edu/src

http://www.phil.frb.org/econ/liv/index.html

For the index of leading indicators, see the Conference Board and the National Bureau of Economic Research (NBER) at:

http://www.conference-board.org/economics/bci/

http://www.nber.org

For forecasts of housing, see:

http://www.forecasts.org/house.htm

http://www.nahb.org/page.aspx/generic/sectionID=150

For gasoline consumption, see:

http://www.eia.doe.gov/oiaf/aeo/gas.html

http://www.eia.doe.gov/emeu/steo/pub/contents.html

For macroeconometric forecasting, see:

http://www.fairmodel.econ.yale.edu

http://www.cbo.gov/showdoc.cfm?index=5151&sequence=2

INTEGRATING CASE STUDY 2
Estimating and Forecasting
the U.S. Demand for Electricity

Estimating and forecasting the demand for electricity is very important since it takes many years to build capacity to meet future needs. One such estimate is provided by Halvorson, who used multiple regression analysis to estimate the market demand equation for electricity with cross-sectional data transformed into natural logarithms for the 48 contiguous states in the United States.

Table 2I-1 reports the estimated elasticity of demand for electricity for residential use in the United States with respect to the price of electricity, per capita income, the price of gas, and the number of customers in the market in 1969. Although the results of the various studies differ somewhat, the results reported below indicate that the amount of electricity for residential use consumed in the United States would fall by 9.74 percent as a result of a 10 percent increase in the price of electricity, would increase by 7.14 percent with a 10 percent increase in per capita income, would increase by 1.59 percent with a 10 percent increase in the price of gas, and is proportional to the number of customers in the market. Thus, the market demand curve for electricity is negatively sloped, electricity is a normal good and a necessity, and gas is a substitute for electricity.

TABLE 2I-1	Elasticities of Demand for Electricity for Residential Use in the United States
Variable	**Elasticity**
Price	−0.974
Per capita income	0.714
Price of gas	0.159
Number of customers	1.000

Source: R. Halvorson, "Demand for Electric Energy in the United States," *Southern Economic Journal* (April 1976).

Using these estimated demand elasticities and projecting the growth in per capita income, in the price of gas, in the number of customers in the market, and in the price of electricity, public utilities could forecast the growth in the demand for electricity in the United States so as to adequately plan new capacity to meet future needs. For example, if we assume that per capita income grows at 3 percent per year, the price of gas at 20 percent per year, the number of customers at 1 percent per year, and the price of electricity at 4 percent per year, we can forecast that the demand for electricity for residential use in the United States will expand at a rate of 2.43 percent per year. This is obtained by adding the products of the value of each elasticity by the projected growth of the corresponding variable, as indicated in the following equation:

$$Q = (0.714)(3\%) + (0.159)(20\%)$$
$$+ (1.000)(1\%) - (0.974)(4\%)$$
$$= 2.142 + 3.180 + 1.000 - 3.896$$
$$= 6.322 - 3.896 = 2.426$$

With different projections on the yearly growth in per capita income, the price of gas, the number of customers in the market, and the price of electricity, we will get correspondingly different results.

The above results are shown in Figure 2I-1, where P_0 and Q_0 are the original price and quantity of electricity demanded in the United States on the hypothetical demand curve D_0 in the base period (say, the current year). Demand curve D' results from the projected increase in per capita income, D'' from the increase in the price of gas and D_1 from the increase in the number of customers in the market. Thus, D_1 takes into account or reflects the cumulative effect of all the growth factors considered.

Were the price of electricity to remain constant, the demand for electricity would rise by 6.322 percent per year (given by the movement from point A on D_0 to point G on D_1 in the figure). The projected increase in the price of electricity by 4 percent per year (from P_0 to P_1), by itself will result in a decline in the quantity demanded of electricity by 3.896 percent (the movement from point G to point F on D_1). The net result of all forces at work gives rise to a net increase in Q of 2.426 percent per year (the movement from point A on D_0 to point F on D_1).

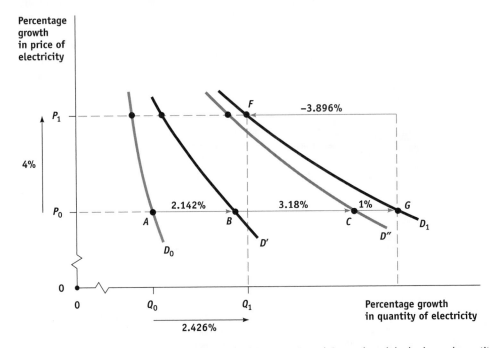

FIGURE 2I-1   Forecast of Electricity in the United States P_0 and Q_0 are the original price and quantity of electricity demanded in the United States on demand curve D_0. D' results from projecting a 3 percent increase in per capita incomes, D'' by also projecting a 20 percent increase in the price of gas, and D_1 from projecting a 1 percent increase in the number of customers in the market as well. If the price of electricity also increases by 4 percent (from P_0 to P_1), the demand for electricity increases by 2.426 percent per year (the movement from point A on D_0 to point F on D_1).

Until the mid-1990s, when the deregulation of the electricity market started in the United States, the nation's regulatory commissions set low electricity rates, and this discouraged the building of new power plants. Electric power companies simply preferred charging higher electricity rates at times of peak demand rather than building the new plants.

All this began to change during the past decade as the electricity market started to be deregulated. Botched up deregulation, however, led to widespread electricity shortages, blackouts or brownouts, and sharply higher electricity prices in California and other western states during 2000 and 2001. This inturn slowed down, put on hold, or even reversed the deregulation process.

In August and November 2003, the Northeast was hit by huge electric power blackouts. Since then, however, enough new capacity came on line to eliminate shortages and keep electricity prices relatively low in the United States. The nation does need to build from 1,300 to 1,900 new power plants to meet future demand, which is expected to grow by 45 percent by the year 2020. Since it takes from 6 to 12 years to build a new plant, electric power companies have no time to waste.

Demand studies have been conducted for practically every major commodity in the United States and are widely used by businesspeople and managers to forecast demand. This, in turn, greatly affects investments in new plants and equipment and the general level of economic activity.

Source: R. Halvorson, "Demand for Electric Energy in the United States," *Southern Economic Journal* (April 1976); Michael Weiner et al., "Value Networks—The Future of the U.S. Electric Utility Industry," *Sloan Management Review* (Summer 1997), pp. 21–34; "The Challenge for Utilities: Increase Capacity and Efficiency," *The Wall Street Journal* (December 18, 2000), p. C6; S. Borenstein, "The Trouble with Energy Markets: Understanding California's Restructuring Disaster," *Journal of Economic Perspectives* (Winter 2002), pp. 191–212; "Enron's Lessons for the Energy Market," *The New York Times* (May 11, 2002), p. 17; "Surplus of Energy Supplies May Persist at Least Until 2005," *The Wall Street Journal* (February 21, 2003), p. A3; and Energy Information Administration, *Annual Energy Outlook* (Washington, D.C.: EIA, 2005).

PART THREE

Production and Cost Analysis

Part Three (Chapters 6 and 7) presents the theory and measurement of the firm's production and costs. These are what lie behind the firm's supply of the commodity. Chapter 6 examines production theory and measurement, or how firms combine inputs to produce goods and services. These concepts are extended in Chapter 7 to derive the short-run and the long-run cost curves of the firm. The rising importance of innovations and global competitiveness, as well as trade in parts and components, are also examined.

CHAPTER 6 Production Theory and Estimation

CHAPTER OUTLINE

Appendix to Chapter 6: Production Analysis with Calculus • Constrained Output Maximization • Constrained Cost Minimization • Profit Maximization • Appendix Problems

Supplementary Readings • Internet Site Addresses

 KEY TERMS (in the order of their appearance)

Production	Marginal revenue product (MRP)	Cobb–Douglas production function
Inputs	Marginal resource cost (MRC)	Product innovation
Fixed inputs	Isoquant	Process innovation
Variable inputs	Ridge lines	Closed innovation model
Short run	Marginal rate of technical substitution (MRTS)	Open innovation model
Long run	Isocost line	Product cycle model
Production function	Expansion path	Just-in-time production system
Total product (TP)	Constant returns to scale	Competitive benchmarking
Marginal product (MP)	Increasing returns to scale	Computer-aided design (CAD)
Average product (AP)	Decreasing returns to scale	Computer-aided manufacturing (CAM)
Output elasticity		
Law of diminishing returns		
Stages I, II, III of production		

In Chapter 1, we defined the firm as an organization that combines and organizes labor, capital, and land or raw materials for the purpose of producing goods and services for sale. The aim of the firm is to maximize total profits or achieve some other related aim, such as maximizing sales or growth. The basic production decision facing the firm is how much of the commodity or service to produce and how much labor, capital, and other resources or inputs to use to produce that output most efficiently. To answer these questions, the firm requires engineering or technological data on production possibilities (the *production function*) as well as economic data on input and output prices. This chapter provides the framework for understanding the economics of production of the firm and derives a set of conditions for efficient production.

The chapter begins with a discussion of the production function, which summarizes the engineering and technological production possibilities open to the firm. This general discussion is extended to the specific case where there is a single variable input or resource (Section 6-2) and examines how much of the variable input the firm should employ to maximize profits (Section 6-3). We then go on to examine the production function when there are two variable inputs (Section 6-4) and to develop the conditions for their efficient combination in production (Section 6-5). In Section 6-6, we discuss returns to scale where all resources or inputs are variable. Section 6-7 discusses the empirical estimation of production functions. Section 6-8 deals with the innovation process. Finally, Section 6-9 deals with technological progress and innovations and their importance for the domestic and global competitiveness of firms. In the Chapter Appendix (which is optional), we use simple calculus to examine the conditions for maximizing output, minimizing costs, or maximizing profits. The nine case studies presented throughout the chapter highlight the importance of production theory to the firm and its great relevance in managerial economics.

| 6-1 |

THE ORGANIZATION OF PRODUCTION AND THE PRODUCTION FUNCTION

In this section, we examine first the organization of production and classify inputs into various broad categories, and then we define the meaning and usefulness of the production function in analyzing the firm's production activity.

The Organization of Production

Production refers to the transformation of inputs or resources into outputs of goods and services. For example, IBM hires workers to use machinery, parts, and raw materials in factories to produce personal computers. The output of a firm can either be a final commodity (such as a personal computer) or an intermediate product, such as semiconductors (which are used in the production of computers and other goods). The output can also be a service rather than a good. Examples of services are education, medicine, banking, communication, transportation, and many others. Note that *production* refers to all of the activities involved in the production of goods and services, from borrowing to setting up or expanding production facilities, to hiring workers, purchasing raw materials, running quality control, cost accounting, and so on, rather than referring merely to the physical transformation of inputs into outputs of goods and services.

Inputs are the resources used in the production of goods and services. As a convenient way to organize the discussion, inputs are classified into labor (including entrepreneurial talent), capital, and land or natural resources. Each of these broad categories, however, includes a great variety of the basic input. For example, labor includes bus drivers, assembly-line workers, accountants, lawyers, doctors, scientists, and many others. Inputs are also classified as fixed or variable. **Fixed inputs** are those that cannot be readily changed during the time period under consideration, except perhaps at very great expense. Examples of fixed inputs are the firm's plant and specialized equipment (it takes several years for IBM to build a new factory to produce computer chips to go into its computers). On the other hand, **variable inputs** are those that can be varied easily and on very short notice. Examples of variable inputs are most raw materials and unskilled labor.

The time period during which at least one input is fixed is called the **short run,** while the time period when all inputs are variable is called the **long run.** The length of the long run (i.e., the time period required for all inputs to be variable) depends on the industry. For some, such as the setting up or expansion of a dry-cleaning business, the long run may be only a few months or weeks. For others, such as the construction of a new electricity-generating plant, it may be many years. In the short run, a firm can increase output only by using more of the variable inputs (say, labor and raw materials) together with the fixed inputs (plant and equipment). In the long run, the same increase in output could likely be obtained more efficiently by also expanding the firm's production facilities (plant and equipment). Thus, we say that the firm operates in the short run and plans increases or reductions in its scale of operation in the long run. In the long run, technology usually improves, so that more output can be obtained from a given quantity of inputs, or the same output from less inputs.

The Production Function

Just as demand theory centers on the concept of the demand function, production theory revolves around the concept of the production function. A **production function** is an equation, table, or graph showing the maximum output of a commodity that a firm can produce per period of time with each set of inputs. Both inputs and outputs are measured in physical rather than in monetary units. Technology is assumed to remain constant during the period of the analysis.

For simplicity we assume here that a firm produces only one type of output (commodity or service) with two inputs, labor (L) and capital (K). Thus, the general equation of this simple production function is

$$Q = f(L, K) \hspace{3cm} [6\text{-}1]$$

Equation 6-1 reads: The quantity of output is a function of, or depends on, the quantity of labor and capital used in production. *Output* refers to the number of units of the commodity (say, automobiles) produced, *labor* refers to the number of workers employed, and *capital* refers to the amount of the equipment used in production. We assume that all units of L and K are homogeneous or identical. An explicit production function would indicate precisely the quantity of output that the firm would produce with each particular set of inputs of labor and capital. Although our discussion will be in terms of a single output produced with only two inputs, the principles that we will develop are general and apply to cases in which the firm uses more than two inputs and produces more than one output (the usual situation).

Table 6-1 gives a hypothetical production function which shows the outputs (the Q's) that the firm can produce with various combinations of labor (L) and capital (K). The table shows that by using 1 unit of labor (1L) and 1 unit of capital (1K), the firm would produce 3 units of output (3Q). With 2L and 1K, output is 8Q; with 3L and 1K, output is 12Q; with 3L and 2K, output is 28Q; with 4L and 2K, output is 30Q, and so on. Note also that labor and

TABLE 6-1	Production Function with Two Inputs						
Capital (K)	6	10	24	31	36	40	39	
	5	12	28	36	40	42	40	
	4	12	28	36	40	40	36	Output (Q)
	3	10	23	33	36	36	33	
↑	2	7	18	28	30	30	28	
K	1	3	8	12	14	14	12	
		1	2	3	4	5	6	
		$L \rightarrow$		Labor (L)				

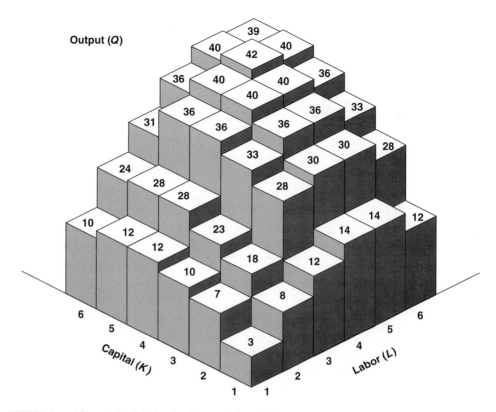

FIGURE 6-1 Discrete Production Surface The height of the bars refers to the maximum output (Q) that can be produced with each combination of labor (L) and capital (K) shown on the axes. Thus, the tops of all the bars form the production surface for the firm.

capital can be substituted for each other in production. For example, 12Q can be produced either with 3L and 1K or with 1L and 4K.[1] Input prices will determine which of these two combinations of labor and capital is cheaper. The output that the firm will want to produce is the one that maximizes its total profits. These questions will be examined and answered later in the chapter.

The production relationships given in Table 6-1 are shown graphically in Figure 6-1, which is three-dimensional. In Figure 6-1, the height of the bars refers to the maximum output that can be produced with each combination of labor and capital shown on the axes. Thus, the tops of all the bars form the production surface for the firm.

If we assume that inputs and outputs are continuously or infinitesimally divisible (rather than being measured in discrete units), we would have an infinite number of outputs, each resulting from one of the infinite number of combinations of labor and capital that could be used in production. This is shown in Figure 6-2, in which the axes forming

---

[1] 12Q could also be produced with 1K and 6L instead of 1K and 3L (see the last entry in the first row of the table), but the firm would certainly not want to use this combination of labor and capital. Similarly, 12Q could be produced with 1L and either 4K or 5K, but the firm would not want to use the latter input combination.

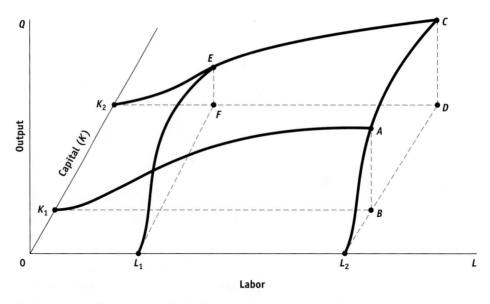

FIGURE 6-2 Continuous Production Surface The horizontal and inclined axes measure, respectively, the labor and capital inputs, while the vertical axis measures the height of the surface or the maximum level of output resulting from each input combination—all assumed to be continuously divisible. The output generated by holding capital constant at K_1 and increasing labor from zero to L_2 units is given by the height of cross section K_1AB (with base parallel to the labor axis).

the base of the figure measure the labor and capital inputs, while the height of the surface gives the (maximum) level of output resulting from each input combination, all assumed to be continuously divisible.

For example, by keeping the quantity of capital used at K_1 in Figure 6-2 and increasing the quantity of labor used from zero to L_2 units (so that we are in the short run), the firm generates the output shown by the height of cross section K_1AB (with base parallel to the labor axis). On the other hand, by increasing the amount of labor used from zero to L_2 units but keeping capital constant at K_2 rather than K_1 (so that we are still in the short run), the firm generates the output shown by the top of cross section K_2CD. If instead the firm kept labor constant at L_1 and increased the quantity of capital used from zero to K_2 units, the firm's output would be the one shown by the top of cross section L_1EF (with base parallel to the capital axis). With labor constant at L_2, on the other hand, the firm's output generated by changing the quantity of capital used from zero to K_2 units would be the one shown by the height of cross section L_2CD.

6-2   THE PRODUCTION FUNCTION WITH ONE VARIABLE INPUT

In this section, we present the theory of production when only one input is variable. Thus, we are in the short run. We begin by defining the total, the average, and the marginal product of the variable input and deriving from these the output elasticity of the variable input.

TABLE 6-2	Total, Marginal, and Average Product of Labor, and Output Elasticity			
(1)	(2)	(3)	(4)	(5)
Labor (number of workers)	Output or Total Product	Marginal Product of Labor	Average Product of Labor	Output Elasticity of Labor
0	0	—	—	—
1	3	3	3	1
2	8	5	4	1.25
3	12	4	4	1
4	14	2	3.5	0.57
5	14	0	2.8	0
6	12	−2	2	−1

We will then examine the law of diminishing returns and the meaning and importance of the stages of production. These concepts will be used in Section 6-3 to determine the optimal use of the variable input for the firm to maximize profits.

Total, Average, and Marginal Product

By holding the quantity of one input constant and changing the quantity used of the other input, we can derive the **total product (*TP*)** of the variable input. For example, by holding capital constant at 1 unit (i.e., with $K = 1$) and increasing the units of labor used from zero to 6 units, we generate the total product of labor given by the last row in Table 6-1, which is reproduced in column 2 of Table 6-2. Note that when no labor is used, total output or product is zero. With one unit of labor ($1L$), total product (*TP*) is 3. With $2L$, $TP = 8$. With $3L$, $TP = 12$, and so on.[2]

From the total product schedule we can derive the marginal and average product schedules of the variable input. The **marginal product (*MP*)** of labor (MP_L) is the change in total product or extra output per unit change in labor used, while the **average product (*AP*)** of labor (AP_L) equals total product divided by the quantity of labor used. That is,[3]

$$MP_L = \frac{\Delta TP}{\Delta L} \qquad [6\text{-}2]$$

$$AP_L = \frac{TP}{L} \qquad [6\text{-}3]$$

Column 3 in Table 6-2 gives the marginal product of labor (MP_L). Since labor increases by 1 unit at a time in column 1, the MP_L in column 3 is obtained by subtracting successive

---

[2] The reason for the decline in *TP* when $6L$ is used will be discussed shortly.
[3] In terms of calculus, $MP_L = \partial TP/\partial L$.

quantities of TP in column 2. For example, TP increases from 0 to 3 units when the first unit of labor is used. Thus, $MP_L = 3$. For an increase in labor from $1L$ to $2L$, TP rises from 3 to 8 units, so that $MP_L = 5$, and so on. Column 4 of Table 6-2 gives the AP_L. This equals TP (column 2) divided by L (column 1). Thus, with 1 unit of labor ($1L$), $AP_L = 3$. With $2L$, $AP_L = 4$, and so on.

Column 5 in Table 6-2 gives the production or **output elasticity** of labor (E_L). This measures the percentage change in output divided by the percentage change in the quantity of labor used. That is,

$$E_L = \frac{\%\Delta Q}{\%\Delta L} \qquad [6\text{-}4]$$

By rewriting Equation 6-4 in a more explicit form and rearranging, we get

$$E_L = \frac{\Delta Q/Q}{\Delta L/L} = \frac{\Delta Q/\Delta L}{Q/L} = \frac{MP_L}{AP_L} \qquad [6\text{-}5]$$

That is, the output elasticity of labor is equal to the ratio of MP_L to AP_L.[4] For example, for the first unit of labor, $E_L = \frac{3}{3} = 1$. This means that from $0L$ to $1L$ (and with $K = 1$), TP or output grows proportionately to the growth in the labor input. For the second unit of labor, $E_L = 1.25$ (i.e., TP or output grows more than proportionately to the increase in L), and so on.

Plotting the total, marginal, and average product of labor of Table 6-2 gives the corresponding product curves shown in Figure 6-3. Note that TP grows to 14 units with $4L$, remains at 14 units with $5L$, and then declines to 12 units with $6L$ (see the top panel of Figure 6-3). The reason for this is that with the addition of the sixth worker, workers begin to get in each other's way and total product declines. In the bottom panel, we see that AP_L rises to 4 units and then declines. Since the marginal product of labor refers to the change in total product per unit change in labor used, each value of the MP_L is plotted halfway between the quantities of labor used. Thus, the MP_L of 3 units of output that results by going from $0L$ to $1L$ is plotted at $0.5L$. The MP_L of 5 that results from increasing labor from $1L$ to $2L$ is plotted at $1.5L$, and so on. The MP_L curve rises to 5 units of output at $1.5L$ and then declines. Past $4.5L$, the MP_L becomes negative.

Had the firm kept capital fixed at $K = 2$, increasing the amount of labor used from $0L$ to $6L$ would have given the TP shown by the second row from the bottom in Table 6-1. This would correspond to the cross section at $K = 2$ in Figure 6-1. From this TP function and curve, we could then derive the MP_L and AP_L functions as done in Table 6-2 and shown in two-dimensional space in Figure 6-3. While the actual values of TP, MP_L, and AP_L for $K = 2$ would differ from the corresponding ones with $K = 1$, the shape of the curves would generally be the same (see Problem 2, with answer at the end of the book).

---

[4] In terms of calculus,

$$E_L = \frac{\partial Q}{\partial L} \cdot \frac{L}{Q}$$

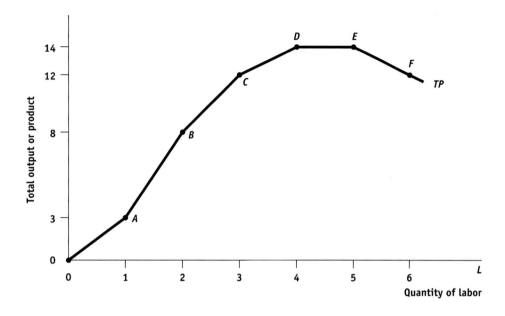

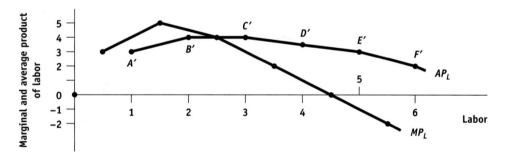

FIGURE 6-3 Total, Marginal, and Average Product of Labor Curves The top panel shows the total product of labor curve. *TP* is highest between 4*L* and 5*L*. The bottom panel shows the marginal and the average product of labor curves. The MP_L is plotted halfway between successive units of labor used. The MP_L curve rises up to 1.5*L* and then declines, and it becomes negative past 4.5*L*. The AP_L is highest between 2*L* and 3*L*.

The Law of Diminishing Returns and Stages of Production

In order to show graphically the relationship between the total product, on the one hand, and the marginal and average products of labor, on the other, we assume that labor time is continuously divisible (i.e., it can be hired for any part of a day). Then the *TP*, MP_L, and AP_L become smooth curves as indicated in Figure 6-4. The MP_L at a particular point on the *TP* curve is given by the slope of the *TP* curve at that point. From Figure 6-4, we see that the slope of the *TP* curve rises up to point *G* (the point of inflection on the *TP* curve), is zero at point *J*, and is negative thereafter. Thus, the MP_L rises up to point *G′*, is zero at point *J′*, and is negative afterward.

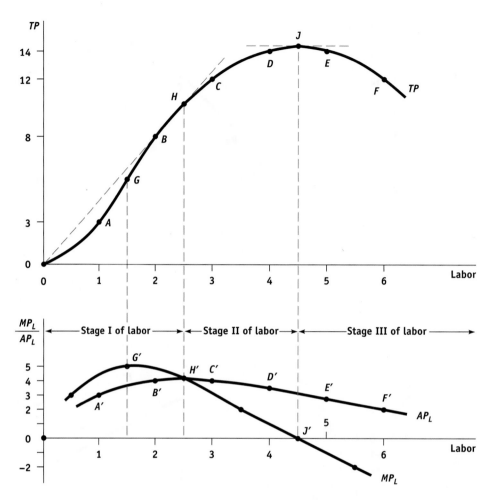

FIGURE 6-4   Total, Marginal, and Average Product Curves, and Stages of Production   With labor time continuously divisible, we have smooth *TP*, *MP*, and *AP* curves. The MP_L (given by the slope of the tangent to the *TP* curve) rises up to point *G′*, becomes zero at *J′*, and is negative thereafter. The AP_L (given by the slope of the ray from the origin to a point on the *TP* curve) rises up to point *H′* and declines thereafter (but remains positive as long as *TP* is positive). Stage I of production for labor corresponds to the rising portion of the AP_L. Stage II covers the range from maximum AP_L to where MP_L is zero. Stage III occurs when MP_L is negative.

The AP_L is given by the slope of a ray from the origin to the *TP* curve. From Figure 6-4, we see that the slope of the *TP* curve rises up to point *H* and falls thereafter but remains positive as long as *TP* is positive. Thus, the AP_L rises up to point *H′* and falls afterward. Note that at point *H* the slope of a ray from the origin to the *TP* curve (or AP_L) is equal to the slope of the *TP* curve (or MP_L). Thus, $AP_L = MP_L$ at point *H′* (the highest point on the AP_L curve). Note also that AP_L rises as long as MP_L is above it and falls when MP_L is below it.

From Figure 6-4, we can also see that up to point *G,* the *TP* curve increases at an increasing rate so that the MP_L rises. Labor is used so scarcely with the 1 unit of capital that the MP_L rises as more labor is used. Past point G, however, the TP curve rises at a decreasing rate so that the MP_L declines. The declining portion of the MP_L curve is a reflection of the **law of diminishing returns.** This postulates that as we use more and more units of the variable input with a given amount of the fixed input, after a point, we get diminishing returns (marginal product) from the variable input. In Figure 6-4, the law of diminishing returns begins to operate after $1.5L$ is used (after point G' in the bottom panel of Figure 6-4). Note that diminishing returns is not a theorem that can be proved or disproved with logic but is a physical law which has been found to be always empirically true. It states that after a point, we will invariably get diminishing returns from the variable input. That is, as the firm uses more and more units of the variable input with the same amount of the fixed input, each additional unit of the variable input has less and less of the fixed input to work with and, after a point, the marginal product of the variable input declines.

The relationship between the MP_L and AP_L curves in the bottom panel of Figure 6-4 can be used to define three stages of production for labor (the variable input). The range from the origin to the point where the AP_L is maximum (point H' at $2.5L$) is **stage I of production** for labor. **Stage II of production** for labor extends from the point where the AP_L is maximum to the point where the MP_L is zero (i.e., from point H' at $2.5L$ to point J' at $4.5L$). The range over which the MP_L is negative (i.e., past point J' or with more than $4.5L$) is **stage III of production** for labor. The rational producer would not operate in stage III of labor, even if labor time were free, because MP_L is negative. This means that a greater output or TP could be produced by using *less* labor! Similarly, he or she will not produce in stage I for labor because (as shown in more advanced texts) this corresponds to stage III of capital (where the MP of capital is negative).[5] Thus, the rational producer will operate in stage II where the MP of both factors is positive but declining. The precise point within stage II at which the rational producer operates will depend on the prices of inputs and output. This is examined in the next section.

6-3   OPTIMAL USE OF THE VARIABLE INPUT

How much labor (the variable input in our previous discussion) should the firm use in order to maximize profits? The answer is that the firm should employ an additional unit of labor as long as the extra revenue generated from the sale of the output produced exceeds the extra cost of hiring the unit of labor (i.e., until the extra revenue equals the extra cost). For example, if an additional unit of labor generates $30 in extra revenue and costs an extra $20 to hire, it pays for the firm to hire this unit of labor. By doing so, the firm adds $30 to its revenues and $20 to its costs, so that its total profits increase. It does not pay, however, for the firm to hire an additional unit of labor if the extra revenue it generates falls short of the extra cost incurred. This is an example or application of the general optimization principle examined in Chapter 2.

---

[5] Stage I of labor corresponds to stage III of capital only under constant returns to scale. This is the case where output changes in the same proportion as the change in all inputs (see Section 6-6).

TABLE 6-3	Marginal Revenue Product and Marginal Resource Cost of Labor			
(1)	(2)	(3)	(4) = (2) × (3)	(5)
Units of Labor	Marginal Product	Marginal Revenue = P	Marginal Revenue Product	Marginal Resource Cost = w
2.5	4	$10	$40	$20
3.0	3	10	30	20
3.5	2	10	20	20
4.0	1	10	10	20
4.5	0	10	0	20

The extra revenue generated by the use of an additional unit of labor is called the **marginal revenue product** of labor (MRP_L). This equals the marginal product of labor (MP_L) times the marginal revenue (MR) from the sale of the extra output produced. That is,

$$MRP_L = (MP_L)(MR) \qquad [6\text{-}6]$$

On the other hand, the extra cost of hiring an additional unit of labor or **marginal resource cost** of labor (MRC_L) is equal to the increase in the total cost to the firm resulting from hiring the additional unit of labor. That is,

$$MRC_L = \frac{\Delta TC}{\Delta L} \qquad [6\text{-}7]$$

Thus, a firm should continue to hire labor as long as $MRP_L > MRC_L$ and until $MRP_L = MRC_L$. We can examine the optimal use of labor (and profit maximization) by the firm facing the short-run production function discussed in Section 6-2 with the aid of Table 6-3.

Column 2 in Table 6-3 gives the marginal product of labor read off from the MP_L curve in stage II of production in the bottom panels of Figures 6-3 and 6-4. The fractional units of labor are based on the assumption that the firm can hire labor for the full or for half a day. Only the MP_L in stage II is given in column 2 because the firm would never produce in stage III of labor (where the MP_L is negative) or in stage I of labor (which corresponds to the stage of negative marginal product for capital). Column 3 gives the marginal revenue of $10 from the sale of each additional unit of the commodity produced, on the assumption that the firm is small and can sell the additional units of the commodity at the given market price (P) of $10. Column 4 gives the marginal revenue product of labor obtained by multiplying the MP_L in column 2 by the $MR = P$ of the commodity in column 3. Note that the MRP_L declines because the MP_L declines. Column 5 gives the marginal resource cost of labor on the assumption that the firm is small and can hire additional units of labor at the constant market wage rate (w) of $20 for each half-day of work.

From Table 6-3, we see that the firm should hire 3.5 units of labor because that is where $MRP_L = MRC_L = \$20$. At less than 3.5L, $MRP_L > MRC_L$, and the firm would be adding more to its total revenues than to its total cost by hiring more labor. For example, with 3L, $MRP_L = \$30$, and this exceeds the MRC_L of $20. By hiring more labor, the firm

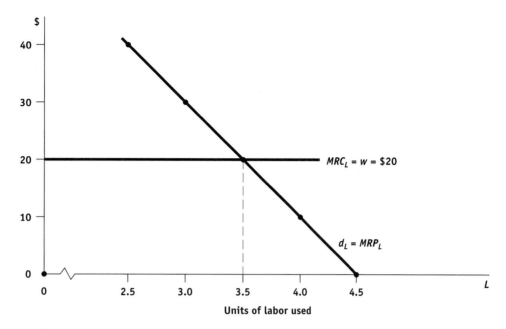

FIGURE 6-5   Optimal Use of Labor It pays for the firm to hire more labor as long as the marginal revenue product of labor (MRP_L) exceeds the marginal resource cost of hiring labor (MRC_L), and until $MRP_L = MRC_L$. With $MRC_L = w = \$20$, the optimal amount of labor for the firm to use is 3.5 units. At 3.5L, $MRP_L = MRC_L = \$20$, and the firm maximizes total profits.

would increase its total profits. On the other hand, if the firm used more than 3.5L, $MRP_L <$ MRC_L, and the firm would be adding more to its total costs than to its total revenue, and its total profits would be lower. For example, with 4L, $MRP_L = \$10$, while $MRC_L = \$20$. The firm could then increase its total profits by hiring less labor. Only with 3.5L will $MRP_L = MRC_L = \$20$, and the firm's profits are maximized. Thus, the optimal use of labor is 3.5 units. Note that the marginal revenue product of labor (MRP_L) schedule in column 4 of Table 6-3 represents the firm's demand schedule for labor. It gives the amount of labor demanded by the firm at various wage rates. For example, if the wage rate per day (w) were \$40, the firm would hire 2.5 units of labor because that would be where $MRP_L = MRC_L = w = \$40$. If $w = \$30$, the firm would demand 3 units of labor. If $w = \$20$, the firm would demand 3.5L, and with $w = \$10$, the firm would demand 4L. This is shown in Figure 6-5, where $d_L = MRP_L$ represents the firm's demand curve for labor. The figure shows that if the wage rate per day (w) were constant at \$20, the firm would demand 3.5L, as indicated above.

This discussion is applicable to any variable input, not just labor. To be noted is that the *MRP* of the variable input can be found not only by multiplying the marginal product of the input by the marginal revenue from the sale of the output produced but it can also be obtained from the change in the total revenue that would result per unit change in the variable input used (see Problem 5, with answer at the end of the book). Case Study 6-1 examines the relationship between labor productivity and total compensation in the United States and abroad.

CASE STUDY 6-1
Labor Productivity and Total Compensation in the U.S. and Abroad

According to the marginal productivity theory, wages equal labor's marginal revenue product, and an increase in labor productivity should be reflected in a similar wage increase. In fact, the increase in total real compensation (wages and fringe benefits) has been 9.0 percent over the 1996–2000 period—almost identical to the increase in total labor productivity of 9.2 percent. Similarly, using 1950 as the base, the increase in the real compensation of U.S. labor from 1950 to 2000 was 151.2 percent as compared with the increase in U.S. labor productivity of 154.1 percent over the same period. Every time a gap arose between the growth in inflation-adjusted compensation and the growth of labor productivity in the United States, it invariably disappeared after a year or two. From 2000 to 2004, however, labor productivity has increased by about 4.1 percent per year while wages have increased by only 1.5 percent. Globalization and the decline in unionization of the U.S. labor force have been blamed for the increase in wages falling short of the increase in labor productivity. It is not clear whether this is a short-term cyclical problem or the beginning of a long-term trend.

The increase in labor productivity in the United States has been greater than in the other Group of Seven (G-7) leading industrial nations (Japan, Germany, France, Britain, Italy, and Canada) since the second half of the 1990s, but not earlier. Since 1996, labor productivity has increased at an annual average of 3.1 percent in the United States, as compared to 1.4 percent for the other G-7 nations. From 1981 to 1995, however, labor productivity increased at an average 1.2 percent per year in the United States and 2.2 percent in the other G-7 nations. This has led to a great deal of wage convergence to the higher U.S. levels in the G-7 countries. The more rapid growth of labor productivity since the second half of the last decade in the United States than in the other G-7 countries has been attributed to a more rapid spread of the "new economy" based on the new information technology and greater flexibility in labor markets and in the economy in general in the United States than abroad.

Source: "Productivity Is All, But It Doesn't Pay Well," *The New York Times* (June 25, 1995), sec. E, p. 3; "As Worker's Pay Lags, Causes Spur a Debate," *The Wall Street Journal* (July 31, 1995), p. A1; "Productivity Developments Abroad," *Federal Reserve Bulletin* (Oct. 2000); and "Salaries Stagnate as Balance of Power Shifts to Employers," *Financial Times,* May 11, 2005, p. 6.

6-4   THE PRODUCTION FUNCTION WITH TWO VARIABLE INPUTS

We now examine the production function when there are two variable inputs. This can be represented graphically by isoquants. In this section we define isoquants and discuss their characteristics. Isoquants will then be used in Section 6-5 to develop the conditions for the efficient combination of inputs in production.

Production Isoquants

An **isoquant** shows the various combinations of two inputs (say, labor and capital) that the firm can use to produce a specific level of output. A higher isoquant refers to a larger

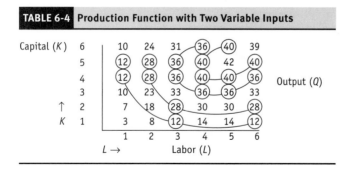

TABLE 6-4 Production Function with Two Variable Inputs

output, while a lower isoquant refers to a smaller output. Isoquants can be derived from Table 6-4, which repeats the production function of Table 6-1 with lines connecting all the labor–capital combinations that can be used to produce a specific level of output. For example, the table shows that 12 units of output (that is, 12*Q*) can be produced with 1 unit of capital (that is, 1*K*) and 3 units of labor (that is, 3*L*) or with 1*K* and 6*L*.[6] The output of 12*Q* can also be produced with 1*L* and 4*K*, and 1*L* and 5*K*. These are shown by the lowest isoquant in Figure 6-6. The isoquant is smooth on the assumption that labor and capital are continuously divisible. Table 6-4 also shows that 28*Q* can be produced with 2*K* and 3*L*, 2*K* and 6*L*, 2*L* and 4*K*, and 2*L* and 5*K* (the second isoquant marked 28*Q* in Figure 6-6). The table also shows the various combinations of *L* and *K* that can be used to produce 36*Q* and 40*Q* (shown by the top two isoquants in the figure). Note that to produce a greater output, more labor, more capital, or more of both labor and capital are required.

Economic Region of Production

While the isoquants in Figure 6-6 (repeated in Figure 6-7) have positively sloped portions, these portions are irrelevant. That is, the firm would not operate on the positively sloped portion of an isoquant because it could produce the same level of output with less capital and less labor. For example, the firm would not produce 36*Q* at point *U* in Figure 6-7 with 6*L* and 4*K* because it could produce 36*Q* by using the smaller quantities of labor and capital indicated by point *V* on the same isoquant. Similarly, the firm would not produce 36*Q* at point *W* with 4*L* and 6*K* because it could produce 36*Q* at point *Z* with less *L* and *K*. Since inputs are not free, the firm would not want to produce in the positively sloped range of isoquants.

Ridge lines separate the relevant (i.e., negatively sloped) from the irrelevant (or positively sloped) portions of the isoquants. In Figure 6-7, ridge line 0*VI* joins points on the various isoquants where the isoquants have zero slope. The isoquants are negatively sloped to the left of this ridge line and positively sloped to the right. This means that starting, for example, at point *V* on the isoquant for 36*Q*, if the firm used more labor, it would also have to use more capital to remain on the same isoquant (compare point *U* to point *V*). Starting from point *V*, if the firm used more labor with the same amount of capital, the level of output would fall (i.e., the firm would fall back to a lower isoquant; see the dashed horizontal line in the figure). The same is true at all other points on ridge line 0*VI*. Therefore, the *MP_L*

---

[6] Since inputs are not free, a firm would produce 12*Q* with 1*K* and 3*L* rather than with 1*K* and 6*L*.

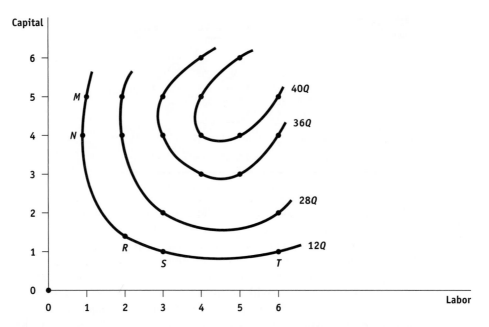

FIGURE 6-6   Isoquants   An isoquant shows the various combinations of two inputs that can be used to produce a specific level of output (Q). From Table 6-4, we can see that 12Q can be produced with 1L and 5K (point M), 1L and 4K (point N), 2L and 1.5K (point R), 3L and 1K (point S), or 6L and 1K (point T). Higher isoquants refer to higher levels of output.

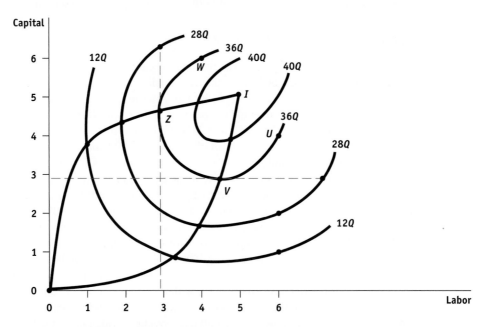

FIGURE 6-7   The Relevant Portion of Isoquants   The economic region of production is given by the negatively sloped segment of isoquants between ridge lines 0VI and 0ZI. The firm will not produce in the positively sloped portion of the isoquants because it could produce the same level of output with both less labor and less capital.

must be negative to the right of this ridge line. This corresponds to stage III of production for labor.

Ridge line $0ZI$ joins points where the isoquants have infinite slope. The isoquants are negatively sloped to the right of this ridge line and positively sloped to the left. This means that starting, for example, at point Z on the isoquant for $36Q$, if the firm used more capital, it would also have to use more labor to remain on the same isoquant (compare point W with point Z). Starting at point Z, if the firm used more capital with the same quantity of labor, the level of output would fall (i.e., the firm would fall back to a lower isoquant; see the dashed vertical line in the figure). The same is true at all other points on ridge line $0ZI$. Therefore, the MP_K must be negative to the left of or above this ridge line. This corresponds to stage III of production for capital.

Thus, we conclude that the negatively sloped portion of the isoquants within the ridge lines represents the relevant economic region of production. This refers to stage II of production for labor and capital, where the MP_L and the MP_K are both positive but declining. Producers will never want to operate outside this region. As a result, in the rest of the chapter we will draw only the negatively sloped portions of isoquants.

Marginal Rate of Technical Substitution

We saw in the previous section that isoquants are negatively sloped in the economically relevant range. This means that if the firm wants to reduce the quantity of capital that it uses in production, it must increase the quantity of labor in order to remain on the same isoquant (i.e., produce the same level of output). For example, the movement from point N to point R on isoquant $12Q$ in Figure 6-8 indicates that the firm can give up $2.5K$ by

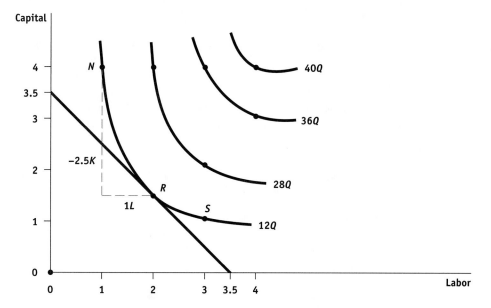

FIGURE 6-8 The Slope of Isoquants   The absolute value of the slope of an isoquant is called the *marginal rate of technical substitution* (*MRTS*). Between points N and R on isoquant $12Q$, *MRTS* = 2.5. Between points R and S, *MRTS* = $\frac{1}{2}$. The *MRTS* at any point on an isoquant is given by the absolute slope of the tangent to the isoquant at that point. Thus, at point R, *MRTS* = 1.

adding $1L$. Thus, the slope of isoquant $12Q$ between points N and R is $-2.5K/1L$. Between points R and S, the slope of isoquant $12Q$ is $-\frac{1}{2}$, and so on.

The absolute value of the slope of the isoquant is called the **marginal rate of technical substitution (MRTS).** For a movement down along an isoquant, the marginal rate of technical substitution of labor for capital is given by $-\Delta K/\Delta L$. We multiply $\Delta K/\Delta L$ by -1 in order to express the $MRTS$ as a positive number. Thus, the $MRTS$ between points N and R on the isoquant for $12Q$ is 2.5. Similarly, the $MRTS$ between points R and S is $\frac{1}{2}$. The $MRTS$ at any point on an isoquant is given by the absolute slope of the isoquant at that point. Thus, the $MRTS$ at point R is 1 (the absolute slope of the tangent to the isoquant at point R; see Figure 6-8).[7]

The $MRTS$ of labor for capital is also equal to MP_L/MP_K. We can prove this by remembering that all points on an isoquant refer to the same level of output. Thus, for a movement down a given isoquant, the gain in output resulting from the use of more labor must be equal to the loss in output resulting from the use of less capital. Specifically, the increase in the quantity of labor used (ΔL) times the marginal product of labor (MP_L) must equal the reduction in the amount of capital used ($-\Delta K$) times the marginal product of capital (MP_K). That is,

$$(\Delta L)(MP_L) = -(\Delta K)(MP_K) \tag{6-8}$$

so that

$$\frac{MP_L}{MP_K} = \frac{-\Delta K}{\Delta L} = MRTS \tag{6-9}$$

Thus, $MRTS$ is equal to the absolute slope of the isoquant and to the ratio of the marginal productivities.

Within the economically relevant range, isoquants are not only negatively sloped but also convex to the origin (see Figure 6-8). The reason for this is that as the firm moves down an isoquant and uses more labor and less capital, the MP_L declines and the MP_K increases (since the firm is in stage II of production for both labor and capital). With the MP_L declining and the MP_K rising as we move down along an isoquant, the $MP_L/MP_K = MRTS$ will fall (thus, the isoquant is convex to the origin).

---

[7] The $MRTS$ at a particular point on an isoquant when labor and capital are continuously divisible (so that the isoquant is a smooth curve) can be obtained by taking the total differential of the production function $Q = f(L, K)$, setting this total differential equal to zero (since output does not change along a given isoquant), and solving for dK/dL (the slope of the isoquant). That is,

$$dQ = \frac{\partial Q}{\partial L} \cdot dL + \frac{\partial Q}{\partial K} \cdot dK = 0$$

so that

$$\frac{dK}{dL} = (-)\frac{\partial Q / \partial L}{\partial Q / \partial K}$$

Since $\partial Q/\partial L = MP_L$ and $\partial Q/\partial K = MP_K$,

$$\frac{dK}{dL} = (-)\frac{MP_L}{MP_K} = MRTS$$

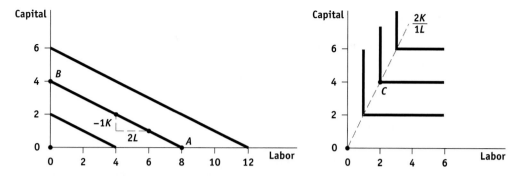

FIGURE 6-9 Perfect Substitutes and Complementary Inputs When an isoquant is a straight line (so that its absolute slope or *MRTS* is constant), inputs are perfect substitutes. In the left panel, 2*L* can be substituted for 1*K* regardless of the point of production on the isoquant. With the right-angled isoquants in the right panel, efficient production can take place only with 2*K*/1*L*. Thus, labor and capital are perfect complements. Using only more labor or only more capital does not increase output (that is, $MP_L = MP_K = 0$).

Perfect Substitutes and Complementary Inputs

The shape of an isoquant reflects the degree to which one input can be substituted for another in production. On one hand, the smaller the curvature of an isoquant, the greater is the degree of substitutability of inputs in production. On the other hand, the greater the curvature of an isoquant, the smaller is the degree of substitutability.

At one extreme are isoquants that are straight lines, as shown in the left panel of Figure 6-9. In this case, labor and capital are perfect substitutes. That is, the rate at which labor can be substituted for capital in production (i.e., the absolute slope of the isoquant or *MRTS*) is constant. This means that labor can be substituted for capital (or vice versa) at the constant rate given by the absolute slope of the isoquant. For example, in the left panel of Figure 6-9, 2*L* can be substituted for 1*K* regardless of the point of production on the isoquant. In fact, point *A* on the labor axis shows that the level of output indicated by the middle isoquant can be produced with labor alone (i.e., without any capital). Similarly, point *B* on the capital axis indicates that the same level of output can be produced with capital only (i.e., without any labor). Examples of near-perfect input substitutability are oil and gas used to operate some heating furnaces, energy and time in a drying process, and fish meal and soybeans used to provide protein in a feed mix.[8]

At the other extreme of the spectrum of input substitutability in production are isoquants that are at a right angle, as in the right panel of Figure 6-9. In this case, labor and capital are perfect complements. That is, labor and capital must be used in the fixed proportion of 2*K*/1*L*. In this case there is zero substitutability between labor and capital in production. For example, starting at point *C* on the middle isoquant in the right panel of Figure 6-9, output remains unchanged if only the quantity of labor used is increased (that is, $MP_L = 0$ along the horizontal portion of the isoquant). Similarly, output remains unchanged if only the quantity of capital is increased (that is, $MP_K = 0$ along the vertical

---

[8] The MP_L also declines because less capital is used. On the other hand, the MP_K increases because more labor is also used.

portion of the isoquant). Output can be increased only by increasing the quantity of both labor and capital used in the proportion of $2K/1L$. Examples of perfect complementary inputs are certain chemical processes that require basic elements (chemicals) to be combined in a specified fixed proportion, engine and body for automobiles, two wheels and a frame for bicycles, and so on. In these cases, inputs can be used only in the fixed proportion specified (i.e., there is no possibility of substituting one input for another in production).

Although perfect substitutability and perfect complementarity of inputs in production are possible, in most cases isoquants exhibit some curvature (i.e., inputs are imperfect substitutes), as shown in Figure 6-8. This means that in the usual production situation, labor can be substituted for capital to some degree. The smaller the degree of curvature of the isoquant, the more easily inputs can be substituted for each other in production. In addition, when the isoquant has some curvature, the ability to substitute labor for capital (or vice versa) diminishes as more and more labor is substituted for capital. This is indicated by the declining absolute slope of the isoquant or *MRTS* as we move down along an isoquant (see Figure 6-8). The ability to substitute one input for another in production is extremely important in keeping production costs down when the price of an input increases relative to the price of another.

6-5   OPTIMAL COMBINATION OF INPUTS

As we have seen in the previous section, an isoquant shows the various combinations of labor and capital that a firm can use to produce a given level of output. In this section we examine isocosts. An **isocost line** shows the various combinations of inputs that a firm can purchase or hire at a given cost. By the use of isocosts and isoquants, we will then determine the optimal input combination for the firm to maximize profits. In this section, we will also examine input substitution in production as a result of a change in input prices.

Isocost Lines

Suppose that a firm uses only labor and capital in production. The total costs or expenditures of the firm can then be represented by

$$C = wL + rK \tag{6-10}$$

where C is total costs, w is the wage rate of labor, L is the quantity of labor used, r is the rental price of capital, and K is the quantity of capital used. Thus, Equation 6-10 postulates that the total costs of the firm (C) equals the sum of its expenditures on labor (wL) and capital (rK). Equation 6-10 is the general equation of the firm's isocost line or equal-cost line. It shows the various combinations of labor and capital that the firm can hire or rent at a given total cost. For example, if $C = \$100$, $w = \$10$, and $r = \$10$, the firm could either hire $10L$ or rent $10K$, or any combination of L and K shown on isocost line AB in the left panel of Figure 6-10. For each unit of capital the firm gives up, it can hire one additional unit of labor. Thus, the slope of the isocost line is -1.

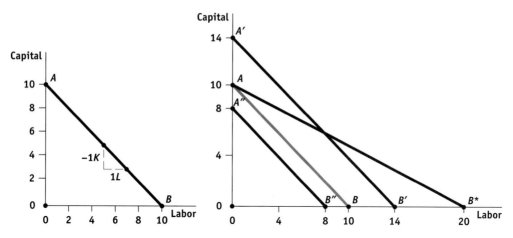

FIGURE 6-10   Isocost Lines   With total cost of $C = \$100$ and $w = r = \$10$, we have isocost line AB in the left panel, with vertical intercept of $C/r = \$100/\$10 = 10K$ and slope of $-w/r = -\$10/\$10 = -1$. With $C' = \$140$ and $w = r = \$10$, we have isocost line $A'\,B'$ in the right panel. With $C'' = \$80$ and $w = r = \$10$, the isocost line is $A''B''$ in the right panel. On the other hand, with $C = \$100$ and $r = \$10$ but $w = \$5$, we have isocost line AB^* in the right panel, with vertical intercept of $10K$ and slope of $-\frac{1}{2}$.

By subtracting wL from both sides of Equation 6-10 and then dividing by r, we get the general equation of the isocost line in the following more useful form:

$$K = \frac{C}{r} - \frac{w}{r} L \qquad [6\text{-}11]$$

where C/r is the vertical intercept of the isocost line and $-w/r$ is its slope. Thus, for $C = \$100$ and $w = r = \$10$, the vertical intercept is $C/r = \$100/\$10 = 10K$, and the slope is $-w/r = -\$10/\$10 = -1$ (see isocost line AB in the left panel of Figure 6-10).

A different total cost by the firm would define a different but parallel isocost line, while different relative input prices would define an isocost line with a different slope. For example, an increase in total expenditures to $C' = \$140$ with unchanged $w = r = \$10$ would give isocost line $A'B'$ in the right panel of Figure 6-10, with vertical intercept $C'/r = \$140/\$10 = 14K$ and slope of $-w/r = -\$10/\$10 = -1$. If total expenditures declined to $C'' = \$80$ with unchanged $w = r = \$10$, the isocost line would be $A''B''$, with vertical intercept of $C''/r = \$80/\$10 = 8K$ and slope of $-w/r = -\$10/\$10 = -1$. On the other hand, with $C = \$100$ and $r = \$10$ but $w = \$5$, we would have isocost line AB^*, with vertical intercept of $C/r = \$100/\$10 = 10K$ and slope of $-w/r = -\$5/\$10 = -\frac{1}{2}$.

Optimal Input Combination for Minimizing Costs or Maximizing Output

The optimal combination of inputs needed for a firm to minimize the cost of producing a given level of output or maximize the output for a given cost outlay is given at the tangency point of an isoquant and an isocost. For example, Figure 6-11 shows that the lowest cost of producing 10 units of output (i.e., to reach isoquant 10Q) is given by point E, where isoquant $10Q$ is tangent to isocost line AB. The firm uses $5L$ at a cost of $\$50$ and $5K$ at a cost of $\$50$

and Equation 6-6 that the marginal revenue product (*MRP*) of an input equals the marginal product of the input (*MP*) times the marginal revenue (*MR*) generated from the sale of the output. Thus, we can rewrite Equations 6-15 and 6-16 as

$$(MP_L)(MR) = w \qquad\qquad [6\text{-}17]$$

$$(MP_K)(MR) = r \qquad\qquad [6\text{-}18]$$

Dividing Equation 6-17 by Equation 6-18 gives

$$\frac{MP_L}{MP_K} = \frac{w}{r} \qquad\qquad [6\text{-}19]$$

Cross-multiplying in Equation 6-19 gives the condition for the optimal combination of inputs given by Equation 6-14:

$$\frac{MP_L}{w} = \frac{MP_K}{r} \qquad\qquad [6\text{-}14]$$

Note that there is an optimal input combination for each level of output (see points *D*, *E*, and *F* in Figure 6-11), but only at one of these outputs (the one where *MRP* of each input equals the input price) will the firm maximize profits. That is, to maximize profits, the firm must produce the profit-maximizing level of output with the optimal input combination. By hiring inputs so that Equations 6-15 and 6-16 are satisfied, however, both conditions are met at the same time. That is, the firm will be producing the best or profit-maximizing level of output with the optimal input combination.

Effect of Change in Input Prices

Starting from an optimal input combination, if the price of an input declines, the firm will substitute the cheaper input for other inputs in production in order to reach a new optimal input combination. For example, Figure 6-12 shows that with $C = \$100$ and $w = r = \$10$, the optimal input combination is $5K$ and $5L$ given by point E, where isoquant $10Q$ is tangent to isocost AB (as in Figure 6-11). At point E, the capital–labor ratio (that is, K/L) is 1.

If r remains at \$10 but w falls to \$5, the isocost line becomes AB^*, and the firm can reach isoquant $14Q$ with $C = \$100$ (point N in Figure 6-12). The firm can now reach isoquant $10Q$ with $C = \$70$. This is given by isocost A^*B', which is parallel to AB^* (that is, $-w/r = -\frac{1}{2}$ for both) and is tangent to isoquant $10Q$ at point R. At point R, the firm uses $3K$ at a cost of \$30 and $8L$ at a cost of \$40, for a total cost of \$70. At point R, $K/L = \frac{3}{8}$ (as compared with $K/L = 1$ at point E before the reduction in w). Thus, with a reduction in w (and constant r), a lower C is required to produce a given level of output. To minimize the production cost of producing $10Q$, the firm will have to substitute L for K in production, so that K/L declines.

The ease with which the firm can substitute L for K in production depends on the shape of the isoquant. As we have seen in Section 6-4, the flatter the isoquant, the easier it is to substitute L for K in production. On the other hand, if the isoquant is at a right angle (as in the right panel of Figure 6-9), no input substitution is possible (that is, $MRTS = 0$). Then, K/L will be constant regardless of input prices. Case Study 6-2 examines the trade-off between consumption and traveling time on the nation's highway.

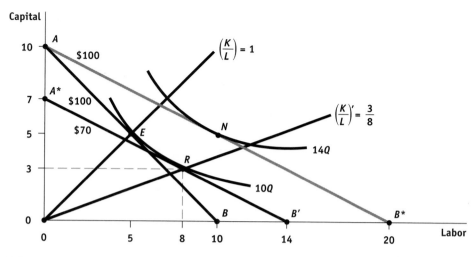

FIGURE 6-12 Input Substitution in Production With $C = \$100$ and $w = r = \$10$, the optimal input combination to produce $10Q$ is $5K$ and $5L$ (point E, where isoquant $10Q$ is tangent to isocost AB). At point E, $K/L = 1$. If r remains at $10 but w falls to $5, the firm can reach isoquant $10Q$ with $C = \$70$. The optimal combination of L and K is then given by point R where isocost $A*B'$ is tangent to isoquant $10Q$, and $K/L = \frac{3}{8}$.

CASE STUDY 6-2
Substitutability between Gasoline Consumption and Driving Time

Higher highway speed reduces driving time but increases gasoline consumption by reducing gas mileage. The trade-off between gasoline consumption and traveling time for a trip of 360 miles can be represented by the isoquant shown in Figure 6-13. The isoquant shows that at 50 miles per hour, the 360 miles can be covered in 7.2 hours (that is, 7 hours and 12 minutes) with 10 gallons of gasoline, at 36 miles per gallon (point A). At 60 miles per hour, the 360 miles can be covered in 6 hours with 12 gallons of gasoline, at 30 miles per gallon (point B). Driving at 60 miles per hour saves 1 hour and 12 minutes of travel time but increases gasoline consumption by 2 gallons. At 72 miles per hour, the trip will take 5 hours and 15 gallons of gasoline, at 24 miles per gallon (point C). Driving at 72 miles per hour saves another 1 hour of travel time but increases gasoline consumption by another 3 gallons.

If the price of gasoline were $2 per gallon and if the individual could have earned $4 per hour by working rather than driving, the optimal combination of the inputs of gasoline and travel time would be at point B where the isoquant is tangent to isocost DE. At point B, the absolute slope of isocost DE is $\frac{1}{2}$ (the ratio of the price of 1 gallon of gasoline to the cost of 1 hour of driving time). The minimum cost for the trip is then $48 (6 hours of driving time at $4 per hour plus 12 gallons of gasoline at $2 per gallon). If the price of gasoline fell from $2 to $1 per gallon, the optimal combination of driving time and gasoline would be given instead by point C where the isoquant is tangent to isocost line FG. At point C the absolute slope of isocost FG is $\frac{1}{4}$ and reflects the new relative price of gasoline ($1 per gallon) and traveling time ($4 per hour). The minimum cost of the trip would then be $35 (5 hours of

Continued . . .

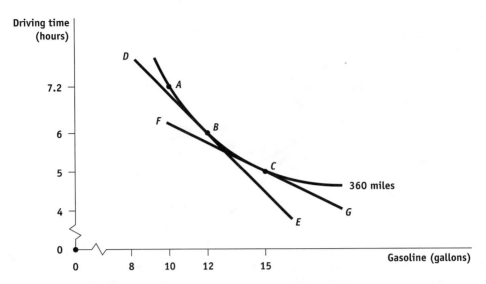

FIGURE 6-13 **The Optimal Combination of Gasoline and Driving Time** At the gasoline price of $2 per gallon and foregone earnings of $4 per hour for driving, the minimum cost of a 360-mile trip is given by point *B*, at which the isoquant is tangent to isocost *DE*. The optimal driving speed is 60 miles per hour so that the trip would take 6 hours and 12 gallons of gasoline at a total cost of $48. If the price of gasoline falls to $1, the minimum cost of the trip is given by point *C*, at which the isoquant is tangent to isocost *FG*. The optimal driving speed is 72 miles per hour so that the trip would take 5 hours and 15 gallons of gasoline at a total cost of $35.

traveling time at $4 per hour plus 15 gallons of gasoline at $1 per gallon).

Thus, the repeal of the 55-miles-an-hour law in 1987 (which had been imposed in 1974 at the start of the petroleum crisis to save gasoline) was a rational response to the decline in gasoline prices (in relation to other prices) and the increase in real wages that

had taken place since 1981. Opposition to the repeal of the 55-miles-an-hour law came primarily from those who believe that lower speed limits save lives. Relatively low gasoline prices from 1986 to 2003 did, however, bring to a halt progress in energy efficiency.

Source: Charles A. Lave, "Speeding, Coordination, and the 55-MPH Limit," *American Economic Review* (December 1985), pp. 1159–1164; "Death Rate on U.S. Roads Reported at a Record Low," *The New York Times* (October 27, 1998), p. 16; "Looking for Ways to Save Gasoline," *The Wall Street Journal* (July 12, 2001), p. A1; "Senate Kills Effort to Raise Cars' Fuel Efficiency," *The Wall Street Journal* (March 14, 2002), p. A2; "Fuel Economy Below 80's Levels, E.P.A. Says," *The New York Times* (October 30, 2002), p. C4; "How Much Is Your Time Worth?" *The New York Times* (February 26, 2003), p. D1; "At $2 a Gallon, Gas Is Still Worth Guzzling," *The New York Times* (May 16, 2004), sec. 4, p. 14; and "New Gas-Mileage Standards May Vary by Vehicle Weight, *The Wall Street Journal* (July 10, 2005), p. A2.

6-6   RETURNS TO SCALE

Returns to scale refers to the degree by which output changes as a result of a given change in the quantity of all inputs used in production. There are three types of returns to scale: constant, increasing, and decreasing. If the quantity of all inputs used in production is increased by a given proportion, we have **constant returns to scale** if output increases in the same proportion; **increasing returns to scale** if output increases by a greater proportion; and **decreasing returns to scale** if output increases by a smaller proportion. That is, suppose that starting with the general production function

$$Q = f(L, K) \qquad\qquad [6\text{-}1]$$

we multiply L and K by h, and Q increases by l, as indicated in Equation 6-20:

$$\lambda Q = f(hL, hK) \qquad\qquad [6\text{-}20]$$

We have constant, increasing, or decreasing returns to scale, respectively, depending on whether $\lambda = h$, $\lambda > h$, or $\lambda < h$.

For example, when all inputs are doubled, we have constant, increasing, or decreasing returns to scale, respectively, if output doubles, more than doubles, or less than doubles. This is shown in Figure 6-14. In all three panels of Figure 6-14, we start with the firm using $3L$ and $3K$ and producing $100Q$ (point A). By doubling inputs to $6L$ and $6K$, the left panel shows that output also doubles to $200Q$ (point B), so that we have constant returns to scale. The center panel shows that output triples to $300Q$ (point C), so that we have increasing returns to scale, while the right panel shows that output only increases to $150Q$ (point D), so that we have decreasing returns to scale. Here h (the increase in L and K) is 100 percent, while (the increase in Q) is 100 percent in the left panel, 200 percent in the middle panel, and 50 percent in the right panel.

Increasing returns to scale arise because as the scale of operation increases, a greater division of labor and specialization can take place and more specialized and productive

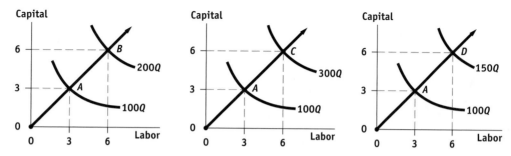

FIGURE 6-14   Constant, Increasing, and Decreasing Returns to Scale   In all three panels of this figure we start with the firm using $3L$ and $3K$ and producing $100Q$ (point A). By doubling inputs to $6L$ and $6K$, the left panel shows that output also doubles to $200Q$ (point B), so that we have constant returns to scale; the center panel shows that output triples to $300Q$ (point C), so that we have increasing returns to scale; while the right panel shows that output only increases to $150Q$ (point D), so that we have decreasing returns to scale.

machinery can be used. Decreasing returns to scale, on the other hand, arise primarily because as the scale of operation increases, it becomes ever more difficult to manage the firm effectively and coordinate the various operations and divisions of the firm. In the real world, the forces for increasing and decreasing returns to scale often operate side by side, with the former usually overwhelming the latter at small levels of output and the reverse occurring at very large levels of output.

For example, in Table 6-1, we saw that with $1L$ and $1K$, we have $3Q$. With $2L$ and $2K$, we have $18Q$. Thus, we have increasing returns to scale over this range of outputs. However, doubling the amount of labor and capital used from $3L$ and $3K$ to $6L$ and $6K$ only increases output from 33 to 39 units, so that we have decreasing returns to scale over this larger range of outputs. In the real world, most industries seem to operate near the range of constant returns to scale where the forces of increasing and decreasing returns to scale are more or less in balance (see Case Study 6-3). But, as Case Study 6-4 shows, General Motors faces decreasing returns to scale and has been shrinking.

CASE STUDY 6-3
Returns to Scale in U.S. Manufacturing Industries

Table 6-5 reports the estimated returns to scale in 18 manufacturing industries in the United States in 1957. A value of 1 refers to constant returns to scale, a value greater than 1 refers to increasing returns to scale, and a value less than 1 refers to decreasing returns to scale. The table shows that for a doubling of (i.e., with a 100 percent increase in) all inputs, output would rise by 111 percent in the furniture industry, by 109 percent in chemicals, but only by 95 percent in petroleum (the last entry in the second column of the table). Although only the textile industry seems to face constant returns to scale exactly, most other industries are very close to it.

TABLE 6-5 Estimated Returns to Scale in U.S. Manufacturing

Industry	Returns to Scale	Industry	Returns to Scale
Furniture	1.11	Stone, clay, etc.	1.03
Chemicals	1.09	Fabricated metals	1.03
Printing	1.08	Electrical machinery	1.03
Food, beverages	1.07	Transport equipment	1.02
Rubber, plastics	1.06	Nonelectrical machinery	1.02
Instruments	1.04	Textiles	1.00
Lumber	1.04	Paper and pulp	0.98
Apparel	1.04	Primary metals	0.96
Leather	1.04	Petroleum	0.95

Source: J. Moroney, "Cobb-Douglas Production Functions and Returns to Scale in U.S. Manufacturing Industry," *Western Economic Journal* (December 1967), pp. 39–51.

CASE STUDY 6-4
General Motors Decides Smaller Is Better

General Motors (GM), the largest carmaker in the world, had a turbulent decade in the 1990s. It started by incurring huge losses of $2 billion in 1990 and $4.5 billion in 1991 as the result of a bloated workforce and management, low capacity utilization, too many divisions and models, and high-cost suppliers. For a corporation that had been extolled as the epitome of a successful company in 1946, this was a dramatic decline indeed! As the data on sales per employee in Table 6-6 seem to indicate, GM was too large and faced strong decreasing returns to scale in 1991. Chrysler, on the other hand, could still have expanded to take advantage of increasing returns to scale (in fact, Chrysler was acquired by Germany's Daimler, to become MercedesChrysler, in 1998). Ford, with the largest sales per employee, seemed to be just about the right size. It was clear that GM required a major restructuring—and this GM has been doing since the early 1990s.

TABLE 6-6	Total Sales, Employees, and Sales per Employee at GM, Ford, and Chrysler		
	Sales (billion dollars)	Employees (thousands)	Sales per Employee (thousand dollars)
General Motors	123.1	756	162.7
Ford	88.3	333	265.4
Chrysler	29.4	123	238.8

Source: The Economist (May 2, 1992), p. 78.

As part of its reorganization plan announced in December 1991, GM closed 21 plants and shed 74,000 workers (50,000 blue-collar and 24,000 white-collar) from 1992 to 1994. The plants closed eliminated GM's excess capacity of 2 million cars and trucks per year and left GM with a 5 to 5.5 million capacity in its North American operation and 33 percent of the U.S. car market, down from 46 percent in 1978 and 35 percent in 1991. Just closing plants and reducing GM's size, however, was not sufficient, and GM went through more restructuring during the mid-1990s. Although these increased efficiency, its competitors did not stand still, and GM productivity still lagged in relation to that of its domestic competitors. For example, in 1998, GM required 34 worker-days to produce its average car, as compared with Chrysler's 32 and Ford's 30, and GM's share of the North American car market declined further to 28 percent.

To close this productivity gap, GM consolidated its North American and international operations; reduced further the number of models it produced; cut average manufacturing time per vehicle; centralized its sales, service, and marketing system; spun off its auto-components group (Delphi Automotive Systems), and outsourced more of the assembly task. As GM was improving, Ford was facing setbacks and in 2002, GM surpassed Ford on vehicle productivity, quality ratings, and profitability. Nevertheless, GM continued to lose market share. In 2005, it employed only 324,000 and its U.S. market share was 25.6 percent, down from 877,000 workers and nearly half of the U.S. market twenty years earlier. The year 2005 was also GM's worst since 1992 with a loss of $8.2 billion, which necessitated still another restructuring plan to eliminate another 30,000 jobs by 2008.

Source: "Automobiles: GM Decides Smaller Is Better," *The Margin* (November/December 1988), p. 29; "GM Posts Record '91 Loss of $4.45 Billion, Sends Tough Message to UAW on Closings," *The New York Times* (February 25, 1992), p. 3; "Reviving GM," *Business Week* (February 1, 1999), pp. 114–122; "GM Outstrips Ford on Vehicle Productivity, Study Shows," *Financial Times* (June 14, 2002), p. 18; "G.M. Posts Worst Loss since 1992," *The New York Times* (January 17, 2006), p. C1; and "Is General Motors Unraveling?" *The Wall Street Journal* (April 8, 2006), p. 7.

6-7 EMPIRICAL PRODUCTION FUNCTIONS

The production function most commonly used in empirical estimation is the power function of the form

$$Q = AK^a L^b \qquad [6\text{-}21]$$

where Q, K, and L refer, respectively, to the quantities of output, capital, and labor, and A, a, and b are the parameters to be estimated empirically. Equation 6-21 is often referred to as the **Cobb–Douglas production function** in honor of Charles W. Cobb and Paul H. Douglas, who introduced it in the 1920s.[9]

The Cobb–Douglas production function has several useful properties. First, the marginal product of capital and the marginal product of labor depend on both the quantity of capital and the quantity of labor used in production, as is often the case in the real world.[10] Second, the exponents of K and L (i.e., a and b) represent, respectively, the output elasticity of labor and capital (E_K and E_L), and the sum of the exponents (i.e., $a + b$) measures the returns to scale. If $a + b = 1$, we have constant returns to scale; if $a + b > 1$, we have increasing returns to scale; and if $a + b < 1$, we have decreasing returns to scale.[11] Third, the Cobb–Douglas production function can be estimated by regression analysis by transforming it into

$$\ln Q = \ln A + a \ln K + b \ln L \qquad [6\text{-}22]$$

which is linear in the logarithms. Finally, the Cobb–Douglas production function can easily be extended to deal with more than two inputs (say, capital, labor, and natural resources or capital, production labor, and nonproduction labor).

The Cobb–Douglas production function can be estimated either from data for a single firm, industry, or nation over time (i.e., using time-series analysis), or for a number of

---

[9] See C. W. Cobb and P. H. Douglas, "A Theory of Production," *American Economic Review* (March 1928), pp. 139–165.

[10] The equation for the marginal product of capital is

$$MP_K = \frac{\partial Q}{\partial K} = aAK^{a-1}L^b = a \cdot \frac{Q}{K}$$

Similarly, the equation for the marginal product of labor is

$$MP_L = \frac{\partial Q}{\partial L} = bAK^a L^{b-1} = b \cdot \frac{Q}{L}$$

The MP_K and MP_L are positive and diminishing throughout (i.e., the Cobb–Douglas production function exhibits only stage II of production for capital and labor).

[11] The output elasticity of capital is

$$E_K = \frac{\partial Q}{\partial K} \cdot \frac{K}{Q} = \frac{(aQ)}{K} \cdot \frac{K}{Q} = a$$

Similarly,

$$E_L = \frac{\partial Q}{\partial L} \cdot \frac{L}{Q} = \frac{(bQ)}{L} \cdot \frac{L}{Q} = b$$

and $E_K + E_L = a + b =$ returns to scale.

firms, industries, or nations at one point in time (i.e., using cross-sectional data). In either case, the researcher faces three potential difficulties:

1. If the firm produces a number of different products, output may have to be measured in monetary rather than in physical units, and this will require deflating the value of output by the price index in time-series analysis or adjusting for price differences for firms and industries located in different regions in cross-sectional analysis.

2. Only the capital consumed in the production of the output should be counted, ideally. Since machinery and equipment are of different types and ages (vintages) and productivities, however, the total stock of capital in existence has to be used instead.

3. In time-series analysis a time trend is also usually included to take into consideration technological changes over time, while in cross-sectional analysis we must ascertain that all firms of industries use the same technology (the best available).

Case Study 6-5 gives the estimated output elasticities of capital, production workers, and nonproduction workers of the U.S. manufacturing industries examined in Case Study 6-3.

CASE STUDY 6-5
Output Elasticities in U.S. Manufacturing Industries

Table 6-7 reports the estimated output elasticities of capital (a), production workers (b), and nonproduction workers (c) for the same 18 manufacturing industries examined in Case Study 6-3. The value of $a = 0.205$ for furniture means that a 1 percent increase in the quantity of capital used (holding the number of production and nonproduction workers constant) results in a 0.205 percent increase in the quantity of furniture produced. The value of $b = 0.802$ means that a 1 percent increase in the number of production workers used (while holding the stock of capital and the number of nonproduction workers used constant) increases Q by 0.802 percent. Finally, the value of $c = 0.102$ means that a 1 percent increase in the number of nonproduction workers used (together with a constant amount of the other inputs) results in Q increasing by 0.102 percent. Increasing all three inputs at the same time by 1 percent leads to Q rising by $a + b + c = 0.205 + 0.802 + 0.102 = 1.11$ percent. This means that we

have slightly increasing returns to scale in furniture production.

The values of a, b, and c reported in Table 6-7 were estimated by regression analysis with cross-sectional data for each of 18 industries for the year 1957, using a Cobb–Douglas production function extended to three inputs and transformed into natural logarithms. All estimated coefficients, with the exception of c for the rubber and plastics industry, were positive, as expected. Of the 54 estimated coefficients, 39 were statistically significant at the 5 percent level and all 18 regressions explained more than 95 percent of the variations in output (i.e., R^2 exceeded 0.95). However, only the first four industries listed in the table and fabricated metals have returns to scale that are statistically different from 1 at the 5 percent level of significance. In all the other industries, constant or near-constant returns to scale seemed to prevail.

Continued...

| TABLE 6-7 | Output Elasticities of Capital (*a*), Production Workers (*b*), and Nonproduction Workers (*c*) in U.S. Manufacturing Industries |

	Output Elasticity of			
Industry	Capital (*a*)	Production Workers (*b*)	Nonproduction Workers (*c*)	Returns to Scale (*a + b + c*)
Furniture	0.205	0.802	0.102	1.110
Chemicals	0.200	0.553	0.336	1.089
Printing	0.459	0.045	0.574	1.078
Food and beverages	0.555	0.439	0.076	1.070
Rubber and plastics	0.481	1.033	−0.458	1.056
Instruments	0.205	0.819	0.020	1.044
Lumber	0.392	0.504	0.145	1.041
Apparel	0.128	0.437	0.477	1.041
Leather	0.076	0.441	0.523	1.040
Stone, clay, etc.	0.632	0.032	0.366	1.030
Fabricated metals	0.151	0.512	0.364	1.027
Electrical machinery	0.368	0.429	0.229	1.026
Transport equipment	0.234	0.749	0.041	1.024
Nonelectrical machinery	0.404	0.228	0.389	1.021
Textiles	0.121	0.549	0.334	1.004
Paper and pulp	0.420	0.367	0.197	0.984
Primary metals	0.371	0.077	0.509	0.957
Petroleum	0.308	0.546	0.093	0.947

Source: J. Moroney, "Cobb–Douglas Production Functions and Returns to Scale in U.S. Manufacturing Industry," *Western Economic Journal* (December 1967), pp. 39–51.

6-8   THE INNOVATION PROCESS

In this section, we examine the meaning and importance of technological progress and the process by which firms get new technology under the closed versus the open innovation model.

Meaning and Importance of Innovations

The introduction of innovations is the single most important determinant of a firm's long-term competitiveness at home and abroad. Innovations are basically of two types—**product innovation** (which refers to the introduction of new or improved products) and **process innovation** (the introduction of new or improved production processes). Contrary to popular belief, most innovations are incremental and involve more or less continuous small improvements in products or processes rather than a major technological breakthrough.[12] Furthermore, most innovations involve the commercial use of ideas that have been around for years. For example, it took a quarter of a century before firms (primarily Japanese ones) were able to perfect the flat video screen (invented in the mid-1960s by George Heilmeier of RCA) and introduce them commercially in portable PCs.

Innovations can be examined with isoquants. A new or improved product requires a new isoquant map showing the various combinations of inputs to produce each level of output of the new or improved product. On the other hand, a process innovation can be shown by a shift toward the origin of product isoquants, showing that each level of output can be produced with fewer inputs after the innovation than before.

Unless a firm aggressively and continuously improves the product or the production process, it will inevitably be overtaken by other more innovative firms. This is how the Xerox Corporation, the inventor of the copier in 1959, lost its competitive edge to Japanese competitors in the 1970s before it shook off its complacency and learned again how to compete during the 1980s. To be successful in today's world, firms must adopt a global competitive strategy, which means that they must continually scout the world for new product ideas and processes. It is also crucial for firms to have a presence, first through exports and then by local production, in the world's major markets. Larger sales mean both improving economies of scale in production and distribution, and being able to spend more on research and development to stay ahead of the competition.

The introduction of innovations is also stimulated by strong domestic rivalry and geographic concentration—the former because it forces firms to constantly innovate or lose market share (and even risk being driven entirely out of the market), the latter because it leads to the rapid spread of new ideas and the development of specialized machinery and other inputs for the industry. It is sharp domestic rivalry and great geographic concentration that made Japanese firms in many high-tech industries such fierce competitors in world markets during the 1980s.[13]

The risk in introducing innovations is usually high. For example, 8 out of 10 new products fail shortly after their introduction. Even the most carefully introduced innovations can fail, as evidenced by the failure of RJR Nabisco Inc.'s "smokeless cigarette" and Coca-Cola's change of its 99-year-old recipe in 1985. In general, the introduction of a new product or concept (such as McDonald's hamburgers and Sony Walkmans) is more likely to succeed than changing an existing product (such as launching a new soup, cheese, or biscuit globally). Product innovations can also die from poor planning and unexpected production problems. This happened, for example, when Weyerhauser (encouraged by market testing, which showed that its product was better than competitors' products and could be produced more cheaply) introduced its UltraSoft diapers in 1990; the project failed within a year because of production problems.[14] Case Study 6-6 examines how firms get new technology.

---

[12] See "Less Glamour, More Profits," *The Economist* (April 24, 2004), p. 11.

[13] See Michael E. Porter, "The Competitive Advantage of Nations," *Harvard Business Review* (March–April 1990), pp. 75–93; Walter B. Wriston, "The State of American Management," *Harvard Business Review* (January–February 1990), pp. 78–83; and "Competition: How American Industry Stacks Up Now," *Fortune* (April 18, 1994), pp. 52–64.

[14] See "Diaper's Failure Shows How Poor Plans, Unexpected Woes Can Kill New Products," *The Wall Street Journal* (October 8, 1990), p. B11.

CASE STUDY 6-6
How Do Firms Get New Technology?

Table 6-8 provides the results of a survey of 650 executives in 130 industries on the methods that U.S. firms use to acquire new technology on process and product innovations, arranged from the most important to the least important. We see that the most important method of acquiring product and process innovations is by independent research and development (R&D) by the firm. The other methods arranged in order of decreasing importance are: licensing technology by the firms that originally developed the technology; publications or technical meetings; reverse engineering (i.e., taking the competitive product apart and devising a method of producing a similar product); hiring employees of innovating firms; patent disclosures (i.e., from the detailed information available from the patent office, which can be used to develop a similar technology or product in such a way as not to infringe on the patent); or information from conversations with employees of innovating firms (who may inadvertently provide secret information in the course of general conversations). For product innovations, reverse engineering becomes more important than licensing, and hiring employees from innovating firms is more important than publications or technical meetings. At least, this was the case in the past.

TABLE 6-8	Methods of Acquiring New Technology	
	Rank	
Method of Acquisition	**Process Innovation**	**Product Innovation**
Independent R&D	1	1
Licensing	2	3
Publications or technical meetings	3	5
Reverse engineering	4	2
Hiring employees of innovating firm	5	4
Patent disclosures	6	6
Conversations with employees of innovating firm	7	7

Source: R. E. Levin, "Appropriability, R&D Spending, and Technological Performance," *American Economic Review* (May 1988), pp. 424–428; P. F. Drucker, "The Discipline of Innovation," *Harvard Business Review* (November–December 1998); "GE Goes Back to the Future," *The Wall Street Journal* (May 7, 2002), p. B1; and "The Way to the Future," *Business Week* (October 11, 2004), pp. 92–97.

The Open Innovation Model

Today companies are, increasingly rethinking the ways in which they get new technology and bring products to market. In the past, in what we may call the **closed innovation model,** companies generated, developed, and commercialized for the most part their own ideas, innovations, or technological breakthroughs. Today, many leading companies are moving toward an **open innovation model**, which involves the commercialization of both, a company's own ideas and innovations, as well as the innovations of other firms, and deploying external as well as internal or in-house pathways to market. Specifically, a firm today seeks to explore ways in which it can utilize external technologies to fill gaps in its businesses and to encourage other firms to use its own technology through licensing agreements, joint ventures, and other arrangements. By doing so, the firm is not constrained by the technologies it develops through its R&D but it can use any technology available to develop and introduce new and innovative products on the market. Similarly, the firm can greatly profit by licensing its own technology to others.

For example, Procter & Gamble (P&G) has recently changed its approach to innovation from the closed to the open model and has since become one of the most aggressive adopter of the latter with the slogan "Connect & Develop." One of the first steps that P&G undertook was to create the position of director of external innovation with the goal of sourcing 50 percent of its innovations from outside the company by 2007, up from an estimated 10 percent in 2002. Recently, P&G introduced the SpinBrush, an electric toothbrush that runs on batteries and sells for about $5. It quickly became the best-selling toothbrush in the United States and was developed not in P&G's labs but by four Cleveland entrepreneurs. P&G also encourages other firms to use its own innovations by instituting the policy that any new idea or innovation that is not used by the firm within three years can be offered to others, even competitors, through a licensing agreement, joint venture, or for a fee, so as not to kill a promising project but to benefit from it.

The ability to rescue "false negatives" or projects that initially do not seem promising to the firm, or that fall outside the firm's main line of business, is an important advantage of the open innovation model over the closed one. The classic example is the Xerox Corporation and its Palo Alto research center (PARC), which developed many computer hardware and software technologies (such as Ethernet and the graphical user interface, or GUI) that were not directly applicable to copiers and printers on which the company focused, but which were subsequently put to brilliant use by Apple Computer and Microsoft, without any benefit to Xerox.

A number of critically important innovations introduced in recent years into copiers, computers, disk drives, semiconductors, telecommunication equipment, pharmaceuticals, biotechnology, and even military weapons and communications systems were developed not in the companies' R&D laboratories but by outside research consortia, start-ups, universities, and other independent inventors. It is clear that the leading companies in these fields are now transitioning from a closed to an open innovation model. They need to do so because of (1) the increasing difficulty that companies are experiencing in controlling their proprietary ideas and expertise due to the dramatic rise in the number and mobility of knowledge workers and (2) growing competition that they are facing from new start-up companies financed by a greater availability of venture capital. The old closed innovation model is not dead, but it is increasingly being integrated into the open model by redirecting the scope of the in-house lab R&D toward utilizing external technologies and finding ways by which firms in other sectors can profitably utilize the firm's own technological breakthroughs.[15]

---

[15] Henry W. Chesbrough, "The Era of Open Innovation," *Sloan Management Review* (Spring 2003), pp. 35–41; "Floodgates Open to a Sea of Ideas," *Financial Times—Special Report on Innovation* (June 8, 2005), p. 1; "An Open Secret," *The Economist* (October 22, 2005), pp. 12–14; and Lorry Huston and Nabil Sakkab, "Connect and Develop," *Harvard Business Review* (March 2006), pp. 58–66.

6-9   INNOVATION AND GLOBAL COMPETITIVENESS

In this section we examine the crucial role that innovations and the new computer-aided production revolution now play in the global competitiveness among American, European, Japanese, and other Asian firms.

Innovations and the International Competitiveness of U.S. Firms

There was hardly a technological breakthrough during the past four decades, from TV to robots, from copiers to fax machines, from semiconductors to flat video screens, that was not made by an American firm or laboratory. According to the **product cycle model,** however, firms that introduce an innovation eventually lose their export market and even their domestic market to foreign imitators who pay lower wages and generally face lower costs. In the meantime, however, technologically leading firms introduce even more advanced products and technologies.

The problem is that the period during which firms can exploit the benefits of innovations is becoming shorter and shorter before foreign imitators take the market away. In fact, in many cases, American discoveries such as the fax machine and the flat video screen were introduced and first exploited commercially by foreign (Japanese) firms. Although many U.S. firms remain world leaders in many high-tech industries (such as Microsoft in software, Intel in computer chips, Boeing in commercial aircraft, IBM in mainframe computers, Hewlett-Packard in laser printers, Coca-Cola in soft drinks, Wal-Mart in general merchandising, and McDonald's in fast food), firms in many other mature industries such as textiles, steel, automobiles, and consumer electronic products lost competitiveness to foreign competitors, especially Japanese ones. One important reason for this is that U.S. firms in these mature industries generally stressed *product* innovation while Japanese firms stressed *process* innovations. Thus, even when U.S. firms were the first to introduce a product, Japanese firms were soon able to produce it better and more cheaply, and in a few years outsold American competitors at home and abroad. This happened in industry after industry, from steel to consumer electronic products to automobiles, especially during the 1970s and 1980s.

During the 1970s and 1980s, Japanese firms became technological leaders in many fields and introduced many successful product and process innovations. For example, Toyota pioneered the **just-in-time production system,** which is based on having every part or component become available just when needed. This avoids carrying costly inventories and double-handling of parts and greatly increases efficiency in general. The time required to switch production from one model to another at Toyota is a fraction of that at competing American automobile plants. U.S. auto producers have learned a great deal from their Japanese competitors and increased efficiency sharply since the mid-1980s, but Japanese firms did not stand still and constantly introduced improvements in product quality and production technology.

One advantage of Japanese firms is that they are often prepared to lose millions of dollars over many years while striving to succeed. American managers and investors, on the other hand, generally have a much shorter time horizon and are excessively concerned with quarterly statements and profits. Japanese firms also face far greater domestic rivalries and geographical concentration than their American and European counterparts, and thus they face a greater stimulus to innovate. Furthermore, as Japanese firms gained a global market share in many industries, their advantages became cumulative.

Under the Japanese competitive threat, American firms, especially the high-tech ones, underwent a fundamental and painful restructuring during the 1980s that returned them to a position of leadership in their industries during the 1990s. Xerox was one of the first U.S. companies to regain its lost competitiveness (see Case Study 6-7). European firms were slower to respond, protected as they were from Japanese competition by tariffs and other trade barriers.

CASE STUDY 6-7
How Xerox Lost and Regained International Competitiveness and Became a Leader in Information Technology

The Xerox Corporation was the first to introduce a copying machine in 1959, based on its patented xerographic technology. Until 1970, Xerox had no competition and thus little incentive to reduce manufacturing costs, improve quality, and increase customer satisfaction. Even when Japanese firms began to take over the low end of the market with better and cheaper copiers in 1970, Xerox did not respond. It concentrated instead on the middle and high end of the market, where profit margins were much higher. Xerox also used the profits from its copier business to expand into computers and office systems. It was not until 1979 that Xerox finally awakened to the seriousness of the Japanese threat. From **competitive benchmarking** missions to Japan to compare relative production efficiency and product quality, Xerox was startled to find that Japanese competitors were producing copiers of higher quality at far lower costs and were positioning themselves to move up to the more profitable middle and high-end segments of the market.

Faced with this life-threatening situation, Xerox, with the help of its Japanese subsidiary (Fuji Xerox), mounted a strong response, which involved reorgan-ization and integration of development and production and an ambitious companywide quality-control effort. Employee involvement was greatly increased, suppliers were brought into the early stages of product design, and inventories and the number of suppliers were greatly reduced. Constant benchmarking was used to test progress in the quality-control program and customer satisfaction. By taking these drastic actions, Xerox reversed the trend toward loss of market share, even in the low segment of the market, during the second half of the 1990s.

History seemed to repeat itself, however, at the beginning of the new decade, when Xerox once again found itself battling Japan's Canon for supremacy in the new digital world of office information technology. This, despite the fact that during the second half of the 1990s Xerox had recast itself as a digital document and solutions company that combines hardware, software, and services into a service and consulting package, industry by industry. It is clear that to remain competitive in today's globalized world requires constant alertness to the competition and continuous innovations on the part of the firm.

Source: The MIT Commission on Industrial Productivity, *Made in America* (Cambridge, Mass.: The MIT Press, 1989), pp. 270–277; "Japan Is Tough, But Xerox Prevails," *The New York Times* (September 3, 1992), p. D1; "Xerox Recasts Itself as a Formidable Force in Digital Revolution," *The Wall Street Journal* (February 2, 1999), p. A1; "Downfall of Xerox," *Business Week* (March 5, 2001), pp. 82–92; "Canon Takes Aim at Xerox," *Fortune* (October 14, 2002), pp. 215–220; and "Xerox Profits Doubles But Falls Short of Estimates," *The New York Times* (July 26, 2005), p. C14.

The New Computer-Aided Production Revolution and the International Competitiveness of U.S. Firms

Since the early 1990s, a veritable revolution in production has been taking place in the United States (and to a much smaller extent in Japan and Europe), based on computer-aided design and computer-aided manufacturing, which greatly increased the productivity and international competitiveness of U.S. firms. **Computer-aided design (CAD)** allows research and development engineers to design a product or component on a computer screen, quickly experiment with alternative designs, and test their strength and reliability—all on the screen. Then, **computer-aided manufacturing (CAM)** issues instructions to a network of integrated machine tools to produce a prototype of the product. These developments allow firms to avoid many production problems, greatly speed up

CASE STUDY 6-8
The New U.S. Digital Factory

Welcome to the new American factory—an information age marvel that is responsible for a quantum leap in speed, flexibility, and productivity resulting from the marriage of computer software and networks in industries as diverse as construction equipment, automobiles, PCs, and pagers. The agility of the digital factory allows it to customize products down to one unit while achieving mass-production speed and efficiency. For example, as a Motorola salesperson specifies an order for a pager for a particular consumer, the digitized data flow to an assembly line, where production begins immediately and is completed in a few minutes, so that the customer can have the customized pager the next day. Another example of this is at Dell computers (see Integrating Case Study 1 at the end of Chapter 2). This is sometimes called software-controlled continuous-flow manufacturing—a process that is basically merging manufacturing and retailing. This much faster time-to-market and customizing capability gives many American firms a tremendous advantage over foreign competitors. As a result, after losing the competitive war (especially to Japan) during the 1980s, the United States regained all of its lost ground, and then some, during the 1990s.

Computer-aided design (CAD) dramatically increases the pace of innovations. For example, a designer can call up on the screen a car door and test opening and closing the door, running the window up and down, experimenting with lighter materials, and directing machinery to make a prototype door. Such CAD allowed DaimlerChrysler to design and build its highly successful Neon subcompact car in 33 months instead of the usual 45. Even more exotically, scientists at Caterpillar, the largest earth-moving equipment builder in the world, test-drive huge machines in virtual reality before they are built. The Boeing 777 jetliner was entirely developed in this way. CAD is even used to design and simulate entire assembly lines, and it can be used to send production orders to suppliers' machines so that, in a sense, they become an extension of the firm's plant. In short, we are likely to be at the dawn of the biggest revolution in manufacturing since the perfection of the industrial lathe in the year 1800. And with the U.S. superiority in software, it is unlikely that foreign competitors will match the new American manufacturing genius any time soon.

Source: "The Digital Factory," *Fortune* (November 14, 1994), pp. 92–110; "Digital Polish for Factory Floor," *The New York Times* (March 22, 1999), p. C1; "The Totally Digital Factory May Not Be So Far Away," *Financial Times* (November 2000), p. XII; "Incredible Shrinking Plants," *The Economist* (February 23, 2002), pp. 71–73; and "The Way to the Future," *Business Week* (October 11, 2004), pp. 92–97.

the time required to develop and introduce products, and reduce the optimal lot size or production runs so as to achieve maximum production efficiency. This revolution, which started earlier and proceeded faster in the United States because of the U.S. superiority in computer software and networks, led to the emergence of the digital factory (see Case Study 6-8). Restructuring and the introduction of these design and production technologies were stimulated in European industries by the introduction of a common currency, the euro, in January 1999 (see Case Study 6-9). In recent years, however, most industries in rich nations have been losing international competitiveness to Chinese firms.

CASE STUDY 6-9
The Euro and the International Competitiveness of European Firms

On January 1, 1999, the euro became the common currency of 11 of the 15 member countries of the European Union (Austria, Belgium, Germany, Finland, France, Ireland, Italy, Luxembourg, Spain, Portugal, and The Netherlands). Britain, Sweden, and Denmark chose not to participate but reserved the right to join later. Greece joined in January 2001. Until January 1, 2002, only the local currencies of the 11 members actually circulated as money, but all prices were expressed both in the local currency and in euros. In January 2002, the local currencies of the 12 participating countries were withdrawn and only the euro circulated. Never before had a large number of sovereign countries voluntarily given up their own monies for a common currency.

The adoption of the euro removed the historical barriers to European competition that resulted from different currencies and volatile exchange rates, and it changed all the relationships between consumers and retailers on the one hand, and between retailers and suppliers on the other. The euro suddenly made price variations transparent across the continent at both the wholesale and the retail levels. Only cross-border price differences that are based on differences in the costs of operation (production and marketing) in the various national markets can now be sustainable. Many retail and wholesale prices are rapidly converging to a falling average, putting the profits of manufacturers and retailers under pressure. Some large price differences do remain, however. Price competition is even greater as a result of the rapid increase in e-commerce, as consumers no longer have to visit other countries to take advantage of price differentials.

Producers of standardized products that compete only on price now have little protection against the price-leveling effect of the euro and face the greatest pressure. In such an environment, only companies that develop products that are sufficiently innovative and diverse to win customers will prosper. The introduction of the euro is also forcing European companies to streamline supply chains, consolidate production capacity, and develop integrated product and market strategies. The single currency is forcing companies to adopt common performance and reporting practices in all facets of their operations from production to marketing. This makes European companies more competitive, just as American companies have been for a long time.

Source: "Managing in the Euro Zone," *Harvard Business Review* (January–February 1999), pp. 47–58; "Converging Prices Mean Trouble in Store," *Financial Times* (June 18, 1999), p. 27; D. Salvatore, "The Euro: Expectations and Performance," *Eastern Economic Journal* (Winter 2002), pp. 121–136; "The Flaw of One Price," *The Economist* (October 18, 2003), p. 18; and "Growth in EU Price Convergence," *Financial Times* (October 31, 2005), p. 4.

SUMMARY

1. *Production* refers to the transformation of inputs or resources into outputs of goods and services. Inputs are broadly classified into labor (including entrepreneurial talent), capital, and land or natural resources. Inputs can also be classified as fixed (if they cannot be readily changed during the time period under consideration) and variable (if they can be varied easily and on very short notice). The time period during which at least one input is fixed is called the "short run." If all inputs are variable, we are in the long run. A production function is an equation, table, or three-dimensional graph that shows the maximum output that a firm can produce per period of time with each set of inputs. If inputs and outputs are measured continuously, the production surface is smooth.

2. Total product (*TP*) is the output produced by using different quantities of an input with fixed quantities of the other(s). Marginal product (*MP*) is the change in total product per unit change in the variable input used. Average product (*AP*) equals total product divided by the quantity of the variable input used. Output elasticity measures the percentage change in output or total product divided by the percentage change in the variable input used. The law of diminishing returns postulates that, after a point, the marginal product of a variable input declines. "Stage I of production" refers to the range of increasing average product of the variable input. "Stage II of production" is the range from the maximum average product of the variable input to where the marginal product of the input is zero. "Stage III of production" refers to the range of negative marginal product of the variable input.

3. The marginal revenue product (*MRP*) of the variable input equals the marginal product (*MP*) of the variable input times the marginal revenue (*MR*) from the sale of the extra output produced. The marginal resource cost (*MRC*) of a variable input is equal to the increase in total costs resulting from hiring an additional unit of the variable input. As long as *MRP* exceeds *MRC*, it pays for the firm to expand the use of the variable input because by doing so, it adds more to its total revenue than to its total cost (so that the firm's total profits rise). On the other hand, the firm should not hire those

units of the variable inputs for which the *MRP* falls short of the *MRC*. The optimal use of the variable input is (i.e., the firm maximizes profits) where *MRP = MRC* for the input.

4. An isoquant shows the various combinations of two inputs that can be used to produce a specific level of output. Ridge lines separate the relevant (i.e., the negatively sloped) from the irrelevant (or positively sloped) portions of the isoquants. The absolute slope of the isoquant is called the "marginal rate of technical substitution" (*MRTS*). This equals the ratio of the marginal products of the two inputs. As we move down along an isoquant, its absolute slope or *MRTS* declines so that the isoquant is convex to the origin. When isoquants are straight lines (so that their absolute slope or *MRTS* is constant), inputs are perfect substitutes. With right-angled isoquants, inputs can be combined only in fixed proportions (i.e., there is zero substitutability of inputs in production).

5. Given the wage rate of labor (w), the rental price of capital (r), and the total costs or expenditures of the firm (C), we can define the isocost line. This shows the various combinations of L and K that the firm can hire. With K plotted along the vertical axis, the Y intercept of the isocost line is C/r and its slope is $-w/r$. In order to minimize production costs or maximize output, the firm must produce where an isoquant is tangent to an isocost. There, $MRTS = w/r$, and $MP_L/w = MP_K/r$. Joining points of optimal input combinations where isoquants are tangent to isocosts, we get the expansion path of the firm. To maximize profits, a firm should hire each input until the marginal revenue product equals the marginal resource cost of the input. If the price of an input declines, the firm will substitute the cheaper input for the more expensive one in order to reach a new optimal input combination.

6. *Constant, increasing,* and *decreasing returns to scale* refer to the situation where output changes, respectively, by the same, by a larger, and by a smaller proportion than inputs. Increasing returns to scale arise because of specialization and division of labor and from using specialized machinery. Decreasing returns to scale arise primarily because as the scale of operation increases, it becomes more and more difficult to manage the firm and

coordinate its operations and divisions effectively. In the real world, most industries seem to exhibit near-constant returns to scale.

7. The most commonly used production function is the Cobb–Douglas in the form of $Q = AK^aL^b$, where a and b are the output elasticities of capital and labor, respectively. If $a + b = 1$, we have constant returns to scale; if $a + b > 1$, we have increasing returns to scale; and if $a + b < 1$, we have decreasing returns to scale. The Cobb–Douglas production function can be estimated from time-series or from cross-sectional data. In either case, difficulties may arise in the measurement of output and capital input. In time-series analysis we must also be concerned with technological change over time, and in cross-sectional analysis we must ascertain that all firms or industries use the same technology.

8. The introduction of innovations is the most important determinant of a firm's long-term competitiveness. *Product innovation* refers to the introduction of new or improved products, while *process innovation* refers to the introduction of new or improved production processes. The introduction of innovations is stimulated by taking a strong global view of competition, as well as the existence of strong domestic rivalry and geographic concentration. Many innovations die because of poor planning and unexpected production problems. The leading firms in many sectors are moving from a closed innovation model to an open innovation model.

9. During the 1970s and 1980s, American firms in many industries lost international competitiveness, especially to Japanese firms, but during the 1990s they regained all of it and then some, based on computer-aided design and computer-aided manufacturing. American, Japanese, and European firms are now facing strong competition from Chinese firms.

DISCUSSION QUESTIONS

1. (*a*) What is meant by production, inputs, fixed inputs, variable inputs, short run, long run? (*b*) How long is the time period of the long run? (*c*) What is a production function? What is its usefulness in the analysis of the firm's production?

2. What is the relationship between the marginal product and the average product curves of a variable input?

3. (*a*) How is the law of diminishing returns reflected in the shape of the total product curve? (*b*) What is the relationship between diminishing returns and the stages of production?

4. If the total product curve increases at a decreasing rate from the very beginning (i.e., from the point where the variable input is zero), what would be the shape of the corresponding marginal and average product curves?

5. (*a*) What is meant by the marginal revenue product of an input? How is it calculated? (*b*) Why does the marginal product of an input decline as more units of the variable input are used?

6. (*a*) What is meant by the marginal resource cost? (*b*) When is the marginal resource cost equal to the input price?

7. What is the principle for the optimal use of a variable input?

8. (*a*) Do isoquants refer to the short run or to the long run? Why? (*b*) In what way are isoquants similar to indifference curves? (*c*) In what way are isoquants different from indifference curves? (*d*) Why can't isoquants intersect?

9. (*a*) What does the shape of an isoquant show? (*b*) Why is this important in managerial economics? (*b*) Does petroleum as an energy source have good substitutes? How is this reflected in the shape of the isoquant for petroleum versus other energy sources? Why was this important during the energy crisis of the 1970s?

10. (*a*) If two firms face the same wage and rental price of capital but spend different amounts on labor and capital, how do their isocost lines differ? What happens to their isocost lines if the wage rate increases? (*b*) If the wage rate increases, what happens to the capital–labor ratio used in production? Why? (*c*) What is the difference between the capital–labor ratio and the expansion path?

11. Minimum wage legislation requires most firms to pay workers no less than the legislated minimum wage per hour. Using marginal productivity theory, explain how a change in the minimum wage affects the employment of unskilled labor.

12. It is always better to hire a more qualified and productive worker than a less qualified and productive one regardless of cost. True or false? Explain.

13. Does the production function of Table 6-1 show constant, increasing, or decreasing returns to scale if the firm increases the quantity of labor and capital used from (a) 2L and 2K to 4L and 4K? (b) 2L and 4K to 3L and 6K?

14. If an estimated Cobb–Douglas production function is $Q = 10K^{0.6}L^{0.8}$ (a) what are the output elasticities of capital and labor? If the firm increases only the quantity of capital or only the quantity of labor used by 10 percent, by how much would output increase? (b) What type of returns to scale does this production function indicate? If the firm increases at the same time both the quantity of capital and the quantity of labor used by 10 percent, by how much would output increase?

15. (a) What is meant by an innovation? What are the different types of innovations? (b) What are some factors that determine the rate at which a firm introduces innovations? (c) What is meant by the closed and open innovation models?

PROBLEMS

1. Assuming that $L_1 = 1$ and $L_2 = 6$, while $K_1 = 1$ and $K_2 = 4$ in Figure 6-2, indicate the number of units of output to which (a) FE, (b) BA, and (c) DC refer by using Table 6-1.

*2. (a) From Table 6-1 construct a table similar to Table 6-2 showing the total product, the marginal product, and the average product of labor, as well as the output elasticity of labor, when capital is kept constant at 4 units rather than at 1 unit. (b) Draw a figure similar to Figure 6-4 showing the total product as well as the marginal and average products of labor from the results in part (a). (c) How do the results in parts (a) and (b) differ from those in Table 6-2 and Figure 6-4 in the text?

3. (a) From Table 6-1 construct a table similar to Table 6-2 showing the total product, and the marginal and the average products of capital, as well as the output elasticity of capital when labor is kept constant at 1 unit. (b) Draw a figure similar to Figure 6-4 showing the total product as well as the marginal and average products of capital from the results in part (a). (c) How much capital would a rational producer use?

4. Ms. Smith, the owner and manager of the Clear Duplicating Service located near a major university, is contemplating keeping her shop open after 4 P.M. and until midnight. In order to do so, she would have to hire additional workers. She estimates that the additional workers would generate the following total output (where each unit of output refers to 100 pages duplicated). If the price of each unit of output is $10 and each worker hired must be paid $40 per day, how many workers should Ms. Smith hire?

Workers hired	0	1	2	3	4	5	6
Total product	0	12	22	30	36	40	42

*5. Find the marginal revenue product of labor for the data in Problem 4 from the change in total revenue resulting from the employment of each additional unit of labor, and show that the number of workers that Ms. Smith should hire is the same as that obtained in Problem 4.

6. From the production function given in the following table, draw a figure showing (a) the isoquants for 8, 12, and 16 units of output and (b) the ridge lines.

Capital (K)	6	4	8	14	16	13	11	
	5	6	12	16	18	15	14	
	4	7	13	16	20	18	16	Output (Q)
	3	8	12	14	16	16	14	
	2	4	7	12	13	12	8	
	1	1	3	8	7	6	5	
	0	1	2	3	4	5	6	
					Labor (L)			

7. Find the marginal rate of technical substitution for the isoquant for 8 units of output (*a*) between (1*L*, 3*K*) and (1.5*L*, 1.5*K*); (*b*) between (1.5*L*, 1.5*K*) and (3*L*, 1*K*); (*c*) at (1.5*L*, 1.5*K*); and (*d*) at (1*L*, 3*K*) and at (3*L*, 1*K*). (*e*) What is the relevant portion of the isoquant for 8 units of output? Why?

8. (*a*) Starting from Figure 6-8 in the text, and assuming that both the wage of labor (*w*) and the rental price of capital (*r*) are $2, draw a figure showing the optimal combination of labor and capital needed to produce 12 units of output. What is the capital–labor ratio at the optimal input combination? What are the total expenditures or costs of the firm required in order to produce 12 units of output with the optimal combination of labor and capital? (*b*) Answer the same questions as in part (*a*) if *w* = $1 and *r* = $3.

*9. Suppose that the marginal product of the last worker employed by a firm is 40 units of output per day and the daily wage that the firm must pay is $20, while the marginal product of the last machine rented by the firm is 120 units of output per day and the daily rental price of the machine is $30. (*a*) Why is this firm not maximizing output or minimizing costs in the long run? (*b*) How can the firm maximize output or minimize costs?

10. John Wilson, the owner of a fast-food restaurant, estimated that he can sell 1,000 additional hamburgers per day by renting more automated equipment at a cost of $100 per day. Alternatively, he estimated that he could sell an extra 1,200 hamburgers per day by keeping the restaurant open for two more hours per day at a cost of $50 per hour. Which of these two alternative ways of increasing output should Mr. Wilson use?

*11. Draw a figure similar to Figure 6-14 in the text showing constant, increasing, and decreasing returns to scale by the quantity of inputs required to double output.

12. Suppose that the production function for a commodity is given by

$$Q = 10\sqrt{LK}$$

where *Q* is the quantity of output, *L* is the quantity of labor, and *K* is the quantity of capital.

(*a*) Indicate whether this production function exhibits constant, increasing, or decreasing returns to scale. (*b*) Does the production function exhibit diminishing returns? If so, when does the law of diminishing returns begin to operate? Could we ever get negative returns?

13. Indicate whether each of the following statements is true or false and give the reason. (*a*) A firm should stop expanding output after reaching diminishing returns and (*b*) if large and small firms operate in the same industry, we must have constant returns to scale.

14. (*a*) What is the difference between technological progress and economies of scale? (*b*) Suppose that technological progress is not neutral (i.e., the productivity of each input does not grow proportionately) but is labor-saving (i.e., the productivity of labor increases proportionately less than the productivity of capital). How can this type of technological progress be shown by isoquants? (*c*) How can we show a capital-saving innovation?

15. **Integrating Problem**

The Rapid Transit Corporation in a city has estimated the following Cobb–Douglas production function using monthly observations for the past two years:

$$\ln Q = 2.303 + 0.40 \ln K + 0.60 \ln L$$
$$\qquad\qquad (3.40)\qquad (4.15)$$
$$+\, 0.20 \ln G$$
$$(3.05)$$
$$R^2 = 0.94 \qquad D\text{–}W = 2.20$$

where *Q* is the number of bus miles driven, *K* is the number of buses the firm operates, *L* is the number of bus drivers it employs each day, and *G* is the gallons of gasoline it uses. The numbers in parentheses below the estimated coefficients are *t* values. With respect to the above results, answer the following questions: (*a*) Estimate *Q* if *K* = 200, *L* = 400, and *G* = 4,000. (*b*) Rewrite the estimated production function in the form of a power function. (*c*) Find the marginal product of capital, labor, and gasoline at *K* = 200, *L* = 400, and *G* = 4,000. (*Hint:* Use the formulas in footnote 10.) Are the *MP_K*, *MP_L*, and *MP_G* positive? Are they diminishing? Why? (*d*) Find the value of the output elasticity of *K*, *L*, and *G*. By how much does output increase by increasing each input by 10 percent, one at a time? (*e*) Determine the economies of scale in production. By how much does output increase if the firm increases the quantity used of all inputs at the same time by 10 percent? (*f*) Suppose the firm operates 200 buses per day, with 400 drivers, and uses 4,000 gallons of gasoline, and the rental price of a bus (*r*) is $40 per day, the wage rate of a driver (*w*) is $30 per day, and the price of gasoline (*g*) is $1 per gallon. Determine whether the firm is using the optimal combination of capital, labor, and gasoline. (*g*) If the firm operated 200 buses with 400 drivers and used 4,000 gallons of gasoline per day, and the average bus ride is 1 mile, what price would the firm have to charge for a bus ride in order to maximize profits? (*h*) Are the estimated coefficients of the Cobb–Douglas production function statistically significant at the 5 percent level? How much of the variation in *Q* does the estimated regression explain? Does the *D–W* statistic indicate the absence of autocorrelation? Does the regression face multicollinearity? Explain.

APPENDIX TO CHAPTER 6: PRODUCTION ANALYSIS WITH CALCULUS

In this appendix we use the Lagrangian multiplier method to examine the condition for a firm to be (1) maximizing output for a given cost outlay and (2) minimizing the cost of producing a given output.

Constrained Output Maximization

Suppose that a firm that uses labor (*L*) and capital (*K*) in production wants to determine the amount of labor and capital that it should use in order to maximize the output (*Q*) produced with a given cost outlay (*C**). That is, the firm wants to

$$\text{Maximize} \qquad Q = f(L, K) \qquad\qquad [6\text{-}1]$$

$$\text{Subject to} \qquad C^* = wL + rK \qquad\qquad [6\text{-}23]$$

where *w* is the wage of labor and *r* is the rental price of capital. This constrained maximization problem can be solved by the Lagrangian multiplier method (see Chapter 2 Appendix).

To do so, we first form the Lagrangian function:

$$Z = f(L, K) + \lambda(C^* - wL - rK) \qquad\qquad [6\text{-}24]$$

To maximize *Z*, we then find the partial derivatives of *Z* with respect to *L*, *K*, and λ and set them equal to zero. That is,

$$\frac{\partial Z}{\partial L} = \frac{\partial f}{\partial L} - \lambda w = 0 \qquad\qquad [6\text{-}25]$$

$$\frac{\partial Z}{\partial K} = \frac{\partial f}{\partial K} - \lambda r = 0 \qquad\qquad [6\text{-}26]$$

$$\frac{\partial Z}{\partial \lambda} = C^* - wL - rK = 0 \qquad\qquad [6\text{-}27]$$

By substituting MP_L for $\partial f/\partial L$ and MP_K for $\partial f/\partial K$, transposing w and r to the right of the equals sign, and dividing Equation 6-25 by Equation 6-26, we have

$$\frac{MP_L}{MP_K} = \frac{w}{r} \qquad\qquad [6\text{-}13]$$

or

$$\frac{MP_L}{w} = \frac{MP_K}{r} \qquad\qquad [6\text{-}14]$$

That is, the firm should hire labor and capital so that the marginal product per dollar spent on each input (λ) is equal. This is the first-order condition for output maximization for the given cost outlay or expenditure of the firm. The second-order condition is for the isoquant to be convex to the origin.

Constrained Cost Minimization

Suppose, on the other hand, that the firm of the previous section wants to determine the amount of labor and capital to use to minimize the cost of producing a given level of output (Q^*). The problem would then be

$$\text{Minimize} \qquad C = wL + rK \qquad\qquad [6\text{-}10]$$
$$\text{Subject to} \qquad Q^* = f(L, K) \qquad\qquad [6\text{-}28]$$

This constrained cost minimization problem can also be solved by the Lagrangian multiplier method. To do so, we first form the Lagrangian function:

$$Z' = wL + rK + \lambda'[Q^* - f(L, K)] \qquad\qquad [6\text{-}29]$$

To minimize Z', we then find the partial derivatives of Z' with respect to L, K, and λ', and set them equal to zero. That is,

$$\frac{\partial Z'}{\partial L} = w - \frac{\lambda' \partial f}{\partial L} = 0 \qquad\qquad [6\text{-}30]$$

$$\frac{\partial Z'}{\partial K} = r - \frac{\lambda' \partial f}{\partial K} = 0 \qquad\qquad [6\text{-}31]$$

$$\frac{\partial Z'}{\partial \lambda'} = Q^* - f(L, K) = 0 \qquad\qquad [6\text{-}32]$$

By substituting MP_L for $\partial f/\partial L$ and MP_K for $\partial f/\partial K$, transposing them to the right of the equal sign, and dividing Equation 6-30 by Equation 6-31, we have

$$\frac{w}{r} = \frac{MP_L}{MP_K} \qquad\qquad [6\text{-}33]$$

or

$$\frac{w}{MP_L} = \frac{r}{MP_K} \qquad\qquad [6\text{-}34]$$

Each term in Equation 6-34 equals λ' and refers to the marginal cost in terms of labor and capital. That is, Equation 6-34 postulates that to minimize the costs of producing Q^*, the firm should use labor and capital in such a way that the extra cost of producing an additional unit of output is the same whether the firm produces it with more labor or more capital. Note that Equation 6-33 and λ' are the inverse of Equation 6-13 and λ. This is the first-order condition for cost minimization. The second-order condition is that the isoquant must be convex to the origin.

Profit Maximization

In general, the firm will want to determine the amount of labor and capital needed to maximize profits rather than to maximize output or minimize costs. Total profit (π) is

$$\pi = TR - TC \tag{6-35}$$

$$= P \cdot Q - wL - rK \tag{6-36}$$

Since $Q = f(L, K)$, we can rewrite the profit function as

$$\pi = P \cdot f(L, K) - wL - rK \tag{6-37}$$

To determine the amount of labor and capital that the firm should use in order to maximize profits, we take the partial derivatives of Equation 6-37 with respect to L and K and set them equal to zero. That is,

$$\frac{\partial \pi}{\partial L} = \frac{P \partial f}{\partial L} - w = 0 \tag{6-38}$$

$$\frac{\partial \pi}{\partial K} = \frac{P \partial f}{\partial K} - r = 0 \tag{6-39}$$

Assuming that the price of the final commodity (P) is constant so that it is equal to marginal revenue (MR), we can rewrite Equations 6-38 and 6-39 as

$$(MP_L)(MR) = MRP_L = w \tag{6-40}$$

$$(MP_K)(MR) = MRP_K = r \tag{6-41}$$

That is, in order to maximize profits, the firm should hire labor and capital until the marginal revenue product of labor equals the wage rate, and until the marginal revenue product of capital is equal to the rental price of capital.

Dividing Equation 6-40 by Equation 6-41, we get Equation 6-19, which we found in Section 6-5:

$$\frac{MP_L}{MP_K} = \frac{w}{r} \tag{6-19}$$

Cross-multiplying in Equation 6-19 gives the condition for the optimal combination of inputs given by Equation 6-14:

$$\frac{MP_L}{w} = \frac{MP_K}{r} \tag{6-14}$$

That is, hiring labor and capital so that Equations 6-40 and 6-41 hold implies that Equation 6-14 for optimal input combinations will also be satisfied.

APPENDIX PROBLEMS

1. Given: $Q = 100K^{0.5}L^{0.5}$, $C^* = \$1,000$, $w = \$30$, and $r = \$40$. Determine the amount of labor and capital that the firm should use in order to maximize output. What is this level of output?

2. Solve Problem 1 with $w = \$50$.

3. Given: $Q = 100K^{0.5}L^{0.5}$, $w = \$50$, and $r = \$40$. Show how to determine the amount of labor and capital that the firm should use in order to minimize the cost of producing 1,118 units of output. What is this minimum cost?

4. Given: $Q = 100K^{0.5}L^{0.5}$, $w = \$30$, and $r = \$40$. Show how to determine the amount of labor and capital that the firm should use in order to minimize the cost of producing 1,444 units of output. What is this minimum cost?

5. Suppose that the production function of a firm is $Q = 100L^{0.5}K^{0.5}$ and $K = 100$, $P = \$1$, $w = \$30$, and $r = \$40$. Determine the quantity of labor that the firm should hire in order to maximize profits. What is the maximum profit of this firm?

6. Solve Problem 5 for $w = \$50$.

SUPPLEMENTARY READINGS

For a more extensive treatment of production theory, see:

Baumol, William J., *Economic Theory and Operations Analysis* (Englewood Cliffs, N.J.: Prentice-Hall, 1977), chap. 11.

Salvatore, Dominick, *Theory and Problems of Microeconomic Theory* 4th ed. (New York: McGraw-Hill, 2006), chap. 6 and secs. 8.1–8.3.

For Innovations, see:

Chesbrough, Henry W., "The Era of Open Innovation," *MIT Sloan Management Review* (Spring 2003).

Drucker, Peter F., "The Discipline of Innovation," *Harvard Business Review* (November–December, 1998), pp. 149–157.

Govindaraja, Vijay, and Chris Trimble, "Strategic Innovation and the Science of Learning," *MIT Sloan Management Review* (Winter 2004).

Kim, Chan W., and Renee Mauborgne, "Strategy, Value Innovation, and the Knowledge Economy," *Sloan Management Review* (Spring 1999), pp. 41–54.

On the empirical estimation of production functions, see:

Atkinson, S. F., and C. Cornwell, "Estimation of Output and Input Technical Efficiency Using a Flexible Functional Form and Panel Data," *International Economic Review* (February 1994), pp. 245–255.

Dhawan, Rajiv, "Firm Size and Productivity Differential: Theory and Evidence from a Panel of US Firms," *Journal of Economic Behavior & Organization* (March 2001).

Douglas, Paul H., "The Cobb–Douglas Production Function Once Again: Its History, Its Testing, and Some New Empirical Values," *Journal of Political Economy* (October 1984), pp. 903–915.

Gold, B., "Changing Perspectives on Size, Scale, and Returns: An Interpretative Survey," *Journal of Economic Literature* (March 1981), pp. 5–33.

For technological progress and international competitiveness, see:

Findlay, Ronald, and Ronald W. Jones, "Input Trade and the Location of Production," *American Economic Review* (May 2001).

Porter, M. J., *The Competitive Advantage of Nations* (New York: Free Press, 1990).

Salvatore, Dominick, *International Economics*, 8th ed. (Hoboken, N.J.: Wiley, 2004), chaps. 6–8, 13.

Salvatore, Dominick, *The Japanese Trade Challenge and the U.S. Response* (Washington, D.C.: Economic Policy Institute, 1990).

INTERNET SITE ADDRESSES

For gasoline consumption and substitution, see:

http://www.eia.doe.gov/emeu/cabs/usa.html

http://www.washingtonwatchdog.org/documents/usc/ttl42/ch134/

http://www.library.thinkquest.org/21794/energysources.html

For production information on General Motors, Ford, Chrysler, and Toyota, see:

General Motors: http://www.gm.com

Ford: http://www.ford.com

Chrysler: http://www.chrysler.com

Toyota: http://www.toyota.com

For competition between Xerox and Canon, see:

Canon: http://www.usa.canon.com

Xerox: http://www.xerox.com

For computer-aided design (CAD) and computer-aided manufacturing (CAM), see:

Microsoft: http://www.microsoft.com

Motorola: http://www.mot.com

Dell: http://www.dell.com

Caterpillar: http://www.caterpillar.com

For information on the euro and the European Union, see:

For data on the euro exchange rate: http://www.x-rates.com/d/EUR/EUR/data120.html

For the European Central Bank: http://www.ecb.int

For the European Commission: http://europa.eu.int

Bloomberg: http://www.bloomberg.co.uk

Reuters: http://www.reuters.com

CHAPTER 7 Cost Theory and Estimation

CHAPTER OUTLINE

KEY TERMS   (in the order of their appearance)

Explicit costs	Average variable cost (*AVC*)	Brain drain
Implicit costs	Average total cost (*ATC*)	Logistics
Alternative or opportunity costs	Marginal cost (*MC*)	Cost–volume–profit or breakeven
Economic costs	Long-run total cost (*LTC*)	analysis
Accounting costs	Long-run average cost (*LAC*)	Contribution margin per unit
Relevant cost	Long-run marginal cost (*LMC*)	Japanese cost-management
Incremental cost	Planning horizon	system
Sunk costs	Economies of scope	Operating leverage
Total fixed costs (*TFC*)	Learning curve	Degree of operating leverage
Total variable costs (*TVC*)	Foreign sourcing of inputs	(*DOL*)
Total costs (*TC*)	New international economies	Engineering technique
Average fixed cost (*AFC*)	of scale	Survival technique

We saw in Section 1-2 that the aim of a firm is generally to maximize profits. Total profits equal the positive difference between total revenue and total costs. The total revenue of the firm was examined in Part Two of the text, which dealt with demand analysis. In this chapter we examine costs and their importance in decision making. The firm's cost functions are derived from the optimal input combinations examined in the preceding chapter and show the minimum cost of producing various levels of output. Clearly, cost is an important consideration in managerial decision making, and cost analysis is an essential and major aspect of managerial economics.

The chapter begins by examining the nature of costs of production. These include explicit and implicit costs, relevant or opportunity costs, and incremental costs. We then derive the firm's short-run and long-run total, average, and marginal cost curves. After that, we examine plant size and economies of scale, economies of scope, and the learning curve. Subsequently, we discuss international trade in inputs and the immigration of skilled labor, as well as logistics or supply chain management. Finally, we discuss breakeven analysis and examine the empirical estimation of cost functions.

7-1   THE NATURE OF COSTS

One crucial distinction in the analysis of costs is between explicit and implicit costs. **Explicit costs** refer to the actual expenditures of the firm to hire, rent, or purchase the inputs it requires in production. These include the wages to hire labor, the rental price of capital, equipment, and buildings, and the purchase price of raw materials and semifinished products. **Implicit costs** refer to the value of the inputs owned and used by the firm in its own production activity. Even though the firm does not incur any actual expenses to use these inputs, they are not free, since the firm could sell or rent them out to other firms. The amount for which the firm could sell or rent out these owned inputs to other firms represents a cost of production of the firm owning and using them. Implicit costs include the highest salary that the entrepreneur could earn in his or her best alternative employment (say, in managing another firm), and the highest return that the firm could receive from investing its capital in the most rewarding alternative use or renting its land and buildings to the highest bidder (rather than using them itself).

In economics, both explicit and implicit costs must be considered. That is, in measuring production costs, the firm must include the **alternative or opportunity costs** of all inputs, whether purchased or owned by the firm. The reason is that the firm could not retain a hired input if it paid a lower price for the input than another firm. Similarly, it would not pay for a firm to use an owned input if the value (productivity) of the input is greater to another firm. These **economic costs** must be distinguished from **accounting costs,** which refer only to the firm's actual expenditures or explicit costs incurred for purchased or rented inputs. Accounting or historical costs are important for financial reporting by the firm and for tax purposes. For managerial decision-making purposes (with which we are primarily interested here), however, economic or opportunity costs are the **relevant cost** concept that must be used. Two examples will clarify this distinction and will highlight its importance in arriving at correct managerial decisions.

One example is from *inventory valuation.* Suppose that a firm purchased a raw material for $100, but its price subsequently fell to $60. The accountant would continue to report the cost of the raw material at its historical price of $100. The economist, however, would value the raw material at its current or replacement value. Failure to do so might lead to the wrong managerial decision. This would occur if the firm decided not to produce a commodity that would lead to a loss if the raw material were valued at its historical cost of $100 but to a profit if the raw material were valued at its current or replacement value of $60. The fact that the firm paid $100 for the input is irrelevant to its current production decision since the firm could only obtain $60 if it sold the input now. The $40 reduction in the price of the raw material is a sunk cost that the firm should not consider in its current managerial decisions.

Another example is given by the *measurement of depreciation cost* for a long-lived asset. Suppose that a firm purchased a machine for $1,000. If the estimated life of the machine is 10 years and the accountant uses a *straight-line depreciation method* (that is, $100 per year), the accounting value of the machine is zero at the end of the tenth year. Suppose, however, that the machine can still be used for (i.e., it would last) another year and that the firm could sell the machine for $120 at the end of the tenth year or use it for another year. The cost of using the machine is zero as far as the accountant is concerned (since the machine has already been fully depreciated), but it is $120 for the economist. Again, incorrectly assigning a zero cost to the use of the machine would be wrong from an economics point of view and could lead to wrong managerial decisions.

In discussing production costs, we must also distinguish between marginal cost and incremental cost. Marginal cost refers to the change in total cost for a 1-unit change in output. For example, if total cost is $140 to produce 10 units of output and $150 to produce 11 units of output, the marginal cost of the eleventh unit is $10. **Incremental cost,** on the other hand, is a broader concept and refers to the change in total costs from implementing a particular management decision, such as the introduction of a new product line, the undertaking of a new advertising campaign, or the production of a previously purchased component. The costs that are not affected by the decision are irrelevant and are called **sunk costs.**

7-2   SHORT-RUN COST FUNCTIONS

In this section we distinguish between fixed and variable costs and derive the firm's total and per-unit cost functions. These cost functions are derived from input prices and the optimal input combinations used to produce various levels of outputs (as explained in the previous chapter).

Short-Run Total and Per-Unit Cost Functions

In Section 6-1 we defined the short run as the time period during which some of the firm's inputs are fixed (i.e., cannot be readily changed, except perhaps at great expense). The total obligations of the firm per time period for all fixed inputs are called **total fixed costs (TFC).** These include interest payments on borrowed capital, rental expenditures on leased plant and equipment (or depreciation associated with the passage of time on owned plant and equipment), property taxes, and those salaries (such as for top management) that are fixed by contract and must be paid over the life of the contract whether the firm produces or not. **Total variable costs (TVC),** on the other hand, are the total obligations of the firm per time period for all the variable inputs that the firm uses. Variable inputs are those that the firm can vary easily and on short notice. Included in variable costs are payments for raw materials, fuels, depreciation associated with the use of the plant and equipment, most labor costs, excise taxes, etc.[1] **Total costs (TC)** equal total fixed costs (TFC) plus total variable costs (TVC). That is,

$$TC = TFC + TVC \qquad [7\text{-}1]$$

Within the limits imposed by the given plant and equipment, the firm can vary its output in the short run by varying the quantity used of the variable inputs. This gives rise to the *TFC*, *TVC*, and *TC* functions of the firm. These show, respectively, the minimum fixed, variable, and total costs of the firm to produce various levels of output in the short run. Cost functions show the minimum costs of producing various levels of output on the assumption that the firm uses the optimal or least-cost input combinations to produce each level of output. Thus, the total cost of producing a particular level of output is obtained by multiplying the optimal quantity of each input used times the input price and then adding all these costs. In defining cost functions, all inputs are valued at their opportunity cost, which includes both explicit and implicit costs. Input prices are assumed to remain constant regardless of the quantity demanded of each input by the firm.

From the total fixed, total variable, and total cost functions, we can derive the corresponding per-unit (average fixed, average variable, average total, and marginal) cost functions of the firm. **Average fixed cost (AFC)** equals total fixed costs (TFC) divided by the level of output (Q). **Average variable cost (AVC)** equals total variable costs (TVC) divided

---

[1] In incremental-cost analysis, *semivariable costs* are often encountered. These are cost changes that arise if output falls outside some specified range. For example, by contract the firm may be able to reduce the salary of top management if output falls sharply or must pay bonuses for large increases in output.

Past point G' (i.e., for output levels greater than 1.5 units in the top panel of Figure 7-1), the law of diminishing returns operates, and the *TVC* curve faces upward or rises at an increasing rate. Since $TC = TFC + TVC$, the *TC* curve has the same shape as the *TVC* curve but is \$60 (the amount of the *TFC*) above it at each output level. These *TVC* and *TC* schedules are plotted in the top panel of Figure 7-1.

The *AFC* values given in column 5 are obtained by dividing the *TFC* values in column 2 by the quantity of output in column 1. *AVC* (column 6) equals *TVC* (column 3) divided by output (column 1). *ATC* (column 7) equals *TC* (column 4) divided by output (column 1). *ATC* also equals *AFC* plus *AVC*. *MC* (column 8) is given by the change in *TVC* (column 3) or in *TC* (column 4) per unit change in output (column 1). Thus, *MC* does not depend on *TFC*. These per-unit cost schedules are plotted in the bottom panel of Figure 7-1. *Note that MC is plotted halfway between the various levels of output.* From Table 7-1 and the bottom panel of Figure 7-1 we see that the *AVC*, *ATC*, and *MC* curves first fall and then rise (i.e., they are U-shaped). Since the vertical distance between the *ATC* and the *AVC* curves equals *AFC*, a separate *AFC* curve is not drawn. Note that *AFC* declines continuously as output expands as the given *total* fixed costs are spread over more and more units of output. Graphically, *AVC* is the slope of a ray from the origin to the *TVC* curve, *ATC* is equal to the slope of a ray from the origin to the *TC* curve, while the *MC* is the slope of the *TC* or *TVC* curves. Note that the *MC* curve reaches its minimum before (i.e., at a lower level of output) and intercepts from below the *AVC* and *ATC* curves at their lowest points.

We can explain the U shape of the *AVC* curve as follows. With labor as the only variable input, *TVC* for any output level (Q) equals the wage rate (w, which is assumed to be fixed) times the quantity of labor (L) used. Thus,

$$AVC = \frac{TVC}{Q} = \frac{wL}{Q} = \frac{w}{Q/L} = \frac{w}{AP_L} \qquad [7\text{-}6]$$

Since the average physical product of labor (AP_L or Q/L) usually rises first, reaches a maximum, and then falls (see Section 6-2), it follows that the *AVC* curve first falls, reaches a minimum, and then rises. Since the *AVC* curve is U-shaped, the *ATC* curve is also U-shaped. The *ATC* curve continues to fall after the *AVC* curve begins to rise as long as the decline in *AFC* exceeds the rise in *AVC*.

The U shape of the *MC* curve can similarly be explained as follows:

$$MC = \frac{\Delta TVC}{\Delta Q} = \frac{\Delta(wL)}{\Delta Q} = \frac{w(\Delta L)}{\Delta Q} = \frac{w}{\Delta Q/\Delta L} = \frac{w}{MP_L} \qquad [7\text{-}7]$$

Since the marginal product of labor (MP_L or $\Delta Q/\Delta L$) first rises, reaches a maximum, and then falls, it follows that the *MC* curve first falls, reaches a minimum, and then rises. Thus, the rising portion of the *MC* curve reflects the operation of the law of diminishing returns. Case Study 7-1 shows the estimated per-unit cost curves in the cultivation of corn on Iowa farms.

CASE STUDY 7-1
Per-Unit Cost Curves in the Cultivation of Corn

Figure 7-2 shows the estimated *AVC*, *ATC*, and *MC* per thousand bushels of corn raised in Iowa farms in 1971. The *AVC*, *ATC*, and *MC* cost curves in the figure have the same general shape as the typical curves examined in the bottom panel of Figure 7-1. Note that once *MC* starts rising in the figure, it does so rapidly. This is true not only in raising corn but also in many other cases in the real world. For example, traveling costs (in terms of travel time) rise steeply during rush hours on highways. Similarly, landing costs (in terms of landing time) at airports also rise rapidly during peak hours (3:00–5:00 P.M.).

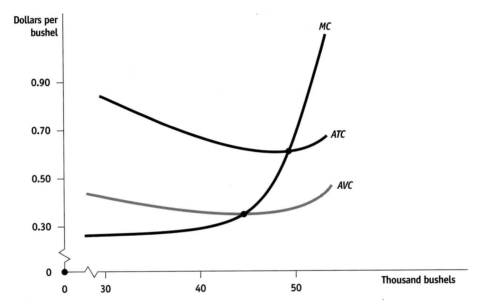

FIGURE 7-2 **Estimated Per-Unit Cost Curves in Corn Cultivation** The estimated *ATC*, *AVC*, and *MC* curves in corn cultivation are U-shaped as are those shown in the bottom panel in Figure 7-1. Once the *MC* curve of corn starts rising, it does so rapidly.

Source: D. Suits, "Agriculture," in W. Adams, *The Structure of the American Economy* (Englewood Cliffs, N.J.: Prentice-Hall, 1995), p. 12; "Road Pricing: The Solution to Highway Congestion," *The Margin* (Spring 1993); A. Carlin and R. Park, "Marginal Cost Pricing of Airport Runway Capacity," *American Economic Review* (June 1970); M. Samuel, "Traffic Congestion: A Solvable Problem," *Issues in Technology* (Spring 1999); "As London Launches Its Congestion Changing Experiment, Gridlocked Cities Around the World Watch with Interest," *Financial Times* (February 13, 2003), p. 9; and "Highway Nirvana, at a Price," *The Wall Street Journal* (July 6, 2005), p. A15.

| 7-3 | **LONG-RUN COST CURVES** |

In this section we derive the firm's long-run total, average, and marginal cost curves. We then show the relationship between the firm's long-run average cost curve and the firm's short-run average cost curves.

Long-Run Total Cost Curves

In Section 6-1 we defined the long run as the time period during which all inputs are variable. Thus, all costs are variable in the long run (i.e., the firm faces no fixed costs). The length of time of the long run depends on the industry. In some service industries, such as dry-cleaning, the period of the long run may be only a few months or weeks. For others that are capital intensive, such as the construction of a new electricity-generating plant, it may be many years. It all depends on the length of time required for the firm to be able to vary all inputs.

The firm's **long-run total cost (*LTC*)** curve is derived from the firm's expansion path and shows the minimum long-run total costs of producing various levels of output. The firm's long-run average and marginal cost curves are then derived from the long-run total cost curve. These derivations are shown in Figure 7-3.

The top panel of Figure 7-3 shows the expansion path of the firm. As explained in Section 6-5 and Figure 6-11, the expansion path shows the optimal input combinations to produce various levels of output. For example, point *A* shows that in order to produce 1 unit of output (1*Q*), the firm uses 4 units of labor (4*L*) and 4 units of capital (4*K*). If the wage of labor (*w*) is $10 per unit and the rental price of capital (*r*) is also $10 per unit, the minimum total cost of producing 1*Q* is

$$(4L)(\$10) + (4K)(\$10) = \$80$$

This is shown as point *A'* in the middle panel, where the vertical axis measures total costs and the horizontal axis measures output. From point *C* on the expansion path in the top panel, we get point *C'* ($100) on the *LTC* curve in the middle panel for 2*Q*. Other points on the *LTC* curve are similarly obtained.[3] Note that the *LTC* curve starts at the origin because there are no fixed costs in the long run.

From the *LTC* curve we can derive the firm's **long-run average cost (*LAC*)** curve. *LAC* is equal to *LTC* divided by *Q*. That is,

$$LAC = \frac{LTC}{Q} \qquad\qquad [7\text{-}8]$$

For example, the *LAC* to produce 1*Q* is obtained by dividing the *LTC* of $80 (point *A'* on the *LTC* curve in the middle panel of Figure 7-3) by 1. This is the slope of a ray from the origin to point *A'* on the *LTC* curve and is plotted as point *A''* in the bottom panel of

---

[3] Point *E'* on the *LTC* curve in the middle panel of Figure 7-3 is based on the assumption that 3*Q* is produced with 5.4*L* and 5.4*K* (not shown on the expansion path in the top panel in order not to clutter the figure), so that *LTC* = $108. The shape of the *LTC* curve will be explained in terms of the *LAC* curve that is derived from it.

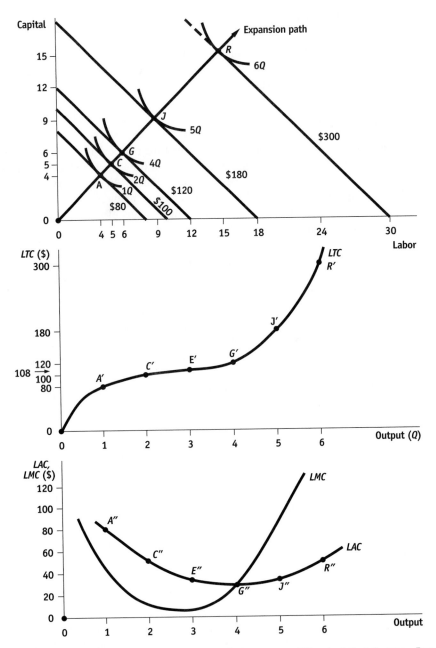

FIGURE 7-3 Derivation of the Long-Run Total, Average, and Marginal Cost Curves   From point *A* on the expansion path in the top panel, and *w* = $10 and *r* = $10, we get point *A′* on the long-run total cost (*LTC*) curve in the middle panel. Other points on the *LTC* curve are similarly obtained. The long-run average cost (*LAC*) curve in the bottom panel is given by the slope of a ray from the origin to the *LTC* curve. The *LAC* curve falls up to point *G″* (4*Q*) because of increasing returns to scale and rises thereafter because of decreasing returns to scale. The long-run marginal cost (*LMC*) curve is given by the slope of the *LTC* curve and intersects the *LAC* curve from below at the lowest point on the *LAC* curve.

Figure 7-3. Other points on the *LAC* curve are similarly obtained. Note that the slope of a ray from the origin to the *LTC* curve declines up to point *G′* (in the middle panel of Figure 7-3) and then rises. Thus, the *LAC* curve in the bottom panel declines up to point *G″* (4*Q*) and rises thereafter.

It is important to keep in mind, however, that while the U shape of the short-run average cost (*SAC*) curve is based on the operation of the law of diminishing returns (resulting from the existence of fixed inputs in the short run), the U shape of the *LAC* curve depends on increasing, constant, and decreasing returns to scale, respectively, as will be explained in Section 7-4.

From the *LTC* curve we can also derive the **long-run marginal cost (*LMC*)** curve. This measures the change in *LTC* per unit change in output and is given by the slope of the *LTC* curve. That is,

$$LMC = \frac{\Delta LTC}{\Delta Q} \qquad [7\text{-}9]$$

For example, increasing output from 0*Q* to 1*Q* increases *LTC* from $0 to $80. Therefore, *LMC* is $80 and is plotted at 0.5 (i.e., halfway between 0*Q* and 1*Q*) in the bottom panel of Figure 7-3. Increasing output from 1*Q* to 2*Q* leads to an increase in *LTC* from $80 to $100, or $20 (plotted at 1.5 in the bottom panel), etc. Note that the relationship between *LMC* and *LAC* is the same as that between the short-run *MC* and *ATC* or *AVC*. That is, the *LMC* curve reaches its lowest point at a smaller level of output than the *LAC* curve and intersects the *LAC* curve from below at the lowest point on the *LAC* curve.

Long-Run Average and Marginal Cost Curves

The long-run average cost (*LAC*) curve shows the lowest average cost of producing each level of output when the firm can build the most appropriate plant to produce each level of output. This is shown in Figure 7-4. The top panel of Figure 7-4 is based on the assumption that the firm can build only four scales of plant (given by *SAC*₁, *SAC*₂, *SAC*₃, and *SAC*₄), while the bottom panel of Figure 7-4 is based on the assumption that the firm can build many more or an infinite number of scales of plant.

The top panel of Figure 7-4 shows that the minimum average cost of producing 1 unit of output (1*Q*) is $80 and results when the firm operates the scale of plant given by *SAC*₁ (the smallest scale of plant possible) at point *A″*. The firm can produce 1.5*Q* at an average cost of $70 by using either the scale of plant given by *SAC*₁ or the larger scale of plant given by *SAC*₂ at point *B** (see the top panel of Figure 7-4). To produce 2*Q*, the firm will use scale of plant *SAC*₂ at point *C″* ($50) rather than the smaller scale of plant *SAC*₁ at point *C** (the lowest point on *SAC*₁, which refers to the average cost of $67). Thus, the firm has more flexibility in the long run than in the short run. To produce 3*Q*, the firm is indifferent between using plant *SAC*₂ or larger plant *SAC*₃ at point *E** ($60). The minimum average cost of producing 4*Q* ($30) is achieved when the firm operates plant *SAC*₃ at point *G″* (the lowest point on *SAC*₃). To produce 5*Q*, the firm operates either plant *SAC*₃ or larger plant *SAC*₄ at point *J** ($60). Finally, the minimum cost of producing 6*Q* is achieved when the firm operates plant *SAC*₄ (the largest plant) at point *R″* ($50).

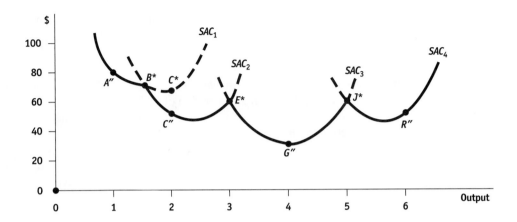

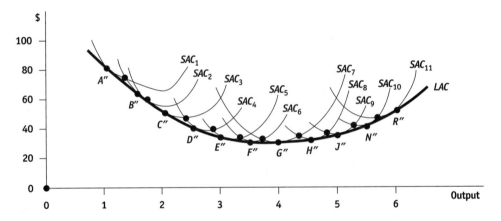

FIGURE 7-4   Relationship Between the Long-Run and Short-Run Average Cost Curves   In the top panel, the *LAC* curve is given by $A''B*C''E*G''J*R''$ on the assumption that the firm can build only four scales of plant (SAC_1, SAC_2, SAC_3, and SAC_4). In the bottom panel, the *LAC* curve is the smooth curve $A''B''C''D''E''F''G''H''J''N''R''$ on the assumption that the firm can build a very large or infinite number of plants in the long run.

Thus, if the firm could build only the four scales of plant shown in the top panel of Figure 7-4, the long-run average cost curve of the firm would be $A''B*C''E*G''J*R''$. If the firm could build many more scales of plant, the kinks at points $B*$, $E*$, and $J*$ would become less pronounced, as shown in the bottom panel of Figure 7-4. In the limit, as the number of scales of plants that the firm can build in the long run increases, the *LAC* curve approaches the smooth curve indicated by the *LAC* curves in the bottom panels of Figures 7-3 and 7-4. Thus, the *LAC* curve is the tangent or "envelope" to the *SAC* curves and shows the minimum average cost of producing various levels of output in the long run, when the firm can build any scale of plant. Note that only at point G'' (the lowest point on the *LAC* curve) does the firm utilize the optimal scale of plant at its lowest point. To the left of point G'', the firm

CASE STUDY 7-2
The Long-Run Average Cost Curve in Electricity Generation

Figure 7-5 shows the estimated *LAC* curve for a sample of 114 firms generating electricity in the United States in 1970. The figure shows that *LAC* is lowest at the output level of about 32 billion kilowatt-hours. The *LAC* curve, however, is nearly L-shaped (the reason for and significance of this are explained in Section 7-4). In order to avoid the increasing costs that they would incur in producing more power themselves to satisfy increasing consumer demand, electric power companies have been buying more and more power from independent power producers. But all of this is changing very rapidly as the industry braces for deregulation and the end of their monopoly power (see Chapter 12). Furthermore, recent technological advances have greatly reduced the average cost of producing electricity with micro-turbine generators, and this may soon provide even small businesses with the choice of generating their own electricity efficiently.

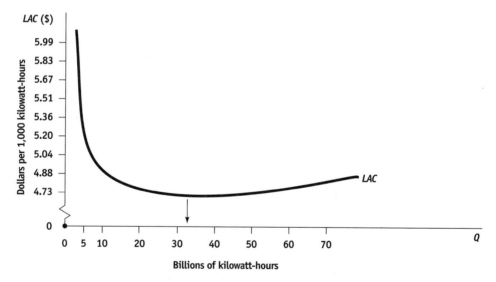

FIGURE 7-5   The Long-Run Average Cost Curve in Electricity Generation   The figure shows the estimated *LAC* curve in the generation of electricity in the United States for a sample of 114 firms in 1970. The lowest *LAC* occurs at the output level of 32 billion kilowatt-hours, but the *LAC* curve is nearly L-shaped.

Source: L. Christensen and H. Green, "Economies of Scale in U.S. Electric Power Generation," *Journal of Political Economy* (August 1976), p. 674; "Electric Utilities Brace for an End to Monopolies," *The New York Times* (August 18, 1994), p. 1; "Energy: Power Unbound," *The Wall Street Journal* (September 14, 1998), pp. R4, R10; The Royal Academy of Engineering, *The Cost of Generating Electricity* (London: The Royal Academy of Engineering, 2004); and OECD, *Projected Costs of Generating Electricity* (Paris: OECD, 2005).

operates on the declining portion of the relevant *SAC* curve, while to the right of point G'' the firm operates on the rising portion of the appropriate *SAC* curve (see the top panel of Figure 7-4).

The long run is often referred to as the **planning horizon** because the firm can build the plant that minimizes the cost of producing any anticipated level of output. Once the plant has been built, the firm operates in the short run. Thus, the firm plans for the long run and operates in the short run (see Case Study 7-2).[4]

| 7-4 | **PLANT SIZE AND ECONOMIES OF SCALE** |

In the bottom panels of Figures 7-3 and 7-4, the *LAC* curves have been drawn as U-shaped. This is based on the assumption that economies of scale prevail at small levels of output and diseconomies of scale prevail at larger levels of output. As pointed out in Section 6-6, "economies of scale" refers to the situation in which output grows proportionately faster than inputs. For example, output more than doubles with a doubling of inputs. With input prices remaining constant, this leads to lower costs per unit. Thus, increasing returns of scale are reflected in a declining *LAC* curve. On the other hand, decreasing returns to scale refers to the situation where output grows at a proportionately slower rate than the use of inputs. With input prices constant, this leads to higher costs per unit. Thus, decreasing returns to scale are reflected in an *LAC* curve that is rising. The lowest point on the *LAC* curve occurs at the output level at which the forces for increasing returns to scale are just balanced by the forces for decreasing returns to scale.

Increasing returns to scale or decreasing costs arise because of technological and financial reasons.[5] At the technological level, economies of scale arise because as the scale of operation increases, a greater division of labor and specialization can take place and more specialized and productive machinery can be used. Specifically, with a large-scale operation, each worker can be assigned to perform a repetitive task rather than numerous different ones. This results in increased proficiency and the avoidance of the time lost in moving from one machine to another. At higher scales of operation, more specialized and productive machinery can also be used. For example, using a conveyor belt to unload a small truck may not be justified, but it greatly increases efficiency in unloading a train or ship. Furthermore, some physical properties of equipment and machinery also lead to increasing returns to scale. For example, doubling the diameter of a pipeline more than doubles the flow without doubling costs, doubling the weight of a ship more than doubles its capacity to transport cargo without doubling costs, and so on. Thus, per-unit costs decline. Firms also need fewer supervisors, fewer spare parts, and smaller inventories per unit of output as the scale of operation increases.

---

[4] If the firm is uncertain about the level of demand and production in the future, it may want to build a more flexible plant for the *range* of anticipated outputs, rather than the optimal plant for producing a *particular* level of output at an even lower cost (see Problem 8, with answer in the back of the book).

[5] The technological forces for economies of scale are sometimes referred to as "plant economies" because they operate at the plant level. On the other hand, the financial reasons for economies of scale are often referred to as "firm economies" because they arise at the firm (as opposed to the plant) level.

Besides the technological reasons for increasing returns to scale or decreasing costs, there are financial reasons that arise as the size of the firm increases. Because of bulk purchases, larger firms are more likely to receive quantity discounts in purchasing raw materials and other intermediate (i.e., semiprocessed) inputs than smaller firms. Large firms can usually sell bonds and stocks more favorably and receive bank loans at lower interest rates than smaller firms. Large firms can also achieve economies of scale or decreasing costs in advertising and other promotional efforts. For all these technological and financial reasons, the *LAC* curve of a firm is likely to decline as the firm expands and becomes larger.

Decreasing returns to scale, on the other hand, arise primarily because as the scale of operation increases, it becomes ever more difficult to manage the firm effectively and coordinate the various operations and divisions of the firm. The number of meetings, the paperwork, and telephone bills increase more than proportionately to the increase in the scale of operation, and it becomes increasingly difficult for top management to ensure that their directives and guidelines are properly carried out by their subordinates. Thus, efficiency decreases and costs per unit tend to rise.

In the real world, the forces for increasing and decreasing returns to scale often operate side by side, with the former prevailing at small levels of output (so that the *LAC* curve declines) and the latter tending to prevail at much larger levels of output (so that the *LAC* curve rises). The lowest point on the *LAC* curve occurs when the forces for increasing and decreasing returns to scale just balance each other. In the real world, however, the *LAC* curve is often found to have a nearly flat bottom and to be L-shaped rather than U-shaped. This implies that economies of scale are rather quickly exhausted and constant or near-constant returns to scale prevail over a considerable range of outputs in many industries. In these industries, small firms coexist with much larger firms.[6]

There are some industries, however, in which the *LAC* curve declines continuously as the firm expands output, to the point where a single firm could satisfy the total market for the product or service more efficiently than two or more firms. These cases are usually referred to as "natural monopolies" and often arise in the provision of such utilities as electricity and public transportation. In such cases the local government often allows a single firm to supply the service to the entire market but subjects the firm to regulation (i.e., regulates the price or rate charged for the service). Three possible shapes of the *LAC* curve (U-shaped, L-shaped, and constantly declining) are shown in Figure 7-6 and examined in various U.S. industries in Case Study 7-3.

Economies of scale have to be distinguished from **economies of scope.** The latter refer to the lowering of costs that a firm often experiences when it produces two or more products together rather than each alone. A smaller commuter airline, for example, can profitably extend into providing cargo services, thereby lowering the cost of each operation alone. Another example is provided by a firm that produces a second product in order to use the by-products (which otherwise the firm had to dispose of at a cost) arising from the production of the first product. Management must be alert to the possibility of profitably extending its product line to exploit such economies of scope.

---

[6] The inability to observe rising *LAC* in the real world may be due to the fact that firms avoid expanding output when *LAC* begins to rise rapidly.

CASE STUDY 7-3
The Shape of the Long-Run Average Cost Curve in Various U.S. Industries

Table 7-2 gives the long-run average cost for small firms as a percentage of the long-run average cost of large firms in six U.S. industries. The table shows that the *LAC* of small hospitals is 29 percent higher than for large hospitals. This implies that small hospitals operate in the falling portion of the *LAC* curve. For most other industries, the *LAC* of small firms is not much different from the *LAC* of large firms in the same industry. These results are consistent with the widespread near-constant returns to scale reported in Table 6-5 and with L-shaped or at least flat-bottomed *LAC* curves. Only in trucking does the *LAC* curve

seem mildly U-shaped (since small firms have lower *LAC* costs than large ones). From Case Study 6-4 we can also infer that the *LAC* curve in automobile manufacturing is U-shaped with a flat bottom, with Ford near the bottom of the *LAC* curve, General Motors (the largest car manufacturer in the world) on the rising arm of its *LAC* curve, while Chrysler, being much smaller than either GM or Ford, on the falling arm of the *LAC* curve in 1991 and thus needed to expand. In fact (see Case Study 6-4), GM did shrink and lowered its long-run average costs below Ford's in 2002 and Chrysler merged with Mercedes-Benz in 1998.

TABLE 7-2 *LAC* of Small Firms as a Percentage of *LAC* of Large Firms	
Industry	**Percentage**
Hospitals	129
Commercial banking	
Demand deposits	116
Installment loans	102
Electric power	112
Airlines (local service)	100
Railroads	100
Trucking	95

Source: H. E. Frech and R. L. R. Mobley, "Resolving the Impasse on Hospital Scale Economies: A New Approach," *Applied Economics* (March 1995); F. Bell and N. Murphy, *Costs in Commercial Banking,* Research Report No. 41 (Boston: Federal Reserve Bank of Boston, 1968); L. Christensen and W. Greene, "Economies of Scale in U.S. Electric Power Generation," *Journal of Political Economy* (August 1976); G. Eads, M. Nerlove, and W. Raduchel, "A Long-Run Cost Function for the Local Service Airline Industry," *The Review of Economics and Statistics* (August 1969); Z. Griliches, "Cost Allocation in Railroad Regulation," *The Bell Journal of Economics and Management Science* (Spring 1972); R. Koenker, "Optimal Scale and the Size Distribution of American Trucking Firms," *Journal of Transport Economics and Policy* (January 1977); "Automobiles: GM Decides Smaller Is Better," *The Margin* (November–December 1988), p. 28; and "GM Outstrips Ford on Vehicle Productivity, Study Finds," *Financial Times* (June 14, 2002), p. 18.

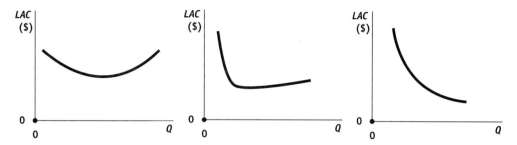

FIGURE 7-6   Possible Shapes of the *LAC* Curve   The left panel shows a U-shaped *LAC* curve, which indicates first increasing and then decreasing returns to scale. The middle panel shows a nearly L-shaped *LAC* curve, which shows that economies of scale quickly give way to constant returns to scale or gently rising *LAC*. The right panel shows an *LAC* curve that declines continuously, as in the case of natural monopolies.

7-5   LEARNING CURVES

As firms gain experience in the production of a commodity or service, their average cost of production usually declines. That is, *for a given level of output per time period,* the increasing *cumulative total output* over many time periods often provides the manufacturing experience that enables firms to lower their average cost of production. The **learning curve** shows the decline in the average input cost of production with rising cumulative total outputs over time. For example, it might take 1,000 hours to assemble the 100th aircraft, but only 700 hours to assemble the 200th aircraft because managers and workers become more efficient as they gain production experience. Contrast this to economies of scale, which refer instead to declining average cost as the firm's output *per time period* increases.

Figure 7-7 shows a learning curve which indicates that the average cost declines from about $250 for producing the 100th unit of the product (point *F*), to about $200 for producing the 200th unit (point *G*), and to about $165 for the 400th unit (point *H*). Note

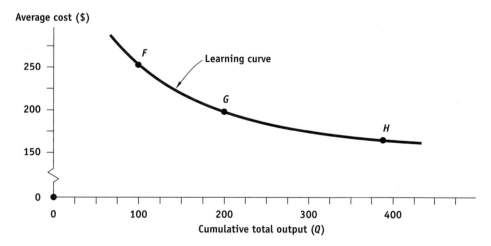

FIGURE 7-7   Learning Curve   Learning curve *FGH* shows that the average cost is about $250 for producing the 100th unit (point *F*), about $200 for the 200th unit (point *G*), and about $165 for the 400th unit (point *H*).

that the average cost declines at a decreasing rate so that the learning curve is convex to the origin. This is the usual shape of learning curves; that is, firms usually achieve the largest decline in average input costs when the production process is relatively new and less decline as the firm matures.

The learning curve can be expressed algebraically as follows:

$$C = aQ^b \qquad [7\text{-}10]$$

where C is the average input cost of the Qth unit of output, a is the average cost of the first unit of output, and b will be negative because the average input cost declines with increases in cumulative total output. The greater the absolute value of b, the faster the average input cost declines. Taking the logarithm of both sides of Equation 7-10 gives

$$\log C = \log a + b \log Q \qquad [7\text{-}11]$$

In the above logarithmic form, b is the slope of the learning curve.

The parameter of the learning curve in the double-log form of Equation 7-11 (i.e., log a and b) can be estimated by regression analysis with historical data on average cost and cumulative output. Suppose that doing this gives the following result:

$$\log C = 3 - 0.3 \log Q \qquad [7\text{-}12]$$

In Equation 7-12, C is expressed in dollars, $\log a = 3$ and $b = -0.3$. Thus, the average input cost of the 100th unit is

$$\log C = 3 - 0.3 \log 100$$

Since the log of 100 is 2 (obtained by simply entering the number 100 in your hand calculator and pressing the "log" key), we have

$$\log C = 3 - 0.3(2)$$
$$= 3 - 0.6$$
$$= 2.4$$

Since the antilog of 2.4 is 251.19, the average input cost (C) of the 100th unit of output is $251.19.

The average input cost for the 200th unit is

$$\log C = 3 - 0.3 \log 200$$
$$= 3 - 0.3 \,(2.30103)$$
$$= 3 - 0.690309$$
$$= 2.309691$$

Therefore, $C = 204.03.

The student can determine in an analogous way that for the 400th unit, $C = 165.72. These are, in fact, the values shown by the learning curve in Figure 7-7.

Learning curves have been documented in many manufacturing and service sectors, ranging from the manufacturing of airplanes, appliances, shipbuilding, refined petroleum products, to the operation of power plants. They have also been used to forecast the needs for personnel, machinery, and raw materials, and for scheduling production, determining the price at which to sell output, and even for evaluating suppliers' price quotations. For example, in its early days as a computer-chip producer, Texas Instruments adopted an aggressive price strategy based on the learning curve. Believing that the learning curve in chip production was steep, it kept unit prices low in order to increase its cumulative total output rapidly and thereby benefit from learning by doing. The strategy was successful, and Texas Instruments became one of the world's major players in this market.

How rapidly the learning curve (i.e., average input costs) declines can differ widely among firms and is greater the smaller the rate of employee turnover, the fewer the production interruptions (which would lead to "forgetting"), and the greater the ability of the firm to transfer knowledge from the production of other similar products. The average cost typically declines by 20 to 30 percent for each doubling of cumulative output for many firms. Firms, however, do not rely only on their production experience to lower costs and are looking farther and farther afield from their industry to gain insights on how to increase productivity (see Case Study 7-4).

CASE STUDY 7-4
To Reduce Costs, Firms Often Look Far Afield

In order to increase productivity and cut costs to better compete, firms often seek creative insights in industries far afield from their own. Of course, in a time of increased global competition, firms routinely scrutinize competitors' practices in their quest for innovative products and processes. But seeking inspiration only in one's own industry has limitations, and so more and more firms are increasingly looking in other industries and fields to come up with new products and better ways of doing things. For example, when Southwest Airlines wanted to improve the turnaround of its aircraft at airports, it did not examine other airlines' practices but went to the Indianapolis 500 to watch how pit crews fuel and service race cars in a matter of seconds. The result was that Southwest was able to cut its turnaround time by 50 percent. Such a drastic increase in productivity could hardly be accomplished by observing other airlines' practices. It is, of course, much more difficult to adapt techniques from other industries, but when it is accomplished, the potential rewards in terms of increased efficiency can be very great.

The key to finding useful insights in seemingly unrelated fields is to focus on processes. After all, all firms do basically the same things—hire employees, buy from suppliers, carry on production processes, sell to customers, and collect payments. For exam-

ple, a firm seeking to speed its production process might look at Domino's Pizza, an outfit that takes an order, produces the pizza, delivers it, and collects the money—often in less than 30 minutes. A major gas utility firm discovered ways to greatly speed the delivery of its fuel to customers by observing how Federal Express delivers packages overnight. Similarly, a firm delivering gravel speeded deliveries by having truck drivers plug a card into a machine to request the quantity of gravel to load—without requiring the driver to get off the truck and fill order forms—just as automated teller machines work at banks.

In 1999, General Motors adapted a system used by the federal Centers for Disease Control and Prevention (CDC) to track down diseases and spot outbreaks to the industrial tasks of debugging its cars, and this is expected to eliminate some nine million claims and save it $1.6 billion in warranty repairs in two years. Motorola is using the biological code DNA to define circuit patterns on semiconductors. To build a better wind turbine, GE built a global team of researchers from Germany, China, India, and the United States; to look for new medicines, Novartis, the Swiss pharmaceutical company, went to a laboratory in Shanghai specializing in ancient remedies; and the technology behind Intel's Centrino, now a $5 billion business, was born in an R&D lab in Israel.

Source: "To Compete Better, Look Far Afield," *The New York Times* (September 18, 1994), sec. 3, p. 11; "GM Takes Advice from Disease Sleuths to Debug Cars," *The Wall Street Journal* (April 8, 1999), p. B1; "Motorola's New Research Efforts Look Far Afield," *The Wall Street Journal* (June 17, 1999), p. B6; and "The World of Ideas," *Fortune* (*July 25, 2005*), pp. 90–96.

| 7-6 |

MINIMIZING COSTS INTERNATIONALLY— THE NEW ECONOMIES OF SCALE

In this section we examine the growing importance of international trade in inputs as a way for firms to minimize costs internationally, as well as the ability of some U.S. firms to satisfy their needs for some skilled labor from abroad.

International Trade in Inputs

During the past decade or so, there has been a sharp increase in international trade in parts and components. Today, more and more products manufactured by international corporations have parts and components made in many countries. The reason is to minimize production costs. For example, the motors of some Ford Fiestas are produced in the United Kingdom, the transmissions in France, and the clutches in Spain; the parts are assembled in Germany for sale throughout Europe. Similarly, Japanese and German cameras are often assembled in Singapore to take advantage of cheaper labor there.

Foreign sourcing of inputs is often not a matter of choice to earn higher profits, but simply a requirement to remain competitive. Firms that do not look abroad for cheaper inputs face loss of competitiveness in world markets and even in the domestic market. For example, $625 of the $860 cost of producing an IBM computer was outsourced abroad, and most of the major components going into the production of a Boeing 777, and even more for the Boeing 787, are made abroad (see Case Study 7-5). U.S. firms now spend more than $100 billion on outsourcing, and by doing so they cut costs 10 to 15 percent.[7] Outsourcing accounts for more than one-third of total manufacturing costs by Japanese firms, saving them more than 20 percent of production costs. Such low-cost offshore purchase of inputs is likely to continue to expand rapidly and is being fostered by joint ventures, licensing arrangements, and other nonequity collaborative arrangements. Indeed, this represents one of the most dynamic aspects of the global business environment of today.

Not only are more and more inputs imported, but also more and more firms are opening production facilities in more and more nations. For example, Nestlé, the largest Swiss company and the world's second largest food company, has production facilities in 59 countries, and America's Gillette has facilities in 22. In 1987, Ford had component factories and assembly plants at 26 industrial sites in the United Kingdom, Germany, Belgium, France, Spain, and Portugal, and it employed more people abroad than in the United States (201,000 people abroad and 181,000 in the United States). Bertelsmann AG, the $7 billion German media empire, not only owns printing plants around the world and the Literary Guild Book Club but also prints books at competitor's plants and sells them through the Time-Warner–owned Book-of-the-Month Club.[8]

---

[7] See "The Outing of Outsourcing," *The Economist* (November 25, 1995), pp. 57–58; "Has Outsourcing Gone Too Far?" *Business Week* (April 1, 1996), pp. 26–28; "The Hidden Costs of Outsourcing," *Sloan Management Review* (Spring 2001), pp. 60–69; and "Out of the Backdoor," *The Economist* (December 1, 2001), pp. 55–56.

[8] See W. H. Davidson and J. de la Torre, *Managing the Global Corporation* (New York: McGraw-Hill, 1989); and "Reengineering 101," *Forbes* (May 13, 2002), pp. 82–88.

CASE STUDY 7-5
The IBM PC and the Boeing 777
and 787 Are All but American!

Table 7-3 shows that of the total manufacturing cost of $860 for the IBM PC in 1985, $625 was for parts and components made abroad (of which $230 was from U.S.-owned plants). Although all the parts made overseas could be manufactured domestically, they would have cost more and would have led to higher PC prices in the United States (and reduced competitiveness of IBM PCs in international markets). Today, even a larger proportion of parts and components going into the IBM PC are made abroad and, in 2004, IBM sold its laptop business to China's Lenovo for $1.75 billion. Only 13 of the 33 major components of the new Boeing 777-330ER jetliner are made in the United States; 7 are made in Japan and another 13 in other countries (England, Italy, South Korea, and Spain). Even less of the brand new Boeing 787 Dreamliner jet is made in the United States.

TABLE 7-3	Distribution of Manufacturing Costs for the IBM PC in the United States and Abroad		
Total manufacturing cost:			$860
Portion made abroad:		$625	
In U.S.-owned plants	$230		
In foreign-owned plants	395		
Distribution of manufacturing costs:			
Monochrome monitor (Korea)	$ 85		
Semiconductors (Japan)	105		
Semiconductors (U.S.)	105		
Power supply (Japan)	60		
Graphics printer (Japan)	160		
Floppy disk drives (Singapore)	165		
Assembly of disk drives (U.S.)	25		
Keyboard (Japan)	50		
Case and final assembly (U.S.)	105		
	$860		

Source: "America's High-Tech Crisis," *Business Week* (March 11, 1985), pp. 56–67; "Outsourcing to the U.S.," *The New York Times* (December 25, 2005), p. C1; Boeing News Release (June 11, 2002); and "A Plastic Dream Machine," *Business Week* (June 20, 2005), pp. 32–35.

So widespread and growing is international trade in inputs and the opening of production facilities abroad that we are rapidly moving toward truly multinational firms with roots in many nations rather than in only one country, as in the past. And this affects more than multinationals. Indeed, firms that until a few years ago operated exclusively in the domestic market are now purchasing increasing quantities of inputs and components and shifting some of their production to foreign nations. For example, Malachi Mixon, an American medical-equipment company, now buys parts and components in half a dozen countries, from China to Colombia; 10 years ago it did all of its shopping at home. The popular Mazda Miata automobile, which is manufactured in Japan, was conceived in Mazda's California design lab by an American engineer at the same time that Mazda opened production facilities for other models in the United States.

The New International Economies of Scale

Firms must constantly explore sources of cheaper inputs and overseas production in order to remain competitive in our rapidly shrinking world. Indeed, this process can be regarded as manufacturing's **new international economies of scale** in today's global economy. Just as companies were forced to rationalize operations within each country in the 1980s, they now face the challenge of integrating their operations for their entire system of manufacturing around the world in order to take advantage of these new international economies of scale.[9] What is important is for the firm to focus on those components that are indispensable to the company's competitive position over subsequent product generations and outsource other components in which outside suppliers have a distinct production advantage.[10]

These new international economies of scale can be achieved in five basic areas: product development, purchasing, production, demand management, and order fulfillment. In product development, the firm can design a core product for the entire world economy, building into the product the possibility of variations and derivatives for local markets. Firms can also achieve new economies of scale by purchasing raw materials, parts, and components globally rather than locally, no matter where their operations are located. Firms can coordinate production in low-cost manufacturing centers with final assembly in high-cost locations near markets. They can also forecast the demand for their products and undertake demand management on a world rather than national basis. Firms can achieve large economies of scale by shipping products from the plants closest to customers, allowing the firms to hold less inventory around the world. These new international economies of scale are likely to become even more important as we move closer to a truly global economy.

---

[9] See "Manufacturing's New Economies of Scale," *Harvard Business Review* (May–June 1992), pp. 94–102; and "The New Dynamics of Global Manufacturing Site Location," *Sloan Management Review* (Summer 1994), pp. 69–80.

[10] See "Strategic Outsourcing," *Harvard Business Review* (November–December 1992), pp. 98–107; "Strategic Outsourcing," *Sloan Management Review* (Summer 1994), pp. 43–55; and "How to Think Strategically About Outsourcing," *Harvard Management Update* (May 2000), pp. 4–6.

Immigration of Skilled Labor

A survey of almost 300 employers by the National Science Foundation (NSF) in 1985 found that 28 percent of them had personnel shortages in science and engineering. This shortage is worse today. Indeed, the NSF had predicted a shortage of 675,000 scientists and engineers in the United States by 2006.[11] This is the result of fewer college-age people in the United States and the decline in the college-age cohort going into science and engineering. Shortages of skilled workers also exist in other fields. Many hospitals are staffed by increasing numbers of foreign-born doctors and nurses. There are also shortages in mathematics and computer science. Although government aid to higher education can induce more students to train in these fields in the long run, in the short run firms will have to turn to foreign workers, and this trend is likely to accelerate during this decade.

Some of the projected shortfall in scientists, engineers, and other highly skilled professionals is likely to be made up by foreign students who attend American universities—many of whom remain in the United States after completing their studies. For example, in recent years more than 30 percent of the students earning doctorates in the United States have been foreigners. The figure is over 40 percent in mathematics and 60 percent in engineering. Changes in U.S. immigration laws in 1998 recognize that the United States now needs "the best and the brightest from other countries in order to compete in the cutthroat world of global markets."[12] The new law nearly doubled (to 115,000) the number of yearly visas granted to sought-after experts and professionals. The number was further increased to 195,000 for 2001–2003, but reverted back to 65,000 since then. With the collapse of communism in the former Soviet Union in the late 1980s and early 1990s, a huge number of chemists, physicists, mathematicians, and computer scientists have flocked to the United States, attracted by higher-paying jobs and better working conditions.

It must be kept in mind, however, that while this represents a gain for the United States, such an inflow of highly skilled personnel represents a loss for the country of emigration. This has been aptly captured by the phrase **brain drain.** But in a world of global competition, the manager must forecast the firm's need for skilled labor and hire it from abroad when not available domestically. If that is not possible, the firm may have to consider moving some of its operations abroad. Since the terrorist attack of September 11, 2001, the United States has tightened visa rules and this is slowing down the vital flow of professionals admitted into the United States. The United States is also slipping in attracting the world's best students.[13]

---

[11] See "Wanted: 675,000 Future Scientists and Engineers," *Science* (June 1989), pp. 1536–1538; and "Supply and Demand for Scientists and Engineers: A National Crisis in the Making," *Science* (April 1990), pp. 425–432.

[12] See "Software Jobs Go Begging, Threatening Technology Boom," *The New York Times* (January 13, 1998), p. 1; "Alien Scientists Take Over USA!" *The Economist* (August 21, 1999), p. 24; "Congress Approves a Big Increase in Visas for Specialized Workers," *The New York Times* (October 4, 2000), p. 1; and Richard Freeman, Emily Jin, and Chia-Yu Shen, "Changing Demographics of U.S. Science-Engineering PhDs.," *NBER Working Paper 10554* (June 2005).

[13] See "Keeping Out the Wrong People," *Business Week* (October 4, 2004), pp. 90–94; "U.S. Slips in Attracting the World's Best Students," *The New York Times* (December 21, 2004), p. 1; D. Salvatore, *International Economics*, 8th ed. (Hoboken, N.J.: Wiley, 2004), sec. 12.6; and "Jobs and Immigrants," *The Wall Street Journal* (August 26, 2005), p. A12.

7-7   LOGISTICS OR SUPPLY-CHAIN MANAGEMENT

Logistics, or supply-chain management, refers to the merging at the corporate level of the purchasing, transportation, warehousing, distribution, and customer services functions, rather than dealing with each of them separately at division levels. Increasingly, logistics or supply-chain management is seen not simply as a way to reduce transportation costs, but as a source of competitive advantage. For example, one health care company was able to substantially increase its market share by establishing overnight delivery to the retailer and next-day service to the customer.

Monitoring the movement of materials and finished products from a central place can reduce the shortages and surpluses that inevitably arise when these functions are managed separately. For example, it would be difficult for a firm to determine the desirability of a sales promotion campaign without considering the cost of the inventory buildup to meet the anticipated increase in demand. Logistics can also help avoid other serious (even amusing) problems. For example, to get rid of an excessive stock of green cars in the mid-1990s, Volvo's marketing department offered attractive deals on green cars. Noting the increase in sales of green cars without knowing about the promotion, the manufacturing department began to produce even more green cars! In short, logistics can increase the efficiency and profitability of the firm.

There are three reasons for the emergence and rapid growth of logistics. First is the development of new and much faster algorithms and ever-faster computers that greatly facilitate the solution of complex logistic problems. The second is the growing use of just-in-time inventory management, which makes the buying of inputs and the selling of the product much more tricky and more closely integrated with all other functions of the firm. The third reason (as seen in Section 7-6) is the increasing trend toward globalization of production and distribution in today's world. With production, distribution, marketing, and financing activities of the leading world corporations scattered around the world, the need for logistic management becomes even more important—and beneficial.

For example, the 3M Corporation saved more than $40 million in 1988 by linking its American logistic operations with those in Europe and the rapidly growing Pacific Rim region. Similarly, Sun Microsystems, a computer maker, saved $15 million and increased revenue by $30 million in the first quarter of 2001 alone by using logistic management that practically eliminated product shortages and hence sales losses, as well as unsold products, which lose value very quickly. By centralizing several logistic functions, companies achieve greater flexibility and savings in ordering inputs and in increased revenues in selling products.

Despite its obvious merits, however, only about 10 percent of small companies now have expertise and are highly sophisticated in logistics; this is certainly likely to change during this decade. Among the companies that are already making extensive use of logistic management are National Semiconductors, 3M Corporation, Saturn, Land O'Lakes Foods, Bergen Brunswing, as well as the express courier companies (DHL, FedEx, and UPS).[14] Case Study 7-6 discusses logistics at National Semiconductors, Saturn, and Compaq.

---

[14] "Logistics: A Trendy Management Tool," *The New York Times* (December 24, 1989), sec. 3, p. 12; "Chain Reaction," *The Economist* (February 2, 2002), pp. 13–14; and "A Moving Story," *The Economist* (December 7, 2002), p. 65.

CASE STUDY 7-6
Logistics at National Semiconductors, Saturn, and Compaq

Since the early 1990s, National Semiconductors, the world's thirteenth largest chipmaker, has become a logistics or supply-chain management expert, and, in the process, it has cut delivery time by 47 percent and reduced distribution costs by 2.5 percent at the same time that its sales increased by 34 percent. National Semiconductors achieved this feat by closing six warehouses around the globe and air-freighting its computer chips from its six production plants (four in the United States, one in England, and one in Israel) to its new world distribution center in Singapore, from where it fills orders from IBM, Toshiba, Compaq, Ford, Siemens, and its other large customers. Earlier, National Semiconductors' distribution network was a nightmare of waste, costly stockpiles, and an inefficient delivery system that often included as many as 10 stopovers for its chips on their way to customers.

From its very beginning Saturn has had a world-class logistics system that links suppliers, factories, and customers so efficiently that it maintains almost no inventory. Its central computer directs truck deliveries from its 339 suppliers located in 39 states at an average distance of more than 500 miles to its 56 receiving docks, 21 hours per day, 6 days per week, in a process that is so smooth that Saturn's assembly line had to be shut only once and for only 18 minutes in 4 years because of the lack of a component. In 1994 (long before it was acquired by Hewlett-Packard), Compaq estimated that it lost $500 million to $1 billion in sales because its computers were not available in the location and at the time customers wanted them. In 1995, Compaq set up a new logistics system that sharply increased the efficiency of its supply-chain management. For one thing, an on-board computer told Compaq's truckers exactly where to go, the best route to take, and the time required.

In short, in many cases there are greater opportunities to cut costs from increasing supply-chain efficiency than from the manufacturing of the product. More and more, logistics is regarded as a crucial strategy for survival and growth in global competition. Today, more than 80 percent of the country's 100 biggest companies use third-party logistics providers, such as C.H. Robinson Worldwide Inc., United Parcel Service, and Deutsche Post AG. The crucial importance of logistics becomes even more evident when there are major supply-chain disruptions, as those caused by Hurricane Katrina, which practically destroyed New Orleans in August 2005.

Source: "Delivering the Goods," *Fortune* (November 28, 1994), pp. 64–78; "Logistics Aspires to Worldly Wisdom," *Financial Times* (June 17, 1999), p. 11; "Supply Chain Logistics Moving Up the Corporate Agenda," *Financial Times* (December 1, 1998), p. I; M. A. Cohen et al., "Saturn Supply-Chain Innovation: High Value in After-Sales Service," *Sloan Management Review* (Summer 2000), pp. 93–101; "Global Goods Jugglers," *The Wall Street Journal* (July 5, 2005), p. A11; "Shippers Warn of Supply Chain Chaos," *Financial Times* (September 1, 2005), p. 2; and "A Distribution System Brought to Its Knees," *The New York Times* (September 1, 2005), p. C1.

7-8

COST–VOLUME–PROFIT ANALYSIS AND OPERATING LEVERAGE

In this section, we examine cost–volume–profit analysis (often called *breakeven analysis*) and operating leverage. These simple analytical techniques are frequently used in managerial decision making and can be quite useful when applied under the proper set of circumstances.

Cost–Volume–Profit Analysis

Cost–volume–profit or **breakeven analysis** examines the relationship among the total revenue, total costs, and total profits of the firm at various levels of output. Cost–volume–profit or breakeven analysis is often used by business executives to determine the sales volume required for the firm to break even and the total profits and losses at other sales levels. The analysis uses a cost–volume–profit chart in which the total revenue (*TR*) and the total cost (*TC*) curves are represented by straight lines, as in Figure 7-8.

In the figure, total revenues and total costs are plotted on the vertical axis, whereas output or sales per time period are plotted on the horizontal axis. The slope of the *TR* curve refers to the constant price of $10 per unit at which the firm can sell its output. The *TC* curve indicates total fixed costs (*TFC*) of $200 (the vertical intercept) and a constant average variable cost of $5 (the slope of the *TC* curve). This is often the case for many firms for small changes in output or sales. The firm breaks even (with $TR = TC = \$400$) at $Q = 40$ per time period (point *B* in the figure). The firm incurs losses at smaller outputs and earns profits at higher output levels.

The cost–volume–profit or breakeven chart is a flexible tool to quickly analyze the effect of changing conditions on the firm. For example, an increase in the price of the commodity can be shown by increasing the slope of the *TR* curve, an increase in total fixed costs of the firm can be shown by an increase in the vertical intercept of the *TC* curve, and an increase in average variable costs by an increase in the slope of the *TC* curve. The chart will then show the change in the breakeven point of the firm and the profits or losses at other output or sales levels (see Problem 11).

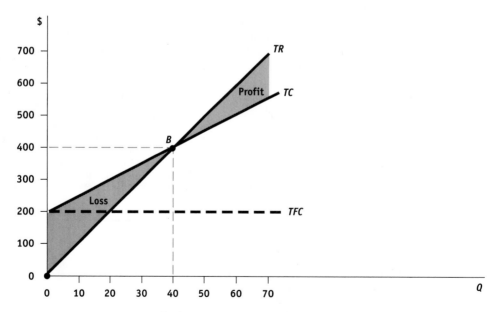

FIGURE 7-8 Linear Cost–Volume–Profit or Breakeven Chart The slope of the total revenue (*TR*) curve refers to the product price of $10 per unit. The vertical intercept of the total cost (*TC*) curve refers to the total fixed costs (*TFC*) of $200, and the slope of the *TC* curve to the average variable cost of $5. The firm breaks even with $TR = TC = \$400$ at the output (*Q*) of 40 units per time period (point *B*). The losses that the firm incurs at smaller output levels and profits at larger output levels can be read off the figure.

Cost–volume–profit analysis can also be performed algebraically, as follows. Total revenue is equal to the selling price (P) per-unit times the quantity of output or sales (Q). That is,

$$TR = (P)(Q) \tag{7-13}$$

Total costs equal total fixed costs plus total variable costs (TVC). Since TVC is equal to the average (per-unit) variable costs (AVC) times the quantity of output or sales, we have

$$TC = TFC + (AVC)(Q) \tag{7-14}$$

Setting total revenue equal to total costs and substituting Q_B (the breakeven output) for Q, we have

$$TR = TC \tag{7-15}$$

$$(P)(Q_B) = TFC + (AVC)(Q_B) \tag{7-16}$$

Solving Equation 7-16 for the breakeven output Q_B, we get

$$(P)(Q_B) - (AVC)(Q_B) = TFC$$

$$(Q_B)(P - AVC) = TFC$$

$$Q_B = \frac{TFC}{P - AVC} \tag{7-17}$$

For example, with $TFC = \$200$, $P = \$10$, and $AVC = \$5$,

$$Q_B = \frac{\$200}{\$10 - \$5} = 40$$

This is the breakeven output shown on the cost–volume–profit chart in Figure 7-8. The denominator in Equation 7-17 (that is, $P - AVC$) is called the **contribution margin per unit** because it represents the portion of the selling price that can be applied to cover the fixed costs of the firm and to provide for profits.

More generally, suppose that the firm wishes to earn a specific profit and wants to estimate the quantity that it must sell to earn that profit. Cost–volume–profit or breakeven analysis can be used in determining the target output (Q_T) at which a target profit (π_T) can be achieved. To do so, we simply add π_T to the numerator of Equation 7-17 and have

$$Q_T = \frac{TFC + \pi_T}{P - AVC} \tag{7-18}$$

For example, if the firm represented in the cost–volume–profit chart in Figure 7-8 wanted to earn a target profit of $100, the target output would be

$$Q_T = \frac{\$200 + \$100}{\$10 - \$5} = \frac{\$300}{\$5} = 60$$

To see that the output of $Q = 60$ does indeed lead to the target profit (π_T) of $100, note that

$$TR = (P)(Q) = (\$10)(60) = \$600$$

$$TC = TFC + (AVC)(Q) = \$200 + (\$5)(60) = \$500$$

and

$$\pi_T = TR - TC = \$600 - \$500 = \$100$$

While linear cost–volume–profit charts and analyses are frequently used by business executives, government agencies, and not-for-profit organizations, care must be exercised to apply them only *when the assumption of constant prices and average variable costs holds.*[15] Cost–volume–profit analysis also assumes that the firm produces a single product or a constant mix of products. Over time, the product mix changes, and it may be difficult to allocate the fixed costs among the various products. Despite these shortcomings, cost–volume–profit analysis can be very useful in managerial decision making.

Note, however, that sometimes Japanese firms turn cost–volume–profit analysis on its head. Instead of designing a new product and then estimating the cost of producing it (as American firms typically do), Japanese firms sometimes start with a target cost based on the market price at which the firm believes consumers will buy the product and then strive to produce the product at the specified targeted cost. Under such **Japanese cost-management systems,** the firm subtracts the desired profit from the expected selling price and then allocates targeted costs to each part, component, and process required to produce the product in such a way as to keep costs within the targeted level.

Operating Leverage

Operating leverage refers to the ratio of the firm's total fixed costs to total variable costs. The higher this ratio, the more leveraged the firm is said to be. As the firm becomes more automated or more leveraged (i.e., substitutes fixed for variable costs), its total fixed costs rise but its average variable costs fall. Because of higher overhead costs, the breakeven output of the firm increases. This is shown in Figure 7-9.

In Figure 7-9, the intersection of *TR* and *TC* defines the breakeven output of $Q_B = 40$ (as in Figure 7-8). If the firm's total fixed costs rise from $200 (the vertical intercept of *TC*) to $300 (the vertical intercept of *TC'*), while average variable costs decline from $AVC = \$5$ (the slope of *TC*) to $AVC' = \$3.33$ (the slope of *TC'*), the breakeven output will rise to $Q_{B'} = 45$ (given by the intersection of *TR* and *TC'*).

Figure 7-9 also shows that the higher the ratio of total fixed costs to total variable costs (i.e., the more leveraged the firm is), the more sensitive are the firm's profits to changes in output or sales. For example, the increase in output or sales from 60 to 70 units increases profits from $100 (the vertical distance between *TR* and either *TC* or *TC'*) to $150 with *TC* and to $166.67 with *TC'*. The responsiveness or sensitivity of the firm's total profits (π) to a change in its output or sales (*Q*) can be measured by the **degree of operating leverage (DOL).** This is nothing other than the sales elasticity of profit and is defined as the percentage change in profit divided by the percentage change in output or sales. That is,[16]

$$DOL = \frac{\%\Delta\pi}{\%\Delta Q} = \frac{\Delta\pi/\pi}{\Delta Q/Q} = \frac{\Delta\pi}{\Delta Q} \cdot \frac{Q}{\pi} \qquad [7\text{-}19]$$

---

[15] If prices and average variable costs are not constant, a nonlinear cost–volume–profit chart and analysis would have to be used. This is similar to the optimization analysis shown in Figure 2-4. The only difference is that the objective of the analysis shifts from the determination of the optimum price and output in optimization analysis to the determination of the output levels at which the firm breaks even or earns a target profit in cost–volume–profit analysis.

[16] In terms of calculus,

$$DOL = \frac{\partial\pi}{\partial Q} \cdot \frac{Q}{\pi}$$

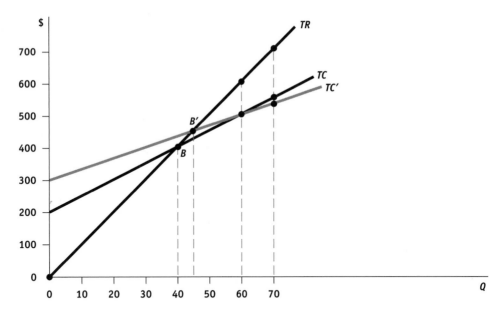

FIGURE 7-9 Operating Leverage, Breakeven Point, and Variability of Profits The intersection of *TR* and *TC* defines the breakeven quantity of $Q_B = 40$ (as in Figure 7-8). With *TC'* (i.e., if the firm becomes more highly leveraged), the breakeven quantity increases to $Q_{B'} = 45$ (given by the intersection of *TR* and *TC'*). The total profits of the firm are also more variable with *TC'* than with *TC*.

But $\pi = Q(P - AVC) - TFC$ and $\Delta\pi = \Delta Q(P - AVC)$. Substituting these values into Equation 7-19, we get

$$DOL = \frac{\Delta Q(P - AVC)Q}{\Delta Q[Q(P - AVC) - TFC]} = \frac{Q(P - AVC)}{Q(P - AVC) - TFC} \qquad [7\text{-}20]$$

The numerator in Equation 7-20 is the total contribution to fixed costs and profits of all units sold by the firm, and the denominator is the total (economic) profit.

For example, for an increase in output from 60 to 70 units, the degree of operating leverage with *TC* is

$$DOL = \frac{60(\$10 - \$5)}{60(\$10 - \$5) - \$200} = \frac{\$300}{\$100} = 3$$

With *TC'* (i.e., when the firm becomes more leveraged), the degree of operating leverage becomes

$$DOL' = \frac{60(\$10 - \$3.33)}{60(\$10 - \$3.33) - \$300} \cong \frac{\$400}{\$100} = 4$$

Thus, the degree of operating leverage (*DOL*) increases as the firm becomes more leveraged or capital intensive. It is also higher the closer we are to the breakeven point because the base in measuring the percentage change in profits (the denominator in Equation 7-19) is close to zero near the breakeven point. Note that when the firm's sales and output are high (greater than 60 units in Figure 7-9), the firm makes larger profits when it is more leveraged (i.e., with *TC'*). But it also incurs losses sooner, and these losses rise more rapidly than when the firm is less highly leveraged (i.e., with *TC*). The larger profits of the more highly leveraged firm when output is high (greater than 60 units in Figure 7-9) can thus be regarded as the return for its greater risk (see Case Study 7-7).

CASE STUDY 7-7
Breakeven Analysis for Lockheed's Tri-Star and Europe's Airbus Industrie

In 1971, Lockheed sought a government guarantee for a bank loan for $250 million in order to complete the development of the L-1011 Tri-Star, a wide-bodied commercial jet aircraft. The debate in the congressional hearings on the question of whether the Tri-Star program was economically sound proceeded almost entirely on the basis of estimated breakeven sales. Lockheed indicated that the breakeven point would be reached at sales of about 200 aircraft, at a price of $15.5 million each at 1968 prices. With firm orders for 103 aircraft and options for 75 others at the time of the congressional hearings, Lockheed was confident it could surpass the breakeven point and earn a profit. Based on this economic rationale of the project, the loan guarantee legislation was passed.

In its calculations, however, Lockheed had not included among its fixed costs the cost of developing the technology and construction facilities to build the aircraft. Had it done so, breakeven sales would have been twice as large as those indicated by Lockheed in the congressional hearings. Since it

was unrealistic (based on the total market for wide-bodied aircraft and competition, at that time, from McDonnell-Douglas and Boeing) for Lockheed to sell that many aircraft, the inclusion of all costs in the calculations would have shown that the project was economically unsound. In fact, only 250 of the L-1011 were sold between 1971 and 1984 and Lockheed phased out the plane in the early 1980s at a total loss of several billion dollars. In the aircraft industry, where development costs are very high, very large sales are usually required before a firm can break even. Indeed, it took 20 years and $26 billion in subsidies by the governments of Germany, France, the United Kingdom, and Spain before Airbus Industrie began to break even in 1990. By the mid-1990s, Airbus had become a fierce (and the only) competitor of Boeing in the market for large commercial jets. In 2001, Airbus was reorganized from a consortium or partnership among four different companies into an independent corporation. Since then, Airbus has made a profit and even surpassed Boeing in aircraft sales.

Source: U. E. Reinhardt, "Break-Even Analysis for Lockheed Tri-Star: An Application of Financial Theory," *The Journal of Finance* (September 1973), pp. 821–838; Lanier C. Benkard, "Learning and Forgetting: The Dynamics of Aircraft Production," *National Bureau of Economic Research,* Working Paper No. 7127 (May 1999); "There Is No Stopping of Europe's Airbus Industrie Now," *The New York Times* (June 23, 1991), sec. 3, p. 1; "Blue Skies for Airbus," *Fortune* (August 2, 1999), pp. 102–108; and "Nose to Nose," *The Economist* (June 25, 2005), pp. 67–79.

| 7-9 | **EMPIRICAL ESTIMATION OF COST FUNCTIONS** |

Empirical estimates of cost functions are essential for many managerial decision purposes. Knowledge of short-run cost functions is necessary for the firm in determining the optimal level of output and the price to charge. Knowledge of long-run cost functions is essential in planning for the optimal scale of plant for the firm to build in the long run. In this section, we examine the most important techniques for estimating the firm's short-run and long-run cost curves, discuss some of the data and measurement problems encountered in estimation, and summarize the results of some empirical studies of short-run and long-run cost functions.

Data and Measurement Problems in Estimating Short-Run Cost Functions

The most common method of estimating the firm's short-run cost functions is regression analysis, whereby total variable costs are regressed against output and a few other variables, such as input prices and operating conditions, during the time period when the size of the plant is fixed. The total variable cost function rather than the total cost function is usually estimated because of the difficulty of allocating fixed costs to the various products produced by the firm. The firm's total cost function can then be obtained by simply adding the best estimate possible of the fixed costs to the total variable costs. The firm's average variable and marginal cost functions can be easily obtained from the total variable cost function as indicated in Section 7-2. Although this sounds simple enough, the estimation of the firm's short-run cost functions is fraught with data and measurement difficulties.

As pointed out earlier in the chapter, the firm's cost functions are based on the assumption of constant input prices. If input prices increase, they will cause an upward shift of the entire cost function. Therefore, input prices will have to be included as additional explanatory variables in the regression analysis in order to identify their independent effects on costs. Other independent variables that may have to be included in the regression analysis are fuel and material costs, the quality of inputs, the technology used by the firm, weather conditions, and changes in the product mix and product quality. The actual independent or explanatory variables included in the regression (besides output) depend on the particular situation under examination. Thus, we can postulate that

$$C = f(Q, X_1, X_2, \ldots , X_n) \qquad [7\text{-}21]$$

where C refers to total variable costs, Q is output, and the X's refer to the other determinants of the firm's costs. Using multiple regression analysis (see Section 4-5) allows us to isolate the effect on costs of changes in each of the independent or explanatory variables. By concentrating on the relationship between costs and output, we can then identify the firm's total variable cost curve.

One fundamental problem that arises in the empirical estimation of cost functions is that opportunity costs must be extracted from the available accounting cost data. That is, each input used in production must be valued at its opportunity cost based on what the input could earn in its best alternative use rather than the actual expenditures for the input. For example, if the firm owns the building in which it operates, the cost of using the building is not zero but is equal to the rent that the firm would obtain by renting the building to the highest bidder. Similarly, inventories used in current production must be valued at current market prices rather than at historical cost. Finally, the part of the depreciation of fixed assets, such as machinery, that is based on the actual usage of the assets (as contrasted to the depreciation of the assets based on the passage of time alone) should be estimated and included in current production costs for each product. These data are often difficult to obtain from the available accounting data.

Not only must costs be correctly apportioned to the various products produced by the firm but care must also be exercised to match costs to output over time (i.e., allocate costs to the period in which the output is produced rather than to the period when the costs were incurred). Specifically, the leads and lags in costs from the corresponding output must be adjusted so as to achieve a correct correspondence between costs and output. For example, while a firm may postpone all but emergency maintenance until a period of slack production, these maintenance costs must be allocated to the earlier production periods.

The manager must also determine the length of time over which to estimate cost functions. While daily, weekly, monthly, quarterly, or yearly data can be used, monthly data over a period of two or three years are usually used. The period of time must be long enough to allow for sufficient variation in output and costs but not long enough for the firm to change plant size (since the firm would then no longer be operating in the short run). Since output is usually measured in physical units (e.g., number of automobiles of a particular type produced per time period) while costs are measured in monetary units, the various costs must be deflated by the appropriate price index to correct for inflation. That is, with input prices usually rising at different rates, the price index for each category of inputs will have to be used to obtain their deflated values to use in the regression analysis.

The Functional Form of Short-Run Cost Functions

Economic theory postulates an S-shaped (cubic) *TVC* curve as indicated in the top left panel of Figure 7-10, with corresponding U-shaped *AVC* and *MC* curve below. The general equations for these functions are, respectively,[17]

$$TVC = a(Q) + bQ^2 + cQ^3 \qquad [7\text{-}22]$$

$$AVC = \frac{TVC}{Q} = a + bQ + cQ^2 \qquad [7\text{-}23]$$

$$MC = a + 2bQ + 3cQ^2 \qquad [7\text{-}24]$$

The top right panel of Figure 7-10 shows a linear approximation to the cubic *TVC* curve, which often gives a good empirical fit of the data points over the observed range of outputs. The estimated equations of the linear approximation to the S-shaped or cubic *TVC* curve and of its corresponding *AVC* and *MC* curves are

$$TVC = a + bQ \qquad [7\text{-}25]$$

$$AVC = \frac{a}{Q} + b \qquad [7\text{-}26]$$

$$MC = b \qquad [7\text{-}27]$$

---

[17] In the empirical estimation of these functions, *a* and *c* will be positive and *b* negative. Also, using calculus, $MC = d(TVC)/dQ$.

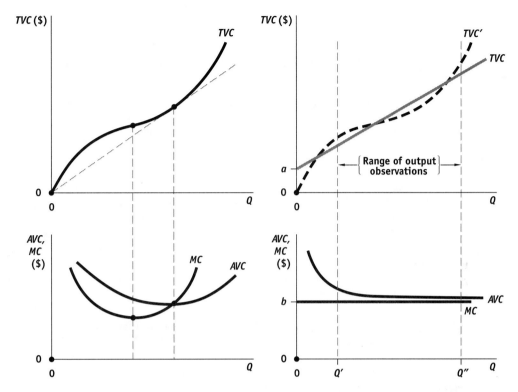

FIGURE 7-10   Theoretical and Empirical Approximation of *TVC*, *AVC*, and *MC* Curves   Economic theory postulates an S-shaped (cubic) *TVC* curve as indicated in the left panel, with corresponding U-shaped *AVC* and *MC* curves. The right panel shows a linear approximation to the cubic *TVC* curve, which often gives a better empirical fit of the data points over the observed range of outputs. Note that the *AVC* curve in the right panel becomes quite flat, approaching the value of *b* (the horizontal *MC* curve) as output expands.

Having estimated the parameters of the *TVC* curve (i.e., the values of *a* and *b* in Equation 7-25), we can use these estimated parameters to derive the corresponding *AVC* and *MC* functions of the firm, as indicated in Equations 7-26 and 7-27. Note that estimated parameter *a* (the constant in estimated regression Equation 7-25) cannot be interpreted as the fixed costs of the firm since we are estimating the *TVC* function. Since $Q = 0$ is usually far removed from the actual observed data points on the *TVC* curve (from Q' to Q'' in the right panels of Figure 7-10), no economic significance can be attached to the estimated parameter *a*. Note also that the *AVC* curve in the bottom right panel becomes quite flat, approaching the value of *b* (the horizontal *MC* curve). This is often observed in the actual empirical estimation (see Case Study 7-8).[18] One possible explanation for this is that while the amount of capital (say, the number of machines)

---

[18] Another nonlinear theoretical form of the *TVC* curve that is often closely approximated by a linear *TVC* is the quadratic form. The quadratic *TVC* curve rises at an increasing rate (i.e., faces diminishing returns) throughout (and so do the corresponding *AVC* and *MC* curves).

CASE STUDY 7-8
Estimates of Short-Run and Long-Run Cost Functions

Table 7-4 summarizes the results of 16 empirical studies on short-run and long-run cost functions, as well as on the method of estimation, reported by A. A. Walters in 1963. The questionnaire's method is based on managers' answers to questions asked by the researcher on the firm's production costs. Most studies found that in the short run *MC* is constant (so that the *AVC* curve approaches the horizontal *MC* curve, as indicated in the right bottom panel of Figure 7-10) in the observed range of outputs. Most studies also indicate the presence of economies of scale (i.e., declining *LAC*) at all observed levels of output. Firms, however, seem to avoid expanding into the range of decreasing returns to scale in the long run. These results are similar to those reported in Case Studies 7-2 and 7-3.

Another empirical study on the extent of economies of scale in specific U.S. industries over the 1967–1970 period by William G. Shepherd found economies of scale to be slight in steel, fabric weaving, shoes, paints, cement, automobile batteries, and petroleum refining; slight to moderate in cigarettes, glass bottles, and bearings; and moderate in beer and refrigerators. Another study of 29 industries in India by V. K. Gupta in 1968 found that 18 industries had L-shaped or nearly L-shaped *LAC* curves, 6 industries had horizontal or nearly horizontal *LAC* curves, and the remaining 5 industries had U-shaped *LAC* curves.

TABLE 7-4   Results of Empirical Studies of Short-Run and Long-Run Cost Functions

Industry	Method*	Period[†]	Result
Manufacturing	Q	SR	*MC* declining
Manufacturing	Q	SR	*AVC* declining
Manufacturing	Q	SR	*MC* below *AVC* at all outputs
Furniture	TS	SR	*MC* constant
Steel	TS	SR	*MC* constant
Hosiery	TS	SR	*MC* constant
Department store	TS	SR	*MC* declining or constant
Electricity[§]	TS	SR	*AVC* falls, approaching constant *MC*
Manufacturing	Q	LR	Small economies of scale
Manufacturing	E	LR	Economies of scale
Metal	E	LR	Economies of scale, then constant
Gas[§]	CS	LR	Economies of scale
Railways	CS	LR	Economies or constant returns
Electricity[§]	CS	LR	Economies of scale
Electricity[§]	CS	LR	Economies of scale
Electricity	CS	LR	Economies and then diseconomies

[*]Q = questionnaire, TS = time series, E = engineering, CS = cross section.
[†]SR = short run, LR = long run.
[§] = United Kingdom, otherwise United States.

Source: A. A. Walters, "Production and Cost Functions: An Econometric Survey," *Econometrica* (January 1963), pp. 48–50; William G. Shepherd, *The Economics of Industrial Organization* (Englewood Cliffs, N.J.: Prentice-Hall, 1997), p. 183; and V. K. Gupta, "Cost Functions, Concentration, and Barriers to Entry in Twenty-Nine Manufacturing Industries in India," *Journal of Industrial Economics* (November 1968), pp. 57–72.

that the firm has is fixed in the short run, the firm may keep some machines idle when output is low and bring them into operation by hiring more labor when it wants to increase output. Since the ratio of machines to output as well as machines to labor tends to remain constant in the face of changes in output, the firm's *AVC* and *MC* tend to remain approximately constant.

Estimating Long-Run Cost Functions with Cross-Sectional Regression Analysis

The empirical estimation of long-run cost curves is even more difficult than the estimation of short-run cost curves. The objective of estimating the long-run cost curves is to determine the best scale of plant for the firm to build in order to minimize the cost of producing the anticipated level of output in the long run. Theoretically, long-run cost curves can be estimated with regression analysis using either time-series data (cost-quantity observations for a given firm or plant over time) or cross-sectional data (cost-quantity data for a number of firms at a given point in time). In fact, time-series data are seldom used to estimate long-run cost functions because the period of observation must be sufficiently long for the firm to have changed its scale of plant several times. But this will inevitably also involve changes in the type of product that the firm produces and the technology it uses to render the correct estimation of the firm's long-run cost curves, with time-series analysis practically impossible.[19] Regression analysis using cross-sectional data is, therefore, used.

Regression analysis using cross-sectional data to estimate long-run cost curves also presents some difficulties, however. For one thing, firms in different geographical regions are likely to pay different prices for their inputs, and so input prices must be included together with the levels of output as independent explanatory variables in the regression.[20] It is even more difficult to reconcile the different accounting and operational practices of the different firms in the sample. For example, some firms pay lower wages but provide more benefits (better health insurance programs, longer vacation, etc.) than other firms that provide smaller benefits to their workers. If only wages are included in labor costs, the former firms will mistakenly seem to have lower labor costs than the latter firms. The various firms in the sample are also likely to follow very different depreciation policies.

It might also be very difficult to determine if each firm is operating the optimal scale of plant at the optimal level of output (i.e., at the point on its *SAC* curve which forms part of its *LAC* curve). Specifically, in order to be able to estimate *LAC* curve *A″C″G″R″* in Figure 7-11, the firms represented by SAC_1, SAC_2, SAC_3, and SAC_4 must operate at points *A″*, *C″*, *G″*, and *R″*, respectively. If in fact the four firms are producing at points *A**, *D**, *G″*, and *R**, respectively, we would be estimating the dashed *LAC′* curve, which overestimates the degree of both the economies and diseconomies of scale. As we have seen in Case Study 7-8, estimated long-run average cost curves seem to indicate sharply increasing returns to scale

---

[19] This is on top of all the other difficulties encountered in the empirical estimation of short-run cost curves with regression analysis using time-series data discussed at the beginning of this section.

[20] Since cross-sectional data refer to one point in time, no adjustment for inflation is necessary.

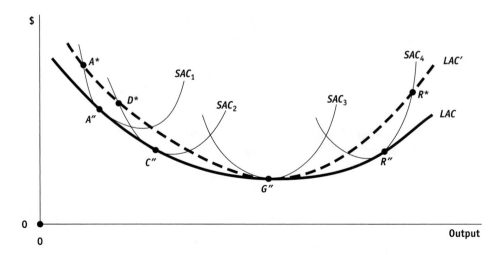

FIGURE 7-11   Efficiency of Operation in Estimating the *LAC* Curve   In order to be able to estimate *LAC* curve *A″C″G″R″*, the firms represented by *SAC₁*, *SAC₂*, *SAC₃*, and *SAC₄* must operate at points *A″*, *C″*, *G″*, and *R″*, respectively. If the firms operated their plants at points *A**, *D**, *G″*, and *R**, respectively, we would be estimating the dashed *LAC′* curve, which overestimates the degree of both the economies and the diseconomies of scale.

(falling *LAC* curve) at low levels of output followed by near-constant returns to scale at higher levels of output (i.e., the *LAC* curve seems to be L-shaped or nearly so).

Estimating Long-Run Cost Functions with Engineering and Survival Techniques

When sufficient data are not available for cross-sectional regression estimation of the long-run cost curves (or as an independent check on that estimation), the engineering or the survival techniques are used. The **engineering technique** uses knowledge of the physical relationship between inputs and output expressed by the production function to determine the optimal input combination needed to produce various levels of output. By multiplying the optimal quantity of each input by the price of the input, we obtain the long-run cost function of the firm, as shown in Figure 7-3. The engineering technique is particularly useful in estimating the cost functions of new products or improved products resulting from the application of new technologies, where historical data are not available.

The advantage of the engineering technique over cross-sectional regression analysis is that it is based on the present technology, thus avoiding mixing old and current technologies used by different firms in cross-sectional analysis. Neither does the problem of different input prices in different geographical regions arise. Many of the difficult cost-allocation and input-valuation accounting problems that plague regression estimation are also avoided. The engineering technique is not without problems, however. These arise because it deals only with the technical aspects of production without considering administrative, financing, and marketing costs; it deals with production under ideal rather than actual real-world conditions; and it is based on current technology, which may soon become obsolete. The engineering technique has been successfully applied to examine the cost-to-output relationship in many industrial sectors, such as petroleum refining and chemical production.[21] The results obtained seem to confirm those obtained with cross-sectional regression analysis. That is, the *LAC* curve seems to be L-shaped.

The **survival technique** was first expounded by John Stuart Mill in the 1850s and was elaborated on by George Stigler a century later. In its original formulation, it simply postulated that if large and small firms coexist in the same industry, in the long run scale economies must be constant or nearly so. With large economies of scale over a wide range of outputs, large and more efficient firms (i.e., those with lower *LAC*) would drive smaller and less efficient firms out of business, leaving only large firms in the long run. Stigler made this concept more operational by proposing to classify firms in an industry according to size and calculate the share of the industry output of the firms in each size classification. If over time the share of the industry output coming from small firms declines while that coming from large firms increases, this is evidence of the presence of significant economies of scale. If the opposite is the case, we would have diseconomies of scale.

Stigler applied this technique to the steel industry and measured the share of industry output of the small, medium, and large firms in the years 1930, 1938, and 1951.[22] He found that the share of the industry output of small and large firms declined over time, while that of medium-sized firms increased. Thus, he concluded that the *LAC* curve in the steel industry was U-shaped but had a flat bottom (i.e., constant returns to scale operated over a wide range of outputs). Stigler also applied the technique to the automobile industry and concluded that economies of scale operated at small outputs, but constant returns to scale operated over the remaining range of outputs (i.e., the *LAC* curve seemed to be L-shaped).

While the survival technique is simple to apply, it implicitly assumes a highly competitive form of market structure in which survival depends only on economic efficiency. If, however, firms are sheltered from competition by government regulation or barriers to entry, inefficient firms can survive, and the survival principle will be distorted or inoperative. Market imperfections, such as product differentiation (i.e., the existence of different brands of a product) or locational advantages, may also allow some firms to survive even if they are relatively inefficient. Furthermore, the survival technique does not allow us to measure the *degree* of economies or diseconomies of scale. Case Study 7-8 gives estimates of short-run and long-run cost functions for a number of industries in the United States, the United Kingdom, and India.

---

[21] See J. Haldi and D. Whitecomb, "Economies of Scale in Industrial Plants," *Journal of Political Economy* (August 1967), pp. 373–385.

[22] See George J. Stigler, "The Economies of Scale," *Journal of Law and Economics* (April 1958), pp. 251–274.

firm at $Q = 60$ and at $Q = 70$. Why is the degree of operating leverage greater for the second than for the first firm? Why is the degree of operating leverage greater at $Q = 60$ than at $Q = 70$?

14. Microsoft wants to estimate the average variable cost function of producing computer diskettes. The firm believes that AVC varies with the level of output and wages. Alan Anderson, the economist in the research department of the firm, collects monthly data on output (the number of diskettes produced), average variable costs, and wage rates paid by the firm over the past two years. He deflates costs and wages by their respective price indexes in order to eliminate inflationary influences. He then regresses total variable costs (TVC) on output (Q) and wages (W) and obtains the following result (where the numbers in parentheses are t values):

$$TVC = 0.14 + 0.80Q + 0.036W$$
$$(2.8) \quad (3.8) \quad (3.3)$$
$$\bar{R}^2 = 0.92 \quad D\text{–}W = 1.9$$

(a) If $W = \$10$, derive the AVC and MC functions of the firm. (b) What are the shapes of the AVC and MC curves of the firm? (c) Why did Anderson fit a linear rather than a quadratic or cubic TVC function? (d) Was this the right choice? Why?

15. **Integrating Problem**
The manager of the Electronic Corporation has estimated the total variable costs and the total fixed cost functions for producing a particular type of camera to be

$$TVC = 60Q - 12Q^2 + Q^3$$
$$TFC = \$100$$

The corporation sells the cameras at the price of $60 each. An engineering study just published estimated that if the corporation employs newly developed technology, the long-run total cost function would be

$$TC = 50 + 20Q + 2w + 3r$$

where $w =$ wage rate and $r =$ rental price of capital. The manager asks you to find (a) the average variable and marginal cost functions of the firm, the output level at which the two curves cross, and a plot of them (Hint: See Equations 7-22 to 7-24); (b) the breakeven output of the firm and the output at which the firm maximizes its total profits; and (c) the long-run average cost and long-run marginal cost functions with the new technology if $w = \$20$ and $r = \$10$, and plot them. Are these curves similar to those found in other empirical studies of the long-run costs? (d) Should the corporation adopt the new technology? If it did, what would be the profit-maximizing level of output if the firm can continue to sell its cameras at the price of $60 per unit?

APPENDIX TO CHAPTER 7: COST ANALYSIS WITH CALCULUS

The general equation of the firm's total cost (TC) function is

$$TC = d + aQ + bQ^2 + cQ^3 \tag{7-28}$$

In the empirical estimation of Equation 7-28, d, a, $c > 0$, and $b < 0$.

Dropping d, the total fixed costs, from Equation 7-28, we get the general equation of the firm's total variable cost (TVC) function:

$$TVC = aQ + bQ^2 + cQ^3 \tag{7-29}$$

The average variable cost (AVC) function of the firm is then

$$AVC = \frac{TVC}{Q} = a + bQ + cQ^2 \tag{7-30}$$

The *AVC* is minimum at the point where

$$\frac{d(AVC)}{dQ} = b + 2cQ = 0 \qquad\qquad [7\text{-}31]$$

and

$$Q = \frac{-b}{2c} \qquad\qquad [7\text{-}32]$$

The second-order condition for a minimum is satisfied (so that the *AVC* curve is U-shaped) because

$$\frac{d^2(AVC)}{dQ^2} = 2c > 0 \qquad\qquad [7\text{-}33]$$

The firm's marginal cost (*MC*) function is

$$MC = \frac{d(TC)}{dQ} = \frac{d(TVC)}{dQ} = a + 2bQ + 3cQ^2 \qquad\qquad [7\text{-}34]$$

The *MC* is minimum at the point where

$$\frac{d(MC)}{dQ} = 2b + 6cQ = 0 \qquad\qquad [7\text{-}35]$$

so that

$$Q = \frac{-b}{3c} \qquad\qquad [7\text{-}36]$$

Since the denominator of Equation 7-36 is larger than the denominator of Equation 7-32, the *MC* curve reaches its minimum point at a smaller level of output than the corresponding *AVC* curve.

The second-order condition for a minimum is satisfied (so that the *MC* curve is U-shaped) because

$$\frac{d^2(MC)}{dQ^2} = 6c > 0 \qquad\qquad [7\text{-}37]$$

To show that the *MC* curve intersects the *AVC* curve at the lowest point of the latter, we set Equation 7-30 for the *AVC* curve equal to Equation 7-34 for the *MC* curve. We then solve for *Q* and find that this is equal to –*b*/2*c* (the output at which the *AVC* curve is minimum). That is,

$$a + bQ + cQ^2 = a + 2bQ + 3cQ^2 \qquad\qquad [7\text{-}38]$$

so that

$$bQ + 2cQ^2 = 0 \qquad\qquad [7\text{-}39]$$

and

$$Q = \frac{-b}{2c} \qquad\qquad [7\text{-}32]$$

To find the value of the *AVC* at its lowest point, we substitute Equation 7-32 for *Q* into Equation 7-30 for the *AVC* curve and solve for the *AVC*. That is,

$$AVC = a + b\left(\frac{-b}{2c}\right) + \frac{c(b^2)}{4c^2} \qquad\qquad [7\text{-}40]$$

$$= \frac{4ac - b^2}{4c}$$

APPENDIX PROBLEMS

1. Given:

$$TC = 100 + 60Q - 12Q^2 + Q^3$$

Find (*a*) the equations of the *TVC*, *AVC*, and *MC* functions and (*b*) the level of output at which *AVC* and *MC* are minimum, and prove that the *AVC* and

MC curves are U-shaped. (*c*) Find *AVC* and *MC* for the level of output at which the *AVC* curve is minimum.

2. Answer the same questions as in Problem 1 if

$$TC = 120 + 50Q - 10Q^2 + Q^3$$

SUPPLEMENTARY READINGS

For a more extensive treatment of cost theory, see:

Salvatore, Dominick, *Microeconomics Theory and Applications*, 4th ed. (New York: Oxford University Press, 2003), chap. 7.

A discussion of economies of scale and economies of scope in some industries is found in:

Frits, K. Phil, and Matthias Holweg, "Exploring Scale," *MIT Sloan Management Review* (Winter 2003).

Gold, B., "Changing Perspective on Size, Scale, and Returns: An Interpretative Essay," *Journal of Economic Literature* (March 1981).

Shepherd, William G., *The Economics of Industrial Organization* (Upper Saddle River, N.J.: Prentice-Hall, 1997), chap. 7.

Teece, David J., "Economies of Scope and the Scope of the Enterprise," *Journal of Economic Behavior and Organization* (September 1980).

For a discussion of cost curves and estimation, see:

Johannes, James M., et al., "Estimating Regional Cost Differences: Theory and Evidence," *Managerial Decision Economics* (June 1985), pp. 70–79.

OECD, *Projected Costs of Generating Electricity* (Paris: OECD, 2005).

The Royal Academy of Engineering, *The Cost of Generating Electricity* (London: The Royal Academy of Engineering, 2004).

The learning curve is discussed in:

Argote, Linda, and Dennis Epple, "Learning Curves in Manufacturing," *Science* (February 23, 1990).

Benkard, Lanier C., "Learning and Forgetting: The Dynamics of Aircraft Production," *National Bureau of Economic Research*, Working Paper No. 7127 (May 1999).

Gruber, Harald, "The Learning Curve in the Production of Semiconductor Memory Chips," *Applied Economics* (August 1992).

Lapre', Michael, and Luk N. Wassenhove, "Learning Across Lines," *Harvard Business Review* (October 2002).

For international trade in inputs and the immigration of skilled labor, see:

Gottfredson, M., R. Puryear, and S. Phillips, "Strategic Sourcing," *Harvard Business Review* (February 2005).

Linder, Janet, "Tranformational Outsourcing," *Sloan Management Review* (Winter 2004).

Salvatore, Dominick, *International Economics*, 8th ed. (Hoboken, N.J.: Wiley, 2004), chap. 12.

For logistics or supply-chain management, see:

Kopczak, Laura R., and M. Eric Johnson, "The Supply-Chain Management Effect," *Sloan Management Review* (Spring 2003).

Lee, Hau L., "The Triple-A Supply Chain," *Harvard Business Review* (October 2004).

Levy, David L., "Lean Production in an International Supply Chain," *Sloan Management Review* (Winter 1997).

Slone, Reuben E., "Leading a Supply Chain Turnaround," *Harvard Business Review* (October 2004).

 ## INTERNET SITE ADDRESSES

For new cost accounting methods for businesses promoted by the Consortium for Advanced Manufacturing-International (CAM-I), visit:

  http://www.cam-i.org

For gasoline consumption and substitution, see:

  http://www.cbo.gov/showdoc.cfm?index=3991 &sequence=0

  http://www.cbo.gov/showdoc.cfm?index=3991 &sequence=1

  http://www.nrdc.org/greengate/air/electricf.asp

For economies or diseconomies of scale at General Motors, Ford, and Chrysler, see:

  http://www.gm.com

  http://www.ford.com

  http://www.chrysler.com

For how far afield companies go to reduce costs, see:

  Southwest Airlines: http://www.southwest.com

  Domino's Pizza: http://www.dominos.com

Federal Express: http://www.fedex.com

GE Information Services: http://www.wbrtv.com/underwriters/ge/

More information on outsourcing is found in:

  http://www.cio.com/research/outsourcing

  http://www.govexec.com/outsourcing

Logistics is examined in:

  http://www.logisticsworld.com/logistics

  http://www.logisticsonline.com

  http://www.logistics.about.com

For learning curves, see:

  National Bureau of Economic Research: http://www.nber.org/papers/w7127

For competition in industry for commercial aircraft, see:

  Lockheed: http://www.lockheedmartin.com

  Boeing: http://www.boeing.com

  Airbus: http://www.airbus.com

INTEGRATING CASE STUDY 3
Production and Cost Functions
in the Petroleum Industry

Introductory **Comment:** In this part of the text (Chapters 6 and 7) we have examined production theory and estimation (Chapter 6) and cost theory and estimation (Chapter 7). We now integrate these topics by starting with production theory, proceeding to cost theory, and then showing the duality or symmetry between production theory and cost theory.

As indicated in Chapter 6, the production function most commonly used in empirical estimation is the Cobb–Douglas of the form:

$$Q = AK^a L^b$$

where Q, K, and L refer, respectively, to the quantities of output, capital, and labor, and A, a, and b are the parameters to be estimated. In order to use regression analysis for the estimation of the parameters, the Cobb–Douglas production function is transformed into

$$\ln Q = \ln A + a \ln K + b \ln L$$

which is linear in logarithms. Such a production function has been estimated for many industries, one of which is the petroleum industry. For the petroleum industry, $a = 0.31$ and $b = 0.64$.[1] Since $a + b = 0.31 + 0.64 = 0.95$ and is smaller than 1, it seems that the petroleum industry operates under slight diseconomies of scale. However, the difference in the estimated value of $a + b$ from 1 was not statistically significant at the 5 percent level, so that the hypothesis of constant returns to scale cannot be rejected.

The marginal product of labor and capital functions for the general formulation of the Cobb–Douglas production function are[2]

$$MP_K = \frac{\partial Q}{\partial K} = aAK^{a-1}L^b$$

$$MP_L = \frac{\partial Q}{\partial L} = bAK^a L^{b-1}$$

For production efficiency,

$$\frac{MP_K}{r} = \frac{MP_L}{w}$$

---

[1] The labor input measures both production and nonproduction workers. They have been aggregated into a single labor input in order to simplify the analysis and deal with only two inputs, L and K.

[2] Those who do not know calculus can simply accept these results since

$$\frac{\partial Q}{\partial K} \cong \frac{\Delta Q}{\Delta K} = MP_K \quad \text{and} \quad \frac{\partial Q}{\partial L} \cong \frac{\Delta Q}{\Delta L} = MP_L$$

where r is the rental price of capital and w is the wage rate of labor. Substituting the values of MP_K and MP_L for the Cobb–Douglas into the above condition, we get

$$\frac{aAK^{a-1}L^b}{r} = \frac{bAK^aL^{b-1}}{w}$$

Solving for K, we have

$$K = \frac{awL}{br}$$

This is the equation of the expansion path for the Cobb–Douglas and shows all efficient combinations of K and L. For the petroleum industry,

$$K = \frac{0.31w}{0.64r}L$$

By substituting the market values of w and r for the petroleum industry into the above equation, we get the equation of the expansion path for this industry. For example, if $w = \$20$ and $r = \$10$, $K \cong L$, which means that the expansion path is a straight line through the origin with slope of about 1.

We can derive the corresponding cost functions and show the duality between production and cost theory. The general equation of the total cost function can be written as

$$TC = rK + wL$$

Substituting the general equation of the expansion path (showing production efficiency) into the TC function, we have

$$TC = r\left(\frac{a}{b} \cdot \frac{w}{r}L\right) + wL$$

which can be rewritten as

$$TC = \left(\frac{a}{b} + 1\right)wL$$

The TC function, however, is usually expressed as a function of output (Q) rather than as a function of L. In order to remove L from the TC function and express TC as a function of Q, we substitute the general equation for the expansion path into the general equation of the Cobb–Douglas and obtain

$$Q = A\left(\frac{aw}{br}L\right)^a L^b = A\left(\frac{aw}{br}\right)^a L^{a+b}$$

Solving for L, we get

$$L^{a+b} = \frac{Q}{A}\left(\frac{aw}{br}\right)^{-a}$$

so that

$$L = \left(\frac{Q}{A}\right)^{1/(a+b)}\left(\frac{aw}{br}\right)^{-a/(a+b)}$$

Substituting the above value of L into the TC function, we get

$$TC = r\left(\frac{aw}{br}L\right) + w\left(\frac{Q}{A}\right)^{1/(a+b)}\left(\frac{aw}{br}\right)^{-a/(a+b)}$$

$$= c\left(\frac{Q}{A}\right)^{1/(a+b)}$$

where c = constant. Thus,

$$TC = c\left(\frac{Q}{A}\right)^{1/(a+b)}$$

is the TC function associated with the Cobb–Douglas $Q = AK^aL^b$.

For the petroleum industry, $a + b \cong 1$, thus,

$$TC = c\frac{Q}{A} = c'Q$$

where $c' = C/A$ = constant. This means that TC is a linear function of Q, and

$$AC = \frac{TC}{Q} = c'$$

and

$$MC = \frac{d(TC)}{dQ} = \frac{\Delta TC}{\Delta C} = c'$$

Thus, $AC = MC \cong c'$ (i.e., the AC and MC curves are horizontal and coincide) and we have (near) constant returns to scale and constant costs in this industry.

Since we have near-constant returns to scale and costs, petroleum prices remained fairly constant over long periods of time before 1973. After 1973, the Organization of Petroleum Exporting Countries (OPEC) was able to increase petroleum prices during periods of high world demand for petroleum by limiting their increase in production and exports (see Case Study 9-3).

Source: J. Moroney, "Cobb–Douglas Production Functions and Returns to Scale in U.S. Manufacturing Industry," *Western Economic Journal* (December 1967), pp. 39–51; A. Manne, *Scheduling of Petroleum Refining Operations* (Cambridge, Mass.: Harvard University Press, 1956); "Delivering the Goods," *Fortune* (November 28, 1994), pp. 64–78; "The New Economics of Oil," *Business Week* (November 3, 1997), pp. 140–144; and "Does OPEC Have Sands in Its Eyes?" *The Economist* (July 1, 2002), p. 60.

PART FOUR

Market Structure and Pricing Practices

P art Four (Chapters 8 through 11) brings together demand analysis (examined in Part Two) and production and cost analysis (examined in Part Three) in order to analyze how price and output are determined under various forms of market organization. Chapter 8 examines how price and output are determined under perfect competition, monopoly, and monopolistic competition. Chapter 9 examines price and output decisions under oligpoly; Chapter 9 also discusses firm architecture in a globalizing world. Chapter 10 deals with strategic behavior and game theory, while Chapter 11 examines some specific pricing practices under monopoly, monopolistic competition, and oligopoly.

CHAPTER 8 — Market Structure: Perfect Competition, Monopoly, and Monopolistic Competition

KEY TERMS (in the order of their appearance)

Market
Market structure
Perfect competition
Monopoly
Monopolistic competition
Oligopoly
Imperfect competition
Price taker

Shut-down point
Short-run supply curve of the
    perfectly competitive firm
Foreign exchange market
Exchange rate
Depreciation
Appreciation
Natural monopoly

Consumers' surplus
Deadweight loss
Differentiated product
Excess capacity
Overcrowding
Product variation
Selling expenses

I n this chapter we bring together demand analysis (examined in Part Two) and production and cost analysis (examined in Part Three) in order to analyze how price and output are determined under perfect competition, monopoly, and monopolistic competition. We begin the chapter by defining the meaning of markets and by identifying the various types of market structure. We go on to examine the meaning of perfect competition and show how the equilibrium price and quantity are determined in a perfectly competitive market. Subsequently, we examine how a perfectly competitive firm determines the optimum level of output in the short run and in the long run. Here, we also examine competition in the international economy by showing the effect of imports on domestic prices and the effect of a change in the dollar exchange rate on the international competitiveness of U.S. firms. We then examine monopoly. After identifying the sources of monopoly power, we examine how the monopolist determines the best level of output and price in the short run and in the long run, and compare monopoly to perfect competition. Finally, we discuss the meaning and importance of monopolistic competition, show how the equilibrium price and quantity are determined in the short run and in the long run, and analyze product variation and selling expenses.

8-1   MARKET STRUCTURE AND DEGREE OF COMPETITION

The process by which price and output are determined in the real world is strongly affected by the structure of the market. A **market** consists of all the actual and potential buyers and sellers of a particular product. **Market structure** refers to the competitive environment in which the buyers and sellers of the product operate.

Four types of market structure are usually identified. These are: perfect competition at one extreme, pure monopoly at the opposite extreme, and monopolistic competition and oligopoly in between. These types of market structure or organization are defined in terms of the number and size of the buyers and sellers of the product, the type of product bought and sold (i.e., standardized or homogeneous as contrasted with differentiated), the degree of mobility of resources (i.e., the ease with which firms and input owners can enter or exit the market), and the degree of knowledge that economic agents (i.e., firms, suppliers of inputs, and consumers) have of prices and costs, and demand and supply conditions.

These market characteristics are used to define the four types of market structure:

1. **Perfect competition** is the form of market organization in which (a) there are many buyers and sellers of a product, each too small to affect the price of the product; (b) the product is homogeneous; (c) there is perfect mobility of resources; and (d) economic agents have perfect knowledge of market conditions.
2. **Monopoly** is the form of market organization in which a single firm sells a product for which there are no close substitutes. Entry into the industry is very difficult or impossible (as evidenced by the fact that there is a single firm in the industry).
3. **Monopolistic competition** refers to the case where there are many sellers of a differentiated product and entry into or exit from the industry is rather easy in the long run.
4. **Oligopoly** is the case where there are few sellers of a homogeneous or differentiated product. Although entry into the industry is possible, it is not easy (as evidenced by the small number of firms in the industry).[1]

Monopoly, monopolistic competition, and oligopoly are often referred to as **imperfect competition** to distinguish them from perfect competition. The definitions of the various types of market structure presented above are examined in detail when the particular market structure is analyzed. In this chapter we examine perfect competition, monopoly, and monopolistic competition. Oligopoly is examined in the next chapter.

8-2   PERFECT COMPETITION

In this section we discuss in detail the meaning of perfect competition, show that under perfect competition the market price and quantity of a product are determined exclusively by the forces of market demand and market supply for the product, and examine how the firm determines its best level of output in the short run and in the long run at the given market price. In the process we also derive the short-run competitive firm and market supply curves for the product.

Meaning and Importance of Perfect Competition

According to the first part of the definition of perfect competition presented above, there are a great number of buyers and sellers of the product, and each seller and buyer is too small in relation to the market to be able to affect the price of the product by his or her own actions. This means that a change in the output of a single firm will not *perceptibly* affect

---

[1] The above definitions of monopoly, monopolistic competition, and oligopoly are expressed in terms of the sellers of the product. Analogous types of market structure can be defined in terms of buyers of the product or input. These are monopsony, monopsonistic competition, and oligopsony. *Monopsony* refers to the market situation in which there is a single *buyer* of a commodity or input for which there are no close substitutes. *Monopsonistic competition* and *oligopsony* are defined in an analogous way. Monopsony and oligopsony are more common in input markets than in commodity markets. They sometimes exist in labor markets dominated by one or a few large employers, in local agricultural markets dominated by one or a few large processors, or in government purchases of large defense systems.

the market price of the product. Similarly, each buyer of the product is too small to be able to extract from the seller such things as quantity discounts and special credit terms.

The product of each competitive firm is homogeneous, identical, or perfectly standardized. An example of this might be grade-A winter wheat. As a result buyers cannot distinguish between the output of one firm and the output of another, so they are indifferent from which firm they buy the product. This refers to not only the physical characteristics of the product but also the "environment" (such as the pleasantness of the seller and the selling location) in which the purchase is made.

Under perfect competition, there is perfect mobility of resources. That is, workers and other inputs can easily move geographically from one job to another and can respond quickly to monetary incentives. No input required in the production of a product is monopolized by its owners or producers. In the long run firms can enter or leave the industry without much difficulty. That is, there are no patents or copyrights, "vast amounts" of capital are not necessary to enter the market, and already established firms do not have any lasting cost advantage over new entrants because of experience or size.

Finally, under perfect competition, consumers, resource owners, and firms in the market have perfect knowledge as to present and future prices, costs, and economic opportunities in general. Thus, consumers will not pay a higher price than necessary for the product. Price differences are quickly eliminated, and a single price will prevail throughout the market for the product. Resources are sold to the highest bidder. With perfect knowledge of present and future prices and costs, producers know exactly how much to produce.

Perfect competition, as defined above, has never really existed. Perhaps the closest we might come today to a perfectly competitive market is the stock market (see Case Study 8-1). Another case where we may have come close to satisfying the first three assumptions of perfect competition is in the market for such agricultural commodities as wheat and corn. The natural gas industry and the trucking industries also approach perfect competition. The fact that perfect competition in its pure form has never really existed in the real world does not reduce the usefulness of the perfectly competitive model. As indicated in Chapter 1, a theory must be accepted or rejected on the basis of its ability to explain and to predict correctly and not on the realism of its assumptions. And the perfectly competitive model does give us some useful (even if at times rough) explanations and predictions of many real-world economic phenomena when the assumptions of the perfectly competitive model are only approximately (rather than exactly) satisfied. In addition, this model helps us evaluate and compare the *efficiency* with which resources are used under different forms of market organization.

Price Determination under Perfect Competition

Under perfect competition, the price of a product is determined at the intersection of the market demand curve and the market supply curve of the product. The market demand curve for a product is simply the horizontal summation of the demand curves of all the consumers in the market, as explained on page 92. As we will see later in this section (see Figure 8-2), the market supply curve of a product is similarly obtained from the horizontal summation of the supply curve of the individual producers of the product.

Given that the market price of a product is determined at the intersection of the market demand and supply curves of the product, the perfectly competitive firm is a **price taker.** That is, the perfectly competitive firm takes the price of the product as given and has no

CASE STUDY 8-1
Competition in the New York Stock Market

The market for stocks traded on the New York and other major stock exchanges is as close as we come today to a perfectly competitive market. In most cases the price of a particular stock is determined by the market forces of demand and supply of the stock, and individual buyers and sellers of the stock have an insignificant effect on price (i.e., they are price takers). All stocks within each category are more or less homogeneous. The fact that a stock is bought and sold frequently is evidence that resources are mobile. Finally, information on prices and quantities traded is readily available.

In general, the price of a stock reflects all the publicly known information about the present and expected future profitability of the stock. This is known as the *efficient market hypothesis*. Funds flow into stocks, and resources flow into uses in which the rate of return, corrected for risk, is highest. Thus, stock prices provide the signals for the efficient allocation of investments in the economy. Despite the fact that the stock market is close to being a perfectly competitive market, imperfections occur even here. For example, the sale of $1 billion worth of stocks by IBM or any other large corporation will certainly affect (depress) the price of its stocks. Furthermore, stock prices can sometimes become grossly overvalued (i.e., we could have a *bubble market*) and thus subject to a subsequent steep correction (fall). This is, in fact, what happened in the New York Stock Exchange at the end of the 1990s.

Today, more and more Americans trade foreign stocks, and more and more foreigners trade American stocks. This has been the result of a communications revolution that linked stock markets around the world into a huge global capital market and around-the-clock trading. Although this provides immense new earning possibilities and sharply increased opportunities for portfolio diversification, it also creates the danger that a crisis in one market will quickly spread to other markets around the world. This actually happened when the collapse of the New York Stock Exchange in October 1987 caused sharp declines in stock markets around the world. It happened again 10 years later (in the fall of 1997), when the collapse of stock markets in Southeast Asia led to a sharp decline in the New York stock market and in stock markets in other nations. In 2002, sharp declines in the New York stock market (as a result of low corporate profits and huge financial scandals) quickly spread to other stock markets around the world.

In recent years, the New York Stock Exchange seems to have lost some of its former ability to predict changing economic conditions and its importance as the central source of capital for corporate America, as the latter borrowed increasing amounts from banks for takeovers and mergers. Indeed, global markets for securities, featuring automated, round-the-world, round-the-clock trading, could eventually eclipse Wall Street's capital-raising dominance.

Source: New York Stock Exchange, *You and the Investment World* (New York: New York Stock Exchange, 1993); "The Future of Wall Street," *Business Week* (November 5, 1990), pp. 119–124; "Luck or Logic? Debate Rages on Over 'Efficient Market Theory'," *The Wall Street Journal* (November 4, 1993), p. C1; "Worrying about World Markets," *Fortune* (July 24, 1995), pp. 43–45; "Unreality Check for the Bull Market," *The Wall Street Journal* (May 25, 1999), p. C1; "Corporate-Profit Fears Put Damper on U.S. Stocks," *The Wall Street Journal* (June 24, 2002), p. C1; and "Another Scandal, Another Scare," *The Economist* (June 29, 2002), pp. 67–69. For 2006 information about the New York Stock Market, see, http://www.nyse.com.

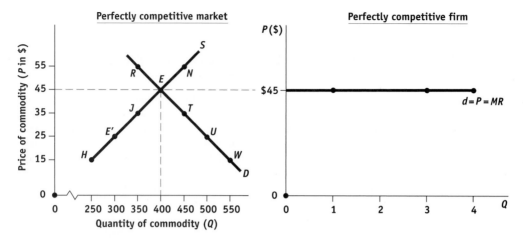

FIGURE 8-1   The Equilibrium Price and the Demand Level Faced by a Perfectly Competitive Firm   The equilibrium price of the product, $P = \$45$, is determined at the intersection of the competitive market demand and supply curves (i.e., at the intersection of D and S) at point E. The perfectly competitive firm is then a price taker and faces the infinitely elastic demand curve, d, at $P = \$45$. Since the firm can sell any quantity of the product at $P = \$45$, the change in total revenue per unit change in output or marginal revenue (MR) also equals $\$45$.

perceptible effect on that price by varying its own level of output and sales of the product. Since the products of all firms are homogeneous, a firm cannot sell at a price higher than the market price of the product; otherwise the firm would lose all its customers. On the other hand, there is no reason for the firm to sell at a price below the market price, since it can sell any quantity of the product at the given market price. As a result, the firm faces a horizontal or infinitely elastic demand curve for the product at the market price determined at the intersection of the market demand and supply curves of the product. For example, a small wheat farmer can sell any amount of wheat at the given market price of wheat. This is shown in Figure 8-1.

In Figure 8-1, D is the market demand curve for the product, and S is the market supply curve of the product. The equilibrium price of the product is $P = \$45$ and is determined at point E at the intersection of D and S. At a price higher than the equilibrium price, say, $P = \$55$, the quantity supplied of the product exceeds the quantity demanded of the product ($QS - QD = RN = 100$), and the price of the product will fall. As P falls, the quantity demanded of the product increases and the quantity supplied declines until the equilibrium price of $P = \$45$ is established, at which the quantity demanded is equal to the quantity supplied (that is, $QD = QS = 400$). By contrast, at a price below the equilibrium price, $QD > QS$ (for example, at $P = \$35$, $QD - QS = JT = 100$), and P rises to the equilibrium $P = \$45$.

The equilibrium price and quantity can be determined algebraically by setting the market demand and supply functions equal to each other and solving for the equilibrium price. Substituting the equilibrium price into the demand or supply functions and solving for Q, we then get the equilibrium quantity. For example, the equations for the market demand and supply curves for the product in Figure 8-1 are

$$QD = 625 - 5P \qquad\qquad\qquad [8\text{-}1]$$

$$QS = 175 + 5P \qquad\qquad\qquad [8\text{-}2]$$

Setting QD equal to QS and solving for P, we have

$$QD = QS$$
$$625 - 5P = 175 + 5P$$
$$450 = 10P$$
$$P = \$45$$

Substituting $P = \$45$ into the demand or supply functions and solving for Q, we have

$$QD = 625 - 5P = 625 - 5(45) = 400$$
$$QS = 175 + 5P = 175 + 5(45) = 400$$

Given the equilibrium price of $P = \$45$, a perfectly competitive firm producing the product faces the horizontal or infinitely elastic demand curve shown by d at $P = \$45$ in Figure 8-1. The perfectly competitive firm only determines what quantity of the product to produce at $P = \$45$ in order to maximize its total profits. How the firm does this is examined in the next section. For the moment, suppose that there are 100 identical firms in this market, each producing 4 units of the product at $P = \$45$. If one such firm expanded its output by 25 percent, the total quantity of product X sold in this market would rise by only 1 unit, from 400 to 401, and P would fall from \$45 to \$44.90. With 1,000 firms, P would fall only from \$45 to \$44.99, and with 10,000 firms to $P = \$44.999$. Of course, if all firms increase their output, the market supply curve of the product would shift to the right and intersect the market demand curve at a lower equilibrium price (see Problem 1). When only one firm changes its output, however, we can safely assume that it will have an imperceptible effect on the equilibrium price (i.e., the firm is a price taker), so that we can draw the demand curve for the product that the firm faces as horizontal. When the product price is constant, the change in the total revenue per unit change in output or marginal revenue (MR) is also constant and is equal to the product price. That is, for a perfectly competitive firm,

$$P = MR \qquad\qquad [8\text{-}3]$$

Short-Run Analysis of a Perfectly Competitive Firm

We saw in Section 1-2 that the aim of a firm is to maximize profits. In the short run, some inputs are fixed, and these give rise to fixed costs, which go on whether the firm produces or not. Thus, it pays for the firm to stay in business in the short run even if it incurs losses, as long as these losses are smaller than its fixed costs.[2] Thus, the best level of output of the firm in the short run is the one at which the firm maximizes profits or minimizes losses.

The best level of output of the firm in the short run is the one at which the marginal revenue (MR) of the firm equals its short-run marginal cost (MC). As pointed out in Figure 2-2, as long as MR exceeds MC, it pays for the firm to expand output because by doing so the firm would add more to its total revenue than to its total costs (so that its total profits

---

[2] In the long run, of course, all costs are variable and the firm will not remain in business if it cannot cover at least all of its costs (so as to break even) and possibly earn a profit.

increase or its total losses decrease). On the other hand, as long as *MC* exceeds *MR*, it pays for the firm to *reduce* output because by doing so the firm will reduce its total costs more than its total revenue (so that, once again, its total profits increase or its total losses decline). Thus, the best level of output of any firm (not just a perfectly competitive firm) is the one at which $MR = MC$. Since a perfectly competitive firm faces a horizontal or infinitely elastic demand curve, $P = MR$, so that the condition for the best level of output can be restated as the one at which $P = MR = MC$.[3] This can be seen in Figure 8-2.

In the top panel of Figure 8-2, *d* is the demand curve for the output of the perfectly competitive firm shown in Figure 8-1, and the marginal and average total cost (i.e., *MC* and *ATC*) curves are those of Figure 7-1. The best level of output of the firm is given at point *E*, where the *MC* curve intersects the firm's *d* or *MR* curve. At point *E*, the firm produces 4 units of output at $P = MR = MC = \$45$. Since at point *E*, $P = \$45$ and $ATC = \$35$, the firm earns a profit of $EA = \$10$ per unit and $EABC = \$40$ in total (the shaded area). This is the largest total profit that the firm can earn. This can be proved as follows. Since at any output level smaller than $Q_X = 4$, $P = MR > MC$, the firm would be adding more to its total revenue than to its total costs (so that its total profits would increase) by expanding output. On the other hand, it does not pay for the firm to expand its output past point *E* (i.e., to be greater than $Q_X = 4$) because $MC > MR = P = \$45$ and the firm would be adding more to its total costs than to its total revenues (so that its total profits would decline). Thus, the best level of output for the firm is $Q_X = 4$, at which $MR = P = MC$ and the total profits of the firm are maximized.[4]

The bottom panel of Figure 8-2 shows that if the market price of the product is $25 instead of $35, so that the demand curve faced by the perfectly competitive firm is *d′*, the best level of output of the firm is 3 units, as indicated by point *E′*, where $P = MR = MC$. At $Q_X = 3$, $P = \$25$ and $ATC = \$35$, so that the firm incurs the loss of $FE' = \$10$ per unit and $FE'C'B = \$30$ in total. If the firm stopped producing the product and left the market, however, it would incur the greater loss of $FA' = \$20$ per unit and $FA'B'B = \$60$ (its total fixed costs). Another way of looking at this is to say that at the best level of output of $Q = 3$, the

---

[3] This can be shown with calculus as follows. Total profits (π) equals total revenue (*TR*) minus total costs *(TC)*. Taking the first derivative of π with respect to Q and setting it equal to zero, we have

$$\frac{d\pi}{dQ} = \frac{d(TR)}{dQ} - \frac{d(TC)}{dQ} = 0$$

Since

$$\frac{d(TR)}{dQ} = MR \quad \text{and} \quad \frac{d(TC)}{dQ} = MC$$

the above condition becomes $MR = MC$. But under perfect competition, the price is given to the firm and is constant. Therefore,

$$\frac{d(TR)}{dQ} = \frac{d(PQ)}{dQ} = P = MR$$

so that the first-order condition for maximization under perfect competition becomes $P = MR = MC$. For the second-order condition, see the appendix to this chapter.

[4] Note that at $Q_X = 3.5$ (point *J* on *ATC* in the top panel of Figure 8-2), the profit *per unit* would be slightly higher than at point *E*, but total profits would be lower, and the aim of the firm is to maximize total profits—not profits per unit of output.

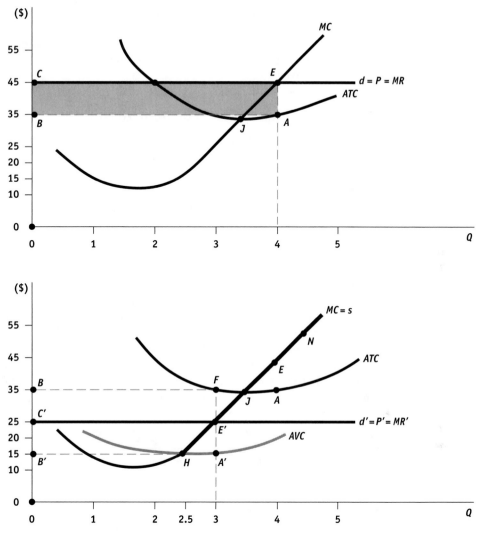

FIGURE 8-2   Short-Run Analysis of a Perfectly Competitive Firm   With *d* the best level of output is 4 units and is shown in the top top panel by point *E*, at which *P* = *MR* = *MC*, and the firm earns profit *EA* = $10 per unit, and *EABC* = $40 in total. With *d* in the bottom panel, the best level of output is 3 units and is given by point *E′* at which the firm incurs a loss of *FE′* = $10 per unit, and *FE′C′B* = $30 in total. At point *E′* the firm minimizes losses. The shut-down point is at point *H*. The rising portion of the *MC* curve above the *AVC* curve (shut-down point) is the firm's short-run supply curve (the heavy portion of the *MC* curve in the bottom panel).

excess of *P* = $25 over the firm's average variable cost (*AVC*) of $15 (also from Figure 7-1) can be applied to cover part of the firm's fixed costs (*FA′* per unit and *FA′B′B* in total). Thus, the firm *minimizes its losses* by continuing to produce its best level of output. If the market price of the product declined to slightly below $15, so that the demand curve facing the firm crossed the *MC* curve at point *H* (see the bottom panel of Figure 8-2), the firm would be indifferent whether to produce or not. The reason is that at point H, $P = AVC$ and the total losses of the firm would be equal to its total fixed costs whether it produced or not. Thus, point H is the **shut-down point** of the firm. Below point H, the firm would not even cover its variable costs, and so by going out of business, the firm would limit its losses to be equal to its total fixed costs.

Short-Run Supply Curve of the Competitive Firm and Market

From what has been said in the preceding, we can conclude that the rising portion of the firm's MC curve above the AVC curve or shut-down point is or represents the **short-run supply curve of the perfectly competitive firm** (the heavier portion of the MC curve labeled s in the bottom panel of Figure 8-2). The reason for this is that the perfectly competitive firm always produces where $P = MR = MC$, as long as $P > AVC$. Thus, at $P = \$55$, the firm produces 4.5 units (point N); at $P = \$45$, $Q = 4$; at $P = \$25$, $Q = 3$; and at $P = \$15$, $Q = 2.5$. That is, given P, we can determine the output supplied by the perfectly competitive firm by the point where $P = MC$. Thus, the rising portion of the competitive firm's MC curve above AVC shows a unique relationship between P and Q, which is the definition of the supply curve.

Given constant prices, the perfectly competitive market supply curve of the product is then obtained by the horizontal summation of the individual firm's supply curves. The market supply curve (S) shown in Figure 8-1 is based on the assumption that there are 100 firms identical to the one shown in Figure 8-2. Thus, S has the same shape as s, but its quantity scale is 100 times larger than for s. At the point where D and S cross, we then have the equilibrium price, which is given to the firm (see Figure 8-1). The circle is now complete—that is, we started with the market, moved on to the firm, and finally returned to the market in a way that is internally consistent and simultaneously determined.

Long-Run Analysis of a Perfectly Competitive Firm

In the long run all inputs and costs of production are variable, and the firm can construct the optimum or most appropriate scale of plant to produce the best level of output. The best level of output is the one at which price equals the long-run marginal cost (LMC) of the firm. The optimum scale of plant is the one with the short-run average total cost ($SATC$) curve tangent to the long-run average cost of the firm at the best level of output.

On one hand, if existing firms earn profits, more firms enter the market in the long run. This increases (i.e., shifts to the right) the market supply of the product and results in a lower product price until all profits are squeezed out. On the other hand, if firms in the market incur losses, some firms will leave the market in the long run. This reduces the market supply of the product until all firms remaining in the market just break even. Thus, when a competitive market is in long-run equilibrium, all firms produce at the lowest point on their long-run average cost (LAC) curve and break even. This is shown by point E^* in Figure 8-3.

Figure 8-3 shows that at $P = \$25$, the best level of output of the perfectly competitive firm is 4 units and is given by point E^*, at which $P = LAC$. Because of free or easy entry into the market, all profits and losses have been eliminated, so that $P = LMC = \text{lowest } LAC$. Thus, for a competitive market to be in long-run equilibrium, all firms in the industry must produce where $P = MR = LMC = \text{lowest } LAC$ (point E^* in Figure 8-3), so that all firms

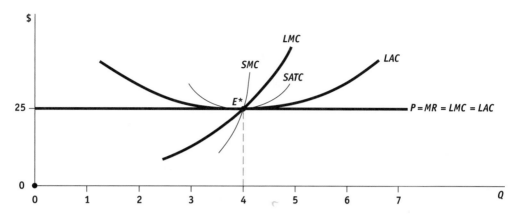

FIGURE 8-3   Long-Run Equilibrium of the Perfectly Competitive Firm and Industry   The best level of output of the perfectly competitive firm at $P = \$25$ is 4 units and is given by point E^*, at which $P = MR = LMC =$ lowest LAC. Because of free or easy entry into the market, all profits and losses have been eliminated, and the firm produces at the lowest point on its LAC curve. The firm operates the scale of plant given by $SATC$ at its lowest point so that $SMC = LMC$ also.

break even. The perfectly competitive firm operates the scale of plant represented by $SATC$ at its lowest point (point E^*), so that its short-run marginal cost (SMC) equals LMC also.

When a perfectly competitive market is in long-run equilibrium, firms break even and earn zero economic profits. Therefore, the owner of the firm receives only a normal return on investment or an amount equal to what he or she would earn by investing his or her funds in the best alternative venture of similar risk. If the owner manages the firm, zero economic profits also include what he or she would earn in the best alternative occupation (i.e., managing the firm for someone else). Thus, zero economic profits means that the total revenues of the firm just cover all costs (explicit and implicit).

It should be noted that perfectly competitive firms need not have identical cost curves (although we assume so for simplicity), but the lowest point on their LAC curves must indicate the same cost per unit. If some firms used more productive inputs and, thus, had lower average costs than other firms in the industry, the more productive inputs would be able to extract from their employer higher rewards (payments) commensurate with their higher productivity, under the threat of leaving to work for others. As a result, their LAC curves would shift upward until the lowest point on the LAC curve of all firms is the same. Thus, competition in the input markets as well as in the commodity market will result in all firms having identical (minimum) average costs and zero economic profits when the industry is in long-run equilibrium.

In the real world, we seldom, if ever, observe markets that are in long-run equilibrium because consumer tastes are constantly changing, market demand curves are shifting, and the technology of production and the prices of inputs change (so that the market supply curve also shifts). Perfectly competitive markets, therefore, seldom if ever reach equilibrium. The fact, however, that they will always be gravitating or moving toward long-run equilibrium is extremely useful to managers in analyzing the effect of changes in market forces and in determining the optimum scale of plants and the best level of output of the firm in the long run (see Case Study 8-2).

CASE STUDY 8-2
Long-Run Adjustment in the
U.S. Cotton Textile Industry

In a study of U.S. industries between the world wars, Lloyd Reynolds found that the U.S. cotton textile industry was the one that came closest to being perfectly competitive. Cotton textiles were practically homogeneous, there were many buyers and sellers of cotton cloth, each was too small to affect its price, and entry into and exit from the industry was easy. Reynolds found that the rate of return on investments in the cotton textile industry was about 6 percent in the South and 1 percent in the North (because of higher costs for raw cotton and labor in the North), as contrasted to an average rate of return of 8 percent for all other manufacturing industries in the United States over the same period of time.

Because of the lower returns, the perfectly competitive model would predict that firms would leave the textile industry in the long run and enter other industries. The model would also predict that because returns were lower in the North than in the South, a greater contraction of the textile industry would take place in the North than in the South. Reynolds found that both of these predictions were borne out by the facts. Capacity in the U.S. textile industry declined by more than 33 percent between 1925 and 1938, with the decline being larger in the North than in the South. Thus, textile firms, cotton farms, and firms using cloth did seem to make use of this knowledge and did respond to these economic forces in their managerial decisions.

Most U.S. textile firms were able to remain in business after World War II only as a result of U.S. restrictions on cheaper textile imports and, subsequently, as a result of the introduction of labor-saving innovations that sharply cut their labor costs. But with the reduction in trade protection negotiated at the Uruguay Round (1986–1993) U.S. and European textile firms have come under renewed pressure, especially from China, which is expected to produce half the world textiles before the end of the decade.

Source: L. Reynolds, "Competition in the Textile Industry," in W. Adams and T. Traywick, eds., *Readings in Economics* (New York: Macmillan, 1948), "Apparel Makes Last Stand," *The New York Times* (September 26, 1990), p. D2; W. McKibbin and D. Salvatore, "The Global Economic Consequences of the Uruguay Round," *Open Economies Review* (April 1995), pp. 111–129; "U.S. Textile Makers Unravel Under Debt, Import Pressure," *The Wall Street Journal* (December 27, 2001), p. A2; "Free of Quota, China Textiles Flood the U.S.," *The New York Times* (March 3, 2005), p. 1; "The Great Stitch-up," *The Economist* (May 28, 2005), p. 61; and "China to Limit Textiles Exports to Europe," *The New York Times* (June 11, 2005), p. C4.

8-3   COMPETITION IN THE GLOBAL ECONOMY

In this section we examine how international competition affects prices in the nation, how the value of the nation's currency affects the nation's international competitiveness, and how a competitive firm in the nation adjusts to international competition.

Domestic Demand and Supply, Imports, and Prices

Domestic firms in most industries face a great deal of competition from abroad. Most U.S.-made goods today compete with similar goods from abroad and, in turn, compete

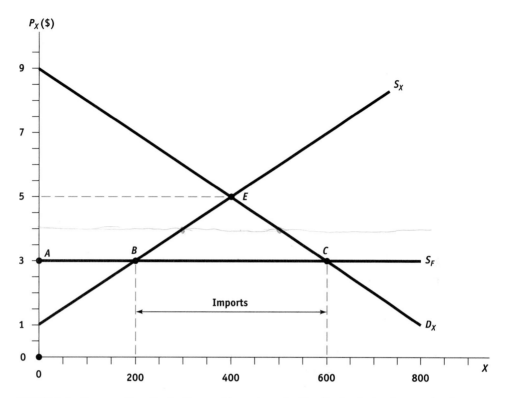

FIGURE 8-4   Consumption, Production, and Imports under Free Trade   In the absence of trade, equilibrium is at point E, where D_X and S_X intersect, so that $P_X = \$5$ and $Q_X = 400$. With free trade at the world price of $P_X = \$3$, domestic consumers purchase $AC = 600X$, of which $AB = 200X$ are produced domestically and $BC = 400X$ are imported.

with foreign-made goods in foreign markets. Steel, textiles, cameras, wines, automobiles, television sets, computers, and aircraft are but a few of the domestic products that compete with foreign products for consumers' dollars in the U.S. economy today. International competition affects the price and the quantity of commodities sold by domestic firms, as shown by Figure 8-4.

In Figure 8-4, D_X and S_X refer to the domestic market demand and supply curves of commodity X. In the absence of trade, the equilibrium price is given by the intersection of D_X and S_X at point E, so that domestic consumers purchase $400X$ (all of which are produced domestically) at $P_X = \$5$. With free trade at the world price of $P_X = \$3$, the price of commodity X to domestic consumers will fall to the world price. The foreign supply curve of this nation's imports, S_F, is horizontal at $P_X = \$3$ *on the assumption that this nation's demand for imports is very small in relation to the foreign supply.* From the figure, we can see that domestic consumers will purchase AC, or $600X$, at $P_X = \$3$ with free trade (and no transportation costs), as compared with $400X$ at $P_X = \$5$ in the absence of trade (given by point E).

Figure 8-4 also shows that with free trade, domestic firms produce only *AB*, or 200*X*, so that *BC*, or 400*X*, is imported at $P_X = \$3$. Resources in the nation will then shift from the production of commodity *X* to the production of other commodities (thus benefiting domestic firms that produce those commodities) in which the nation is relatively more efficient or has a comparative advantage. With tariffs or other trade restrictions, the price of commodity *X* in the nation will be higher than the free-trade price of $3, and the nation's imports will be smaller than 400*X*. However, tariffs and other restrictions to the flow of international trade have been reduced sharply over the past decades and have been all but eliminated for trade among the 15-nation European Union (EU) and in North America (by the North American Free Trade Agreement, or NAFTA).

In the final analysis, a firm will import a commodity as long as the domestic currency price of the imported commodity is lower than the price of the identical domestically produced commodity, and until they are equal (in the absence of transportation costs, tariffs, or other obstructions to the flow of trade). In order to make the payment, however, the domestic importer will have to exchange the domestic currency for the foreign currency. Since the U.S. dollar is also used as an international currency, a U.S. importer could also pay in dollars. In that case, it is the foreign exporter that will have to exchange dollars into the local currency. In any event, importing or exporting a commodity or service will necessarily involve the exchange of one currency for another and depends also on the rate at which currencies are exchanged.

The Dollar Exchange Rate and the International Competitiveness of U.S. Firms

The market where one currency is exchanged for another is called the foreign exchange market. The **foreign exchange market** for any currency, say the U.S. dollar, is formed by all the locations (such as London, Tokyo, and Frankfurt, as well as New York) where dollars are bought and sold for other currencies. These international monetary centers are connected by a telecommunication network and are in constant contact with one another. The rate at which one currency is exchanged for another is called the **exchange rate.** This is the price of a unit of the foreign currency in terms of the domestic currency. For example, the exchange rate (R) between the U.S. dollar and the euro ($\euro$), the currency of 12 nations of the European Monetary Union (Austria, Belgium, Finland, France, Germany, Greece, Ireland, Italy, Luxembourg, Netherlands, Portugal, and Spain), is the number of dollars required to purchase one euro. That is, $R = \$/\euro$. Thus, if $R = \$/\euro = 1$, this means that one dollar is required to purchase one euro.

Under a flexible exchange rate system of the type we have today, the dollar price of the euro (R) is determined (just like the price of any other commodity in a competitive market) by the intersection of the market demand and supply curves of euros. This is shown in Figure 8-5, where the vertical axis measures the dollar price of euros, or the exchange rate ($R = \$/\euro$), and the horizontal axis measures the quantity of euros. The market demand and supply curves for euros intersect at point E, defining the equilibrium exchange rate of $R = 1$, at which the quantity of euros demanded and the quantity of euros supplied are equal at $\euro300$ million per day. At a higher exchange rate, the quantity of euros supplied exceeds the quantity demanded, and the exchange rate will fall toward the

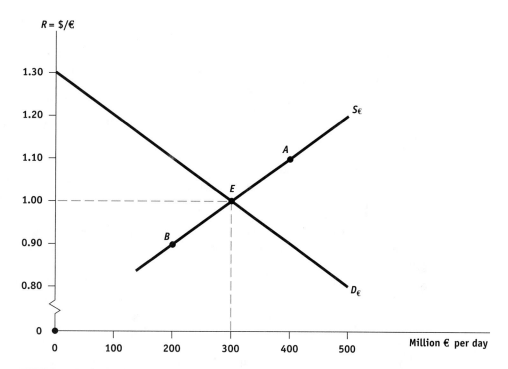

FIGURE 8-5   The Foreign Exchange Market and the Dollar Exchange Rate   The vertical axis measures the dollar price of euros ($R = \$/€$) and the horizontal axis measures the quantity of euros. Under a flexible exchange rate system, the equilibrium exchange rate is $R = 1$ and the equilibrium quantity of euros bought and sold is €300 million per day. This is given by point E, at which the U.S. demand and supply curves for euros intersect.

equilibrium rate of $R = 1$. At an exchange rate lower than $R = 1$, the quantity of euros demanded exceeds the quantity supplied, and the exchange rate will be bid up toward the equilibrium rate of $R = 1$.

The U.S. demand for euros is negatively inclined, indicating that the lower the exchange rate (R), the greater is the quantity of euros demanded by the United States. The reason is that the lower is the exchange rate (i.e., the fewer the number of dollars required to purchase one euro), the cheaper it is for the United States to import from and invest in the European Monetary Union (EMU), and thus the greater is the quantity of euros demanded by U.S. residents. On the other hand, the U.S. supply of euros is usually positively inclined, indicating that the higher the exchange rate (R), the greater is the quantity of euros earned by or supplied to the United States. The reason is that at higher exchange rates, residents of the EMU receive more dollars for each of their euros. As a result, they find U.S. goods and investments cheaper and spend more in the United States, thus supplying more euros to the United States.

If the U.S. demand curve for euros shifted up (e.g., as a result of increased U.S. tastes for EMU's goods) and intersected the U.S. supply curve for euros at point A (see Figure 8-5), the equilibrium exchange rate would be $R = 1.10$, and the equilibrium quantity would be €400 million per day. The dollar is then said to have depreciated, since it now requires $1.10 (instead of the previous $1.00) to purchase one euro. **Depreciation** thus refers to an increase in the domestic price of the foreign currency. On the other hand, if through time the U.S. demand for euros shifted down so as to intersect the U.S. supply curve of euros at point B (see Figure 8-5), the equilibrium exchange rate would fall to $R = 0.90$ and the dollar is said to have appreciated (because fewer dollars are now required to purchase one euro). An **appreciation** thus refers to a decline in the domestic price of the foreign currency. Shifts in the U.S. supply curve of euros through time would similarly affect the equilibrium exchange rate and equilibrium quantity of euros.

In the absence of interferences by national monetary authorities, the foreign exchange market operates just like any other competitive market, with the equilibrium price and quantity of the foreign currency determined at the intersection of the market demand and supply curves for the foreign currency. Sometimes, monetary authorities attempt to affect exchange rates by a coordinated purchase or sale of a currency on the foreign exchange market. For example, U.S. and foreign monetary authorities might sell dollars for foreign currencies to induce a dollar depreciation (which makes U.S. goods cheaper to foreigners) in order to reduce the U.S. trade deficit. These official foreign exchange market interventions are only of limited effectiveness, however, because the foreign exchange resources at the disposal of national monetary authorities are very small in relation to the size of daily transactions on the foreign exchange market (now estimated to be more than $1 trillion per day!). Such a huge volume of transactions has been made possible by sharp improvements in telecommunications and the existence of a 24-hour foreign exchange market around the world.

Case Study 8-3 gives the foreign exchange quotations of the dollar with respect to other currencies, while Case Study 8-4 examines the relationship between the exchange rate of the dollar and the profitability of U.S. firms.

CASE STUDY 8-3
Foreign Exchange Quotations of the Dollar

Table 8-1 gives the exchange rates for various currencies with respect to the U.S. dollar for Wednesday, May 24, 2006, and for Tuesday, May 23, 2006—defined first as the dollar price of the foreign currency (as in the text) and then, alternatively, as the foreign currency price of the dollar. For example, next to Europe, we find that the exchange rate of the euro (€) was $1.2773/€1 on Wednesday and $1.2861 on Tuesday. On the same line, we find that the euro price of the dollar was €0.7829/$1 on Wednesday and €0.7775 on Tuesday. On the next three lines under Europe, we find the 30-day forward rate (i.e., the rate for a transaction entered upon today but with the foreign currency delivered in 30 days) and the 60- and 90-day forward rates. The 30-day forward rate of the euro is higher than the spot rate, meaning that the market expects the euro to be stronger in 30 days (and still stronger in 60 and 90 days because the 60- and 90-day forward rates are higher and the spot rate than the 30-day forward rate).

TABLE 8-1	**Foreign Exchange Quotations**

Foreign Exchange Quotations for Wednesday May 24, 2006

Currency	Foreign Currency in Dollars		Dollars in Foreign Currency		Currency	Foreign Currency in Dollars		Dollars in Foreign Currency	
	Wed.	Tue.	Wed.	Tue.		Wed.	Tue.	Wed.	Tue.
ASIA/PACIFIC					Sweden (Krona)	.1369	.1378	7.3031	7.2573
Australia (Dollar)	.7518	.7582	1.3301	1.3189	Switzerland (Franc)	.8226	.8288	1.2156	1.2066
China (Yuan)	.1247	.1247	8.0210	8.0175	30-day fwd	.8249	.8312	1.2123	1.2031
Hong Kong (Dollar)	.1289	.1289	7.7558	7.7550	60-day fwd	.8276	.8339	1.2083	1.1992
India (Rupee)	.0219	.0220	45.570	45.380	90-day fwd	.8304	.8368	1.2043	1.1950
Indonesia (Rupiah)	.000107	.000108	9360.00	9250.00	Turkey (Lira)	.6416	.6669	1.5585	1.4995
Japan (Yen)	.008874	.008983	112.69	111.32					
30-day fwd	.008918	.009036	112.13	110.67	**MIDDLE EAST/AFRICA**				
60-day fwd	.008956	.009072	111.66	110.23	Bahrain (Dinar)	2.6525	2.6546	.3770	.3767
90-day fwd	.009052	.009193	110.47	108.78	Egypt (Pound)	.1746	.1746	5.7275	5.7275
Malaysia (Ringgit)	.2747	.2768	3.6400	3.6130	Israel (Shekel)	.2209	.2229	4.5265	4.4860
New Zealand (Dollar)	.6337	.6277	1.5780	1.5931	Jordan (Dinar)	1.4110	1.4110	.7087	.7087
Pakistan (Rupee)	.0167	.0167	59.98	59.98	Kenya (Shilling)	.0139	.0139	72.20	72.20
Philippines (Peso)	.0190	.0190	52.75	52.65	Kuwait (Dinar)	3.4590	3.4590	.2891	.2891
Singapore (Dollar)	.6290	.6340	1.5899	1.5774	Lebanon (Pound)	.000666	.000666	1501.00	1501.00
So. Korea (Won)	.001054	.001060	949.20	943.80	Saudi Arabia (Riyal)	.2667	.2667	3.7501	3.7500
Taiwan (Dollar)	.0313	.0313	32.00	31.98	So. Africa (Rand)	.1495	.1540	6.6900	6.4935
Thailand (Baht)	.02593	.02616	38.57	38.23	U.A.E. (Dirham)	.2723	.2725	3.6720	3.6702
EUROPE					**NORTH AMERICA/CARIBBEAN**				
Britain (Pound)	1.8717	1.8843	.5343	.5307	Canada (Dollar)	.8929	.8943	1.1199	1.1182
30-day fwd	1.8716	1.8839	.5343	.5308	30-day fwd	.8916	.8972	1.1216	1.1146
60-day fwd	1.8725	1.8847	.5340	.5306	60-day fwd	.8924	.8972	1.1206	1.1146
90-day fwd	1.8736	1.8857	.5337	.5303	90-day fwd	.8932	.8979	1.1196	1.1137
Czech Rep (Koruna)	.0453	.0456	22.09	21.92	Dominican Rep (Peso)	.0308	.0307	32.49	32.54
Denmark (Krone)	.1713	.1724	5.8381	5.7999	Mexico (Peso)	.088498	.089350	11.2997	11.1920
Europe (Euro)	1.2773	1.2861	.7829	.7775					
30-day fwd	1.2791	1.2882	.7818	.7763	**SOUTH AMERICA**				
60-day fwd	1.2814	1.2904	.7804	.7750	Argentina (Peso)	.3245	.3257	3.0820	3.0705
90-day fwd	1.2841	1.2930	.7788	.7734	Brazil (Real)	.4194	.4409	2.3845	2.2680
Hungary (Forint)	.0048	.0049	206.24	203.52	Chile (Peso)	.001874	.001893	533.50	528.35
Norway (Krone)	.1632	.1639	6.1280	6.0996	Columbia (Peso)	.000394	.000401	2540.95	2495.00
Poland (Zloty)	.3215	.3268	3.11	3.06	Peru (New Sol)	.3060	.3067	3.268	3.261
a-Russia(Ruble)	.0370	.0371	27.0115	26.9862	Uruguay (New Peso)	.0418	.0418	23.9000	23.9250
Slovak Rep (Koruna)	.0336	.0341	29.76	29.35	Venezuela (Bolivar)	.000466	.000466	2147.30	2147.30

Source: Reprinted by permission of *The New York Times* ©. All rights reserved worldwide.

CASE STUDY 8-4
The Exchange Rate of the U.S. Dollar
and the Profitability of U.S. Firms

A depreciation of the dollar, by making U.S. goods and services cheaper to foreigners in terms of their currency, allows U.S. firms to sell more abroad without lowering the dollar price of their products, and thus increases their profits and their share of foreign markets. U.S. firms also receive more dollars for their foreign-currency profits earned abroad. Against these benefits are the higher dollar prices that U.S. firms must pay for imported inputs. How much a U.S. firm gains from a depreciation of the dollar, therefore, depends on the amount of its foreign sales as opposed to its expenditures on imported inputs.

For example, the Black & Decker Corporation, a maker of power tools and appliances with about half of its sales abroad, found that the depreciation of the dollar during 1990 led to a 5 percent increase in its foreign sales and earnings. In contrast, the Gillette Corporation, which has plants in many countries and uses almost exclusively local inputs to supply each market, benefited mostly through the repatriation of foreign profits. Merck & Company, which has plants in 19 nations and conducts most of its business in local currencies, was in a similar position. In between was Compaq, which found some of its price advantage abroad resulting from the depreciation of the dollar eaten away by the higher cost of its imported disk drives and circuit-board parts.

The 20 percent appreciation of the dollar vis-a-vis the euro from the time of its launching at the beginning of 1999 until January 2002 meant that U.S. exporters received 20 percent fewer dollars per euro earned in Europe, while U.S. importers paid 20 percent less for imports from Europe. Thus, a change in the exchange rate benefits some and harms others, but affects all firms with foreign transactions and all individuals (Americans and foreigners) traveling abroad. The subsequent depreciation of the dollar eliminated all of the previous appreciation (and overvaluation) and then some, and it was very much appreciated by U.S. exporters, but not by U.S. importers.

Source: "How Dollar's Plunge Aids Some Companies, Does Little for Others," *The Wall Street Journal* (October 22, 1990), p. A1; "Exporters in U.S. Confront a New Reality," *The Wall Street Journal* (April 28, 1998), p. A2; "Japan Car Makers Find a Friend in a Weaker Yen—Up to a Point," *The Wall Street Journal* (January 28, 2002), p. A12; D. Salvatore, "The Euro: Expectations and Performance," *Eastern Economic Journal* (January 2002); "Dollar Dive Helps U.S. Companies," *The Wall Street Journal* (April 21, 2003); and "Struggling with Falling Dollar," *The New York Times* (January 15, 2004), p. C7.

8-4   MONOPOLY

In this section we discuss the sources of monopoly, examine how the monopolist determines the best level of output and price in the short run and in the long run, and compare monopoly with perfect competition.

Sources of Monopoly

As defined in Section 8-1, monopoly is the form of market organization in which a single firm sells a product for which there are no close substitutes. Thus, the monopolist represents the market and faces the market's negatively sloped demand curve for the product. As opposed to a perfectly competitive firm, a monopolist can earn profits in the long run because entry into the industry is essentially blocked. Thus, monopoly is at the opposite extreme from perfect competition in the spectrum or range of market organizations.

There are four basic reasons that can give rise to monopoly. *First,* the firm may control the entire supply of raw materials required to produce the product. For example, until World War II, the Aluminum Company of America (Alcoa) controlled almost every source of bauxite (the raw material required to produce aluminum) and thus had a monopoly over the production of aluminum in the United States (see Case Study 8-5).

Second, the firm may own a patent or copyright that precludes other firms from using a particular production process or producing the same product. For example, when cellophane was introduced, Du Pont had monopoly power in its production based on patents. Similarly, Xerox had a monopoly on copying machines and Polaroid on instant cameras. Patents are granted by the government for a period of 17 years as an incentive to inventors.

Third, in some industries, economies of scale may operate (i.e., the long-run average cost curve may fall) over a sufficiently large range of outputs as to leave only one firm supplying the entire market. Such a firm is called a **natural monopoly.** Examples of these are public utilities (electric, gas, water, and local transportation companies). To have more than one such firm in a given market would lead to duplication of supply lines and to much higher costs per unit. To avoid this, local governments usually allow a single firm to operate in the market but regulate the price of the services provided, so as to allow the firm only a normal return on investment.

Fourth, a monopoly may be established by a government franchise. In this case, the firm is set up as the sole producer and distributor of a product or service but is subjected to governmental regulation. The best example of a monopoly established by government franchise is the post office. Local governments also require a license to operate many types of businesses, such as liquor stores, taxis, broadcasting, medical offices, and private health care clinics. The aim of these licenses is to ensure minimum standards of competence, but since the number of licenses is usually restricted, their effect is also to restrict competition and to provide monopoly profits to license owners.

Aside from regulated monopolies, cases of pure monopoly have been rare in the past and are forbidden today by U.S. antitrust laws. Even so, the pure monopoly model is often useful in explaining observed business behavior in cases approximating pure monopoly and also gives insights into the operation of other types of imperfectly competitive markets (i.e., monopolistic competition and oligopoly). To be noted is that a monopolist does not have unlimited market power. The monopolist faces indirect competition for the consumer's dollar from all other commodities. Furthermore, although there are no *close* substitutes for the product sold by the monopolist, substitutes may nevertheless exist. For example, even when Alcoa had a monopoly over the production and sale of aluminum in the United States, aluminum faced competition from steel, plastics, copper, and other materials. Fear of government prosecution and the threat of potential competition also act as a check on the monopolist's market power. In general, all monopoly power based on barriers to entry is subject to decay in the long run, except that based on government franchise.

CASE STUDY 8-5
Barriers to Entry and Monopoly by Alcoa

The Aluminum Company of America (Alcoa) is a classic example of how a monopoly was created and maintained for almost 50 years. The monopoly was created in the late nineteenth century when Alcoa acquired a patent on the method to remove oxygen from bauxite to obtain aluminum. This patent expired in 1906, but in 1903, Alcoa had patented another, more efficient method to produce aluminum. This patent expired in 1909. By that time, Alcoa had signed long-term contracts with producers of bauxite, prohibiting them from selling bauxite to any other American firm. At the same time, Alcoa entered into agreements with foreign producers of aluminum not to export aluminum into each other's market. Alcoa even went as far as purchasing electricity only from those power companies that agreed not to sell energy for the production of aluminum to any other firm.

In 1912, the courts invalidated all of these contracts and agreements. Nevertheless, Alcoa retained monopoly power by always expanding productive capacity in anticipation of any increase in demand and by pricing aluminum in such a way as to discourage new entrants. The monopoly was finally broken after World War II, when Alcoa was not allowed to purchase government-financed aluminum plants built during the war. This is how Reynolds and Kaiser aluminum came into existence. During the 1960s, Reynolds diversified into plastics, gold, and consumer products, while Alcoa stuck to pure aluminum.

But on May 3, 2000, Alcoa acquired Reynolds Metals Company, thus remaining the world's largest producer of aluminum, with 2001 revenues of $23 billion, 142,000 workers, operations in 37 countries, and nearly 16 percent of the world aluminum market.

During the early 1990s, the world price of aluminum declined by almost 50 percent because of oversupply resulting, in part, from the sharp increase in aluminum exports by Russia, as internal demand by its military-industrial complex vanished after the collapse of communism. In response to this price collapse, the representatives of 17 nations, including Russia, the European Union countries, the United States, and other major aluminum exporters agreed in January 1994 to voluntarily cut production for two years, and this led to a partial recovery in aluminum prices. In agreeing to voluntarily cut production, the major exporting nations came very close to behaving like an international monopoly (cartel, see Chapter 9). Despite the relatively high concentration in the aluminum market (e.g., together Alcoa and Canadian-European APA have a 27.4 percent share of the world market), prices rose and fell during the rest of the 1990s and early 2000s, primarily because of demand and supply considerations. In 2002, China became the largest producer of primary aluminum, with nearly 60 percent of world output. Rapidly growing internal demand, however, absorbed most of its increase in supply without affecting much the world price.

Source: R. Lanzilotti, "The Aluminum Industry," in W. Adams, ed., *The Structure of American Industry* (New York: Macmillan, 1961); "Reynolds Metals, Alcoa Split on Strategy," *The Wall Street Journal* (November 7, 1990), p. A4; "Aluminum Pact Set to Curb World Output," *The Wall Street Journal* (January 31, 1994); "Global Merger Could Steady Aluminum Market," *The Wall Street Journal* (August 11, 1999), p. A13; "Alcoa's Outlook Is Bright Due to Cost Cuts, Shortages," *The Wall Street Journal* (January 1, 2000), p. B4; and "The China Factor: Aluminum Industry Impact," *Journal of Minerals (JOM)* (September 2004), pp. 1–6.

Short-Run Price and Output Determination under Monopoly

A monopolist, as contrasted to a perfect competitor, is not a price taker but can set the price at which it sells the product. In this section, we see how the monopolist sets the price to maximize profits or minimize losses in the short run. In the following section we see how

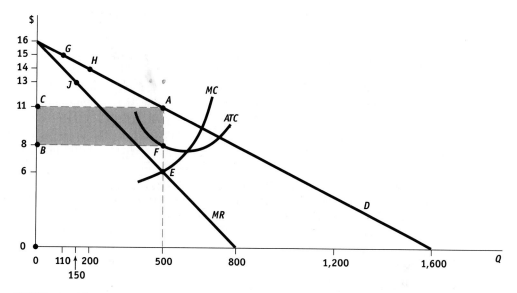

FIGURE 8-6   Short-Run Price and Output Determination by a Monopolist   The best level of output for the monopolist in the short run is 500 units and is given by point *E*, where *MR* = *MC*. At *Q* = 500, *P* = $11 (point *A* on the *D* curve), and *ATC* = $8 (point *F*), so that the monopolist earns a profit of *AF* = $3 per unit and *AFBC* = $1,500 in total (the shaded area).

the monopolist adjusts the scale of plant and sets the price in order to maximize profits in the long run.

Since a monopolist is the sole seller of a product for which there are no close substitutes, the monopolist faces the negatively sloped market demand curve for the product. This means that the monopolist can sell more units of the product only by lowering its price. Because of this, the marginal revenue is smaller than the product price and the marginal revenue curve is below the demand curve that the monopolist faces. This is shown in Figure 8-6.

In Figure 8-6, *D* is the market demand curve faced by the monopolist, and *MR* is the corresponding marginal revenue curve. To see why the *MR* curve is below the *D* curve, note that the monopolist can sell 100 units of the product at *P* = $15 (point *G* on the *D* curve), so that *TR* = $1,500. To sell 200 units, the monopolist must lower its price to *P* = $14 on all units sold (point *H*), so that *TR* = $2,800. The change in *TR* per unit change in output or *MR* is

$$MR = \frac{\Delta TR}{\Delta Q} = \frac{\$1,300}{100} = \$13$$

(point *J*, plotted halfway between 100 and 200 units of output on the *MR* curve in Figure 8-6). Thus, with *D* negatively sloped, the *MR* curve must be below it. From Figure 8-6 we can also see that when the demand curve (*D*) is linear, the absolute slope of the *MR* curve is twice that of the D curve so that the MR curve lies everywhere halfway between the D curve and the price axis.[5]

The best level of output in the short run is 500 units and is given by point E in Figure 8-6 at which $MR = MC$. At $Q < 500$, $MR > MC$ and the total profits of the monopolist will increase by expanding output. On the other hand, at $Q > 500$, $MC > MR$ and the total profits of the monopolist will increase by *reducing* output. The price at which the monopolist should sell its best level of output is then given on the D curve. In Figure 8-6, $P = \$11$ at $Q = 500$. Since at $Q = 500$, $ATC = \$8$ (point F in the figure), the monopolist earns a profit of $AF = \$3$ per unit and $AFBC = \$1,500$ in total (the shaded area in the figure). This is the largest profit that the monopolist can earn in the short run. Note that, as contrasted with the case under perfect competition, $P > MR$ at the best level of output under monopoly because the demand curve is above the marginal revenue curve.

While the monopolist of Figure 8-6 is earning short-run profits, a monopolist (just like a perfect competitor) could also break even or incur losses in the short run. It all depends on the height of the ATC at the best level of output. If $ATC = P$ at the best level of output, the monopolist breaks even, and if $ATC > P$ at the best level of output, the monopolist incurs a loss. Again, as in the case of perfect competition, it pays for a monopolist to remain in business in the short run even if it incurs losses, as long as $P > AVC$. In that case, the excess of P over AVC can be used to cover part of the fixed costs of the monopolist. Were the monopolist to go out of business, it would incur the larger loss equal to its total fixed costs. Thus, the aim of the monopolist in the short run is the same as that of a perfect competitor, that is, to maximize profits or minimize losses.[6]

Long-Run Price and Output Determination under Monopoly

In the long run, all inputs and costs of production are variable, and the monopolist can construct the optimal scale of plant to produce the best level of output. As in the case of perfect competition, the best level of output of the monopolist is given at the point at which $MR = LMC$, and the optimum scale of plant is the one with the $SATC$ curve tangent to the LAC curve at the best level of output. As contrasted with perfect competition,

---

[5] This can easily be shown mathematically, as follows. Let the monopolist's demand function be

$$Q = \frac{a - P}{b} \qquad \text{or} \qquad P = a - bQ$$

where a is the vertical or price intercept and $-b$ is the slope of the demand curve. Then $TR = PQ = (a - bQ)Q = aQ - bQ^2$ and

$$MR = \frac{d(TR)}{dQ} = a - 2bQ$$

Thus, the MR curve has the same vertical or price intercept as the D curve, but its absolute slope $(2b)$ is twice the slope of the D curve (b).

[6] Note that since at the best level of output $MR = MC < P$ under monopoly and a given MR can be associated with different P's, depending on the price elasticity of demand, there is no unique relationship between P and Q under monopoly (i.e., we cannot derive the supply curve of the monopolist from the rising portion of its MC curve above the AVC curve, as was done for a perfectly competitive firm).

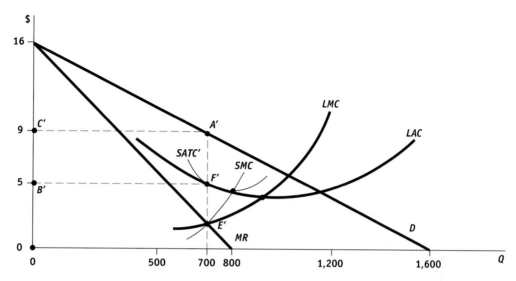

FIGURE 8-7   Long-Run Price and Output Determination by the Monopolist   The best level of output for the monopolist in the long run is 700 units and is given by point E', at which $MR = LMC$. At $Q = 700$, $P = \$9$ (point A' on the D curve). The monopolist operates the optimal scale of plant (given by the $SATC$ curve in the figure) at point F' at an average cost of $\$5$. The monopolist earns a long-run profit of $A'F' = \$4$ per unit, and $A'F'B'C' = \$2,800$ in total.

however, entrance into the market is blocked under monopoly, and so the monopolist can earn economic profits in the long run. Because of blocked entry, the monopolist is also not likely to produce at the lowest point on its *LAC* curve. This is shown in Figure 8-7.

Figure 8-7 shows that the best level of output for the monopolist in the long run is 700 units and is given by point E', at which $MR = LMC$. At $Q = 700$, $P = \$9$ (point A' on the D curve). The monopolist has had time in the long run to build the optimum scale of plant given by the *SATC* curve tangent to the *LAC* curve at $Q = 700$ (point F' in Figure 8-7). Operating the optimum scale of plant at F' at the best level of output of $Q = 700$, the monopolist has $SATC = LAC = \$5$ (point F'). Thus, the monopolist is earning a long-run profit of $A'F' = \$4$ per unit and $A'F'B'C' = \$2,800$ in total (as compared to $\$1,500$ in the short run). Because entry into the market is blocked, the monopolist will continue to earn these profits in the long run as long as the demand it faces and its cost curves remain unchanged (see Case Study 8-6).

To be noted is that when the monopolist is in long-run equilibrium (point E' in Figure 8-7), it is also and necessarily in short-run equilibrium (i.e., $MR = SMC$), but the reverse is not true. Also to be noted is that the monopolist of Figure 8-7 does not produce at the lowest point on its *LAC* curve (as competition forces the perfectly competitive firm to do). Only in the unusual situation when the *MR* curve of the monopolist goes through the lowest point on its *LAC* curve would the monopolist (as the perfect competitor) produce at the lowest point on its *LAC* curve. In that case, however, the monopolist would still charge a price that is higher than its *LAC* and earn a profit in the long run.

CASE STUDY 8-6
The Market Value of Monopoly Profits in the New York City Taxi Industry

New York City, as most other municipalities (cities) in the United States, requires a license (medallion) to operate a taxi. Since medallions are limited in number, this confers a monopoly power (i.e., the ability to earn economic profits) to owners of medallions. The value of owning a medallion is equal to the present discounted value of the future stream of earnings from the ownership of a medallion—a process called *capitalization*. For example, the number of medallions in New York City remained at 11,787 from 1937 until 1996, when it was increased by only 400 to 12,187. It was increased by another 900 to 13,087 from 2004 to 2006, and the value of a medallion rose from $10 in 1937 to over nearly $300,000 in 2005, or by about 18 percent per year. The price of a medallion is lower (and sometimes much lower) in other cities, reflecting the lower earning powers there. It is about $210,000 in Boston and $55,000 in Chicago, where taxis are less scarce.

Proposals to increase the number of medallions in New York City have been blocked by the taxi industry lobby. Were the city to freely grant a license to operate a taxi for the asking, the price of the medallion would drop to zero. Although not doing that, New York City has allowed a sharp growth during the 1980s in the number of radio cabs, which can respond only to radio calls and cannot cruise the streets for passengers. This sharply increased competition in the New York City taxi industry and reduced profits to taxi owners from 32 percent in 1993 to 11 percent in 2001.

Source: "Owners Bewail Flood of Cabs in New York," *The New York Times* (April 10, 1989), p. B1; "Panel Clears Plan to Enlarge Taxicab Fleet," *The New York Times* (January 27, 1996), p. B1; "Medallion Financial Sees Growth in Taxi Tops," *The Wall Street Journal* (July 19, 1999), p. B7A; "Yellow Taxis Battle to Keep Livery Cabs Off Their Turf," *The New York Times* (May 10, 2001), p. 1; "Taken for a Ride?" *The Economist* (April 24, 2004), p. 30; and "Medallion Prices," http://www.Schallerconsult.com/taxi/fb/fb4.htm.

Comparison of Monopoly and Perfect Competition

We saw on page 330 that when a perfectly competitive industry is in long-run equilibrium, each firm produces at the lowest point on its *LAC* curve and charges a price equal to the lowest *LAC*, so that each firm earns zero economic profits. Under monopoly, on the other hand, production is not likely to take place at the lowest point on the *LAC* curve, and, because of blocked entry, the monopolist is also likely to earn profits in the long run. We cannot conclude from this, however, that perfect competition is necessarily "better" or more efficient than monopoly.

Perfect competition is more efficient than monopoly only if the lowest point on the *LAC* curve occurs at an output level that is very small in relation to the market demand, so as to allow many firms to operate and, if the product is homogeneous, so that perfect competition is possible. Often this is not the case. That is, a very large scale of operation is often required to produce most products efficiently, and this permits only a few firms to operate. For example, economies of scale operate over such a large range of outputs that steel, aluminum, automobiles, mainframe computers, aircraft, and many other products and services can be produced efficiently only by very large firms, so that a handful of such firms can meet the entire market demand for the product or service. Perfect competition under such conditions would either be impossible or lead to prohibitively high production costs. One could only imagine how high the cost per unit would be if automobiles were produced by 100 or more firms instead of by three or four very large firms.

There are also those who believe that the ability to earn profits in the long run because of restricted entry provides the monopolist with the resources and the incentive to undertake research and development. Since the greater part of the increase in the standards of living in industrial countries today arises from technological progress, this is a very important consideration.

There is, however, a great deal of disagreement as to whether monopoly leads to more technological change than perfect competition. There are those who believe that a monopolist, sheltered as it is from competition, does not have much of an incentive to innovate and that many technological advances are in fact introduced by very small firms.

Only if we abstract from technological progress and if we assume that the technology used in the production of the product allows many firms to operate efficiently, can we prove that perfect competition is better than monopoly from the point of view of society as a whole. This can be shown with the aid of Figure 8-8.

In Figure 8-8, we assume that the *LMC* curve is constant and equal to the perfectly competitive firm's and the monopolist's *LAC*. Under perfect competition, the *LAC* = *LMC* curve represents the market supply curve. The equilibrium price of $6 and the equilibrium quantity of 1,000 units are given by point *E*, at which the *D* and the *LMC* (the long-run

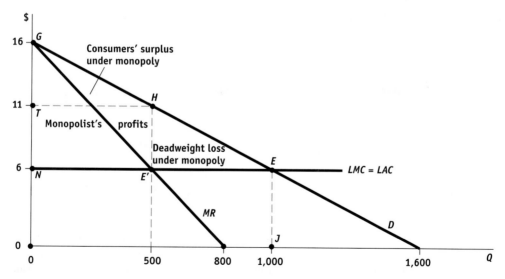

FIGURE 8-8   The Social Cost of Monopoly   Under perfect competition, the *LMC* = *LAC* curve represents the market supply curve. Therefore, equilibrium is at point *E*, at which *Q* = 1,000 units, *P* = $6 (point *E* on the *D* curve), *ENG* = $5,000 represents the consumers' surplus (i.e., the difference between what consumers are willing to pay and what they actually pay for 1,000 units of the product), and all firms break even. If the market is monopolized, the best level of output is 500 and is given by point *E'*, at which *MR* = *LMC*, and *P* = $11 (point *H* on the *D* curve). The monopolist's profits are *HE'NT* = $2,500, consumers' surplus is *HTG* = $1,250, and the true deadweight loss to society (resulting from a less efficient use of resources) is *EE'H* = $1,250.

market supply) curves under perfect competition cross. All the many competitive firms in the market together supply 1,000 units of the product at $P = \$6$ and break even. Consumers pay a total of $EJON = \$6,000$ for 1,000 units of the product. They would have been willing to pay $EJOG = \$11,000$ (the total area under the D curve up to point E) if the product were sold 1 unit at a time and if the seller sold each unit at the highest price possible. The difference between what consumers would have been willing to pay for 1,000 units of the product (that is, $EJOG = \$11,000$) and what they actually pay (that is, $EJON = \$6,000$) is called **consumers' surplus.** The consumers' surplus in this case is $ENG = \$5,000$.

Suppose that now the market were suddenly monopolized and the monopolist faced the same demand and cost conditions as the perfectly competitive firms. The best level of output of the monopolist is now 500 units (given by point E' at which $MR = LMC$). The monopolist would charge $P = \$11$ (point H on the D curve) and earn profits of $HE' = \$5$ per unit and $HE'NT = \$2,500$ in total. Only $HTG = \$1,250$ of the original consumers' surplus of $ENG = \$5,000$ would remain to consumers. $HE'NT = \$2,500$ would be transferred to the monopolist in the form of profits, and $EE'H = \$1,250$ represents the true or **deadweight loss** from monopoly. The transfer of some of the consumers' surplus to the profits of the monopolist ($HE'NT$) does not necessarily represent a loss to society (for example, the monopolist could use the profits for research and development). There is no disagreement, however, that the deadweight loss ($EE'H$) is a true loss to society because consumers are willing to pay $\$11$ for the last unit produced under monopoly (point H on the D curve), but the cost of producing that unit is only $\$6$ (point E' on the LMC curve). The monopolist restricts output and charges too high a price. Some resources will be transferred to the production of other products which are valued less by society, and so triangle $EE'H$ represents the loss of efficiency in the use of society's resources resulting from the monopolization of the market.

8-5   MONOPOLISTIC COMPETITION

In this section we discuss in detail the meaning and importance of monopolistic competition, show how the equilibrium price and quantity are determined in the short run and in the long run, and examine product variation and selling expenses.

Meaning and Importance of Monopolistic Competition

In Section 8-1 we defined *monopolistic competition* as the form of market organization in which there are many sellers of a heterogeneous or differentiated product, and entry into and exit from the industry are rather easy in the long run. **Differentiated products** are those that are similar but not identical and satisfy the same basic need. Examples are the numerous brands of breakfast cereals, toothpaste, cigarettes, detergents, and cold medicines. The differentiation may be real (for example, the various breakfast cereals may have greatly different nutritional and sugar contents) or imaginary (for example, all brands of aspirin contain the same basic ingredients). Product differentiation may also be based on a more convenient location or more courteous service.

As the name implies, monopolistic competition is a blend of competition and monopoly. The competitive element results from the fact that in a monopolistically competitive market (as in a perfectly competitive market), there are many sellers of the differentiated product, each too small to affect others. The monopoly element arises from product differentiation (i.e., from the fact that the product sold by each seller is somewhat different from the product sold by any other seller). The resulting monopoly power is severely limited, however, by the availability of many close substitutes. Thus, if the seller of a particular brand of aspirin increased its price even moderately, it would stand to lose a great deal of its sales.

Monopolistic competition is most common in the retail and service sectors of our economy. Clothing, cotton textiles, and food processing are the industries that come close to monopolistic competition at the national level. At the local level, the best examples of monopolistic competition are fast-food outlets, shoe stores, gasoline stations, beauty salons, drugstores, video rental stores, and pizza parlors, all located in close proximity to one another. Firms in each of these businesses have some monopoly power over their competitors based on the uniqueness of their product, better location, better service, greater range of product varieties, and slightly lower prices, but their market power is severely limited by the availability of many close substitutes (see Case Study 8-7).

Since each firm sells a somewhat different product under monopolistic competition, we cannot derive the market demand curve and the market supply curve of the product as we did under perfect competition, and we do not have a single equilibrium price for the differentiated products but a cluster of prices. Our analysis must, therefore, necessarily be confined to that of the "typical" or "representative" firm. The graphical analysis will also

---

CASE STUDY 8-7
The Monopolistically Competitive
Restaurant Market

The restaurant market in any city has all the characteristics of monopolistic competition. There are usually thousands of restaurants in any large city, catering to all types of foods, tastes, incomes, and sectors. Some restaurants are luxurious and expensive, while others are simple and inexpensive. Some restaurants provide entertainment, while others do not. Some are located in the theater district and serve pre-theater dinner and after-theater supper, while others are located in residential areas and cater to the family business.

In one block in mid-Manhattan, there are 19 restaurants: 5 Italian, 4 French, 3 Chinese, and 1 each Brazilian, Indian, Japanese, Korean, Mexican, Pakistani, and Spanish. In a recent issue of *New York Magazine* were advertisements for more than 100 restaurants of all types, and these are only a small fraction of the restaurants in the city. Entry into the restaurant business is also relatively easy (witness the hundreds of restaurants that open each year and the about equal number that close in any large city during the same year). Since each restaurant offers a somewhat differentiated product, many advertise their existence, location, and menu, together with the usual claim (which no one really takes seriously) of superiority over all other restaurants in the same class.

Source: New York Magazine (March 2006).

be greatly simplified by assuming (with Edward Chamberlin, the originator of the monopolistically competitive model[7]) that all firms selling similar products face identical demand and cost curves. This is unrealistic because the production of differentiated products is likely to lead to somewhat different demand and cost curves. Making such an assumption, however, will greatly simplify the analysis.

As contrasted to a perfectly competitive firm, a monopolistically competitive firm can determine the characteristics of the products and the amount of selling expenses (such as advertising) to incur, as well as the price and quantity of the product. In the next section we assume first that the monopolistically competitive firm has already decided on the characteristics of the product and on the selling expenses to incur, so that we can concentrate on its pricing and output decisions in the short run and in the long run. Subsequently, we examine how the firm determines the optimal expenditures on product variation and selling effort.

Short-Run Price and Output Determination under Monopolistic Competition

Since a monopolistically competitive firm produces a differentiated product, the demand curve it faces is negatively sloped, but since there are many close substitutes for the product, the demand curve is highly price elastic. The price elasticity of demand is higher the smaller is the degree of product differentiation. As in the case of monopoly, since the demand curve facing a monopolistic competitor is negatively sloped and linear, the corresponding marginal revenue curve is below it, with the same price intercept and twice the absolute slope. As in the case of firms in the other forms of market structure examined, the best level of output of the monopolistically competitive firm in the short run is given by the one at which marginal revenue equals marginal cost, provided that price (determined on the demand curve) exceeds the average variable cost. This is shown in Figure 8-9.

Figure 8-9 shows that the best level of output of the typical or representative monopolistically competitive firm in the short run is 6 units and is given by point E, at which $MR = MC$. At $Q < 6$, $MR > MC$, and the total profits of the firm increase by expanding output. At $Q > 6$, $MC > MR$, and the total profits of the firm increase by *reducing* output. To sell the best level of output (that is, 6 units), the firm charges a price of $9 per unit (point A on the D curve). Since at $Q = 6$, $ATC = \$7$ (point F in the figure), the monopolistic competitor earns a profit of $AF = \$2$ per unit and $AFBC = \$12$ in total (the shaded area in the figure).[8] As in the case of a perfectly competitive firm and monopolist, the monopolistic competitor can earn profits, break even, or incur losses in the short run. If at the best level of output, $P > ATC$, the firm earns a profit; if $P = ATC$, the firm breaks even; and if $P < ATC$, the firm incurs losses, but it minimizes losses by continuing to produce as long as $P > AVC$. Finally,

---

[7] Edward H. Chamberlin, *The Theory of Monopolistic Competition* (Cambridge, Mass.: Harvard University Press, 1962).

[8] Note that Figure 8-9 is similar to Figure 8-6 for the monopolist. The only difference is that the monopolistic competitor's D curve is more price elastic than the monopolist's D curve.

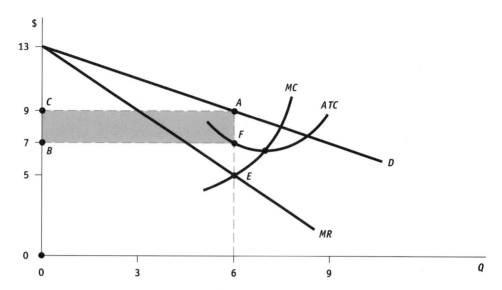

FIGURE 8-9   Short-Run Price and Output Determination under Monopolistic Competition   The best level of output of the monopolistic competitor in the short run is 6 units and is given by point *E*, where *MR = MC*. At *Q* = 6, *P* = $9 (point *A* on the *D* curve) and *ATC* = $7 (point *F*), so that the monopolistic competitor earns a profit of *AF* = $2 per unit and *AFBC* = $12 in total (the shaded area).

since the demand curve facing a monopolistic competitor is negatively sloped, $MR = MC < P$ at the best level of output so that (as in the case of monopoly) the rising portion of the MC curve above the AVC curve does not represent the short-run supply curve of the monopolistic competitor.

Long-Run Price and Output Determination under Monopolistic Competition

If firms in a monopolistically competitive market earn profits in the short run (or would earn profits in the long run by building optimal scales of plants to produce their best level of output), more firms will enter the market in the long run. This shifts the demand curve facing each monopolistic competitor to the left (as its market share decreases) until it becomes tangent to the firm's LAC curve. Thus, in the long run all monopolistically competitive firms break even and produce on the negatively sloped portion of their LAC curve (rather than at the lowest point, as in the case of perfect competition). This is shown in Figure 8-10.

In Figure 8-10, D' is the demand curve facing a typical or representative monopolistically competitive firm in the long run. Demand curve D' is lower and more price elastic than demand curve D that the firm faced in the short run. That is, as more firms enter the monopolistically competitive market in the long run (attracted by the profits that can be earned), each monopolistic competitor is left with a smaller share of the market and a more price elastic demand curve because of the greater range of competition (products) that becomes available in the long run. Note that demand curve D' is tangent to the LAC and $SATC'$ curves at point A', the output at which $MR' = LMC = SMC'$ (point E' in the figure). Thus, the monopolistic competitor sells 4 units of the product at the price of $6 per unit and

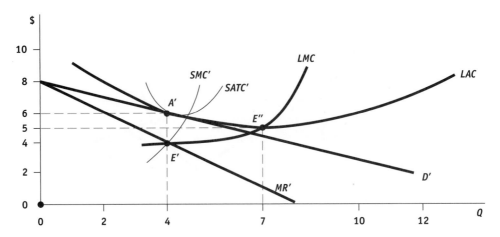

FIGURE 8-10   Long-Run Price and Output Determination under Monopolistic Competition   The best level of output of the monopolistically competitive firm in the long run is 4 units and is given by point E', at which $MR' = LMC = SMC'$ and $P = LAC = SATC' = \$6$ (point A'), so that the firm breaks even. This compares to the best level of output of 7 units given by point E'', at which $MR' = LMC$ and $P = LAC = \$5$ (point E'') under long-run perfectly competitive market equilibrium.

breaks even in the long run (as compared to $Q = 6$ at $P = \$9$ and profits of \$2 per unit and \$12 in total in the short run). At any other price the monopolistically competitive firm would incur losses in the long run, and with a different number of firms it would not break even.[9]

The fact that the monopolistically competitive firm produces to the left of the lowest point on its LAC curve when it is in long-run equilibrium means that the average cost of production and price of the product under monopolistic competition are higher than under perfect competition (\$6 at point A' as compared with \$5 at point E'', respectively, in Figure 8-10). This difference is not large because the demand curve faced by the monopolistic competitor is very elastic. In any event, the slightly higher LAC and P under monopolistic competition than under perfect competition can be regarded as the cost of having a variety of differentiated products appealing to different consumer tastes, rather than a single undifferentiated product. The fact that each monopolistic competitor produces to the left of the lowest point on its LAC curve means that each firm operates with **excess capacity** and that there are many more firms (i.e., there is some **overcrowding**) when the market is organized along monopolistically competitive rather than along perfectly competitive lines.

Product Variation and Selling Expenses under Monopolistic Competition

Under monopolistic competition a firm can increase its expenditures on product variation and selling effort in order to increase the demand for its product and make it more price inelastic. **Product variation** refers to changes in some of the characteristics of the product

---

[9] Mathematically, we could determine the best level of output (Q) and price (P) for a monopolistic competitor in long-run equilibrium by setting the price equal to LAC and solving for Q and P (see point A' in Figure 8-10 and Problem 14 with answer at the end of the book).

CASE STUDY 8-8
Advertisers Are Taking on Competitors by Name . . . and Being Sued

Since 1981 when the National Association of Broadcasters abolished its guidelines against making disparaging remarks against competitors' products, advertisers have taken their gloves off and have begun to praise the superior qualities of their products, not compared to "brand X" as before 1981 but by identifying competitors' products by name. The Federal Trade Commission welcomed the change because it anticipated that this would increase competition and lead to better-quality products at lower prices. Some of these hopes have in fact been realized. For example, the price of eyeglasses was found to be much higher in states that prohibited advertising by optometrists and opticians than in states that allowed such advertising, without any increase in the probability of having the wrong eyeglass prescription. Similarly, the price of an uncontested divorce dropped from $350 to $150 in Phoenix, Arizona, after the Supreme Court allowed advertising for legal services.

Although the actions are less sportsmanlike and may result in legal suits, advertisers have been willing to take on competitors by name because the technique seems effective. For example, sales soared when Burger King began to attack McDonald's by name, when AT&T attacked MCI pricing, and when Unilever named Proctor & Gamble's competitive products specifically. Sectors where comparative advertising are most common include food, retail, automobiles, airlines and, more recently, law. U.S. and European courts have generally allowed comparison advertising, unless dishonest or inaccurate. Thus, the courts threw out the suit and countersuit between Gillette and Wilkinson allowing each to claim superior blades, RBS Bank's claiming its credit cards superior to Barkleys', and Rayner claiming a lot cheaper tickets than British Airways'. A Belgian Court, however, ruled against Rayner's advertisement with a picture of the Brussels landmark the "Mannequin Pis," a statue of a boy urinating, with the line "Pissed off by Sabena's high fares?" as defamatory.

Source: "Advertisers Remove the Cover from Brand X," *U.S. News & World Report* (December 19, 1983), pp. 75–76; L. Benham, "The Effect of Advertising on the Price of Eyeglasses," *Journal of Law and Economics* (October 1973), pp. 337–352; "Lawyers Are Facing Surge in Competition as Courts Drop Curbs," *The Wall Street Journal* (October 18, 1978), p. 1; "Long-Distance Risks of AT&T MCI War," *The Wall Street Journal* (April 14, 1993), p. B9; "MCI WorldCom Unveils Rate Reduction on Long Distance to Five Cents a Minute," *The Wall Street Journal* (August 9, 1999), p. A2; "Marketeers Increasingly Dispute Health Claims of Rivals' Products," *The Wall Street Journal* (April 4, 2002), p. B1; and F. Barigozzi and M. Peitz at: http://papers.ssrn.com/sol3/papers.cfm?abstract_id=69958.

that a monopolistic competitor undertakes in order to make its product more appealing to consumers. For example, producers may reduce the sugar content of breakfast cereals and include a small surprise gift in each package. **Selling expenses** are all those expenses that the firm incurs to advertise the product, increase its sales force, provide better servicing for its product, etc. Product variation and selling expenses can increase the firm's sales and profits, but they also lead to additional costs and legal problems (see Case Study 8-8). A firm should spend more on product variation and selling effort as long as the *MR* from these efforts exceeds the *MC*, and until *MR = MC*. While spending more on product variation and selling effort can increase profits in the short run, monopolistically competitive firms will break even in the long run because of imitation by other firms and the entrance of new firms. This is shown in Figure 8-11.

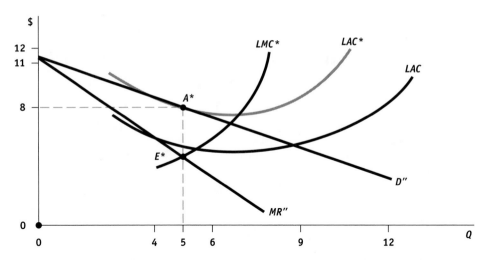

FIGURE 8-11   Long-Run Equilibrium of the Monopolistically competitive Firm with Selling Expenses   Curves *D″* and *MR″*, as well as *LAC** and *LMC**, are higher than in Figure 8-10 because of greater expenses on product variation and selling effort. While these efforts can increase the firm's profits in the short run, in the long run the firm breaks even. This is shown by point *A**, at which *Q* = 5 units and *P* = *LAC* = \$8, and *MR″* = *LMC** (point *E**).

In Figure 8-11, *D″* and *MR″* are demand and marginal revenue curves that are higher than *D′* and *MR′* in Figure 8-10 as a result of greater product variation and selling expenses. The *LAC* curve is that of Figure 8-10, while *LAC** and *LMC** are the long-run average and marginal cost curves resulting from greater product variation and selling expenses. Note that the vertical distance between *LAC** and *LAC* increases on the (realistic) assumption that to sell greater quantities of the product requires larger expenses per unit on product variation and selling effort. While these efforts can lead to larger short-run profits, however, our typical or representative firm will break even in the long run. This is shown by point *A** in Figure 8-11, at which *Q* = 5 and *P* = *LAC** = \$8, and *MR″* = *LMC** (point *E**). Note that at point *A** the firm charges a higher price and sells a greater quantity than at point *A′* in Figure 8-10, but the firm will nevertheless break even in the long run. If all firms selling similar products increase their expenses on product variation and selling effort, each firm may retain only its share of an expanding market in the long run.

SUMMARY

1. The process by which price and output are determined in the real world is strongly affected by the structure of the market. A market consists of all the actual and potential buyers and sellers of a particular product. Market structure refers to the competitive environment in which the buyers and sellers of the product operate. Four different types

of market structure are usually identified: perfect competition at one extreme, pure monopoly at the opposite extreme, and monopolistic competition and oligopoly in between.

2. The perfectly competitive firm is a price taker (i.e., it faces an infinitely elastic demand curve for the product). The best level of output for a perfectly

competitive firm in the short run is at the point where $P = MR = MC$, provided that $P > AVC$. The rising portion of the firm's MC curve above the AVC curve is the competitive firm's short-run supply curve of the product. If input prices are constant, the market supply curve is obtained by the horizontal summation of the competitive firms' supply curves. In the long run, the firm can construct the optimal scale of plant to produce the best level of output. If profits can be earned in the industry, more firms will enter the industry in the long run until all profits are eliminated and all firms produce at the lowest point on their LAC curve. If firms in the industry incur losses, some firms will leave the industry in the long run until the remaining firms break even.

3. Domestic firms in most industries face a great deal of competition from imports. International trade leads to a decline in the domestic price of the commodity, and to larger domestic consumption and lower domestic production of the commodity than in the absence of trade. The exchange rate refers to the dollar price of a unit of the foreign currency. In the absence of government intervention, the exchange rate of the dollar is determined by the intersection of the market demand and supply for the foreign currency. A depreciation of the dollar allows U.S. firms to increase foreign sales and profits but will also increase their cost of imported inputs.

4. Monopoly is the form of market organization in which a single firm sells a product for which there are no close substitutes. Thus, the monopolist faces the market's negatively sloped demand curve for the product and $MR < P$. As in the case of perfect competition, the best level of output for the monopolist in the short run is given by the point at which $MR = MC$, provided that $P > AVC$. In the long run, the monopolist will construct the optimal scale of plant to produce the best level of output (given by the point at which $P = LMC$). Because of blocked entry into the market, however, the monopolist can earn profits in the long run and is not likely to produce at the lowest point on the LAC curve. Perfect competition represents a better use of society's resources only when technology allows many firms to operate efficiently in the market.

5. Monopolistic competition is the form of market organization in which there are many sellers of a differentiated product, and entry into and exit from the industry are rather easy in the long run. Monopolistic competition is most common in the retail sector of the economy. Because of the availability of many close substitutes, the demand curve faced by a monopolistically competitive firm is highly elastic. The best level of output in the short run is where $MR = MC$, provided $P > AVC$. Monopolistically competitive firms should spend on product variation and selling expenses until $MR = MC$. If monopolistically competitive firms earn profits in the short run, more firms enter the market in the long run. This shifts the demand curve facing each firm to the left until all firms break even. In monopolistic competition, P and LAC are somewhat higher than under perfect competition and firms operate with excess capacity.

DISCUSSION QUESTIONS

1. A certain car manufacturer regards his business as highly competitive because he is keenly aware of his rivalry with the other car manufacturers. Like the other manufacturers, he undertakes vigorous advertising campaigns seeking to convince potential buyers of the superior quality and better style of his automobiles and reacts very quickly to claims of superiority by rivals. Is this the meaning of perfect competition from an economics point of view? Explain.

2. (*a*) Under what condition should a firm continue to produce in the short run if it incurs losses at the best level of output? (*b*) Are the normal returns on investment included as part of costs or as part of profits in managerial economics? Why?

3. (*a*) Is the market supply curve for a product more or less price elastic than the supply curve of one of the firms in the market? Why? (*b*) How is an increase in input prices shown on the firm's short-run marginal cost curve? Will this affect the competitive firm's

short-run supply curve? (*c*) Is the competitive firm's short-run supply curve affected by a change in the firm's fixed costs? Why?

4. (*a*) What is the best level of output of a perfectly competitive firm in the long run? (*b*) What is the optimal scale of plant of a perfectly competitive firm when the firm is in long-run equilibrium? (*c*) What is the best level of output and the optimal scale of plant when the competitive market and firm are in long-run equilibrium?

5. (*a*) If a competitive firm is in short-run equilibrium, must it also be in long-run equilibrium? (*b*) If a competitive firm is in long-run equilibrium, must it also be in short-run equilibrium?

6. (*a*) How can an import tariff be shown in Figure 8-4? (*b*) What is the size of a prohibitive tariff (i.e., one that would stop all trade) in Figure 8-4?

7. Assuming a two-currency world, the U.S. dollar and the euro, what does a depreciation of the dollar mean for the euro? Explain.

8. What happens to the dollar price that a U.S. (*a*) importer pays and (*b*) exporter receives if prices are agreed in euros and the dollar then appreciates by 10 percent with respect to the euro?

9. (*a*) What are the reasons for the existence of monopoly? (*b*) Which of these did Alcoa use to establish and retain a monopoly?

10. (*a*) Can a monopolist incur losses in the short run? Why? (*b*) Can a monopolist earning short-run profits increase those profits in the long run? Why? (*c*) Would a monopolist ever operate in the inelastic portion of the demand curve it faces? Why?

11. Can we derive the supply curve of the monopolist from its marginal cost curve in the same way that it was derived for a perfectly competitive firm? Why?

12. Under what conditions can we be sure that perfect competition leads to a more efficient use of society's resources than monopoly? How prevalent are these conditions in the real world?

13. (*a*) What are the choice-related variables for a firm under monopolistic competition? (*b*) What is nonprice competition? (*c*) Product variation? (*d*) Selling expenses?

14. Many firms under monopolistic competition set their advertising budgets at a fixed percentage of their anticipated sales. Does this mean that these firms behave in a nonmaximizing manner? Why?

15. Excess capacity is inversely related to the price elasticity of demand faced by a monopolistically competitive firm. True or false? Explain.

PROBLEMS

*1. The market demand and supply functions for pizza in Newtown were

$$QD = 10,000 - 1,000P$$

$$QS = -2,000 + 1,000P$$

(*a*) Determine algebraically the equilibrium price and quantity of pizza and (*b*) plot the market demand and supply curves, label the equilibrium point *E,* and draw the demand curve faced by a single pizza shop in this market on the assumption that the market is perfectly competitive. Show also the marginal revenue of the firm on the figure.

2. Starting with the market demand and supply functions in Problem 1, determine algebraically the new equilibrium price and quantity if (*a*) the demand function changes to $QD' = 12,000 - 1,000P$

or to $QD'' = 8,000 - 1,000P$, or (*b*) the market supply function changes to $QS^* = -4,000 + 1,000P$ or to $QS^{**} = 1,000P.$ (*c*) Draw a figure for parts (*a*) and (*b*) and label *E'* and *E''*, respectively, the equilibrium point resulting when the market demand changes to QD' or QD''; label *E** and *E***, respectively, the equilibrium point resulting when the market supply function changes to QS^* or QS^{**}; on the same figure, label *F* the equilibrium point resulting with QD' and QS^*, label *G* the equilibrium resulting with QD'' and QS^{**}, label *H* the equilibrium resulting with QD'' and QS^{**}, and label *J* the equilibrium resulting with QD'' and QS^*.

*3. Emily Rivera, a consultant hired by the Unisex Hair Styling Corporation, a beauty salon in New York City, has estimated the cost curves shown in Figure 8-12 for hair styling. Determine the

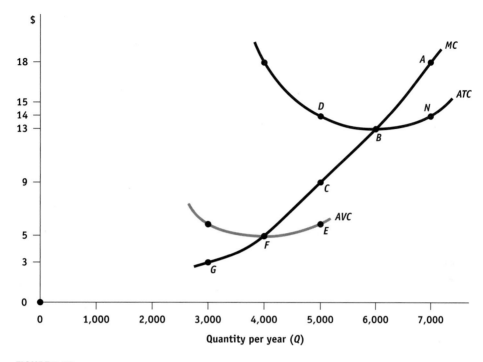

FIGURE 8-12

company's best level of output and its total profits if the price of hair styling is (*a*) $18, (*b*) $13, (*c*) $9, (*d*) $5, and (*e*) $3.

4. (*a*) Draw the supply curve for the perfectly competitive firm of Problem 3. Also draw the industry short-run supply curve on the assumptions that there are 100 identical firms in the industry and that input or factor prices remain unchanged as industry output expands (and thus more factors are used). (*b*) Explain the graph of part (*a*). (*c*) What quantity of the service will be supplied by each firm and the industry at the price of $9? At $18? At prices below $5?

*5. John Gilledeau, an economist in the research department of the Computer Parts Corporation, one of many producers of hard disks for personal computers, has estimated the short-run and long-run per-unit cost curves for the company, given in Figure 8-13. Suppose that the market is close to being perfectly competitive and that the company has the scale of plant indicated by SAC_1 and the short-run equilibrium price is $16. (*a*) What output will this firm produce and sell in the short run? Is

the firm making a profit or a loss at this level of output? (*b*) Discuss the adjusted prices for this firm in the long run, *if only this firm* and no other firm in the industry *adjusted to the long run.*

6. With regard to Problem 5, (*a*) explain the long-run adjustment process for the firm and the market in the figure. (*b*) What implicit assumption about factor prices was made in the solution to 5(*a*)? What would happen if input prices increase as more firms enter the market and demand more inputs?

7. From Figure 8-4, determine the effect of a 33 percent import tariff on commodity X.

8. The Halloran Specialty Food Company imports specialty foods from Europe and pays for imports in euros. The financial officer of the company notices that the dollar/euro exchange rate fluctuates continuously, sometimes even by several percentage points in the course of a few days. (*a*) What risk does the company face? (*b*) How can the company cover this risk?

9. Starting from Figure 8-6 showing the short-run price and output determination by the monopolist,

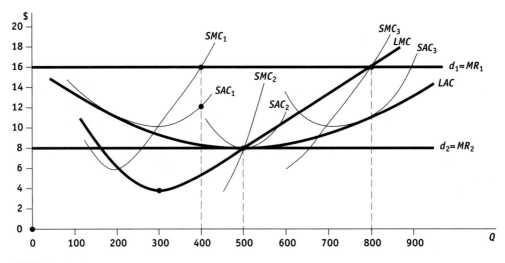

FIGURE 8-13

suppose that the average fixed costs of the monopolist increase by $5 and that its AVC is $6 less than the new ATC at the best level of output. Draw a figure showing the best level of output and price, the amount of profit or loss per unit and in total, and whether it pays for the monopolist to produce.

10. Starting from Figure 8-7 showing the monopolist in long-run equilibrium, draw a figure showing that (*a*) the monopolist would break even if costs rose sufficiently in the long run and (*b*) the change in demand that would result in the monopolist's producing at the lowest point on its LAC curve.

11. Most book publishers pay authors a percentage of the revenue from book sales. Explain the conflict that this creates between publishers and authors.

12. Unisex International Haircutters, Inc., faces the following demand function for haircuts per day:

$$QD = 240 - 20P$$

(*a*) Draw a figure showing the demand curve and the corresponding marginal revenue curve of the firm. On the same figure draw typical MC, ATC, and AVC curves showing that the best level of output is 80 haircuts per day, and that $ATC = \$10$ and $AVC = \$6$ at $Q = 80$. (*b*) How much profit or loss per haircut does the firm have? Does the firm remain in business in the short run? Why?

13. (*a*) Draw a figure similar to Figure 8-10 for the firm of Problem 1 showing the best level of output in the

long run based on the assumption that the demand curve facing the firm shifts in the long run but remains parallel to demand curve D in Problem 1. On the same figure show the best level of output and price of the product if the market had been organized along perfectly competitive lines. (Omit the short-run per-unit cost curves from the figure to avoid overcrowding the figure.) (*b*) What is the amount of excess capacity of the monopolistically competitive firm in the long run? How does this affect the number of firms in the market? (*c*) Can you conclude from your figure in part (*a*) that perfect competition is more efficient than monopolistic competition?

*14. In Akron, Ohio, the movie market is monopolistically competitive. The demand function for daily attendance and the long-run average cost function at the Plaza Movie House are, respectively,

$$P = 9 - 0.4Q$$

and

$$AC = 10 - 0.06Q + 0.0001Q^2$$

(*a*) Calculate the price that the Plaza Movie House will charge for admission to movies in the long run. What will be the number of patrons per day at that price? (*b*) What is the value of the LAC that the firm will incur? How much profit will the firm earn?

15. **Integrating Problem**

Suppose that in a city there are 100 identical self-service gasoline stations selling the same type of gasoline. The total daily market demand function for gasoline in the market is $QD = 60,000 - 25,000P$, where P is expressed in dollars per gallon. The daily market supply curve is $QS = 25,000P$ for $P > \$0.60$. (*a*) Determine algebraically the equilibrium price and quantity of gasoline. (*b*) Draw a figure showing the market supply curve and the market demand curve for gasoline, and the demand curve and the supply curve of one firm in the market on the assumption that the market is nearly perfectly competitive. (*c*) Explain why your figure of the market and the firm in part (*b*) is consistent. (*d*) Suppose that now the market is monopolized (e.g., a cartel is formed that determines the price and output as a monopolist would and allocates production equally to each member). Draw a figure showing the monopolist's equilibrium output and price. (*e*) How many gasoline stations would the monopolist operate? (*f*) Can we say that the monopoly leads to a less efficient use of resources than perfect competition? What is the amount of the deadweight loss, if any?

APPENDIX TO CHAPTER 8: PROFIT MAXIMIZATION WITH CALCULUS

A firm usually wants to produce the output that maximizes its total profits. Total profits (π) are equal to total revenue (TR) minus total costs (TC). That is,

$$\pi = TR - TC \qquad [8\text{-}4]$$

where π, TR, and TC are all functions of output (Q).

Taking the first derivative of π with respect to Q and setting it equal to zero gives

$$\frac{d\pi}{dQ} = \frac{d(TR)}{dQ} - \frac{d(TC)}{dQ} = 0 \qquad [8\text{-}5]$$

so that

$$\frac{d(TR)}{dQ} = \frac{d(TC)}{dQ} \qquad [8\text{-}6]$$

Equation 8-6 indicates that in order to maximize profits, a firm must produce where marginal revenue (*MR*) equals marginal cost (*MC*). Since for a perfectly competitive firm P is constant and $TR = (P)(Q)$ so that

$$\frac{d(TR)}{dQ} = MR = P$$

the first-order condition for profit maximization for a perfectly competitive firm becomes $P = MR = MC$.

Equation 8-6 is only the first-order condition for maximization (and minimization). The second-order condition for profit maximization requires that the second derivative of π with respect to Q be negative. That is,

$$\frac{d^2\pi}{dQ^2} = \frac{d^2(TR)}{dQ^2} - \frac{d^2(TC)}{dQ^2} < 0 \qquad [8\text{-}7]$$

so that

$$\frac{d^2(TR)}{dQ^2} < \frac{d^2(TC)}{dQ^2} \qquad\qquad [8\text{-}8]$$

According to Equation 8-8, the algebraic value of the slope of the *MC* function must be greater than the algebraic value of the *MR* function. Under perfect competition, *MR* is constant (i.e., the *MR* curve of the firm is horizontal) so that Equation 8-8 requires that the *MC* curve be rising at the point where *MR* = *MC* for the firm to maximize its total profits (or to minimize its total losses). With imperfect competition, the firm's demand curve (and therefore its *MR* curve) is negatively sloped, so that Equation 8-8 requires that the *MC* curve be either rising or falling less rapidly than the *MR* curve for the second-order condition for maximization to be satisfied.

For example, if the demand function faced by a firm is

$$Q = 90 - 2P$$

or

$$P = 45 - 0.5Q$$

so that

$$TR = PQ = (45 - 0.5Q)Q = 45Q - 0.5Q^2$$

and if

$$TC = Q^3 - 8Q^2 + 57Q + 2$$

the total profit function is then

$$\begin{aligned}
\pi = TR - TC \\
= (45Q - 0.5Q^2) - (Q^3 - 8Q + 57Q + 2) \\
= 45Q - 0.5Q^2 - Q^3 + 8Q^2 - 57Q - 2
\end{aligned}$$

To determine the level of output at which the firm maximizes π, we proceed as follows:

$$\begin{aligned}
\frac{d\pi}{dQ} = -3Q^2 + 15Q - 12 = 0 \\
= (-3Q + 3)(Q - 4) = 0
\end{aligned}$$

therefore,

$$Q = 1 \qquad \text{and} \qquad Q = 4$$

$$\frac{d^2\pi}{dQ^2} = -6Q + 15$$

At $Q = 1$,

$$\frac{d^2\pi}{dQ^2} = -6(1) + 15 = 9$$

and π is minimum. At $Q = 4$,

$$\frac{d^2\pi}{dQ^2} = -6(4) + 15 = -9$$

and π is maximum. Therefore, π is maximized at $Q = 4$, and from the original π function we can determine that

$$\pi = -(4)^3 + 7.5(4)^2 - 12(4) - 2$$
$$= -64 + 120 - 48 - 2$$
$$= \$6$$

APPENDIX PROBLEMS

1. Determine the best level of output for the above example by the *MR* and *MC* approach.

2. Determine the best level of output for a perfectly competitive firm that sells its product at $P = \$4$ and faces $TC = 0.04Q^3 - 0.9Q^2 + 10Q + 5$. Will the firm produce this level of output? Why?

SUPPLEMENTARY READINGS

For a more extensive theoretical analysis of perfect competition, monopoly, and monopolistic competition, see:

Salvatore, Dominick, *Microeconomics: Theory and Applications*, 3rd ed. (New York: Oxford University Press, 2003), chaps. 8 and 9 and secs. 10.1 and 10.2.

Salvatore, Dominick, *Theory and Problems of Microeconomic Theory*, 4th ed., Schaum Outline Series (New York: McGraw-Hill, 2006), chaps. 8–10 and secs. 11.1 to 11.3.

Other readings on markets and industrial structure are:

Adams, W., and J. Brock, eds., *The Structure of American Industry* (Upper Saddle River, N.J.: Prentice-Hall, 2001).

Carlton, D. W., and J. M. Perloff, *Modern Industrial Organization* (Reading, Mass.: Addison-Wesley, 2000).

Fama, Eugene F., "Market Efficiency, Long-Term Returns, and Behavioral Finance," *Journal of Financial Economics* (September 1998), pp. 283–306.

Jim, Jim F., "Monopolistic Competition and Bounded Rationality," *Journal of Economic Organization and Behavior* (June 2001), pp. 175–184.

Martin, Stephen, "Market Power or Efficiency?" *Review of Economics and Statistics* (February 1986), pp. 84–95.

Porter, Michael, "The Competitive Advantage of Nations," *Harvard Business Review* (March–April 1990), pp. 73–93.

For the economic effects of product variation and advertising, see:

Comanor, William S., and Thomas A. Wilson, "The Effect of Advertising on Competition: A Survey," *Journal of Economic Literature* (June 1979), pp. 453–476.

Lancaster, Kelvin, "Competition and Product Variety," *Journal of Business* (July 1980), pp. S79–S105.

Silk, A. J., L. R. Klein, and E. R. Berndt, "The Emerging Position of the Internet as an Advertising Medium," *Netnomics,* no. 3 (2001), pp. 129–148.

Stageman, Mark, "Advertising in Competitive Markets," *American Economic Review* (March 1991), pp. 210–233.

Stansell, R. S., C. P. Harper, and R. P. Wilder, "The Effects of Advertising Expenditures: Evidence from an Analysis of Major Advertisers," *Review of Business and Economic Research* (Fall 1984), pp. 86–95.

For the effect of international competition and imports on domestic demand, supply, and prices, see:

Salvatore, Dominick, *International Economics*, 8th ed. (Hoboken, N.J.: Wiley, 2004), sec. 4.2.

A detailed discussion of the foreign exchange market and exchange rate determination is found in:

Salvatore, Dominick, *International Economics*, 8th ed. (Hoboken, N.J.: Wiley, 2004), chap. 14.

Salvatore, Dominick, "The Euro-Dollar Exchange Rate Defies Prediction," *Journal of Policy Modeling* (June 2005), pp. 455–464.

For comparative advertising, see:

Barigozzi, Francesca, and Martin Peitz, "Comparative Advertising and Competition Policy," http:// papers. ssrn.com/sol3/papers.cfm?abstract_id = 699583.

 ## INTERNET SITE ADDRESSES

For information on the New York Stock Exchange, see:

http://www.nyse.com

Information on Alcoa and aluminum prices is found in:

http://www.alcoa.com

http://www.metals.about.com/cs/utilities/l/ blprices.htm

http://www.minerals.usgs.gov.minerals/pubs/ commodity/aluminum/050798.pdf

http://www.Ime.co.uk/aluminum.asp

http://www.Tocom.or.jp/souba/aluminum

http://www.tms.org/pubs/journals/JOM/0409/ Hunt-0409.html

For information on the taxi market and the price of a medallion in New York, Boston, and Chicago, see:

http://www.schallerconsult.com/taxi/fb/fb4.htm

http://www.nyc.gov/html/tlc/medallion/downloads/ pdf/brochure.pdf

For a discussion of the economic effects of an import tariff, see:

http://www.economics.about.com/cs/taxpolicy/a/ tariffs_2.htm

Data on exchange rates between any two currencies can be obtained by clicking on "currencies" and "currency calculator" on the Bloomberg Web site at:

http://www.bloomberg.com

The monthly trade-weighted exchange rate of the dollar can be obtained from the Federal Reserve Bank of St. Louis Web site at:

http://www.stls.frb.org/fred/data/exchange/ twexmmth

For comparative advertising, see:

http://www.inta.org/policy/res_compad.html

http://www.law.com/jsp/article.jsp?id =1115111119049

http://www.papers.ssrn.com/sol3/papers.cfm? abstract_id=699583

CHAPTER 9 Oligopoly and Firm Architecture

CHAPTER OUTLINE

KEY TERMS (in the order of their appearance)

Oligopoly	Cournot model	Sales maximization model
Duopoly	Bertrand model	Firm architecture
Pure oligopoly	Kinked demand curve model	Creative company
Differentiated oligopoly	Collusion	Virtual corporation
Nonprice competition	Market-sharing cartel	Relationships enterprises
Limit pricing	Centralized cartel	Reaction function
Concentration ratios	Price leadership	Cournot equilibrium
Herfindahl index (*H*)	Barometric firm	Nash equilibrium
Theory of contestable markets	Porter's strategic framework	

In this chapter we examine oligopoly and firm architecture. We begin by discussing the meaning and sources of oligopoly, examining various models of oligopoly pricing and output, and evaluating the profitability and efficiency implications of oligopoly. We will see that there is no general theory of oligopoly but a number of models of various degrees of realism. We then go on to discuss the sales maximization model and the growth of global oligopolists. Subsequently, we examine the architecture of the ideal firm, the evolution of the creative company, as well as the virtual corporation and relationship enterprises.

9-1 OLIGOPOLY AND MARKET CONCENTRATION

In this section we examine the meaning and sources of oligopoly, discuss measures of market concentration, and present the theory of contestable markets.

Oligopoly: Meaning and Sources

In Section 8-1 we defined **oligopoly** as the form of market organization in which there are few sellers of a homogeneous or differentiated product. If there are only two sellers, we have a **duopoly.** If the product is homogeneous, we have a **pure oligopoly.** If the product is differentiated, we have a **differentiated oligopoly.** Although entry into an oligopolistic industry is possible, it is not easy (as evidenced by the fact that there are only a few firms in the industry).

Oligopoly is the most prevalent form of market organization in the manufacturing sector of industrial nations, including the United States. Some of the oligopolistic industries in the United States are automobiles, primary aluminum, steel, electrical equipment, glass, breakfast cereals, cigarettes, and soaps and detergents. Some of these products (such as steel and aluminum) are homogeneous, while others (such as automobiles, cigarettes, breakfast cereals, and soaps and detergents) are differentiated. Oligopoly exists also when transportation costs limit the market area. For example, even though there are many cement producers in the United States, competition is limited to the few local producers in a particular area.

Since there are only a few firms selling a homogeneous or differentiated product in oligopolistic markets, the action of each firm affects the other firms in the industry and vice versa. For example, when General Motors introduced price rebates in the sale of its automobiles, Ford immediately followed with price rebates of its own. Furthermore, since price competition can lead to ruinous price wars, oligopolists usually prefer to compete on the basis of product differentiation, advertising, and service. These are referred to as **nonprice competition.** Yet, even here, if GM mounts a major advertising campaign, Ford is likely to soon respond in kind. When Pepsi mounted a major advertising campaign in the early 1980s, Coca-Cola responded with a large advertising campaign of its own.

From what has been said, it is clear that the distinguishing characteristic of oligopoly is the interdependence or rivalry among firms in the industry. This is the natural result of fewness. Since an oligopolist knows that its own actions will have a significant impact on the other oligopolists in the industry, each oligopolist must consider the possible reaction of competitors in deciding its pricing policies, the degree of product differentiation to introduce, the level of advertising to undertake, the amount of service to provide, and so on. Since competitors can react in many ways (depending on the nature of the industry, the type of product, etc.), we do not have a single oligopoly model but many—each based on the particular behavioral response of competitors to the actions of the first. Because of this interdependence, managerial decision making is much more complex under oligopoly than under other forms of market structure. In this chapter we present some of the most important oligopoly models. We must keep in mind, however, that each model is, at best, incomplete and more or less unrealistic.

The sources of oligopoly are generally the same as for monopoly. That is, (1) economies of scale may operate over a sufficiently large range of outputs as to leave only a few firms supplying the entire market; (2) huge capital investments and specialized inputs are usually required to enter an oligopolistic industry (say, automobiles, aluminum, steel, and similar industries), and this acts as an important natural barrier to entry; (3) a few firms may own a patent for the exclusive right to produce a commodity or to use a particular production process; (4) established firms may have a loyal following of customers based on product quality and service (brands) that new firms would find very difficult to match (see Case Study 9-1); (5) a few firms may own or control the entire supply of a raw material required in the production of the product; and (6) the government may give a franchise to only a few firms to operate in the market. These are not only the sources of oligopoly but they also represent the barriers to other firms entering the market in the long run. If entry were not so restricted, the industry could not remain oligopolistic in the long run. A further barrier to entry is provided by **limit pricing,** whereby existing firms charge a price low enough to discourage entry into the industry. By doing so, they voluntarily sacrifice short-run profits in order to maximize long-run profits.

Concentration Ratios, the Herfindahl Index, and Contestable Markets

The degree by which an industry is dominated by a few large firms is measured by **concentration ratios.** These give the percentage of total industry sales of the 4, 8, or 12 largest firms in the industry (see Case Study 9-2). An industry in which the four-firm concentration ratio is close to 100 is clearly oligopolistic, and industries in which this ratio is higher

CASE STUDY 9-1
Brands: Thrive or Die

Brands seem to either thrive or die under the pressure of private labels in the highly competitive world of today. Private-label consumer products have become more and more like brand-name products in quality, looks, and taste, but cost from 15 percent to 40 percent less. During the 1980s, private labels took markets away from established brands and caused profit margins to fall, but they seemed to have plateaued at about 14 percent of U.S. supermarket sales volume during the 1990s (the percentages in 2005 were 22 in Europe, 16 in North America, and less than 5 elsewhere), as brand names fought back with product improvements, increased advertising, lower prices, and the introduction of their own private-label products.

For example, Hellmann's reduced the fat content of its mayonnaise, Heinz introduced a 20-ounce squeezable and recyclable plastic ketchup bottle, and Procter & Gamble introduced a diaper that is 50 percent thinner. Most makers of brand-name products have also increased their advertising expenditures to shore up brand loyalty. Makers of brand-name products have also reduced prices. For example, Philip Morris lowered the price of its premium Marlboro cigarettes by 20 percent in April 1993 to better compete with private-label cigarettes. Procter & Gamble cut prices of Pampers diapers several times over the years to keep generics at bay. Finally, many brand-name product manufacturers such as Heinz, Campbell Soup, Nestlé, 3M, and every major U.S. cigarette maker are also churning out their own private-label versions of their brand-name products (even though margins are lower) in order to fight loss of market share, on the theory that "if you can't beat them, join

them." But they have to be careful not to slight their prestigious brands or price their private labels too low, which would further erode their profit margins. Private labels can help a manufacturer preserve market share when it decides to increase the price of its brand-name product or take market share from the market leader in a category. They are likely to make the most sense when entry barriers are low, when substantial economies of scale exist, and when the price elasticity of demand for the brand-name product is low.

Clearly brand names do serve useful purposes for consumers and sellers. For consumers, they provide assurance of quality, reduce search costs, and confer status and prestige. For producers, brand names permit premium pricing and strengthen consumer loyalty. They also facilitate repeat purchases, promotional efforts, the introduction of new products, and market segmentation. The brands that have fared best are those based on clear higher quality and superior technology, and those that have not gouged consumers on prices in the past. The world's 10 most valuable brands in 2005 were: Coca-Cola, Microsoft, IBM, GE, Intel, Nokia, Disney, McDonald's, Toyota, and Marlboro. Note that 8 of the top 10 brands are American (U.S.) and five of the top six are in technology (in the past they were mostly in food products). In the future, only the number 1 and number 2 brands plus a private label are likely to survive in any given market. There is simply no room on most store shelves for more brands. It's thrive or die! Makers of the number 3, 4, or 5 brands will either have to become the number 1 or number 2 brand, move to a private label, or leave the market.

Source: D. Dunne and C. Narasimhan, "The New Appeal of Private Labels," *Harvard Business Review* (May–June 1999), pp. 41–52; "Retailers Pack New Punch in Battle with the Brands," *Financial Times* (January 16, 2004), p. 22; "How Brands Compete," *Harvard Business Review* (September 2004), pp. 68–75; "Achieving the Ideal Brand Portfolio," *MIT Sloan Management Review* (Winter 2005), pp. 85–90; "The Rise of the Superbrands," *The Economist* (February 5, 2005), pp. 63–65; and "The 100 Top Brands," *Business Week* (August 1, 2005), pp. 90–94.

CASE STUDY 9-2
Industrial Concentration in the United States

Table 9-1 gives the four-firm and the eight-firm concentration ratios for various industries in the United States from the 2002 Census of Manufacturers (the latest available).

There are several reasons, however, for using these concentration ratios cautiously. First, in industries where imports are significant, concentration ratios might greatly overestimate the relative importance of the largest firms in the industry. For example, since automobile imports represent about 29 percent of the U.S. auto sales, the real four-firm concentration ratio in the automobile industry (which includes Honda's U.S. output as the fourth largest U.S. producer) is not 81 percent (as indicated in the table) but 58 percent (i.e., 81 percent times 0.71). Second, concentration ratios refer to the nation as a whole, even though the relevant market might be local. For example, the four-firm concentration ratio for the cement industry is 39 percent, but because of very high transportation costs, only two or three firms may actually compete in many local markets. Third, how broadly or narrowly a product is defined is also very important. For example, the concentration ratio in the office machines industry as a whole is smaller than in the personal computer segment of the market. Fourth, and as postulated by the theory of contestable markets, concentration ratios do not give any indication of potential entrants into the market and of the degree of actual and potential competition in the industry. In short, concentration ratios provide only one dimension of the degree of competition in the market, and although useful, they must be used with great caution.

TABLE 9-1 Concentration Ratios in the United States, 2002		
Industry	**Four-Firm Ratio**	**Eight-Firm Ratio**
Cigarettes	95	99
Breweries	91	94
Electric lamp bulbs and parts	89	94
Aircraft	81	94
Motor vehicles	81	91
Breakfast cereals	78	91
Office machines	75	86
Tires	73	87
Soap and detergents	61	72
Soft drinks	52	64
Computers	50	65
Men's clothing	49	62
Iron and steel mills	44	58
Cement	39	60
Petroleum refining	41	64
Book printing	38	54
Pharmaceuticals and medicines	34	49
Stationary	29	45
Canned fruits and vegetables	24	38
Women's dresses	22	32

Source: U.S. Bureau of Census, 2002 Census of Manufacturers, *Concentration Ratios in Manufacturing* (Washington, D.C.: Government Printing Office, May 2006), Table 2, pp. 2–65.

than 50 or 60 percent are also likely to be oligopolistic. The four-firm concentration ratio for most manufacturing industries in the United States is between 20 and 80 percent. As discussed in Case Study 9-2, however, concentration ratios must be used and interpreted with great caution since they may greatly overestimate the market power of the largest firms in an industry.

Another method of estimating the degree of concentration in an industry is the **Herfindahl index (H).** This is given by the sum of the squared values of the market shares of all the firms in the industry. The higher the Herfindahl index, the greater is the degree of concentration in the industry. For example, if there is only 1 firm in the industry, so that its market share is 100 percent, $H = 100^2 = 10,000$. If there are 2 firms in an industry, one with a 90 percent share of the market and the other with a 10 percent share, $H = 90^2 + 10^2 = 8,200$. If each firm had a 50 percent share of the market, $H = 50^2 + 50^2 = 5,000$. With four equal-sized firms in the industry, $H = 2,500$. With 100 equal-sized firms in the (perfectly competitive) industry, $H = 100$. This points to the advantage of the Herfindahl index over the concentration ratios discussed before. Specifically, the Herfindahl index uses information on all the firms in the industry—not just the market share by the largest 4, 8, or 12 firms in the market. Furthermore, by squaring the market share of each firm, the Herfindahl index appropriately gives a much larger weight to larger than to smaller firms in the industry. The Herfindahl index has become of great practical importance since 1982, when the Justice Department announced new guidelines for evaluating proposed mergers based on this index (see Section 12-5).

In fact, according to the **theory of contestable markets** developed during the 1980s, even if an industry has a single firm (monopoly) or only a few firms (oligopoly), it would still operate as if it were perfectly competitive if entry is "absolutely free" (i.e., if other firms can enter the industry and face exactly the same costs as existing firms) and if exit is "entirely costless" (i.e., if there are no sunk costs so that the firm can exit the industry without facing any loss of capital).[1] An example of this might be an airline that establishes a service between two cities already served by other airlines, if the new entrant faces the same costs as existing airlines and could subsequently leave the market by simply reassigning its planes to other routes without incurring any loss of capital. When entry is absolutely free and exit is entirely costless, the market is contestable. Firms will then operate as if they were perfectly competitive and sell at a price which only covers their average costs (so that they earn zero economic profit) even if there is only one firm or a few of them in the market.

9-2   OLIGOPOLY MODELS

In this section we present some of the most important oligopoly models: the Cournot model, the kinked demand curve model, cartel arrangements, and the price leadership model. As we will see, each of these models focuses on one particular aspect of oligopoly but overlooks others. As a result, they have limited applicability and are more or less unrealistic.

---

[1] See William J. Baumol, "Contestable Markets: An Uprising in the Theory of Industrial Structure," *American Economic Review* (March 1982), pp. 1–5.

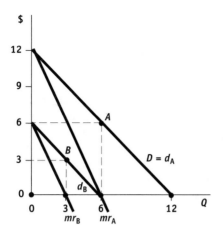
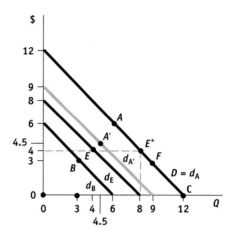

FIGURE 9-1   The Cournot Model   In the left panel, D is the market demand curve for spring water. The marginal cost of production is assumed to be zero. When only firm A is in the market, $D = d_A$ and the firm maximizes profits by selling $Q = 6$ at $P = \$6$ (point A, given by $mr_A = MC = 0$). When firm B enters the market, it will face d_B (given by shifting market demand curve D to the left by the 6 units sold by A). Firm B maximizes profits by selling $Q = 3$ at $P = \$3$ (point B, the midpoint, of d_B at which $mr_B = MC = 0$). Duopolist A now faces $d_{A'}$ (given by $D - 3$ in the right panel) and maximizes profits by selling $Q = 4.5$ at $P = \$4.50$ (point A'). The process continues until each duopolist is at point E on d_E and sells $Q = 4$ at $P = \$4$.

The Cournot Model

The French economist Augustin Cournot introduced the first formal oligopoly model (that bears his name) more than 160 years ago.[2] The Cournot model is useful in highlighting the interdependence that exists among oligopolistic firms.

For simplicity, Cournot assumed that there were only two firms (duopoly) selling identical spring water. Consumers came to the springs with their own containers, so that the marginal cost of production was zero for the two firms. With these assumptions, the analysis is greatly simplified without losing the essence of the model.[3] Moreover, it sets the stage for more realistic, more complicated models.

The basic behavioral assumption made in the **Cournot model** is that each firm, while trying to maximize profits, assumes that the other duopolist holds its *output* constant at the existing level. The result is a cycle of moves and countermoves by the duopolists until each sells one-third of the total industry output (if the industry were organized along perfectly competitive lines). This is shown in Figure 9-1.

In the left panel of Figure 9-1, D is the market demand curve for spring water. Initially, firm A is the only firm in the market, and thus, it faces the total market demand curve. That is, $D = d_A$. The marginal revenue curve of firm A is then mr_A (see the figure). Since the marginal cost is zero, the MC curve coincides with the horizontal axis. Under these

---

[2] A. Cournot, *Recherches sur les principes mathématiques de la théorie de richesse* (Paris: 1838). English translation by N. Bacon, *Researches into the Mathematical Principles of the Theory of Wealth* (New York: Macmillan, 1897). A more advanced and mathematical treatment of the Cournot model is provided in the appendix to this chapter.

[3] The model, however, can be extended to deal with more than two firms and nonzero marginal costs.

circumstances, firm A maximizes total profits where $mr_A = MC = 0$. Firm A sells 6 units of spring water at $P = \$6$ so that its total revenue (TR) is \$36 (point A in the left panel). This is the monopoly solution. Note that point A is the midpoint of demand curve $D = d_A$, at which price elasticity is 1 and TR is maximum (see Section 3-2). With total costs equal to zero, total profits equal $TR = \$36$.

Next, assume that firm B enters the market and believes that firm A will continue to sell 6 units. The demand curve that firm B faces is then d_B in the left panel, which is obtained by subtracting from market demand curve D the 6 units sold by firm A (i.e., shifting D 6 units to the left). The marginal revenue curve of firm B is then mr_B. Firm B maximizes total profits where $mr_B = MC = 0$. Therefore, firm B sells 3 units at $P = \$3$ (point B, the midpoint of d_B). This is also shown in the right panel of Figure 9-1. Assuming that firm B continues to sell three units, firm A reacts and faces d_A in the right panel of Figure 9-1 (obtained by subtracting from market demand curve D the three units supplied by firm B). Firm A will then maximize profits by selling 4.5 units (point A', at the midpoint of d_A in the right panel). Firm B now reacts once again and maximizes profits on its new demand curve, which is obtained by shifting market demand curve D to the left by the 4.5 units supplied by firm A (not shown in the right panel of Figure 9-1).

The process continues until each duopolist faces demand curve d_E and maximizes profits by selling 4 units at $P = \$4$ (point E in the right panel of Figure 9-1).[4] This is equilibrium, because whichever firm faces demand curve d_E and reaches point E first, the other will also face d_E (obtained by subtracting the 4 units sold by the first duopolist from market demand curve D) and also maximizes profits at point E. With each duopolist selling 4 units, a combined total of 8 units will be sold in the market at $P = \$4$ (point E^* on D in the right panel of Figure 9-1). If the market had been organized along perfectly competitive lines, sales would have been 12 units, given by point C, where market demand curve D intercepts the horizontal axis. The reason for this is that since we have assumed costs to be zero, price will also have to be zero for each competitive firm to break even, as required, when the perfectly competitive industry is in long-run equilibrium.

Thus, the duopolists supply one-third, or 4 units each (and two-thirds or 8 units together), of the total perfectly competitive market quantity of 12 units. Note that the Cournot duopoly outcome of $P = \$4$ and $Q = 8$ lies between the monopoly equilibrium of $P = \$6$ and $Q = 6$ and the competitive equilibrium of $P = \$0$ and $Q = 12$. The final Cournot equilibrium reflects the interdependence between the duopolists, even though they (rather naively) do not recognize it.

In a more advanced treatment, we could show that with three oligopolists, each would supply one-fourth (i.e., 3 units) of the perfectly competitive market of 12 units and three-fourths (i.e., 9 units) in total. Note that when $Q = 9$, $P = \$3$ on market demand curve D (point F in the right panel of Figure 9-1). Thus, as the number of firms increases, the total combined output of all the firms together increases and price falls (compare equilibrium point A with only firm A in the market, with equilibrium point E^* with firms A and B, and equilibrium point F with three firms). Eventually, as more firms enter, the market will no

---

[4] How this equilibrium is reached is shown in the appendix to this chapter. All that is important at this point is to show that when each duopolist faces demand curve d_E and sells 4 units at $P = \$4$ (i.e, is at point E), each duopolist and the market as a whole are in equilibrium.

longer be oligopolistic. In the limit, with many firms, total output will approach 12 units and price will approach zero (the perfectly competitive solution—point *C* in the right panel of Figure 9-1).

The same result (i.e., zero profit) would occur even with only two firms (duopoly), if each firm assumed that the other kept its *price* rather than its quantity constant (as in the Cournot model). In that case, the first firm enters the market and maximizes its profits by producing 6 units at the price of $6. The second firm, assuming that the first will keep its price constant, will lower its price just a little and captures the entire market (because the product is homogeneous). The first firm will then react by lowering its price even more and recaptures the entire market. If the duopolists do not recognize their interdependence (as in the Cournot model), the process will continue until each firm sells 6 units at zero price and makes zero profits. This is the **Bertrand model**,[5] which is a forerunner of the price war models.

The Kinked Demand Curve Model

The **kinked demand curve model** was introduced by Paul Sweezy in 1939 in an attempt to explain the price rigidity that was often observed in many oligopolistic models.[6] Sweezy postulated that if an oligopolist raised its price, it would lose most of its customers because other firms in the industry would not follow by raising their prices. On the other hand, an oligopolist could not increase its share of the market by lowering its price because its competitors would quickly match price cuts. As a result, according to Sweezy, oligopolists face a demand curve that has a kink at the prevailing price and is highly elastic for price increases but much less elastic for price cuts. In this model, oligopolists recognize their interdependence but act without collusion in keeping their prices constant, even in the face of changed cost and demand conditions—preferring instead to compete on the basis of quality, advertising, service, and other forms of nonprice competition. The Sweezy model is shown in Figure 9-2.

In Figure 9-2, the demand curve facing the oligopolist is *D*—including points *ABC*—and has a kink at the prevailing price of $6 and quantity of 40 units (point *B*). Note that the *D* curve is much more elastic above the kink than below, on the assumption that competitors will not match price increases but will quickly match price cuts. The marginal revenue curve is *MR*, or *AGEHJ*; *AG* is the segment of the marginal revenue curve corresponding to the *AB* portion of the demand curve; *HJ* corresponds to the *BC* portion of the demand curve. The kink at point *B* on the demand curve causes the *BH* discontinuity in the marginal revenue curve. The best level of output of the oligopolist with marginal cost curve *MC* is 40 units and is given by point *E* at which the *MC* curve intersects the vertical portion of the *MR* curve. The oligopolist will then charge the price of $6 given by point *B* (at the kink on the demand curve). As in other forms of market organization, the firm under oligopoly can earn profits, break even, or incur losses in the short run, and it will continue to produce as long as $P > AVC$.[7]

---

[5] J. Bertrand, "Théorie Mathématique de la Richesse Sociale," *Journal de Savantes* (1983).

[6] P. Sweezy, "Demand under Conditions of Oligopoly," *Journal of Political Economy* (August 1939), pp. 568–573.

[7] For the mathematical presentation of the model shown in Figure 9-2, see the appendix to this chapter.

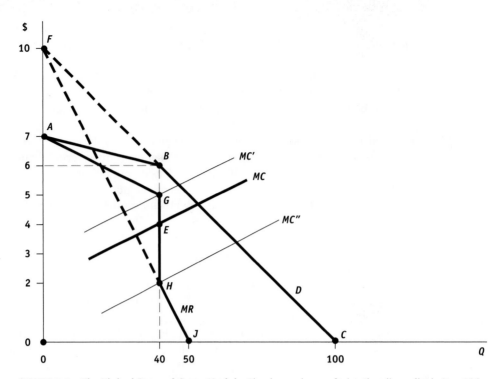

FIGURE 9-2   The Kinked Demand Curve Model   The demand curve facing the oligopolist is *D* or *ABC* and has a kink at the prevailing market price of $6 and quantity of 40 units (point *B*), on the assumption that competitors match price cuts but not price increases. The marginal revenue curve is *MR* or *AGEHJ*. The best level of output of the oligopolist is 40 units and is given by point *E* at which the *MC* curve intersects the discontinuous portion of the *MR* curve. At *Q* = 40, *P* = $6 (point *B* on the *D* curve). Any shift in the *MC* curve from *MC′* to *MC″* would leave price and output unchanged.

From Figure 9-2 we can also see that the oligopolist's marginal cost curve can rise or fall anywhere within the discontinuous portion of the *MR* curve (i.e., from *MC′* to *MC″*) without inducing the oligopolist to change the prevailing price of $6 and sales of 40 units (as long as *P* > *AVC*).[8] Only if the *MC* curve shifts above the *MC′* curve will the oligopolist be induced to increase its price and reduce quantity, or only if the *MC* curve shifts below *MC″* will the oligopolist lower price and increase quantity. With a rightward or a leftward shift in the demand curve, sales will increase or fall, respectively, but the oligopolist will keep the price constant as long as the kink on the demand curve will remain at the same price and the *MC* curve continues to intersect the discontinuous or vertical portion of the *MR* curve.

When the kinked demand curve model was introduced 60 years ago, it was hailed as a general theory of oligopoly. Subsequently, however, two serious criticisms were raised against the model. First, Stigler found no evidence that oligopolists readily matched price

---

[8] The shift in the oligopolist's *MC* curve will change only the level of profits or losses.

cuts but not price increases, thus seriously questioning the existence of the kink.[9] Thus, the model may be applicable only in a new industry and in the short run, when firms have no clear idea as to how competitors might react to price changes. Even more serious is the criticism that while the kinked demand curve model can rationalize the existence of rigid prices, it cannot explain or predict at what price the kink will occur in the first place.

Cartel Arrangements

In the kinked demand curve model, oligopolists did not collude to restrict or eliminate competition in order to increase profits. **Collusion** can be overt or explicit, as in centralized and market-sharing cartels, or tacit or implicit, as in price leadership models. Overt collusion as well as tacit collusion (if it can be proven) are illegal in the United States under the Sherman Antitrust Act of 1890, but they are legal in many parts of the world. U.S. corporations can, however, belong to international cartel arrangements, such as the International Air Transport Association (IATA), which sets uniform fares for transatlantic flights. Some cartellike arrangements are also sanctioned by the U.S. government, as in the sale of certain farm products such as milk. Similarly, many professional associations, such as the American Medical Association and the New York Taxi and Limousine Commission, restrict entrance into their respective markets to ensure monopoly profits for their members. In this section we deal with overt collusion or cartels while in the next section we deal with tacit collusion or price leadership models.

There are two types of cartels: the centralized cartel and the market-sharing cartel. As the name implies, the **market-sharing cartel** gives each member the exclusive right to operate in a particular geographical area. The most notorious of the market-sharing cartels was the one under which Du Pont of the United States and Imperial Chemicals of the United Kingdom agreed in the early part of last century to divide the market for some chemicals in such a way that Du Pont had the exclusive right to sell in North and Central America (except for British possessions) and Imperial Chemical had the exclusive rights in the British Empire and Egypt. The most well-known type of cartel, however, is the **centralized cartel.** This is a formal agreement among the oligopolistic producers of a product to set the monopoly price, allocate output among its members, and determine how profits are to be shared. This was attempted by OPEC, the Organization of Petroleum Exporting Countries (see Case Study 9-3). Figure 9-3 shows a simple, two-firm centralized cartel.

In Figure 9-3, D is the total market demand curve, and MR is the corresponding MR curve for the homogeneous product produced by the two firms forming the centralized cartel. The ΣMC curve for the entire cartel is obtained by summing horizontally the MC curves of the two firms. The centralized cartel authority will set $P = \$8$ and sell $Q = 50$ units (given by point E, at which ΣMC intersects the MR curve of the cartel). To minimize production costs, the centralized authority will have to allocate 20 units of output to firm 1 and 30 units of output to firm 2 (given, respectively, by point E_1 at which $MC_1 = MR$ and by point E_2 at which $MC_2 = MR$).[10] If $MC_1 > MC_2$ at the point of production, the total costs of

---

[9] G. J. Stigler, "The Kinky Oligopoly Demand Curve and Rigid Prices," *Journal of Political Economy* (October 1947), pp. 432–449.

[10] For a mathematical analysis of the centralized and market-sharing cartels, see the appendix to this chapter.

CASE STUDY 9-3
The Organization of Petroleum Exporting Countries (OPEC) Cartel

The Organization of Petroleum Exporting Countries (OPEC) is a cartel of petroleum exporters that seeks to increase the petroleum earnings of its members. Eleven nations are presently members of OPEC: Algeria, Indonesia, Iran, Iraq, Kuwait, Libya, Nigeria, Qatar, Saudi Arabia, the United Arab Emirates, and Venezuela (OPEC used to have 13 members, but Ecuador and Gabon withdrew).

As a result of supply shocks during the Arab–Israeli war in the fall of 1973 and the Iranian revolution during 1979–1980, OPEC was able to increase the price of petroleum from $2.50 per barrel in 1973 to more than $40 per barrel in 1980. This stimulated conservation in developed nations (by lowering thermostats, switching to small, fuel-efficient automobiles, etc.), expanded exploration and production (by the United Kingdom and Norway in the North Sea, by the United States in Alaska, by Mexico in newly discovered fields, and by Canada from the tar sands in Alberta), and led to the switching to other energy sources (such as coal). As a result, from 1974 to 2005, OPEC's share of world oil production fell from 55 percent to 40 percent, and its share of world petroleum exports declined from more than 90 percent to 50 percent. Although OPEC meets regularly for the purpose of setting petroleum prices and production quotas, petroleum prices remained below $20 per barrel under the conditions of excess supply that generally prevailed from 1985 to 1999 (except during Iraq's invasion of Kuwait in 1991). The price of petroleum was between $20 and $30 from 2000 to 2003, but then rose to an average of $41 in 2004 and $55 in 2005.

There are several reasons for the sharp increase in crude prices since the beginning of 2004, the most important being the sharp increase in petroleum consumption (especially by China) relative to production, the war in Iraq, the fear of supply disruption from a terrorist attack on production facilities in the Middle East, and the political turmoil in Nigeria and Venezuela. To this, we have to add hurricane Katrina's disruption of oil extraction in the Gulf of Mexico at the end of August 2005, which caused a temporary spike in the price of petroleum to over $70 per barrel. How high petroleum prices will be in the future depends on how strong world demand grows relative to supply, the political situation in the Middle East and in other petroleum-exporting countries, and on how successful and willing OPEC (with the cooperation of other non-OPEC oil exporters, such as Russia, Mexico, and Norway) will be to meet the world's growing demand of crude oil.

Source: "OPEC's Painful Lessons," *The New York Times* (December 29, 1985), p. F3; "OPEC Sets New Policy on Quota," *The New York Times* (November 29, 1989), p. D1; "OPEC Plan to Lift Oil Prices Goes Awry," *The Wall Street Journal* (March 3, 1995), p. A2; "Mid East and Venezuela Turmoil Sends Oil Prices into Wild Swing," *The New York Times* (April 9, 2002), p. 1; "Fuel Gold," *The Economist* (March 12, 2005), p. 71; "Katrina's Destructive Swell Carries Crude Over the $70 a Barrel Barrier," *Financial Times* (August 30, 2005), p. 23; and "OPEC Is Confident Oil Will Stay over $50," *Financial Times* (December 12, 2005), p. 1.

the cartel as a whole can be reduced by shifting production from firm 1 to firm 2 until $MC_1 = MC_2$. At the cartel price of $P = \$8$, firm 1 then earns a profit of $B_1F_1 = \$1$ per unit and $20 in total (the shaded area) and firm 2 earns a profit of $B_2F_2 = \$2$ per unit and $60 in total. The result would be the same for a multiplant monopolist operating plants 1 and 2. Firm 1, however, may demand a more equitable share of profits under the threat of withdrawing from the cartel, and herein lies an important weakness of most cartels and the

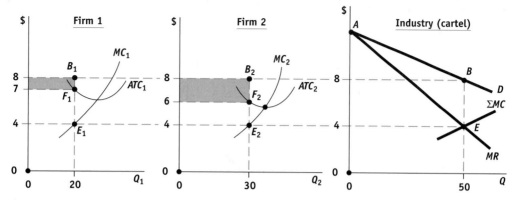

FIGURE 9-3 The Centralized Cartel *D* is the total market demand curve, and *MR* is the corresponding marginal revenue curve for the two-firm centralized cartel. The ΣMC for the cartel is obtained by summing horizontally the *MC* curves of the two member firms. The centralized authority will set $P = \$8$ and sell $Q = 50$ units (given by point *E* at which the ΣMC curve intersects the *MR* curve). If firm 1 sells 20 units at a profit of $1 per unit and $20 in total (the shaded area) and firm 2 sells 30 units at a profit of $2 per unit and $60 in total, we have the monopoly solution. The share of each firm could, however, be determined by bargaining.

reason for their failure. Cartel members also have a strong incentive to cheat by selling more than their quota. The existence of monopoly profits is also likely to attract other firms into the market. As indicated next, all these factors operated to bring OPEC to near collapse after 1985.

Price Leadership

One way of making necessary adjustments in oligopolistic markets without fear of starting a price war and without overt collusion is by **price leadership.** With price leadership, the firm that is recognized as the price leader initiates a price change and then the other firms in the industry quickly follow. The price leader is usually the largest or the dominant firm in the industry. It could also be the low-cost firm or any other firm (called the **barometric firm**) recognized as the true interpreter or barometer of changes in industry demand and cost conditions warranting a price change. An orderly price change is then accomplished by the other firms in the industry following the leader. In the dominant-firm price leader-ship model, the dominant firm sets the product price that maximizes its total profits, allows all the other firms (the followers) in the industry to sell all they want at that price, and then it comes in to fill the market. Thus, the follower firms behave as perfect competitors or price takers, and the dominant firm acts as the residual monopolistic supplier of the product. This is shown in Figure 9-4.

In Figure 9-4, D_T (*ABCFG*) is the total market demand curve for the homogeneous product sold in the oligopolistic market, and curve ΣMC_F is the horizontal summation of the marginal cost curves of the follower firms in the industry. Since the follower firms be-have as perfect competitors, they produce where price (set by the leader) equals ΣMC_F. Then $D_T - \Sigma MC_F = D_L$ is the demand curve faced by the leader or dominant firm. For ex-ample, if the leader sets $P = \$7$, the followers supply $HB = 50$ units of the product, leaving

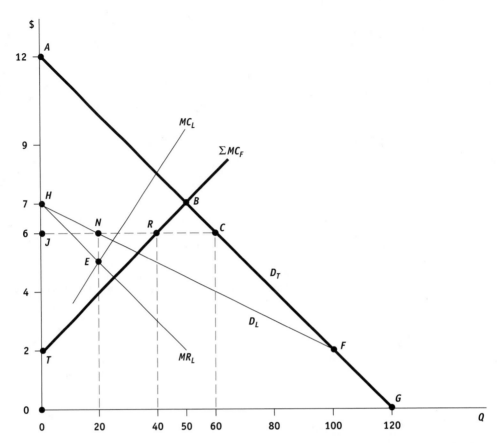

FIGURE 9-4 **Price Leadership by the Dominant Firm** D_T (*ABCFG*) is the market demand curve for the product, and ΣMC_F is the marginal cost curve of all the follower firms in the industry. Since the followers always produce where $P = \Sigma MC_F$, $D_T - \Sigma MC_F = D_L$ (*HNFG*) is the demand curve faced by the dominant leader firm, and MR_L is the corresponding marginal revenue curve. With MC_L as the marginal cost curve of the leader, the leader will set $P = \$6$ (given by point N at which $MC_L = MR_L$) in order to maximize its total profits. At $P = \$6$, the followers will supply $JR = 40$ units of the product and the leader $RC = RN = 20$ units.

nothing to be supplied by the leader. This gives the vertical intercept (point H) on D_L. If the leader sets $P = \$6$, $\Sigma MC_F = JR = 40$ units, leaving $RC = JN = 20$ units to be supplied by the leader (point N on D_L). At $P = \$2$, $\Sigma MC_F = 0$ (point T), and the leader would face the total quantity demanded in the market (point F). Thus, the demand curve faced by the leader is D_L (*HNFG*) and its marginal revenue curve is MR_L. If the marginal cost curve of the leader is MC_L, the leader will set $P = \$6$ (given by point N on D_L at which $MC_L = MR_L$) in order to maximize its total profits. At $P = \$6$, the followers will supply $JR = 40$ units (see the figure), and the leader fills the market by selling $RC = JN = 20$ units.

Among the firms that operated as price leaders in their respective industries in the U.S. economy were General Motors, U.S. Steel, Alcoa, American Tobacco, Goodyear Tire and Rubber, Gulf Oil, and the Chase Manhattan Bank (in setting the prime rate). For example, during the auto sales slumps of 1981 to 1982, 1985 to 1986, 1990 to 1991, and 2000 to

2002, a cash rebate program initiated by one automaker was invariably matched by the others in a matter of days. The role of the price leader can also shift from one firm to another over time.

9-3   PROFITABILITY AND EFFICIENCY IMPLICATIONS OF OLIGOPOLY

We now examine the relationship between profitability and efficiency for firms in oligopoly markets. We begin by presenting Porter's strategic framework of industry competition and profitability and then go on to discuss the efficiency implications of oligopoly.

Porter's Strategic Framework

Michael Porter of the Harvard University Business School developed the conceptual framework for identifying the five structural determinants of the intensity of competition and of the profitability of firms in oligopolistic industries.[11] These are: (1) the threat from substitute products, (2) the threat of entry, (3) the bargaining power of buyers, (4) the bargaining power of suppliers, and (5) the intensity of rivalry among existing competitors, as shown in Figure 9-5. These five forces of **Porter's strategic framework** represent the strategic challenges facing firm managers as they seek to maximize profits in oligopolistic markets. The firm will tend to earn higher than average industry profits if it does not face

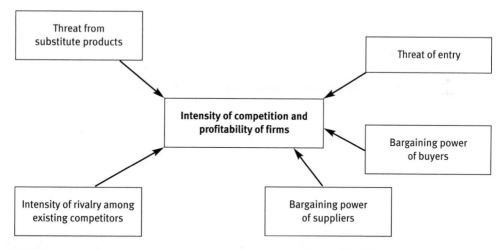

FIGURE 9-5   Porter's Competitive Framework   Porter's five structural determinants of the intensity of competition and of the profitability of firms in oligopolistic industries: threat from substitute products, threat of entry, bargaining power of buyers, bargaining power of suppliers, and intensity of rivalry among existing competitors.

---

[11] Michael E. Porter, *Competitive Strategy* (New York: The Free Press, 1998); and Henry Mintzberg, Bruce Ahlstrand, and Joseph Lampel, *Strategy Safari: A Guided Tour through the Wilds of Strategic Management* (New York: The Free Press, 1998).

much of a threat from substitute products and from the entry of potential competitors, if buyers and suppliers do not exert much market power over the firm, and if there is low intensity of rivalry and competition among existing firms.

The greater the differentiation and uniqueness of the product the firm sells and the greater the brand loyalty of consumers for the firm's product, the higher is the markup that the firm can apply and the greater are its profits. For example, there are few and imperfect substitutes for Microsoft's Windows Operating System, and this allows high profits for the incumbent. There is also limited threat of new entrants into the field because of the very high cost of doing so and also because of the barriers that Microsoft raised by preinstalling Windows on all new computers sold. Similarly, airlines increase the cost of switching to other airlines for their regular passengers by establishing frequent-flier programs. In the grocery market, not only huge size and brand loyalty, but also limited shelf space severely limit potential entrants.

The profitability of a firm in oligopolistic markets is also affected by the bargaining power of buyers and suppliers. The smaller the concentration (and hence market power) of buyers and suppliers, the higher is likely to be the profitability of the firm. Because of its huge size, Wal-Mart can squeeze the lowest price from its many suppliers. At the same time, Wal-Mart can sell at a price which, although lower than that of its competitors, allows it to earn an enviable rate of profit because it sells to unorganized consumers with little individual market power.

Finally, Porter indicates that an oligopolist's profit depends also on the intensity of rivalry with other firms in the market. Rivalry tends to be less (and hence profits higher) the greater (1) the degree of concentration in the market, (2) nonprice versus price competition, (3) exit barriers, (4) the ratio of fixed to total costs, (5) switching costs, and (6) the growth rate of the industry. For example, because of the high degree of concentration in the soft drinks market, Coca-Cola and Pepsi have learned to compete more on product differentiation and advertising than on price. Furthermore, because exit barriers and the ratio of fixed to total costs are high, because switching distribution channels (independent beverage resellers, vending machine companies, company-owned beverage resellers, and others) from one to the other is very expensive, and because the growth of the market was high (until recently), the rate of profits of Coca-Cola and Pepsi has been much higher than it would have been if rivalry between them was more intense. Case Study 9-4 examines the relationship between firm size and profitability.

Efficiency Implications of Oligopoly

Most of our analysis of oligopoly until this point has referred to the short run. In the short run, an oligopolist, just as a firm under any other form of market organization, can earn a profit, break even, or incur a loss. Even if incurring a loss, it pays for an oligopolist to continue to produce in the short run as long as $P > AVC$. In the long run, the oligopolistic firm will leave the industry unless it can earn a profit (or at least break even) by constructing the best scale of plant to produce the anticipated best long-run level of output. However, in view of the uncertainty generally surrounding oligopolistic industries, it is even more difficult than under other forms of market organization for firms to determine their best level of output and plant in the long run.

CASE STUDY 9-4
Firm Size and Profitability

Do larger firms, because of their size and possible market power, earn larger profits than smaller firms? This question has been of great interest to both business and government, and it has been hotly debated over the years. To answer this question, the rank correlation was calculated between size (measured by sales) and profits in 2005 for the 20 largest U.S. corporations from the data shown in Table 9-2. The rank correlation, which can range from 0 to 100 percent, was found to be only 39.3 percent. Thus, profits were only weakly associated with size in 2005 in the United States. It should be noted that life at the top is also slippery—from 30 to 50 companies are displaced from the *Fortune 500* in a typical year.

TABLE 9-2	Sales and Profits for the 20 Largest U.S. Corporations in 2005 (in millions of dollars)	
Company	**Sales**	**Profits**
Exxon Mobil	339,938	36,130
Wal-Mart Stores	315,654	11,231
General Motors	192,604	(10,600)
Chevron	189,481	14,099
Ford Motor	177,210	2,024
ConocoPhillips	166,683	13,529
General Electric	157,153	16,353
Citigroup	131,045	24,589
American International Group	108,905	10,477
IBM	91,134	7,934
Hewlett-Packard	86,696	2,398
Bank of America Corp.	83,980	16,465
Berkshire-Hathaway	81,663	8,528
Home Depot	81,511	5,838
Valero Energy	81,362	3,590
McKesson	80,515	(157)
J.P. Morgan Chase & Co.	79,902	8,483
Verizon Communications	75,112	7,397
Cardinal Health	74,915	1,051
Altria Group	69,148	10,435

Source: "Fortune 500 Largest U.S. Corporations," *Fortune* (April 17, 2006), pp. F-1 to F-20. The value in parenthesis refer to losses.

In the long run, oligopoly may lead to the following harmful effects: (1) as in monopoly, price usually exceeds *LAC* so that profits in oligopolistic markets can persist in the long run because of restricted entry; (2) oligopolists usually do not produce at the lowest point on their *LAC* curve as perfectly competitive firms do; (3) because the demand curves facing oligopolists are negatively sloped, $P > LMC$ at the best level of output (except by the followers in a price leadership model by the dominant firm) and so there is an underallocation of the economy's resources to the firms in an oligopolistic industry; and (4) when oligopolists produce a differentiated product, too much may be spent on advertising and model changes.

These statements on the harmful effects of oligopoly must be highly qualified, however. For technological reasons (economies of scale), many products (such as automobiles, steel, and aluminum) could not possibly be produced under conditions of perfect competition (or their cost of production would be prohibitive). In addition, oligopolists spend a great deal of their profits on research and development, and many economists believe that this leads to much faster technological advance and higher standards of living than if the industry were organized along perfectly competitive lines. Finally, some advertising is useful because it informs consumers, and some product differentiation has economic value in satisfying different consumers' tastes.

The reason that we cannot be more specific in evaluating the efficiency implications of oligopoly is that, as mentioned at the beginning of the chapter, we have no general theory of oligopoly but a number of specific models, each focusing on one particular aspect of oligopoly but overlooking others. This is unfortunate in view of the fact that oligopoly is the most prevalent form of market organization in production in all modern economies. It is also unlikely that major new developments will take place on the oligopoly theory front in the near future. Case Study 9-5 discusses the pure efficiency of operating units.

CASE STUDY 9-5
Measuring the Pure Efficiency of Operating Units

A serious problem faced by any large business with hundreds or thousands of units is how to measure and maximize the real performance or pure efficiency of each store, branch, or office. There are, of course, many traditional methods of measuring and comparing the efficiency of each unit, such as sales, sales growth, profits, market share, labor and other costs per unit or the product or service, profit per employee, revenues per square foot, and so on. All of these methods, however, use overall average performance as the benchmark for comparison. Much more useful is to measure the real performance or pure efficiency of each unit after adjusting for all the important differences between the specific unit and

all the other units. For example, a particular unit may earn more profit than another unit, but when its better location, new equipment, and better trained labor force are taken into consideration, the unit may, in fact, be seen as underperforming in relation to another unit earning less but operating under much less favorable conditions.

The real performance or pure efficiency of a unit can now be measured more accurately with a relatively new operations research technique called *data envelopment analysis* (*DEA*), which utilizes the technical apparatus of linear programming. DEA takes into account all the most important measurable factors under which each unit or branch operates—the type of technology it uses, its level of capacity utilization, the degree of competition it faces, the quality of its inputs, and so on—in measuring the real performance or pure efficiency of each unit or branch. That is, DEA compares the performance of each unit or branch to that of a standardized peer unit or branch with similar attributes. Thus, DEA might show that a particular unit with high profits does operate with high efficiency. Another unit might have high profits but be underperforming in relation to its potential. A third unit might be earning low profits because of inefficiencies and, therefore, might be a candidate for managerial help to bring it up to its potential. Still another unit might be efficient and earning low profits and, thus, be a candidate for closing or disinvestment. DEA has been profitably used by such companies as Citigroup, British Airways, and Pizza Hut, and it is increasingly being used to identify the best site or location for new units or branches of a firm. Although DEA was developed several decades ago, it is only with the advent of very powerful PCs since the early 1990s that it has become feasible because of its very high computational intensity.

Source: "Which Offices or Stores Really Perform Best? A New Tool Tells," *Fortune* (October 31, 1994), p. 38; "The Balanced Score Card," *Harvard Business Review* (July August 2005), pp. 172–180; for recent developments in DEA, see http://www.banxia.com.

9-4 THE SALES MAXIMIZATION MODEL

In the study of market structure in this and in the previous chapter, we have assumed that the firm seeks to maximize profits or the value of the firm. This has been criticized as being much too narrow and unrealistic. In its place, broader theories of the firm have been proposed. The most prominent among these is the **sales maximization model** proposed by William Baumol, which postulates that managers of modern corporations seek to maximize sales after an adequate rate of return has been earned to satisfy stockholders.[12] Baumol argued that a larger firm may feel more secure, may be able to get better deals in the purchase of inputs and lower rates in borrowing money, and may have a better image with consumers, employees, and suppliers. Furthermore, and as pointed out in Section 1-3, some early empirical studies found that a strong correlation existed between executives' salaries and sales, but not between sales and profits. More recent studies, however, have found the opposite. The sales maximization model is presented here because it is particularly relevant in oligopolistic markets. The model can be shown with Figure 9-6.

In Figure 9-6, *TR* refers to the total revenue, *TC* to the total costs, and π to the total profits of the firm. $\pi = TR - TC$ and is maximized at \$90 at $Q = 40$ units where the positive difference between *TR* and *TC* is greatest (i.e., where the *TR* and *TC* curves are parallel). On the other hand, *TR* is maximum at \$250 where $Q = 50$, at which the slope of the *TR* curve or *MR* is zero and $\pi = \$70$ (see the figure). If the firm had to earn a profit of at least \$70 to satisfy the minimum profit constraint, the firm would produce 50 units of output and maximize *TR* at \$250 with $\pi = \$70$. The same would be true as long as the minimum profit requirement of the firm was equal to or smaller than \$70.

---

[12] W. J. Baumol, *Business Behavior, Value and Growth* (New York: Macmillan, 1959).

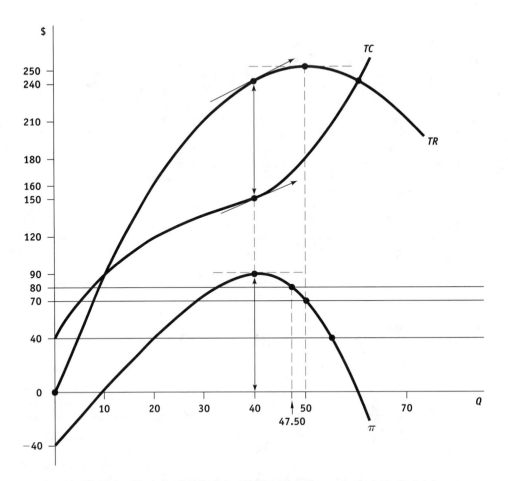

FIGURE 9-6 The Sales Maximization Model *TR*, *TC*, and π refer, respectively, to the total revenue, total cost, and total profits of the oligopolistic firm. $\pi = TR - TC$ and is maximized at $90 when $Q = 40$ and $TR = \$240$. On the other hand, *TR* is maximum at $250 when $Q = 50$ and $\pi = \$70$. A minimum profit requirement above $70 would be binding, and the firm would produce less than 50 units of output. For example, if the minimum profit requirement were $80, the firm would produce 47.50 units of output with *TR* of nearly $250.

With a minimum profit requirement between $70 and $90, however, the profit constraint would be binding. For example, to earn a profit of at least $80, the firm would have to produce an output of about 47.50 units (see Figure 9-5). Finally, if the minimum profit requirement were higher than $90, all that the firm could do would be to produce $Q = 40$ and maximize π at $90 with $TR = \$240$.[13]

While these alternative and broader theories of the firm stress some relevant aspect of the operation of the modern corporation, they do not provide a satisfactory alternative to

---

[13] For a mathematical presentation of the sales maximization model, see the appendix to this chapter.

the theory of the firm postulated in Section 1-3. Indeed, the stiff competition prevailing in most product and resource markets as well as in managerial and entrepreneurial talent today forces managers to pay close attention to profits—lest the firm go out of business or they be replaced.

9-5   THE MARCH OF GLOBAL OLIGOPOLISTS

During the past decade the trend toward the formation of global oligopolies has accelerated as the world's largest corporations have been getting bigger and bigger through internal growth and mergers. Indeed, in more and more industries and sectors the pressure to become one of the largest global players seems irresistible. No longer are corporations satisfied to be the largest or the next-to-largest national company in their industry or sector. More and more corporations operate on the belief that their very survival requires that they become one of a handful of world corporations or global oligopolists in their sector. Many smaller corporations are merging with larger ones in the belief that either they grow or they become a casualty of the sharply increased global competition. Strong impetus toward globalization has been provided by the revolution in telecommunications and transportation, the movement toward the globalization of tastes, and the reduction of barriers to international trade and investments. Rapid globalization has occurred in practically every sector from industry, banking, entertainment and telecommunications, consumer products, food, drugs, electronics, and commercial aircraft.

In industry, the total sales in real terms (i.e., after taking inflation into account) of the world's 25 largest *industrial* corporations increased 70 percent faster than the combined index of real total industrial production in all industrial countries during the past 30 years. Thus, there has been a clear tendency for the largest industrial corporations to become larger.[14] The movement toward globalization is very clear in automobiles, where only a handful of global independent players are likely to survive (see Case Study 9-6). Globalization has proceeded even more rapidly in tires, where Bridgestone (Japanese), Michelin (French), and Goodyear (American) command more than half of the total world sales, and further consolidation is expected.

The sector in which the size of the largest firm has grown the most during the past decades is international banking. From 1966 to 2005, the total deposits of the world's 10 largest banks grew from $87 billion to more than $12,000 billion. Even after accounting for the quadrupling of prices and exchange rate changes (to convert local currency values into dollar values), this meant that the size of the world's 10 largest banks increased by more than 16 times during the past three decades. It is often pointed out, however, that after a certain size, stability and profitability are more important than size per se. Nevertheless, the growth in the size of the world's largest banks has been nothing but spectacular (see Case Study 9-7).

Another sector where corporations have grown sharply in size and gone global has been in the entertainment and communications industry. The merger of Time Inc. with Warner Communications and its subsequent acquisition by America Online (AOL) for

---

[14] *Source:* "The Fortune Global 500," *Fortune* (August 1970, May 1980, July 1990, and July 2005).

CASE STUDY 9-6
The Globalization of the Automobile Industry

The automotive industry is rapidly globalizing, with six companies producing 60 percent of the total world sales of automobiles of about 60 million units (see Table 9-3). From the more than 40 independent producers during the 1980s, only about 10 or so remain today. General Motors has acquired Saab and Daewoo; Ford acquired Jaguar, Volvo, and Mazda; Renault merged with Nissan; Volkswagen acquired Seat, Skoda, and Audi; Daimler-Benz absorbed Chrysler. Only Toyota grew without mergers. There remains only a handful of smaller independent automakers in the market today: BMW, Honda, PSA, and Fiat. These are not likely to survive without rapid growth (as BMW, Honda, and PSA are trying to do) or with a merger (e.g., Fiat). The reason is that economies of scale are so pervasive that a company needs to produce more than 2 or 3 million cars to be able to survive. This is one reason that Renault merged with Nissan and Daimler absorbed Chrysler. There are, of course, some very small highly luxurious and expensive makes, but even these are owned by some of the larger companies (for example, Rolls Royce is owned by BMW and Ferrari is part of Fiat). All the other automakers are members of an alliance with one of the majors (see Case Study 9-11). Toyota is the undisputed best automobile company in the world: it makes the best quality cars, earns huge profits, and continues to grow very rapidly (and in a year or two is likely to replace GM as the world's largest automaker).

TABLE 9-3	World's Largest Auto Producers in 2005
Company	**Vehicles Produced (millions)**
General Motors	8.90
Ford	7.73
Toyota	7.30
Renault/Nissan	5.85
Volkswagen	5.09
DaimlerChrysler	4.27
Total	39.14

Source: CMS Worldwide (2005).

Source: "U.S. Car Makers Lose Market Share," *The Wall Street Journal* (January 6, 2004), p. A3; "The Quick and the Dead," *The Economist* (January 29, 2005), pp. 10–11; "GM on the Skids," *Fortune* (April 4, 2005), pp. 71–74; "The Car Company in Front," *The Economist* (January 29, 2005), pp. 65–67; "A Hard Lesson in Globalization," *The Economist* (April 30, 2005), p. 63; and "Toyota Set to Take GM's Top Slot," *Financial Times* (October 27, 2005), p. 16.

CASE STUDY 9-7
Rising Competition in Global Banking

This decade is likely to be an era of aggressively intensified competition in the high-stakes world of international banking, with fewer than 10 of the 40 to 45 large international banks now aspiring to become global powerhouses attaining their goal. From the 1950s through the 1970s, world banking was dominated by U.S. banks, while in the 1980s Japanese banks made a run for the top.

American banks were weakened by soured loans on real estate and to developing countries during the 1980s and for highly leveraged takeovers during the 1990s. Japanese banks suffered from years of bad loans, low profits, and antiquated technology during the 1990s and were generally less competitive than European Banks and much less efficient than U.S. banks. European banks entered into the 1990s in better shape than their American counterparts. They were better capitalized and made much fewer bad loans than U.S. banks to developing countries, especially in Latin America, during the 1980s. They were also not restricted by law—as U.S. banks were until 1999—from entering the insurance and securities fields. European banks, however, generally lagged in technology and in the introduction of new financial instruments, such as derivatives, when compared with U.S. banks. European banks were also much more exposed in—and incurred much higher losses than U.S. banks from—the financial and economic crisis in Southeast Asia during the latter part of the 1990s. The European banking sectors did start to consolidate in the mid-1990s, but mergers generally

took place within countries rather than across countries because of persisting nationalism.

In 2005, the world's largest bank (with assets of $2.0 trillion) was created from the merger of Japan's Mitsubishi Tokyo Financial Group (MTFG) and UFJ. Citigroup (United States) was second, with $1.5 trillion in assets. Of the world's top ten largest banks, three were American (Citigroup, JP Morgan Chase, and Bank of America), two were Japanese, and one each British, German, French, Dutch, and Swiss. Size is important in banking because with deregulation, each bank must increasingly compete with foreign banks at home and abroad to be successful. Global banks must be able to meet the rising financial needs for lending, underwriting, currency and security trading, insurance, financial advice, and other financial services for customers and investors with increasingly global operations (i.e., they must provide one-stop banking for global corporations.) But size is not everything in banking, and once a bank is, say, one of the top 10 largest in the world, efficiency is what matters the most. Global banks must also be highly innovative and introduce new financial products and technologies to meet changing customer needs. Overcapacity—too many banks chasing too few customers—will also increase competition. Large U.S. banks are strong on innovations, and with the repeal of the 1933 Glass–Steagal Act (which prevented them from entering the insurance and securities fields), they are now able to compete with foreign banks more effectively at home and abroad.

Source: "Competition Rises in Global Banking," *The Wall Street Journal* (March 25, 1991), p. A1; "International Banking Survey," *The Economist* (April 30, 1994), pp. 1–42; "Congress Passes Wide-Ranging Bill Easing Bank Laws," *The New York Times* (November 5, 1999), p. 1; "In Face of Growing U.S. Rivals, Europe's Banks Balk at Talk that Consolidation Is Needed," *The Wall Street Journal* (June 29, 2004), p. C1; and "The World's Biggest Bank Opens in Japan," *Free Republic* (January 3, 2006), p. 1.

$110 billion to form Time Warner, Viacom's acquisitions (CBS, MTV, Infinity Broadcasting, Simon & Schuster, Blockbuster, and Paramount Pictures), and Walt Disney's acquisition of Capital Cities formed, respectively, the world's first, second, and third largest communications companies (all three American).[15] Many mergers involved the purchase of American companies by foreigners: Japan's Sony Corporation's purchase of American CBS Records and MGM; Germany's Bertelsmann acquired RCA Records as well as Doubleday and Bantam Books; Ruppert Murdoch's (from Australia but now residing in the United States) News Corporation owns Harper & Row Publishers, Triangle Publications, and Twentieth-Century Fox, and Vivendi (French) acquired Seagram and US Networks. The industry is now dominated by AOL Time Warner, Walt Disney, Viacom CBS, News Corporation, Bertelsmann (German), and Vivendi (French). The reason given for most mergers in the entertainment and communications industry is to become more competitive globally. "Competitive," according to the current conventional wisdom, means "being equipped to become one of the five to eight giant corporations expected to dominate the industry worldwide. These enterprises, the reasoning goes, will be able to produce and distribute information and entertainment in virtually any medium: books, magazines, news, television, movies, videos, cinemas, electronic data networks, and so on." This is expected to provide important synergies or cross benefits from joint operation.[16]

The same type of globalization has been taking place in consumer products, food, drugs, electronics, and commercial aircraft. In 1990, Gillette introduced its new Sensor razor, which took 20 years and $300 million to develop, and captured an incredible 71 percent of the world razor market by 1999, when it introduced its Mach3. In 2005, Gillette was acquired by Procter & Gamble. Nestlé, the world's largest food company, has production plants in 59 countries and sells its food products in more than 100 countries. America's Procter & Gamble, Switzerland's Nestlé, and Britain's Unilever are among the world's 100 largest corporations. Coca-Cola has 40 percent of the U.S. market and an incredible 33 percent of the world's soft drink market. Despite the need to cater to local food tastes (Nestlé has more than 200 blends of Nescafé to cater to different local tastes), there is a clear trend toward global supermarkets. The same is true in chemicals, electronics, commercial aircraft, petroleum, and drugs (see Case Study 9-8), where a handful of huge corporations literally control the world market.

It no longer makes any sense to talk about or be concerned only with national rather than global competition in these sectors. A large corporation can even be a monopolist in the national market and face deadly competition from larger and more efficient global

---

[15] In 2005, however, Viacom, reversing direction, decided to split itself into a radio and broadcast TV operation (which includes CBS network) from its MTV cable network and Paramount film studio in order to better meet the competition from new technologies, which include the Internet, satellite radio, and digital video recorders. In 2006, the Cedant Corporation plans to split into four main business units (real estate, travel, hotels, and car rentals), and Tyco will spin off its electronics and health-care businesses. See, "Viacom Board Agrees to Split of Company," *The New York Times* (June 15, 2005), p. C4; and "Time to Slice the Mergers," *The Wall Street Journal* (January 10, 2006), p. C1.

[16] "Media Mergers: An Urge to Get Bigger and More Global," *The New York Times* (March 19, 1989), p. 7; "Corporations' Dreams Converge in One Idea: It's Time to Do a Deal," *The Wall Street Journal* (February 26, 1997), p. A1; "The New Media Colossus," *The Wall Street Journal* (December 15, 2000), p. B1; and "The Urge to Merge," *Fortune* (February 21, 2005), pp. 21–26.

CASE STUDY 9-8
The Globalization of the Pharmaceutical Industry

The past decade has witnessed more than a dozen huge mergers of large pharmaceutical companies—as well as many failed attempts. The largest merger was Pfizer's (the largest drug company in the world, American) acquisition of Pharmacia (the eighth largest, also American) for $60 billion in 2001. In 2004, Pfizer had annual sales of nearly $53 billion, with GlaxoSmithKlein's (the second largest drug company in the world, British) sales of $37 billion. Indeed, all of the world's 10 largest pharmaceutical companies have been the result of one or more mergers. The only exception is Merck, the fourth largest drug company in the world (American), with 2004 sales of $23 billion. Still, the top 12 pharmaceutical companies control less than 50 percent of total world drug sales, and so there still seems to be a great deal of room for further mergers in the industry in the future.

There are three major reasons for the urge to merge in the pharmaceutical industry. The first and most important arises from the incredibly high cost (about $900 million in 2005) of developing and marketing new drugs. Despite average profit rates of about 15 percent in the industry, these huge development costs are getting out of the reach of even the largest drug companies, hence the need for further consolidation and globalization in the industry, even by today's largest industry players. The second reason is that management typically expects savings

equivalent to 10 percent of the combined sales of the merged company. These can run in the billions of dollars per year for the largest companies. The third reason is that the combined sales force of the merged company can reach that many more doctors and hospitals and thus increase sales. Although making a great deal of sense theoretically, most mergers in the pharmaceutical industry did not deliver the benefits expected. In all cases the merged company lost market share and faced reduced profits after the merger.

Because of price regulation (and thus lower profit margins) and fragmented national markets, European drug companies are losing international competitiveness to U.S. firms. All companies now face very strong competition from generics as patents (usually granted for twenty years from the date the application is filed) expire on many blockbuster drugs. Generic drugs usually sell for as little as 10 to 20 percent of the patented drug. By 2005, about 50 percent of all prescriptions were filled by generic drugs (up from 20 percent in 1984) in the United States (saving consumers more than $10 billion). In recent years several drug companies were also hit by huge lawsuits for the alleged harmful side effects of their drugs. In 2004, Merck was forced to withdraw from the market its painkiller Vioxx (that had brought in $2.5 billion per year in revenues) for causing heart attacks and faced thousands of lawsuits with potentially billions of dollars in damages.

Source: "Drug Makers See 'Branded Generics' Eating Into Profits," *The Wall Street Journal* (April 18, 2003), p. A1; "Delicate Balance Needed in Uniting of Drug Companies," *The New York Times* (April 27, 2004), p. C1; "An Overdose of Bad News," *The Economist* (March 15, 2005), pp. 73–75; and "Merck to Pay $253 Million after Losing Vioxx Suit," *Financial Times* (August 21, 2005), p. 1.

oligopolists. The ideal global corporation is today strongly decentralized to allow local units to develop products that fit into the local cultures and yet at its core is very centralized to coordinate activities around the globe.[17]

[17] "A View from the Top: Survival Tactics for the Global Business Arena," *Management Review* (October 1992), pp. 49–53; "The Fallout from Merger Mania," *Fortune* (March 2, 1998), pp. 26–27; "If at First," *The Economist* (September 3, 2005), p. 13; and "Europe's Nascent Merger Boom," *The Economist* (September 3, 2005), p. 46.

9-6

THE ARCHITECTURE OF THE IDEAL FIRM AND THE CREATIVE COMPANY

In this section we examine some new ideas on the architecture of the ideal firm and on the evolution of the creative company. These ideas are at the frontier of modern managerial economics and are already being applied by some of the most dynamic companies, such as Procter & Gamble and General Electric in the United States.

The Architecture of the Ideal Firm

The term **firm architecture** refers to the way the firm is organized, operates, and responds to changes in the markets. The ideal firm specializes in its core competencies and outsources all other activities so as to maximize the creation of value by the firm. It is a learning organization that rapidly innovates and creates new competencies around its core ones; it has a flat organizational structure and short lines of command to facilitate communication and interaction; it operates factories that are highly specialized and capable of shifting rapidly to produce new products; it seamlessly combines the physical with the virtual; it is a real-time enterprise; and, above all, the ideal firm is agile and able to respond quickly to changing market conditions. Although these conditions are difficult to satisfy, there are indications that leading firms, such as General Electric, Microsoft, IBM, Dell, Boeing, and even Ford and General Motors, seem to be moving in this direction.[18]

- *The ideal firm concentrates on its core competencies and outsources all other activities.* The ideal firm concentrates on designing the product or service, advertising its brand, and taking orders from customers, while outsourcing the actual assembling and distribution functions. Wholesalers and distributors specialize and have lower costs in performing those tasks. To some extent, this is already happening in the computer industry, where Ingram Micro Inc. assembles and ships some computers to customers for IBM, Hewlett-Packard-Compaq, and Apple. This is sometimes referred to as the direct-sales model, compared with the traditional model and the hybrid model (followed by Dell). Ford and GM are reorganizing in that direction, and so are the leading firms in many other industries. For standardized products or commodities, we may soon see the equivalent of Amazon.com, whereby the company simply operates a Web site that displays repackaged listings from distributors' catalogs, with prices only slightly higher to cover its operating and shipping costs—and a small profit.

---

[18] "Remember when Companies Used to Make Things?" *The Wall Street Journal* (September 18, 1997), p. C1; "The Totally Digital Factory May Not Be So Far Away," *Financial Times* (November 1, 2000), p. XII; "How About Now?" *The Economist* (February 2, 2002), pp. 3–5; "Incredible Shrinking Plants," *The Economist* (February 23, 2002), pp. 71–73; "GE Goes Back to the Future," *The Wall Street Journal* (May 7, 2002), p. B1; "Bye-Bye, American Car," *Forbes* (May 27, 2002), pp. 70–72; "Process Outsourcing Catches on in Europe," *The Wall Street Journal* (June 6, 2002), p. B4; and "GE Likely to Unload Traditional Businesses," *Financial Times* (September 14, 2005).

- *The ideal firm is a learning organization.* The ideal firm will also be a learning organization that engages in systems thinking on how to deepen its core competencies and develop new ones. It is a firm that develops a shared vision of its strategy and how to carry it out. It will have team leadership, with many decisions made collegially by a team of top executives. It will have a flat organizational structure, with a blurred line between its various departments so that engineers, production people, and sales personnel will all work together on every aspect of the product, from its original design to its final sale. Communications will be easy and rapid, facilitating the cross-fertilization of ideas.

- *The ideal firm will operate extremely efficient factories or plants.* These will be generally smaller than they are today, more flexible, and able to shift gears quickly; they will be closer to markets and more focused, producing one or a very few related products. Recent technological advances, such as computer-aided design and computer-aided manufacturing, have greatly reduced optimal lot sizes or the production runs necessary to achieve maximum production efficiency. The average new factory is likely to employ from 400 to 600 workers, down from 1,200 workers today. Shorter production runs also mean that, often, it will not be wise for the firm to completely automate all of its production processes if the product will not be around long enough for the firm to recoup all of the capital invested in automation. Capital investment will also be dictated by the need for the firm to shift quickly to the production of different or related products, as required by changes in consumer demand.

  Factories will also be located closer to markets in order to speed deliveries and, even more importantly, in order to have rapid customer feedback on product performance and to anticipate changes in consumer tastes. The global firm will have a manufacturing network of decentralized plants in each large, sophisticated regional market for its product, such as the United States, Europe, and Asia. The specific location of factories will depend on the availability of the manufacturing infrastructure (i.e., on where the labor force has the necessary skill and on where there is easy accessibility to raw materials, transportation, and communications).

- *The ideal firm seamlessly combines the physical with the virtual.* The ideal firm will have a convergent architecture that fully and seamlessly integrates the physical (bricks and mortar) and the virtual (Internet) worlds to maximize the benefits of each, as well as (and perhaps most importantly) the synergies that exist between them. For example, when e-commerce started, many people thought that Internet firms would drive the traditional bricks-and-mortar retailers out of business. In recent years, however, traditional retailers have been able to also enter e-commerce, and by so doing they have been able to reap the synergies that exist between the two. (Consumers can navigate the Internet for product information and pricing, and then they can visit a real store to physically inspect the product and possibly purchase it.)

- *The ideal firm is real-time enterprise.* It will use information technology to become a *real-time enterprise*—an organization that is able to react instantaneously to changes in its business. It is as much a "new" as a "now" enterprise.

General Electric estimated that its digitization efforts saves it $1.6 billion per year. A real-time enterprise is like a giant spreadsheet in which new information, like a new order, percolates through the firm's computer system and that of its suppliers. Not only does it immediately permit answering the status request of an order but also it fully integrates in real time all aspects of the business, thus making the firm agile enough to immediately seize emerging opportunities and quickly respond to changes in consumers' tastes. Sluggishness in responding to changing tastes from analog to digital technology in cellular telephones cost Motorola market leadership in the United States and abroad in the mid-1990s. That this could happen to Motorola, one of the best-run and most dynamic companies in the world, shows how crucial it is to identify emerging consumer trends and then quickly market products that address those needs sooner and better than any competitor.

In short, the ideal firm concentrates on making its core competency the best in the world; it is a learning organization with a flat organizational structure; it operates specialized and efficient plants; it seamlessly integrates the physical with the virtual worlds; it is a real-time enterprise, and it anticipates and quickly responds to changes in the market. Many firms are moving in this direction, and the one that comes closest to its goals will likely claim the industry's richest rewards. Needless to say, the ideal firm must have good governance and must be managed ethically (see Section 1-5). Case Study 9-9 examines the relationship between firm architecture and organizational competitiveness.

The Evolution of the Creative Company

The *Knowledge Economy* is now being eclipsed by the *Creative Economy*. This is giving rise to the **creative company,** whose new core competency is creativity rather than six sigma, or efficiency in production. Knowledge is today fast becoming commoditized and moving to the most dynamic emerging markets, such as China and India, which possess lots of scientists and engineers and have learned or are rapidly learning how to make refrigerators, automobiles, computers, and all types of products cheaper and of the same or better quality than advanced countries.

The leading companies in advanced countries can compete effectively by designing and creating new products based on their intimate understanding of consumer culture, even before world consumers can articulate their unmet desires. In short, the creative company is based on design strategy and consumer-centric innovations, or CENCOR (calibrate, explore, create, organize, and realize)—the post-sigma-six that Jeff Immelt, who followed Jack Welch as GE's CEO in 2001, is pushing among GE managers, and which is elevating GE to new heights.

Although the creative company has been evolving for some time (old electronic stores have been replaced by new Apple outlets, corner coffee shops by Starbucks, traditional radio by satellite radio, and so on) it is only very recently that the idea of the creative company has been spreading widely, especially in the United States and Japan. It is with the power of design and creativity and moving to an open innovation model (see Section 6-8) that P&G's CEO A.G. Lafley transformed the company from a stagnant brand manager to a

CASE STUDY 9-9
Firm Architecture and Organizational Competitiveness

Table 9-4 shows the results of a large survey conducted by the American Management Association (AMA) on the 16 key business issues (from a list of 65) that North American corporations believe they will face with regard to firm architecture and organizational competitiveness in the future. The highest rankings go to customer service, quality control, acquiring new technologies, innovations, product development, business partnerships and alliances, and team-based approach, in that order. The lowest rankings go to political lobbying, reliance on consulting services, and foreign language training. To be noted is that even the lowest-ranked issues received absolute score values above 5 on a scale from 1 to 10 (they are, after all, in the top 16 out of 65 issues identified in the survey). The results shown in Table 9-4 refer to North American (mostly U.S.) corporations, but they are similar to those of corporations from 36 other countries that were also polled. The results presented in Table 9-4 differ somewhat from those in Table 2-4 in Case Study 2-3 (also from the same AMA survey), which examined the most important *general* objectives of global corporations, as opposed to the most important issues of *firm architecture* and *organizational competitiveness* examined here.

TABLE 9-4	Key Business Issues for Firm Architecture and Organizational Competitiveness That North American Corporations Believe They Will Face	
Rank	**Business Issue**	**Average Rating**
1	Customer service	9.42
2	Quality control and assurance	8.86
3	Acquiring new technologies	8.63
4	Innovations	8.51
5	R&D/new product development	8.24
6	Business partnerships and alliances	7.75
7	Team-based approach	7.54
8	Study and use of best practices	7.43
9	Manpower planning	7.41
10	Environmentally sound practices	7.35
11	Reengineering business processes	6.63
12	Outsourcing and contracting	6.59
13	Mergers and acquisitions	6.02
14	Reliance on consulting services	5.55
15	Foreign language training	5.42
16	Political lobbying	5.00

Source: AMA Global Survey on Key Business Issues (New York: American Management Association, 1998).

CASE STUDY 9-10
The Top Innovative Companies in the World

Table 9-5 lists the world's top 20 innovative companies and the reason for their selection based on the percentage of respondents that voted the company as the most innovative in the world in a 2005 poll of 940 senior executives in 68 countries. The table shows that 12 of the 20 companies (including the top 4) are American, two are Japanese (Sony and Toyota), and one each is Finnish (Nokia), British (Virgin), Korean (Samsung), and BMW (German).

TABLE 9-5 Top Innovative Companies in the World in 2005

Company	Responses (percent)	Reason
1. Apple	24.84	Great consumer experience with outstanding design
2. 3M	11.77	Internal culture of creativity with formal incentives
3. Microsoft	8.53	Management pushes continuous improvement of products
4. GE	8.53	Practices that are ahead of competition
5. Sony	5.94	Understanding of importance of media convergence
6. Dell	5.62	Ruthless cost-cutting and innovations
7. IBM	5.29	Uses its powerful IT base to solve customers' problems
8. Google	5.18	New tools and services provide simple solutions
9. P&G	4.21	Product innovation based on consumer lifestyles
10. Nokia	4.21	Design, rapid model change, and added features
11. Virgin	4.00	Air travel as a lifestyle trend
12. Samsung	3.89	Catches the pulse of the consumer
13. Wal-Mart	3.24	Supply-chain and logistics superiority
14. Toyota	3.02	Advanced technology
15. eBay	2.92	Customer power, cheap prices, and community
16. Intel	2.70	Dynamic business model
17. Amazon	2.70	Internet technology and a focus on the consumer experience
18. Ideo	2.16	Consultant on the innovation process
19. Starbucks	2.05	Coffee business as a lifestyle brand
20. BMW	1.73	Sleek design, advanced technology, and Web-based marketing

Source: "Top 20 Innovative Companies in the World," *Business Week* (August 1, 2005), p. 64.

creative company that far outperforms industry rivals. The challenge is how to change corporate structure to stimulate creativity so as to increase innovation productivity from the dismally low rate of success of less than 1 in 20 for traditional innovations.[19]

---

[19] "Getting Creative," *Business Week* (August 1, 2005), pp. 60–68; and "Creative Models Shaped by Education," *Financial Times,* Special Report on Innovation (June 8, 2005), pp. 6–7.

9-7	# THE VIRTUAL CORPORATION # AND RELATIONSHIP ENTERPRISES

In order to fully exploit opportunities and meet competition, the ideal firm is also becoming a virtual corporation and a relationship enterprise. The virtual corporations and relationship enterprises extend the concept of firm architecture to beyond the individual firm to involve other firms in the industry or sector.

The Virtual Corporation

A **virtual corporation** is a temporary network of independent companies (suppliers, customers, and even rivals) coming together, with each contributing its core competence to quickly take advantage of a fast-changing opportunity. In today's world of fierce global competition, the possibility of taking advantage of fast-moving opportunities is often so frustratingly brief as to make it impossible for a single firm to have all the in-house expertise to quickly launch complex products in diverse markets. By temporarily banding together to take advantage of a specific market opportunity and with each company bringing what it is best at, the virtual firm is a "best-of-everything organization." Information networks and electronic contracts will permit far-flung partners to work together on a particular project and then disband when the opportunity has been fully exploited. The virtual corporation may very well be the blueprint of the ideal firm of the future.

In a virtual firm, one of the partners might have the idea for a new product, another might design the product, another may produce it, and still another might market it. For example, IBM, Apple Computer, and Motorola came together to develop a new operating system and computer chip for a new generation of computers. During the 1990s, MCI Communications entered into partnerships with as many as 100 companies to provide a one-stop package of telecommunications hardware and services based on MCI competencies in network integration and software development with the strength of other companies making all kinds of telecommunications equipment.

Although power, flexibility, and quickness are crucial advantages, the virtual corporation model does face two real risks. First, a company joining such a network may lose control of its core technology. Second, by abandoning manufacturing, the company may become "hollow" and unable to resume the manufacture of its traditional product when the network dissolves. Some observers point out that IBM's desire to quickly enter the personal computer (PC) market in 1981 by relying on Intel for computer chips and Microsoft for the operating software left IBM without control of the market and encouraged hundreds of clone makers to eventually enter the market with lower prices and better products.

Thus, not everyone is sold on the virtual firm model. In order to work, (1) the virtual corporation will have to be formed by partners that are dependable and are the best in their field, (2) the network will have to serve the interest of all partners in a win–win situation, (3) each company has to put its best and brightest people in the network to show its partners that its link with them is important to the company, (4) the objective of the network and what each partner is expected to gain must be clearly defined, and (5) the network must build a common telecommunications network and other infrastructures so that each partner can be in constant touch with the others to anticipate problems and review progress. Creating and successfully operating a virtual firm is not easy, but it might very well be the way of the future.[20]

Relationship Enterprises

Relationship enterprises are networks of independent firms that form strategic alliances to build the capabilities and to have the geographic presence needed to be global leaders in their field. Relationship enterprises or business alliances are based fundamentally on a complementarity of capabilities and resources among the partner firms. They create value by leveraging this complementarity. These are *long-term, more stable and broader* relationships than virtual corporations, which are *more limited and temporary* networks of independent companies (as indicated above). There are about 20,000 such relationship enterprises in the world today. The top 500 multinationals have an average of 60 major strategic alliances each. The largest and most important ones are in the aerospace, airline, telecommunications, and automobile industries (see Case Study 9-11).

It has been estimated that alliances now account for 30 to 40 percent of revenues for the top American and European companies. Relationship enterprises often extend beyond market or contractual obligations and share information, knowledge, and learning. They attempt to reduce risk and increase profits by collaborating across the supply chain. As a result, competition is less among individual firms and more among entire supply chains. Not all alliances are successful, and many break up after a while. In recent years, almost half of them failed. But when alliances fail, it is primarily because of a poor or damaged working relationship rather than because of poor strategy or vision.[21]

In relationship enterprises, the partners are bonded together by a common mission and a shared strategic agenda, with each contributing capabilities desired by the network. Relationship enterprises operate as a single company on issues related to their common mission by adopting a common strategy, sharing resources and profits, melding capabilities, and providing a single range of products or services. Relationship enterprises have several crucial advantages over mergers. For one thing, regulations and nationalism often make it impossible for one company to buy another. For example, no foreign company is allowed by law to acquire more than 25 percent of an American airline, and it is unthinkable that Deutsche Telekom could purchase France's Telecom or a foreigner buy a national airline.

A second advantage of a relationship enterprise over a merger is that a company might not have the resources to purchase all the large competitors necessary to operate globally, and, in any event, they might not be available or be willing to be acquired. Other advantages of

---

[20] "The Virtual Firm," *Business Week* (February 8, 1993), pp. 98–102; C. Wardell, "The Art of Managing Virtual Teams: Eight Key Lessons," *Harvard Business Review* (November 1998), pp. 4–5; M. Hammer, "The Superefficient Company," *Harvard Business Review* (September 2001), pp. 82–91; and "Outsourcing," *Business Week* (March 21, 2005), pp. 84–94.

[21] "Strategic Alliances," *Financial Times* (January 2000), pp. 6–8; "Making Alliances Work: Improving 'Return' on Relationships," *Global Finance* (September 2001), pp. 73–74; "When Internal Bounderies Become Network Relationships," *Financial Times* (November 2001), pp. 6–7; "When to Ally and When to Acquire," *Harvard Business Review* (July–August 2004), pp. 109–115; and "Your Alliances Are Too Stable," *Harvard Business Review* (June 2005), pp. 133–141.

CASE STUDY 9-11
Relationship Enterprises in Aerospace, Airlines, Telecommunications, and Automobiles

The aerospace industry is today controlled by two huge networks (duopoly), those of Boeing and of Airbus, each consisting of more than 100 partners scattered around the world. In the airline industry, there are three major alliances. The Star Alliance includes United Airlines, U.S. Airways, Air Canada; Lufthansa, BMI, Austrian Airlines, Spanair, TAP Portugal, Scandinavian Airline System (SAS), LOT Polish Airlines; Varig (Brazilian Airline); ANA, Asiana Airlines, Singapore Airlines, THAI; and Air New Zealand. The Oneworld alliance includes American Airlines, British Airways, Aer Lingus, Cathay Pacific, Finnair, Iberia, LanChile, and Quantas Airways. The SkyTeam Alliance includes Air France (which acquired KLM in 2004), Delta Airlines, Alitalia, Korean Air, Aeromexico, and CSA Czech Airlines. These provide the international traveler with nearly seamless airline service around the world.

In telecommunications, Verizon (formed by the $60 billion merger of GTE and Bell Atlantic in 2000) acquired MCI in 2005; the regional Bell SBC acquired AT&T (thus putting an end to independent long-distance telephony in the United States); and Sprint merged with Nextel Communications Inc., thus leaving four major telephone companies in the United States in 2005: BellSouth, Qwest, SBC (which adopted the name of AT&T after its acquisition of AT&T), and Verizon (Sprint Nextel is now primarily a cellular phone company). Few weeks before SBC's Acquisition of AT&T, Cingular acquired AT&T Wireless for $41 billion, creating the nation's largest cellular service with more than 49 million subscribers. But Cingular is itself owned by SBC and

BellSouth, and Vedafone Group PLC of the United Kingdom owns 45 percent of Verizon Wireless. In 2006, a reborn AT&T acquired BellSouth further reducing the number of major U.S. telephone companies to three. Although less dramatic, consolidation is also occurring in Europe. In the meantime, the massive transformation sweeping the telecom industry, as it shifts to digital technology, is rapidly eroding the barriers between the telephone companies, cable providers, and other tech companies, and is pushing phone companies to forge partnerships with satellite-TV companies, such as EchoStar Communications Corp. and Direct TV Group Inc. Soon they will all be in the same business (see Integrating Case Study 6 at the end of Part Five).

In automobiles, Ford went for complete ownership of other automobile companies (it acquired British Jaguar, Swedish Volvo, and Japanese Mazda). General Motors went for alliances in which it has management control without ownership of Saab of Sweden, Susuki, Isuzu of Japan, Daewoo of Korea, Shanghai GM and Jinbei GM Automotive Co. of China, and AvtoVAZ of Russia (in 2004, GM acquired all of Saab of Sweden and Daewoo of Korea, but in 2005 it discontinued its alliance with Fiat of Italy and sold its interest in Suzuki and Isuzu). Toyota went for a different type of alliance with its numerous suppliers. Although independent and not owned by Toyota, suppliers agreed to let Toyota design the parts it needs and inspect and essentially direct their manufacturing operations. Of course, not all relationship enterprises are as large and well developed as the above, but that is the unmistakable direction that global competition is taking.

Sources: "Two New Airline Alliances Are Aimed at Sharpening Competition," *The New York Times* (June 25, 1999), p. C1; "Turbulent Skies," *The Economist* (July 10, 2004), pp. 61–63; "The Shifting Telecom Landscape," *Business Week* (February 28, 2005), pp. 36–37; "Global Motors," *Forbes* (January 12, 2004), pp. 62–68; "The War of Wires," *The Economist* (July 30, 2005), pp. 53–54; "Justice Department Approves Two Big Telecom Deals," *The New York Times* (October 28, 2005), p. C4; "SBC to Resurrect AT&T Name," *Financial Times* (October 28, 2005), p. 1; "Strategy of Growth by Conquest Has Fallen Firmly Out of Favor," *Financial Times, Motor Industry* (February 28, 2006), p. 1; and "A Reborn AT&T to Buy BellSouth," *The Wall Street Journal* (March 6, 2006), p. A1.

relationship enterprises are that they are not directly accountable to the company's share-holders and that they allow the company to avoid the high risk of owning subsidiaries in emerging market economies, which are more prone to financial crises, such as the one that afflicted Southeast Asia in the late 1990s. Successful relationship enterprises or network businesses have been found to create more value, to be more efficient, to need less capital, and to maintain their advantage over peers even in a broad market decline.

 ## SUMMARY

1. Oligopoly is the form of market organization in which there are few sellers of a homogeneous or differentiated product, and entry into or exit from the industry is possible but difficult. Oligopoly is the most prevalent form of market organization in the manufacturing sector. The distinguishing characteristic of oligopoly is the independence or rivalry among the firms in the industry. The sources of oligopoly are similar to those of monopoly. The degree by which an industry is dominated by a few large firms can be measured by concentration ratios and the Herfindahl index. According to the theory of contestable markets, vigorous competition can take place even among few sellers if entry into the market is absolutely free and exit is entirely costless.

2. The Cournot model shows that if each firm assumes that the other keeps its output constant, each firm will sell one-third of the perfectly competitive output. If each firm assumes instead that the other will keep its price constant (the Bertrand model), the perfectly competitive solution arises even with only two firms. The kinked demand curve model attempts to explain the price rigidity often encountered in oligopolistic markets by postulating a demand curve with a kink at the prevailing price. A centralized cartel can reach the monopoly solution. Another form of market collusion is the market-sharing cartel. An example of tacit collusion is price leadership by the dominant or barometric firm.

3. Porter's five structural determinants of the intensity of competition and of the profitability of firms in oligopolistic industries are: threat from substitute products, threat of entry, bargaining power of buyers, bargaining power of suppliers, and intensity of rivalry among existing competitors. Oligopoly may lead to many of the

same harmful effects as monopoly. In addition, oligopolists generally spend too much on advertising and model changes. However, economies of scale make large-scale production and oligopoly inevitable in many industries and may even lead to more technological change than alternative forms of market organization.

4. The sales maximization model postulates that oligopolistic firms seek to maximize sales after they have earned a satisfactory rate of profit to satisfy stockholders. In the past, evidence was introduced that executives' salaries were correlated more with sales than with profits (thus, providing support for the sales maximization model). More recently, the opposite has been found. In general, the profit rather than the sales maximization model provides the best vantage point from which to study the behavior of firms.

5. During the past decade, the trend toward the formulation of global oligopolies has accelerated as the world's largest corporations have been getting bigger and bigger through internal growth and mergers. Today, more and more corporations operate on the belief that their very survival requires that they become one of a handful of world corporations, or global oligopolists, in their sector.

6. Firm architecture refers to the way the firm is organized, operates, and responds to changes in markets. The ideal firm specializes in its core competencies; it is a learning organization; it has a flat organizational structure and short lines of command; it operates factories that are highly specialized and capable of rapidly shifting to produce new products; and, above all, the ideal firm is agile and able to quickly respond to changing market conditions. The knowledge economy is now being eclipsed by the creative economy. This is giving rise to the creative

company, whose new core competency is creativity rather efficiency in production.

7. A virtual corporation is a temporary network of independent companies (suppliers, customers, and even rivals) coming together with each contributing its core competence to quickly

take advantage of a fast-changing opportunity. A relationship enterprise is a network of independent firms that form strategic alliances to build the capabilities and have the geographic presence needed to be global leaders in their field.

DISCUSSION QUESTIONS

1. (a) What is the distinguishing characteristic of oligopoly in relation to other forms of market organizations? What is the significance of this? (b) In which sector of the U.S. economy is oligopoly most prevalent? Why?

2. (a) What are the advantages of the Herfindahl index over concentration ratios in measuring the degree of concentration in an industry? (b) What is the disadvantage of both?

3. What is the difference between limit pricing and contestable markets?

4. (a) What is meant by the Cournot model? (b) Why do we study it if it is unrealistic?

5. What is the Bertand model? What is its relationship to the Cournot model?

6. (a) What alleged pricing behavior of oligopolists does the kinked demand curve seek to explain? (b) How does the model seek to accomplish this? (c) What criticism does the model face?

7. (a) Why do we study cartels if they are illegal in the United States? (b) Why are cartels unstable and often fail?

8. In what way does OPEC resemble a cartel? How successful is it?

9. (a) What are the five forces in Porter's strategic framework? (b) What are the long-run efficiency implications of oligopoly?

10. (a) What does the sales maximization model postulate? (b) Under what conditions does this model give the same results as the profit maximization model? When does it not? (c) How relevant or useful is the sales maximization model?

11. What is the most important reason for the rise and rapid spread of global oligopolists?

12. (a) What is meant by *firm architecture?* (b) What is the architecture of the ideal firm? (c) What is meant by a *creative company?*

13. (a) What is meant by *virtual corporation?* (b) What are its advantages over traditional corporations?

14. (a) What is a relationship enterprise? (b) What is the relationship between the virtual corporation and relationship enterprises?

15. What are the advantages of relationship enterprises over mergers?

PROBLEMS

1. Find the Herfindahl index for an industry composed of (a) three firms—one with 70 percent of the market, and the other two with 20 and 10 percent of the market, respectively; (b) one firm with a 50 percent share of the market and 10 other equal-sized firms; (c) 10 equal-sized firms.

*2. Suppose that the market demand curve is given by $Q = 10 - P$ and that production costs are zero for each of four oligopolists. (a) Determine the level of output of each of the

four oligopolists according to the Cournot model. (b) What general rule can you deduce from your answer to part (a)?

3. (a) Determine the price at which each oligopolist of Problem 2 would sell. (b) If there had been only three oligopolists in Problem 2, what would be the price at which each would sell?

4. (a) The equation $Q_A = 1/2(12 - Q_B)$ is the so-called reaction function of duopolist A in a Cournot model because given the value of Q_B, Q_A gives the

best or profit maximizing level of sales of oligopolist A (reaction functions are derived in the first section of the appendix to this chapter). Show that this is the case with reference to Figure 9-1. (*b*) What is the reaction function of oligopolist B?

5. Starting with the reaction functions of duopolists A and B from Problem 4, find the Cournot solution algebraically.

*6. The research department of the Computer Supplies Corporation, a producer of computer diskettes, has estimated that the demand function facing the firm for price increases and price declines from the prevailing price are, respectively,

$$Q = 210 - 30P \quad \text{and} \quad Q' = 90 - 10P$$

The marginal and average total cost functions of the firm were also estimated to be, respectively,

$$MC = 3.5 + Q/30 \quad \text{and} \quad ATC = 3.5 + Q/60$$

(*a*) Draw the demand, marginal revenue, marginal cost, and average total cost curves of the firm. (*b*) Determine the best level of output of the firm, the price at which the firm sells its output, as well as the profit per unit and in total. (*c*) Within what range can the *MC* curve of the firm shift without inducing it to change its price and output?

7. Suppose that the demand function for price increases for the firm in Problem 2 shifts to $Q^* = 15 - 30P$. (*a*) Draw a figure showing the best level of output, price, and profits per unit and in total. (*b*) Has the price of the firm changed or remained the same? Why?

*8. A two-firm cartel producing industrial diamonds faces the following demand function:

$$Q = 120 - 10P \quad \text{or} \quad Q = 12 - 0.1P$$

The marginal cost and average total cost functions of each firm are, respectively,

$$MC_1 = 4 + 0.2Q_1 \quad \text{and} \quad ATC_1 = 4 + 0.1Q_1$$

$$MC_2 = 2 + 0.2Q_2 \quad \text{and} \quad ATC_2 = 2 + 0.1Q_2$$

Draw a figure showing the best level of output and price for the cartel, and the output of each firm to minimize the total costs of production for the cartel. Calculate the profits per unit and in total for each firm.

9. A two-equal-size-firm cartel faces demand function $Q = 20 - 2P$ and each firm faces marginal cost function $MC = 2Q$. Derive (*a*) the *MR* function of

the cartel and (*b*) the *MC* function for the entire cartel (i.e., $\Sigma\,MC$).

10. Find the algebraic solution to Problem 9 (i.e., determine the equilibrium *Q* and *P* for the cartel).

11. Plains, an isolated farming town, is cut in half by a highway, and each side of town has a supplier of fertilizer. John, one of the suppliers, learned that the other, Joe, was planning to open a store on his side of town. John called Joe to arrange a meeting in which he threatened to open another store on Joe's side of town. Joe took the threat seriously and agreed with John that each would remain only on his side of town, thus basically setting up a market-sharing cartel. Suppose that the total market demand for fertilizer in Plains is $Q = 120 - 10P$, where *Q* is in pounds and *P* is in dollars. John and Joe face *MC* and *ATC* functions equal to $MC = 0.2$ and $ATC = 0.1Q$. (*a*) Draw a figure showing the best level of output, price, and profit of each firm. (*b*) Explain why this market-sharing cartel reaches the monopoly solution. Is this realistic in the real world? Why?

12. Assume that (1) the 10 identical firms in a purely oligopolistic industry form a centralized cartel; (2) the total market demand function facing the cartel is $Q = 240 - 10P$, where *P* is given in dollars; and (3) each firm's marginal cost function is $MC = \$1$ for $Q > 4$ units, and input or factor prices remain constant. Find (*a*) the best level of output and price for this cartel, (*b*) how much each firm should produce if the cartel wants to minimize costs of production, and (*c*) how much profit the cartel will make if $ATC = \$12$ at the best level.

13. Assume that (1) two firms selling a homogeneous product share the market equally, (2) the total market demand schedule facing each firm is $Q = 240 - 10P$, and (3) the cost schedules of each firm are the ones shown below. (*a*) What would be the total profit of each firm if each were producing its best level of output? (*b*) What is the most likely result? (*c*) What other result is possible?

Q_1	40	50	60	80	Q_2	50	70	100
$MC_1(\$)$	8	10	12	16	$MC_2(\$)$	4	6	9
$ATC_1(\$)$	13	12.30	12	13	$ATC_2(\$)$	7	6	7

14. Since under price leadership by the dominant firm, the firms in the industry following the leader behave as perfect competitors or price takers by

always producing where the price set by the leader equals the sum of their marginal cost curves, the followers break even in the long run. True or false? Explain.

15. **Integrating Problem**
In Bayonne, New Jersey, there is a large beauty salon and a number of smaller ones. The total demand function for hair styling per day is $Q = 180 - 10P$, where P is in dollars. The marginal cost function of all the small salons together is $SMC_F = 4 + 0.1Q$, and the marginal cost function of the dominant or leading salon is $MC_L = 7 + 0.1Q$. (a) Draw a figure showing D_T, SMC_F, MC_L, D_L, MR_T, MR_L, and the horizontal summation of SMC_F and MC_L. (b) Determine the best level of output and price for hair styling for the dominant and for

the smaller salons if the large or dominant salon operates as the price leader. How many stylings will the large salon supply per day? How many will the small salons supply together? (c) If the large salon forms a centralized cartel, what would be the best level of output per day and price? How much will be supplied by the dominant salon and by all the small salons together if the cartel wants to minimize the total costs of producing the best level of output for the cartel as a whole? (d) What would be the equilibrium output level and price if the large salon did not exist and the small salons operated as perfect competitors? (e) What would be the best level of output and price if the large salon did exist in the market but operated as a perfect competitor, just like the small salons?

APPENDIX TO CHAPTER 9: OLIGOPOLY THEORY MATHEMATICALLY

In this appendix we examine mathematically some of the oligopoly models presented graphically in the text. The models examined in this appendix are the Cournot model, the kinked demand curve model, the centralized cartel model, the market-sharing cartel, and the sales maximization model.

The Cournot Model

In this part of the appendix we present a more advanced and complete treatment of the Cournot model presented in Section 9-2.

We begin by writing the equation for market demand curve D shown in both panels of Figure 9-1 as

$$Q = 12 - P$$

where Q is the total quantity of spring water sold in the market per unit of time (say per week) and P is the market price. For example, applying the above formula, $Q = 0$ when $P = \$12$ (the vertical intercept of market demand curve D in the right panel of Figure 9-1, repeated here for ease of reference as the left panel of Figure 9-7). When $P = \$0$, $Q = 12$ (point C on market demand curve D in the left panel of Figure 9-7).

Given the quantity of spring water supplied by duopolist B (Q_B), duopolist A will supply one-half of the difference between 12 (the total that would be supplied to the market at $P = \$0$) and Q_B in order to maximize total profits. That is,

$$Q_A = \frac{12 - Q_B}{2}$$

For example, when $Q_B = 0$, $Q_A = 12/2 = 6$ (point A and d_A in the left panel of Figure 9-7). On the other hand, when $Q_B = 3$, $Q_A = (12 - 3)/2 = 4.5$ (point A' on d_A in the left panel of Figure 9-7). With total costs equal to zero, duopolist A always maximizes total revenue and total profits by producing one-half of 12 minus the amount supplied by duopolist B (see the above formula). The reason is that (as shown in the left panel of Figure 9-1) this is the quantity at which $mr = MC = 0$.

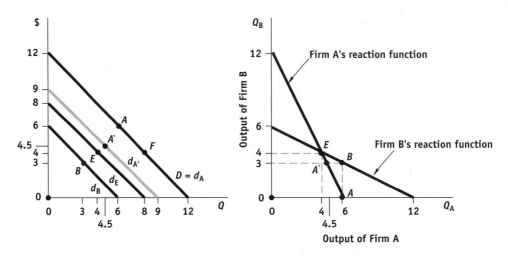

FIGURE 9-7 **Duopolists' Demand Curves and Reaction Functions in the Cournot Model** The left panel shows the demand curves faced by duopolists A and B and the quantity sold by each, given the quantity sold by the other (exactly as in the right panel of Figure 9-1). The right panel shows duopolist A's and B's reaction functions. The intersection of the two reaction functions at point E gives the Cournot equilibrium of $Q_A = Q_B = 4$ (in the right panel), so that $Q_A + Q_B = 8$ and $P = \$4$ (point F in the left panel).

The last equation above is duopolist A's **reaction function** because it shows how duopolist A reacts to duopolist B's action. It is plotted in the right panel of Figure 9-7. It shows that if $Q_B = 0$, $Q_A = 6$ (given by point A at which duopolist A's reaction function crosses the horizontal or Q_A axis in the right panel of Figure 9-7) in order for duopolist A to maximize total revenue and total profits. If $Q_B = 3$, $Q_A = 4.5$ (point A' on duopolist A's reaction function).

Similarly, duopolist B maximizes total revenue and total profits by selling

$$Q_B = \frac{12 - Q_A}{2}$$

For example, when $Q_A = 6$, $Q_B = (12 - 6)/2 = 3$ (point B on d_B in the left panel of Figure 9-7) because (as shown in the left panel of Figure 9-1) that is the quantity at which $mr = MC = 0$.

The last equation above is duopolist B's reaction function. It is also plotted in the right panel of Figure 9-7. It shows that if $Q_A = 6$, $Q_B = 3$ (given by point B on duopolist B's reaction function in the right panel of Figure 9-7) in order for duopolist B to maximize total revenue and total profits. Thus, a duopolist's reaction function shows the quantity that the duopolist should sell to maximize its total profits, given the amount sold by the other duopolist.

The two reaction functions intersect at point E, giving the **Cournot equilibrium** of $Q_A = Q_B = 4$. That is, if $Q_B = 4$, then $Q_A = 4$ (point E on duopolist A's reaction function) for duopolist A to maximize total profits. Similarly, if $Q_A = 4$, then $Q_B = 4$ (point E on duopolist B's reaction function) for duopolist B to maximize total profits. Thus, point E (where the two reaction functions intersect) is the Cournot equilibrium point, because there is no tendency for either duopolist to change the quantity it sells. A situation such as the Cournot equilibrium where each player's strategy is optimal, given the strategy chosen by the other player, is called a **Nash equilibrium.**

The right panel of Figure 9-7 can also be used to show the time path or movement toward equilibrium. With $Q_B = 0$, $Q_A = 6$ (point A on duopolist A's reaction function). With $Q_A = 6$, $Q_B = 3$ (point B on duopolist B's reaction function). With $Q_B = 3$, $Q_A = 4.5$ (point A' on duopolist A's reaction function). Note how the direction of the arrows from point A to point B and from point B to point A' moves the duopolists toward the final Cournot equilibrium point E at the intersection of the two reaction functions.

The Cournot equilibrium point E can be obtained algebraically by substituting duopolist B's reaction function (i.e., the last equation above) into duopolist A's reaction function (the previous equation). Doing this, we get

$$Q_A = \frac{12 - (12 - Q_A)/2}{2}$$
$$= \frac{12 - 6 + Q_A/2}{2}$$
$$= 3 + Q_A/4$$

Multiplying both sides by 4, we get

$$4Q_A = 12 + Q_A$$

so that

$$3Q_A = 12$$

and

$$Q_A = 4$$

With $Q_A = 4$

$$Q_B = \frac{12 - 4}{2}$$

so that

$$Q_A = 4 = Q_B \text{ (Cournot equilibrium)}$$

and

$$Q = Q_A + Q_B = 4 + 4 = 8$$

Solving the equation $Q = 12 - P$ for P, we get

$$P = 12 - Q$$

With $Q = 8$ at Cournot equilibrium, the price at which each duopolist will sell spring water is

$$P = 12 - 8 = \$4$$

which is shown by point F in the left panel of Figure 9-7.

The Kinked Demand Curve Model

Suppose that the demand functions for price increases and for price cuts facing an oligopolist are, respectively,

$$Q_1 = 280 - 40P_1 \quad \text{or} \quad P_1 = 7 - 0.025Q_1$$
$$Q_2 = 100 - 10P_2 \quad \text{or} \quad P_2 = 10 - 0.1Q_2$$

where Q is output and P is price in dollars.

Suppose that the firm's total cost function is

$$TC = 2Q + 0.025Q^2$$

We can calculate MR_1, MR_2, and MC as follows:

$$TR_1 = P_1Q_1 = (7 - 0.25Q_1)Q_1$$
$$= 7Q_1 - 0.25Q_1^2$$
$$MR_1 = \frac{d(TR_1)}{dQ_1} = 7 - 0.05Q_1$$
$$TR_2 = P_2Q_2 = (10 - 0.1Q_2)Q_2$$
$$= 10Q_2 - 0.1Q_2^2$$
$$MR_2 = \frac{d(TR_2)}{dQ_2} = 10 - 0.2Q_2$$
$$MC = \frac{d(TC)}{dQ} = 2 + 0.05Q$$

To find the kink, or point of intersection of demand curves D_1 and D_2, we set $Q_1 = Q_2 = Q$ and get

$$7 - 0.25Q = 10 - 0.1Q$$
$$0.075Q = 3$$
$$Q = 40$$

and

$$P = 7 - 0.025(40) = \$6$$

The upper and lower limits of the MR gap are

$$MR_1 = 7 - 0.5(40) = 7 - 2 = 5$$
$$MR_2 = 10 - 0.2(40) = 10 - 8 = 2$$

Since

$$MC = 2 + 0.05(40) = 4$$

the MC curve intersects the vertical portion of the MR curve. The total profits (π) of the firm are

$$\pi = TR - TC = PQ - 2Q - 0.025Q^2$$
$$= 6(40) - 2(40) - 0.025(40)^2 = \$120$$

The level of π could also have been found from

$$\pi = (P - ATC)Q$$
$$ATC = \frac{TC}{Q} = \frac{2Q + 0.025Q^2}{Q}$$
$$= 2 + 0.25Q = 2 + 0.025(40) = 3$$

so that

$$\pi = (6 - 3)(40) = \$120$$

The graphical solution for this problem is shown in Figure 9-2.

The Centralized Cartel Model

Suppose that a two-firm cartel faces the following demand function:

$$Q = 120 - 10P \quad \text{or} \quad P = 12 - 0.1Q$$

and the total cost function of each member firm is, respectively,

$$TC_1 = 4Q_1 + 0.1Q_1^2$$
$$TC_2 = 2Q_2 + 0.1Q_2^2$$

We can calculate MR, MC_1, and MC_2 as follows:

$$TR = PQ = (12 - 0.1Q)Q$$
$$= 12Q - 0.1Q^2$$
$$MR = \frac{d(TR)}{dQ} = 12 - 0.2Q$$
$$MC_1 = \frac{d(TC_1)}{dQ_1} = 4 + 0.2Q_1$$
$$MC_2 = \frac{d(TC_2)}{dQ_2} = 2 + 0.2Q_2$$

In order to add MC_1 and MC_2 horizontally to find ΣMC, we solve for Q_1 and Q_2 and get

$$Q_1 = -20 + 5MC_1$$
$$Q_2 = -10 + 5MC_2$$

so that

$$Q = -30 + 10 \, \Sigma MC$$

Solving for ΣMC, we have

$$\Sigma MC = \frac{Q + 30}{10} = 3 + 0.1Q$$

(Strictly speaking, this is the average ΣMC function. It does not show the kink at $Q = 10$ in Figure 16 in the answer to Problem 8 at the end of the book.)

Setting $\Sigma MC = MR$, we get

$$3 + 0.1Q = 12 - 0.2Q$$

so that

$$9 = 0.3Q$$

and

$$Q = 30$$

Then

$$P = 12 - 0.1(30) = \$9$$

At $Q = 30$,

$$MR = 12 - 0.2\,(30) = 12 - 6 = \$6$$

Setting MC_1 and MC_2 equal to MR, we have

$$4 = 0.2Q_1 = 6 \quad \text{so that} \quad Q_1 = 10$$

and

$$2 + 0.2Q_2 = 6 \quad \text{so that} \quad Q_2 = 20$$

and

$$Q = Q_1 + Q_2 = 10 + 20 = 30$$

Therefore,

$$\pi_1 = TR_1 - TC_1 = PQ_1 - 4Q_1 - 0.1Q_1^2$$
$$= 9(10) - 4(10) - 0.1(10)^2$$
$$= 90 - 40 - 10 = \$40$$

$$\pi_2 = TR_2 - TC_2 = PQ_2 - 2Q_2 - 0.1Q_2^2$$
$$= 9(20) - 2(20) - 0.1(20)^2$$
$$= 180 - 40 - 40 = \$100$$

and

$$\pi = \pi_1 + \pi_2 = \$40 + \$100 = \$140$$

The graphical solution of this problem is shown in Figure 16 in the answer to Problem 8 at the end of the text.

The Market-Sharing Cartel

Suppose that the market demand function for a two-firm equal-market-sharing cartel is

$$Q = 120 - 10P$$

and that the total cost function of duopolist 1 is

$$TC' = 0.1Q^2$$

The half-share market faced by each duopolist is then

$$Q' = 60 - 5P \quad \text{or} \quad P' = 12 - 0.2Q$$

so that

$$TR' = P'Q' = (12 - 0.2Q')Q'$$
$$= 12Q' - 0.2Q'^2$$

and

$$MR' = \frac{d(TR')}{dQ'} = 12 - 0.4Q'$$

The marginal and average total cost of each duopolist is

$$MC' = \frac{d(TC')}{dQ'} = 0.2Q'$$

$$ATC' = \frac{TC'}{Q'} = \frac{0.1Q'^2}{Q'} = 0.1Q'$$

Setting MC' equal to MR', we get

$$0.2Q' = 12 - 0.4Q'$$
$$0.6Q' = 12$$
$$Q' = 20$$

and

$$P' = 12 - 0.2(20) = \$8$$

Therefore,

$$TR' = 12(20) - 0.2(20)^2 = 240 - 80 = \$160$$

and

$$\pi' = TR' - TC' = 160 - 0.1(20)^2$$
$$= 160 - 40 = \$120$$
$$\pi = 2(\pi') = \$240$$

The Sales Maximization Model

Suppose that the demand function faced by an oligopolist is

$$Q = 100 - 10P \quad \text{or} \quad P = 10 - 0.1Q$$

so that the total revenue function of the firm is

$$TR = PQ = (10 - 0.1Q)Q = 10Q - 0.1Q^2$$

If the total cost function of the firm is given by

$$TC = 70 + 2Q$$

then the total profit of the firm is

$$\pi = TR - TC = 10Q - 0.1Q^2 - 70 - 2Q$$
$$= -70 + 8Q - 0.1Q^2$$

On one hand, the firm maximizes profits where

$$\frac{d\pi}{dQ} = 8 - 0.2Q = 0$$

so that $Q = 40$ and $P = 10 - 0.1(40) = \$6$.

$$TR = 10(40) - 0.1(40)^2 = 400 - 160 = \$240$$
$$\pi = -70 + 8(40) - 0.1(40)^2$$
$$= -70 + 320 - 160 = \$90$$

On the other hand, the firm maximizes sales or total revenue where

$$\frac{d(TR)}{dQ} = 10 - 0.2Q = 0$$

so that $Q = 50$ and $P = 10 - 0.1(50) = \$5$.

$$TR = 10(50) - 0.1(50)^2$$
$$= 500 - 250 = \$250$$
$$\pi = -70 + 8(50) - 0.1(50)^2$$
$$= -70 + 400 - 250 = \$80$$

To find Q, P, and TR if the minimum profit constraint of the firm is $\pi = \$85$, we proceed as follows:

$$\pi = -70 + 8Q - 0.1Q^2 = \$85$$
$$0.1Q^2 - 8Q + 155 = 0$$

Gordon, Mark, and Julie Salganik, "Making Alliances Work: Improving 'Return on Relationship,'" *Global Finance* (September 2001), pp. 73–74.

Gulati, R., N. Hohria, and A. Zaheer, "Strategy Networks," *Strategic Journal Management* (March 2000), pp. 203–216.

Hacki, Reno, and Julian Leighton, "The Future of the Network Company," *The McKinsey Quarterly,* no. 3 (2001), pp. 21–27.

Hammer, Michael, "The Superefficient Company," *Harvard Business Review* (September 2001), pp. 82–91.

Storey, John, "When Internal Boundaries Become Network Relationships," *Financial Times* (November 19, 2001), pp. 6–7.

Wardell, Charles, "The Art of Managing Virtual Teams: Eight Key Lessons," *Harvard Business Review* (November 1998), pp. 4–5.

 ## INTERNET SITE ADDRESSES

For concentration ratios in U.S. manufacturing industries, see:

> http://www.census.gov/epcd/www/concentration. html and then click on manufacturing

For OPEC, see:

> http://www.opec.org
>
> http://www.en.wikipedia.org/wiki/OPEC

For the Fortune Global 500 companies, see:

> http://www.fortune.com/global500

For business architecture, see:

> American Management Association International: http://www.amanet.org

For business architecture and its application in the computer industry, see:

> Ingram Computers: http://www.ingrammicro.com
>
> Apple: http://www.apple.com
>
> Hewlett-Packard: http://www.hp.com
>
> IBM: http://www.ibm.com
>
> Dell: http://www.dell.com

For competition in international banking, see:

> Bank of America: http://www.bankamerica.com
>
> Citigroup: http://www.citigroup.com
>
> Deutsche Bank: http://www.deutschebank.com

> J.P. Morgan Chase: http://www.jpmorganchase.com
>
> Union Bank of Switzerland: http://www.ubs.com

For competition in the pharmaceutical industry, see:

> Bristol-Meyers Squibb: http://www.bms.com
>
> Johnson & Johnson: http://www.jj.com
>
> Merck: http://www.merck.com
>
> Novartis: http://www.novartis.com
>
> Pfizer: http://www.pfizer.com
>
> Procter & Gamble: http://www.pg.com
>
> Sanofi-Aventis: http://www.sanofi-aventis@com

The virtual company and relationship enterprises or strategic alliances are examined in:

> http://www.skyrme.com/insights/2virtorg.htm
>
> http://www.opengroup.org/opencomments/ winter96/1_text.htm
>
> http://www.entreplanet.org/vc_e/level01/ whatsvc.html
>
> http://www.openwave.com/alliances/strategic
>
> http://www.lawyers.com/lawyers/A~1001955~LD S/Strategic+Business++Alliances+FAQS.html
>
> http://www.irc.caltech.edu/courses/Strategic_ Partnerships_Business_Alliances.htm

CHAPTER **10** Game Theory and Strategic Behavior

CHAPTER OUTLINE

KEY TERMS (in the order of their appearance)

Strategic behavior	**Payoff matrix**	**Prisoners' dilemma**
Game theory	**Zero-sum game**	**Repeated games**
Players	**Nonzero-sum game**	**Tit-for-tat**
Strategies	**Dominant strategy**	**Decision tree**
Payoff	**Nash equilibrium**	

I n this chapter, we extend our analysis of firm behavior in oligopolistic markets using game theory. Game theory offers many insights into oligopolistic interdependence and strategic behavior that could not be examined with the traditional tools of analysis presented in the previous chapter.

The chapter begins with a discussion of the meaning and usefulness of game theory. It then defines a dominant strategy and a Nash equilibrium, and it examines their usefulness in the analysis of oligopolistic behavior. Next, the chapter describes the prisoners' dilemma and its applicability to the analysis of price and nonprice competition as well as cartel cheating. Finally, the chapter discusses multiple and strategic moves in domestic and international competition, with and without risk. The examples and applications presented in the chapter clearly highlight the importance of game theory to the understanding of many aspects of oligopolistic behavior that could not otherwise be explained.

10-1   STRATEGIC BEHAVIOR AND GAME THEORY

Strategic behavior refers to the plan of action or behavior of an oligopolist, after taking into consideration all possible reactions of its competitors, as they compete for profits or other advantages. Since there are only a few firms in the industry, the actions of each affects the others, and the reaction of the others must be kept in mind by the first in charting its best course of action. Thus, each oligopolist changes the product price, the quantity of the product that it sells, the level of advertising, and so on, so as to maximize its profits after having considered all possible reactions of its competitors to each of its courses of action. Some have likened the behavior of oligopolists to that of players in a game and to the strategic actions of warring factions (see Case Study 10-1). The study of such strategic behavior is the subject matter of game theory.

Game theory was pioneered by the mathematician John von Neumann and the economist Oskar Morgenstern in 1944 and it was soon hailed as a breakthrough in the study of oligopoly.[1] In general, game theory is concerned with the choice of the best or optimal strategy in conflict situations. For example, game theory can help a firm determine the conditions under which lowering its price would not trigger a ruinous price war, whether

---

[1] J. von Neumann and O. Morgenstern, *Theory of Games and Economic Behavior* (Princeton, N.J.: Princeton University Press, 1944). A more in-depth presentation of game theory with applications to economics and management is found in Prajit K. Dutta, *Strategies and Games* (Cambridge, Mass.: MIT Press, 1999).

CASE STUDY 10-1
Military Strategy and Strategic Business Decisions

According to William E. Peacock, the former president of two St. Louis companies and assistant secretary of the army in the Carter administration, decision making in business has much in common with military strategy and can thus be profitably analyzed using game theory. Although business managers' actions are restricted by laws and regulations to prevent unfair practices, and although the objective of managers, of course, is not to literally destroy the competition, there is much that they can learn from military strategists. Peacock points out that throughout history, military conflicts have produced a set of basic Darwinian principles that can serve as an excellent guideline to business managers about how to compete in the marketplace. Neglecting these principles can make the difference between business success and failure.

In business, as in war, it is crucial for the organization to have a clear objective and to explain this objective to all of its employees. The benefits of a simple marketing strategy that all employees can understand are clearly evidenced by the success of McDonald's. Both business and war also require the development of a strategy for attacking. Being aggressive is important because few competitions are ever won by being passive. Furthermore, both business and warfare require unity of command to pinpoint responsibility. Even in decentralized companies with informal lines of command, there are always key individuals who must make important decisions. Finally, in business as in war, the element of surprise and security (keeping your strategy secret) is crucial. For example, Lee Iacocca stunned the competition in 1964 by introducing the immensely successful (high payoff) Mustang. Finally, in business as in war, spying to discover a rival's plans or to steal a rival's new technological breakthrough is becoming more common.

More than ever before, today's business leaders must learn how to tap employees' ideas and energy, manage large-scale rapid change, anticipate business conditions 5 or 10 years down the road, and muster the courage to steer the firm in radical new directions when necessary. Above all, firms must think and act strategically in a world of increasing global competition. Game theory can be particularly useful and can offer important insights in the analysis of oligopolistic independence. Indeed, more and more firms are making use of war-game simulations in their decision making.

Source: W. E. Peacock, *Corporate Combat* (New York: Facts on File Publication, 1984); "The Valley of Spies," *Forbes* (October 26, 1992), pp. 200–204; "Business War Games Attract Big Warriors," *The Wall Street Journal* (December 22, 1994), p. B1; "The Right Game: Use Game Theory to Shape Strategy," *Harvard Business Review* (July–August 1995), pp. 57–71; "From Battlefield to Boardroom," *Financial Times* (February 10, 2003), p. 7; "Global Gamesmanship," *Harvard Business Review* (May 2003), pp. 62–71; and "A Question of Management," *The Economist* (June 11, 2005), p. 74.

the firm should build excess capacity to discourage entry into the industry, even though this lowers the firm's short-run profits, and why cheating in a cartel usually leads to its collapse. In short, game theory shows how an oligopolistic firm makes strategic decisions to gain a competitive advantage over a rival or how it can minimize the potential harm from a strategic move by a rival.

Every game theory model includes players, strategies, and payoffs. The **players** are the decision makers (here, the managers of oligopolist firms) whose behavior we are trying to explain and predict. The **strategies** are the choices to change price, develop new products, undertake a new advertising campaign, build new capacity, and all other such actions that affect the sales and profitability of the firm and its rivals. The **payoff** is the outcome or consequence of each strategy. For each strategy adopted by a firm, there are usually a number of strategies (reactions) available to a rival firm. The payoff is the outcome or consequence of each combination of strategies by the two firms. The payoff is usually expressed in terms of the profits or losses of the firm that we are examining as a result of the firm's strategies and the rivals' responses. The table giving the payoffs from all the strategies open to the firm and the rivals' responses is called the **payoff matrix.**

We must distinguish between zero-sum games and nonzero-sum games. A **zero-sum game** is one in which the gain of one player comes at the expense and is exactly equal to the loss of the other player. An example of this occurs if firm A increases its market share at the expense of firm B by increasing its advertising expenditures (in the face of unchanged advertising by firm B). On one hand, if firm B also increased its advertising expenditures, firm A might not gain any market share at all. On the other hand, if firm A increased its price and firm B did not match it, firm A might lose market to firm B. Games of this nature, where the gains of one player equal the losses of the other (so that total gains plus total losses sum to zero) are called zero-sum games. If the gains or losses of one firm do not come at the expense of or provide equal benefit to the other firm, however, we have a **nonzero-sum game.** An example of this might arise if increased advertising leads to higher profits of both firms and we use profits rather than market share as the payoff. In this case, we would have a *positive-sum game.* If, however, increased advertising raises costs more than revenues and the profits of both firms decline, we have a case of *negative-sum game.*

10-2   DOMINANT STRATEGY AND NASH EQUILIBRIUM

We now discuss the meaning of a dominant strategy and the Nash equilibrium and examine their usefulness in the analysis of oligopolistic interdependence.

Dominant Strategy

To see how players chose strategies to maximize their payoffs, let us begin with the simplest type of game in an industry (duopoly) composed of two firms, firm A and firm B, and a choice of two strategies for each—advertise or don't advertise. Firm A, of course, expects to earn higher profits if it advertises than if it doesn't. But the actual level of profits of firm A depends also on whether firm B advertises or not. Thus, each strategy by firm A (i.e., advertise or don't advertise) can be associated with each of firm B's strategies (also to advertise or not to advertise).

The four possible outcomes for this simple game are illustrated by the payoff matrix in Table 10-1. The first number of each of the four cells refers to the payoff (profit) for firm A, while the second is the payoff (profit) for firm B. From Table 10-1, we see that if both firms advertise, firm A will earn a profit of 4, and firm B will earn a profit of 3 (the top left cell of the payoff matrix).[2] The bottom left cell of the payoff matrix, on the other hand, shows that if firm A doesn't advertise and firm B does, firm A will have a profit of 2, and firm B will have a profit of 5. The other payoffs in the second column of the table can be similarly interpreted.

---

[2] The profits of 4 and 3 could refer, for example, to $4 million and $3 million, respectively.

TABLE 10-1	Payoff Matrix for an Advertising Game		
		Firm B	
		Advertise	Don't Advertise
Firm A	Advertise	(4, 3)	(5, 1)
	Don't Advertise	(2, 5)	(3, 2)

What strategy should each firm choose? Let us consider firm A first. If firm B does advertise (i.e., moving down the left column of Table 10-1), we see that firm A will earn a profit of 4 if it also advertises and 2 if it doesn't. Thus, firm A should advertise if firm B advertises. If firm B doesn't advertise (i.e., moving down the right column in Table 10-1), firm A would earn a profit of 5 if it advertises and 3 if it doesn't. Thus, firm A should advertise whether firm B advertises or not. Firm A's profits would always be greater if it advertises than if it doesn't regardless of what firm B does. We can then say that advertising is the dominant strategy for firm A. The **dominant strategy** is the optimal choice for a player no matter what the opponent does.

The same is true for firm B. Whatever firm A does (i.e., whether firm A advertises or not), it would always pay for firm B to advertise. We can see this by moving across each row of Table 10-1. Specifically, if firm A advertises, firm B's profit would be 3 if it advertises and 1 if it does not. Similarly, if firm A does not advertise, firm B's profit would be 5 if it advertises and 2 if it doesn't. Thus, the dominant strategy for firm B is also to advertise.

In this case, both firm A and firm B have the dominant strategy of advertising, and this will, therefore, be the final equilibrium. Both firm A and firm B will advertise regardless of what the other firm does and will earn a profit of 4 and 3, respectively (the top left cell in the payoff matrix in Table 10-1). Note that in this case, the advertising solution or final equilibrium for both firms holds whether firm A or firm B chooses its strategy first, or if both firms decide on their best strategy simultaneously.

Nash Equilibrium

Not all games have a dominant strategy for each player. In fact, it is more likely in the real world that one or both players do not have a dominant strategy. An example of this is shown in the payoff matrix in Table 10-2. This is the same as the payoff matrix in Table 10-1,

TABLE 10-2	Payoff Matrix for the Advertising Game		
		Firm B	
		Advertise	Don't Advertise
Firm A	Advertise	(4, 3)	(5, 1)
	Don't Advertise	(2, 5)	(6, 2)

except that the first number in the bottom right cell was changed from 3 to 6. Now firm B has a dominant strategy, but firm A does not. The dominant strategy for firm B is to advertise whether firm A advertises or not, exactly as above, because the payoffs for firm B are the same as in Table 10-1. Firm A, however, has no dominant strategy now. The reason is

---

CASE STUDY 10-2
Dell Computers and Nash Equilibrium

Dell Computers of Austin, Texas, a company created by 27-year-old Michael Dell in 1984, ended the 2004 fiscal year with revenues of $49.2 billion, making it the third largest computer company in the nation (and the largest seller of PCs in the United States and the world). By offering a 30-day money-back guarantee on next-day, free on-site service through independent contractors for the first year of ownership, and unlimited calls to a toll-free technical support line, Dell established a solid reputation for reliability, thus taking the fear and uncertainty out of mail-order computers. Dell will even mail a $25 check to any customer who does not get a Dell technician within five minutes of calling Dell's technical support line! Ordering a computer from Dell by mail is now like ordering a Big Mac at McDonald's—you know exactly what you will get. By eliminating retailers, Dell was also able to charge lower prices than its larger and more established competitors. For example, Dell's selling and administrative expenses were 14 cents for each dollar of sales, compared with 24 cents for Apple and 30 cents for IBM. Dell ships computers by mail by adding only a 2 percent shipping charge to the sale price. When receiving a mail order, Dell technicians simply pick up the now-standard components from the shelf to assemble the particular PC ordered. It is simple, quick, and inexpensive. Thus, Dell has developed a dominant strategy—one that is optimal, regardless of what competitors do. By doing so, Dell has become a kind of high-tech Wal-Mart.

Until the early 1990s, traditional computer firms such as IBM, Hewlett-Packard/Compaq, Apple, and others always thought that customers were willing to pay a substantial retail markup for the privilege of being able to go to a store and feel and touch the machine before buying it. Some customers still do. But by reducing fears and uncertainty from ordering computers through the mail, Dell was able to convince a growing number of customers to bypass the retailers and order directly from Dell by mail at lower prices. Today, more than 20 percent of PCs are sold by mail in the United States. Given Dell's dominant and profitable strategy, IBM, Hewlett-Packard/Compaq, and Apple quickly followed and set up their own mail-order departments and 800 phone lines in 1993 and 1994. Their dominant strategy of selling exclusively through retail outlets was knocked out by Dell's new market strategy, and so we now can say that the computer industry is in Nash equilibrium. Given Dell's dominant strategy, the other major computer companies have decided to change their strategy and also sell by mail. Dell, however, is more adept at selling computers through the mail and retains almost 50 percent of the mail-order computer business. By 2005, Dell had 19 percent of the world PC market and 32 percent (and aiming at 40 percent) of the U.S. market, and it was growing and earning profits while other PC makers were shrinking and incurring losses. In fact, at the beginning of 2002 IBM announced that it was leaving the PC market, and at the end of 2004 it sold its laptop business to Lenovo of China.

Source: "The Computer Is in the Mail (Really)," *Business Week* (January 23, 1995), pp. 76–77; "Michael Dell Turns the PC World Inside Out," *Fortune* (September 8, 1997), pp. 76–86; "IBM Plans to Stop Selling Its PC's in Retail Outlets," *The New York Times* (October 20, 1999), p. C6; "Dell Domination," *Fortune* (January 21, 2002), pp. 71–75; "IBM Strikes a Deal with Rival Lenovo," *The Wall Street Journal* (December 9, 2004), p. A3; and "Technology's Mr. Predictable," *The Economist* (September 24, 2005), p. 82.

that if firm B advertises, firm A earns a profit of 4 if it advertises and 2 if it does not. Thus, if firm B advertises, firm A should also advertise. On the other hand, if firm B does not advertise, firm A earns a profit of 5 if it advertises and 6 if it does not.[3] Thus, firm A should advertise if firm B does, and it should not advertise if firm B doesn't. Firm A no longer has a dominant strategy. What firm A should do now depends on what firm B does.

In order for firm A to determine whether to advertise, firm A must first try to determine what firm B will do, and advertise if firm B does and not advertise if firm B does not. Since firm A knows the payoff matrix, it can figure out that firm B has the dominant strategy of advertising. Therefore, the optimal strategy for firm A is also to advertise (because firm A will earn a profit of 4 by advertising and 2 by not advertising—see the first column of Table 10-2). This is the Nash equilibrium, named after John Nash, the Princeton University mathematician and 1994 Nobel Prize winner who first formalized the notion in 1951.[4]

The **Nash equilibrium** is the situation where each player chooses his or her optimal strategy, *given the strategy chosen by the other player.* In our example, the high advertising strategy for firm A and firm B is the Nash equilibrium because, given that firm B chooses its dominant strategy of advertising, the optimal strategy for firm A is also to advertise. Note that when both firms had a dominant strategy, each firm was able to choose its optimal strategy regardless of the strategy adopted by its rival. Here, only firm B has a dominant strategy. Firm A does not. As a result, firm A cannot choose its optimal strategy independently of firm B's strategy. Only when each player has chosen its optimal strategy given the strategy of the other player do we have a Nash equilibrium. In short, a dominant strategy equilibrium is always a Nash equilibrium, but a Nash equilibrium is not necessarily a dominant strategy equilibrium. Case Study 10-2 examines how Dell Computers developed a dominant strategy that is also a Nash equilibrium for the computer industry.

10-3   THE PRISONERS' DILEMMA

Oligopolistic firms often face a problem called the **prisoners' dilemma.** This refers to a situation in which each firm adopts its dominant strategy but each could do better (i.e., earn larger profits) by cooperating. To understand this, consider the following situation. Two suspects are arrested for armed robbery, and if convicted, each could receive a maximum sentence of 10 years' imprisonment. However, unless one or both suspects confess, the evidence is such that they could be convicted only of possessing stolen goods, which carries a maximum sentence of 1 year in prison. Each suspect is interrogated separately, and no communication is allowed between the two suspects. The district attorney promises each suspect that by confessing, he will go free while the other suspect (who does not confess) will receive the full 10-year sentence. If both suspects confess, each gets a reduced sentence of 5 years' imprisonment. The (negative) payoff matrix in terms of years of detention is given in Table 10-3.

---

[3] This might result, for example, if firm A's advertisement is not effective or if advertising adds more to firm A's cost than to its revenues.

[4] "You've Seen the Movie. Now Just Exactly What Was It that John Nash Had on His Beautiful Mind?" *The New York Times* (April 11, 2002), p. C2.

TABLE 10-3	Negative Payoff Matrix (Years of Detention) for Suspect A and Suspect B		
		Individual B	
		Confess	Don't Confess
Individual A	Confess	(5, 5)	(0, 10)
	Don't Confess	(10, 0)	(1, 1)

From Table 10-3, we see that confessing is the best or dominant strategy for suspect A no matter what suspect B does. The reason is that if suspect B confesses, suspect A receives a 5-year sentence if he confesses and a 10-year jail sentence if he does not. Similarly, if suspect B does not confess, suspect A goes free if he confesses and receives a 1-year jail sentence if he does not. Thus, the dominant strategy for suspect A is to confess. Confessing is also the best or dominant strategy for suspect B. The reason is that if suspect A confesses, suspect B gets a 5-year jail sentence if he also confesses and a 10-year jail sentence if he does not. Similarly, if suspect A does not confess, suspect B goes free if he confesses and gets 1 year if he does not. Thus, the dominant strategy for suspect B is also to confess.

With each suspect adopting his dominant strategy of confessing, each ends up receiving a 5-year jail sentence. But if each suspect did not confess, each would get only a 1-year jail sentence. Each suspect, however, is afraid that if he does not confess, the other will confess, so that he would end up receiving a 10-year jail sentence. Only if each suspect was sure the other would not confess and he himself does not confess would each get away with only a 1-year sentence. Since it is not possible to reach agreement not to confess (remember, the suspects are already in jail and cannot communicate), each suspect adopts his dominant strategy to confess and receives a 5-year jail sentence. Note that even if an agreement not to confess could be reached, the agreement could not be enforced. Therefore, each suspect will end up confessing and receiving a 5-year jail sentence—at least this is what the theory predicts.

10-4   PRICE AND NONPRICE COMPETITION, CARTEL CHEATING, AND PRISONERS' DILEMMA

We now use the concept of the prisoners' dilemma to examine price and nonprice competition, as well as cartel cheating in oligopolistic markets.

Price Competition and the Prisoners' Dilemma

The concept of the prisoners' dilemma can be used to analyze price and non-price competition in oligopolistic markets, as well as the incentive to cheat (i.e., the tendency to secretly cut price or sell more than one's allocated quota) in a cartel. Oligopolistic price competition in the presence of the prisoners' dilemma can be examined with the payoff matrix in Table 10-4.

TABLE 10-4	Payoff Matrix for a Pricing Game	
	Firm B	
	Low Price	High Price
Firm A Low Price	(2, 2)	(5, 1)
High Price	(1, 5)	(3, 3)

The payoff matrix of Table 10-4 shows that if firm B charged a low price (say, $6), firm A would earn a profit of 2 if it also charged the low price ($6) and 1 if it charged a high price (say, $8). Similarly, if firm B charged a high price ($8), firm A would earn a profit of 5 if it charged the low price and 3 if it charged the high price. Thus, firm A should adopt its dominant strategy of charging the low price. Turning to firm B, we see that if firm A charged the low price, firm B would earn a profit of 2 if it charged the low price and 1 if it charged the high price. Similarly, if firm A charged the high price, firm B would earn a profit of 5 if it charged the low price and 3 if it charged the high price. Thus, firm B should also adopt its dominant strategy of charging the low price. However, both firms could do better (i.e., earn the higher profit of 3) if they cooperated and both charged the high price (the bottom right cell).

Thus, the firms are in a prisoners' dilemma: Each firm will charge the low price and earn a smaller profit because if it charges the higher price, it cannot trust its rival to also charge the high price. Specifically, suppose that firm A charged the high price in the expectation that firm B would also charge the high price (so that each firm would earn a profit of 3). Given that firm A has charged the high price, however, firm B has now an incentive to charge the low price because by doing so it can increase its profits to 5 (see the bottom left cell). The same is true if firm B started by charging the high price in the expectation that firm A would also do so. The net result is that each firm charges the low price and earns a profit of only 2. Only if the two firms learned to cooperate and both charged the high price would they earn the higher profit of 3 (and overcome their dilemma). Case Study 10-3 shows that the airlines' fare war is an example of the prisoners' dilemma.

Nonprice Competition, Cartel Cheating, and the Prisoners' Dilemma

Although the payoff matrix of Table 10-4 was used to examine oligopolistic price competition in the presence of the prisoners' dilemma, by simply changing the heading of the columns and rows of the payoff matrix we can use the same payoff matrix to examine nonprice competition and cartel cheating. For example, if we changed (penciled in) the heading of "low price" to "advertise" and changed the heading of "high price" to "don't advertise" in the columns and rows of the payoff matrix of Table 10-4, we can use the same payoff matrix of Table 10-4 to analyze advertising as a form of nonprice competition in the presence of the prisoners' dilemma. We would then see that each firm would adopt its dominant strategy of advertising and (as in the case of charging a low price) would earn a profit

CASE STUDY 10-3
The Airlines' Fare War and the Prisoners' Dilemma

In April 1992, American Airlines, then the nation's largest carrier with a 20 percent share of the domestic market, introduced a new, simplified fare structure that included only 4 kinds of fares instead of 16, and it lowered prices for most business and leisure travelers. Coach fares were cut by an average of 38 percent and first-class fares were lowered by 20 to 50 percent. Other domestic airlines quickly announced similar fare cuts. American and other carriers hoped that the increase in air travel resulting from the fare cuts would more than offset the price reductions and eventually turn losses into badly needed profits (during 1990 and 1991, domestic airlines lost more than $6 billion, Pan Am and Eastern Airlines went out of business, and Continental, TWA, and America West filed for bankruptcy protection).

Rather than establishing price discipline, however, American's new fare structure started a process of competitive fare cuts that led to another disastrous price war during the summer of 1992. It started when TWA, operating under protection from creditors and badly needing quick revenues, began to undercut American's fares by 10 to 20 percent as soon as they were announced. American and other airlines responded by matching TWA's price cuts. Then, on May 26, 1992, Northwest, in an effort to stimulate summer leisure travel, announced that an adult and child could travel on the same flight within the continental United States for the price of one ticket. The next day, American countered by cutting all fares by 50 percent. The other big carriers immediately matched American's 50 percent price cut for all summer travel. Another full-fledged price war had been unleashed.

Even though deep price cuts increased summer travel sharply, all airlines incurred losses (i.e., the low fares failed to cover the industry average cost). Three attempts to increase air fares by 30 percent above presale levels in the fall of 1992 failed when one or more of the carriers did not go along. Having become used to deep discounts, passengers were simply unwilling to pay higher fares, especially in a weak economy. Similar price wars erupted in the summers of 1993 and 1994. In short, U.S. airlines seemed to be in a prisoners' dilemma and, unable to cooperate, faced heavy losses. Only with the strong rebound in air travel in 1995 did airlines refrain from engaging in another disastrous price war and thus earned profits.

But tranquility and profits did not last long. With the very low marginal cost of adding passengers to a flight after it has been scheduled, there is a strong incentive for all airlines to cut fares to fill all seats on a flight. In addition, economic recession in the second half of 2001 and the terrorist attack on the World Trade Center in September of that year resulted in a sharp decline in air travel, prompting the U.S. Congress to extend $10 billion in loan guarantees to the nation's airlines to prevent their collapse. But pressure from low-cost carrier Southwest and the emergence of discount carriers, such as America West, JetBlue, and AirTran, sparked renewed fare wars in 2001 and 2002, leading to total industry losses of $40 billion from 2001 to 2005. This, together with the doubling of jet fuel prices in 2005, caused Delta and Northwest to join United and U.S. Airways into Chapter 11 bankruptcy in 2005.

Source: "American Air Cuts Most Fares in Simplification of Rate System," *The New York Times* (April 10, 1992), p. 1; "The Airlines Are Killing Each Other Again," *Business Week* (June 8, 1992), p. 32; "Airlines Cut Fares by Up to 45%," *The New York Times* (September 14, 1993), p. D1; "Come Fly the Unfriendly Skies," *The Economist* (November 5, 1994), pp. 61–62; "How High Can the Airlines Fly?" *Business Week* (August 7, 1995), pp. 24–25; "The Age of 'Wal-Mart' Airlines Crunches the Biggest Carriers," *The Wall Street Journal* (June 18, 2002), p. A1; "Losses Widen at Nation's Major Airlines," *The Wall Street Journal* (July 19, 2002), p. B4; "Flying on Empty," *The Economist* (September 17, 2005), pp. 59–60; and "The Law of Gravity Doesn't Apply," *NewsWeek* (September 26, 2005), p. 49.

of 2. Both firms, however, would do better by not advertising because they would then ea... (as in the case of charging a high price) the higher profit of 3. The firms then face the prisoners' dilemma. Only by cooperating in not advertising would each increase its profits to 3. For example, when cigarette advertising on television was banned in 1971, all tobacco companies benefited by spending less on advertising and earning higher profits. While the intended effect of the law was not to encourage people to smoke, the law also had the unintended effect of solving the prisoners' dilemma for cigarette producers.

Similarly, if we now changed the heading of "low price" or "advertise" to "cheat" and the heading of "high price" or "don't advertise" to "don't cheat" in the columns and rows of the payoff matrix of Table 10-4, we could use the same payoffs in Table 10-4 to analyze the incentive for cartel members to cheat in the presence of the prisoners' dilemma. In this case, each firm adopts its dominant strategy of cheating and (as in the case of charging the low price or advertising) earns a profit of 2. But by not cheating, each member of the cartel would earn the higher profit of 3. The cartel members then face the prisoners' dilemma. Only if cartel members do not cheat will each share the higher cartel profits of 3. A cartel can prevent or reduce the probability of cheating by monitoring the sales of each member and punishing cheaters. However, the greater the number of members of the cartel and the more differentiated the product, the more difficult it is for the cartel to do this and prevent cheating.

10-5 REPEATED GAMES AND TIT-FOR-TAT STRATEGY

We have seen how two firms facing the prisoners' dilemma can increase their profits by cooperating. Such cooperation, however, is not likely to occur in the type of prisoners' dilemma games discussed until now, which are played only once (i.e., that involve a single move or action by each player). Cooperation is more likely to occur in repeated games, or games involving many consecutive moves by each player. These types of games are more realistic in the real world. For example, oligopolists do not decide on their pricing strategy only once but many times over many years.

In **repeated games** (i.e., in games involving many consecutive moves and countermoves by each player), the best strategy for each player is tit-for-tat. **Tit-for-tat** behavior can be summarized as follows: Do to your opponent what he has just done to you. That is, you begin by cooperating and continue to cooperate as long as your opponent cooperates. If he betrays you, the next time you betray him back. If he then cooperates, the next time you also cooperate. This strategy is retaliatory enough to discourage noncooperation, but forgiving enough to allow a pattern of mutual cooperation to develop. In computer simulation as well as in actual experiments, a tit-for-tat behavior was found to be consistently the best strategy (i.e., the one that resulted in the largest benefit) for each player over time.[5]

For a tit-for-tat strategy to be best, however, certain conditions must be met. First, it requires a reasonably stable set of players. If the players change frequently, there is little chance for cooperative behavior to develop. Second, there must be a small number of players (otherwise, it becomes very difficult to keep track of what each is doing). Third, it is

---

[5] See R. Axelrod, *The Evolution of Cooperation* (New York: Basic Books, 1984).

assumed that each firm can quickly detect (and is willing and able to quickly retaliate for) cheating by other firms. Cheating that can go undetected for a long time encourages cheating. Fourth, demand and cost conditions must be relatively stable (for if they change rapidly, it is difficult to define what is cooperative behavior and what is not). Fifth, we must assume that the game is repeated indefinitely, or at least a very large and *uncertain* number of times. If the game is played for a finite number of times, each firm has an incentive not to cooperate in the final period since it cannot be harmed by retaliation. However, each firm knows this and thus will not cooperate on the next-to-the-last move. Indeed, in an effort to gain a competitive advantage by being the first to start cheating, the entire situation will unravel, and cheating begins from the first move.[6]

There are, of course, times when a firm finds that it is to its advantage not to cooperate. For example, if a supplier is near bankruptcy, a firm may find every excuse for not paying its bills to the near-bankrupt firm (claiming, for example, that supplies were defective or did not meet specifications) in the hope of avoiding payment altogether if the firm does go out of business. It is the necessity to deal with the same suppliers and customers in the future and their ability to retaliate for noncooperative behavior that often forces a firm to cooperate. With a tit-for-tat strategy, however, it is possible for firms to cooperate without actually resorting to collusion. As we will see in Chapter 12, this can be a nightmare for antitrust officials.

10-6   STRATEGIC MOVES

In this section, we examine games involving threats, commitments, credibility, and entry deterrence. These concepts greatly enrich game theory and provide an important element of realism and relevance.

Threat, Commitments, and Credibility

Oligopolistic firms often adopt strategies to gain a competitive advantage over their rivals even if it means constraining their own behavior or temporarily reducing their own profits. For example, an oligopolist may threaten to lower its prices if its rivals lower theirs, even if this means reducing its own profits. This threat can be made credible, for example, by a written commitment to customers to match any lower price by competitors.

For example, suppose that the payoff matrix of firms A and B is given by Table 10-5. This payoff matrix indicates that firm A has the dominant strategy of charging a high price. The reason is that if firm B charged a low price, firm A would earn a profit of 2 if it charged a low price and a profit of 3 if it charged a high price. Similarly, if firm B charged a high price, firm A would earn a profit of 2 if it charged a low price and a profit of 5 if it charged a high price. Therefore, firm A charges a high price regardless of what firm B does. Given that firm A charges a high price, firm B will want to charge a low price

---

[6] See D. Kreps, P. Milgron, J. Roberts, and R. Wilson, "Rational Cooperation in the Finitely Repeated Prisoners' Dilemma," *Journal of Economic Theory* (1982), pp. 245–252.

TABLE 10-5	Payoff Matrix for Pricing Game with a Threat	
		Firm B	
		Low Price	High Price
Firm A	Low Price	(2, 2)	(2, 1)
	High Price	(3, 4)	(5, 3)

because by doing so it will earn a profit of 4 (instead of 3 with a high price). This is shown by the bottom left cell of Table 10-5. Now firm A can threaten firm B to lower its price and also charge a low price. However, firm B does not believe this threat (i.e., the threat is not credible) because by lowering its price, firm A would lower its profits from 3 (with a high price) to 2 with the low price (the top left cell in the table).

One way to make this threat credible is for firm A to develop a *reputation* for carrying out its threats—even at the expense of profits. This may seem irrational. However, if firm A actually carried out its threat several times, it would earn a reputation for making credible threats, and this is likely to induce firm B to also charge a high price, thus possibly leading to higher profits for firm A in the long run. In that case, firm A would earn a profit of 5 and firm B a profit of 3 (the bottom right cell) as opposed to a profit of 3 for firm A and 4 for firm B (the bottom left cell). Note that even if firm B earns a profit of 3 by charging the high price (as compared with a profit of 4 by charging the low price), this is still higher than the profit of 2 that it would earn if firm A carried out the threat of charging the low price if firm B does (see the top left cell of the table). By showing a commitment to carry out its threats, firm A makes its threats credible and increases its profits over time.

Entry Deterrence

One important strategy that an oligopolist can use to deter market entry is to threaten to lower its price and thereby impose a loss on the potential entrant. Such a threat, however, works only if it is credible. *Entry deterrence* can be examined with the payoff matrices of Tables 10-6 and 10-7. Let us start with the payoff matrix of Table 10-6.

The payoff matrix of Table 10-6 shows that firm A's threat to lower its price is not credible and does not discourage firm B from entering the market. The reason is that firm A earns

TABLE 10-6	Payoff Matrix without Credible Entry Deterrence	
		Firm B	
		Enter	Do Not Enter
Firm A	Low Price	(4, −2)	(6, 0)
	High Price	(7, 2)	(10, 0)

TABLE 10-7	Payoff Matrix with Credible Entry Deterrence	
		Firm B	
		Enter	Do Not Enter
Firm A	Low Price	(4, −2)	(6, 0)
	High Price	(3, 2)	(8, 0)

CASE STUDY 10-4
Wal-Mart's Preemptive Expansion Marketing Strategy

Rapid expansion during the 1980s (from 153 stores in 1976 to more than 3,773 in 2005) propelled Wal-Mart, the discount retail-store chain started by Sam Walton in 1969, to become the nation's (and the world's) largest and most profitable retailer, at a time when most other retailers were making razor-thin profits or incurring losses as a result of stiff competition. How did Wal-Mart do it? By opening retail discount stores in small towns across America and adopting an everyday low-price strategy. The conventional wisdom had been that a discount retail outlet required a population base of at least 100,000 people to be profitable. Sam Walton showed otherwise—by relying on size, low costs, and high turnover, Wal-Mart earned high profits even in towns of only a few thousand people. Since a small town could support only one large discount store, Wal-Mart did not have to worry about competition from other national chains (which would drive prices and profit margins down). At the same time, Wal-Mart was able to easily undersell small local specialized stores out of existence (Wal-Mart has been labeled the "Merchant of Death" by local retailers), thereby establishing a virtual local retailing monopoly.

The success of Wal-Mart did not go unnoticed by other national discount retailers such as Kmart and Target, and so a frantic race started to open discount stores in rural America ahead of the competition. By adopting such an aggressive expansion or *preemptive investment strategy*, Wal-Mart has continued to expand at breathtaking speed and to beat the competition most of the time. Sales at Wal-Mart increased from $80 billion in 1994 to $288 billion in 2004 (thus heading the list of the Fortune 500 companies) and are projected to continue to rise rapidly in the future. Pricier than Wal-Mart and dowdier than Target, Kmart, instead, filed for bankruptcy in January 2002 and merged with Sears Roebuck to form Kmart Holdings in 2004.

Since 1992, Wal-Mart has also expanded abroad, first in Canada and Mexico (where it is already the largest retailer), then in Argentina, Brazil, China, Korea, and Puerto Rico, and more recently in Germany, England, and Japan. In 2005, Wal-Mart had 1,643 stores abroad, which generated 21 percent of its total revenue. Regarded as one of the most successful and aggressive retailers in the United States, Wal-Mart is now also shaking up the industry abroad in the nations in which it is operating by its winning low-price strategy, long store hours, friendly service, private-label brands, and a superefficient distribution system.

During the next few years, Europe is likely to be the fiercest battleground as Wal-Mart tries to expand across the continent and attempts to duplicate its American success. For example, Wal-Mart has yet to turn a profit in Germany. European retailers are responding by also consolidating. In fall 1999, French retailers Carrefour and Promedes merged, creating Europe's biggest and the world's second largest retailer with annual sales of $90 billion and operating more than 6,000 stores in 28 countries in 2004. Despite its great market success at home, however, Wal-Mart is facing a tougher commercial battleground abroad, especially in Continental Europe.

Source: "Big Discounters Duel Over Hot Market," *The Wall Street Journal* (August 23, 1995), p. A8; "French Retailers Create New Wal-Mart Rival," *The Wall Street Journal* (August 31, 1999), p. A14; "Wal-Mart Around the World," *The Economist* (December 8, 2001), pp. 55–57; "Kmart Takeover of Sears Is Set," *The New York Times* (November 11, 2004), p. 1; "Wal-Mart," *Forbes* (April 12, 2005), pp. 77–85; and "Carrefour at the Crossroad," *The Economist* (October 31, 2005), p. 71.

a profit of 4 if it charges the low price and a profit of 7 if it charges the high price. Unless firm A makes a credible commitment to fight entry even at the expense of profits, it would not deter firm B from entering the market. Firm A could make a credible threat by expanding its capacity before it is needed (i.e., to build excess capacity). The new payoff matrix might then look like the one indicated in Table 10-7.

The payoff matrix of Table 10-7 is the same as in Table 10-6, except that firm A's profits are now lower when it charges a high price because idle or excess capacity increases firm A's costs without increasing its sales. On the other hand, in the payoff matrix of Table 10-7, we assume that charging a low price would allow firm A to increase sales and utilize its newly built capacity so that costs and revenues increase, leaving firm A's profits the same as in Table 10-6 (i.e., the same as before firm A expanded capacity).[7] Building excess capacity in anticipation of future needs now becomes a credible threat because with excess capacity firm A will charge a low price and earn a profit of 4 instead of a profit of 3 if it charged the high price. By now charging a low price, however, firm B would incur a loss of 2 if it entered the market, and so firm B would stay out. Entry deterrence is now credible and effective. An alternative to building excess capacity could be for firm A to cultivate a reputation for irrationality in deterring entry by charging a low price even if this means lower profits indefinitely.[8] Case Study 10-4 examines Wal-Mart's winning preemptive marketing strategy.

10-7 | STRATEGIC BEHAVIOR AND INTERNATIONAL COMPETITIVENESS

Game theory can also be used to examine strategic trade and industrial policies that a nation can use to gain a competitive advantage over other nations, particularly in the high-technology field. We can best show this by an example.

Suppose that Boeing (the American commercial aircraft company) and Airbus Industrie (a consortium of German, French, English, and Spanish companies) are both deciding whether to produce a new aircraft. Suppose also that because of the huge cost of developing the aircraft, a single producer would have to have the entire world market for itself to earn a profit, say, of $100 million. If both firms produce the aircraft, each loses $10 million. This information is shown in Table 10-8. The case where both firms produce the aircraft and each incurs a loss of $10 million is shown in the top left cell of Table 10-8. If only Boeing produces the aircraft, Boeing makes a profit of $100 million while Airbus makes a zero profit (the top right cell of the table). On the other hand, if Boeing does not produce the aircraft while Airbus does, Boeing makes zero profit while Airbus makes a profit of $100 million (the bottom left cell). Finally, if neither firm produces the aircraft, each makes a zero profit (the bottom right cell).

---

[7] Revenues and profits need not increase exactly by the same amount, so that profits can change even when firm A charges a low price. The conclusion would remain the same, however (i.e., firm B would be deterred from entering the market) as long as firm A earns a higher profit with a low price than with a high price after increasing its capacity.

[8] For a more detailed analysis of the use of excess capacity to deter entry, see J. Tirole, *The Theory of Industrial Organization* (Cambridge, Mass.: MIT Press, 1988).

TABLE 10-8	Two-Firm Competition and Strategic Trade Policy	

		Airbus	
		Produce	Don't Produce
Boeing	Produce	$(-10, -10)$	$(100, 0)$
	Don't Produce	$(0, 100)$	$(0, 0)$

Suppose that for whatever reason Boeing enters the market first and earns a profit of $100 million (we might call this the *first-mover advantage*). Airbus is now locked out of the market because it could not earn a profit. This is the case shown in the top right cell of the table. If Airbus entered the market, both firms would incur a loss (and we would have the case shown in the top left column of the table). Suppose that now European governments give a subsidy of $15 million per year to Airbus. Then Airbus will produce the aircraft even though Boeing is already producing the aircraft because with the $15 million subsidy Airbus would turn a loss of $10 million into a profit of $5 million. Without a subsidy, Boeing will go from making a profit of $100 million (without Airbus in the market) to incurring a loss of $10 million afterward (we are still in the top left corner of the table, but with the Airbus entry changed from −10 without the subsidy to +5 with the subsidy). Because of its unsubsidized loss, Boeing will stop producing the aircraft and leave the entire market to Airbus, which will then make a profit of $100 million without any further subsidy (the bottom left cell of the table).[9]

The U.S. government could, of course, retaliate with a subsidy of its own to keep Boeing producing the aircraft. Except in cases of national defense, however, the U.S. government is much less disposed to grant subsidies to firms than European governments. Although the real world is certainly much more complex than this example, we can see how a nation could overcome a market disadvantage and acquire a strategic comparative advantage in a high-tech field by using an industrial and strategic trade policy.

One serious shortcoming of the above analysis is that it is usually very difficult to accurately forecast the outcome of government industrial and trade policies (i.e., get the data to fill a table such as Table 10-8). Even a small change in the table could completely change the results. For example, suppose that if both Airbus and Boeing produce the aircraft, Airbus incurs a loss of $10 million (as before) but Boeing makes a profit of $10 million (without any subsidy), say, because of superior technology. Then, even if Airbus produces the aircraft with the subsidy, Boeing will remain in the market because it is able to earn a profit without any subsidy. Then, Airbus would require a subsidy indefinitely, year after year, in order to continue to produce the aircraft. In this case, giving a subsidy to Airbus does not seem to be such a good idea. Thus, it is extremely difficult to carry out this type of analysis in the real world. Getting the analysis wrong, however, can be very harmful and may even result in the firm's failure (see Case Study 10-5). This is the reason

---

[9] This type of analysis was first introduced into international trade by James Brander and Barbara Spencer. See their "International R & D Rivalry and Industrial Strategy," *Review of Economic Studies* (October 1983), pp. 707–722; see also M. Porter, *The Competitive Advantage of Nations* (New York: Free Press, 1990).

CASE STUDY 10-5
Companies' Strategic Mistakes and Failures

Nearly 100,000 businesses failed in the United States during 1992 (a recession year) as compared with about 35,000 in 2000 (the last year of the boom of the 1990s) and nearly 40,000 in 2001 (a recession year). Although the reasons businesses fail are many and the details differ from case to case, several general underlying causes can be identified. *First*, many business failures arise because senior executives do not fully understand the fundamentals of their business or the core expertise of the firm. Then the company drifts (often through mergers and acquisitions) into lines of business about which it knows little. This, for example, happened to Kodak when it diversified from its core camera and film business into pharmaceuticals and consumer health products during the 1990s.

The *second* basic reason for business failures is lack of vision, or the inability of top management to anticipate or foresee serious problems that the business may face down the road. For example, U.S. automakers (General Motors, Ford, and Chrysler) failed to understand early enough the seriousness of the competitive challenge coming from Japan and almost willingly ceded the small-car market to Japan (because of the low profits per car earned in that market) during the 1970s. They erroneously believed that Japan would never be able to compete effectively in the medium-range segment of the market (where profit per automobile was much higher and American automakers were stronger). This resulted in huge losses for U.S. automakers during the second half of the 1980s and early 1990s and almost drove Chrysler out of business (this is examined in Case

Study 12–10). Another example is provided by Sears, which was unable or unwilling to understand the kind of sea of change going on in consumer preferences. This eventually propelled Wal-Mart to replace it as the nation's top marketeer. Most dangerous are latent or stealthy competitors, who as a result of some major and quick technological or market change can devastate the firm in its very core business. A clear example of this is IBM's inability to recognize early enough the importance and dramatic growth of the PC market in the mid-1980s and subsequent signing of Microsoft to develop the software and Intel to supply the chips for its PCs.

A *third* reason for business failures is the loading of the firm with a heavy debt burden (usually to carry out a program of merger and acquisitions, often at overpriced terms), which then robs the firm of its strength in a market downturn. This is precisely what happened (together with greed, deceit, and financial chicanery) to WorldCom (one of the world's largest telecommunications companies), which filed the largest U.S. claim for bankruptcy in July 2002.

Fourth, business failures arise when firms vainly try to recapture their past glories, become stuck on an obsolete strategy, and are unable to respond to new and major competitive challenges. This is, to some extent, what happened to General Motors and IBM during the past decade before the brutal forces of the market shook them out of their complacency. It is often more difficult to keep a business great than to build it in the first place. *Finally*, a company may fail as a result of strikes and hostilities from unhappy workers.

Source: "Dinosaurs?" *Fortune* (May 3, 1994), pp. 36–42; "Why Companies Fail," *Fortune* (November 14, 1994), pp. 52–68; "How Good Companies Go Bad," *Harvard Business Review* (July–August 1999), pp. 42–52; "Why Enron Went Bust," *Fortune* (December 24, 2001), pp. 58–68; "WorldCom Files for Bankruptcy: Largest U.S. Case," *The New York Times* (July 22, 2002), p. 1; "Why Companies Fail," *Business Week* (May 22, 2002), pp. 50–62; and "A Question of Management," *The Economist* (June 11, 2005), p. 74.

that most U.S. economists are today against industrial policy and still regard free trade as the best policy.[10]

10-8 SEQUENTIAL GAMES AND DECISION TREES

Until now, we have examined games in which players selected their best strategies and moved at the same time. Some strategic choices or games, however, are sequential in nature in that the best strategy or move for each player depends on the other player's previous move. Sequential games can be shown by *game* or *decision trees.* A **decision tree** is a diagram with *nodes* and *branches:* the nodes depict points at which decisions are made and the branches show the outcome of each decision in sequential games. The construction of decision trees begin with the earliest decision and moves forward in time through a series of subsequent decisions. At every point that a decision must be made, the tree branches out until all the possible outcomes of the game have been depicted. The possible outcomes of the game are given by the payoffs on the right side of the figure or tree.

For example, Figure 10-1 shows the decision tree that firm (duopolist) A can use to determine whether to adopt a high-price or a low-price strategy (circle A on the left-hand side of the figure). Circle B depicts competitor (duopolist) B's reactions to firm A's price strategy. Firm A estimates that if it adopts a high-price strategy (the top branch of the figure), it will make a profit of $100 if firm B reacts by also charging a high price and a profit of $130 if firm B reacts by charging a low price (see the first column labeled firm A on the right-hand side of the figure). When firm A charges a high price, firm B will make

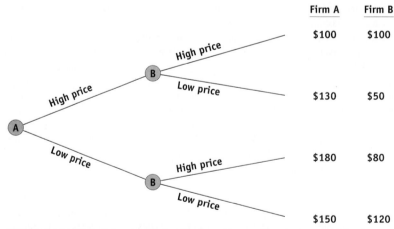

FIGURE 10-1 High-Price, Low-Price Strategy Game The strategy or highest payoff for firm A is to adopt a low-price strategy (the bottom branch node) rather than a high-price strategy (the top branch node). Given firm A's decision, firm B's best payoff is to also adopt a low-price strategy.

---

[10] "Remember Clinton's Industrial Policy? O.K. Now Forget It," *Business Week* (December 12, 1994), p. 53; P. Krugman, "Is Free Trade Passe?" *The Journal of Economic Perspectives* (Fall 1987), pp. 131–144; "Games or Serious Business?" *Financial Times* (March 26, 2002), p. 8; and "Free Trade," *Global Finance* (July 2002), p. 14.

a profit of $100 if it also charges a high price and a profit of $50 if it charges a low price (see the second column labeled firm B on the right-hand side of the figure). If firm A adopts a low-price strategy (the bottom branch of the figure), firm A estimates that it will make a profit of $180 if firm B reacts by charging a high price and a profit of $150 if firm B reacts by also charging a low price. When firm A charges a low price, firm B will make a profit of $80 if it charges a high price and a profit of $120 if it also charges a low price.

The game begins when firm A decides to follow a high- or a low-price strategy. Firm B moves next by deciding to respond with a high- or low-price strategy of its own. If firm A decides on a high-price strategy, the game moves along the upper branch; if firm A decides on a low-price strategy, the games moves along the lower branch. There are thus four possible outcomes: (1) firm A follows a high-price strategy and firm B responds with a high price of its own; (2) firm A follows a high-price strategy and firm B responds by charging a low price; (3) firm A follows a low-price strategy and firm B responds with a high price; (4) firm A follows a low-price strategy and firm B responds with a low price of its own. The profits of each firm are shown on the right-hand of the figure next to each of the four possible outcomes.

How is the game solved? Firm A wants to adopt the pricing strategy that leads to the highest payoff, but this depends on firm B's reaction to firm A's decision. Figure 10-1 shows that if firm A chooses a high-price strategy, firm B enters the game at the upper decision node and faces a payoff of $100 if it also charges a high price or $50 if it charges a low price. Thus, if firm A followed a high-price strategy, it knows that firm B would respond with a high-price strategy of its own and firm A would get a payoff of $100. However, if firm A chooses a low-price strategy, firm B follows the lower decision node and faces a payoff of $80 if it charges a high price or $120 if it charges a low price. Thus, if firm A followed a low-price strategy, it knows that firm B would respond with a low price-strategy of its own and firm A would get a payoff of $150. Comparing the outcome of these two pricing strategies, firm A knows that it would get a payoff of $100 if it charged a high price and a payoff of $150 if it charged a low price. Thus, firm A chooses to charge a low price (i.e., the lower decision node) and receives a payoff of $150, and firm B decides to respond with a low price of its own (i.e., the lower branch) and receives a payoff of $120.

Note that the above game has been solved by starting with the best payoffs shown on the right-hand side of the figure and then moving leftward along the branches—a process called *backward induction*—to determine the firm's best strategy. Since the best payoffs for firm A are on the lower branches, its strategy would be to follow a low-price strategy. Given firm A's strategy, the highest payoff for firm B on the lower branches occurs when it also charges a low price. This type of sequential game is called *extensive form game*. Extensive form games may or may not have Nash equilibria, but they are usually characterized by equilibrium strategies that involve a sequence of strategic decisions by each player.

In the real world, extensive form games are much more complex and are represented by decision trees that are much more extensive than that shown in Figure 10-1. They often involve also uncertainty about the payoffs. These are discussed in Section 13-5. Case Study 10-6 shows how Airbus might have decided on building the superjumbo jet A380 and how Boeing responded with plans to build its sonic cruiser.

CASE STUDY 10-6
Airbus's Decision to Build the A380 and Boeing's Sonic Cruiser Response and the 747-8

In 2000, Airbus decided to build its superjumbo A380 capable of transporting 550 passengers, to be ready by 2006 at a cost of over $10 billion, and thus compete head-on with the Boeing 747 (which has been in service since 1969 and can carry up to 475 passengers). Boeing greeted Airbus's decision to build its A380 by announcing in 2001 plans to build a new "sonic cruiser" jet that can transport, nonstop, 250 passengers to any point on earth at close to the speed of sound by 2008. Boeing believes that passengers prefer arriving at their destinations sooner and avoid congested hubs and the hassle and delays of intermediate stops.

We can use the decision tree of Figure 10-2 to examine how Airbus might have decided to build its A380 plane and Boeing's response with plans to build its "sonic cruiser" jet. The figure shows that the best payoff (shown on the right-hand side of the figure) for Airbus is to build the A380 (the top branch node) rather than not to build it (the bottom branch node). By building the A380, Airbus would earn a profit of $50 if Boeing decided also to build a superjumbo jet and a profit of $120 if Boeing decided instead to build the sonic cruiser (by 2000, it had become clear that the market for the superjumbo was larger than previously estimated and that both Airbus and Boeing could probably earn a profit if both built the plane). If instead Airbus decided not to build the superjumbo jet, it would earn zero profits from this project, regardless of what Boeing decided to do (the bottom branch of the decision tree). Thus, Airbus decided to build the superjumbo jet. Given Airbus's decision, Boeing decided to build the sonic cruiser and earn a profit of $100 instead of building its own superjumbo jet and earn a profit of only $50 million. In November 2005, however, Boeing surprised Airbus by also announcing a new version of its Boeing 747 (the 747-8) to enter service in 2009.

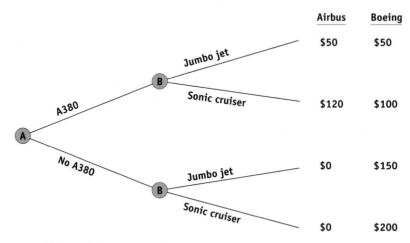

FIGURE 10-2   Airbus's Strategic Decision to Build the A380 and Boeing's Sonic Cruiser Response   The best payoff for Airbus is to build the A380 (the top branch node) rather than not to build it (the bottom branch node). Given Airbus's decision, Boeing's best payoff is to build the sonic cruiser.

Source: "The Birth of a Giant," *Business Week* (July 10, 2000), pp. 170–176; "Boeing Opts to Build New Class of 'Sonic Cruiser' Jet," *Financial Times* (March 30, 2001), p. 1; "Boeing Flight to Safety," *Business Week* (July 29, 2002), pp. 70–71; "After Four Years in the Rear, Boeing Is Set to Jet Past Airbus," *The Wall Street Journal* (June 6, 2005), p. A1; "Boeing New Tailwind," *Newsweek* (December 5, 2005), p. 45; and "Boeing Updates 747 in Battle with Airbus," *The Wall Street Journal* (November 16, 2005), p. A10.

SUMMARY

1. Strategic behavior is concerned with the choice of an optimal strategy in conflict situations and is analyzed with game theory. Every game theory model includes players, strategies, and payoffs. A game in which the gain of one player or firm comes at the expense and is exactly equal to the loss of the other player or firm is called a zero-sum game. A game in which the gains or losses of one player or firm do not come at the expense of or provide equal benefit to the other player or firm is a nonzero-sum game.

2. The dominant strategy is the best or optimal choice for a player no matter what the opponent does. The Nash equilibrium occurs when each player has chosen his or her optimal strategy, given the strategy chosen by the other player.

3. Oligopolistic firms often face a problem called the prisoners' dilemma. This refers to a situation in which each firm adopts its dominant strategy but could do better (i.e., earn a larger profit) by cooperating.

4. Oligopolistic firms deciding on their pricing or advertising strategy, or on whether to cheat in a cartel, may face the prisoners' dilemma. In those cases, both firms would gain by shifting from a noncooperative to a cooperative game.

5. The best strategy for repeated or multiple-move prisoners' dilemma games is tit-for-tat, which refers to doing to your opponent what he or she has just done to you. A player must show a commitment to carry out a threat for it to be credible.

6. Oligopolists often make strategic moves. A strategic move is one in which a player constrains its own behavior in order to make a threat credible so as to gain a competitive advantage over a rival. The firm making the threat must be committed to carrying it out for the threat to be credible. This may involve accepting lower profits or building excess capacity.

7. Just like firms, nations can behave strategically by protecting and subsidizing some high-tech industry in order to gain a competitive advantage over other nations. It is very difficult, however, to carry out a successful industrial policy, and so free trade remains the best policy in most cases.

8. Sequential games can be shown by game or decision trees. A decision tree is a diagram with nodes and branches used to depict points at which decisions are made and the outcome or payoffs of each decision.

 DISCUSSION QUESTIONS

1. In what way does game theory extend the analysis of oligopolistic behavior presented in Chapter 9?

2. What is meant by (*a*) Strategy? (*b*) Payoff? (*c*) Payoff matrix?

3. What is meant by (*a*) Zero-sum game? (*b*) Nonzero-sum game?

4. (*a*) Can game theory be used only for analyzing oligopolistic interdependence? (*b*) In what way is game theory similar to playing chess?

5. Do we have a Nash equilibrium when each firm chooses its dominant strategy?

6. (*a*) Why is the Cournot equilibrium a Nash equilibrium? (*b*) In what way does the Cournot equilibrium differ from the Nash equilibrium given in Table 10-2?

7. In what way is the prisoners' dilemma related to the choice of dominant strategy by the players in a game and to the concept of Nash equilibrium?

8. How can the concept of the prisoners' dilemma be used to analyze price competition?

9. How can introducing yearly style changes lead to a prisoners' dilemma for automakers?

10. (*a*) What is the incentive for the members of a cartel to cheat on the cartel? (*b*) What can the cartel do to prevent cheating? (*c*) Under what conditions is a cartel more likely to collapse?

11. Do the duopolists in a Cournot equilibrium face a prisoners' dilemma? Explain.

12. How did the 1971 law that banned cigarette advertising on television solve the prisoners' dilemma for cigarette producers?

13. (*a*) What is the meaning of tit-for-tat in game theory? (*b*) What conditions are usually required for tit-for-tat strategy to be the best strategy?

14. (*a*) How is a strategic move differentiated from a Nash equilibrium? (*b*) What is a credible threat? When is a threat not credible?

15. What is a decision tree? When is a decision tree useful?

PROBLEMS

1. From the following payoff matrix, where the payoffs are the profits or losses of the two firms, determine (*a*) whether firm A has a dominant strategy, (*b*) whether firm B has a dominant strategy, and (*c*) the optimal strategy for each firm.

		Firm B	
		Low Price	High Price
Firm A	Low Price	(1, 1)	(3, −1)
	High Price	(−1, 3)	(2, 2)

2. From the following payoff matrix, where the payoffs are the profits or losses of the two firms, determine (*a*) whether firm A has a dominant strategy, (*b*) whether firm B has a dominant strategy, (*c*) the optimal strategy for each firm, and (*d*) the Nash equilibrium, if there is one.

		Firm B	
		Low Price	High Price
Firm A	Low Price	(1, 1)	(3, −1)
	High Price	(−1, 3)	(4, 2)

*3. From the following payoff matrix, where the payoffs are the profits or losses of the two firms, determine (*a*) whether firm A has a dominant strategy, (*b*) whether firm B has a dominant strategy, (*c*) the optimal strategy for each firm, and (*d*) the Nash equilibrium. (*e*) Under what conditions is the situation indicated in the payoff matrix likely to occur?

		Firm B	
		Small Cars	Large Cars
Firm A	Small Cars	(4, 4)	(−2, −2)
	Large Cars	(−2, −2)	(4, 4)

4. Provide a hypothetical payoff matrix for Case Study 10-2 in this chapter.

5. From the following payoff matrix, where the payoffs (the negative values) are the years of possible imprisonment for individuals A and B, determine (*a*) whether individual A has a dominant strategy, (*b*) whether individual B has a dominant strategy, and (*c*) the optimal strategy for each individual. (*d*) Do individuals A and B face a prisoners' dilemma?

		Individual B	
		Confess	Don't Confess
Individual A	Confess	(−5, −5)	(−1, −10)
	Don't Confess	(−10, −1)	(−2, −2)

6. Explain why the payoff matrix in Problem 1 indicates that firms A and B face the prisoners' dilemma.

7. Do firms A and B in Problem 2 face the prisoners' dilemma? Why?

*8. From the following payoff matrix, where the payoffs refer to the profits that firms A and B earn by cheating and not cheating in a cartel, (*a*) determine whether firms A and B face the prisoners' dilemma. (*b*) What would happen if we changed the payoff in the bottom left cell to (5, 5)?

		Firm B	
		Cheat	Don't Cheat
Firm A	Cheat	(4, 3)	(8, 1)
	Don't Cheat	(2, 6)	(6, 5)

*9. Starting with the payoff matrix of Problem 1, show what the tit-for-tat strategy would be for the first five of an infinite number of games if firm A starts by cooperating but firm B does not cooperate in the next period.

10. Given the following payoff matrix, (*a*) indicate the best strategy for each firm. (*b*) Why is the entry-deterrent threat by firm A to lower the price not credible to firm B? (*c*) What could firm A do to make its threat credible without building excess capacity?

		Firm B	
		Enter	Don't Enter
Firm A	Low Price	(3, −1)	(3, 1)
	High Price	(4, 5)	(6, 3)

11. Show how the payoff matrix in the table for Problem 10 might change if firm A were to make a credible threat to lower the price by building excess capacity to deter firm B from entering the market.

12. What strategic industrial or trade policy would be required (if any) in the United States and in Europe if the entries in the top left cell of the payoff matrix in Table 10-8 were changed to (*a*) (10, 10)? (*b*) (5, 0)? (*c*) (5, −10)?

13. Given the following decision tree in which Boeing, not Airbus, makes the first move, determine (*a*) Boeing's best strategy and (*b*) Airbus's best strategy. See Figure 10-3.

14. (*a*) What is the difference between Case Study 10-6 in the text and the situation in Problem 13? (*b*) What would the result be if the payoff for Boeing building the sonic cruiser were $150 million if Airbus builds the superjumbo jet and $120 million if Airbus does not build the superjumbo jet?

15. **Integrating Problem**
Determine (*a*) firm A's best strategy, (*b*) firm B's best strategy from the following decision tree. (*c*) How could the decision tree be expanded further? See Figure 10-4.

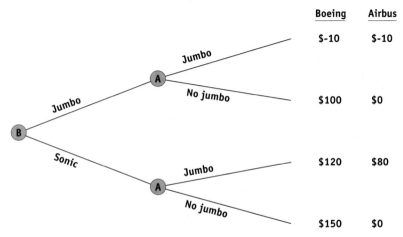

FIGURE 10-3

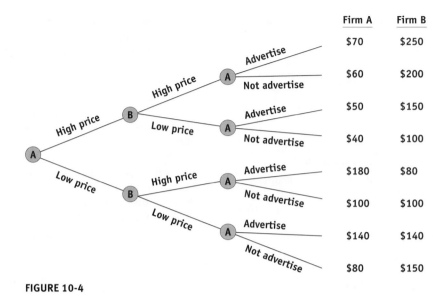

	Firm A	Firm B
Advertise	$70	$250
Not advertise	$60	$200
Advertise	$50	$150
Not advertise	$40	$100
Advertise	$180	$80
Not advertise	$100	$100
Advertise	$140	$140
Not advertise	$80	$150

FIGURE 10-4

SUPPLEMENTARY READINGS

The original work that introduced game theory to economics is:

von Neumann, John, and Oskar Morgenstern, *Theory of Games and Economic Behavior* (Princeton, N.J.: Princeton University Press, 1944).

More recent presentations of game theory with applications to economics are found in:

Camerer, C., "Progress in Behavioral Game Theory," *Journal of Economic Perspectives* (Summer 1997), pp. 159–174.

Coate, Malcolm B., "Market Structure and Competition Policy: Game-Theoretic Approaches," *Managerial & Decision Economics* (December 2001), pp. 465–466.

Dutta, Prajit K., *Strategies and Games* (Cambridge, Mass.: MIT Press, 1999).

Friedman, James W., *Game Theory with Applications to Economics* (New York: Oxford University Press, 1990).

Fudenberg, D., and Tirole, J., *Game Theory* (Cambridge, Mass.: MIT Press, 2000).

McMillan, James, *Games, Strategies, and Managers* (New York: Oxford University Press, 1996).

For repeated games, see:

Axelrod, R., *The Evolution of Cooperation* (New York: Basic Books, 1984).

Strategic moves are examined in:

Porter, Michael E., *Competitive Strategy* (New York: Free Press, 1980).

Schelling, Thomas C., *The Strategy of Conflict* (Cambridge, Mass.: Harvard University Press, 1990).

A detailed analysis of the use of excess capacity to deter entry is found in:

Tirole, Jean, *The Theory of Industrial Organization* (Cambridge, Mass.: MIT Press, 1988).

On the competition between Airbus and Boeing, see:

Irwin, Douglas A., and Nina Pavcnik, "Airbus Versus Boeing Revisited: International Competition in the Aircraft Market," *Journal of International Economics* (December 2004), pp. 223–245.

For strategic moves to increase the international competitiveness of nations, see:

Krugman, Paul, "Is Free Trade Passe?" *Journal of Economic Perspectives* (Fall 1987), pp. 131–144.

Porter, Michael, *The Competitive Advantage of Nations* (New York: Free Press, 1990).

Salvatore, Dominick, *The Japanese Trade Challenge and the U.S. Response* (Washington, D.C.: The Economic Policy Institute, 1990).

 INTERNET SITE ADDRESSES

For an excellent presentation of game theory, see:

http://www.raven.stern.nyu.edu/networks/5.html

For game strategies used by firms as reported in press, see:

http://www.gametheory.net/news/concept.pl

For more information on John Nash (as well as John Harsanyi and Reinhard Selten who shared the Nobel Prize for Game Theory with John Nash in 1994), see:

http://www.almaz.com/nobel/economics/1994a.html

You can play an interactive online prisoners' dilemma game at:

http://www.princeton.edu/~mdaniels/PD/PD.html

http://www.combabgames.com

For the Fortune Global 500 companies, see:

http://www.fortune.com/global500

Data on business failures are found in:

http://www.BankruptcyData.com

For competition in the computer industry, see:

Apple: http://www.apple.com

Hewlett-Packard: http://www.hp.com

IBM: http://www.ibm.com

Dell: http://www.dell.com

For competition in the commercial aircraft industry, see:

Lockheed Martin: http://www.lockheedmartin.com

Boeing: http://www.boeing.com

Airbus: http://www.airbus.com

For competition in the airline industry, see:

American Airlines: http://www.aa.com

U.S. Airways: http://www.usair.com

Continental Airlines: http://www.continental.com

Delta Air Lines: http://www.delta-air.com

United Airlines: http://www.ual.com

CHAPTER **11**   Pricing Practices

CHAPTER OUTLINE

KEY TERMS (in the order of their appearance)

Demand interrelationships	Cost-plus pricing	Prestige pricing
Price discrimination	Fully allocated average cost	Price lining
First-degree price discrimination	Markup on cost	Skimming
Consumers' surplus	Profit margin	Value pricing
Second-degree price discrimination	Incremental analysis	Price matching
Third-degree price discrimination	Two-part tariff	Electronic scanners
Dumping	Peak-load pricing	Auction pricing
Transfer pricing	Tying	
	Bundling	

We saw in Chapters 8 and 9 that in order to maximize profits, a firm produces where marginal revenue (MR) equals marginal cost (MC) and then charges the price indicated on the demand curve it faces. This is true under all types of market structures, except perfect competition, where the firm is a price taker and maximizes profits by producing the output level at which $P = MR = MC$. Throughout our presentation, however, we assumed that the firm produced only one product, sold its product in only one market, was organized as a centralized entity, and had precise knowledge of the demand and cost curves it faced. None of these assumptions is generally true for most firms today. That is, most firms produce more than one product, sell products in more than one market, are organized (at least large corporations) into a number of decentralized or semiautonomous divisional profit centers, and have only a general rather than a precise knowledge of the demand and cost curves they face. As a result, our discussion of the pricing decision presented in Chapters 8 and 9 must be expanded to take into consideration actual pricing practices.

In this chapter, we examine the firm's pricing of multiple products, price discrimination or the pricing of products sold by the firm in different markets, transfer pricing or the pricing of (intermediate) products transferred between the firm's divisions, and cost-plus pricing (a rule of thumb used by firms to approximate the $MR = MC$ rule when precise data on demand and cost curves are usually unavailable). We conclude the chapter with some other recent pricing practices.

11-1 PRICING OF MULTIPLE PRODUCTS

Most modern firms produce a variety of products rather than a single product. This requires that we expand our simple pricing rule examined in Chapters 8 and 9 to consider demand and product interdependencies. In this section, we examine the firm's pricing of multiple products with interdependent demands, plant capacity utilization and optimal product pricing, and the optimal pricing of joint products produced in fixed or in variable proportions.

Pricing of Products with Interrelated Demands

The products sold by a firm may be interrelated as substitutes or complements. For example, Saturns and Chevrolets produced by General Motors are substitutes, while the various options (such as air conditioning, power windows, etc.) produced by GM are complementary to its automobiles. In the pricing of interrelated products, a firm needs to consider the effect of a change in the price of one of its products on the demand for the others. The reason for this is that a reduction in the price of a product (say, Saturns) leads to a reduction in the demand for a substitute product (Chevrolets) sold by the same firm, and to an increase in the demand for complementary products (options for Saturns). Thus, profit maximization requires that the output levels and prices of the various products produced by the firm be determined jointly rather than independently.

Demand interrelationships influence the pricing decisions of a multiple product firm through their effect on marginal revenue. For a two-product (A and B) firm, the marginal revenue functions of the firm are[1]

$$MR_A = \frac{\Delta TR_A}{\Delta Q_A} + \frac{\Delta TR_B}{\Delta Q_A} \qquad [11\text{-}1]$$

$$MR_B = \frac{\Delta TR_B}{\Delta Q_B} + \frac{\Delta TR_A}{\Delta Q_B} \qquad [11\text{-}2]$$

From the two equations above, we see that the marginal revenue for each product has two components, one associated with the change in the total revenue from the sale of the product itself, and the other associated with the change in the total revenue from the other product. The second term on the right-hand side of each equation, thus, reflects the demand interrelationships. For example, the term $(\Delta TR_B)/(\Delta Q_A)$ in Equation 11-1 measures the effect on the firm's revenues from product B resulting from the sale of an additional unit of product A by the firm. Similarly, $(\Delta TR_A)/(\Delta Q_B)$ in Equation 11-2 measures the effect on the firm's total revenue from product A resulting from the sale of an additional unit of product B by the firm. If the second term on the right-hand side of each equation is positive, indicating that increased sales of one product stimulates sales of the other, the two products are complementary. If, on the other hand, the second term in each equation is negative, indicating that increased sales of one product leads to reduced sales of the other, the two products are substitutes. For example, increased sales of Saturns leads to increased sales of options for Saturns (complements) but reduced sales of Chevrolets (substitutes for Saturns).

Optimal pricing and output decisions on the part of the firm, therefore, require that the total effect (i.e., the direct as well as the cross-marginal effects) of the change in the price of a product on the firm be taken into consideration. Failure to do so leads to suboptimal pricing and output decisions. For example, suppose that products A and B are complements so that the term $(\Delta TR_B)/(\Delta Q_A)$ in Equation 11-1 is positive. If the firm disregards this term and produces where $MR_A = (\Delta TR_A)/(\Delta Q_A) = MC_A$, the firm will be producing too little of product A to maximize profits. On the other hand, suppose that products A and B are substitutes, so that $(\Delta TR_B)/(\Delta Q_A)$ is negative. If the firm disregards this term and produces where $MR_A = (\Delta TR_A)/(\Delta Q_A) = MC_A$, the firm will be producing too much of product A to be maximizing profits.

---

[1] In terms of calculus,

$$MR_A = \frac{\partial(TR_A)}{\partial Q_A} + \frac{\partial(TR_B)}{\partial Q_A} \qquad \text{and} \qquad MR_B = \frac{\partial(TR_B)}{\partial Q_B} + \frac{\partial(TR_A)}{\partial Q_B}$$

Plant Capacity Utilization and Optimal Product Pricing

One important reason that firms produce more than one product is to make fuller use of their plant and production capacities. A firm that would have idle capacity after producing the best level of output of a single product can search for other products to produce so as to make fuller (which does not necessarily mean 100 percent) use of its plant and production capacity.[2] As long as the marginal revenue from these products exceeds their marginal cost, the profits of the firm will increase. Thus, instead of producing a single product at the point where $MR = MC$ and be left with a great deal of idle capacity, the firm will introduce new products (or different varieties of existing products), in the order of their profitability, until the marginal revenue of the least profitable product produced equals its marginal cost to the firm. The quantity produced of the more profitable products is then determined by the point at which their marginal revenue equals the marginal revenue and marginal cost of the last unit of the least profitable product produced by the firm. The price of each product is then determined on its respective demand curve. This process is shown in Figure 11-1.

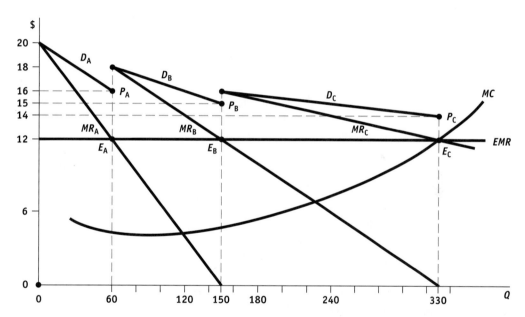

FIGURE 11-1   Optimal Outputs and Prices of Multiple Products by a Firm D_A, D_B, and D_C are the demand curves for products A, B, and C sold by the firm, and MR_A, MR_B, and MR_C are the corresponding marginal revenue curves. The firm maximizes profits when $MR_A = MR_B = MR_C = MC$. This is shown by points E_A, E_B, and E_C, where the equal marginal revenue (EMR) curve, at the level at which $MR_C = MC$, crosses the MR_A, MR_B, and MR_C curves. Thus, $Q_A = 60$ and $P_A = \$16$; $Q_B = 90$ (from $150 - 60$) and $P_B = \$15$; and $Q_C = 180$ (from $330 - 150$) and $P_C = \$14$. Note that each successive demand curve is more elastic and that the price of each successive product is lower, while its MC is higher.

---

[2] In fact, Clemens has convincingly argued that it is more realistic to regard the firm as selling its unique productive capacity than specific products. See Eli Clemens, "Price Discrimination and the Multiple Product Firm," *Review of Economic Studies*, no. 29 (1950–1951), pp. 1–11.

Figure 11-1 shows the situation of a firm selling three products (A, B, and C) with respective demand curves D_A, D_B, and D_C, and corresponding marginal revenue curves MR_A, MR_B, and MR_C. The firm maximizes profits when it produces the quantity of each product at which $MR_A = MR_B = MR_C = MC$. This is shown by points E_A, E_B, and E_C, at which the equal marginal revenue (EMR) line from the level at which $MR_C = MC$ crosses the MR_A, MR_B, and MR_C curves. Thus, in order to maximize profits, the firm should produce 60 units of product A and sell them at the price of $P_A = \$16$ on the D_A curve (see the figure); 90 units of product B (the horizontal distance between points E_B and E_A, or $150 - 60$) and sell them at $P_B = \$15$ on the D_B curve; and 180 units of product C (from $330 - 150$) and sell them at $P_C = \$14$ on the D_C curve. Note that each successive demand curve is more elastic and that the price of each successive product introduced is lower, while its marginal cost is higher (so that per-unit profits decline).

Four things must be pointed out with respect to the above analysis and figure:

1. It would be profitable for the firm to introduce still other products until the price of the last product introduced is equal to its marginal cost (so that the firm would be a perfect competitor in the market for this product), or the firm's productive capacity has been reached.

2. It is assumed that the firm's production facilities can easily be adapted to the production of other products and that the firm's marginal cost curve reflects any increase in costs resulting from the introduction of additional products.

3. Figure 11-1 assumes that the demand curve for each product sold by the firm is independent rather than interrelated, or that the figure shows the total and final effect of all demand interrelationships.

4. A firm may produce a product on which it makes little or no profit in order to offer a full range of products, to use it as a *loss leader* (i.e., to attract customers), to retain customers' goodwill, to keep channels of distribution open, or to keep the firm's resources in use while awaiting more profitable opportunities (as in the case of construction companies). This is related to the first point. For example, supermarkets earn very thin profit margins on staples (soaps, detergents, coffee, sodas, potatoes, etc.), which have very elastic demands and are heavily advertised. They earn much more on specialty products, which are often bought on impulse and with which customers have much less pricing experience.

Optimal Pricing of Joint Products Produced in Fixed Proportions

The products produced by a firm can be related not only in demand but also in production. Production interdependence arises when products are jointly produced. Products can be jointly produced in fixed or variable proportions. An example of joint production in fixed proportions is cattle raising, which provides both beef and hides in the ratio of one-to-one. An example of joint production with variable proportions is provided by petroleum refining, which results in gasoline, fuel oils, and other products in proportions which, within a range, can be varied by the firm. Such production interdependence must be considered by the firm in order to reach optimal output and pricing decisions. We will consider joint production in fixed proportions in this section and joint production in variable proportions in the next section.

When products are jointly produced in fixed proportions, they should be thought of as a single production package. There is then no rational way of allocating the cost of producing the package to the individual products in the package. For example, the cost of raising cattle cannot be allocated in any rational way to beef and hides, since they are jointly produced. On the other hand, the jointly produced products may have independent demands and marginal revenues. For example, the demand and marginal revenue for beef are separate and independent of the demand and marginal revenue for hides. The best level of output of the joint product is then determined at the point where the vertical summation of the marginal revenues of the various jointly produced products equals the single marginal cost of producing the entire product package. This is shown in Figure 11-2.

In the left panel of Figure 11-2, D_A and D_B refer, respectively, to the demand curves of products A and B, which are jointly produced in the proportion of one-to-one. We could think of product A as beef and product B as hides, which results in the ratio of one-to-one from the slaughter of each cow. Thus, the horizontal axis of the figure measures at the same time the quantity (Q) of cattle, beef, and hides. Despite the fact that beef and hides are jointly produced, their demand curves are independent because they are unrelated in consumption. The corresponding marginal revenue curves are MR_A and MR_B in the figure. The total marginal revenue (MR_T) curve is obtained by summing vertically the MR_A and MR_B curves because the firm receives marginal revenues from the sale of both products. Note that starting at the output level of $Q = 45$ units, at which $MR_B = 0$, the MR_T curve coincides

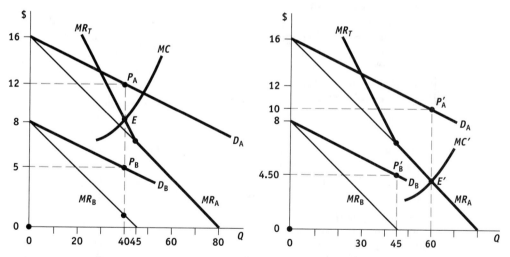

FIGURE 11-2   Optimal Output and Prices of Joint Products Produced in Fixed Proportions   In both panels, D_A and MR_A, and D_B and MR_B refer, respectively, to the demand and marginal revenue curves for products A and B, which are jointly produced in fixed proportions. The total marginal revenue (MR_T) curve is obtained from the vertical summation of the MR_A and MR_B curves. When the marginal cost of the jointly produced production package is MC (see the left panel), the best level of output of products A and B is 40 units and is given by point E, at which $MR_T = MC$. At $Q = 40$, $P_A = \$12$ on D_A and $P_B = \$5$ on D_B. On the other hand, with MC' (see the right panel), the best level of output of the joint product package is 60 units and is given by point E', at which $MR_T = MC'$. At $Q = 60$, $P'_A = \$10$ on D_A, but since MR_B is negative for $Q_B > 45$, the firm sells only 45 units of product B at $P'_B = \$4.50$ (at which TR_B is maximum at $MR_B = 0$) and disposes of the remaining 15 units of product B.

with the MR_A curve. The best level of output of both beef and hides is 40 units and is given by point E, at which the MC curve for cattle (both beef and hides together) crosses the MR_T curve of the firm. At $Q = 40$, $P_A = \$12$ on the D_A curve and $P_B = \$5$ on the D_B curve.

In the left panel of Figure 11-2, both MR_A and MR_B are positive at the best level of output of $Q = 40$. In contrast, in the right panel of Figure 11-2, MR_B is negative at the best level of output of $Q = 60$ given by point E', at which the lower MC' curve crosses the same MR_T curve. This means that selling more than 45 units of product B (hides) reduces the firm's total revenue and profits. In such a case the firm produces 60 units of the joint product (cattle), sells 60 units of product A (beef) at $P'_A = \$10$ but sells only 45 units of product B (hides) at $P'_B = \$4.50$ (at which TR_B is maximum and $MR_B = 0$). That is, the firm withholds from the market and disposes of the extra 15 units of product B jointly produced with the 60 units of product A in order not to sell them at a negative marginal revenue.[3] An example of this was provided by the destruction of excess pineapple juice that jointly resulted from the production of sliced pineapples for canning. Until use was found for it, the excess pineapple juice was simply destroyed in order not to depress its price below the point at which its marginal revenue became negative.[4]

Optimal Pricing and Output of Joint Products Produced in Variable Proportions

Although the case of products that are produced jointly in fixed proportions (i.e., that are complementary in production) is possible, more common is the case of products that are jointly produced in variable proportions (i.e., that are substitutes in production). We can determine the profit-maximizing combination of products that are jointly produced in variable proportions with the aid of Figure 11-3.

In Figure 11-3, the curved lines are product transformation curves and show the various combinations of products A and B that the firm can produce at each level of input use and total cost. For example, the lowest curve shows that with $TC = \$100$, the firm can produce 40 units of product A and 60 units of product B (point G), 20 units of product A and 80 units of product B (point H), or any combination of products A and B shown on the curve. Higher product transformation curves refer to the various larger combinations of products A and B that can be produced at each higher level of TC. Production transformation curves are concave to the origin because the firm's production resources are not perfectly adaptable in (i.e., cannot be perfectly transferred between) the production of products A and B.

Figure 11-3 also shows *isorevenue lines.* They represent all combinations of outputs of products A and B that generate the same total revenue for the firm. For example, the lowest isorevenue line shows all the combinations of products A and B that lead to $TR = \$120$ with $P_A = \$1.50$ and $P_B = \$1.00$. For example, at point G (40A, 60B),

---

[3] For the mathematical analysis of optimal pricing of joint products produced in fixed proportions, see Problem 3, with answer at the end of the book.

[4] When the firm incurs a significant cost in disposing of the excess quantity of a jointly produced product, the cost is added to the MC function of the firm, thereby reducing the optimal level of output. Significant disposal costs, however, provide strong incentives for the firm to find uses for the excess products that are jointly produced.

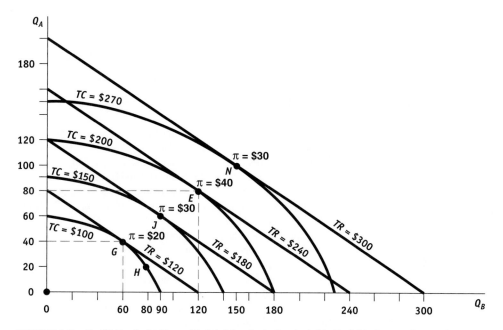

FIGURE 11-3 Profit Maximization with Joint Products Produced in Variable Proportions The curved lines are product transformation curves showing the various combinations of products A and B that the firm can produce at each level of total cost (*TC*). The curvature arises because the firm's productive resources are not perfectly adaptable in the production of products A and B that give rise to the same total revenue (*TR*) to the firm when sold at constant prices. The tangency point of an isorevenue to a *TC* curve gives the combination of products A and B that leads to the maximum profit (π) for the firm for the specific *TC*. The overall maximum profit of the firm is π = $40. This is earned by producing and selling 80A and 120B (point *E*) with *TR* = $240 and *TC* = $200.

$TR = (40)(\$1.50) + (60)(\$1.00) = \$120$. The higher isorevenue lines refer to the higher levels of *TR* that the firm receives by selling larger quantities of products A and B at constant P_A and P_B. The isorevenue lines are straight on the assumption that the prices of products A and B are constant (as in the case of a perfectly competitive firm).[5]

Looking at both the product transformation curves and the isorevenue lines in Figure 11-3, we can see that for a given *TC*, the firm maximizes profits by reaching the isorevenue line that is tangent to the particular *TC* curve. For example, with *TC* = $100, the highest total profit (π) possible is $20, which is reached by producing 40A and 60B and reaching the *TR* = $120 isorevenue line. With *TC* = $150, the maximum π = $30, which is reached by producing 60A and 90B and reaching the *TR* = $180 isorevenue line at point *J*. The overall highest profit that the firm can earn is π = $40. This is reached by producing 80A and 120B at *TC* = $200 and reaching the *TR* = $240 isorevenue line at point *E* (see Figure 11-3).[6] Case Study 11-1 examines pricing and output decisions by Gillette.

---

[5] Note that isorevenue lines are parallel and that their absolute slope is $P_B/P_A = \$1/\$1.50 = 2/3$. If P_A and P_B were not constant, the isorevenue lines would not be straight, but the analysis remains basically the same.

[6] Note that this is an example of constrained maximization and can easily be solved by linear programming.

CASE STUDY 11-1
Optimal Pricing and Output by Gillette

The Gillette Company is one of many firms producing and selling numerous varieties of many products. The U.S. subsidiary of the Gillette Company sells many types of razors, razor blades, shaving creams, deodorants, hair conditioners, batteries, and many other products for personal care, while Braun, the European subsidiary, sells more than 400 other products. Many of these products are interdependent in demand or consumption as well as in production. For example, razor blades and shaving creams are complementary with razors, so that lowering the price of one product (say, razors) increases the quantity demanded of that product (and the total revenue from that product if its demand is price elastic) and also increases the demand and total revenue from complementary products (such as razor blades and shaving creams). Indeed, Gillette's strategy seems to be to keep the price of razors relatively low and the prices of razor blades and shaving creams relatively high—and it is the latter products that contribute the most to the company's revenues and profits. However, lowering the price of one type of razor reduces the demand for the other types of (substitute) razors sold by the company. Thus, the firm must keep these demand interdependencies in mind in devising the optimal pricing and output strategy for its many products.

During the 1970s, Gillette diversified into many other related and unrelated product lines in order to fully exploit demand interdependencies and to achieve a fuller utilization of its productive resources. By 1977, Braun produced more than 600 products. That diversification, however, was not successful, so Gillette's top management ordered nearly one-third of

the products sold by Braun (such as pocket calculators, digital watches, and small electrical appliances) to be discontinued. Gillette was further reorganized in 1988 into a North Atlantic unit (responsible for blades and razors, and personal care and stationery businesses in North America and Europe) and another division (handling international operations outside Europe, as well as Braun small appliances), and further streamlined its product offerings.

Another reorganization in 1993 restructured the company into six global business management units, each responsible for its own product development and manufacturing, and reporting to two executive vice presidents. Gillette went through still another reorganization in 1998, which closed 14 plants and 12 warehouses, and eliminated or consolidated 30 office facilities worldwide. This saved Gillette $200 million and completed its makeover into a truly global company.

But even this latest restructuring did not succeed, and in October 2000 Gillette forced the resignation of its CEO. James Kilts, its new chairman brought in from Nabisco, put the company through another big restructuring aimed at cutting the 75 percent of Gillette's products that accounted for only 5 percent of its sales. Gillette focused attention on its highly profitable products, such as its premium razors (see Case Study 3-8) and batteries, and would phase out most of its less profitable ones such as disposable razors, basic batteries, and some toiletries. In 2005, Gillette was acquired by Procter & Gamble and went through another major reorganization to integrate its product line with that of the merged company.

Source: "Gillette After the Diversification That Failed," *Business Week* (February 28, 1977), pp. 58–62; "Gillette Takes a Shave and a Big Haircut," *Business Week* (October 12, 1998), p. 44; "Gillette Ousts CEO as Profit Barely Budges," *The Wall Street Journal* (October 20, 2000), p. A3; "Gillette's New Chief Is Critical of the Company's Missteps," *The New York Times* (June 7, 2001), p. C4; "Gillette Shows First Signs of Turnround," *Financial Times* (April 24, 2002), p. 17; and "P&G/Gillette Expects to Make More Savings," *Financial Times* (October 4, 2005), p. 23.

11-2 | PRICE DISCRIMINATION

In this section we examine the optimal pricing of a product sold by the firm in multiple markets. First, we define the meaning of "price discrimination" and examine the conditions under which it arises. Then, we deal with first- and second-degree price discrimination. Finally, we examine third-degree price discrimination graphically and algebraically.

Meaning of and Conditions for Price Discrimination

Price discrimination refers to the charging of different prices for different quantities of a product, at different times, to different customer groups or in different markets, when these price differences are not justified by cost differences. For example, telephone companies usually charge a given price per call for a given number of calls and a lower price for additional batches of calls, charge higher prices for calls during business hours than in evenings and on holidays, and charge higher prices to businesses than to households. The incentive for this is that the firm can increase its total revenue and profits for a given level of sales and total costs by practicing price discrimination.

Other examples of price discrimination are (1) power (i.e., electrical and gas) companies charging lower prices to commercial than to residential users; (2) medical and legal professions charging lower fees to low-income than to high-income people; (3) companies charging lower prices abroad than at home for a variety of products and services, ranging from books and medicines to movies; (4) entertainment companies charging lower prices for afternoon than for evening performances of movies, theaters, and sports events; (5) service industries charging lower prices for children and the elderly for haircuts, public transportation, and airline tickets; (6) hotels charging lower rates for conventions, and so on. These examples are an indication of the pervasiveness of price discrimination in our economy.

To be remembered, however, is that price differences based on cost differences in supplying a product or service in different quantities, at different times, to different customer groups, or in different markets, are not forms of price discrimination. To be a price discrimination, the price differences must not be based on cost differences. Also, price discrimination does not have a negative connotation in economics (as contrasted with the case of law). That is, in economics, price discrimination is neutral and benefits some (those paying a price for the product lower than in the absence of price discrimination) and harms others, and as such, it is often difficult or impossible to determine whether, on balance, it is beneficial or harmful for society as a whole.

Three conditions must be met for a firm to be able to practice price discrimination. (1) The firm must have some control over the price of the product (i.e., the firm must be an imperfect competitor). A perfectly competitive firm has no control over the price of the product it sells (i.e., it is a price taker) and thus cannot possibly practice price discrimination. (2) The price elasticity of demand for the product must differ for different quantities of the product, at different times, for different customer groups, or in different markets. As we will see later, if the price elasticities of demand are equal, the firm cannot increase its revenues and profits by practicing price discrimination. (3) The quantities of the product or service, the times when they are used or consumed, and the customer groups or markets for the product must be separable (i.e., the firm must be able to segment the market). Otherwise, individuals or firms will purchase the product or service where they are cheap and resell them where they are more expensive, thereby undermining the firm's effort to charge different prices for the same product (i.e., practice price discrimination). In the case of electricity, gas, and water consumption, meters on business premises or in homes keep the markets separate. Transportation costs and trade restrictions keep domestic and foreign markets separate. In the case of services, markets are naturally separated by the fact that most services (e.g., doctors' visits, legal advice, haircuts, and public transportation passes for the elderly) cannot easily or possibly be transferred or resold to other people.

First- and Second-Degree Price Discrimination

There are three types of price discrimination: first, second, and third degree. By practicing any type of price discrimination, the firm can increase its total revenue and profits by capturing all or part of the consumer's surplus. **First-degree price discrimination** involves selling each unit of the product separately and charging the highest price possible for each unit sold. By doing so, the firm extracts all of the consumers' surplus from consumers and maximizes the total revenue and profits from the sale of a particular quantity of the product. This is shown in Figure 11-4.

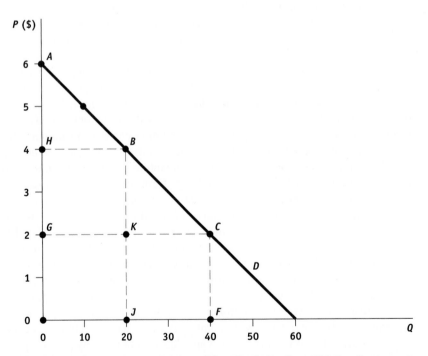

FIGURE 11-4 First- and Second-Degree Price Discrimination   With D as the demand curve faced by a monopolist, the firm could sell $Q = 40$ at $P = \$2$ for a $TR = \$80$ (the area of rectangle $CF0G$). Consumers, however, would be willing to pay $ACF0 = \$160$ for 40 units of the product. The difference of $80 (the area of triangle ACG) is the consumer's surplus. With first-degree price discrimination (i.e., by selling each unit of the product separately at the highest price possible), the firm can extract all the consumers' surplus from consumers. If, however, the firm charged the price of $P = \$4$ per unit for the first 20 units of the product and $2 per unit on the next 20 units, the total revenue of the firm would be $120 (the sum of the areas of rectangles $BJOH$ and $CFJK$), so that the firm would extract $40 (the area of rectangle $BKGH$), or half of the consumers' surplus from consumers. This is second-degree price discrimination.

In Figure 11-4, D is the demand curve faced by a monopolistic firm. The firm can sell 40 units of the product at the price of $2 per unit and receive a total revenue of $80 (the area of rectangle $CF0G$). Consumers, however, are willing to pay $ACF0 = \$160$ for 40 units of the product. That is, demand curve D indicates that the firm can sell the first unit of the product at the price of $6. To sell additional units of the product, the firm would have to lower the price a little on each additional unit sold. For example, the firm could sell the second unit of the product for slightly less than $6 per unit, it could sell the 20th unit at the price of $4, and the 40th unit at the price of $2 (see the figure). Thus, if the firm sold each unit of the product separately and charged the highest price possible, the firm would generate the total revenue of $ACF0 = \$160$. In the absence of first-degree price discrimination, however, the firm will charge the price of $2 (only as much as consumers are willing to pay for the 40th unit of the product) for all the 40 units of the product and receive a total revenue of only $CF0G = \$80$. The difference between what consumers are willing to pay ($ACF0 = \$160$) and what they actually pay ($CF0G = \$80$) is the **consumers' surplus** (triangle $ACG = \$80$). Thus, by practicing first-degree price discrimination (i.e., by selling each unit of the product separately and charging the highest price possible for each unit), the firm can extract all the consumers' surplus from buyers and increase its total revenues from $80 to $160. Since the total cost of producing the 40 units of the product is not affected by the price at which the product is sold, the total profits of the firm rise sharply by practicing first-degree price discrimination.

First-degree price discrimination is seldom encountered in the real world, however, because to practice it, the firm needs to have precise knowledge of each individual consumer's demand curve and charge the highest possible price for each separate unit of the product sold. This is practically impossible. One situation in which this does seem to occur is when independent colleges and universities adjust the amount of financial aid based on detailed data on family income, mortgage payments, and savings, and charge the highest price possible. More practical and common is **second-degree price discrimination.** This refers to the charging of a uniform price per unit for a specific quantity or block of the product sold to each customer, a lower price per unit for an additional batch or block of the product, and so on. By doing so, the firm will extract part, but not all, of the consumers' surplus. For example, suppose that the firm of Figure 11-4 sets the price of $4 per unit on the first 20 units of the product and the price of $2 per unit on the next batch or block of 20 units of the product. The total revenue of the firm would then be $BJ0H = \$80$ from the first batch of 20 units of the product and $CFJK = \$40$ from the next batch or block of 20 units, for the overall total revenue of $120 (as compared to $160 with first-degree price discrimination and $80 without any price discrimination). Thus, the firm can extract one-half or $40 (the area of rectangle $BKGH$) of the total consumers' surplus from consumers by practicing second-degree price discrimination in this market. The remaining consumers' surplus of $40 is given by the sum of the areas of triangles ABH and BCK (see the figure).

Although second-degree price discrimination is more common than first-degree price discrimination, it is also somewhat limited to cases where products and services are easily metered, such as kilowatt-hours of electricity, cubic feet of gas and water, number of copies duplicated, minutes of CPU (central processing unit of a computer) time used, and so on. Thus, second-degree price discrimination is often encountered in the pricing of electric, gas, water, and other public utilities, in the renting of photocopying machines, in the use of computers, and so on.

Third-Degree Price Discrimination Graphically

Third-degree price discrimination refers to the charging of different prices for the same product in different markets until the marginal revenue of the last unit of the product sold in each market equals the marginal cost of producing the product. For example, if the firm sells a product in two markets (market 1 and market 2), the firm will maximize its total profits by selling the product in each market until $MR_1 = MR_2 = MC$. If $MR_1 > MR_2$, it pays for the firm to redistribute sales from the second to the first market until the condition for profit maximization is met. On the other hand, if $MR_1 < MR_2$, it pays for the firm to transfer sales from the first to the second market until $MR_1 = MR_2$. As pointed out earlier, in order for the firm to be able to practice this or any other type of price discrimination, the firm must have some monopoly power, the price elasticity of demand for the product must be different in the different markets, and the markets must be separable. The rule that, in order to maximize total profits, the firm must sell in each market until $MR_1 = MR_2 = MC$ will then involve selling the product at a higher price in the market with the less elastic demand than in the market with the more elastic demand. This is shown in Figure 11-5.

Panel a in Figure 11-5 shows D_1 and MR_1 (the demand and marginal revenue curves for the product that the firm faces in market 1); panel b shows D_2 and MR_2 (the demand and marginal revenue curves that the firm faces in market 2); and panel c shows D and MR (the total demand and marginal revenue curves for the product that the firm faces in both markets together). The total market demand curve (D) is obtained from the horizontal summation of the demand curves in market 1 and in market 2 (that is, $D = \Sigma D_{1+2}$). Note that up to $Q = 60$, $D = D_1$. Similarly, the total marginal revenue curve (MR) is obtained from the horizontal summation of MR_1 and MR_2 (that is, $MR = \Sigma MR_{1+2}$). Note, also, that up to $Q = 30$, $MR = MR_1$.

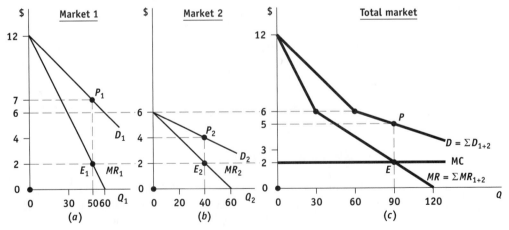

FIGURE 11-5   Third-Degree Price Discrimination   Panel a shows D_1 and MR_1 (the demand and marginal revenue curves faced by the firm in market 1), panel b shows D_2 and MR_2, and panel c shows D and MR (the total demand and marginal revenue curves for the two markets together). $D = \Sigma D_{1+2}$, and $MR = \Sigma MR_{1+2}$, by horizontal summation. The best level of output of the firm is 90 units and is given by point E in panel c at which $MR = MC = \$2$. The firm sells 50 units of the product in market 1 and 40 units in market 2, so that $MR_1 = MR_2 = MR = MC = \$2$ (see points E_1, E_2, and E). For $Q = 50$, $P_1 = \$7$ on D_1 in market 1, and for $Q_2 = 40$, $P_2 = \$4$ on D_2 in market 2. With an average total costs of \$3 per unit for $Q = 90$, the firm earns a profit of \$4 per unit and \$200 in total in market 1, and \$1 per unit and \$40 in total in market 2, for an overall total profit of \$240 in both markets. In the absence of price discrimination, $Q = 90$, $P = \$5$ (see panel c), so that profits are \$2 per unit and \$180 in total.

The best level of output of the firm is 90 units of the product and is given by point E in panel c, at which $MR = \Sigma MR_{1+2} = MC = \$2$. To maximize profits, the firm should then sell 50 units of the product in the first market and the remaining 40 units of the product in the second market, so that $MR_1 = MR_2 = MR = MC = \$2$ (see, respectively, points E_1, E_2, and E in the three panels of Figure 11-5). For $Q = 50$, $P_1 = \$7$ on D_1 in market 1, and for $Q_2 = 40$, $P_2 = \$4$ on D_2 in market 2. Note that the price is higher in the market with the more inelastic demand. Thus, the firm generates total revenues of \$350 in market 1 and \$160 in market 2, for an overall total revenue of \$510 in both markets together.

If the average total cost (ATC) of the firm is \$3 at the best level of output of 90 units (50 units for market 1 and 40 units for market 2), then the firm earns a profit of $P_1 - ATC = \$7 - \$3 = \$4$ per unit and \$200 in total in market 1, and $P_2 - ATC = \$4 - \$3 = \$1$ per unit and \$40 in total in market 2, for a total profit of \$240 in both markets together.[7] In the absence of price discrimination, the firm would sell the best level of output of $Q = 90$ at $P = \$5$ (see panel c) and generate a total revenue of \$450 (as compared to $TR = \$510$ with third-degree price discrimination). With $ATC = \$3$ for $Q = 90$, the firm would earn a profit of $P - ATC = \$5 - \$3 = \$2$ per unit and \$180 in total. Thus, given the best level of output and costs, the firm can increase its total revenue and profits significantly by practicing third-degree price discrimination.

There are many examples of third-degree price discrimination in our economy. One of these is provided by electric power companies, which usually charge higher rates to residential than to commercial users of electricity (see Case Study 11-2). The reason for this is that the price elasticity of demand for electricity is higher for the latter than for the former because the latter could generate their own electricity if its price rose above the cost of building and running their own power plants. This choice is generally not available to households. The commercial and residential markets for electricity are then kept separate or segmented by meters installed in offices and homes. Other examples of third-degree price discrimination are the higher airfares charged by airlines to business travelers than to vacationers, the higher prices that college bookstores charge students than professors for books, the higher price charged for milk to households than to cheese makers, the higher price charged by telephone companies during business hours than at other times, and the higher prices charged for many services to all customers except children and the aged. In each case, the higher price is charged in the market with the less elastic demand (i.e., the one in which there are fewer substitutes for the product) and the markets are kept separated or segmented by various methods.

Third-Degree Price Discrimination Algebraically

The graphical analysis of price discrimination shown in Figure 11-5 can easily be shown algebraically.[8] From Figure 11-5, we can determine that the demand and marginal revenue functions of the firm in each market are, respectively,

$$Q_1 = 120 - 10P_1 \quad \text{or} \quad P_1 = 12 - 0.1Q_1 \quad \text{and} \quad MR_1 = 12 - 0.2Q_1$$
$$Q_2 = 120 - 20P_2 \quad \text{or} \quad P_2 = 6 - 0.05Q_2 \quad \text{and} \quad MR_2 = 6 - 0.1Q_2$$

---

[7] An $ATC = \$3$ for $Q = 90$ and a constant $MC = \$2$ for any output level implies a total cost function of $TC = 90 + 2Q$, so that the TC curve (not shown in Figure 11-5) is a straight line with vertical intercept or total fixed costs of \$90 and a constant slope or marginal cost of \$2.

[8] For the analysis of third-degree price discrimination using calculus, see the appendix to this chapter.

CASE STUDY 11-2
Price Discrimination by Con Edison

Table 11-1 gives the price per kilowatt-hour (kWh) that Con Edison charged residential users and small and large commercial users for various quantities of electricity consumed in New York City in June through September and in other months in 2005. Since Con Edison charged different rates for different categories of customers and for different quantities of electricity purchased, it is clear that Con Edison practiced both second- and third-degree price discrimination.

Another way for a seller to practice third-degree price discrimination is by offering coupons to consumers for the purchase of some products (such as a box of breakfast cereal) at a discount. This allows a firm to sell the product at a lower price to only the 20 to 30 percent of consumers who bother to clip, save, and use coupons. (These are the consumers who have a higher price elasticity of demand.) In 2005, more than $300 billion of grocery coupons were distributed in the United States, but only a small percentage of them were redeemed. Offering coupons is a form of third-degree price discrimination that the firm can use to increase profits. Firms often offer rebates, airlines charge many different fares for a given trip for the same reason, and colleges offer varying tuition discounts in the form of financial aid.

TABLE 11-1	Electricity Rates Charged by Con Edison in 2005 (cents per kilowatt-hour)			
	kWh	Cents/kWh	kWh	Cents/kWh
Residential Rates (Single Residence)				
June–September	0–250	5.18	Above 250	5.83
Other months	0–250	5.18	Above 250	4.76
Commercial Rates (Small Business)				
June–September	0–900	6.97	Above 900	6.23
April	0–900	5.96	Above 900	5.23
Commercial Rates (Large Business)				
Low tension	0–15,000	1.42	Above 15,000	1.42
High tension	0–15,000	1.33	Above 15,000	1.32

Source: Con Edison, New York City (2005).

Source: Con Edison, *Electric Rates* (New York, 2005); C. Narasimhan, "A Price Discriminatory Theory of Coupons," *Marketing Science* (Spring 1984); "The Art of Devising Air Fares," *The New York Times* (March 8, 1987), p. D1; and "Colleges Clamp Down on Financial Aid, Making Haggling a Difficult Approach," *The Wall Street Journal* (April 11, 2002).

With third-degree price discrimination, the condition for profit maximization is

$$MR_1 = MR_2 = MR = MC$$

Setting $MR_1 = MC$ and $MR_2 = MC$, we get

$$MR_1 = 12 - 0.2Q_1 = 2 = MC \qquad \text{and} \qquad MR_2 = 6 - 0.1Q_2 = 2 = MC$$

so that

$$0.2Q_1 = 10 \qquad 0.1Q_2 = 4$$

and

$$Q_1 = 50 \qquad Q_2 = 40$$

The price that the firm should charge for the product in each market is then

$$P_1 = 12 - 0.1(50) = \$7 \qquad \text{and} \qquad P_2 = 6 - 0.05(40) = \$4$$

so that

$$TR_1 = P_1Q_1 = (\$7)(50) = \$350 \qquad \text{and} \qquad TR_2 = P_2Q_2 = (\$4)(40) = \$160$$

and

$$TR = TR_1 + TR_2 = \$350 + \$160 = \$510$$

If the firm's total cost function is

$$TC = 90 + 2(Q_1 + Q_2)$$

the total cost for 90 units of output is

$$TC = 90 + 2(50 + 40) = \$270$$

and the total profits (π) of the firm are

$$\pi = TR_1 + TR_2 - TC$$
$$= \$350 + \$160 - \$270$$
$$= \$240$$

In the absence of price discrimination, the firm will sell the product at the same price in both markets (that is, $P_1 = P_2 = P$). The total market demand faced by the firm for prices below $6 (for which $Q_2 > 0$) is

$$Q = Q_1 + Q_2$$
$$= 120 - 10P_1 + 120 - 20P_2$$
$$= 120 - 10P + 120 - 20P$$
$$= 240 - 30P$$

so that $P = 8 - 0.0333Q$, $TR = 8Q - 0.0333Q^2$, and $MR = 8 - 0.0667Q$. Setting $MR = MC$, we get

$$MR = 8 - 0.0667Q = 2 = MC$$

so that

$$0.0667Q = 6$$

and

$$Q = 89.955 \cong 90$$

At $Q = 90$, $P = 8 - 0.0333(90) = 8 - 2.997 \cong \$5$ so that $TR = (P)(Q) = (\$5)(90) = \$450$ (as compared to $TR = \$510$ with third-degree price discrimination). The total profits of the firm are then

$$\pi = TR - TC$$
$$= \$450 - \$270$$
$$= \$180$$

(as compared to $\$240$ with third-degree price discrimination). These results are the same as those shown in Figure 11-5.

11-3   INTERNATIONAL PRICE DISCRIMINATION AND DUMPING

Price discrimination can also be practiced between the domestic and the foreign market. International price discrimination is called **dumping.** This refers to the charging of a lower price abroad than at home for the same commodity because of the greater price elasticity of demand in the foreign market. By so doing, the monopolist earns higher profits than by selling the best level of output at the same price in both markets. The price elasticity of demand for the monopolist's product abroad is higher than that at home because of the competition from producers from other nations in the foreign market. Foreign competition is usually restricted at home by import tariffs or other trade barriers. These import restrictions serve to segment the market (i.e., keep the domestic market separate from the foreign market) and prevent the re-export of the commodity back to the monopolist's home country (which would undermine the monopolist's ability to sell the commodity at a higher price at home than abroad). International price discrimination can be viewed with Figure 11-5 if D_1 refers to the demand curve faced by the monopolist in the domestic market and D_2 refers to the demand curve that the monopolist faces in the foreign market.

Besides dumping resulting from international price discrimination (often referred to as *persistent dumping*), there are two other forms of dumping. These are predatory dumping and sporadic dumping. *Predatory dumping* is the *temporary* sale of a commodity at below cost or at a lower price abroad in order to drive foreign producers out of business, after which prices are raised abroad to take advantage of the newly acquired monopoly power. *Sporadic dumping* is the *occasional* sale of the commodity at below cost or at a lower price abroad than domestically in order to unload an unforeseen and temporary surplus of a commodity without having to reduce domestic prices.

Trade restrictions to counteract predatory dumping are justified and allow to protect domestic industries from unfair competition from abroad. These restrictions usually take the form of antidumping duties to offset price differentials. However, it is often difficult to determine the type of dumping and domestic producers invariably demand protection against any form of dumping. In fact, the very threat of filing a dumping complaint discourages imports and leads to higher domestic production and profits. This is referred to as the "harassment thesis." Persistent and sporadic dumping benefit domestic consumers (by allowing them to purchase the commodity at a lower price) and these benefits may exceed the possible losses of domestic producers.

Over the past decade, Japan was accused of dumping steel, television sets, and computer chips in the United States, and Europeans of dumping cars, steel, and other products.

Most industrial nations (especially those of the European Union) have a tendency of persistently dumping surplus agricultural commodities arising from their farm support programs. Export subsidies are also a form of dumping which, though illegal by international agreement, often occur in disguised forms. When dumping is proved, the violating firm usually chooses to raise its prices (as Volkswagen did in 1976 and Japanese TV exporters did in 1977) rather than face antidumping duties. Case Study 11-3 discusses Kodak's antidumping dispute with Fuji.

CASE STUDY 11-3
Kodak Antidumping Disputes with Fuji

In August 1993, the Eastman Kodak Company of Rochester, New York, charged that the Fuji Photo Film Company of Japan had violated U.S. federal law by selling paper and chemicals for color-film processing in the United States at less than one-third of the price that it charges in Japan and that this had materially injured Kodak. Specifically, Kodak charged that Fuji used its excessive profits from its near monopoly in photographic supplies in Japan to dump photographic supplies in the United States in order to undermine the competitive position of Kodak and other U.S. competitors. By 1993, Fuji had captured more than 10 percent of the U.S. photographic supply market, mostly from Kodak. Kodak asked the U.S. Commerce Department to impose stiff tariffs on Fuji's imports of these products into the United States. In August 1994, Fuji signed a five-year agreement under which it agreed to sell color paper and chemical components at or above a fair price determined quarterly by the U.S. Department of Commerce from Fuji cost of production figures in Japan and the Netherlands, where Fuji produces the photographic supplies exported to the United States. This "fair" price was about 50 percent higher than the pre-agreement price that Fuji charged in the United States. The immediate effect of the agreement was higher prices for photographic supplies for U.S. consumers.

In the face of continued loss of U.S. market share, Kodak again accused Fuji in 1995 of unfairly restricting its access to the Japanese market and again demanded the imposition of stiff tariffs on Fuji photographic exports to the United States. However, the World Trade Organization (the institution created in 1993 to regulate international trade and adjudicate trade disputes among its member nations) dismissed the case in 1997. Although Kodak retains nearly 70 percent of the U.S. photographic market (compared to Fuji's 19 percent), it has been steadily losing market share to Fuji over the past decade because of the latter's low-price policy. In the meantime, Fuji spent more than $1 billion on new plants to produce photographic supplies in the United States, which makes Fuji a domestic supplier and, to a large extent, no longer subject to U.S. antidumping rules. Kodak, on the other hand, has gone through a series of restructuring moves from 1998 to 2005 that cut costs by nearly $2 billion by eliminating 35,000 jobs, or about 35 percent of its worldwide labor force, and shifting to higher-end products, such as digital cameras. But the sharp decline in traditional film products as the market moves toward digital technology continues to put pressure on Kodak.

Source: "Kodak Asks 25% Tariffs on Some Fuji Imports," *The New York Times* (August 31, 1993), p. D1; "Fuji Photo Pact on U.S. Prices," *The Wall Street Journal* (August 22, 1994), p. A4; "Kodak Is Loser in Trade Ruling on Fuji Dispute," *The New York Times* (December 6, 1997), p. 1; "Kodak Losing U.S. Market Share to Fuji," *The Wall Street Journal* (May 28, 1999), p. A3; "Kodak Will Offer Its Staff Chance to Upgrade Options," *The Wall Street Journal* (November 11, 2001), p. B7; and "Great Pictures, But Where Are the Profits?" *Financial Times* (September 1, 2005), p. 15.

11-4 TRANSFER PRICING

In this section we discuss the meaning and importance of transfer pricing, and we examine the rules for optimal transfer pricing when no external market for the transfer or intermediate product exists, when such a market exists and is perfectly competitive, and when it is imperfectly competitive.

Meaning and Nature of Transfer Pricing

The rapid rise of modern large-scale enterprises has been accompanied by decentralization and the establishment of semiautonomous profit centers. This was made necessary by the need to contain the tendency toward increasing costs for communications and coordination among the various divisions. Decentralization and the establishment of semiautonomous profit centers also gave rise to the need for **transfer pricing,** or the need to determine the price of intermediate products sold by one semiautonomous division of a large-scale enterprise and purchased by another semiautonomous division of the same enterprise. For example, if a steel company owned its own coal mine, the questions would arise as to how much coal the coal mine should sell to the parent steel company and how much to outsiders, and at what prices. Similarly, the parent steel company must determine how much coal to purchase from its own coal mine and how much from outsiders, and at what prices. These are some of the most complex and troublesome questions that arise in the operation of large-scale enterprises today.

Transfer pricing is of crucial importance to the efficient operation of the individual divisions of the enterprise, as well as to the enterprise as a whole. There are two reasons for this. First, the price paid by a division of the enterprise for intermediate products produced by another division affects the output of each division and, therefore, the output of the entire enterprise. If wrong transfer prices are set, the various divisions of the firm involved in the transaction, and the firm as a whole, will not produce the optimum or profit-maximizing level of output. Second, transfer prices affect the profitability of the divisions involved in the transfer of the intermediate products, and, as such, they serve as incentives and rewards for the efficient operation of the various divisions of the enterprise. Too-low transfer prices artificially reduce the profitability of the producing division and artificially increase the profitability of the purchasing division, and these can undermine the morale of the managers, officers, and workers of the former because salary increases and bonuses, and sometimes even their jobs, depend on the profitability of the division.

In what follows, we will examine how the appropriate transfer prices are determined in cases where an external market for the transfer or intermediate product does not exist, when it exists and is perfectly competitive, and when it exists and is imperfectly competitive. To simplify our discussion, we assume throughout that the firm has two divisions, a production division (indicated by the subscript p) and a marketing division (indicated by the subscript m). The production division sells the intermediate product to the marketing division, as well as to outsiders, if an outside market for the intermediate product exists. The marketing division purchases the intermediate product from the production division, completes the production process, and markets the final product for the firm. Also, to simplify the presentation, we will assume throughout that 1 unit of the transfer or intermediate product is required to produce each unit of the final product sold by the marketing division. While our discussion is necessarily limited in scope (since transfer pricing is covered in other business courses), it does indicate the nature of the problem and outlines the rules for optimal transfer pricing.

Transfer Pricing with No External Market for the Intermediate Product

When there is no external demand for the intermediate product, the production division can sell the intermediate product only internally to the marketing division of the firm, and the marketing division can purchase the intermediate product only from the production division of the firm. Since 1 unit of the intermediate product is used to produce each unit of the final product, the outputs of the intermediate product and of the final product are equal. Figure 11-6 shows how the transfer price of the intermediate product is determined when there is no external market for the intermediate product.

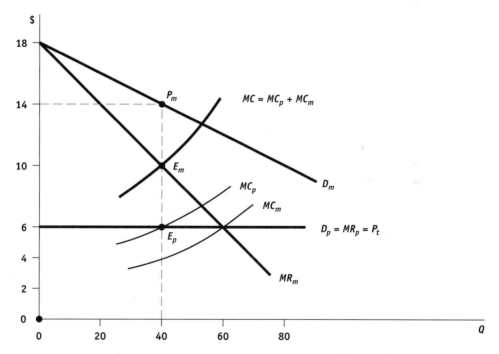

FIGURE 11-6   Transfer Pricing of the Intermediate Product with No External Market MC, the marginal cost of the firm, is equal to the vertical summation of MC_p and MC_m, the marginal cost curves of the production and the marketing divisions of the firm, respectively. D_m is the external demand for the final product faced by the marketing division of the firm, and MR_m is the corresponding marginal revenue curve. The firm's best level of output of the final product is 40 units and is given by point E_m, at which $MR_m = MC$, so that $P_m = \$14$. Since the production of each unit of the final product requires 1 unit of the intermediate product, the transfer price for the intermediate product, P_t, is set equal to MC_p at $Q_p = 40$. Thus, $P_t = \$6$. With $D_p = MR_p = P_t = MC_p = \$6$ at $Q_p = 40$ (see point E_p), $Q_p = 40$ is the best level of output of the intermediate product for the production division.

In Figure 11-6, MC_p and MC_m are the marginal cost curves of the production and marketing divisions of the firm, respectively, while MC is the vertical summation of MC_p and MC_m, and it represents the total marginal cost curve for the firm as a whole. The figure also shows the external demand curve for the final product sold by the marketing division (D_m) and its corresponding marginal revenue curve (MR_m). The firm's best or profit-maximizing level of output for the final product is 40 units and is given by point E_m, at which $MR_m = MC$. Therefore, $P_m = \$14$. Since 40 units of the intermediate product are required (i.e., are demanded by the marketing division of the firm in order to produce the best level of 40 units of the final product), the transfer price for the intermediate product (P_t) is set equal to the marginal cost of the intermediate product (MC_p) at $Q_p = 40$. Thus, $P_t = \$6$ and is given by point E_p at which $Q_p = 40$. The demand and marginal revenue curves faced by the production division of the firm are then equal to the transfer price (that is, $D_p = MR_p = P_t$). Note that $Q_p = 40$ is the best level of output of the intermediate product by the production division of the firm because at $Q_p = 40$, $D_p = MR_p = P_t = MC_p = \$6$. Thus, we can conclude that the correct transfer price for an intermediate product for which there is no external market is the marginal cost of production.

Transfer Pricing with a Perfectly Competitive Market for the Intermediate Product

When an external market for the intermediate product does exist, the output of the production division need not be equal to the output of the final product. On one hand, if the optimal output of the production division exceeds the quantity of the intermediate product demanded internally by the marketing division, the excess of the intermediate product produced can be sold on the external market for the intermediate product. On the other hand, if the marketing division of the firm demands more than the best level of output of the production division, the excess demand can be covered by purchases of the intermediate product in the external market. The transfer price, however, depends on whether or not the external market for the intermediate product is perfectly competitive. The determination of the transfer price when the external market is perfectly competitive is shown in Figure 11-7.

Figure 11-7 is identical to Figure 11-6, except that the marginal cost curve of the production division MC is lower than in Figure 11-6. The production division then produces more of the intermediate product than the marketing division demands and sells the excess in the perfectly competitive external market for the intermediate product. With a perfectly competitive market for the intermediate product, the production division faces horizontal demand curve D_p for its output at the given market price P_t for the intermediate product. Since D_p is horizontal, $D_p = MR_p = P_t$ (see Figure 11-7). The best or profit-maximizing level of output of the intermediate product by the production division of the firm is 50 units and is given by point E'_p at which $D_p = MR_p = P_t = MC = \$6$.

Since the marketing division can purchase the *intermediate* product either internally or externally at $P_t = \$6$, its total marginal cost curve is given by MC_t, which is the vertical sum of its own marginal cost of assembling and marketing the product (MC_m) and the price of the intermediate product (P_t). Thus, the best level of output of the *final* product by the marketing division of the firm is 40 units (the same as when there was no external market for

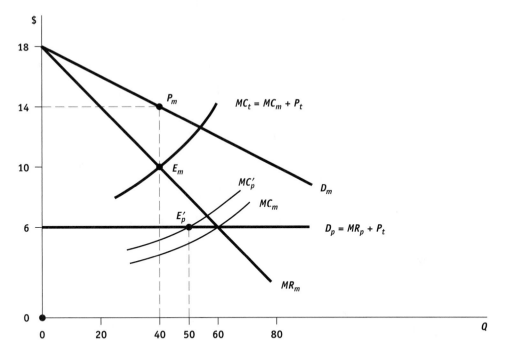

FIGURE 11-7   Transfer Pricing of the Intermediate Product with a Perfectly Competitive Market
This figure is identical to Figure 11-6, except that MC is lower than MC_p. At the perfectly competitive external price of $P_t = \$6$ for the intermediate product, the production division of the firm faces $D_p = MR_p = P_t = \$6$. Therefore, the best level of output of the intermediate product is $Q_p = 50$ and is given by point E_p' at which $D_p = MR_p = P_t = MC = \$6$. Since the marketing division can purchase the intermediate product (internally or externally) at $P_t = \$6$, its total marginal cost curve, MC_t, is equal to the vertical summation of MC_m and P_t. Thus, the best level of output of the final product by the marketing division is 40 units and is given by point E_m, at which $MR_m = MC_t$, so that $P_m = \$14$ (as in Figure 11-6).

the intermediate product) and is given by point E_m at which $MR_m = MC_t$. At $Q_m = 40$, $P_m = \$14$ (the same as in Figure 11-6).

Thus, the production division of the firm produces 50 units of the intermediate product, sells 40 units internally to the marketing division at $P_t = \$6$, and sells the remaining 10 units in the external market, also at $P_t = \$6$. The marketing division will not pay more than the external price of $6 per unit for the intermediate product, while the production division will not sell the intermediate product internally to the marketing division for less than $6 per unit. Thus, when a perfectly competitive external market for the intermediate product exists, the transfer price for intracompany sales of the intermediate product is given by the external competitive price for the intermediate product.

The analysis shown graphically in Figure 11-7 can also be undertaken algebraically, as follows. The demand and marginal revenue curves for the final product faced by the marketing division in Figure 11-7 can be represented algebraically as

$$Q_m = 180 - 10P_m \quad \text{or} \quad P_m = 18 - 0.1Q_m$$

and

$$MR_m = 18 - 0.2Q_m$$

Assuming that the marginal cost functions of the production and marketing divisions of the firm are, respectively,

$$MC'_p = 1 + 0.1Q_p \quad \text{and} \quad MC_m = 0.1Q_m$$

and that the perfectly competitive external price for the transfer product is $P_t = \$6$, we can find the best level of output of the intermediate product for the production division by setting its marginal cost equal to the transfer price. That is,

$$MC'_p = 1 + 0.1Q_p = \$6 = P_t$$

so that
$$0.1Q_p = 5$$
and
$$Q_p = 50$$

The best level of output of the *final product* for the marketing division is determined by finding the total marginal cost of the marketing division (MC_t) and setting it equal to its marginal revenue. That is,

$$MC_t = MC_m + P_t$$
$$= 0.1Q_m + 6$$

Then

$$MC_t = 0.1Q_m + 6 = 18 - 0.2Q_m = MR_m$$
$$0.3Q_m = 12$$

so that
$$Q_m = 40$$
and
$$P_m = 18 - 0.1(40) = \$14$$

Thus, the production division sells 40 units of the intermediate product internally to the marketing division and the remaining 10 units on the external competitive market, all at $P_t = \$6$. The marketing division uses the 40 units of the intermediate product purchased internally from the production division at $P_t = \$6$ to produce 40 units of the final product to be sold on the external market at $P_m = \$14$. These are the same results obtained graphically in Figure 11-7, except that we have assumed linear rather than curvilinear MC functions in the above algebraic solution.

Transfer Pricing with an Imperfectly Competitive Market for the Intermediate Product

When an imperfectly competitive external market for the intermediate product exists, the transfer price of the intermediate product for intrafirm sales will differ from the price of the intermediate product on the imperfectly competitive external market. The determination of the internal and external prices of the intermediate product by the production division of the firm becomes one of third-degree price discrimination. This is shown in Figure 11-8.

Panel *a* of Figure 11-8 shows the marginal revenue of the marketing division of the firm (that is, MR_m) after subtracting from it the transfer price of the intermediate product

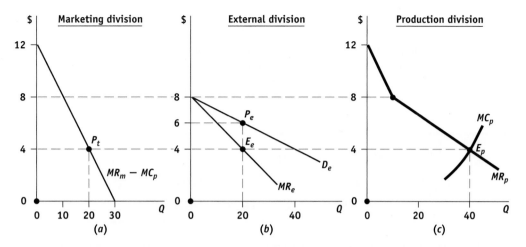

FIGURE 11-8   Transfer Pricing of the Intermediate Product with an Imperfectly Competitive Market
Panel *a* presents the net marginal revenue ($MR_m - MC_p$) curve of the marketing division for the intermediate product, panel *b* shows the external demand and marginal revenue curves (that is, D_e and MR_e) for the intermediate product, while panel *c* shows the $MR_p = MR_m - MC_p + MR_e$ and MC_p curves of the production division. The best level of output of the intermediate product by the production division is 40 units and is given by E_p, at which $MR_p = MC_p$ in panel *c*. The optimal distribution of $Q_p = 40$ is 20 units to the marketing division and 20 units to the external market (given by points P_t and E_e, respectively), at which $MR_m - MC_p = MR_e = MR_p = MC_p = \$4$. The transfer price to the marketing division is then $P_t = MC_p = \$4$, and the price of the intermediate product for sales on the external market is $P_e = \$6$.

(P_t), which is equal to the marginal cost of the production division (MC_p). Thus, the $MR_m - MC_p$ curve in the left panel shows the net marginal revenue of the marketing division. Panel *b* presents the negatively sloped demand curve for the intermediate product of the firm on the imperfectly competitive external market (D_e) and its corresponding marginal revenue curve (MR_e). In panel *c*, on one hand, the MR_p curve is the total revenue curve of the production division of the firm, which is equal to the horizontal summation of the net marginal revenue curves for internal sales to the marketing division of the firm and to the external market (that is, $MR_p = MR_m - MC_p + MR_e$). The MC_p curve, on the other hand, shows the marginal cost to the production division of the firm of producing the intermediate product for internal sales to the marketing division of the firm and to the external market.

The best level of output of the intermediate product by the production division of the firm is 40 units and is given by point E_p, at which $MR_p = MC_p$ in panel *c*. The optimal distribution of the 40 units of the intermediate product produced by the production division of the firm is 20 units internally to the marketing division of the firm (given by point P_t in panel *a*) and 20 units to the external market (given by point E_e in panel *b*), so that $MR_m - MC_p = MR_e = MR_p = MC_p = \$4$. Thus, the production division of the firm operates as the monopolist seller of the intermediate product in the segmented internal and external markets for the intermediate product. Setting the internal transfer price at $P_t = MC_p = \$4$ ensures that the marketing division of the firm (in panel *a*) demands 20 units of the intermediate product, which leads to profit maximization for the marketing division and for the firm as a whole. With optimal sales of 20 units of the intermediate product in the external market (given by point E_e in panel *b*), the market-clearing price for the intermediate product is $P_e = \$6$. Case Studies 11-4 and 11-5 examine how multinational corporations use transfer pricing to avoid paying taxes in high-tax countries, thereby greatly increasing their profits.

CASE STUDY 11-4
Transfer Pricing by Multinationals Operating in Emerging Markets

When an enterprise operates across national borders, additional profit opportunities and risks arise because of different rates of corporate taxes in different countries. By artificially overpricing intermediate products shipped to a semiautonomous division of the firm in a higher-tax nation and underpricing products shipped from the division in the high-tax nation, a multinational corporation can minimize its tax bill and increase its profits. Governments of high-tax countries seek to minimize the loss of tax and customs revenues resulting from transfer pricing by generally applying an *arm's-length test*. "Arm's-length" is defined as the price an unrelated party would pay for the products under the same circumstances. This test, however, provides general guidance only and is vague on many issues. As a result, multinational corporations retain a great deal of leeway in setting transfer prices so as to minimize their overall taxes and maximize profits. This is especially true in developing countries since they generally have less effective legal controls on the transfer pricing practices of multinational corporations than developed countries.

A 1986 study in Bangladesh pointed out that multinational enterprises have many important advantages over local competitors. These include economies of scale in production, high research

and development expenditures by the parent company, sophisticated and efficient marketing techniques, access to sources of finance on a worldwide basis, superior marketing skills, and so on. Because of these important economic advantages, the authors expected that semiautonomous divisions of multinational corporations would have higher profit rates than local competitors. They found the reverse to be the case, however. The average net profit as a percentage of total sales of the division of multinational corporations was 3.4 percent as compared to 5.4 percent for the local competitors over the period 1975 to 1979 of the study. The authors then examined the price of intermediate products imported by semiautonomous divisions of multinational pharmaceutical corporations and the price of the same products imported by their local competitors and found that, on the average, the former were 194 percent higher than the later. Since this difference was not caused by differences in transportation costs, the authors concluded that multinational pharmaceutical firms operating in Bangladesh used transfer pricing to transfer large profits abroad. Governments in many emerging markets, such as Poland, are now cracking down on transfer pricing by multinationals operating in their countries.

Source: M. Z. Rahman and R. W. Scapens, "Transfer Pricing by Multinationals: Some Evidence from Bangladesh," *Journal of Business and Financial Accounting* (Autumn 1986), pp. 383–391; and "Poland to Crack Down on Transfer Pricing," *Financial Times* (December 12, 2001), p. 8.

CASE STUDY 11-5
Transfer Pricing in Advanced Countries

The U.S. Internal Revenue Service, bolstered by new auditing powers, is investigating many American subsidiaries of foreign firms on the suspicion that they have underpaid U.S. corporate income taxes by as much as $12 billion. Indirect evidence of this is given by the fact that the ratio of income tax payments to total receipts of foreign-controlled U.S. corporations was less than half that of U.S. corporations. Even more incredible is the fact that of the nearly 37,000 foreign-owned companies filing returns in 1986, more than half reported no taxable income! In 1991, the IRS adopted an "advance pricing agreement" with an increasing number of multinational corporations on the range of prices at which to value the various products that these multinationals import to the United States, so as to avoid transfer pricing disputes. But such disputes continue.

In 1993, Nissan had to pay $144 million to the U.S. Internal Revenue Service to settle claims arising from transfer pricing; in 1996, Japan filed claims for nearly $500 million in back taxes for transfer pricing against more than 50 multinational corporations; in

2000 DaimlerChrysler had to pay an extra $46 million in taxes to Japan because of transfer pricing, and in the same year Nissan also had to pay extra taxes to the United Kingdom for the same reason. The foreign profits of the six largest U.S. drug companies rose from 38 percent of their overall income in 1994 to more than 65 percent in 2003 even though the share of overseas sales grew only slightly. As a result, taxes on corporate profits for those companies fell from the 31 percent rate on domestic profits to the 17.5 percent rate on foreign profits. By far the largest transfer pricing case to date is the one going to trial in the United States in 2006 against the pharmaceutical group GlaxoSmithKline seeking to recoup $4.6 billion in unpaid taxes and $2.5 billion in penalty interest. Starting in 2002, the United States began to aggressively crackdown on a new type of transfer pricing used by U.S. and foreign computer and pharmaceutical companies arising from their transfer of intellectual property (such as trademarks and patents) to tax havens to avoid paying taxes on the income generated from those properties.

Source: "I.R.S. Investigating Foreign Companies for Tax Cheating," *The New York Times* (February 10, 1990), p. 1; "Big Japan Concern Reaches an Accord on Paying U.S. Tax," *The New York Times* (November 11, 1992), p. 1; "Why Do Foreign Companies Report Such Low Profits on Their U.S. Operations?" *The Wall Street Journal* (November 2, 1994), p. A1; "Japan's Tax Man Leans on Foreign Firms," *The Wall Street Journal* (November 25, 1966), p. C21; "DaimlerChrysler Japan Forced to Pay More Tax," *Financial Times* (October 10, 2000), p. 22; "Nissan's U.K. Arm Hit by Tax Charges," *Financial Times* (November 8, 2000), p. 27; "A New Twist in Tax Avoidance: Firms Send Best Ideas Abroad," *The Wall Street Journal* (June 24, 2002), p. A1; and "Treasury Cracks Down on Companies Shifting Profits to Low-Tax Jurisdictions," *Financial Times* (August 25, 2005), p. 1.

11-5   PRICING IN PRACTICE

In this section we examine some of the actual pricing practices followed by firms in the real world. The most common of these is cost-plus pricing. Here, we explain this practice, examine its advantages and disadvantages, and show that it approximates the profit-maximizing pricing rule. We complete this section with an examination of incremental analysis in pricing, peak-load pricing, two-part tariff, tying, bundling, and other real-world pricing practices.

Cost-Plus Pricing

In the real world, firms may not be able (and it may be too expensive) to collect precise marginal revenue (*MR*) and marginal cost (*MC*) data to determine the optimal level of output and price at the point at which *MR* = *MC*. Therefore, firms have developed rules of thumb or short-cut methods for pricing their products. The most widely used of such pricing rules is **cost-plus pricing** (also called "markup pricing" and "full-cost pricing"). The usual method is for the firm to first estimate the average variable cost (*AVC*) of producing or purchasing and marketing the product for a normal or standard level of output (usually taken to be between 70 and 80 percent of capacity). The firm then adds to the *AVC* an average overhead charge (usually expressed as a percentage of *AVC*), so as to get the estimated fully allocated average cost (*C*). To this **fully allocated average cost,** the firm then adds a markup on cost (*m*) for profits.

The formula for the **markup on cost** can, thus, be expressed as

$$m = \frac{P - C}{C} \qquad\qquad [11\text{-}3]$$

where *m* is the markup on cost, *P* is the product price, and *C* is the fully allocated average cost of the product. The numerator of Equation 11-3 (that is, *P* − *C*) is called the **profit margin.** Solving Equation 11-3 for *P*, we get the price of the product in a cost-plus pricing scheme. That is,

$$P = C(1 + m) \qquad\qquad [11\text{-}4]$$

For example, suppose that a firm takes 80 percent of its capacity output of 125 units as the normal or standard output, that it projects total variable and overhead costs for the year to be, respectively, $1,000 and $600 for the normal or standard output, and that it wants to apply a 25 percent markup on cost. Then the normal or standard output is 100 units, the *AVC* = $10, and the average overhead cost is $6. Thus, *C* = $16 and *P* = 16(1 + 0.25) = $20 with *m* = ($20 − $16)/$16 = 0.25. Markups of 25 percent have been traditional in some major industries, such as automobiles, electrical equipment, and aluminum, in order for firms in these industries to achieve a target rate of return on investment for the normal or standard level of output.

Evaluation of Cost-Plus Pricing

The widespread use of cost-plus pricing in the real world can be explained by the several important advantages that it provides. First, cost-plus pricing generally requires less information and less precise data than the rule of setting price at the output level at which marginal revenue equals marginal cost. Second, cost-plus pricing seems easy and simple to use. This apparent simplicity, however, is misleading since it may be very difficult to correctly estimate and project total variable costs, and it may actually be impossible to appropriately allocate total overhead charges to the various products produced by the firm. Third, cost-plus pricing usually results in relatively stable prices when costs do not vary very much over time. This is an advantage because it is costly to change prices. Price changes may also lead to uncertain price responses in oligopolistic markets. Finally, cost-plus pricing can provide a clear justification for price increases when costs rise.

Despite these important advantages and widespread use, cost-plus pricing is criticized on several important grounds. One criticism is that cost-plus pricing is based on accounting and historical costs, rather than on replacement and opportunity costs. Although this is a serious criticism of how cost-plus pricing is usually conducted in practice, it is not a criticism of cost-plus pricing itself, since the firm could (and should) base its calculations on the correct replacement or opportunity cost basis rather than on incorrect accounting and historical costs. Another important criticism is that cost-plus pricing is based on the average, rather than on the marginal, cost of production. To the extent, however, that marginal cost is constant or nearly constant over the normal or standard level of output of the firm, marginal cost is approximately equal to (the fully allocated) average cost. Therefore, cost-plus pricing would not lead to product prices that are much different from prices based on the $MR = MC$ rule.

Finally, cost-plus pricing is criticized because it ignores conditions of demand. Since it has been shown, however, that firms usually apply higher markups to products facing less elastic demand than to products with more elastic demand, it can be demonstrated that cost-plus pricing leads to approximately the profit-maximizing price. To show this, we begin with Equation 3-12, repeated below as Equation 11-5:

$$MR = P\left(1 + \frac{1}{E_p}\right) \quad [11\text{-}5]$$

where MR is the marginal revenue, P is the product price, and E_p is the price elasticity of demand. Solving for P, we get

$$P = \frac{MR}{1 + 1/E_p} = \frac{MR}{(E_p + 1)/E_p} = MR\frac{E_p}{E_p + 1} \quad [11\text{-}6]$$

Since profits are maximized where $MR = MC$, we can substitute MC for MR in the above equation and get

$$P = MC\frac{E_p}{E_p + 1}$$

To the extent that the firm's MC is constant over the normal or standard level of output, $MC = C$, where C is the fully allocated average cost of the product. Substituting C for MC into the above equation, we get

$$P = C\frac{E_p}{E_p + 1} \quad [11\text{-}7]$$

Setting Equations 11-4 and 11-7 equal to each other, we have

$$C(1 + m) = C\frac{E_p}{E_p + 1}$$

or

$$1 + m = \frac{E_p}{E_p + 1}$$

so that the optimal markup is

$$m = \frac{E_p}{E_p + 1} - 1 \qquad\qquad [11\text{-}8]$$

From Equation 11-8 we can calculate that if $E_p = -1.5$, $m = 2$, or 200 percent; if $E_p = -2$, $m = 1$, or 100 percent; if $E_p = -3$, $m = 0.5$, or 50 percent; and if $E_p = -4$, $m = 0.33$, or 33 percent. We can thus conclude that the optimal markup is lower the greater is the price elasticity of demand of the product.[9]

This fact has often been observed in the real world.[10] That is, firms have been found to apply a higher markup to products with inelastic demand than to products with elastic demand, and when increased competition has increased the price elasticity of demand, they have been found to reduce their markup. For example, the markup on cost is much lower (between 10 and 12 percent) in the grocery business, where price elasticity of demand is very high, than for industrial machinery where the price elasticity is lower. We can, therefore, conclude that cost-plus pricing does take demand considerations into account in actual practice and does lead to approximately profit-maximizing prices. In a world of inadequate and imprecise data on demand and costs, firms may simply use cost-plus pricing as the rule-of-thumb method for determining the profit-maximizing prices.

Incremental Analysis in Pricing

Correct pricing and output decisions require **incremental analysis.** That is, a firm should change the price of a product or its output, introduce a new product, or a new version of a given product, accept a new order, and so on, if the increase in total revenue or incremental revenue from the action exceeds the increase in total or incremental cost. For example, an airline should introduce a new flight if the incremental revenue from the flight exceeds the incremental cost (see Case Study 11-6). When excess capacity exists in the short run, overhead or fixed costs are irrelevant in determining whether a firm should undertake a particular course of action. Since overhead or fixed costs have already been covered, any action on the part of the firm that increases revenues more than costs leads to an increase in the total profits of the firm and should be undertaken.

If, however, the firm is already producing at capacity, lowering a product's price to increase sales or introducing a new product will lead to the expansion of all costs, including those for plant and equipment. In this case, full-cost and incremental-cost pricing lead to the same results. Even when the firm is operating with idle capacity, the long-run implications of a particular course of action must be taken into consideration in order for the firm to reach correct pricing and output decisions. For example, if a firm lowers the price of a product in order to increase sales or introduces a new product in order to take advantage of idle capacity, these actions may require the expansion of capacity if the firm

---

[9] Note that an imperfectly competitive firm (i.e., one facing a negatively sloped demand) will operate only in the elastic portion of the demand curve for the product (i.e., in the range of the demand curve for which $E_p > |{-}1|$) so that MR is positive and equals MC.

[10] See R. M. Cyert and J. G. March, *A Behavioral Theory of the Firm* (Englewood Cliffs, N.J.: Prentice-Hall, 1963).

CASE STUDY 11-6
Incremental Pricing at Continental Airlines

A classic example of incremental analysis is the decision process followed by Continental Airlines to add or to cancel a particular flight from its schedule. Continental—and the airline industry in general—face high overhead costs for depreciation, interest charges, and ground, office, and flight crews. Continental follows the rule of adding a flight to its schedule as long as the increase in total revenue or the incremental revenue from the flight exceeds the increase in out-of-pocket expenses or incremental cost. The excess of incremental revenue over incremental cost thus makes a contribution toward covering the firm's overhead or fixed costs. Great care is exercised to uncover all incremental revenues and costs in deciding whether to add a particular flight.

In determining the net incremental revenue from the flight, Continental considers not only the extra revenue that the flight itself is expected to generate but also the effect of adding the flight on competing and connecting flights. For example, the direct incremental revenue from the proposed flight might fall short of the incremental cost, but if the flight feeds passengers into Continental's long-haul service and the overall direct and indirect incremental revenue exceeds the overall direct and indirect incremental costs, the airline would add the flight. Similarly, Continental sometimes schedules late-evening flights from New York to Houston without a single passenger to avoid the higher overnight hangar rental cost in New York than in Houston (its home base). By doing these things, Continental succeeded in lowering its marginal and average cost per seat mile below those of other major U.S. airlines.

On some of its routes, Continental also introduced fares sufficiently low to discourage other airlines from entering the market and servicing the route. This is an example of *limit pricing* examined in Section 9-1. But the emergence of discount carriers such as America West and JetBlue at the beginning of the decade led to renewed fare wars in 2001 and 2002 and huge losses for the traditional airlines, except low-cost Southwest (refer back to Case Study 10-3). In recent years, incremental pricing has been greatly refined with the use of advanced computers and is now practiced by all airlines under the name of *yield management* (see Integrating Case Study Five at the end of this chapter).

Source: "Airline Takes the Marginal Route," *Business Week* (April 20, 1963), pp. 111–114; "Continental Airlines Grounds Airbus Fleet in Cost-Cutting Move," *The Wall Street Journal* (December 22, 1994), p. C18; "Bandits at Nine O'Clock," *The Economist* (February 7, 1996), pp. 57–58; "The Age of 'Wal-Mart' Airlines Crunches the Biggest Carriers," *The Wall Street Journal* (June 18, 2002), p. A1; "Losses Widen at Nation's Major Airlines," *The Wall Street Journal* (July 19, 2002), p. B4; and "Continental Sees Significant Loss in 2005," *The New York Times* (September 10, 2005), p. C3.

expects the demand for its products to increase in the long run. Incremental analysis must, then, take these long-run effects into consideration.

Correct incremental analysis requires that all direct and indirect changes in revenues and costs resulting from a particular course of action be taken into consideration. For example, in calculating the incremental revenue from lowering the price of a product or from the introduction of a new product, the firm must consider all demand interrelationships between the product in question and all other complementary and substitute products sold by the firm. For example, the incremental revenue from lowering the price of photographic film by Kodak may very well be smaller than the incremental cost, but when the increase in sales of Kodak cameras resulting from the reduction in the price of the film is taken into consideration, the action may prove to be highly profitable for the firm. Similarly, increasing the production of a particular product or the introduction of a new product may lower the cost of a jointly produced product so much that the overall incremental cost from the action may be much lower than the overall incremental revenue, so that the decision may lead to much higher profits for the firm.

From what has been said above, it should be clear that a firm could not price all its products on an incremental basis since in the aggregate, the firm must also cover all its overhead and fixed costs, at least in the long run. But it is not necessary and it would be inappropriate for a firm to price each of its products on a fully allocated average cost basis. Particularly in the short run and in the presence of idle capacity, it would be very advantageous (i.e., it would increase total profits or reduce total losses) if the firm accepted a price on some additional sales that was below fully allocated average costs, as long as the price exceeded average incremental costs. Such incremental pricing policies provide the firm with much more flexibility and are clearly in evidence in the pricing policies followed by "excellently managed firms."[11] These firms take into consideration not only the short-run but also the long-run implications of their pricing policies, and they consider all important demand and production interrelationships.

Peak-Load Pricing, Two-Part Tariff, Tying, and Bundling

Peak-load pricing refers to the charging of a higher price for a good or service during peak times than at off-peak times. The demand for some services (such as electricity) is higher during some periods (such as in the evening and in the summer) than at other times (such as during the day or in the spring). Electricity is also a nonstorable service (i.e., it must be generated when it is needed). In order to satisfy peak demand, electric power companies must bring into operation older and less efficient equipment and thus incur higher marginal costs and charge higher prices. Such price differences would be based on cost differences, so they are not technically price discrimination (nevertheless, they have sometimes been referred to as *intertemporal* price discrimination—see Case Study 11-7).

Two-part tariff refers to the pricing practice in which consumers pay an initial fee for the right to purchase a product or service, as well as a usage fee or price for each unit of the product they purchase. Oligopolistic and monopolistic firms sometimes use this pricing method as a way to increase their profits. Examples are provided by some amusement parks, where visitors are charged a general admission fee as well as a fee or price for each ride they take; telephone companies, which charge a monthly fee plus a message-unit fee; computer companies, which charge monthly rentals plus a usage fee for renting their mainframe computers; and golf and tennis clubs, which charge an annual membership fee plus a fee for each round or game played.[12]

Tying refers to the requirement that a consumer who buys or leases a product also purchases another product needed in the use of the first. For example, when the Xerox

---

[11] See J. S. Early, "Marginal Policies in Excellently Managed Firms: A Survey," *American Economic Review* (March 1956), pp. 44–70; and "Flexible Pricing," *Business Week* (December 12, 1977), pp. 66–76.

[12] For a more in-depth discussion of two-part tariff, see W. Oi, "A Disneyland Dilemma: Two-Part Tariff for a Mickey Mouse Monopoly," *Quarterly Journal of Economics* (February 1971), pp. 77–96.

CASE STUDY 11-7
Peak-Load Pricing by Con Edison

Table 11-2 gives the higher price per kilowatt-hour (kWh) that Con Edison charged residential users and small and large commercial users of electricity for voluntary-time-of-day or peak hours (8 A.M. to 10 P.M. on weekdays) than for off-peak hours in New York City in June through September and in other months in 2005. To be noted is that peak-load pricing is different from third-degree price discrimination because higher peak electricity rates are based on or reflect the higher costs of generating electricity at peak hours when older and less efficient plants and equipment have to be brought into operation.

TABLE 11-2	Electricity Rates Charged by Con Edison in 2005 for Peak and Off-Peak Hours (cents per kilowatt-hour)	
	Peak Hours	**Off-Peak Hours**
Residential Rates, 0–250 kWh (single residence)		
June–September	18.26	0.63
Other months	6.57	0.63
Commercial Rates, 0–900 kWh (small business)		
June–September	13.55	0.48
Other months	6.66	0.48
Delivery Charges (Plus $/kWh) for Low and High Tension (large business)		
June–September	10.24 (0.52)	5.47 (0.52)
Other months	7.55 (0.52)	3.27 (3.17)

Source: Con Edison, New York City (2005).

Corporation was the only producer of photocopiers in the 1950s, it required companies leasing its machines to also purchase paper from Xerox. Similarly, until it was ordered by the court to discontinue the practice, IBM required by contract that the users of its computers purchase IBM punch cards. Sometimes tying of purchases is done to ensure that the correct supplies are used for the equipment to function properly or to ensure a level of quality. More often, it is used as a form of two-part tariff to earn higher profits. The courts, however, often intervene to forbid these restrictions on competition. For example, McDonald's was forced to allow its franchises to purchase their materials and supplies from any McDonald's-approved supplier rather than only from McDonald's. This increased competition, while still ensuring quality and protection of the brand name.[13]

---

[13] See B. Klein and L. F. Saft, "The Law and Economics of Franchise Tying Contracts," *Journal of Law and Economics* (May 1985), pp. 345–361.

Bundling is a common form of tying in which the firm requires customers buying or leasing one of its products or services to also buy or lease another product or service *when customers have different tastes* but the firm cannot price discriminate (as in tying). By selling or leasing the product or service as a package or bundle rather than separately, the monopolist can increase its total profits. This is examined in Case Study 11-8.

CASE STUDY 11-8
Bundling in the Leasing of Movies

Table 11-3 shows the prices that theater 1 and theater 2 would be willing to pay to lease movie A and movie B. If the film company cannot price discriminate and it leases each movie separately to the two theaters, it will have to lease each movie at the lower of the two prices at which each theater is willing to lease each film. Specifically, the film company would have to charge $10,000 for movie A and $3,000 for movie B, for a total of $13,000 to lease both movies to each theater (if the film company charged more for each movie, one of the theaters would not lease the movie). But theater 1 would have been willing to pay $15,000 to lease both movies, and theater 2 would have been willing to pay $14,000 for both movies. The film company can thus lease both movies as a package or a *bundle* for $14,000 (the lowest of the total amounts at which the two theaters are willing to lease the two movies) rather than individually for $13,000. Thus, by leasing the two movies together as a bundle rather than individually, the film company can extract some of the surplus from theater 1 without price discriminating between the two theaters.

Such profitable bundling is possible only when one theater is willing to pay more for leasing one movie but less for leasing the other movie with respect to the other theater (i.e., when the *relative* valuation for the movies differs between the two theaters or the demand for the two movies by each theater is negatively correlated). If, in our example, both theaters had been willing to pay only $9,000 to lease movie A, then the maximum price that the film company could charge either theater without price discrimination would be $12,000, whether it leased the movies as a bundle or separately. For bundling to be profitable one theater must be willing to pay more for one movie and less for another movie with respect to the other theater. This occurs only if the two theaters serve different audiences with different tastes and have different relative valuations for the two movies.

Other examples of bundling are complete dinners versus a la carte pricing at restaurants, travel packages (which often include flights, hotel accommodations and meals), and the sale of wire and wireless telephone services, Internet access, and cable TV as a single package by telecommunications companies.

TABLE 11-3	Maximum Price Each Theater Would Pay to Lease Each Film Separately and as Bundle	
	Theater 1	Theater 2
Movie A	$12,000	$10,000
Movie B	3,000	4,000

Source: R. L. Schmalensee, "Commodity Bundling by Single-Product Monopolies," *Journal of Law and Economics* (April 1982), pp. 67–71; A. Lewbel, "Bundling of Substitutes or Complements," *International Journal of Industrial Organization* (no. 3, 1985), pp. 101–107; and "The Benefits of Bundling," *Economic Intuition* (Winter 1999), pp. 6–7.

Other Pricing Practices

Many other pricing practices are often used in the real world. Some of these are prestige pricing, price lining, skimming, and value pricing. A new pricing technology based on the use of electronic scanners is also spreading rapidly in supermarkets.

Prestige pricing refers to deliberately setting high prices to attract prestige-oriented consumers. For example, many people pay prices ranging from $30,000 to $70,000 to drive Mercedes rather than similar lower-priced automobiles for the prestige that they get from doing so. There are more people buying furs costing $10,000 than similar furs costing $4,000 because of the snob appeal they get from the more expensive furs. Consumers often pay high prices for some goods when very similar, much cheaper substitutes exist because they often equate price with quality. This occurs particularly when it is difficult to obtain objective information on product quality. Recognizing this fact, producers sometimes package the same basic product differently—one to appear of higher quality than another—and sell the first at a much higher price.

Price lining is another pricing practice sometimes observed. This refers to the setting of a price target by a firm and then developing a product that would allow the firm to maximize total profits at that price. Instead of deciding first on the type of product to produce and then on the price to charge so as to maximize the firm's total profits (as usual), the order is reversed. For example, GM's Cadillac line of automobiles sells at the highest price range and appeals to the wealthiest and most quality-conscious consumers. GM also sells the Buick line of midsized automobiles at a lower price range to consumers of average income. Finally, GM has the compact-car line, which sells at the lowest price range. GM automobile lines compete with similar lines of automobiles from Ford, Chrysler, and imports. Trying to increase the quality and price of Buicks outside the established range would probably not be profitable, because consumers have become accustomed to viewing Buicks as being of midrange quality and price.

Skimming refers to the setting of a high price when a product is introduced and gradually lowering its price. This occurs most often in durable goods such as refrigerators, washing machines, and personal computers. The reason and the rationale for this are that it is often difficult to determine exactly the strength of demand when a product is introduced and, therefore, the best price to charge. Starting with a high price allows the firm to sell the product to those consumers who are willing to pay the high price. The firm then lowers the price, both to increase sales and to discourage entrants if the initial high price leads to large profits. Skimming is particularly useful if the firm has initially limited production capacity. In that case, it pays for the firm to sell its limited output at the highest price it can fetch. As the firm becomes convinced that it can sell a greater quantity at a lower price, it will expand capacity and lower its price.

Value pricing refers to the selling of quality goods at much lower prices than previously. This is old-fashioned price cutting but with manufacturers redesigning the product to keep or enhance quality while lowering costs so as to still earn a profit. It is offering more for a lot less. For example, PepsiCo Inc.'s Taco Bell chain saw its fourth quarter 1990 sales jump 15 percent in response to a "value" menu offering 59-cent tacos and 14 other items for either 59 cents or 79 cents. This forced McDonald's and Wendy's to respond with a value menu of their own. Similarly, Toyota redesigned its lowest-price automobile, the Tercel, to offer more horsepower and a quieter ride than its

CASE STUDY 11-9
No-Haggling Value Pricing in Car Buying

During the past decade, General Motors (GM) has been gradually moving toward no-haggling value pricing for some of its cars. Other carmakers have also been experimenting with this policy in the United States. Although some Americans find it stimulating, most consider the time-honored business of haggling over the price of a new car intimidating and even humiliating. One-price selling was first instituted at GM's Saturn division when it began building cars in 1990. Ford has also started experimenting with one-price selling on a few of its vehicles, and in 2001 DaimlerChrysler began to phase in its new N.F.P. policy (*negotiation-free process*). Although no-haggle pricing in car buying may yet become the rule in the future, as of 2006, only the Saturn division of General Motors has successfully adopted the approach on a large scale. Dealers' great fear of one-price selling is that customers will simply take the offer elsewhere and use it to negotiate a better deal. Advocates of one-price selling respond that dealers can avoid being undercut by combining one-price selling with value pricing and accepting smaller

profit margins. They believe that customers are not going to go to other dealers to haggle over $40 or $50 if they know that they are already getting good value for their money.

GM moved to value pricing for some of its cars (besides the Saturn) with the 1994 model year. This involved the selling of well-equipped 1994 cars at lower prices than similarly equipped 1993 models. For example, the 1994 Pontiac Grand Prix was offered at a lower price than the 1993 model, even though the newer model had dual airbags while the 1993 model came with no airbags. GM's hope, of course, was to increase market share and profits. The strategy seemed to work. For example, by lowering the price of a well-equipped Buick LeSabre from $21,000 for the 1993 model to $18,995 for a similarly equipped 1994 model, GM boosted sales of the model by about 15 percent, but profit margins fell. With more and more information available and more automobiles sold on the Internet, value pricing or lower prices are in, but some haggling still takes place in most automobile purchases.

Source: "GM Stresses Value Pricing for '94 Models," *The Wall Street Journal* (July 12, 1993), p. A3; "Buying Without Haggling as Cars Get Fixed Prices," *The New York Times* (February 1, 1994), p. 1; "At Car Dealers, a No-Haggle Policy Sets Off a Battle," *The New York Times* (August 29, 1999), sec. 3, p. 4; "Meet Your Local GM Dealer: GM," *Business Week* (October 11, 1999), p. 48; "The Web Doesn't Sell Cars But Lets Buyers Build Their Own," *The New York Times* (September 26, 2001), p. 10; "The Best Way to Buy a Car," *The Wall Street Journal* (November 12, 2001), p. R4; "It's a Match," *The Wall Street Journal* (July 25, 2005), p. R4; and "GM, Ford Shift Gears on Pricing," *The Wall Street Journal* (August 2, 2005), p. D2.

predecessor at a lower price and still make money on it. Value pricing is likely to spread as companies cater to increasingly sophisticated bargain-conscious consumers (see Case Study 11-9).[14]

Price matching is the pricing strategy in which a firm advertises a price for its product or services and promises to match any lower price offered by a competitor. The firm's advertisement for mattresses may read: "Our price for the mattress is $200. If you can find a better price in the market, we will match it. We will not be undersold!" Price matching allows a firm to sell at a higher price because it sounds like a good deal to

---

[14] "Setting the Right Price at the Right Time," *Harvard Management Update* (December 2003), pp. 4–5.

CASE STUDY 11-10
Name Your Price at Priceline

In just a few years, Priceline has become one of three icons of e-commerce. The others are Amazon.com and eBay. Amazon.com sells books, videos, and gifts by traditional methods— only without the bricks and mortar of storefronts (see Case Study 3-10). In October 1999, Amazon opened its Web site to merchants of all kinds, essentially becoming an Internet shopping bazaar. eBay's auctions originally matched buyers and sellers of collectibles, such as Beanie Babies and baseball cards, but they now include most products. eBay has now more than 150 million customers in over 15 countries around the world, and in the United States it opened 50 regional marketplaces for large items, such as cars, boats, and refrigerators, that are not well suited for its national Web site.

Priceline allows buyers to name the price they are willing to pay for flights, hotel rooms, mortgages, cars, and groceries. The only condition is that the buyer be flexible as to seller or brand name. For example, in the purchase of an airline ticket to a certain city the buyer cannot specify the airline or the time of flight, but has to take what is offered by the carrier that accepts the bid. This allows airlines to sell empty seats without losing their regular customers. As customers learned to make realistic bids, and as Priceline added more airlines and flights, more and more bids have been successful (although they are still less than half). Students at the University of Pennsylvania's Wharton School of Business registering for elective courses have even been able to log on to

Wharton's course auction Web site and bid on the courses they want.

In fall 1999 in New York City, Priceline introduced the WebHouse Club, which was a name-your-price scheme for groceries. Customers specified how much they will spend for various items, such as colas, detergents, batteries, etc., but they could not specify the exact brand. If their price was accepted (answers came within minutes), the item was charged to their credit card and the customer got a voucher to "pay" for the items at the more than 600 participating local stores. Despite the fact that WebHouse Club and other similar online grocery businesses (such as Webvan and Streamline) failed for lack of sufficient participation, others such as FreshDirect in New York City and Safeway in Phoenix have been created. Several new smaller sites have also been established that not only led to lower prices than at Priceline but even identify the price of the winning bid and the company that accepted the bid—something that Priceline won't (really cannot) do because it has promised the companies not to do so. More recently, some consumers have engaged in collective bargain hunting at FatWallett.com and SlickDels.net. Now, a new crop of start-ups, such as Become.com, Smarter.com, and BuySafe, is pushing the price-comparison concept even further, offering extra discounts, greater convenience, and protection against fraud. The Net has certainly been a fertile ground for launching entirely new ways of doing business!

Source: "Wired for the Bottom Line," *Newsweek* (September 20, 1999), pp. 43–49; "eBay Plans to Open 50 Web Markets for Regional Use," *The Wall Street Journal* (October 1, 1999), p. B6; "New Battlefield for Priceline Is Diapers, Tuna," *The Wall Street Journal* (September 22, 1999), p. B1; "Business School Puts Courses in the Hands of an On-Line Market," *The New York Times* (September 9, 1999), p. G3; "The Brave New World of Pricing," *Financial Times* (August 2, 2001), p. 2; "How to Beat Priceline: New Sites Post Secret Bids," *The Wall Street Journal* (April 9, 2002), p. D1; "Priceline's Ex-CEO Puts Eggs in Basket of an Online Grocer," *The Wall Street Journal* (June 2, 2005), p. B7; "The Next Generation of Price-Comparison Sites," *The Wall Street Journal* (September 14, 2005), p. D1; and "Collective Bargain Hunting," *The New York Times Magazine* (September 18, 2005), p. 32 .

consumers (who may feel it is futile for them to search for a better price) and because it also discourages competitors from undercutting any given rival's price. Price matching is becoming increasingly popular among car dealers, office supply stores, electronic stores, and other retailers.[15]

Pricing technology at supermarkets is being revolutionized by the use of **electronic scanners.** Most of the nation's supermarkets already use such electronic scanners at checkout counters to ring up prices for barcoded items. The use of scanners drastically cuts costs by allowing supermarkets to avoid item-by-item pricing and repricing of grocery items on the shelves and allowing them to use less skilled and less costly sales clerks at checkout counters. Although it is expensive to install scanners, with profit margins already very thin, competition has forced almost all supermarkets to adopt this innovation in order to remain in business.

Auction pricing is the pricing strategy where buyers and sellers make bids for the goods on sale. One type of auction price on the Internet is where the consumer posts the price that he or she is willing to pay for a good or service and the site facilitates a match with the seller (see Case Study 11-10).

SUMMARY

1. When a firm produces more than one product, the firm must consider demand interdependence (substitutability and complementarity, which are reflected in the marginal revenue function of each product), for optimal pricing and output decisions. Firms produce more than one product in order to make fuller use of their production facilities. They introduce products in order of their profitability until $MR_A = MR_B = MC_C = MC$, where product C is the least profitable product for the firm. The best level of output of products that are jointly produced in fixed proportions is given by the point at which total marginal revenue (MR_T) equals the marginal cost for the joint products. Prices are then determined on the respective demand curves for the jointly produced products. A firm will sell a jointly produced product, however, only up to the point at which $MR = 0$. The optimal output of products that are jointly produced in variable proportions is given at the tangency point of the isorevenue line and the product transformation or total cost curve that leads to the overall maximum profits for the firm.

2. *Price discrimination* refers to the charging of different prices for different quantities of a product, at different times, to different customer groups, or in different markets, when these price differences are not justified by cost differences. Three conditions must be met for a firm to be able to practice price discrimination: (1) The firm must have some monopoly power, (2) the price elasticities of demand for the product in different markets must differ, and (3) the markets must be separable or able to be segmented. *First-degree price discrimination* refers to the selling of each unit of the product separately and charging the highest price possible for each unit sold. *Second-degree price discrimination* refers to the charging of a uniform price per unit for a specific quantity or block of the product, a lower price per unit for an additional batch or block of the product, and so on. *Third-degree price discrimination* refers to the charging of different prices for the same product in different markets until the marginal revenue of the last unit of the product sold in each market equals the marginal cost of the product.

---

[15] See J. D. Hess and E. Gerstner, "Price-Matching Policies: An Empirical Case," *Managerial and Decision Economics* (December 1991), pp. 305–315.

3. International price discrimination is called (persistent) dumping. Under this type of dumping the monopolist sells the commodity at a higher price at home (where the market demand curve is less elastic) than abroad, where the monopolist faces competition from other nations and the market demand curve for the monopolist's product is more elastic.

4. *Transfer pricing* refers to the determination of the price of the intermediate products sold by one semiautonomous division of a firm to another semiautonomous division of the same enterprise. Appropriate transfer pricing is essential in determining the optimal output of each division and of the firm as a whole, and in evaluating divisional performance and determining divisional rewards. The correct transfer price for an intermediate product for which there is no external market is the marginal cost of production. When a perfectly competitive external market for the intermediate product exists, the transfer price for intracompany sales of the intermediate product is given by the external competitive price for the intermediate product. When an intermediate product can be sold in an imperfectly competitive market, the (internal) transfer price of the intermediate product is given at the point at which the net marginal revenue of the marketing division

of the firm is equal to the marginal cost of the production division at the best total level of output of the intermediate product, and the price charged in the external market is given on the external demand curve.

5. Because it may be too expensive or impossible to collect precise marginal revenue and marginal cost data, most firms use cost-plus pricing. This involves calculating the average variable cost of producing the normal or standard level of output (usually between 70 and 80 percent of capacity), adding an average overhead charge so as to get the fully allocated average cost for the product, and then adding to this a markup on cost for profits. Since firms usually apply higher markups for products facing less elastic demand than for products with more elastic demand, it can also be demonstrated that cost-plus pricing leads to approximately the profit-maximizing price. Correct pricing and output decisions by the firm involve incremental analysis or comparison of the incremental revenue to the incremental cost of the managerial decisions. Other real-world pricing practices are two-part tariff, tying, bundling, prestige pricing, price lining, value pricing, skimming, auction pricing, and price matching. Pricing technology at supermarkets is also being revolutionized by the use of electronic scanners.

DISCUSSION QUESTIONS

1. (*a*) What is meant by demand interrelationships for a multiproduct firm? (*b*) How are demand interrelationships measured? (*c*) Why must a multiproduct firm take into consideration demand interrelationships in its pricing and output decisions?

2. (*a*) Why do most firms produce more than one product? (*b*) What is the rule for profit maximization for a multiproduct firm? (*c*) Why would a firm produce a product on which it makes zero profits?

3. Why should jointly produced products in fixed proportions be (*a*) regarded as a single production package? (*b*) treated separately in demand?

4. (*a*) How can a firm determine the best level of output and price for products that are jointly

produced in fixed proportions? (*b*) Under what circumstances would a firm produce a product and then destroy it?

5. Although the case of products jointly produced in variable proportions is more common than the case of products jointly produced in fixed proportions, Figure 11-3 is based on a somewhat inappropriate assumption. Can you identify what that assumption is?

6. (*a*) How would the shape of the isorevenue lines in Figure 11-3 change if we did not assume that P_A and P_B are constant? (*b*) How does this change the analysis?

7. Quantity discounts are not a form of price discrimination because the firm saves on handling large orders. True or false? Explain.

8. (*a*) Why are first- and second-degree price discrimination less common than third-degree price discrimination? (*b*) Are lower airline fares at midweek an example of third-degree price discrimination? (*c*) Under what conditions would it not be useful to charge different prices in different markets (i.e., practice third-degree price discrimination) even if possible?

9. (*a*) Is persistent dumping good or bad for the receiving country? (*b*) Against what type of dumping would the nation want to protect itself? Why?

10. (*a*) What has stimulated the growth of the large-scale modern enterprise? (*b*) What organizational development was introduced in order to contain the tendency toward rising costs? (*c*) To what problem did this lead? (*d*) Why is it important to solve this problem?

11. How is the transfer price of an intermediate product determined when (*a*) there is no external market for the intermediate product, (*b*) a perfectly competitive external market for the intermediate product exists, and (*c*) an imperfectly competitive external market for the intermediate product exists?

12. (*a*) Indicate in Figure 11-6 the shape and location of the total marginal cost curve of the marketing division of the firm. (*b*) Can you explain why such a curve was not shown in Figure 11-6?

13. What are (*a*) the advantages and (*b*) the disadvantages of cost-plus pricing? (*c*) Why is incremental cost pricing the correct pricing method? Why is full-cost pricing equal to it?

14. What is meant by (*a*) peak-load pricing? (*b*) two-part tariff? (*c*) Tying? (*d*) Bundling? (*e*) Prestige pricing? (*f*) Price lining? (*g*) Skimming? (*h*) Value pricing? (*i*) Price matching? (*j*) Auction pricing?

15. Peak-load pricing can be regarded as an application of the marginal principle? True or false? Explain.

PROBLEMS

*1. The Bike Corporation of America produces four types of bicycles (A, B, C, and F) in declining order of sophistication, price, and profitability. In fact, in the sale of model F, the firm is a perfect competitor. Draw a figure showing the best level of output and price of each type of bicycle produced by the firm.

2. The Bel Monte Canning Company cans pineapples and sells the juice that results as a byproduct of peeling and slicing pineapples. Each 10-pound basket of pineapples results in a 5-pound can of pineapples and in a 5-quart can of pineapple juice. The demand and marginal revenue functions that the firm faces for canned pineapple (product A) and pineapple juice (product B) are, respectively,

$$Q_A = 80 - 5P_A \quad \text{or} \quad P_A = 16 - 0.2Q_A$$
$$\text{and} \quad MR_A = 16 - 0.4Q_A$$
$$Q_B = 50 - 5P_B \quad \text{or} \quad P_B = 10 - 0.2Q_B$$
$$\text{and} \quad MR_B = 10 - 0.4Q_B$$

Two alternative marginal cost functions for the total pineapple "package" are, respectively,

$$MC = 8 + 0.1Q \quad \text{or} \quad MC' = \frac{2Q}{35}$$

Determine graphically the best level of output and price of canned pineapple and pineapple juice with each alternative *MC* function.

*3. Solve Problem 2 algebraically.

4. Suppose that the marginal cost functions in Figure 11-2 were not the ones indicated on that figure but were instead:

$$MC = 1 + 0.2Q \quad \text{and} \quad MC' = 1 + 0.05Q$$

Solve the problem of Figure 11-2 mathematically.

5. The Dairy Farm Company, a small producer of milk and cheese, has estimated the quantities of milk and cheese that it can produce with three levels of total expenditures or total costs. These are indicated in the following table. If the price of milk (product A) and the price of cheese (product B)

that the firm receives are $1 each per unit of the products, draw a figure showing the maximum total profit (π) that the firm can earn at each level of TC and the overall maximum profit that the firm can earn for the three different levels of TC.

TC = $70		TC = $90	
Product A	**Product B**	**Product A**	**Product B**
80	0	100	0
70	40	90	60
50	70	70	90
20	90	30	120
0	95	0	130

TC = $140	
Product A	**Product B**
130	0
110	70
80	120
40	150
0	160

6. Show graphically the maximum total profit that the firm of Problem 5 earns if the price of milk (product A) falls to $0.50 while the price of cheese (product B) remains at $1.

*7. The Saga Food Company produces one type of frozen dinner sold directly to consumers and to restaurants. The demand and marginal revenue functions for Saga's frozen dinner by consumers (market 1) and restaurants (market 2) are, respectively,

$$Q_1 = 160 - 10P_1 \quad \text{or} \quad P_1 = 16 - 0.1Q_1$$
$$\text{and} \quad MR_1 = 16 - 0.2Q_1$$
$$Q_2 = 200 - 20P_2 \quad \text{or} \quad P_2 = 10 - 0.05Q_2$$
$$\text{and} \quad MR_2 = 10 - 0.1Q_2$$

Saga's total cost function is

$$TC = 120 + 4Q$$

Draw a figure showing (a) the demand, marginal revenue, and marginal cost curves faced by the firm; (b) the best level of output of the firm and how the firm should distribute sales in each market in order to maximize total profits with third-degree price discrimination; (c) the price and total revenue of the firm in each market with third-degree price

discrimination; (d) the profit per unit and in total with third-degree price discrimination; and (e) the output, price, total revenue, and profit per unit and in total in the absence of price discrimination.

8. Solve Problem 7 algebraically.

9. The Digital Clock Corporation is composed of two semiautonomous divisions—a production division that manufactures the moving mechanism for digital clocks and a marketing division that assembles and markets the clocks. There is no external market for the moving parts of the clocks manufactured by the production division. The external demand and marginal revenue functions for the finished product (i.e., the clock) sold by the marketing division of the firm are, respectively,

$$Q_m = 160 - 10P_m \quad \text{or} \quad P_m = 16 - 0.1Q_m$$
$$\text{and} \quad MR_m = 16 - 0.2Q_m$$

The marginal cost functions of the production and marketing divisions of the firm are, respectively,

$$MC_p = 3 + 0.1Q_p \quad \text{and} \quad MC_m = 1 + 0.1Q_m$$

Draw a figure showing (a) the firm's best level of output and price for the finished product (the clock) and (b) the transfer price and output of the intermediate product (the moving parts of the clock).

10. Starting with the given information of Problem 9, except that

$$MC_p' = 2 + 0.1Q_p$$

and that a perfectly competitive market exists for the intermediate product at $P_t = \$6$, determine graphically the profit-maximizing outputs for the production and marketing divisions of the firm and the optimal transfer price for the intermediate product and the price of the final product.

*11. Solve Problem 10 algebraically.

12. (a) Will a monopolist's total revenue be larger with second-degree price discrimination when the batches on which it charges a uniform price are larger or smaller? Why? (b) How does a two-part tariff differ from bundling?

13. The San Francisco Power Company faces a total cost function of

$$P = (1/2)Q^2 + 100,000$$

where prices are in cents/kilowatt-hour and quantities are in millions of kilowatt-hours.

The demand function of San Francisco residents for off-peak hours is:

$$D^o: \quad P = 4 - Q \qquad \text{or} \qquad D^{o'}: \quad Q = 4 - P$$

The demand function of San Francisco residents for peak hours is:

$$D^p: \quad P = 8 - Q \qquad \text{or} \qquad D^{p'}: \quad Q = 8 - P$$

Calculate (a) The short-run marginal cost function (SMC); (b) the equilibrium price (P_o) and quantity demanded (Q_o) during off-peak hours; (c) the equilibrium price (P_p) and quantity demanded (Q_p) during peak hours; (d) the total demand for electricity ($Q_o + Q_p$).

14. Assume that the San Francisco Power Authority of Problem 13 has set a rate of 3 cents per kilowatt-hour for both peak and off-peak hours. Calculate (a) the new equilibrium quantity demanded during off-peak hours ($Q_p{}^*$); (b) the new equilibrium quantity demanded during peak hours ($Q_p{}^*$); (c) the new total demand for electricity ($Q_o{}^* + Q_p{}^*$).

15. **Integrating Problem**

The California Instruments Corporation, a producer of electronic equipment, makes pocket calculators in a plant that is run autonomously. The plant has a capacity output of 200,000 calculators per year, and the plant's manager regards 75 percent of capacity as the normal or standard output. The projected total variable costs for the normal or standard level of output are $900,000, while the total overhead or fixed costs are estimated to be 120 percent of total variable costs. The plant manager wants to apply a 20 percent markup on cost. (a) What price should the manager charge for the calculators? (b) If the price set is the profit-maximizing price, what is the price elasticity of demand for calculators faced by the plant? (c) If the price elasticity of demand were 24, what would be the optimum markup on cost that the manager should apply? (d) If during the year the plant manager receives an order for an additional 20,000 of its calculators from a school system to be delivered in four months for the price of $10, should the manager accept the order? (e) If California Instruments wants to add the pocket calculator to its own product line, what should be the transfer price of the pocket calculators?

(f) Suppose that in the future the plant will sell pocket calculators to the marketing division of California Instruments and on the external imperfectly competitive market, where the price elasticity of demand is $E_p = -2$. What would be the net marginal revenue of the marketing division of the firm for the pocket calculators? At what price should the calculators be sold on the external market?

APPENDIX TO CHAPTER 11: THIRD-DEGREE PRICE DISCRIMINATION WITH CALCULUS

A monopolist selling a commodity in two separate markets must decide how much to sell in each market in order to maximize his or her total profits. The total profits of the monopolist (π) are equal to the sum of the total revenue that he or she receives from selling the commodity in the two markets (that is, $TR_1 + TR_2$) minus the total cost (TC) of producing the total output. That is,

$$\pi = TR_1 + TR_2 - TC \qquad [11\text{-}9]$$

Taking the first partial derivative of π with respect to Q_1 (the quantity sold in the first market) and Q_2 (the amount sold in the second market) and setting them equal to zero, we get

$$\frac{\partial \pi}{\partial Q_1} = \frac{\partial (TR_1)}{\partial Q_1} - \frac{\partial (TC)}{\partial Q_1} = 0$$

and

$$\frac{\partial \pi}{\partial Q_2} = \frac{\partial (TR_2)}{\partial Q_2} - \frac{\partial (TC)}{\partial Q_2} = 0$$

$$[11\text{-}10]$$

or

$$MR_1 = MR_2 = MC \qquad [11\text{-}11]$$

That is, in order to maximize his or her total profits, the monopolist must distribute sales between the two markets in such a way that the marginal revenue is the same in both markets and equals the common marginal cost. Equations 11-10 and 11-11 represent the first-order condition for profit maximization. The second-order condition is that

$$\frac{\partial^2 \pi}{\partial Q_1^2} < 0 \quad \text{and} \quad \frac{\partial^2 \pi}{\partial Q_2^2} < 0 \qquad [11\text{-}12]$$

Since we know from Equation 3-12 that

$$MR = P\left(1 + \frac{1}{E_p}\right) \qquad [11\text{-}13]$$

profit maximization requires that $MR_1 = MR_2$ or

$$P_1\left(1 + \frac{1}{E_{p1}}\right) = P_2\left(1 + \frac{1}{E_{p2}}\right) \qquad [11\text{-}14]$$

where P_1 and P_2 are the prices in market 1 and market 2, respectively, and E_{p1} and E_{p2} are the coefficients of price elasticity of demand in market 1 and market 2 (which are negative). If $|E_{p1}| < |E_{p2}|$, Equation 11-14 will hold only if $P_1 > P_2$. That is, in order to maximize total profits, the monopolist must sell the commodity at a higher price in the market with the lower price elasticity of demand (see Figure 11-5).

For example, if

$$Q_1 = 120 - 10P_1 \quad \text{so that} \quad P_1 = 12 - 0.1Q_1$$

and

$$Q_2 = 120 - 20P_2 \quad \text{so that} \quad P_2 = 6 - 0.05Q_2$$

then

$$TR_1 = P_1Q_1 = (12 - 0.1Q_1)Q_1$$
$$= 12Q_1 - 0.1Q_1^2$$

and

$$TR_2 = P_2Q_2 = (6 - 0.05Q_2)Q_2$$
$$= 6Q_2 - 0.05Q_2^2$$

If $TC = 90 + 2(Q_1 + Q_2)$, then

$$\pi = TR_1 + TR_2 - TC$$
$$= 12Q_1 - 0.1Q_1^2 + 6Q_2 - 0.05Q_2^2$$
$$- 90 - 2(Q_1 + Q_2)$$

and

$$\frac{\partial \pi}{\partial Q_1} = 12 - 0.2Q_1 - 2 = 0$$

$$\frac{\partial \pi}{\partial Q_2} = 6 - 0.1Q_2 - 2 = 0$$

so that

$$0.2Q_1 = 10 \qquad 0.1Q_2 = 4$$

and

$$Q_1 = 50 \qquad Q_2 = 40$$

Since

$$\frac{\partial^2 \pi}{\partial Q_1^2} = -0.2 < 0$$

and

$$\frac{\partial^2 \pi}{\partial Q_2^2} = -0.1 < 0$$

the monopolist maximizes his or her total profits by selling $Q_1 = 50$ and $Q_2 = 40$. Then

$$P_1 = 12 - 0.1(50) = \$7$$

and

$$P_2 = 6 - 0.05(40) = \$4$$

and

$$\pi = 12(50) - 0.1(50)^2 + 6(40) - 0.05(40)^2 - 90 - 2(50) - 2(40) = \$240$$

with third-degree price discrimination.

In the absence of price discrimination,

$$Q = Q_1 + Q_2 = 240 - 30P$$

and

$$P = 8 - 0.0333Q$$

$$TR = (P)(Q) = (8 - 0.0333Q)Q$$

$$= 8Q - 0.0333Q^2$$

$$\pi = TR - TC$$

$$= 8Q - 0.0333Q^2 - 90 - 2Q$$

$$\frac{d\pi}{dQ} = 8 - 0.0667Q - 2 = 0$$

$$0.0667Q = 6$$

$$Q = 89.96 \cong 90$$

$$\frac{d^2\pi}{dQ^2} = -0.0667 < 0$$

Since

the monopolist maximizes profits at $Q = 90$ in the absence of price discrimination. Then

$$P = 8 - 0.0333Q = 8 - 0.0333(90)$$
$$= 8 - 2.997 \cong \$5$$

and

$$\pi = 8(90) - 0.0333(90)^2 - 90 - 2(90)$$
$$= \$180$$

APPENDIX PROBLEMS

1. Calculate the price that the monopolist would charge and the quantity of the product that he or she would sell with third-degree price discrimination in the above example if the monopolist's total cost curve were $TC = 20 + 4(Q_1 + Q_2)$. How much profit would the monopolist earn?

2. Estimate the price that the monopolist would charge and the quantity of the product that he or she would sell in the absence of third-degree price discrimination in Problem 1. How much profit would the monopolist earn?

SUPPLEMENTARY READINGS

Readings on pricing are:

Blinder, A. S., "Why Are Prices Sticky? Preliminary Results from an Interview Study," *American Economic Review* (May 1991), pp. 89–96.

Coats, K. S., "Third-Degree Price Discrimination in Oligopoly: All-Out Competition and Strategic Commitment," *Rand Journal of Economics* (Summer 1998) pp. 306–323.

Friedman, James, "Oligopoly Pricing: Old Ideas and New Tools," *Journal of Economic Literature* (June 2001), pp. 573–575.

Hanson, W., "The Dynamics of Cost-Plus Pricing," *Managerial and Decision Economics* (March–April 1992), pp. 149–161.

Hess, J. D., and E. Gerstner, "Price-Matching Policies: An Empirical Case," *Managerial and Decision Economics* (1991), pp. 305–315.

Layson, S. K., "Third-Degree Price Discrimination under Economies of Scale," *Southern Economic Journal* (October 1994), pp. 323–327.

Levy, D., et al., "Price Adjustment at Multiproduct Retailers," *Managerial and Decision Economics* (1998), pp. 81–120.

Manes, Rene P., Francoise Shoumaker, and Peter A. Silhan, "Demand Relationships and Pricing Decisions for Related Products," *Managerial and Decision Economics* (June 1984), pp. 120–122.

Sudhir, K., "Competitive Pricing Behavior in the Auto Market: A Structural Analysis," *Marketing Science* (Winter 2001), pp. 42–60.

Yamawaki, Hideki, "Price Reactions to New Competition: A Study of the U.S. Luxury Car Market," *International Journal of Industrial Organization* (January 2002), pp. 19–39.

On transfer pricing, see:

Gresik, T.A., "The Taxing Task of Taxing Transnationals," *Journal of Economic Literature* (September 2001), pp. 800–838.

Kim, S. H., "International Transfer Pricing," in R. Z. Aliber and R. W. Click, eds., *Readings in International Business* (Cambridge, Mass.: MIT Press, 1993), pp. 407–421.

Mataloni, R. J., "An Examination of Low Rates of Return on Foreign-Owned U.S. Companies," *Survey of Current Business* (March 2000), pp. 5–73.

OECD, *Transfer Pricing and Multinational Enterprises* (Paris, 1979).

OECD, *Transfer Pricing Guidelines for Multinational Enterprises and Tax Administrations: 1999 Update* (Paris, 1999).

Prusa, T. J., "An Incentive Compatible Approach to the Transfer Pricing Problem," *Journal of International Economics* (February 1990), pp. 155–172.

Rugaman, A. M., and L. Eden, eds., *Multinationals and Transfer Pricing* (New York: St. Martin's, 1985).

For a more extensive discussion of international price discrimination and dumping, see:

Salvatore, Dominick, *International Economics*, 8th ed. (Hoboken, N.J.: Wiley, 2004), chap. 9. See also the references for chaps. 9 and 10.

INTERNET SITE ADDRESSES

Third degree price discrimination is examined in:

http://www.coned.com

http://www.coolsaving.com

For electricity pricing by Con Edison in New York City, see:

http://www.coned.com/documents/elec/MSCMAC statement080105.pdf

For articles on transfer pricing in the OECD site:

http://www.oecd.org and click transfer pricing

http://www.econ.iastate.edu/classes/econ355/choi/mnc.htm

For more information on value-based pricing, see the article by Kevin Guthrie at:

http://www.arl.org/scomm/scat/guthries.html

For yield management, go to:

http://www.hotel-online.com/Trends/IDeaS/YieldMeasurement.html

http://www.luc.edu/faculty/eventa/archive/su483we/yield.htm

The Internet sites of the companies discussed in this chapter (Gillette, Con Edison, Kodak, Fuji, Continental, GM, and Mercedes-Chrysler) are:

http://www.gillette.com

http://www.coned.com

http://www.kodak.com

http://www.fujifilm.co.jp

http://www.gm.com

http://www.mbusa.com

For e-commerce at Amazon, e-auctions at eBay, and auction pricing at Priceline, go to:

http://www.Amazon.com

http://www.ebay.com

http://www.priceline.com

INTEGRATING CASE STUDY 4
eBay and Competition on the Internet

Ten years ago, Pierre Omidyar, a software engineer working in California's Silicon Valley, began thinking about how to use the Internet for a trading system in which buyers and sellers could establish a genuine market price. Over a long holiday weekend he wrote the computer code. At first, a trickle of users arrived at his Web site—including his girlfriend, who traded PEZ candy dispensers. By the end of 1995, several thousand auctions had been completed and interest in eBay was growing. And it grew and grew. From this modest beginning, eBay has become a global giant, with around 150 million registered users worldwide who are set to buy and sell goods worth more than $40 billion this year.

The remarkable tale of eBay's growth points to some important lessons for any business trying to operate on line—and today that includes, one way or another, most firms. The commercial opportunities presented by an expanding global Web seem almost limitless. But the pace of change is rapid, and so is the ferocity of competition. To succeed, firms need agility, an open mind, and the ability to reinvent themselves repeatedly. Most of all, they need to listen carefully to their customers, paying close attention to what they do and don't want.

Such qualities, of course, would be valuable in any kind of business. Yet for on-line firms they are not a luxury, but necessary for mere survival. This is true for a variety of reasons. The Internet is not only growing, but changing rapidly, which, in turn, changes the rules of the game for any business relying on it. The barriers to entry are still low compared with those for most off-line businesses, which means that just keeping track of your existing rivals is not enough. These may not represent the greatest competitive threat tomorrow or the next day. That could come from a number of directions—a firm in a different type of on-line business; one that does not yet exist; or even from one of your own customers. On top of all this, the behavior of many consumers is constantly changing as well, as individuals discover new ways to shop and interact with each other via the Web.

No Safe Havens

All these factors make the Internet a dangerous place to do business, as well as one full of promise. eBay's history demonstrates both of those things. It is probably safe to say that nothing like eBay could have existed without the Internet—or could have grown so fast. Even though there have been signs of the firm's blistering pace slowing a bit in America, its most "mature" market, there remain vast opportunities overseas, particularly, some argue, in China. Meg Whitman, eBay's chief executive, believes the company is still only at the beginning of what it could achieve.

And yet just getting as far as it has is quite an achievement. Like the other on-line giants, Google, Yahoo!, and Amazon, eBay is the survivor of a brutal shake-out. A decade ago, the Internet had less than 20 million users. By 1999, when it had reached 150 million users, dotcoms were being formed every day. But when the technology bubble burst in 2001, thousands of firms were swept away.

The survivors now operate in a market with close to one billion users worldwide and growing. But to flourish these firms have had to remake their businesses over and over again. eBay, for example, is no longer solely an auctioneer; Google has become more than a search engine; Yahoo! is adding yet more services to its web portal; Amazon sells a lot more than just books, and both firms now offer auctions. New features and new strategies are being embraced as these firms fight each other, and a horde of others, for the e-commerce pie.

Customers behind the Wheel

Driving the strategy of all these firms is the shifting behavior of consumers. eBay's business, in particular, has been molded by its users. Second-hand cars now account for 30 percent of sales on its sites, something that managers never expected. They discovered that it was possible to sell cars on their site only when customers started listing them on the section for toy cars. eBay has since followed its customers into lots of other areas, including new clothes, cosmetics, and high-priced medical and industrial machinery. Moreover, some 30 percent of its sales are now at fixed prices, rather than from auctions.

With their ability to aggregate vast audiences, could eBay and other e-commerce giants turn into semimonopolies like Microsoft? In theory this seems possible. Network effects, for example, mean that the bigger eBay gets, the more addictive it becomes for both buyers and sellers. And much the same can be said about Google's emerging role as the on-line advertising agency of choice, with firms paying for search links to ensure their products can be "Googled."

It is not impossible that some kind of monopoly might emerge, wielding true pricing power, but right now it looks unlikely. eBay's managers, for example, admit that customers are shaping its business more than they are, and seem acutely aware that groups of customers could easily depart together to set up their own specialist auction or sales sites if eBay charges too much for its services or lets them down. This month it paid $620 million to buy Shopping.com, a shopping comparison site, to help its customers offer auctioned items to an even wider audience. The fact that the biggest Web firms such as eBay, Yahoo!, Google, and Amazon are so keen to invade each other's turf shows that none of them feels secure in their niche, or considers the others as well-protected from new competition.

The relatively low barriers to entry remain one of the most alluring features of the Internet—and the greatest threat to any incumbent firm. Millions of people have already set up small Web businesses, and millions more will do so, many of them using services provided by eBay, Amazon, Google, and Yahoo!. A few, it seems safe to predict, will become the giant-killers of tomorrow. For managers of any business, the lessons of eBay are both exhilarating and daunting: the prizes offered by the Internet are dazzling by any measure, but only those who can satisfy the demanding and changing tastes of consumers, the Internet's true sovereigns, will survive to enjoy them.

Source: "Anniversary Lessons from e-Bay," *The Economist* (June 11, 2005), p. 9. Adapted with permission from *The Economist.*

INTEGRATING CASE STUDY 5
The Art of Devising Airfares

Introductory Comment: The following selection illustrates most of the concepts presented in this part of the text as they are applied in the real world, and, thus, it serves as an excellent integrating case study. It shows the importance of market structure in output and pricing decisions, price leadership, price discrimination, and the pricing of multiple products, and how they are all interrelated to incremental analysis in pricing as it is conducted in a major industry.

The Art of Devising Airfares

In the airline business, it is sometimes called the *dark science.* Fare wars, however, have put a spotlight on how carriers use state-of-the-art computer software, complex forecasting techniques, and a little intuition to divine how many seats and at what prices they will offer on any given flight.

The aim of this inventory, or yield management, is to squeeze as many dollars as possible out of each seat and mile flown. That means trying to project just how many tickets to sell at a discount without running out of seats for the business traveler, who usually books at the last minute and therefore pays full fare. Too many wrong projections can lead to huge losses of revenue, or even worse. The inability of the People Express airline to manage its inventory of seats properly, for example, was one of the major causes of its demise.

"It's a sophisticated guessing game," said Robert E. Martens, vice president of pricing and production planning at American Airlines, which has the most sophisticated technology for yield management, according to airline analysts and consultants. "You don't sell a seat to a guy for $69 when he is willing to pay $400."

With the industry now adopting very low discount but nonrefundable fares, the complex task of managing seat inventory may become easier because airlines will be better able to predict how many people will show up for a flight. Some airlines have already seen a drop in their no-shows, which means they can overbook less and bump fewer customers. The nonrefundable fares could also enable carriers to sell more discount seats weeks before a flight, rather than putting them on sale at the last minute in an effort to fill up the plane.

American's inventory operation illustrates just how complicated the process can be. At the airline's corporate headquarters, 90 yield managers are linked by terminals to five IBM mainframe computers in Tulsa, Oklahoma. The managers monitor and adjust the fare mixes on 1,600 daily flights, as well as 528,000 future flights involving nearly 50 million passengers. Their work is hectic: A fare's average life span is two weeks, and industrywide about 200,000 fares change daily.

FEW DISCOUNTS ON FRIDAYS   American and the other airlines base their forecasts largely on historical profiles on each flight. Business travelers, for example, book heavily on many Friday afternoon flights, but often not until the day of departure. The airlines reserve blocks of seats for those frequent fliers. Few, if any, discounts are made available. "Good luck in getting a 'Q fare' from New York to

Chicago on Friday afternoon," said James J. Hartigan, president of United Airlines, using the industry parlance for the low-priced, supersaver ticket. "It's like winning the New York lottery." The same route at midday on a Wednesday, however, begs for passengers, so the airline might discount more than 80 percent of its seats to draw leisure travelers and others with more flexible schedules.

PASSENGERS ANGERED   Many passengers, attracted by advertisements trumpeting deep discounts but unaware that fare allocations change from flight to flight, have expressed anger at the carriers and travel agents when the cheap seats were unavailable. To help clear up the confusion, Continental Airlines has run ads noting the relative demand for certain routes, thus giving some sense of the supply of discount seats. Overbooking, too, is based on the computerized history of flights and their no-shows and involves myriad factors that include destination, time of day, and cost of ticket.

The airlines have used inventory management for decades, but its importance in helping carriers enhance their revenue coincides with new software developed in the past three or four years, analysts and airline executives said. Some of the software has been developed in-house; other systems have been from such companies as the Unis Corporation and the Control Data Corporation. "It's probably the No. 1 management tool required to compete properly in this highly competitive airline environment," said Lee R. Howard, executive vice president of Airline Economics, a Washington-based consulting firm.

Effective inventory management alone can improve an airline's revenues by 5 to 20 percent annually, analysts estimated. Mr. Martens said American's system was worth "hundreds of millions of dollars" a year to the airline. The airline's total sales exceeded $6 billion last year. "The revenue implications for yield management are enormous," said Julius Maltudis, airline analyst at Salomon Brothers. Inventory management improves a carrier's load factor, or ratio of seats filled. Every 1 percent increase in the load factor translates into $10 million in revenues for the typical major carrier, analysts said.

CRYSTAL-BALL GAZING   As sophisticated as it is, however, yield management is still subject to variables beyond its control. "Yield management is about 70 percent technology and 30 percent crystal-ball gazing," said Robert W. Cuggin, assistant vice president of marketing development at Delta Air Lines. Bad weather or a last-minute switch to a plane of a different size can wreak havoc with weeks of planning, he said.

At American, inventory management begins 330 days before departure. Yield managers use the profiles of a flight's history to parcel out an alphabet soup of fares, rationing full-fare seats first, then moving down the price scale. In the following weeks, the computer alerts the managers if sales in a particular fare class pick up unexpectedly. If a travel agent booked a large group of passengers, for example, the computer would flag the large order, and yield managers would restrict or expand the number of seats in that category. Otherwise, managers begin checking all fare mixes regularly 180 days before departure, adding or subtracting seats in each according to demand.

The process continues right up to two hours before boarding, according to American's director of yield management, Dennis McKaige. Airlines typically put more discount seats on sale just before an advance purchase requirement expires, he said. Therefore, a new batch of cheap tickets that require a 30-day advance purchase might go on sale 31 days before departure. A cut-rate fare offered on Monday might be sold out by Wednesday, then suddenly reoffered hours before takeoff on Thursday if passenger projections based on previous flights fail to materialize, Mr. McKaige said.

There are some instances when an airline actually gives preference to discount travelers over customers paying full fare. American has recently developed software to increase the yield on flights through its hubs. American gives preference to a passenger flying on a discount fare from Austin, Texas, to London through Dallas/Fort Worth, over another passenger paying full fare from Austin to Shreveport, Louisiana, through Dallas/Fort Worth. The London passenger, who pays $241 each way, is worth more to the airline than the passenger flying to Shreveport, who pays the full fare of $87 each way. For the bargain hunter, finding a discount will increasingly depend on the season, day and time of travel, the destination, and the length of stay.

THE NEW FARE CUTS   Continental, a unit of Texas Air, ignited one round of rock-bottom fares with "Maxsaver tickets," which require a minimum two-day advance purchase and are nonrefundable. "The spread between our highest and lowest fares is much lower than with other airlines," said James O'Donnel, vice president of marketing at Continental. "While our yield management job is no less important than other airlines', it is easier." Mr. O'Donnel said the carrier's system was more automated than those used by some of its competitors.

The two-day purchase requirement has siphoned off some business travelers who would otherwise have paid full fare. (American and several other airlines abandoned plans to raise their lowest discount fares and increase the advance purchase requirement on the cheapest tickets to 30 days, from 2. The airlines backed away from the change when support for the proposal collapsed.) Airline officials said that nonrefundable tickets were here to stay. Mr. Martens said that since the nonrefundable, Maxsaver-type fares were introduced, American's no-show rate had dropped "substantially below" the usual range of 12 to 15 percent. Passengers who are willing to commit themselves to a particular flight in exchange for lower prices allow yield managers to refine their operations by concentrating on the remaining coach seats.

Concluding Remarks

Yield management (i.e., the idea of selling as many tickets as possible at high fares and filling the rest of the seats at cut rates) is here to stay in the pricing of airline tickets and is constantly being refined with the use of ever more powerful computers and software. Indeed, yield management is considered the single most important technological improvement in airline management in the past decade and is often credited with making the difference between profit and loss for many airlines. For example, *The New York Times* found that on a single flight in 1997, the 33 passengers who held Chicago–Los Angeles tickets paid 27 different fares, ranging from $87 to $728. Yield management is now spreading also to hotels, cruise lines, and truck rentals. The great variety and frequent changes in airfares is, however, creating great confusion and frustration for air travelers as they are routinely unable to book seats at the lowest advertised fares. This led to increasing complaints of false advertisement, which the Transportation Department (the sole authority charged with regulating the airline industry since it was deregulated in 1978) has regularly investigated. In 1998, the Transportation Department also started to investigate the major airlines' practices of slashing fares to drive newcomers (i.e., start-up airlines) out or to discourage their entering the market. This type of "predatory pricing," illegal under U.S. antitrust laws, will be examined in Chapter 12. As more and more travelers use the Internet to shop around for the lowest airfares available, the number of passengers paying full fare has now sharply declined, leading to tremendous yield erosion for the regular airlines.

Source: Eric Schmidt, "The Art of Devising Air Fares," *The New York Times* (March 4, 1987), pp. D1–D2. Reprinted by permission of the *New York Times Corporation.* See also "Computers as Price Setters Complicate Travelers' Lives," *The New York Times* (January 24, 1994), p. 1; "Special Offers by Airlines Come Under U.S. Review," *The New York Times* (January 23, 1995), p. 10; "So, How Much Did You Pay for Your Ticket?" *The New York Times* (April 12, 1998), sec. 4, p. 2; "Prying Open the Open Skies," *Business Week* (February 9, 1998), p. 39; "U.S. Expands Airline Investigation of Possible Monopolization of Airports," *The Wall Street Journal* (February 26, 1998), p. A3; "Airlines Now Offer 'Last Minute' Fare Bargains Weeks Before Flights," *The Wall Street Journal* (March 15, 2002), p. B1; and "Airline Seats Have Become a Commodity," *Financial Times* (July 13, 2005), p. 5.

PART FIVE

Regulation, Risk Analysis, and Capital Budgeting

Part Five (Chapters 12 through 14) examines regulation and antitrust, risk analysis, and long-term capital investment decisions. Chapter 12 on regulation and antitrust examines the rationale for government intervention in the economy, presents the method or vehicle by which the government intervenes in the economy, evaluates the cost and benefits of such intervention, and examines the regulation of international competition and taxation. Chapter 13 extends the basic model of the firm presented in Chapter 1 to include risk (both domestic and international) and to deal with the economics of information. Finally, Chapter 14 examines capital budgeting, or the process by which firms make decisions involving costs and giving rise to revenues over a number of years. It also examines foreign capital inflows and the cost of capital in the United States.

CHAPTER 12 · Regulation and Antitrust: The Role of Government in the Economy

CHAPTER OUTLINE

KEY TERMS (in the order of their appearance)

Economic theory of regulation	External economies of consumption	Dissolution and divestiture
Licensing	Natural monopoly	Injunction
Patent	Public utilities	Consent decree
Public interest theory of regulation	Averch–Johnson (A–J) effect	Conscious parallelism
	Sherman Act (1890)	Predatory pricing
Market failures	Clayton Act (1914)	Import tariff
Externalities	Federal Trade Commission Act (1914)	Import quota
External diseconomies of production	Robinson–Patman Act (1936)	Voluntary export restraint (VER)
External economies of production	Wheeler–Lea Act (1938)	Uruguay round
External diseconomies of consumption	Celler–Kefauver Antimerger Act (1950)	Border taxes
		Foreign sales corporation (FSC)

In this chapter we examine regulation and antitrust, or the role of government in the economy. The government's traditional role of maintaining law and order and providing for national defense has greatly expanded over time, particularly during the past few decades, so that today it affects most industries, firms, and consumers. It is important, therefore, that managers be sufficiently familiar with business laws and regulations to know when to seek legal help in the conduct of their business and to be able to recognize when competitors are harming the firm through illegal business practices.

According to one theory of government involvement in the economy, regulation is the result of pressures from business, consumers, and environmental groups and results in regulation, which supports business and protects consumers, workers, and the environment. This theory of regulation is examined in the first section of the chapter. According to more traditional theory, however, regulation is undertaken to ensure that the economic system operates in a manner consistent with the public interest and to overcome market failures. This is discussed in Sections 12-2 and 12-3 of this chapter. Section 12-4 summarizes U.S. antitrust laws, which are designed to enhance competition and forbid anticompetitive actions on the part of business firms. Section 12-5 examines the enforcement of antitrust laws and the recent deregulation movement. Section 12-6 deals with the regulation of international competition. Finally, Section 12-7 examines the effect of taxation on business decisions.

12-1 GOVERNMENT REGULATION TO SUPPORT BUSINESS AND TO PROTECT CONSUMERS, WORKERS, AND THE ENVIRONMENT

According to the **economic theory of regulation** (sometimes called the "capture theory of regulation") expounded by Stigler and others,[1] regulation is the result of pressure-group action and results in laws and policies to support business and to protect

---

[1] G. Stigler, "The Theory of Economic Regulation," *Bell Journal of Economics and Management Science* (Spring 1971), pp. 3–21; J. Buchanan and G. Tullock, *The Calculus of Consent* (Ann Arbor: University of Michigan Press, 1962); and R. Posner, "Theories of Economic Regulation," *Bell Journal of Economics and Management Science* (Autumn 1974), pp. 335–358.

consumers, workers, and the environment. In this section, we examine regulations that shelter firms from competition and protect consumers against unfair business practices, workers against hazardous working conditions, and the environment against pollution and degradation.

Government Regulations that Restrict Competition

Hundreds of pressure groups from business, agriculture, trades, and the professions have been successful in having government (local, state, and federal) adopt many regulations which, in effect (though perhaps not always and entirely by intent), restrict competition and create artificial market power. These regulations include licensing, patents, restrictions on price competition, and restrictions on the free flow of international trade. These are briefly discussed in turn.

A license is often required to enter and remain in many businesses (such as operating a radio or TV station or a liquor store), professions (such as medicine or law), and trades (such as driving a cab or being a dietitian). **Licensing** is usually justified to ensure a minimum degree of competence and to protect the public against fraud and harm in cases in which it is difficult for the public to gather independent information about the quality of the product or service, and the potential for harm is quite large. Inevitably, however, licensing becomes a method to restrict entry into the business, profession, or trade and to restrict competition. Sometimes licensing seems to serve no other function than to restrict entry and competition.

Examples of this range from unnecessarily high standards for admission into some craft unions, the serious limitations that the American Medical Association (AMA) enforced for many decades on admissions into medical schools in this country and on the use of paramedical personnel to perform many routine functions, to the limitation on the number of customers that a trucking firm could have or on the size of the brush that a painter could use. Even when a clear need for licensing exists, the inevitable result is also to restrict entry and competition, thereby increasing prices to consumers and profits to license holders. This is an important reason that most business, professional, and trade associations strongly support licensing and regulation and actively lobby against deregulation. For example, prices and profits in the trucking industry declined sharply in the early 1980s as a result of deregulation of the trucking industry (as well as the recession in the economy) and the American Truckers' Association petitioned Congress to bring back regulation.

Patents are another means by which competition and entry into an industry, profession, or trade is restricted by government action. A **patent** is the right granted by the federal government to an inventor for the exclusive use of the invention for a period of 17 years. The patent holder (individual or firm) can use the patent directly or grant a license for others to use the invention in exchange for royalty payments. The granting of a limited monopoly to the inventor is aimed at encouraging inventions, but it also leads to output restrictions and higher prices. To be sure, the monopoly power resulting from a patent is limited, not only by time, but also because other firms try to develop similar products and processes. Sometimes this is not possible, however, because large firms often hold so many patents on a particular product or process as to completely dominate a field and exclude others long after the original patents have expired. This has been the case in such industries as aluminum, shoe manufacturing, photographic equipment, and many others. Even if restricted by antitrust action, this monopoly power is sometimes further reinforced by cross-licensing agreements, whereby a firm allows other firms in related fields to use some of its patents in exchange for being allowed to use theirs. The result is a cartel-like agreement indirectly made possible by the government, under which a few firms dominate technology in the field.

There are also many restrictions on price competition that are the direct result of government action. These include government-guaranteed parity prices in agriculture, trucking freight rates and airline fares before deregulation, ocean shipping rates, and many others (see Case Study 12-1). One aspect of the *Robinson–Patman Act* passed in 1936 to amend the *Clayton Act* (discussed in Section 12-4) also restricted price competition by forbidding selling more cheaply to one buyer or in one market than to others, or selling at "unreasonably low prices" with the intent of destroying competition or eliminating a competitor. The act sought to protect small retailers (primarily independent grocery stores and drugstores) from price competition from chain-store retailers, based on the latter's ability to obtain lower prices and brokerage concession fees on bulk purchases from suppliers. Judging from the continuous decline in the number of small independent grocers, drugstores, and other retail businesses, and the expansion in the number and size of supermarkets, the act was not very successful.

There are many other actions undertaken by the government to directly support some sectors of the economy, particularly agriculture, transportation, and energy with subsidies and special tax treatment. Agriculture has been aided with price supports and many other programs costing billions of dollars per year to consumers and taxpayers. Railroads were granted free lands along their right-of-way as well as direct subsidies, the maritime industry has been greatly helped with large direct subsidies, airlines have greatly benefited from government-sponsored aerospace military research, and the energy (oil, gas, and coal) sectors have benefited from depletion allowances. Although all these actions on the part of the government in support of business have been justified on the basis of the national interest, they often represented the government response to strong lobbying pressure from industry seeking support to restrict entry and competition.

Government Regulations to Protect Consumers, Workers, and the Environment

Government also intervenes in the economy in order to protect consumers against unfair business practices, workers against hazardous working conditions, and the environment against pollution and degradation. These laws and regulations are often passed or adopted in response to political pressure brought to bear by some consumer group, workers' association, or environmental group. Often these have the effect of restricting competition.

The first type of policy designed to protect consumers is that of *requiring truthful disclosure and forbidding the misrepresentation of products*. The *Food and Drug Act of 1906* forbids adulteration and mislabeling of foods and drugs sold in interstate commerce. The act was strengthened to also include cosmetics in 1938. More recent amendments require that drugs and chemical additives to food be proven safe for human use and that herbicides and pesticides be tested for toxicity. The *Federal Trade Commission Act of 1914* was designed to protect firms against unfair methods of competition based on product

CASE STUDY 12-1
Restrictions on Competition in the Pricing of Milk in New York City and the Nation

Retail milk prices in New York State have been kept artificially high by an antiquated law passed during the Great Depression of the 1930s that required milk dealers to obtain a license to operate in any local market in the state. The commissioner of agriculture, appointed by the governor, had the responsibility of granting these licenses, except when they led to "destructive competition in a market already adequately served." In practice, however, commissioners did not issue licenses if these threatened the profits of established local dairies. The result was the retail milk prices in New York were about 20 percent higher than in neighboring New Jersey. In 1986, the commissioner finally allowed a New Jersey dairy firm to sell milk in Staten Island (a borough of New York City), and immediately the price of milk in the borough declined by 20 percent. The commissioner, however, under strong pressure from local dairies (which contended that they could not tolerate more competition because their costs were higher), rejected the application for a license from the same New Jersey dairy firm to sell milk in two other boroughs of New York City.

These state regulations are in addition to federal regulations that have set minimum prices for fluid milk since the time of the Great Depression with the intent of stabilizing milk prices, thereby ensuring reliable supplies across the country. Under federal law, the country was divided into 31 regions, with the U.S. Department of Agriculture setting the minimum price that farmers in each region could charge for milk each month. Minimum prices were set higher the farther the region is from Eau Claire, Wisconsin, historically the center of the dairy industry. Then, the 1996 Freedom to Farm Act instructed the secretary of agriculture to develop a more market-oriented dairy system by 1999. In July 1997, the Northeast Interstate Dairy Compact (a cartel) was allowed to set a minimum wholesale price for milk above the federal minimum price in the six Northeastern states. Five other Atlantic states (New York State, New Jersey, Pennsylvania, Delaware, and Maryland) also applied to join the Northeast Interstate Dairy Compact, and Southern states indicated their intent to form a dairy cartel of their own.

In spring 2002, however, Congress refused to extend the law allowing the Dairy Compact to exist but included a new subsidy program in the farm bill signed into law in spring 2002. The 2002 farm bill (continued in 2005) provides farmers a subsidy when the market price of milk falls below the price that the Dairy Compact would have set. But taxpayers, instead of consumers, will foot the bill and the new program will be administered by the U.S. Department of Agriculture rather than by the Dairy Compact in the affected states. The dairy industry is but one clear case in which government regulations (both state and federal) restricted entry and competition and led to higher prices for consumers and profits for firms in the industry.

Source: "The Price of Monopoly Milk," *The New York Times* (February 10, 1986), p. 22; "The Milk Cartel," *The New York Times* (September 1, 1987), p. 22; "The OPEC of Milk," *The Wall Street Journal* (June 20, 2001), p. A18; "Reversing Course, Bush Signs Bill Raising Farm Subsidies," *The New York Times* (May 14, 2002), p. 16; and "Senate Panel Extends Milk Subsidy Amid Farm Cuts," *The Wall Street Journal* (October 20, 2005), p. A4.

misrepresentation, but it also provided significant protection to consumers. Among the practices that were forbidden by the act were misrepresenting (1) the price of products (such as claiming that prices have been slashed after first artificially raising them, or falsely claiming to be selling at below cost); (2) the origin of products (such as claiming that the product was manufactured in the United States when in fact it was produced abroad); (3) the usefulness of the product (such as claiming, for example, that a product can prevent arthritis when it does not); and (4) the quality of the product (such as claiming that glass is crystal). The act was amended by the *Wheeler–Lea Act of 1938,* which forbids false or deceptive advertisement of foods, drugs, corrective devices, and cosmetics entering interstate commerce. The federal laws have been supplemented by similar state and local laws and regulations. By authority of the *1990 Nutrition Labeling Act,* the Food and Drug Administration (FDA) mandated more strict labeling requirements on all foods sold in the United States (see Case Study 12-2).

A second type of regulation designed to protect consumers is the *truth-in-lending law.* This is based on the *Consumer Credit Protection Act of 1968,* which requires lenders to make a complete and accurate disclosure, in easy-to-understand language, of the precise terms of credit, particularly the absolute amount of interest and other credit charges and the annual interest rate on the unpaid balance. A third type of consumer protection is provided by the *Consumer Product Safety Commission,* which was established in 1972 to (1) protect consumers against risk and injury associated with the use of some products, (2) provide information to consumers for comparing and evaluating the relative safety in the use of various products, and (3) develop uniform safety standards for many products. During the first five years of operation, the commission recalled more than 20 million units of various products but has been criticized by consumer groups for concentrating on unimportant products and by business for unreasonably high standards of product safety and for the very high cost of compliance.

Other laws designed to protect consumers are (1) the *Fair Credit Reporting Act of 1971,* which grants credit applicants the right to examine their credit file and to know the reason for the rejection of a credit application, and forbidding credit discrimination based on race, religion, sex, marital status, or age; (2) the *Warranty Act of 1975,* which requires warranties to be written in plain English, indicate which parts are covered, and explain how the consumer can exercise the rights granted by the warranty; (3) creation of the *National Highway Traffic Safety Administration (NHTSA),* which imposes safety standards on highway traffic; and (4) laws that require mail-order houses to fill orders within 30 days or refund the customer's money.

Some of the laws and regulations protecting workers are (1) the *Occupational Safety and Health Administration (OSHA),* which specifies safety standards for noxious gases and chemicals, noise levels, and other hazards; (2) the *Equal Employment Opportunity Commission (EEOC),* which regulates business hiring and firing practices; and (3) minimum wage laws, which put a floor on wages that businesses can pay to hired labor.

Environmental pollution and degradation are regulated by the *Environmental Protection Agency (EPA).* Since its creation in 1970, the EPA has become one of the most powerful of the federal regulatory agencies, and it is credited with substantially reducing environmental deterioration (see Case Study 12-3). The EPA monitors the air, water, toxic chemicals, pesticides, and waste materials, and it oversees grants for sewage treatment plants throughout the United States. Business, however, has often bitterly complained

CASE STUDY 12-2
The FDA Steps Up Regulation of the Food and Drug Industry

The passage of the *1990 Nutrition Labeling Act* empowered the Food and Drug Administration (FDA) to impose more stringent labeling, production, and quality standards on all foods and drugs sold in the United States. For example, in 1991, the FDA forced food companies to remove from their labels misleading claims regarding cholesterol and to discontinue their claims that bottled water was superior to tap water, and it ordered the removal of the word "fresh" in describing sauces and juices made from concentrate. In 1992, it pulled most breast implants off the market for safety reasons. In 1993, it forced the Warner-Lambert Corporation to temporarily halt production of its drugs and over-the-counter products (including Listerine, Rolaids, and Benadryl) that did not meet FDA specifications. In 1996, the FDA imposed strict limits on pesticide residues in food, in 1997 it approved the irradiation of red meat to eliminate dangerous bacteria and proposed sweeping regulations of the organic food industry, in 1999 it limited the use of pesticides, and over time it ordered a number of drugs off the market because of dangerous side effects.

These are only a few of the many actions that a more active FDA has taken since 1990. It is not that industry practices have deteriorated, but that the FDA has adopted a more rigorous and demanding standard since 1990. In the Warner-Lambert case, the FDA found the company's plants did not meet the agency's production, quality control, and testing procedures. It found that the company's anti-anxiety drug Centrax did not dissolve as specified, Tedral (the asthma medicine) did not meet sustained-release requirements, and Ergostat (the migraine drug) was below potency in the FDA's lab tests. The FDA has also been sending hundreds of letters to the top executives of some of the nation's largest drug makers, such as Merck, Johnson & Johnson, Pfizer, and Abbott Laboratories, warning them to rigorously follow the agency-defined acceptable production, testing, and marketing practices. The industry has certainly taken note, and compliance has increased sharply. Nevertheless, despite internal company concerns about the cardiovascular risks to patients taking the painkiller Vioxx, Merck sold it to millions of people in the United States and abroad, until it voluntarily withdrew it in September 2004, but is now facing billions of dollars in punitive damages in thousands of lawsuits filed against it by people or their relatives for allegedly being harmed or killed by Vioxx.

Source: "Strong Medicine," *Business Week* (September 6, 1993), pp. 20–21; "Serving Up a Safer Food Supply," *U.S. News & World Report* (August 5, 1996); "Irradiating Red Meat Approved as Means to Kill Deadly Germs," *The New York Times* (December 3, 1997), p. 1; "U.S. to Subject Organic Foods, Long Ignored, to Federal Rules," *The New York Times* (December 15, 1997), p. 1; "Citing Children, E. P. A. Is Limiting Use of Pesticides," *The New York Times* (August 3, 1999), p. 1; "Merck Legal Bill for Vioxx Could Hit $10 billion," *Financial Times* (October 2, 2005), p. 8; and "Punishment for Merck," *The New York Times* (August 23, 2005), p. 16.

about too stringent air and water pollution regulations. These have added several hundreds of billions of dollars to costs of production in three decades. The *Clean Air Act of 1990* requires a phased reduction in overall pollution and established a generalized market for pollution permits. Many other laws and regulations designed to protect consumers, workers, and the environment exist. Those discussed here are only some of the most important ones.

CASE STUDY 12-3
Regulation Greatly Reduced Air Pollution

There is now clear evidence that regulations enforced by the Environmental Protection Agency sharply reduced the level of air pollution in some of America's largest and most congested cities. In hot weather, air pollutants react with sunlight to form ozone. Stagnant air makes the problem worse. Since the passage of the Clean Air Act of 1990, the number of summer ozone-advisory days has declined sharply. For example, during summer 1993, Philadelphia had just 7 days of ozone advisories, compared with 23 during the summer of 1988, even though summer 1993 was almost as hot as the summer of 1988. New York City had just 4 days of ozone advisories during the summer of 1993, compared with 21 days during the summer of 1988, while Washington had just 1 day in summer 1993, compared with 12 days in summer 1988. In Los Angeles, ozone readings declined steadily during the past decade, carbon-monoxide pollution went down 30 percent, sulfur dioxide declined 20 percent, and airborne lead fell almost 90 percent.

Great progress was also made against carbon monoxide, which causes respiratory problems and is the most serious winter pollutant. For example, New York City was out of compliance with the EPA standard for carbon monoxide for 71 days during 1985 but none in 1992. Since automobiles and trucks are responsible for two-thirds of smog emission, the replacement of older, more polluting cars with newer and less-polluting ones was the biggest contributor to the sharply reduced level of air pollution in American cities. For example, the average 1999 automobile emits less than 1 percent of the pollution emitted by the average 1970 automobile.

Since 1996, the EPA has been pushing a plan for much higher clean air standards. The plan calls for (1) a sharp reduction of sulfur (the main pollutant) in gasoline, (2) requiring sport utility vehicles, minivans, and pickup trucks (which now emit three times more pollutants than automobiles) to meet the same tailpipe emission requirements as automobiles, as well as reducing further automobile emissions, and (3) requiring electrical generating plants to use cleaner energy sources (such as gas, hydroelectric power, wind, sun, and petroleum, instead of coal, which creates much more pollution). Removing 90 percent of the sulfur from gasoline is estimated to cost the oil refining industry from $3 billion to $6 billion per year and increase retail gasoline prices. Compliance with the motor vehicle emission standard was estimated to increase the price of new automobiles by $100 and that of minivans, sport vehicles, and light trucks by $200. Using cleaner energy sources cost electrical utilities for the 22 states east of the Mississippi from $2 billion to $3 billion more per year and increased the price of electricity for consumers by about 20 percent. More than half of the U.S. electricity is generated today by burning coal, and this accounts for one-third of the country's air pollution. In 1999, New York State sued 17 electric utilities in the Midwest for refusing to stop burning coal, which contributes most of the pollution that blows into New York and makes people ill and kills trees and fish.

The effort to reduce pollution further is clearly reaching diminishing returns (in terms of sharply rising costs for each additional amount of pollution removed) and many industry spokespeople feel that the extra benefits do not justify the extra costs. Environmentalists, on the other hand, disagree and point to some studies that seem to show that the annual savings in medical bills from respiratory ailments alone far exceed the cost of cleaner air—and so the debate continues.

By 2005, the U.S. Justice Department had reached a settlement in 8 of the 15 cases that it had brought against power companies in the eastern half of the country since 1999 for violating the Clean Air Act. The settlements required power companies to install new pollution controls costing hundreds of millions of dollars. In March 2005, the EPA announced new rules to cut air pollution in the eastern half of the country by more than 60 percent by 2015 at a cost of more than $50 billion over the next decade, but estimated to result in up to $100 billion in annual health benefits.

Source: "Winning the War on Smog," *Newsweek* (August 23, 1993), p. 29; "E.P.A. Advocating Higher Standards to Clean the Air," *The New York Times* (November 25, 1996), p. 1; "E.P.A. Acts to Require Big Cut in Air Emissions by 22 States," *The New York Times* (October 11, 1997), p. 9; "California to Toughen Its Emission Standards," *The New York Times* (November 6, 1998), p. C2; "The Regulation Toll," *The Wall Street Journal* (September 13, 1999), p. R9; "E. P. A. Is Ordering 392 Plants to Cut Pollution in Half," *The New York Times* (December 18, 1999), p. 1; "Files Detail Debate in E. P. A. on Clean Air," *The New York Times* (March 21, 2002), p. 32; "Utility to Spend $500 Million on Cleanup," *The New York Times* (March 3, 2005), p. 14; and "E.P.A. Sets Rules to Cut Pollution," *The New York Times* (March 11, 2005), p. 1.

12-2   EXTERNALITIES AND REGULATION

According to the **public interest theory of regulation,** government regulation is under-taken to overcome **market failures,** so as to ensure that the economic system operates in a manner consistent with the public interest. Market failures arise because of externalities and from the monopoly power that exists in imperfectly competitive markets. In this sec-tion, we examine externalities and ways to overcome them. Monopoly power, as another type of market failure, is examined in the rest of this chapter.

The Meaning and Importance of Externalities

The production and consumption of some products may give rise to some harmful or ben-eficial side effects that are borne by firms or people not directly involved in the production or consumption of the product. These are called **externalities.** There are external disec-onomies and economies of production and consumption. **External diseconomies of production** are uncompensated costs imposed on some firms by the expansion of output by other firms. For example, the increased discharge of waste materials by some firms along a waterway may result in antipollution legislation that increases the cost of disposing of waste materials for all firms in the area. **External economies of production** are un-compensated benefits conferred on some firms by the expansion of output by other firms. An example of this arises when some firms train workers and some of these workers go to work for other firms (which, therefore, save on training costs). **External diseconomies of consumption** are uncompensated costs imposed on some individuals by the consumption expenditures of other individuals. For example, smoking in a public place has a harmful effect (i.e., imposes a cost) on nonsmokers in the place. Finally, **external economies of consumption** are uncompensated benefits conferred on some individuals by the increased consumption of a product by other individuals. For example, increased expenditures to maintain a lawn by a homeowner increases the value of the neighbor's home also.

When the private and social costs or benefits do not coincide (i.e., in the presence of externalities), too much or too little of a product or service is produced or consumed from society's point of view. Specifically, if social costs exceed private costs, too much of the product is being produced, while if social benefits exceed private benefits, too lit-tle of the product is being consumed. These are shown in Figure 12-1.

In the left panel of Figure 12-1, MPB_A refers to the marginal private benefit that indi-vidual A receives for each additional hour of making furniture at home in the evening after a regular full-time day job. If individual A is willing to work on a piece of furniture for only 1 hour per evening, he or she will accept work only from the best-paying customer (i.e., \$12). If individual A is willing to work for more hours per evening, he or she will have to accept work from customers who are willing to pay less and less, as indicated by the MPB_A curve. The left panel of Figure 12-1 shows also the MPC_A, or the marginal private cost, that individual A incurs in working each additional hour per evening. The best number of hours that individual A is then willing to work per evening is 4 and is given by point E_A, at which the MPB_A and MPC_A curves intersect.

By making furniture at home in the evening, however, individual A creates noise with power tools and other equipment, which drives his or her neighbor to eat out or to go to a movie or a bar. Suppose that the private marginal cost imposed on individual B from each

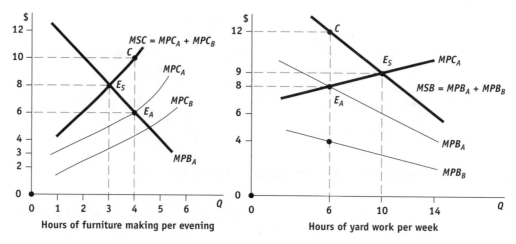

FIGURE 12-1 **Private and Social Costs and Benefits of Production and Consumption** The left panel shows that the best number of hours of furniture making per evening for individual A is 4 and is given by point E_A, at which the marginal private benefit to individual A (MPB_A) equals the private marginal cost to individual A (MPC_A). Evening work by individual A, however, also creates noise and a cost for individual B. The marginal social cost (MSC) is thus given by the vertical summation of the MPC_A and MPC_B curves. From society's point of view, the best level of work by individual A is 3 hours per evening and is given by point E_S, at which $MPB_A = MSC = \$8$. In the right panel, the best number of hours for individual A to work in his or her yard is 6 hours per week and is given by point E_A, at which $MPB_A = MPC_A$. Individual A's yard work, however, generates an external benefit to individual B. The marginal social benefit, MSB, equals $MPB_A + MPB_B$. The best level of yard work by individual A is 10 hours per week, as shown by point E_S, at which $MSB = MPC_A = MSC = \$9$.

additional hour of evening work by individual A is given by the MPC_B curve. The marginal social cost of evening work by individual A is then given by the MSC curve, which is the vertical summation of the MPC_A and MPC_B curves. At the best number of 4 hours of evening work by individual A, the MSC of \$10 (point C) exceeds the MPB_A of \$6 (point E_A). It is, therefore, economically inefficient from society's point of view for individual A to work 4 hours. From society's point of view, individual A should work only 3 hours per evening, which is given by point E_S, at which $MSC = MPB_A = \$8$.[2]

In the right panel of Figure 12-1, the MPB_A gives the marginal private benefit that individual A receives for each additional hour per week devoted to tending his or her yard (i.e., cutting grass, planting flowers, etc.), thereby increasing the value of individual A's home and providing relaxation. The private marginal cost incurred by individual A for tending the yard (the depreciation on the lawn mowers, the cost of seeds, etc.) is given by the MPC_A curve. Therefore, the best number of hours to spend tending the yard is 6 hours per week and is given by point E_A, at which the MPB_A and MPC_A curves cross. By improving his or her yard, however, individual A also confers a benefit to individual B (i.e., it also increases the value of individual B's home). If the marginal private benefit conferred on individual B is given by the MPB_B curve, the total marginal social benefit is then given by the MSB curve, which is the vertical summation of the MPB_A and the MPB_B curves. The

---

[2] Since $MPB_B = 0$, $MPB_A = MSB$, where MSB refers to the marginal social benefit. Therefore, 3 hours of evening woodworking by individual A is socially efficient because $MSC = MSB$.

best number of 6 hours per week spent working in the yard by individual A is not socially efficient, however, because $MSB = \$12$, while $MPC_A = MSC = \$8$. From society's point of view, the most efficient number of hours for individual A to work in his or her yard is 10 hours per week and is given by point E_S, at which $MPC_A = MSC = MSB = \$9$. In cases such as these where the private costs and benefits do not coincide with the social costs and benefits, government intervention in the economy is justified in order to induce the production and/or the consumption of the product or service until the marginal social cost is equal to the marginal social benefit (i.e., until $MSC = MSB$).

Policies to Deal with Externalities

One way that a market failure or inefficiency resulting from external economies can be overcome is by government prohibition or regulation. By forbidding an activity that gives rise to an external diseconomy, the external diseconomy can be avoided. For example, by prohibiting the use of automobiles, auto emissions can be eliminated. Similarly, by forbidding evening woodworking at home by individual A in the left panel of Figure 12-1, the noise externality that such woodworking creates for individual B would be avoided. Such prohibitions, however, also eliminate the benefit that results from the activities that give rise to the externalities. More reasonable, therefore, is regulation that allows the activity that leads to the externality up to the point at which the marginal social benefit from the activity is equal to the marginal social cost. For example, the government could allow individual A to make furniture only 3 hours per evening in the left panel of Figure 12-1, so that the marginal private (and social) benefit of evening furniture making to individual A equals the marginal social cost (i.e., the marginal cost to individual A plus the marginal cost to individual B—see point E_S in the figure). Since direct regulation, however, often specifies the production technique to be used in order to limit the external diseconomies, it is usually not cost-efficient.

More efficient in limiting externalities to the level at which the marginal social benefit from an externality-producing activity is equal to the marginal social cost are taxes or subsidies. This is shown in Figure 12-2, which is an extension of Figure 12-1. In the left panel of Figure 12-2, the dashed MPC_{A+t} curve is obtained when the government imposes a tax of $t = \$3$ per hour of evening woodworking on individual A. Since the MPC_{A+t} curve intersects the MPB_A curve at point E_S, individual A will be induced to work the socially optimal number of hours per evening (3 hours), so that the marginal social benefit (MSB, which now coincides with MPB_A) equals the marginal social cost (that is, $MSC = MSC_A + MSC_B$).

In the right panel of Figure 12-2, the dashed MPB_{A+s} curve is obtained when the government gives individual A a subsidy of $s = \$3$ per hour for tending his or her yard. Since the MPB_{A+s} curve intersects the MPC_A curve at point E_S, individual A will be induced to work the socially optimal number of hours (that is, 10 hours) per week in his or her yard, so that the marginal social benefit ($MSB = MPB_A + MPB_B$) equals the marginal social cost ($MSC = MPC_A$).[3] Other taxes used to overcome negative externalities or external diseconomies (and raise revenues to provide government services) are liquor, cigarette, and gasoline taxes.

---

[3] The same result can be reached by a $3 downward shift in the MPC_{A+s} curve, not shown in Figure 12-2.

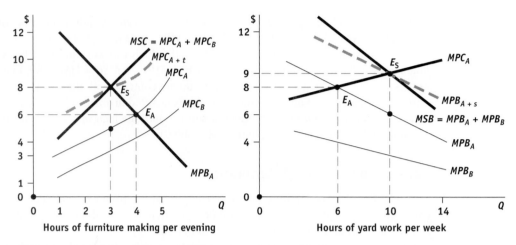

FIGURE 12-2   A Tax or Subsidy to Overcome a Negative or Positive Externality   The left panel shows that the socially optimal level of 3 hours of evening work is reached when the government imposes a tax of $t = \$3$ per hour on evening woodworking on individual A. This shifts the MPC_A curve up by $3 so that the MPC_{A+t} curve intersects the MPB_A curve at point E_S, at which $MPB_A = MSB = MSC$. The right panel shows that individual A can be induced to demand or consume the socially optimal home improvement that results from tending his or her yard for 10 hours per week by giving him or her a consumption subsidy of $s = \$3$ per hour. This shifts the MPB_A curve up by $3, so that the MPB_{A+t} curve intersects the MPC_A curve at point E_S, at which $MSB = MPC_A = MSC$.

Other subsidies used to correct for positive externalities or external economies are investment tax credits to promote investments, depletion allowances to promote natural resource development, and aid to education.

Besides prohibition and regulation, and taxes and subsidies, negative and positive externalities can sometimes be overcome by *voluntary payments.* For example, if a firm pollutes the air and produces a foul odor, the residents of the area can get together and contribute to the cost of introducing pollution-abatement equipment by the firm, or the firm can contribute to the cost of relocating the area residents.[4] This method, however, is impractical when there are many people residing in an area. Still another method of overcoming external diseconomies imposed by some firms is to allow or foster *mergers,* so that the external diseconomies are internalized and explicitly taken into consideration by the merged firm. For example, if a paper mill is located upstream from a brewery, the discharges from the paper mill into the stream represent an external diseconomy for the brewery because the latter incurs the additional cost of purifying the water that it uses in beer making. If the paper mill and the brewery merge, however, the cost of purifying the water for beer making becomes an explicit and direct cost that the merged firm will have to take into consideration in its production (milling and brewing) decisions.

A radically different method of limiting the amount of a negative externality to the level that is socially optimal is by the *sale of pollution rights* by the government (see Case Study 12-4). Under such a system, the government decides on the amount of pollution that it thinks

---

[4] See R. Coase, "The Problem of Social Cost," *Journal of Law and Economics* (October 1960), pp. 1–44.

CASE STUDY 12-4
The Market for Dumping Rights

The Clean Air Act of 1990 led to the establishment of a market for dumping rights. In such a market, the Environmental Protection Agency decides how much pollution it wants to allow and then issues marketable rights for that quantity of pollution. Since these dumping rights are marketable (i.e., can be bought and sold by firms), they are likely to be used in those activities in which they are most valuable. For example, suppose that the EPA has imposed specific dumping restrictions on two firms. If the cost of reducing emission by 1 unit is $10,000 for one firm and $50,000 for a second firm, the first firm could sell the right to dump that unit of emission to the second firm for a price between $10,000 and $50,000. The result would be that both firms (and society) would gain without any overall increase in pollution. In fact, the only way that a new firm can build a plant that pollutes the air in an area that does not meet federal air-quality standards is to purchase the right to a specific amount of pollution from an already existing and polluting firm in the area. The EPA can then gradually lower the level of overall pollution by reducing the amount of right-to-pollute credits or pollution allowances it issues, while allowing each firm to decide to comply with the law by installing antipollution equipment or buying right-to-pollution credits from other firms that have some to spare.

Since 1992, when the first right-to-pollute credits were traded, the market grew rapidly and we now have pollution-rights banks, which act as brokers between firms that want to sell pollution rights and firms that want to purchase them. The concept of marketable pollution rights has also been extended by the so-called bubble policy. Under this policy, a firm with several plants operating in a single air pollution area is given a total permissible emission level for all its plants rather than a limit for each one. This allows the firm to concentrate its emission reduction efforts in plants where it can be done more cheaply. As a result of such a program, electric utilities now emit about 25 percent fewer tons of sulfur oxide in the atmosphere while producing 41 percent more electricity and also saving $3 billion. In January 2000, the number of generating units participating in the program rose from 445 to 2,200, and the cap on sulfur emissions was reduced by another 25 percent.

The establishment of a market for pollution permits represents a significant victory for economists (who have been advocating this for many years) and changes the direction of antipollution efforts in the United States for decades to come. In July 2001, a historic accord that set targets for industrialized countries to cut the emission of greenhouse gases that contribute to global warming was signed as part of the implementation of the *Kyoto Protocol* on climate change signed in 1997. The United States refused to sign the agreement, calling its targets arbitrary and too costly for the United States to comply. The Kyoto Protocol stimulated the development of a market for emission trading on a global scale. After trading unofficially since 2003, the European Union's carbon-trading program formally started on January 1, 2005, and is expected to be valued at billions of dollars annually. The right to release one ton of carbon monoxide into the atmosphere increased from $6 in 2003 to $35 in 2005 in this market. In July 2005, the United States, Japan, Australia, China, India, and Korea announced a new pact to combat global warming, which emphasized technology transfer to reduce emissions of greenhouse gases rather than the fixed targets of the Kyoto Protocol (which has been signed by only Japan and Korea out of the six countries of the group).

Source: "A Market Place for Pollution Rights," *U.S. News & World Report* (November 12, 1990), p. 79; "New Rules Harness the Power of Free Markets to Curb Air Pollution," *The Wall Street Journal* (April 4, 1992), p. A1; "Cheapest Protection of Nature May Lie in Taxes, Not Laws," *The New York Times* (November 24, 1992), p. C1; "How Much Is the Right to Pollute Worth?" *The Wall Street Journal* (August 1, 2001), p. A15; "New Limits on Pollution Herald Change in Europe," *The New York Times* (January 1, 2005), p. C2; "Carbon Trading—Revving Up," *The Economist* (July 19, 2005), pp. 64–65; and "An Alternative to Kyoto," *The Economist* (July 30, 2005), p. 39.

is socially desirable (based on the benefits that result from the activities that generate the pollution) and then auctions off licenses to firms to generate pollution up to the specified amount. Pollution costs are thus internalized (i.e., considered as part of regular production costs) by firms, and the allowed amount of pollution is used in activities in which it is most valuable. This and other methods of dealing with externalities, however, are based on the assumption that the private and social benefits and costs of any activity leading to externalities can be measured or estimated fairly accurately. This is seldom the case. Nevertheless, the policies that we have examined do give an indication of what needs to be measured and the procedure for reaching socially optimal decisions or policies in cases involving externalities.

12-3 PUBLIC UTILITY REGULATION

In this section we define public utilities and natural monopoly, and we examine the need for their regulation and the dilemma usually faced in determining the appropriate method and degree of regulation.

Public Utilities as Natural Monopolies

In some industries, economies of scale operate (i.e., the long-run average cost curve may fall) continuously as output expands, so that a single firm could supply the entire market more efficiently than any number of smaller firms. Such a large firm supplying the entire market is called a **natural monopoly.** The distinguishing characteristic of a natural monopoly is that the firm's long-run average cost curve is still declining when the firm supplies the entire market. Monopoly in this case is the natural result of a larger firm having lower costs per unit than smaller firms and being able to drive the latter out of business. Examples of natural monopolies are **public utilities** (electric, gas, water, and local transportation companies). To have more than one such firm in a given market would lead to duplication of supply lines and to much higher costs per unit. To avoid this, local governments usually allow a single firm to operate in the market but regulate the price and quality of the services provided, so as to allow the firm only a normal risk-adjusted rate of return on its investment. This is shown in Figure 12-3.

In Figure 12-3, the D and MR curves are, respectively, the market demand and marginal revenue curves for the service faced by the natural monopolist, while the LAC and LMC curves are its long-run average and marginal cost curves. If unregulated, the best level of output of the monopolist in the long run would be 3 million units per time period and is given by point E, at which the LMC and MR curves intersect. For $Q = 3$ million units, the monopolist would charge the price of $6 (point A on the D curve) and incur at $LAC = \$5$ (point B on the LAC curve), thereby earning a profit of $1 ($AB$) per unit and $3 million (the area of rectangle $ABCF$) in total. Note that at $Q = 3$ million units, the LAC curve is still declining. Note also that at the output level of 3 million units, $P > LMC$, so that more of the service is desirable from

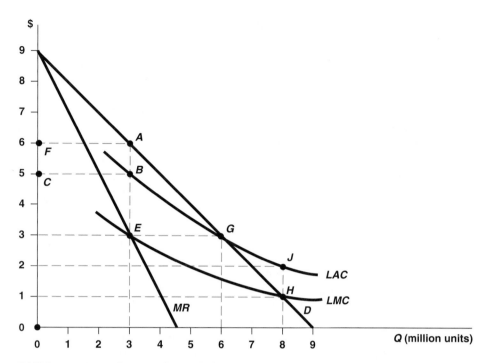

FIGURE 12-3   Natural Monopoly Regulation   A regulatory commission usually sets $P = LAC = \$3$ (point G), at which output is 6 million units per time period and the public utility breaks even in the long run. At $Q = 6$ million, however, $P > LMC$, and more of the service is desirable from society's point of view. The best level of output from society's point of view is 8 million units per time period and is given by point H, at which $P = LMC = \$1$. However, that would result in a loss of $\$1$ (JH) per unit and $\$8$ million in total, and the public utility company would not supply the service in the long run without a subsidy of $\$1$ per unit.

society's point of view. That is, the marginal cost of the last unit of the service supplied is smaller than the value of the service to society, as reflected by the price of the service. There is, however, no incentive for the unregulated monopolist to expand output beyond $Q = 3$ million units per time period because its profits are maximized at $Q = 3$ million.

To ensure that the monopolist earns only a normal rate of return on its investment, the regulatory commission usually sets the price at which $P = LAC$. In Figure 12-3, this is given by point G, at which $P = LAC = \$3$ and output is 6 million units per time period. While the price is lower and the output is greater than at point A, $P > LMC$ at point G. The best level of output from society's point of view would be 8 million units per time period, as shown by point H, at which $P = LMC = \$1$. At $Q = 8$ million, however, the $LAC = \$2$ (point J on the LAC curve), and the public utility company would incur a loss of $\$1$ (JH) per unit and $\$8$ million per time period. As a result, the public utility would not supply the service in the long run without a per-unit subsidy of $\$1$ per unit. In general, regulatory commissions set $P = LAC$ (point G in Figure 12-3) so that the public utility company breaks even in the long run without a subsidy.

Difficulties in Public Utility Regulation

While the previous discussion of public utility regulation seems fairly simple and straightforward, the actual determination of prices (rates) for public utility services by regulatory commissions (often called the *rate case*) is very complex. For one thing, it is difficult to determine the value of the plant or fixed assets on which to allow a normal rate of return. Should it be the original cost of the investment or the replacement cost? More often than not, regulatory commissions decide on the former. Furthermore, since public utility companies supply the service to different classes of customers, each with different price elasticities of demand, many different rate schedules could be used to allow the public utility company to break even. Even more troublesome is the fact that a public utility company usually provides many services that are jointly produced, and so it is impossible to allocate costs in any rational way to the various services provided and customers served.

Regulation can also lead to inefficiencies. These result from the fact that, having been guaranteed a normal rate of return on investment, public utility companies have little incentive to keep costs down. For example, managers may decide on salary increases for themselves in excess of what they would get in their best alternative employment and provide luxurious offices and large expense accounts for themselves. Regulatory commissions must, therefore, scrutinize costs to prevent such abuses.

Other inefficiencies arise because if rates are set too high, public utilities will overinvest in fixed assets and use excessively capital-intensive production methods to avoid showing above-normal returns (which would lead to rate reductions). On the other hand, if public utility rates are set too low, public utility companies will underinvest in fixed assets (i.e., in plant and equipment) and overspend on variable inputs, such as labor and fuel, and tend to reduce the quality of services. Overinvestment or underinvestment in plant and equipment resulting from the wrong public utility rates being set is known as the **Averch–Johnson** or **A–J effect** (from Harvey Averch and Leland Johnson, who first identified this problem) and can lead to large inefficiencies.[5] And yet, it is difficult indeed for regulatory commissions to come up with correct utility rates in view of the difficulty of valuing the fixed assets of public utilities and because of the long planning and gestation period of public utility investment projects.[6]

Finally, there is usually a lag of 9 to 12 months from the time the need for a rate change is recognized and the time it is granted. This *regulatory lag* results because public hearings must be conducted before a regulatory commission can approve a requested rate change. Since the members of the regulatory commissions are either political appointees or elected officials and are thus subject to political pressures from consumer groups, they usually postpone a rate increase as long as possible and tend to grant rate increases which are smaller than necessary. During inflationary periods, this leads to underinvestment in fixed assets and to the inefficiencies discussed above. To avoid these regulatory lags, rates are sometimes tied to fuel costs and are automatically adjusted as variable costs change. However, most public utilities are now in the process of deregulation (see Case Study 12-5).

---

[5] Harvey Averch and Leland Johnson, "Behavior of the Firm under Regulatory Constraint," *American Economic Review* (December 1962), pp. 1052–1069.

[6] In recent years regulatory commissions have begun to pay more attention to the structure of rates so as to avoid undue price discrimination against any class of customers.

CASE STUDY 12-5
Regulated Electricity Rates for Con Edison

In February 1983, and after nearly six months of public hearings and deliberations, the New York Public Service Commission approved a 6.5 percent increase in electricity rates for the 2.7 million customers served by the Consolidated Edison Company. This rate increase, which took effect in March 1983, increased the basic monthly electricity charge by $2.60 in New York City and $3.75 in Westchester County, where the average resident uses more electricity. The increase in the monthly electricity charge was about half of the 12.4 percent that Con Edison had asked for and far lower than the 15.5 percent increase that the commission granted Con Edison in 1981. The commission indicated that the decision to grant rate increases that would generate additional revenues of only $240 million per year for Con Edison rather than the requested $491 million was based on the fact that the borrowing and operating costs of the public utility had fallen sharply since it had made the request for a rate increase as the result of the decline in fuel costs, interest rates, and inflation.

Both Con Edison and consumer advocates immediately criticized the rate increase—the former as inadequate and the latter as too high. Because of even lower fuel costs, greater demand for electricity, and higher productivity increases than anticipated, the rate increase actually generated $267 million in additional revenues per year for Con Edison, and this represented a 15.2 percent return on its investment, instead of the projected 13.67 percent return. In 1986, the city administration threatened to sue Con Edison to have the excess profits returned to customers but dropped its plan when Con Edison agreed not to seek another rate increase until March 1987. In fact, Con Edison did not get another rate increase until 1992. The rate increases that it got from 1992 to 1995 were very small, and from 1996 to 1999 rates declined slightly. Con Edison and other electric utilities in New York State and in about one-third of the United States have now been deregulated, thus allowing customers to choose their power company and bargain for rates, just as they do for telephone services. Furthermore, while in the past electric utility companies produced, delivered, metered, and billed for the electricity they sold, with deregulation, these functions were taken over (for the most part) by separate and more specialized companies. Deregulation increased the efficiency of the electric industry, but this did not translate into lower rates for every type of user. In fact, deregulation brought blackouts and sharply higher electricity bills in California in 2000 and 2001 and in the Northeast in 2003, and this (together with the collapse of Enron, one of the world's largest energy traders at the end of 2001) convinced many states to delay deregulation until enough generating capacity was built to ensure ample supply with low and stable electricity rates. In the meantime, the European Union is scheduled to fully liberalize the electricity market.

Source: "Con Edison Wins 6.5% Rise in Rates, Half of Its Request," *The New York Times* (February 24, 1983), p. B4; "Con Edison Puts Freeze on Its Electricity Rates," *The New York Times* (January 13, 1986), p. B1; Paul L. Joskow, "Restructuring, Competition and Regulatory Reform in the U.S. Electric Sector," *Journal of Economic Perspectives* (Summer 1997), pp. 119–138; "Con Edison Customers Get Tough Lesson on Deregulation," *The Wall Street Journal* (August 23, 2000), p. B6; "California Moving Toward Re-regulating Energy," *The New York Times* (September 21, 2001), p. 16; "Collapse May Reshape the Battlefield of Deregulation," *The New York Times* (December 4, 2001), p. C1; "Experts Assess Deregulation as Factor in 2003 Blackout," *The New York Times* (September 16, 2005), p. 20; and "European Utilities–Energetic Efforts," *The Economist* (September 10, 2005), p. 60.

<table>
<tr><td>**12-4**</td><td># ANTITRUST: GOVERNMENT REGULATION OF MARKET STRUCTURE AND CONDUCT</td></tr>
</table>

The late nineteenth century saw a rapid increase in concentration of economic power in the United States in the form of trusts. Under a trust agreement, the voting rights of the stock of the firms in an (oligopolistic) industry are transferred to a legal trust, which manages the firms as a cartel, restricting output, charging monopoly prices, and earning monopoly profits. The most notorious of these trusts were the Standard Oil Trust, the Tobacco Trust, and several railroad and coal trusts, all of which were in operation in the United States in the 1880s. Public indignation over the rapid increase in the concentration of economic power and the abuses that resulted from it led to the passage of antitrust laws, starting with the Sherman Act of 1890. The intent of these antitrust laws was to prevent monopoly or undue concentration of economic power, to protect the public against the abuses and inefficiencies resulting from monopoly or the concentration of economic power, and to maintain a workable degree of competition in the economy.

In this section we summarize the provisions of the most important antitrust laws. These are the **Sherman Act (1890)**, the **Clayton Act (1914)**, the **Federal Trade Commission Act (1914)**, the **Robinson–Patman Act (1936)**, the **Wheeler–Lea Act (1938),** and the **Celler–Kefauver Antimerger Act (1950)**. The two basic statutes of antitrust legislation are the Sherman and Clayton acts. They prohibited "monopolization," "restraints of trade," and "unfair competition." Being very broad in nature, however, the Sherman Act and the Clayton Act left a great deal to judicial interpretation based on economic analysis and led to the passage of the subsequent legislation to spell out more precisely what business behavior was in fact prohibited by the antitrust laws and close loopholes in the original legislation.

Sherman Act (1890)

This is the first federal antitrust law. Sections 1 and 2 state:

1. Every contract, combination in the form of a trust or otherwise, or conspiracy, in restraint of trade or commerce among the several states, and with foreign nations is hereby declared to be illegal.
2. Every person who shall monopolize, or combine or conspire with any other person or persons, to monopolize any part of the trade or commerce among the several states, or with foreign nations, shall be deemed guilty of a misdemeanor.

Thus, Section 1 made any contract or combination in restraint of trade (such as price fixing) illegal, while Section 2 made any attempt to monopolize a market illegal. In 1903, the Antitrust Division of the U.S. Department of Justice was established to enforce the act. A 1974 amendment to the Sherman Act made violations felonies rather than misdemeanors, increased maximum penalties from $50,000 to $1 million for corporations and from $50,000 and one year in prison to $100,000 and three years in prison for individuals, and made it possible for those injured by antitrust violations to collect triple damages in civil suits.

Clayton Act (1914)

This act listed four types of unfair competition that were illegal: price discrimination, exclusive and tying contracts, intercorporate stock holdings, and interlocking directorates:

1. Section 2 of the act makes it illegal for sellers to discriminate in price among buyers, when such discrimination has the effect of substantially lessening competition or tends to create a monopoly. Price discrimination is *otherwise* permissible when it is based on differences in grade, quality or quantities sold, or selling or transportation costs and when lower prices are offered in good faith to meet competition.

2. Section 3 of the act makes it illegal for sellers to lease, sell, or contract for the sale of a commodity on the condition that the lessee or buyer does not purchase, lease, or deal in the commodity of a competitor, if such an exclusive or tying contract substantially lessens competition or tends to create a monopoly.

3. Section 7 of the act makes it illegal for a corporation engaged in commerce to acquire the stocks of a competing corporation or the stocks of two or more corporations that compete with one another if such intercorporate stock holdings substantially lessen competition or tend to create a monopoly.

4. Section 8 of the act makes it illegal for the same individual to be on the board of directors of two or more corporations (interlocking directorate) if the corporations are competitive and if any has capital, surplus, or undivided profits in excess of $1 million.

Note that while price discrimination, exclusive and tying contracts, and intercorporate stock holdings are illegal only if they *substantially lessen competition or tend to create a monopoly,* interlocking directorates are illegal per se, without any need to show that they lead to a reduction in competition.

Federal Trade Commission Act (1914)

This act supplemented the Clayton Act and simply stated that "unfair methods of competition were unlawful." The act also established the Federal Trade Commission (FTC) to prosecute violators of the antitrust laws and to protect the public against false and misleading advertisements (see Section 12-1). Determination of what constitutes *unfair competition* beyond that specified by the Clayton Act was left to the FTC, but it was now no longer necessary to wait for private parties to sue at their own expense when injured by unfair and monopolistic practices.

Robinson–Patman Act (1936)

As pointed out in Section 12-1, this act, passed to amend the Clayton Act, made it illegal to sell more cheaply to one buyer or in one market than to others or to sell at "unreasonably low prices" with the intent of destroying competition or eliminating a competitor. The act sought to protect small retailers (primarily independent grocery stores and drugstores) from price competition from chain-store retailers, based on the latter's ability to obtain lower prices and brokerage concession fees on bulk purchases from suppliers.

Wheeler–Lea Act (1938)

As pointed out in Section 12-1, this act amended the Federal Trade Commission Act and forbade false or deceptive advertisement of foods, drugs, corrective devices, and cosmetics entering interstate commerce. Its main purpose was to protect consumers against false or deceptive advertisement.

Celler–Kefauver Antimerger Act (1950)

This act closed a loophole in Section 7 of the Clayton Act, which made it illegal to acquire the stock of a competing corporation but allowed the purchase of the *assets* of a competing corporation. The Celler–Kefauver Antimerger Act closed this loophole by making it illegal to purchase not only the stock but also the assets of a competing corporation if such a purchase substantially lessens competition or tends to create a monopoly. Thus, the act forbids all types of mergers: horizontal (i.e., firms producing the same type of products, such as steel mills), vertical (firms at various stages of production, such as steel mills and coal mines), and conglomerate (firms in unrelated product lines, such as breakfast cereals and magazines) if their effect lessens competition substantially or tends to create a monopoly.

12-5   ENFORCEMENT OF ANTITRUST LAWS AND THE DEREGULATION MOVEMENT

In this section we discuss the enforcement of antitrust laws, first in general and then from the point of view of market structure and market conduct. Finally, we examine the recent deregulation movement.

Enforcement of Antitrust Laws: Some General Observations

The enforcement of antitrust laws has been the responsibility of the Antitrust Division of the Department of Justice and the Federal Trade Commission (FTC). In general, the Justice Department enforces the Sherman Act and Section 7 (the antimerger section) of the Clayton Act with criminal proceedings, while the FTC enforces other sections of the Clayton Act with civil proceedings. Antitrust action can be initiated by the Justice Department, the FTC, state attorneys general (based on states' antitrust legislation), and private parties (individuals and firms). Of the roughly 2,000 antitrust suits currently filed in the United States each year, over 90 percent are initiated by private parties.

Since U.S. antitrust laws are often broad, a great deal of judicial interpretation based on economic analysis has often been required in the enforcement of antitrust laws. The problems of defining what is meant by "substantially lessening competition," defining the relevant product and geographical markets, and deciding when competition is "unfair" have not been easy to determine and often could not be resolved in a fully satisfactory and uncontroversial way. The fact that many antitrust cases lasted many years, involved thousands of pages of testimony, and cost millions of dollars to prosecute is ample evidence of their great complexity. In one area, however, the antitrust laws are very clear: Price collusion among firms is clearly and unequivocally prohibited.

Antitrust violations or alleged violations have been resolved by (1) dissolution and divestiture, (2) injunction, or (3) consent decree. **Dissolution and divestiture** have been used in monopoly and antimerger cases. With these, the firm is ordered either to dissolve (thereby losing its identity) or to divest itself of (i.e., sell) some of its assets. An **injunction** is a court order requiring that the defendant refrain from certain anticompetitive actions or take some specified competitive actions. A **consent decree** is an agreement, without a court trial, between the defendant (without, however, admitting guilt) and the Justice Department under which the defendant agrees to abide by the rules of business behavior set down in the decree. Most antitrust actions have been settled with consent decrees. Antitrust violations have also been punished by fines and jail sentences (see the discussion of the Sherman Act in Section 12-4).

Enforcement of Antitrust Laws: Structure

Enforcement of the antitrust laws to break up or prevent the emergence of an anticompetitive industry structure involved the application of Section 2 of the Sherman Act prohibiting monopolization and attempts or conspiracies to monopolize, and application of Section 7 of the Clayton Act, and the Celler–Kefauver Act, which prohibit mergers that substantially lessen competition.

Until 1945, the U.S. Supreme Court held that size per se was not illegal. The illegal use of monopoly power was required for successful prosecution. Thus, in the 1911 Standard Oil case, the Supreme Court argued that Standard Oil of New Jersey had acquired and used a 90 percent control in the refining and sale of petroleum products by illegal actions (such as using profits from one market to sell at below cost in another market to drive competitors out) and ordered its dissolution into 30 independent firms. On the other hand, in the 1920 U.S. Steel case, the Supreme Court ruled that size, in and of itself, was no offense and in the absence of conclusive proof of illegal actions, refused to order the dissolution of U.S. Steel. The same was true in the International Harvester case in 1927.

Starting with the 1945 Alcoa case, however, the Supreme Court ruled that size per se was an offense, irrespective of illegal acts. The fact that Alcoa had achieved 90 percent control of the aluminum market by efficient operation and by maintaining low profit margins was no defense.[7] In the 1982 IBM and AT&T cases (see Case Study 12-6), however, the Court took an intermediate position in its interpretation of Section 2 of the Sherman Act. While the Court backed away from the ruling that size per se was illegal, it ruled that size, together with practices that by themselves or when used by smaller firms did not represent an offense, were illegal when used by a very large firm. Thus, the Court ordered AT&T to divest itself of 22 local telephone companies under a consent decree but decided to drop its case against IBM. Overall, Section 2 of the Sherman Act may have been more effective in preventing monopolization than in breaking it up after its occurrence.

The Supreme Court recognized that the structure of an industry was also affected by mergers. Section 7 of the Clayton Act and the Celler–Kefauver Act prohibit mergers that "substantially lessen competition" or tend to lead to monopoly. According to its 1984 guidelines, the Justice Department did not usually challenge a horizontal merger (i.e., a

---

[7] For a more detailed discussion of this and other antitrust cases, see the readings in the selected bibliography at the end of the chapter.

CASE STUDY 12-6
The IBM and AT&T Cases

In 1969, the Justice Department filed suit against IBM under Section 2 of the Sherman Act for monopolizing the computer market, for using exclusive and tying contracts, and for selling new equipment at below cost. The government sought the dissolution of IBM. After 13 years of litigation, more than 104,000 trial transcript pages, $26 million cost to the government (and $300 million incurred by IBM to defend itself), however, the Justice Department dropped its suit against IBM in 1982. The rapid technological change, increased competition in the field of computers, and changed marketing methods since the filing of the suit had so weakened the government case that the Justice Department felt it could not win. In 1995, IBM was a struggling giant in a highly competitive market rather than the near monopolist it had been accused of being in 1969. It was only in the second half of the 1990s that IBM seemed to find its way again. While prospering in computer hardware (mainframe computers), by 2006 IBM had also become a service powerhouse.

In 1974, the Justice Department filed suit (also under Section 2 of the Sherman Act) against AT&T for illegal practices aimed at eliminating competitors in the market for telephone equipment and for long-distance telephone service. At the time, AT&T was the largest private firm in the world. After 8 years of litigation and a cost of $25 million to the government (and $360 million incurred by AT&T to defend itself), the case was settled on January 8, 1982 (the

same day that the government dropped its case against IBM). By consent decree, AT&T agreed to divest itself of the 22 local telephone companies (which represented two-thirds of its total assets) and lose its monopoly on long-distance telephone service. In return, AT&T was allowed to retain Bell Laboratories and its manufacturing arm, Western Electric, and was allowed to enter the rapidly growing fields of cable TV, electronic data transmission, video-text communications, and computers. The settlement also led to an increase in local telephone charges (which had been subsidized by long-distance telephone service by AT&T) and a reduction in long-distance telephone charges.

By the end of 2001, competitors had captured more than 40 percent of the long-distance telephone market from AT&T. Furthermore, the sharp increase in competition and the price wars resulted in much lower profits for AT&T and the other long-distance telephone companies. AT&T sold its cable-TV business to Comcast at the end of 2001 for $44 billion, thus ending its frenzied and costly three-year effort to transform itself into a telecommunications powerhouse, and returning to being just a long-distance telephone company. Then, in 2005, AT&T itself was acquired by the regional bell SBC, which subsequently adopted the name of AT&T and put an end to long-distance telephony in the United States. (See Case Study 9-11 and Integrating Case Study 6.)

Source: "Windup for Two Super Suits," *Time* (January 18, 1982), pp. 38–40; "Ma Bell's Big Breakup," *Newsweek* (January 18, 1982), pp. 58–63; "Gertner's IBM Revival: Impressive, Incomplete," *The Wall Street Journal* (March 25, 1997), p. B1; "IBM's Giant Gamble," *Forbes* (October 4, 1999), pp. 95; "Inside Sam's $100 Billion Growth Miracle," *Fortune* (June 14, 2004), pp. 81–98; "Congress Votes to Reshape the Communications Industry," *The New York Times* (February 2, 1996), p. 1; "Telecoms in Trouble," *The Economist* (December 16, 2000), pp. 77–79; "Justice Department Approves Two Big Telecom Deals," *The New York Times* (October 28, 2005), p. C4; and "SBC to Resurrect AT&T Name," *Financial Times* (October 28, 2005), p. 1.

---

merger of firms in the same product line) during the 1980s and early 1990s if the postmerger Herfindahl index (defined in Section 9-1) was less than 1,000. If the postmerger index was between 1,000 and 1,800 and the increase in the index as a result of the merger was less than 100 points, the merger usually also went unchallenged. But if the postmerger index was between 1,000 and 1,800 and the merger led to an increase in the index of more than 100 points, or if the postmerger index was more than 1,800 and the merger led to an increase in the index of more than 50 points, the Justice Department was likely to challenge the merger.

These guidelines based on the Herfindahl index were not the only factors that the Justice Department considered in horizontal mergers during the 1980s, however. The Justice Department was more likely to bend its Herfindahl-index guidelines if the merger prevented the failure of the acquired firm, if entry into the industry was easy, if the degree of foreign competition was strong, and if the acquisition led to substantial economies of scale.[8] Less clear-cut were the guidelines on vertical and conglomerate mergers. As a result of the relaxed guidelines and in the face of sharply increased foreign competition, especially from Japan, the number and size of corporate acquisitions in the United States increased sharply during the 1980s. For example, as many as 143 of the 500 largest corporations in the United States in 1980 had been purchased by 1989. These were made possible by the easy accessibility of funds and the hands-off antitrust policy of the 1980s. Most takeovers occurred by firms in the same line of business and made corporations more focused and efficient, after years of diversification. When conglomerates were taken over, the various business lines were often sold off to buyers in the same line of business.[9]

The wave of mergers since the early 1990s was different from that of the 1980s, and so was the enforcement of antitrust laws. Whereas in the 1980s many mergers were among firms of unrelated industries raising few antitrust concerns, the merger wave since the early 1990s often involved the merging of competitors, giving the combined companies the power to dominate their industries and, in theory, control prices and the availability of products. Starting from the second half of the 1990s, the enforcement of antitrust laws changed its focus from the doctrine that bigness led to power and unfair behavior to that of protecting consumers and thus refusing to approve a merger that reduced competition and was likely to increase prices to consumers (see Case Study 12-7).

Enforcement of Antitrust Laws: Conduct

Antitrust policy was also directed against anticompetitive industry conduct. The Supreme Court ruled against price collusion outright and ruled against price discrimination if it substantially lessened competition or tended to create a monopoly. Specifically, the Court ruled illegal not only cartels but also any informal understanding or collusion to share the market, fix prices, or establish price leadership schemes. **Conscious parallelism** (i.e., the adoption of similar policies by oligopolists in view of their recognized interdependence) was ruled to be illegal when reflecting collusion. Thus, the Supreme Court ruled against the three large tobacco companies in the 1946 Tobacco case (conscious parallelism was believed to have been the result of collusion in the form of price leadership), but ruled to drop the suit in the 1954 Theater Enterprises case (collusion could not be inferred from conscious parallelism).

The most difficult aspect in enforcing Section 1 of the Sherman Act has been to prove tacit or informal collusion. Sometimes the case was clear-cut. For example, in 1936, the

---

[8] See "Symposium on Mergers and Antitrust," *Journal of Economic Perspectives* (Fall 1987), pp. 3–54; and W. E. Kovaric and Carl Shapiro, "Antirust Policy: A Century of Economic and Legal Thinking," *Journal of Economic Perspectives* (Winter 2000), pp. 43–60.

[9] See Andrei Sheifer and Robert W. Vishny, "The Takeover Wave of the 1980s," *Science* (August 17, 1990), pp. 745–749.

CASE STUDY 12-7
Antitrust and the New Merger Boom

Since the early 1990s there has been a huge merger boom in the United States and abroad. The year 2000 was the biggest year for mergers and acquisitions in history with deals valued at more than $1.8 trillion. During the 1990s, megadeals occurred in telecommunications, defense, railroads, pharmaceuticals, retailing, health care, banking, entertainment, publishing, computers, consulting, and in many other industries (see Section 9-5). The biggest merger in history was the America Online (AOL) acquisition of Time Warner for $110 billion in 2000. There were several forces that fueled this urge to merger. The most important were massive technological changes, increased international competition, and deregulation. Firms are under strong pressure to reduce excessive capacity and cut costs, and to become major players in the global marketplace. Only with the U.S. recession in 2001 did the merger boom subside, but it then resumed in 2004 and spread to Europe in 2005.

The new merger wave was also different from that of the 1980s and so has been the enforcement of antitrust laws. Whereas in the 1980s many mergers were among firms in unrelated industries (thus creating conglomerates) and raising few antitrust concerns, the merger wave since the early 1990s often involved the merger of competitors, potentially giving the combined companies the power to dominate their industries and, in theory, control prices and the availability of products. Starting from the second half of the 1990s, the enforcement of antitrust laws thus changed its focus from the doctrine that bigness led to power and unfair behavior to that of protecting consumers, and thus refusing to approve mergers that reduced competition and that were likely to increase prices. In short, enforcement has become pro-competition and pro-consumer.

For example, the Federal Trade Commission (FTC) did not approve the proposed merger of Staples and Office Depot, two chains of office-supply superstores, in 1997 because it found that Staples had lower prices in those locations where there was also an Office Depot outlet, thus concluding that their merger would very likely have led to higher consumer prices. Not approved for the same reason were many other proposed mergers, among them WorldCom purchase of Sprint in 2000, United Airlines' acquisition of American West, and General Electric's acquisition of Honeywell in 2001 (which was blocked by the European Commission, even though the two companies are American and the merger had been cleared by the U.S. Justice Department).

Whether, in fact, the recent merger boom led companies to reduce costs and increase efficiency and revenue depends on the type of merger taking place. In the defense and health care fields, the promise of reduced costs and increased efficiency has been or can be realized. In others sectors, it is not too certain. Often the acquiring company paid a premium over the market price because of synergies that the acquiring company's management saw but the market did not. When such synergies failed to materialize or did not live up to expectations, the acquiring company and its stockholders suffered, especially if the company took on huge debt loads to make the acquisitions. The biggest loss resulted from the 2000 merger of AOL/Time Warner ($200 billion loss in stock-market value and $54 billion write-down in the worth of the combined company assets).

Source: "The New Merger Boom," *Fortune* (November 28, 1994), pp. 95–106; "Aiding Consumers Is Now the Thrust of Antitrust Push," *The New York Times* (March 22, 1998), p. 1; "Corporate Governance and Merger Activity in the United States: Making Sense of the 1980s and 1990s," *Journal of Economic Perspectives* (Spring 2001), pp. 121–144; "Volatile Markets and Global Slowdown Cool Corporate Desire to Merge," *The Wall Street Journal* (January 2, 2002), p. R10; "They Shopped—Now They've Dropped," *Business Week* (February 25, 2002), pp. 36–37; "Mergers: Why Most Don't Pay Off," *Business Week* (October 14, 2002), pp. 60–70; "What Mergers Are Good For," *The New York Times Magazine* (June 5, 2005), pp. 56–62; and "Europe's M&A Boom Is Set to Hit $930 Billion by End of the Year," *Financial Times* (November 7, 2005), p. 1.

U.S. Engineer's Office received 11 closed bids to supply 6,000 barrels of cement, each quoting a price of $3.286854 per barrel! The probability of identical prices, down to the sixth decimal, occurring without some form of collusion is practically zero. One of the most important collusive agreements uncovered and successfully prosecuted was the "electrical machinery conspiracy" in which General Electric, Westinghouse, and a number of smaller companies producing electrical equipment pleaded guilty in 1961 to violation of antitrust laws for price fixing and dividing up the market. The companies were fined a total of $2 million and had to pay over $400 million in damages to customers in civil suits, 7 of their executives were sent to jail, and 23 others received suspended sentences.[10]

Predatory pricing was ruled to be illegal under Section 1 of the Sherman Act. **Predatory pricing** refers to the case where a firm uses the profits earned in one market to sell a product or service below its average variable cost in another market in order to drive competitors out of the latter market or to discourage the entrance of new firms by threatening to lower prices below costs. Besides predatory pricing, the Court ruled that any other form of price discrimination or price behavior that substantially lessened competition or tended to create a monopoly was illegal under the Clayton Act and the Robinson–Patman Act.

In determining illegal antitrust conduct, the definition of the relevant product market has been very important. For example, in the well-known *cellophane case,* DuPont was accused of monopolizing the market for cellophane. In its defense, DuPont argued that cellophane was just one of many flexible packaging materials that included cellophane, waxed paper, aluminum foil, and many others. Based on the high cross-price elasticity of demand between cellophane and these other products, DuPont successfully argued that the relevant market was not cellophane but flexible packaging materials. Since DuPont had less than 20 percent of this market, the Supreme Court ruled in 1953 that DuPont had not monopolized the market. The most celebrated antitrust case of the 1990s was the one against Microsoft (see Case Study 12-8).

The Deregulation Movement

The *public interest theory* postulates that regulation is undertaken to overcome market failures, so as to ensure that the economic system operates in a manner consistent with the public interest (see Section 12-2). By contrast, the *economic theory of regulation* expounded by Stigler and others postulates that regulation is the result of pressure-group action and results in laws and policies that restrict competition and promote the interest of the firms that they are supposed to regulate (this is the *capture theory* discussed in Section 12-1).

Regulation is also attacked because of the heavy cost it imposes on society. Estimates have put this cost at more than $100 billion in the year 1979 (of which about 5 percent were administrative costs and the rest were the costs of compliance) and more than $200 billion a year in the 1990s.[11] Although these estimates have been challenged as grossly

---

[10] "The Incredible Electrical Conspiracy," *Fortune* (April 1961), p. 132, and (May 1961), p. 161.

[11] Murray Weidenbaum, "The High Cost of Government Regulation," *Challenge* (November–December 1979), pp. 32–39; and "A New Project Will Measure the Cost and Effect of Regulation," *The New York Times* (March 30, 1998), p. D2.

CASE STUDY 12-8
The Microsoft Antitrust Case

Soon after its introduction in 1995, Microsoft's Windows 95 operating systems captured nearly 90 percent of the U.S. (and world) PC market and faced only weak competition from Apple Macintosh and IBM OS/2 operating systems. Inevitably, the threat from Windows 95 gave rise to predictable cries of monopoly from competitors. The introduction of Windows 95 put at risk especially small software companies that provided such specialized programs as hooking up to the Internet, retrieving lost files, turning the PC into a fax machine, and allocating memory inside the PC efficiently—since most of these programs were now provided as part of Windows 95. This was good news for computer users but drove many small software companies out of business and represented a serious threat to the others.

In fall 1998, the U.S. Justice Department sued Microsoft accusing it of illegally using its Windows operating system near monopoly to overwhelm rivals and hurt consumers. In April 2000, the federal district judge trying the case ruled that Microsoft had violated antitrust laws with predatory behavior and in June of the same year the same judge ordered the breakup of Microsoft. The company, however, appealed and in November 2001 the U.S. Justice Department and Microsoft reached a settlement agreement that not only left Microsoft intact but also continued to permit Microsoft's strategy of "bundling" applications with its Windows operating

system. Both represented substantial victories for Microsoft. In 2004, the federal appeals court upheld the 2001 ruling, thus putting an end to Microsoft antitrust problems in the United States. But Microsoft also faced an antitrust suit in Europe. In 2004, the European Commission (the European antitrust regulator) fined Microsoft $600 million, ordered it to offer a version of the Windows operating system without its media player software, and to share more technical information with other software makers.

Besides antitrust problems on both sides of the Atlantic, Microsoft also faced many private suits. One of the largest was that brought by the Netscape Communications Corporation in 2002. Netscape was the commercial pioneer in the Web browsing software whose fortune faded as a result of the competition from Microsoft and was acquired by AOL in 1999. Netscape's broad antitrust suit charged that its decline had been the direct result of Microsoft's illegal tactics. This suit was settled in March 2003 with Microsoft paying AOL $750 million in penalty, granting AOL a seven-year royalty-free license to its Internet browsing software, and a long-term license to its software for delivering music and video over the Internet. By the end of 2005, Microsoft payouts to settle all antitrust and private suits exceeded $4.2 billion dollars, but with over $50 billion in cash at hand, Microsoft was hardly hurt.

Source: "Windows 95," *Business Week* (July 10, 1995), pp. 94–107; "U.S. Judge Says Microsoft Violated Antitrust Laws with Predatory Behavior," *The New York Times* (April 4, 2000), p. 1; "Microsoft Breakup Ordered for Antitrust Law Violations," *The New York Times* (June 8, 2000), p. 1; "Settlement or Sellout," *Business Week* (November 19, 2001), p. 114; "An AOL Unit Sues Microsoft, Saying Tactics Were Illegal," *The New York Times* (January 23, 2002), p. C1; "Microsoft to Pay AOL $750 Million to End Long War," *The New York Times* (May 30, 2003), p. 1; "Europeans Rule Against Microsoft," *The New York Times* (March 25, 2004), p. C1; "Court Lets Settlement Stand in Microsoft Antitrust Case," *The New York Times* (July 1, 2004), p. C7; and "Microsoft Payouts Set to Top $4.5 Billion," *Financial Times* (April 12, 2005), p. 21.

exaggerated,[12] compliance costs are surely very high, particularly in the area of social regulation, such as job safety, energy and the environment, and consumer safety and health.[13] In any event, since it is even more difficult to measure the full private and social benefits of regulation, it is practically impossible to determine on a strict benefit–cost basis whether regulation is economically justified.

Be that as it may, a growing deregulation movement has sprung up in the United States since the 1970s that led to deregulation in the air travel, trucking, railroad, banking, and telecommunications industries. The *Airline Deregulation Act of 1978* removed all restrictions on entry, scheduling, and pricing in domestic air travel in the United States, and so did the *Motor Carrier Act of 1980* in the trucking industry. The *Depository Institutions Deregulation and Monetary Control Act of 1980* allowed banks to pay interest on checking accounts and increased competition for business loans. The *Railroad Revitalization and Regulatory Reform Act of 1976* greatly increased the flexibility of railroads to set prices and to determine levels of service and areas of operation. The settlement of the *AT&T Antitrust Case in 1982* opened competition in long-distance telephone service and in telecommunications. Natural gas pipelines and oil are now deregulated, and the banking and electric power industries are now in the process of being deregulated.

The general purpose of deregulation is to increase competition and efficiency in the affected industries and lead to lower prices without sacrificing the quality of service. Most observers would probably conclude that, on balance, the net effect has been positive. Competition has generally increased, and prices have fallen in industries that were deregulated. As expected, however, deregulation has also resulted in some difficulties and strains in the industries. Many economists think that what is needed is more vigilance and enforcement rather than more regulation.[14] Nowhere is this more evident than in the airline industry (see Case Study 12-9).

12-6 REGULATION OF INTERNATIONAL COMPETITION

There are many ways by which national governments regulate international trade. Some of these are tariffs, quotas, voluntary export restraints, antidumping duties, as well as technical, administrative, and other regulations. An **import tariff** is simply a tax on imports.[15] As such, it increases prices to domestic consumers, reduces the quantity demanded of the commodity at home and imports from abroad, and encourages the

---

[12] See William K. Tabb, "Government Regulation: Two Sides of the Story," *Challenge* (November–December 1980), pp. 40–48.

[13] Regulation often leads to inefficiencies because regulators do not specify the desired result but only the method of compliance (such as the type of pollution-abatement equipment to use) in the absence of adequate information and expertise. It would be much better if regulators specified the results wanted and left to industry the task of determining the most efficient way to comply. In recent years, there has been a significant movement along this direction (see Case Study 12-4).

[14] See "Race Is on for Tougher Regulation," *The New York Times* (February 10, 2002), sec. 3, p. 1; and "Mood Swings in Favor of Regulation," *The Wall Street Journal* (March 29, 2002), p. A14.

[15] The U.S. Constitution forbids tariffs on exports.

CASE STUDY 12-9
Deregulation of the Airline Industry: An Assessment

By 2001 all but one (America West) of the 16 air carriers that had been started since the 1978 deregulation had gone out of business or had merged with established carriers. Several mergers took place among large established carriers (such as American Airlines' acquisition of TWA in 2001), and Eastern Airline and Pan Am went out of business. The result was that in 2001 seven carriers handled 93 percent of all domestic air travel in the United States (as compared with 11 carriers handling 87 percent of the traffic in 1978). From 1985 to 2001, the market share of the top five carriers jumped from 61 percent to 77 percent. Instead of the large number of small and highly competitive airlines envisioned by deregulation, the airline industry has become even more concentrated than it was before deregulation.

Entry into the industry was restricted by established airlines by (1) long-term leasing of the limited number of gates at most airports, (2) frequent flier programs that tie passengers to a given airline, (3) computerized reservations systems, which give a competitive advantage in attracting customers to the airlines owning such a system, (4) the "hub and spoke" operations in which airlines funnel passengers through centrally located airports, and (5) predatory pricing practices under which established airlines lower the price and increase flights to drive new entrants out.

From 2001 to 2006, however, new discount airlines came into existence which, with their low-price strategy, began taking market away from the established airlines. This, together with the more than doubling of jet fuel price, led to huge losses for the traditional airlines and landed United, US Airways, Delta, and Northwest into Chapter 11 bankruptcy in 2005 (see case Study 10-3).

It is true that with deregulation, airfares, after adjusting for inflation, have declined by an average of more than 30 percent, and that this greatly stimulated domestic air travel (from about 250 million passengers in 1976 to more than 600 million in 2005). But it is also true that airlines cannot charge fares so low and continue to incur huge losses. Furthermore, delays at airports and passenger complaints about lost luggage, canceled flights, overbooking, and the general decline in the quality of service are fueling demands to reimpose some type of regulation in the industry. Clearly, some restructuring of the U.S. airline industry seems required in order to reduce overcapacity (read: some airlines must be allowed to go out of business), reduce costs, and avoid price wars.

Since the deregulation of the industry in 1997, established European airlines have been facing the same problems as American airlines from new discount airlines. Despite the deregulation of the domestic airline industry, however, international air travel remains governed by intergovernmental deals, which dictate which airline can fly where, how many seats they can offer, and, in many cases, what fares to charge. At the end of 2005, the United States and the European Union (EU) were negotiating to replace the bilateral agreements which the United States has with each individual EU member with a U.S.–EU-wide agreement and liberalize somewhat air travel over the Atlantic.

Source: "Airline Deregulation," *Federal Reserve Bank of San Francisco Review* (March 9, 1990); "Predatory Pricing: Cleared for Takeoff," *Business Week* (May 4, 2001), p. 50; "Airlines and Antitrust: A New World. Or Not," *The New York Times* (November 18, 2001), sec. 3, p. 1; "Airlines under Siege," *The Economist* (March 27, 2004), pp. 67–69; "The Discount Jet-Set: Europe's Budget Airlines," *The Wall Street Journal* (April 27, 2004), p. D1; "Coffee, Tea or Regulation?" *The New York Times* (January 23, 2005), sec. 3, p. 1; "For U.S. Airlines, a Shakeout Runs into Heavy Turbulence," *The Wall Street Journal* (September 19, 2005), p. A1; and "U.S. and Europe Move Closer to an Open-Skies Agreement," *The New York Times* (October 22, 2005), p. C2.

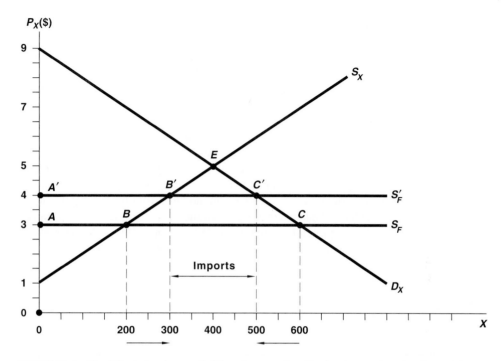

FIGURE 12-4   The Effect of an Import Tariff on Consumption, Production, and Imports D_X and S_X refer to the domestic demand and supply curves of commodity X, while S_F and S_F' refer, respectively, to the foreign supply curve of the nation's imports of commodity X with and without an import tariff of $1 per unit. With the import tariff (i.e., with S_F') $P_X = \$4$ for domestic consumers (compared with $P_X = \$3$ without the tariff), domestic consumers purchase $AC' = 500X$ (compared with $AC = 600X$ without the tariff), domestic producers produce $AB' = 300X$ (instead of $AB = 200X$), and the government collects $200 in revenues ($1 per unit on each of the $200X$ imported).

domestic production of import substitutes. The nation also collects tariff revenues. This is seen by examining Figure 12-4 (which is an extension of Figure 9-4).

In Figure 12-4, D_X and S_X refer to the domestic demand and supply curves of commodity X, while S_F is the horizontal foreign supply curve of the nation's imports (on the assumption that the nation is too small to affect the world price of commodity X). If the nation imposes a $1 tariff on each unit of commodity X imported, the new foreign supply curve of imports to the nation shifts up to S_F'. From the figure, we see that with the tariff (i.e., with S_F') $P_X = \$4$ for domestic consumers (compared with $P_X = \$3$ without the tariff), domestic consumers purchase $AC' = 500X$ (compared with $AC = 600X$ without the tariff), domestic producers produce $AB' = 300X$ (instead of $AB = 200X$), and the government collects $200 in revenues ($1 per unit on each of the $200X$ imported).

An **import quota** of $200X$ would have the same effect as the $1 tariff per unit of commodity X imported. Although foreign producers could increase their exports by reducing the price of commodity X when they face an import tariff, however, they cannot with an equivalent import quota. Thus, an import quota is a more stringent restriction. In any event, import tariffs, quotas, and other trade restrictions protect domestic producers from foreign competition, thereby allowing them to produce more and charge higher prices. Import restrictions are invariably demanded by trade associations in order to protect their members from "unfair" foreign competition. In reality, they are often a convenient and effective way to restrict competition and increase prices.

Another form of trade restriction is the **voluntary export restraint (VER).** This refers to the case in which an importing country induces another nation to reduce its exports of a commodity "voluntarily," under the threat of higher all-around trade restrictions, when these exports threaten an entire domestic industry. Voluntary export restraints have been negotiated by the United States and other industrial countries to curtail exports of textiles, automobiles, steel, shoes, and other commodities from Japan and other nations. VERs have allowed industrial nations making use of them to save at least the appearance of continued support for the principle of free trade. When successful, VERs have all the economic effects of equivalent import tariffs, except that they are administered by the exporting country, and so the revenue effect or monopoly profits are captured by foreign exporters. Foreign exporters are also likely to fill their quota with higher-quality and higher-priced units of the product over time (see Case Study 12-10).

CASE STUDY 12-10
Voluntary Export Restraints on Japanese Automobiles to the United States

From 1977 to 1981, U.S. automobile production fell by about one-third, the share of imports rose from 18 to 29 percent, and nearly 300,000 autoworkers in the United States lost their jobs. In 1980 the Big Three U.S. automakers (GM, Ford, and Chrysler) suffered combined losses of $4 billion. As a result, the United States negotiated an agreement with Japan that limited Japanese automobile exports to the United States to 1.68 million units per year from 1981 to 1983 and to 1.85 million units for 1984 and 1985. Japan "agreed" to restrict its automobile exports out of fear of still more stringent import restrictions by the United States.

U.S. automakers generally used the time from 1981 to 1985 wisely to lower breakeven points and improve quality, but the cost improvements were not passed on to consumers, and Detroit reaped profits of nearly $6 billion in 1983, $10 billion in 1984, and $8 billion in 1985. Japan gained by exporting higher priced autos and earning higher profits. The big loser

was the American public, which had to pay about $660 more for U.S.-made automobiles and $1,300 more for Japanese cars in 1984. The total cost of the agreement to U.S. consumers has been estimated to be $15.7 billion from 1981 through 1984 and 44,000 U.S. automakers' jobs were saved at the cost of more than $100,000 each.

Since 1985, the United States has not asked for a renewal of the VER agreement, but Japan unilaterally limited its auto exports (to 2.3 million from 1986 to 1991 and 1.65 million afterward) in order to avoid more trade frictions with the United States. Since the late 1980s, Japan has invested heavily to produce automobiles in the United States in so-called transplant factories, and by 1996 Japan was producing more than 2 million cars in the United States and had captured 23 percent of the U.S. auto market. By 2005, the Japanese automakers' share of the U.S. market had reached 30 percent (between domestic production and imports) out of a total of 43 percent for all foreign automakers. Following the U.S. lead, Canada and Germany also negotiated restrictions on Japanese exports (France and Italy already had very stringent quotas). A 1991 agreement to limit the Japanese share of the European Union's auto market to 16 percent expired at the end of 1999, when the share of Japanese cars (imports and production in Europe) was 11.4 percent of the European market. That share reached 13.2 in 2005 and is expected to continue to rise in the future.

Source: U.S. International Trade Commission, *A Review of Recent Developments in the U.S. Automobile Industry Including an Assessment of the Japanese Voluntary Restraint Agreements* (Washington, D.C.: February 1985); "Japanese Car Makers Plan Major Expansion of American Capacity," *The Wall Street Journal* (September 12, 1997), p. A1; "Japanese Carmakers Accelerate in Europe," *Financial Times* (September 15, 2003), p. 8; "Foreign Auto Makers Aim to Boost U.S. Market Share," *The Wall Street Journal* (January 12, 2005), p. A1; "Japanese Cars Set Europe Sales Record," *The Japan Times* (January 16, 2005), p. 1; and "G.M. Posts Worst Loss since 1992," *The New York Times* (January 17, 2006), p. C1.

Another method of regulating (restricting) international trade is by antidumping complaints that are deliberately used to harass exporters to the nation (see Section 11-3). Still other methods are *safety regulations* for automobile and electrical equipment, *health regulations* for the hygienic production and packaging of imported food products, and *labeling requirements* showing origin and contents. While many of these regulations serve legitimate purposes, some (such as the restriction on the showing of foreign films in some European Union countries) are thinly veiled disguises for restricting imports.

The United States is now extending the reach of U.S. antitrust laws beyond U.S. borders to strike at such practices as bid rigging, price fixing, industrial subsidies, and other cartel behavior by foreign companies that hurt U.S. international competitiveness. Since 1984, the United States has also granted joint U.S. research-and-development ventures limited immunity from antitrust suits, including exemption from treble damages for private lawsuits against such ventures, in order to counter strategic trade policies and targeting by other nations and regions, particularly Japan and the members of the European Union.[16] These and other trade restrictions, however, were greatly reduced as a result of the **Uruguay Round** of multilateral trade negotiations, which took effect in April 1995 and was fully implemented by 2004.

12-7 THE EFFECT OF TAXATION ON BUSINESS DECISIONS

Governments tax individuals and businesses in order to provide services (such as education, defense, police, and so on). Most importantly, governments use taxes and subsidies to redistribute income from the rich to the poor. As we have seen, governments also use taxes to discourage the consumption of certain commodities such as alcohol and tobacco and provide incentives for the consumption of other commodities such as housing and education. Thus, taxes and subsidies affect personal and business decisions and economic efficiency in general.

[16] "Antitrust Extension Is Weighted," *The New York Times* (April 16, 1990), pp. 54–55; and "Uncle Sam's Helping Hand," *The Economist* (April 2, 1994), pp. 77–79.

CASE STUDY 12-11
Corporate Tax Rates around the World

Table 12-1 shows the maximum corporate tax rates calculated on profit before tax in 10 advanced nations and 10 emerging markets in 2005. From the table we see that Ireland has by far the smallest corporate tax rate on profits among the advanced nations listed in the table. At 35 percent, the U.S. corporate tax rate on profits is only lower than that of Canada, Germany, and Japan. Among the emerging nations, Poland has the lowest rate, followed by Russia, Brazil, and Korea. The highest rate (35.88 percent) is in India. Nations with higher tax rates discourage domestic and foreign investments and tend to lose tax revenues through transfer pricing.

TABLE 12-1	**Maximum Corporate Tax Rate on Profits Calculated before Tax in Some Advanced and Emerging Nations in 2005**		
Advanced Nation	**Tax Rate (%)**	**Emerging Nation**	**Tax Rate (%)**
Ireland	12.50	Poland	19.00
Australia	30.00	Russia	24.00
United Kingdom	30.00	Brazil	25.00
Italy	33.00	Korea	27.00
France	34.42	South Africa	30.00
Spain	35.00	Mexico	32.00
United States	35.00	Philippines	32.00
Canada	41.10	China	33.00
Germany	41.63	Argentina	35.00
Japan	46.29	India	35.88

Source: IMD, *World Competitiveness Yearbook* (Lausanne, Switzerland, 2005), p. 490.

High personal and business taxes discourage work and investments and may lead corporations to practice transfer pricing and to shift their operations to lower tax nations (see Case Study 12-11). By taxing wages and capital income rather than consumption, the present U.S. tax system discourages work, savings, and investments, and reduces the economic efficiency of the nation. A fundamental tax reform to tax consumption rather than income (as the countries of the European Union do) is thus needed in the United States.[17] To overcome the disadvantage that U.S. corporations have on the world market resulting from the present U.S. tax system, the government has been providing billions of dollars of tax rebates per year (subsidies) to U.S. exporters. These have been found to be illegal by the World Trade Organization (WTO), and the United States was required to remove them (see Case Study 12-12).

---

[17] See "America Needs a Tax System that Reflects Its Values," *Financial Times* (October 27, 2005), p. 13.

CASE STUDY 12-12
U.S. Border Taxes and Export Subsidies

Price competition among nations is affected by **border taxes.** These are rebates for internal *indirect taxes* given to exporters of a commodity and imposed (in addition to the tariff) on importers of a commodity. Examples of indirect taxes are excise and sales taxes in the United States and the value-added tax (VAT) in Europe. Since most government revenues are raised through direct taxes (such as income taxes) in the United States and through indirect taxes (such as the value-added tax) in Europe, United States exporters receive much lower rebates than European exporters (or no rebate at all) and are thus at a competitive disadvantage.

The problem was overcome by the U.S. **Foreign Sales Corporation (FSC)** provisions of the U.S. tax code. These have been used since 1971 by some 3,600 U.S. corporations (including Boeing, Microsoft, and Caterpillar) to set up overseas subsidiaries to enjoy partial exemption from U.S. tax laws on income earned from exports. This provision saved American

companies from $4 to $5 billion in taxes each year. In 1999, the World Trade Organization (WTO) ruled that such tax relief was a form of export subsidy and ordered the United States to repeal it. In 2004, the United States repealed the FSC scheme, but did not eliminate all export subsidies, and so the WTO authorized the countries of the European Union to impose tariffs on $300 million of U.S. exports to the E.U. in 2005.

The new tax law (the *Homestead Investment Act of 2004*) also gave U.S. companies a one-time opportunity to bring back into the United States during 2005 a total of as much as $500 billion in foreign profits and pay a tax rate of only 5.25 percent instead of the standard corporate tax rate of 35 percent if they pledged to invest in activities that created jobs at home. During 2005, U.S. corporations did in fact repatriate more than $300 billion in foreign profits but used them mostly to buy back their own stock.

Sources: "WTO Setback for US Tax Break," *Financial Times* (October 1, 2005), p. 3; "Trade Group Says U.S. Tax Breaks Are Illegal," *The New York Times* (October 1, 2005), p. C4; "Foreign-Profit Tax Break Is Outlawed," *The New York Times* (January 14, 2005), p. C1; "Homecoming Victory," *The Wall Street Journal* (October 17, 2005), p. A18; and "Rising Stock Buybacks Align with Repatriated Profits," *The Wall Street Journal* (October 21, 2005), p. A2.

SUMMARY

1. According to the economic theory of regulation expounded by Stigler and others, regulation arises from pressure-group action and results in laws and policies in support of business, and to protect consumers, workers, and the environment. Some of the policies designed to support business restrict entry and competition. These are licensing, patents, restrictions on price competition, import restrictions (tariffs and quotas), as well as subsidies and special tax treatments to aid such sectors as agriculture, transportation, airlines, and

energy. Consumers are protected by requiring truthful disclosure by firms and by forbidding misrepresentation of products, and by laws requiring truth in lending, fairness in evaluating credit applications, clarity in warranties, safety on highways, and many others. Workers are protected by laws that specify safety standards, equal employment opportunity, and minimum wages, while air, water, and other environmental pollution are regulated by the Environmental Protection Agency.

2. According to the public interest theory of regulation, government regulation is undertaken to overcome market failures, so that the economic system can operate in a manner consistent with the public interest. One type of market failure is due to externalities. These are uncompensated costs and benefits borne or received by firms or individuals other than those producing or consuming the product or service. Thus, we have external economies and diseconomies of production and consumption. When private and social costs or benefits do not coincide (i.e., in the presence of externalities), too much or too little of a product or service is being produced or consumed from society's point of view. In such cases, government intervention is justified in order to induce the production or consumption of the product or service until the marginal social cost is equal to the marginal social benefit. Market failures due to externalities can be overcome by prohibition or regulation, taxes or subsidies, by voluntary payments, by mergers, or the sale of pollution rights. Prohibition and regulation are preferred by regulatory agencies, but they are not the most efficient methods of dealing with externalities.

3. In some industries, economies of scale may operate continuously as output expands, so that a single firm can supply the entire market more efficiently than any number of smaller firms. Such natural monopolies are common in the provision of electrical, gas, water, and local transportation services (public utilities). In cases such as these, the government usually allows a single firm to operate but regulates it by setting $P = LAC$ (so that the firm breaks even and earns only a normal return on investment). Economic efficiency, however, requires that $P = LMC$, but this would result in a loss so that the company would not supply the service in the long run without a subsidy. Therefore, P is usually set equal to LAC. Public utility regulation faces many difficulties. These arise from the difficulty in determining the value of the fixed assets of the company, in setting rates for each type of customer, in allocating costs for the jointly produced services, in ensuring that public utilities keep costs as low as possible, from over- or underinvestments in fixed assets (the Averch–Johnson effect), and from regulatory lags.

4. Starting with the Sherman Act of 1890, a number of antitrust laws were passed to prevent monopoly or undue concentration of economic power, protect the public against the abuses and inefficiencies resulting from monopoly or the concentration of economic power, and maintain a workable degree of competition in the American economy. *The Sherman Act (1890)* prohibited monopolization and restraints of trade in commerce among the states and with foreign nations. *The Clayton Act (1914)* prohibited price discrimination, exclusive and tying contracts, and intercorporate stock holdings if they substantially lessened competition or tended to create a monopoly, and prohibited outright interlocking directorates. *The Federal Trade Commission Act (1914),* passed to supplement the Clayton Act, made unfair methods of competition illegal and established the Federal Trade Commission (FTC) to prosecute violators of the antitrust laws and protect the public against false and misleading advertisements. *The Robinson–Patman Act (1936)* sought to protect small retailers from price competition from large chain-store retailers, based on the latter's ability to obtain lower prices and brokerage concession fees on bulk purchases from suppliers if the intent was to destroy competition or eliminate a competitor. *The Wheeler–Lea Act (1938)* amended the Federal Trade Commission Act and forbade false or deceptive advertisement of foods, drugs, corrective devices, and cosmetics entering interstate commerce. *The Celler–Kefauver Antimerger Act (1950)* closed a loophole in the Clayton Act by making it illegal to acquire not only the stock but also the assets of competing corporations if such purchases substantially lessen competition or tend to create a monopoly.

5. Enforcement of antitrust laws has been the responsibility of the Antitrust Division of the Department of Justice and the Federal Trade Commission (FTC). Antitrust violations have been resolved by (1) dissolution and divestiture, (2) injunction, or (3) consent decree. Fines and jail sentences have also been imposed. Starting with the 1945 Alcoa case, the Supreme Court ruled that size per se was an offense, irrespective of illegal acts. Today, both size and some anticompetitive behavior seem to be required for successful prosecution. The Court has generally challenged horizontal mergers between large direct

competitors, but not vertical and conglomerate mergers unless they would lead to increased horizontal market power. The Court has used the Sherman Act to prosecute not only attempts to set up a cartel but also any informal collusion to share the market, fix prices, or establish price leadership schemes. The Court has ruled that conscious parallelism is illegal when it reflects collusion. The Court has also attacked predatory pricing and price discrimination and other price behavior when it substantially lessened competition or tended to create a monopoly. Since the mid-1970s, the government has deregulated airlines and trucking and has reduced the level of regulation for financial institutions, telecommunications, and railroads in order to increase competition and avoid some of the heavy compliance costs of regulation. Deregulation seems to have led to increased competition and lower prices, but it has also resulted in some problems.

6. Nations regulate international trade by tariffs, quotas, voluntary export restraints, and antidumping duties, as well as technical, administrative, and other regulations. An import tariff is simply a tax on imports. As such, it increases prices to domestic consumers, reduces the quantity demanded of the commodity at home and imports from abroad, and encourages the domestic production of import substitutes. The nation also collects tariff revenues. An import quota is a quantitative restriction on imports. A voluntary export restraint is used by an importing country to induce another nation to reduce its exports of a commodity "voluntarily," under the threat of higher all-around trade restrictions, when these exports threaten an entire domestic industry. Other regulations are antidumping duties and safety, health, and labeling regulations when they are used to restrict imports. Trade restrictions were reduced by the Uruguay Round.

7. High personal and business taxes discourage work and investments and may lead corporations to practice transfer pricing and to shift their operations to lower tax nations. By taxing wages and capital income rather than consumption, the present U.S. tax system discourages work, savings, and investments and puts U.S. corporations at a competitive disadvantage on world markets. To overcome this problem, the U.S. government has been providing billions of dollars of tax rebates per year (subsidies) to U.S. exporters though the Foreign Sales Corporation, which has been found illegal by the World Trade Organization.

 ## DISCUSSION QUESTIONS

1. Name two theories that seek to explain the rationale for government intervention in the economy. What do they postulate? Which is the prevailing theory today?

2. In what way do licensing, patents, import taxes, and import quotas restrict competition?

3. What are some of the direct restrictions on price competition resulting from government regulation?

4. What are the pros and cons of regulating oil and natural gas prices?

5. Why is it likely that in a system of private education (i.e., a system in which individuals pay for their own education) there will be underinvestment in education?

6. (a) How much of a tax of $3 per hour for evening furniture making imposed on individual A in the left panel of Figure 12-2 actually falls on (i.e., is

actually paid by) individual A, and how much of the tax falls on those who demand the services of individual A? (b) On what does the incidence of a per-unit tax (i.e., the relative share of the tax burden) depend in general?

7. (a) Why can a per-hour subsidy given to individual A for tending his or her yard be shown by a downward shift in the MPC_A curve in the right panel of Figure 12-2? (b) Explain why the result of a subsidy of $3 per hour given to individual A for tending his or her yard shown by shifting the MPC_A curve down by $3 is the same as the result obtained by shifting the MPB_A curve up by $3.

8. What is the basic difference between using a subsidy to induce producers to install antipollution equipment and a tax on producers who pollute?

9. (*a*) How could a regulatory commission induce a public utility company to operate as a perfect competitor in the long run? (*b*) To what difficulty would this lead? (*c*) What compromise does a regulatory commission usually adopt?

10. Given the difficulties that the regulation of public utilities faces, would it not be better to nationalize public utilities, as some European countries have done? Explain your answer.

11. How does government decide whether to subject a very large firm to regulation or antitrust action?

12. Which are the basic antitrust laws? Why were other laws passed subsequently?

13. Has the Supreme Court interpreted size as illegal per se in enforcing the antitrust laws? Explain.

14. The settlement of the AT&T antitrust case in January 1982 involved both good news and bad news for AT&T and its customers. What were (*a*) the bad news and good news for AT&T? (*b*) the good news and bad news for users of telephone services?

15. From Figure 12-4, determine the effect of an import tariff of (*a*) $0.50 per unit and (*b*) $2 per unit.

16. What is meant by (a) border taxes and (b) Foreign Sales Corporation?

PROBLEMS

1. The perfectly competitive industry demand and supply functions for a special type of computer memory chip are, respectively,

$$Q_d = 7,000 - 5P \quad \text{and} \quad Q_s = -22,000 + 10P$$

where P is in dollars. The production of each computer chip, however, results in a pollution cost of 10 cents. Draw a figure showing the equilibrium price and quantity for this special type of memory chip, as well as the socially optimal price and quantity.

*2. Draw a figure showing the corrective tax or subsidy that would induce the industry of Problem 1 to produce the socially optimal quantity of the product. What is the net price received by the producers?

3. Suppose that the production of each computer chip in Problem 1 results in an external benefit (economy of production) of 6 cents (instead of a pollution cost of 10 cents). Draw a figure showing the socially optimal price and quantity of the computer chips, as well as the corrective tax or subsidy needed to achieve them. What is the net price received by the producers?

4. The market demand and supply functions for canned soft drinks in Smithtown are, respectively,

$$Q_d = 18,000 - 10,000P$$

and

$$Q_s = 0.6 + 0.0001P$$

where P is in dollars. The market is nearly perfectly competitive. Since the consumption of each can of soft drink, however, leads to the need to collect and recycle empty soft-drink cans, the demand curve showing the marginal social benefit of canned soft drinks has the same vertical intercept but twice the absolute slope of D. Draw a figure showing the equilibrium price and quantity, as well as the socially optimal price and quantity for cans of soft drinks in Smithtown.

*5. Draw a figure showing the corrective tax or subsidy that would induce consumers in Smithtown to consume the socially optimal number of cans of soft drinks. What is the net price now paid by consumers for each can of soft drink?

6. Suppose that each empty can of soft drink collected can be sold for scrap metal so that the demand curve showing the marginal social benefit of canned soft drinks has the same vertical intercept but half the absolute slope of *D* in Problem 4. Draw a figure showing the socially optimal price and quantity, as well as the corrective tax or subsidy needed to achieve them. What is the net price paid by consumers for each can of soft drink that they purchase?

*7. Suppose that the market demand curve for the public utility service shown in Figure 12-3 shifts to the right by 1 million units at each price level but the *LAC* and *LMC* curves remain unchanged. Draw a figure showing the price of the service that the public utility commission would set and the quantity of the service that would be supplied to the market at that price.

8. Suppose that the market demand curve for the public utility service shown in Figure 12-3 shifts to the right by 1 million units at each price level and, at the same time, the *LAC* curve of the public utility company shifts up by $1 throughout because of production inefficiencies that escape detection by the public utility commission. Draw a figure showing the price of the service that the public utility commission would set and the quantity of the service that would be supplied to the market at that price.

9. Sears sells under its trademark steel-belted tires that are manufactured by the Pneumatic Tire Company under an exclusive contract. Two years before that contract expires, the Pneumatic Tire Company merges with a nationally known firm that competes with Sears in the sale of steel-belted tires and breaks the contract with Sears. During the years before the Pneumatic Tire Company broke the contract, Sears sold on the average $100 million worth of tires with a net (i.e., after taxes, depreciation, etc.) profit margin of 30 percent. Sears expected to have the same revenue from the sale of tires in the remaining two years of the contract with the Pneumatic Tire Company, but after the latter breaks the contract and Sears starts to buy tires from another supplier, Sears's sales fall by 25 percent in the first year and by another 25 percent in the second year. Sears's net profit

margin on tire sales, however, remains at 30 percent in both years. (*a*) Indicate which antitrust law Sears could accuse the Pneumatic Tire Company of having broken, and (*b*) measure the total economic loss that Sears can allege to have sustained from the Pneumatic Tire Company's breaking its contract with Sears.

10. Suppose that the long-run marginal revenue curve for electricity in a locality intersects the long-run average cost curve for electricity at its lowest point of $0.04 per kWh and the electricity market is a regulated public utility. Determine the best price that the public utility can charge for electricity.

11. Explain why the problems arising in public-utility regulation do not arise in the case of a monopoly that is not a natural monopoly.

12. Determine whether the Justice Department would challenge a merger between two firms in an industry with 10 equal-sized firms, based on its 1984 Herfindahl-index guidelines only.

13. (Library research) Explain (*a*) in what way the U.S. trucking industry exemplified the capture theory hypothesis of government regulation prior to the passage of the *Motor Carrier Act of 1980* and (*b*) the result of the passage of the Motor Carrier Act in 1980.

*14. (Library research) During the 1970s the average rate of return on stockholders' equity in the U.S. banking industry was consistently higher than the average rate of return in other U.S. industries, while the opposite was the case in the 1980s. Identify the most important reasons for this.

15. **Integrating Problem**
   From the following figure referring to a natural monopolist, indicate (*a*) the best level of output, price, and profits per unit and in total for the monopolist, (*b*) the best level of output and price with a lump sum tax that would eliminate all the monopolist's profits, (*c*) the best level of output, price, and profits per unit and in total with a $3 per unit tax collected from the monopolist, (*d*) the best level of output and profit per unit and in total if the government sets the price of the product or service at $10. (*e*) Which is the best method of controlling monopoly power. Why? (See Figure 12-5.)

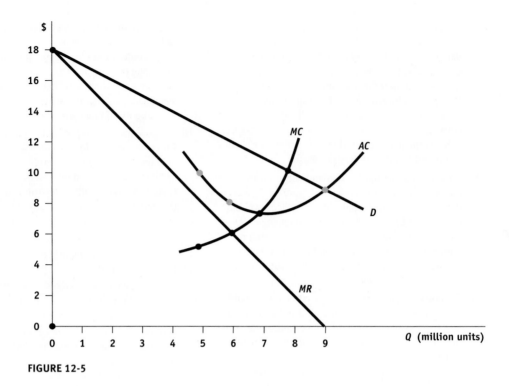

FIGURE 12-5

SUPPLEMENTARY READINGS

The topics examined in this chapter are also discussed in:

Viscusi, W. Kip, John M. Vernon, and Joseph E. Harrington, *Economics of Regulation and Antitrust* (Cambridge, Mass.: MIT Press, 2000).

For government regulations that restrict competition, see:

Buchanan, James, and G. Tullock, *The Calculus of Consent* (Ann Arbor: University of Michigan Press, 1962).

Posner, Richard, "Theories of Economic Regulation," *Bell Journal of Economics and Management Science* (Autumn 1974), pp. 335–358.

Stigler, George J., "The Theory of Economic Regulation," *Bell Journal of Economics and Management Science* (Spring 1971), pp. 3–21.

Externalities are examined in:

Bator, Francis M., "The Anatomy of Market Failure," *Quarterly Journal of Economics* (August 1958), pp. 351–379.

Coase, Ronald R., "The Problem of Social Costs," *Journal of Law and Economics* (October 1960), pp. 1–44.

Crooper, M. L., and W. E. Oats, "Environmental Economics: A Survey," *Journal of Economic Literature* (June 1992), pp. 675–740.

Gray, Wayne B., and Ronald J. Shadbegian, "Environmental Regulation, Investment Timing, and Technology Choice," *Journal of Industrial Economics* (June 1998), pp. 235–256.

Misham, Ezra J., "The Postwar Literature on Externalities: An Interpretative Essay," *Journal of Economic Literature* (March 1971), pp. 395–409.

Schmalensee, Richard, et al., "An Interim Evaluation of Sulfur Dioxide Emissions Trading," *Journal of Economic Perspectives* (Summer 1998), pp. 69–88.

For public utility regulations, see:

Averch, Harvey, and Leland Johnson, "Behavior of the Firm under Regulatory Constraint," *American Economic Review* (December 1962), pp. 1052–1069.

Kahn, Alfred E., *The Economics of Regulation* (New York: Wiley, 1971).

Phillips, Charles F., *The Regulation of Public Utilities* (Arlington, Va.: Public Utilities Report, 1984).

An evaluation of regulation and the deregulation movement is found in:

Baker, Jonathan B., "The Case for Antitrust Enforcement," *Journal of Economic Perspectives* (Fall 2003), pp. 27–50.

Crandall, Robert W., and Clifford Winston, "Does Antitrust Policy Improve Consumer Welfare? Assessing the Evidence," *Journal of Economic Perspectives* (Fall 2003), pp. 3–26.

Kahn, Alfred E., "Surprises of Airline Deregulation," *American Economic Review* (May 1988), pp. 316–322.

Peltzman, Sam, "The Economic Theory of Regulation after a Decade of Regulation," *Brookings Papers on Economic Activity* (1989), pp. 2–41.

Viscusi, W. K., "Economic Foundations of the Current Regulatory Reform Efforts," *Journal of Economic Perspectives* (Summer 1996), pp. 119–134.

Winston, Clifford, "U.S. Industry Adjustment to Economic Deregulation," *Journal of Economic Perspectives* (Summer 1998), pp. 89–110.

For regulation of international trade, see:

Fox, Eleonor M., "Antitrust Regulation across National Borders: The United States of Boeing versus the European Union of Airbus," *Brookings Review* (Winter 1998), pp. 30–32.

Salvatore, Dominick, *International Economics,* 9th ed. (Hoboken, N.J.: Wiley, 2007), chaps. 8–9.

Salvatore, Dominick, ed., *Protectionism and World Welfare* (New York: Cambridge University Press, 1993).

INTERNET SITE ADDRESSES

The Internet site for the U.S. Patent and Trademark Office is:

> http://www.uspto.gov

For pricing by Con Edison, see:

> http://www.conedison.com

For information on antitrust on the Internet, see:

> http://www.usdoj.gov/atr/index.html

For the texts of the Sherman Antitrust Act, the Clayton Act, and other U.S. antitrust laws, see:

> http://www4.law.cornell.edu/uscode/15/ch1.html

Comprehensive antitrust Internet links to the U.S. Department of Justice, the Federal Trade Commission, case summaries, journals, etc., are found at:

> http://www.findlaw.com/01topics/01antitrust/index.html

For information on the antitrust case against Microsoft and on other pending cases, see:

> http://www.usdoj.gov/atr/index.html
>
> http://www.findlaw.com/01topics/01antitrust/microsoft.html

For conditions, deregulation, and antitrust cases in the airline industry, see:

> American Airlines: http://www.aa.com
>
> U.S. Airways: http://www.usairway.com
>
> Continental Airlines: http://www.continental.com
>
> Delta Airlines: http://www.delta.com
>
> United Airlines: http://www.ual.com

For information on the companies discussed in this chapter (IBM, SBC (AT&T), Con Edison, and Microsoft), see:

> http://www.ibm.com
>
> http://www.att.com
>
> http://www.conedison.com
>
> http://www.microsoft.com

Information on international trade regulations and rulings is found on the Internet site of the World Trade Organization at:

> http://www.wto.org

CHAPTER 13   Risk Analysis

CHAPTER OUTLINE

KEY TERMS (in the order of their appearance)

Certainty	Risk neutral	Minimax regret criterion
Risk	Risk averter	Foreign-exchange rate
Uncertainty	Diminishing marginal utility	Hedging
State of nature	of money	Forward contract
Probability	Util	Futures contract
Probability distribution	Expected utility	Asymmetric information
Expected profit	Risk-adjusted discount rate	Adverse selection
Discrete probability distribution	Risk–return trade-off function	Moral hazard
Continuous probability	Risk premium	Principal–agent problem
distribution	Certainty-equivalent coefficient (α)	Golden parachute
Standard deviation (σ)	Decision tree	English auction
Variance (σ^2)	Conditional probability	First-price sealed-bid auction
Standard normal distribution	Simulation	Second-price sealed-bid auction
Coefficient of variation (V)	Sensitivity analysis	Dutch auction
Risk seeker	Maximin criterion	Winner's curse

ntil now we have examined managerial decision making under conditions of certainty. In such cases, the manager knows exactly the outcome of each possible course of action. Many managerial decisions are, indeed, made under conditions of certainty, especially in the short run. For example, suppose that the firm had borrowed $100,000 at a 7 percent interest rate on a note that still has 30 days to maturity. Suppose also that the firm has just generated $100,000 in surplus cash that it can invest in a 30-day Treasury bill with a yield of 3 percent. The manager of the firm can determine with certainty that the firm would earn $329 more by using the cash to prepay the loan.[1]

In many managerial decisions, however, the manager often does not know the exact outcome of each possible course of action. For example, the return on a long-run investment depends on economic conditions in the future, the degree of future competition, consumer tastes, technological advances, the political climate, and many other such factors about which the firm has only imperfect knowledge. In such cases, we say that the firm faces "risk" or "uncertainty." Most strategic decisions of the firm are of this type. Thus, it is essential to extend the basic model of the firm presented in Chapter 1 to include risk and uncertainty.

We begin this chapter by distinguishing between risk and uncertainty and introducing some of the concepts essential for risk analysis. Then we examine methods for measuring risk and for analyzing the manager's attitude toward risk. Subsequently, we show how to adjust the valuation model of the firm for risk, and how to use decision trees and simulation to aid complex managerial decision making subject to risk. Finally, we examine decision making under uncertainty, including that resulting from fluctuating values of foreign currencies and from lack of (or inadequate) information.

---

[1] The $329 higher earnings in prepaying the loan rather than investing in Treasury bills is obtained as follows:

$$(7\% - 3\%)(\$100,000)(30/365) = \$329$$

13-1 RISK AND UNCERTAINTY IN MANAGERIAL DECISION MAKING

Managerial decisions are made under conditions of certainty, risk, or uncertainty. **Certainty** refers to the situation where there is only one possible outcome to a decision and this outcome is known precisely. For example, investing in Treasury bills leads to only one outcome (the amount of the yield), and this is known with certainty. The reason is that there is virtually no chance that the federal government will fail to redeem these securities at maturity or that it will default on interest payments. On the other hand, when there is more than one possible outcome to a decision, risk or uncertainty is present.

Risk refers to a situation in which there is more than one possible outcome to a decision and the probability of each specific outcome is known or can be estimated. Thus, risk requires that the decision maker know all the possible outcomes of the decision and have some idea of the probability of each outcome's occurrence. For example, in tossing a coin, we can get either a head or a tail, and each has an equal (i.e., a 50–50) chance of occurring (if the coin is balanced). Similarly, investing in a stock or introducing a new product can lead to one of a set of possible outcomes, and the probability of each possible outcome can be estimated from past experience or from market studies. In general, the greater the variability (i.e., the greater the number and range) of possible outcomes, the greater is the risk associated with the decision or action.

Uncertainty is the case when there is more than one possible outcome to a decision and where the probability of each specific outcome occurring is not known or even meaningful. This may be due to insufficient past information or instability in the structure of the variables. In extreme forms of uncertainty not even the outcomes themselves are known. For example, drilling for oil in an unproven field carries with it uncertainty if the investor does not know either the possible oil outputs or their probability of occurrence.[2]

In the analysis of managerial decision making involving risk, we will use such concepts as strategy, states of nature, and payoff matrix.[3] A *strategy* refers to one of several alternative courses of action that a decision maker can take to achieve a goal. For example, a manager may have to decide on the strategy of building a large or a small plant in order to maximize profits or the value of the firm. **States of nature** refer to conditions in the future that will have a significant effect on the degree of success or failure of any strategy, but over which the decision maker has little or no control. For example, the economy may be booming, normal, or in a recession in the future. The decision maker has no control over the states of nature that will prevail in the future but the future states of nature will certainly affect the outcome of any strategy that he or she may adopt. The particular decision made will depend, therefore, on the decision maker's knowledge or estimation of how a particular future state of nature will affect the outcome or result of each particular strategy (such as investing in a large or in a small plant). Finally, a *payoff matrix* is a table that shows the possible outcomes or results of each strategy under each state of nature. For example, a payoff matrix may show the level of profit that would result if the firm builds a large or a small plant and if the economy will be booming, normal, or recessionary in the

---

[2] Although the distinction between risk and uncertainty is theoretically important, in this chapter, we follow the usual convention (when introducing this topic) of using these two terms interchangeably.

[3] The concepts of strategy and payoff matrix were already encountered in Chapter 10 in the discussion of game theory.

CASE STUDY 13-1
The Risk Faced by Coca-Cola in Changing
Its Secret Formula

On April 23, 1985, the Coca-Cola Company announced that it was changing its 99-year-old recipe for Coke. Coke is the leading soft drink in the world, and the company took an unusual risk in tampering with its highly successful product. The Coca-Cola Company felt that changing its recipe was a necessary strategy to ward off the challenge from Pepsi-Cola, which had been chipping away at Coke's market lead over the years. The new Coke, with its sweeter and less fizzy taste, was clearly aimed at reversing Pepsi's market gains. Coca-Cola spent more than $4 million to develop its new Coke, and it conducted taste tests on more than 190,000 consumers over a three-year period. These tests seemed to indicate that consumers preferred the new Coke over the old Coke by 61 percent to 39 percent. Coca-Cola then spent more than $10 million to advertise its new product.

When the new Coke was finally introduced in May 1985, there was nothing short of a consumers' revolt against the new Coke, and in what is certainly one of the most stunning multimillion-dollar about-faces in the history of marketing, the company felt compelled to bring back the old Coke under the brand name Coca-Cola Classic. The irony is that with the Classic and new Coke sold side by side, Coca-Cola regained some of the market share that it had lost to Pepsi.

Although some people believed that Coca-Cola intended all along to reintroduce the old Coke and that the whole thing was part of a shrewd marketing strategy, most marketing experts are convinced that Coca-Cola had underestimated consumers' loyalty to the old Coke. This did not come up in the extensive taste tests conducted by Coca-Cola because the consumers tested were never informed that the company intended to *replace* the old Coke with the new Coke rather than sell them side by side. This example clearly shows that even a well-conceived strategy is risky and can lead to results estimated to have a small probability of occurrence. Although Coca-Cola recuperated from the fiasco, most companies are not so lucky! In the meantime, the perennial cola battle for market supremacy between Coke and Pepsi rages on.

Source: "Coca-Cola Changes Its Secret Formula in Use for 99 Years," *The New York Times* (April 24, 1985), p. 1; "'Old' Coke Coming Back After Outcry by Faithful," *The New York Times* (July 11, 1985), p. 13; "Flops," *Business Week* (August 16, 1993), pp. 76–82; "Facing Slow Sales, Coke and Pepsi Gear Up for new Battle," *The Wall Street Journal* (April 16, 2001), p. B4; and "A Better Model? Diversified Pepsi Steals Some of Coke's Sparkle," *Financial Times* (February 28, 2005), p. 15.

future. Case Study 13-1 examines the risk that Coca-Cola faced in changing its secret formula. Case Study 13-2 then examines the biggest business failures in the United States during the past 20 years.

13-2   MEASURING RISK WITH PROBABILITY DISTRIBUTIONS

In the previous section we defined risk as the situation where there is more than one possible outcome to a decision and the probability of each possible outcome is known or can be estimated. In this section we examine the meaning and characteristics of probability distributions, and then we use these concepts to develop a precise measure of risk.

CASE STUDY 13-2
The Biggest Business Failures

Table 13-1 shows the 12 biggest business failures in the United States during the past two decades and the prebankruptcy total assets of the failing firms. Note that the largest failures occurred during and immedi-ately after the recession of 2001 and the stock market crash of 1987. The reasons that companies fail were discussed in Case Study 10-5.

TABLE 13-1   The Dozen Biggest Failures in the United States

Company	Bankruptcy Date	Total Assets (in billion dollars)
WorldCom	July 2002	$103.9
Enron Corp.	Dec. 2001	63.4
Conseco	Dec. 2002	61.4
Texaco, Inc.	April 1987	35.9
Financial Corp. of America	Sept. 1988	33.9
Refco Inc.	Oct. 2005	33.3
Global Crossing Ltd.	Jan. 2002	30.2
Pacific Gas and Electric Co.	April 2001	29.8
UAL Corp.	Dec. 2002	25.2
Delta Airlines, Inc.	Sept. 2005	21.8
Adelphia Communications	June 2002	21.5

Source: BankruptcyData.com

Probability Distributions

The **probability** of an event is the chance or odds that the event will occur. For example, if we say that the probability of booming conditions in the economy next year is 0.25, or 25 percent, this means that there is 1 chance in 4 for this condition to occur. By listing all the possible outcomes of an event and the probability attached to each, we get a **probability distribution.** For example, if only three states of the economy are possible (boom, normal, or recession) and the probability of each occurring is specified, we have a probability

TABLE 13-2   Probability Distribution of States of the Economy

State of the Economy	Probability of Occurrence
Boom	0.25
Normal	0.50
Recession	0.25
Total	1.00

TABLE 13-3	Calculation of the Expected Profits of Two Projects			
Project	(1) State of Economy	(2) Probability of Occurrence	(3) Outcome of Investment	(4) Expected Value (2) × (3)
	Boom	0.25	$600	$150
A	Normal	0.50	500	250
	Recession	0.25	400	100
		Expected profit from project A		$500
	Boom	0.25	$800	$200
B	Normal	0.50	500	250
	Recession	0.25	200	50
		Expected profit from project B		$500

distribution such as the one shown in Table 13-2. Note that the sum of the probabilities is 1, or 100 percent, since one of the three possible states of the economy must occur with certainty.

The concept of probability distributions is essential in evaluating and comparing investment projects. In general, the outcome or profit of an investment project is highest when the economy is booming and smallest when the economy is in a recession. If we multiply each possible outcome or profit of an investment by its probability of occurrence and add these products, we get the expected value or profit of the project. That is,

$$\text{Expected profit} = E(\pi) = \bar{\pi} = \sum_{i=1}^{n} \pi_i \cdot P_i \qquad [13\text{-}1]$$

where π_i is the profit level associated with outcome i, P_i is the probability that outcome i will occur, and $i = 1$ to n refers to the number of possible outcomes or states of nature. Thus, the **expected profit** of an investment is the weighted average of all possible profit levels that can result from the investment under the various states of the economy, with the probability of those outcomes or profits used as weights. The expected profit of an investment is a very important consideration in deciding whether to undertake the project or which of two or more projects is preferable.[4]

For example, Table 13-3 presents the payoff matrix of project A and project B and shows how the expected value of each project is determined. In this case the expected value of each of the two projects is $500, but the range of outcomes for project A (from $400 in recession to $600 in boom) is much smaller than for project B (from $200 in

---

[4] Although the discussion is in terms of profits and we have defined the expected profit, the concepts are general. Specifically, the expected value or mean of the possible outcomes of any strategy or experiment is given by

$$\text{Expected value of } X = E(X) = \bar{X} = \sum_{i=1}^{n} X_i \cdot P_i$$

where X_i is outcome i, P_i is the probability of outcome i, and $i = 1$ to n refers to the number of possible outcomes.

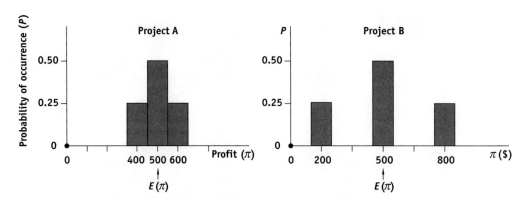

FIGURE 13-1 Probability Distribution of Profits from Project A and Project B The expected profit, $E(\pi)$, is $500 for both projects A and B, but the range of profits (and therefore the risk) is much smaller for project A than for project B. For project A the range of profits is from $400 in a recession to $600 in a boom. For project B, the range of profits is from $200 in a recession to $800 in a boom.

recession to $800 in boom). Thus, project A is less risky than and, therefore, preferable to project B.[5]

The expected profit and the variability in the outcomes of project A and project B are shown in Figure 13-1, where the height of each bar measures the probability that a particular outcome (measured along the horizontal axis) will occur. Note that the relationship between the state of the economy and profits is much tighter (i.e., less dispersed) for project A than for project B. Thus, project A is less risky than project B. Since both projects have the same expected profit, project A is preferable to project B if the manager is risk averse (the usual case).

So far, we have identified only three possible states of the economy and obtained a step-like **discrete probability distribution** of profits. As we specify more and more different states of nature (gradients of boom, normal business conditions, and recession—and their respective probabilities and profits), each bar becomes thinner and thinner and approaches a vertical line in the limit. We then approach the **continuous probability distributions** shown in Figure 13-2. Note that the probability distribution for project A is again tighter or less dispersed from its expected value than the probability distribution of project B and that it reflects the smaller risk associated with project A than with project B.[6]

---

[5] Note that the expected value of a probability distribution need not equal any of the possible outcomes (although in this case it does). The expected value is simply a weighted average of all the possible outcomes if the decision or experiment were repeated a very large number of times. Had the expected value of project A been lower than that of project B, the manager would have had to decide whether the lower expected profit from project A was compensated by its lower risk. In Section 13-3 we will show how a manager makes such decisions.

[6] With a continuous probability distribution there is theoretically an infinite number of outcomes, and so the probability of occurrence of each specific outcome is zero. We can determine, however, the probability that a particular outcome falls within a particular range, say, the profit will be $400 and $500. This is given by the area under the curve within the range of outcomes (profits) specified. How this is done is shown is Section 13-2.

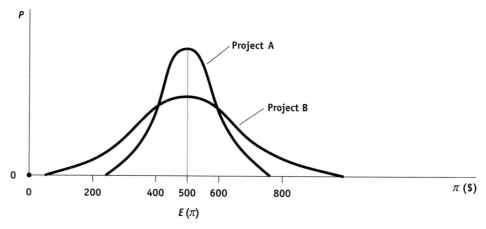

FIGURE 13-2 **Continuous Probability Distribution of Profits from Project A and Project B** By specifying many states of nature, the steplike probability distribution of profits from project A and project B of Figure 13-1 becomes smooth and continuous.

An Absolute Measure of Risk: The Standard Deviation

We have seen that the tighter or the less dispersed a probability distribution, the smaller is the risk of a particular strategy or decision. The reason is that there is a smaller probability that the actual outcome will deviate significantly from the expected value. We can measure the tightness or the degree of dispersion of a probability distribution by the standard deviation, which is indicated by the symbol σ (sigma). Thus, the **standard deviation (σ)** measures the dispersion of possible outcomes from the expected value. The smaller the value of σ, the tighter or less dispersed is the distribution, and the lower the risk.[7]

To find the value of the standard deviation (σ) of a particular probability distribution, we follow three steps:

1. Subtract the expected value or the mean ($\bar{X}$) of the distribution from each possible outcome (X_i) to obtain a set of deviations (d_i) from the expected value. That is,

$$d_i = X_i - \bar{X} \qquad [13\text{-}2]$$

2. Square each deviation, multiply the squared deviation by the probability of its expected outcome, and then sum these products. This weighted average of squared deviations from the mean is the **variance** of the distribution (σ^2). That is,

$$\text{Variance} = \sigma^2 = \sum_{i=1}^{n} (X_i - \bar{X})^2 \cdot P_i \qquad [13\text{-}3]$$

3. Take the square root of the variance to find the standard deviation (σ):

$$\text{Standard deviation} = \sigma = \sqrt{\sum_{i=1}^{n} (X_i - \bar{X})^2 \cdot P_i} \qquad [13\text{-}4]$$

---

[7] If all the outcomes were identical, then σ and risk would be zero.

under the standard normal curve corresponding to a profit of below $500) plus 0.4222 (the area between $z = 0$ and $z = 1.42$, corresponding to a profit between $500 and $600). Thus, the probability of profits being below $600 is 0.9222, or 92.22 percent. Finally, the probability of a profit higher than $600 (or lower than $400) is $1 - 0.9222$, which is 0.0778, or 7.78 percent. The probability of profit falling within any other range can be similarly found (see Problem 2, with answer at the end of the book).

A Relative Measure of Risk: The Coefficient of Variation

The standard deviation is not a good measure to compare the dispersion (relative risk) associated with two or more probability distributions with different expected values or means. The distribution with the largest expected value or mean may very well have a larger standard deviation (absolute measure of dispersion) but not necessarily a larger *relative* dispersion. To measure relative dispersion, we use the **coefficient of variation (V)**. This is equal to the standard deviation of a distribution divided by its expected value or mean. That is,

$$\text{Coefficient of variation} = V = \frac{\sigma}{\bar{X}} \qquad [13\text{-}6]$$

The coefficient of variation, thus, measures the standard deviation per dollar of expected value or mean. As such, it is dimension-free, or, in other words, it is a pure number that can be used to compare the relative risk of two or more projects. The project with the largest coefficient of variation will be the most risky.

For example, if the expected value or mean and standard deviation of project A were, respectively, $\bar{X}_A = \$5,000$ and $\sigma_A = \$707.11$ (instead of the $500 and $70.71, respectively, calculated in Tables 13-3 and 13-4) while $\bar{X}_B = \$500$ and $\sigma_B = \$212.13$ (as calculated in Tables 13-3 and 13-4), the standard deviation or absolute measure of dispersion for project A would be more than three times that for project B ($707.11 for project A compared with $212.13 for project B). However, the coefficient of variation (V) as a measure of relative dispersion or risk would still be smaller for project A than for project B. That is,

$$V_A = \frac{\sigma_A}{X_A} = \frac{\$707.11}{\$5,000} = 0.14 \qquad \text{while} \qquad V_B = \frac{\sigma_B}{X_B} = \frac{\$212.13}{\$500} = 0.42$$

Thus, project A would have less dispersion relative to its mean (i.e., it would be less risky) than project B.[9] One more specific method for measuring risk, as well as actual measures of risk, in investing or holding bonds, stocks, and foreign currencies is RiskMetrics by J. P. Morgan (see Case Study 13-3).

---

[9] Using the expected value or mean of $500 and standard deviation of $70.71 for project A found in Tables 13-3 and 13-4 to calculate the coefficient of variation for project A gives the same result as that obtained above. That is,

$$V_A = \frac{\sigma_A}{X_A} = \frac{\$70.71}{\$500} = 0.14$$

In fact, in that case, since the expected value or mean of projects A and B would be equal ($500), there would be no need to calculate the coefficient of variation to determine that project A is less risky than project B. Comparing the standard deviation of the two projects would suffice.

CASE STUDY 13-3
RiskMetrics: A Method of Measuring Value at Risk

From 1994 until 1998, J. P. Morgan, the large New York bank, offered a free service to promote *value-at-risk* (VaR) as a risk management tool. As part of the service, J. P. Morgan published daily estimates of volatility of more than 300 bond, equity, and currency prices, as well as the thousands of correlations among them. Morgan published not only the data but also the entire methodology it used in measuring risk, including all the assumptions and the equations on which it was based. Morgan believed that its system, called RiskMetrics, captured 95 percent of the risk involved in major global stock, bond, and currency markets. Morgan's aim was to establish a common standard for measuring risk that would allow comparisons and become the benchmark by which banks, corporations, and institutional investors measure risk. Other banks and investment institutions, such as Bankers Trust, Goldman Sachs, Merrill Lynch, and Lehman Brothers, also offered risk-management services to their clients, but only Morgan offered its risk calculations as well as its entire methodology to all, and for free, on the Internet, CompuServe, and Dow Jones/Telerate. In 1998 RiskMetrics became an independent company, extended the service it provided (for a fee), and went on to become the largest independent financial risk-management firm.

The importance of managing risk has sharply increased during the past decade as a result of the growing globalization of financial markets and the increasing complexity of the new financial instruments that have been created to cover such risk. Even the best risk-management strategy cannot ensure against occasional losses, but RiskMetrics can help firms or investors understand and measure the kind and amount of risks they face. For example, RiskMetrics allows a firm or investor to measure the value at risk, or the amount of money a firm or investor can lose by holding a position for a given period of time. It can also help in evaluating the performance of traders and money managers based on returns in relation to the amount of risks they assume. This is better than simply evaluating performance based on returns or risks separately, as was generally done until 1994. Thus, a firm can now use RiskMetrics to design its own risk-management system.

Many banks, corporations, and institutional investors use RiskMetrics today to design their own risk-management systems and measure the market and credit risks that they face. This represents an important attempt to overcome the "black box" feeling that often surrounds risk-management services offered to investors, and it proposes an objective benchmark for measuring and managing risk in general. This and similar value-at-risk models have led in the last few years to credit-risk models that seek to calculate the probability that any one of the firm's borrowers will default and that any number of them, or all of them, will default at the same time. Today, the two credit-risk models receiving the most attention are J. P. Morgan Chase CreditMetrics and Credit Suisse Financial Products' (CSFP) CreditRisk+.

Source: "Morgan Unveils the Way It Measures Market Risk," *The Wall Street Journal* (October 11, 1994), p. C1; "A Framework for Risk Management," *Harvard Business Review* (November–December 1994), pp. 91–102; "Model Behavior," *The Economist* (February 28, 1999), p. 80; "Total Strategies for Company-Wide Risk Control," *Financial Times* (May 9, 2000), pt. III, pp. 2–4; "A Route through the Hazards of Business," *Financial Times Special Report* (June 10, 2005), pp. 4–5; and "RiskMetrics," *News Release* (November 2, 2005).

| 13-3 | **UTILITY THEORY AND RISK AVERSION** |

Most managers, faced with two alternative projects of equal expected value of profit but different coefficients of variation or risk, will generally prefer the less risky project (i.e., the one with the smaller coefficient of variation). Although it is true that some managers may very well choose the more risky project (i.e., are **risk seekers**) and some are indifferent to risk (i.e., are **risk neutral**), most managers are **risk averters.** The reason for this is to be found in the principle of **diminishing marginal utility of money.** The meaning of diminishing, constant, and increasing marginal utility of money can be explained with the aid of Figure 13-4.

In Figure 13-4, money income or wealth is measured along the horizontal axis while the utility or satisfaction of money (measured in **utils**) is plotted along the vertical axis.[10] From the figure, we can see that $10,000 in money or wealth provides 2 utils of utility to a particular individual (point *A*), while $20,000 provides 3 utils (point *B*), 4 utils (point *C*), or 6 utils (point *D*), respectively, depending on the *total* utility of money curve for this individual being concave or facing down, a straight line, or convex or facing up. If the *total* utility curve is concave or faces down, doubling the individual's income or wealth from $10,000 to $20,000 only increases his or her utility from 2 to 3 utils, so that the *marginal* utility of money (the slope of the total utility curve) diminishes for this individual. If the

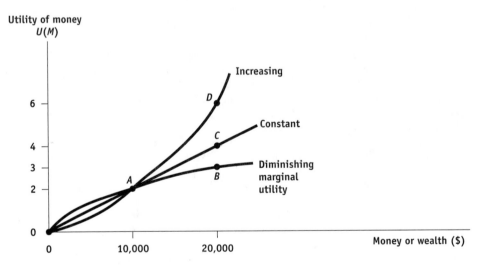

FIGURE 13-4   Diminishing, Constant, and Increasing Marginal Utility of Money   A $10,000 money income or wealth provides 2 utils of utility to a particular individual (point *A*), while $20,000 provides 3 utils (point *B*) if the total utility of money curve of the individual is concave or faces down (so that the marginal utility of money declines), 4 utils (point *C*) if the total utility curve is a straight line (so that the marginal utility is constant), and 6 utils (point *D*) if the total utility curve is convex or faces up (so that marginal utility increases). The individual would then be, respectively, a risk averter, risk neutral, or a risk seeker.

---

[10] A *util* is a fictitious unit of utility. For the moment we assume that the utility or satisfaction that a particular individual receives from various amounts of money income or wealth can be measured in terms of utils.

total utility of money curve is a straight line, doubling income also doubles utility, so that the marginal utility of money is constant. Finally, if the total utility of money curve is convex or faces up, doubling income more than doubles utility, so that the marginal utility of money income increases.

Most individuals are risk averters because their marginal utility of money diminishes (i.e., they face a total utility curve that is concave or faces down). To see why this is so, consider the offer to engage in a bet to win $10,000 if a head turns up in the tossing of a coin or to lose $10,000 if a tail comes up. The expected value of the money won or lost is

$$\text{Expected value of money} = E(M)$$
$$= 0.5(\$10,000) + 0.5(-\$10,000) \qquad [13\text{-}7]$$
$$= 0$$

Even though the expected value of such a *fair game* is zero, a risk averter (an individual facing diminishing marginal utility of money) would gain less utility by winning $10,000 than he or she would lose by losing $10,000. Starting from point A in Figure 13-4, we see that by losing $10,000, the risk-averting individual loses 2 utils of utility but gains only 1 util of utility if he or she wins $10,000. Even though the bet is fair (i.e., there is a 50–50 chance of winning or losing $10,000), the **expected utility** of the bet is negative. That is,

$$\text{Expected utility} = E(U) = 0.5(1 \text{ util}) + 0.5(-2 \text{ utils}) = -0.5 \qquad [13\text{-}8]$$

In such a case, the individual will refuse a fair bet.[11] From this, we can conclude that a risk-averting manager will not necessarily accept an investment project with positive expected value or a positive net profit. To determine whether or not the manager should accept the project, we need to know his or her utility function of money.

For example, suppose that a manager has to decide whether or not to introduce a new product that has a 40 percent probability of providing a net return (profit) of $20,000, and a 60 percent probability of resulting in a loss of $10,000. Since the *expected monetary return* of such a project is positive (see Table 13-5), a risk-neutral or a risk-seeking manager would undertake the project. However, if the manager is risk averse (the usual

TABLE 13-5 Expected Return of Project

State of Nature	(1) Probability	(2) Monetary Outcome	(3) Expected Return (1) × (2)
Success	0.40	$20,000	$8,000
Failure	0.60	−10,000	−6,000
		Expected return	$2,000

---

[11] With constant utility, $E(U) = 0.5(2 \text{ utils}) + 0.5(-2 \text{ utils}) = 0$, and the individual is risk neutral and indifferent to the bet. With increasing marginal utility, $E(U) = 0.5(4 \text{ utils}) + 0.5(-2 \text{ utils}) = 1$, and the individual is a risk seeker and would accept the bet.

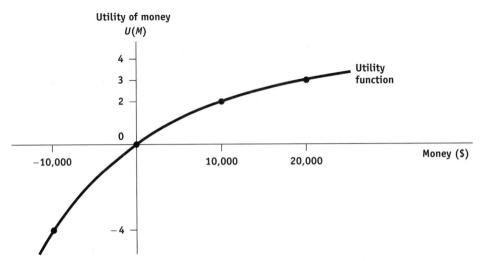

FIGURE 13-5 **The Utility Function of a Risk-Averse Manager** A project with a 40 percent probability of providing a return of $20,000 (3 utils of utility) and a 60 percent probability of resulting in a loss of $10,000 (–4 utils of utility) has an expected utility of (0.4)(3 utils) + (0.6)(–4 utils) = –1.2 utils and would not be undertaken by the manager.

TABLE 13-6	Expected Utility of Project			
	(1)	**(2)**	**(3)**	**(4)**
State of		**Monetary**	**Associated**	**Expected Utility**
Nature	**Probability**	**Outcome**	**Utility**	**(1) × (3)**
Success	0.40	$20,000	3	1.2
Failure	0.60	–10,000	–4	–2.4
			Expected utility	–1.2

case) and his or her utility function is as indicated in Figure 13-5, the manager would not undertake the same project because the *expected utility* from the project is negative (see Table 13-6). Thus, even if the expected *monetary* return is positive, a risk-averse manager will not undertake the project if the expected *utility* from the project is negative.[12] Needless to say, different managers have different utility functions and face marginal utilities of money that diminish at different rates. Case Study 13-4 utilizes the above analysis to explain why the same individual might gamble and buy insurance at the same time—a seeming contradiction.

---

[12] Only for a risk-neutral manager does maximizing the expected monetary value or return correspond to maximizing expected utility. Thus, a risk-neutral manager need not go through the difficult task of attempting to derive his or her own utility function in order to reach correct managerial decisions.

CASE STUDY 13-4
The Purchase of Insurance and Gambling by the Same Individual—A Seeming Contradiction

In the real world, we often observe individuals purchasing insurance and also gambling. For example, many people insure their homes against fire and also purchase lottery tickets. This behavior may seem contradictory. Why should the same individual act as a risk avoider (purchase insurance) and at the same time as a risk seeker (gamble)? One possible explanation for this seemingly contradictory behavior is provided by Friedman and Savage, who postulate that the total utility of money curve may look like that in Figure 13-6. This total utility curve is concave or faces down (so that the marginal utility of money diminishes) at low levels of money income, and it is convex or faces up (so that the marginal utility of

money increases) at higher levels of income. An individual with an income at or near the point of inflection on the total utility curve (point A) will find it advantageous both to spend a small amount of money to insure himself or herself against the small chance of a large loss (say, through a fire that destroys his or her home) and to purchase a lottery ticket providing a small chance of a large win. Starting with an income level at or near A', the individual would act as a risk avoider for declines in income and as a risk seeker for increases in income. Financial planners and brokers make use of these concepts in trying to assess their clients' tolerance for risk in providing financial advice.

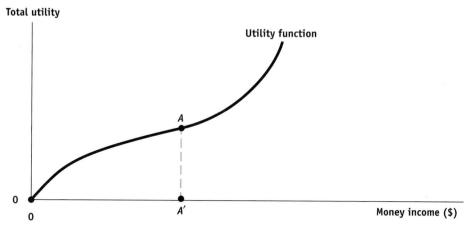

FIGURE 13-6   Utility Function of an Individual Who Purchases Insurance and Gambles   An individual whose income is at or near point A', which is directly below the point of inflection (point A) on the total-utility curve, will act as a risk averter and will spend a small amount of money to purchase insurance against the small chance of a large loss of income, and at the same time will act as a risk seeker and gamble a small amount of money (say, to purchase a lottery ticket) to have a small chance of a large win.

Source: Milton Friedman and Leonard J. Savage, "The Utility Analysis of Choices Involving Risk," *Journal of Political Economy* (August 1948); "Finding the Right Levels of Risk," *The New York Times* (November 12, 1988), p. 36; "Dealing with Risk," *Business Week* (January 17, 2000), pp. 102–112; "Gauging Investors' Appetite for Risk," *The Wall Street Journal* (September 18, 2001), p. C14; and "Against the Odds," *U.S. News & World Report* (May 23, 2005), pp. 47–53.

13-4	## ADJUSTING THE VALUATION MODEL FOR RISK

In Section 1-3 of Chapter 1 we presented the valuation model for the firm:

$$\text{Value of firm} = \sum_{t=1}^{n} \frac{\pi_t}{(1 + r)^t} \qquad [13\text{-}9]$$

where π_t refers to the expected profit in each of the n years considered, r is the appropriate discount rate used to calculate the present value of the future profits, and Σ refers to the sum of the present discounted value of future profits. In this section, we extend the above valuation model to deal with an investment project subject to risk. Two of the most commonly used methods of doing this are risk-adjusted discount rates and the certainty-equivalent approach.

Risk-Adjusted Discount Rates

One method of adjusting the valuation model of Equation 13-9 to deal with an investment project subject to risk is to use **risk-adjusted discount rates.** These reflect the manager's or investor's trade-off between risk and return, as shown, for example, by the **risk–return trade-off functions** of Figure 13-7. In the figure, risk, measured by the standard deviation of profit or returns, is plotted along the horizontal axis while the rate of return on investment is plotted along the vertical axis. The risk–return trade-off function or indifference curve labeled R (the middle curve in the figure) shows that the manager or investor is indifferent among a 10 percent rate of return on a riskless asset with $\sigma = 0$ (point A), a 20 percent rate of return on an investment with $\sigma = 1.0$ (point C), and a rate of return of 32 percent for a very risky asset with $\sigma = 1.5$ (point D).

The difference between the expected or required rate of return on a risky investment and the rate of return on a riskless asset is called the **risk premium** on the risky investment. For example, the middle risk–return trade-off function labeled R in Figure 13-7 shows that a risk premium of 4 percent is required to compensate for the level of risk given by $\sigma = 0.5$ (the 14 percent required on the risky investment with $\sigma = 0.5$ minus the 10 percent rate on the riskless asset). A 10 percent risk premium is required for an investment with risk given by $\sigma = 1.0$, and a 22 percent risk premium for an investment with $\sigma = 1.5$. The risk–return trade-off curve would be steeper (R' in Figure 13-7) for a more risk-averse manager or investor, and less steep (R'' in Figure 13-7) for a less risk-averse manager or investor. Thus, the more risk-averse manager facing curve R' would require a risk premium of 22 percent (point C') for an investment with risk given by $\sigma = 1.0$, while a less risk-averse investor with curve R'' would require a risk premium of only 4 percent for the same investment.

We can adjust the valuation model of the firm given by Equation 13-9 above to deal with an investment project subject to risk by using a risk-adjusted discount rate, as follows:

$$\text{Net present value } (NPV) \text{ of investment project} = \sum_{t=1}^{n} \frac{R_t}{(1 + k)^t} - C_0 \qquad [13\text{-}10]$$

where R_t refers to the net cash flow or return from the investment project in each of the n time periods considered, k is the risk-adjusted discount rate, Σ refers to the sum of the present discounted value of all the future net cash flows from the investment, and C_0 is the initial cost of the investment. Note that the risk-adjusted discount rate (k) in Equation 13-10 is

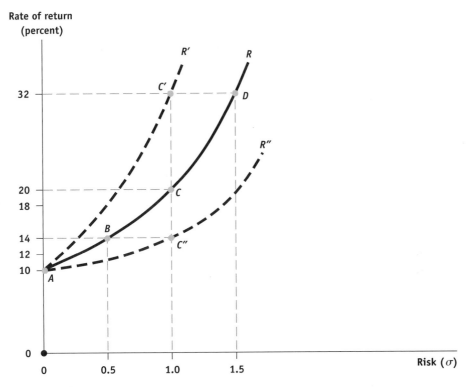

FIGURE 13-7 Risk–Return Trade-Off Functions Risk–return trade-off function or indifference curve *R* indicates that the manager or investor is indifferent among a 10 percent rate of return on a riskless asset with σ = 0 (point *A*), a 14 percent rate of return on an investment with risk of σ = 0.5 (point *B*), a 20 percent rate of return on an investment with σ = 1.0, and a 32 percent rate of return on an investment with σ = 1.5. Thus, the risk premium is 4 percent (i.e., 14 – 10 percent) at point *B*, 10 percent at point *C*, and 22 percent at point *D*. A more risk-averse manager or investor (curve *R'*) requires a higher premium, while a less risk-averse one (with curve *R''*) requires a smaller risk premium for each level of risk (σ).

equal to the risk-free discount rate (*r*) used in the valuation model of the firm of Equation 13-9 plus the risk premium involved. An investment project is undertaken if its *NPV* is greater than or equal to zero, or larger than that for an alternative project.

For example, suppose that a firm is considering undertaking an investment project that is expected to generate a net cash flow or return of $45,000 for the next five years and costs initially $100,000. If the risk-adjusted discount rate of the firm for this investment project is 20 percent, we have[13]

---

[13] The value of 2.9906 for

$$\sum_{t=1}^{5} \frac{1}{(1.20)^t}$$

in the calculations that follow is obtained from Table B-4 on the present value of an annuity in Appendix B at the end of the book. Specifically, the interest factor of 2.9906 is obtained by moving across Table B-4 until we reach the column headed 20 percent, and then moving down five rows for *n* = 5. A review of present value concepts is found in Appendix A. Students who are not familiar with present value concepts may want to read Appendix A at this time.

$$NPV = \sum_{t=1}^{5} \frac{R_t}{(1.20)^t} - C_0$$

$$= \sum_{t=1}^{5} \frac{\$45,000}{(1.20)^t} - \$100,000$$

$$= \$45,000 \left(\sum_{t=1}^{5} \frac{1}{(1.20)^t} \right) - \$100,000$$

$$= \$45,000(2.9906) - \$100,000$$

$$= \$34,577$$

If the firm perceived this investment project as much more risky and used the risk-adjusted discount rate of 32 percent to adjust for the greater risk, the *NPV* of the investment project would be instead

$$NPV = \sum_{t=1}^{5} \frac{\$45,000}{(1.32)^t} - \$100,000$$

$$= \$45,000 \left(\sum_{t=1}^{5} \frac{1}{(1.32)^t} \right) - \$100,000$$

$$= \$45,000(2.3452) - \$100,000$$

$$= \$5,534$$

With the risk-adjusted discount rate of 32 percent, the investment project is still acceptable, but the *NPV* of the project is much lower than if the firm perceived the project as less risky and used the risk-adjusted discount rate of 20 percent. A risk-adjusted discount rate of 20 percent may be appropriate for the firm for the expansion of a given line of business, while the high rate of 32 percent might be required to reflect the much higher risk involved in moving into a totally new line of business. This method, however, has the serious shortcomings that risk-adjusted discount rates are subjectively assigned by managers and investors, and variations in net cash flows or returns are not explicitly considered. This approach is most useful for the evaluation of relatively small and repetitive investment projects. A better method for adjusting the valuation model for risk is the certainty-equivalent approach.

Certainty-Equivalent Approach

The risk-adjusted discount rate presented above modified the discount rate in the denominator of the valuation model to incorporate risk. The certainty-equivalent approach, on the other hand, uses a risk-free discount rate in the denominator and incorporates risk by modifying the numerator of the valuation model, as follows:

$$NPV = \sum_{t=1}^{n} \frac{\alpha R_t}{(1+r)^t} - C_0 \qquad [13\text{-}11]$$

where R_t is the *risky* net cash flow or return from the investment (as in Equation 13-10), r is the *risk-free* discount rate, and α is the **certainty-equivalent coefficient.**[14] The latter is the certain sum (i.e., the sum received with certainty that is equivalent to the expected risky sum or return on the project) divided by the expected risky sum. That is,

$$\alpha = \frac{\text{equivalent certain sum}}{\text{expected risky sum}} = \frac{R_t^*}{R_t} \qquad [13\text{-}12]$$

Specifically, the manager or investor must specify the certain sum that yields to him or her the same utility or satisfaction of (i.e., that is equivalent to) the expected risky sum or return from the investment. The value of α ranges from 0 to 1 for a risk-averse decision maker and reflects his or her attitude toward risk. A value of 0 for α means that the project is viewed as too risky by the decision maker to offer any effective return. On the other hand, a value of 1 for α means that the project is viewed as risk-free by the decision maker. Thus, the smaller the value of α, the greater is the risk perceived by the manager for the project.

For example, if the manager or investor regarded the sum of $36,000 with certainty as equivalent to the expected (risky) net cash flow or return of $45,000 per year for the next five years (on the investment project discussed in the previous section and costing initially $100,000), the value of α is

$$\alpha = \frac{\$36,000}{\$45,000} = 0.8$$

Using the risk-free discount rate of 10 percent, we can then find the net present value of the investment project, as follows[15]:

$$
\begin{aligned}
NPV &= \sum_{t=1}^{n} \frac{\alpha R_t}{(1+r)^t} - C_0 \\
&= \sum_{t=1}^{5} \frac{(0.8)(\$45,000)}{(1.10)^t} - \$100,000 \\
&= \$36,000 \left[\sum_{t=1}^{5} \frac{1}{(1.10)^t} \right] - \$100,000 \\
&= \$36,000(3.7908) - \$100,000 \\
&= \$36,468.80
\end{aligned}
\qquad [13\text{-}13]
$$

---

[14] The other symbols have the same meaning as before.

[15] The interest factor of 3.7908 for

$$\sum_{t=1}^{5} \frac{1}{(1.10)^t}$$

in the calculations that follow is obtained from Table B-4 in Appendix B at the end of the book by moving across the table until we reach the column headed 10 percent, and then moving down five rows for $n = 5$.

This is close to the result obtained by using the risk-adjusted discount rate of 20 percent in the previous section. If, on the other hand, the firm perceived the project as much more risky and applied the certainty-equivalent coefficient of 0.62, we would have

$$NPV = \sum_{t=1}^{5} \frac{(0.62)(\$45,000)}{(1.10)^t} - \$100,000$$

$$= \$27,900 \left[\sum_{t=1}^{5} \frac{1}{(1.10)^t} \right] - \$100,000$$

$$= \$27,900(3.7908) - \$100,000$$

$$= \$5,763.32$$

This is close to the result obtained by using the risk-adjusted discount rate of 32 percent in the previous section. Case Study 13-5 examines the methods that U.S. firms actually used to adjust the valuation model for risk.

CASE STUDY 13-5
Adjusting the Valuation Model for Risk in the Real World

A study by Gitman and Forrester reported the results of a survey that they conducted on the capital budgeting techniques used by U.S. firms. Using a sample of 268 major U.S. firms, the authors asked, among other things, whether the firms did take risk into consideration in their investment decisions, and, if so, which method they used. Of the 103 respondents (thus giving a response rate of 38 percent), 71 percent answered that they did take risk explicitly into consideration in their investment decisions, while 29 percent answered that they did not. Of the respondents that answered that they did take risk explicitly into consideration in their investment decisions, 43 percent indicated that they used the risk-adjusted discount rate method, and 26 percent answered that they used the certainty-equivalent approach. The remainder of 31 percent of the respondents indicated that they used other more subjective methods. Thus, the risk-adjusted discount rate method appears to be the most common method that major firms use to deal with risk. This is not surprising in view of the fact that the risk-adjusted discount rate method is one of the easiest approaches available for dealing with risk. Today, most firms take risk explicitly into consideration in their investment decisions and use more sophisticated methods of measuring and dealing with risk (see Case Study 13-3).

Source: L. G. Gitman and J. R. Forrester, "A Survey of Capital Budgeting Techniques Used by Major U.S. Firms" *Financial Management* (Fall 1977), pp. 66–71; "Risky Business," *Financial Executive* (September/October 1999), pp. 30–32; "Dealing with Risk," *Business Week* (January 17, 2000), pp. 102–112; "Total Strategies for Company-Wide Risk Control," *Financial Times* (May 9, 2000), pt. III, pp. 2–4; and "A Route through the Hazards of Business," *Financial Times Special Report* (June 10, 2005), pp. 4–5.

| 13-5 | **OTHER TECHNIQUES FOR INCORPORATING RISK INTO DECISION MAKING** |

Most real-world managerial decisions are much more complex than the ones already examined. Two methods of organizing and analyzing these more complex, real-world situations involving risk are decision trees and simulation. These are examined in turn.

Decision Trees

Managerial decisions involving risk are often made in stages, with subsequent decisions and events depending on the outcome of earlier decisions and events. A **decision tree** shows the sequence of possible managerial decisions and their expected outcomes under each set of circumstances or states of nature. Since the sequence of decisions and events is represented graphically as the branches of a tree, this technique has been named *decision tree*. The construction of decision trees begins with the earliest decision and moves forward in time through a series of subsequent events and decisions. At every point that a decision must be made or a different event can take place, the tree branches out until all the possible outcomes have been depicted. In the construction of decision trees, boxes are used to show decision points, while circles show states of nature. Branches coming out of boxes depict the alternative strategies of courses of action open to the firm. On the other hand, the branches coming out of circles show the various states of nature (and their probability of occurrence) that affect the outcome.

For example, Figure 13-8 shows a decision tree that a firm can use to determine whether to adopt a high-price or a low-price strategy (the box on the left of the figure). Since the firm has control over this strategy (i.e., whether to charge a high or a low price), no probabilities are attached to these branches (see section 1 of the figure). Next (section 2 of the figure) is the competitors' reaction to the firm's pricing strategy. This is an uncontrollable event for the firm, and so probabilities are attached to each possible price response of competitors. The firm estimates that if it adopts a high-price strategy (the top branch of the figure), there is a 60 percent probability that competitors will respond with a high price of their own, and 40 percent that they will respond with a low price. On the other hand, if the firm adopts a low-price strategy (the bottom branch of the figure), there is a 20 percent probability that competitors will respond with a high price, and 80 percent with a low price. Note that probabilities are entered in parentheses on the appropriate branches, and the sum of the probabilities of competitors' responses to each pricing strategy of the firm adds up to 1.0 or 100 percent.

Next we see that each pricing strategy on the part of the firm and the competitors' price response (reaction) can occur under three states of the economy: boom, normal, and recession (section 3 of the figure), with probabilities of 30, 50, and 20 percent, respectively. Thus, we have 12 possible outcomes, 6 for the high-price strategy of the firm (the top branch of the figure), and 6 for the low-price strategy (the bottom branch). The probability of each of these 12 possible outcomes is shown in section 4 of the figure. The probability of occurrence of each possible outcome is a joint or **conditional probability** and is obtained by multiplying the probability of a particular state of the economy by the probability of a specific price reaction of competitors. For example, the probability of both booming conditions in the economy and a high price by competitors is equal to the probability of

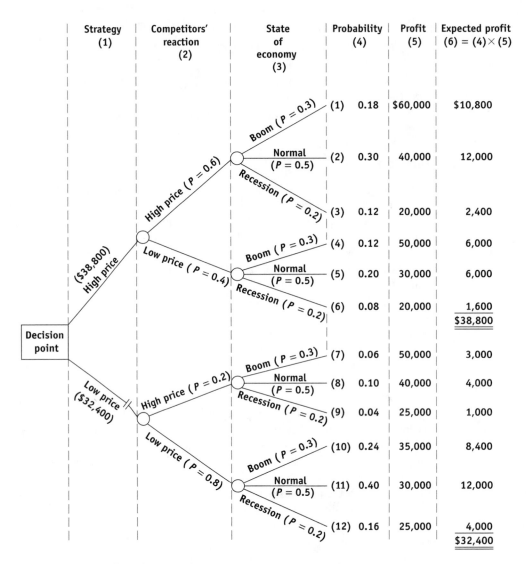

Strategy (1)	Competitors' reaction (2)	State of economy (3)		Probability (4)	Profit (5)	Expected profit (6) = (4) × (5)
		Boom (P = 0.3)	(1)	0.18	$60,000	$10,800
	High price (P = 0.6)	Normal (P = 0.5)	(2)	0.30	40,000	12,000
		Recession (P = 0.2)	(3)	0.12	20,000	2,400
		Boom (P = 0.3)	(4)	0.12	50,000	6,000
($38,800) High price	Low price (P = 0.4)	Normal (P = 0.5)	(5)	0.20	30,000	6,000
		Recession (P = 0.2)	(6)	0.08	20,000	1,600
						$38,800
		Boom (P = 0.3)	(7)	0.06	50,000	3,000
	High price (P = 0.2)	Normal (P = 0.5)	(8)	0.10	40,000	4,000
		Recession (P = 0.2)	(9)	0.04	25,000	1,000
Low price ($32,400)		Boom (P = 0.3)	(10)	0.24	35,000	8,400
	Low price (P = 0.8)	Normal (P = 0.5)	(11)	0.40	30,000	12,000
		Recession (P = 0.2)	(12)	0.16	25,000	4,000
						$32,400

Decision point

FIGURE 13-8   Decision Tree for Pricing Decisions   Starting at the left of the figure, we see that the firm can adopt either a high- or a low-price strategy (section 1 of the figure). Each of these strategies can lead to either a high- or a low-price response (reaction) by competitors, each with a particular probability of occurrence (section 2). Each strategy and the competitors' reaction can take place under each of three possible states of the economy (boom, normal, or recession) with specific probabilities of occurrence (section 3). The probability of each joint outcome is obtained by multiplying the probability of each state of the economy by the probability of each competitor's price response. The expected profit of each outcome (section 6) is then obtained by multiplying the probability of occurrence by its associated profit. Assuming that the firm already considered the difference in risk in estimating the net present value of profits of the two strategies, it will choose the high-price strategy. The low-price strategy is, thus, slashed off as suboptimal.

boom (0.3) times the probability of a high price by competitors (0.6). Thus, the probability of both boom and a high price by competitors (outcome 1) is 0.18, or 18 percent. Similarly, the probability of both normal conditions in the economy and a high competitors' price (outcome 2) is given by 0.5 times 0.6, or 0.3 or 30 percent, and so on.

Section 5 of the figure then gives the estimated net present value of the profits of the firm associated with each of the 12 possible outcomes. By multiplying the probability of occurrence of each possible outcome by the profit associated with that particular outcome, we get the corresponding expected profit (section 6 of the figure). For example, the expected profit of boom and high competitors' price (outcome 1) is equal to the joint or conditional probability of occurrence (0.18) times the profit ($60,000), or $10,800. Similarly, the expected profit of outcome 2 (normal business conditions and high competitors' price) is equal to the probability of occurrence (0.30) times the profit ($40,000), or $12,000, and so on. By then adding the expected profit associated with each of the first 6 outcomes, we get the expected profit of $38,800 associated with the firm's high-price strategy (and noted in parentheses under this strategy in section 1 of the figure). Similarly, by adding all the expected profits associated with the last 6 outcomes, we get the expected profit of $32,400 associated with the firm's low-price strategy (and noted in parentheses under this strategy). Assuming that the firm already considered the difference in risk in estimating the net present value of profits of the two strategies, it will choose the high-price strategy. The low-price strategy is, thus, slashed off (in section 1) on the decision tree to indicate that it is suboptimal.

Several additional things need to be pointed out with respect to the above decision tree. First, the sum of the joint probabilities of the 6 possible outcomes (outcomes 1 through 6) resulting from the firm's high-price strategy is equal to 1, and so is the sum of the joint probabilities of the 6 possible outcomes (outcomes 7 through 12) resulting from the firm's low-price strategy. Second, while the construction of a decision tree starts at the left with the earliest decision and moves forward in time to the right through a series of subsequent events and decisions, the analysis of a decision tree begins at the right at the end of the sequence and works backward to the left. Third, while in the decision tree of Figure 13-8, the firm makes only one decision (the box leading to the high- and low-price strategies at the beginning of the tree at the left), there can be several decision points in between several states of nature (see the decision tree for Problem 10). Indeed, for many real-world business decisions, decision trees can become much more elaborate and complex than the one shown in Figure 13-8.

Simulation

Another method for analyzing complex, real-world decision-making situations involving risk is **simulation.** The first step in simulation is the construction of a mathematical model of the managerial decision-making situation that we seek to simulate. For example, an aerospace engineer constructs a miniature model plane and wind tunnel to test the strength and resistance of the model plane to change in wind speed and direction. This modeling mimics the essential features of the real-world situation and allows the engineer to simulate the effect of changes in wind speed and direction on a real aircraft. Similarly, the firm might construct a model for the strategy of expanding the output of a commodity. The model would specify in mathematical (i.e., equational) form the relationship between the output of the commodity and its price; output, input prices, and costs of production; output and depreciation;

output, selling costs, and revenue; output, revenues, and taxes; and so on. The manager could then substitute likely values or best estimates for each variable into the model and estimate the firm's profit. By then varying the value of each variable substituted into the model, the firm can get an estimate of the effect of the change in the variable on the output of the model or profit of the firm. This simplest type of simulation is often referred to as **sensitivity analysis.**

In full-fledged simulation models, the model builder needs to estimate or specify the probability distribution of each variable in the model. For example, in order to fully simulate the strategy to expand output, the firm needs the probability distribution of output, commodity prices, input prices, costs of production, depreciation, selling costs, revenue, taxes, and so on. Randomly selected values of each variable of the model are then fed into the computer program to generate the present value of the firm's profits. This process is then repeated a large number of times. Each time (i.e., for each computer run), a new randomly selected value for each variable is fed into the computer program, and the net present value of the firm's profit is recorded. A large number (often in the hundreds) of such trials, or *iterations,* are conducted, so as to generate the probability distribution of the firm's profit. The probability distribution of the firm's profits so generated can then be used to calculate the expected profit of the firm and the standard deviation of the distribution of profits (as a measure of risk). Finally, the firm can use this information to determine the optimal strategy to adopt (as shown earlier in this chapter).

Full-scale simulation models are very expensive and are generally used only for large projects when the decision-making process is too complex to be analyzed by decision trees. The simulation techniques are very powerful and useful, however, because they explicitly and simultaneously consider all the interactions among the variables of the model. For the evaluation of alternative business strategies involving risk where millions of dollars are involved, computer simulation is becoming more and more widely used today.

13-6   DECISION MAKING UNDER UNCERTAINTY

In Section 13-1, we defined *uncertainty* as the case where there is more than one possible outcome to a decision and the probability of each specific outcome occurring is not known or even meaningful. As a result, decision making under uncertainty is necessarily subjective. Some specific decision rules are available, however, if the decision maker can identify the possible states of nature and estimate the payoff for each strategy. Two specific decision rules applicable under uncertainty are the maximin criterion and the minimax regret criterion. These are discussed next, as are some more informal and less precise methods of dealing with uncertainty.

The Maximin Criterion

The **maximin criterion** postulates that the decision maker should determine the worst possible outcome of each strategy and then pick the strategy that provides the best of the worst possible outcomes. The maximin criterion can be illustrated by applying it to the example in Table 13-5, where the firm could follow the strategy of introducing a new product that would provide a return of $20,000 if it succeeded or lead to a loss of $10,000 if it failed, or

TABLE 13-7 **Payoff Matrix for Maximin Criterion**			

	State of Nature		
Strategy	**Success**	**Failure**	**Maximin**
Invest	$20,000	−$10,000	−$10,000
Do not invest	0	0	0*

* The strategy of not investing.

choose not to invest in the venture, with zero possible return or loss. This matrix is shown in Table 13-7. Note that no probabilities are given in Table 13-7 because we are now dealing with uncertainty. That is, we now assume that the manager does not know and cannot estimate the probability of success and failure of investing in the new product. Therefore, he or she cannot calculate the expected payoff or return and risk of the investment.

To apply the maximin criterion to this investment, the manager first determines the worst possible outcome of each strategy (row). This is −$10,000 in the case of failure for the investment strategy and 0 for the strategy of not investing. These worst-possible outcomes are recorded in the last or maximin column of the table. Then, he or she picks the strategy that provides the best (maximum) of the worst (minimum) possible outcomes (i.e., maximin). This is the strategy of not investing, which is indicated by the asterisk next to its zero return or loss in the last column of the table (compared with the loss of $10,000 in the case of failure with the introduction of the new product). Thus, the maximin criterion picks the strategy of not investing, which has the maximum of the minimum payoffs.

By examining only the most pessimistic outcome of each strategy for the purpose of avoiding the worst of all possible outcomes, it is obvious that the maximin criterion is a very conservative decision rule and that the decision maker using it views the world pessimistically. This criterion is appropriate, however, when the firm has a very strong aversion to risk, as, for example, when the survival of a small firm depends on avoiding losses. The maximin criterion is also appropriate in the case of oligopoly, where the actions of one firm affect the others. Then, if one firm lowers its price, it can expect the others to soon lower theirs, thus reducing the profits of all.

The Minimax Regret Criterion

Another specific decision rule under uncertainty is the **minimax regret criterion.** This postulates that the decision maker should select the strategy that minimizes the maximum regret or opportunity cost of the wrong decision, whatever the state of nature that actually occurs. Regret is measured by the difference between the payoff of a given strategy and the payoff of the best strategy *under the same state of nature.* The rationale for measuring regret this way is that if we have chosen the best strategy (i.e., the one with the largest payoff) for the particular state of nature that has actually occurred, then we have no regret. But if we have chosen any other strategy, the regret is the difference between the payoff of the best strategy under the specific state of nature that has occurred and the payoff of the strategy chosen. After determining the maximum regret for each strategy under each state of nature, the decision maker then chooses the strategy with the minimum regret value.

TABLE 13-8	Payoff and Regret Matrices for the Maximum Regret Criterion				
	State of Nature		Regret Matrix		
Strategy	Success	Failure	Success	Failure	Maximum Regret
Invest	$20,000	$ –10,000	$ 0	$10,000	$10,000*
Do not invest	0	0	20,000	0	20,000

* The strategy with the minimum regret value.

To apply the minimax regret criterion, the decision maker must first construct a regret matrix from the payoff matrix. For example, Table 13-8 presents the payoff and regret matrices for the investment problem of Table 13-5 that we have been examining. The regret matrix is constructed by determining the maximum payoffs for each state of nature (column) and then subtracting each payoff in the same column from that figure. These differences are the measures of regrets. For example, on one hand, if the manager chooses to invest in the product and the state of nature that occurs is the one of success, he or she has no regret because this is the correct strategy. Thus, the regret value of zero is appropriately entered at the top of the first column in the regret matrix in Table 13-8. On the other hand, if the firm had chosen not to invest, so that it had a zero payoff under the same state of nature of success, the regret is $20,000. This regret value is entered at the bottom of the first column of the regret matrix. Moving to the state of failure column in the payoff matrix, we see that the best strategy (i.e., the one with the largest payoff) is not to invest. This has a payoff of zero. Thus, the regret value of this strategy is zero (the bottom of the second column in the regret matrix). If the firm undertook the investment under the state of nature of failure, it would incur a loss and a regret of $10,000 (the top of the second column of the regret matrix). Note that the regret value for the best strategy under each state of nature is always zero and that the other regret values in the regret matrix must necessarily be positive since we are always subtracting smaller payoffs from the largest payoff under each state of nature (column).

After constructing the regret matrix (with the maximum regret for each strategy under each state of nature), the decision maker then chooses the strategy with the minimum regret value. In our example, this is the strategy of investing, which has the minimum regret value of $10,000 (indicated by the asterisk in the maximum regret column of Table 13-8). This compares with the maximum regret of $20,000 resulting from the strategy of not investing. Thus, while the best strategy for the firm according to the maximin criterion is not to invest, the best strategy according to the minimax regret criterion is to invest. The choice as to which of these two decision rules the firm might apply under conditions of uncertainty depends on the firm's objectives and on the particular investment decision that it faces.

Other Methods of Dealing with Uncertainty

Besides the above formal investment criteria, there are a number of less formal methods that are commonly used by decision makers to reduce uncertainty or the dangers arising from uncertainty. Some of these are the acquisition of additional information, referral to authority, attempting to control the business environment, and diversification. We now briefly examine each of these in turn.

Decision makers often attempt to deal with uncertainty by gathering additional information. This can go a long way toward reducing the uncertainty surrounding a particular strategy or event and the dangers arising from it. Gathering more information is costly, however, and the manager should treat it as any other investment. That is, as pointed out in optimization analysis (see Section 2-3), the manager should continue to gather information until the marginal benefit (return) from it is equal to the marginal cost.

The decision maker can sometimes deal with uncertainty by requesting the opinion of a particular authority (such as the Internal Revenue Service on tax questions, the Securities and Exchange Commission on financial investments, the Labor Relations Board on labor questions, or a particular professional association on matters of its particular competence). Although this might remove uncertainty on some specific questions, one could hardly expect referrals to authority to eliminate the uncertainty inherent in most managerial decisions, especially those regarding long-term investments.

Another method by which decision makers sometimes seek to deal with uncertainty is by trying to control the business environment in which they operate. Thus, firms often attempt to gain monopoly control over a product by means of patents, copyrights, exclusive franchises, and so on. Competition through imitation as well as antitrust laws, however, severely limit firms' attempts to gain monopoly power, especially in the long run.

Diversification in the types of products produced, in the composition of security portfolios, and in different lines of business by a conglomerate corporation is another important method by which investors attempt to reduce risk. In such cases, if the demand for one product, the return on one particular asset, or the profit on one line of business falls, then the existence of the firm, the profitability of the entire portfolio, and the survival of the corporation, respectively, are not endangered. Diversification is an example of the old saying, "Don't put all your eggs in one basket," and it is a common way of dealing with uncertainty (see Case Study 13-6).

CASE STUDY 13-6
Spreading Risks in the Choice of a Portfolio

Since investors are risk averse, on the average, they will hold a more risky portfolio (stocks and bonds) only if it provides a higher return. Suppose for simplicity that there exist only two assets, with risk and return given by points E and F in Figure 13-9. If the risk of assets E and F are independent of each other, the investor can choose any mixed portfolio of assets E and F shown on the frontier or curve ECF.

To understand the shape of frontier ECF, note that the return on a mixed portfolio will be between the return on asset E and on asset F alone, depending on the particular combination of the two assets in the portfolio. As far as risk is concerned, there are portfolios (such as that indicated by point C) on frontier ECF that have lower risks than those composed exclusively of either asset E or asset F. The reason for this can be gathered by assuming that the probability of a low return is .50 on asset E and .25 on asset F, and that, for the moment, we take the probability of a low return as a measure of risk. If these probabilities are independent of each other, the probability of a low return on both assets E and F at the same time is $(.50)(.25) = .125$, which is smaller than for either asset E or F separately.

Continued . . .

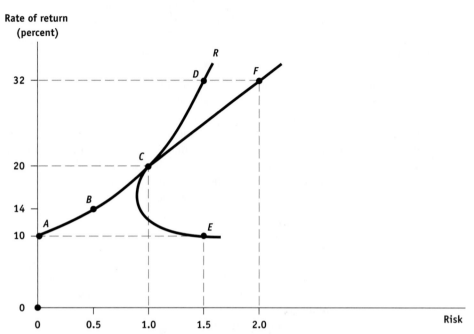

FIGURE 13-9   Choosing a Portfolio   The risk–return trade-off function or indifference curve R is the same as in Figure 13-7. It shows the various risk–return trade-off combinations among which the investor is indifferent. On the other hand, frontier ECF represents the combinations of risk and return that are obtainable with mixed portfolios of asset E and asset F, with independent risk. The optimum portfolio for the investor is represented by point C, where the risk–return trade-off function or indifference curve R is tangent to frontier ECF.

Given the risk–return trade-off function or indifference curve R in Figure 13-9, we can see that the optimum portfolio for this investor is the mixed portfolio indicated by point C in the figure, where risk–return indifference curve R is tangent to frontier ECF. Indeed, market evidence shows that a well-diversified portfolio containing various mixes of stocks, bonds, Treasury bills, real estate, and foreign securities can even out a lot of the ups and downs of investing without sacrificing much in the way of returns. Of course, the type of portfolio that an investor actually chooses depends on his/her tolerance for risk.

Source: H. M. Markowitz, "Portfolio Selection," *Journal of Finance* (March 1952), pp. 77–91; "What's Your Risk Tolerance?" *The Wall Street Journal* (January 23, 1998), p. CIW; "Dealing with Risk," *Business Week* (January 17, 2000), pp. 102–112; "Gauging Investor's Appetite for Risk," *The Wall Street Journal* (September 18, 2001), p. C14; "Just How Risky Is Your Portfolio?" *Fortune* (November 26, 2001), pp. 219–224; and "Why Do Stocks Pay So Much More than Bonds?" *The New York Times* (February 26, 2006), p. 4.

13-7   FOREIGN-EXCHANGE RISKS AND HEDGING

Portfolios with domestic and foreign securities usually enjoy lower overall volatility and higher dollar returns than portfolios with U.S. securities only (see Case Study 13-7). Many experts have traditionally recommended as much as 40 percent of a portfolio to be in

CASE STUDY 13-7
How Foreign Stocks Have Benefited a Domestic Portfolio

Foreign stocks provided higher returns and higher risks in comparison to U.S. stocks over the 1984–1994 decade. Therefore, a portfolio that included domestic and foreign stocks faced lower risks and higher returns than a portfolio that included only domestic stocks. This is shown by Figure 13-10. The figure shows that a portfolio that included only (i.e., 100 percent) U.S. stocks faced relatively low volatility (measured by the standard deviation as a measure of risk) and provided an average annual dollar rate of return of about 15 percent from June 1984 to June 1994. A portfolio that included 20 percent foreign and 80 percent U.S. stocks would have provided a lower volatility and an average annual return of 16 percent over the same 10 years. For about the same volatility but with 40 percent foreign stocks, the portfolio would have given an average annual rate of return of almost 17 percent. Finally, a portfolio of

100 percent foreign stocks would have provided an average annual dollar rate of return of over 18 percent but with much higher volatility (risk).

From 1995 to 1998, the U.S. stock market did much better than most foreign stock markets, and so a diversified portfolio that included domestic and foreign stocks generally provided lower risks but not higher returns than a portfolio that included only U.S. stocks. Note that with a diversified portfolio that includes foreign stocks, the investor needs to cover the foreign exchange risks that arise from first having to exchange the domestic currency for the foreign currency (in order to purchase the foreign stocks) and subsequently from the need to convert the foreign currency back into the domestic currency when the investor sells the foreign stock and repatriates his/her capital. From 1999 to 2005, foreign stocks have generally outperformed U.S. stocks in dollar terms.

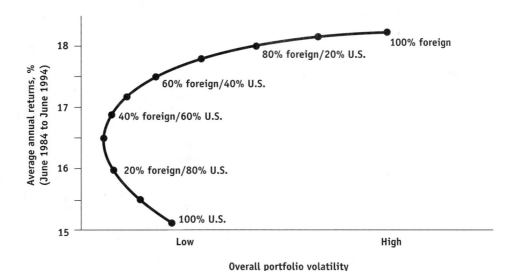

FIGURE 13-10   Average Return and Risk for Portfolios of U.S. and Foreign Stocks

Source: "Three Steps to Intelligent Overseas Investing," *The Wall Street Journal* (October 13, 1994), p. C3; "Going Global: Is It Time to Take the Plunge?" *Business Week* (April 6, 1998), pp. 136–138; "World Markets Stumble, Leaving Investors Cautious," *The Wall Street Journal* (January 2, 2002), p. R21; and "How Worldly Is Your Portfolio?" *Business Week* (June 27, 2005), pp. 96–102.

foreign securities. Investing in foreign securities, however, gives rise to a foreign-exchange risk because the foreign currency can depreciate or decrease in value during the time of the investment.[16]

For example, suppose that the return on European Monetary Union (EMU) securities is 15 percent, compared with 10 percent at home. As a U.S. investor, you might then want to invest part of your portfolio in EMU. To do so, however, you must first exchange dollars for euros (€), the currency of the EMU, in order to make the investment. If the **foreign-exchange rate** is $1 to the euro (that is, $1/€1), you can, for example, purchase €10,000 of EMU securities for $10,000. In a year, however, the exchange rate might be $0.90/€1, indicating a 10 percent depreciation of the euro (i.e., each euro now buys 10 percent fewer dollars). In that case, you will earn 15 percent on your investment in terms of euros, but lose 10 percent on the foreign-exchange transaction, for a net *dollar* gain of only 5 percent (compared with 10 percent on U.S. securities). Of course, the exchange rate at the end of the year might be $1.10/€1, which means that the euro appreciated by 10 percent, or that you would get 10 percent more dollars per euro. In that case, you would earn 15 percent on the euro investment *plus* another 10 percent on the foreign-exchange transaction. As an investor (rather than a speculator), however, you would probably want to avoid the risk of a large foreign-exchange loss, and you would not invest in the EMU unless you can hedge or cover the foreign-exchange risk.

Hedging refers to the covering of a foreign-exchange risk. Hedging is usually accomplished with a **forward contract.** This is an agreement to purchase or sell a specific amount of a foreign currency at a rate specified today for delivery at a specific future date. For example, suppose that a U.S. exporter expects to receive €1 million in 3 months. At today's exchange rate of $1/€1, the exporter expects to receive $1 million in three months. To avoid the risk of a large dollar depreciation by the time the exporter is to receive payment (and thus receive much fewer dollars than anticipated), the exporter hedges his foreign-exchange risk. He does so by selling €1 million forward at today's forward rate for delivery in three months, so as to coincide with the receipt of the €1 million from his exports. Even if today's forward rate is $0.99/€1, the exporter willingly "pays" 1 cent per euro to avoid the foreign-exchange risk. In 3 months, when the U.S. exporter receives the €1 million, he will be able to immediately exchange it for $990,000 by fulfilling the forward contract (and thus avoid a possible large foreign-exchange loss). An importer avoids the foreign-exchange risk by doing the opposite (see Problem 13).

Hedging can also be accomplished with a **futures contract.** This is a standardized forward contract for *predetermined quantities* of the currency and *selected calendar dates* (e.g., for €25,000 for March 15 delivery). As such, futures contracts are more liquid than forward contracts. There is a forward market in many currencies and a futures market in the world's most important currencies (U.S. dollar, euro, Japanese yen, British pound, Swiss franc, and Canadian dollar). Futures markets exist not only in currencies but also in many other financial instruments or derivatives (a broad class of transactions whose value is based on, or derived from, a financial market like stocks or interest rates, as well as currencies) and commodities (corn, oats, soybeans, wheat, cotton; cocoa, coffee, orange juice; cattle, hogs, pork bellies; copper, gold, silver, and platinum). Hedging in forward or futures

---

[16] D. Salvatore, *International Economics,* 8th ed. (Hoboken, N.J.: John Wiley & Sons, 2004), chap. 14.

markets reduces transaction costs and risks and increases the volume of domestic and foreign trade in the commodity, currency, or other financial instrument. Of course, forward and futures contracts can also be used for speculation, where they can lead to very large wins or huge losses (see Case Study 13-8).

CASE STUDY 13-8
Information, Risk, and the Collapse of Long-Term Capital Management

A company known as Long-Term Capital Management (LTCM) collapsed in September 1998 as a result of massive speculative bets gone wrong in the high-risk and secretive world of hedge funds. Investors in LTCM had little or no information on the fund's investment strategy and no idea of its huge leverage (the ratio of borrowed funds to the firm's capital).

LTCM was created by John W. Meriwether when the famous bond trader left Salomon Brothers in 1994. The bulk of LTCM's (speculative) investments were *convergence trades,* or gambles that interest rate spreads between risky bonds (e.g., mortgage-backed securities) and low-risk bonds (U.S., Japanese, and European government securities) had widened beyond a sustainable level and would soon narrow and return to more normal spreads. The actual investment strategy used was based on the asset-pricing model (see Section 14-4) developed by Nobel Prize winners Myron Scholes and Robert Merton, both of whom were also part of LTCM's management team. At the beginning of 1998, with capital of $4.8 billion, LTCM managed a balance-sheet position of $120 billion in borrowed funds, implying a leverage ratio of 25, on derivative contracts with a total gross notional (book) value of $1.3 trillion (about the size of Britain's GDP). The returns to LTCM's investors (a restricted number of wealthy individuals and institutions, each investing a minimum of $10 million) were 43 percent in 1995, 41 percent in 1996, and 20 percent in 1997. But then the trouble started.

Contrary to LTCM's expectations, interest rate spreads widened throughout 1998, first as a result of the financial crisis in Southeast Asia (Thailand, Korea, Malaysia, Indonesia, and the Philippines) and then (in the summer of 1998) as a result of the financial and economic collapse of Russia. The losses associated with this divergence of spreads wiped out 90 percent of the fund's equity (net asset value), which fell to just $600 million in September 1998, implying a balance sheet leverage of 167.

At this point the Federal Reserve Bank of New York (FRBNY) felt it had to step in to organize a private rescue of LTCM in order to avoid the risk of widespread spillovers and contagion to other financial organizations and markets at a time when the international financial system was already in great turmoil. In September 1998, the FRBNY helped to organize and coordinate a $3.6 billion rescue of LTCM by a consortium of 14 major international financial institutions (Banker's Trust, Barkley's, Chase Manhattan, Citicorp, Credit Suisse First Boston, Deutsche Bank, J. P. Morgan, Goldman Sachs, Merrill Lynch, Morgan Stanley Dean Witter, Paribas, Société Générale, Travelers, and Union Bank of Switzerland). Each participating institution contributed from $125 million to $300 million and assumed 90 percent control of LTCM (leaving just 10 percent to Meriwether and the other original investors) for three years in order to undertake an orderly unwinding of LTCM's positions.

The FRBNY was criticized for organizing this rescue operation, but in its defense it pointed out that no public funds were used and that it could not just sit idly by in such a dangerous situation where the sudden and disorderly liquidation of LTCM could have disrupted financial markets around the globe. By the end of 1999, 72 percent of LTCM had been liquidated, with the remainder liquidated in the first quarter of 2000.

But how could the LTCM collapse have occurred, one may ask? There were several reasons. First of all, LTCM was a highly speculative venture to begin

Continued . . .

with. Secondly, LTCM and other hedge funds are, for the most part, unregulated. For example, since LTCM dealt with bonds, it did not come under the financial regulations that limit buying stocks on margin, and LTCM exploited this loophole to become highly leveraged. Finally, LTCM was not required to provide any information to investors—and it did not. It was the high-risk operation, lack of transparency, loopholes in financial regulations, high leverage, and

financial crises in Asia and Russia that brought LTCM down. Congress is now considering legislation to require more disclosure by large hedge funds on the theory that public disclosure will lower the risk of an LTCM-type collapse in the future. By the end of 2005, little seemed to have changed, with almost $1 trillion invested in hedge funds—three times the amount in the middle of 1998 before the trouble started.

Source: "The LTCM Episode," *Annual Report* (Basle: Bank for International Settlements, 1999), pp. 99–102; "Long-Term Capital to Make Payment to Bailout Group," *The Wall Street Journal* (September 29, 1999), p. C19; "Hedge Funds Managers Are Back, Profiting in Others' Bad Times," *The New York Times* (July 26, 2002), p. C1; "Clues to a Hedge Fund Collapse," *The New York Times* (September 18, 2005), p. 1; "Refco Chief Charged with Fraud," *Financial Times* (October 13, 2005), p. 15; "Take My Hedge Fund . . . Please," http://www.cnn.com/2005/10/14/technology/hedgefunds; and "Hedge Fund Fraud Much Higher in US," http://www.cnn.com/2005/10/27/markets/hedge_fund.

13-8   INFORMATION AND RISK

Risk often results from lack of or inadequate information. The relationship between information and risk can be analyzed by examining asymmetric information, adverse selection, moral hazard, principal–agent problem, and auctions.

Asymmetric Information and the Market for Lemons

One party to a transaction (i.e., the buyer or seller of a product or service) often has less information than the other party with regard to the quality of the product or service. This is a case of **asymmetric information.** An example of this is the market for "lemons" (i.e., a defective product, such as a used car, that will require a great deal of costly repairs and is not worth its price).

Specifically, sellers of used cars know exactly the quality of the cars that they are selling but prospective buyers do not. As a result, the market price for used cars will depend on the quality of the average used car available for sale. The owners of lemons would then tend to receive a higher price than their cars are worth, while the owners of high-quality used cars would tend to get a lower price than their cars are worth. The owners of high-quality used cars would therefore withdraw their cars from the market, thus lowering the average quality and price of the remaining cars available for sale. Sellers of the now above-average-quality cars withdraw their cars from the market, further reducing the quality and price of the remaining used cars offered for sale. The process continues until only the lowest-quality cars are sold in the market at the appropriate very low price. Thus, the end result is that low-quality cars drive high-quality cars out of the market. This is known as **adverse selection.**

The problem of adverse selection that arises from asymmetric information can be overcome or reduced by the acquisition of more information by the party lacking it. For example, in the used-car market, a prospective buyer can have the car evaluated at an independent automotive service center, or the used car dealer can *signal* above-average-quality cars by providing guarantees.

The Insurance Market and Adverse Selection

The problem of adverse selection arises not only in the market for used cars, but in any market characterized by asymmetric information, such as the market for individual health insurance. Here the individual knows much more about the state of her health than an insurance company can ever find out, even with a medical examination. As a result, when an insurance company sets the insurance premium for the average individual (i.e., an individual of average health), unhealthy people are more likely to purchase insurance than healthy people. Because of this adverse selection problem, the insurance company is forced to raise the insurance premium, thus making it less advantageous for healthy people to purchase insurance. This increases even more the proportion of unhealthy people in the pool of insured people, thus requiring still higher insurance premiums. In the end, insurance premiums would have to be so high that even unhealthy people would stop buying insurance. Why buy insurance if the premium is as high as the cost of personally paying for an illness?

The problem of adverse selection arises in the market for any type of insurance (i.e., for accidents, fire, floods, and so on). In each case, only higher-risk individuals buy insurance, and this forces insurance companies to raise their premiums. The worsening adverse selection problem can lead to insurance premiums being so high that in the end no one would buy insurance. Insurance companies try to overcome the problem of adverse selection by requiring medical checkups, charging different premiums for different age groups and occupations, and offering different rates of coinsurance, levels of deductibles, lengths of contracts, and so on.

The Problem of Moral Hazard

Another problem that arises in the insurance market is that of **moral hazard.** This refers to the increase in the probability of an illness, fire, or other accident when an individual is insured than when she is not. With insurance, the loss from an illness, fire, or other accident is shifted from the individual to the insurance company. Therefore, the individual will take fewer precautions to avoid the illness, fire, or other accident, and when a loss does occur, she will tend to inflate the amount of the loss. With auto insurance, an individual may drive more recklessly (thus increasing the probability of a car accident) and then is likely to exaggerate the injury and inflate the property damage that he suffers if he does get into an accident. Similarly with fire insurance, a firm may take fewer reasonable precautions (such as the installation of a fire detection system, thereby increasing the probability of a fire) than in the absence of fire insurance; and then the firm is likely to inflate the property damage suffered if a fire does occur.

If the problem of moral hazard is not reduced or somehow contained, it could lead to unacceptably high insurance rates and costs and thus defeat the very reason for insurance. One method by which insurance companies try to overcome the problem of moral hazard is by specifying the precautions that an individual or firm must take as a condition for buying insurance. For example, an insurance company might require yearly physical checkups as a condition for continuing to provide health insurance to an individual, increase insurance premiums for drivers involved in accidents, and require the installation of a fire detector before providing fire insurance to a firm. By doing this, the insurance company tries to limit the possibility of illness, accident, or fire, and thereby reduce the number and amount of possible claims it will face. Another way used by insurance companies to overcome or reduce the problem of moral hazard is *coinsurance.* This refers to insuring only part of the possible loss or value of the property being insured. The idea is that if the individual or firm shares a significant portion of a potential loss with the insurance company, the individual or firm will be more prudent and will take more precautions to avoid losses from illness or accidents.

The Principal–Agent Problem

A firm's managers act as the *agents* for the owners or stockholders (legally referred to as the *principals*) of the firm. Because of this separation of ownership from control in the modern corporation, a **principal–agent problem** arises.[17] This refers to the fact that while the owners of the firm want to maximize the total profits or the present value of the firm, the managers or agents want to maximize their own personal interests, such as their salaries, tenure, influence, and reputation.[18] The principal–agent problem often becomes evident in the case of takeover bids for a firm by another firm. Although the owners or stockholders of the firm may benefit from the takeover if it raises the value of the firm's stock, the managers may oppose it for fear of losing their jobs in the reorganization of the firm that may follow the takeover.

One way of overcoming the principal–agent problem and ensuring that the firm's managers act in the stockholders' interests is by providing managers with **golden parachutes.** These are large financial settlements paid out by a firm to its managers if they are forced out or choose to leave as a result of the firm being taken over. With golden parachutes, the firm is in essence buying the firm managers' approval for the takeover (see Case Study 13-9). Even though golden parachutes may cost a firm millions of dollars, they may be more than justified by the sharp increase in the value of the firm that might result from a takeover. Note that a principal–agent problem may also arise in the acquiring firm. Specifically, the agents or managers of a firm may initiate and carry out a takeover bid more for personal gain (in the form of higher salaries, more secure tenure, and the enhanced reputation and prestige in directing the resulting larger corporation) than to further the stockholders' interest. In fact, the managers of the acquiring firm may be carried away by their egos and bid too much for the firm being acquired.

More generally (and independent of takeovers) a firm can overcome the principal–agent problem by offering big bonuses to its top managers based on the firm's long-term performance and profitability or a generous deferred-compensation package, which provides relatively low compensation at the beginning and very high compensation in the future. This would induce managers to stay with the firm and strive for its long-term success. In the case of public enterprises such as a public-transportation agency, or in a nonprofit enterprise such as a hospital, an inept manager can be voted out or removed.

---

[17] E. F. Fama, "Agency Problems of the Theory of the Firm," *Journal of Political Economy* (April 1980), pp. 288–307.

[18] W. Baumol, *Business Behavior, Value, and Growth* (New York: Harcourt-Brace, 1967); and O. Williamson, *Corporate Control and Business Behavior* (Englewood Cliffs, N.J.: Prentice-Hall, 1964).

CASE STUDY 13-9
Do Golden Parachutes Reward Failure?

The proliferation and size of golden parachutes has sharply increased during the great wave of mergers that has taken place in the United States since the early 1980s. Some of the largest and most controversial golden parachutes (amounting to a total of nearly $100 million) were set up for ten of Primerica's executives for retiring as a result of its friendly merger with the Commercial Credit Corporation in 1988. These golden parachutes represented 6 percent of Primerica's $1.7 billion book value and cost stockholders $1.88 a share. Gerald Tsai, Jr., the chairman of Primerica, who arranged the merger, was to receive $19.2 million as severance pay, $8.6 million to defray the excise taxes resulting from the compensation agreement, and several other millions of dollars from Primerica's long-term incentive, life insurance, and retirement benefits program—for an overall total of nearly $30 million!

Even before the final approval of the merger in December 1988, some of Primerica's stockholders filed suit in New York State Supreme Court charging that Primerica's top executives had violated their fiduciary role and had acted in their own interest and against the stockholders' interests; they demanded that the termination agreements for the ten executives be canceled. The lawsuit pointed out that golden parachutes were originally set up in 1985 for six of Primerica's executives to cover only hostile takeovers; they were then extended to ten executives in 1987; and finally they were revised in 1988, three months after Primerica agreed to the merger, to also cover friendly takeovers.

It has been estimated that 15 percent of the nation's largest corporations offered golden parachutes to its top executives in 1981. This figure rose to 33 percent in 1985 and to nearly 50 percent in 1990.

Indeed, golden parachutes are no longer confined to the corporation's top executives. They are offered farther and farther down the corporate ladder to middle-level management and sometimes even to all employees. This has resulted in a public outcry and has led the Securities and Exchange Commission to rule that a firm must hold a shareholder vote on its golden parachute plans. Until the early 1990s, corporations typically did not make public their offers of golden parachutes. Not only are they now required to do so, but some companies are even beginning to demand restitution.

The practice of giving golden parachutes, nevertheless, continues. Indeed, after observing huge severance packages given to CEOs who "were let go" in 2000, Dean Foust of *Business Week* (see the reference below) remarked that "failure has never looked more lucrative." For example, in August 2000, Procter & Gamble gave Durk Jager, its just-ousted CEO, a $9.5 million bonus, even though he had been at P&G less than one and one-half years and P&G's stock had fallen by 50 percent during his tenure. Also in 2000, Conseco Inc. gave a $49.3 million going-away gift to CEO Stephen Hilbert, who practically bankrupted the company with his ill-fated move into subprime lending. Similarly, Ford gave Jacques Nasser, its ousted CEO, a compensation package worth $23 million in 2001, even though the company lost $5.5 billion that year, and John Eyler, Toys "R" Us CEO received a $63 million payout upon selling the company in 2005. And this is not only an American problem. For example, Percy Barnevik's $87 million pension payment from ABB, the Swiss engineering group, was called into question in February 2002, especially after his admission of partial responsibility for ABB's worsening performance. In fact, ABB asked for restitution.

Source: "Ten of Primerica Executives' Parachutes Gilded in $98.2 Million Severance Pay," *The Wall Street Journal* (November 29, 1988), p. A3; "Primerica Holders File Lawsuit to Halt 'Golden Parachutes'," *The Wall Street Journal* (December 2, 1988), p. A9; "Ruling by SEC May Threaten Parachute Plans," *The Wall Street Journal* (January 10, 1990), p. A3; "CEO Pay: Nothing Succeeds Like Failure," *Business Week* (September 11, 2000), p. 46; "Golden Parachutes' Emerge in European Deals," *The Wall Street Journal* (February 14, 2000), p. A17; "Ex-Ford Chief Receives $23 million in 2001," *The New York Times* (April 10, 2002), p. C6; "Barnevik's Role on GM Board to Be Reviewed," *Financial Times* (February 18, 2002), p. 17; and "What Are Mergers Good For?" *The New York Times Magazine* (June 5, 2005), pp. 56–62.

Auctions

One of the most important applications of decision making under uncertainty and the oldest forms of economic exchange are auctions. An auction is a market in which potential buyers compete for the right to purchase a good, service, or anything of value. Managers need to understand auctions because they may want to auction off some goods and services or bid for some inputs. The advent of the Internet greatly stimulated the use of auctions as a trading system in the United States during the past decade, and from there it rapidly spread around the world (see Integrating Case Study 4 on eBay). There are four types of auctions: (1) the English or ascending bid, (2) the first-price sealed bid, (3) the second-price sealed-bid, and (4) the Dutch or descending bid. These differ on whether the bidding is simultaneous or sequential, sealed or unsealed, and on the amount that the bidder is required to pay.

In the **English auction** an item is sold to the highest bidder. The auction begins with an opening bid, and the bidding continues until no one is willing to pay a higher price. The item will then go to the highest (the only remaining) bidder. Thus, the English auction is a sequential, ascending-bid auction. In the **first-price sealed-bid auction** the auctioneer collects the bids made on slips of papers and awards the item to the highest bidder. This is the same as the English auction, except that the bidding is simultaneous and the bidders do not know what the others are bidding. The **second-price sealed-bid auction** is the same as the first-price sealed-bid auction, except that the participant who wins by submitting the highest bid has to pay only the amount of the second highest bid. Finally, in the **Dutch auction** the auctioneer starts with a very high price and then gradually lowers the price until one participant agrees to buy the item. The auction is then over and the bidder buys the item at the last announced price. The Dutch auction is thus a descending-bid where the bidders do not know the bids of the other participants (as in the first-price sealed bid).[19]

Bidders at auctions face the danger of a **winner's curse,** or overpaying for an item by placing the winning bid. This is more likely to occur in first-price sealed-bid and Dutch auctions than in the English auction, where the information revealed in the bidding process may lead a participant to reduce the amount that he or she is willing to bid. The flower market in Holland uses the Dutch auction and so do Treasuries in the United States and in other countries in selling bonds. The winner's curse is also somewhat reduced in second-price sealed-bid auctions, precisely because the bid winner pays only the amount of the second highest bid. Bidding on eBay and Priceline (see Case Study 11-10) are examples of second-price auctions. Here, the dominant strategy is for a participant to submit early the maximum "reservation price" that he or she is willing to pay. [20]

The winner's curse is more likely to arise in first-price sealed-bid and Dutch auctions because if the average for all the bids equals the true (but unknown) value of the item, then the price paid by the highest bidder would exceed the average bid and the true value of the

[19] P. Milgrom, "Auctions and Bidding: A Primer," *Journal of Economic Perspectives* (Summer 1989); "The Heyday of the Auction," *The Economist* (July 24, 1999), pp. 67–68; and "Bidding Adieu?" *The Economist* (June 29, 2002), p. 74.

[20] S. Thiel, "Some Evidence on the Winner's Curse," *American Economic Review* (December 1988); J. H. Kagel and Dan Levin, "The Winner's Curse and Public Information," *American Economic Review* (December 1986); and "Going, Going, Gone, Sucker!" *Business Week* (March 20, 2000), pp. 124–125.

item. This is exactly what happened in the bidding for oil leases in the Gulf of Mexico during the 1950s and 1960s. The winner's curse can also arise when publishers bid for a novel. The most optimistic company is likely to be the highest bidder, and its bid will exceed the average bid and true value of the asset. The only way to avoid the winner's curse is for an individual or company to adopt a prudent bidding approach and not overbid. In auctioning airwaves, the Federal Communications Commission (FCC) used a variety of auctioning strategies (see Case Study 13-10).

CASE STUDY 13-10
Auctioning of the Airwaves

Since the time of its creation in 1927 until December 1994, the Federal Communications Commission (FCC) handed out airwaves (radio frequency) licenses free of charge through either lotteries or merit-based hearings, favoring local radio and TV stations on the theory that they would be more attuned to community programming needs. During the 1980s, pressure began to mount to scrap the old system and allow market forces to allocate these scarce resources (airwaves). Between December 5, 1994, and March 1995, the U.S. Government auctioned off to the highest bidder thousands of licenses to blanket the nation with new personal communications services (PCS) for the huge sum of $7.7 billion.

Although similar to an art auction—except that all licenses rather than a single one were up for bidding at the same time—auctioning airwaves licenses was unlike anything ever done before. The plan carved the nation into 51 regions and 492 subregions (metropolitan areas) and auctioned two licenses for each of the 51 regions and up to five licenses for each of the 492 subregions. A large company or group of companies could bid for a nationwide license by combining bids for a license for each region. Thus, each metropolitan area could have as many as seven new wireless services (five for the metropolitan area alone and another two from the region of which the metropolitan area is part) and each of these would

compete with the one or two already established cellular telephone companies (which were allowed and did bid for some of the new wireless licenses).

Since March 1995, 13 other auctions of wireless licenses were held, which netted the government an additional $40 billion, and more auctions are planned for the future. It is estimated that during this decade more than 100 million Americans will create a $100 billion-a-year industry for wireless services. Such large revenues are needed in order for the industry to recoup the original investments. These include the nearly $50 billion already paid for the licenses as well as the even larger investments that wireless companies are collectively making in order to set up the new digital transmission systems. Thus, it may take a decade before wireless companies can break even and possibly turn profitable. In the end, the difference between a profit and a loss could be the price of the license itself. Wireless companies may simply have paid too much for these licenses (winner's curse). Evidence of this is that, starting in 1996, several of the less known large bidders for the licenses started to default on payments. The government then reauctioned these licenses. Legislation has also been proposed to require TV broadcasters to go all-digital by the end of 2008 and relinquish their analog airwaves, so that they can also be auctioned off by the government at an estimated price of $10 billion.

Source: "U.S. Lays Out Rules for a Big Auction of Radio Airwaves," *The New York Times* (September 24, 1993), p. 1; "Winners of Wireless Auctions to Pay $7 Billion," *The New York Times* (March 14, 1995), p. D1; "Clinton Orders a New Auction of Airwaves," *The New York Times* (October 14, 2001), p. 1; and "Everybody Wants a Piece of the Air," *Business Week* (July 4, 2005), pp. 38–39.

SUMMARY

1. Most strategic managerial decisions are made in the face of risk or uncertainty. *Risk* refers to the situation in which there is more than one possible outcome to a decision and the probability of each specific outcome is known or can be estimated. Under uncertainty, on the other hand, the probability of each specific outcome is not known or even meaningful. Managerial decisions involving risk use such concepts as strategy, states of nature, and payoff matrix.

2. The probability of an event is the chance or odds that the event will occur. A probability distribution lists all the possible outcomes of a decision and the probability attached to each. The expected value of an event is obtained by multiplying each possible outcome of the event by its probability of occurrence and then adding these products. As the number of possible outcomes specified increases, we approach a continuous probability distribution. The standard deviation (σ) measures the dispersion of possible outcomes from the expected value and is used as an absolute measure of risk. The probability that an outcome will fall within a specified range of outcomes can be determined by measuring the area under the standard normal curve that lies within this range, for outcomes that are approximately normally distributed. A relative measure of risk is provided by the coefficient of variation (V), which is given by the standard deviation of the distribution divided by its expected value or mean.

3. Although some managers are risk neutral or risk seekers, most are risk averters. Risk aversion is based on the principle of diminishing marginal utility of money, which is reflected in a total utility of money curve that is concave or faces down. A risk averter would not accept a fair bet, a risk-neutral individual would be indifferent to it, while a risk seeker would accept even some unfair bets. In managerial decisions subject to risk, a risk-averse manager seeks to maximize expected utility rather than monetary returns. The expected utility of a decision or strategy is the sum of the product of the utility of each possible outcome and the probability of its occurrence.

4. One method of adjusting the valuation model of the firm to deal with a project subject to risk is to use risk-adjusted discount rates. This involves adding a risk premium to the risk-free rate of interest or discount used to find the present value of the net cash flow or return of the investment. A similar method that explicitly incorporates the decision maker's attitude toward risk is the certainty-equivalent approach. This uses a risk-free discount rate in the denominator and incorporates risk by multiplying the net cash flow or return in the numerator of the valuation model by the certainty-equivalent coefficient. This is the ratio of the equivalent certain sum to the expected risky sum or net return from the investment.

5. Managerial decisions involving risk are often made in stages, with subsequent decisions or events depending on earlier decisions or events. Such decision processes can be analyzed with decision trees. The construction of a decision tree begins at the left with the earliest decision and moves forward in time to the right through a series of subsequent events and decisions. Boxes show decision points, and circles show possible states of nature. The analysis of decision trees starts at the right at the end of the sequence and moves backward to the left. For the evaluation of even more complex managerial decisions involving risk, simulation is often used. This involves the use of a computer program that explicitly and simultaneously considers all the interactions among the variables of the model to determine the expected outcome and risk of a particular business strategy.

6. One decision rule under uncertainty is the maximin criterion. This conservative and pessimistic rule postulates that the decision maker should determine the worst possible outcome of each strategy and then pick the strategy that provides the best of the worst possible outcomes. Another decision rule under uncertainty is the minimax regret criterion. This postulates that the decision maker should select the strategy that minimizes the maximum regret or opportunity cost of the wrong decision, whatever the state of nature that occurs. Other more informal and less precise methods of dealing with uncertainty involve the acquisition of additional information, referral to authority, attempting to control the business environment, and diversification.

7. Including foreign securities in an investment portfolio can reduce risk (through diversification)

and increase the rate of return, but also gives rise to a foreign-exchange risk because the foreign currency can depreciate during the time of the investment. Such foreign-exchange risk can be covered by hedging. This is usually accomplished with a forward or a futures contract. A forward contract is an agreement to purchase or sell a specific amount of a foreign currency at a rate specified today for delivery at a specific future date. A futures contract is a standardized forward contract for *predetermined quantities of the currency* and *selected calendar dates.*

8. Risk often results from lack of or inadequate information. Asymmetric information (i.e., when one party to a transaction has less information on the quality of the product or service offered for sale than the other party) gives rise to the problem of adverse selection (low-quality products or services driving high-quality products or services out of the market). The problem of adverse selection can be overcome by acquiring or providing more information. Moral hazard refers to the increased probability of a loss when an economic agent can shift some of its costs to others. Insurance companies try to overcome this problem by specifying the precautions that an individual or firm must take as a condition for insurance. A principal–agent problem arises because the agents (managers) of a firm may seek to maximize their own benefits (such as salaries) rather than the profits or value of the firm, which is the owners' or principals' interest. The problem can be overcome by the firm offering big bonuses to its top managers based on the firm's long-term performance and profitability. There are four types of auctions: (1) the English or ascending bid (2) the first-price sealed bid, (3) the second-price sealed bid, and (4) the Dutch or descending bid. These differ on whether the bidding is simultaneous or sequential, sealed or unsealed, and on the amount that the bidder is required to pay. Auctions can give rise to the winner's curse, or overpaying for an item by placing the winning bid. This can be avoided by adopting a prudent bidding approach and not overbidding.

DISCUSSION QUESTIONS

1. What is the meaning of: risk, uncertainty, expected value, probability distribution, standard deviation, coefficient of variation?

2. What is the distinction between a discrete and a continuous probability distribution? How is the probability that an outcome will fall within a given range of outcomes determined? What is the usefulness of probability distributions in risk analysis?

3. What is the value of the standard deviation and coefficient of variation if all the outcomes of a probability distribution are identical? Why is this so? What does this mean? How does the maximization decision of a manager differ in the case of certainty and risk?

4. What is the meaning of diminishing, constant, and increasing marginal utility of money?

5. Why is maximization of the expected value not a valid criterion in decision making subject to risk?

Under what conditions would that criterion be valid?

6. What is the expected utility of a project with a 40 percent probability of gaining 6 utils and a 60 percent probability of losing 1 util? Should the manager undertake this project? What if the payoff of the project were the same as above, except that the utility lost were 4 utils?

7. What is the meaning of a risk-adjusted discount rate? A risk–return trade-off function? A risk premium? What is their usefulness in adjusting the valuation model of the firm or of a project for risk?

8. What is the meaning of the certainty-equivalent coefficient? What is its relationship to utility theory and risk aversion? How is the certainty-equivalent coefficient used to adjust the valuation model for risk?

9. What is the number of possible outcomes in a decision tree depicting the choice between five

different plant sizes and four possible ways that competitors may react under each of three different economic conditions? How is the probability of each outcome determined?

10. What is meant by *simulation?* By *sensitivity analysis?* When is simulation most useful and used?

11. Why is decision making under uncertainty necessarily subjective? Why is the maximin criterion a very conservative decision rule? Under what conditions might this decision rule be appropriate?

12. What is the rationale behind the minimax regret rule? What are some less formal and precise methods of dealing with uncertainty? When are these useful?

13. Why does an importer usually face a foreign-exchange risk? How can the importer hedge the foreign-exchange risk by purchasing the foreign currency today to have it by the time the foreign-currency payment is due? Why does hedging usually take place with a forward contract?

14. Why does an exporter face a foreign exchange risk? How can the exporter hedge its foreign exchange risk?

15. How does the adverse selection problem arise in the credit-card market? How do credit-card companies reduce the adverse selection problem that they face? To what complaint does this give rise?

16. What is the principal–agent problem? How can it be minimized?

17. What are the different types of auctions? What problem can the participant to an auction face? How can this problem be avoided or reduced?

PROBLEMS

1. An investor has two investment opportunities, each involving an outlay of $10,000. The present value of possible outcomes and their respective probabilities are

	Investment I		Investment II		
Outcome	$4,000	$6,000	$3,000	$5,000	$7,000
Probability	0.6	0.4	0.4	0.3	0.3

(*a*) Calculate the expected value of each investment. (*b*) Draw a bar chart for each investment. (*c*) Calculate the standard deviation of each project. (*d*) Determine which of the two investments the investor should choose.

*2. Using Table C-1 for the standard normal distribution in Appendix C at the end of the book, determine (*a*) that 68.26 percent of the area under the standard normal curve is found within plus or minus 1 standard deviation of the mean, 95.44 percent within $\pm 2\sigma$, and 99.74 percent within $\pm 3\sigma$; (*b*) the probability that profit will fall between $500 and $650 for project A in Section 13-2 of the text (with expected value of $500 and standard deviation of $70.71); (*c*) the probability that profit for project A will fall between $300 and $650, below $300, above $650.

3. An individual is considering two investment projects. Project A will return a loss of $45 if conditions are poor, a profit of $35 if conditions are good, and a profit of $155 if conditions are excellent. Project B will return a loss of $100 if conditions are poor, a profit of $60 if conditions are good, and a profit of $300 if conditions are excellent. The probability distribution of conditions are:

Conditions:	Poor	Good	Excellent
Probability:	40%	50%	10%

(*a*) Calculate the expected value of each project and identify the preferred project according to this criterion. (*b*) Calculate the standard deviation of the expected value of each project and identify the project with the highest risk.

4. A software company has to decide which of two advertising strategies to adopt: TV commercials or newspaper ads. The marketing department has

estimated that sales and their probability under each alternative plan are as given in the table below:

Strategy A (TV Commercials)		Strategy B (Newspaper Ads)	
Sales	Probability	Sales	Probability
$ 8,000	0.2	$ 8,000	0.3
10,000	0.3	12,000	0.4
12,000	0.3	16,000	0.3
14,000	0.2		

The firm's profit is 50 percent of sales. (*a*) Calculate the expected profit under each promotion strategy. (*b*) Calculate the standard deviation of the distribution of profits for each promotion strategy. (*c*) Which of the two promotion strategies is more risky? (*d*) Which promotion strategy should the firm choose?

*5. An oil-drilling venture offers the chance of investing $10,000 with a 20 percent probability of a return of $40,000 if the venture is successful (i.e., oil is found). If unsuccessful, the $10,000 investment will be lost. (*a*) What is the expected monetary return of this investment? (*b*) If the utility schedule of individuals A, B, and C is as indicated below, what is the expected utility of the project for each? Which individual(s) would invest in the venture? Why?

Money	−$10,000	0	$10,000
Utility of A	−5	0	4
B	−5	0	5
C	−5	0	6
	$20,000	$30,000	$40,000
Utility of A	7	9	10
B	10	15	20
C	13	21	30

6. A manager must determine which of two products to market. From market studies the manager constructed the following payoff matrix of the

present value of all future net profits under all the different possible states of the economy:

State of the Economy	Probability	Profit
Product 1		
Boom	0.2	$50
Normal	0.5	20
Recession	0.3	0
Product 2		
Boom	0.2	$30
Normal	0.4	20
Recession	0.4	10

The manager's utility for money function is

$$U = 100M - M^2$$

where M refers to dollars of profit. (*a*) Is the manager a risk seeker, risk neutral, or risk averter? Why? (*b*) If the manager's objective were profit maximization regardless of risk, which product should he or she introduce? (*c*) Evaluate the risk associated per dollar of profit with each product. (*d*) If the manager's objective were utility maximization, which product should he or she introduce?

*7. The manager of the Quality Products Company is faced with two alternative investment projects. Project A involves the introduction of a higher-quality version of its basic shaving cream, and project B, the introduction of a men's hair lotion (a new line of business for the company). The two projects involve the following expected streams of net cash flows and initial outlays:

	Net Cash Outflows			
Investment	Year 1	Year 2	Year 3	Initial Outlay
A	$40,000	$60,000	$40,000	$110,000
B	30,000	80,000	50,000	104,000

(*a*) Calculate the net present value of each investment project with the basic risk-free discount rate of 8 percent. (*b*) Which of the two projects should the manager adopt if the risk premium is 2 percent on project A and 6 percent on project B?

8. The Beach Resort Hotel must decide which of two vending machines, the Refreshing or the Cooling, to install on its beach front. The net cash flow remains the same for each machine in each of the four years that each machine lasts. The purchase price, the salvage value, and the payoff matrix for each machine are indicated in the table below:

	Refreshing		
Purchase price	$10,000		
Salvage value after 4 years	0		
Expected net cash flow in each of 4 years	$6,000	$5,000	$4,000
Probability of occurrence	0.25	0.50	0.25

	Cooling		
Purchase price	$11,000		
Salvage value after 4 years	0		
Expected net cash flow in each of 4 years	$7,000	$5,000	$3,000
Probability of occurrence	0.25	0.50	0.25

The risk-free discount rate is 10 percent. The risk premium applied by the hotel is as follows:

σ	**Risk Premium**
$ 0–$ 999	0%
1,000–1,999	4
2,000–2,999	10
3,000–3,999	20

Prepare an analysis to determine which of the two machines the hotel should install.

9. Suppose that the certainty-equivalent coefficient for each machine of Problem 7 is as indicated below:

	Certainty-Equivalent Coefficient			
	Year 1	**Year 2**	**Year 3**	**Year 4**
Refreshing machine	0.90	0.85	0.75	0.70
Cooling machine	0.96	0.92	0.90	0.85

Calculate the net present value of each machine.

*10. The Fitness World Sporting Company wants to move into a new sales region and must determine which of two plants to build. It can build a large plant that costs $4 million or a small plant that costs $2 million. The company estimated that the probability that the economy will be booming, normal, or in a recession is 30 percent, 40 percent, and 30 percent, respectively. The company also estimated the present value of net cash flows for each type of plant under each state of the economy to be as indicated in the following payoff matrix. Construct a decision tree for the firm to show which of the two plants the company should build. Assume that the company is risk neutral.

Present Value of Net Cash Flows (in millions)		
	Large Plant	**Small Plant**
Boom	$10	$4
Normal	6	3
Recession	2	2

11. Suppose that the Beauty Company faces the choice of introducing a new beauty cream or investing the same amount of money in Treasury bills with a return of $10,000. If the company introduces the beauty cream, there is an 80 percent probability that a competing firm will introduce a similar product and a 20 percent chance that it will not. Whether or not the competitor responds with a similar product, the company has a choice of charging a high, a medium, or a low price. In the absence of competition this is the end of the story. In the presence of competition, the competitive firm can react to each price strategy of the Beauty Company with a high, medium, or low price of its own. The probability and the present value of the company's profit under each competitor's price response for the company strategy of high price (HP), medium price (MP), and low price (LP) are indicated in the table below. Construct a decision tree and determine whether the Beauty Company should introduce the new beauty cream or use its funds to purchase Treasury bills.

12. Given the following payoff matrix for investment projects A, B, and C, determine the best investment project for the firm according to (*a*)

Competition	Company's Price Strategy	Competitor's Price Response	Probability	Present Value of Company's Profit
		HP	0.5	$12,000
	HP	MP	0.3	10,000
		LP	0.2	8,000
		HP	0.3	12,000
Yes	MP	MP	0.5	10,000
		LP	0.2	6,000
		HP	0.0	25,000
	LP	MP	0.4	15,000
		LP	0.6	10,000
	HP	—	—	40,000
No	MP	—	—	30,000
	LP	—	—	20,000

the maximin criterion and (b) the minimax regret criterion.

	State of Nature		
Project	Recession	Normal	Boom
A	$50	$75	$ 85
B	40	80	100
C	30	70	70

13. A U.S. firm imports €100,000 worth of goods from the European Monetary Union and agrees to pay in three months. The exchange rate is $1/€1 and the three-month forward rate is $1.01/€1. Explain how the importer can hedge his foreign exchange risk.

14. For the givens of Problem 13, indicate how an exporter who expects to receive a payment of €1 million in three months can hedge the foreign exchange risk.

15. **Integrating Problem**

The Food Products Company has decided to introduce a new brand of breakfast cereals and is contemplating building either a $10 million or a $6 million plant to produce the new breakfast cereals. If the company builds the $10 million plant, there is a 70 percent chance that competitors will respond with a large increase in their advertising and a 30 percent probability that competitors will respond with a small increase in their advertising. On the other hand, if the company builds the $6 million plant, there is a 40 percent probability that competitors will respond with a large increase in their advertising and a 60 percent probability that competitors will respond with a small increase in their advertising.

Whether the company builds the $10 million or the $6 million plant and whether competitors will respond with a large or a small increase in their advertising, the general demand conditions that the company will face can be high, medium, or low. The probability and the net cash flow that the company faces under each plant it can build and competitors' responses are indicated in the table below. Since the variability of the net cash flows is higher with the $10 million plant, the company uses the risk-adjusted discount rate of 20 percent to calculate the present value of the net cash flows. On the other hand, the company uses the risk-adjusted discount rate of 14 percent to calculate the present value of the net cash flows of the $6 million plant.

Construct a decision tree, and determine whether the Food Products Company should build the $10 million or the $6 million plant. Round all calculations to the nearest dollar.

Plant	Competitors' Advertising Reaction	Conditions of Demand	Probability	Net Cash Flows for Year (in millions)		
				1	2	3
		High	0.4	$6	$6	$5
	Large	Normal	0.4	4	5	4
		Low	0.2	3	4	2
$10 million						
		High	0.4	7	7	7
	Small	Normal	0.4	5	5	5
		Low	0.2	4	4	4
		High	0.4	3	4	3
	Large	Normal	0.4	3	3	2
		Low	0.2	2	2	2
$6 million						
		High	0.4	5	4	4
	Small	Normal	0.4	4	3	3
		Low	0.2	3	3	2

SUPPLEMENTARY READINGS

For the measuring of risk with probability distributions, see:

Salvatore, Dominick, and Derrick Reagle, *Theory and Problems of Statistics Econometrics,* 2nd ed. (New York: McGraw-Hill, 2002), chaps. 2 and 3.

Skaperdas, S., "Conflicts and Attitudes Toward Risk," *American Economic Review* (May 1991), pp. 116–120.

Weiss, Neil A., *Introductory Statistics* (Reading, Mass.: Addison Wesley Longman, 1999), chaps. 4–7.

Utility theory and risk aversion are discussed in:

Salvatore, Dominick, *Microeconomic Theory and Applications,* 4th ed. (New York: Oxford University Press, 2003), sec. 6.4.

Schoemaker, P. J. H., "The Expected Utility Model: Its Variants, Purposes, Evidence and Limitations," *Journal of Economic Literature* (1982).

Machina, M., "Choice Under Uncertainty: Problems Solved and Unsolved," *Journal of Economic Perspectives* (Summer 1987), pp. 121–154.

For adjusting the valuation model for risk, see:

Butler, J. S., and Barry Schachter, "The Investment Decision: Estimating Risk and Risk-Adjusted Discount Rates," *Financial Management* (Winter 1989), pp. 13–22.

Sick, Gordon, "A Certainty-Equivalent Approach to Capital Budgeting," *Financial Management* (Winter 1986), pp. 23–32.

A discussion of decision trees is found in:

Hespos, Richard F., and Paul A. Strassman, "Stochastic Decision Trees for the Analysis of Investment Decisions," *Management Science* (1965).

Magee, John F. "Decision Trees for Decision Making," *Harvard Business Review* (1964).

Sharpe, Paul, and Tom Keelin, "How SmithKline Beecham Makes Better Resource-Allocation Decisions," *Harvard Business Review* (March–April 1998), pp. 45–57.

For decision making under uncertainty, see:

Markowitz, Harry, *Portfolio Selection: Efficient Diversification of Investments* (New York: Wiley, 1959).

Neuman, John von, and Oscar Morgenstern, *Theory of Games and Economic Behavior,* 3rd ed. (Princeton, N.J.: Princeton University Press, 1953).

Sauer, Raymond D., "The Economics of Wagering Markets," *Journal of Economic Literature* (December 1998), pp. 2021–2064.

Foreign-exchange risks and hedging are examined in:

Salvatore, Dominick, *International Economics,* 8th ed. (Hoboken, N.J.: Wiley, 2004), chap. 14.

On the relationship between risk and information, see:

Ackerlof, George A., "The Market for 'Lemons': Qualitative Uncertainty and the Market Mechanism," *Quarterly Journal of Economics* (August 1970), pp. 488–500.

Lind, Barry, and Charles Plott, "The Winner's Curse: Experiments with Buyers and Sellers," *American Economic Review* (March 1991), pp. 335–346.

Lucking-Reiley, David., "Auctions on the Internet: What's Being Auctioned and How?" *Journal of Industrial Economics* (September 2000), pp. 227–252.

Klemperer, Paul: "Spectrum Auctions," *European Economic Review* (Summer 2002), pp. 829–845.

McAfee, R. P., and J. McMillan, "Analyzing the Airwaves Auctions," *Journal of Industrial Perspectives,* (Spring 1996), pp. 159–176.

Miller, Kent D., "Economic Exposure and Risk Management," *Strategic Management Journal* (May 1998), pp. 497–514.

"Symposium on Auctions," *Journal of Economic Perspectives* (Summer 1989), pp. 3–50.

"Symposium on the Spectrum Auctions," *Journal of Economics and Management Strategy* (Fall 1997), pp. 431–675.

Thiel, S., "Some Evidence on the Winner's Curse," *American Economic Review* (December 1988).

INTERNET SITE ADDRESSES

For a discussion of risk analysis, see the Decision Analysis Society, a subdivision of the Institute of Operations Research and the Management Sciences, at:

http://www.fuqua.duke.edu/faculty/daweb

For DecisionPro, a software package for management decision analysis with a decision tree component created by the Vanguard Software Corporation, see:

http://www.vanguardsw.com

An analysis of what Coca-Cola is doing to meet its competition, see:

http://www.coke.com

The method of measuring risk used by J. P. Morgan is examined at:

http://www.jpmorgan.com

http://www.contingencyanalysis.com/glossary modernportfoliotheory.html

For futures trading and hedging, see the Commodity Futures Trading Commission Web site at:

http://www.cftc.gov

For the Hedge Fund home page, and Long Term Capital Management, see:

http://www.gao.gov/new.items/gg00003.pdf

http://www.bits2atoms.com/addvalue/hedge_ funds.html

Asymmetric information is examined in:

http://www.nobel.se/economics/laureates/2001/ ecoadv.pdf

Market signaling is examined in:

http://www.berkeley.edu/berkeleyan/2001/10/17_ asyme.html

For moral hazard, see:

http://www.en.wikipedia.org/wiki/Moral_ hazard

http://www.economist.com/research/Economics/
alphabetic.cfm?TERM=MARKET%20FAILURE

For the principal–agent problem, see:

http://www.economics.about.com/od/economics
glossary/g/principalag.htm

http://www.ideas.repec.org/p/cpr/ceprdp/5119.html

http://www2.chass.ncsu.edu/garson/pa765/agent.htm

http://www.en.wikipedia.org/wiki/Principal-
agent_problem

A discussion of auctions and the winner's curse is
given in:

http//:www.ebay.com

http://www.priceline.com

http://www.auctionwatch.com

http://www.slate.msn.com/id/21810

http://www.nuff.ox.ac.uk/users/klemperer/
readingauction.pdf

CHAPTER 14 Long-Run Investment Decisions: Capital Budgeting

CHAPTER OUTLINE

579

KEY TERMS (in the order of their appearance)

Capital budgeting	Internal rate of return (*IRR*)	Capital asset pricing model
Net cash flow from a project	on a project	(CAPM)
Time value of money	Profitability index (*PI*)	Beta coefficient (β)
Net present value (*NPV*)	Cost of debt	Composite cost of capital
of a project	Dividend valuation model	

In previous chapters we were primarily interested in examining how firms organize production within existing facilities in order to maximize profits during a given year. In this chapter we shift attention to the analysis of a firm's investment opportunities. These may involve expansion of the firm's capacity in a given line of business or entrance into entirely different lines of business. The distinguishing characteristic of investment decisions is that they involve costs and give rise to revenues over a number of years rather than for one year only. Since $1 paid or received next year is worth less than $1 paid or received today, discounting and present value concepts need to be used in order to properly evaluate and compare different investment projects. These concepts are reviewed in Appendix A at the end of the book.[1]

In this chapter, we first present an overview of the capital budgeting process and then examine the various steps involved in capital budgeting and the key roles that the marketing, production, and financing departments of the firm play in the process. The chapter ends with a discussion of the relationship between cost of capital and international competitiveness.

14-1   CAPITAL BUDGETING: AN OVERVIEW

In this section we discuss the meaning and importance of capital budgeting, we classify the different types of investment projects, and we provide an overview of the capital budgeting process. In the remainder of the chapter, we will provide a more detailed look at the various steps involved in capital budgeting.

Meaning and Importance of Capital Budgeting

Capital budgeting refers to the process of planning expenditures that give rise to revenues or returns over a number of years. Capital budgeting is of crucial importance to a firm. The application of new technological breakthroughs may lead to new and more efficient production techniques, changes in consumer tastes may make a firm's existing product line

---

[1] Since knowledge of compounding, discounting, and present value concepts is essential for understanding the material in this chapter, the student is urged to review or study the material in Appendix A before proceeding further with this chapter. The more advanced student can read F. Shane, G. Loewenstein, and T. Donoghue, "Time Discounting and Time Preference: A Critical Review," *Journal of Economic Literature* (June 2002), pp. 351–401.

obsolete and give rise to the demand for entirely different products, and merger with other firms may significantly strengthen a firm's position vis-à-vis its competitors. The firm's management must constantly be on the alert to explore these and other opportunities. The firm's profitability, growth, and its very survival in the long run depend on how well management accomplishes these tasks. Capital budgeting is also crucial because major capital investment projects are for the most part irreversible (e.g., after a specialized type of machinery has been installed, it has a very small secondhand value if the firm reverses its decision).

Capital budgeting is used not only to plan for the replacement of worn-out capital and equipment, for the expansion of production facilities, or for entering entirely new product lines but also in planning major advertising campaigns, employee training programs, research and development, decisions to purchase or rent production facilities or equipment, and any other investment project that would result in costs and revenues over a number of years. In general, firms classify investment projects into the following categories:

1. *Replacement.* Investments to replace equipment that is worn out in the production process.
2. *Cost reduction.* Investments to replace working but obsolete equipment with new and more efficient equipment, expenditures for training programs aimed at reducing labor costs, and expenditures to move production facilities to areas where labor and other inputs are cheaper.
3. *Output expansion of traditional products and markets.* Investments to expand production facilities in response to increased demand for the firm's traditional products in traditional or existing markets.
4. *Expansion into new products and/or markets.* Investments to develop, produce, and sell new products and/or enter new markets.
5. *Government regulation.* Investments made to comply with government regulations. These include investment projects required to meet government health and safety regulations, pollution control, and to satisfy other legal requirements.

In general, investment decisions to replace worn-out equipment are the easiest to make since management is familiar with the specifications, productivity, and operating and maintenance costs of existing equipment and with the time when it needs to be replaced. Investment projects to reduce costs and expand output in traditional products and markets are generally more complex and usually require more detailed analysis and approval by higher-level management. Familiarity with the product and the market, however, does not usually make these projects among the most challenging that management is likely to face.

Investment projects to produce new products and move into new markets are likely to be very complex because of the much greater risk involved. They are also likely to be the most essential and financially rewarding in the long run, since a firm's product line tends to become obsolete over time and its traditional market may shrink or even disappear (witness the market for slide rules, which were practically replaced entirely by handheld calculators). Finally, investment projects to meet government regulations often give rise to special legal, evaluation, and monitoring problems requiring outside expert assistance.

From what has been said, it is clear that the generation of ideas and proposals for new investment projects is crucial to the future profitability of the firm and to its very survival over time. In well-managed and dynamic firms, all employees are encouraged to come up with new investment ideas. Most large firms, however, are likely to have a research and development division especially entrusted with the responsibility of coming up with proposals for new investment projects. Such a division is likely to be staffed by experts in product development, marketing research, industrial engineering and so on, and they may regularly meet with the heads of other divisions in brainstorming sessions to examine new products, markets, and strategies.

Although the final decision to undertake or not to undertake a major investment project is made by the firm's top management, especially for investment projects that involve entering into new product lines and markets, the capital budgeting process is likely to involve most of the firm's divisions. The marketing division will need to forecast the demand for the new or modified products that the firm plans to sell; the production, engineering, personnel, and purchasing departments must provide feasibility studies and estimates of the cost of the investment project; and the financing department must determine how the required investment funds are to be raised and their cost to the firm. Thus, capital budgeting can truly be said to integrate the operation of all the major divisions of the firm.

Overview of the Capital Budgeting Process

Capital budgeting is essentially an application of the general principle that a firm should produce the output or undertake an activity until the marginal revenue from the output or activity is equal to its marginal cost. In a capital budgeting framework, this principle implies that the firm should undertake additional investment projects until the marginal return from the investment is equal to its marginal cost. The schedule of the various investment projects open to the firm, arranged from the one with the highest to the lowest return, represents the firm's demand for capital. The marginal cost of capital schedule, on the other hand, gives the cost that the firm faces in obtaining additional amounts of capital for investment purposes.[2] The intersection of the demand and marginal cost curves for capital that the firm faces determines how much the firm will invest. This is shown in Figure 14-1.

In Figure 14-1, the various lettered bars indicate the amount of capital required for each investment project that the firm can undertake and the rate of return expected on each investment project. Thus, project A requires an investment of $2 million and is expected to generate an 18 percent rate of return. Project B requires an investment of $3 million (the total of $5 million minus the $2 million required for project A along the horizontal axis) and is expected to generate a 16 percent rate of return, and so on. The top of each bar, thus, represents the firm's demand for capital. Note that the projects are arranged from the one that is expected to provide the highest return to the firm to the one that is expected to provide the lowest return. The marginal cost of capital (*MCC*) curve shows that the firm can raise about $2 million of capital at the rate (cost) of 10 percent, but if it wants to raise additional amounts, it faces increasingly higher costs. How this *MCC* curve is derived and the reason for its shape are discussed in Section 14-4. At this point, we simply take it as a given to the firm.

---

[2] The cost of capital is the rate that the firm must pay on money raised externally (i.e., by borrowing or selling stock) and the opportunity cost or the return foregone on internal funds that the firm could have invested outside the firm. More will be said on this in Section 14-4.

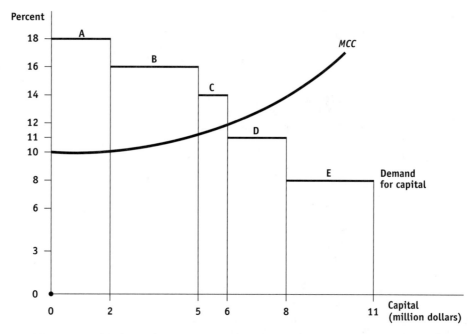

FIGURE 14-1 Graphical Overview of the Capital Budgeting Process The various lettered bars indicate the amount of capital required for each investment project and the rate of return on the investment. The top of each bar, thus, represents the firm's demand for capital. The marginal cost of capital (*MCC*) curve shows the rising cost of raising additional amounts of capital that the firm faces. The firm will undertake projects A, B, and C because the expected rates of return on these projects exceed the cost of raising the capital to make these investments. On the other hand, the firm will not undertake projects D and E because the expected rates of return are lower than their capital costs.

Faced with the demand for capital and marginal cost of capital curves shown in Figure 14-1, the firm will undertake projects A, B, and C because the expected rates of return on these projects exceed the cost of capital to make these investments. Specifically, the firm will undertake project A because it expects a return of 18 percent from the project as compared with its capital cost of only 10 percent. Similarly, the firm undertakes project B because it expects a return of 16 percent as compared with a capital cost of between 10 and 11 percent for the project. The firm also undertakes project C because its expected return of 14 percent exceeds its capital cost of nearly 12 percent. On the other hand, the firm will not undertake projects D and E because the expected rate of return on these projects is lower than the cost of raising the capital to make these investments. For example, project D provides an expected return of only 11 percent, as compared to a capital cost exceeding 12 percent. For project E the excess of capital cost over expected return is even greater. If the firm invested in projects D and E, it would face lower overall profits in the long run and the value of the firm would decline. Case Study 14-1 discusses the cost–benefit analysis of the supersonic transport plane (SST), while Case Study 14-2 examines the investment in the Eurotunnel.

CASE STUDY 14-1
Cost–Benefit Analysis and the SST

After a cost–benefit analysis, the development of the supersonic transport plane (SST) was abandoned by the United States in 1971. The benefits were simply not large enough to justify the costs. The French and British governments, however, jointly pursued the project and built the Concorde at a huge cost. Only a handful of such planes were built, and they were operated exclusively by the British and French national airlines in flights between New York and Paris or London from 1976 until it was grounded in 2003. With operating costs more than 4 times higher than the Boeing 747, the Concorde must be classified as a clear market failure. Specifically, a one-way seat from New York to London was $6,000 and from New York to Paris it was $5,000 on the Concorde, which was more than the roundtrip price from New York to London or Paris on the Boeing 747. This meant that passengers paid more than $1,000 for each hour saved by traveling on the Concorde. Modern people may be hurried today but not that hurried!

British Airways and Air France insisted all along that the Concorde broke even. Even so, the huge development cost of $8 billion was never recouped.

And business on the Concorde was not brisk—British Airways and Air France found it increasingly difficult to fill the Concorde. It seems that in their zeal to fly the only supersonic plane, the British and French greatly overestimated the benefits and grossly underestimated the costs of building and running the Concorde in their cost–benefit analysis. This is an example of how imprecise cost–benefit analysis and how costly national pride can sometimes be.

Be that as it may, the Concorde was a marvel of air travel with no rival in sight. A European project to build a Concorde 2 with double the capacity of the past Concorde was scrapped in 1995. Similarly, a 10-year study on the feasibility of building an American supersonic passenger plane by the National Aeronautics and Space Administration and involving Boeing and engine makers General Electric and Pratt & Whitney that cost $1.8 billion was shut down in 1998. Only France and Japan are still jointly trying to develop a supersonic commercial plane. The problem is not technological but economic. It seems that at present there is still no possibility of building a supersonic passenger aircraft that could be operated at a profit.

Source: "The Concorde's Destination," *The New York Times* (September 28, 1979), p. 26; "Supersonic on the Back Burner," *The Economist* (March 6, 1999), p. 74; "Concorde Successor Faces Many Hurdles," *Financial Times* (December 12, 2001), p. V; and "France and Japan Seek Concorde Alternative," *The New York Times* (June 16, 2005), p. C4.

14-2   THE CAPITAL BUDGETING PROCESS

In this section we discuss how the firm projects the cash flows from an investment project, how it calculates the net present value of and the internal rate of return on the project, and how the two are related.

Projecting Cash Flows

One of the most important and difficult aspects of capital budgeting is the estimation of the **net cash flow from a project.** This is the difference between cash receipts and cash expenditures over the life of a project. Since cash receipts and expenditures occur in the future, a great deal of uncertainty is inevitably involved in their estimation. Some general guidelines must be followed in estimating cash flows. *First,* cash flows should be measured

CASE STUDY 14-2
The Eurotunnel: Another Bad French–British Investment?

In 1987, the French and the British launched the Eurotunnel, another grandiose cooperative project to provide a rail link under the channel separating France and England, thereby cutting travel time from London to Paris to three hours and from London to Brussels to 3 hours and 15 minutes. The project was expected to be completed in 1993 at a cost $7 billion and generate enough revenues to pay the interest on the amount borrowed from a consortium of 225 banks and also to provide a return to stockholders from the 15 million passengers it was expected to transport each year. Instead, the project was completed in 1995 at a cost of $15 billion, and it had only 7 million passengers per year.

Because of much higher costs (especially interest charges) and lower revenues than anticipated, Eurotunnel, the Anglo-French operator of the English Channel tunnel, declared a moratorium on most of its staggering $14 billion debt in September 1995. After two years of often difficult negotiations with creditor banks, a restructuring plan was approved, which cut by nearly half the Eurotunnel annual servicing costs, partly through a debt-for-equity conversion that gave the creditor banks 45.5 percent of the company's capital, and partly through reduced interest charges on the remaining debt. By the end of 2005, however, Eurotunnel was again near bankruptcy, burdened as it was by $11 billion in debt and with its revenues

covering not enough to pay even the interest on the debt. The new management that ousted the Eurotunnel board in April 2004 has asked creditors to write off two-thirds of the debt if they wanted to avoid bankruptcy.

There are several reasons for the financial troubles of the Eurotunnel project. First, there is the problem that while high-speed rail links have been built on the French side of the tunnel, the British have not yet done so. This means that the trip from Paris on Brussels to London now takes much longer than originally scheduled. Second, passengers would have liked to drive through rather than load their automobiles on rail cars. Channel ferries survived the competition and now retain half of the market and, while taking longer to make the crossing, provide a more enjoyable ride. Third, there are now many budget flights from Paris and Brussels that cost much less than the train ticket.

But at this point, one may still want to ask, what is the use of cost–benefit analysis if it can be so egregiously wrong? The answer is that if the assumptions on which the analysis is based are wrong, the outcome will also be wrong. In other words: garbage in, garbage out. Firms generally do a much better job than governments in their cost–benefit analysis, but in this case, investors were suckered in by relying on governments analyses and guarantees.

Source: "More Money Down the Hole," *The Economist* (October 16, 1993), pp. 77–78; "Eurotunnel, Citing Start-Up Delays, Says Revenues to Fall Short of Forecasts," *The Wall Street Journal* (October 18, 1994), p. A2; "Eurotunnel Plan Avoids Bankruptcy," *The New York Times* (November 27, 1997), p. D4; "Eurotunnel Narrows Its Loss but Sees New Problems Ahead," *The New York Times* (July 24, 2001), p. W1; "A Tunnel Too Far," *The New York Times* (May 10, 2005), p. 21; "Eurotunnel Seeks Write-off of Debt," *Financial Times* (April 27, 2005), p. 17; and "Eurotunnel Urges New Deadline for Debt Pact," *The Wall Street Journal* (April 13, 2006), p. 88.

on an *incremental basis.* That is, the cash flow from a given project should be measured by the difference between the stream of the firm's cash flows with and without the project. Any increase in the expenditures or reduction in the receipts of other divisions of the firm resulting from the adoption of a given project must be considered. For example, the firm must subtract from the estimated gross cash receipts resulting from the introduction of a new product any anticipated reduction in the cash receipts of other divisions of the firm selling competitive products. *Second,* cash flows must be estimated on an *after-tax* basis, using the firm's marginal tax rate. *Third,* as a noncash expense, depreciation affects the firm's cash flow only through its effect on taxes.

A typical project involves making an initial investment and generates a series of net cash flows over the life of the project. The initial investment to add a new product line may include the cost of purchasing and installing new equipment, reorganizing the firm's production processes, providing additional working capital for inventory and accounts receivable, and so on. The net cash flows are equal to cash inflows minus cash outflows in each year during the life of the project. The cash inflows are, of course, the incremental sales revenues generated by the project plus the salvage value of the equipment at the end of its economic life, if any, and recovery of working capital at the end of the project. The cash outflows usually include the incremental variable costs, fixed costs, and taxes resulting from the project.

For example, suppose that a firm estimates that it needs to make an initial investment of $1 million in order to introduce a new product. The marketing division of the firm expects the life of the product to be five years. Incremental sales revenues are estimated to be $1 million during the first year of operation and to rise by 10 percent per year until the fifth year, when the product will be replaced. The production department projects that the incremental variable costs of producing the product will be 50 percent of incremental sales revenues and that the firm would also incur additional fixed costs of $150,000 per year. The finance department anticipates a marginal tax rate of 40 percent for the firm. The finance department of the firm would use the straight-line depreciation method so that the annual depreciation charge would be $200,000 per year for five years. The salvage value of the initial equipment is estimated to be $250,000, and the firm also expects to recover $100,000 of its working capital at the end of the fifth year. The cash flows from this project are summarized in Table 14-1.

TABLE 14-1	Estimated Cash Flow from Project				
	Year				
	1	**2**	**3**	**4**	**5**
Sales Less:	$1,000,000	$1,100,000	$1,210,000	$1,331,000	$1,464,100
Variable costs	500,000	550,000	605,000	665,500	732,050
Fixed costs	150,000	150,000	150,000	150,000	150,000
Depreciation	200,000	200,000	200,000	200,000	200,000
Profit before taxes	$ 150,000	$ 200,000	$ 255,000	$ 315,500	$ 382,050
Less: Income tax	60,000	80,000	102,000	126,200	152,820
Profit after tax	$ 90,000	$ 120,000	$ 153,000	$ 189,300	$ 229,230
Plus: Depreciation	200,000	200,000	200,000	200,000	200,000
Net cash flow	$ 290,000	$ 320,000	$ 353,000	$ 389,300	$ 429,230
				Plus: Salvage value of equipment	250,000
				Recovery of working capital	100,000
				Net cash flow in year 5	$ 779,230

The question now is whether the firm should undertake the investment. In order to answer this question, the firm must compare the net cash flow over the five years of the project indicated in Table 14-1 to the initial $1 million cost of the project. Since $1 received in future years is worth less than $1 spent today (this is referred to as the **time value of money**), the net cash flow from the project must be discounted to the present before comparing it to the initial cost of the investment. Alternatively, the firm could find the internal rate of return on the project. These methods of evaluating an investment project are next examined in turn.

Net Present Value (*NPV*)

One method of deciding whether or not a firm should accept an investment project is to determine the net present value of the project. The **net present value (*NPV*) of a project** is equal to the present value of the expected stream of net cash flows from the project, discounted at the firm's cost of capital, minus the initial cost of the project. As pointed out in Equation 13-10 in Chapter 13, the net present value (*NPV*) of a project is given by

$$NPV = \sum_{t=1}^{n} \frac{R_i}{(1+k)^t} - C_0 \qquad [14\text{-}1]$$

where R_t refers to the estimated net cash flow from the project in each of the n years considered, k is the risk-adjusted discount rate, Σ refers to the sum, and C_0 is the initial cost of the project. The value of the firm will increase if the *NPV* of the project is positive and decline if the *NPV* of the project is negative. Thus, the firm should undertake the project if its *NPV* is positive and should not undertake it if the *NPV* of the project is negative.

For example, if k (the risk-adjusted discount rate) or cost of capital of the project to the firm is 12 percent, the net present value of the project with the estimated net cash flow given in Table 14-1, and the initial cost of $1 million is

$$NPV = \frac{\$290,000}{(1+0.12)^1} + \frac{\$320,000}{(1+0.12)^2} + \frac{\$353,000}{(1+0.12)^3} + \frac{\$389,300}{(1+0.12)^4}$$
$$+ \frac{\$779,230}{(1+0.12)^5} - \$1,000,000$$
$$= \$1,454,852 - \$1,000,000$$
$$= \$454,852$$

This project would thus add $454,852 to the value of the firm, and the firm should undertake it.[3] If the firm had used instead the risk-adjusted discount rates of 10 percent and 20 percent, respectively, the net present value of the project would have been $543,012 and $169,078 (see the answer to Problem 3 at the end of the book). Thus, even if $k = 20$ percent, the firm should undertake the project.

---

[3] The values of the term $1/(1+0.12)^t$ for $t = 1$ to $t = 5$ in the above calculations can be obtained with a calculator and are equal to the first five terms in the column headed 12 percent in Table B-2 in Appendix B, as explained in Section A-2 in Appendix A at the end of the book.

Internal Rate of Return (*IRR*)

Another method of determining whether a firm should accept an investment project is to calculate the internal rate of return on the project. The **internal rate of return (*IRR*) on a project** is the discount rate that equates the present value of the net cash flow from the project to the initial cost of the project. This is obtained by solving Equation 14-2 for k^*, the internal rate of return (*IRR*).

$$\sum_{t=1}^{n} \frac{R_t}{(1 + k^*)^t} = C_0 \qquad\qquad [14\text{-}2]$$

Although the internal rate of return ($IRR = k^*$) on a project can easily be obtained with a computer or a sophisticated handheld calculator, it can also be obtained by trial and error by using Table B-2 in Appendix B at the end of the book. Specifically, we begin by using an arbitrary discount rate to calculate the present value of the net cash flows from the project. If the present value of the net cash flow exceeds the initial cost of the project, we increase the discount rate and repeat the process. On the other hand, if the present value of the net cash flows from the project is smaller than the initial cost of the project, we reduce the discount rate. The process is continued until the rate of discount is found that equates the present value of the net cash flow from the project to the initial cost of the project (so that Equation 14-2 holds). The discount rate found is the internal rate of return ($IRR = k^*$) on the project.

The firm should undertake the project if the internal rate of return on the project ($IRR = k^*$) exceeds or is equal to the marginal cost of capital or risk-adjusted discount rate (k) that the firm uses, and it should not undertake the project if the internal rate of return is smaller than the marginal cost of capital.[4] For example, using Table B-2, we can find that the present value of the net cash flow from the project shown in Table 14-1 is $1,057,631 with $k = 24$ percent and $961,986 with $k = 28$ percent, as compared to the initial cost of the project of $1 million. Since the present value of the net cash flow from the project exceeds the initial cost of the project at $k = 24$ percent and is smaller at $k = 28$ percent, the internal rate of return on this project (k^*) must be between 24 and 28 percent. It is in fact 26.3 percent.[5]

Comparison of *NPV* and *IRR*

When evaluating a single or independent project, the *NPV* and *IRR* methods will always lead to the same accept–reject decision. The reason for this is that the *NPV* is positive only if the *IRR* on the project exceeds the marginal cost of capital or risk-adjusted discount rate used by the firm. Similarly, the *NPV* is negative only when the *IRR* is smaller than the marginal cost of capital. For mutually exclusive projects (i.e., when only one of

---

[4] This is nothing else than the application of the marginal analysis presented in Figure 14-1, where the internal rates of return on the various projects open to the firm, arranged from the highest to the lowest, represent the firm's demand for capital.

[5] This was obtained with a hand calculator. Other investment criteria include the payback period and the average rate of return. Since they do not involve discounting the net cash flow from the investment, however, they are inferior to the *NPV* and *IRR* methods and are not discussed here.

TABLE 14-2 Net Present Value and Internal Rate of Return on Two Mutually Exclusive Investment Projects		
	Project A	**Project B**
Initial cost	$1,000,000	$1,000,000
Net cash flow (years)		
Year 1	−100,000	350,000
Year 2	0	350,000
Year 3	500,000	350,000
Year 4	500,000	350,000
Year 5	1,400,000	350,000
Net present value (*NPV*) at 12% discount rate	$1,378,720	$1,261,680
Internal rate of return (*IRR*)	20.3%	22.1%

two or more projects can be undertaken), however, the *NPV* and the *IRR* methods may provide contradictory signals as to which project will add more to the value of the firm. That is, the project with the higher *NPV* may have a lower *IRR* than an alternative project, and vice versa.

For example, Table 14-2 shows that project A has a higher net present value but a lower internal rate of return than project B. The reason this situation may arise is that under the *NPV* method, the net cash flows generated by the project are implicitly and conservatively assumed to be reinvested at the firm's cost of capital or risk-adjusted discount rate used by the firm. On the other hand, under the *IRR* method, the net cash flows generated by the project are implicitly assumed to be reinvested at the same higher internal rate of return earned on the project. Since there is no certainty that the firm can reinvest the net cash flows generated by a project at the same higher internal rate of return earned on the given project, it is generally better to use the *NPV* method in deciding which of two mutually exclusive investment projects to undertake. That is, it is preferable for the firm to undertake the project with the higher *NPV* rather than the one with the higher *IRR* when the two methods provide contradictory signals. Case Study 14-3 examines Pennzoil's $3 billion capital budgeting challenge, while Case Study 14-4 discusses capital budgeting for investments in human capital.

14-3   CAPITAL RATIONING AND THE PROFITABILITY INDEX

We saw in the previous section that in the case of mutually exclusive projects the *NPV* and the *IRR* methods may lead to contradictory investment signals. If that happens, the *NPV* method is generally preferable. Even the *NPV* investment rule, however, may lead to difficulties in the case of mutually exclusive investment projects of *unequal* size. That is, a smaller project may lead to a lower *NPV* than an alternative larger project, but the ratio of the present value of the net cash flows to the initial cost of the project (i.e., the profitability per dollar of investment) may be higher on the former than on the latter project.

CASE STUDY 14-3
Pennzoil's $3 Billion Capital Budgeting Challenge

In December 1987, after four years of litigation, Pennzoil settled its case against Texaco, the third-largest U.S. energy company, for $3 billion in cash. Texaco agreed to pay the $3 billion in cash to Pennzoil in lieu of an earlier $10.3 billion court judgment against Texaco for illegally inducing Getty Oil to break a merger agreement with Pennzoil. The $3 billion, which Pennzoil received in 1988 (compared with Pennzoil's $2.6 billion in total assets and $1.9 billion sales prior to the settlement), catapulted Pennzoil from No. 394 to No. 220 among all publicly traded companies in the United States.

The capital budgeting challenge faced by Pennzoil in 1988 was what to do with the $2.5 billion that it had left after paying $400 million in legal expenses and $100 million in taxes. Pennzoil had several options. One option was to put the money into Treasury bills, another option was to retire Pennzoil debt, a third option was to pay a one-time dividend of about $40, and a fourth option was to triple Pennzoil oil reserves through acquisitions. Of these four options, only the fourth provided the opportunity to avoid the large lump-sum tax penalty. The reason was that income from using the cash settlement to acquire oil and gas properties or similar assets would be taxed over the subsequent 20 or 30 years.

After scouting the economic landscape in general and the energy sector in particular, preparing various investment projects, and estimating the net present value and the internal rate of return of each, Pennzoil did a little of each of the above in 1989. It used $400 million to repurchase 5.3 million shares of its stock, raised the common stock dividend by 36 percent to $3 per share, and used nearly $2 billion of the remaining $2.2 billion (and the interest earned on the

capital during 1988) to acquire an 8.8 percent stake in the Chevron Corporation (another petroleum company) to shelter it from taxes. Pennzoil argued that Chevron stock represented an investment in replacement property similar to that lost to Texaco and that such a property was, therefore, not to be treated as taxable property. The Internal Revenue Service (IRS), however, thought otherwise, and Pennzoil finally settled at the end of 1994 by agreeing to pay $454 million ($265 million in additional taxes and $189 million in interest), or half of what the IRS had originally sought. Thus, came to an end a 10-year investment-litigation saga.

In September 1987, Pennzoil fought off a $4.2 billion hostile takeover by Union Pacific Resources, and in April 1998 it acquired for $727 million Quaker State, the second-largest motor oil company (after Pennzoil).

In 2002, Pennzoil was acquired by Royal Dutch Shell, the Anglo-Dutch oil giant, for $1.8 billion. Shell also took over Pennzoil's debt of $1.1 billion. Thus, the net worth of Pennzoil-Quaker was only $0.7 billion. Had Pennzoil invested its net worth of $2.6 billion in 1987 plus the $2.5 billion net received from the Texaco settlement in Treasury bills, it would have had about $10 billion in 2002, instead of a net worth of only $0.7 billion!

In fall 2004, Google, the California-based Internet search-engine firm, faced a similar enviable challenge as Pennzoil faced 17 years earlier, namely, how to utilize the nearly $2 billion cash that it raised from going public. By 2005, it seemed clear that Google was using the cash to strengthen its core competency against the encroachment by Microsoft and Yahoo.

Source: "A $3 Billion Question for Pennzoil," *The New York Times* (December 12, 1987), p. D1; "Problem Facing Pennzoil Company in Deciding Where to Invest," *The New York Times* (July 30, 1989), sec. 3, p. 1; "Pennzoil Agrees to Settle IRS's Texaco Claim," *The Wall Street Journal* (October 27, 1994), p. A4; "Pennzoil and Quaker State Plan a Two-Stage Merger," *The New York Times* (April 16, 1998), p. D4; "Shell Acquires Pennzoil-Quaker for $3 billion," *Financial Times* (March 26, 2002), p. 1; and "Nice Problem: How Will Google Use Its $2 billion?" *The Wall Street Journal* (August 17, 2004), B1.

CASE STUDY 14-4
Capital Budgeting for Investments in Human Capital

Expenditures on education, job training, migration to areas of better job opportunities, health, and so on are often referred to as investments in *human capital.* As for other investments, these involve costs and provide returns. For example, college students incur out-of-pocket expenses or explicit costs for tuition, books, and living expenses and even larger implicit costs for the earnings forgone by attending college rather than working. A college education, however, also leads to higher lifetime earnings. Thus, the valuation model can be used to determine the net present value of any investment in human capital, such as an investment in a college education.

Using the valuation model, it was estimated that the return to a college education was about 10 to 15 percent per year during the 1950s and the 1960s. This was substantially higher than the return on similarly risky investments (such as the purchase of a stock). Thus, getting a college education during the 1950s and 1960s, besides its intrinsic value, was also a good investment that made much economic sense. During the 1970s, however, as a result of sharp tuition increases and lower starting salaries,

the return to a college education declined to 7 or 8 percent per year. It then rose to between 10 to 13 percent during the 1980s and 1990s, but it has declined somewhat since then.

These studies face a number of statistical problems. For example, some of the expenditures included among the costs of attending college are more in the nature of consumption than investment (as, for example, when an engineering student takes a philosophy course). In addition, some of the higher lifetime earnings attributed to a college education may in fact result from the higher presumed intelligence of individuals attending college and would probably result even without a college education. There are then some benefits to a college education that are not easily measurable, such as college graduates suffering fewer mental problems, having happier marriages, and so on, than those without a college education. Despite these measurement difficulties, the concept and measurement of human capital is very important and commonly used (e.g., to determine damages to award to injury victims).

Source: Gary S. Becker, *Human Capital*, 2nd ed. (New York: Columbia University Press, 1975); Richard B. Freeman, "The Decline in the Economic Rewards to College Education," *Review of Economic and Statistics* (February 1977), pp. 18–29; "The Soaring Payoff from Higher Education," *The Margin* (January/February 1990), p. 6; "The New Math of Higher Education," *Business Week* (March 18, 1996), p. 39; and "College Degree Still Pays, but It's Leveling off," *The New York Times* (January 13, 2005), p. C1.

In cases of capital rationing (i.e., when the firm cannot undertake all the projects with positive *NPV*), the firm should rank projects according to their profitability index and choose the projects with the highest profitability indexes rather than those with the highest *NPV*s. The **profitability index (*PI*)** of a project is measured by

$$PI = \frac{\sum_{t=1}^{n} [R_t/(1 + k)^t]}{C_0} \qquad [14\text{-}3]$$

	Project A	Project B	Project C
TABLE 14-3 Comparison of *NPV* and *PI* Rankings of Projects with Unequal Costs			
Present value of net cash flows (*PVNCF*)	$2,600,000	$1,400,000	$1,400,000
Initial cost of project (C_0)	2,000,000	1,000,000	1,000,000
$NPV = PVNCF - C_0$	$ 600,000	$ 400,000	$ 400,000
$PI = \dfrac{PVNCF}{C_0}$	1.3	1.4	1.4

where R_t is the net cash flow in year t of the project, and C_0 is the initial cost of the project. With capital rationing, the firm should choose the projects with the highest relative profitability, or highest profitability per dollar of cost or investment (i.e., those whose *PI* exceeds 1 by the greatest amount) in order to avoid bias in favor of larger projects.

For example, the data in Table 14-3 show that while project A has a higher *NPV* than either project B or C and would, therefore, be the only project undertaken according to the *NPV* investment rule if the firm could invest only $2 million, the profitability indexes for projects B and C are greater than for project A, and the firm should undertake both of these projects instead of project A. That is, jointly, projects B and C increase the value of the firm by more than project A, but they would not be undertaken if the firm followed the *NPV* rule and could invest only $2 million. Although this example is simplistic, it does show that with capital rationing, the profitability index or relative *NPV* rule may lead to a different *ranking* or order in which projects are to be undertaken. Of course, in the absence of capital rationing, the firm will undertake all projects with a positive *NPV* or profitability index larger than 1.

Capital rationing may arise for several reasons. First, undertaking all the projects with positive *NPV* may involve such rapid expansion as to strain the managerial, personnel, and other resources of the firm. As a result, top management may impose a limit on the number and size of the investment projects to be undertaken during a given period of time. Second, a firm may be reluctant to borrow heavily to supplement internal funds because of the risk to which the firm would be exposed in case of an unexpected economic downturn. Top management may also be reluctant to raise additional capital by selling stocks because of fear of losing control of the firm. Third, top management may arbitrarily limit the capital budget of its various divisions.

14-4 THE COST OF CAPITAL

In this section we examine how the firm estimates the cost of raising the capital to invest. As we saw in Section 14–1, this is an essential element of the capital budgeting process. The firm can raise investment funds internally (i.e., from undistributed profits) or externally (i.e., by borrowing and from selling stocks). The cost of using internal funds is the opportunity cost or foregone return on these funds outside the firm. The cost of external funds is the lowest rate of return that lenders and stockholders require to lend to or invest their funds in the firm. In this section we examine how the cost of debt (i.e., the cost of raising capital by borrowing) and the cost of equity capital (i.e., the cost of raising capital by selling stocks) are determined. On one hand, the estimation of the cost of debt is fairly straightforward. On the other hand, there are at least three methods of estimating the cost of equity capital: the risk-free rate plus premium, the dividend valuation model, and the capital asset pricing model (CAPM). These methods will be examined in turn. The estimation of the cost of capital to the firm is studied in detail in financial management courses. What follows is only an introduction to this topic.

The Cost of Debt

The **cost of debt** is the return that lenders require to lend their funds to the firm. Since the interest payments made by the firm on borrowed funds are deductible from the firm's taxable income, the *after-tax* cost of borrowed funds to the firm (k_d) is given by the interest paid (r) multiplied by 1 minus the firm's marginal tax rate (t). That is,

$$k_d = r(1-t) \qquad\qquad [14\text{-}4]$$

For example, if the firm borrows at a 12.5 percent interest rate and faces a 40 percent marginal tax rate on its taxable income, the after-tax cost of debt capital to the firm is

$$k_d = 12.5\%(1-0.40) = 7.5\%$$

To be noted is that if the firm has no taxable income after all costs are deducted during a particular year, the firm's after-tax cost of debt is equal to its pretax interest rate charged on borrowed funds. Also to be noted is that we are interested in the cost of new or marginal debt, not the average cost of debt, since it is the marginal cost of debt that is used to determine whether the firm should or should not undertake a particular investment project.

The Cost of Equity Capital: The Risk-Free Rate Plus Premium

As pointed out earlier, the cost of equity capital is the rate of return that stockholders require to invest in the firm. The cost of raising equity capital externally usually exceeds the cost of raising equity capital internally by the flotation costs (i.e., the cost of issuing the stock). For simplicity, we disregard these costs in the following analysis and treat both types of equity capital together. Since dividends paid on stocks (as opposed to the interest paid on bonds) are not deductible as a business expense (i.e., dividends are paid out after corporate taxes have been paid), there is no tax adjustment in determining the equity cost of capital.

One method employed to estimate the cost of equity capital (k_e) is to use the risk-free rate (r_f) plus a risk premium (r_p). That is,

$$k_e = r_f + r_p \qquad\qquad [14\text{-}5]$$

The risk-free rate (r_f) is usually taken to be the six-month U.S. Treasury bill rate.[6] The reason for this is that the obligation to make payments of the interest and principal on government

---

[6] Some security analysts prefer to use instead the long-term government bond rate for r_f.

securities is assumed to occur with certainty. The risk premium (r_p) that must be paid in raising equity capital has two components. The first component results because of the greater risk that is involved in investing in a firm's securities (such as bonds) as opposed to investing in federal government securities. The second component is the additional risk resulting from purchasing the common stock rather than the bonds of the firm. Stocks involve a greater risk than bonds because dividends on stocks are paid only after the firm has met its contractual obligations to make interest and principal payments to bondholders. Since dividends vary with the firm's profits, stocks are more risky than bonds so that their return must include an additional risk premium. If the premiums associated with these two types of risk are labeled p_1 and p_2, we can restate the formula for the cost of equity capital as

$$k_e = r_f + p_1 + p_2 \qquad\qquad [14\text{-}6]$$

The first type of risk (that is, p_1) is usually measured by the excess of the rate of interest on the firm's bonds (r) over the rate of return on government bonds (r_f). The additional risk involved in purchasing the firm's stocks rather than bonds (that is, p_2) is usually taken to be about 4 percentage points. This is the historical difference between the average yield (dividends plus capital gains) on stocks as opposed to the average yield on bonds issued by private companies. For example, if the risk-free rate of return on government securities is 8 percent and the firm's bonds yield 11 percent, the total risk premium (r_p) involved in purchasing the firm's stocks rather than government bonds is

$$r_p = p_1 + p_2 = (11\% - 8\%) + 4\% = 3\% + 4\% = 7\%$$

so that the firm's cost of equity capital is

$$k_e = r_f + p_1 + p_2 = 8\% + 3\% + 4\% = 15\%$$

The Cost of Equity Capital: The Dividend Valuation Model

The equity cost of capital to a firm can also be estimated by the **dividend valuation model.** To derive this model, we begin by pointing out that, with perfect information, the value of a share of the common stock of a firm should be equal to the present value of all future dividends expected to be paid on the stock, discounted at the investor's required rate of return (k_e). If the dividend per share (D) paid to stockholders is expected to remain constant over time, the present value of a share of the common stock of the firm (P) is then

$$P = \sum_{t=1}^{\infty} \frac{D}{(1 + k_e)^t} \qquad\qquad [14\text{-}7]$$

If dividends are assumed to remain constant over time and to be paid indefinitely, Equation 14-7 is nothing else than an annuity (see Section A-4 in Appendix A at the end of the book) and can be rewritten as

$$P = \frac{D}{k_e} \qquad\qquad [14\text{-}8]$$

If dividends are instead expected to increase over time at the annual rate of g, the price of a share of the common stock of the firm will be greater and is given by

$$P = \frac{D}{k_e - g} \qquad \text{[14-9]}$$

Solving Equation 14-9 for k_e, we get the following equation to measure the equity cost of capital equation to the firm:

$$k_e = \frac{D}{P} + g \qquad \text{[14-10]}$$

That is, the investor's required rate of return on equity is equal to the ratio of the dividend paid on a share of the common stock of the firm to the price of a share of the stock (the so-called dividend yield) plus the expected growth rate of dividend payments by the firm (g). The value of g is the firm's historic growth rate or the earnings growth forecasts of security analysts (based on the expected sales, profit margins, and competitive position of the firm) published in *Business Week, Forbes,* and other business publications.

For example, if the firm pays a dividend of $20 per share on common stock that sells for $200 per share and the growth rate of dividend payments is expected to be 5 percent per year, the cost of equity capital for this firm is

$$k_e = \frac{\$20}{\$200} + 0.05 = 0.10 + 0.05 = 0.15 \qquad \text{or } 15\%$$

The Cost of Equity Capital: The Capital Asset Pricing Model (CAPM)

Another method commonly used to estimate the equity cost of capital is the **capital asset pricing model (CAPM).** This takes into consideration not only the risk differential between common stocks and government securities but also the risk differential between the common stock of the firm and the average common stock of all firms or broad-based market portfolio. The risk differential between common stocks and government securities is measured by $(k_m - r_f)$, where k_m is the average return on all common stocks and r_f is the return on government securities.

The risk differential between the common stock of the firm and the common stock of all firms is given by the **beta coefficient (β).** This is the ratio of the variability in the return on the common stock of the firm to the variability in the average return on the common stocks of all firms. Beta coefficients can be obtained by regressing the variability in the return of the stock of the firm on the variability in the average return of common stocks (as measured by the Standard & Poor's 500 Index or the New York Stock Exchange Index) over a given period of time. More commonly, beta coefficients for individual stocks are obtained from the Value Line Investment Survey, Merrill Lynch, or other brokerage firms.

A beta coefficient of 1 means that the variability in the returns on the common stock of the firm is the same as the variability in the returns on all stocks. Thus, investors holding the stock of the firm face the same risk as holding a broad-based market portfolio of all stocks. A beta coefficient of 2 means that the variability in the returns on (i.e., risk of holding) the stock of the firm is twice that of the average stock. On the other hand, holding a stock with a beta coefficient of 0.5 is half as risky as holding the average stock.

The cost of equity capital to the firm estimated by the capital asset pricing model is measured by

$$k_e = r_f + \beta(k_m - r_f) \qquad\qquad [14\text{-}11]$$

where k_e is the cost of equity capital to the firm, r_f is the risk-free rate, β is the beta co-efficient, and k_m is the average return on the stock of all firms. Thus, the CAPM postu-lates that the cost of equity capital to the firm is equal to the sum of the risk-free rate plus the beta coefficient (β) times the risk premium on the average stock ($k_m - r_f$). Note that multiplying β by ($k_m - r_f$) gives the risk premium on holding the common stock of the particular firm.

For example, suppose that the risk-free rate (r_f) is 8 percent, the average return on common stocks (k_m) is 15 percent, and the beta coefficient (β) for the firm is 1. The cost of equity capital to the firm (k_e) is then

$$k_e = 8\% + 1(15\% - 8\%) = 15\%$$

That is, since a beta coefficient of 1 indicates that the stock of this firm is as risky as the av-erage stock of all firms, the equity cost of capital to the firm is 15 percent (the same as the average return on all stocks). If $\beta = 1.5$ for the firm (so that the risk involved in holding the stock of the firm is 1.5 times larger than the risk on the average stock), the equity cost of capital to the firm would be

$$k_e = 8\% + 1.5(15\% - 8\%) = 18.5\%$$

On the other hand, if $\beta = 0.5$,

$$k_e = 8\% + 0.5(15\% - 8\%) = 11.5\%$$

In this example and in the examples using the risk-free rate plus premium and the dividend valuation model, the equity cost of capital was found to be the same (15 percent). This is seldom the case. That is, the different methods of estimating the equity cost of capital to a firm are likely to give somewhat different results. Firms are, thus, likely to use all three methods and then attempt to reconcile the differences and arrive at a consensus equity cost of capital for the firm.

The Weighted Cost of Capital

In general, a firm is likely to raise capital from undistributed profits, by borrowing, and by the sale of stocks, and so the marginal cost of capital to the firm is a weighted average of the cost of raising the various types of capital.

Since the interest paid on borrowed funds is tax deductible while the dividends paid on stocks are not, the cost of debt is generally less than the cost of equity capital. The risk involved in raising funds by borrowing, however, is greater than the risk on equity capital because the firm must regularly make payments of the interest and principal on borrowed funds before paying dividends on stocks. Thus, firms do not generally raise funds only by borrowing but also by selling stock (as well as from undistributed profits).

Firms often try to maintain or achieve a particular long-term capital structure of debt to equity. For example, public utility companies may prefer a capital structure involving 60 percent debt and 40 percent equity, while auto manufacturers may prefer 30 percent debt and 70 percent equity. The particular debt/equity ratio that a firm prefers reflects the risk preference of its managers and stockholders and the nature of the firm's business. Public utilities accept the higher risk involved in a higher debt/equity ratio because of their more stable flow of earnings than automobile manufacturers. When a firm needs to raise investment capital, it borrows and it sells stocks so as to maintain or achieve a desired debt/equity ratio.

The **composite cost of capital** to the firm (k_c) is then a weighted average of the cost of debt capital (k_d) and equity capital (k_e) as given by

$$k_c = w_d k_d + w_e k_e \qquad [14\text{-}12]$$

where w_d and w_e are, respectively, the proportion of debt and equity capital in the firm's capital structure. For example, if the (after-tax) cost of debt is 7.5 percent, the cost of equity capital is 15 percent, and the firm wants to have a debt/equity ratio of 40:60, the composite or weighted marginal cost of capital to the firm will be

$$k_c = (0.40)(7.5\%) + (0.60)(15\%) = 3\% + 9\% = 12\%$$

This is the composite marginal cost of capital that we have used to evaluate all the proposed investment projects that the firm faced in Section 14-1 and Figure 14-1. That is, the proportion of debt to equity that the firm seeks to achieve or maintain in the long run is not usually defined for individual projects but for all the investment projects that the firm is considering. Note that the marginal cost of capital eventually rises (i.e., the *MCC* curve in Figure 14-1 becomes positively sloped) as the firm raises additional amounts of capital by borrowing and selling stocks because of the higher risk that lenders and investors' face as the firm's debt/equity ratio rises. Case Study 14-5 examines firms' choice between equity and debt in Britain, while Case Study 14-6 discusses capital budgeting techniques used by major U.S. firms.

14-5   REVIEWING INVESTMENT PROJECTS AFTER IMPLEMENTATION

It is important to review projects after they have been implemented. Such a review involves comparing the actual cash flow and return from a project with the expected or predicted cash flow and return on the project, as well as an explanation of the observed differences between predicted and actual results. In reviewing projects after their implementation, it is important, however, to recognize that some differences between predicted

CASE STUDY 14-5
The Choice between Equity and Debt

In a study published in the *Journal of Finance,* Paul Marsh used regression analysis to identify and determine the relative importance of the factors that influence firms' decisions to raise new capital by debt or equity. The author used data on 748 issues of debt and equity made by U.K. companies from 1959 through 1970. The author found that (1) companies that are below their long-term debt targets are more likely to issue debt than equity; (2) smaller companies, those with few fixed assets, and those facing a greater risk of bankruptcy are more likely to issue equity than debt; (3) firms that have recently experienced unusually large increases in the value of their stocks tend to favor equity over debt; and (4) firms are more likely to issue equity than debt after periods of strong stock market performance, and they are more likely to issue debt than equity when interest rates are low and are expected to increase. The author tested the predictive ability of the model using a sample of 110 debt and

equity issues made by U.K. companies between 1971 and 1974. The author found that the model classified 75 percent of the new issues correctly between debt and equity over that period.

A 2001 study by Graham and Harvey based on a 1999 survey sample of 392 U.S. CEOs found that U.S. firms do not seem to target specific debt ratios. The most important consideration affecting debt decisions is management's desire for "financial flexibility" and to overcome insufficient internal funds. The authors also found that U.S. firms are reluctant to issue common stock when they perceive that it is undervalued and are more likely to issue stock after their stock price has increased. On the other hand, U.S. firms are more likely to issue debt when interest rates are low in relation to long rates and to borrow abroad when interest rates are lower there. In general, U.S. firms rely less on debt than European firms (20 percent and 30 percent, respectively).

Source: J. R. Graham and Campbell Harvey, "The Theory and Practice of Finance: Evidence from the Field," *Journal of Financial Economics* (Fall 2001), pp. 187–243; and *Vernimmen.Com Letter* (June 2005), at http://www.vernimmen.com/letter/html/letter_7.html.

or estimated and actual results are to some extent inevitable in view of the uncertainty surrounding future cash flows. Some differences between predicted and actual results may also be due to unforeseen events (such as the downturn in the airline industry following the 9/11 terrorist attack and subsequent security challenge in 2001 and 2002) over which a firm has no control.

Comparing and explaining differences between the predicted and the actual results of an investment project after its implementation is, nevertheless, very useful. The reason is that if decision makers know that their investment projects will be reviewed and evaluated after implementation and compared with predicted outcomes, they are likely to draw up investment plans more carefully and also to work harder to ensure that their predictions are fulfilled. It has been found, for example, that the best-run companies are those that place great importance on *post-audits* and that decision makers' estimates improve when they know that post-audit reviews are routinely conducted. Post-audit reviews must be used carefully, however, to avoid discouraging decision makers from proposing very risky but potentially very profitable investment projects.

CASE STUDY 14-6
Capital Budgeting Techniques of Major U.S. Firms

Table 14-4 gives the results of a survey conducted on the capital budgeting techniques used by major U.S. firms in 1959 and in 1985. The firms surveyed could choose among the following capital budgeting techniques: net present value, internal rate of return, payback period, or other method. The first two methods (discussed in Section 14-2) are sophisticated in the sense that they consider the time value of money, while the third (i.e., the payback period) is unsophisticated because it simply involves the estimation of the number of years it takes for the project to generate enough revenue to fully cover the cost of the project, without discounting. The "other" methods used were also unsophisticated.

The table shows that 21 percent of firms surveyed used the net present value as their primary capital budgeting evaluating method in 1985 (up from 7 percent in 1959), 49 percent used the internal rate of return in 1985 (up from practically zero in 1959), 19 percent used the payback method in 1985 (down from 42 percent in 1959), and 11 percent used some other unsophisticated method in 1985 (down from 51 percent in 1959). Thus, in 1985, 70 percent of the firms surveyed used either the net present value or the internal rate of return as their primary capital budgeting evaluating method while the re-maining 30 percent used either the payback period or some other unsophisticated method. This is to be contrasted with 93 percent of the firms surveyed using the payback period or other unsophisticated method as their primary evaluating method in 1959.

As far as their secondary evaluating method, 24 percent of the firms used the net present value in 1985 (up from 1 percent in 1959), 15 percent used the internal rate of return in 1985 (up from 1 percent in 1959), 35 percent used the payback period (up from 15 percent in 1959), and 26 percent used some other method (down from 85 percent in 1959). Thus, aside from the increase in the use of the payback period as the secondary evaluating method from 1959 to 1985, the capital budgeting evaluating method used by U.S. firms became much more sophisticated over time by the inclusion of the time value of money in the calculation, especially in the primary evaluating method used. In fact a 2001 study by Graham and Harvey based on a 1999 survey sample of 392 CEOs found that about three-quarters of large companies used either the net present value or the internal rate of return about three-quarters of the time. Small companies, however, especially if managed by older CEOs without an MBA, use the payback period about half of the time.

TABLE 14-4 Capital Budgeting Techniques Used (percent of respondents)		
Primary Evaluating Method	**1959**	**1985**
Net present value	7	21
Internal rate of return	—	49
Payback period	42	19
Other	51	11
Secondary Evaluating Method	**1959**	**1985**
Net present value	1	24
Internal rate of return	1	15
Payback period	15	35
Other	82	26

Source: Suk H. Kim, Trevor Crick, and Seung H. Kim, "Do Executives Practice What Academics Preach?" *Management Accounting* (November 1986), pp. 49–52; and J. R. Graham and Campbell Harvey, "The Theory and Practice of Finance: Evidence from the Field," *Journal of Financial Economics* (Fall 2001), pp. 187–243.

| **14-6** | ## THE COST OF CAPITAL AND INTERNATIONAL COMPETITIVENESS |

During most of the 1980s, the cost of capital was much higher in the United States than in Japan and in many other major industrial nations, and this was one of the factors that undermined the international competitiveness of U.S. firms. Having to pay even one additional percentage point in interest charges could add hundreds of thousands or even millions of dollars to the capital cost of a large firm and hurt its ability to compete both at home and abroad.[7] Table 14-5 shows the average nominal and real (i.e., inflation-adjusted) lending rates charged

TABLE 14-5 Real and Nominal Bank Lending Rates in the United States and Japan (in percentages per year: 1981–2004)

Year	United States			Japan			U.S.–Japanese Differentials	
	Nominal	CPI*	Real	Nominal	CPI	Real	Nominal	Real
1981	18.9	10.3	8.6	7.9	4.9	3.0	11.0	5.6
1982	14.9	6.2	8.7	7.3	2.7	4.6	7.6	4.1
1983	10.8	3.2	7.6	7.1	1.9	5.2	3.7	2.4
1984	12.0	4.3	7.7	6.8	2.2	4.5	5.2	3.2
1985	9.9	3.6	3.3	6.6	2.0	4.6	3.3	−1.3
1986	8.4	1.9	6.5	6.0	0.6	5.4	2.4	1.1
1987	8.2	3.7	4.5	5.2	0.1	5.2	3.0	−0.7
1988	9.3	4.0	5.3	5.0	0.7	4.3	4.3	1.0
1989	10.9	4.8	6.1	5.3	2.3	3.0	5.6	3.1
1990	10.1	5.4	4.7	7.0	3.1	3.9	3.1	0.8
1991	8.5	4.2	4.3	7.5	3.3	4.2	1.0	0.1
1992	6.3	3.0	3.3	6.2	1.7	4.5	0.1	−1.2
1993	6.0	3.0	3.0	4.4	1.3	3.1	1.6	−0.1
1994	7.1	2.6	4.5	4.1	0.7	3.4	3.0	1.1
1995	8.8	2.8	6.0	3.5	−0.1	3.5	5.4	2.5
1996	8.3	2.9	5.4	2.7	0.1	2.6	5.6	2.8
1997	8.4	2.3	6.1	2.5	1.7	0.8	5.9	5.3
1998	8.4	1.6	6.8	2.3	0.7	1.7	6.1	5.1
1999	8.0	2.2	5.8	2.2	−0.3	1.9	5.8	3.9
2000	9.2	3.4	5.8	2.1	−0.7	1.5	7.1	4.3
2001	6.9	2.8	4.1	2.0	−0.7	1.3	4.9	2.8
2002	4.7	1.6	3.1	1.9	−0.9	2.8	2.8	0.3
2003	4.1	2.3	1.8	1.8	−0.3	2.1	2.3	−0.3
2004	4.3	2.7	1.6	1.8	0.0	1.8	2.5	−0.2

Source: IMF, *International Financial Statistics Yearbook 2005* (Washington, D.C.: IMF, 2005).

* CPI refers to the consumer price index as a measure of the rate of inflation.

---

[7] To be noted is that Japanese firms, just like their U.S. counterparts, borrowed heavily during the 1980s. Thus, it was the higher real cost of capital rather than the borrowing itself that undermined the international competitiveness of U.S. firms vis-à-vis Japanese firms during the 1980s.

by banks for short- and medium-term loans to the private sector in the United States and Japan from 1981 to 2004. During this period, Japan was the main competitor of the United States in most high-tech goods both at home and around the world. Long-term lending rates are related to short- and medium-term rates and generally move in tandem with them.

Table 14-5 shows that nominal lending rates were higher in the United States than in Japan in every year from 1981 to 2004. Real (i.e., inflation-adjusted) lending rates (which are the ones that really count for international competitiveness) were higher from 1981 to 1984, and this was the period of greatest loss of U.S. international competitiveness to Japan. While there were other forces at work, the higher cost of capital in the United States relative to Japan was certainly one important contributing factor. From 1985 to 1994, U.S.–Japanese real lending rate differentials were mixed and U.S. firms recaptured some of the competitiveness that they had lost during the early 1980s. From 1995 to 2001, real interest rates have once again become much higher in the United States than in Japan. Despite this, the United States continued to gain in competitiveness in relation to Japan. Obviously, the other forces at work (such as much greater efficiency of the service and financial sectors in the United States than in Japan) more than overwhelmed its real interest rates. From 2002 to 2004, real interest rates were about the same in the United States and Japan.

The reason for the higher nominal and real interest or lending rates in the United States than in Japan was the much higher demand for borrowing and the much lower supply of loanable funds in the former than in the latter. One of the reasons for the higher demand for borrowing in the United States was its huge budget deficit during the 1980s and the excellent investment opportunities during the 1990s. At the same time, the savings rate was very low in the United States and very high in Japan. With the demand for loanable funds very large relative to its supply in comparison to Japan, it should not be surprising to find interest rates higher in the United States than in Japan throughout most of the period.

SUMMARY

1. In this chapter we examined capital budgeting. This refers to the process of planning expenditures that give rise to revenues or returns over a number of years. Investment projects can be undertaken to replace worn-out equipment, reduce costs, expand output of traditional products in traditional markets, expand into new products and/or markets, or meet government regulations. The firm's profitability, growth, and its very survival in the long run depend on how well management accomplishes these tasks. Capital budgeting integrates the operation of all the major divisions of the firm. The basic principle involved in capital budgeting is for the firm to undertake additional investment projects until the marginal return from the investment is equal to its marginal cost.

2. The net cash flow from a project is the difference between cash receipts and cash expenditures over the life of a project. Net cash flows should be measured on an incremental and after-tax basis, and depreciation charges should be used only to calculate taxes. A firm should undertake a project only if the net present value (*NPV*) of the project is positive. The *NPV* is equal to the present value of the estimated stream of net cash flows from the project, discounted at the firm's cost of capital, minus the initial cost of the project. Alternatively, the project should be undertaken only if the internal rate of return (*IRR*) on the project exceeds the cost of capital to the firm. The *IRR* is the rate of discount that equates the present value of the net cash flows from the project to the initial cost of the project. For a single or independent project, the *NPV* and *IRR* methods will always lead to the same accept-reject investment decision. For mutually exclusive projects, however, they may provide contradictory signals. In that case the project with the higher *NPV* should be chosen.

3. In cases of capital rationing (i.e., when the firm cannot undertake all the projects with positive *NPV*), the firm should rank projects according to their relative profitability rather than according to their *NPV*. The profitability index (*PI*) of a project is measured by the ratio of the present value of the net cash flows from a project to the cost of the investment. Capital rationing may be imposed by top management to avoid over-expansion, over-borrowing, and possibly losing control of the firm by selling more stocks to raise additional capital.

4. A firm can raise investment funds internally or externally. The cost of using internal funds is the forgone return on these funds outside the firm. The cost of external funds is the rate of return that lenders and stockholders require to lend or invest funds in the firm. Since interest paid on borrowed funds is tax deductible, the after-tax cost of borrowed funds is given by the interest paid times 1 minus the firm's marginal tax rate. The cost of equity capital can be measured by (1) the risk-free rate plus a risk premium for holding the firm's stock rather than government bonds; (2) the dividend per share of the stock divided by the price of the stock, plus the expected growth rate of dividend payments; and (3) the risk-free rate plus the beta coefficient (β) times the risk premium on the average stock. This last named is the capital asset pricing model (CAPM). β is the ratio of the variability on the return on the stock of the firm to the variability in the average return on all stocks. Firms generally use more than one method to estimate the equity cost of capital. The composite cost of capital is the weighted average of the cost of debt and equity capital.

5. It is very important to review projects after they have been implemented. Such a review involves comparing the actual cash flow and return from the project with the expected or predicted cash flow and return, as well as an explanation of the observed differences between predicted and actual results. If decision makers know that their investment projects will be evaluated, they are likely to draw up investment plans more carefully and to work harder to ensure that their predictions are fulfilled.

6. During most of the 1980s, the cost of capital was much higher in the United States than in Japan and in many other major industrial nations, and this was one of the factors that undermined the international competitiveness of U.S. firms during this period. Higher interest rates also required somewhat higher returns on stock to attract domestic and foreign equity capital. It also kept the international value of the dollar higher than it would otherwise have been and thus further contributed to the loss of international competitiveness of U.S. firms. During the early 1990s, however, interest rates rose faster in Japan and Germany, thus reducing or eliminating this competitive disadvantage of U.S. firms.

DISCUSSION QUESTIONS

1. In what way can it be said that capital budgeting is nothing more than the application of the theory of the firm to investment projects?

2. What general guidelines should a firm follow in properly estimating the net cash flow from an investment?

3. (*a*) What is the difference between the profit flow and the cash flow from an investment project? (*b*) Why do firms use the net cash flow to estimate the net present value of a project?

4. (*a*) How are depreciation charges taken into consideration in estimating the net cash flow from a project? (*b*) Why?

5. (*a*) What effect does the use of a higher risk-adjusted discount rate have on the net present value of a project? (*b*) Why?

6. What is the relationship between the *NPV* and the *IRR* methods of evaluating investment projects?

7. (*a*) When can the *NPV* and the *IRR* methods of evaluating investment projects provide contradictory results? (*b*) How can this arise? (*c*) Which method should then be used? Why?

8. (*a*) Why might a firm face capital rationing? (*b*) What investment criteria should the firm follow when it faces capital rationing? (*c*) Why?

9. Explain (*a*) why the cost of debt capital is usually lower than equity capital to the firm and (*b*) why firms do not rely exclusively on debt financing.

10. (*a*) How can a firm raise equity capital internally? (*b*) What is the cost to the firm of this type of capital? (*c*) Must the firm pay dividends to raise equity capital internally or externally? (*d*) Why is internal equity capital generally less costly to the firm than external equity capital?

11. (*a*) Why are government securities taken to be risk free? What is used as the risk-free rate? (*b*) What additional risks do the stockholders of a firm face in comparison to holders of government securities?

12. Why do different firms choose different debt/equity ratios?

13. Why is the marginal cost schedule of most firms upward sloping?

14. What is the relationship between the cost of capital and public utility regulation?

15. In what ways do higher interest rates in the United States than abroad interfere with the international competitiveness of U.S. firms?

 PROBLEMS

*1. As a result of a great deal of analysis and input from its various divisions, the Computer Software Corporation has concluded that it can undertake the projects indicated in the following table, and it has estimated that it could raise $2.5 million of capital at the rate (cost) of 9 percent, an additional $3 million at 12 percent, and another $3.5 million at 16 percent. Draw a figure to show which projects the firm should undertake and which it should not.

Capital Projects	Required Investment (millions)	Rate of Return
A	$1.0	18%
B	2.0	16
C	1.5	13
D	2.5	11
E	2.0	9

2. (*a*) Redraw Figure 14-1, and draw on it a smooth curve approximating the firm's demand curve for capital and marginal cost curve of capital. (*b*) Under what conditions would these smooth curves hold? (*c*) How much would the firm invest with these smooth curves? What would be the return on and cost of the last dollar invested?

*3. Show the calculations needed to estimate the net present value of the project discussed in Section 14-2 and Table 14-1 if the firm uses the

risk-adjusted discount rate of (*a*) 10 percent and (*b*) 20 percent. (*c*) By how much would the value of the firm increase if the firm uses the risk-adjusted discount rates of 10 percent and 20 percent?

4. Gregory Burton, the manager of the Toybest Company, would like to introduce a new toy, and he has received the following estimates of costs and sales from the various divisions of the firm. The cost of purchasing, delivering, and installing the new machinery that is required to manufacture the toy is estimated to be $10 million. The expected life of the toy is four years. Incremental sales revenues are estimated to be $10 million in the first year of operation, are expected to rise by 20 percent in the second year and another 20 percent in the third year, but they are expected to remain unchanged in the fourth and final year. The incremental variable costs of producing the toy are estimated to be 40 percent of incremental sales revenues. The firm is also expected to incur additional fixed costs of $1 million per year. The marginal tax rate of the firm is 40 percent. The firm uses the straight-line depreciation method. The machinery purchased will have no salvage value but the firm is expected to recuperate $1.5 million of its working capital at the end of the four years. (*a*) Construct a table similar to Table 14-1 summarizing the cash flows from the project. (*b*) Calculate the net present value of the project if the firm uses the risk-adjusted

discount rate of 20 percent. (*c*) Should the firm undertake the project? If so, by how much would the value of the firm increase?

*5. Suppose that the net cash flow from the investment project of Problem 4 is $5 million in each year and the firm does not recover any working capital at the end of the four years. Use Table B-4 in Appendix B at the end of the book to determine whether the firm should undertake the project if the firm uses the risk-adjusted discount rate of 20 percent.

6. Determine the internal rate of return for the project of Problem 4.

7. The Cosmetics Company has to decide whether to introduce beauty cream A or beauty cream B on the market. The initial cost of introducing each cream is $1 million and the net cash flows generated by each are indicated in the following table. Using the discount rate of 10 percent, determine (*a*) the net present value and (*b*) the internal rate of return on investment projects A and B. (*c*) Which project (cream) should the firm undertake? Why?

Net Present Value and Internal Rate of Return on Two Mutually Exclusive Investment Projects

	Project A	Project B
Initial cost	$1,000,000	$1,000,000
Net cash flows (years)		
Year 1	300,000	−100,000
Year 2	300,000	10,000
Year 3	300,000	300,000
Year 4	300,000	300,000
Year 5	300,000	1,400,000

8. John Piderit, the general manager of the Western Tool Company, is considering introducing some new tools to the company's product line. The top management of the firm has identified three types of tools (referred to as projects A, B, and C). The various divisions of the firm have provided the data given in the following table on these three possible projects. The company has a limited capital budget of $2.4 million for the coming year.

(*a*) Which project(s) would the firm undertake if it used the *NPV* investment criterion? (*b*) Is this the correct decision? Why?

	Project A	Project B	Project C
Present value of net cash flows (*PVNCF*)	$3,000,000	$1,750,000	$1,400,000
Initial cost of project (*C₀*)	2,400,000	1,300,000	1,100,000

9. The Optical Instruments Corporation can sell bonds at an interest rate of 9 percent. The interest rate on government securities is 7 percent. Calculate the cost of equity capital for this firm.

10. The MacBurger Company, a chain of fast-food restaurants, expects to earn $200 million after taxes for the current year. The company has a policy of paying out half of its net after-tax income to the holders of the company's 100 million shares of common stock. A share of the common stock of the company currently sells for eight times current earnings. Management and outside analysts expect the growth rate of earnings and dividends for the company to be 7.5 percent per year. Calculate the cost of equity capital to this firm.

*11. Suppose that the Eldridge Manufacturing Company pays an interest rate of 11 percent on its bonds, the marginal income tax rate that the firm faces is 40 percent, the rate on government bonds is 7.5 percent, the return on the average stock of all firms in the market is 11.55 percent, the estimated beta coefficient for the common stock of the firm is 2, and the firm wishes to raise 40 percent of its capital by borrowing. Determine (*a*) the cost of debt, (*b*) the cost of equity capital, (*c*) the composite cost of capital for this firm.

12. (*a*) From a library or Internet search try to find the average real rate of return and standard deviation (as a measure of risk) from the 1920s until the present for (1) common stock, (2) long-term corporate bonds, and (3) U.S. Treasury bills. (*b*) Do the values that you found confirm your expectations as to the different rates of return for the three types of investments?

13. With regard to foreign direct investment inflows into the United States, determine (*a*) the benefits to the United States, (*b*) the dangers or costs, and (*c*) the net effect (i.e., where foreign direct investments beneficial or harmful to the United States?).

14. (a) From the Survey of Current Business, find the value of foreign direct investments inflows into the United States from 1980 to 2001. (b) Were foreign direct investment inflows into the United States cyclical?

15. **Integrating Problem**

The Laundromat Corporation is considering opening another coin-operated laundry in a city. It has estimated that opening the laundry would involve an initial cost of $100,000 and would generate a net cash flow of $32,000 in each of five years, with no salvage value for the equipment and no recovery of operating expenses at the end of the five years. The corporation estimates that it would have to pay a rate of interest of 12 percent on its bonds and that it would face a marginal income tax rate of 40 percent. The interest on government securities is 10 percent. During the current year, the corporation expects to pay a dividend of $20 dollars on each share of its common stock, which sells for 10 times current earnings. Management and outside analysts expect the growth rate of earnings and dividends of the corporation to be 7 percent per year. The return on the average stock of all firms in the market is 14 percent, and the estimated beta coefficient for the common stock of the corporation is 1.25. The corporation wants to maintain a capital structure of 30 percent debt. Determine (a) the internal rate of return for the proposed project, (b) the cost of debt for the corporation, (c) the cost of equity capital by the risk-free rate plus premium method, (d) the cost of equity capital by the dividend valuation model, (e) the cost of equity capital by the capital asset pricing model, (f) the composite cost of capital if the firm uses the average of the cost of equity capital determined by each of the three methods, and (g) whether or not the corporation should undertake the project.

SUPPLEMENTARY READINGS

A general discussion of capital budgeting is found in:

Bernardo, Antonio, Hongbin Cai, and Jiang Luo, "Capital Budgeting and Compensation with Asymmetric Information and Moral Hazard," *Journal of Financial Economics* (September 2001), pp. 311–344.

Luehrman, Timothy, "Using APV: A Better Tool for Valuing Operations," *Harvard Business Review* (May–June 1997), pp. 145–154.

Mukherjee, Tarun K., and Glenn V. Henderson, "The Capital Budgeting Process: Theory and Practice," *Interfaces* (March–April 1987), pp. 78–90.

Pollak, Robert A., "Imagined Risk and Cost-Benefit Analysis," *American Economic Review Papers and Proceedings* (May 1998), pp. 376–380.

The cost of capital is examined in:

Fisher, L., and J. H. Lorie, "Rates of Return on Investments in Common Stock: 1926–1965," *Journal of Business* (July 1968), pp. 291–316.

Froot, Kenneth A., and Jeremy C. Stein, "Risk Management, Capital Budgeting, and Capital Structure Policy for Financial Institutions: An Integrated Approach," *Journal of Financial Economics* (January 1998), pp. 55–82.

Graham, J. R., and Harvey Campbell, "The Theory and Practice of Finance: Evidence from the Field," *Journal of Financial Economics* (Fall 2001), pp. 187–243.

Hall, Robert E., "The Stock Market and Capital Accumulation," *American Economic Review* (December 2001), pp. 1185–1202.

Harris, M., and A. Raviv, "The Theory of Capital Structure," *Journal of Finance* (March 1991), pp. 297–355.

Harris, R. S., "Using Analysts' Growth Forecasts to Estimate Shareholder Required Rates of Return," *Financial Management* (Spring 1986), pp. 58–67.

Le Thuan and Kevin P. Sheehan, "Measuring the Relative Marginal Cost of Debt and Capital for Banks," *Federal Reserve Bank of New York Economic Policy Review* (October 1998), pp. 45–49.

Markowitz, H. M., "Portfolio Selection," *Journal of Finance* (March 1952), pp. 77–91.

Modigliani, F., and M. H. Miller, "The Cost of Capital, Corporation Finance and the Theory of Investment," *American Economic Review* (June 1958), pp. 261–297.

Sick, Gordon A., "A Certainty-Equivalent Approach to Capital Budgeting," *Financial Management* (Winter 1986), pp. 23–32.

Talmor, E., and H. E. Thompson, "Technology, Dependent Investments, and Discounting Rules for Corporate Investment Decisions," *Managerial and Decision Economics* (March–April 1992), pp. 101–109.

For the presentation and evaluation of the capital asset pricing model, see:

Fama, Eugene F., and Kenneth R. French, "The Capital Asset Pricing Model: Theory and Evidence," *Journal of Economic Perspectives* (Summer 2004), pp. 25–46.

Perold, Andre F., "The Capital Asset Pricing Model," *Journal of Economic Perspectives* (Summer 2004), pp. 3–24.

For the effect of international interest rate differentials on international competitiveness, see:

Gitman, Lawrence, *Principles of Managerial Finance,* 11th ed. (Reading, Mass.: Addison-Wesley, 2005), chaps. 5, 8–9.

Hill, Charles W. L., *International Business,* 5th ed. (Boston: Irwin–McGraw-Hill, 2005), chap. 20.

Salvatore, Dominick, *International Economics,* 8th ed. (Hoboken, N.J.: Wiley, 2004), chaps. 14 and 19.

 ## INTERNET SITE ADDRESSES

An excellent and useful financial Web site is:

http://www.money.cnn.com

Financial calculators that can be used to calculate present discounted values can be found at:

http://www.biznizportal.com/calculators/bus10/java/BusinessValuation.html

For cost–benefit analysis software provided free by Legacy System Research, see:

http://www.legacy-systems-research.com-download.net

For more information on the supersonic transport plane (SST), see the Internet sites for British Airways and Air France, the only two airlines that flew the Concorde, at:

http://www.airfrance.fr

http://www.british-airways.com

Information on the company running the Eurotunnel is found at:

http://www.eurotunnel.com

More information on the internal rate of return is found in an article by Ray Martin at:

http://www.riskworld.com/Nreports

A good source of information on corporate finance is the Vernimmen letter, such as the June 2005 issue at:

http://www.vernimmen.com/letter/html/letter_7.html

For more information on Pennzoil's capital budgeting, see:

http://www.pennzoil.com

For cost of capital analysis for over 300 industries, see the site of the Ibbotson Associates' *Cost of Capital Quarterly* at:

http://www.ibbotson.com/content/cc_lvl1.asp

http://www.yahoo.com and select "stock quotes"

For the economic and financial situation of the world's leading telecom companies (American Verizon, SBC Communications, MCI, Cingular, and Sprint; Japan's NTT; Deutsche Telekom; France's Alcatel; British Telecom; Spanish Telefonica, and Telecom Italia), see:

http://www.verizon.com/

http://www.sbc.com

http://www.mci.com

http://www.cingular.com

http://www.sprint.com

http://www.ntt.co.jp

http://www.dtag.de

http://www.alcatel.com

http://www.bt.com

http://www.telefonica.es

http://www.telecomitalia.it

INTEGRATING CASE STUDY 6
Deregulation, Risk, Capital Budgeting, and the Telecom Crisis

Introductory Comment: The following selection illustrates how deregulation, risk, and capital budgeting are interrelated with technological change and competition as established telecom companies fight an increasingly bitter battle, not only among themselves, but especially against innovative attackers, thus serving as an excellent integrating case study for Part 5 of the text.

The War of the Wires

"We're not a telephone company anymore; I sort of resent that," says Lea Ann Champion, an executive at SBC, America's second-largest "Baby Bell." "We're a communications and entertainment company." Well, maybe. Ms. Champion is in charge of "lightspeed," an SBC project to deliver TV, movies, and other entertainment to customers via hugely enhanced broadband connections using Internet protocol—a service known in short as IPTV. Lightspeed, which will cost $4 billion, has hit technological and legal snags recently that could slow its rollout, scheduled to begin at the end of 2006. But sooner or later IPTV will happen, if only because telecom companies all over the world are betting on it. And when it does, it will be controversial.

That is because IPTV forms part of a larger, and quite desperate, defensive strategy now being adopted by telecom firms against fierce attacks on multiple fronts. On one front are cable giants, such as America's Comcast, which are luring customers with an enticing "triple-play bundle" of TV, broadband, and telephony services. On a second front are mobile-phone operators, which young customers in particular are using increasingly to "cut the cord" from their fixed-line company.

But arguably most dangerous of all is the third front, where traditional telecom firms are under attack from "voice-over-Internet-protocol" (VOIP) providers, which use the Internet to carry conversations that would previously have taken place via a conventional phone. TeleGeography, a research firm, estimates that the number of subscribers to VOIP services such as Vonage, which let users plug their traditional phones into a gadget connected to the Internet, will grow from 1.8 million at the start of 2006 to 4 million by the end of December in America alone; by 2010 it projects over 17 million American subscribers. This does not count the world's largest VOIP provider, Skype, which uses a small and simple software application to let users make free calls between computers—so far, it has been downloaded 141 million times.

Hanging on the Telephone

Traditional telecom firms are doing their best to respond to these threats by adopting Internet technologies themselves. In July 2005, VSNL, the top operator in India for international calls, said it would buy Teleglobe, the world's largest international wholesale VOIP carrier. Every big telecom firm is investing to migrate from old circuit-switched networks to new Internet-based ones, with Britain's BT probably moving fastest. The threat from VOIP would then be neutralized, as the telecom firms themselves would be providing it. Even so, VOIP makes already grim revenue forecasts for old-style telecom firm look truly depressing.

Hence IPTV—a sort of last-ditch charge by a cornered beast. By switching to fast new Internet-based networks, telecom companies will also be able to catch up with their cable rivals by offering entertainment, Internet access, and voice services over their networks. Better yet, those telecom firms that also own mobile-phone subsidiaries might outdo their cable rivals by adding cellular service to create a "quadruple-play bundle."

Yet IPTV is an extremely risky strategy. To deliver it, the telecom firms must first provide huge bandwidth to their customers. Some, such as BT, are doing this by souping up their existing copper lines into homes, which is costly, while others, such as America's Verizon and SBC, are also laying new fiber in the ground, which is outrageously costly. The firms will then put a box, called a "residential gateway," into customers' garages or basements, which will connect at blazing speeds to computers and telephones as well as to a set-top box by the TV. Family members can then make phone calls, surf the Web, and watch movies simultaneously, all via one "pipe."

Technological glitches are possible. The bandwidth may prove insufficient, or the digital-rights and compression formats could prove too fiddly. But the industry is playing down such risks. "The issues are not technical but regulatory and cultural," says Tim Krause, a manager at Alcatel, a firm that supplies the necessary infrastructure to IPTV operators such as SBC.

The main cultural risk, says Albert Lin of American Technology Research, a consultancy, is that telecom firms, which have not hitherto been seated at the best tables in Hollywood restaurants, will not be able to buy rights to films and shows that anybody actually wants to watch. This suggestion infuriates the telecom firms. The doubters "are just plain wrong," says Michael Coe, a spokesman for SBC. "There are no barriers to acquiring content. The only question is: what will it cost?"

Having literally sunk their billion-dollar investments in the ground, the telecom firms will need to get a decent return on them. But in their nightmare scenario, customers may simply sign up to their huge bandwidth and then use it not to buy the services touted by the telecom firms but instead to obtain independent or Web-based services, such as Skype for making calls or (when the service is launched) Netflix for downloading movies. Can the telecom firms do anything to stop that?

Stoyan Kenderov, an IPTV expert at Amdocs, a firm that makes back-office software for telecom companies, says that the telecom firms are building into their residential gateways new technology that will inspect the packets of zeros and ones passing through. This will let them identify traffic from third-party rivals, which might then end up at the back of the queue and thus be slow and patchy. The only hint that users might have of that going on, says Mr. Kenderov, would be some very fine print on their bills explaining, in turgid legalese, that the provider guarantees the quality of its own services only.

The telecom firms counter such suggestions with well-rehearsed indignation. In a hearing before the judiciary committee of America's Senate in March 2005, Edward Whitacre, SBC's chairman, said in emphatic Texan that "SBC would not block any Vonage traffic or anybody else's and has never done that, would not do that. That's not the way we do business, and it's just not going to happen."

Cyrus Mewawalla of Westhall Capital, a brokerage, predicts that "at some point the world VOIP market will experience a massive security scare," when viruses or other banes of the Internet make themselves felt in the world of the new services. At that point, Mr. Mewawalla says, customers will "flock in droves back to the big boys who own their own networks," such as SBC or BT, and "desert those who use the public Internet," like Skype or Vonage.

The packet-monitoring technology that the telecom firms are installing can be used—legitimately—to enhance security and quality. It can also be used—though it will be hard to prove—to degrade the services of rivals. The only true protection against that outcome is more competition between broadband access providers (cable and telecom firms; new technologies such as WiMax, a wireless system that, one day, may cover entire cities; and broadband over power lines). But given the tactics of the incumbent telecom firms, it may fall to regulators to ensure that this essential competition develops.

Concluding Remarks

In September 2005, eBay acquired Skype, a small firm whose software allows people to make free telephone calls to other Skype users over the Internet and very cheap calls to traditional telephones. Voice over the Internet protocol (VOIP) is going to lead to the death of the trillion dollar traditional telephone business, as the marginal cost of making telephone calls falls inexorably to zero or near zero (as for e-mail messages). With broadband connection, VOIP not only allows consumers to choose the telephony provider but also to get other services, such as voicemail, conference calling, and video from the provider.

The threat of VOIP not only exists in the United States but is looming in Europe, Japan, and other parts of the world, where Microsoft, Google, AOL, and Yahoo are likely to make big inroads in the near future. European telecoms have responded by resuming the process of mergers and acquisitions from the peak reached in the year 2000. In fact, three big transactions occurred in 2005: Spain's Telefonica's $3.5 billion purchase of a 51 percent stake in Cesky Telecom (the Czech Republic's dominant telecommunications company), the purchase by France's Telecom of Ameda (the Spanish mobil opertator for $2.6 billion), and Telefonica's $24 billion acquisition of KPN of the Netherlands. In the biggest deal of all, Telefonica proposed a $31.5 billion acquisition of the mobile-phone operator O2 (which is likely to lead to other large mergers in Europe).

Source: "The War of the Wires," *The Economist* (July 30, 2005), pp. 53–54. © 2005 The Economist Newspaper Ltd. All rights reserved. See also, "How the Internet Killed the Phone Business," *The Economist* (September 17, 2005), p. 11; "European Phone Industry Split on the Need to Bulk Up," *The New York Times* (October 4, 2005), p. C4; "Rewired and Ready for Combat," *Business Week* (November 7, 2005), pp. 110–113; and "Survival of the Biggest," *The Economist* (November 5, 2005), pp. 65–66.

Appendixes

APPENDIX A

Compounding, Discounting, and Present Value

I n this appendix, we examine compounding, discounting, and the present value of money. These concepts are widely used in all aspects of business and economics and especially in managerial economics. Specifically, it is important to recognize that $1 received today is worth more than $1 received next year because $1 deposited in a bank today will earn interest and grow to more than $1 by the end of the year. Similarly, $1 received next year is worth less than $1 received today because an amount less than $1 deposited in a bank today will grow (with the interest earned) to $1 by the end of the year. This is often referred to as the *time value of money*.

A-1   FUTURE VALUE AND COMPOUNDING

The process of determining the amount to which a sum will accumulate or grow over a specified number of periods of time at a given interest rate per time period is called *compounding*. For example, $100 deposited in a bank savings account that pays 12 percent interest per year will grow to ($100)(1.12) = $112 by the end of the year. If the $112 is left on deposit for another year, it will grow to ($112)(1.12) = $125.44 by the end of the second year.

We can easily derive a formula for determining the amount to which a sum will accumulate or grow at the end of any number of years when the account is left untouched and each year's interest is compounded on the previous year's ending balance. We can derive the formula for determining the future or compound value of a sum by defining the following terms:

PV = present value or beginning amount deposited
i = interest rate earned on the account, expressed as a decimal per year
FV_n = future value or ending amount of the account at the end of n years, after the interest has been added or compounded

At the end of the first year,

$$FV_1 = PV + PV(i) = PV(1 + i) \qquad \text{[A-1]}$$

For example, $100 deposited in a savings account that pays 12 percent (i.e., 0.12) interest per year will have grown by the end of the year to

$$FV_1 = \$100(1 + 0.12)$$
$$= \$100(1.12) = \$112$$

This is equal to the $100 deposit plus the $12 interest earned and is shown in the first row of Table A-1.

At the end of the second year,

$$FV_2 = FV_1(1 + i) = PV(1 + i)(1 + i)$$
$$= PV(1 + i)^2$$

Thus, by the end of the second year the $100 deposited will have grown to

$$FV_2 = \$100(1.12)^2 = \$100(1.2544)$$
$$= \$125.44$$

This is shown in the second row of Table A-1.

Continuing, we see that FV_3, the balance after three years, is

$$FV_3 = FV_2(1 + i) = PV(1 + i)(1 + i)(1 + i)$$
$$= PV(1 + i)^3$$

Thus, by the end of the third year the $100 will have grown to

$$FV_3 = \$100(1.12)^3 = \$100(1.4049)$$
$$= \$140.49$$

This is shown in the third row of Table A-1.

Generalizing, we can say that FV_n, the future value at the end of n years, is

$$FV_n = PV(1 + i)^n \qquad \text{[A-2]}$$

For example, by the end of five years the $100 deposited in the savings account paying 12 percent interest compounded annually will have grown to

$$FV_5 = \$100(1.12)^5 = \$100(1.7623)$$
$$= \$176.23$$

The value of 1.7623 for $(1.12)^5$ was obtained by $(1.12)(1.12)(1.12)(1.12)(1.12)$. Such a time-consuming calculation is not necessary, however, because a table has been constructed for the compound value of the interest factor $(1 + i)^n$ for many values of i and n. This is Table B-1 in Appendix B. In Table B-1, $FVIF_{i, n}$ (the future value interest factor) equals $(1 + i)^n$. Thus, $FV_n = PV(1 + i)^n = PV(FVIF_{i, n})$. For $i = 12$ percent and $n = 5$, the $FVIF_{12, 5}$ is obtained by moving across Table B-1 until we reach the column headed 12 percent and then moving down five rows for $n = 5$. The value we get is 1.7623 (the same obtained by multiplying 1.12 by itself five times). Thus,

$$FV_5 = \$100(FVIF_{12, 5}) = \$100(1.7623)$$
$$= \$176.23$$

(the same amount found in the fifth row of Table A-1 below).

Using Table B-1, we can find that if the interest rates had been 10 percent and 14 percent, respectively,

TABLE A-1   Compound Interest Calculations

Year	Beginning Amount (*PV*)	1 + *i*	Ending Amount (*FV*)
1	$100.00	1.12	$112.00
2	112.00	1.12	125.44
3	125.44	1.12	140.49
4	140.49	1.12	157.35
5	157.35	1.12	176.23

the $100 deposit would have grown by the end of the fifth year to

$$FV_5 = \$100(FVIF_{10, 5}) = \$100(1.6105)$$
$$= \$161.05$$

and

$$FV_5 = \$100(FVIF_{14, 5}) = \$100(1.9254)$$
$$= \$192.54$$

On the other hand, with the interest rate of 12 percent, the $100 would have grown by the end of the tenth year to

$$FV_{10} = \$100(FVIF_{12, 10}) = \$100(3.1058)$$
$$= \$310.58$$

Thus, the higher the interest rate, the greater is the rate of growth of the deposit, and the greater the number of years that the sum is left on deposit, the larger will be the amount accumulated or compounded.

A-2   PRESENT VALUE AND DISCOUNTING

The *present value* of a sum due in n years is the amount that, if invested today at a specified rate of interest, would grow to the future sum in n years. For example, since $100 invested today at 12 percent interest per year will grow to $176.23 in five years (see Section A-1 and Table A-1), $100 is the present value of $176.23 due in five years when the interest rate is 12 percent per year. Thus, finding the present value, or *discounting,* is the reverse of finding the future value of compounding. The interest rate used in such calculations is called the *discount rate* because the present value is smaller than the future value by the specific percentage each year.

The formula to find the present value (PV) can easily be derived from Equation A-2, which was used to find the future value (FV). Specifically, by solving equation

$$FV_n = PV(1 + i)^n$$

for *PV,* we get

$$PV = \frac{FV_n}{(1 + i)^n} = FV_n\left[\frac{1}{(1 + i)^n}\right] \qquad \text{[A-3]}$$

The term in square brackets in Equation A-3 is called the *present value interest factor* (PVIF). Table B-2 in

Appendix B gives the value of the present value interest factor for each value of i and n (that is, $PVIF_{i, n}$). For example, by moving across Table B-2 until we reach the column headed 12 percent and then moving down five rows for $n = 5$, we get the value of $PVIF_{12, 5} = 0.5674$, to be used to find the present value of $176.23 to be received in five years and discounted at the annual rate of 12 percent. That is,

$$PV = FV_n(PVIF_{i, n})$$
$$= FV_5(PVIF_{12, 5})$$
$$= \$176.23(0.5674)$$
$$= \$99.99 \text{ or } \$100$$

Using Table B-2 we can find that if the discount rate had been 10 percent and 14 percent, respectively, the $176.23 to be received in five years would have a present value of

$$PV = FV_5(PVIF_{10, 5}) = \$176.23(0.6209)$$
$$= \$109.42$$

and

$$PV = FV_5(PVIF_{14, 5}) = \$176.23(0.5194)$$
$$= \$91.53$$

On the other hand, with the discount rate of 12 percent, $176.23 to be received in 10 years would have a present value of

$$PV = FV_{10}(PVIF_{12, 10}) = \$176.23(0.3220)$$
$$= \$56.75$$

Thus, the higher the discount rate and the longer the discounting period, the smaller is the present value of a sum to be received in the future. From Table B-2, it can be seen that the present value of a sum to be received in 25 years or more and discounted at the rate of 10 percent or more per year is less than $\frac{1}{10}$ of the value of the future sum.

A-3   FUTURE VALUE OF AN ANNUITY

An *annuity* is a fixed sum that is received at the end of each year for a specified number of years into the future. The value of an annuity is the sum to which such year-end receipts would accumulate or grow if left in an account at a specified rate of interest compounded annually. For example, the future value of a five-year annuity (FVA_5) of $100 left in an account paying 12 percent interest compounded annually is $635.28. This is obtained as follows:

$$FVA_5 = \underbrace{\$100(1.12)^4}_{\text{from year 1}} + \underbrace{\$100(1.12)^3}_{\text{from year 2}}$$

$$+ \underbrace{\$100(1.12)^2}_{\text{from year 3}} + \underbrace{\$100(1.12)^1}_{\text{from year 4}}$$

$$+ \underbrace{\$100(1.12)^0}_{\text{from year 5}} = \$635.28$$

Note that since the first sum is received at the end of the first year, interest is compounded for only four years on this sum. Interest is compounded for three years on the second sum, two years on the third sum, one year on the fourth sum, and zero years on the fifth sum (since it is received at the end of the fifth year).

More generally, letting FVA_n be the future value of the annuity, R the yearly receipts, and n the number of years of the annuity, we can derive the formula for FVA_n as follows:

$$FVA_n = R(1+i)^{n-1} + R(1+i)^{n-1}$$

$$+ \cdots + R(1+i)^1 + R(1+i)^0$$

$$= R[(1+i)^{n-1} + (1+i)^{n-1}$$

$$+ \cdots + (1+i)^1 + (1+i)^0]$$

$$= R\sum_{t=1}^{n}(1+i)^{n-t} = R\sum_{t=1}^{n}(1+i)^{t-1}$$

$$= R(FVIFA_{i,n}) \qquad \text{[A-4]}$$

where $FVIFA_{i,\,n}$ is the future value interest factor for an annuity with interest i compounded annually for n years. Table B-3 in Appendix B gives the values of $FVIFA_{i,\,n}$ for various values of i and n. For example, by moving across Table B-3 until we reach the column headed 12 percent and then moving down five rows for $n = 5$, we get the value of $FVIFA_{12,\,5} = 6.3528$ to be used to find the future value of $635.28 for $i = 12$ percent and $n = 5$ years. That is,

$$FVA_n = R(FVIFA_{i,\,n})$$

$$= \$100(FVIFA_{12,\,5})$$

$$= \$100(6.3528)$$

$$= \$635.28$$

This is the same answer that we obtained above by long-hand calculation. From Table B-3, we can see that the value of $FVIFA_{i,\,n}$ is always equal to or larger than n.

A-4   PRESENT VALUE OF AN ANNUITY

The present value of a five-year annuity (PVA_5) of $100 discounted at the annual rate of 12 percent is $360.48. This is obtained as follows:

$$PVA_5 = \frac{\$100}{(1.12)^1} + \frac{\$100}{(1.12)^2} + \frac{\$100}{(1.12)^3}$$

$$+ \frac{\$100}{(1.12)^4} + \frac{\$100}{(1.12)^5}$$

$$= \$360.48$$

This means that investing $360.48 today at 12 percent will return exactly $100 at the end of each of the next five years.

More generally, letting PVA_n be the present value of the annuity, R the yearly receipts, and n the number of years of the annuity, we can derive the formula for PVA_n as follows:

$$FVA_n = \frac{R}{(1+i)^1} + \frac{R}{(1+i)^2} + \cdots + \frac{R}{(1+i)^n}$$

$$= R\left[\frac{1}{(1+i)^1} + \frac{1}{(1+i)^2} + \cdots + \frac{1}{(1+i)^n}\right]$$

$$= R\sum_{t=1}^{n}\frac{1}{(1+i)^t}$$

$$= R(PVIFA_{i,\,n}) \qquad \text{[A-5]}$$

where $PVIFA_{i,\,n}$ is the present value interest factor for an annuity discounted at the annual rate of i for n years. Table B-4 in Appendix B gives the values of $PVIFA_{i,\,n}$ for various values of i and n. For example, for $i = 12$ percent and $n = 5$ years, $PVIFA_{12,\,5} = 3.6048$. Thus, the present value of a five-year annuity of $100 discounted at the annual rate of 12 percent is

$$PVA_n = R(PVIFA_{i,\,n})$$

$$= \$100(PVIFA_{12,\,5})$$

$$= \$100(3.6048)$$

$$= \$360.48$$

This is the same answer that we obtained above by long-hand calculation. From Table B-4, we can see that the value of $PVIFA_{i,n}$ is always smaller than n.

A-5 COMPOUNDING AND DISCOUNTING PERIODS

Until now we assumed that interest was compounded or earned annually or at the end of each year. Some bonds, however, compound or pay interest semiannually, some banks pay interest quarterly, and some cash receipts and payments occur monthly. The more frequently interest is compounded or earned, the larger will be the future value of a sum and the smaller its present value for a given interest rate.

For example, a sum deposited at 12 percent interest compounded *semiannually* will earn 6 percent interest at the end of every six months or half year. Thus, $100 deposited at the beginning of the year will grow to $100(1.06) = $106 at the end of the first six months and then by another 6 percent, or to $106(1.06) = $112.36, by the end of the second six-month period (i.e., by the end of the first year), as compared to $112 at the rate of 12 percent compounded annually. Thus, a 12 percent interest rate compounded semiannually is equivalent to an *effective* annual rate of ($112.36/$100) − 1 = 0.1236, or 12.36 percent, compounded annually. The more frequently interest is compounded or earned, the greater is the effective annual rate corresponding to a given *nominal or stated* annual rate (i.e., interest rate compounded annually).

To find the future value of a sum when compounding occurs more frequently than once a year, we use the following formula:

$$FV_n = PV\left(1 + \frac{i}{m}\right)^{mn} \qquad [\text{A-6}]$$

where m is the number of times per year that compounding occurs. Equation A-6 is obtained by dividing i by m and multiplying n by m in Equation A-2. For example, for $100 deposited for 1 year at the nominal or stated interest rate of 12 percent compounded semiannually, $m = 2$ so that $i/m = 12$ percent/2 = 6 percent, and $mn = 2(1) = 2$. From Table B-1 in Appendix B, we find that $FVIF_{6,2} = 1.1236$, so that $100 grows to $100(1.1236) = $112.36 (the same result obtained above by long-hand calculation).

If the $100 had been deposited for 5 years at the nominal or stated interest rate of 12 percent compounded

semiannually, $m = 2$, $i/m = 12$ percent/2 = 6 percent, $mn = 2(5) = 10$, so that $FVIF_{6,10} = 1.7908$, and $100 grows to $100(1.7908) = $179.08 (as compared with $176.23 found in Section A-1 for $100 deposited at 12 percent per year compounded annually). Finally, for $100 deposited for five years at the nominal or stated interest rate of 12 percent compounded quarterly, we have $m = 4$, $i/m = 12$ percent/4 = 3 percent, $mn = 4(5) = 20$, so that $FVIF_{3,20} = 1.8061$, and $100 grows to $100(1.8061) = $180.61.

The same method is used in discounting. For example, to find the present value of $176.23 to be received in five years and discounted semiannually at the nominal or stated annual rate of 12 percent, $m = 2$, $i/m = 12$ percent/2 = 6 percent, $mn = 2(5) = 10$, $PVIF_{6,10} = 0.5584$ (from Table B-2 in Appendix B), so that the present value of $176.23 is $176.23(0.5584) = $98.41 (as compared with $100 found with annual discounting in Section A-2). The same general procedure is used to find the future or present value of an annuity with other than annual compounding or discounting.

A-6 DETERMINING THE INTEREST RATE

Sometimes we know the present value and the future value of a sum or an annuity and we want to determine or solve for the implied rate of interest. For example, suppose you borrow $100 and promise to repay $176.23 at the end of five years. Since $100 is the present value of $176.23, the implied rate of interest that you are paying can be found as follows:

$$PVA_5 = FV_n \frac{1}{(1+i)^n} \qquad [\text{A-7}]$$

$$= FV_n(PVIF_{i,n})$$

$$\$100 = \$176.23(PVIF_{i,5})$$

$$\frac{\$100}{\$176.23} = PVIF_{i,5}$$

$$PVIF_{i,5} = 0.5674$$

By then moving across the fifth row (for $n = 5$ years) in Table B-2 in Appendix B, we find that 0.5674 is under the 12 percent column. Thus, you are paying a 12 percent interest rate.

Similarly, if you borrow $100,000 today to purchase a home and sign a mortgage agreement to pay $12,750 at the end of each of the next 25 years, the implied interest rate that you are paying can be found by first recognizing that $100,000 is the present value of a 25-year, $12,750 annuity. Thus,

$$PVA_n = R(PVIFA_{i,n}) \qquad [\text{A-8}]$$

$$\$100,000 = \$12,750(PVIF_{i,25})$$

$$\frac{\$100,000}{\$12,750} = PVIF_{i,25}$$

$$PVIF_{i,25} = 7.8431$$

By then moving across the twenty-fifth row (for $n = 25$ years) in Table B-4 in Appendix B, we find that 7.8431 is under the 12 percent column. Thus, you are paying a 12 percent interest rate on your mortgage loan.

If the yearly payments in the above mortgage loan had been $13,000 instead of $12,750, the implied interest rate that you would be paying can be found as follows:

$$\frac{\$100,000}{\$13,000} = 7.6923 = PVIF_{i,25}$$

Moving across the twenty-fifth row in Table B-4, we find 7.8431 under the 12 percent column and 6.8729 under the 14 percent column. Since $PVIF_{i,\,25} = 7.6923$ lies between these two values, the implied interest rate is between 12 percent and 14 percent and is found by interpolation to be

$$i = 12\%$$

$$+ \frac{7.8431 - 7.6923}{(7.8431 - 7.6923) + (7.6923 - 6.8729)}$$

$$\times (14\% - 12\%)$$

$$= 12\% + \frac{0.1508}{0.9702}(2\%)$$

$$= 12.31\%$$

A-7 PERPETUITIES

Sometimes we are interested in finding the present value of an annuity for an infinite number of years, or *perpetuity*. The present value of a perpetuity of R equal cash flows and interest rate i is given by

$$PVA_\infty = \sum_{t=1}^{\infty} \frac{R}{(1+i)^t} = R \sum_{t=1}^{\infty} \frac{1}{(1+i)^t}$$

However, it can be shown that the above expression reduces to

$$PVA_\infty = \frac{R}{i} \qquad [\text{A-9}]$$

For example, the present value of $100 to be received each year in perpetuity, discounted at 12 percent, is $100/0.12 = $833.33. At $i = 10$ percent, the present value of the perpetuity would be $100/0.1 = $1,000, and at $i = 14$ percent, it would be $100/0.14 = $714.29.

APPENDIX B   Interest Factor Tables

TABLE B-1 Compound Value of $1: $FVIF_{i,n} = (1 + i)^n$

Period	1%	2%	3%	4%	5%	6%	7%	8%	9%	10%	12%	14%	15%	16%	18%	20%	24%	28%	32%	36%
1	1.0100	1.0200	1.0300	1.0400	1.0500	1.0600	1.0700	1.0800	1.0900	1.1000	1.1200	1.1400	1.1500	1.1600	1.1800	1.2000	1.2400	1.2800	1.3200	1.3600
2	1.0201	1.0404	1.0609	1.0816	1.1025	1.1236	1.1449	1.1664	1.1881	1.2100	1.2544	1.2996	1.3225	1.3456	1.3924	1.4400	1.5376	1.6384	1.7424	1.8496
3	1.0303	1.0612	1.0927	1.1249	1.1576	1.1910	1.2250	1.2597	1.2950	1.3310	1.4049	1.4815	1.5209	1.5609	1.6430	1.7280	1.9066	2.0972	2.3000	2.5155
4	1.0406	1.0824	1.1255	1.1699	1.2155	1.2625	1.3108	1.3605	1.4116	1.4641	1.5735	1.6890	1.7490	1.8106	1.9388	2.0736	2.3642	2.6844	3.0360	3.4210
5	1.0510	1.1041	1.1593	1.2167	1.2763	1.3382	1.4026	1.4693	1.5386	1.6105	1.7623	1.9254	2.0114	2.1003	2.2878	2.4883	2.9316	3.4360	4.0075	4.6526
6	1.0615	1.1262	1.1941	1.2653	1.3401	1.4185	1.5007	1.5869	1.6771	1.7716	1.9738	2.1950	2.3131	2.4364	2.6996	2.9860	3.6352	4.3980	5.2899	6.3275
7	1.0721	1.1487	1.2299	1.3159	1.4071	1.5036	1.6058	1.7138	1.8280	1.9487	2.2107	2.5023	2.6600	2.8262	3.1855	3.5832	4.5077	5.6295	6.9826	8.6054
8	1.0829	1.1717	1.2668	1.3686	1.4775	1.5938	1.7182	1.8509	1.9926	2.1436	2.4760	2.8526	3.0590	3.2784	3.7589	4.2998	5.5895	7.2058	9.2170	11.703
9	1.0937	1.1951	1.3048	1.4233	1.5513	1.6895	1.8385	1.9990	2.1719	2.3579	2.7731	3.2519	3.5179	3.8030	4.4355	5.1598	6.9310	9.2234	12.166	15.916
10	1.1046	1.2190	1.3439	1.4802	1.6289	1.7908	1.9672	2.1589	2.3674	2.5937	3.1058	3.7072	4.0456	4.4114	5.2338	6.1917	8.5944	11.805	16.059	21.646
11	1.1157	1.2434	1.3842	1.5395	1.7103	1.8983	2.1049	2.3316	2.5804	2.8531	3.4785	4.2262	4.6524	5.1173	6.1759	7.4301	10.657	15.111	21.198	29.439
12	1.1268	1.2682	1.4258	1.6010	1.7959	2.0122	2.2522	2.5182	2.8127	3.1384	3.8960	4.8179	5.3502	5.9360	7.2876	8.9161	13.214	19.342	27.982	40.037
13	1.1381	1.2936	1.4685	1.6651	1.8856	2.1329	2.4098	2.7196	3.0658	3.4523	4.3635	5.4924	6.1528	6.8858	8.5994	10.699	16.386	24.758	36.937	54.451
14	1.1495	1.3195	1.5126	1.7317	1.9799	2.2609	2.5785	2.9372	3.3417	3.7975	4.8871	6.2613	7.0757	7.9875	10.147	12.839	20.319	31.691	48.756	74.053
15	1.1610	1.3459	1.5580	1.8009	2.0789	2.3966	2.7590	3.1722	3.6425	4.1772	5.4736	7.1379	8.1371	9.2655	11.973	15.407	25.195	40.564	64.358	100.71
16	1.1726	1.3728	1.6047	1.8730	2.1829	2.5404	2.9522	3.4259	3.9703	4.5950	6.1304	8.1372	9.3576	10.748	14.129	18.488	31.242	51.923	84.953	136.96
17	1.1843	1.4002	1.6528	1.9479	2.2920	2.6928	3.1588	3.7000	4.3276	5.0545	6.8660	9.2765	10.761	12.467	16.672	22.186	38.740	66.461	112.13	186.27
18	1.1961	1.4282	1.7024	2.0258	2.4066	2.8543	3.3799	3.9960	4.7171	5.5599	7.6900	10.575	12.375	14.462	19.673	26.623	48.038	85.070	148.02	253.33
19	1.2081	1.4568	1.7535	2.1068	2.5270	3.0256	3.6165	4.3157	5.1417	6.1159	8.6128	12.055	14.231	16.776	23.214	31.948	59.567	108.89	195.39	344.53
20	1.2202	1.4859	1.8061	2.1911	2.6533	3.2071	3.8697	4.6610	5.6044	6.7275	9.6463	13.743	16.366	19.460	27.393	38.337	73.864	139.37	257.91	468.57
21	1.2324	1.5157	1.8603	2.2788	2.7860	3.3996	4.1406	5.0338	6.1088	7.4002	10.803	15.667	18.821	22.574	32.323	46.005	91.591	178.40	340.44	637.26
22	1.2447	1.5460	1.9161	2.3699	2.9253	3.6035	4.4304	5.4365	6.6586	8.1403	12.100	17.861	21.644	26.186	38.142	55.206	113.57	228.35	449.39	866.67
23	1.2572	1.5769	1.9736	2.4647	3.0715	3.8197	4.7405	5.8715	7.2579	8.9543	13.552	20.361	24.891	30.376	45.007	66.247	140.83	292.30	593.19	1178.6
24	1.2697	1.6084	2.0328	2.5633	3.2251	4.0489	5.0724	6.3412	7.9111	9.8497	15.178	23.212	28.625	35.236	53.108	79.496	174.63	374.14	783.02	1602.9
25	1.2824	1.6406	2.0938	2.6658	3.3864	4.2919	5.4274	6.8485	8.6231	10.834	17.000	26.461	32.918	40.874	62.668	95.396	216.54	478.90	1033.5	2180.0
26	1.2953	1.6734	2.1566	2.7725	3.5557	4.5494	5.8074	7.3964	9.3992	11.918	19.040	30.166	37.856	47.414	73.948	114.47	268.51	612.99	1364.3	2964.9
27	1.3082	1.7069	2.2213	2.8834	3.7335	4.8223	6.2139	7.9881	10.245	13.110	21.324	34.389	43.535	55.000	87.259	137.37	332.95	784.63	1800.9	4032.3
28	1.3213	1.7410	2.2879	2.9987	3.9201	5.1117	6.6488	8.6271	11.167	14.421	23.883	39.204	50.065	63.800	102.96	164.84	412.86	1004.3	2377.2	5483.8
29	1.3345	1.7758	2.3566	3.1187	4.1161	5.4184	7.1143	9.3173	12.172	15.863	26.749	44.693	57.575	74.008	121.50	197.81	511.95	1285.5	3137.9	7458.0
30	1.3478	1.8114	2.4273	3.2434	4.3219	5.7435	7.6123	10.062	13.267	17.449	29.959	50.950	66.211	85.849	143.37	237.37	634.81	1645.5	4142.0	10143.
40	1.4889	2.2080	3.2620	4.8010	7.0400	10.285	14.974	21.724	31.409	45.259	93.050	188.88	267.86	378.72	750.37	1469.7	5455.9	19426.	66520.	*
50	1.6446	2.6916	4.3839	7.1067	11.467	18.420	29.457	46.901	74.357	117.39	289.00	700.23	1083.6	1670.7	3927.3	9100.4	46890.	*	*	*
60	1.8167	3.2810	5.8916	10.519	18.679	32.987	57.946	101.25	176.03	304.48	897.59	2595.9	4383.9	7370.1	20555.	56347.	*	*	*	*

*$FVIF > 99,999$.

TABLE B-2 Present Value of \$1: $PVIF_{i,n} = 1/(1 + i)^n = 1/FVIF_{i,n}$

Period	1%	2%	3%	4%	5%	6%	7%	8%	9%	10%	12%	14%	15%	16%	18%	20%	24%	28%	32%	36%
1	.9901	.9804	.9709	.9615	.9524	.9434	.9346	.9259	.9174	.9091	.8929	.8772	.8696	.8621	.8475	.8333	.8065	.7813	.7576	.7353
2	.9803	.9612	.9426	.9246	.9070	.8900	.8734	.8573	.8417	.8264	.7972	.7695	.7561	.7432	.7182	.6944	.6504	.6104	.5739	.5407
3	.9706	.9423	.9151	.8890	.8638	.8396	.8163	.7938	.7722	.7513	.7118	.6750	.6575	.6407	.6086	.5787	.5245	.4768	.4348	.3975
4	.9610	.9238	.8885	.8548	.8227	.7921	.7629	.7350	.7084	.6830	.6355	.5921	.5718	.5523	.5158	.4823	.4230	.3725	.3294	.2923
5	.9515	.9057	.8626	.8219	.7835	.7473	.7130	.6806	.6499	.6209	.5674	.5194	.4972	.4761	.4371	.4019	.3411	.2910	.2495	.2149
6	.9420	.8880	.8375	.7903	.7462	.7050	.6663	.6302	.5963	.5645	.5066	.4556	.4323	.4104	.3704	.3349	.2751	.2274	.1890	.1580
7	.9327	.8706	.8131	.7599	.7107	.6651	.6227	.5835	.5470	.5132	.4523	.3996	.3759	.3538	.3139	.2791	.2218	.1776	.1432	.1162
8	.9235	.8535	.7894	.7307	.6768	.6274	.5820	.5403	.5019	.4665	.4039	.3506	.3269	.3050	.2660	.2326	.1789	.1388	.1085	.0854
9	.9143	.8368	.7664	.7026	.6446	.5919	.5439	.5002	.4604	.4241	.3606	.3075	.2843	.2630	.2255	.1938	.1443	.1084	.0822	.0628
10	.9053	.8203	.7441	.6756	.6139	.5584	.5083	.4632	.4224	.3855	.3220	.2697	.2472	.2267	.1911	.1615	.1164	.0847	.0623	.0462
11	.8963	.8043	.7224	.6496	.5847	.5268	.4751	.4289	.3875	.3505	.2875	.2366	.2149	.1954	.1619	.1346	.0938	.0662	.0472	.0340
12	.8874	.7885	.7014	.6246	.5568	.4970	.4440	.3971	.3555	.3186	.2567	.2076	.1869	.1685	.1372	.1122	.0757	.0517	.0357	.0250
13	.8787	.7730	.6810	.6006	.5303	.4688	.4150	.3677	.3262	.2897	.2292	.1821	.1625	.1452	.1163	.0935	.0610	.0404	.0271	.0184
14	.8700	.7579	.6611	.5775	.5051	.4423	.3878	.3405	.2992	.2633	.2046	.1597	.1413	.1252	.0985	.0779	.0492	.0316	.0205	.0135
15	.8613	.7430	.6419	.5553	.4810	.4173	.3624	.3152	.2745	.2394	.1827	.1401	.1229	.1079	.0835	.0649	.0397	.0247	.0155	.0099
16	.8528	.7284	.6232	.5339	.4581	.3936	.3387	.2919	.2519	.2176	.1631	.1229	.1069	.0930	.0708	.0541	.0320	.0193	.0118	.0073
17	.8444	.7142	.6050	.5134	.4363	.3714	.3166	.2703	.2311	.1978	.1456	.1078	.0929	.0802	.0600	.0451	.0258	.0150	.0089	.0054
18	.8360	.7002	.5874	.4936	.4155	.3503	.2959	.2502	.2120	.1799	.1300	.0946	.0808	.0691	.0508	.0376	.0208	.0118	.0068	.0039
19	.8277	.6864	.5703	.4746	.3957	.3305	.2765	.2317	.1945	.1635	.1161	.0829	.0703	.0596	.0431	.0313	.0168	.0092	.0051	.0029
20	.8195	.6730	.5537	.4564	.3769	.3118	.2584	.2145	.1784	.1486	.1037	.0728	.0611	.0514	.0365	.0261	.0135	.0072	.0039	.0021
21	.8114	.6598	.5375	.4388	.3589	.2942	.2415	.1987	.1637	.1351	.0926	.0638	.0531	.0443	.0309	.0217	.0109	.0056	.0029	.0016
22	.8034	.6468	.5219	.4220	.3418	.2775	.2257	.1839	.1502	.1228	.0826	.0560	.0462	.0382	.0262	.0181	.0088	.0044	.0022	.0012
23	.7954	.6342	.5067	.4057	.3256	.2618	.2109	.1703	.1378	.1117	.0738	.0491	.0402	.0329	.0222	.0151	.0071	.0034	.0017	.0008
24	.7876	.6217	.4919	.3901	.3101	.2470	.1971	.1577	.1264	.1015	.0659	.0431	.0349	.0284	.0188	.0126	.0057	.0027	.0013	.0006
25	.7798	.6095	.4776	.3751	.2953	.2330	.1842	.1460	.1160	.0923	.0588	.0378	.0304	.0245	.0160	.0105	.0046	.0021	.0010	.0005
26	.7720	.5976	.4637	.3607	.2812	.2198	.1722	.1352	.1064	.0839	.0525	.0331	.0264	.0211	.0135	.0087	.0037	.0016	.0007	.0003
27	.7644	.5859	.4502	.3468	.2678	.2074	.1609	.1252	.0976	.0763	.0469	.0291	.0230	.0182	.0115	.0073	.0030	.0013	.0006	.0002
28	.7568	.5744	.4371	.3335	.2551	.1956	.1504	.1159	.0895	.0693	.0419	.0255	.0200	.0157	.0097	.0061	.0024	.0010	.0004	.0002
29	.7493	.5631	.4243	.3207	.2429	.1846	.1406	.1073	.0822	.0630	.0374	.0224	.0174	.0135	.0082	.0051	.0020	.0008	.0003	.0001
30	.7419	.5521	.4120	.3083	.2314	.1741	.1314	.0994	.0754	.0573	.0334	.0196	.0151	.0116	.0070	.0042	.0016	.0006	.0002	.0001
35	.7059	.5000	.3554	.2534	.1813	.1301	.0937	.0676	.0490	.0356	.0189	.0102	.0075	.0055	.0030	.0017	.0005	.0002	.0001	*
40	.6717	.4529	.3066	.2083	.1420	.0972	.0668	.0460	.0318	.0221	.0107	.0053	.0037	.0026	.0013	.0007	.0002	.0001	*	*
45	.6391	.4102	.2644	.1712	.1113	.0727	.0476	.0313	.0207	.0137	.0061	.0027	.0019	.0013	.0006	.0003	.0001	*	*	*
50	.6080	.3715	.2281	.1407	.0872	.0543	.0339	.0213	.0134	.0085	.0035	.0014	.0009	.0006	.0003	.0001	*	*	*	*
55	.5785	.3365	.1968	.1157	.0683	.0406	.0242	.0145	.0087	.0053	.0020	.0007	.0005	.0003	.0001	*	*	*	*	*

*The factor is zero to four decimal places.

| TABLE C-4 | Durbin–Watson Statistic for 1 Percent Significance Points of d_L and d_U |

	$k' = 1$		$k' = 2$		$k' = 3$		$k' = 4$		$k' = 5$	
n	d_L	d_U	d_L	d_U	d_L	d_U	d_L	d_U	d_L	d_U
15	0.81	1.07	0.70	1.25	0.59	1.46	0.49	1.70	0.39	1.96
16	0.84	1.09	0.74	1.25	0.63	1.44	0.53	1.66	0.44	1.90
17	0.87	1.10	0.77	1.25	0.67	1.43	0.57	1.63	0.48	1.85
18	0.90	1.12	0.80	1.26	0.71	1.42	0.61	1.60	0.52	1.80
19	0.93	1.13	0.83	1.26	0.74	1.41	0.65	1.58	0.56	1.77
20	0.95	1.15	0.86	1.27	0.77	1.41	0.68	1.57	0.60	1.74
21	0.97	1.16	0.89	1.27	0.80	1.41	0.72	1.55	0.63	1.71
22	1.00	1.17	0.91	1.28	0.83	1.40	0.75	1.54	0.66	1.69
23	1.02	1.19	0.94	1.29	0.86	1.40	0.77	1.53	0.70	1.67
24	1.04	1.20	0.96	1.30	0.88	1.41	0.80	1.53	0.72	1.66
25	1.05	1.21	0.98	1.30	0.90	1.41	0.83	1.52	0.75	1.65
26	1.07	1.22	1.00	1.31	0.93	1.41	0.85	1.52	0.78	1.64
27	1.09	1.23	1.02	1.32	0.95	1.41	0.88	1.51	0.81	1.63
28	1.10	1.24	1.04	1.32	0.97	1.41	0.90	1.51	0.83	1.62
29	1.12	1.25	1.05	1.33	0.99	1.42	0.92	1.51	0.85	1.61
30	1.13	1.26	1.07	1.34	1.01	1.42	0.94	1.51	0.88	1.61
31	1.15	1.27	1.08	1.34	1.02	1.42	0.96	1.51	0.90	1.60
32	1.16	1.28	1.10	1.35	1.04	1.43	0.98	1.51	0.92	1.60
33	1.17	1.29	1.11	1.36	1.05	1.43	1.00	1.51	0.94	1.59
34	1.18	1.30	1.13	1.36	1.07	1.43	1.01	1.51	0.95	1.59
35	1.19	1.31	1.14	1.37	1.08	1.44	1.03	1.51	0.97	1.59
36	1.21	1.32	1.15	1.38	1.10	1.44	1.04	1.51	0.99	1.59
37	1.22	1.32	1.16	1.38	1.11	1.45	1.06	1.51	1.00	1.59
38	1.23	1.33	1.18	1.39	1.12	1.45	1.07	1.52	1.02	1.58
39	1.24	1.34	1.19	1.39	1.14	1.45	1.09	1.52	1.03	1.58
40	1.25	1.34	1.20	1.40	1.15	1.46	1.10	1.52	1.05	1.58
45	1.29	1.38	1.24	1.42	1.20	1.48	1.16	1.53	1.11	1.58
50	1.32	1.40	1.28	1.45	1.24	1.49	1.20	1.54	1.16	1.59
55	1.36	1.43	1.32	1.47	1.28	1.51	1.25	1.55	1.21	1.59
60	1.38	1.45	1.35	1.48	1.32	1.52	1.28	1.56	1.25	1.60
65	1.41	1.47	1.38	1.50	1.35	1.53	1.31	1.57	1.28	1.61
70	1.43	1.49	1.40	1.52	1.37	1.55	1.34	1.58	1.31	1.61
75	1.45	1.50	1.42	1.53	1.39	1.56	1.37	1.59	1.34	1.62
80	1.47	1.52	1.44	1.54	1.42	1.57	1.39	1.60	1.36	1.62
85	1.48	1.53	1.46	1.55	1.43	1.58	1.41	1.60	1.39	1.63
90	1.50	1.54	1.47	1.56	1.45	1.59	1.43	1.61	1.41	1.64
95	1.51	1.55	1.49	1.57	1.47	1.60	1.45	1.62	1.42	1.64
100	1.52	1.56	1.50	1.58	1.48	1.60	1.46	1.63	1.44	1.65

Note: n = number of observations; k' = number of independent variables.

Source: J. Durbin and G. S. Watson, "Testing for Serial Correlation in Least Squares Regression," *Biometrica,* vol. 38, 1951, pp. 159–177. Reprinted with the permission of the authors and the trustees of *Biometrica.*

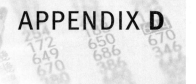

APPENDIX D Answers to Selected (Asterisked) Problems

Chapter 1

3.
$$PV = \frac{\$100}{(1.15)^1} + \frac{\$100}{(1.15)^2} + \frac{\$800}{(1.15)^2}$$

$$= \frac{\$100}{1.15} + \frac{\$100}{1.3225} + \frac{\$800}{1.3225}$$

$$= \$86.96 + \$75.61 + \$604.91$$

$$= \$767.48$$

(The computer-generated solution gives $767.47 as the answer because of a difference in rounding. The same may be true for some of the other solutions.)

5. Project 1:
$$PV = \frac{\$100,000}{1.10} + \frac{\$100,000}{(1.10)^2}$$

$$+ \frac{\$100,000}{(1.10)^3} + \frac{\$100,000}{(1.10)^4}$$

$$= \frac{\$100,000}{1.10} + \frac{\$100,000}{1.21}$$

$$+ \frac{\$100,000}{1.331} + \frac{\$100,000}{1.4641}$$

$$= \$316,986.55$$

Project 2:
$$PV = \frac{\$75,000}{1.10} + \frac{\$75,000}{(1.10)^2}$$

$$+ \frac{\$75,000}{(1.10)^3} + \frac{\$75,000}{(1.10)^4}$$

$$+ \frac{\$75,000}{(1.10)^5} + \frac{\$75,000}{(1.10)^6}$$

$$= \$326,644.55$$

The manager should choose project 2.

8. The explicit costs are $6,000 for tuition, plus $2,000 for the room, plus $1,500 for meals, plus $500 for books and supplies, for a total of $10,000 per year. The implicit costs are given by the sum of $15,000, which the student could have earned by getting a job instead of going to college and the $1,000 of interest foregone on the $10,000 of expenses for a year, for a total of $16,000. The total economic cost of attending college for a year by this student equals the sum of its explicit costs of $10,000 and the implicit costs of $16,000, or $26,000.

14. See Chapter 1 in the Web site for this text.

Chapter 2

5. The average profit $(\bar{\pi})$ and marginal profit $(\dot{\pi})$ schedules are derived in Table 1.

6. (a) The π, $\bar{\pi}$, and $\dot{\pi}$ schedules of Table 1 are plotted in Figure 1.

(b) The slope of a ray from the origin to the π curve, or $\bar{\pi}$, is negative at first but rises up to almost $Q = 3$, after which it declines, becomes zero at $Q = 4$, and negative thereafter (because π is once again negative). On the other hand, the slope of the π curve, or $\dot{\pi}$, is zero at $Q = 1$, but it rises up to $Q = 2$ (the point of inflection) and declines thereafter, in such a way that $\bar{\pi}$ is zero at $Q = 1$ and $Q = 3$ (where the π curve has zero slope). As the $\bar{\pi}$ curve rises, reaches its highest point, and declines, the $\dot{\pi}$ curve is above it, intersects it, and is below it, respectively. Note that $\bar{\pi}$ is highest at a smaller level of output than the one $(Q = 3)$ at which π is maximum.

15. (a) In Figure 2, the profit-maximizing output is $Q = 3$. This is the level of output at which the MC curve intersects the MR curve from below. We can explain why the firm maximizes total profits (π) at $Q = 3$ by showing that it pays for

631

TABLE 1			
Q	**π**	**π̄ = π/Q**	**π̇ = Δπ/ΔQ**
0	$–20	—	—
1	–50	$–50	$–30
2	0	0	50
3	30	10	30
4	0	0	–30

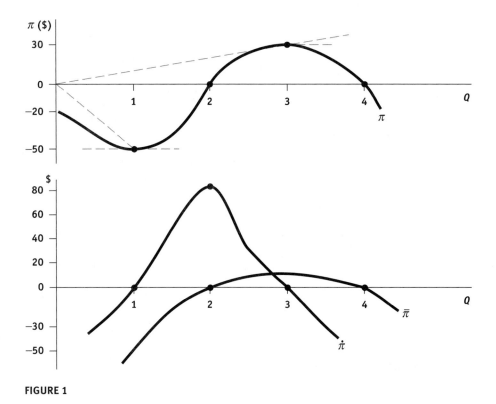

FIGURE 1

the firm to expand an output smaller than 3 units and reduce a larger output. For example, at $Q = 2$, $MR > MC$. Therefore, the firm is adding more to its *TR* than to its *TC,* and so π increases by expanding output. On the other hand, at $Q = 4$, $MR < MC$. Therefore, the firm is adding less to its *TR* than to its *TC,* and so increases by *reducing* output. At $Q = 3$, $MR = MC$. Therefore, the firm is adding as much to *TR* as to *TC* and π is maximum. Note, however, that

$MR = MC$ at $Q = 1$ also. But at $Q = 1$, the firm has produced all the (fractional) units of the commodity for which $MC > MR$, and so the firm maximizes its total loss. To distinguish between the loss-maximizing and the profit-maximizing level of output (since at both levels of output $MR = MC$), we seek the level of output at which $MR = MC$ and the *MC* curve intersects the *MR* curve from below. This corresponds to looking for the level of output at which the π curve has

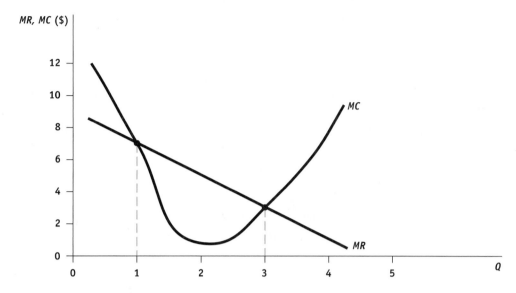

MR, MC ($)

FIGURE 2

zero slope and faces down (i.e., its slope diminishes, from positive, to zero, to negative).

(b) The answer to part (a) is an example of marginal analysis and optimization behavior in general because it shows that an organization (say, a business firm) should pursue an activity (say, expand output) as long as the marginal benefit (say, marginal revenue) from the activity exceeds the marginal cost and until the marginal benefit equals the marginal cost. By doing so, the organization (firm) maximizes the benefit (total profit) from the activity. Marginal analysis, therefore, is a most important tool of optimizing behavior on the part of any organization, and especially of a business firm.

Chapter 3

2. (a) The number of Chevrolets purchased per year (Q_C) declines by 100 units for each $1 increase in the price of Chevrolets (P_C), increases by 2,000 units for each 1 million increase in population (N), increases by 50 units for each $1 increase in per capita disposable income (I), and increases by 30 units for each dollar increase in the price of Fords (P_F). On the other hand, Q_C declines by 1,000 for each 1 cent increase in the price of gasoline (P_G), increases

by 3 units for each $1 increase in advertising expenditures on Chevrolets (A), and increases by 40,000 units for each 1 percentage point reduction in the rate of interest charged to borrow to purchase Chevrolets (P_I).

(b) To find the value of Q_C, we substitute the average value of the independent or explanatory variables into the estimated demand function. Thus, for $P_C = \$9,000$, $N = 200$ million, $I = \$10,000$, $P_F = \$8,000$, $P_G = 80$ cents, $A = \$200,000$, and $P_I = 1$ percentage point, we have

$$\begin{aligned}
Q_C = \;& 100,000 - 100(9,000) \\
& + 2,000(200) + 50(10,000) \\
& + 30(8,000) - 1,000(80) \\
& + 3(200,000) + 40,000(1) \\
= \;& 100,000 - 900,000 \\
& + 400,000 + 500,000 \\
& + 240,000 - 80,000 \\
& + 600,000 + 40,000 \\
= \;& 900,000
\end{aligned}$$

(c) To derive the equation for the demand curve for Chevrolets, we substitute into the estimated demand equation the average value of all the independent or explanatory variables given

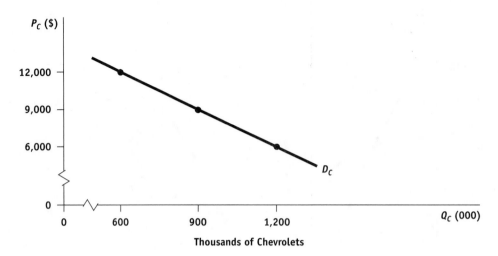

FIGURE 3

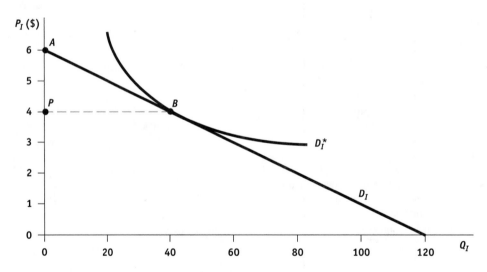

FIGURE 4

above, with the exception of P_C. Thus, the equation of the demand curve for Chevrolets is

$$Q_C = 100,000 - 100P_C$$
$$+ 2,000(200) + 50(10,000)$$
$$+ 30(8,000) - 1,000(80)$$
$$+ 3(200,000) + 40,000(1)$$
$$= 1,800,000 - 100P_C$$

(*d*) To derive the demand curve for Chevrolets (D_C), we substitute the hypothetical values of

$12,000, $9,000, and $6,000 for P_C into the equation of the demand curve found in part (*c*). This gives, respectively, $Q_C = 600,000$, $Q_C = 900,000$, and $Q_C = 1,200,000$. Plotting these price-quantity values, we get the demand curve for Chevrolets, D_C, shown in Figure 3.

5. Figure 4 shows how Michael could have found the price elasticity of demand for ice cream graphically at $P_I = \$4$. We can also use Figure 4 to show that the price elasticity of demand at $P_I = \$4$ would have

been the same if the demand curve for ice cream had been curvilinear but tangent to the linear demand curve given in Problem 4 at $P_I = \$4$. For linear demand curve D_I, E_P at $P_I = \$4$ is given by

$$E_P = \frac{P}{P-A} = \frac{\$4}{\$4 - \$6} = \frac{\$4}{-\$2} = -2$$

where P is the price of the commodity at which we want to find E_P, and A is the price of the commodity at which $Q = 0$ (see footnote 10 in Section 3-2 in the text). The value of E_P at other points on D_I can be similarly obtained. If the demand curve were curvilinear (D_I^* in Figure 4) and tangent to D_I at $P_I = \$4$, $E_P = -2$ at $P_I = \$4$, as for D_I.

8. (a) The income elasticity of demand (E_I) is given by

$$\frac{\Delta Q}{\Delta I} \cdot \frac{I}{Q}$$

where ΔQ is the change in quantity, and ΔI is the change in income. The estimated coefficient of I in the regression of Q on I and other explanatory variables is 10. That is,

$$\frac{\Delta Q}{\Delta I} = 10$$

Thus, with income of $10,000 and sales of 80,000 units, $E_I = 10(10,000/80,000) = 1.25$.

(b) For an increase in sales from 80,000 to 90,000 units and an increase in consumers' income from $10,000 to $11,000,

$$E_I = \frac{Q2 - Q1}{I2 - I1} \cdot \frac{I2 + I1}{Q2 + Q1}$$

$$= \frac{90,000 - 80,000}{\$11,000 - \$10,000}$$

$$\cdot \frac{\$11,000 + \$10,000}{90,000 + 80,000}$$

$$= 1.24$$

Since E_I is positive, the good is normal, and since E_I exceeds 1, the good is a luxury.

12. (a) Since $E_P = -2$, if the firm increased the price of steel by 6 percent, its sales would change by $(-2)(6 \text{ percent}) = -12$ percent. With $E_I = 1$, the forecasted increase in income of 4 percent,

by itself, would result in a (1) (4 percent) = 4 percent increase in the steel sold by the firm. Finally, since $E_{XY} = 1.5$, a *reduction* in the price of aluminum of 2 percent, by itself, will result in a $(1.5)(-2) = -3$ percent change in steel sales. Therefore, the net effect of a 6 percent increase in the price of steel by the firm, a 4 percent increase in income, and a 2 percent reduction in the price of aluminum would result in a net decline in the sales of the firm of -12 percent + 4 percent $-$ 3 percent = -11 percent. Thus, the steel sales of the firm next year would be $1,200 - (1,200)(-11 \text{ percent}) = 1,200 - 132 = 1,068$ tons.

(b) By themselves (i.e., without any increase in the price of steal), the increase in income and the reduction in the price of aluminum would result in a 1 percent increase in the steel sales of the firm. Thus, in order to keep sales unchanged, the firm can only increase the price of the steel so that, by itself, it would reduce the demand for steel by 1 percent. Since the price elasticity of demand of the steel is -2, the firm can increase the price of the steel by only 0.5 percent.

13. (a) Using Equation 3-12, we get,

$$MR = \$10 \ (1 - \tfrac{1}{2}) = \$5.$$

(b) Using Equation 3-12, we get

$$\$12 = \$16 \ (1 - 1/E_p)$$
$$\$12 = \$16 - \$16/E_p$$
$$-\$4 = -\$16/E_p$$
$$E_p = 4$$

(c) From Figure 2-4, we see that a firm maximizes its total profits when it produces where $MR = MC$. Since $MR = \$12$ for the firm in part (b), $MC = \$12$ also.

Chapter 4

2. (a) See Figure 5.

(b) See Figure 6.

(c) Because of changing and varying weather conditions, the supply curve of agricultural commodities is likely to shift much more than the demand curve (since most foods are necessities). Thus, it may be easier to derive or identify the demand curve than the supply curve of agricultural commodities from the observed

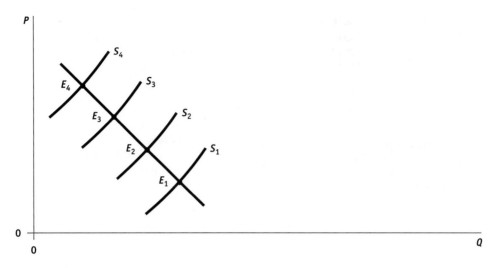

FIGURE 5

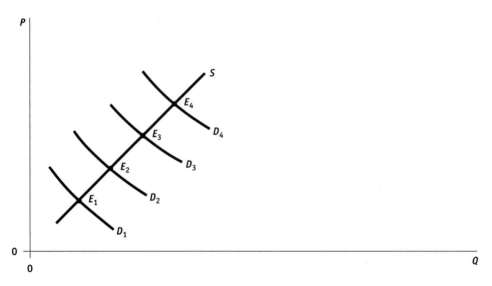

FIGURE 6

price–quantity data points. The same may be true in the markets for commodities, such as pocket calculators, where rapid technological change shifted the supply curve of pocket calculators in a short time during which demand conditions did not change much. In the case of most industrial commodities, however, the demand curve is more likely to shift than the supply curve because of business cycles. Thus, it may be easier to derive or identify the supply curve than the demand curve from the observed price–quantity data points.

3. (a) Since the price elasticity of demand for Florida Indian River oranges is –3.07, a 10 percent decrease in the price of these oranges would increase their quantity demanded by (–10 percent) × (–3.07) = 30.7 percent. Since the price elasticity of demand for Florida interior

TABLE 2	Calculations to Estimate Regression Line of Sales on Quality Control					
Year	Y_t	Z_t	$Y_t - \bar{Y}$	$Z_t - \bar{Z}$	$(Z_t - \bar{Z})(Y_t - \bar{Y})$	$\Sigma (Z_t - \bar{Z})^2$
1	44	3	-6	-2	12	4
2	40	4	-10	-1	10	1
3	42	3	-8	-2	16	4
4	46	3	-4	-2	8	4
5	48	4	-2	-1	2	1
6	52	5	2	0	0	0
7	54	6	4	1	4	1
8	58	7	8	2	16	4
9	56	7	6	2	12	4
10	60	8	10	3	30	9
$n = 10$	$\Sigma Y_t = 500$	$\Sigma Z_t = 50$	$\Sigma (Y_t - \bar{Y}) = 0$	$\Sigma (Z_t - \bar{Z}) = 0$	$\Sigma (Z_t - \bar{Z})(Y_t - \bar{Y})$	$\Sigma (Z_t - \bar{Z})^2$
	$\bar{Y} = 50$	$\bar{Z} = 5$			$= 110$	$= 32$

oranges is –3.01, a 10 percent decrease in the price of these oranges would increase their quantity demanded by $(-10 \text{ percent}) \times (-3.01) =$ 30.1 percent. Since the price elasticity of demand for California oranges is –2.76, a 10 percent decrease in the price of these oranges would increase their quantity demanded by $(-10 \text{ percent}) \times (-2.76) = 27.6$ percent.

(b) Since the demand for all three types of oranges is price elastic, a decline in price will increase the total revenue of the sellers of all three types of oranges because the percentage increase in quantity sold exceeds the percentage decrease in their prices. Specifically, for the sellers of Florida Indian River oranges, the 10 percent decrease in price would result in an increase in the quantity sold of 30.7 percent, so that their total revenue would increase by 30.7 percent – 10 percent = 20.7 percent. For the sellers of Florida interior oranges, the 10 percent decrease in price would result in an increase in the quantity sold of 30.1 percent, so that their total revenue would increase by 30.1 percent – 10 percent = 20.1 percent. For the sellers of California oranges, the 10 percent decrease in price would result in an increase in the quantity sold of 27.6 percent, so that their total revenue would increase by 27.6 percent – 10 percent = 17.6 percent.

(c) Total profits are equal to the total revenue minus the total costs. We know from part (b)

that the sellers' total revenue increases, but their total costs will also increase (to grow, transport, and sell more oranges). Their profits will increase if the increase in their total revenue exceeds the increase in their total costs. Since we do not know by how much total costs increase by selling more oranges, we cannot answer this question more precisely.

5. (a) Table 2 shows the calculations to find a and b for the data in Table 4-6 in the text on sales revenues of the firm (Y) and its expenditures on quality control (for simplicity, label this Z rather than X_2 here).

$$\hat{b} = \frac{\sum_{t=1}^{n}(Z_t - \bar{Z})(Y_t - \bar{Y})}{\sum_{t=1}^{n}(Z_t - \bar{Z})}$$

$$= \frac{110}{32} = 3.44$$

By then using the value of $\hat{b}$ found above and the values of Y and Z found in Table 2, we get the value of $\hat{a}$

$$\hat{a} = \bar{Y} - \hat{b}\bar{Z} = 50 - 3.44(5) = 32.80$$

Thus, the equation of the regression line is

$$\hat{Y}_t = 32.80 + 3.44Z_t$$

(b) With quality-control expenditures of $3 million as in the first observation year (i.e., with

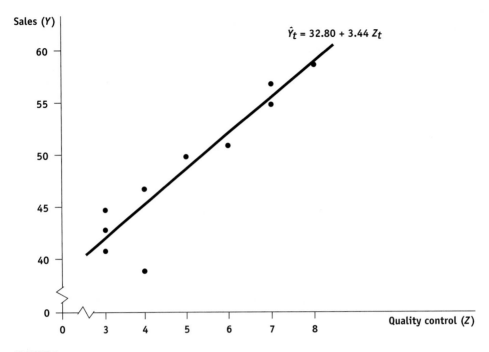

FIGURE 7

Z_1 = \$3 million), Y_1 = \$32.80 + \$3.44(3) = \$43.12 million. On the other hand, with Z_{10} = \$8 million, Y_{10} = \$32.80 + \$3.44(8) = \$60.32 million. Plotting these two points [(3, 43.12) and (8, 60.32)] and joining them by a straight line, we have the regression line plotted in Figure 7.

(c) If the firm's expenditure on quality control were \$2 million, its estimated sales revenue would be

$$\hat{Y}_t = 32.80 + 3.44(2) = \$39.68 \text{ million}$$

On the other hand, if the firm's expenditure on quality control were \$9 million, its estimated sales revenue would be

$$\hat{Y}_t = 32.80 + 3.44(9) = \$63.76 \text{ million}$$

These results are greatly biased because, as we have seen in the text, the sales revenues of the firm also depend in an important way on its advertising expenditures. By including only the firm's quality-control expenditures in estimating the regression line, we obtain biased estimates for the a and b parameters and, therefore,

biased values for the forecast of the firm's sales revenues. The same, of course, is the case when sales revenues are regressed only on the firm's advertising expenditures (as was done in the text). The only reason for running these simple regressions is to make it easier for the student to understand how regression analysis is performed and how its results are interpreted.

6. (a)
$$\hat{Y}_t = 114.074 - 9.470X_{1t} + 0.029X_{2t}$$
$$(-5.205) \quad (4.506)$$
$$R^2 = 0.96822 \qquad \bar{R}^2 = 0.96448$$
$$F = 258.942$$

The value of $b_1 = -9.47$ indicates that a \$1 decline in the price of the commodity will lead to a 9.47-unit increase in the quantity demanded of the commodity. On the other hand, the value of $b_2 = 0.029$ indicates that a \$100 increase in consumer's income will increase the quantity demanded of the commodity by 2.9 units.

(b) Since the t statistic for both b_1 and b_2 exceeds the critical t value of 2.110 for 17 df, both slope coefficients are statistically significant at the 5 percent level.

(c) The unadjusted and adjusted coefficients of determination are $R^2 = 0.96822$ and $\bar{R}^2 = 0.96448$, respectively. This means that the variation in price and income explains 96.82 percent of the variation in the quantity demanded of the commodity when no adjustment is made for degrees of freedom and 96.45 percent when such an adjustment is made.

(d) Since the value of the F statistic exceeds the critical F value of 3.59 with $k - 1 = 3 - 1 = 2$ and $n - k = 20 - 3 = 17$ df, we accept the hypothesis that the regression explains a significant proportion of the variation in the quantity demanded of the commodity (Y) at the 5 percent level of significance.

Chapter 5

1. (a) Regressing gasoline sales (S_t) on time, from $t = 1$ for the first quarter of 1995 to $t = 16$ for the last quarter of 1998, we get

$$S_t = 22,902.05 + 117.06t \quad R^2 = 0.42$$
$$(36.83)$$

Using these regression results to forecast gasoline sales (in thousands of gallons) for each quarter of 1999, we get

$$S_{17} = 22,902.05 + 117.06(17) = 24,892.07$$
in the first quarter of 1999

$$S_{18} = 22,902.05 + 117.06(18) = 25,009.13$$
in the second quarter of 1999

$$S_{19} = 22,902.05 + 117.06(19) = 25,126.19$$
in the third quarter of 1999

$$S_{20} = 22,902.05 + 117.06(20) = 25,243.25$$
in the fourth quarter of 1999

(b) Regressing the logarithm of gasoline sales (ln S_t) on time, from $t = 1$ for the first quarter of 1995 to $t = 16$ for the last quarter of 1998, we get:

$$\ln S_t = 10.04 + 0.0049t \quad R^2 = 0.41$$
$$(3.15)$$

Since the estimated parameters are based on the logarithms of the data, however, they must be converted into their antilogs to be interpreted in terms of the original data. The antilog of ln $S_0 = 10.04$ is $S_0 = 22,925.38$ and the antilog of $\ln(1 + g) = 0.0049$ gives $(1 + g) = 1.0049$. Substituting these values back into the equation, we get:

$$S_t = 22,925.38(1.0049)^t$$

where $S_0 = 22,925.38$ in thousands of gallons is the estimated sales of petroleum in the United States in the fourth quarter of 1994 (i.e., at $t = 0$) and the estimated growth rate is 1.0049, or 0.49 percent per quarter. To estimate sales (in thousands of gallons) in any future quarter, we substitute into the above equation the value of t for the quarter for which we are seeking to forecast S and solve for S_t. Thus,

$$S_{17} = 22,925.38(1.0049)^{17} = 24,910.72$$
$$S_{18} = 22,925.38(1.0049)^{18} = 25,034.51$$
$$S_{19} = 22,925.38(1.0049)^{19} = 25,156.02$$
$$S_{20} = 22,925.38(1.0049)^{20} = 25,279.82$$

(c) Since the value of the t statistic is higher for the linear trend than for the constant logarithmic trend, the former seems to fit the data marginally better. However, both fits are very poor (i.e., they "explain" less than 50 percent of the variation in the quarterly sales of gasoline).

   If we used either trend projection to forecast gasoline sales for 1999, they would be very poor because they do not take into consideration the strong seasonal factor in the data.

3. Taking the last quarter as the base-period quarter and defining dummy variable D_1 by a time series with ones in the first quarter of each year and zero in other quarters, D_2 by a time series with ones in the second quarter of each year and zero in other quarters, and D_3 by ones in the third quarter and zero in other quarters, we obtain the following results by running a regression of housing starts on the seasonal dummy variables and the linear time trend:

$$S_t = 381.53 + 8.51D_{1t} - 7.98D_{2t}$$
$$(0.57) \quad (-0.54)$$
$$- 4.71D_{3t} + 4.11D_{4t}$$
$$(-0.32) \quad (5.39)$$
$$R^2 = 0.78$$

None of the estimated coefficients for the dummy variables are statistically significant at the 5 percent level and the regression "explains" 78 percent of the variation in new housing starts (more than for the regression Equation 5-8). With none of the estimated coefficients for the dummy variables statistically significant at the 5 percent level, we would not be justified in using this method for introducing the seasonal variation into the forecasts. If we did, however, we would get the following forecasts for housing starts in each quarter of 2005:

$S_{25} = 381.53 + 8.51 + (25)4.11 = 492.79$ in 2005.1

$S_{26} = 381.53 - 7.98 + (26)4.11 = 480.41$ in 2005.2

$S_{27} = 381.53 - 4.71 + (27)4.11 = 487.78$ in 2005.3

$S_{28} = 381.53 \qquad + (28)4.11 = 496.61$ in 2005.4

These forecast values are similar to those obtained by the ratio-to-trend method shown in Case Study 5-2.

9. (a) By substituting the given values of the independent or explanatory variables and $t = 24$ for 1972 in the estimated demand equation, we get the quantity demanded (sales) of sweet potatoes in the United States in 1972 of

$$QD_S = 7,609 - 1,606(4.10) + 59(208.78)$$
$$+ 947(3.19) + 479(2.41) - 271(24)$$
$$= 11,013.74 \text{ in thousands}$$
$$(11.01 \text{ millions}) \text{ hundredweight}$$

(b) By substituting the given values of the independent or explanatory variables and $t = 25$ for 1973 in the estimated demand equation, we get the quantity demanded (sales) of sweet potatoes in the United States in 1973 of

$$QD_S = 7,609 - 1,606(4.00) + 59(210.90)$$
$$+ 947(3.55) + 479(2.40) - 271(25)$$
$$= 11,364.55 \text{ in thousands}$$
$$(11.36 \text{ millions}) \text{ hundredweight}$$

Of course, the accuracy of these results depends on the accuracy of the forecasted values of the independent or explanatory variables. The greater the errors in forecasting the latter, the greater will be the forecasting error in the former.

11. (a) The reduced-form equation for C_t is obtained by substituting Equation 5-23 for GNP_t into Equation 5-21 for C_t. That is, substituting Equation 5-23 for GNP_t into Equation 5-21 for C_t (and omitting u_{1t} because its expected value is zero), we get

$$C_t = a_1 + b_1(C_t + I_t + G_t) \qquad [5\text{-}24']$$
$$= a_1 + b_1 C_t + b_1 I_t + b_1 G_t \qquad [5\text{-}24'']$$

By then substituting Equation 5-22 for I_t into Equation 5-24″ (and omitting u_{2t}), we have

$$C_t = a_1 + b_1 C_t + b_1(a_2 + b_2\pi_{t-1} + b_1 G_t$$
$$[5\text{-}25']$$
$$= a_1 + b_1 C_t + b_1 a_2 + b_1 b_2 \pi_{t-1} + b_1 G_t$$
$$[5\text{-}25'']$$

Collecting the C_t terms to the left in Equation 5-25″ and isolating C_t, we have

$$C_t(1 - b_1) = a_1 + b_1 a_2 + b_1 b_2 \pi_{t-1} + b_1 G_t$$
$$[5\text{-}26']$$

Dividing both sides of Equation 5-26′ by $1 - b_1$, we finally obtain

$$C_t = \frac{a_1}{1 - b_1} + \frac{b_1 a_1}{1 - b_1} + \frac{b_1 b_2 \pi_{t-1}}{1 - b_1} + \frac{b_1 G_t}{1 - b_1}$$
$$[5\text{-}27']$$

Equation 5-27′ is the reduced-form equation for C_t. It is expressed only in terms of π_{t-1} and G_t (the exogenous variables of the model) and can be used in forecasting C_{t+1} by substituting the known value of π_t and the predicted value of G_{t+1} into Equation 5-27′ and solving for C_{t+1}.

(b) Equation 5-22 is already in reduced form because π_{t-1} is exogenous (i.e., it is known in period t). The lagged (and therefore known) value of a variable is sometimes known as a "predetermined variable."

Chapter 6

2. (a) See Table 3.

(b) See Figure 8.

(c) When capital is fixed at 4 units rather than 1 unit, the MP_L and AP_L are both greater than when capital is held constant at 1 unit. This is reasonable. With more capital to work with, each unit of labor is more productive, so that both the MP_L and the AP_L are higher, and diminishing returns sets in later (i.e., after more units of labor have been used).

5. We can find the marginal revenue product of each additional worker hired by calculating the change in total revenue that results from the sale of the output produced by the additional worker. This is shown in Table 4.

Since Mr. Smith can hire additional workers at the given daily wage (w) of \$40, $MRC = w = \$40$

(1) Labor (Number of Workers)	(2) Output or Total Product	(3) Marginal Product of Labor	(4) Average Product of Labor	(5) Output Elasticity of Labor
0	0	—	—	—
1	12	12	12	1
2	28	16	14	$\frac{8}{7}$
3	36	8	12	$\frac{2}{3}$
4	40	4	10	$\frac{2}{5}$
5	40	0	8	0
6	36	−4	6	$-\frac{2}{3}$

TABLE 3   Total, Marginal, and Average Products of Labor, and Output Elasticity

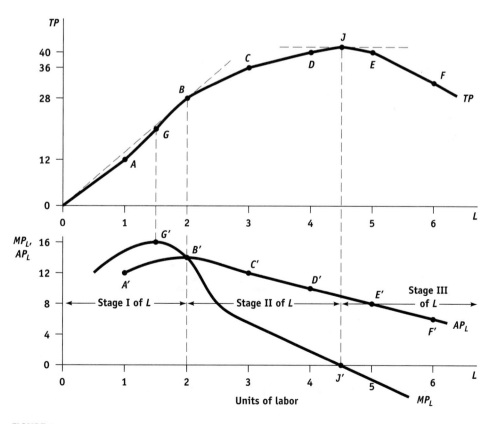

FIGURE 8

(column 6 in Table 4), and the firm's total profits will be maximum when it hires five workers so that $MRP = MRC = \$40$. The result is the same as that obtained in Problem 4, where the MRP was obtained by multiplying the MP of labor by the MR or P of the commodity. This is shown in Figure 9. Note that the MRP values are plotted at the midpoint of each additional unit of labor used in Figure 9.

9. (a) The firm is not maximizing output or minimizing costs (i.e., the firm is not using the optimal input combination) because $MP_L/w = 40/\$20 = 2$ is not equal to $MP_K/r = 120/\$30 = 4$.

(b) The firm can maximize output or minimize costs by hiring fewer workers and renting more machines. Since the firm produces in stage II of production for both labor and capital, as the firm employs fewer workers, the MP

TABLE 4

(1) Number of Workers (L)	(2) TP	(3) P	(4) $TR = (TP)(P)$	(5) $MRP_L = \Delta TR/\Delta L$	(6) $MRC_L = w$
0	0	$10	$ 0	—	$40
1	12	10	120	$120	40
2	22	10	220	100	40
3	30	10	300	80	40
4	36	10	360	60	40
5	40	10	400	40	40
6	42	10	420	20	40

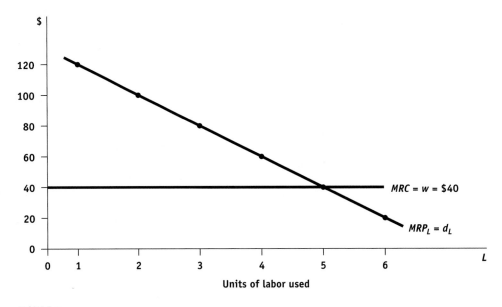

FIGURE 9

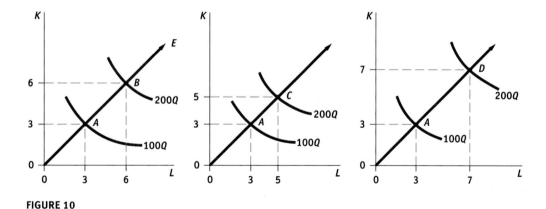

FIGURE 10

of the last remaining worker rises. On the other hand, as the firm rents more machines, the MP of the last machine rented declines. This process should continue until $MP_L/w = MP_K/r$. One such point of output maximization or cost minimization might be where

$$\frac{MP_L}{w} = \frac{60}{\$20} = \frac{MP_K}{r} = \frac{90}{\$30} = 3$$

11. Figure 10 shows constant, increasing, and decreasing returns to scale from the quantity of inputs required to double output. The left panel shows constant returns to scale. Here, doubling inputs from $3L$ and $3K$ to $6L$ and $6K$ doubles output from 100 (point A) to 200 (point B). Thus, $0A = AB$ along ray $0E$. The middle panel shows increasing returns to scale. Here, output can be doubled by less than doubling the quantity of inputs. Thus, $0A > AC$, and the isoquants become closer together. The right panel shows decreasing returns to scale. Here, output changes proportionately less than labor and capital, and $0A < AD$.

Chapter 7

1. (a) The explicit costs are $10,000 + $20,000 + $15,000 + $5,000 = $50,000.
   (b) The accounting costs would be equal to the explicit costs of $50,000. The implicit costs are $60,000 (the earnings that would be foregone from his present occupation). The economic

costs are the sum of the explicit costs of $50,000 and implicit costs of $60,000, or $110,000.
   (c) Since the estimated total revenues from opening his own law practice are $100,000 while the total estimated economic costs are $110,000, John McAuley should not start his own law practice.

8. With constant returns to scale, the LTC curve is a straight line through the origin. This is shown in the left panel of Figure 11. Since the LTC curve is a straight line through the origin, $LAC = LMC$ and equals the constant slope of the LTC curve. This is shown in the middle panel of Figure 11. Finally, since the LAC is horizontal the SAC curves are tangent to the LAC curve at the lowest points on the SAC curves (see the right panel of Figure 11).

9. See Figure 12. The figure shows that to produce output level Q_2, the plant represented by SAC is better (i.e., it leads to lower per-unit costs) than the plant indicated by SAC'. However, for outputs smaller than Q_1 or larger than Q_3, plant SAC' leads to lower per-unit costs. Thus, if the firm is not sure that its output will be between Q_1 and Q_3, it may prefer to build plant SAC'.

13. (a) The breakeven outputs for the first firm (Q_B) and the second firm ($Q_{B'}$) are

$$Q_B = \frac{TFC}{P - AVC} = \frac{\$100}{\$10 - \$6} = 25$$

$$Q_{B'} = \frac{TFC'}{P - ACV'} = \frac{\$300}{\$10 - \$3.33} = 45$$

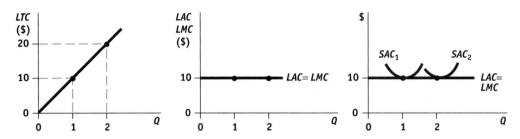

FIGURE 11

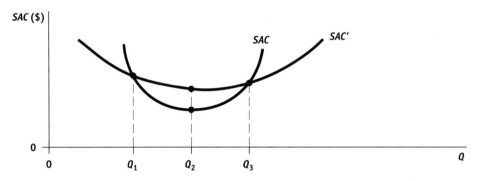

FIGURE 12

These are shown in Figure 13. The breakeven output of the second firm (i.e., the more highly leveraged firm) is larger than that for the first firm because the second firm has larger overhead costs. Thus, it takes a greater level of output for the second firm to cover its larger overhead costs.

(b) At $Q = 60$, the degrees of operating leverage of firm 1 (DOL) and firm 2 (DOL') are

$$DOL = \frac{Q(P - AVC)}{Q(P - AVC) - TFC}$$

$$= \frac{60(\$10 - \$6)}{60(\$10 - \$6) - \$100}$$

$$= \frac{\$240}{\$140} = 1.71$$

$$DOL' = \frac{Q(P - AVC')}{Q(P - AVC') - TFC'}$$

$$= \frac{60(\$10 - \$3.33)}{60(\$10 - \$3.33) - \$300}$$

$$= \frac{\$400}{\$100} = 4$$

Thus, the more highly leveraged firm has a higher DOL (i.e., a greater variability of profits) than the less highly leveraged firm. The reason for this is that firm 2 has a larger contribution margin per unit (that is, $P - AVC$) than firm 1. Graphically, this is reflected in a larger difference between the slopes of TR and TC' than between TR and TC. At $Q = 70$, DOL and DOL' are, respectively,

$$DOL = \frac{70(\$10 - \$6)}{70(\$10 - \$6) - \$100}$$

$$= \frac{\$280}{\$180} = 1.56$$

$$DOL' = \frac{70(\$10 - \$3.33)}{70(\$10 - \$3.33) - \$300}$$

$$= \frac{\$467}{\$167} = 2.8$$

Thus, the larger the level of output, the smaller are DOL and DOL'. The reason for this is that the farther we are from the breakeven point, the smaller is the percentage change in profits (since the level of profits is higher).

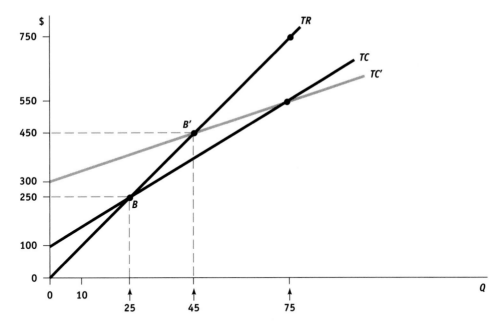

FIGURE 13

Chapter 8

1. (a)
$$QD = QS$$
$$10{,}000 - 1{,}000P = -2{,}000 + 1{,}000P$$
$$12{,}000 = 2{,}000P$$
$$P = \$6$$

(equilibrium price)

Substituting the equilibrium price into either the market demand or supply function, we get the equilibrium quantity. That is,

$$QD = 10{,}000 - 1{,}000(\$6) = 4{,}000$$

or

$$QS = -2{,}000 + 1{,}000(\$6) = 4{,}000$$

(b) See Figure 14.
3. (a) When $P = \$18$, the best or optimum level of output is 7,000 units (given by point A). The firm earns \$4 of profit per unit (AN) and a total profit of \$28,000. This represents the maximum total profit that the firm can make at this price.
(b) When $P = \$13$, the best level of output is 6,000 units (point B), and the firm breaks even.

(c) When $P = \$9$, the best level of output is 5,000 units (point C). At this level of output, the firm incurs a loss of \$5 per unit (CD) and \$25,000 in total. If the firm went out of business, however, it would incur a total loss to its TFC of \$40,000 (obtained by multiplying the AFC of DE or \$8 per unit times 5,000 units). Thus, the firm would minimize its total losses in the short run by staying in business.
(d) When $P = \$5$, the best level of output is 4,000 (point F). However, since $P = AVC$ and thus $TR = TVC$ ($= \$20{,}000$), the firm is indifferent whether it produces or not. In either case, the firm would incur a short-run loss equal to its TFC of \$40,000. Point F is thus the shutdown point.
(e) Since P is smaller than AVC, TR (\$9,000) does not cover TVC (\$18,000). Therefore, the firm would incur a total loss equal to its TFC (\$40,000) *plus* the \$9,000 amount by which TVC exceeds TR (\$18,000 − \$9,000 = \$9,000). Thus, it pays for the firm to shut down and minimize its total losses at \$40,000 (its TFC) over the period of the short run.

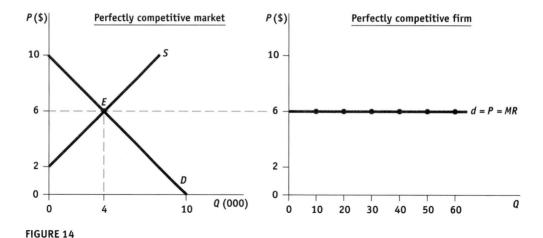

FIGURE 14

5. (a) The best or optimum level of output for this firm in the short run is given by the point where $P = SMC_1$. At this level of output (400 units), the firm earns a profit of $4 per unit and $1,600 in total.

(b) If only this firm adjusts to the long run (a simplifying and unrealistic assumption for a perfectly competitive market), this firm will produce where $P = SMC_3 = LMC$. The firm will build the scale of plant indicated by SAC_3 and will produce and sell 800 units of output. The firm will earn a profit of $5 per unit and $4,000 in total per time period. Note that since we are dealing with a perfectly competitive firm, we can safely assume that if only this firm expanded its output, the effect on the equilibrium price would be imperceptible.

14. (a) Since the movie market is monopolistically competitive, $P = LAC$ in the long run. Thus,

$$9 - 0.04Q = 10 - 0.06Q + 0.001Q^2$$
$$1 - 0.02Q + 0.001Q^2 = 0$$
$$10,000 - 200Q + Q^2 = 0$$

which can be factored as

$$(Q - 100)(Q - 100) = 0$$

so that $Q = 100$. Substituting $Q = 100$ into the demand function, we have

$$P = 9 - 0.04(100) = \$5$$

(b) At $Q = 100$,

$$AC = 10 - 0.06(100) + 0.0001(100)^2$$
$$= 10 - 6 + 1$$
$$= \$5$$

Since $P = LAC = \$5$, the Plaza Movie House breaks even in the long run.

Chapter 9

2. (a) Each oligopolist would produce one fifth of the perfectly competitive equilibrium. The reason is that, as we saw in the text, with two firms, each produces one third of the perfectly competitive output; with three firms, each produced one quarter of the perfectly competitive output, and so, by extension, each of four firms would produce one fifth of the perfectly competitive equilibrium. In this case, since production costs are zero and firms break even in the long run, price is zero and the perfectly competitive output is 10 (see the demand equation). Thus each of the four oligopolists would produce $\frac{1}{5}(10) = 2$.

(b) The general rule that we can deduce is that each oligopolists would produce $1/(n-1)$ of the perfectly competitive output according to the Cournot model. We assume, for simplicity, that production costs are zero.

6. (a) See Figure 15.

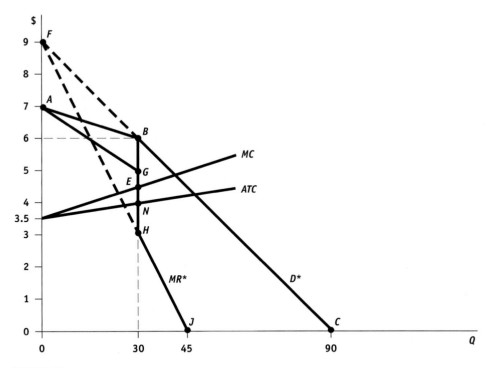

FIGURE 15

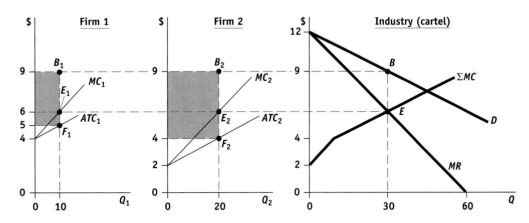

FIGURE 16

(b) The best level of output is 30 units and is given by point E at which $MR^* = MC$. At $Q = 30$, $P = 6 (point B in Figure 18), $ATC = 4, and profits are $BN = 2 per unit and $60 in total.

(c) The firm's MC curve can shift up to $MC = 5 and down to $MC = 3 (i.e., within the vertical

segment GH of the MR curve) without inducing the firm to change its best level of output of 30 units and price of $6.

8. See Figure 16. The best level of output for the cartel is 30 units and is given by point E at which $\Sigma MC = MR$. For $Q = 30$, the output of firm 1 is

10 units (given by point E_1 at which $MC_1 = MR$), and the output of firm 2 is 20 units (given by point E_2 at which $MC_2 = MR$). The profits are $B_1F_1 = \$4$ per unit and $40 in total (the shaded area for firm 1), and $B_2F_2 = \$5$ per unit and $100 in total for firm 2.

Chapter 10

3. (a) If firm B produces small cars, firm A will earn a profit of 4 if it produces large cars and has a payoff of –2 (i.e., incurs a loss of 2) if it produces small cars. If firm B produces large cars, firm A will incur a loss of 2 if it also produces large cars and it earns a profit of 4 if it produces small cars. Therefore, firm A does not have a dominant strategy.

   (b) If firm A produces large cars, firm B will earn a profit of 4 if it produces small cars and has a payoff of –2 (i.e., incurs a loss of 2) if it also produces large cars. If firm A produces small cars, firm B will incur a loss of 2 if it also produces small cars and it earns a profit of 4 if it produces large cars. Therefore, firm B does not have a dominant strategy.

   (c) The optimal strategy is for one firm to produce small cars and the other to produce large cars. In that case, each firm earns a profit of 4. If both firms produce either small cars or large cars, each incurs a loss of 2.

   (d) In this case we have two Nash equilibria: either firm A produces large cars and firm B produces small cars (the top left cell in the given pay-off matrix), or firm A produces small cars and firm B produces large cars (the bottom right cell in the payoff matrix).

   (e) A situation such as that indicated in the payoff matrix of this problem might arise if each firm does not have the resources to invest in the plant and equipment necessary to produce both large and small cars, and the demand for either small or large cars is not sufficient to justify the production of small or large cars by both firms. Specifically, if both firms produced the same type of car, the oversupply of that type of car will result in low car prices and losses for both firms.

8. (a) Each firm adopts its dominant strategy of cheating (the top left cell), but could do better by cooperating not to cheat (the bottom right

cell). Thus the firms face the prisoners' dilemma.

   (b) If the payoff in the bottom right cell were changed to (5, 5), the firms would still face the prisoners' dilemma by cheating.

9. The tit-for-tat strategy for the first 5 of an infinite number of games for the payoff matrix of Problem 1—when firm A begins by cooperating but firm B does not cooperate in the next period—is given by the following table:

Period	Firm A	Firm B
1	2	2
2	–1	3
3	1	1
4	3	–1
5	2	2

The above table shows that in the first period, firm A sets a high price (i.e., cooperates) and so does firm B (so that each firm earns a profit of 2). If in the second period firm B does not cooperate and sets a low price while firm A is still cooperating and setting a high price, firm B earns a profit of 3 and firm A incurs a loss of 1. In the third period, firm A retaliates and also sets a low price. As a result, each firm earns a profit of only 1 in period 3. In period 4, firm B cooperates again by setting a high price. With firm A still setting a low price, firm A earns a profit of 3 while firm B incurs a loss of 1. In the fifth period, firm A cooperates again and sets a high price. Since both firms are now setting a high price, each earns a profit of 2.

Chapter 11

1. See Figure 17.

3. Adding the MR_A and MR_B functions together, we get

$$MR_T = MR_A + MR_B$$
$$= 16 - 0.4Q_A + 10 - 0.4Q_B$$
$$= 26 - 0.8Q$$

Setting $MR_T = MC$, we get

$$MR_T = 26 - 0.8Q = 8 + 0.1Q = MC$$
$$0.9Q = 18$$
$$Q = 20$$

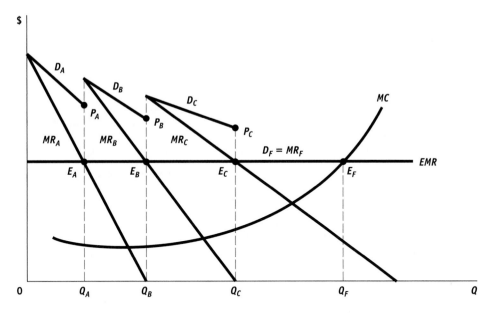

FIGURE 17

Since at $Q = 20$,

$$MR_A = 16 - 0.4(20) = 8 > 0$$

and

$$MR_B = 10 - 0.4(20) = 2 > 0$$

$Q = 20$ is the profit-maximizing level of output and sales of each product. On the other hand, with MC', we have

$$MR_T = 26 - 0.8Q = \frac{2Q}{35} = MC'$$

$$0.8Q + \frac{2Q}{35} = 26$$

$$\frac{(28 + 2)Q}{35} = 26$$

$$30Q = 910$$

$$Q = 30.3$$

However, setting $MR_B = 0$, we get

$$MR_B = 10 - 0.4Q_B = 0$$

$$Q_B = 25$$

Therefore, $MR_B < 0$ for $Q_B = Q > 25$, and so $MR_T = MR_A$ for $Q > 25$. Setting MR_A equal to MC', we have

$$MR_A = 16 - 0.4Q = \frac{2Q}{35} = MC'$$

$$0.4Q + \frac{2Q}{35} = 16$$

$$\frac{(14 + 2)Q}{35} = 16$$

$$16Q = 560$$

$$Q = 35$$

Thus, the best level of *sales* (as opposed to output) is 35 units of product A but only 25 units of product B (i.e., the firm disposes of or keeps off the market 10 units of product B in order not to sell it at $MR_B < 0$). At sales of $Q_A = 35$, $P_{A'} = 16 - 0.2(35) = \$9$. At sales of $Q_B = 25$, $P_{B'} = 10 - 0.2(25) = \$5$.

7. See Figure 18. D_1 and MR_1 in part (a) are the demand and marginal revenue curves that the firm faces in market 1, D_2 and MR_2 in part (b) are the demand and marginal revenue curves that the firm faces in market 2, and D and MR in part (c) are the overall

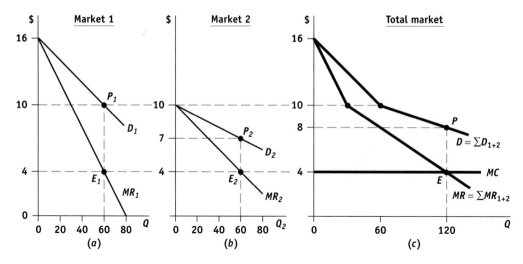

FIGURE 18

total demand and marginal revenue curves faced by the firm for the two markets together. $D = \Sigma D_{1+2}$, and $MR = \Sigma MR_{1+2}$, by horizontal summation. The total cost function, $TC = 120 + 4Q$, indicates that the firm faces total fixed costs of $120 and a marginal cost of $4. The best level of output of the firm is 120 units and is given by point E in part (c) at which $MR = MC = \$4$. With third-degree price discrimination, the firm should sell 60 units of the product in each market, so that $MR_1 = MR_2 = MR = MC = \$4$ (points E_1, E_2, and E). For $Q_1 = 60$, $P_1 = \$10$ (on D_1) in market 1, so that $TR_1 = \$600$. For $Q_2 = 60$, $P_2 = \$7$ (on D_2) in market 2, so that $TR_2 = \$420$. Thus, the overall total revenue of the firm is $TR = TR_1 + TR_2 = \$600 + \$420 = \$1,020$. For $Q = 120$, $TC = 120 + 4(120) = \$600$, so that

$$ATC = \frac{TC}{Q} = \frac{\$600}{120} = \$5$$

Thus, the firm earns a profit of $P_1 - ATC = \$10 - \$5 = \$5$ per unit and $300 in total in market 1, and a profit of $P_2 - ATC = \$7 - \$5 = 2$ per unit and $120 in total in market 2. Thus, the overall total profit of the firm is $\pi = \pi_1 + \pi_2 = \$300 + \$120 = \$420$. In the absence of third-degree price discrimination, $Q = 120$, $P = \$8$ (in part (c)), $TR = (8)(120) = \$960$, and profits are $3 per unit and $360 in total.

11. The demand and marginal revenue curves for the final product faced by the marketing division of

the firm in Figure 19 can be represented algebraically as

$$Q_m = 160 - 10P_m$$

or

$$P_m = 16 - 0.1Q_m$$

and

$$MR_m = 16 - 0.2Q_m$$

The marginal cost functions of each division are, respectively,

$$MC_p' = 2 + 0.1Q_p$$

and

$$MC_m = 1 + 0.1Q_m$$

Since $P_t = \$6$, the total marginal cost function of the marketing division (MC_t) is

$$MC_t = MC_m + P_t = 1 + 0.1Q_m + 6$$
$$= 7 + 0.1Q_m$$

The best level of output of the intermediate product by the production division is given by the point at which $MC_p' = P_t$. Thus,

$$MC_p' = 2 + 0.1Q_p = 6 = P_t$$

so that

$$0.1Q_p = 4$$

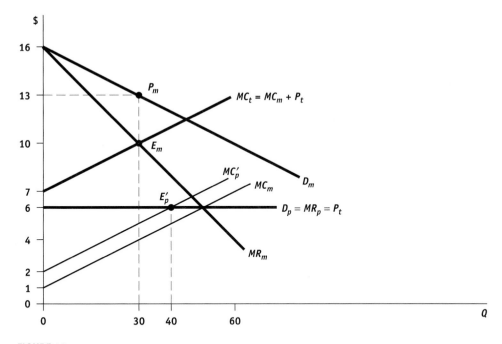

FIGURE 19

and

$$Q_p = 40$$

The best level of output of the *final product* by the marketing division is given by the point at which $MC_t = MR_m$. Thus,

$$MC_t = 7 + 0.1Q_m = 16 - 0.2Q_m$$

$$= MR_m$$

so that

$$0.3Q_m = 9$$

and

$$Q_m = 30$$

$$P_m = 16 - 0.1(30) = \$13$$

Chapter 12

2. Figure 20 shows that a corrective tax of $300 per unit collected from producers will make S″ the new industry supply curve. With S′, P = $800 and Q = 3,000 (given by the intersection of the D and S′ curves at point E′). Producers now receive a

net price of $500 (P = $800 minus the $300 tax per unit).

5. Figure 21 shows that the corrective tax of $0.40 per can of soft drink imposed on consumers will make D″ the new market demand curve. With D′, P = $1.00 and Q = 4,000 (given by the intersection of D″ and S at point E′). Consumers now pay $1.00 plus the $0.40 tax per can for soft drinks, or a net price of $1.40 (as compared with the price of $1.20 before the imposition of the tax).

7. In Figure 22, D and D′ are, respectively, the original and new market demand curves. With the new demand curve D′ and the unchanged LAC curve, the regulatory commission would set P′ = LAC = $2 (point G′), and the public utility company would supply 8 million units of the service per time period (as compared with P = LAC = $3 with Q = 6 million units per time period shown by point G on D). In either case, the public utility company breaks even.

14. During the 1970s, entrance into the banking industry in the United States was highly restricted, and banks were not allowed to pay interest on checking deposits or higher than specified interest

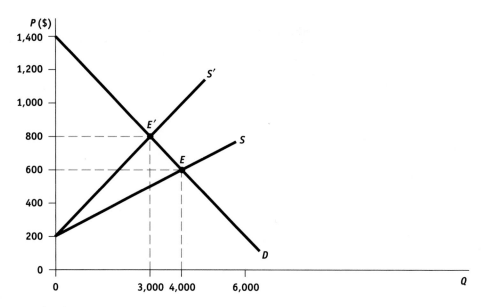

FIGURE 20

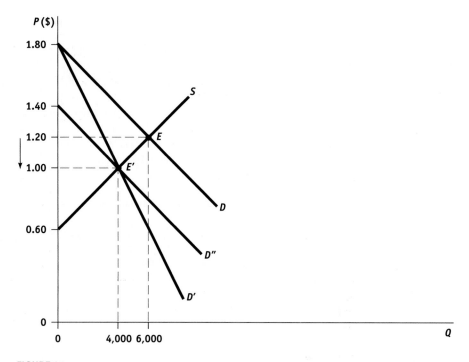

FIGURE 21

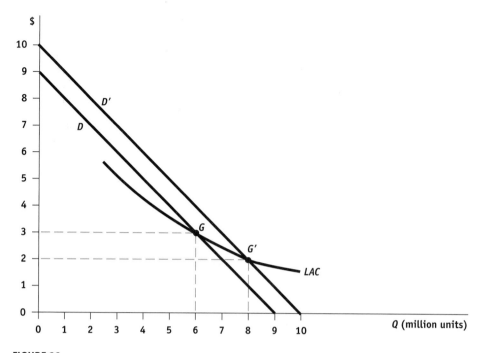

FIGURE 22

rates on savings deposits (the so-called Regulation *Q*). Banks were also the only financial institutions that could make commercial loans. In the face of such restrictions on competition, the banking industry earned rates of return on stockholders' equity during the 1970s that were higher than the average rates of return (about 15 percent) in other industries. During the 1980s, however, the reverse was the case. That is, the banking industry earned rates of return that were consistently lower than for other U.S. industries. One reason for this was that the *Depository Institutions Deregulation and Monetary Control Act of 1980* deregulated many aspects of banking in the United States and greatly increased the competition for business loans. Another reason was that many of the loans that large U.S. commercial banks made in developing countries (primarily to such Latin American countries as Brazil, Argentina, and Venezuela) had to be written off as noncollectible.

Chapter 13

2. (*a*) To determine that the area under the standard normal distribution within ±1σ is 68.26 per-

cent, we look up the value of $z = 1.0$ in Table C-1. This is 0.3413. This means that the area to the right of the zero mean of the standard normal distribution to $z = 1$ is 0.3413, or 34.13 percent. Because of symmetry, the area between the mean and $z = 21$ is also 0.3413, or 34.13 percent. Therefore, the area between $z = ±1σ$ under the standard normal distribution is double 0.3413, which is 0.6826, or 68.26 percent. From Table C-1, we get the value of 0.4772 for $z = 2$. Thus, the area under the standard normal curve between $z = ±2σ$ is 2(0.4772), which equals 0.9544, or 95.44 percent. From Table C-1, we get the value of 0.4987 for $z = 3$. Thus, the area under the standard normal curve between $z = ±3σ$ is 0.9974, or 99.74 percent.

(*b*) For $650,

$$z = \frac{\$650 - \$500}{\$70.71} = 2.12$$

which from Table C-1 gives 0.4830, or 48.30 percent.

(c) For $300,

$$z = \left| \frac{\$300 - \$500}{\$70.71} \right| = \frac{\$200}{\$70.71} = 2.83$$

which from Table C-1 gives 0.4977. This is the area between $300 and $500 (i.e., the probability that profit will fall between $300 and $500). Therefore, the probability that profit will fall between $300 and $650 is equal to the probability that profit will fall between $300 and $500 (49.77 percent) plus the probability that profit will fall between $500 and $650 (found earlier to be 48.30 percent), or 98.07. The probability that profit will be lower than $300 is equal to 1.0 minus 0.9977, which is 0.0023, or 0.23 percent. The probability that profit will be higher than $650 is 1.0 – 0.9830, which is 0.017, or 1.7 percent.

5. (a) The expected monetary return of this investment (R) is

Expected return = $E(R)$
$$= 0.2(\$40{,}000) + 0.8(-\$10{,}000)$$
$$= \$8{,}000 - \$8{,}000$$
$$= 0$$

(b) The expected utilities of the project for individuals A, B, and C are

$E(U)$ of $A = 0.2(10 \text{ utils}) + 0.8(-5 \text{ utils})$
$$= 2 \text{ utils} - 4 \text{ utils} = -2 \text{ utils}$$
$E(U)$ of $B = 0.2(20 \text{ utils}) + 0.8(-5 \text{ utils})$
$$= 4 \text{ utils} - 4 \text{ utils} = 0 \text{ utils}$$
$E(U)$ of $C = 0.2(30 \text{ utils}) + 0.8(-5 \text{ utils})$
$$= 6 \text{ utils} - 4 \text{ utils} = 2 \text{ utils}$$

Only individual C (the only individual for whom the marginal utility for money increases) will invest in the venture because only for him or her is the expected utility of the project positive. Because the marginal utility for money increases, individual C is a risk seeker. Individual B is indifferent to the venture because the expected utility of the project is zero. For individual B, the marginal utility for money is constant, so that he or she is risk neutral. Individual A will not invest in the venture because the expected utility of the project

is negative. For individual A, the marginal utility for money diminishes, so that he or she is a risk averter.

7. (a) The net present values of project A and project B at the risk-free discount rate of 8 percent are

$$NPV_A = \sum_{t=1}^{n} \frac{R_t}{(1+r)^t} - C_0$$
$$= \frac{\$40{,}000}{1.08} + \frac{\$60{,}000}{(1.08)^2}$$
$$+ \frac{\$40{,}000}{(1.08)^3} - \$110{,}000$$
$$= \frac{\$40{,}000}{1.08} + \frac{\$60{,}000}{1.1664}$$
$$+ \frac{\$40{,}000}{1.259712} - \$110{,}000$$
$$= \$37{,}037.04 + \$51{,}440.33$$
$$+ \$31{,}753.29 - \$110{,}000$$
$$= \$10{,}230.66$$

$$NPV_B = \frac{\$30{,}000}{1.08} + \frac{\$80{,}000}{(1.08)^2}$$
$$+ \frac{\$50{,}000}{(1.08)^3} - \$104{,}000$$
$$= \$27{,}777.78 + \$68{,}587.11$$
$$+ \$39{,}691.61 - \$104{,}000$$
$$= \$32{,}056.50$$

(b) With a risk premium of 2 percent for project A, the risk-adjusted discount rate is $8 + 2 = 10$ percent. Thus,

$$NPV_A = \frac{\$40{,}000}{1.10} + \frac{\$60{,}000}{(1.10)^2}$$
$$+ \frac{\$40{,}000}{(1.10)^3} - \$110{,}000$$
$$= \frac{\$40{,}000}{1.10} + \frac{\$60{,}000}{1.21}$$
$$+ \frac{\$40{,}000}{1.331} - \$110{,}000$$
$$= \$36{,}363.64 + \$49{,}586.78$$
$$+ \$30{,}052.59 - \$110{,}000$$
$$= \$6{,}003.01$$

On the other hand, with a risk premium of 6 percent for project B, the risk-adjusted discount rate is $8 + 6 = 14$ percent. Thus,

$$NPV_B = \frac{\$30,000}{1.14} + \frac{\$80,000}{(1.14)^2}$$

$$+ \frac{\$50,000}{(1.14)^3} - \$104,000$$

$$= \frac{\$30,000}{1.14} + \frac{\$80,000}{1.2996}$$

$$+ \frac{\$50,000}{1.481544} - \$104,000$$

$$= \$26,315.79 + \$61,557.40$$

$$+ \$33,748.58 - \$104,000$$

$$= \$17,621.77$$

Even though project B is more risky than project A, it still gives a higher risk-adjusted NPV than project A. Therefore, the manager should undertake project B rather than project A.

10. The decision tree for the Fitness World Sporting Company to build either a large or small plant is given in Figure 23. Being risk neutral, the company should choose the strategy with the largest expected present value. Thus, it should build the large plant. This results in the expected net present value of $2,000,000 as compared with $1,000,000 for the small plant. The strategy of building the small plant is then slashed off on the decision tree to indicate that it is suboptimal.

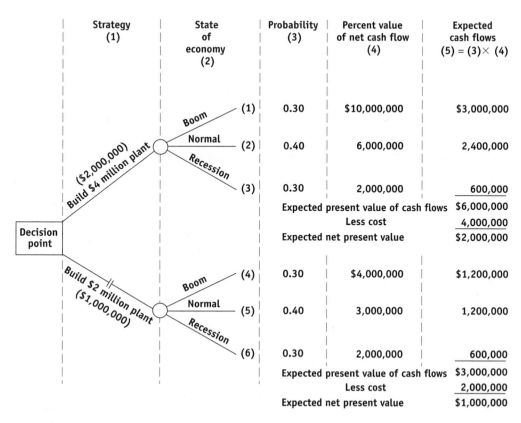

Strategy (1)	State of economy (2)		Probability (3)	Percent value of net cash flow (4)	Expected cash flows (5) = (3)× (4)
	Boom	(1)	0.30	$10,000,000	$3,000,000
	Normal	(2)	0.40	6,000,000	2,400,000
	Recession	(3)	0.30	2,000,000	600,000
			Expected present value of cash flows		$6,000,000
			Less cost		4,000,000
			Expected net present value		$2,000,000
	Boom	(4)	0.30	$4,000,000	$1,200,000
	Normal	(5)	0.40	3,000,000	1,200,000
	Recession	(6)	0.30	2,000,000	600,000
			Expected present value of cash flows		$3,000,000
			Less cost		2,000,000
			Expected net present value		$1,000,000

Decision point

Build $4 million plant ($2,000,000)

Build $2 million plant ($1,000,000)

FIGURE 23

Chapter 14

1. In Figure 24, the top of the lettered bars gives the firm's demand for capital, while the step *MCC* curve gives the marginal cost of capital to the firm. From Figure 24 we can determine that the firm should undertake projects *A, B,* and *C* because the rates of return expected from these projects exceed the marginal cost of raising the capital required to undertake them. On the other hand, the firm would not undertake projects *D* and *E* because the rates of return that these projects are expected to generate are below the cost of capital.

3. (*a*) If the firm uses the risk-adjusted discount rate (*k*) of 10 percent, the net present value (*NPV*) of the project is

$$NPV = \frac{\$290,000}{(1.10)^1} + \frac{\$320,000}{(1.10)^2} + \frac{\$353,000}{(1.10)^3}$$
$$+ \frac{\$389,300}{(1.10)^4} + \frac{\$779,230}{(1.10)^5} - \$1,000,000$$
$$= \frac{\$290,000}{1.1} + \frac{\$320,000}{1.21} + \frac{\$353,000}{1.331}$$
$$+ \frac{\$389,300}{1.4641} + \frac{\$779,230}{1.61051} - \$1,000,000$$
$$= \$263,636 + \$264,463 + \$265,214$$
$$+ \$265,897 + \$483,841 - \$1,000,000$$
$$= \$1,543,051 - \$1,000,000$$
$$= \$543,051$$

(*b*) If the firm uses instead the risk-adjusted discount rate (*k*) of 20 percent, the net present value (*NPV*) of the project is

$$NPV = \frac{\$290,000}{(1.20)^1} + \frac{\$320,000}{(1.20)^2}$$
$$+ \frac{\$353,000}{(1.20)^3} + \frac{\$389,300}{(1.20)^4}$$
$$+ \frac{\$779,230}{(1.20)^5} - \$1,000,000$$
$$= \frac{\$290,000}{1.2} + \frac{\$320,000}{1.44} + \frac{\$353,000}{1.728}$$
$$+ \frac{\$389,300}{2.0736} + \frac{\$779,230}{2.48832}$$
$$- \$1,000,000$$
$$= \$241,657 + \$222,222 + \$204,282$$
$$+ \$187,741 + \$313,155$$
$$- \$1,000,000$$
$$= \$1,169,067 - \$1,000,000$$
$$= \$169,067$$

The same value could have been obtained more readily by multiplying the net cash flow from the project in each year by the present value interest factor (*PVIF*) for $i = k = 20$ percent and from $n = t = 1$ to $n = t = 5$ given in Table B-2 in Appendix B, as explained in Appendix A at the end of the book.

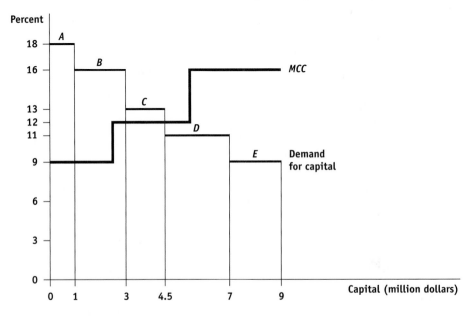

FIGURE 24

(c) The value of the firm would increase by $543,051 (the net present value of the project) if the firm used the risk-adjusted discount rate of 10 percent and would increase by $169,067 if the firm used the risk-adjusted discount rate of 20 percent. Since the net present value of the project is positive in either case, the firm should undertake the project.

5. The net present value of the project is obtained from

$$NPV = \sum_{t=1}^{n} \frac{R_t}{(1+k)^t} - C_0$$

$$= \sum_{t=1}^{4} \frac{\$5,000,000}{(1+0.20)^t} - \$10,000,000$$

$$= \$5,000,000(PVIFA_{20,4})$$

$$- \$10,000,000$$

$$= \$5,000,000(2.5887)$$

$$- \$10,000,000$$

$$= \$12,943,500 - \$10,000,000$$

$$= \$2,943,500$$

Since $NPV > 0$ the firm should undertake the project.

Note that $PVIFA_{20,4}$ refers to the present value interest factor of an annuity of $1 for 4 years discounted at 20 percent (see Section A-4 of Appendix A).

11. (a) The cost of debt (k_d) is given by the interest rate that the firm must pay on its bonds (r) times 1 minus the firm's marginal income tax rate. That is,

$$k_d = r(1 - t) = 11\%(1 - 0.4)$$

$$= 6.6\%$$

(b) The cost of equity capital (k_e) found by the capital asset pricing model (CAPM) is given by

$$k_e = r_f + \beta(k_m - r_f)$$

where r_f is the risk-free rate (i.e., the interest rate on government securities), k_m is the return on the average stock of all firms in the market, and β is the estimated beta coefficient for the common stock of this firm. With $r_f = 7.5$ percent, $k_m = 11.55$ percent, and $\beta = 2$, the cost of equity capital for this firm found with the CAPM is

$$k_e = 7.5\% + 2(11.55\% - 7.5\%)$$

$$= 15.6\%$$

(c) The composite cost of capital (k_c) is given by

$$k_c = w_d k_d + w_e k_e$$

where w_d and w_e are, respectively, the proportion of debt and equity capital in the firm's capital structure. With $w_d = 0.4$, $w_e = 0.6$, $k_d = 6.6$ percent, and the cost of equity capital of $k_e = 15.6$ percent, the composite cost of capital for this firm is

$$k_c = 0.4(6.6\%) + 0.6(15.6\%)$$

$$= 12.0\%$$

GLOSSARY

Accounting costs   Historical explicit costs.

Adjusted R^2 ($\bar{R}^2$)   The coefficient of multiple determination adjusted for the reduction in degrees of freedom as more independent variables are included in the regression.

Adverse selection   The situation in which low-quality products or services drive high-quality products or services out of the market as a result of asymmetric information between buyers and sellers.

Alternative or opportunity costs   The cost to the firm of using a purchased or owned input, which is equal to what the input could earn in its best alternative use.

Analysis of variance   A test of the overall explanatory power of the regression using the F statistic.

Appreciation   A decrease in the domestic-currency price of the foreign currency.

Arc cross-price elasticity of demand   The cross-price elasticity of demand for commodity X between two price levels of commodity Y; it is measured by

$$\frac{Q_{X_2} - Q_{X_1}}{P_{Y_2} - P_{Y_1}} \cdot \frac{P_{Y_2} + P_{Y_1}}{Q_{X_2} + Q_{X_1}}$$

Arc income elasticity of demand   The income elasticity of demand between two levels of income; it is measured by

$$\frac{Q_2 - Q_1}{I_2 - I_1} \cdot \frac{I_2 + I_1}{Q_2 + Q_1}$$

Arc price elasticity of demand   The price elasticity of demand between two points on the demand curve; it is measured by

$$\frac{Q_2 - Q_1}{P_2 - P_1} \cdot \frac{P_2 + P_1}{Q_2 + Q_1}$$

Asymmetric information   The situation in which one party to a transaction has more information than the other party on the quality of the product or service offered for sale.

Auction pricing   The pricing strategy for Internet purchases in which the consumer names the price that he or she is willing to pay for an item without being able to choose the seller or the brand.

Autocorrelation   The problem that can arise in regression analysis with time-series data, where consecutive errors have the same sign or change sign frequently; it leads to exaggerated t statistics and to an unreliable R^2 and F statistic.

Average fixed cost (AFC)   Total fixed costs divided by output.

Average product (AP)   The total product divided by the quantity of the variable input used.

Average total cost (ATC)   Total costs divided by output. Also equals $AFC + AVC$.

Average variable cost (AVC)   Total variable costs divided by output.

Averch–Johnson (A–J) effect   The overinvestments and underinvestments in plant and equipment resulting when public utility rates are set too high or too low.

Bandwagon effect   The situation in which some people demand a commodity because other people purchase it (i.e., in order to "keep up with the Joneses").

Barometric firm   The oligopolistic firm that is recognized as the true interpreter or barometer of changes in demand and cost conditions warranting a price change in the industry.

Barometric forecasting   The method of forecasting turning points in business cycles by the use of leading economic indicators.

Benchmarking   Finding out, in an open and above-board way, how other firms may be doing something better (cheaper) so that your firm can copy, and possibly improve on, their technique.

Bertrand model The oligopoly model where each firm assumes that the other will keep its price constant. It leads to the perfectly competitive solution even with only two firms.

Beta coefficient (β) The ratio of the variability of the return on the common stock of the firm to the variability of the average return on all stocks.

Border taxes Rebates for internal *indirect taxes* given to exporters of a commodity and imposed (in addition to the tariff) on importers of a commodity.

Brain drain The emigration of highly skilled workers from poorer nations to the United States and leading industrial countries in Europe.

Broadbanding The elimination of multiple salary grades to foster movement among jobs within the firm.

Bundling The form of tying in which the firm requires customers buying or leasing one of its products or services to also buy or lease another product or service when customers have different tastes but the firm cannot price discriminate (as in tying).

Business ethics The code or guidelines that prescribe acceptable behavior in business behavior and business transactions.

Business profit The revenue of the firm minus its explicit or accounting costs.

Capital asset pricing model (CAPM) The method of measuring the equity cost of capital as the risk-free rate plus the beta coefficient (β) times the risk premium on the average stock.

Capital budgeting The process of planning expenditures that give rise to revenues or returns over a number of years.

Celler–Kefauver Antimerger Act (1950) The law that closed a loophole in the Clayton Act by making it illegal to acquire not only the stock but also the assets of competing corporations if such purchases substantially lessen competition or tend to create a monopoly.

Centralized cartel A formal agreement among oligopolists to set the monopoly price, allocate output among member firms, and share profits.

Certainty The situation in which there is only one possible outcome to a decision and this outcome is known precisely; risk-free.

Certainty-equivalent coefficient (α) The ratio of the certain sum equivalent to the expected risky sum or net return from the investment that is used to adjust the valuation model for risk.

Change in demand A shift in the demand curve of a commodity as a result of a change in the consumer's income, in the price of related commodities, tastes, or in any of the determinants of demand other than the price of the commodity.

Change in the quantity demanded The movement along a particular demand curve resulting from a change in the price of the commodity, while holding everything else constant.

Circular flow of economic activity The flow of resources from resource owners to business firms and the reverse flow of goods and services from the latter to the former. Money flows from firms to resource owners to pay for resources and back to firms in payment for goods and services.

Clayton Act (1914) The law that prohibits price discrimination, exclusive and tying contracts, and intercorporate stock holdings if they substantially lessen competition or tend to create a monopoly and that prohibits outright interlocking directorates.

Closed innovation model The situation where companies generate, develop, and commercialize their own ideas, innovations, or technological breakthroughs.

Cobb–Douglas production function A production function of the form $Q = AK^aL^b$ where Q, K, and L are physical units of output, labor, and capital, and A, a, and b are the parameters to be estimated empirically.

Coefficient of correlation (r) The measure of the degree of covariation between two variables; the positive or negative square root of the coefficient of determination in simple regression analysis.

Coefficient of determination (R^2) The proportion of the explained to the total variation in the dependent variable in regression analysis.

Coefficient of variation (V) The standard deviation of the distribution divided by the expected value or mean.

Coincident indicators Time series that move in step or coincide with movements in the level of general economic activity.

Collusion A formal or informal agreement among oligopolists to adopt policies to restrict or eliminate competition and increase profits.

Competitive benchmarking The comparison of the efficiency of a firm's production methods relative to its competitors.

Composite cost of capital The weighted average of the cost of debt and equity capital to the firm.

Composite indexes Indexes formed by a weighted average of the individual indicators. There are composite indexes for the 12 leading, the 4 roughly coincident, and the 6 lagging indicators.

Computer-aided design (CAD)   The technique that allows research and development engineers to design a new or changed product or component on a computer screen.

Computer-aided manufacturing (CAM)   The technique that allows research and development engineers to issue instructions to a network of integrated machine tools to produce a prototype of the new or changed product.

Concentration ratios   The percentage of total industry sales of the 4, 8, and 20 largest firms in the industry.

Conditional probability   The probability that an event will occur given that another event has already occurred.

Confidence interval   The range within which we are confident (usually at the 95 percent level) that the true value of the parameter lies.

Conscious parallelism   The adoption of similar policies by oligopolistic firms in view of their recognized interdependence.

Consent decree   An agreement, made without a court trial, between the defendant and the Justice Department under which the defendant (without admitting guilt) agrees to abide by the rules of business behavior set down in the decree.

Constant returns to scale   The case in which output changes in the same proportion as inputs.

Constrained optimization   The maximizing or the minimizing of an objective function subject to some constraints.

Consumer clinics   Laboratory experiments in which the participants are given a sum of money and asked to spend it in a simulated store to see how they react to changes in the commodity price and other determinants of demand.

Consumer demand theory   The study of the determinants of consumer demand for a commodity.

Consumer surveys   The questioning of a sample of consumers about how they would respond to particular changes in the price and other determinants of the demand for the commodity.

Consumers' surplus   The difference between what consumers are willing to pay for a specific quantity of a product and what they actually pay.

Continuous probability distribution   The smooth bell-like curve that can be used to determine the probability that an outcome will fall within a specific range of outcomes.

Contribution margin per unit   The excess of the selling price of the product over the average variable costs

of the firm (that is, $P - AVC$), which can be applied to cover the fixed costs of the firm and to provide profits.

Cost of debt   The net (after-tax) interest rate paid by a firm to borrow funds.

Cost-plus pricing   The most common pricing practice by firms today, whereby a markup is added to the fully allocated average cost of the product.

Cost–volume–profit or breakeven analysis   A method of determining the output at which a firm breaks even or earns a target profit from the total revenue and total cost functions of the firm.

Cournot model   The oligopoly model in which each firm assumes that the other keeps its output constant. With two firms, each firm will sell one-third of the perfectly competitive output.

Creative company   A firm whose new core competence is creativity rather than production efficiency.

Critical value   The value found from the table of a distribution (say, the t distribution) that is used to conduct a significance test.

Cross-price elasticity of demand (E_{XY})   The percentage change in the demand for commodity X divided by the percentage change in the price of commodity Y, while holding constant all other variables in the demand function.

Cross-sectional data   Data on a sample of families, firms, or other economic units at a particular point in time, say, for a given year.

Customer relationship management (CRM)   The mix of business strategy, process, and information technology to try to increase business with customers the firm already has, especially the most profitable ones, as well as doing its best to attract new customers by trying to learn everything possible about its customers and making them feel that they are receiving personal attention.

Cyclical fluctuations   The major expansions and contractions in most economic time series that recur every number of years.

Deadweight loss   The loss of efficiency in the use of society's resources arising from monopoly.

Decision tree   A diagram of a figure with nodes and branches depicting points at which decisions are made and the outcome of each decision; used for showing or analyzing sequential games.

Decision variables   The variables that the firm can vary in order to optimize the objective function.

Decreasing returns to scale   The case in which output changes by a smaller proportion than inputs.

Definitional equations   The equations in a multiple-equation model that are identities and true by definition.

Degree of operating leverage (*DOL*)   The percentage change in the firm's profits divided by the percentage change in output or sales; the sales elasticity of profits.

Degrees of freedom (df)   The number of data points or sample observations minus the number of estimated parameters in regression analysis.

Delphi method   The forecasting method based on polling the firm's top executives or outside experts separately and then providing feedback in the hope that they would reach a consensus forecast.

Demand function faced by a firm   The relationship that identifies the determinants of the demand for a commodity faced by a firm. These include the price of the commodity, the number of consumers in the market, consumers' incomes, the price of related commodities, tastes, and other forces that are specific to the particular industry and firm.

Demand interrelationship   The relationship of substitutability or complementarity among the products produced by the firm.

Depreciation   An increase in the domestic-currency price of the foreign currency.

Derivative of *Y* with respect to *X* (*dY/dX*)   The limit of the ratio $\Delta Y/\Delta X$, as ΔX approaches zero; that is, $dY/dX = \lim_{\Delta X \to 0} \Delta Y/\Delta X$.

Derived demand   The firm's demand for the inputs or factors of production required in the production of the commodity that the firm sells.

Differentiated oligopoly   An oligopoly in which the products of the firms in the industry are differentiated.

Differentiated products   Products that are similar and that satisfy the same basic need.

Differentiation   The process of determining the derivative of a function.

Diffusion index   An index that measures the percentage of the 12 leading indicators moving upward.

Diminishing marginal utility of money   The decline in the extra utility received from each dollar increase in income.

Direct business model   The situation in which a firm deals directly with the consumer, eliminating distributors.

Discrete probability distribution   The steplike bar chart showing the probability of each possible outcome of a decision or strategy.

Dissolution and divestiture   A court order in monopoly and antimerger cases under which the firm is ordered to dissolve (thereby losing its identity) or to divest itself of (i.e., sell) some of its assets.

Dividend valuation model   The method of measuring the equity cost of capital to the firm with the ratio of the dividend per share of the stock to the price of the stock, plus the expected growth rate of dividend payments.

Dominant strategy   The best or optimal strategy for a player regardless of what the other player does.

Dual problem   The inverse of the primal linear programming problem.

Duality theorem   The postulate that the optimal value of the primal objective function is equal to the optimal value of the dual objective function.

Dumping   Refers to international price discrimination or the sale of a commodity at a lower price abroad than at home.

Duopoly   An oligopoly of two firms.

Durable goods   Goods that can be stored, as well as other products that provide services not only during the year that they are purchased but also in subsequent years.

Durbin–Watson statistic (*d*)   The statistic used for the test to detect auto-correlation.

Dutch auction   The auction where the auctioneer starts with a very high price and then gradually lowers the price until one participant agrees to buy the item.

E-commerce   The production, advertising, sale, and distribution of products and services business-to-business and business-to-consumer through the Internet.

Econometrics   The empirical estimation and testing of economic relationships and models.

Economic costs   Alternative or opportunity costs.

Economic profit   The revenue of the firm minus its economic costs.

Economic theory   The study of microeconomics and macroeconomics.

Economic theory of regulation   The theory that regulation results from pressure-group action to support business and to protect consumers, workers, and the environment.

Economies of scope   The lowering of costs that a firm often experiences when it produces two or more products together rather than producing each product separately.

Electronic scanners   The automatic ringing up of prices for bar-coded items at supermarket checkout counters.

Endogenous variables   Those variables whose values are determined by the solution of a multiple-equation model.

Engineering technique   The method of estimating the long-run average cost curve of the firm from the determination of the optimal input combinations used to produce various levels of output from the present technology and from input prices.

English auction An auction where an item is sold to the highest bidder.

Excess capacity The difference between the quantity that a monopolistically competitive firm and a perfectly competitive firm would sell when the market is in long-run equilibrium.

Exchange rate The price of a unit of the foreign currency in terms of the domestic currency.

Exogenous variables Those variables whose values are determined outside (and must be provided to solve) a multiple-equation model.

Expansion path The line joining tangency points of isoquants and isocosts with input prices held constant and which shows optimal input combinations.

Expected profit A weighted average of all possible profit levels that can result from an investment, with the probability of occurrence of each profit level used as weights.

Expected utility The sum of the product of the utility of each possible outcome of a decision or strategy and the probability of its occurrence.

Expected value The sum of the products of each possible outcome of a decision or strategy and the probability of its occurrence.

Explained variation The sum of the squared deviations of each *estimated* value of the dependent variable ($\hat{Y}$) from its mean ($\bar{Y}$).

Explicit costs The actual expenditures of the firm required to hire or purchase inputs.

Exponential smoothing The smoothing technique in which the forecast for a period is a *weighted* average of the actual and forecast values of the time series in the previous period.

External diseconomies of consumption Uncompensated costs imposed on some individuals by the consumption expenditures of some other individual.

External diseconomies of production Uncompensated costs imposed on some firms by the expansion of output by other firms.

External economies of consumption Uncompensated benefits conferred on some individuals by the consumption expenditures of some other individual.

External economies of production Uncompensated benefits conferred on some firms by the expansion of output by other firms.

Externalities Harmful or beneficial effects borne or received by firms or individuals other than those producing or consuming a product or service.

F **statistic** The ratio of the explained variance divided by $k-1$ df to the unexplained variance divided by $n-k$ df, where k is the number of estimated parameters and n is the number of observations.

Fair game A game or bet in which there is a 50–50 chance of winning or losing.

Feasible region The area that includes all the solutions that are possible with the given constraints.

Federal Trade Commission Act (1914) A supplement to the Clayton Act, which made unfair methods of competition illegal and which established the Federal Trade Commission (FTC) to prosecute violators of the antitrust laws and protect the public against false and misleading advertisements.

Firm An organization that combines and organizes resources for the purpose of producing goods and/or services for sale.

Firm architecture The way the firm is organized, operates, and responds to market changes.

First-degree price discrimination The selling of each unit of a product separately and charging the highest price possible for each unit sold.

First-price sealed-bid auction The auction where the auctioneer collects the bids made on slips of papers and awards the item to the highest bidder.

Fixed inputs Inputs that cannot be changed readily during the time period under consideration.

Foreign-exchange market The market where national currencies are bought and sold.

Foreign-exchange rate The price of a unit of a foreign currency in terms of the domestic currency.

Foreign Sales Corporation (FSC) Provisions of the U.S. tax code used by U.S. corporations since 1971 to enjoy partial exemption from U.S. tax laws on income earned from exports.

Foreign sourcing of inputs The purchase of parts and components abroad in order to keep production costs down and meet the competition.

Forward contract An agreement to purchase or sell a specific amount of a foreign currency at a rate specified today for delivery at a specified future date.

Fully allocated average cost The sum of the average variable cost of producing the normal or standard level of output and an average overhead charge.

Functional areas of business administration studies The academic disciplines of accounting, finance, marketing, personnel, and production.

Futures contract A standardized forward contract for predetermined quantities of the currency and selected calendar dates.

Game theory   The theory that examines the choice of the best or optimal strategies in conflict situations.

Giffen good   An inferior good for which the positive substitution effect is smaller than the negative income effect so that less of the good is purchased when its price falls.

Globalization of economic activity   The setting up of production facilities and/or the purchase of components and parts, as well as the sale of commodities in other nations.

Golden parachute   A large financial settlement paid out by a firm to its managers if they are forced or choose to leave as a result of a takeover that greatly increases the value of the firm.

Hedging   The covering of a foreign-exchange risk.

Herfindahl index (H)   A measure of concentration in an industry given by the sum of the squared values of the market shares of all the firms in the industry.

Heteroscedasticity   The problem that can arise in regression analysis on cross-sectional data, where the error term is not constant; it leads to biased standard errors and incorrect statistical tests.

Identification problem   The difficulty of deriving the demand curve for a commodity from observed price-quantity points that result from the intersection of different and unobserved demand and supply curves for the commodity.

Imperfect competition   Monopoly, monopolistic competition, and oligopoly.

Implicit costs   The value (from their best alternative use) of the inputs owned and used by the firm.

Import quota   A quantitative restriction on imports.

Import tariff   A per-unit tax on imports.

Income effect   The increase in the quantity demanded of a commodity resulting only from the increase in real income that accompanies a price decline.

Income elasticity of demand (E_I)   The percentage change in the demand for a commodity divided by the percentage change in consumers' income, while holding constant all the other variables in the demand function.

Increasing returns to scale   The case in which output changes by a larger proportion than inputs.

Incremental analysis   The comparison of the incremental revenue to the incremental cost in managerial decision making.

Incremental costs   The total increase in costs from implementing a particular managerial decision.

Individual's demand curve   The graphical relationship between the price and the quantity demanded of a commodity by an individual per time period.

Individual's demand schedule   The tabular relationship between the price and the quantity demanded of a commodity by an individual per time period.

Inequality constraints   Limitations on the use of some inputs or certain minimum requirements that must be met.

Inferior goods   Goods of which the consumer purchases less with an increase in income.

Information superhighway   The ability of researchers, firms, and consumers to hook up with libraries, databases, and marketing information through a national high-speed computer network and have at their fingertips a vast amount of information as never before.

Injunction   A court order requiring that the defendant refrain from certain anticompetitive actions or take some specified competitive actions.

Inputs   Resources used in the production of goods and services.

Internal rate of return (IRR) on a project   The rate of discount that equates the present value of the net cash flows to the initial cost of a project.

Internet   A collection of thousands of computers and businesses, and millions of people throughout the world linked together in a service called World Wide Web.

Irregular or random influences   The unpredictable variations in the data series resulting from wars, natural disasters, strikes, or other unforeseen events.

Isocost line   It shows the various combinations of two inputs that the firm can hire with a given total cost outlay.

Isoquant   A curve showing the various combinations of two inputs that can be used to produce a specific level of output.

Iteration   A computer run or trial of a simulation model with one set of randomly chosen values of the variables of the model.

Japanese cost-management system   The production system in which the firm starts with a target cost based on the market price at which the firm believes consumers will buy the product and then strives to produce the product at the specified targeted cost.

Just-in-time production system   The production system introduced by Toyota in which every part and component of a product becomes available just when needed.

Kinked demand curve model   The model that seeks to explain price rigidity by postulating a demand curve with a kink at the prevailing price.

Lagging indicators   Time series that follow or lag movements in the level of general economic activity.

Lagrangian function   A function formed by the original objective function that the firm seeks to maximize or minimize plus l (the Lagrangian multiplier) times the constraint function set equal to zero.

Lagrangian multiplier method   A technique for solving a constrained optimization problem by forming a Lagrangian function and treating it as an unconstrained problem.

Law of demand   The inverse relationship between the price and the quantity demanded of a commodity per time period.

Law of diminishing returns   A physical law, always empirically true, stating that after a point, the marginal product of a variable input declines.

Leading economic indicators   Time series that tend to precede (lead) changes in the level of general economic activity.

Learning curve   The curve showing the decline in average cost with rising cumulative total outputs over time.

Learning organization   An organization that values continuing learning, both individual and collective, and believes that competitive advantage derives from and requires continuous learning in our information age.

Least-squares method   The statistical technique for estimating a regression line that minimizes the sum of the squared vertical deviations or errors of the observed points from the regression line.

Licensing   The requirement of a franchise or permission to enter or remain in a business, profession, or trade.

Limit pricing   The charging of lower than the profit-maximizing price by a firm in order to discourage the entrance of other firms into the market.

Linear programming   A mathematical technique for solving constrained maximization and minimization problems when there are many constraints and the objective function to be optimized as well as the constraints faced are linear.

Logistics   Supply chain management or the merging at the corporate level of the purchasing, transportation, warehousing, distribution, and customer services functions, rather than dealing with each of them separately at division levels.

Long run   The time period when all inputs are variable.

Long-run average cost (*LAC*)   The minimum per-unit cost of producing any level of output when the firm can build any desired scale of plant; $LAC = LTC/Q$.

Long-run marginal cost (*LMC*)   The change in long-run total costs per unit change in output; $LMC = \Delta LTC/\Delta Q$.

Long-run total cost (*LTC*)   The minimum total costs of producing various levels of output when the firm can build any desired scale of plant.

Macroeconomics   The study of the total or aggregate level of output, income, employment, consumption, investment, and prices for the economy *viewed as a whole.*

Managerial economics   The application of economic theory and the tools of decision science to examine how an organization can achieve its aims or objectives most efficiently.

Marginal analysis   The postulate that optimization occurs when the marginal benefit of an activity equals the marginal cost.

Marginal cost (*MC*)   The change in total costs or in total variable costs per unit change in output.

Marginal product (*MP*)   The change in total product per unit change in the variable input used.

Marginal rate of technical substitution (*MRTS*)   The absolute value of the slope of the isoquant. It equals the ratio of the marginal products of the two inputs.

Marginal resource cost (*MRC*)   The increase in total cost from hiring an additional unit of the variable input.

Marginal revenue (*MR*)   The change in total revenue per unit change in quantity sold.

Marginal revenue product (*MRP*)   The marginal product of the variable input times the marginal revenue from the sale of the extra output produced.

Market   All the actual and potential buyers and sellers of a particular product.

Market demand function   The relationship that identifies the determinants of the total or aggregate demand for a commodity.

Market experiments   Attempts by the firm to estimate the demand for the commodity by changing price and other determinants of the demand for the commodity in the actual marketplace.

Market failure   Economic inefficiencies arising from the existence of monopoly power in imperfectly competitive markets, from externalities, and from the existence of public goods.

Market-sharing cartel   An agreement among oligopolists to divide the market.

Market structure   The competitive environment in which the buyers and sellers of the product operate.

Markup on cost   The ratio of the profit margin to the fully allocated average cost of the product.

Mathematical economics   The study of the formal (equational) relationships among economic variables in economic models and their theoretical implications.

Maximin criterion   The decision rule under uncertainty that postulates that the decision maker should determine the worst possible outcome of each strategy and then pick the strategy that provides the best of the worst possible outcomes.

Microeconomics   The study of the economic behavior of *individual* decision-making units, such as individual consumers, resource owners, and business firms, in a free-enterprise system.

Micromarketing   Detailed point-of-sale information to identify store by store the types of products with the greatest potential appeal for the specific customers in the area.

Minimax regret criterion   The decision rule under uncertainty that postulates that the decision maker should select the strategy that minimizes the maximum regret or opportunity cost of the wrong decision, whatever the state of nature that occurs.

Model   A formal or mathematical statement of an economic theory.

Monopolistic competition   The form of market organization in which there are many sellers of a differentiated product and entry into or exit from the industry is rather easy in the long run.

Monopoly   The form of market organization in which a single firm sells a product for which there are no close substitutes.

Moral hazard   The increased probability of a loss when an economic agent can shift some of its costs to others.

Moving average   The smoothing technique in which the forecast value of a time series in a given period is equal to the average value of the time series in a number of previous periods.

Multicollinearity   The problem in regression analysis that arises when two or more explanatory variables are highly correlated; it leads to exaggerated standard errors and biased statistical tests.

Multiple regression analysis   The regression analysis with more than one independent or explanatory variable.

Nash equilibrium   The equilibrium situation in which each player has chosen his or her optimal strategy, given the strategy chosen by the other player.

Natural monopoly   The case in which economies of scale result in a single firm's supplying the entire market.

Net cash flow from a project   The difference between cash receipts and cash expenditures over the life of a project.

Net present value (*NPV*) of a project   The present value of the estimated stream of net cash flows from the project, discounted at the firm's cost of capital, minus the initial cost of the project.

Networking   The forming of temporary strategic alliances in which each firm contributes its best competency.

New international economies of scale   The increased productivity resulting from the firm's integration of its entire system of manufacturing operations around the world.

Nonnegativity constraints   Limits that preclude negative values for the solution in a linear programming problem.

Nonprice competition   Competition based on product variation, advertising, and service rather than on price.

Nonzero-sum game   A game in which the gain of one player or firm does not come at the expense of the other player or firm.

Normal goods   Goods of which the consumer purchases more with an increase in income.

Objective function   The function to be optimized in linear programming.

Observational research   The gathering of information on consumer preferences by watching them buying and using products.

Oligopoly   The form of market organization in which there are few sellers of a homogeneous or differentiated product and entry into or exit from the industry is difficult.

Open innovation model   The situation where companies commercialize both, their own ideas and innovations, as well as the innovations of other firms, and deploy external as well as internal or in-house pathways to market.

Operating leverage   The ratio of the firm's total fixed costs to its total variable costs.

Optimal solution   The best of the feasible solutions.

Output elasticity   The percentage change in output or total product divided by the percentage change in the variable input used.

Overcrowding   The larger number of firms present in a monopolistically competitive market than if the market were perfectly competitive because of excess capacity in monopolistically competitive markets.

Partial derivative   The marginal effect on the dependent or left-hand variable of a multivariate function resulting from changing one of the independent or right-hand variables while holding all the others constant.

Patent   The right granted to an inventor by the federal government for the exclusive use of an invention for a period of 17 years.

Payoff   The outcome or consequence of each combination of strategies by the players in game theory.

Payoff matrix   A table that shows the possible outcome or result of each strategy under each state of nature.

Peak-load pricing   The firm's charging of a higher price during peak times than at off-peak times.

Perfect competition   The form of market organization in which there are many firms selling a homogeneous or identical product and each firm is too small to affect the price of the commodity.

Performance management   The holding of executives and their subordinates accountable for delivering the desired results and superior competitive performance.

Planning horizon   The period of time of the long run when the firm can build any desired scale of plant.

Players   The decision makers in the theory of games (here the oligopolistic firms or its managers) whose behavior we are trying to explain and predict.

Point cross-price elasticity of demand   The cross-price elasticity of demand for commodity X at a particular price of commodity Y; it is measured by

$$\frac{\Delta Q_X}{\Delta P_Y} \cdot \frac{P_Y}{Q_X}$$

Point income elasticity of demand   The income elasticity of demand at a particular level of income; it is measured by

$$\frac{\Delta Q}{\Delta I} \cdot \frac{I}{Q}$$

Point price elasticity of demand   The price elasticity of demand at a particular point on the demand curve; it is measured by

$$\frac{\Delta Q}{\Delta P} \cdot \frac{P}{Q}$$

Porter's strategic framework   The conceptual framework for identifying the structural determinants of the intensity of competition and the profitability of firms in oligopolistic industries.

Predatory pricing   Selling at below average variable cost in order to drive a competitor out of the market or discourage new entrants.

Prestige pricing   The pricing method of deliberately setting high prices to attract prestige-oriented consumers.

Price discrimination   The charging of different prices for different quantities of a product, at different times, to different customer groups, or in different markets, when these price differences are not justified by cost differences.

Price elasticity of demand (E_P)   The percentage change in the quantity demanded of a commodity divided by the percentage change in its price, while holding constant all the other variables in the demand function.

Price leadership   The form of market collusion in oligopolistic firms whereby the firm that serves as the price leader initiates a price change and the other firms in the industry soon match it.

Price lining   The pricing practice of setting a price target and then developing a product that would allow the firm to maximize total profits at that price.

Price matching   The pricing strategy where a firm advertises a price for the product or services that it sells and promises to match any lower price offered by a competitor.

Price taker   The situation under perfect competition whereby each firm has no effect on the price of the product it sells and can sell any quantity at the given market price.

Pricing power   The ability of a firm to raise prices faster than the rise in its costs or to lower its costs faster than the fall in the prices at which the firm sells—thus increasing its profits.

Primal problem   The original maximization (e.g., profit) or minimization (e.g., cost) linear programming problem.

Principal–agent problem   The problem that arises because the agents (managers) of a firm may seek to maximize their own benefits (such as salaries) rather than the profits or value of the firm, which is the owners' or principals' interest.

Prisoners' dilemma   The situation in which each player in an oligopolistic game adopts his or her dominant strategy but could do better by cooperating.

Probability   The chance or odds that an event will occur.

Probability distribution   The list of all possible outcomes of a decision or strategy and the probability attached to each.

Process innovation   The introduction of a new or improved production process.

Process management   The coordination or integration under a single umbrella of all the firm's performance-improvement initiatives, such as benchmarking, reengineering, TQM, and Six Sigma.

Producers' goods   The raw materials, capital equipment, and other inputs used by the firm to produce the goods and services demanded by consumers.

Product cycle model   The theory that firms that introduce an innovation eventually lose their export market and even their domestic market to foreign imitators facing lower production costs.

Product innovation   The introduction of a new or improved product.

Product variation   Differences in some of the characteristics of differentiated products.

Production   The transformation of inputs or resources into output of goods and services.

Production function   An equation, table, or graph that shows the maximum output that a firm can produce per period of time with each set of inputs.

Production process   The various capital/labor ratios that a firm can use to produce a commodity; it is depicted by a ray from the origin in input space.

Profit margin   The difference between the price and the fully allocated average cost of the product.

Profitability index (*PI*)   The ratio of the present value of the net cash flows from a project to its initial cost.

Public interest theory of regulation   The theory that regulation is undertaken to ensure that the economic system operates in a manner consistent with the public interest and to overcome market failures.

Public utilities   Natural monopolies supplying electricity, water, gas, local telephone, and local transportation services.

Pure oligopoly   An oligopoly in which the products of the firms in the industry are homogeneous.

Reaction function   The equation showing how a duopolist reacts to the other duopolist's action.

Reduced-form equations   The equations that represent the solution of a multiple-equation model and express the endogenous variables of the model in terms of the exogenous variables only.

Reengineering   The radical redesign of all of the firm's processes to achieve major gains in speed, quality, service, and profitability.

Regression analysis   A statistical technique for estimating the quantitative relationship between the economic variable that we seek to explain (the dependent variable) and one or more independent or explanatory variables.

Regression line   The line obtained by minimizing the sum of the squared vertical deviations of all data points from the line.

Relationship enterprises   A network of independent firms that form strategic alliances to build the capabilities and have the geographic presence needed to be global leaders in their field.

Relevant costs   The costs that should be considered in making a managerial decision; opportunity costs.

Repeated games   Prisoners' dilemma games of more than one move.

Ridge lines   The lines that separate the relevant (i.e., the negatively sloped) from the irrelevant (or positively sloped) portions of the isoquant.

Risk   The situation in which there is more than one possible outcome to a decision and the probability of each possible outcome is known or can be estimated.

Risk-adjusted discount rate   The higher rate of discount used to calculate the present value of the net cash flow or return of an investment project in order to compensate for risk.

Risk averter   An individual for whom the marginal utility of money diminishes; he or she would not accept a fair bet.

Risk neutral   An individual for whom the marginal utility of money is constant; he or she is indifferent to a fair bet.

Risk premium   The excess in the expected or required rate of return on a risky investment over the rate of return on a riskless asset in order to compensate for risk.

Risk–return trade-off function   A curve showing the various risk–return combinations among which a manager or investor is indifferent.

Risk seeker   An individual for whom the marginal utility of money increases; he or she would accept a fair bet and even some unfair bets.

Robinson–Patman Act (1936)   The law that protects small retailers from price competition from chain-store retailers, based on the latter's ability to obtain lower prices and brokerage concession fees on bulk purchases from suppliers if the intent is to destroy competition or eliminate a competitor.

Root-mean-square error (*RMSE*) The measure of the weighted average error of a forecast.

Sales maximization model The model that postulates that oligopolistic firms seek to maximize sales after an adequate rate of profit has been earned to satisfy stockholders.

Sarbanes–Oxley Act The law passed in July 2002 in response to financial scandals, such as Enron, which provides much tougher regulations on corporate governance and accounting oversight.

Satisficing behavior The theory of the firm that postulates that managers are not able to maximize profits but can strive only for some satisfactory goal in terms of sales, profits, growth, market share, and so on.

Scatter diagram A figure with the plots of the data points.

Seasonal variation The regularly recurring fluctuations in economic activity during each year because of weather and social customs.

Second-degree price discrimination The charging of a uniform price per unit for a specific quantity or block of a product, a lower price per unit for an additional batch or block of the product, and so on.

Second derivative The derivative of the derivative; it is found by the same rules of differentiation used to find the (first) derivative.

Second-price sealed-bid auction The auction where the auctioneer collects the bids made on slips of paper and awards the item to the highest bidder, who has to pay only the amount of the second highest bid.

Secular trend The long-run increase or decrease in a data series.

Selling expenses Expenditures (such as advertising) that a firm incurs in order to induce consumers to purchase more of its product.

Sensitivity analysis The statistical technique for measuring the effect of a variation in each variable of a model on the outcome of a simulation exercise.

Shadow price The marginal valuation of an input or output to the firm.

Sherman Act (1890) The law that prohibits monopolization and restraints of trade in commerce among the states and with foreign nations.

Short run The time period when at least one input is fixed.

Short-run supply curve of the perfectly competitive firm The rising portion of the firm's short-run marginal cost curve above its average variable cost curve.

Shut-down point The level of output at which the price of the product equals the average variable cost of the firm.

Significance test The test to determine if there is a statistically significant relationship between the dependent and the independent variable(s) in regression analysis.

Simple regression analysis The regression analysis with only one independent or explanatory variable.

Simplex method A mathematical technique for solving linear programming problems.

Simulation The statistical technique for replicating and analyzing a real-world event or situation.

Skimming Setting a high price when a product is first introduced and then gradually lowering its price later.

Slack variable A variable that is not fully used at a particular point.

Small-word model The idea or theory that a corporate giant can be made to operate as a small firm by linking well-connected individuals from each level of the organization to one another.

Smoothing techniques A method of naive forecasting in which future values of a time series are forecast on the basis of some average of its past values only.

Snob effect The situation where some people demand a smaller quantity of a commodity as more people consume it, in order to be different and exclusive.

Stage I of production The range of increasing average product of the variable input.

Stage II of production The range from the maximum average product of the variable input to where the marginal product of the input is zero.

Stage III of production The range of negative marginal product of the variable input.

Standard deviation (σ) A measure of the dispersion of possible outcomes from the expected value of a distribution; the square root of the variance.

Standard error (*SE*) of the regression The standard error of the dependent variable (Y) from the regression line.

Standard normal distribution A normal distribution with zero mean and standard deviation of 1.

States of nature Conditions in the future that will have a significant effect on the degree of success or failure of any strategy, but over which the decision maker has little or no control.

Strategic behavior The plan of action of a player or oligopolist, after taking into consideration all possible reactions of the others, as they compete for profits or other advantages.

Strategic development The idea that assessment and action should be under continuous review and provide a direction and an agenda or continuous strategic development, rather than a strategic plan.

Strategies   The potential choices that can be made by the players (firms) in the theory of games.

Structural (behavioral) equations   The equations that seek to explain (i.e., to identify the determinants of) the relationships of the model.

Substitution effect   The increase in the quantity demanded of a commodity resulting only from the decline in its price and independent of the change in real income.

Sunk costs   The costs that are not affected by a particular managerial decision.

Survival technique   The method of determining the existence of increasing, decreasing, or constant returns to scale depending on whether the share of industry output coming from large firms (as compared to the share of industry output coming from small firms) increases, decreases, or remains the same over time.

t **statistic**   The ratio of the value of the estimated parameter to its standard deviation or error.

t **test**   The significance test for an estimated parameter using the *t* distribution.

Theory of contestable markets   The theory that postulates that even if an industry has only one or a few firms, it would still operate as if it were perfectly competitive if entry is absolutely free and exit is entirely costless.

Theory of the firm   The postulate that the primary goal or objective of the firm is to maximize wealth or the value of the firm.

Third-degree price discrimination   The charging of different prices for the same product in different markets until the marginal revenue of the last unit of the product sold in each market equals the marginal cost of the product.

Time-series analysis   The technique of forecasting future values of a time series by examining past observations of the time-series data only.

Time-series data   The values of a variable arranged chronologically by days, weeks, months, quarters, or years.

Time value of money   The recognition that $1 received or paid in the future is worth less than $1 paid or received today.

Tit-for-tat   The strategy in repeated prisoners' dilemma games of doing to your opponent what he or she has just done to you.

Total costs (*TC*)   Total fixed costs plus total variable costs.

Total fixed costs (*TFC*)   The total obligations of the firm per time period for all the fixed inputs used.

Total product (*TP*)   The output produced by using different quantities of an input with fixed quantities of other(s).

Total quality management (*TQM*)   The effort to constantly improve the quality of products and the firm's processes so as to consistently deliver increasing value to customers. It constantly asks how something can be done cheaper, faster, or better by benchmarking and teamwork.

Total revenue (*TR*)   The price per unit of the commodity times the quantity sold.

Total variable costs (*TVC*)   The total obligations of the firm per time period for all the variable inputs the firm uses.

Total variation   The sum of the squared deviations of each *observed* value of the dependent variable (Y) from its mean ($\overline{Y}$).

Transaction costs   The extra cost (beyond the price of the purchase) in terms of money, time, or inconvenience of conducting a transaction. Firms exist to avoid many transaction costs.

Transfer pricing   The determination of the price of intermediate products sold by one semiautonomous division of a firm to another semiautonomous division of the same enterprise.

Two-part tariff   The pricing practice in which consumers pay an initial fee for the right to purchase a product or service, as well as a usage fee or price for each unit of the product they purchase.

Tying   The requirement that a consumer who buys or leases a product also purchases another product needed in the use of the first.

Uncertainty   The situation where there is more than one possible outcome to a decision and the probability of each specific outcome is not known or even meaningful.

Unexplained variation   The sum of the squared deviations of each *observed* value of the dependent variable (Y) from its corresponding *estimated* value ($\hat{Y}$).

Uruguay Round   The multilateral trade agreement concluded in December 1993 under which trade restrictions are to be reduced.

Util   The arbitrary unit of measure of utility.

Value of the firm   The present value of all expected future profits of the firm.

Value pricing   The selling of quality goods at lower prices than previously.

Variable inputs   Inputs that can be varied easily and on a very short notice.

Variance (σ^2)   The weighted average of the squared deviations from the mean of a distribution.

Virtual corporation   A temporary network of independent companies (suppliers, customers, and even rivals) coming together with each contributing its core competence to quickly take advantage of a fast-changing opportunity.

Virtual integration   The blurring of the traditional boundaries and roles between the manufacturer, its suppliers, and its customers.

Virtual management   The ability of a manager to simulate consumer behavior using computer models based on the emerging science or theory of complexity.

Virtual shopping   A sample of consumers shopping in a virtual retail store recreated on a computer screen.

Voluntary export restraint   A restriction on exports voluntarily agreed-upon by a nation under the threat of higher all-around trade restrictions by the importing nation.

Wheeler–Lea Act (1938)   The amendment to the Federal Trade Commission Act that forbids false or deceptive advertisement of foods, drugs, corrective devices, and cosmetics entering interstate commerce.

Winner's curse   The danger that a participant to an auction overpays for an item by placing the winning bid.

Zero-sum game   A game in which the gain of one player or firm comes at the expense and is exactly equal to the loss of the other player or firm.

INDEX